Fundamentals of
INVESTING

The Prentice Hall Series in Finance

Alexander/Sharpe/Bailey
Fundamentals of Investments

Bear/Moldonado-Bear
Free Markets, Finance, Ethics, and Law

Bekaert/Hodrick
International Financial Management

Berk/ DeMarzo
*Corporate Finance**

Berk/DeMarzo
*Corporate Finance: The Core**

Berk/DeMarzo/ Harford
*Fundamentals of Corporate Finance**

Bierman/ Smidt
The Capital Budgeting Decision: Economic Analysis of Investment Projects

Bodie/Merton/Cleeton
Financial Economics

Brooks
*Financial Management: Core Concepts**

Click/Coval
The Theory and Practice of International Financial Management

Copeland/Weston/Shastri
Financial Theory and Corporate Policy

Cox/ Rubinstein
Options Markets

Dorfman
Introduction to Risk Management and Insurance

Dietrich
Financial Services and Financial Institutions: Value Creation in Theory and Practice

Dufey/Giddy
Cases in International Finance

Eakins
Finance in .learn

Eiteman/Stonehill/Moffett
Multinational Business Finance

Emery/Finnerty/Stowe
Corporate Financial Management

Fabozzi
Bond Markets: Analysis and Strategies

Fabozzi/Modigliani
Capital Markets: Institutions and Instruments

Fabozzi/Modigliani/Jones
Foundations of Financial Markets and Institutions

Finkler
Financial Management for Public, Health, and Not-for-Profit Organizations

Francis/Ibbotson
Investments: A Global Perspective

Frasca
Personal Finance: An Integrated Planning Approach

Fraser/Ormiston
Understanding Financial Statements

Geisst
Investment Banking in the Financial System

Gitman
*Principles of Managerial Finance**

Gitman
*Principles of Managerial Finance—Brief Edition**

Gitman/Joehnk/Smart
*Fundamentals of Investing**

Gitman/Madura
Introduction to Finance

Guthrie/Lemon
Mathematics of Interest Rates and Finance

Haugen
The Inefficient Stock Market: What Pays Off and Why

Haugen
Modern Investment Theory

Haugen
The New Finance: Overreaction, Complexity, and Uniqueness

Holden
Excel Modeling and Estimation in the Fundamentals of Corporate Finance

Holden
Excel Modeling and Estimation in the Fundamentals of Investments

Holden
Excel Modeling and Estimation in Investments

Holden
Excel Modeling and Estimation in Corporate Finance

Hughes/MacDonald
International Banking: Text and Cases

Hull
Fundamentals of Futures and Options Markets

Hull
Options, Futures, and Other Derivatives

Hull
Risk Management and Financial Institutions

Keown/Martin/Petty/Scott
Financial Management: Principles and Applications

Keown/Martin/Petty/Scott
Foundations of Finance: The Logic and Practice of Financial Management*

Keown
Personal Finance: Turning Money into Wealth*

Kim/Nofsinger/Mohr
Corporate Governance

Levy/ Post
Investments

May/May/Andrew
Effective Writing: A Handbook for Finance People

Madura
Personal Finance*

Marthinsen
Risk Takers: Uses and Abuses of Financial Derivatives

McDonald
Derivatives Markets

McDonald
Fundamentals of Derivatives Markets

Megginson
Corporate Finance Theory

Melvin
International Money and Finance

Mishkin/Eakins
Financial Markets and Institutions

Moffett
Cases in International Finance

Moffett/Stonehill/Eiteman
Fundamentals of Multinational Finance

Nofsinger
Psychology of Investing

Ogden/Jen/O'Connor
Advanced Corporate Finance

Pennacchi
Theory of Asset Pricing

Rejda
Principles of Risk Management and Insurance

Schoenebeck
Interpreting and Analyzing Financial Statements

Scott/Martin/Petty/Keown/Thatcher
Cases in Finance

Seiler
Performing Financial Studies: A Methodological Cookbook

Shapiro
Capital Budgeting and Investment Analysis

Sharpe/Alexander/Bailey
Investments

Solnik/McLeavey
Global Investments

Stretcher/Michael
Cases in Financial Management

Titman/Martin
Valuation: The Art and Science of Corporate Investment Decisions

Trivoli
Personal Portfolio Management: Fundamentals and Strategies

Van Horne
Financial Management and Policy

Van Horne
Financial Market Rates and Flows

Van Horne/Wachowicz
Fundamentals of Financial Management

Vaughn
Financial Planning for the Entrepreneur

Welch
Corporate Finance: An Introduction*

Weston/Mulherin/Ahern
Takeovers, Restructuring, and Corporate Governance

Fundamentals of
INVESTING

ELEVENTH EDITION

LAWRENCE J. GITMAN, CFP®
San Diego State University

MICHAEL D. JOEHNK, CFA
Arizona State University

SCOTT B. SMART
Indiana University

Prentice Hall

Boston   Columbus   Indianapolis   New York   San Francisco   Upper Saddle River
Amsterdam   Cape Town   Dubai   London   Madrid   Milan   Munich   Paris   Montreal   Toronto
Delhi   Mexico City   Sao Paulo   Sydney   Hong Kong   Seoul   Singapore   Taipei   Tokyo

DEDICATED TO
ROBIN F. GITMAN,
CHARLENE W. JOEHNK,
AND SUSAN R. SMART

Editorial Director: Sally Yagan
Editor in Chief: Donna Battista
Acquisitions Editor: Noel Kamm Seibert
Director of Marketing: Patrice Jones
Senior Marketing Manager: Elizabeth A. Averbeck
Marketing Assistant: Ian Gold
Managing Editor: Nancy H. Fenton
Senior Production Project Manager: Nancy Freihofer
Project Manager: Kerri McQueen
Senior Manufacturing Buyer: Carol Melville
Permissions Project Supervisor: Michael Joyce
Cover Designer: Linda Knowles

Cover Photograph: © Frank Krahmer/ Getty Images
Media Director: Susan Schoenberg
Content Leads, MyFinanceLab: Douglas A. Ruby and Miguel Leonarte
Media Producer: Nicole Sackin
Supplements Editor: Alison Eusden
Text Design: Sally Steele
Production Coordination and Composition: Nesbitt Graphics, Inc.
Printer/Binder: Courier Kendallville
Cover Printer: Lehigh Phoenix
Text Font: Sabon

Credits and acknowledgments borrowed from other sources and reproduced, with permission, in this textbook appear on appropriate page within text and on pages C1–C2.

Library of Congress Cataloging-in-Publication Data

Gitman, Lawrence J.
    Fundamentals of investing / Lawrence J. Gitman, Michael D. Joehnk, Scott Smart. — 11th ed.
      p. cm.
    Includes bibliographical references and index.
    ISBN 0-136-11704-X; 978-0-136-11704-9 (alk. paper)
    1. Investments. 2. Portfolio management. 3. Investments—Problems, exercises, etc.
      I. Joehnk, Michael D.   II. Title.

  HG4521.G547   2011
  332.6--dc22

10 9 8 7 6 5 4 3

Prentice Hall
is an imprint of

www.pearsonhighered.com

ISBN 10: 0-136-11704-X
ISBN 13: 978-0-136-11704-9

Brief Contents

Contents

CHAPTER 3

Investment Information and Securities Transactions 68

ETHICS IN INVESTING
Did Martha Stewart Cross the
Line? PAGE 97

MARKETS IN CRISIS
Tech Stocks and Online Trading
Go Bust PAGE 101

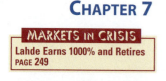

Part Four · Investing in Fixed-Income Securities · 361

CHAPTER 10 · Fixed-Income Securities 362

MARKETS IN CRISIS
Yield Spreads Approach Records   PAGE 365

MARKETS IN CRISIS
Rating Agencies Miss a Big One   PAGE 376

MARKETS IN CRISIS
Implicit Guarantee Becomes Explicit   PAGE 379

CHAPTER 11 · Bond Valuation 404

MARKETS IN CRISIS
Signs of a Recession
PAGE 406

Part Five

Portfolio Management   443

CHAPTER 12

MARKETS IN CRISIS
Mutual Fund Vulnerability
PAGE 446

ETHICS IN INVESTING
**When Mutual Funds Behaved
Badly** PAGE 450

Preface

" **Great firms aren't great investments unless the price is right.** " Those words of wisdom come from none other than Warren Buffett, who is, without question, one of the greatest investors ever. The words of Mr. Buffett sum up very nicely the essence of this book—namely, to help students learn to make *informed investment decisions*, not only when buying stocks, but also when investing in bonds, mutual funds, or any other type of investment.

The fact is, investing may sound simple, but it's not. Investors in today's turbulent financial markets confront many challenges when deciding how to invest their money. After the 2008 meltdown in financial markets, investors have become more wary of risk than they have been in many years. This book is designed to help students understand the risks inherent in investing and to give them the tools they need to answer the fundamental questions that help shape a sound investment strategy. For example, students want to know, what are the best investments for me? Should I buy individual securities or mutual funds? What's the market outlook in the next few years? What about risk? Do I need professional help with my investments, and can I afford it? Clearly, investors need answers to questions like these to make informed decisions.

The language, concepts, vehicles, and strategies of investing are foreign to many. In order to become informed investors, students must first become conversant with the many aspects of investing. Building on that foundation, they can learn how to make informed decisions in the highly dynamic investment environment. This eleventh edition of *Fundamentals of Investing* provides the information and guidance needed by individual investors to make such informed decisions and to achieve their investment goals.

This book meets the needs of professors and students in the first investments course offered at colleges and universities, junior and community colleges, professional certification programs, and continuing education courses. Focusing on both individual securities and portfolios, *Fundamentals of Investing* explains how to develop, implement, and monitor investment goals after considering the risk and return of both markets and investment vehicles. A conversational tone and liberal use of examples guide students through the material and demonstrate important points.

New for the Eleventh Edition

Our many adopters are interested in how we have changed the content from the tenth to the eleventh edition. We hope that that this same information will also interest potential adopters, because it indicates our mandate to stay current in the field of investments and to continue to craft a book that will truly meet the needs of students and professors.

The most dramatic change in the eleventh edition is the addition of **Scott Smart** to the author team. Scott received his Ph.D. from Stanford University in 1991, and he has been a member of the finance faculty at Indiana University since then. His scholarly articles have appeared in the *Journal of Financial Economics, Financial Management,* the *Financial Review,* the *Journal of Accounting and Economics,* and other scholarly journals. He has been recognized as an outstanding teacher by *Business Week*, and he has won more than a dozen teaching awards. Readers will see Scott's imprint on every page.

The table on pages xxi–xxiii outlines in detail the chapter-by-chapter revisions we have made to the eleventh edition and the benefits that we think accrue as a result of these changes. Some of the major changes made in the eleventh edition are the following:

- Updated all real-world data through 2008 or early 2009, including text, tables, and figures.

- Updated numerous Investor Facts boxes from the tenth edition and incorporated entirely new ones in each chapter.

- Added a new Markets in Crisis feature highlighting various aspects of the recent financial crisis and recession.

- Step-by-step video tutorials featuring author Scott Smart can be found in MyFinanceLab as a learning aid for select end-of-chapter questions.

- Added a new feature on MyFinanceLab called Smart's Tour of the Web, which features interesting and useful websites related to investments topics. This feature replaces the former Hotlinks boxes which appeared in the margins of the tenth edition, resulting in a more streamlined appearance in this edition.

- Expanded the use of real-world data in examples.

- Expanded and updated coverage of behavioral finance, particularly but not exclusively in Chapter 9.

- Revised or replaced every chapter opener, and in many chapters, included an end-of-chapter problem, chapter-opening problem, that ties back to the chapter opener.

- Added a list of key terms at the end of each chapter, to help students focus on vocabulary to master. Additionally, the end-of-chapter summary and key terms are now presented in an easy-to-read table that helps students focus on what they need to know and where to go in MyFinanceLab for additional help and practice.

Hallmarks of *Fundamentals of Investing*

Using information gathered from both academicians and practicing investment professionals, plus feedback from adopters, the eleventh edition reflects the realities of today's investment environment. At the same time, the following characteristics provide a structured framework for successful teaching and learning.

Clear Focus on the Individual Investor

Today, about half of all U.S. households own stock either directly or indirectly through mutual funds or participation in 401(k)s. That percentage has been growing for many years and is likely to continue to do so despite the upheaval in the U.S. stock market in 2008. The focus of *Fundamentals of Investing* has always been on the individual investor. This focus gives students the information they need to develop, implement, and monitor a successful investment program. It also provides students with a solid foundation of basic concepts, tools, and techniques. Subsequent courses can build on that foundation by presenting the advanced concepts, tools, and techniques used by institutional investors and money managers.

Comprehensive Yet Flexible Organization

The text provides a firm foundation for learning by first describing the overall investment environment, including the various investment markets, information, and transactions. Next, it presents conceptual tools needed by investors—the concepts of return and risk and the basic approaches to portfolio management. It then examines the most popular types of investments—common stocks, bonds, and mutual funds. Following this series of chapters on investment vehicles is a chapter on how to construct and administer one's own portfolio. The final section of the book focuses on derivative securities—options and futures—which require more expertise. Although the first two parts of the textbook are best covered at the start of the course, instructors can cover particular investment types in just about any sequence. The comprehensive yet flexible nature of the book enables instructors to customize it to their own course structure and teaching objectives.

We have organized each chapter according to a decision-making perspective, and we have been careful always to point out the pros and cons of the various vehicles and strategies we present. With this information, individual investors can select the investment actions that are most consistent with their objectives. In addition, we have presented the various investment vehicles and strategies in such a way that students learn the decision-making implications and consequences of each investment action they contemplate.

Timely Topics

Various issues and developments constantly reshape financial markets and investment vehicles. Virtually all topics in this book take into account changes in the investment environment. For example, in every chapter we've included a new feature called *Markets in Crisis*. This feature highlights various aspects of the recent and historic financial crisis, the government's response to that crisis, and the deep recession that followed the crisis. Fundamentally, investing is about the tradeoff between risk and return, and the Markets in Crisis feature serves as a reminder to students that they should not focus exclusively on an investment's returns.

Globalization

One issue that is reshaping the world of investing is the growing globalization of securities markets. As a result, *Fundamentals of Investing* continues to stress the global aspects of investing. We initially look at the growing importance of international markets, investing in foreign securities (directly or indirectly), international investment performance, and the risks of international investing. In later chapters, we describe popular international investment opportunities and strategies as part of the coverage of each specific type of investment vehicle. This integration of international topics helps students understand the importance of maintaining a global focus when planning, building, and managing an investment portfolio. Global topics are highlighted by a globe icon in the margin.

Comprehensive, Integrated Learning System

Another feature of the eleventh edition is its comprehensive and integrated learning system, which makes clear to students what they need to learn in the chapter and helps them focus their study efforts as they progress through the chapter. For more detailed discussion of the learning system, see the feature walkthrough later in the preface (beginning on page xxiv).

CFA Questions

We are pleased to include CFA questions in the eleventh edition. CFA exam questions appear at the end of five of the book's six parts. Due to the nature of the material in some of the early chapters, the CFA questions for Parts One and Two are combined and appear at the end of Part Two. These questions offer students an opportunity to test their investment knowledge against that required for the CFA Level I exam. These questions are taken from the 2010 Level I curriculum and the *CFA Candidate Study Notes, Level 1, Volume 4*, by Cengage Learning. Answers are included for immediate reinforcement.

myfinancelab

MyFinanceLab is a fully integrated online homework and tutorial system. MyFinanceLab offers flexible instructor tools like the easy-to-use homework manager for test, quiz, or homework assignments, automatic grading, and a powerful online Gradebook. Students can take pre-loaded Sample Tests for each chapter and their results generate an individualized Study Plan that helps focus and maximize their study time. Students will find ample opportunities to solve problems (some with help from author Scott Smart on video) and to explore investments-related content on the Internet through features like Smart's Tour of the Web. Please visit www.myfinancelab.com for more information or to register.

Online Trading and Investment Simulator—OTIS

A component of our teaching and learning system is OTIS, a powerful trading and investment simulator, developed at the Alfred P. West, Jr., Learning Lab at the Wharton School of the University of Pennsylvania. This Web-based simulator makes the student a virtual fund manager. The simulator enables students to make trades, view holdings, assess performance, and evaluate performance against that of classmates. Through activities in OTIS, students can experience the mechanics, risks, and requirements of margin trading; appreciate the benefits of short selling; grasp the concept of liquidity as it applies to meeting short- and long-term needs; and learn how to construct and manage portfolios. OTIS will quickly propel students into a hands-on, interactive learning environment.

REVISIONS	BENEFITS

PART ONE: Preparing to Invest

	REVISIONS	BENEFITS
Chapter 1 **The Investment** **Environment**	Added new section on career opportunities in the investments field. Added new Investor Facts box on the long-run performance of collectible stamps as an investment. Added new section discussing hedge funds and comparing them to mutual funds. Substantially revised section on Investments and the Business Cycle. Added new Markets in Crisis feature describing how governments around the world raised their deposit insurance limits to prevent bank runs during the financial crisis. Added new current and historical data on direct stock ownership around the world which highlight the declining role of individual investors and the increasing role of institutions in markets around the world.	Sets the scene for the course, with up-to-date information and greater clarity.
Chapter 2 **Securities Markets** **and Transactions**	Updated chapter-opener to better highlight the global nature of the New York Stock Exchange. Coverage of major stock exchanges reflects mergers and acquisitions in the industry that occurred since the tenth edition. Updated IPO data through 2008, and noted the near collapse of the IPO market in 2007–2008. Added a new *Investor Fact* box on prohibitions on short sales during the financial crisis.	Focuses on the structure, operation, and regulation of the securities markets.
Chapter 3 **Investment** **Information and** **Securities** **Transactions**	Revised chapter opener. Added new information on some of the best free information sites and other popular investment sites. Updated data in discussions of market averages and indexes. Updated *Ethics in Investing* box about Martha Stewart and ImClone trading. Updated/added *Investor Facts* boxes on election returns. Added Investor Facts boxes describing research that documents the generally poor performance of online traders and investment clubs. Added Markets in Crisis feature describing the collapse of day trading following the tech-stock bubble's collapse in 2000.	Provides a clear and up-to-date description of the primary traditional and online sources of investment information. Outlines services available to individual investors.

PART TWO: Important Conceptual Tools

	REVISIONS	BENEFITS
Chapter 4 **Return and Risk**	Added new chapter opener that uses data on house prices to illustrate the link between risk and return in investments. A new exercise at the end of the chapter ties back to the data in the opener. Added a longer time series of historical Investment returns that also includes some foreign markets. In many places throughout the chapter replaced hypothetical data with real-world examples. New Markets In Crisis features explain that the inflation rate in the United States briefly turned negative during the recent recession and that firms made unusually large dividend cuts during that period. Moved away from using financial tables for time value of money problems in favor of using algebra, financial calculators, or Excel. Added new Investor Facts box describing Treasury Inflation-Protected Securities (TIPS).	Revised chapter better highlights the core concepts of return and risk. Separate appendix on time value of money allows those who do not want to cover this topic to isolate it.
Chapter 5 **Modern Portfolio** **Concepts**	New chapter opener introduces the concept of beta, and a new end-of-chapter problem ties back to the opener. Extensively replaced hypothetical numbers with real-world data, both in text and in tables and figures. New Investment Facts box on the cost of investing in mutual funds in different countries. Markets In Crisis feature discusses that betas of financial institutions and auto firms spiked during the financial crisis and recession. Another new Investor Facts box cautions students by showing that different Internet sites report very different betas for the same companies.	Increases reader understanding of the key concepts underlying modern portfolio theory.

REVISIONS	BENEFITS

PART THREE: Investing in Common Stocks

**Chapter 6
Common Stocks**

New chapter opener describing GE's first dividend cut since the Great Depression and linking that to dividend reductions by many firms in 2008. A new end-of-chapter problem prompts students to calculate how much GE saved by cutting its dividend and how that compares to the loss in GE's market value when the cut was announced. Revised section on technology stock bubble to focus instead on real estate market bubble. Added new Investor Facts box about dividend practices around the world. Updated many figures and tables with more recent data. Added new Markets In Crisis feature on the recent bear market.

Presents clear view of the current investment environment and of the impact that the market and issues like dividends can have on investor returns.

**Chapter 7
Analyzing Common Stocks**

New chapter opener discusses the impact of an analyst's upgrade of Dell Computer on the firm's stock price. A new end-of-chapter problem asks students to verify whether one of the analyst's predictions came true. New Markets In Crisis features discuss how a hedge fund manager earned spectacular returns betting against real-estate-backed securities and how the crisis led to liquidity problems at certain firms. Updated Ethics in Investing box to reflect the recent Satyam Computer Services scandal in India.

Maintains a clear and well-defined focus on the role that the economy, the industry, and the company play in security analysis and stock valuation.

**Chapter 8
Stock Valuation**

New chapter opener shows how information revealed by Winn-Dixie corporate executives caused a dramatic drop in the stock price. A new end-of-chapter problem asks students to use information revealed in the call to estimate the value of Winn-Dixie stocks in different ways. A new figure and accompanying Markets In Crisis feature show the P/E ratio of the S&P500 over a long time horizon and how that ratio spiked during the recent market crisis as corporate earnings fell sharply. New Investor Facts box applies the dividend growth model to value a company that paid a constant dividend for many years.

Provides a concise discussion of fundamental analysis and valuation, from the generation of the variables used in the valuation process to the various stock valuation models.

**Chapter 9
Market Efficiency, Behavioral Finance, and Technical Analysis**

Changed chapter title to reflect new structure and emphasis on behavioral finance. New chapter opener uses the TV show Who Wants to be a Millionaire to illustrate that the consensus opinion of a large group is likely to be right most of the time. This illustrates the principle of market efficiency. New Markets in Crisis feature offers a behavioral finance explanation of why transactions volume dries up in real estate markets when prices fall. Updated Investor Facts box on returns during the third year of a president's term. Most importantly, behavioral finance material updated and expanded.

Focuses on market behavior, the principles and procedures used to assess the market, and the major theories that describe how prices are set in the market and how investors select securities.

PART FOUR: Investing in Fixed-Income Securities

**Chapter 10
Fixed-Income Securities**

New chapter opener discusses the loss of a AAA credit rating by GE and Berkshire Hathaway and discusses the broader pattern of downgrades during the recession. An end-of-chapter problem links back to the opener by asking students to examine a time series graph of rating upgrades and downgrades and to comment on the patterns revealed in that graph. A new Markets in Crisis feature discusses the near-record levels of junk bond spreads in 2008. Several tables and figures have updated data on bond returns. Updated Investor Facts box on junk bonds. New Markets in Crisis feature discusses how rating agencies failed to warn investors about the credit quality of "toxic" mortgage-backed debt. Another Markets in Crisis feature explains the government takeover of Fannie Mae and Freddie Mac.

Explains the practical side of the bond market and emphasizes the variables that drive bond price behavior and the wide array of securities available in the bond market.

	REVISIONS	BENEFITS
Chapter 11 Bond Valuation	New chapter opener discusses how U.S. interest rates fell to nearly 0% during the recession. Introduced effective duration to complement existing coverage of other duration concepts. Revised numerous figures and tables. Substantially revised discussion of the expectations hypothesis. New Markets in Crisis feature discusses the predictive link between yield curve inversions and subsequent recessions.	Increases readers' understanding of the principles and properties of bond valuation, as well as the uses and limitations of the popular yield and price volatility measures.

PART FIVE: Portfolio Management

	REVISIONS	BENEFITS
Chapter 12 Mutual Funds: Professionally Managed Portfolios	Updated chapter opener on Vanguard 500 Index fund. Updated all mutual fund performance data and market statistics through 2008 or early 2009. New Markets in Crisis feature discusses the impact of the financial crisis and recession on the mutual fund industry. New Investor Facts box describes long-term downward trend in costs associated with mutual fund investments.	Maintains the strong focus on mutual funds as investment vehicles, the roles that these securities can play in an investment program, and the mutual fund selection process.
Chapter 13 Managing Your Own Portfolio	Updated chapter opener on Warren Buffett. Updated several Investor Facts boxes to reflect more recent data and trends. New Markets in Crisis feature outlines how the financial crisis and market meltdown have led many baby boomers to delay retirement.	Gives readers insight into asset allocation and how to evaluate, monitor, and assess the performance of both individual investments and portfolios.

PART SIX: Derivative Securites

	REVISIONS	BENEFITS
Chapter 14 Options: Puts and Calls	New chapter opener explain how a CEO offered to work for a salary of $1 in exchange for a large stock options grant. New end-of-chapter problem asks students to calculate the value of these options several months after the deal was struck. Added new section on Black and Scholes option pricing model. New Markets in Crisis illustrates how the VIX market volatility index shot up during the financial crisis. New Ethics in Investing box discusses the recent widespread optoins backdating scandal. Updated Investor Facts box on options trading volume.	Clearly presents how options are valued and how the options market works. Increases understanding of the uses of various types of options as investment vehicles.
Chapter 15 Commodities and Financial Futures	Updated chapter opener. Numerous updates to tables and figures. New Investor Facts box on weather futures contracts. Updated Ethics in Investing box to reflect the fate of the principal figures in the Enron scandal. New Markets in Crisis features shows the turbulence in the oil futures markets in 2007–2008.	Focuses on the basic properties and uses of commodities and financial futures.

WEB CHAPTERS

	REVISIONS	BENEFITS
Chapter 16 Investing in Preferred Stocks	New chapter opener and Investor Facts box. Numerous minor changes throughout chapter.	Describes the basic features of preferred stock. Addresses valuation and investment strategies for preferred stock.
Chapter 17 Tax-Advantaged Investments	New chapter opener. Updates throughout to reflect changes in tax laws.	Presents tax fundamentals and basic strategies for tax avoidance, tax deferral, and how to earn tax-favored income.
Chapter 18 Real Estate and Other Tangible Investments	Updated chapter opener to include more recent data. New Markets in Crisis feature focusing on decline in REITs in recent years. Updates to Investor Facts boxes, tables, and figures.	Describes and demonstrates valuation techniques for real estate. Discusses the appeal of REITs. Presents tangible investments such as precious metals.

The Gitman,
Joehnk & Smart

PROVEN
TEACHING/LEARNING/MOTIVATIONAL
SYSTEM

Users of *Fundamentals of Investing* have praised the effectiveness of the Gitman/Joehnk/Smart teaching and learning system, which has been hailed as one of its hallmarks. In the eleventh edition we have retained and polished the system, which is driven by a set of carefully developed learning goals. Users have also praised the rich motivational framework that underpins each chapter. Key elements of the pedagogical and motivational features are illustrated and described below.

THE LEARNING GOAL SYSTEM

The Learning Goal system begins each chapter with **six Learning Goals**, labeled with numbered icons. These goals anchor the most important concepts and techniques to be learned. The Learning Goal icons are then tied to key points in the chapter's structure, including

- First-level headings
- Summary
- Discussion Questions
- Problems
- Cases

This tightly knit structure provides a clear roadmap for students—they know what they need to learn, where they can find it, and whether they've mastered it by the end of the chapter.

An **opening story** sets the stage for the content that follows by focusing on an investment situation involving a real company or real event, which is in turn linked to the chapter topics. Students see the relevance of the vignette to the world of investments.

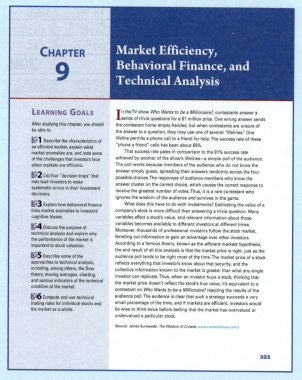

In many cases, an end-of-chapter problem draws students back to the chapter opener and asks them to use the data in the opener to make a calculation or draw a conclusion to demonstrate what they learned in the chapter.

MORE LEARNING TOOLS

ETHICS IN INVESTING

Did Martha Stewart Cross the Line?

On March 5, 2004, a jury returned a guilty verdict convicting homemaking queen Martha Stewart and her former stockbroker, Peter Bacanovic, of obstructing justice and lying about a well-timed stock sale. According to the prosecution, Martha Stewart committed illegal insider trading when she sold stock in biotech company ImClone Systems and then made false statements to federal investigators. The government also accused Stewart and Bacanovic of creating an alibi for her ImClone sales and attempting to obstruct justice during investigations into her trades. Stewart found herself tarred by the scandal, during which she resigned as chair of the board and CEO of her company. In addition, the stock of her company dropped more that 20%, and her holdings took nearly a $200 million hit, wiping out more than a quarter of her net worth.

The government alleged that Bacanovic tipped off Stewart that two of his other clients, ImClone's CEO Samuel Waksal and Waksal's daughter, had just placed orders to sell their ImClone stock. Waksal, a long-time friend of Stewart, had obtained information that the U.S. Food and Drug Administration (FDA) was about to reject ImClone's new cancer product, Erbitux. Stewart promptly sold all 3,928 shares of her ImClone stock, thus avoiding about $50,000 in losses. The very next day, ImClone announced that the FDA had rejected its application for Erbitux. Quickly, the price of ImClone stock dropped 16%, to $46 per share. According to authorities, Stewart and Bacanovic fabricated an alibi for Stewart's trades—that she and her broker had decided earlier that she would sell if the price fell below $60 per share.

As a result of the conviction, Martha Stewart spent five months in jail and another five months under house arrest. Interestingly, she was not convicted on a more serious charge of insider trading—which the judge dismissed—but for obstructing the federal investigation. By an ironic twist of fate, in February 2004 the drug at the heart of the scandal received FDA approval to treat certain forms of cancer.

Critical Thinking Question In light of the *Insider Trading and Fraud Act of 1988*, does Martha Stewart, or any other investor, have the right to sell stock any time a broker advises him or her to?

Although her incarceration ended on March 4, 2005, and her house arrest was complete five months later, it was not until August 2006 that the Securities and Exchange Commission announced that it had reached an agreement with Stewart on a settlement of the civil case against her. Under the settlement, Stewart agreed to a five-year ban from serving as a director, as a CEO, as a CFO, or in any officer role, where she would be responsible for preparing, auditing, or disclosing financial results, of any public company. Thus, not until late 2011 will Stewart be eligible to again serve as the chairwoman, president, and CEO of her own company.

Ethics boxes—short, boxed discussions of real-life scenarios in the investments world that focus on ethics—appear in eight selected chapters and on the book's Web site. Many ethics boxes contain a Critical Thinking Question for class discussion, with guideline answers given in the Instructor's Manual.

Each chapter features a short **Markets in Crisis** item that discusses some element of the recent financial crisis and the recession that followed. These items help students see the breadth of the financial crisis and the depth of its impact around the world.

MARKETS IN CRISIS

Bulging Betas

Ford Motor Company has always been considered a cyclical stock whose fortunes rise and fall with the state of the economy. But as the table on page 177 shows, in August 2009 Yahoo! Finance reported a beta for Ford Motor of 2.80, indicating that Ford common stock was extremely sensitive to movements in the broad market. That high sensitivity was a result of the financial crisis and recession from 2007–2009, which hit automakers hard and prompted them to seek government assistance.

Ford's high beta in 2009 meant that investors believed the company would rebound quickly if and when the economy improved, but if the economy failed to improve, Ford might find itself in bankruptcy with General Motors, which had filed for bankruptcy a few months earlier. Notice that Bank of America, another firm in an industry hit hard by the recession, had a beta in 2009 of 2.61, indicating that it too was extremely sensitive to movements in the overall economy.

Each chapter contains a handful of **Investor Facts**—brief sidebar items that give an interesting statistic or cite an unusual investment experience. These facts add a bit of seasoning to the concepts under review and capture a real-world flavor. Among the many snapshots provided by the Investor Facts are recent increases in dividend payouts, costs of mutual funds that trade globally, indicators of poor financial health, and free cash flow.

INVESTOR FACTS

WRESTLE WITH DIVIDENDS— In August 2009, the stock of World Wrestling Entertainment (WWE) sold for about $15 per share, exactly the same price that an investor would have paid to buy it a year earlier in August 2008. Although it might appear that WWE investors made no money during that time, in fact, WWE paid quarterly dividends totalling $1.44, which represented a return of 9.6% on a $15 investment.

Key Equations are screened in green throughout the text to help readers identify the most important mathematical relationships.

Equation 4.1	$\dfrac{\text{Required return}}{\text{on investment } j} = \dfrac{\text{Real rate}}{\text{of return}} + \dfrac{\text{Expected inflation}}{\text{premium}} + \dfrac{\text{Risk premium}}{\text{for investment } j}$
Equation 4.1a	$r_i = r^* + IP + RP_i$

Calculator Keystrokes At appropriate spots in the text the student will find sections on the use of financial calculators, with marginal calculator graphics that show the inputs and functions to be used.

Smart's Tour of the Web is a short video discussion (included as part of MyFinanceLab) of several Web sites that have useful information related to content in each chapter.

Smart's Tour of the Web
To watch author Scott Smart discuss key websites for this chapter visit www.myfinancelab.com

Concepts in Review questions appear at the end of each section of the chapter. These review questions allow students to test their understanding of each section before moving on to the next section of the chapter. Answers for these questions are available at the book's Web site, and by review of the preceding text.

CONCEPTS IN REVIEW
Answers available at www.pearsonhighered.com/gitman

3.1 Discuss the impact of the Internet on the individual investor and summarize the types of resources it provides.

3.2 Identify the four main types of online investment tools. How can they help you become a better investor?

3.3 What are some of the pros and cons of using the Internet to choose and manage your investments?

STILL MORE LEARNING TOOLS

The **end-of-chapter summary** makes *Fundamentals of Investing* an efficient study tool by integrating chapter contents with online learning resources available in **MyFinanceLab**. A thorough summary of the key concepts—What You Should Know—is directly linked with the text and online resources—Where To Practice. **Learning Goal** icons precede each summary item which begins with a bold-faced restatement of the learning goal.

myfinancelab

Here is what you should know after reading this chapter. **MyFinanceLab** will help you identify what you know, and where to go when you need to practice.

What You Should Know	Key Terms	Where To Practice
LG1 Identify the basic types of securities markets and describe their characteristics. Short-term investment vehicles trade in the money market; longer-term securities, such as stocks and bonds, trade in the capital market. New security issues are sold in the primary market. Investors buy and sell existing securities in the secondary markets.	ask price, p. 41 bear markets, p. 43 bid price, p. 41 broker market, p. 38 bull markets, p. 43 capital market, p. 33 dealer market, p. 38	MyFinanceLab Study Plan 2.1
LG2 Explain the initial public offering (IPO) process. The first public issue of a company's common stock is an initial public offering (IPO). The company selects an investment banker to sell the IPO. The lead investment banker may form a syndicate with other investment bankers and then create a selling group to sell the issue. The IPO process includes filing a registration statement with the Securities and Exchange Commission (SEC), getting SEC approval, promoting the offering to investors, pricing the issue, and selling the shares.	designated market maker (DMM), p. 40 dual listing, p. 40 electronic communications network (ECN), p. 43 fourth market, p. 43 initial public offering (IPO), p. 33 investment banker, p. 34 market makers, p. 38 money market, p. 33	MyFinanceLab Study Plan 2.2
LG3 Describe broker markets and dealer markets, and discuss how they differ from alternative trading systems. In dealer markets, buy/sell orders are executed by market makers. The market makers are securities dealers who "make markets" by offering to buy or sell certain securities at stated bid/ask prices. Dealer markets also serve as primary markets for both IPOs and secondary distributions. Over-the-counter transactions in listed securities take place in the third market. Direct transactions between buyers and sellers are made in the fourth market. Market conditions are commonly classified as "bull" or "bear," depending on whether securities prices are generally rising or falling.	Nasdaq market, p. 38 over-the-counter (OTC) market, p. 38 primary market, p. 33 private placement, p. 33 prospectus, p. 34 public offering, p. 33 red herring, p. 34 rights offering, p. 33 secondary distributions, p. 41 secondary market, p. 37	MyFinanceLab Study Plan 2.3

Discussion Questions, keyed to Learning Goals, guide students to integrate, investigate, and analyze the key concepts presented in the chapter. Many questions require that students apply the tools and techniques of the chapter to investment information they have obtained, and then make a recommendation with regard to a specific investment strategy or vehicle. These project-type questions are far broader than the Concepts in Review questions within the chapter. Answers to odd-numbered questions are available to students at the book's Web site.

Discussion Questions

LG1 Q6.1 Look at the record of stock returns in Table 6.1, particularly the return performance during the 1970s, 1980s, 1990s, and 2000–2008.

a. How would you compare the returns during the 1970s with those produced in the 1980s? How would you characterize market returns in the 1990s? Is there anything that stands out about this market? How does it compare with the market that existed from early 2000 through 2008?

b. Considering the average annual returns that have been generated over holding periods of five years or more, what rate of return do you feel is typical for the stock market in general? Is it unreasonable to expect this kind of return, on average, in the future? Explain.

LG2 Q6.2 Given the information in the *Wall Street Journal* quote in Figure 6.4 (page 216), answer the following questions for Harley Davidson Inc.

a. On what day did the trading activity occur?

b. At what price did the stock sell at the end of the day on Thursday, September 3, 2009?

c. What is the firm's price/earnings ratio? What does that indicate?

d. What is the last price at which the stock traded on the date quoted?

e. What was the divide payout per share for the previous year?

f. What are the highest and lowest prices at which the stock traded during the latest 52-week period?

Expanded Problem Sets—offer additional review and homework opportunities and are keyed to Learning Goals. Answers to odd-numbered Problems are available to students at the book's Web site, while all answers/solutions are available for instructors in the Instructor's Manual.

Problems

All problems are available on **www.myfinancelab.com**

LG3 P6.1 An investor owns some stock in General Refrigeration & Cooling. The stock recently underwent a 5-for-2 stock split. If the stock was trading at $50 per share just before the split, how much is each share most likely selling for after the split? If the investor owned 200 shares of the stock before the split, how many shares would she own afterward?

LG3 P6.2 An investor deposits $20,000 into a new brokerage account. The investor buys 1,000 shares of Tipco stock for $19 per share. Two weeks later, the investor sells the Tipco stock for $20 per share. When the investor receives his brokerage account statement, he sees that there is a balance of $20,900 in his account:

Item	Number	Price per Share	Total Transaction	Account Balance
1. Deposit			$20,000	$20,000
2. Tipco purchase	1,000 shares	$19	($19,000)	$20,000
3. Tipco sale	1,000 shares	$20	$20,000	$21,000
4.				
5. Balance				$20,900

What belongs in item 4 on this statement?

Two **Case Problems**, keyed to the Learning Goals, encourage students to use higher-level critical thinking skills: to apply techniques presented in the chapter, to evaluate alternatives, and to recommend how an investor might solve a specific problem. Again, Learning Goals show the student the chapter topics on which the case problems focus.

Case Problem 2.1   *Dara's Dilemma: What to Buy?*

LG6

Dara Simmons, a 40-year-old financial analyst and divorced mother of two teenage children, considers herself a savvy investor. She has increased her investment portfolio considerably over the past five years. Although she has been fairly conservative with her investments, she now feels more confident in her investment knowledge and would like to branch out into some new areas that could bring higher returns. She has between $20,000 and $25,000 to invest.

Attracted to the hot market for technology stocks, Dara was interested in purchasing a tech IPO stock and identified "NewestHighTech.com," a company that makes sophisticated computer chips for wireless Internet connections, as a likely prospect. The one-year-old company had received some favorable press when it got early-stage financing and again when its chip was accepted by a major cell phone manufacturer.

Dara also was considering an investment in 400 shares of Casinos International common stock, currently selling for $54 per share. After a discussion with a friend who is an economist with a major commercial bank, Dara believes that the long-running bull market is due to cool off and that economic activity will slow down. With the aid of her stockbroker, Dara researches Casinos International's current financial situation and finds that the future success of the company may hinge on the outcome of pending court proceedings on the firm's application to open a new floating casino on a nearby river. If the permit is granted, it seems likely that the firm's stock will experience a rapid increase in value, regardless of economic conditions. On the other hand, if the company fails to get the permit, the falling stock price will make it a good candidate for a short sale.

Dara felt that the following alternatives were open to her:

Alternative 1: Invest $20,000 in NewestHighTech.com when it goes public.

Alternative 2: Buy Casinos International now at $54 per share and follow the company closely.

Excel with Spreadsheets problems, appearing at the end of all chapters, challenge students to solve financial problems and make decisions through the creation of spreadsheets. In Chapter 1 students are directed to the Web site, **www.myfinancelab.com**, where they can complete a spreadsheet tutorial, if needed. In addition, this tutorial and selected tables within the text carrying a spreadsheet icon are available in spreadsheet form on the text's Web site.

Excel with Spreadsheets

You have just learned about the mechanics of margin trading and want to take advantage of the potential benefits of financial leverage. You have decided to open a margin account with your broker and to secure a margin loan. The specifics of the account are as follows:

- Initial margin requirement is 70%.

- Maintenance margin is 30%.

- You are informed that if the value of your account falls below the maintenance margin, your account will be subject to a margin call.

You have been following the price movements of a stock over the past year and believe that it is currently undervalued and that the price will rise in the near future. You feel that the opening of a margin account is a good investment strategy. You have decided to purchase three round lots (i.e., 100 shares per round lot) of the stock at its current price of $25 per share.

Create a spreadsheet similar to the spreadsheet for Table 2.3, which can be viewed at www. myfinancelab.com, to model and analyze the following market transactions.

Questions

a. Calculate the value of the investment in the stock as if you did not make use of margin trading. In other words, what is the value of the investment if it is funded by 100% cash equity?

b. Calculate the debit balance and the cash equity in the investment at the time of opening a margin account, adhering to the initial margin requirement.

c. If you use margin and the price of the stock rises by $15 to $40/share, calculate the capital gain earned and the return on investor's equity.

d. What is the current margin percentage based on question **b**?

e. If you use margin and the price of the stock falls by $15 to $10/share, calculate the capital loss and the respective return on investor's equity.

f. What is the new margin percentage based on question **e**, and what is the implication for you, the investor?

New to this edition, **CFA questions** from 2010 Level One Curriculum and the *CFA Candidate Study Notes, Level 1, Volume 4* (Cengage Learning) are now at the end of each part of the book, starting at Part Two. These questions are also assignable in MyFinanceLab.

INTERACTIVE LEARNING

myfinancelab is a fully integrated homework and tutorial system which solves one of the biggest teaching problems in finance courses—students learn better with lots of practice, but grading complex multipart problems is time-consuming for the instructor. In MyFinanceLab, students can work the end-of-chapter problems with algorithmically-generated values for unlimited practice and instructors can create assignments that are automatically graded and recorded in an online Gradebook.

New in the eleventh edition, MyFinanceLab contains brief videos of author Scott Smart walking students through step-by-step solutions of select end-of-chapter problems.

MyFinanceLab: hands-on practice, hands-off grading.

Trading Online with OTIS. The world of electronic investing comes alive with the addition of OTIS—the Online Trading and Investment Simulator, developed at the Alfred West, Jr. Learning Lab at the Wharton School of the University of Pennsylvania. OTIS, enables students to become "fund managers" and to buy and sell equities using real data from today's markets. By doing the OTIS activities, students learn such key concepts as portfolio management, benchmarking, liquidity, and pricing in a hands-on environment. Instructors have the option to bundle OTIS with the textbook. Please contact your local Pearson sales rep for more details, or visit **www.pearsonhighered.com/wharton**

Supplemental Materials

We recognize the key role of a complete and creative package of materials to supplement a basic textbook. We believe that the following materials, offered with the eleventh edition, will enrich the investments course for both students and instructors.

Fundamentals of Investing Companion Website

The book's Companion Website offers students and professors an up-to-date source of supplemental materials. This resource is located at **www.pearsonhighered.com/gitman**. Visitors will find calculator keystrokes tutorials; answers to concepts in review; answers to odd-numbered Discussion Questions and Problems; and other readings and material that are beyond the normal scope of the first-level investments course.

Also at the book's Web site are three complete chapters that appeared in the book in earlier editions: "Investing in Preferred Stocks," "Tax-Advantaged Investments," and "Real Estate and Other Tangible Investments." These highly informative chapters have been substantively updated and moved to the Web site in response to user, reviewer, and our own preference that the text focus solely on securities investing. In addition to its improved focus, moving these chapters to the Web site allows us both to tighten and improve a number of text discussions and to shorten the text's overall length. We feel this change improves the text's effectiveness in terms of both content and length.

Study Guide

The Study Guide to accompany *Fundamentals of Investing,* Eleventh Edition, prepared by Karin B. Bonding, CFA, lecturer at the McIntire School at University of Virginia and President of Capital Markets Institute, Inc., Ivy, Virginia, has been completely revised. Each chapter of the *Study Guide* contains a chapter summary, a chapter outline, and a self-test that consists of true-false and multiple-choice questions with answers. Also contained in the self-test are problems with detailed solutions and, where appropriate, calculator key strokes and/or Excel input to solve certain problems. All elements are similar in form and content to those found in the book.

Instructor's Manual

Revised by Joe Greco of California State University, Fullerton, the *Instructor's Manual* contains chapter outlines; lists of key concepts discussed in each chapter; detailed chapter overviews; answers/suggested answers to all Concepts in Review and Discussion Questions, Problems, and Critical Thinking Questions to *Ethics in Investing* boxes; solutions to the Case Problems; and ideas for outside projects. The Instructor's Manual is error-free thanks to accuracy checker Thomas Krueger of the University of Wisconsin-La Cross.

Test Item File

Revised for the eleventh edition by Robert J. Hartwig of Worcester State College, the *Test Item File* includes a substantial number of new questions. Each chapter features true-false and multiple-choice questions, as well as several problems and short-essay questions. The *Test Item File* is also available in Test Generator Software (TestGen with

QuizMaster). Fully networkable, this software is available for Windows and Macintosh. TestGen's graphical interface enables instructors to easily view, edit, and add questions; export questions to create tests; and print tests in a variety of fonts and forms. Search and sort features let the instructor quickly locate questions and arrange them in a preferred order. QuizMaster, working with your school's computer network, automatically grades the exams, stores results on disk, and allows the instructor to view or print a variety of reports.

PowerPoint Lecture Slides

To facilitate classroom presentations, PowerPoint slides of all text images and class-room lecture notes are available for Windows and Macintosh. A PowerPoint viewer is provided for use by those who do not have the full software program. The slides were revised by textbook author Scott Smart.

CourseSmart for Instructors

CourseSmart goes beyond traditional expectations providing instant, online access to the textbook's and course materials you need at a lower cost to students. And, even as students save money, you can save time and hassle with a digital textbook that allows you to search the most relevant content at the very moment you need it. Whether it's evaluating textbooks or creating lecture notes to help students with difficult concepts, CourseSmart can make life a little easier. See how when you visit **www.coursesmart.com/instructors**.

CourseSmart for Students

CourseSmart goes beyond traditional expectations providing instant, online access to the textbooks and course materials students need at a lower cost. They can also search, highlight, and take notes anywhere at any time. See all the benefits to students at **www.coursesmart.com/students**.

Acknowledgments

Many people gave their generous assistance during the initial development and revisions of *Fundamentals of Investing*. The expertise, classroom experience, and general advice of both colleagues and practitioners have been invaluable. Reactions and suggestions from students throughout the country—comments we especially enjoy receiving—sustained our belief in the need for a fresh, informative, and teachable investments text.

A few individuals provided significant subject matter expertise in the initial development of the book. They are Terry S. Maness of Baylor University, Arthur L. Schwartz, Jr., of the University of South Florida at St. Petersburg, and Gary W. Eldred. Their contributions are greatly appreciated. In addition, Pearson obtained the advice of a large group of experienced reviewers. We appreciate their many suggestions and criticisms, which have had a strong influence on various aspects of this volume. Our special thanks go to the following people, who reviewed all or part of the manuscript for the previous ten editions of the book.

Kevin Ahlgrim
M. Fall Ainina
Joan Anderssen
Felix O. Ayadi
Gary Baker
Harisha Batra
Richard B. Bellinfante
Cecil C. Bigelow
Robert J. Boldin
Paul Bolster
A. David Brummett
Gary P. Cain
Gary Carman
Daniel J. Cartell
P. R. Chandy
Steven P. Clark
David M. Cordell
Timothy Cowling
Robert M. Crowe
Richard F. DeMong
Clifford A. Diebold
James Dunn
Betty Marie Dyatt
Steven J. Elbert
Imad Elhaj
Thomas Eyssell
Frank J. Fabozzi
Robert A. Ford
Albert J. Fredman
John Gerlach

Tom Geurts
Chaim Ginsberg
Joel Gold
Terry Grieb
Frank Griggs
Brian Grinder
Harry P. Guenther
Tom Guerts
Robert Hartwig
Mahboubul Hassan
Gay Hatfield
Robert D. Hollinger
Sue Beck Howard
Roland Hudson, Jr.
Raad Jassim
Donald W. Johnson
Samuel Kyle Jones
Ravindra R. Kamath
Bill Kane
Daniel J. Kaufmann, Jr.
Nancy Kegelman
Phillip T. Kolbe
Sheri Kole
Christopher M. Korth
Marie A. Kratochvil
Thomas M. Krueger
George Kutner
Blake LeBaron
Robert T. LeClair
Chun I. Lee

William Lepley
Steven Lifland
Ralph Lim
James Lock
Larry A. Lynch
Weston A. McCormac
David J. McLaughlin
Anne Macy
James Mallett
Keith Manko
Timothy Manuel
Kathy Milligan
Warren E. Moeller
Homer Mohr
Majed R. Muhtaseb
Joseph Newhouse
Michael Nugent
Joseph F. Ollivier
Michael Palermo
John Palffy
John Park
Thomas Patrick
Michael Polakoff
Barbara Poole
Ronald S. Pretekin
Stephen W. Pruitt
S. P. Umamaheswar Rao
Rathin Rathinasamy
William A. Richard
Linda R. Richardson

William A. Rini
Roy A. Roberson
Edward Rozalewicz
William J. Ruckstuhl
David Russo
Arthur L. Schwartz, Jr.
William Scroggins
Daniel Singer
Keith V. Smith
Pat R. Stout
Nancy E. Strickler
Glenn T. Sweeney
Amir Tavakkol
Phillip D. Taylor
Wenyuh Tsay
Robert C. Tueting
Howard E. Van Auken
P. V. Viswanath
John R. Weigel
Sally Wells
Peter M. Wichert
John C. Woods
Michael D. Woodworth
Robert J. Wright
Richard H. Yanow
Ali E. Zadeh
Edward Zajicek

The following people provided extremely useful reviews and input to the eleventh edition:

Steven Dolvin, Butler University
Robert Eldridge, Southern Connecticut State University
Ping Hsiao, San Fransicso State University
Rajiv Kalra, Minnesota State University Moorhead
Burhan Kawosa, Wright State University
Wendy Ku, University of Illinois Chicago
Mark Pyles, College of Charleston
Tammy Rogers, University of Central Arkansas
Doug Waggle, University of West Florida

Because of the wide variety of topics covered in the book, we called upon many experts for advice. We thank them and their firms for allowing us to draw on their insights and awareness of recent developments, to ensure that the text is as current as possible. In particular, we want to mention Jeff Buetow, CFA, BFRC Services, Charlottesville, VA; Bill Bachrach, Bachrach & Associates, San Diego, CA; John Markese, President, American Association of Individual Investors, Chicago, IL; Frank Hatheway, CFA, Chief Economist, Nasdaq, New York, NY; George Ebenhack,

Oppenheimer & Co., Los Angeles, CA; Mark D. Erwin, ChFC, Commonwealth Financial Network, San Diego, CA; Martin P. Klitzner, Sunrise Capital Management, Del Mar, CA; David M. Love, C.P. Eaton and Associates, La Jolla, CA; David H. McLaughlin, Chase Investment Counsel Corp., Charlottesville, VA; Michael R. Murphy, Sceptre Investment Counsel, Toronto, Ontario, Canada; Mark S. Nussbaum, CFP®, Wells Fargo Advisors, Inc., La Jolla, CA; Richard Russell, Dow Theory Letters, La Jolla, CA; and Michael J. Steelman, Bank of America, San Diego, CA.

Special thanks to Karin Bonding of the University of Virginia for her excellent revision of the *Study Guide;* Robert Hartwig of Worcester State College for revising and updating the *Test Item File;* Joe Greco of California State University, Fullerton, for his revision of the *Instructor's Manual;* and Tom Krueger of the University of Wisconsin–La Crosse, for his thorough accuracy check of the material.

The staff at Pearson, particularly Noel Seibert, contributed their creativity, enthusiasm, and commitment to this textbook. Pearson Project Manager Kerri McQueen managed and pulled together the various strands of the project. Other dedicated Pearson staff, including production supervisor Nancy Freihofer, designer Linda Knowles, media producer Nicole Sackin, content lead for MyFinanceLab Miguel Leonarte, marketing manager Elizabeth Averbeck, and supplements coordinator Alison Eusden warrant special thanks for shepherding the project through the development, production, marketing, and Web site construction stages. Without their care and concern, this text would not have evolved into the teachable and interest text and package we believe it to be.

Finally, our wives, Robin, Charlene, and Susan, played important roles by providing support and understanding during the book's development, revision, and production. We are forever grateful to them, and we hope that this edition will justify the sacrifices required during the many hours we were away from them working on this book.

LAWRENCE J. GITMAN

MICHAEL D. JOEHNK

SCOTT B. SMART

Preparing to Invest

The Investment Environment

LEARNING GOALS

After studying this chapter, you should be able to:

LG1 Understand the meaning of the term *investment* and the factors used to differentiate types of investments.

LG2 Describe the investment process and types of investors.

LG3 Discuss the principal types of investments.

LG4 Describe the steps in investing, review fundamental tax considerations, and discuss investing over the life cycle.

LG5 Describe the most common types of short-term investments.

LG6 Describe some of the main careers open to people with financial expertise and the role that investments play in each.

You have worked hard for your money. Now it is time to make your money work for you. Welcome to the world of investments. There are literally thousands of investments, from all around the world, from which to choose. How much should you invest, when should you invest, and which investments are right for you? The answers depend upon the knowledge and financial circumstances of each individual investor.

There is plenty of financial news available, and finding that information has become easier than ever. At one time, the only exposure most people had to investment news was a 10-second announcement on the evening news about the change in the Dow Jones Industrial Average that day. Today, Americans are bombarded with financial news: Cable TV networks such as CNBC specialize in business and financial news, and network newscasters feature business news more prominently. In print, in addition to *The Wall Street Journal,* you can subscribe to *Investor's Business Daily, Barron's, Kiplinger's Personal Finance Magazine, Money, Smart Money,* and many other publications that focus on investing.

Today, approximately half of all Americans own stocks or stock mutual funds, and many of those people are new investors. The Internet has played a major role in opening the world of investing to them. It makes enormous amounts of information readily available and enables investors to trade securities with the click of a mouse button. In short, technology makes investing much easier. Access to tools formerly restricted to investment professionals helps create a more level playing field—yet at the same time, such easy access can increase the risks for inexperienced investors.

Regardless of whether you conduct transactions online or use a traditional broker, the same investment fundamentals apply. Chapter 1 introduces the various types of investments, the investment process, key investment vehicles, the role of investment plans, the importance of meeting liquidity needs, and careers in finance. Becoming familiar with investment alternatives and developing realistic investment plans should greatly increase your chance of achieving financial success.

Investments and the Investment Process

LG 1 LG 2

You are probably already an investor. If you have money in a savings account, you already have at least one investment to your name. An **investment** is simply any asset into which funds can be placed with the expectation that it will generate positive income and/or preserve or increase its value.

The rewards, or **returns**, from investing come in two basic forms: income and increased value. Money invested in a savings account provides *income* in the form of periodic interest payments. A share of common stock also provides income (in the form of dividends), but investors often buy stock because they expect its price to rise. That is, common stock offers both income and the chance of an *increased value*. Since 1900, the average annual return on a savings account has been a little more than 3%. The average annual return on common stock has been just over 11%. Of course, during major market downturns (such as the one that occurred in 2008), the returns on nearly all investment vehicles fall well below these long-term historical averages.

Is cash placed in a simple (no-interest) checking account an investment? No, because it fails both tests of the definition: It does not provide added income, nor does its value increase. In fact, over time, inflation erodes the purchasing power of money left in a non-interest-bearing checking account.

We begin our study of investments by looking at types of investments and at the structure of the investment process.

Types of Investments

When you invest, the organization in which you invest—whether it is a company or a government entity—offers you an expected future benefit in exchange for the use of your funds. Organizations compete for the use of your funds. The one that will get your investment dollars is the one that offers a benefit you judge to be better than any competitor offers. Different investors judge benefits differently. As a result, investments of every type are available, from "sure things" such as earning 1% interest on your bank savings account to the possibility of tripling your money fast by investing in a newly issued biotech stock. The investments you choose will depend on your resources, your goals, and your willingness to take risk. We can differentiate types of investments on the basis of a number of factors.

Securities or Property **Securities** are investments issued by firms, governments, or other organizations that represent a financial claim on the resources of the issuer. The most common types of securities are stocks and bonds, but more exotic types, such as stock options, are available as well. The focus of this book is primarily on the most basic types of securities, particularly common stocks.

Property, on the other hand, consists of investments in real property or tangible personal property. *Real property* refers to land, buildings, and that which is permanently affixed to the land. *Tangible personal property* includes items such as gold, artwork, antiques, and other collectibles.

Direct or Indirect A **direct investment** is one in which an investor directly acquires a claim on a security or property. If you buy shares of common stock in a company such as IBM, then you have made a direct investment, and you are a part owner of that firm. Direct ownership of common stock has been on the decline in the United States for many years. For example, in 1945,

FIGURE 1.1

Direct Stock Ownership by Households

The figure shows the percentage of common stocks in each country that is owned directly by households. In most countries, households' direct ownership accounts for less than one-quarter of listed common stocks in the country. (Source: Kristian Rydqvist, Joshua Spizman, and Ilya Strebulav, "The Evaluation of Aggregate Stock Ownership: A Unified Explanation." CEPR Discussion Paper No. 7356, July 2009.)

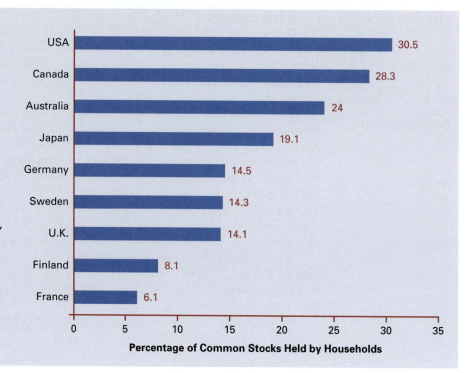

households owned (directly) 93.1% of all common stocks listed in the United States. By 2006, that percentage had dropped to just 30.5%. The same trend has occurred in most of the world's larger economies. Figure 1.1 shows the percentage of direct stock ownership by households in several different countries as of 2006.

An **indirect investment** is an investment in a collection of securities or properties managed by a professional investor. For example, when individuals send their money to a mutual fund company such as Vanguard or Fidelity, they are making indirect investments in the assets held by these mutual funds. Just as direct stock ownership by households has been falling, indirect ownership has been rising. One way to examine this trend is to look at the direct ownership held by institutions that manage money on behalf of households. In 1945, pension funds and mutual funds combined held just 1.5% of the outstanding stock in the United States, but by 2006, their direct ownership had risen to 43.1%.

Debt, Equity, or Derivative Securities Most investments fall into one of two broad categories—debt or equity. **Debt** is simply a loan that obligates the borrower to make periodic interest payments and to repay the full amount of the loan by some future date. When companies or governments need to borrow money, they issue debt instruments called *bonds*. When you buy a debt instrument such as a *bond*, in effect you lend money to the issuer. The issuer agrees to pay you interest for a specified time, at the end of which the issuer will repay the original loan.

Equity represents ongoing ownership in a business or property. An equity investment may be held as a security or by title to a specific property. The most common type of equity security is *common stock*.

Derivative securities are neither debt nor equity. Instead, they derive their value from an underlying security or asset. Stock *options* are an example. A stock option is an investment that grants the right to purchase (or sell) a share of stock in a company at a fixed price for a limited period of time. The value of this option depends on the market price of the underlying stock.

Low- or High-Risk Investments Investments also differ on the basis of risk. **Risk** reflects the uncertainty surrounding the return that a particular investment will generate. The broader the range of possible values or returns associated with an investment, the greater is its risk.

Investors are confronted with a continuum of investments that range from low risk to high risk. For example, stocks are generally considered riskier than bonds because stock returns vary over a much wider range and are harder to predict than are bond returns. However, it is not difficult to find high-risk bonds that are riskier than the stock of a financially sound firm.

Low-risk investments provide a relatively predictable, but also relatively low, return. *High-risk investments* provide much higher returns, on average, but they also have the potential for much larger losses. **Speculation** offers highly uncertain returns, and because of this greater risk, the returns associated with speculation are expected to be greater.

Short- or Long-Term Investments The life of an investment can be described as either short or long term. **Short-term investments** typically mature within one year. **Long-term investments** are those with longer maturities or, like common stock, with no maturity at all.

NOTE Discussions of international investing are highlighted by this icon.

Domestic or Foreign As recently as 25 years ago, U.S. citizens invested almost exclusively in purely **domestic investments**: the debt, equity, and derivative securities of U.S.-based companies and governments. Today, investors routinely also look for **foreign investments** (both direct and indirect) that might offer more attractive returns than purely domestic investments. Information on foreign companies is now readily available, and it is now relatively easy to make foreign investments.

The Structure of the Investment Process

The investment process brings together *suppliers* who have extra funds with *demanders* who need funds. Suppliers and demanders of funds usually come together by means of a financial institution or a financial market. **Financial institutions** are organizations, such as banks and insurance companies, that pool the savings of governments, businesses, and individuals and channel them into loans and other types of assets. **Financial markets** are forums in which suppliers and demanders of funds trade financial assets, typically with the assistance of intermediaries such as securities brokers and dealers. All types of investments, including stocks, bonds, commodities, and foreign currencies, trade in financial markets.

The dominant financial market in the United States is the *securities market*. It includes stock markets, bond markets, and options markets. Similar markets exist in most major economies throughout the world. Their common feature is that the price of an investment vehicle at any point in time results from an equilibrium between the forces of supply and demand. As new information about returns and risk becomes available, the changes in supply and demand may result in a new equilibrium or *market price*. Financial markets streamline the process of bringing together suppliers and

FIGURE 1.2

The Investment Process

Financial institutions participate in the financial markets as well as transfer funds between suppliers and demanders. Although the arrows go only from suppliers to demanders, for some transactions (e.g., the sale of a bond or a college loan), the principal amount borrowed by the demander from the supplier (the lender) is eventually returned.

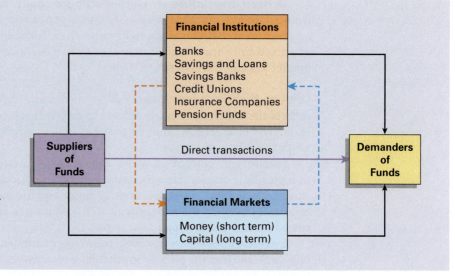

demanders of funds, and they allow transactions to be made quickly and at a fair price. They also publicize security prices.

Figure 1.2 is a diagram of the investment process. Note that the suppliers of funds may transfer their resources to the demanders through financial institutions, through financial markets, or in direct transactions. As the broken lines show, financial institutions can participate in financial markets as either suppliers or demanders of funds.

Suppliers and Demanders of Funds   Government, business, and individuals are the key participants in the investment process. Each may act as a supplier or a demander of funds. For the economy to grow and prosper, funds must flow to individuals and businesses with attractive investment opportunities. If individuals began suddenly hoarding their excess funds rather than putting them to work in financial institutions and markets, then organizations in need of funds would have difficulty obtaining them. As a result, government spending, business expansion, and consumer purchases would decline, and economic activity would slow.

Government   All levels of government—federal, state, and local—require vast sums of money to finance long-term projects related to the construction of public facilities and to keep the government running. Occasionally, governments run budget surpluses, allowing them to invest excess funds. In general, though, government is a *net demander of funds*—meaning that it demands more funds than it supplies because government spending often exceeds tax revenues. The huge amount of money borrowed by governments has the potential to "crowd out" private investment by increasing the cost and decreasing the amount of funds available to individuals and businesses.

Business   Most business firms require large sums of money to support operations. Like government, business has both long- and short-term financial needs. Businesses issue a wide variety of debt and equity securities to finance these needs. They also supply funds when they have excess cash. But like government, business firms in general are *net demanders of funds*.

Individuals You might be surprised to learn that even though individuals demand funds in the form of loans to pay for property (e.g., houses and automobiles) and education, as a group, individuals are *net suppliers of funds*. Through their savings, individuals put more into the financial system than they take out.

Types of Investors When we refer to individuals in the investment process, we do so to differentiate households from government and business. We can further characterize the participation of individuals in the investment process in terms of who manages the funds. **Individual investors** manage their own funds to achieve their financial goals. Individual investors usually concentrate on earning a return on idle funds, building a source of retirement income, and providing security for their families.

Individuals who lack the time or expertise to make investment decisions often employ **institutional investors**—investment professionals who earn their living by managing other people's money. These professionals trade large volumes of securities for individuals, businesses, and governments. Institutional investors include financial institutions—such as banks, life insurance companies, mutual funds, and pension funds. For example, a life insurance company invests the premiums it receives from policyholders to earn returns that will cover death benefits paid to beneficiaries.

Both individual and institutional investors apply similar fundamental principles when deciding how to invest money. However, institutional investors generally control larger sums of money and have more sophisticated analytical skills than do most individual investors. *The information presented in this textbook is aimed primarily at individual investors*. It represents only the first step toward developing the expertise needed to qualify as an institutional investor.

CONCEPTS IN REVIEW

Answers available at
www.pearsonhighered.com/
gitman

NOTE The Concepts in Review questions at the end of each text section encourage you, before you move on, to test your understanding of the material you've just read.

1.1 Define the term *investment*, and explain why individuals invest.

1.2 Differentiate among the following types of investments, and cite an example of each: (a) securities and property investments; (b) direct and indirect investments; (c) debt, equity, and derivative securities; and (d) short-term and long-term investments.

1.3 Define the term *risk*, and explain how risk is used to differentiate among investments.

1.4 What are *foreign investments*, and what role do they play today for the individual investor?

1.5 Describe the structure of the overall investment process. Explain the role played by *financial institutions* and *financial markets*.

1.6 Classify the role of (a) government, (b) business, and (c) individuals as net suppliers or net demanders of funds.

1.7 Differentiate between *individual investors* and *institutional investors*.

Investment Vehicles

 A wide variety of investments is available to individual investors. Investments differ in terms of maturities (lives), costs, return and risk characteristics, and tax considerations. We devote the bulk of this book—Chapters 6 through 15—to describing the characteristics, special features, returns and risks, and possible investment strategies of the vehicles available to individual investors. Here we will introduce these investment vehicles. Table 1.1 (on page 8) summarizes the information presented in this section.

TABLE 1.1	Major Types of Investments		
Type	Description	Examples	Where Covered in This Book
Short term	Savings instruments with lives of 1 year or less. Used to warehouse idle funds and to provide liquidity.	Deposit accounts, Series EE savings bonds, U.S. Treasury bills (T-bills), Certificates of deposit (CDs), Commercial paper, Banker's acceptances, Money market mutual funds	Ch. 1
Common stock	Equity investments that represent ownership in a corporation.		Chs. 6–9
Fixed-income securities	Investments that make fixed cash payments at regular intervals.	Bonds Convertible securities Preferred stock	Chs. 10, 11 Ch. 10 Web Ch. 16
Mutual funds	Companies that pool money from many different investors and invest funds in a diversified portfolio of securities.		Ch. 12
Derivatives	Securities that are neither debt nor equity but are structured to exhibit the characteristics of the underlying assets from which they derive their value.	Options Futures	Ch. 14 Ch. 15
Miscellaneous	Various other investment vehicles that are widely used by investors.	Tax-advantaged investments Real estate Tangibles	Web Ch. 17 Web Ch. 18 Web Ch. 18

Short-Term Investments

Short-term investments include savings instruments that usually have lives of one year or less. Short-term vehicles generally carry little or no risk. Investors use these instruments as a temporary "warehouse" for idle funds before transferring the money into a long-term investment. Short-term investments are also popular among conservative investors who may be reluctant to lock up their funds in long-term assets such as stocks or bonds.

Short-term investments also provide **liquidity**. That is, they can be converted into cash quickly and with little or no loss in value. Provision for liquidity is an important part of any financial plan. We discuss the role of short-term vehicles in financial planning and the key features of the most popular short-term vehicles later in this chapter.

Common Stock

Common stock is an equity investment that represents ownership in a corporation. Each share of common stock represents a fractional ownership interest in the firm. For example, one share of common stock in a corporation that has 10,000 shares outstanding would represent 1/10,000 ownership interest. Next to short-term investments and residential real estate, common stock is the most popular form of investment vehicle. Today, roughly half of all U.S. households own some common stock, either directly or indirectly.

The return on investment in common stock comes from two sources: dividends and capital gains. **Dividends** are quarterly payments the corporation makes to its shareholders. **Capital gains** result from selling the stock (or any asset) at a price that *exceeds* its original purchase price.

For example, say you purchased a single share of Walmart common stock for $45 on January 1, 2008. During 2008, you received $0.95 in cash dividends. At the end of the year, you sold the stock for $55. You earned $0.95 in dividends and $10 in capital gains ($55 sale price — $45 purchase price) for a total return of $10.95. On a percentage basis, the return on Walmart shares in 2008 was 24.3% ($10.95/$45).

As mentioned earlier, since 1900, the average annual rate of return on common stocks has been a little more than 11%, so 2008 was a particularly good year for Walmart. As a retailer that focuses on low-priced goods, Walmart performs well when the economy is doing poorly (as it was in 2008) and consumers are trying to stretch every dollar in their budgets.

Fixed-Income Securities

Fixed-income securities are investments that offer a fixed periodic cash payment. Some offer contractually guaranteed returns. Others have specified, but not guaranteed, returns. Because of their fixed returns, fixed-income securities tend to be popular during periods of high interest rates when investors seek to "lock in" high returns. The key forms of fixed-income securities are bonds, convertible securities, and preferred stock.

Bonds   **Bonds** are long-term debt instruments (IOUs) issued by corporations and governments. A bondholder has a contractual right to receive periodic interest payments plus return of the bond's *face value* (the stated value given on the certificate) at maturity (typically 20 to 40 years).

If you purchased a $1,000 bond paying 9% interest in semiannual installments, you would receive $45 (9% × ½ year × $1,000) every six months. At maturity you would receive the $1,000 face value of the bond. Depending on the bond, you may be able to buy or sell it prior to maturity.

Since 1900, the average annual rate of return on long-term government bonds has been about 5.5%. Because they are not backed by the full faith and credit of the U.S. government, corporate bonds are riskier and, therefore, tend to offer slightly higher returns than government bonds provide.

Convertible Securities   A **convertible security** is a special type of fixed-income obligation. It has a feature permitting the investor to convert it into a specified number of shares of common stock. Convertibles provide the fixed-income benefit of a bond (interest) while offering the price-appreciation (capital gain) potential of common stock.

Preferred Stock   Like common stock, **preferred stock** represents an ownership interest in a corporation and has no maturity date. Unlike common stock, preferred stock has a fixed dividend rate. Firms are generally required to pay dividends on preferred shares before they are allowed to pay dividends on their common shares. Furthermore, if a firm is having financial difficulties and decides to stop paying preferred dividends, it must usually make up all of the dividend payments that it skipped before paying dividends on common shares. Investors typically purchase preferred stock for the dividends it pays, but it may also provide capital gains.

INVESTOR FACTS

THE FEELING'S MUTUAL!—In 2008, the more than 8,800 mutual funds in the United States accounted for investment assets of more than $10.3 trillion and employed around 168,000 people. They owned 27% of all stocks and 33% of all bonds issued by state and local government entities. Approximately 52.5 million households own mutual funds, which represents 45% of all households. Mutual funds manage 19% of all household financial assets.

(Source: 2009 Investment Company Factbook downloaded from www. ici.factbook.org, accessed September 28, 2009.)

Mutual Funds

A company that pools money from many different investors and invests the funds in a diversified portfolio of stocks or bonds is called a **mutual fund**. Investors in the fund own an interest in the fund's collection of securities. When investors send money to a mutual fund, they literally buy shares in the fund (as opposed to shares in the companies in which the fund invests), and the prices of the mutual fund shares reflect the value of the assets that the fund holds. Because mutual funds provide an inexpensive means for investors to hold well-diversified and professionally managed portfolios of securities, the mutual fund industry has experienced tremendous growth. The number of equity mutual funds (i.e., funds that invest mainly or exclusively in common stock) has more than quadrupled since 1980. **Money market mutual funds** (also called **money funds**) are mutual funds that invest solely in short-term investment vehicles.

Hedge Funds

Like mutual funds, **hedge funds** are investment funds that pool resources from many different investors and invest those funds in securities. Hedge funds are generally open to a narrower group of investors than are mutual funds. For example, the minimum investment required by a mutual fund might be a few hundred dollars whereas the minimum investment required to participate in a hedge fund runs into the tens of thousand of dollars.

Hedge funds are not as closely regulated as are mutual funds, and they tend to invest in riskier and less liquid securities. The very name "hedge fund" suggests that these funds try to limit or hedge the risks that they take, and, indeed, some hedge funds do operate with that goal in mind. However, some hedge funds adopt very high-risk investment strategies. Nonetheless, the hedge fund industry experienced dramatic growth in the last decade.

Smart's Tour of the Web
To watch author Scott Smart discuss key websites for this chapter visit www.myfinancelab.com

Derivative Securities

As noted earlier, *derivative securities* derive their value from an underlying security or asset. Many derivatives are among the most risky financial assets because they are designed to magnify price changes of the underlying asset. For example, when the price of oil moves up or down by $1 per barrel, the value of an oil futures contract moves in the same direction . . . but by $1,000 rather than $1. Investors may buy or sell derivatives to speculate on the future movements of another asset, but corporations also buy and sell derivatives to hedge against some of the risks they face. For example, a cereal company may purchase wheat futures contracts as a kind of insurance against the possibility that wheat prices will rise.

Options Options are securities that give the investor an opportunity to sell or buy another security at a specified price over a given period of time. Investors purchase options to take advantage of an anticipated change in the price of common stock. However, the purchaser of an option is not guaranteed a return and could even lose the entire amount invested if the option does not become attractive enough to use. Two common types of options are *puts* and *calls*.

Futures Futures are legally binding obligations stipulating that the seller of the futures contract will make delivery and the buyer of the contract will take delivery of an asset at some specific date and at a price agreed on at the time the contract is sold. Examples of *commodities futures* include soybeans, pork bellies, platinum, and cocoa contracts. Examples of *financial futures* are contracts for Japanese yen, U.S. Treasury securities, interest rates, and stock indexes. Trading in commodity and financial futures is generally a highly specialized, high-risk proposition.

Other Popular Investments

Because the federal income tax rate for an individual can be as high as 35% (a figure that many expect to rise in the future), many investors look for **tax-advantaged investments**. These are investment vehicles and strategies designed to provide higher after-tax returns by reducing the amount of taxes that investors must pay. For instance, municipal bonds, which are bonds issued by state and local governmental bodies, make interest payments that are not subject to federal income taxation. Because investors do not have to pay taxes on the interest they receive on municipal bonds, they will accept lower interest rates on these investments than they would on similar bonds that made taxable interest payments.

Real estate consists of assets such as residential homes, raw land, and a variety of forms of income property, including warehouses, office and apartment buildings, and condominiums. The appeal of real estate investment is the potential returns in the form of rental income, tax write-offs, and capital gains.

Tangibles are investment assets, other than real estate, that can be seen or touched. They include gold and other precious metals, gemstones, and collectibles such as coins, stamps, artwork, and antiques. People purchase these assets as investments in anticipation of price increases.

CONCEPTS IN REVIEW

Answers available at
www.pearsonhighered.com/
gitman

1.8   What are *short-term investments?* How do they provide *liquidity?*

1.9   What is *common stock,* and what are its two sources of potential return?

1.10 Briefly define and differentiate among the following investments. Which offer fixed returns? Which are derivative securities? Which offer professional investment management?

a. Bonds   b. Convertible securities

c. Preferred stock   d. Mutual funds

e. Hedge funds   f. Options

g. Futures

Making Investment Plans

LG4 Investing can be carried out in a logical progression of steps. Here we outline those steps and then consider three other key aspects of making your own investment plans: the impact of personal taxes, your stage in the life cycle, and the changing economic environment.

Steps in Investing

Investing can be conducted on a strictly intuitive basis or on the basis of plans carefully developed to achieve specific goals. Evidence favors the planned approach. It begins with establishing a set of overall financial goals and then developing and executing an investment program consistent with those goals. The following overview of the steps in investing provides a framework for the concepts, tools, and techniques presented throughout the book.

Step 1: Meeting Investment Prerequisites   Before investing, you must make certain that you have adequately provided for the *necessities of life*. This includes funds for housing, food, transportation, taxes, and clothing. In addition, you should have a pool of easily accessible funds for meeting emergency cash needs.

Another prerequisite is adequate protection against various "common" risks. Protection against such risks can be acquired through life, health, property, and liability insurance.

Step 2: Establishing Investment Goals   Once you have satisfied the prerequisites, the next step is to establish *investment goals*. **Investment goals** are the financial objectives you wish to achieve by investing. Clearly, your investment goals will determine the types of investments you will make. Common investment goals include:

1. *Accumulating retirement funds.* Accumulating funds for retirement is the *single most important reason for investing*. The earlier in life you assess your retirement needs, the greater your chance of accumulating sufficient funds to meet them.

2. *Enhancing income.* Investments enhance income by earning dividends or interest. Retirees frequently choose investments offering *high income at low risk*.

3. *Saving for major expenditures.* Families often put aside money over the years to accumulate the funds needed for major expenditures such as a down payment on a home, college tuition, vacation travel, and capital to start a business.

4. *Sheltering income from taxes.* Federal income tax law contains provisions that allow individuals to either defer or avoid paying personal income taxes on certain types of investments.

Step 3: Adopting an Investment Plan   Once you have established your general goals, you should adopt an **investment plan**—a written document describing how you will invest funds. You can develop a series of supporting investment goals for each long-term goal. For each goal, specify the target date for achieving it and the amount of tolerable risk. The more specific you can be in your statement of investment goals, the easier it will be to establish an investment plan consistent with your goals.

Step 4: Evaluating Investment Vehicles   Next you will want to evaluate investments by assessing the potential return and risk of each investment option. (Chapter 4 offers a general discussion of the procedures for measuring these key dimensions of potential investments.)

Step 5: Selecting Suitable Investments   You now gather additional information and use it to select specific investments consistent with your goals. You must assess factors such as expected return, risk, and tax considerations. Careful selection of investment vehicles is essential to successful investing.

Step 6: Constructing a Diversified Portfolio   To achieve your investment goals, you will assemble an investment **portfolio** of suitable investments. You will use **diversification**, the inclusion of a number of different investments in a portfolio, to earn higher returns, to reduce risk, or to do a little of both. Diversification is the financial term for the age-old advice, "Don't put all your eggs in one basket." (Chapter 5 includes discussions of diversification and other modern portfolio concepts.)

Many individual investors buy mutual funds to achieve diversification and receive the benefit of professional management (see Chapter 12); others will construct and manage their own portfolios (see Chapter 13).

Step 7: Managing the Portfolio Once you have constructed your portfolio, you should measure its actual behavior in relation to expected performance. If the investment results are not consistent with your objectives, you may need to take corrective action.

Considering Personal Taxes

A knowledge of the tax laws can help you reduce taxes and increase the amount of after-tax dollars available for investing. Because tax laws are complicated and subject to frequent revision, we present only the key concepts and how they apply to popular investment transactions.

Basic Sources of Taxation The two major types of taxes are those levied by the federal government and those levied by state and local governments. The federal *income tax* is the major form of personal taxation. Federal rates currently range from 10% to 35% of taxable income, although with rising federal budget deficits, many experts believe that those tax rates will rise in the future.

State and local taxes vary from area to area. Some states have income taxes that range as high as 15% or more. Some cities, especially large East Coast cities, also have local income taxes that typically range between 1% and 5%. In addition to income taxes, state and local governments rely heavily on sales and property taxes as a source of revenue.

Income taxes at the federal, state, and local levels have a great impact on the returns that investors earn from security investments. Property taxes can have a sizable impact on real estate and other forms of property investment.

Types of Income The income of individuals is classified into one of *three basic categories*:

1. *Active income* consists of everything from wages and salaries to bonuses, tips, pension income, and alimony. Active income is made up of income earned on the job as well as most other forms of *noninvestment* income.

2. *Portfolio income* includes earnings generated from various types of investments. This category covers most (but not all) types of investments from savings accounts, stocks, bonds, and mutual funds to options and futures. For the most part, portfolio income consists of interest, dividends, and capital gains (the profit on the sale of an investment).

3. *Passive income* is a special category of income composed chiefly of income derived from real estate, limited partnerships, and other forms of tax-advantaged investments.

Tax laws limit the amount of deductions (write-offs) that can be taken for each category, particularly for portfolio and passive income. The amount of allowable deductions for portfolio and passive income is *limited to the amount of income derived from these two sources*. For example, if you had a total of $380 in portfolio income for the year, you could deduct no more than $380 in investment-related interest expense. For deduction purposes, the portfolio and passive income categories cannot be mixed or combined with each other or with active income. *Investment-related expenses can be used only to offset portfolio income,* and (with a few exceptions) *passive investment expenses can be used only to offset the income from passive investments.*

TABLE 1.2	Tax Rates and Income Brackets for Individual and Joint Returns (2009)	
	Taxable Income	
Tax Rates	**Individual Returns**	**Joint Returns**
10%	$0 to $8,350	$0 to $16,700
15	$8,351 to $33,950	$16,701 to $67,900
25	$33,951 to $82,250	$67,901 to $137,050
28	$82,251 to $171,550	$137,051 to $208,850
33	$171,551 to $372,950	$208,851 to $372,950
35	Over $372,950	Over $372,950

Ordinary Income   Regardless of whether it's classified as active, portfolio, or passive, ordinary income is taxed at the federal level at one of six rates: 10%, 15%, 25%, 28%, 33%, or 35%. There is one structure of tax rates for taxpayers who file *individual* returns and another for those who file *joint* returns with a spouse. Table 1.2 shows the 2009 tax rates and income brackets for these two categories. Note that the rates are *progressive*. That is, taxpayers with taxable income above a specified amount are taxed at a higher rate.

An example will demonstrate how ordinary income is taxed. Consider the Ellis sisters, Joni and Cara. Both are single. Joni's taxable income is $25,000. Cara's is $50,000. Using Table 1.2, we can calculate their taxes as follows:

Joni:

$$(0.10 \times \$8,350) + [0.15 \times (\$25,000 - \$8,350)] = \$835 + \$2,498 = \underline{\underline{\$3,333}}$$

Cara:

$$(0.10 \times \$8,350) + [0.15 \times [\$33,950 - \$8,350]]$$
$$+ [0.25 \times (\$50,000 - \$33,950)] = \$835 + \$3,840 + \$4,013 = \underline{\underline{\$8,688}}$$

The progressive nature of the federal income tax structure means that Cara pays a higher fraction of her income in taxes—although her taxable income is twice Joni's, Cara's income tax is about 2.6 times Joni's.

Capital Gains and Losses   A *capital asset* is property owned and used by the taxpayer for personal reasons, pleasure, or investment. The most common types are securities and real estate, including one's home. A *capital gain* represents the amount by which the proceeds from the sale of a capital asset *exceed* its original purchase price. How heavily capital gains should be taxed is a contentious political issue, so tax rates on gains change frequently, especially when political power shifts between parties as it did in 2008. At the time this book was going to press in late 2009, capital gains were taxed at two different rates, depending on the holding period.

The capital gains tax rate is 15% if the asset is held for more than 12 months. This 15% capital gains tax rate assumes that you're in the 25%, 28%, 33%, or 35% tax bracket. If you're in the 10% or 15% tax bracket, then the capital gains tax rate on an asset held for more than 12 months is just 5%. *Note that under 2009 tax law, dividends received on stock in domestic corporations are taxed as long-term capital gains rather than ordinary income.* If the asset is held for less than 12 months, then the amount of any capital gain realized is added to other sources of income, and the total is taxed at the rates given in Table 1.2.

For example, imagine that James McFail, a single person who has other taxable income totaling $75,000, sold 500 shares of stock at $12 per share. He originally purchased this stock at $10 per share. The total capital gain on this transaction was $1,000 [500 shares × ($12/share – $10/share)]. Thus, James's taxable income would total $76,000, which puts him in the 25% tax bracket (see Table 1.2).

If the $1,000 capital gain resulted from an asset that was held for more than 12 months and because James is in the 25% tax bracket, the capital gain would be taxed at the maximum rate of 15%. His total tax would be calculated as follows:

Ordinary income ($75,000)

$$(0.10 \times \$8,350) + [0.15 \times (\$33,950 - \$8,350)]$$
$$+ [0.25 \times (\$75,000 - \$33,950)] = \$835 + \$3,840 + \$10,263 = \$14,938$$

Capital gain ($1,000)

$(0.15 \times \$1,000) =$ $ 150

Total tax $15,088

James's total tax would be $15,088. Had his other taxable income been below $33,951 (i.e., in the 15% bracket), the $1,000 capital gain would have been taxed at 5% rather than 15%. Had James held the asset for less than 12 months, his $1,000 capital gain would have been taxed as ordinary income, which in James's case would result in a 25% rate.

Capital gains are appealing because they are not taxed until actually realized. For example, if you own a stock originally purchased for $50 per share that at the end of the tax year has a market price of $60 per share, you have a "paper gain" of $10 per share. This *paper (unrealized) gain* is not taxable because you still own the stock. *Only realized gains are taxed.* If you sold the stock for $60 per share during the tax year, you would have a realized—and therefore taxable—gain of $10 per share.

A **capital loss** results when a capital asset is sold for *less than* its original purchase price. Before taxes are calculated, all gains and losses must be netted out. Taxpayers can apply up to $3,000 of **net losses** against ordinary income in any year. Losses that cannot be applied in the current year may be carried forward and used to offset future income, subject to certain conditions.

Investments and Taxes The opportunities created by the tax laws make tax planning important in the investment process. **Tax planning** involves looking at your earnings, both current and projected, and developing strategies that will defer and minimize the level of taxes. The tax plan should guide your investment activities so that over the long run, you will achieve maximum after-tax returns for an acceptable level of risk.

For example, the fact that capital gains are not taxed until actually realized allows you to defer tax payments on them as well as control the timing of these payments. However, investments that are likely to lead to capital gains income generally have higher risk than those that provide only current investment income. Therefore, the choice of investments cannot be made solely on the basis of the possible reduction of tax payments. The levels of both return and risk need to be viewed in light of their tax effects. *It is the after-tax return and associated risk that matter.*

Tax-Advantaged Retirement Vehicles The federal government over the years has established a number of types of retirement vehicles. Those that are employer sponsored include profit-sharing plans, thrift and savings plans, and 401(k) plans. These plans are often *voluntary* and allow employees to both increase the amount of money held for retirement and enjoy attractive tax-deferral benefits. Individuals can also set up their own tax-sheltered retirement programs—for example, Keogh plans and SEP-IRAs for self-employed people. Individual retirement accounts (IRAs), both deductible and nondeductible, and Roth IRAs, can be set up by just about anybody subject to certain qualifications. In general, these plans allow individuals to defer taxes, typically on both the contributions and the earnings on them, until retirement. Clearly, the individual investor should take advantage of these vehicles when they are available and appropriate to achieving his or her investment goals.

Investing Over the Life Cycle

Investors tend to follow different investment philosophies as they move through different stages of the life cycle. Generally speaking, most investors tend to be more aggressive when they're young and more conservative as they grow older. Typically, investors move through these investment stages:

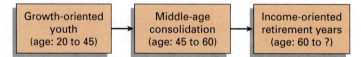

Most young investors, in their twenties and thirties, tend to prefer growth-oriented investments that stress *capital gains* rather than current income. Often young investors don't have much in the way of investable funds, so capital gains are viewed as the quickest (if not necessarily the surest) way to build capital. Young investors tend to favor growth-oriented and speculative vehicles, particularly high-risk common stocks.

As investors approach the middle-age consolidation stage of life (the mid-forties), family demands and responsibilities such as educational expenses and retirement contributions become more important. The whole portfolio goes through a transition to *higher-quality securities*. Low-risk growth and income stocks, high-grade bonds, preferred stocks, convertibles, and mutual funds are all widely used at this stage.

Finally, when investors approach their retirement years, preservation of capital and current income become the principal concerns. A secure, high level of income is paramount. Capital gains are viewed as merely a pleasant, occasional by-product of investing. The investment portfolio now becomes *highly conservative*. It consists of low-risk income stocks and mutual funds, high-yielding government bonds, quality corporate bonds, bank certificates of deposit (CDs), and other short-term vehicles. At this stage, investors reap the rewards of a lifetime of saving and investing.

Investments and the Business Cycle

Common stocks and other equity-related securities (convertible securities, stock mutual funds, stock options, and stock index futures) are highly responsive to conditions in the economy. The *business cycle* refers to the recurring sequence of growth and decline, boom and recession, that characterizes the U.S. economy. The business cycle reflects the current status of a variety of economic variables, including gross domestic product (GDP), industrial production, personal disposable income, the unemployment rate, and more.

A strong economy is reflected in an expanding business cycle. Stocks tend to be a leading indicator of the business cycle, meaning that stock prices tend to rise prior to periods when business is good and profits are up. Growth-oriented and speculative stocks tend to do especially well in strong markets. To a lesser extent,

ETHICS IN INVESTING

The Price for Behaving Badly

In recent years, business headlines were full of allegations of massive financial fraud committed by prominent business leaders. These allegations shocked the investment community and resulted in spectacular bankruptcies of some of the largest U.S. corporations. High-profile indictments and court convictions soon followed. Among the list of convicted felons were Jeff Skilling and Ken Lay of Enron, Bernard Ebbers of WorldCom, Dennis Kozlowski of Tyco International, Martha Stewart of Martha Stewart Omnimedia, and John Rigas of Adelphia Communications.

In many cases, the primary weapon of fraudulent CEOs was the use of corporate accounting to report huge, fictitious profits. When the fraud was discovered, a catastrophic crash of the stock price followed. This is what happened at Enron, WorldCom, and Global Crossing. In some cases,

accounting firms and Wall Street bankers aided in the schemes. Phony profits helped dishonest CEOs reap fantastic benefits in the form of huge performance bonuses and cash stock options. Many corporate crooks also used their companies as personal piggy banks, as was the case at Tyco International and Adelphia. These executives were able to defeat or completely dismantle internal and external supervision mechanisms and to manipulate their boards of directors to their advantage.

Fraudulent CEOs showed the ability to fool investors, securities analysts, and government regulators for years. In 2002, the U.S. Congress passed the Sarbanes-Oxley Act in the hope of preventing future corporate financial frauds.

Critical Thinking Question Why did accounting "irregularities" become such a widespread problem plaguing public companies in recent years?

NOTE Ethics boxes, which appear in many chapters, focus on the ethical dimensions of particular situations and issues in the investments world. Each box includes a Critical Thinking Question for discussion.

so do low-risk and income-oriented stocks. In contrast, stock values often fall several months before periods when economic activity is declining. The reason that stocks tend to move ahead of changes in the business cycle is that stock prices reflect investors' beliefs about the future prospects of companies. When investors believe that business conditions will deteriorate, stock prices will fall even before those poor business conditions materialize. Of course, the same thing happens in reverse when investors believe the economy will perform better. Stock prices rise in anticipation of strong future economic performance.

Bonds and other forms of fixed-income securities (bond funds and preferred stocks) are also sensitive to the business cycle because they are highly sensitive to movements in interest rates. In fact, interest rates represent the single most important variable in determining bond price behavior and returns to investors. Interest rates and bond prices move in opposite directions (as will be explained in Chapters 10 and 11). Therefore, rising interest rates are unfavorable for bonds already held in an investor's portfolio. Of course, high interest rates enhance the attractiveness of new bonds because these bonds must offer high returns to attract investors.

CONCEPTS IN REVIEW

Answers available at www.pearsonhighered.com/gitman

1.11 What should an investor first establish before developing and executing an investment program? Briefly describe each of the seven steps involved in investing.

1.12 What are four common investment goals?

1.13 Define and differentiate among the following. Explain how each is related to federal income taxes.

   a. Active income   b. Portfolio and passive income

   c. Capital gain   d. Capital loss

   e. Tax planning   f. Tax-advantaged retirement vehicles

(Continued)

1.14 Describe the differing investment philosophies typically applied during each of the following stages of an investor's life cycle.

a. Youth (ages 20 to 45)

b. Middle age (ages 45 to 60)

c. Retirement years (age 60 on)

1.15 Discuss the relation between stock prices and the business cycle.

Meeting Liquidity Needs: Investing in Short-Term Vehicles

LG5 As discussed earlier, you should ensure that you have adequate liquidity. This provision is a prerequisite to implementing long-term investment goals. *Liquidity* is the ability to convert an investment into cash quickly and with little or no loss in value. A checking account is highly liquid. Stocks and bonds are less liquid because there is no definite assurance that you will be able to quickly sell them without having to cut the price dramatically to attract a buyer.

The Role of Short-Term Investments

Short-term investments represent an important part of most savings and investment programs. They generate income—which can be quite high during periods of high interest rates. However, their primary function is to provide a pool of reserves for emergencies or simply to accumulate funds for some specific purpose. As a rule of thumb, financial planners often suggest that you hold cash reserves equivalent to three to six months of your after-tax salary, and typically this type of emergency fund would be invested in safe, liquid, short-term investments.

Some individuals choose to hold short-term vehicles because they simply do not want to take the risk inherent in many types of long-term investments. In fact, this approach has considerable merit during periods of economic and investment instability. Regardless of your motives for holding short-term vehicles, you should evaluate them in terms of their risk and return, just as you would longer-term investments.

Interest on Short-Term Investments   Short-term investments earn interest in one of two ways. Some investments, such as savings accounts, pay a *stated rate of interest*. In this case, you can easily find the interest rate—it's the stated rate on the account.

Alternatively, some short-term investments earn interest on a **discount basis**. This means that the security is purchased at a price below its redemption value (or face value), and the difference between what you pay to acquire the asset and what you receive when it matures is the interest the investment will earn. U.S. Treasury bills (T-bills), for example, are issued on a discount basis.

Risk Characteristics   Short-term investments are generally considered low in risk. Their primary risk results from *inflation risk*—the loss of potential purchasing power that occurs when the rate of return on these investments falls short of the inflation rate. This has often been the case with such vehicles as passbook savings accounts, the traditional bank savings accounts that generally pay a low rate of interest and have no minimum balance. Most other short-term investments have rates of return that are slightly higher than the inflation rate.

The *risk of default*—nonpayment—is almost nonexistent with short-term investments. The reason is that issuers of most short-term vehicles are highly reputable

MARKETS IN CRISIS

Your Money Back, Guaranteed

During the financial crisis that began in 2007, depositors began to question the safety of banks and other financial institutions, not only in the United States but also in many other countries. In an attempt to reassure depositors and to prevent a classic "bank run," several countries increased the limit on their deposit insurance programs. On October 3, 2008, the Federal Deposit Insurance Corporation (FDIC) increased the amount of insured deposits from $100,000 to $250,000. That same month, Greece, Poland, Sweden, Denmark, and the United Kingdom all increased their limits on insured deposits. Most of those countries doubled the limit on insured deposits, and in Greece and Ireland, the limit was entirely eliminated, committing those governments to cover 100% of customers' deposits at insured financial institutions.

institutions, such as the U.S. Treasury, large banks, and major corporations. In addition, government agencies insure deposits in commercial banks, savings and loans, savings banks, and credit unions for up to $250,000 per account. Finally, because the value of short-term investments does not change much in response to changing interest rates, exposure to capital loss is correspondingly low.

Advantages and Disadvantages of Short-Term Investments As noted, the major advantages of short-term investments are their high liquidity and low risk. Most are available from local financial institutions and can be readily converted to cash with minimal inconvenience. Finally, because the returns on most short-term investments vary with inflation and market interest rates, investors can readily capture higher returns as rates move up. On the negative side, when interest rates go down, returns drop as well.

Although a decline in market rates has undesirable effects on most short-term vehicles, perhaps their biggest disadvantage is their relatively low return. Because these securities are generally so low in risk, you can expect the returns on short-term investments to average less than the returns on long-term investments.

Popular Short-Term Investments

A variety of short-term investments are available to the individual investor. Some are deposit-type accounts in which investors can place money, earn a relatively low rate of interest, and conveniently withdraw funds at their discretion. Part A of Table 1.3 on page 20 summarizes the popular deposit-type accounts. Another group of short-term investments are those issued by the federal government. The more popular of those instruments are summarized in Part B of Table 1.3. The final group of short-term investments includes nongovernment instruments, typically issued by a financial institution or a corporation. Part C of Table 1.3 summarizes some of the more popular nongovernment issues.

Investment Suitability

Individual investors use short-term investments for both savings and investment. They use these assets to maintain a desired level of savings that will be readily available if the need arises—in essence, to provide *safety and security*. For this purpose, high yield is less important than safety, liquidity, and convenience. Passbook savings accounts, NOW accounts, and Series EE savings bonds are the most popular savings vehicles.

When investors use short-term vehicles for *investment purposes*, the yield that these instruments provide is often just as important as their liquidity. Most investors will hold at least a part of their portfolio in short-term, highly liquid securities, if for no

TABLE 1.3   Popular Short-Term Investments

Part A. Deposit-Type Accounts

Type of Account	Description	Minimum Balance	Interest Rate	Federal Insurance
Passbook savings account	Savings accounts offered by banks.* Used primarily for convenience or if investors lack sufficient funds to purchase other short-term vehicles.	Typically none	0.5%–4% depending on economy	Yes, up to $250,000 per deposit.
NOW (negotiated order of withdrawal) account	Bank checking account that pays interest on balances.	No legal minimum but often set at $500 to $1,000	At or near passbook rates	Yes, up to $250,000 per deposit.
Money market deposit account (MMDA)	Bank deposit account with limited check-writing privileges.	No legal minimum, but often set at about $2,500	Typically slightly above passbook rate	Yes, up to $250,000 per deposit.
Asset management account	Deposit account at bank, brokerage house, mutual fund, or insurance company that combines checking, investing, and borrowing. Automatically "sweeps" excess balances into short-term investments and borrows to meet shortages.	Typically $5,000 to $20,000	Similar to MMDAs	Yes, up to $250,000 per deposit in banks. Varies in other institutions.

Part B. Federal Government Issues

Security	Issuer	Description	Initial Maturity	Risk and Return
Series EE savings bonds	U.S. Treasury	Savings bonds issued by the U.S. Treasury in varying denominations, at 50% of face value; earn a fixed rate of interest (set every 6 months in May and December) compounded semiannually for 30 years from issue date.	None	Lowest, virtually risk free
Treasury bills	U.S. Treasury	Issued weekly at auction; sold at a discount; strong secondary market; exempt from local and state income taxes.	1 year or less	Lowest, virtually risk free

Part C. Nongovernment Issues

Certificates of deposit (CDs)	Commercial banks	Represent specific cash deposits in commercial banks; amounts and maturities tailored to investor needs.	1 month and longer	Higher than U.S. Treasury issues and comparable to commercial paper.
Commercial paper	Corporation with a high credit standing	Unsecured note of issuer; large denominations.	3 to 270 days	Higher than U.S. Treasury issues and comparable to CDs.

Security	Issuer	Description	Initial Maturity	Risk and Return
Banker's acceptances	Banks	Results from a bank guarantee of a business transaction; sold at a discount from maturity value.	30 to 180 days	About the same as CDs and commercial paper but higher than U.S. Treasury issues.
Money market mutual funds (money funds)	Professional portfolio management companies	Professionally managed portfolios of marketable securities; provide instant liquidity.	None—depends on wishes of investor	Vary, but generally higher than U.S. Treasury issues and comparable to CDs and commercial paper.

*The term *bank* refers to commercial banks, savings and loans (S&Ls), savings banks, and credit unions.

other reason than to be able to act on unanticipated investment opportunities. Some investors, in fact, devote all or most of their portfolios to such securities.

Investors also use short-term securities as a temporary place to "park" funds before deciding where to invest the money on a long-term basis. For example, if you have just sold some stock but do not have a suitable long-term investment alternative, you might place the proceeds in a money fund until you find a longer-term use for them. Or if you feel that interest rates are about to rise sharply, you might sell your long-term bonds and use the proceeds to buy T-bills. The higher-yielding securities— like money market deposit accounts (MMDAs), CDs, commercial paper, banker's acceptances, and money funds—are generally preferred for this warehousing function, as are asset management accounts at major brokerage firms.

To decide which securities are most appropriate for a particular situation, you need to consider such characteristics as availability, safety, liquidity, and yield. Although all investments we have discussed satisfy the basic liquidity demand, they do so to varying degrees. A NOW account is unquestionably the most liquid of all. You can write as many checks on the account as you wish and for any amount. A certificate of deposit, on the other hand, is not so liquid because early redemption involves an interest penalty. Table 1.4 summarizes the key characteristics of the short-term investments

TABLE 1.4	A Scorecard for Short-Term Investment Vehicles			
Savings or Investment Vehicle	Availability	Safety	Liquidity	Typical Rate
Passbook savings account	A+	A+	A	D (0.6%)
NOW account	A−	A+	A+	F (0.5)
Money market deposit account (MMDA)	B	A+	A	B− (0.7)
Asset management account	B−	A	A+	B (1.0)
Series EE savings bond	A+	A++	C−	B+ (3.7)
U.S. Treasury bill (91 day)	B−	A++	A−	A− (5.0)
Certificate of deposit (3 month, large denomination)	B	A+	C	A (5.4)
Commercial paper (90 day)	B−	A−	C	A− (5.3)
Banker's acceptance (90 day)	B−	A	B	A− (5.3)
Money market mutual fund (money fund)	B	A/A+	B+	A− (4.7)

described in Table 1.3. The letter grade assigned for each characteristic reflects an estimate of the investment's quality in that area. For example, money market mutual funds (MMMFs) rate only a B+ on liquidity because withdrawals must usually be made in a minimum amount of $250 to $500. NOW accounts are somewhat better in this respect because a withdrawal can be for any amount. Rates on short-term investments tend to be low. Among the investments listed in Table 1.4, the rates on NOW and passbook savings accounts are typically lowest, and the rates on large, three-month CDs are the highest. However, in August 2009 as the economy was still struggling through a recession, rates on all of these instruments were barely above zero. For example, a large, three-month CD offered investors a return of roughly 1%. You should note, though, that if an investment scores lower on availability, safety, or liquidity, it will generally offer a higher rate.

CONCEPTS IN REVIEW

Answers available at
www.pearsonhighered.com/gitman

1.16 What makes an asset liquid? Why hold liquid assets? Would 100 shares of IBM stock be considered a liquid investment? Explain.

1.17 Explain the characteristics of short-term investments with respect to purchasing power and default risk.

1.18 Briefly describe the key features and differences among the following deposit accounts.

   a. Passbook savings account

   b. NOW account

   c. Money market deposit account

   d. Asset management account

1.19 Define, compare, and contrast the following short-term investments.

   a. Series EE savings bonds

   b. U.S. Treasury bills

   c. Certificates of deposit

   d. Commercial paper

   e. Banker's acceptances

   f. Money market mutual funds (money funds)

Careers in Finance

LG6 Regardless of the job title, a career in finance requires an understanding of the investment environment. The principles presented throughout this book will provide an initial foundation in investments essential to pursuing one of the many rewarding career paths within the field of finance. If you are well prepared and enthusiastic about a career in finance, you will find a wide variety of job opportunities available to you. The following overview provides a brief introduction to some careers in finance.

Commercial Banking Commercial banks provide banking services to individuals and businesses alike. In spite of considerable consolidation within the banking sector, more people work in commercial banking than in any other area of the financial services industry. Some of the long-standing commercial banks include J. P. Morgan Chase & Company (New York, N.Y.), Wells Fargo & Company (San Francisco,

Calif.), U.S. Bancorp (Minneapolis, Minn.), and Bank of the New York Mellon Corp. (New York, N.Y.).

Due to the vast range of services provided by commercial banks, there exists a tremendous range of finance career opportunities within commercial banking, many of which require training in investments. Some of the finance-related areas found within commercial banks include mortgage lending, mortgage underwriting, corporate lending, asset management, leasing, consumer credit, trade credit, and international finance. Some of the job titles common in the commercial banking sector include personal banker, portfolio manager, short-term securities manager, financial analyst, credit analyst, home loan officer, corporate loan officer, and mortgage underwriter.

Corporate Finance Within the corporate finance setting, you will find several rewarding job opportunities. Among other things, corporations require financial professionals to manage cash and short-term investments, raise and manage long-term financing resources, evaluate and undertake investment opportunities, and interface with investors and the financial community. These critical finance functions exist within virtually every firm regardless of size, public status, or international presence.

The top finance job within a corporation is that of the chief financial officer (CFO). The CFO's primary responsibilities are to manage the firm's capital resources and capital investments. Managing the firm's capital resources includes managing its internal financing, such as cash and retained earnings, and interacting with the financial markets to acquire external financing, such as debt or equity. Investment principles are important to CFOs because so much of a CFO's job revolves around communication with investors. A CFO must understand how investors view the firm and value the securities the firm has issued.

Corporate finance jobs are typically focused on a firm's long-term goals aimed at increasing its value through successful investment decisions. More so than any other finance-related job, corporate finance jobs require a broad understanding of the various functional areas within the corporate setting (e.g., operations, marketing, and accounting) and how these areas contribute to the corporate finance goals.

Financial Planning A financial planner consults clients on how to deal with their specific situations and meet their specific goals, both short term and long term. When consulting with individuals, a personal financial planner provides advice relating to education, retirement, investment, insurance, tax, and estate planning—in most cases this means providing investment advice. Business owners will consult financial planners on issues such as cash flow management, investment planning, risk management and insurance planning, tax planning, and business succession planning. The investment concepts discussed in the book represent the financial planner's primary tools.

An ability to clarify objectives, assess risks, and develop strategic plans is essential for financial planners. For example, if a client desires to send a child to college someday, what savings or investment strategies are best suited to meet that client's goals? Financial planners can work within a large financial services company such as ING, within a small practice, or for themselves as a sole proprietorship. In all of these work environments, it is beneficial to obtain the Certified Financial Planner (CFP®) designation. To become a CFP®, you must pass an exam administered by the CFP® Board of Standards. The exam covers more than 175 topics in investing and financial planning. Obtaining this designation serves to demonstrate your proficiency as a financial planner and provides a comparative advantage relative to those who do not hold the CFP® designation. Chartered Wealth Manager is a designation that is common outside the United States.

Insurance   The insurance business is a trillion-dollar industry that serves both individual and business client needs. There are two prominent finance jobs in insurance; one involves assisting individuals or businesses in managing risk, and the second involves asset management. Individuals and businesses invest in risk management in order to protect themselves from catastrophic losses or to guarantee certain outcomes. While insurers collect premiums and fees for the services they provide, their goal is to develop investment strategies intended to neutralize the risk assumed from their clients. The insurance industry has vast sums under management and therefore requires highly trained investment specialists.

Investment Banking   Investment banks assist firms and governments when issuing financial securities, such as stocks and bonds, and they facilitate the purchase of securities by both institutional and retail investors. Their in-house security analysts provide research on both equity and fixed-income securities. Investment banks also make markets for financial securities (e.g., stocks and bonds), provide financial advice to and manage financial assets for high net worth individuals, firms, institutions, and governments. Investment banks even provide their clients with technical analysis or program trading and consultation on mergers and acquisitions.

The investment banking industry changed dramatically during the recent financial crisis. Many investment banks invested heavily in securities tied to U.S. real estate values, and when home prices began to drop, the losses on banks' investments began to mount. Several prominent investment banks either went bankrupt or were acquired by other banks. On September 22, 2008, to survive the U.S. financial crisis, Goldman Sachs and Morgan Stanley, the last two major investment banks on Wall Street, elected to convert their charters to traditional depository commercial banks and become fully regulated by the Federal Reserve.

Investment Management   As the name implies, investment management is all about managing money for clients. The role of an investment manager includes elements of financial analysis, asset selection, security (e.g., stock or bond) selection, and investment implementation and monitoring. Most investment management is done on behalf of a pool of investors whose investments comprise a fund. Some common examples of managed funds are bank trust funds, pension funds, mutual funds, exchange-traded funds, and hedge funds.

Investment management comes in two basic flavors, passive or active. Investment managers engaged in *passive investment management* simply try to create a portfolio whose performance will mimic that of a major stock index like the Standard and Poor's 500. Such a strategy tends to be very cost effective because the fund does not expend resources trying to analyze stocks to determine which will perform best in the future.

If you are an adrenaline junkie, then *active investment management* is likely to satisfy your craving. Although active investment management encompasses an unbounded set of possible investment strategies, all active investment management strategies share the same overarching goal of earning above-average returns. Some active investment managers take advantage of the latest and most sophisticated quantitative techniques whereas others rely on well-established analytical methods in addition to the portfolio manager's instincts.

Each money manager has his or her own unique style. Many money managers buy and hold fixed-income securities including mortgaged-backed securities, corporate bonds, municipal bonds, agency securities, and asset-backed securities. Others focus on equities, including small stocks, large caps, and emerging market stocks.

Investment management is a challenging and competitive career, so any additional preparation or edge that you can acquire will likely enhance your chances for success. The Chartered Financial Analyst (CFA) certification is one such advantage that you might consider obtaining. One of the most respected financial certifications, it is administered by The CFA Institute, which also administers the Certificate in Investment Performance Measurement (CIPM) program. Either the CFA or the CIPM designation will enhance you qualifications for a career in finance.

CONCEPTS IN REVIEW		
CONCEPTS IN REVIEW Answers available at www.pearsonhighered.com/gitman	**1.20**	Why is an understanding of investment principles important to a senior manager working in corporate finance?
	1.21	Why do insurance companies need employees with advanced training in investments?

Here is what you should know after reading this chapter. **MyFinanceLab** will help you identify what you know, and where to go when you need to practice.

What You Should Know	Key Terms	Where To Practice
NOTE The end-of-chapter Summaries restate the chapter's Learning Goals and review the key points of information related to each goal.	NOTE A list of Key Terms gathers in one place the new vocabulary presented in each chapter.	
LG1 Understand the meaning of the term *investment* and the factors used to differentiate types of investments. An investment is any asset into which investors can place funds with the expectation of generating positive income and/or of preserving or increasing their value. The returns from investing are received either as income or as increased value. Types of investments are securities or property; direct or indirect; debt, equity, or derivative; low risk or high risk; short term or long term; and domestic or foreign.	debt, *p. 4* derivative securities, *p. 5* direct investment, *p. 3* domestic investments, *p. 5* equity, *p. 4* financial institutions, *p. 5* financial markets, *p. 5* foreign investments, *p. 5* indirect investments, *p. 4* individual investors, *p. 7* institutional investors, *p. 7*	MyFinanceLab Study Plan 1.1
LG2 Describe the investment process and types of investors. Financial institutions and financial markets bring together suppliers and demanders of funds. The dominant U.S. financial market is the securities market for stocks, bonds, and options. The participants in the investment process are government, business, and individuals. Only individuals are net suppliers of funds. Investors can be either individual investors or institutional investors.	investment, *p. 3* long-term investments, *p. 5* property, *p. 3* returns, *p. 3* risk, *p. 5* securities, *p. 3* short-term investments, *p. 5* speculation, *p. 5*	MyFinanceLab Study Plan 1.2
LG3 Discuss the principal types of investments. Short-term investments have low risk. They are used to earn a return on temporarily idle funds, to serve as a primary vehicle for conservative investors, and to provide liquidity. Common stocks offer dividends and capital gains. Fixed-income securities—bonds, convertible securities, and preferred stock—offer fixed periodic	bonds, *p. 9* capital gains, *p. 9* common stock, *p. 8* convertible security, *p. 9* dividends, *p. 9* fixed-income securities, *p. 9*	MyFinanceLab Study Plan 1.3

What You Should Know	Key Term	Where To Practice
returns with some potential for gain in value. Mutual funds allow investors to buy or sell interests in a professionally managed, diversified group of securities. Hedge funds are similar to mutual funds except that they are open only to relatively wealthy investors, they tend to make riskier investments, and they are subject to less regulation compared to mutual funds. Derivative securities such as options and futures are high-risk vehicles. Options offer an opportunity to buy or sell another security at a specified price over a given period of time. Futures are contracts between a seller and a buyer for delivery of a specified commodity or financial instrument, at a specified future date, at an agreed-on price. Other popular investment vehicles include tax-advantaged investments, real estate, and tangibles.	futures, *p. 10* hedge fund, *p. 10* liquidity, *p. 8* money funds, *p. 10* money market mutual funds, *p. 10* mutual fund, *p. 10* options, *p. 10* preferred stock, *p. 9* real estate, *p. 11* tangibles, *p. 11* tax-advantaged investments, *p. 11*	
LG4 Describe the steps in investing, review fundamental tax considerations, and discuss investing over the life cycle. Investing should be driven by well-developed plans established to achieve specific goals. It involves a set of steps: meeting investment prerequisites, establishing investment goals, adopting an investment plan, evaluating investment vehicles, selecting suitable investments, constructing a diversified portfolio, and managing the portfolio. Investors must also consider the tax consequences associated with various investment vehicles and strategies. The key dimensions are ordinary income, capital gains and losses, tax planning, and the use of tax-advantaged retirement vehicles. The investment vehicles selected are affected by the investor's stage in the life cycle and by economic cycles. Younger investors tend to prefer growth-oriented investments that stress capital gains. As they age, investors move to higher-quality securities. As they approach retirement, they become even more conservative. Some investments, such as stocks, behave as leading indicators of the state of the economy.	capital loss, *p. 15* diversification, *p. 12* investment goals, *p. 12* investment plan, *p. 12* net losses, *p. 15* portfolio, *p. 12* tax planning, *p. 15*	MyFinanceLab Study Plan 1.4 Video Learning Aid for Problems P1.1, P1.2
LG5 Describe the most common types of short-term investments. Liquidity needs can be met by investing in various short-term investments, which can earn interest at a stated rate or on a discount basis. They typically have low risk. Banks, the government, and brokerage firms offer numerous short-term vehicles. Their suitability depends on the investor's attitude toward availability, safety, liquidity, and rate of return.	discount basis, *p. 18*	MyFinanceLab Study Plan 1.5

What You Should Know	Key Term	Where To Practice
LG6 Describe some of the main careers open to people with financial expertise and the role that investments play in each. Exciting and rewarding career opportunities in finance are available in many different fields such as commercial banking, corporate finance, financial planning, insurance, investment banking, and money management.		MyFinanceLab Study Plan 1.6

Log into **MyFinanceLab**, take a chapter test, and get a personalized Study Plan that tells you which concepts you understand and which ones you need to review. From there, **MyFinanceLab** will give you further practice, tutorials, animations, videos, and guided solutions.
Log into www.myfinancelab.com

Discussion Questions

NOTE The Discussion Questions at the end of the chapter ask you to analyze and synthesize information presented in the chapter. These questions, like all other end-of-chapter assignment materials, are keyed to the chapter's learning goals.

LG4   Q1.1 Assume that you are 35 years old, are married with two young children, are renting a condo, and have an annual income of $90,000. Use the following questions to guide your preparation of a rough investment plan consistent with these facts.

    a. What are your key investment goals?
    b. How might personal taxes affect your investment plans? Use current tax rates to assess their impact.
    c. How might your stage in the life cycle affect the types of risk you might take?

LG5   Q1.2 What role, if any, will short-term vehicles play in your portfolio? Why? Complete the following table for the short-term investments listed. Find their yields in a current issue of *The Wall Street Journal*, and explain which, if any, you would include in your investment portfolio.

Savings or Investment Vehicle	Minimum Balance	Interest Rate	Federal Insurance	Method and Ease of Withdrawing Funds
a. Passbook savings account	None		Yes	In person or through teller machines; very easy
b. NOW account				Unlimited check-writing privileges
c. Money market deposit account (MMDA)				
d. Asset management account				
e. Series EE savings bond	Virtually none			
f. U.S. Treasury bill				
g. Certificate of deposit (CD)				
h. Commercial paper				
i. Banker's acceptance				
j. Money market mutual fund (money fund)				

Problems

All problems are available on **www.myfinancelab.com**

LG4

P1.1 Sonia Gomez, a 45-year-old woman, wishes to accumulate $250,000 over the next 15 years to supplement the retirement programs that are being funded by the federal government and her employer. She expects to earn an average annual return of about 8% by investing in a low-risk portfolio containing about 20% short-term securities, 30% common stock, and 50% bonds.

Sonia currently has $31,500 that at an 8% annual rate of return will grow to about $100,000 at the end of 15 years (found using time-value techniques that will be described in Chapter 4 Appendix). Her financial adviser indicated that for every $1,000 Sonia wishes to accumulate at the end of 15 years, she will have to make an annual investment of $36.83. (This amount is also calculated on the basis of an 8% annual rate of return using the time-value techniques that are described in the Chapter 4 Appendix.) Sonia plans to accumulate needed funds by making equal, annual, end-of-year investments over the next 15 years.

a. How much money does Sonia need to accumulate by making equal, annual, end-of-year investments to reach her goal of $250,000?

b. How much must Sonia deposit annually to accumulate at the end of year 15 the sum calculated in part **a**?

LG4

P1.2 During 2009, the Allens and the Zells both filed joint tax returns. The Allens' taxable income was $130,000, and the Zells had total taxable income of $65,000 for the tax year ended December 31, 2009.

a. Using the federal tax rates given in Table 1.2, calculate the taxes for both the Allens and the Zells.

b. Calculate and compare the ratio of the Allens' to the Zells' taxable income and the ratio of the Allens' to the Zells' taxes. What does this demonstrate about the federal income tax structure?

LG4

P1.3 Jason Consalvo, a 53-year-old software engineer, and his wife, Kerri, have $50,000 to invest. They will need the money at retirement in 10 years. They are considering two investments. The first is a utility company common stock that costs $50 per share and pays dividends of $2 per share per year (a 4% dividend yield). Note that these dividends will be taxed at the same rates that apply to long-term capital gains. The Consalvos do not expect the value of this stock to increase. The other investment under consideration is a highly rated corporate bond that currently sells for $1,000 and pays annual interest at a rate of 5%, or $50 per $1,000 invested. After 10 years, these bonds will be repaid at par, or $1,000 per $1,000 invested. Assume that the Consalvos keep the income from their investments but do not reinvest it (they keep the cash in a non-interest-bearing bank account). They will, however, need to pay income taxes on their investment income. They will sell the stock after 10 years if they buy it. If they buy the bonds, in 10 years they will get back the amount they invested. The Consalvos are in the 33% tax bracket.

a. How many shares of the stock can the Consalvos buy?

b. How much will they receive after taxes each year in dividend income if they buy the stock?

c. What is the total amount they would have from their original $50,000 if they purchased the stock and all went as planned?

d. How much will they receive after taxes each year in interest if they purchase the bonds?

e. What is the total amount they would have from their original $50,000 if they purchased the bonds and all went as planned?

f. Based only on your calculations and ignoring other risk factors, should they buy the stock or the bonds?

LG4

P1.4 Mike and Julie Bedard are a working couple. They will file a joint income tax return. This year, they have the following taxable income:

1. $125,000 from salary and wages (ordinary income).
2. $1,000 in interest income.

3. $3,000 in dividend income.
4. $2,000 in profit from sale of a stock they purchased two years ago.
5. $2,000 in profit from a stock they purchased this year and sold this year.

Use the federal income tax rates given in Table 1.2 to work this problem.
   a. How much will Mike and Julie pay in federal income taxes on 2 above?
   b. How much will Mike and Julie pay in federal income taxes on 3 above? (*Note:* Remember that dividend income is taxed differently than ordinary income.)
   c. How much will Mike and Julie pay in federal income taxes on 4 above?
   d. How much will Mike and Julie pay in federal income taxes on 5 above?

Visit **www.myfinancelab.com** for web exercises, spreadsheets, and other online resources.

Case Problem 1.1   *Investments or Golf?*

LG1 LG2 LG3

NOTE Two Case Problems appear at the end of every chapter. They ask you to apply what you have learned in the chapter to a hypothetical investment situation.

Judd Read and Judi Todd, senior accounting majors at a large midwestern university, have been good friends since high school. Each has already found a job that will begin after graduation. Judd has accepted a position as an internal auditor in a medium-size manufacturing firm. Judi will be working for one of the major public accounting firms. Each is looking forward to the challenge of a new career and to the prospect of achieving success both professionally and financially.

Judd and Judi are preparing to register for their final semester. Each has one free elective to select. Judd is considering taking a golf course offered by the physical education department, which he says will help him socialize in his business career. Judi is planning to take a basic investments course. She has been trying to convince Judd to take investments instead of golf. Judd believes he doesn't need to take investments because he already knows what common stock is. He believes that whenever he has accumulated excess funds, he can invest in the stock of a company that is doing well. Judi argues that there is much more to it than simply choosing common stock. She feels that exposure to the field of investments would be more beneficial than learning how to play golf.

Questions

a. Explain to Judd the structure of the investment process and the economic importance of investing.

b. List and discuss the other types of investment vehicles with which Judd is apparently unfamiliar.

c. Assuming that Judd already gets plenty of exercise, what arguments would you give to convince Judd to take investments rather than golf?

Case Problem 1.2   *Preparing Carolyn Bowen's Investment Plan*

LG4 LG5

Carolyn Bowen, who just turned 55, is employed as a administrative assistant for the Xcon Corporation where she has worked for the past 20 years. She is in good health, lives alone, and has two grown children. A few months ago, her husband died. Carolyn's husband left her with only their home and the proceeds from a $75,000 life insurance policy. After she paid medical and funeral expenses, $60,000 of the life insurance proceeds remained. In addition to the life insurance proceeds, Carolyn has $37,500 in a savings account, which she had accumulated over the past 10 years. Recognizing that she is within 10 years of retirement, Carolyn wishes to use her limited resources to develop an investment program that will allow her to live comfortably once she retires.

Carolyn is quite superstitious. After consulting with a number of psychics and studying her family tree, she feels certain she will not live past 80. She plans to retire at either 62 or 65, whichever will better allow her to meet her long-run financial goals. After talking with a number of knowledgeable individuals—including, of course, the psychics—Carolyn estimates that to live comfortably, she will need $45,000 per year before taxes once she retires. This amount will be required annually for each of 18 years if she retires at 62 or for each of 15 years if she retires at 65. As part of her financial plans, Carolyn intends to sell her home at retirement and rent an apartment. She has estimated that she will net $112,500 if she sells the house at 62 and $127,500 if she sells it at 65. Carolyn has no financial dependents and is not concerned about leaving a sizable estate to her heirs.

If Carolyn retires at age 62, she will receive from Social Security and an employer-sponsored pension plan a total of $1,359 per month ($16,308 annually); if she waits until age 65 to retire, her total retirement income will be $1,688 per month ($20,256 annually). For convenience, Carolyn has already decided that to convert all her assets at the time of retirement into a stream of annual income, she will at that time purchase an annuity by paying a single premium. The annuity will have a life just equal to the number of years remaining until her 80th birthday. If Carolyn retires at age 62 and buys an annuity at that time, for each $1,000 that she puts into the annuity she will receive an annual benefit equal to $79 for the subsequent 18 years. If she waits until age 65 to retire, each $1,000 invested in the annuity will produce an annual benefit of $89.94 for the next 15 years.

Carolyn plans to place any funds currently available into a savings account paying 6% compounded annually until retirement. She does not expect to be able to save or invest any additional funds between now and retirement. For every dollar that Carolyn invests today, she will have $1.50 by age 62, or if she leaves the money invested until age 65, she will have $1.79 for each dollar invested today.

Questions

a. Assume that Carolyn places currently available funds in the savings account. Determine the amount of money Carolyn will have available at retirement once she sells her house if she retires at (1) age 62 and (2) age 65.

b. Using the results from **a**, determine the level of annual income that will be provided to Carolyn through purchase of an annuity at (1) age 62 and (2) age 65.

c. With the results found in the preceding questions, determine the total annual retirement income Carolyn will have if she retires at (1) age 62 and (2) age 65.

d. From your findings, do you think Carolyn will be able to achieve her long-run financial goal by retiring at (1) age 62 or (2) age 65? Explain.

e. Evaluate Carolyn's investment plan in terms of her use of a savings account and an annuity rather than some other investment vehicles. Comment on the risk and return characteristics of her plan. What recommendations might you offer Carolyn? Be specific.

Excel with Spreadsheets

NOTE Excel spreadsheet exercises at the end of each chapter will assist you in learning some useful applications of this tool in the personal investing process.

In the following chapters of this text, you will be asked to solve spreadsheet problems using Microsoft Excel®. While each person's skill and experience with Excel will vary, we assume that you understand its basics. This includes entering text and numbers, copying or moving a cell, moving and copying using "drag and drop," inserting and deleting rows and columns, and checking your spelling. The review in this chapter focuses on entering and editing data in the worksheet.

To complete the spreadsheet review, go to www.myfinancelab.com and to "Student Resources." Click on "Spreadsheet Review." There you will be asked to **create a spreadsheet** and perform the following tasks.

Questions

a. Add and subtract data with a formula.

b. Multiply and divide data with a formula.

c. Total cells using the sum function and calculate an average.

d. Use the average function.

e. Copy a formula using the "drag and drop" method.

CHAPTER 2

Securities Markets and Transactions

LEARNING GOALS

After studying this chapter, you should be able to:

LG1 Identify the basic types of securities markets and describe their characteristics.

LG2 Explain the initial public offering (IPO) process.

LG3 Describe broker markets and dealer markets, and discuss how they differ from alternative trading systems.

LG4 Review the key aspects of the globalization of securities markets, and discuss the importance of international markets.

LG5 Discuss trading hours and the regulation of securities markets.

LG6 Explain long purchases, margin transactions, and short sales.

"Wall Street" is an early 17th century testament to the global beginnings of U.S. financial markets. Wall Street was originally the northern boundary of a Dutch colonial settlement founded in 1625 called New Amsterdam, which after coming under English rule in 1664 became New York City. The U.S. financial markets that we know today began to take shape in the late 18th century as stockbrokers and speculators informally gathered on Wall Street under a buttonwood tree to trade. In 1792 twenty-four stockbrokers signed the Buttonwood Agreement, agreeing to trade securities on a commission basis, thus becoming the first organized American securities exchange. In 1817 the Buttonwood organization renamed itself the New York Stock & Exchange Board and rented rooms on Wall Street to establish the first centralized exchange location of what in 1863 became known as the New York Stock Exchange (NYSE).

Jumping ahead one hundred forty-three years, the NYSE and Archipelago Holdings, Inc. merged in 2006 to create the NYSE Group, Inc., a publicly traded company. Archipelago Holdings was comprised of the Archipelago Exchange and Pacific Stock Exchange. Although the merger with Archipelago was the largest ever among securities exchanges at the time, it was to be outdone. NYSE Euronext was formed in 2007 through a merger of NYSE Group, Inc., and Euronext N.V., thus creating the first global stock exchange. Euronext brought a consortium of European exchanges to the merger, including the Paris, Brussels, Lisbon, and Amsterdam stock exchanges and the London-based electronic derivatives market Euronext.liffe. Further expansion occurred in 2008 when NYSE Euronext acquired the American Stock Exchange. As a result of the acquisition, more than 500 Amex-listed companies joined NYSE Euronext. Through a series of acquisitions and mergers, the Buttonwood Agreement has become the world's largest and most liquid exchange group.

From the trading under a buttonwood tree in a Dutch colonial settlement in 1792 to the NYSE's introduction of 3D trading floors in 1999, to the launch of the NYSE Euronext's Universal Trading Platform in 2008, to the more than 4,000 NYSE-listed companies with an aggregate market capitalization of more than $10 trillion in 2009, Wall Street remains a truly global marketplace.

(Sources: "Timeline www.nyse.com, accessed August 22, 2009; "Wall Street," en.wikipedia.org/wiki/Wall_street, accessed August 22, 2009; and "NYSE Group and Euronext N.V. Agree to a Merger of Equals," NYSE press release, dated June 2, 2006, www.nyse.com, accessed August 22, 2009.)

Securities Markets

LG1 LG2 LG3   **Securities markets** are forums that allow suppliers and demanders of *securities* to make financial transactions. Their goal is to permit such transactions to be made quickly and at a fair price. In this section we will look at the various types of securities markets and their general characteristics.

Types of Securities Markets

In general, securities markets are broadly classified as either **money markets** or **capital markets**. The money market is the market where *short-term* debt securities (with maturities less than one year) are bought and sold. Investors use the money market for *short-term* borrowing and lending. Investors turn to the capital market to buy and sell *long-term* securities (with maturities of more than one year), such as stocks and bonds. In this book we will devote most of our attention to the capital market. There investors can make transactions in a wide variety of financial securities, including stocks, bonds, mutual funds, exchange traded funds, options, and futures. Capital markets are classified as either *primary* or *secondary,* depending on whether securities are being sold initially to investors by the issuer (*primary* market) or resold among investors.

The Primary Market The market in which *new issues* of securities are sold to investors is the **primary market.** In the primary market, the issuer of the equity or debt securities receives the proceeds of sales. In 2008, due in large part to a turbulent economy, only 21 companies sold stock to the public for the first time in the primary market in the United States. As this book was going to press, it appeared that number would more than double in 2009, but these numbers still compared unfavorably with the 477 companies that "went public" just ten years earlier in 1999. The most significant transaction in the primary market is the **initial public offering (IPO),** which marks the first public sale of a company's stock and results in the company's taking on a public status. The primary markets also provide a forum for the sale of additional stock, called *seasoned equity issues,* by already public companies.

Before offering its securities for public sale, the issuer must register them with and obtain approval from the **Securities and Exchange Commission (SEC).** This federal regulatory agency must confirm both the adequacy and the accuracy of the information provided to potential investors before a security is publicly offered for sale. In addition, the SEC regulates the securities markets.

To sell its securities in the primary market, a firm has three choices. It may make (1) a **public offering,** in which the firm offers its securities for sale to public investors; (2) a **rights offering,** in which the firm offers shares to existing stockholders on a pro rata basis; or (3) a **private placement** in which the firm sells securities directly without SEC registration to select groups of private investors such as insurance companies, investment management funds, and pension funds.

Going Public: The IPO Process Most companies that go public are small, fast-growing companies that require additional capital to continue expanding. For example, LogMeIn, Inc., a company that allows its customers to leave their laptop computers behind and instead use the company's remote access software, raised about $85 million when it went public in June 2009 at $16 per share. Alternatively, large companies may decide to spin off a unit into a separate public corporation. McDonald's did this when it spun off its Chipotle Mexican Grill, a 489-location, Mexican-food restaurant chain, in January 2006, raising about $174 million at $22 per share.

When a company decides to go public, it first must obtain the approval of its current shareholders, the investors who own its privately issued stock. Next, the company's auditors and lawyers must certify that all financial disclosure documents for the company are legitimate. The company then finds an investment bank willing to *underwrite* the offering. This bank is the lead underwriter and is responsible for promoting the company's stock and facilitating the sale of the company's IPO shares. The lead underwriter often brings in other investment banking firms to help underwrite and market the company's stock. We'll discuss the role of the investment banker in more detail in the next section.

The underwriter also assists the company in filing a registration statement with the SEC. One portion of this statement is called the **prospectus.** It describes the key aspects of the securities to be issued, the issuer's management, and the issuer's financial position. While waiting for the registration statement's SEC approval, prospective investors may receive a preliminary prospectus. This preliminary version is called a **red herring** because a notice printed in red on the front cover indicates the tentative nature of the offer. The cover of the preliminary prospectus describing the 2009 stock issue of LogMeIn, Inc., appears in Figure 2.1 on page 35. Note the red herring printed across the top of the front page.

After the SEC approves the registration statement, the investment community can begin analyzing the company's prospects. However, from the time the company files its preliminary registration statement until at least one month after the IPO is complete, the company and the company's auditors, lawyers, and underwriters must observe a *quiet period,* during which there are restrictions on what can be said about the company. The purpose of the quiet period is to make sure that all potential investors have access to the same information about the company—that which is presented in the preliminary prospectus—but not to any unpublished data that might provide an unfair advantage.

During the registration period and prior to the actual IPO date, the investment bankers and company executives promote the company's stock offering through a *road show*, which consists of a series of presentations to potential investors—typically institutional investors—around the country and sometimes overseas. In addition to providing investors with information about the new issue, road show sessions help the investment bankers gauge the demand for the offering and set an expected price range. Once all of the issue terms have been set, including the price, the SEC must approve the offering before the IPO can commence.

Table 2.1 (on page 36) shows the number of offerings, the average first-day return, and the gross proceeds raised in each year between 1999 and 2008. Note the exceptionally high first-day returns and large number of offerings during 1999 and 2000 caused by the technology-stock-driven bull market that ended in 2000. Since then, the number of offerings and the first-day returns have declined dramatically, consistent with the precipitous market decline that occurred in 2001 and 2002.

Investing in IPOs is risky business, particularly for individual investors who can't easily acquire shares at the offering price. Most of those shares go to institutional investors and brokerage firms' best clients. Although news stories may chronicle huge first-day gains, IPO stocks are not necessarily good long-term investments.

The Investment Banker's Role Most public offerings are made with the assistance of an investment banker. The **investment banker** is a financial intermediary (such as Goldman, Sachs & Co.) that specializes in assisting companies to issue new securities and advising firms with regard to major financial transactions. The main activity of the

FIGURE 2.1

Cover of a Preliminary Prospectus for a Stock Issue

Some of the key factors related to the 2009 common stock issue by LogMeIn, Inc., are summarized on the cover of the prospectus. The disclaimer statement across the top of the page is normally printed in red, which explains its name "red herring." (Source: LogMeIn, Inc., June 26, 2009, p. 1.)

Subject to Completion, dated June 26, 2009

Prospectus

6,666,667 Shares

LogMeIn, Inc.

Common Stock

This is the initial public offering of common stock by LogMeIn, Inc. We are offering 5,000,000 shares of common stock. The selling stockholders identified in this prospectus, including our chief executive officer and chief technology officer, are offering an additional 1,666,667 shares of common stock. We will not receive any proceeds from the sale of shares by the selling stockholders.

The estimated initial public offering price is between $14.00 and $16.00 per share. Currently, no public market exists for the shares. Our shares of common stock have been approved for listing on The NASDAQ Global Market under the symbol "LOGM."

Investing in our common stock involves risks. See "Risk Factors" beginning on page 8 of this prospectus.

	Per Share	Total
Initial public offering price	$	$
Underwriting discounts	$	$
Proceeds to us (before expenses)	$	$
Proceeds to selling stockholders (before expenses)	$	$

We and the selling stockholders have granted the underwriters a 30-day option to purchase up to an additional 1,000,000 shares (750,000 shares from us and 250,000 shares from the selling stockholders) on the same terms and conditions as set forth above if the underwriters sell more than 6,666,667 shares of common stock in this offering.

Neither the Securities and Exchange Commission nor any state securities commission has approved or disapproved of these securities or determined if this prospectus is truthful or complete. Any representation to the contrary is a criminal offense.

The underwriters expect to deliver the shares on or about   , 2009.

J.P. Morgan   **Barclays Capital**

Thomas Weisel Partners LLC   **Piper Jaffray**   **RBC Capital Markets**

Prospectus dated   , 2009

investment banker is **underwriting**. This process involves purchasing the securities from the issuing firm at an agreed-on price and bearing the risk of reselling them to the public. The investment banker also provides the issuer with advice about pricing and other important aspects of the issue.

In the case of large security issues, the lead investment banker brings in other bankers as partners to form an **underwriting syndicate**. The syndicate shares the financial risk associated with buying the entire issue from the issuer and reselling the new securities to the public. The lead or originating investment banker and the syndicate members put together a **selling group**, normally made up of themselves and a large

TABLE 2.1	Annual IPO Data, 1999–2008		
		Aggregate	
Year	Number of IPOS	Average First-Day Return (%)	Gross proceeds ($ billion)
1999	487	69.6	65.07
2000	385	55.4	65.63
2001	81	13.7	34.37
2002	70	8.6	22.14
2003	68	12.4	10.12
2004	186	12.2	32.38
2005	169	9.8	28.68
2006	164	11.3	30.69
2007	160	13.5	35.20
2008	21	6.4	22.76

(Source: Jay R. Ritter, "Some Factoids About the 2008 IPO Market," Retrieved August 20, 2009, from bear.cba.ufl.edu/ritter/IPOs2008sorts.pdf, table 8.)

number of brokerage firms. Each member of the selling group is responsible for selling a certain portion of the issue and is paid a commission on the securities it sells. The selling process for a large security issue is depicted in Figure 2.2.

The relationships among the participants in this process can also be seen on the cover of the June 26, 2009, preliminary prospectus for the common stock offering for LogMeIn, Inc., in Figure 2.1 on page 35. The layout of the prospectus cover indicates the roles of the various participating firms. Isolated firm names or a larger typeface differentiates the originating underwriter or underwriting syndicate members (J. P. Morgan and Barclays Capital) from the selling group, whose names appear in a smaller font below.

Compensation for underwriting and selling services typically comes in the form of a discount on the sale price of the securities. For example, an investment banker may pay the issuing firm $24 per share for stock that will be sold for $26 per share. Next,

MARKETS in CRISIS

No Time to Go Public

Starting in 2004 and lasting through 2007, the IPO markets became more active. Their improvement was primarily the result of a strengthening of the public equity markets. However, due largely to the outbreak of the financial crisis in 2007, IPO volume dropped to a 29-year low in 2008. When financial markets are in crisis, issuing new securities to the public can be difficult for companies. This is because during times of crisis, investors and regulators alike take actions that make selling new securities more difficult. Investors tend to withdraw from the markets during times of crisis because they are more unsure than usual about the future prospects of publicly listed companies—in other

words, which ones will weather the storm. Regulators, meanwhile, tend to impose new regulatory requirements during times of crisis. It often takes companies a while to fully comprehend the impact of new regulations, and until they do, they may opt to avoid issuing new securities. Typically, smaller firms are the ones most affected by a financial crisis since they often lack the track record necessary to reassure the financial market's creditors and investors. Table 2.1 supports this notion. Notice that the average IPO size, calculated by dividing the yearly aggregate gross proceeds by the yearly number of IPOs, in 2008 is on average five times larger than that of the other nine years.

FIGURE 2.2

The Selling Process for a Large Security Issue

The investment banker hired by the issuing firm may form an underwriting syndicate. The underwriting syndicate buys the entire security issue from the issuing corporation at an agreed-on discount to the public offering price. The underwriter then bears the risk of reselling the issue to the public at a public offering price. The investment banks' profit is the difference between the price they guaranteed the issuer and the public offering price. Both the originating investment banker and the other syndicate members put together a selling group to sell the issue on a commission basis to investors.

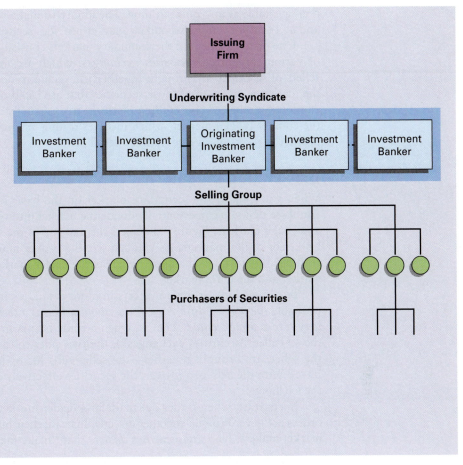

the underwriting syndicate members may then sell the shares to members of the selling group for $25.25 per share. This difference is referred to as the *gross spread,* which comprises the lead underwriter's management fee, the syndicate underwriters' discounts, and the selling group's selling concession. Having guaranteed the issuer $24 per share, the originating underwriter may then sell the share to the underwriting syndicate members for $24.25 per share. The 25 cents per share difference represents the lead underwriter's management fee. The difference between the $24.25 per share the investment banks in the underwriting syndicate paid and the $25.25 per share they sold to the selling group represents the underwriters' discount, which is their profit per share. The members of the selling group earn a selling concession of 75 cents for each share they sell ($26 sale price − $25.25 purchase price). Although the issuer places some primary security offerings directly, the majority of new issues are sold through public offering via the process just described.

Secondary Markets The **secondary market,** or the *aftermarket,* is the market in which securities are traded *after they have been issued.* Unlike the primary market, secondary-market transactions do not involve the corporation that issued the securities. Instead, the secondary market permits an investor to sell his or her holdings to another investor. The secondary market provides an environment for continuous pricing of securities that helps to ensure that securities reflect their true value on the basis of the best information then available at any point in time. The ability to make securities transactions quickly and at a fair price in the secondary market provides securities traders with *liquidity*.

One major segment of the secondary markets consists of the securities listed on one of various organized *securities exchanges*, which are forums where the buyers and sellers of securities are brought together to execute trades. Another major segment of the market is made up of those securities that are listed on the **Nasdaq market**, which employs an all-electronic trading platform to execute trades. Finally, there is the **over-the-counter (OTC) market**, which involves trading in smaller, unlisted securities. Each of these markets is covered in more detail next.

Broker Markets and Dealer Markets

When you look at the secondary market on the basis of how securities are traded, you'll see that you can essentially divide the market into two segments: broker markets and dealer markets. Figure 2.3 depicts the makeup of the secondary market in terms of broker or dealer markets. As you can see, the **broker market** consists of national and regional "securities exchanges," whereas the **dealer market** is made up of the Nasdaq market and the OTC market.

Before we look at these markets in more detail, it's important to understand that probably *the biggest difference in the two markets is a technical point dealing with the way trades are executed*. That is, when a trade occurs in a broker market (on one of the so-called "securities exchanges"), the two sides to the transaction, the buyer and the seller, are brought together—the seller sells his or her securities directly to the buyer. With the help of a *broker*, the securities effectively change hands on the floor of the exchange.

In contrast, when trades are made in a dealer market, buyers' orders and sellers' orders are never brought together directly. Instead, their buy/sell orders are executed by **market makers**, who are *securities dealers* that "make markets" by offering to buy or

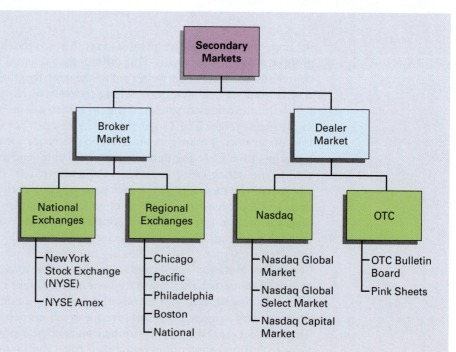

FIGURE 2.3

Broker and Dealer Markets

On a typical trading day, the secondary market is a beehive of activity, where literally billions of shares change hands. The market consists of two distinct parts—the *broker market* and the *dealer market*. As shown, each of these markets is made up of various exchanges and trading venues.

sell a certain amount of securities at stated prices. Essentially, two separate trades are made: The seller sells his or her securities (for example, in Intel Corp.) to a dealer, and the buyer buys his or her securities (in Intel Corp.) from another, or possibly even the same, dealer. Thus, there is always a dealer (*market maker*) on one side of a dealer-market transaction.

Smart's Tour of the Web
To watch author Scott Smart discuss key websites for this chapter visit www.myfinancelab.com

Broker Markets If you're like most people, when you think of the "stock market," the first thing that comes to mind is the New York Stock Exchange (NYSE), which is a national exchange. Actually, the NYSE is the dominant broker market. Also included in this market are the NYSE Amex (formally the American Stock Exchange), another *national exchange*, and several so-called *regional exchanges*. Regional exchanges are national stock exchanges that reside outside New York City, such as the Chicago Stock Exchange. One of the things that these exchanges have in common is that all the trading takes place on centralized trading floors. These exchanges account for about 60% of the *total dollar volume* of all shares traded in the U.S. stock market.

The NYSE is, in fact, the largest securities exchange in the world. Known as "the Big Board," it accounts for over 350 billion shares of stock that in 2009 had an aggregate market value of more than $10 trillion. It has very stringent listing requirements, and in 2009, more than 4,000 firms from around the world listed their shares on the NYSE.

The NYSE Amex is the second largest U.S. stock exchange in terms of the number of listed companies. However, when it comes to the dollar volume of trading, the NYSE Amex is actually smaller than the largest regional exchange—the Chicago Stock Exchange. NYSE Amex is home to more than 500 listed stocks and handles about 4% of the total annual dollar volume of shares traded on all U.S. securities exchanges. In contrast, the NYSE handles around 90% of all common shares traded on organized exchanges, so the NYSE Amex is far smaller than the NYSE in terms of size or stature. Even so, the NYSE Amex has created a strong market niche for itself through listing and trading the very popular exchange-traded funds (ETFs), a type of index-based mutual fund that we will discuss in Chapter 12.

In addition to the NYSE and NYSE Amex, a handful of so-called *regional exchanges* are part of the broker market. The number of securities listed on each of these exchanges is typically in the range of 100 to 500 companies. As a group, they handle around 6% of all shares traded on organized exchanges. The best known of these are the Chicago, Pacific, Philadelphia, Boston, and National stock exchanges. The largest of these exchanges is the Chicago Stock Exchange, which is actually larger than the NYSE Amex in terms of the dollar volume of trading. These exchanges deal primarily in securities with local and regional appeal. Most are modeled after the NYSE, but their membership and listing requirements are considerably more lenient. To enhance their trading activity, regional exchanges often list securities that are also listed on the NYSE or NYSE Amex.

Other broker markets include foreign stock exchanges that list and trade shares of firms in their own foreign markets. Also, separate domestic exchanges exist for trading in options and in futures. Here we consider the basic structure, rules, and operations of each of the major exchanges in the broker markets. We'll discuss foreign exchanges later.

The New York Stock Exchange Most securities exchanges are modeled after the New York Stock Exchange. Before the NYSE became a for-profit, publicly traded company in 2006, an individual or firm had to own or lease one of the 1,366 "seats" on the exchange to become a member of the exchange. The word "seat" comes from the fact that until the 1870s, members sat in chairs while trading. On December 30,

2005, in anticipation of becoming a publicly held company, the NYSE ceased having member seats. Each existing seat owner received $500,000 cash and 77,000 shares in the newly public NYSE Group, Inc., for its seat. Now the NYSE sells one-year trading licenses to trade directly on the exchange. As of January 1, 2009, a one-year trading license cost $44,000. Investment banks and brokerage firms comprise the majority of trading license holders, and each typically holds more than one trading license.

Firms such as Merrill Lynch designate officers to hold trading licenses. Only such designated individuals can make transactions on the floor of the exchange. The two main types of floor brokers are commission brokers and independent brokers. *Commission brokers* execute orders for their firm's customers. An *independent broker* works for himself or herself and handles orders on a fee basis, typically for smaller brokerage firms or large firms that are too busy to handle their own orders.

Trading Activity The floor of the NYSE is an area about the size of a football field. Its operation is typical of the various exchanges (although details vary). The NYSE floor has trading posts. Certain stocks trade at each post. (Bonds and less active stocks are traded in an annex.) Around the perimeter are telephones and electronic equipment that transmit buy and sell orders from brokers' offices to the exchange floor and back again after members execute the orders.

All transactions on the floor of the exchange occur through an auction process. The goal is to fill all buy orders at the lowest price and to fill all sell orders at the highest price with supply and demand determining the price. The actual auction takes place at the post where the particular security trades. Members interested in purchasing a given security publicly negotiate a transaction with members interested in selling that security. The job of the **designated market maker (DMM)**—an exchange member who specializes in making transactions in one or more stocks—is to manage the auction process. The DMM buys or sells (at specified prices) to provide a continuous, fair, and orderly market in those securities assigned to her or him.

Listing Policies To list its shares on a stock exchange, a firm must file an application and meet certain listing requirements. As noted earlier, some firms have **dual listing**, or listings on more than one exchange.

To be listed on the NYSE, a U.S. firm must have at least 400 stockholders owning 100 or more shares and a minimum of 1.1 million shares of publicly held stock outstanding; aggregate pretax earnings of at least $10 million over the previous three years, of at least $2 million in the previous two years and positive for the first of the last three years (an alternative earnings test of aggregate pretax earnings of at least $12 million over the previous three years, of at least $5 million in the most recent year, and of at least $2 million in the next most recent year), and a minimum market value of public shares of $100 million (a $60 million minimum market value is acceptable for IPOS and spin offs). Foreign companies are subject to similar listing requirements under the domestic listing criteria. The firm also must pay an original listing fee between $150,000 and $250,000. Once the NYSE accepts a firm's securities for listing, the company must continue to meet SEC requirements for exchange-listed securities. Listed firms that fail to meet specified requirements may be *delisted* from the exchange.

NYSE Amex The NYSE Amex has organization and procedures similar to those of the NYSE. Because its listing requirements are less stringent, many smaller and younger firms choose to list on the NYSE Amex, which has approximately 500 listed stocks.

In recent years the NYSE Amex has reinvented itself to focus on more specialized market instruments. Today about two-thirds of its daily volume comes from *exchange-traded funds (ETFs)*, a security pioneered by NYSE Amex more than 13 years ago. These funds are baskets of securities that are designed to generally track an index of the broad stock or bond market, a stock industry sector, or an international stock, but that trade like a single stock. Trading in stock options accounts for another large segment of the NYSE Amex's business.

Regional Stock Exchanges Most regional exchanges are modeled after the NYSE, but their membership and listing requirements are considerably more lenient. Trading costs are also lower. The majority of securities listed on regional exchanges are also listed on the NYSE or the NYSE Amex. About 100 million NYSE shares pass through one of the regional exchanges on a typical trading day. This dual listing may enhance a security's trading activity. In addition, the *Intermarket Trading System (ITS)* links nine markets—five regional exchanges, the NYSE, the NYSE Amex, the Nasdaq market (Nasdaq Global Select Market; Nasdaq Global Market; and Nasdaq Capital Market), and the Chicago Board Options Exchange—through an electronic communications network that allows brokers and dealers to make transactions at the best prices.

Options Exchanges *Options* allow their holders to sell or to buy another security at a specified price over a given period of time. The dominant options exchange is the Chicago Board Options Exchange (CBOE). Options are also traded on the NYSE Amex, on the Boston, Pacific, and Philadelphia exchanges, and on the International Securities Exchange (ISE). Usually, an option to sell or buy a given security is listed on all five options exchanges. Options exchanges deal only in security options. Other types of options (not discussed in this text) result from private transactions made directly between sellers and buyers.

Futures Exchanges *Futures* are contracts that guarantee the delivery of a specified commodity or financial instrument at a specific future date at an agreed-on price. The dominant exchange for trading commodity and financial futures is the Chicago Board of Trade (CBT). There are numerous other futures exchanges, some of which specialize in certain commodities and financial instruments rather than handling the broad spectrum listed on the CBT. The largest of these exchanges are the New York Mercantile Exchange; the Chicago Mercantile Exchange; the Deutsche Terminboerse; the London International Financial Futures and Options Exchange; the New York Coffee, Sugar & Cocoa Exchange; the New York Cotton Exchange; the Kansas City Board of Trade; and the Minneapolis Grain Exchange.

Dealer Markets One of the key features of the *dealer market* is that it has no centralized trading floors. Instead, it is made up of a large number of market makers who are linked together via a mass telecommunications network. Each market maker is actually a securities dealer who makes a market in one or more securities by offering to buy or sell them at stated bid/ask prices. The **bid price** and **ask price** represent, respectively, the highest price offered to purchase a given security and the lowest price offered to sell a given security. An investor pays the ask price when *buying* securities and receives the bid price when *selling* them. The dealer market is made up of both the Nasdaq and the OTC markets, which account for about 40% of all shares traded in the U.S. market—with the Nasdaq accounting for the overwhelming majority of those trades. As an aside, the *primary market* is also a dealer market because all new issues—*IPOs* and **secondary distributions**, which involve the public sale of large blocks of previously issued securities held by large investors—are sold to the investing public by securities dealers, acting on behalf of the investment banker.

The largest dealer market is made up of a large list of stocks that are listed and traded on the *National Association of Securities Dealers Automated Quotation System*, typically referred to as *Nasdaq*. Founded in 1971, Nasdaq had its origins in the OTC market but is today considered *a totally separate entity that's no longer a part of the OTC market*. In fact, in 2006 the Nasdaq was formally recognized by the SEC as a "listed exchange," giving it pretty much the same stature and prestige as the NYSE.

To be traded on the Nasdaq, all stocks must have at least two market makers, although the bigger, more actively traded stocks, like Cisco Systems, will have many more than that. These dealers electronically post all their bid/ask prices so that when investors place market orders, they are immediately filled at the best available price.

The Nasdaq listing standards vary depending on the Nasdaq listing market. The 1,000 or so stocks traded on the *Nasdaq Global Select Market* meet the world's highest listing standards. Created in 2006, the Global Select Market is reserved for the biggest and the "bluest"—highest quality—of the Nasdaq stocks. The listing requirements are also fairly comprehensive for the roughly 1,000 stocks traded on the *Nasdaq Global Market*. Stocks included on these two markets are all widely quoted, actively traded, and, in general, have a *national following*. The trades, all executed electronically, are every bit as efficient as they are on the floor of the NYSE. Indeed, the big-name stocks traded on the Nasdaq Global Select Market, and to some extent, on the Nasdaq Global Market, receive as much national visibility and are as liquid as those traded on the NYSE. As a result, just as the NYSE has its list of big-name players (like ExxonMobil, GE, Citigroup, Walmart, Pfizer, IBM, Procter & Gamble, Coca-Cola, Home Depot, and UPS), so too does Nasdaq. Its list includes companies like Microsoft, Intel, Cisco Systems, Dell, eBay, Google, Yahoo!, Apple, Starbucks, and Staples. Make no mistake, Nasdaq competes head-to-head with the NYSE for listings. In 2008, eight companies with a combined market capitalization of $79.9 billion moved their listings from the NYSE to Nasdaq. DreamWorks Animation SKG did the same in 2009. The *Nasdaq Capital Market* is still another Nasdaq market; it makes a market in about 600 or 700 stocks that, for one reason or another, are not eligible for the *Nasdaq Global Market*. In total, 50 countries are represented by the more than 3,800 companies listed on Nasdaq as of 2009.

The other part of the dealer market is made up of securities that trade in the *over-the-counter (OTC) market*. These non-Nasdaq issues include mostly small companies that either cannot or do not wish to comply with Nasdaq's listing requirements. They trade on either the *OTC Bulletin Board (OTCBB)* or in the so-called "*Pink Sheets*." The OTCBB is an electronic quotation system that links the market makers who trade the shares of small companies. The Bulletin Board is regulated by the SEC, which, among other things, requires all companies traded on this market to file audited financial statements and comply with federal securities law.

In sharp contrast, the OTC Pink Sheets is the *unregulated* segment of the market, where the companies are not even required to file with the SEC. This market is broken into two tiers. The biggest is populated by many small and often questionable companies that provide little or no information about their operations. The top, albeit smaller, tier is reserved for those companies that choose to provide audited financial statements and other required information. While the name comes from the color of paper these quotes used to be printed on, the "pinks" today use an electronic quotation system. Even so, liquidity is often minimal or almost nonexistent, and the market, especially the bottom tier, is littered with scores of nearly worthless stocks. It is definitely not a market for the prudent individual investor.

Alternative Trading Systems

Some individual and institutional traders now make direct transactions outside of the broker and dealer markets in the *third* and *fourth markets*. The **third market** consists of over-the-counter transactions made in securities listed on the NYSE, the NYSE Amex, or one of the other exchanges. These transactions are typically handled by market makers that are not members of a securities exchange. They charge lower commissions than the exchanges and bring together large buyers and sellers. Institutional investors, such as mutual funds, pension funds, and life insurance companies, are thus often able to realize sizable savings in brokerage commissions and to have minimal impact on the price of the transaction.

The **fourth market** consists of transactions made through a computer network, rather than on an exchange, directly between large institutional buyers and sellers of securities. Unlike third-market transactions, fourth-market transactions bypass the market maker. **Electronic communications networks (ECNs)** are at the heart of the fourth market. Archipelago (part of the NYSE Group), Bloomberg Tradebook, Island, Instinet, and MarketXT are some of the many ECNs that handle these trades.

ECNs are most effective for high-volume, actively traded securities, and they play a key role in after-hours trading, discussed later in this chapter. They automatically match buy and sell orders that customers place electronically. If there is no immediate match, the ECN, acting like a broker, posts its request under its own name on an exchange or with a market maker. The trade will be executed if another trader is willing to make the transaction at the posted price.

ECNs can save customers money because they charge only a transaction fee, either per share or based on order size. For this reason, money managers and institutions such as pension funds and mutual funds with large amounts of money to invest favor ECNs. Many also use ECNs or trade directly with each other to find the best prices for their clients.

General Market Conditions: Bull or Bear

Conditions in the securities markets are commonly classified as "bull" or "bear," depending on whether securities prices are rising or falling over time. Changing market conditions generally stem from changes in investor attitudes, changes in economic activity, and government actions aimed at stimulating or slowing down economic activity. **Bull markets** are markets normally associated with rising prices, investor optimism, economic recovery, and government stimulus. **Bear markets** are markets normally associated with falling prices, investor pessimism, economic slowdown, and government restraint. The beginning of 2003 marked the start of a generally bullish market cycle that peaked before turning sharply bearish in October 2007. Although far from having fully recovered, the bearish market appears to have bottomed out in March 2009 and has since been trying to establish a bullish momentum.

In general, investors experience higher (or positive) returns on common stock investments during a bull market. However, some securities are bullish in a bear market or bearish in a bull market. Market conditions are difficult to predict and usually can be identified only after they exist. In Chapter 3, we describe sources of information that can be used to assess market conditions. Chapters 7 through 9 discuss how to apply such information to the analysis and the evaluation of common stock.

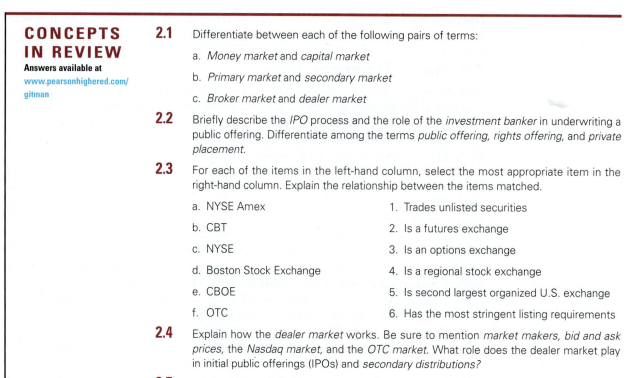

CONCEPTS IN REVIEW
Answers available at
www.pearsonhighered.com/gitman

2.1 Differentiate between each of the following pairs of terms:

a. *Money market* and *capital market*

b. *Primary market* and *secondary market*

c. *Broker market* and *dealer market*

2.2 Briefly describe the *IPO* process and the role of the *investment banker* in underwriting a public offering. Differentiate among the terms *public offering*, *rights offering*, and *private placement*.

2.3 For each of the items in the left-hand column, select the most appropriate item in the right-hand column. Explain the relationship between the items matched.

a. NYSE Amex   1. Trades unlisted securities

b. CBT   2. Is a futures exchange

c. NYSE   3. Is an options exchange

d. Boston Stock Exchange   4. Is a regional stock exchange

e. CBOE   5. Is second largest organized U.S. exchange

f. OTC   6. Has the most stringent listing requirements

2.4 Explain how the *dealer market* works. Be sure to mention *market makers, bid and ask prices,* the *Nasdaq market,* and the *OTC market.* What role does the dealer market play in initial public offerings (IPOs) and *secondary distributions?*

2.5 What are the *third* and *fourth markets?*

2.6 Differentiate between a *bull market* and a *bear market.*

Globalization of Securities Markets

LG4

Today investors, issuers of securities, and securities firms look beyond the markets of their home countries to find the best returns, lowest costs, and best international business opportunities. The basic goal of most investors is to earn the highest return with the lowest risk. This outcome is achieved through **diversification**—the inclusion of a number of different securities in a portfolio to increase returns and/or reduce risk. An investor can greatly increase the potential for diversification by holding (1) a wider range of industries and securities, (2) securities traded in a larger number of markets, and (3) securities denominated in different currencies, and the diversification is even greater if the investor does these things for a mix of domestic and foreign securities. The smaller and less diversified an investor's home market is, the greater the potential benefit from prudent international diversification. However, even investors from the United States and other highly developed markets can benefit from global diversification.

In short, globalization of the securities markets enables investors to seek out opportunities to profit from rapidly expanding economies throughout the world. Here we consider the growing importance of international markets, international investment performance, ways to invest in foreign securities, and the risks of investing internationally.

Growing Importance of International Markets

Securities exchanges now operate in over 100 countries worldwide. Both large (Tokyo) and small (Fiji), they are located not only in the major industrialized nations such as

Japan, Great Britain, Canada, and Germany but also in emerging economies such as Brazil, Chile, India, South Korea, Malaysia, Mexico, Poland, Russia, and Thailand. The top four securities markets worldwide (based on dollar volume) are the New York, Nasdaq, London, and Tokyo stock exchanges. Other important foreign exchanges include Shanghai, Paris, Osaka, Toronto, Montreal, Sydney, Hong Kong, Zurich, and Taiwan.

The economic integration of the European Monetary Union (EMU), along with pressure from financial institutions that want an efficient process for trading shares across borders, is changing the European securities market environment. Instead of many small national exchanges, countries are banding together to create cross-border markets and to compete more effectively in the pan-European equity-trading markets. The Paris, Amsterdam, Brussels, and Lisbon exchanges, plus a derivatives exchange in London, merged to form Euronext, and the Scandinavian markets formed Norex. In mid-2006, Euronext and the NYSE Group—the NYSE parent—signed an agreement to combine their businesses in a merger of equals. Some stock exchanges—for example, Tokyo and Australia—are forming cooperative agreements. Others are discussing forming a 24-hour global market alliance, trading the stocks of selected large international companies via an electronic order-matching system. Nasdaq, with joint ventures in Japan, Hong Kong, Canada, and Australia, plans to expand into Latin America and the Middle East. The increasing number of mergers and cooperative arrangements represent steps toward a worldwide stock exchange.

Bond markets, too, have become global, and more investors than ever before regularly purchase government and corporate fixed-income securities in foreign markets. The United States dominates the international government bond market, followed by Japan, Germany, and Great Britain.

International Investment Performance

A motive for investing overseas is the lure of high returns. In fact, only once since 1980 did the United States finish first among the major stock markets of the world in the rate of increase in its stock price index. For example, in 2005, an overall good year, investors would have earned higher returns in many foreign markets. During that year the Dow Jones Global Index in U.S. dollars for South Korea increased 58%; for Mexico, 40%; for Japan, 25%; for Finland, 14%; for France, 9%; for Germany, 8%; and for Thailand, 5%. By comparison, the U.S. stock price index increased about 4%. Of course, foreign securities markets tend to be riskier than U.S. markets.

A market with high returns in one year may not do so well in the next. However, even in 2008, one of the worst years on record for stock market investors, more than a dozen foreign exchanges earned returns higher than the NYSE Euronext.

Investors can compare activity on U.S. and foreign exchanges by following market indexes that track the performance of those exchanges. For instance, the Dow Jones averages and the Standard & Poor's indexes are popular measures of the U.S. markets, and indexes for more than 20 different stock markets are available. (We'll discuss indexes in more detail in Chapter 3.) *The Wall Street Journal* publishes daily reports on most major indexes, trading activity in selected stocks on major foreign exchanges, and currency exchange rates. Also, *The Wall Street Journal*'s "World Stock Markets" in Section C frequently compares the performance of the U.S. exchanges with that of selected foreign markets.

Ways to Invest in Foreign Securities

Investors can make foreign security transactions either indirectly or directly. One form of *indirect* investment is to purchase shares of a U.S.-based multinational with substantial foreign operations. Many U.S.-based multinational firms, such as ExxonMobil, IBM, Citigroup, Dow Chemical, Coca-Cola, Colgate-Palmolive, and Hewlett-Packard, receive more than 50% of their revenues from overseas operations. By investing in the securities of such firms, an investor can achieve a degree of international diversification. Purchasing shares in a mutual fund that invests primarily in foreign securities is another way to invest indirectly. Investors can make both of these indirect foreign securities investment transactions through a stockbroker, as explained in Chapter 3 and in Chapter 12 (on mutual funds).

To make *direct* investments in foreign companies, investors have three options. They can purchase securities on foreign exchanges, buy securities of foreign companies that trade on U.S. exchanges, or buy American depositary receipts (ADRs).

The first way—purchasing securities on foreign exchanges—involves additional risks because foreign securities do not trade in U.S. dollars and, thus, investors must cope with currency fluctuations. This approach is not for the timid or inexperienced investor. Investors also encounter different securities exchange rules, transaction procedures, accounting standards, and tax laws in different countries. Direct transactions are best handled either through brokers at major Wall Street firms with large international operations or through major banks, such as JPMorgan Chase and Citibank, that have special units to handle foreign securities transactions. Alternatively, investors can deal with foreign broker-dealers, but such an approach is more complicated and riskier.

The second form of direct investment is to buy the securities of foreign companies that trade on both organized and over-the-counter U.S. exchanges. Transactions in foreign securities that trade on U.S. exchanges are handled in the same way as exchange-traded domestic securities. These securities are issued by large, well-known foreign companies. Stocks of companies such as Alcan (Canada), DaimlerChrysler (Germany), France Telecom (France), Head (Netherlands), Sony (Japan), and Unilever (United Kingdom) trade directly on U.S. exchanges. In addition, **Yankee bonds**, U.S. dollar-denominated debt securities issued by foreign governments or corporations and traded in U.S. securities markets, trade in both broker and dealer markets.

Finally, foreign stocks also trade on U.S. exchanges in the form of **American depositary shares (ADSs)**. These securities have been created to permit U.S. investors to hold shares of non-U.S. companies and trade them on U.S. stock exchanges. They are backed by **American depositary receipts (ADRs)**, which are U.S dollar-denominated receipts for the stocks of foreign companies that are held in the vaults of banks in the companies' home countries. Today more than 2,000 ADRs representing more than 50 different home countries are traded (as ADSs) on U.S. exchanges. About one-fourth of them are actively traded. Included are ADSs of well-known companies such as Cadbury Schweppes, Hitachi, Nippon, LG Philips, Pearson, Reed Elseivier, and Siemans. ADSs, which trade in the same way as standard domestic securities, are further discussed in Chapter 6.

Risks of Investing Internationally

Investing abroad is not without pitfalls. In addition to the usual risks involved in any security transaction, investors must consider the risks of doing business in a particular foreign country. Changes in trade policies, labor laws, and taxation may affect operating conditions for the country's firms. The government itself may not be stable. You must track similar environmental factors in each foreign market in which you invest. This is clearly more difficult than following your home market.

U.S. securities markets are generally viewed as highly regulated and reliable. Foreign markets, on the other hand, may lag substantially behind the United States in both operations and regulation. Additionally, some countries place various restrictions on foreign investment. In Korea and Taiwan, for example, mutual funds are the only way for foreigners to invest. Mexico has a two-tier market, with certain securities restricted to foreigners. Some countries make it difficult for foreigners to get their funds out, and many impose taxes on dividends. For example, Swiss taxes are about 20% on dividends paid to foreigners. Other difficulties include illiquid markets and an inability to obtain reliable investment information because of a lack of reporting requirements.

Furthermore, accounting standards vary from country to country. Differences in accounting practices can affect a company's apparent profitability, conceal assets (such as the hidden reserves and undervalued assets that are permitted in many countries), and fail to disclose other risks. As a result, it is difficult to compare the financial performance of firms operating in different foreign countries. Although the accounting profession has agreed on a set of international accounting standards, it will be years until all countries have adopted them and even longer until all companies apply them.

Another concern stems from the fact that international investing involves securities denominated in foreign currencies. Trading profits and losses are affected not only by a security's price changes but also by changes in currency exchange rates. The values of the world's major currencies fluctuate with respect to each other on a daily basis. The relationship between two currencies on a specified date is called the **currency exchange rate.** On April 3, 2009, the currency exchange rate for the European Monetary Union euro (€) and the U.S. dollar (US$) was expressed as follows:

$$\text{US\$} = \text{€ } 0.7418 \quad \text{€} = \text{US\$ } 1.3481$$

On that day, if you had purchased 100 shares of Heineken, which was trading for € 18.75 per share on Euronext Amsterdam, it would have cost you $2,527.69.

Changes in the value of a particular foreign currency with respect to the U.S. dollar—or any other currency—are called *appreciation* and *depreciation*. For example, on August 21, 2009, the euro/US$ exchange rate was 0.6975. From April to August, the European Monetary Union euro *appreciated* relative to the dollar (and the dollar *depreciated* relative to the euro). On August 21 it took fewer euros to buy $1 (0.6975 versus 0.7418), so each euro was worth more in dollar terms ($1.4337 versus $1.3481). Had the European Monetary Union euro instead *depreciated* (and the dollar *appreciated* relative to the euro), each euro would have been worth less in dollar terms.

Currency exchange risk is the risk caused by the varying exchange rates between the currencies of two countries. For example, assume that on August 21, 2009, you sold your 100 shares of Heineken, which was trading for € 28.315 per share on Euronext Amsterdam; sale proceeds would have been $4,059.52.

In this example you had a win–win outcome since both the original purchase price in euros increased and the euro/US$ exchange rate decreased. In dollar terms the transaction resulted in a gain of $1,531.83 ($4,059.52 − $2,527.69). Investors in foreign securities must be aware that the value of the foreign currency in relation to the dollar can have a profound effect on returns from foreign security transactions.

**CONCEPTS
IN REVIEW**
Answers available at
www.pearsonhighered.com/
gitman

2.7 Why is globalization of securities markets an important issue today? How have international investments performed in recent years?

2.8 Describe how foreign security investments can be made, both indirectly and directly.

2.9 Describe the risks of investing internationally, particularly *currency exchange risk*.

Trading Hours and Regulation of Securities Markets

LG5 Understanding the structure of domestic and international securities markets is an important foundation for developing a sound investment program. Now let's look at market trading hours and the regulation of U.S. securities markets.

Trading Hours of Securities Markets

The regular trading session for organized U.S. exchanges runs from 9:30 A.M. to 4:00 P.M. eastern time. However, trading is no longer limited to these hours. Nasdaq and ECNs offer extended trading sessions before and after regular hours. Most of the after-hours markets are **crossing markets** in which orders are filled only if they can be matched. That is, buy and sell orders are filled only if they can be matched with identical opposing sell and buy orders at the desired price. These allow U.S. securities markets to compete more effectively with foreign securities markets, in which investors can execute trades when U.S. markets are closed.

The NYSE has two short electronic-trading sessions that begin after the 4:00 P.M. closing bell. One session, from 4:15 to 5:00 P.M., trades stocks at that day's closing prices via a computer matching system. Transactions occur only if a match can be made and are handled on a first-come, first-served basis. The other session lasts from 4:00 to 5:15 P.M. and allows institutional investors to trade large blocks of stock valued at $1 million or more. Since their inception, the NYSE has experienced increased volume in both sessions.

Nasdaq has its own extended-hours electronic-trading sessions from 4:00 to 6:30 P.M. eastern time, as well as two SelectNet trading sessions, from 8:00 to 9:30 A.M. eastern time and from 4:00 to 5:15 P.M. eastern time. Regional exchanges have also moved to after-hours trading sessions. Now individual investors can participate in after-hours trading activity. Many large brokerage firms, both traditional and online, offer after-hours trading services for their individual clients.

Regulation of Securities Markets

U.S. securities laws protect investors and participants in the financial marketplace. A number of state and federal laws require that investors receive adequate and accurate disclosure of information. Such laws also regulate the activities of participants in the securities markets. State laws that control the sale of securities within state borders are commonly called *blue sky laws* because they are intended to prevent investors from being sold nothing but "blue sky." These laws typically establish procedures for regulating both security issues and sellers of securities doing business within the state. Most states have a regulatory body, such as a state securities commission, that is charged with enforcing the related state statutes. Table 2.2 (on page 49) summarizes the most important securities laws enacted by the federal government (listed in chronological order).

TABLE 2.2	Important Federal Securities Laws
Act	**Brief Description**
Securities Act of 1933	Passed to ensure full disclosure of information about new security issues. Requires the issuer of a new security to file with the Securities and Exchange Commission (SEC) a registration statement containing information about the new issue. The firm cannot sell the security until the SEC approves the registration statement, which usually takes about 20 days. Approval of the registration statement by the SEC merely indicates that the facts presented in the statement appear to reflect the firm's true position.
Securities Exchange Act of 1934	Formally established the SEC as the agency in charge of administering federal securities laws. The act gave the SEC the power to regulate the organized exchanges and the OTC market; their members, brokers, and dealers; and the securities traded in these markets. Each of these participants must file reports with the SEC and periodically update them. The 1934 act has been amended several times over the years.
Maloney Act of 1938	An amendment to the Securities Exchange Act of 1934, it provided for the establishment of trade associations to self-regulate the securities industry. Only one such trade association, the National Association of Securities Dealers (NASD), has been formed. NASD members include nearly all of the nation's securities firms that do business with the public. The NASD, operating under SEC supervision, establishes standardized procedures for securities trading and ethical behavior, monitors and enforces compliance with these procedures, and serves as the industry spokesperson. Today any securities firms that are not members of the NASD must agree to direct SEC supervision.
Investment Company Act of 1940	Established rules and regulations for investment companies and formally authorized the SEC to regulate their practices and procedures. It required investment companies to register with the SEC and to fulfill certain disclosure requirements. An *investment company* obtains funds by selling its shares to investors and uses the proceeds to purchase securities. The dominant type of investment company is the *mutual fund*. A 1970 amendment prohibits investment companies from paying excessive fees to advisers and from charging excessive commissions to purchasers of company shares.
Investment Advisers Act of 1940	Requires *investment advisers*, persons hired by investors to advise them about security investments, to disclose all relevant information about their backgrounds, conflicts of interest, and any investments they recommend. Advisers must register and file periodic reports with the SEC. A 1960 amendment extended the SEC's powers to permit inspection of the records of investment advisers and to revoke the registration of advisers who violate the act's provisions.
Securities Acts Amendments of 1975	Requires the SEC and the securities industry to develop a competitive national system for trading securities. First, the SEC abolished fixed-commission schedules, thereby providing for negotiated commissions. Second, it established the *Intermarket Trading System (ITS),* an electronic communications network linking nine markets and trading over 4,000 eligible issues, that allows trades to be made across these markets wherever the network shows a better price for a given issue.
Insider Trading and Fraud Act of 1988	Established penalties for *insider trading,* using *nonpublic* information to make profitable securities transactions. Insiders include anyone who obtains nonpublic information, typically a company's directors, officers, major shareholders, bankers, investment bankers, accountants, or attorneys. The SEC requires corporate insiders to file monthly reports detailing all transactions made in the company's stock. Recent legislation substantially increased the penalties for insider trading and gave the SEC greater power to investigate and prosecute claims of illegal insider-trading activity.
Sarbanes-Oxley Act of 2002	Passed to protect investors against corporate fraud, particularly accounting fraud. It created an oversight board to monitor the accounting industry, tightened audit regulations and controls, toughened penalties against executives who commit corporate fraud, strengthened accounting disclosure requirements and ethical guidelines for financial officers, established corporate board structure and membership guidelines, established guidelines for analyst conflicts of interest, and increased the SEC's authority and budgets for auditors and investigators. The act also mandated instant disclosure of stock sales by corporate executives.

The intent of these federal securities laws is to protect investors. Most of these laws were passed in response to observed damaging abuses by certain market participants. Congress passed two laws recently in response to public concern over corporate financial scandals: The *Insider Trading and Fraud Act of 1988* aims at stopping **insider trading,** the use of *nonpublic* information about a company to make profitable securities transactions. The *Sarbanes-Oxley Act of 2002* focuses on eliminating corporate fraud related to accounting and other information releases. Both of these acts heightened the public's awareness of **ethics**—standards of conduct or moral judgment—in business. The government and the financial community are continuing to develop and enforce ethical standards that will motivate market participants to adhere to laws and regulations. Getting market participants to adhere to ethical standards, whether through law enforcement or incentives, remains an ongoing challenge.

CONCEPTS IN REVIEW

Answers available at
www.pearsonhighered.com/
gitman

2.10 How are after-hours trades typically handled? What is the outlook for after-hours trading?

2.11 Briefly describe the key requirements of the following federal securities laws:

a. Securities Act of 1933.

b. Securities Exchange Act of 1934.

c. Maloney Act of 1938.

d. Investment Company Act of 1940.

e. Investment Advisers Act of 1940.

f. Securities Acts Amendments of 1975.

g. Insider Trading and Fraud Act of 1988.

h. Sarbanes-Oxley Act of 2002.

Basic Types of Securities Transactions

LG6 An investor can make a number of basic types of security transactions. Each type is available to those who meet certain requirements established by government agencies as well as by brokerage firms. Although investors can use the various types of transactions in a number of ways to meet investment objectives, we describe only the most popular use of each transaction here, as we consider the long purchase, margin trading, and short selling.

Long Purchase

The **long purchase** is a transaction in which investors buy securities in the hope that they will increase in value and can be sold at a later date for profit. The object, then, is to *buy low and sell high*. A long purchase is the most common type of transaction. Because investors generally expect the price of a security to rise over the period of time they plan to hold it, their return comes from any dividends or interest received during the ownership period, *plus* the difference (capital gain or loss) between the purchase and selling prices. Transaction costs, of course, reduce this return.

Ignoring any dividends and transaction costs, we can illustrate the long purchase by a simple example. After studying Varner Industries, you are convinced that its common stock, which currently sells for $20 per share, will increase in value over the next few years. You expect the stock price to rise to $30 per share within two years. You place an order and buy 100 shares of Varner for $20 per share. If the stock price rises to, say, $40 per share, you will profit from your long purchase. If it drops below $20 per share, you will experience a loss on the transaction. Obviously, one of the major motivating factors in making a long purchase is an expected rise in the price of the security.

Margin Trading

Security purchases do not have to be made on a cash basis; investors can use borrowed funds instead. This activity is referred to as **margin trading**. It is used for one basic reason: to magnify returns. As peculiar as it may sound, the term *margin* refers to the amount of equity (stated as a percentage) in an investment, or the amount that is *not* borrowed. If an investor uses 75% margin, for example, it means that 75% of the investment position is being financed with the person's own funds and the balance (25%) with borrowed money. Brokers must approve margin purchases. The brokerage firm then lends the purchaser the needed funds and retains the purchased securities as collateral. It is important to recognize that margin purchasers must pay a specified rate of interest on the amount they borrow.

The Federal Reserve Board (the "Fed") sets the **margin requirement,** specifying the minimum amount of equity that must be the margin investor's own funds. The margin requirement for stocks has been at 50% for some time. By raising and lowering the margin requirement, the Fed can depress or stimulate activity in the securities markets.

A simple example will help to clarify the basic margin transaction. Assume that you wish to purchase 70 shares of common stock, which is currently selling for $63.50 per share. With the prevailing margin requirement of 50%, you need put up only $2,222.50 in cash ($63.50 per share × 70 shares × 0.50). Your brokerage firm will lend you the remaining $2,222.50. You will, of course, have to pay interest on the amount you borrow, plus the applicable brokerage fees. With the use of margin, you can purchase more securities than you could afford on a strictly cash basis. In this way, you can magnify your returns (as demonstrated in the next section).

Although margin trading can lead to increased returns, it also presents substantial risks. One of the biggest is that the issue may not perform as expected. If this occurs, no amount of margin trading can correct matters. Margin trading can only magnify returns, not produce them. And if the security's return is negative, margin trading magnifies the loss. Because the security being margined is always the ultimate source of return, choosing the right securities is critical to this trading strategy.

Essentials of Margin Trading Investors can use margin trading with most kinds of securities. They regularly use it, for example, to buy common and preferred stocks, most types of bonds, mutual funds, options, warrants, and futures. It is not normally used with tax-exempt municipal bonds because the interest paid on such margin loans is not deductible for income tax purposes. It is also possible to use margin on certain foreign stocks and bonds that meet prescribed criteria and appear on the Fed's "List of Foreign Margin Stocks," which is published semiannually. For simplicity, we will use common stock as the vehicle in our discussion of margin trading.

Magnified Profits and Losses With an investor's equity serving as a base, the idea of margin trading is to employ **financial leverage**—the use of debt financing to magnify investment returns.

Here is how it works: Suppose you have $5,000 to invest and are considering the purchase of 100 shares of stock at $50 per share. If you do not margin, you can buy

TABLE 2.3 The Effect of Margin Trading on Security Returns				EXCEL WITH SPREADSHEETS
	Without Margin (100% Equity)	With Margins of		
		80%	65%	50%
Number of $50 shares purchased	100	100	100	100
Cost of investment	$5,000	$5,000	$5,000	$5,000
Less: Borrowed money	0	1,000	1,750	2,500
Equity in investment	$5,000	$4,000	$3,250	$2,500
A. Investor's position if price rises by $30 to $80/share				
Value of stock	$8,000	8,000	8,000	$8,000
Less: Cost of investment	5,000	5,000	5,000	5,000
Capital gain	$3,000	3,000	3,000	$3,000
Return on investor's equity (capital gain/equity in investment)	60%	75%	92.3%	120%
B. Investor's position if price falls by $30 to $20/share				
Value of stock	$2,000	2,000	2,000	$2,000
Less: Cost of investment	5,000	5,000	5,000	5,000
Capital loss*	($3,000)	(3,000)	(3,000)	($3,000)
Return on investor's equity (capital loss/equity in investment)*	(60%)	(75%)	(92.3%)	(120%)

*Both the capital loss and the return on investor's equity are *negative* as noted by the parentheses.

exactly 100 shares of the stock (ignoring brokerage commissions). If you margin the transaction—for example, at 50%—you can acquire the same $5,000 position with only $2,500 of your own money. This leaves you with $2,500 to use for other investments or to buy on margin another 100 shares of the same stock. Either way, by margining you will reap greater benefits from the stock's price appreciation.

Table 2.3 illustrates the concept of margin trading. It shows an unmargined (100% equity) transaction, along with the same transaction using various margins. Remember that the margin rates (e.g., 65%) indicate the investor's equity in the investment. When the investment is unmargined and the price of the stock goes up by $30 per share (see Table 2.3, part A), the investor enjoys a very respectable 60% rate of return. However, observe what happens when margin is used: The rate of return shoots up as high as 120%, depending on the amount of equity in the investment. This occurs because the gain is the same ($3,000) *regardless of how the investor finances the transaction.* Clearly, as the investor's equity in the investment *declines* (with lower margins), the rate of return *increases* accordingly.

Three facets of margin trading become obvious from the table:

1. The price of the stock will move in whatever way it is going to, regardless of how the position is financed.

2. The lower the amount of the investor's equity in the position, the *greater the rate of return* the investor will enjoy when the price of the security rises.

3. The *loss is also magnified* (by the same rate) when the price of the security falls (see Table 2.3, part B).

Note that Table 2.3 has an "Excel with Spreadsheets" icon. Throughout the text, tables with this icon indicate that they are available as spreadsheets on www. myfinancelab.com. The use of electronic spreadsheets in finance and investments, as well as in all functional areas of business, is pervasive. We use spreadsheets from time to time throughout the text to demonstrate how the content has been constructed or calculated. As you know from Chapter 1, we include Excel spreadsheet exercises at the end of most chapters to give you practice with spreadsheets and help you develop the ability to clearly set out the logic needed to solve investment problems.

Advantages and Disadvantages of Margin Trading A magnified return is the major advantage of margin trading. The size of the magnified return depends on both the price behavior of the security and the amount of margin used. Another, more modest benefit of margin trading is that it allows for greater diversification of security holdings because investors can spread their limited capital over a larger number of investments.

The major disadvantage of margin trading, of course, is the potential for magnified losses if the price of the security falls. Another disadvantage is the cost of the margin loans themselves. A **margin loan** is the official vehicle through which the borrowed funds are made available in a margin transaction. All margin loans are made at a stated interest rate, which depends on prevailing market rates and the amount of money being borrowed. This rate is usually 1% to 3% above the **prime rate**—the interest rate charged to creditworthy business borrowers. For large accounts, it may be at the prime rate. The loan cost, which investors pay, will increase daily, reducing the level of profits (or increasing losses) accordingly.

Making Margin Transactions To execute a margin transaction, an investor must establish a **margin account** with a minimum of $2,000 in equity or 100% of the purchase price, whichever is less, in the form of either cash or securities. The broker will retain any securities purchased on margin as collateral for the loan.

The margin requirement established by the Federal Reserve Board sets the minimum amount of equity for margin transactions. Investors need not execute all margin transactions by using exactly the minimum amount of margin; they can use more than the minimum if they wish. Moreover, it is not unusual for brokerage firms and the major exchanges to establish their own margin requirements, which are more restrictive than those of the Federal Reserve. Brokerage firms also may have their own lists of especially volatile stocks for which the margin requirements are higher. There are basically two types of margin requirements: initial margin and maintenance margin.

Initial Margin The minimum amount of equity that must be provided by the investor *at the time of purchase* is the **initial margin**. It prevents overtrading and excessive speculation. Generally, this is the margin requirement to which investors refer when discussing margin trading. All securities that can be margined have specific initial requirements, which the governing authorities can change at their discretion. Table 2.4 (on page 54) shows initial margin requirements for various types of securities. The more stable investment vehicles, such as U.S. government issues, generally have substantially lower margin requirements and thus offer greater opportunities to magnify returns. Stocks traded on the Nasdaq National Market can be margined like listed securities; OTC stocks are considered to have no collateral value and therefore cannot be margined.

As long as the margin in an account remains at a level equal to or higher than prevailing initial requirements, the investor may use the account in any way he or she wants. However, if the value of the investor's holdings declines, the margin in his or her account will also drop. In this case, the investor will have what is known as a **restricted account,** one whose equity is less than the initial margin requirement. It does not mean that the investor must put up additional cash or equity. However, as long as the

TABLE 2.4	Initial Margin Requirements for Various Types of Securities
Security	Minimum Initial Margin (Equity) Required (%)
Listed common and preferred stock	50
OTC stocks traded on Nasdaq	50
Convertible bonds	50
Corporate bonds	30
U.S. government bills, notes, and bonds	10 of principal
U.S. government agencies	24 of principal
Options	Option premium plus 20 of market value of underlying stock
Futures	2 to 10 of the value of the contract

account is restricted, the investor may not make further margin purchases and must bring the margin back to the initial level when securities are sold.

Maintenance Margin The absolute minimum amount of margin (equity) that an investor must maintain in the margin account at all times is the **maintenance margin**. When an insufficient amount of maintenance margin exists, an investor will receive a **margin call**. This call gives the investor a short period of time (perhaps 72 hours) to bring the equity up above the maintenance margin. If this doesn't happen, the broker is authorized to sell enough of the investor's margined holdings to bring the equity in the account up to this standard.

Margin investors can be in for a surprise if markets are volatile. When the Nasdaq stock market fell 14% in one day in early April 2000, brokerages made many more margin calls than usual. Investors rushed to sell shares, often at a loss, to cover their margin calls—only to watch the market bounce back a few days later.

The maintenance margin protects both the brokerage house and investors: Brokers avoid having to absorb excessive investor losses, and investors avoid being wiped out. The maintenance margin on equity securities is currently 25%. It rarely changes, although it is often set slightly higher by brokerage firms for the added protection of brokers and customers. For straight debt securities such as government bonds, there is no official maintenance margin except that set by the brokerage firms themselves.

The Basic Margin Formula The amount of margin is always measured in terms of its relative amount of equity, which is considered the investor's collateral. A simple formula can be used with all types of long purchases to determine the amount of margin in the transaction at any given time. Basically, only two pieces of information are required: (1) the prevailing market value of the securities being margined and (2) the **debit balance**, which is the amount of money being borrowed in the margin loan. Given this information, we can compute margin according to Equation 2.1.

Equation 2.1

$$\text{Margin} = \frac{\text{Value of securities} - \text{Debit balance}}{\text{Value of securities}}$$

Equation 2.1a

$$= \frac{V - D}{V}$$

To illustrate, consider the following example. Assume you want to purchase 100 shares of stock at $40 per share at a time when the initial margin requirement is 70%. Because 70% of the transaction must be financed with equity, you can finance the (30%) balance with a margin loan. Therefore, you will borrow 0.30 × $4,000, or $1,200. This amount, of course, is the *debit balance*. The remainder ($4,000 − $1,200 = $2,800) represents your equity in the transaction. In other words, equity is represented by the numerator $(V − D)$ in the margin formula.

What happens to the margin as the value of the security changes? If over time the price of the stock moves to $65, the margin is then

$$\text{Margin} = \frac{V - D}{V} = \frac{\$6,500 - \$1,200}{\$6,500} = 0.815 = \underline{\underline{81.5\%}}$$

Note that the margin (equity) in this investment position has risen from 70% to 81.5%. *When the price of the security goes up, your margin also increases.*

On the other hand, *when the price of the security goes down, so does the amount of margin.* For instance, if the price of the stock in our illustration drops to $30 per share, the new margin is only 60% [($3,000 − $1,200) ÷ $3,000]. In that case, we would be dealing with a *restricted account* because the margin level would have dropped below the prevailing initial margin of 70%.

Finally, note that although our discussion has been couched largely in terms of individual transactions, the same margin formula applies to margin accounts. The only difference is that we would be dealing with input that applies to the account *as a whole*—the value of all securities held in the account and the total amount of margin loans.

Return on Invested Capital When assessing the return on margin transactions, you must take into account the fact that you put up only part of the funds. Therefore, you are concerned with the *rate of return* earned on only the portion of the funds that you provided. Using both current income received from dividends or interest and total interest paid on the margin loan, we can apply Equation 2.2 to determine the return on invested capital from a margin transaction.

Equation 2.2

$$\begin{array}{c}\text{Return on} \\ \text{invested capital} \\ \text{from a margin} \\ \text{transaction}\end{array} = \dfrac{\begin{array}{c}\text{Total} \\ \text{current} \\ \text{income} \\ \text{received}\end{array} - \begin{array}{c}\text{Total} \\ \text{interest} \\ \text{paid on} \\ \text{margin loan}\end{array} + \begin{array}{c}\text{Market} \\ \text{value of} \\ \text{securities} \\ \text{at sale}\end{array} - \begin{array}{c}\text{Market} \\ \text{value of} \\ \text{securities} \\ \text{at purchase}\end{array}}{\text{Amount of equity at purchase}}$$

We can use this equation to compute either the expected or the actual return from a margin transaction. To illustrate: Assume you want to buy 100 shares of stock at $50 per share because you feel it will rise to $75 within six months. The stock pays $2 per share in annual dividends, and during your six-month holding period, you will receive half of that amount, or $1 per share. You are going to buy the stock with 50% margin and will pay 10% interest on the margin loan. Therefore, you are going to put up $2,500 equity to buy $5,000 worth of stock that you hope will increase to $7,500 in six months. Because you will have a $2,500 margin loan outstanding at 10% for six months, you will pay $125 in total interest costs ($2,500 × 0.10 × 6/12 = $125).

We can substitute this information into Equation 2.2 to find the expected return on invested capital from this margin transaction:

$$\text{Return on invested capital from a margin transaction} = \frac{\$100 - \$125 + \$7,500 - \$5,000}{\$2,500} = \frac{\$2,475}{\$2,500} = 0.99 = \underline{\underline{99\%}}$$

Keep in mind that the 99% figure represents the rate of return earned over a six-month holding period. If you wanted to compare this rate of return to other investment opportunities, you could determine the transaction's annualized rate of return by multiplying by 2 (the number of six-month periods in a year). This would amount to an annual rate of return of 198% (99% × 2 = 198%).

Uses of Margin Trading Investors most often use margin trading in one of two ways. As we have seen, one of its uses is to magnify transaction returns. The other major margin tactic is called *pyramiding*, which takes the concept of magnified returns to its limits. **Pyramiding** uses the paper profits in margin accounts to partly or fully finance the acquisition of additional securities. This allows investors to make such transactions at margins below prevailing initial margin levels, sometimes substantially so. In fact, with this technique it is even possible to buy securities with no new cash at all. Rather, they can all be financed entirely with margin loans. The reason is that the paper profits in the account lead to **excess margin**—more equity in the account than required. For instance, if a margin account holds $60,000 worth of securities and has a debit balance of $20,000, it is at a margin level of 66⅔% [($60,000 − $20,000) ÷ $60,000]. This account would hold a substantial amount of excess margin if the prevailing initial margin requirement were only 50%.

The principle of pyramiding is to use the excess margin in the account to purchase additional securities. The only constraint—and the key to pyramiding—is that when the additional securities are purchased, your margin account must be at or above the prevailing required initial margin level. Remember that it is the *account*, not the individual transactions, that must meet the minimum standards. If the account has excess margin, you can use it to build up security holdings. Pyramiding can continue as long as there are additional paper profits in the margin account and as long as the margin level exceeds the initial requirement that prevails when purchases are made. The tactic is somewhat complex but is also profitable, especially because it minimizes the amount of new capital required in the investor's account.

In general, margin trading is simple, but it is also risky. Risk is primarily associated with potential price declines in the margined securities. A decline in prices can result in a *restricted account*. If prices fall enough to cause the actual margin to drop below the maintenance margin, the resulting margin call will force you to deposit additional equity into the account almost immediately. In addition, losses (resulting from the price decline) are magnified in a fashion similar to that demonstrated in Table 2.3, part B. Clearly, the chance of a margin call and the magnification of losses make margin trading riskier than nonmargined transactions. Margin should be used only by investors who fully understand its operation and appreciate its pitfalls.

Short Selling

In most cases, investors buy stock hoping that the price will rise. What if you expect the price of a particular security to fall? By using short selling, you may be able to profit from falling security prices. Almost any type of security can be "shorted": common and preferred stocks, all types of bonds, convertible securities, listed mutual funds, options, and warrants. In practice, though, the short-selling activities of most investors are limited almost exclusively to common stocks and to options. (However, investors are prohibited from using short selling to *protect* themselves from falling security prices, a strategy called *shorting-against-the-box*.)

Essentials of Short Selling **Short selling** is generally defined as the practice of selling borrowed securities. Unusual as it may sound, selling borrowed securities is (in most cases) legal and quite common. Short sales start when an investor borrows securities from a broker and sells these securities in the marketplace. Later, when the price of the issue has declined, the short seller buys back the securities and then returns them to the lender. A short seller must make an initial equity deposit with the broker, subject to rules similar to those for margin trading. The deposit plus the proceeds from sale of the borrowed shares assure the broker that sufficient funds are available to buy back the shorted securities at a later date, even if their price increases. Short sales, like margin transactions, require investors to work through a broker.

Making Money When Prices Fall Making money when security prices fall is what short selling is all about. Like their colleagues in the rest of the investment world, short sellers are trying to make money by *buying low and selling high*. The only difference is that they reverse the investment process: *They start the transaction with a sale and end it with a purchase.*

Table 2.5 shows how a short sale works and how investors can profit from such transactions. (For simplicity, we ignore transaction costs.) The transaction results in a net profit of $2,000 as a result of an initial sale of 100 shares of stock at $50 per share (step 1) and subsequent covering (purchase) of the 100 shares for $30 per share (step 2). The amount of profit or loss generated in a short sale depends on the price at which the short seller can buy back the stock. Short sellers earn profit only when the proceeds from the sale of the stock are higher than the cost of buying it back.

Who Lends the Securities? Acting through their brokers, short sellers obtain securities from the brokerage firm or from other investors. (Brokers are the principal source of borrowed securities.) As a service to their customers, brokers lend securities held in their portfolios or in *street-name* accounts. It is important to recognize that when the brokerage firm lends street-name securities, it is lending the short seller the securities of other investors. Individual investors typically do not pay fees to the broker for the privilege of borrowing the shares; in exchange, investors do not earn interest on the funds they leave on deposit with the broker.

Margin Requirements and Short Selling To make a short sale, the investor must make a deposit with the broker that is equal to the initial margin requirement (currently 50%) applied to the short-sale proceeds. In addition, the broker retains the proceeds from the short sale.

TABLE 2.5 The Mechanics of a Short Sale	EXCEL WITH SPREADSHEETS
Step 1—Short sale initiated	
100 shares of borrowed stock are sold at $50/share: Proceeds from sale to investor	$5,000
Step 2—Short sale covered	
Later, 100 shares of the stock are *purchased* at $30/share and returned to broker from whom stock was borrowed:	
Cost to investor	3,000
Net profit	$2,000

MARKETS in CRISIS

SEC Bans Short Selling

In September 2008, as the financial crisis grew deeper, the Securities and Exchange Commission announced a temporary ban on short sales of almost 800 financial stocks from September 19 to October 9. Research shows that the prices of stocks affected by the ban rose significantly, but those price increases were largely reversed when the ban was lifted.

To demonstrate, assume that you sell short 100 shares of Smart, Inc., at $50 per share at a time when the initial margin requirement is 50% and the maintenance margin on short sales is 30%. The values in lines 1 through 4 in column A in Table 2.6 indicate that your broker would hold a total deposit of $7,500 on this transaction. Note in columns B and C that regardless of subsequent changes in Smart's stock price, your deposit with the broker would remain at $7,500 (line 4).

By subtracting the cost of buying back the shorted stock at the given share price (line 5), you can find your equity in the account (line 6) for the current (column A) and two subsequent share prices (columns B and C). We see that at the initial short sale price of $50 per share, your equity would equal $2,500 (column A). If the share price subsequently drops to $30, your equity would rise to $4,500 (column B). If the share price subsequently rises to $70, your equity would fall to $500 (column C). Dividing these account equity values (line 6) by the then-current cost of buying back the stock (line 5), we can calculate the actual margins at each share price (line 7). We see that at the current $50 price the actual margin is 50%, whereas at the $30 share price it is 150%, and at the $70 share price it is 7.14%.

TABLE 2.6	Margin Positions on Short Sales			
		A	B	C
Line	Item	Initial Short Sale Price	Subsequent Share Prices	
1	Price per share	$50	$30	$70
2	Proceeds from initial short sale [(1) × 100 shares]	$5,000		
3	Initial margin deposit [0.50 × (2)]	2,500		
4	Total deposit with broker [(2) + (3)]	$7,500	$7,500	$7,500
5	Current cost of buying back stock [(1) × 100 shares]	5,000	3,000	7,000
6	Account equity [(4) − (5)]	$2,500	$4,500	$ 500
7	Actual margin [(6) ÷ (5)]	50%	150%	7.14%
8	Maintenance margin position [(7) > 30%?]	OK	OK	Margin call*

*Investor must either (a) deposit at least an additional $1,600 with the broker to bring the total deposit to $9,100 ($7,500 + $1,600), which would equal the current value of the 100 shares of $7,000 plus a 30% maintenance margin deposit of $2,100 (.30 × $7,000) or (b) buy back the 100 shares of stock and return them to the broker.

As noted in line 8, given the 30% maintenance margin requirement, your margin would be okay at the current price of $50 (column A) or lower (column B). But at the $70 share price, the 7.14% actual margin would be below the 30% maintenance margin, thereby resulting in a margin call. In that case (or whenever the actual margin on a short sale falls below the maintenance margin), you must respond to the margin call either by depositing additional funds with the broker or by buying the stock and covering (i.e., closing out) the short position.

If you wished to maintain the short position when the share price has risen to $70, you would have to deposit an additional $1,600 with the broker. Those funds would increase your total deposit to $9,100 ($7,500 + $1,600)—an amount equal to the $7,000 value of the shorted stock plus the 30% maintenance margin, or $2,100 (.30 × $7,000). Buying back the stock to cover the short position would cost $7,000, thereby resulting in the return of the $500 of equity in your account from your broker. Clearly, margin requirements tend to complicate the short-sale transaction and the impact of an increase in the shorted stock's share price on required deposits with the broker.

Advantages and Disadvantages The major advantage of selling short is, of course, the chance to profit from a price decline. The key disadvantage of many short-sale transactions is that the investor faces limited return opportunities along with high-risk exposure. The price of a security can fall only so far (to zero or near zero), yet there is really no limit to how far such securities can rise in price. (Remember, a short seller is hoping for a price *decline*; when a security goes up in price, a short seller loses.) For example, note in Table 2.5 (on page 57) that the stock in question cannot possibly fall by more than $50, yet who is to say how high its price can go?

A less serious disadvantage is that short sellers never earn dividend (or interest) income. In fact, short sellers owe the lender of the shorted security any dividends (or interest) paid while the transaction is outstanding. That is, if a dividend is paid during the course of a short-sale transaction, the short seller must pay an equal amount to the lender of the stock. (The mechanics of these payments are taken care of automatically by the short seller's broker.)

Uses of Short Selling Investors short sell primarily to seek speculative profits when they expect the price of a security to drop. Because the short seller is betting against the market, this approach is subject to a considerable amount of risk. The actual procedure works as demonstrated in Table 2.5. Note that had you been able to sell the stock at $50 per share and later repurchase it at $30 per share, you would have generated a profit of $2,000 (ignoring dividends and brokerage commissions). However, if the market had instead moved against you, all or most of your $5,000 investment could have been lost.

CONCEPTS IN REVIEW

Answers available at
www.pearsonhighered.com/gitman

2.12 What is a *long purchase?* What expectation underlies such a purchase? What is *margin trading,* and what is the key reason why investors sometimes use it as part of a long purchase?

2.13 How does margin trading magnify profits and losses? What are the key advantages and disadvantages of margin trading?

2.14 Describe the procedures and regulations associated with margin trading. Be sure to explain *restricted accounts,* the *maintenance margin,* and the *margin call.* Define the term *debit balance,* and describe the common uses of margin trading.

2.15 What is the primary motive for *short selling?* Describe the basic short-sale procedure. Why must the short seller make an initial equity deposit?

(Continued)

2.16 What relevance do margin requirements have in the short-selling process? What would have to happen to experience a margin call on a short-sale transaction? What two actions could be used to remedy such a call?

2.17 Describe the key advantages and disadvantages of short selling. How are short sales used to earn speculative profits?

 **myfinancelab**

Here is what you should know after reading this chapter. **MyFinanceLab** will help you identify what you know, and where to go when you need to practice.

What You Should Know	Key Terms	Where To Practice
LG1 **Identify the basic types of securities markets and describe their characteristics.** Short-term investment vehicles trade in the money market; longer-term securities, such as stocks and bonds, trade in the capital market. New security issues are sold in the primary market. Investors buy and sell existing securities in the secondary markets.	ask price, *p. 41* bear markets, *p. 43* bid price, *p. 41* broker market, *p. 38* bull markets, *p. 43* capital market, *p. 33* dealer market, *p. 38* designated market maker (DMM), *p. 40* dual listing, *p. 40* electronic communications network (ECN), *p. 43* fourth market, *p. 43* initial public offering (IPO), *p. 33* investment banker, *p. 34* market makers, *p. 38* money market, *p. 33* Nasdaq market, *p. 38* over-the-counter (OTC) market, *p. 38* primary market, *p. 33* private placement, *p. 33* prospectus, *p. 34* public offering, *p. 33* red herring, *p. 34* rights offering, *p. 33* secondary distributions, *p. 41* secondary market, *p. 37* Securities and Exchange Commission (SEC), *p. 33* securities markets, *p. 33* selling group, *p. 35* third market, *p. 43* underwriting, *p. 35* underwriting syndicate, *p. 35*	MyFinanceLab Study Plan 2.1
LG2 **Explain the initial public offering (IPO) process.** The first public issue of a company's common stock is an initial public offering (IPO). The company selects an investment banker to sell the IPO. The lead investment banker may form a syndicate with other investment bankers and then create a selling group to sell the issue. The IPO process includes filing a registration statement with the Securities and Exchange Commission (SEC), getting SEC approval, promoting the offering to investors, pricing the issue, and selling the shares.		MyFinanceLab Study Plan 2.2
LG3 **Describe broker markets and dealer markets, and discuss how they differ from alternative trading systems.** In dealer markets, buy/sell orders are executed by market makers. The market makers are securities dealers who "make markets" by offering to buy or sell certain securities at stated bid/ask prices. Dealer markets also serve as primary markets for both IPOs and secondary distributions. Over-the-counter transactions in listed securities take place in the third market. Direct transactions between buyers and sellers are made in the fourth market. Market conditions are commonly classified as "bull" or "bear," depending on whether securities prices are generally rising or falling. Broker markets bring together buyers and sellers to make trades. Included are the New York Stock Exchange (NYSE), the NYSE Amex, regional stock exchanges, foreign stock exchanges, options exchanges, and future exchanges. In these markets the forces of supply and demand drive the transactions on the floor of the exchange and determine prices. These securities exchanges are secondary markets where existing securities trade.		MyFinanceLab Study Plan 2.3

What You Should Know	Key Term	Where To Practice
LG4 Review the key aspects of the globalization of securities markets, and discuss the importance of international markets. Securities exchanges operate in over 100 countries—both large and small. Foreign security investments can be made indirectly by buying shares of a U.S.-based multinational with substantial foreign operations or by purchasing shares of a mutual fund that invests primarily in foreign securities. Direct foreign investment can be achieved by purchasing securities on foreign exchanges, by buying securities of foreign companies that are traded on U.S. exchanges, or by buying American depositary shares (ADSs). International investments can enhance returns, but they entail added risk, particularly currency exchange risk.	American depositary receipts (ADRs), *p. 46* American depositary shares (ADSs), *p. 46* currency exchange rate, *p. 47* currency exchange risk, *p. 47* diversification, *p. 44* Yankee bonds, *p. 46*	MyFinanceLab Study Plan 2.4 Video Learning Aid for Problem P2.3
LG5 Discuss trading hours and the regulation of securities markets. Investors now can trade securities outside regular market hours (9:30 A.M. to 4:00 P.M., eastern time). Most after-hours markets are crossing markets, in which orders are filled only if they can be matched. Trading activity during these sessions can be quite risky. The securities markets are regulated by the federal Securities and Exchange Commission (SEC) and by state commissions. The key federal laws regulating the securities industry are the Securities Act of 1933, the Securities Exchange Act of 1934, the Maloney Act of 1938, the Investment Company Act of 1940, the Investment Advisers Act of 1940, the Securities Acts Amendments of 1975, the Insider Trading and Fraud Act of 1988, and the Sarbanes-Oxley Act of 2002.	crossing markets, *p. 48* ethics, *p. 50* insider trading, *p. 50* long purchase, *p. 50*	MyFinanceLab Study Plan 2.5
LG6 Explain long purchases, margin transactions, and short sales. Most investors make long purchases—buy low, sell high—in expectation of price increases. Many investors establish margin accounts to use borrowed funds to enhance their buying power. The Federal Reserve Board establishes the margin requirement—the minimum investor equity in a margin transaction. The return on capital in a margin transaction is magnified for both positive returns *and* negative returns. Paper profits can be used to pyramid a margin account by investing its excess margin. The risks of margin trading are the chance of a restricted account or margin call and the consequences of magnified losses due to price declines. Short selling is used when a decline in security prices is anticipated. It involves selling securities, typically borrowed from the broker, to earn a profit by repurchasing them at a lower price in the future. The short seller makes an initial equity deposit with the broker. If the price of a shorted stock rises, the investor may receive a margin call and must then either increase the deposit with the broker or buy back the stock to cover the short position. The	debit balance, *p. 54* excess margin, *p. 56* financial leverage, *p. 51* initial margin, *p. 53* maintenance margin, *p. 54* margin account, *p. 53* margin call, *p. 54* margin loan, *p. 53* margin requirement, *p. 51* margin trading, *p. 51* prime rate, *p. 53* pyramiding, *p. 56* restricted account, *p. 53* short selling, *p. 57*	MyFinanceLab Study Plan 2.6 Excel Tables 2.3, 2.5 Video Learning Aid for Problem P2.19

What You Should Know	Key Term	Where To Practice
major advantage of selling short is the chance to profit from a price decline. The disadvantages of selling short are the unlimited potential for loss and the fact that short sellers never earn dividend (or interest) income. Short selling is used primarily to seek speculative profits.		

Log into **MyFinanceLab**, take a chapter test, and get a personalized Study Plan
that tells you which concepts you understand and which ones you need to
review. From there, **MyFinanceLab** will give you further practice, tutorials,
animations, videos, and guided solutions.
Log into **www.myfinancelab.com**

Discussion Questions

LG2 **Q2.1** From 1990 to 2005, the average IPO rose by more than 20% in its first day of trading. In 1999, 117 deals doubled in price on the first day, compared to only 39 in the previous 24 years combined. Since 2000, no deals doubled on the first day. What factors might contribute to the huge first-day returns on IPOs? Some critics of the current IPO system claim that underwriters may knowingly underprice an issue. Why might they do this? Why might issuing companies accept lower IPO prices? What impact do institutional investors have on IPO pricing?

LG1 LG3 **Q2.2** Why do you think some large, well-known companies such as Cisco Systems, Intel, and Microsoft prefer to trade on the Nasdaq National Market rather than on a major securities exchange such as the NYSE (for which they easily meet the listing requirements)? Discuss the pros and cons of listing on a major securities exchange.

LG1 LG2 LG4 **Q2.3** On the basis of the current structure of the world's financial markets and your knowledge of the NYSE and Nasdaq markets, describe the key features, functions, and problems that would be faced by a single global market (exchange) on which transactions can be made in all securities of all of the world's major companies. Discuss the likelihood of such a market developing.

LG5 **Q2.4** Critics of longer trading hours believe that expanded trading sessions turn the stock market into a casino and place the emphasis more on short-term gains than on long-term investment. Do you agree? Why or why not? Is it important to have a "breathing period" to reflect on the day's market activity? Why are smaller brokerages and ECNs, more than the NYSE and Nasdaq, pushing for longer trading hours?

LG6 **Q2.5** Describe how, if at all, conservative and aggressive investors might use each of the following types of transactions as part of their investment programs. Contrast these two types of investors in view of these preferences.

   a. Long purchase
   b. Margin trading
   c. Short selling

Problems

All problems are available on **www.myfinancelab.com**

 P2.1 The current exchange rate between the U.S. dollar and the Japanese yen is 116.915 (yen/$). How many dollars would you get for 1,000 Japanese yen?

 P2.2 An investor recently sold some stock that was a Eurodollar investment for 20,000 euros. The U.S.$/euro exchange rate is currently 1.100. How many U.S. dollars will the investor receive?

 P2.3 In each of the following cases, calculate the price of one share of the foreign stock measured in United States dollars (US$).

    a. A Belgian stock priced at 103.2 euros (€) when the exchange rate is .8595 €/US$.

    b. A Swiss stock priced at 93.3 Swiss francs (Sf) when the exchange rate is 1.333 Sf/US$.

    c. A Japanese stock priced at 1,350 yen (¥) when the exchange rate is 110 ¥/US$.

P2.4 Erin McQueen purchased 50 shares of BMW, a German stock traded on the Frankfurt Exchange, for 64.5 euros (€) per share exactly one year ago when the exchange rate was .78 €/US$. Today the stock is trading at 68.4 € per share, and the exchange rate is .86 €/US$.

    a. Did the € *depreciate* or *appreciate* relative to the US$ during the past year? Explain.

    b. How much in US$ did Erin pay for her 50 shares of BMW when she purchased them a year ago?

    c. For how much in US$ can Erin sell her BMW shares today?

    d. Ignoring brokerage fees and taxes, how much profit (or loss) in US$ will Erin realize on her BMW stock if she sells it today?

 P2.5 An investor believes that the U.S. dollar will rise in value relative to the Japanese yen. The same investor is considering two investments with identical risk and return characteristics: One is a Japanese yen investment and the other is a U.S. dollar investment. Should the investor purchase the Japanese yen investment?

 P2.6 Elmo Inc.'s stock is currently selling at $60 per share. For each of the following situations (ignoring brokerage commissions), calculate the gain or loss that Courtney Schinke realizes if she makes a 100-share transaction.

    a. She sells short and repurchases the borrowed shares at $70 per share.

    b. She takes a long position and sells the stock at $75 per share.

    c. She sells short and repurchases the borrowed shares at $45 per share.

    d. She takes a long position and sells the stock at $60 per share.

P2.7 Assume that an investor buys 100 shares of stock at $50 per share, putting up a 60% margin.

    a. What is the *debit balance* in this transaction?

    b. How much equity capital must the investor provide to make this margin transaction?

P2.8 Assume that an investor buys 100 shares of stock at $50 per share, putting up a 60% margin. If the stock rises to $60 per share, what is the investor's new margin position?

P2.9 Assume that an investor buys 100 shares of stock at $50 per share, putting up a 70% margin.

    a. What is the *debit balance* in this transaction?

    b. How much equity funds must the investor provide to make this margin transaction?

    c. If the stock rises to $80 per share, what is the investor's new margin position?

 P2.10 Miguel Torres purchased 100 shares of Can'tWin.com for $50 per share, using as little of his own money as he could. His broker has a *50% initial margin* requirement and a *30% maintenance margin* requirement. The price of the stock falls to $30 per share. What does Miguel need to do?

P2.11 Jerri Kingston bought 100 shares of stock at $80 per share using an *initial margin* of 60%. Given a *maintenance margin* of 25%, how far does the stock have to drop before Jerri faces a margin call? (Assume that there are no other securities in the margin account.)

 P2.12 An investor buys 200 shares of stock selling at $80 per share using a margin of 60%. The stock pays annual dividends of $1 per share. A margin loan can be obtained at an annual interest cost of 8%. Determine what return on invested capital the investor will realize if the price of the stock increases to $104 within six months. What is the *annualized* rate of return on this transaction?

P2.13 Marlene Bellamy purchased 300 shares of Writeline Communications stock at $55 per share using the prevailing minimum *initial margin* requirement of 50%. She held the stock for exactly four months and sold it without any brokerage costs at the end of that period. During the four-month holding period, the stock paid $1.50 per share in cash dividends. Marlene was charged 9% annual interest on the margin loan. The minimum *maintenance margin* was 25%.

    a. Calculate the initial value of the transaction, the *debit balance*, and the equity position on Marlene's transaction.

    b. For each of the following share prices, calculate the actual margin percentage, and indicate whether Marlene's margin account would have excess equity, would be restricted, or would be subject to a margin call.

        1. $45

        2. $70

        3. $35

    c. Calculate the dollar amount of (1) dividends received and (2) interest paid on the margin loan during the four-month holding period.

    d. Use each of the following sale prices at the end of the four-month holding period to calculate Marlene's *annualized* rate of return on the Writeline Communications stock transaction.

        1. $50

        2. $60

        3. $70

 P2.14 Not long ago, Jack Edwards bought 200 shares of Almost Anything Inc. at $45 per share; he bought the stock on margin of 60%. The stock is now trading at $60 per share, and the Federal Reserve has recently lowered *initial margin* requirements to 50%. Jack now wants to do a little *pyramiding* and buy another 300 shares of the stock. What is the minimum amount of equity that he'll have to put up in this transaction?

 P2.15 An investor short sells 100 shares of a stock for $20 per share. The initial margin is 50%. How much equity will be required in the account to complete this transaction?

P2.16 An investor short sells 100 shares of a stock for $20 per share. The initial margin is 50%. Ignoring transaction costs, how much will be in the investor's account after this transaction if this is the only transaction the investor has undertaken and the investor has deposited only the required amount?

P2.17 An investor short sells 100 shares of a stock for $20 per share. The *initial margin* is 50%, and the *maintenance margin* is 30%. The price of the stock falls to $12 per share. What is the margin, and will there be a *margin call*?

P2.18 An investor short sells 100 shares of a stock for $20 per share. The *initial margin* is 50%, and the *maintenance margin* is 30%. The price of the stock rises to $28 per share. What is the margin, and will there be a *margin call*?

P2.19 Calculate the profit or loss per share realized on each of the following short-sale transactions.

Transaction	Stock Sold Short at Price/Share	Stock Purchased to Cover Short at Price/Share
A	$75	$83
B	30	24
C	18	15
D	27	32
E	53	45

P2.20 Charlene Hickman expected the price of Bio International shares to drop in the near future in response to the expected failure of its new drug to pass FDA tests. As a result, she sold short 200 shares of Bio International at $27.50. How much would Charlene earn or lose on this transaction if she repurchased the 200 shares four months later at each of the following prices per share?

    a. $24.75
    b. $25.13
    c. $31.25
    d. $27.00

Visit www.myfinancelab.com for web exercises,
spreadsheets, and other online resources.

Case Problem 2.1   *Dara's Dilemma: What to Buy?*

Dara Simmons, a 40-year-old financial analyst and divorced mother of two teenage children, considers herself a savvy investor. She has increased her investment portfolio considerably over the past five years. Although she has been fairly conservative with her investments, she now feels more confident in her investment knowledge and would like to branch out into some new areas that could bring higher returns. She has between $20,000 and $25,000 to invest.

Attracted to the hot market for technology stocks, Dara was interested in purchasing a tech IPO stock and identified "NewestHighTech.com," a company that makes sophisticated computer chips for wireless Internet connections, as a likely prospect. The one-year-old company had received some favorable press when it got early-stage financing and again when its chip was accepted by a major cell phone manufacturer.

Dara also was considering an investment in 400 shares of Casinos International common stock, currently selling for $54 per share. After a discussion with a friend who is an economist with a major commercial bank, Dara believes that the long-running bull market is due to cool off and that economic activity will slow down. With the aid of her stockbroker, Dara researches Casinos International's current financial situation and finds that the future success of the company may hinge on the outcome of pending court proceedings on the firm's application to open a new floating casino on a nearby river. If the permit is granted, it seems likely that the firm's stock will experience a rapid increase in value, regardless of economic conditions. On the other hand, if the company fails to get the permit, the falling stock price will make it a good candidate for a short sale.

Dara felt that the following alternatives were open to her:

Alternative 1: Invest $20,000 in NewestHighTech.com when it goes public.

Alternative 2: Buy Casinos International now at $54 per share and follow the company closely.

Alternative 3: Sell Casinos short at $54 in anticipation that the company's fortunes will change for the worse.

Alternative 4: Wait to see what happens with the casino permit and then decide whether to buy or short the Casinos International stock.

Questions

a. Evaluate each of these alternatives. On the basis of the limited information presented, recommend the one you feel is best.

b. If Casinos International's stock price rises to $60, what will happen under alternatives 2 and 3? Evaluate the pros and cons of these outcomes.

c. If the stock price drops to $45, what will happen under alternatives 2 and 3? Evaluate the pros and cons of these outcomes.

Case Problem 2.2   *Ravi Dumar's High-Flying Margin Account*

 Ravi Dumar is a stockbroker who lives with his wife, Sasha, and their five children in Milwaukee, Wisconsin. Ravi firmly believes that the only way to make money in the market is to follow an aggressive investment posture—for example, to use margin trading. In fact, Ravi himself has built a substantial margin account over the years. He currently holds $75,000 worth of stock in his margin account, though the *debit balance* in the account amounts to only $30,000. Recently, Ravi uncovered a stock that, on the basis of extensive analysis, he feels is about to take off. The stock, Running Shoes (RS), currently trades at $20 per share. Ravi feels it should soar to at least $50 within a year. RS pays no dividends, the prevailing *initial margin* requirement is 50%, and margin loans are now carrying an annual interest charge of 10%. Because Ravi feels so strongly about RS, he wants to do some *pyramiding* by using his margin account to purchase 1,000 shares of the stock.

Questions

a. Discuss the concept of pyramiding as it applies to this investment situation.

b. What is the present margin position (in percent) of Ravi's account?

c. Ravi buys the 1,000 shares of RS through his margin account (bear in mind that this is a $20,000 transaction).
   1. What will the margin position of the account be after the RS transaction if Ravi follows the prevailing initial margin (50%) and uses $10,000 of his money to buy the stock?
   2. What if he uses only $2,500 equity and obtains a margin loan for the balance ($17,500)?
   3. How do you explain the fact that the stock can be purchased with only 12.5% margin when the prevailing initial margin requirement is 50%?

d. Assume that Ravi buys 1,000 shares of RS stock at $20 per share with a minimum cash investment of $2,500 and that the stock does take off and its price rises to $40 per share in 1 year.
   1. What is the *return on invested capital* for this transaction?
   2. What return would Ravi have earned if he had bought the stock without margin—that is, if he had used all his own money?

e. What do you think of Ravi's idea to pyramid? What are the risks and rewards of this strategy?

Excel with Spreadsheets

You have just learned about the mechanics of margin trading and want to take advantage of the potential benefits of financial leverage. You have decided to open a margin account with your broker and to secure a margin loan. The specifics of the account are as follows:

- Initial margin requirement is 70%.

- Maintenance margin is 30%.

- You are informed that if the value of your account falls below the maintenance margin, your account will be subject to a margin call.

You have been following the price movements of a stock over the past year and believe that it is currently undervalued and that the price will rise in the near future. You feel that the opening of a margin account is a good investment strategy. You have decided to purchase three round lots (i.e., 100 shares per round lot) of the stock at its current price of $25 per share.

Create a spreadsheet similar to the spreadsheet for Table 2.3, which can be viewed at www. myfinancelab.com, to model and analyze the following market transactions.

Questions

a. Calculate the value of the investment in the stock as if you did not make use of margin trading. In other words, what is the value of the investment if it is funded by 100% cash equity?

b. Calculate the debit balance and the cash equity in the investment at the time of opening a margin account, adhering to the initial margin requirement.

c. If you use margin and the price of the stock rises by $15 to $40/share, calculate the capital gain earned and the return on investor's equity.

d. What is the current margin percentage based on question b?

e. If you use margin and the price of the stock falls by $15 to $10/share, calculate the capital loss and the respective return on investor's equity.

f. What is the new margin percentage based on question e, and what is the implication for you, the investor?

CHAPTER 3

Investment Information and Securities Transactions

Millions of Web pages devoted to stocks and investment strategies put everything at your fingertips—literally—and most of it is free. Here are some basic steps to follow in finding and using that information.

First, determine your investment objectives and do some initial research to identify your risk tolerance and investment time horizon. Consider taking the risk tolerance surveys at **www.fizone.com/Investing/RiskTolerance.asp** and at **www.wellsfargo.com/retirement_tools/risk_tolerance**; they can help you determine your investing style. Next, visit financial portal sites such as those offered by Yahoo! Finance (**finance.yahoo.com**), Morningstar (**www.morningstar.com**), and CNN/Money (**money.cnn.com**). These sites can help you familiarize yourself with what's happening currently in the markets.

With the recent high fuel prices, you might be interested in investing in oil company stocks. Free stock screening tools at sites like **StockCharts.com** and Morningstar will help narrow the field. For example, with Morningstar's Stock Screener (go to **screen.morningstar.com/StockSelector.html**) you can define search criteria such as energy stocks with a return on equity (ROE) greater than 20%, 5-year total return that meets or exceeds the S&P 500, price/earnings (P/E) ratio of 15 or less. Within a few seconds, you'll have a list of stocks that meet your parameters.

Then, head to each company's Web site to find the latest annual report and press releases. More detailed Securities and Exchange Commission (SEC) filings are available online at **www.sec.gov** and at **www.freeedgar.com**. Find out what the securities analysts say: You can buy individual stock research reports at Yahoo! Finance or Reuters Business & Finance (go to **www.reuters.com/finance/**, then click on [Analyst Research]). Armed with this information, you can evaluate your candidates and make your selection.

In reality, picking stocks may not be quite that easy. Nevertheless, the power of the Internet enables you to access in minutes information that in the past was either unavailable to the average investor or would take weeks to accumulate. In this chapter, you'll learn more about the many sources of investment information, both online and offline, as well as how to make transactions.

Online Investing

LG1 Today the Internet is a major force in the investing environment. It provides individual investors with access to tools formerly restricted to professionals. With these tools you can find and process a wealth of information online and also trade many types of securities. This information ranges from real-time stock price quotes to securities analysts' research reports to techniques for investment analysis. The time and money savings from online investing are huge. Instead of wading through reams of paper, you can quickly sort through vast databases to determine appropriate investments, make securities transactions to acquire your investments, and monitor the progress of your investments—all without leaving your computer.

Because new Web sites appear every day and existing ones change constantly, it's impossible to catalog all the good ones. Rather, our intent is to give you a sampling of Web sites that will introduce you to the wealth of investing information available on the Internet. The bottom line is that you can find plenty of cool, comprehensive, and sophisticated investment resources online to help you invest.

Getting Started in Online Investing

To successfully navigate the cyberinvesting universe, open your Web browser and explore the multitude of investing sites. These sites typically include a combination of resources for novice and experienced investors alike. For example, look at brokerage firm TD Ameritrade's homepage (**www.tdameritrade.com**), shown in Figure 3.1 (on page 70). With a few mouse clicks you can learn about TD Ameritrade's services, open an account, and begin trading. In addition, you will find the day's and week's market activity, price quotes, news, analysts' research reports, and more.

Although exceedingly valuable, the vast quantity of investment information available on the Internet can be overwhelming and intimidating. The good news is the Internet itself can help you work through the maze of information and become a wise Internet investor. Educational sites are a good place to start, and once you master what they have to offer you can confidently check out the many online investment tools. In the following section, we'll discuss how to use the Internet wisely to become a smarter investor.

Investment Education Sites The Internet offers many articles, tutorials, and online classes to educate the novice investor. Even experienced investors can find sites that will expand their investing knowledge. Although most investing-oriented Web sites and financial portals (described later) include many educational resources, here are a few good sites that feature investing fundamentals.

- *Investing Online Resource Center* (**www.investingonline.org**) is an educational site that provides a wealth of information for those getting started online as well as those already investing online. It includes an online quiz that, based on your answers, will categorize your readiness for trading online. There is even an investment simulator that creates an online interactive learning experience that allows the user to "test drive" online trading.

- *InvestorGuide.com* (**www.investorguide.com**) is a free educational site offering InvestorGuide University, which is a collection of educational articles about investing and personal finance. In addition, the site provides access to quotes and charts, portfolio tracking software, research, news and commentary, and a glossary through **InvestorWords.com** (**www.investorwords.com**).

FIGURE 3.1

TD Ameritrade Web Site

TD Ameritrade's Web site www.tdameritrade.com provides a wealth of investment resources. You can open an account, assess market activity, obtain news, access analysts' research, and more. (Source: TD Ameritrade www.eSignal.com. Reprinted with permission.)

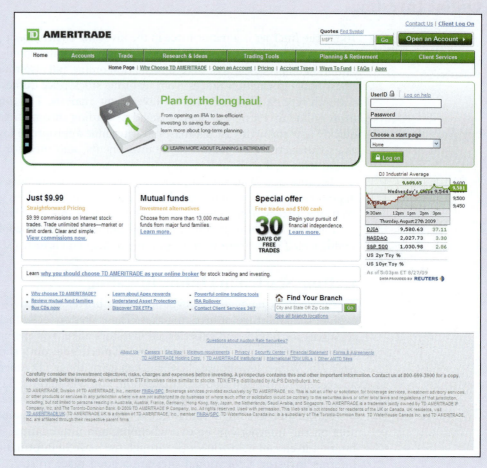

- *The Motley Fool* (**www.fool.com**) has sections on investing basics, mutual fund investing, choosing a broker, and investment strategies and styles, as well as lively discussion boards and more.

- Investopedia (**www.investopedia.com**) is an educational site featuring tutorials on numerous basic and advanced investing and personal finance topics, a dictionary of investing terms, and other useful investment aids.

- *WSJ.com* (**www.wsj.com**), a free site from the *Wall Street Journal,* is an excellent starting place to learn what the Internet can offer investors.

- Nasdaq (**www.nasdaq.com**) has both an Investing and a Personal Finance section that provides links to a number of investment education resources.

Other good educational sites include leading personal finance magazines such as *Money* (**money.cnn.com**), *Kiplinger's Personal Finance Magazine* (**kiplinger.com**), and *Smart Money* (**www.smartmoney.com**).

Investment Tools Once you are familiar with investing basics, you can use the Internet to develop financial plans and set investment goals, find securities that meet your objectives, analyze potential investments, and organize your portfolio. Many of

FIGURE 3.2

Stock Investing Financial Calculator

At sites like Kiplinger.com, you'll find many calculators that you can use to solve specific problems. At right is the screen listing, in question form, of several investment-related stock calculators available at Kiplinger's site. (Source: Kiplinger.com Tools & Calculators, www.kiplinger.com/tools/. Screenshot courtesy of Kiplinger's ©2009 The Kiplinger Washington Editors.)

these tools, once used only by professional investment advisers, are free online. You can find financial calculators and worksheets, screening and charting tools, and stock quotes and portfolio trackers at general financial sites (described in the later section on financial portals) and at the Web sites of larger brokerage firms. You can even set up a personal calendar that notifies you of forthcoming earnings announcements and can receive alerts when one of your stocks has hit a predetermined price target.

Planning Online calculators and worksheets help you find answers to your financial planning and investing questions. Using them you can figure out how much to save each month for a particular goal, such as the down payment for your first home, a college education for your children, or retiring when you are 60. For example, the brokerage firm Fidelity (**www.fidelity.com**) has a number of planning tools: college planning, retirement planning, and research tools. One of the best sites for financial calculators is Kiplinger's Tools & Calculators (**kiplinger.com/tools**). It includes numerous calculators for investing, money management, retirement, and spending wisely. Figure 3.2 lists, in question form, several calculators specifically related to investing in stocks. For example, one calculator helps you answer the question "what stock price achieves my target rate of return?" Click on the calculator question and input the values for your situation, and the calculator will show you the selling price at which you will earn the desired return on your stock investment. Other investment-related calculators focus on funds and bonds. Because not all calculators give the same answer, you may want to try out those at several sites.

FIGURE 3.3

Zacks Predefined Screens

Search for stocks based on popular investment strategies. The predefined searches allow selection from a list of predefined criteria such as "52 Week Highs" or "52 Week Lows." Zacks stock screening tool will give you a list of stocks that meet your specifications. (Source: Zacks, **www.zacks .com/screening/ custom/ predefined_index .php**. Screenshot courtesy of Zacks. Reprinted with permission from Zacks Investment Research. ©2009 Zacks Investment Research.)

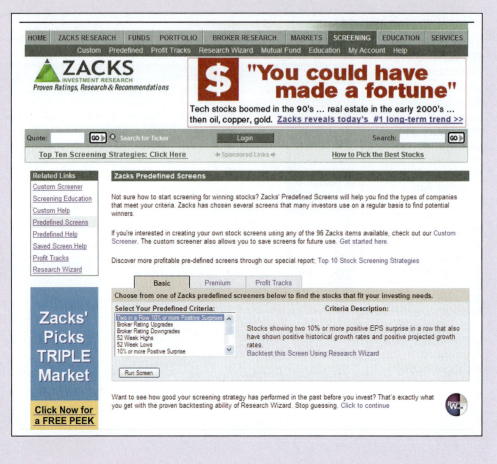

Screening With screening tools, you can quickly sort through huge databases of stocks, bonds, and mutual funds to find those that have specific characteristics. For stocks, you can specify low or high price/earnings ratios, small market value, high dividend return, specific revenue growth, and/or a low debt-to-equity ratio. For bonds, you can specify a given industry, maturity date, or yield. For mutual funds, you might specify low minimum investment, a particular industry or geographical sector, and low fees. Each screening tool uses a different method to sort. You answer a series of questions to specify the type of stock or fund, performance criteria, cost parameters, and so on. The result is a list of securities that meet your investment criteria. Then if necessary you can do additional research on the individual stocks, bonds, or mutual funds to determine which ones best meet your investment objectives.

Zacks.com provides some of the best free tools. Figure 3.3 shows the opening page for Zacks "Predefined Screens" that lists searches based on the predefined investment strategies. The "Custom Stock Screener" contains more than 145 items from the proprietary Zacks database. MSN Money also offers some excellent screening tools, both "Power Searches" (**moneycentral.msn.com/investor/finder/predefstocks.aspx**) that offer a number of preset searches and "Custom Search" (**moneycentral.msn.com/investor/ finder/customstocksdl.asp**) that allow you to create your own stock search. Yahoo!

FIGURE 3.4

Stock Chart for Qualcomm

At Morningstar's Web site you can plot a chart tracking the performance of a stock or mutual fund over several different time horizons. (Source: © 2009 Morningstar, Inc. All rights reserved. Reprinted with permission of Morningstar, Inc.)

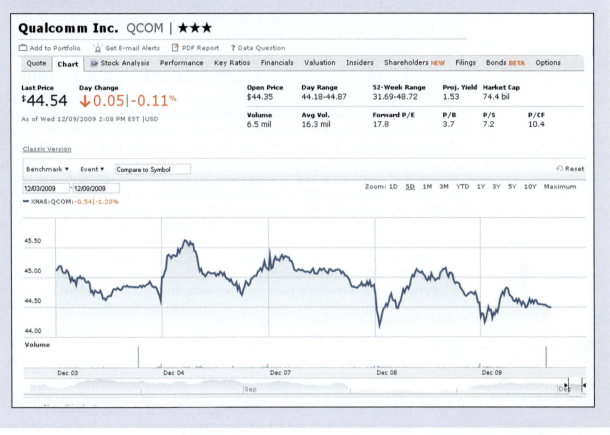

Finance offers screening tools for stocks (**screener.finance.yahoo.com/stocks.html**), mutual funds (**screener.finance.yahoo.com/funds.html**), and bonds (**screener.finance.yahoo.com/bonds.html**). You can check out the site's preset screens—for example, "Large Cap Value" stocks and "Bargain Growth" stocks. Morningstar (**www.morningstar.com**) also offers a variety of screeners: stock (**screen.morningstar.com/ StockSelector.html**), mutual funds (**screen.morningstar.com/FundSelector.html**), and exchange traded fund (ETF) (**screen.morningstar.com/screener_etf/etf_screener_version1.aspx**).

Charting Charting is a technique that plots the performance of securities over a specified time period, from months to decades or beyond. Looking at the 1-year stock chart for Qualcomm (QCOM) in Figure 3.4, it's obvious that charting can be tedious and therefore expensive. But by going online, you can see the chart for a selected stock in just seconds. With another click you can compare one company's price performance to that of other companies, industries, sectors, or market indexes, choosing the type of chart, time frame, and indicators. Several good sites are Barchart (**barchart.com**), BigCharts (**bigcharts.marketwatch.com**), and **StockCharts.com**. All three offer free, comprehensive charting features.

Stock Quotes and Portfolio Tracking Almost every investment-related Web site includes stock quotation and portfolio tracking tools. Simply enter the stock symbol to get the price, either in real time or delayed several minutes. Once you create a portfolio of stocks in a portfolio tracker, the tracker automatically updates your portfolio's value every time you check. Usually, you can even link to more detailed information about each stock; many sites let you set up multiple portfolios. The features, quality, and ease of use of stock and portfolio trackers vary, so check several to find the one that best meets your needs. Yahoo! Finance, MSN.Money, and Morningstar have portfolio trackers that are easy to set up and customize.

Pros and Cons of Using the Internet as an Investment Tool

The power of the Internet as an investing tool is alluring. "Do-it-yourself" investing is readily available to the average investor, even to novices who have never before bought stock. However, online investing also carries risks. Trading on the Internet requires that investors exercise the same—and possibly more—caution than they would if they were getting information from and placing orders with a human broker. You don't have the safety net of a live broker suggesting that you rethink your trade. The ease of point-and-click investing can be the financial downfall of inexperienced investors. Drawn by stories of others who have made lots of money, many novice investors take the plunge before they acquire the necessary skills and knowledge—often with disastrous results.

Online or off, the basic rules for smart investing are the same. Know what you are buying, from whom, and at what level of risk. Be skeptical. If it sounds too good to be true, it probably is! Always do your own research; don't accept someone else's word that a security is a good buy. Perform your own analysis before you buy, using the skills you will develop in later chapters of this book.

Here is some additional advice:

- Don't let the speed and ease of making transactions blind you to the realities of online trading. More frequent trades mean higher total transaction costs. Although some brokers advertise per-trade costs as low as $3, the average online transaction fee is higher (generally about $10 to $15). If you trade often, it will take longer to recoup your costs. Studies reveal that the more often you trade, the harder it is to beat the market. In addition, on short-term trades of less than one year, you'll pay taxes on profits at the higher, ordinary income tax rates, not the lower capital gains rate.

- Don't believe everything you read on the Internet. It's easy to be impressed with a screen full of data touting a stock's prospects or to act on a hot tip you find on a discussion board or in an online chat (more on this later). But what do you know about the person who posts the information? He or she could be a shill for a dealer, posing as an enthusiastic investor to push a stock. Stick to the sites of major brokerage firms, mutual funds, academic institutions, and well-known business and finance publications.

- If you get bitten by the online buying bug, don't be tempted to use margin debt to increase your stock holdings. As noted in Chapter 2, you may instead be magnifying your losses.

We will return to the subject of online investment fraud and scams and will discuss guidelines for online transactions in subsequent sections of this chapter.

INVESTOR FACTS

TOO MUCH OF A GOOD THING—A recent study looked at the investment performance of a group of individual investors who switched from trading by phone to online trading in the mid 1990s. As phone traders, these investors did very well, earning returns that were well above average. But after switching to online trading, they traded more often and more aggressively, generating much higher transactions costs in the process. As a result, their returns after going online dropped by roughly 5% per year compared to what they had previously achieved.

(Source: Brad M. Barber & Terrance Odean. (2002). Online Investors: Do the Slow Die First? *Review of Financial Studies, 15*(2), 455-487.)

3.1 Discuss the impact of the Internet on the individual investor and summarize the types of resources it provides.

3.2 Identify the four main types of online investment tools. How can they help you become a better investor?

3.3 What are some of the pros and cons of using the Internet to choose and manage your investments?

Types and Sources of Investment Information

LG2 As you learned in Chapter 1, becoming a successful investor starts with developing investment plans and meeting your liquidity needs. Once you have done that, you can search for the right investments to implement your investment plan and monitor your progress toward achieving your goals. Whether you use the Internet or print sources, you should examine various kinds of investment information to formulate expectations of the risk–return behaviors of potential investments. This section describes the key types and sources of investment information.

Investment information can be either descriptive or analytical. **Descriptive information** presents factual data on the past behavior of the economy, the market, the industry, the company, or a given investment. **Analytical information** presents projections and recommendations about potential investments based on available current data. The sample page from *Value Line* included in Figure 3.5 (on page 76) provides both descriptive and analytical information on Walmart Stores. We have marked items that are primarily descriptive with a D, and analytical items with an A. The key below the *Value Line* page explains the marked items. Examples of descriptive information are the company's capital structure (7D) and monthly stock price ranges for the past 13 years (13D). Examples of analytical information are rank for timeliness (1A) and projected price range and associated annual total returns for the next 3 years (4A).

Some forms of investment information are free; others must be purchased individually or by annual subscription. You'll find free information on the Internet, in newspapers, in magazines, at brokerage firms, and at public, university, and brokerage firm libraries. Alternatively, you can subscribe to free and paid services that provide periodic reports summarizing the investment outlook and recommending certain actions. Many Internet sites now offer free e-mail newsletters and alerts. You can even set up your own personalized home page at many financial Web sites so that stock quotes, portfolio tracking, current business news, and other information on stocks of interest to you appear whenever you visit the site or are sent automatically to you via e-mail. Other sites charge for premium content, such as brokerage research reports, whether in print or online form.

Although the Internet has increased the amount of free information, it may still make sense to pay for services that save you time and money by gathering and processing relevant investment information for you. But first consider the value of potential information: For example, paying $40 for information that increases your return by $27 would not be economically sound. The larger your investment portfolio, the easier it is to justify information purchases, because they are usually applicable to a number of investments.

FIGURE 3.5

A Report Containing Descriptive and Analytical Information

Value Line's full-page report on Walmart Stores from August 7, 2009, contains both descriptive (marked D) and analytical (marked A) information. (Source: Adapted from *The Value Line Investment Survey*, Ratings and Reports, August 7, 2009. ©Value Line Publishing, Inc., www.valueline.com. ©2009 Reproduced with the permission of Value Line Publishing, Inc.)

WAL-MART STORES NYSE-WMT — RECENT PRICE **48.92** — P/E RATIO **13.6** (Trailing: 14.3; Median: 25.0) — RELATIVE P/E RATIO **0.83** — DIV'D YLD **2.3%** — VALUE LINE

BUSINESS: Wal-Mart Stores, Inc. is the world's largest retailer, operating 891 discount stores, 2,612 supercenters (includes sizable grocery departments), 602 Sam's Clubs, and 153 Neighborhood Markets in the U.S., plus 3,615 foreign stores in Latin America, Asia, Canada, and the U.K. as of 1/31/09. Total store space: about 920 million square feet. Most stores are owned and are within 400 miles of an expanding network of distribution centers. Groceries accounted for 49% of U.S. sales; sales per square foot in 2008 and 2007: $461 and $450, resp. Has 2,100,000 employees. Off./ dir. own 43.6% of shares (4/09 proxy). Chairman: S. Robson Walton. CEO and Pres.: Michael Duke. Inc.: DE. Addr.: Box 116, Bentonville, AR 72716. Tel.: 479-273-4000. Net: walmartstores.com.

We've raised our fiscal 2009 (ends January 31, 2010) and fiscal 2010 share-net estimates for Wal-Mart by $0.05 and $0.10, respectively. As expected, the negative impact of foreign exchange rate fluctuations clipped earnings by $0.04 a share in the first quarter. That said, the improved near-term top- and bottom-line prospects include significant market-share gains among households with annual incomes above $50,000. That trend was evident in the latter half of 2008, but it appears to have accelerated in 2009's first quarter. Due to the current economic weakness, consumers in all income brackets are generally more amenable to the giant discounter's relatively low costs. Too, the company's expanded annual store-refurbishment program includes enhanced presentation of high-end electronics, wider aisles, and improved sight lines. Our fiscal 2010 earnings estimate assumes less of a drag from currency exchange rates, along with a lower unemployment rate.

The percentage of SG&A expenses to sales will likely remain at an elevated level for a while. The rise from 16.9% in fiscal 1999 to 19% currently reflects, to a large degree, higher costs per employee. Too, Wal-Mart's settlement last year of class action suits related to the underpayment of employees, as well as broader health insurance coverage, suggest that the SG&A-to-sales ratio will continue to be held in check for a while. Meanwhile, expenses for MIS (management information systems) upgrades have been elevated lately, but benefits from these measures might help improve the operating margin slightly next year.

The International division is slated to expand at a faster pace than U.S. operations over the coming 3 to 5 years. Wal-Mart has reduced its annual domestic expansion plans several times over the past 18 months. The retailer plans to open some 130 supercenters in the U.S. this year, versus the peak expansion, in fiscal 2006, of 276 such facilities. We expect the division's selling space to increase 10%–15% per annum through fiscal 2012, with the focus on Latin America and China. This high-quality stock's Timeliness rank slipped one notch, to 3 (Average), on July 31st.

David R. Cohen — August 7, 2009

(A) Fiscal year ends Jan. 31st of following calendar year. Sales exclude rentals from licensed depts. (B) Based on diluted shares. Excludes extraord. (losses) and gains: '99, $0.07; '01, ($0.01); '05, $0.03; '08, ($0.07). Excl. gain (loss) from discontinued operation: '03, $0.04; '06, ($0.21); '07, ($0.03); '08, $0.04. Next earnings report due late August. (C) Dividend payments historically in early January, April, July, and October. (D) Dividend reinvestment plan available. (D) In millions, adjusted for stock split.

	Company's Financial Strength	A++
	Stock's Price Stability	100
	Price Growth Persistence	30
	Earnings Predictability	100

To subscribe call 1-800-833-0046.

© 2009, Value Line Publishing, Inc. All rights reserved. Factual material is obtained from sources believed to be reliable and is provided without warranties of any kind. THE PUBLISHER IS NOT RESPONSIBLE FOR ANY ERRORS OR OMISSIONS HEREIN. This publication is strictly for subscriber's own, non-commercial, internal use. No part of it may be reproduced, resold, stored or transmitted in any printed, electronic or other form, or used for generating or marketing any printed or electronic publication, service or product.

Key:

1. Rank for timeliness (price performance in next 12 months)—from 1 (highest) to 5 (lowest)
2. Rank for long-term safety—1 (highest) down to 5 (lowest)
3. Beta (the stock's sensitivity to market fluctuation—NYSE average = 1.00)
4. Projected price range and associated annual returns—3 years ahead
5. Insider decisions
6. Institutional decisions
7. Company's capital structure
8. Pension liability
9. Working capital
10. Growth rates
11. Quarterly sales, earnings, dividends—actual past, estimated future
12. Footnotes—including estimated constant dollar earnings, dividend payment dates
13. Monthly price ranges—past 15 years and value line (cash flow line)
14. Statistical milestones—on a per share basis and a company basis— historical past and estimated future
15. Brief summary of company's business
16. Critique—of recent developments and prospects
17. Company's financial strength
18. Important indices of quality

Types of Information

Investment information can be divided into five types, each concerned with an important aspect of the investment process.

1. *Economic and current event information:* Includes background and forecast data related to economic, political, and social trends on both domestic and global scales. Such information provides a basis for assessing the environment in which decisions are made.

2. *Industry and company information:* Includes background and forecast data on specific industries and companies. Investors use such information to assess the outlook for a given industry or a specific company. Because of its company orientation, it is most relevant to stock, bond, or options investments.

3. *Information on alternative investment vehicles:* Includes background and forecast data for securities other than stocks, bonds, and cash, such as real estate, private equity, or commodities.

4. *Price information:* Includes price quotations on investment securities. These quotations are commonly accompanied by statistics on the recent price behavior of the security.

5. *Information on personal investment strategies:* Includes recommendations on investment strategies, or specific purchase or sale recommendations. In general, this information tends to be educational or analytical rather than descriptive.

Sources of Information

The discussion in this section focuses on the most common online and traditional sources of information on economic and current events, industries and companies, and prices, as well as other online sources. Beyond the discussion in this section, however, there are countless sources of investment information available to investors.

Economic and Current Event Information Investors who are aware of current economic, political, and business events tend to make better investment decisions. Popular sources of economic and current event information include financial journals, general newspapers, institutional news, business periodicals, government publications, and special subscription services. These are available in print and online versions; often the online versions are free but may have limited content. Most offer free searchable article archives and charge a nominal fee for each article downloaded.

Financial Journals The **Wall Street Journal** is the most popular source of financial news. Published daily Monday through Saturday in U.S., European, and Asian editions, the *Journal* also has an online version called the *WSJ Online* (**online.wsj.com**), which is updated frequently throughout the day and on the weekends. In addition to giving daily price quotations on thousands of investment securities, the *Journal* reports world, national, regional, and corporate news. The first page of its third section usually contains a column called "Heard on the Street" that focuses on specific market and company events. In addition, a fourth section containing articles that address personal finance issues and topics is included in the Tuesday, Wednesday, and Thursday editions, and an expanded version of that section, called "Weekend Journal," is included in Friday's edition. *WSJ Online* includes features such as quotes and news that provide stock and mutual fund charting, company profiles, financials,

Smart's Tour of the Web
To watch author Scott Smart discuss key websites for this chapter visit www.myfinancelab.com

and analyst ratings; article searches; special online-only articles; and access to the Dow Jones article archives.

A second popular source of financial news is *Barron's*, which is published weekly. *Barron's* generally offers lengthier articles on a variety of topics of interest to individual investors. Probably the most popular column in *Barron's* is "Up & Down Wall Street," which provides a critical, and often humorous, assessment of major developments affecting the stock market and business. *Barron's* also includes current price quotations and a summary of statistics on a range of investment securities. Subscribers to *WSJ Online* also have access to *Barron's* online edition (**online.barrons.com**) because both are published by Dow Jones & Company.

Investor's Business Daily is a third national business newspaper published Monday through Friday. It is similar to the *Wall Street Journal* but contains more detailed price and market data. Its Web site (**investors.com**) has limited free content. Another source of financial news is the *Financial Times* (**www.ft.com**), with U.S., U.K., European, and Asian editions.

General Newspapers Major metropolitan newspapers such as the *New York Times, Washington Post, Los Angeles Times*, and *Chicago Tribune* provide investors with a wealth of financial information in their print and online editions. Most major newspapers contain stock price quotations for major exchanges, price quotations on stocks of local interest, and a summary of the major stock market averages and indexes. Local newspapers are another convenient source of financial news. In most large cities, the daily newspaper devotes at least a few pages to financial and business news.

Another popular source of financial news is *USA Today*, the national newspaper published daily Monday through Friday. It is available in print and online versions (**usatoday.com**). Each issue contains a "Money" section (Section B) devoted to business and personal financial news and to current security price quotations and summary statistics.

Institutional News The monthly economic letters of the nation's leading banks, such as Bank of America (based in Charlotte, North Carolina), Northern Trust (Chicago), and Wells Fargo (San Francisco), provide useful economic information. Wire services such as Dow Jones, Bloomberg Financial Services, AP (Associated Press), and UPI (United Press International) provide economic and business news feeds to brokerages, other financial institutions, and Web sites that subscribe to them. Bloomberg has its own comprehensive site (**www.bloomberg.com**). Business.com (**www.business.com**) offers industry-by-industry news, targeted business searches, and employment resources by industry. Web sites specializing in financial news include CNNMoney (**money.cnn.com**) and MarketWatch (**www.marketwatch.com**).

Business Periodicals Business periodicals vary in scope. Some present general business and economic articles, others cover securities markets and related topics, and still others focus solely on specific industries. Regardless of the subject matter, most business periodicals present descriptive information, and some also include analytical information. They rarely offer recommendations.

The business sections of general-interest periodicals such as *Newsweek, Time,* and *U.S. News & World Report* cover business and economic news. Strictly business- and finance-oriented periodicals, including *Business Week, Fortune,* and *The Economist*, provide more in-depth articles. These magazines also have investing and personal finance articles.

Some financial periodicals specialize in securities and marketplace articles. The most basic, commonsense articles appear in *Forbes, Kiplinger's Personal Finance, Money,*

Smart Money, and *Worth.* Published every two weeks, *Forbes* is the most investment-oriented. *Kiplinger's Personal Finance, Money, Smart Money,* and *Worth* are published monthly and contain articles on managing personal finances and on investments.

All these business and personal finance magazines have Web sites with free access to recent, if not all, content. Most include a number of other features. For example, *Smart Money* has interactive investment tools, including a color-coded "Market Map 1000" that gives an aerial view of 1,000 U.S. and international stocks so that you can see which sectors and stocks are hot.

Government Publications A number of government agencies publish economic data and reports useful to investors. The annual *Economic Report of the President,* which can be found at the U.S. Government Printing Office (**www.gpo.gov**), provides a broad view of the current and expected state of the economy. This document reviews and summarizes economic policy and conditions and includes data on important aspects of the economy.

The *Federal Reserve Bulletin,* published monthly by the Board of Governors of the Federal Reserve System, and periodic reports published by each of the 12 Federal Reserve District Banks, provide articles and data on various aspects of economic and business activity. Visit **www.federalreserve.gov** to read many of these publications.

A useful Department of Commerce publication is the *Survey of Current Business* (**www.bea.gov/scb**). Published monthly, it includes indicators and data related to economic and business conditions. A good source of financial statement information on all manufacturers, broken down by industry and asset size, is the *Quarterly Financial Report for U.S. Manufacturing, Mining, and Wholesale Trade Corporations* (**www .census.gov/csd/qfr/view/qfr_mg.html**), published by the Department of Commerce.

Special Subscription Services Investors who want additional insights into business and economic conditions can subscribe to special services. These reports include business and economic forecasts and give notice of new government policies, union plans and tactics, taxes, prices, wages, and so on. One popular service is the *Kiplinger Washington Letter,* a weekly publication that provides a wealth of economic information and analyses.

Industry and Company Information Of special interest to investors is information on particular industries and companies. Often, after choosing an industry in which to invest, an investor will want to analyze specific companies. A recent change in disclosure rules, discussed following, gives individual investors access to more company information than before. General business periodicals such as *Business Week, Forbes,* the *Wall Street Journal,* and *Fortune* carry articles on the activities of specific industries and individual companies. Trade publications such as *Chemical Week, American Banker, Computerworld, Industry Week, Oil and Gas Journal,* and *Public Utilities Fortnightly* provide more focused industry and company information. *Red Herring, PC Magazine, Business 2.0,* and *Fast Company* are magazines that can help you keep up with the high-tech world; all have good Web sites.

The Internet makes it easy to research specific industries and companies at the company's Web site, a publication's archive search, or database services such as the Dow Jones Publications Library. Company Web sites typically offer a wealth of information about the company—investor information, annual reports, filings, and financial releases, press releases, and more. Table 3.1 presents several free and subscription resources that emphasize industry and company information.

TABLE 3.1	Online Sources for Industry and Company Information	
Web Site	Description	Cost
Hoover's Online (**www.hoovers.com**)	Reports and news on public and private companies with in-depth coverage of 43,000 of the world' top firms.	Varies according to level of service
CNET (**news.cnet.com**)	One of the best sites for high-tech news, analysis, breaking news, great search capabilities, links.	Free
Yahoo! Finance (**finance.yahoo.com**)	Provides information on companies from around the Web: stock quotes, news, investment ideas, research, financials, analyst ratings, insider trades, and more.	Free
Market Watch (**www.marketwatch.com**)	Latest news from various wire services. Searchable by market or industry. Good for earnings announcements and company news.	Free

Fair Disclosure Rules In August 2000, the SEC passed the **fair disclosure rule**, known as **Regulation FD**, a rule requiring senior executives to disclose material information such as earnings forecasts and news of mergers and new products simultaneously to investment professionals and the public via press releases or SEC filings. Companies may limit contact with analysts if they are unsure whether the information requires a press release. However, Regulation FD does not apply to communications with journalists and securities ratings firms like Moody's Investors Service and Standard & Poor's. Violations of the rule carry injunctions and fines but are not considered fraud.

Stockholders' Reports An excellent source of data on an individual firm is the **stockholders' report,** or **annual report,** published yearly by publicly held corporations. These reports contain a wide range of information, including financial statements for the most recent period of operation, along with summarized statements for several prior years. These reports are free and may be obtained from the companies themselves, from brokers, or downloaded from the company's Web site. The cover and a sample page from Walmart Stores, Inc. 2009 Stockholders' Report are shown in Figure 3.6 (on page 81). From page 14 of Walmart's 2009 Annual Report, it is easy to see the wealth of information available to investor in companies' annual reports. Most companies now place their annual reports on their Web sites. **AnnualReports.com** (**www.annualreports .com**) boasts having the most complete listing of annual reports on the Internet.

In addition to the stockholders' report, many serious investors review a company's **Form 10-K.** This is a statement that firms with securities listed on a securities exchange or traded in the OTC market must file annually with the SEC. Finding 10-K and other SEC filings is now a simple task, thanks to SEC/EDGAR (Electronic Data Gathering and Analysis Retrieval), which has reports filed by all companies traded on a major exchange. You can read them free either at the SEC's Web site (**www.sec.gov/edgar .shtml**) or at EDGAR Online's FreeEdgar site (**www.freeedgar.com**).

Comparative Data Sources Sources of comparative data, typically broken down by industry and firm size, are a good tool for analyzing the financial condition of companies. Among these sources are Dun & Bradstreet's *Key Business Ratios*, RMA's *Annual*

FIGURE 3.6   Pages from a Stockholders' Report

The "Financial Review" on the right-hand page from the 2009 Annual Report of Walmart Stores, Inc., quickly acquaints the investor with some key information on the firm's operations over the past year. The cover of the Annual Report is shown on the left-hand page. The actual Annual Report is available at Walmart's Web site **walmartstores.com/Investors/7666.aspx**.
(Source: Walmart Stores, Inc. 2009 Annual Report; Walmart Stores, Inc., Investor Relations, 479-273-8446, Walmart Stores, Inc., Bentonville, AR 72716-8611.)

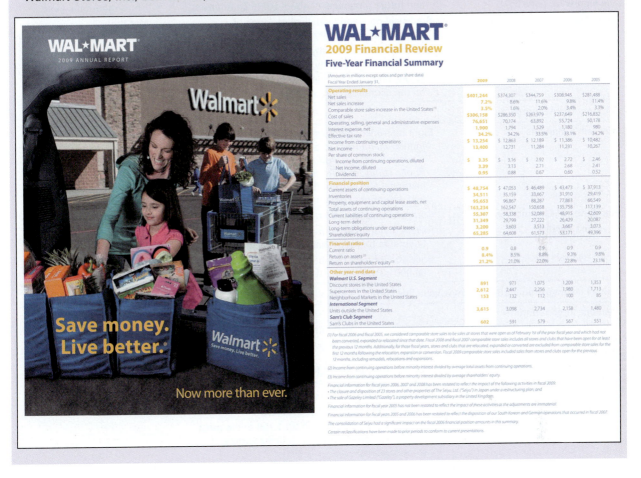

Statement Studies, the *Quarterly Financial Report for U.S. Manufacturing, Mining, and Wholesale Trade Corporations* (cited earlier), and the *Almanac of Business & Industrial Financial Ratios*. These sources, which are typically available in public and university libraries, are a useful benchmark for evaluating a company's financial condition.

Subscription Services A variety of subscription services provide data on specific industries and companies. Today, many of these services are available on the Internet. Generally, a subscriber pays a basic fee to access the service's information and can purchase premium services for greater depth or range. The major subscription services provide both descriptive and analytical information, but they generally do not make recommendations. Most investors, rather than subscribing to these services, access

TABLE 3.2	Popular Offerings of the Major Subscription Services	
Subscription Service/Offerings	**Coverage**	**Frequency of Publication**
Standard & Poor's Corporation (www2.standardandpoors.com)		
Corporation Records	Detailed descriptions of publicly traded securities of over 12,000 public corporations.	Annually with updates throughout the year
Stock Reports (sample shown in Figure 7.1, page 257)	Summary of financial history, current finances, and future prospects of about 5,000 companies.	Annually with updates throughout the year
Stock Guide	Statistical data and analytical rankings of investment desirability for major stocks.	Monthly
Bond Guide	Statistical data and analytical rankings of investment desirability of over 10,000 bonds.	Monthly
The Outlook	Analytical articles with investment advice on the economy, market, and investments.	Weekly magazine
Mergent (www.mergent.com)		
Mergent's Manuals	Eight reference manuals—*Bank and Finance, Industrial, International, Municipal and Government, OTC Industrial, OTC Unlisted, Public Utility,* and *Transportation*—with historical and current financial, organizational, and operational data on major firms.	Annually with monthly print updates (weekly online updates)
Handbook of Common Stocks	Common stock data on nearly 900 NYSE companies.	Quarterly
Dividend Record	Recent dividend announcements and payments on more than 30,000 securities.	Twice weekly, with annual summary
Bond Record	Price and interest rate behavior of over 68,000 issues.	Monthly
Value Line Investment Survey (www.valueline.com)		
Includes three reports:		Weekly
1. *Ratings and Reports* (sample shown in Figure 3.5, page 76)	Full-page report including financial data, descriptions, analysis, and ratings for each of about 130 stocks.	
2. *Selection and Opinion*	A 12- to 16-page report featuring a discussion of the U.S. economy and the stock market, sample portfolios for different types of investors, and an in-depth analysis of selected stocks.	
3. *Summary and Index*	A 40-page update listing about 1,700 of the most widely held stocks. Also includes a variety of stock screens.	

them through their stockbrokers or a large public or university library. The Web sites for most services offer some free information and charge for the rest.

The dominant subscription services are those offered by Standard & Poor's, Mergent, and Value Line. Table 3.2 summarizes the most popular services of these companies. **Standard & Poor's Corporation (S&P) (www2.standardandpoors.com)** offers a large number of different financial reports and services. Its Investing Web site, owned by *Business Week* (**www.businessweek.com/investor**), is geared toward individual investors. Although basic news and market commentary is free, *Business Week* subscribers obtain access to premium online services. **Mergent** (formerly Moody's Financial Information Services Division) (**www.mergent.com**) also publishes a variety of material, including its equity and bond portraits, corporate research, well-known reference manuals on eight industries, and numerous other products. The *Value Line Investment Survey* (**www.valueline.com**) is one of the most popular subscription services used by individual investors. It is available at most libraries and provides online access to additional services including data, graphing, portfolio tracking, and technical indicators.

Brokerage Reports Brokerage firms often make available to their clients reports from the various subscription services and research reports from their own securities analysts. They also provide clients with prospectuses for new security issues and *back-office research reports*. As noted in Chapter 2, a *prospectus* is a document that describes in detail the key aspects of the issue, the issuer, and its management and financial position. The cover of the preliminary prospectus describing the 2009 stock issue of LogMeIn, Inc., was shown in Figure 2.1 (on page 35). **Back-office research reports** include the brokerage firm's analyses of and recommendations on prospects for the securities markets, specific industries, or specific securities. Usually a brokerage firm publishes lists of securities classified by its research staff as either "buy," "hold," or "sell." Brokerage research reports are available on request at no cost to existing and potential clients.

Securities analysts' reports are now available on the Web, either from brokerage sites or from sites that consolidate research from many brokerages. At Reuters Investing (**www.investor.reuters.com**), a leading research site, over 1.5 million reports on companies and industries from over 700 brokerage and research firms are available. Investors can use Zacks's (**www.zacks.com**) Research Digest Reports to find and purchase analyst reports on over 700 widely followed stocks or to read free brokerage report abstracts with earnings revisions and recommendations.

Investment Letters Investment letters are newsletters that provide, on a subscription basis, the analyses, conclusions, and recommendations of experts in securities investment. Some letters concentrate on specific types of securities; others are concerned solely with assessing the economy or securities markets. Among the more popular investment letters are *Blue Chip Advisor, Dick Davis Digest, The Dines Letter, Dow Theory Letters,* the *Growth Stock Outlook, Louis Rukeyser's Wall Street, The Prudent Speculator,* and *Zacks Advisor.* Most investment letters come out weekly or monthly. Advertisements for many of these investment letters can be found in *Barron's* and in various business periodicals.

The *Hulbert Financial Digest* (**store.marketwatch.com/webapp/wcs/stores/servlet/premiumNewsletters_HulbertFinancialDigest**) monitors the performance of investment letters. It is an excellent source of objective information on investment letters and a good place to check out those that interest you. Many investment letters now offer online subscriptions. Use a general search engine or Newsletter Access (**www.newsletteraccess.com**), a searchable database of newsletters that lists about 370 investment newsletters.

Price Information Price information about various types of securities is contained in their **quotations**, which include current price data and statistics on recent price behavior. The Web makes it easy to find price quotes for actively traded securities, and many financially oriented sites include a stock price look-up feature or a stock ticker running across the screen, much like the ones that used to be found only in brokerage offices. The ticker consolidates and reports stock transactions made on the NYSE, NYSE Amex, regional exchanges, and Nasdaq market systems as they occur. Cable TV subscribers in many areas can watch the ticker at the bottom of the screen on certain channels, including Bloomberg TV, CNBC, and CNN Headline News. Table 3.3 (on page 84) lists the ticker symbols for some well-known companies.

TABLE 3.3	Symbols for Some Well-Known Companies		
Company	Symbol	Company	Symbol
Amazon.com	AMZN	Lucent Technologies	LU
Apple Computer	AAPL	McDonald's Corporation	MCD
AT&T	T	Microsoft	MSFT
Bank of America	BAC	Nike	NKE
Cisco	CSCO	Oracle	ORCL
The Coca-Cola Company	KO	PepsiCo, Inc.	PEP
Dell	DELL	Reebok	RBK
Eastman Kodak	EK	Sears Holdings	SHLD
ExxonMobil	XOM	Starbucks	SBUX
FedEx	FDX	Sun Microsystems	JAVA
General Electric	GE	Texas Instruments	TXN
Google	GOOG	Time Warner	TWX
Hewlett-Packard	HP	United Parcel Service	UPS
Intel	INTC	Walmart Stores	WMT
Int'l. Business Machines	IBM	Yahoo!	YHOO

Investors can easily find the prior day's security price quotations in the published news media, both nonfinancial and financial. They also can find delayed or real-time quotations for free at numerous Web sites, including *financial portals* (described below), most business periodical Web sites, and brokerage sites. The Web site for CNBC TV has real-time stock quotes, as do sites that subscribe to their news feed.

The major published source of security price quotations is the *Wall Street Journal,* which presents quotations for each previous business day's activities in all major markets. (We'll explain how to read and interpret actual price quotations in later chapters.)

Other Online Investment Information Sources   Many other excellent Web sites provide information of all sorts to increase your investment knowledge and skills. Let's now look at financial portals, sites for bonds and mutual funds, international sites, and investment discussion forums. Table 3.4 (on page 85) lists some of the most popular financial portals, bond sites, and mutual fund sites. We'll look at online brokerage and investment adviser sites later in the chapter.

Financial Portals   **Financial portals** are supersites that bring together a wide range of investing features, such as real-time quotes, stock and mutual fund screens, portfolio trackers, news, research, and transaction capabilities, along with other personal finance features. These sites want to be your investing home page.

Some financial portals are general sites such as Yahoo! and Excite that offer a full range of investing features along with their other services, or they may be investing-oriented sites. You should check out several to see which best suits your needs, because their strengths and features vary greatly. Some portals, to motivate you to stay at their site, offer customization options so that your start page includes the data you want. Although finding one site where you can manage your investments is indeed appealing, you may not be able to find the best of what you need at one portal. You'll want to explore several sites to find the ones that meet your needs. Table 3.4 (on page 85) summarizes the features of several popular financial portals.

Bond Sites   Although many general investment sites include bond and mutual fund information, you can also visit sites that specialize in these investments. Because Internet bond-trading activity is fairly limited at the present time, there are fewer online resources for individuals. Some brokerage firms are starting to allow clients

TABLE 3.4	Popular Investment Web Sites

The following Web sites are just a few of the thousands of sites that provide investing information. Unless otherwise mentioned, all are free.

Web Site	Description
Financial Portals	
America Online (proprietary portal) (**money.aol.com**)	Subscriber-only Money & Finance channel includes Investing and Personal Finance areas containing business news, market and stock quotes, stocks, mutual funds, investment research, retirement, saving and planning, credit and debt, banking and loans, and more. Each area offers education, tools, and message boards. Ease of use is a big plus.
Excite (**www.excite.com**)	Offers a money and investing channel that provides news, market data, and research capabilities along with a variety of links for tracking stocks, portfolios, screening stocks, participating in conference calls, and obtaining SEC filings.
MSN MoneyCentral Investor (**www.moneycentral.msn.com**)	More editorial content than many sites; good research and interactive tools like Research Wizard; can consolidate accounts in portfolio tracker. (Many tools don't run on Macintosh.)
Motley Fool (**www.fool.com**)	Comprehensive and entertaining site with educational features, research, news, and message boards. Model portfolios cover a variety of investment strategies. Free but offers premium services such as its *Stock Advisor* monthly newsletter for $149 per year.
Yahoo! Finance (**finance.yahoo.com**)	Simple design, content-rich; easy to find information quickly. Includes financial news, price quotes, portfolio trackers, bill paying, personalized home page, and a directory of other major sites.
Yodlee (**www.yodlee.com**)	Aggregation site that collects financial account data from banking, credit card, brokerage, mutual fund, mileage, and other sites. One-click access saves time and enables users to manage and interact with their accounts; offers e-mail accounts; easy to set up and track finances. Security issues concern potential users; few analytical tools.
Bond Sites	
Investing in Bonds (**www.investinginbonds.com**)	The Bond Market Association's Web site; good for novice investors. Bond education, research reports, historical data, and links to other sites. Searchable database.
BondsOnline (**www.bondsonline.com**)	Comprehensive site for news, education, free research, ratings, and other bond information. Searchable database. Some charges for newsletters and research.
CNNMoney.com Bonds (**www.money.com/markets/bondcenter**)	Individual investors can search for bond-related news, market data, and bond offerings.
Bureau of the Public Debt Online (**www.publicdebt.treas.gov**)	Run by U.S. Treasury Department; information about U.S. savings bonds and Treasury securities; can also buy Treasury securities online through Treasury Direct program.
Mutual Fund Sites	
Morningstar (**www.morningstar.com**)	Profiles of over 3,000 funds with ratings; screening tools, portfolio analysis and management; fund manager interviews, e-mail newsletters; educational sections. Advanced screening and analysis tools are $14.95 a month or $135 per year.
Mutual Fund Investor's Center (**www.mfea.com**)	Not-for-profit, easy-to-navigate site from the Mutual Fund Education Alliance with investor education, search feature, and links to profiles of funds, calculators for retirement, asset allocation, and college planning.
Fund Alarm (**www.fundalarm.com**)	Takes a different approach and identifies underperforming funds to help investors decide when to sell; alerts investors to fund manager changes. Lively commentary from the site founder, a CPA.
MAXfunds (**www.maxfunds.com**)	Offers several custom metrics and data points to help find the best funds and give investors tools other than past performance to choose funds. Covers more funds than any other on- or offline publication. MAXadvisor Powerfund Portfolios, a premium advisory service, costs $24.95 per 90 days.
IndexFunds.com (**www.indexfunds.com**)	Comprehensive site covering only index funds.
Personal Fund (**www.personalfund.com**)	Especially popular for its Mutual Fund Cost Calculator that shows the true cost of ownership, after fees, brokerage commissions, and taxes. Suggests lower-cost alternatives with similar investment objectives.

access to bond information that formerly was restricted to investment professionals. In addition to the sites listed in Table 3.4, other good sites for bond and interest rate information include **Bloomberg.com**'s Market Data Rates & Bonds (**bloomberg.com/ markets/rates/index.html**) and **WSJ.com** (**wsj.com**).

The sites of the major bond ratings agencies—Moody's Investors Services (**www.moodys.com**), Standard & Poor's (**www.standardandpoors.com**), and Fitch (**www.fitchibca.com**)—provide ratings lists, recent ratings changes, and information about how they determine ratings.

Mutual Fund Sites With thousands of mutual funds, how do you find the ones that match your investment goals? The Internet makes this task much easier, offering many sites with screening tools and worksheets. Almost every major mutual fund family has its own Web site as well. Some allow visitors to hear interviews or participate in chats with fund managers. Fidelity (**www.fidelity.com**) is one of the most comprehensive sites, with educational articles, fund selection tools, fund profiles, and more. Portals and brokerage sites also offer these tools. Table 3.4 includes some independent mutual fund sites that are worth checking out.

International Sites The international reach of the Internet makes it a natural resource to help investors sort out the complexity of global investing, from country research to foreign currency exchange. Site-by-Site! International Investment Portal & Research Center (**www.site-by-site.com/index_july14_2009.htm**) is a comprehensive portal just for international investing. Free daily market data, news, economic insights, research, and analysis and commentary covering numerous countries and investment vehicles are among this site's features. For more localized coverage, check out Euroland European Investor (**www .europeaninvestor.com**), UK-Invest (**www.uk-invest.com**), LatinFocus (**www.latin-focus .com**), and similar sites for other countries and regions. J. P. Morgan's ADR site (**www.adr .com**) is a good place to research American depositary receipts and learn about their financial positions. For global business news, the *Financial Times* site (**www.ft.com**) gets high marks. Dow Jones's MarketWatch (**www.marketwatch.com/news**) has good technology and telecommunications news, as well as coverage of global markets.

Investment Discussion Forums Investors can exchange opinions about their favorite stocks and investing strategies at the *online discussion forums* (message boards and chat rooms) found at most major financial Web sites. However, remember that the key word here is *opinion*. You don't really know much about the qualifications of the person posting the information. *Always do your own research before acting on any hot tips!* The Motley Fool's (**www.fool.com**) discussion boards are among the most popular, and Fool employees monitor the discussions. Message boards at Yahoo! Finance (**messages.yahoo.com**) are among the largest online, although many feel that the quality is not as good as at other sites. The Raging Bull (**ragingbull.com**) includes news and other links along with its discussion groups. Technology investors flock to Silicon Investor (**siliconinvestor.advfn.com**), a portal site whose high-tech boards are considered among the best.

Avoiding Online Scams Just as the Internet increases the amount of information available to all investors, it also makes it easier for scam artists and others to spread false news and manipulate information. Anyone can sound like an investment expert online, posting stock tips with no underlying substance. As mentioned earlier, you may not know the identity of the person touting or panning a stock on the message boards. The person panning a stock could be a disgruntled former employee or a short seller. For example, the ousted former chief executive of San Diego's Avanir Pharmaceuticals posted negative remarks on stock message boards, adversely affecting share price. The company sued and won a court order prohibiting him from ever posting derogatory statements about the company on any Internet message boards.

In the fast-paced online environment, two types of scams turn up frequently: "pump-and-dump" and "get-rich-quick" scams. In *pump-and-dump* scams, perpetrators buy select stocks and then falsely promote or hype the stocks to the public. The false promotion quickly pumps the prices sky-high, at which point the scam artist dumps the stocks at inflated prices. In *get-rich-quick* scams, promoters sell worthless investments to naïve buyers.

One well-publicized pump-and-dump scam demonstrates how easy it is to use the Internet to promote stocks. In September 2000, the SEC caught a 15-year-old boy who had made over $270,000 by promoting small-company stocks. The self-taught young investor/scam artist would buy a block of a company's shares and then send out a barrage of false and/or misleading e-mail messages and message board postings singing the praises of that stock and the company's prospects. Once this misinformation pushed up the stock price, he sold and moved on to a new target company. His postings were so articulate that other investors at Silicon Investor's message boards thought he was a 40-year-old.

To crack down on cyber-fraud, in 1998 the SEC formed the Office of Internet Enforcement. Its staff members quickly investigate reports of suspected hoaxes and prosecute the offenders. Former SEC Chairman Arthur Levitt cautions investors to remember that the Internet is basically another way to send and receive information, one that has no controls for accuracy or truthfulness. The SEC Web site (**www.sec.gov/investor/pubs/scams.htm**) includes tips to avoid investment scams. Three key questions that investors should ask are:

- *Is the investment registered?* Check the SEC's EDGAR database (**www.sec.gov/edgar/quickedgar.htm**) and with your state securities regulator (**www.nasaa.org.QuickLinks/ContactYourRegulator.efm**).

- *Is the person licensed and law-abiding?* Make sure the seller is licensed in your state. Check with the NASD for any record of complaints or fraud.

- *Does the investment sound too good to be true?* Then it probably is. Just being on the Web doesn't mean it's legitimate.

Another source of information regarding online frauds is the various state securities commissions, which typically provide useful advice regarding online investment fraud and how to avoid it.

CONCEPTS IN REVIEW

Answers available at
www.pearsonhighered.com/gitman

3.4 Differentiate between *descriptive information* and *analytical information*. How might one logically assess whether the acquisition of investment information or advice is economically justified?

3.5 What popular financial business periodicals would you use to follow the financial news? General news? Business news? Would you prefer to get your news from print sources or online, and why?

3.6 Briefly describe the types of information that the following resources provide.

    a. Stockholders' report   b. Comparative data sources
    c. Standard & Poor's Corporation   d. Mergent
    e. *Value Line Investment Survey*

3.7 How would you access each of the following types of information, and how would the content help you make investment decisions?

a. Prospectuses   b. Back-office research reports
c. Investment letters   d. Price quotations

3.8 Briefly describe several types of information that are especially well suited to being made available on the Internet. What are the differences between the online and print versions, and when would you use each?

Understanding Market Averages and Indexes

LG3 The investment information we have discussed in this chapter helps investors understand when the economy is moving up or down and how individual investments have performed. You can use this and other information to formulate expectations about future investment performance. It is also important to know whether market behavior is favorable or unfavorable. The ability to interpret various market measures should help you to select and time investment actions.

A widely used way to assess the behavior of securities markets is to study the performance of market averages and indexes. These measures allow you to conveniently (1) gauge general market conditions; (2) compare your portfolio's performance to that of a large, diversified (market) portfolio; and (3) study market cycles, trends, and behaviors in order to forecast future market behavior. Here we discuss key measures of stock and bond market activity. In later chapters, we will discuss averages and indexes associated with other investment securities. Like price quotations, measures of market performance are available at many Web sites.

Stock Market Averages and Indexes

Stock market averages and indexes measure the general behavior of stock prices over time. Although the terms *average* and *index* tend to be used interchangeably when people discuss market behavior, technically they are different types of measures. **Averages** reflect the arithmetic average price behavior of a representative group of stocks at a given point in time. **Indexes** measure the current price behavior of a representative group of stocks in relation to a base value set at an earlier point in time.

Averages and indexes provide a convenient method of capturing the general mood of the market. Investors can also compare these measures at different points in time to assess the relative strength or weakness of the market. Current and recent values of the key averages and indexes are quoted daily on financial Web sites, in the financial news, in most local newspapers, and on many radio and television news programs. Figure 3.7 (on page 89) shows "U.S. Indexes," a version of which is published daily at *WSJ Online* (**online.wsj.com/mdc/page/marketsdata.html**) in the Market Data Center, which provides summary statistics on the major U.S. stock market averages and indexes.

The Dow Jones Averages Dow Jones & Company, publisher of the *Wall Street Journal*, prepares four stock averages. The most popular is the **Dow Jones Industrial Average (DJIA)**. This average is made up of 30 stocks selected for total market value and broad public ownership. The group consists of high-quality stocks whose behaviors are believed to reflect overall market activity. The list at the bottom of Figure 3.8 (on page 90) includes the 30 stocks in the DJIA as of August 2009.

FIGURE 3.7

Major Stock Market Averages and Indexes (August 26, 2009)

The "U.S. Indexes" summarizes the key stock market averages and indexes. It includes statistics showing the last recorded level, the change in level since the previous day's closing level, and the percentage change since the previous day's closing level. The asterisks next to the index names indicate that the last levels reported in the table are end-of-day closing levels. Notice that if you view this table from the Market Data Center of the *WSJ Online* Web site you can roll over the index name with your cursor for a pop-up chart showing the index. (Source: *WSJ Online* Market Data Center, August 26, 2009. ©Dow Jones & Company, Inc. All rights reserved.)

U.S. INDEXES

Dow Jones Indexes (Roll over for charts) — 4:34 p.m. EDT 08/26/09

	Last	Change	% Chg
DJIA*	9543.52	4.23	0.04
DJ Transportation Average*	3723.96	-48.77	-1.29
DJ Utility Average*	378.16	-1.23	-0.32
DJ Composite Average*	3279.92	-13.94	-0.42
DJ Total Stock Market*	10571.13	0.21	0.00
DJ Broad Stock Market*	2491.98	0.08	0.00
DJ Large-Cap Growth TSM*	2353.67	0.07	0.00
DJ Large-Cap Value TSM*	2271.01	-0.05	0.00
DJ Mid-Cap Growth TSM*	3254.48	-5.42	-0.17
DJ Mid-Cap Value TSM*	3361.55	1.87	0.06
DJ Small-Cap Growth TSM*	2897.31	-1.17	-0.04
DJ Small-Cap Value TSM*	4316.85	4.22	0.10
DJ Micro-Cap TSM*	5489.04	42.55	0.78
DJ Select REIT*	124.98	0.62	0.50
DJ U.S. Select Dividend*	289.83	-0.22	-0.08
DJ Internet*	92.22	-0.41	-0.44
Barron's 400*	233.96	-0.51	-0.22

Nasdaq Stock Market (Roll over for charts)

	Last	Change	% Chg
Nasdaq*	2024.43	0.20	0.01
Nasdaq 100*	1637.00	-2.90	-0.18
Nasdaq Biotech*	819.75	5.99	0.74
Nasdaq Computer*	986.16	-0.73	-0.07
Nasdaq Industrials*	1529.38	-1.51	-0.10
Nasdaq Insurance*	3459.33	4.18	0.12
Nasdaq Banks*	1716.54	7.02	0.41
Nasdaq Telecommunications*	205.97	0.11	0.05

Standard & Poor's (Roll over for charts)

	Last	Change	% Chg
S&P 500*	1028.12	0.12	0.01
S&P 100*	477.95	0.46	0.10
S&P Industrials*	1312.63	1.01	0.08
S&P 400 Mid-Cap*	659.48	-0.69	-0.10
S&P 600 Small-Cap*	308.29	-0.18	-0.06
S&P 1500 SuperComp*	234.66	0.00	0.00

New York Stock Exchange (Roll over for charts)

	Last	Change	% Chg
NYSE Composite*	6687.94	-9.28	-0.14
NYSE Arca Tech 100*	788.44	1.04	0.13
NYSE Financial*	4765.96	-3.16	-0.07
NYSE Health Care*	5812.05	-16.62	-0.29
NYSE Energy*	10484.58	-5.75	-0.05

Occasionally, a merger, bankruptcy, or extreme lack of activity causes a change in the makeup of the average. For example, SBC Communications' 2005 merger with AT&T moved it (AT&T) to the DJIA. Changes to the 30 stocks also occur when Dow Jones believes that the average does not reflect the broader market. For example, in 2004 pharmaceutical company Pfizer and technology company Verizon replaced Eastman Kodak and International Paper. Most recently, on June 8, 2009, General Motors and Citigroup were replaced by Cisco Systems and Travelers Cos. When a new

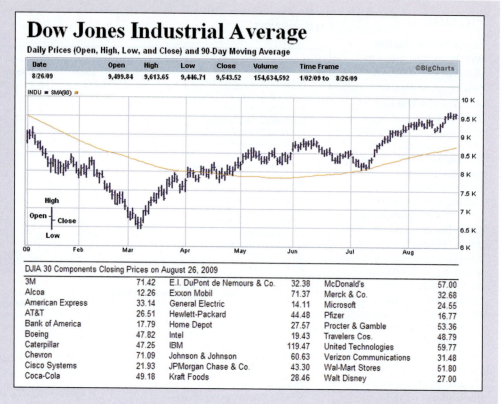

FIGURE 3.8

The DJIA from January 2, 2009 to August 26, 2009

For the first two months of 2009, the market remained bearish following the 2008 financial market crisis, but after finding a bottom in early March it began rebounding. (Source: *WSJ Online* Market Data Center, August 26, 2009. ©Dow Jones & Company, Inc. All rights reserved.)

stock is added, the average is readjusted so that it continues to behave in a manner consistent with the immediate past.

The value of the DJIA is calculated each business day by substituting the closing share prices of each of the 30 stocks in the DJIA into the following equation:

Equation 3.1

$$\text{DJIA} = \frac{\begin{array}{c}\text{Closing share price} \\ \text{of stock 1}\end{array} + \begin{array}{c}\text{Closing share price} \\ \text{of stock 2}\end{array} + \cdots + \begin{array}{c}\text{Closing share price} \\ \text{of stock 30}\end{array}}{\text{DJIA divisor}}$$

The value of the DJIA is merely the sum of the closing share prices of the 30 stocks included in it, divided by a "divisor." The purpose of the divisor is to adjust for any stock splits, company changes, or other events that have occurred over time. Without the divisor, whose calculation is very complex, the DJIA value would be totally distorted. The divisor makes it possible to use the DJIA to make time-series comparisons. On August 26, 2009, the sum of the closing prices (shown in Figure 3.8) of the 30 industrials was 1262.79 and the DJIA divisor at the time was 0.132319125. Using Equation 3.1, you can divide the sum of the closing prices of the 30 industrials by the DJIA divisor and arrive at the DJIA closing value of 9543.52 shown in Figure 3.8.

Because the DJIA results from summing the prices of the 30 stocks, higher-priced stocks tend to affect the index more than do lower-priced stocks. For example, a 5% change in the price of a $50 stock (i.e., $2.50) has less impact on the index than a 5%

change in a $100 stock (i.e., $5.00). In spite of this and other criticisms leveled at the DJIA, it remains the most widely cited stock market indicator.

The actual value of the DJIA is meaningful only when compared to earlier values. For example, the DJIA on August 26, 2009, closed at 9543.52. This value is meaningful only when compared to the previous day's closing value of 9539.29, a change of about 0.04%. Many people mistakenly believe that one DJIA "point" equals $1 in the value of an average share. Actually, one point currently translates into about 0.44 cents in average share value. Figure 3.8 shows the DJIA over the first eight months of 2009. For the first two months of 2009, the market remained bearish following the 2008 financial market crisis, but after finding a bottom in early March it began rebounding. At the beginning of 2009, it started at about 9034.69 and then dropped to a year-to-date low of 6547.05 on March 9th. Over the next three months, the market steadily rose to 8770.92 on June 11, 2009, before sliding back down to summer a low of 8146.52 on July 10th. Since hitting the summer low, the market has been mostly bullish.

The three other Dow Jones averages are the transportation, utilities, and composite. The *Dow Jones Transportation Average* is based on 20 stocks, including railroads, airlines, freight forwarders, and mixed transportation companies. The *Dow Jones Utilities Average* is computed using 15 public-utility stocks. The *Dow Jones 65 Stocks Composite Average* is made up of the 30 industrials, the 20 transportations, and the 15 utilities. Like the DJIA, each of the other Dow Jones averages is calculated using a divisor to allow for continuity of the average over time. The transportation, utilities, and 65-stocks composite are often cited along with the DJIA, as shown in Figure 3.7.

Dow Jones also publishes numerous indexes as seen in Figure 3.7. The first one listed, the **DJ U.S. Total Stock Market Index**, is a market-weighted index. "Market-weighted" means that companies with large total market values have the most effect on the index's movement. The Dow Jones U.S. Total Stock Market Index measures the performance of all equity securities issued by U.S. companies that have readily available price data. As of July 31, 2009, it represents the dollar value (in billions of dollars) of 4,376 actively traded stocks with a combined market value of $11,739.1 billion.

Standard & Poor's Indexes Standard & Poor's Corporation, another leading financial publisher, publishes six major common stock indexes. One oft-cited S&P index is the 500-stock composite index. **Standard & Poor's indexes** are calculated each business day by substituting the *closing market value of each stock* (closing price × number of shares outstanding) into the following equation:

Equation 3.2

$$\text{S\&P Index} = \frac{\begin{array}{c}\text{Current closing} \\ \text{market value} \\ \text{of stock 1}\end{array} + \begin{array}{c}\text{Current closing} \\ \text{market value} \\ \text{of stock 2}\end{array} + \cdots + \begin{array}{c}\text{Current closing} \\ \text{market value} \\ \text{of last stock}\end{array}}{\begin{array}{c}\text{Base period} \\ \text{closing market} \\ \text{value of stock 1}\end{array} + \begin{array}{c}\text{Base period} \\ \text{closing market} \\ \text{value of stock 2}\end{array} + \cdots + \begin{array}{c}\text{Base period} \\ \text{closing market} \\ \text{value of last stock}\end{array}} \times 10$$

The value of the S&P index is found by dividing the sum of the market values of all stocks included in the index by the market value of the stocks in the base period and then multiplying the resulting quotient by the base value for the respective S&P indexes. To ensure continuity in index values, the base period values for index stocks are adjusted as necessary through time to account for changes in share capital. For example, on August 26, 2009, the ratio of the closing market values of the S&P 500 composite stocks to the 1941–1943 base-period closing market values was 102.812, which, when multiplied by the base value of the S&P 500 index of 10, results in an index value of 1028.12 (as shown in Figure 3.7).

Certain of the S&P indexes contain many more shares than the Dow averages do, and all of them are based on *market values* rather than *share prices*. Therefore, many investors feel that the S&P indexes provide a more broad-based and representative measure of general market conditions than do the Dow averages. Although some technical computational problems exist with these indexes, they are widely used—frequently as a basis for estimating the "market return," an important concept that is introduced in Chapter 4.

Like the Dow averages, the S&P indexes are meaningful only when compared to values in other time periods or to their respective base-period value. For example, the August 26, 2009, value of the S&P 500 Stock Composite Index of 1028.12 means that the market values of the stocks in the index increased by a factor of 102.812 (1028.12 ÷ 10) since the 1941–1943 period.

The six major common stock indexes published by Standard & Poor's are the following:

- The *S&P 500 Index*, comprised of 500 large-sized companies.

- The *S&P 100 Index*, comprised of 100 large-sized companies with individual stock options required for each constituent.

- *The industrials index*, made up of the common stock of 400 industrial firms.

- The *S&P 400 MidCap Index*, comprised of 400 medium-sized companies.

- The *S&P 600 SmallCap Index*, comprised of 600 small-sized companies.

- The *1500 SuperComp Index,* comprised of all stocks in the S&P 500, 400 MidCap, and 600 SmallCap indexes.

Like the Dow averages and indexes, many of the S&P indexes are frequently quoted in the financial news, as shown in Figure 3.7.

Although the Dow Jones averages and S&P indexes tend to behave in a similar fashion over time, their day-to-day magnitude and even direction (up or down) can differ significantly because of the differences in how the indexes are constructed.

NYSE, Amex, and Nasdaq Indexes Three indexes measure the daily results of the New York Stock Exchange (NYSE), the NYSE Amex Exchange, and the National Association of Securities Dealers Automated Quotation (Nasdaq) system. Each reflects the movement of stocks listed on its exchange.

The **NYSE composite index** includes about 2,100 or so stocks listed on the "Big Board." The index's base of 5000 reflects the December 31, 2002, value of stocks listed on the NYSE. In addition to the composite index, the NYSE publishes indexes for financial and other subgroups. The behavior of the NYSE composite index is normally similar to that of the DJIA and the S&P 500 indexes.

The **Amex composite index** reflects the price of all shares traded on the NYSE Amex Exchange, relative to a base of 550 set at December 29, 1995. Although it does not always closely follow the S&P and NYSE indexes, the Amex index tends to move in the general direction they do.

The **Nasdaq Stock Market indexes** reflect Nasdaq stock market activity. The most comprehensive of the Nasdaq indexes is the *composite index,* which is calculated using the more than 4,000 domestic common stocks traded on the Nasdaq stock market. It is based on a value of 100 set at February 5, 1971. Also important is the *Nasdaq 100,* which includes 100 of the largest domestic and international nonfinancial companies listed on Nasdaq. It is based on a value of 125, set on January 1, 1994. The other two commonly quoted Nasdaq indexes are the *biotech* and *computer indexes.* Although their degrees of responsiveness may vary, the Nasdaq indexes tend to move in the same direction at the same time as the other major indexes.

Value Line Indexes Value Line publishes a number of stock indexes constructed by equally weighting the price of each stock included. This is accomplished by considering only the percentage changes in stock prices. This approach eliminates the effects of differing market price and total market value on the relative importance of each stock in the index. The **Value Line composite index** includes the about 1,700 stocks in the *Value Line Investment Survey* that are traded on the NYSE, NYSE Amex, and OTC markets. The base of 100 reflects the stock prices on June 30, 1961. In addition to its composite index, Value Line publishes other specialized indexes.

Other Averages and Indexes A number of other indexes are available. Frank Russell Company, a pension advisory firm, publishes three primary indexes. The *Russell 1000* includes the 1,000 largest companies, the most widely quoted *Russell 2000* includes 2,000 small- to medium-sized companies, and the *Russell 3000* includes all 3,000 companies in the Russell 1000 and 2000.

In addition, the *Wall Street Journal* publishes a number of global and foreign stock market indexes summarized in the "International Stocks & Indexes" section, normally in Section C. Included are Dow Jones indexes for countries in the Americas, Europe, Africa, Asia, and the Pacific region that are based on a value of 100 set at December 31, 1991. About 35 foreign stock market indexes are also given for major countries, including a *World Index* and the *Europe/Australia/Far East (EAFE MSCI) Index.* Like the purely domestic averages and indexes, these international averages and indexes measure the general price behavior of the stocks that are listed and traded in the given market. Useful comparisons of the market averages and indexes over time and across markets are often made to assess both trends and relative strengths of foreign markets throughout the world.

Bond Market Indicators

A number of indicators are available for assessing the general behavior of the bond markets. A "Bond Market Data Bank" that includes a wealth of return and price index data for various types of bonds and various domestic and foreign markets is published daily in the *Wall Street Journal.* However, there are fewer indicators of overall bond market behavior than of stock market behavior. The key measures of overall U.S. bond market behavior are bond yields and bond indexes.

Bond Yields A **bond yield** is the return an investor would receive on a bond if it were purchased and held to maturity. Bond yields are reported as annual rates of return. For example, a bond with a yield of 5.50% would provide its owner with a total return from periodic interest and capital gain (or loss) that would be equivalent to a 5.50%

annual rate of earnings on the amount invested (i.e., the bond's purchase price), if the bond were purchased and held to maturity.

Typically, bond yields are quoted for a group of bonds that are similar with respect to type and quality. For example, *Barron's* quotes the yields on the Dow Jones bond averages of 10 high-grade corporate bonds, 10 medium-grade corporate bonds, and a confidence index that is calculated as a ratio of the high-grade to medium-grade indexes. In addition, like the *Wall Street Journal,* it quotes numerous other bond indexes and yields, including those for Treasury and municipal bonds. Similar bond yield data are available from S&P, Moody's, and the Federal Reserve. Like stock market averages and indexes, bond yield data are especially useful when viewed over time.

Bond Indexes   There are a variety of bond indexes. The **Dow Jones Corporate Bond Index** includes 96 bonds—32 industrial, 32 financial, and 32 utility/telecom bonds. It reflects the simple mathematical average of the *closing prices* for the bonds. It is based on a value of 100 set at December 31, 1996. The Index is published daily in the *Wall Street Journal* and summarized weekly in *Barron's.*

CONCEPTS IN REVIEW

Answers available at
www.pearsonhighered.com/gitman

3.9   Describe the basic philosophy and use of stock market averages and indexes. Explain how the behavior of an average or index can be used to classify general market conditions as bull or bear.

3.10   List each of the major averages or indexes prepared by (a) Dow Jones & Company and (b) Standard & Poor's Corporation. Indicate the number and source of the securities used in calculating each average or index.

3.11   Briefly describe the composition and general thrust of each of the following indexes.

   a. NYSE composite index
   b. Amex composite index
   c. Nasdaq Stock Market indexes
   d. Value Line composite index

3.12   Discuss each of the following as they are related to assessing bond market behavior.

   a. Bond yields
   b. Bond indexes

Making Securities Transactions

LG4   **LG5**   Now that you know how to find information to help you locate attractive security investments, you need to understand how to make securities transactions. Whether you decide to start a self-directed online investment program or to use a traditional stockbroker, you must first open an account with a brokerage service. In this section, we will look at the role stockbrokers play and how that role has changed with the growth in online investing. We will also explain the basic types of orders you can place, the procedures required to make regular and online securities transactions, the costs of investment transactions, and investor protection.

The Role of Stockbrokers

Stockbrokers—also called *account executives, investment executives,* and *financial consultants*—act as intermediaries between buyers and sellers of securities. They typically charge a commission to facilitate these securities transactions. Stockbrokers must be licensed by both the SEC and the securities exchanges on which they place orders and must follow the ethical guidelines of those bodies.

Although the procedure for executing orders in broker markets may differ from that in dealer markets, it starts the same way: An investor places an order with his or her stockbroker. The broker works for a brokerage firm that maintains memberships on the securities exchanges, and members of the securities exchange execute orders that the brokers in the firm's various sales offices transmit to them. For example, the largest U.S. brokerage firm, Bank of America (which recently acquired Merrill Lynch), transmits orders for listed securities from its offices in most major cities throughout the country to the main office of Bank of America (BofA) and then to the floor of the broker market exchanges (NYSE and NYSE Amex), where BofA exchange members execute them. Confirmation of the order goes back to the broker placing the order, who relays it to the customer. This process can take a matter of seconds with the use of sophisticated telecommunications networks and Internet trading.

For a dealer market securities transaction (Nasdaq and OTC markets), brokerage firms transmit orders to *market makers*. Normally, dealer market transactions are executed rapidly, since there is considerable competition among dealers for the opportunity to execute brokerage orders. The revenue that market makers generate from executing orders is offset by the cost of maintaining inventories of the securities in which they deal.

Brokerage Services The primary activity of stockbrokers is to route clients' buy and sell orders to market venues where they will be executed at the best possible price. The speed with which brokers can get clients' orders executed is enhanced by the fact that brokerage firms typically hold their clients' security certificates for safekeeping. Securities kept by the firm in this manner are said to be held in **street name**. Because the brokerage house issues the securities in its own name and holds them in trust for the client (rather than issuing them in the client's name), the firm can transfer the securities at the time of sale without the client's signature. Street name is actually a common way of buying securities, because most investors do not want to be bothered with the handling and safekeeping of stock certificates. In such cases, the brokerage firm records the details of the client's transaction and keeps track of his or her investments through a series of bookkeeping entries. Dividends and notices received by the broker are forwarded to the client who owns the securities.

In addition to order routing and certificate storage, stockbrokers offer clients a variety of other services. For example, the brokerage firm normally provides free information about investments. Quite often, the firm has a research staff that periodically issues reports on economic, market, industry, or company behavior and makes recommendations to buy, sell, or hold certain securities. You will also receive a statement describing your transactions for the month and showing commission and interest charges, dividends and interest received, and detailed listings of your current holdings.

Today, most brokerage firms will invest surplus cash left in a client's account in a money market mutual fund, allowing the client to earn a reasonable rate of interest on these balances. Such arrangements help the investor earn as much as possible on temporarily idle funds.

Types of Brokerage Firms Just a few years ago, there were three distinct types of brokerage firms: full-service, premium discount, and basic discount. No longer are the lines between these categories clear-cut. Most brokerage firms, even the most traditional ones, now offer online services. And many discount brokers now offer services, like research reports for clients, that were once available only from a full-service broker.

The traditional broker, or so-called **full-service broker**, in addition to executing clients' transactions, offers investors a full array of brokerage services: providing investment advice and information, holding securities in street name, offering online brokerage services, and extending margin loans.

Investors who wish merely to make transactions and are not interested in taking advantage of other services should consider either a premium or basic discount broker.

Premium discount brokers focus primarily on making transactions for customers. They charge low commissions and provide limited free research information and investment advice. The investor visits the broker's office, calls a toll-free number, or accesses the broker's Web site to initiate a transaction. The broker confirms the transaction in person or by phone, e-mail, or regular mail. Premium discount brokers like Charles Schwab, the first discount broker, now offer many of the same services that you'd find at a full-service broker. Other premium discounters are similar.

Basic discount brokers, also called *online brokers* or *electronic brokers,* are typically deep-discount brokers through which investors can execute trades electronically online via a commercial service, on the Internet, or by phone. The investor accesses the basic discount broker's Web site to open an account, review the commission schedule, or see a demonstration of the available transactional services and procedures. Confirmation of online trades can take mere seconds, and most trades occur within one minute. Most basic discount brokers operate primarily online, but also provide telephone and live broker backup in case there are problems with the Web site or the customer is away from his or her computer. In response to the rapid growth of online investors, particularly among young investors who enjoy surfing the Web, most brokerage firms now offer online trading. These firms usually charge higher commissions when live broker assistance is required.

The rapidly growing volume of business done by both premium and basic discount brokers attests to their success. Today, many full-service brokers, banks, and savings institutions are making discount and online brokerage services available to their customers and depositors who wish to buy stocks, bonds, mutual funds, and other investment securities. Some of the major full-service, premium discount, and basic discount brokers are listed in Table 3.5.

Selecting a Stockbroker If you decide to start your investing activities with the assistance of either a full-service or premium discount stockbroker, select the person you believe best understands your investment goals. Choosing a broker whose disposition toward investing is similar to yours is the best way to establish a solid working relationship. Your broker should also make you aware of investment possibilities that are consistent with your objectives and attitude toward risk.

TABLE 3.5 Major Full-Service, Premium Discount, and Basic Discount Brokers		
Full-Service Broker	Premium Discount Broker	Basic Discount Broker
A.G. Edwards	Bank of America	Firstrade
Morgan Stanley	Charles Schwab	Scottrade
UBS Financial Services	E*Trade	Thinkorswim
Wells Fargo	Fidelity.com	TradeKing
	TD Ameritrade	Wall Street*E
	WellsTrade	

ETHICS IN INVESTING

Did Martha Stewart Cross the Line?

On March 5, 2004, a jury returned a guilty verdict convicting homemaking queen Martha Stewart and her former stockbroker, Peter Bacanovic, of obstructing justice and lying about a well-timed stock sale. According to the prosecution, Martha Stewart committed illegal insider trading when she sold stock in biotech company ImClone Systems and then made false statements to federal investigators. The government also accused Stewart and Bacanovic of creating an alibi for her ImClone sales and attempting to obstruct justice during investigations into her trades. Stewart found herself tarred by the scandal, during which she resigned as chair of the board and CEO of her company. In addition, the stock of her company dropped more that 20%, and her holdings took nearly a $200 million hit, wiping out more than a quarter of her net worth.

The government alleged that Bacanovic tipped off Stewart that two of his other clients, ImClone's CEO Samuel Waksal and Waksal's daughter, had just placed orders to sell their ImClone stock. Waksal, a long-time friend of Stewart, had obtained information that the U.S. Food and Drug Administration (FDA) was about to reject ImClone's new cancer product, Erbitux. Stewart promptly sold all 3,928 shares of her ImClone stock, thus avoiding about $50,000 in losses. The very next day, ImClone announced that the FDA had rejected its application for Erbitux. Quickly, the price of ImClone stock dropped 16%, to $46 per share. According to authorities, Stewart and Bacanovic fabricated an alibi for Stewart's trades—that she and her broker had decided earlier that she would sell if the price fell below $60 per share.

As a result of the conviction, Martha Stewart spent five months in jail and another five months under house arrest. Interestingly, she was not convicted on a more serious charge of insider trading—which the judge dismissed—but for obstructing the federal investigation. By an ironic twist of fate, in February 2004 the drug at the heart of the scandal received FDA approval to treat certain forms of cancer.

Critical Thinking Question In light of the *Insider Trading and Fraud Act of 1988*, does Martha Stewart, or any other investor, have the right to sell stock any time a broker advises him or her to?

Although her incarceration ended on March 4, 2005, and her house arrest was complete five months later, it was not until August 2006 that the Securities and Exchange Commission announced that it had reached an agreement with Stewart on a settlement of the civil case against her. Under the settlement, Stewart agreed to a five-year ban from serving as a director, as a CEO, as a CFO, or in any officer role, where she would be responsible for preparing, auditing, or disclosing financial results, of any public company. Thus, not until late 2011 will Stewart be eligible to again serve as the chairwoman, president, and CEO of her own company.

You should also consider the cost and types of services available from the firm with which the broker is affiliated, in order to receive the best service at the lowest possible cost to you. The premium discount brokerage service is primarily transactional, and the basic discount brokerage service is *purely* transactional. Contact with a broker for advice or research assistance is generally only available at a higher price. Investors must weigh the added commissions they pay a full-service broker against the value of the advice they receive, because the amount of available advice is the only major difference among the three types of brokers.

Referrals from friends or business associates are a good way to begin your search for a stockbroker. (Don't forget to consider the investing style and goals of the person making the recommendation.) However, it is not important—and often not even advisable—to know your stockbroker personally. In this age of online brokers, you may never meet your broker face to face. A strictly business relationship eliminates the possibility that personal concerns will interfere with the achievement of your investment goals. For an example of a stockbroker-client business relationship that crossed the line, see the *Ethics* box above on Martha Stewart.

However, your broker's main interest should not be commissions. Responsible brokers do not engage in **churning**—that is, causing excessive trading of their clients' accounts to increase commissions. Churning is both illegal and unethical under SEC and exchange rules, although it is often difficult to prove.

Opening an Account To open an account, you will fill out various documents that establish a legal relationship between yourself and the brokerage firm. A signature card and personal data card provide the information needed to identify your account. The stockbroker must also have a reasonable understanding of your personal financial situation to assess your investment goals—and to be sure that you can pay for the securities purchased. You also provide the broker with instructions regarding the transfer and custody of securities. Customers who wish to borrow money to make transactions must establish a margin account (described following). If you are acting as a custodian, a trustee, an executor, or a corporation, the brokerage firm will require additional documents. Today, all of this can be done online with most brokerage firms.

Investors may have accounts with more than one stockbroker. Many investors establish accounts at different types of firms to obtain the benefit and opinions of a diverse group of brokers and to reduce their overall cost of making buy and sell transactions.

Next you must select the type of account best suited to your needs. We will briefly consider several of the more popular types.

Single or Joint A brokerage account may be either single or joint. Joint accounts are most common between husband and wife or parent and child. The account of a minor (a person younger than 18 years of age) is a **custodial account**, in which a parent or guardian must be part of all transactions. Regardless of the form of the account, the name(s) of the account holder(s) and an account number are used to identify it.

Cash or Margin A **cash account**, the more common type, is one in which the customer can make only cash transactions. Customers can initiate cash transactions via phone or online and are given three business days in which to transmit the cash to the brokerage firm. The firm is likewise given three business days in which to deposit the proceeds from the sale of securities in the customer's cash account.

A **margin account** is an account in which the brokerage firm extends borrowing privileges to a creditworthy customer. By leaving securities with the firm as collateral, the customer can borrow a prespecified proportion of the securities' purchase price. The brokerage firm will, of course, charge the customer a stated rate of interest on borrowings. (The mechanics of margin trading are covered in Chapter 2.)

Wrap The **wrap account** (also called a *managed account*) allows brokerage customers with large portfolios (generally $100,000 or more) to shift stock selection decisions conveniently to a professional money manager, either in-house or independent. In return for a flat annual fee, commonly between 1% and 3% of the portfolio's total asset value, the brokerage firm helps the investor select a money manager, pays the manager's fee, and executes the money manager's trades. Initially the investor, broker, and/or manager discuss the client's overall goals.

Wrap accounts are appealing for a number of reasons other than convenience. The annual fee in most cases covers commissions on all trades, virtually eliminating the chance of the broker churning the account. In addition, the broker monitors the manager's performance and provides the investor with detailed reports, typically quarterly.

Odd-Lot or Round-Lot Transactions Investors can buy stock in either odd or round lots. An **odd lot** consists of fewer than 100 shares of a stock. A **round lot** is a 100-share unit. You would be dealing in an odd lot if you bought, say, 25 shares of stock, but in round lots if you bought 200 shares. A trade of 225 shares would be a combination of an odd lot and two round lots.

Transactions in odd lots require either additional processing by the brokerage firm or the assistance of a specialist. For odd lots, an added fee—known as an *odd-lot differential*—is tacked on to the normal commission charge, driving up the per share costs of these small trades. Small investors in the early stages of their investment programs are primarily responsible for odd-lot transactions since they often lack the financial resources sufficient to purchase round lots.

Basic Types of Orders

Investors can use different types of orders to make security transactions. The type placed normally depends on the investor's goals and expectations. The three basic types of orders are the market order, the limit order, and the stop-loss order.

Market Order   An order to buy or sell stock at the best price available at the time the investor places the order is a **market order**. It is generally the quickest way to fill orders, because market orders are usually executed as soon as they reach the exchange floor or are received by the market maker. Because of the speed with which market orders are executed, the buyer or seller of a security can be sure that the price at which the order is transacted will be very close to the market price prevailing at the time the order was placed.

Limit Order   A **limit order** is an order to buy at or below a specified price (a limit buy order) or to sell at or above a specified price (a limit sell order). When the investor places a limit order, the broker transmits it to a market maker dealing in the security. The market maker notes the number of shares and price of the limit order in his or her book and executes the order as soon as the specified limit price (or better) exists. The market maker must first satisfy all other orders with precedence—similar orders received earlier, buy orders at a higher specified price, or sell orders at a lower specified price. Investors can place a limit order in one of the following forms:

1. A *fill-or-kill order,* which is canceled if not immediately executed.

2. A *day order,* which if not executed is automatically canceled at the end of the day.

3. A *good-'til-canceled (GTC) order,* which generally remains in effect for 6 months unless executed, canceled, or renewed.

Assume, for example, that you place a limit order to buy, at a limit price of $30, 100 shares of a stock currently selling at $30.50. Once the specialist clears all similar orders received before yours, and once the market price of the stock falls to $30 or less, he or she executes your order. It is possible, of course, that your order might expire (if it is not a GTC order) before the stock price drops to $30.

Although a limit order can be quite effective, it can also keep you from making a transaction. If, for instance, you wish to buy at $30 or less and the stock price moves from its current $30.50 price to $42 while you are waiting, you have missed the opportunity to make a profit of $11.50 per share ($42 − $30.50). If you had placed a *market order* to buy at the best available price ($30.50), the profit of $11.50 would have been yours. Limit orders for the sale of a stock are also disadvantageous when the stock price closely approaches, but does not attain, the minimum sale price limit before dropping substantially. Generally speaking, limit orders are most effective when the price of a stock fluctuates greatly, because there is then a better chance that the order will be executed.

Stop-Loss Order   When an investor places a **stop-loss order** or **stop order,** the broker tells the market maker to sell a stock when its market price reaches or drops below a specified level. Stop-loss orders are *suspended orders* placed on stocks; they are activated when and if the stock reaches a certain price. The stop-loss order is placed on the market maker's book and becomes active once the stock reaches the stop price. Like limit orders, stop-loss orders are typically day or GTC orders. When activated, the stop order becomes a *market order* to sell the security at the best price available. Thus it is possible for the actual price at which the sale is made to be well below the price at which the stop was initiated. Investors use these orders to protect themselves against the adverse effects of a rapid decline in share price.

For example, assume you own 100 shares of Ballard Industries, which is currently selling for $35 per share. Because you believe the stock price could decline rapidly at any time, you place a stop order to sell at $30. If the stock price does in fact drop to $30, the market maker will sell the 100 shares at the best price available at that time. If the market price declines to $28 by the time your stop-loss order comes up, you will receive less than $30 per share. Of course, if the market price stays above $30 per share, you will have lost nothing as a result of placing the order, because the stop order will never be initiated. Often investors raise the level of the stop as the price of the stock rises. Such action helps to lock in a higher profit when the price is increasing.

Investors can also place stop orders to *buy* a stock, although buy orders are far less common than sell orders. For example, you may place a stop order to buy 100 shares of MJ Enterprises, currently selling for $70 per share, once its price rises to, say, $75 (the stop price). These orders are commonly used either to limit losses on short sales (discussed in Chapter 2) or to buy a stock just as its price begins to rise.

To avoid the risk of the market moving against you when your stop order becomes a market order, you can place a *stop-limit order,* rather than a plain stop order. This is an order to buy or sell stock at a given price, or better, once a stipulated stop price has been met. For example, in the Ballard Industries example, had a stop-limit order been in effect, then when the market price of Ballard dropped to $30, the broker would have entered a limit order to sell your 100 shares at $30 a share or *better.* Thus you would have run no risk of getting less than $30 a share for your stock—unless the price of the stock kept right on falling. In that case, as is true for any limit order, you might miss the market altogether and end up with stock worth much less than $30. Even though the stop order to sell was triggered (at $30), the stock will not be sold, with a stop-limit order, if it keeps falling in price.

Online Transactions

The competition for your online business increases daily as more players enter an already crowded arena. Brokerage firms are encouraging customers to trade online and offering a variety of incentives to get their business, including free trades! However, low cost is not the only reason to choose a brokerage firm. As with any financial decision, you must consider your needs and find the firm that best matches them. One investor may want timely information, research, and quick, reliable trades from a full-service broker like Bank of America or a premium discounter like Charles Schwab or TD Ameritrade. Another, who is an active trader, will focus on cost and fast trades rather than research and so will sign up with a basic discounter like Firstrade or Wall Street*E. Ease of site navigation is a major factor in finding a basic discount broker to

MARKETS IN CRISIS

Tech Stocks and Online Trading Go Bust

Prior to the global recession that began in late 2007, the last recession in the United States occurred shortly after the sharp decline in stock prices, especially tech stock prices, from 1999–2000. As tech stocks and the broader Nasdaq index soared through 1999, so did the volume of online trading. But stocks peaked in March 2000, and online trading volume began a long, steep decline, taking the prices of online trading firms along for the ride. For example, E*trade stock peaked in May 1999, but by July 2002, the value of E*trade shares had fallen more than 90%.

use in executing online transactions. Some online brokers also offer online trading of bonds and mutual funds.

Day Trading For some investors, online stock trading is so compelling that they become day traders. The opposite of buy-and-hold investors with a long-term perspective, **day traders** buy and sell stocks quickly throughout the day. They hope that their stocks will continue to rise in value for the very short time they own them—sometimes just seconds or minutes—so they can make quick profits. Some also sell short, looking for small price decreases. True day traders do not own any stocks overnight—hence the term "day trader"—because they believe that the extreme risk of prices changing radically from day to day will lead to large losses.

Day trading is not illegal or unethical, but it *is* highly risky. To compound their risk, day traders usually buy on margin in order to leverage their potential profits. But as we saw in Chapter 2, margin trading also increases the risk of large losses.

Because the Internet makes investment information and transactions accessible to the masses, day trading has grown in popularity. It's a very difficult task—essentially a very stressful, full-time job. Although sales pitches for day trading make it seem like an easy route to quick riches, quite the reverse is more generally true. Day traders typically incur major financial losses when they start trading. In addition, they have high expenses for brokerage commissions, training, and computer equipment. They must earn sizable trading profits annually to break even on fees and commissions alone. Some never achieve profitability.

Technical and Service Problems As the number of online investors increases, so do the problems that beset brokerage firms and their customers. During the past few years most brokerage firms have upgraded their systems to reduce the number of service outages. But the potential problems go beyond the brokerage sites. Once an investor places a trade at a firm's Web site, it goes through several other parties to be executed. Most online brokers don't have their own trading desks and have agreements with other trading firms to execute their orders on the *New York Stock Exchange* or *Nasdaq Stock Market*. Slowdowns at any point in the process can create problems confirming trades. Investors, thinking that their trades had not gone through, might place the order again—only to discover later that they have bought the same stock twice. Online investors who don't get immediate trade execution and confirmation use the telephone when they can't get through online or to solve other problems with their accounts, and they often face long waiting times on hold.

Tips for Successful Online Trades   Successful online investors take additional precautions before submitting their orders. Here are some tips to help you avoid some of the common problems:

- *Know how to place and confirm your order before you begin trading.* This simple step can keep you from having problems later.

- *Verify the stock symbol of the security you wish to buy.* Two very different companies can have similar symbols. Some investors have bought the wrong stock because they didn't check before placing their order.

- *Use limit orders.* The order you see on your computer screen may not be the one you get. With a limit order, you avoid getting burned in fast-moving markets. Although limit orders cost more, they can save you thousands of dollars. For example, customers eager to get shares of a hot IPO stock placed market orders. Instead of buying the stock near the offering price of $9, some were shocked to find that their orders were filled at prices as high as $90 during the stock's first trading day. Investors who were aware of the price run-up tried to cancel orders but couldn't get through to brokers. Because of this, some brokers accept only limit orders for online IPO purchases on the first day of trading.

- *Don't ignore the online reminders that ask you to check and recheck.* It's easy to make a typo that adds an extra digit to a purchase amount.

- *Don't get carried away.* It's easy to churn your own account. In fact, new online investors trade about twice as much as they did before they went online. To control impulse trading, have a strategy and stick to it.

- *Open accounts with two brokers.* This protects you if your online brokerage's computer system crashes. It also gives you an alternative if one brokerage is blocked with heavy trading volume.

- *Double-check orders for accuracy.* Make sure each trade was completed according to your instructions. It's very easy to make typos or use the wrong stock symbol, so review the confirmation notice to verify that the right number of shares was bought or sold and that the price and commissions or fees are as quoted. Check your account for "unauthorized" trades.

Transaction Costs

Making transactions through brokers or market makers is considerably easier for investors than it would be to negotiate directly, trying to find someone who wants to buy what you want to sell (or vice versa). To compensate the broker for executing the transaction, investors pay transaction costs, which are usually levied on both the purchase and the sale of securities. When making investment decisions, you must consider the structure and magnitude of transaction costs, because they affect returns.

Since the passage of the *Securities Acts Amendments of 1975*, brokers have been permitted to charge whatever brokerage commissions they deem appropriate. Most firms have established **fixed-commission schedules** that apply to small transactions, the ones most often made by individual investors. On large institutional transactions, the client and broker may arrange a **negotiated commission**—a commission to which both parties agree. Negotiated commissions are also available to individual investors who maintain large accounts, typically above $50,000. The commission structure varies with the type of security and the type of broker. In subsequent chapters we'll describe the basic commission structures for various types of securities.

Because of the way brokerage firms charge commissions on stock trades, it is difficult to compare prices precisely. Traditional brokers generally charge on the basis of number of shares and the price of the stock at the time of the transaction. Internet brokers usually charge flat rates, often for transactions up to 1,000 shares, with additional fees for larger or more complicated orders. However, many traditional brokerage firms have reduced their commissions on broker-assisted trades and have instituted annual flat fees (on wrap accounts) set as a specified percentage of the value of the assets in the account. Unless you are a very active trader, you are probably better off paying commissions on a per-transaction basis.

Obviously, premium and basic discount brokers charge substantially less than full-service brokers for the same transaction. However, some discounters charge a minimum fee to discourage small orders. The savings from the discounter can be substantial. Depending on the size and type of transaction, premium and basic discount brokers can typically save investors between 30% and 80% of the commission charged by the full-service broker.

Investor Protection: SIPC and Arbitration

Although most investment transactions take place safely, it is important for you to know what protection you have if things *don't* go smoothly. As a client, you are protected against the loss of the securities or cash held by your broker. The **Securities Investor Protection Corporation (SIPC)**, a nonprofit membership corporation, was authorized by the *Securities Investor Protection Act of 1970* to protect customer accounts against the consequences of financial failure of the brokerage firm. The SIPC currently insures each customer's account for up to $500,000, with claims for cash limited to $100,000 per customer. Note that SIPC insurance does not guarantee that the investor will recover the dollar value of the securities; it guarantees only that the securities themselves will be returned. Some brokerage firms also insure certain customer accounts for amounts in excess of $500,000. Certainly, in light of the diversity and quality of services available among brokerage firms, this may be an additional service you should consider when you select a firm and an individual broker.

The SIPC provides protection in case your brokerage firm fails. But what happens if your broker gave you bad advice and, as a result, you lost a lot of money on an investment? Or what if you feel your broker is *churning* your account? In either case, the SIPC won't help. It's not intended to insure you against bad investment advice or churning. Instead, if you have a dispute with your broker, the first thing you should do is discuss the situation with the managing officer at the branch where you do business. If that doesn't do any good, then contact the firm's compliance officer and the securities regulator in your home state.

If you still don't get any satisfaction, you can use litigation (judicial methods in the courts) to resolve the dispute. Alternative dispute-resolution processes that may avoid litigation include **mediation** and **arbitration**. Mediation is an informal, voluntary approach in which you and the broker agree to a mediator, who facilitates negotiations between the two of you to resolve the case. The mediator does not impose a solution on you and the broker. The Financial Industry Regulatory Authority (FINRA) and securities-related organizations encourage investors to mediate disputes rather than arbitrate them, because mediation can reduce costs and time for both investors and brokers.

If mediation is not pursued or if it fails, you may have no choice but to take the case to arbitration, a formal process whereby you and your broker present the two sides of the argument before an arbitration panel. The panel then decides the case.

Many brokerage firms require you to resolve disputes by *binding arbitration*; in this case, you don't have the option to sue. You must accept the arbitrator's decision, and in most cases you cannot go to court to review your case. Before you open an account, check whether the brokerage agreement contains a binding-arbitration clause.

Mediation and arbitration proceedings typically cost less and are resolved more quickly than litigation. Recent legislation has given many investors the option of using either securities industry panels or independent arbitration panels such as those sponsored by the American Arbitration Association (AAA). Independent panels are considered more sympathetic toward investors. In addition, only one of the three arbitrators on a panel can be connected with the securities industry. On their Web site, FINRA reports that in 2008 approximately 74% of customer claimant cases resulted, through settlements or awards, in monetary or non-monetary recovery for the investor.

Probably the best thing you can do to avoid the need to mediate, arbitrate, or litigate is to select your broker carefully, understand the financial risks involved in the broker's recommendations, thoroughly evaluate the advice he or she offers, and continuously monitor the volume of transactions that he or she recommends and executes. Clearly, it is much less costly to choose the right broker initially than to incur later the financial and emotional costs of having chosen a bad one.

If you have a problem with an online trade, immediately file a written—not e-mail—complaint with the broker. Cite dates, times, and amounts of trades, and include all supporting documentation. File a copy with the Financial Industry Regulatory Authority (**www.finra.org**) and with your state securities regulator. If you can't resolve the problems with the broker, you can try mediation and then resort to arbitration, litigation being the last resort.

CONCEPTS IN REVIEW

Answers available at
www.pearsonhighered.com/
gitman

3.13 Describe the types of services offered by brokerage firms, and discuss the criteria for selecting a suitable stockbroker.

3.14 Briefly differentiate among the following types of brokerage accounts:

a. Single or joint
b. Custodial
c. Cash
d. Margin
e. Wrap

3.15 Differentiate among *market orders, limit orders,* and *stop-loss orders.* What is the rationale for using a stop-loss order rather than a limit order?

3.16 Differentiate between the services and costs associated with *full-service, premium discount,* and *basic discount* brokers. Be sure to discuss online transactions.

3.17 What is *day trading,* and why is it risky? How can you avoid problems as an online trader?

3.18 In what two ways, based on the number of shares transacted, do brokers typically charge for executing transactions? How are online transaction fees structured relative to the degree of broker involvement?

3.19 What protection does the *Securities Investor Protection Corporation (SIPC)* provide for securities investors? How are mediation and arbitration procedures used to settle disputes between investors and their brokers?

Investment Advisers and Investment Clubs

LG6 Many investors feel that they have neither the time nor the expertise to analyze financial information and make decisions on their own. Instead, they turn to an **investment adviser**, an individual or firm that provides investment advice, typically for a fee. Alternatively, some small investors join **investment clubs**. Here we will discuss using an investment adviser and then briefly cover the key aspects of investment clubs.

Using an Investment Adviser

The "product" provided by an investment adviser ranges from broad, general advice to detailed, specific analyses and recommendations. The most general form of advice is a newsletter published by the adviser. These letters comment on the economy, current events, market behavior, and specific securities. Investment advisers also provide complete individualized investment evaluation, recommendation, and management services.

Regulation of Advisers As we noted in Chapter 2, the *Investment Advisers Act of 1940* ensures that investment advisers make full disclosure of information about their backgrounds, conflicts of interest, and so on. The act requires professional advisers to register and file periodic reports with the SEC. A 1960 amendment permits the SEC to inspect the records of investment advisers and to revoke the registration of those who violate the act's provisions. However, financial planners, stockbrokers, bankers, lawyers, and accountants who provide investment advice in addition to their main professional activity are not regulated by the act. Many states have also passed similar legislation, requiring investment advisers to register and to abide by the guidelines established by the state law.

Be aware that the federal and state laws regulating the activities of professional investment advisers do not guarantee competence. Rather, they are intended to protect the investor against fraudulent and unethical practices. It is important to recognize that, at present, no law or regulatory body controls entrance into the field. Therefore, investment advisers range from highly informed professionals to totally incompetent amateurs. Advisers who possess a professional designation are usually preferred because they have completed academic courses in areas directly or peripherally related to the investment process. Such designations include CFA (Chartered Financial Analyst), CIMA (Certified Investment Management Analyst), CIC (Chartered Investment Counselor), CFP® (Certified Financial Planner™), ChFC (Chartered Financial Consultant), CLU (Chartered Life Underwriter), and CPA (Certified Public Accountant).

Online Investment Advice You can also find financial advice online. Whether it's a retirement planning tool or advice on how to diversify your assets, automated financial advisers may be able to help you. If your needs are specific rather than comprehensive, you can find good advice at other sites. For example, T. Rowe Price has an excellent college planning section (**www.troweprice.com/college**). Financial Engines (**www.financialengines.com**), AdviceAmerica (**www.adviceamerica.com**), and DirectAdvice (**www.directadvice.com**) are among several independent advice sites that offer broader planning capabilities. Many mutual fund Web sites have online financial advisers. For example, The Vanguard Group (**www.vanguard.com**) has a personal investors section that helps you choose funds for specific investment objectives, such as retirement or financing a college education.

The Cost and Use of Investment Advice The annual costs of obtaining professional investment advice typically run between 0.25% and 3% of the dollar amount of money being managed. For large portfolios, the fee is typically in the range of 0.25% to 0.75%. For small portfolios (less than $100,000), an annual fee ranging from 2% to 3% of the dollar amount of funds managed would not be unusual. These fees generally cover complete management of a client's money, excluding any purchase or sale commissions. The cost of periodic investment advice not provided as part of a subscription service could be based on a fixed-fee schedule or quoted as an hourly charge for consultation. Online advisers are much less expensive; they either are free or charge an annual fee.

Whether you choose a traditional investment advisory service or decide to try an online service, some are better than others. More expensive services do not necessarily provide better advice. It is best to study carefully the track record and overall reputation of an investment adviser before purchasing his or her services. Not only should the adviser have a good performance record, but he or she also should be responsive to your personal goals.

How good is the advice from online advisers? It's very hard to judge. Their suggested plans are only as good as the input. Beginning investors may not have sufficient knowledge to make wise assumptions on future savings, tax, or inflation rates or to analyze results thoroughly. A good face-to-face personal financial planner will ask lots of questions to assess your investing expertise and explain what you don't know. Automated tools for these early-stage questions may take too narrow a focus and not consider other parts of your investment portfolio. For many investors, online advisers lack what leads them to get help in the first place—the human touch. They want handholding, reassurance, and gentle nudging to follow through on their plans.

Investment Clubs

Another way to obtain investment advice and experience is to join an investment club. This route can be especially useful for those of moderate means who do not want to incur the cost of an investment adviser. An investment club is a legal partnership binding a group of investors (partners) to a specified organizational structure, operating procedure, and purpose. The goal of most clubs is to earn favorable long-term returns by making investments in accordance with the group's investment objectives.

Individuals with similar goals usually form investment clubs to pool their knowledge and money in a jointly owned and managed portfolio. Certain members are responsible for obtaining and analyzing data on a specific investment strategy. At periodic meetings, the members present their findings for discussion and further analysis by the members. Once discussed, the group decides whether to pursue the proposed strategy. Most clubs require members to make scheduled contributions to the club's treasury, thereby regularly increasing the pool of investable funds. Although most clubs concentrate on investments in stocks and bonds, some may concentrate on specialized investments such as options or futures. Membership in an investment club provides an excellent way for the novice investor to learn the key aspects of portfolio construction and investment management, while (one hopes) earning a favorable return on his or her funds.

As you might expect, investment clubs have also joined the online investing movement. By tapping into the Internet, clubs are freed from geographical restrictions. Now investors around the world, many who have never met, can form a club and discuss investing strategies and stock picks just as easily as if they gathered in person. Finding a time or place to meet is no longer an issue. Some clubs are formed by friends; others are strangers who have similar investing philosophies and may have met online. Online clubs conduct business via e-mail or set up a private Web site. Members of the *Better Investing Community,* a not-for-profit organization, have access to educational materials, investment tools, and other investment features.

Better Investing, which has over 200,000 individual and club investors and over 16,000 investment clubs, publishes a variety of useful materials and also sponsors regional and national meetings. To learn how to start an investment club, visit the Better Investing Web site at **www.betterinvesting.org.**

CONCEPTS IN REVIEW

Answers available at
www.pearsonhighered.com/
gitman

3.20 Describe the services that professional investment advisers perform, how they are regulated, online investment advisers, and the cost of investment advice.

3.21 What benefits does an *investment club* offer the small investor? Why do investment clubs regularly outperform the market and the pros? Would you prefer to join a regular or an online club, and why?

Here is what you should know after reading this chapter. **MyFinanceLab** will help you identify what you know, and where to go when you need to practice.

What You Should Know	Key Terms	Where To Practice
LG 1 Discuss the growth in online investing and the pros and cons of using the Internet as an investment tool. The Internet has empowered individual investors by providing information and tools formerly available only to investing professionals and by simplifying the investing process. The time and money savings it provides are huge. Investors get the most current information, including real-time stock price quotes, market activity data, research reports, educational articles, and discussion forums. Tools such as financial planning calculators, stock-screening programs, charting, and stock quotes and portfolio tracking are free at many sites. Buying and selling securities online is convenient, relatively simple, inexpensive, and fast.		MyFinanceLab Study Plan 3.1
LG 2 Identify the major types and sources of traditional and online investment information. Investment information, descriptive or analytical, includes information about the economy and current events, industries and companies, and alternative investment vehicles, as well as price	analytical information, *p. 75* back-office research reports, *p. 83* *Barron's, p. 78*	MyFinanceLab Study Plan 3.2

What You Should Know	Key Terms	Where To Practice
information and personal investment strategies. It can be obtained from financial journals, general newspapers, institutional news, business periodicals, government publications, special subscription services, stockholders' reports, comparative data sources, subscription services, brokerage reports, investment letters, price quotations, and electronic and online sources. Most print publications also have Web sites with access to all or part of their content. Financial portals bring together a variety of financial information online. Investors will also find specialized sites for bond, mutual fund, and international information, as well as discussion forums that discuss individual securities and investment strategies. Because it is hard to know the qualifications of those who make postings on message boards, participants must do their own homework before acting on an online tip.	descriptive information, *p. 75* fair disclosure rule (Regulation FD), *p. 80* financial portals, *p. 84* Form 10-K, *p. 80* investment letters, *p. 83* Mergent, *p. 82* quotations, *p. 83* Standard & Poor's Corporation (S&P), *p. 82* stockholders' (annual) report, *p. 80* *Value Line Investment Survey*, *p. 83* *Wall Street Journal*, *p. 77*	
LG3 **Explain the key aspects of the commonly cited stock and bond market averages and indexes.** Investors commonly rely on stock market averages and indexes to stay abreast of market behavior. The most often cited are the Dow Jones averages, which include the Dow Jones Industrial Average (DJIA). Also widely followed are the Standard & Poor's indexes, the NYSE composite index, the NYSE Amex composite index, the Nasdaq Stock Market indexes, and the Value Line indexes. Numerous other averages and indexes, including a number of global and foreign market indexes, are regularly reported in financial publications. Bond market indicators are most often reported in terms of bond yields and bond indexes. The Dow Jones Corporate Bond Index is among the most popular. Yield and price index data are also available for various types of bonds and various domestic and foreign markets. Both stock and bond market statistics are published daily in the *Wall Street Journal* and summarized weekly in *Barron's*.	Amex composite index, *p. 93* averages, *p. 88* bond yield, *p. 93* DJ U.S. Total Stock Market Index, *p. 91* Dow Jones Corporate Bond Index, *p. 94* Dow Jones Industrial Average (DJIA), *p. 88* indexes, *p. 88* Nasdaq Stock Market indexes, *p. 93* NYSE composite index, *p. 92* Standard & Poor's indexes, *p. 91* Value Line composite index, *p. 93*	MyFinanceLab Study Plan 3.3 Video Learning Aid for Problem P3.2
LG4 **Review the role of stockbrokers, including the services they provide, selection of a stockbroker, opening an account, and transaction basics.** Stockbrokers facilitate buying and selling of securities, and provide other client services. An investor should select a stockbroker who has a compatible disposition toward investing and whose firm offers the desired services at competitive costs. Today the distinctions among full-service, premium discount, and basic discount (online) brokers are blurring. Most brokers now offer online trading capabilities, and many no-frills brokers are expanding their services to include research and advice. Investors can open a variety of types of brokerage accounts, such as single, joint, custodial, cash, margin, and wrap.	basic discount broker, *p. 96* cash account, *p. 98* churning, *p. 98* custodial account, *p. 98* full-service broker, *p. 96* margin account, *p. 98* odd lot, *p. 98* premium discount broker, *p. 96* round lot, *p. 98* stockbrokers, *p. 94* street name, *p. 95* *wrap account*, *p. 98*	MyFinanceLab Study Plan 3.4

What You Should Know	Key Terms	Where To Practice
Transactions take place in odd-lot (less than 100 shares) or round-lot (100 shares or multiples thereof). Odd-lot transactions usually incur an added fee.		
LG5 Describe the basic types of orders, online transactions, transaction costs, and the legal aspects of investor protection. A market order is an order to buy or sell stock at the best price available. A limit order is an order to buy at a specified price or below, or to sell at a specified price or above. Stop-loss orders become market orders as soon as the minimum sell price or the maximum buy price is hit. Limit and stop-loss orders can be placed as fill-or-kill orders, day orders, or good-'til-canceled (GTC) orders. On small transactions, most brokers have fixed-commission schedules; on larger transactions, they will negotiate commissions. Commissions also vary by type of security and type of broker. The Securities Investor Protection Corporation (SIPC) insures customers' accounts against the brokerage firm's failure. Mediation and arbitration procedures are frequently employed to resolve disputes. These disputes typically concern the investor's belief that the broker either gave bad advice or churned the account.	arbitration, *p. 103* day trader, *p. 101* fixed-commission schedules, *p. 102* limit order, *p. 99* market order, *p. 99* mediation, *p. 103* negotiated commissions, *p. 102* Securities Investor Protection Corporation (SIPC), *p. 103* stop-loss (stop) order, *p. 100*	MyFinanceLab Study Plan 3.5 Video Learning Aid for Problem P3.10
LG6 Discuss the roles of investment advisers and investment clubs. Investment advisers charge an annual fee ranging from 0.25% to 3% of the dollar amount being managed and are often regulated by federal and state law. Web sites that provide investment advice are now available as well. Investment clubs provide individual investors with investment advice and help them gain investing experience. Online clubs have members in various geographical areas and conduct business via e-mail or at a private Web site.	investment adviser, *p. 105* investment club, *p. 105*	MyFinanceLab Study Plan 3.6

Log into **MyFinanceLab**, take a chapter test, and get a personalized Study Plan
that tells you which concepts you understand and which ones you need to
review. From there, **MyFinanceLab** will give you further practice, tutorials,
animations, videos, and guided solutions.
Log into www.myfinancelab.com

Discussion Questions

LG2 **Q3.1** Thomas Weisel, chief executive of a securities firm that bears his name, believes that individual investors already have too much information. "Many lose money by trading excessively on stray data," he says. Other industry professionals oppose the SEC's fair disclosure rule (Regulation FD) for the same reason. The Securities Industry Association's general counsel expressed concern that the rule restricts rather than encourages the flow of information. Other securities professionals argue that individual investors aren't really capable of interpreting much of the information now available to them. Explain why you agree or disagree with these opinions.

LG2 **Q3.2** Innovative Internet-based bookseller **Amazon.com** has expanded into other retail categories. Gather appropriate information from relevant sources to assess the following with an eye toward investing in **Amazon.com**.
   a. Economic conditions and the key current events during the past 12 months.
   b. Information on the status and growth (past and future) of the bookselling industry and specific information on **Amazon.com** and its major competitors.
   c. Brokerage reports and analysts' recommendations with respect to **Amazon.com**.
   d. A history of the past and recent dividends and price behavior of **Amazon.com**, which is traded on the Nasdaq National Market.
   e. A recommendation with regard to the advisability of investing in **Amazon.com**.

LG2 **LG6** **Q3.3** Visit four financial portals or other financial information Web sites listed in Table 3.4. Compare them in terms of ease of use, investment information, investment tools, advisory services, and links to other services. Also catalog the costs, if any, of obtaining these services. Which would you recommend, and why?

LG3 **Q3.4** Gather and evaluate relevant market averages and indexes over the past six months to assess recent stock and bond market conditions. Describe the conditions in each of these markets. Using recent history, coupled with relevant economic and current event data, forecast near-term market conditions. On the basis of your assessment of market conditions, would you recommend investing in stocks, in bonds, or in neither at this time? Explain the reasoning underlying your recommendation.

LG4 **Q3.5** Prepare a checklist of questions and issues you would use when shopping for a stockbroker. Describe both the ideal broker and the ideal brokerage firm, given your investment goals and disposition. Discuss the pros and cons of using a full-service rather than a premium discount or basic discount broker. If you plan to trade online, what additional questions would you ask?

LG4 **Q3.6** Find and visit the sites of two basic discount brokerages listed in Table 3.5 or any others you know. After exploring the sites, compare them for ease of use, quality of information, availability of investing tools, reliability, other services, and any other criteria important to you. Summarize your findings and explain which you would choose if you were to open an account, and why.

LG5 **Q3.7** Describe how, if at all, a conservative and an aggressive investor might use each of the following types of orders as part of their investment programs. Contrast these two types of investors in view of these preferences.
   a. Market
   b. Limit
   c. Stop-loss

LG5 **Q3.8** Learn more about day trading at sites such as Edgetrade (**www.edgetrade.com**), Daytradingthemarkets.com (**www.daytradingthemarkets.com**), TrendVue (**www.1daytradingstockadviceandpicks.com**), and The Rookie DayTrader (**www.rookiedaytrader.com**). On the basis of your research, summarize how day trading works, some strategies for day traders, the risks, and the rewards. What type of person would make a good day trader?

LG6 Q3.9 Differentiate between the financial advice you would receive from a traditional investment adviser and one of the new online planning and advice sites. Which would you personally prefer to use, and why? How could membership in an investment club serve as an alternative to a paid investment adviser?

Problems

All problems are available on **www.myfinancelab.com**

LG2 P3.1 Chris LeBlanc estimates that if he does 5 hours of research using data that will cost $75, there is a good chance that he can improve his expected return on a $10,000, 1-year investment from 8% to 10%. Chris feels that he must earn at least $20 per hour on the time he devotes to his research.
   a. Find the cost of Chris' research.
   b. By how much (in dollars) will Chris' return increase as a result of the research?
   c. On a strict economic basis, should Chris perform the proposed research?

LG3 P3.2 Imagine that the Mini-Dow Average (MDA) is based on the closing prices of five stocks. The divisor used in the calculation of the MDA is currently 0.765. The closing prices for each of the five stocks in the MDA today and exactly a year ago, when the divisor was 0.790, are given in the accompanying table.

Stock	Closing Stock Price	
	Today	One Year Ago
Ace Computers	$65	$74
Coburn Motor Company	37	34
National Soap & Cosmetics	110	96
Ronto Foods	73	72
Wings Aircraft	96	87

   a. Calculate the MDA today and that of a year ago.
   b. Compare the values of the MDA calculated in part **a** and describe the apparent market behavior over the last year. Was it a bull or a bear market?

LG3 P3.3 The SP-6 index (a fictitious index) is used by many investors to monitor the general behavior of the stock market. It has a base value set equal to 100 at January 1, 1975. In the accompanying table, the closing market values for each of the six stocks included in the index are given for three dates.

Stock	Closing Market Value of Stock		
	June 30, 2010 (Thousands)	January 1, 2010 (Thousands)	January 1, 1975 (Thousands)
1	$430	$460	$240
2	1,150	1,120	630
3	980	990	450
4	360	420	150
5	650	700	320
6	290	320	80

a. Calculate the value of the SP-6 index on both January 1, 2010, and June 30, 2010, using the data presented here.

b. Compare the values of the SP-6 index calculated in part **a** and relate them to the base index value. Would you describe the general market condition during the six-month period January 1 to June 30, 2010, as a bull or a bear market?

 P3.4 Deepa Chungi wishes to develop an average or index that can be used to measure the general behavior of stock prices over time. She has decided to include six closely followed, high-quality stocks in the average or index. She plans to use August 15, 1984, her birthday, as the base and is interested in measuring the value of the average or index on August 15, 2008, and August 15, 2011. She has found the closing prices for each of the six stocks, A through F, at each of the three dates and has calculated a divisor that can be used to adjust for any stock splits, company changes, and so on that have occurred since the base year, which has a divisor equal to 1.00.

	Closing Stock Price		
Stock	August 15, 2011	August 15, 2008	August 15, 1984
A	$46	$40	$50
B	37	36	10
C	20	23	7
D	59	61	26
E	82	70	45
F	32	30	32
Divisor	0.70	0.72	1.00

Note: The number of shares of each stock outstanding has remained unchanged at each of the three dates. Therefore, the closing stock prices will behave identically to the closing market values.

a. Using the data given in the table, calculate the market average, using the same methodology used to calculate the Dow averages, at each of the three dates— August 15, 1984, 2008, and 2011.

b. Using the data given in the table and assuming a base index value of 10 on August 15, 1984, calculate the market index, using the same methodology used to calculate the S&P indexes, at each of the three dates.

c. Use your findings in parts **a** and **b** to describe the general market condition—bull or bear—that existed between August 15, 2008, and August 15, 2011.

d. Calculate the percentage changes in the average and index values between August 15, 2008, and August 15, 2011. Why do they differ?

P3.5 Al Cromwell places a *market order* to buy a round lot of Thomas, Inc., common stock, which is traded on the NYSE and is currently quoted at $50 per share. Ignoring brokerage commissions, how much money would Cromwell probably have to pay? If he had placed a market order to sell, how much money will he probably receive? Explain.

P3.6 Imagine that you have placed a *limit order* to buy 100 shares of Sallisaw Tool at a price of $38, although the stock is currently selling for $41. Discuss the consequences, if any, of each of the following.

a. The stock price drops to $39 per share two months before cancellation of the limit order.

b. The stock price drops to $38 per share.

c. The minimum stock price achieved before cancellation of the limit order was $38.50. When the limit order was canceled, the stock was selling for $47.50 per share.

 P3.7 If you place a *stop-loss order* to sell at $23 on a stock currently selling for $26.50 per share, what is likely to be the minimum loss you will experience on 50 shares if the stock price rapidly declines to $20.50 per share? Explain. What if you had placed a *stop-limit order* to sell at $23, and the stock price tumbled to $20.50?

LG5 **P3.8** You sell 100 shares of a stock short for $40 per share. You want to limit your loss on this transaction to no more than $500. What order should you place?

LG5 **P3.9** You have been researching a stock that you like, which is currently trading at $50 per share. You would like to buy the stock if it were a little less expensive—say, $47 per share. You believe that the stock price will go to $70 by year-end, and then level off or decline. You decide to place a limit order to buy 100 shares of the stock at $47, and a limit order to sell it at $70. It turns out that you were right about the direction of the stock price, and it goes straight to $75. What is your current position?

LG5 **P3.10** You own 500 shares of Ups&Downs, Inc., stock. It is currently priced at $50. You are going on vacation, and you realize that the company will be reporting earnings while you are away. To protect yourself against a rapid drop in the price, you place a stop-limit order to sell 500 shares at $40. It turns out the earnings report was not so good, and the stock price fell to $30 right after the announcement. It did, however, bounce back, and by the end of the day it was back to $42. What happened in your account?

LG5 **P3.11** You have $5,000 in a 50% margin account. You have been following a stock that you think you want to buy. The stock is priced at $52. You decide that if the stock falls to $50, you would like to buy it. You place a limit order to buy 300 shares at $50. The stock falls to $50. What happens?

Visit **www.myfinancelab.com** for web exercises, spreadsheets, and other online resources.

Case Problem 3.1   *The Perezes' Good Fortune*

LG2 **LG4** **LG6** Angel and Marie Perez own a small pool hall located in southern New Jersey. They enjoy running the business, which they have owned for nearly three years. Angel, a retired professional pool shooter, saved for nearly 10 years to buy this business, which he and his wife own free and clear. The income from the pool hall is adequate to allow Angel, Marie, and their two children, Mary (age 10) and José (age 4), to live comfortably. Although he lacks formal education beyond the tenth grade, Angel has become an avid reader. He enjoys reading about current events and personal finance, particularly investing. He especially likes *Money* magazine, from which he has gained numerous ideas for better managing the family's finances. Because of the long hours required to run the business, Angel can devote three to four hours a day (on the job) to reading.

Recently, Angel and Marie were notified that Marie's uncle had died and left them a portfolio of stocks and bonds with a current market value of $300,000. They were elated to learn of their good fortune but decided it would be best not to change their lifestyle as a result of this inheritance. Instead, they want their newfound wealth to provide for their children's college education as well as their own retirement. They decided that, like their uncle, they would keep these funds invested in stocks and bonds.

Angel felt that in view of this plan, he needed to acquaint himself with the securities currently in the portfolio. He knew that to manage the portfolio himself, he would have to stay abreast of the securities markets as well as the economy in general. He also realized that he would need to follow each security in the portfolio and continuously evaluate possible alternative securities that could be substituted as conditions warranted. Because Angel had plenty of time in which to follow the market, he strongly believed that with proper information, he could manage the portfolio. Given the amount of money involved, Angel was not too concerned with the information costs; rather, he wanted the best information he could get at a reasonable price.

Questions

a. Explain what role the *Wall Street Journal* and/or *Barron's* might play in meeting Angel's needs. What other general sources of economic and current event information would you recommend to Angel? Explain.

b. How might Angel be able to use the services of Standard & Poor's Corporation, Mergent, and the *Value Line Investment Survey* to learn about the securities in the portfolio? Indicate which, if any, of these services you would recommend, and why.

c. Recommend some specific online investment information sources and tools to help Angel and Marie manage their investments.

d. Explain to Angel the need to find a good stockbroker and the role the stockbroker could play in providing information and advice. Should he consider hiring a financial adviser to manage the portfolio?

e. Give Angel a summary prescription for obtaining information and advice that will help to ensure the preservation and growth of the family's newfound wealth.

Case Problem 3.2 *Paul and Deborah's Choices of Brokers and Advisers*

LG4 LG5 LG6 Paul Chang and Deborah Barry, friends who work for a large software company, decided to leave the relative security of their employer and join the staff of OnlineSpeed Inc., a 2-year-old company working on new broadband technology for fast Internet access. Paul will be a vice president for new-product development; Deborah will be treasurer. Although they are excited about the potential their new jobs offer, they recognize the need to consider the financial implications of the move. Of immediate concern are their 401(k) retirement plans. On leaving their current employer, each of them will receive a lump-sum settlement of about $75,000 that they must roll over into self-directed, tax-deferred retirement accounts. The friends met over lunch to discuss their options for investing these funds.

Paul is 30 years old and single, with a bachelor's degree in computer science. He rents an apartment and would like to buy a condominium fairly soon but is in no rush. For now, he is happy using his money on the luxuries of life. He considers himself a bit of a risk taker and has dabbled in the stock market from time to time, using his technology expertise to invest in software and Internet companies.

Deborah's undergraduate degree was in English, followed by an M.B.A. in finance. She is 32, is married, and hopes to start a family very soon. Her husband is a physician in private practice.

Paul is very computer-savvy and likes to pick stocks on the basis of his own Internet research. Although Deborah's finance background gives her a solid understanding of investing fundamentals, she is more conservative and has thus far stayed with blue-chip stocks and mutual funds. Among the topics that come up during their lunchtime conversation are stockbrokers and financial planners. Paul is leaning toward a bare-bones basic discount broker with low cost per online trade that is offering free trades for a limited time. Deborah is also cost-conscious but warns Paul that the low costs can be deceptive if you have to pay for other services or find yourself trading more often. She also thinks Paul is too focused on the technology sector and encourages him to seek financial advice to balance his portfolio. They agree to research a number of brokerage firms and investment advisers and meet again to compare notes.

Questions

a. Research at least two different full-service, premium discount, and basic discount stock brokerage firms, and compare the services and costs. What brokers would suit Paul's needs best, and why? What brokers would suit Deborah's needs best, and why? What are some key questions each should ask when interviewing potential brokers?

b. What factors should Paul and Deborah consider before deciding to use a particular broker? Compare the pros and cons of getting the personal attention of a full-service broker with the services provided by the discount brokers.

c. Do you think that a broker that assists in making transactions and focuses on personal attention would be a good choice for either Paul or Deborah?

d. Paul mentioned to Deborah that he had read an article about *day trading* and wanted to try it. What would you advise Paul about the risks and rewards of this strategy?

e. Prepare a brief overview of the traditional and online sources of investment advice that could help Paul and Deborah create suitable portfolios. Which type of adviser would you recommend for Paul? For Deborah? Explain your reasoning.

Excel with Spreadsheets

Peter Tanaka is interested in starting a stock portfolio. He has heard many financial reporters talk about the Dow Jones Industrial Average (DJIA) as being a proxy for the overall stock market. From visiting various online investment sites, Peter is able to track the variability in the Dow. Peter would like to develop an average or index that will measure the price performance of his selected portfolio over time. He has decided to create a price-weighted index, similar to the Dow, where the stocks are held in proportion to their share prices. He wishes to form an index based on the following 10 high-quality stocks and has designated October 13, 1977, as the base year. The number of shares outstanding has remained constant over the time period 1977 through 2011. The implication is that the closing stock prices will behave just like the closing market values. Given the data below, **create a spreadsheet** to model and analyze the use of an index.

	Prices		
Stocks	10/13/2011	10/13/2007	10/13/1977
A	45	50	55
B	12	9	15
C	37	37	37
D	65	66	67
E	36	42	48
F	26	35	43
G	75	68	59
H	35	38	30
I	67	74	81
J	84	88	92

Questions

a. The divisor is 1.00 on October 13, 1977, 0.75 on October 13, 2007, and 0.85 on October 13, 2011. Using this information and the data supplied above, calculate the market average, using the same methodology used to calculate the Dow averages, on each of the three dates—October 13, 1977, 2007, and 2011.

b. The DJIA is the most widely cited stock market indicator, yet there are criticisms of the model. One criticism is that the higher-priced securities in the portfolio will impact the Dow more than the relatively lower-priced stocks. Assume that Stock J increases by 10%. Recalculate the market averages on each of the three dates.

c. Next, assume Stock J is back to its original level and Stock B increases by 10%. Recalculate the market averages on each of the three dates. Compare your findings in all three scenarios. Do you find support for the criticism of the Dow? Explain.

Return and Risk

An old saying often attributed to Mark Twain advises, "Buy land—they're not making it anymore." That bit of folk wisdom gained enormous popularity during the U.S. real estate boom. According to the S&P/Case-Shiller Index, which tracks home prices in 20 large cities, U.S. homeowners saw their property values increase almost 70% from 2002–2005. Over the same four years, the U.S. stock market eked out a meager 16% gain.

Moreover, the tantalizing returns on real estate seemed to come without much risk. The average home price rose every single month from July 1996 to May 2006. No wonder, then, that investing in real estate became fashionable, as evidenced by the introduction of television shows such as A&E's *Flip This House*.

Unfortunately, home prices declined in June 2006, and their fall continued through May 2009. Over that period, average home prices dropped 32%, and foreclosures skyrocketed, reminding homeowners that investing in real estate had both rewards and risks. The drop in home prices prompted Congress to enact a tax credit for first-time homebuyers, and that appeared to provide a boost to the market. Home prices rose on average in June, July, and August, and Congress extended the tax credit through mid 2010.

(Source: S&P/Case-Shiller price indexes downloaded from standardandpoors.com.)

The Concept of Return

LG1 **LG2** People are motivated to invest in a given asset by its expected return. The **return** is the level of profit from an investment—that is, the reward for investing. Suppose you have $1,000 in an insured savings account paying 2% annual interest, and a business associate asks you to lend her that much money. If you lend her the money for one year, at the end of which she pays you back, your return will depend on the amount of interest you charge. If you make an interest-free loan, your return will be zero. If you charge 2% interest, your return will be $20 (0.02 × $1,000). Because you are already earning a safe 2% on the $1,000, it seems clear that to equal that return you should charge your associate a minimum of 2% interest.

Some investments guarantee a return, but most do not. The return on a bank deposit insured by the federal government is virtually certain. The return earned on a loan to your business associate might be less certain. The size and the certainty of the expected return are important factors in choosing a suitable investment.

> ### INVESTOR FACTS
>
> **WRESTLE WITH DIVIDENDS—** In August 2009, the stock of World Wrestling Entertainment (WWE) sold for about $15 per share, exactly the same price that an investor would have paid to buy it a year earlier in August 2008. Although it might appear that WWE investors made no money during that time, in fact, WWE paid quarterly dividends totaling $1.44, which represented a return of 9.6% on a $15 investment.

Components of Return

The return on an investment may come from more than one source. The most common source is periodic payments, such as dividends or interest. The other source of return is the change in the investment's price. We call these two sources of return *current income* and *capital gains* (or *capital losses*), respectively.

Income Income may take the form of dividends from stocks or mutual funds, or interest received on bonds. To be considered income, it must be in the form of cash or be readily convertible into cash. For our purposes, an investment's **income** is usually cash that investors periodically receive as a result of owning an investment.

Using the data in Table 4.1, we can calculate the income from investments A and B, both purchased for $1,000, over a one-year period of ownership. Investment A provides income of $80, and investment B pays $120. Solely on the basis of the income received over the one-year period, investment B seems preferable.

Capital Gains (or Losses) The second dimension of return focuses on the change in an investment's market value. As noted in Chapter 1, the amount by which the proceeds from the sale of an investment exceed its original purchase price is a *capital gain*. If an investment sells for less than its original purchase price, a *capital loss* results.

TABLE 4.1 Profiles of Two Investments		
	Investment	
	A	B
Purchase price (beginning of year)	$1,000	$1,000
Cash received		
1st quarter	$ 10	$ 0
2nd quarter	20	0
3rd quarter	20	0
4th quarter	30	120
Total income (for year)	80	$120
Sale price (end of year)	$1,100	$ 960

TABLE 4.2	Total Returns of Two Investments	
	Investment	
Return	A	B
Income	$ 80	$120
Capital gain (loss)	100	(40)
Total return	$180	$ 80

We can calculate the capital gain or loss of the investments shown in Table 4.1. Investment A experiences a capital gain of $100 ($1,100 sale price − $1,000 purchase price) over the one-year period. For investment B, a $40 capital loss results ($960 sale price − $1,000 purchase price).

Combining the capital gain (or loss) with the income (calculated in the preceding section) gives the **total return**. Table 4.2 shows the total return for investments A and B over the year. Investment A earns a $180 total returns, compared to just $80 earned by investment B.

It is generally preferable to use *percentage returns* rather than dollar returns. Percentages allow direct comparison of different sizes and types of investments. Investment A earned an 18% return ($180 ÷ $1,000); B produced only an 8% return ($80 ÷ $1,000). At this point investment A appears preferable, but as we'll see, differences in risk might cause some investors to prefer B.

Why Return Is Important

An asset's return is a key variable in the investment decision because it indicates how rapidly an investor can build wealth. Naturally, because most people prefer to have more wealth rather than less, they prefer investments that offer high returns rather than low returns if all else is equal. However, we've already said that the returns on most investments are uncertain, so how do investors distinguish assets that offer high returns from those likely to produce low returns? One way to make this kind of assessment is to examine the returns that different types of investments have produced in the past.

Historical Performance   Most people recognize that future performance is not guaranteed by past performance, but past data often provide a meaningful basis for future expectations. A common practice in the investment world is to look closely at the historical record when formulating expectations about the future.

Interest rates and other measures of financial return are most often cited on an annual basis. Evaluation of past investment returns is typically done on the same basis. Consider the data for ExxonMobil Corp. presented in Table 4.3. Exxon paid dividends in every year from 1999–2008 (and has continued to do so since then). Exxon's stock price generally rose during this decade, starting at $36.56 and ending at $79.83. Despite the overall upward trend, the company's stock fell slightly in 2001 and 2002 (largely due to the September 11 terrorist attack and the recession that followed), and it declined again in 2008 (as oil prices plunged from over $140 per barrel that summer to less than $40 in December).

Two aspects of these data are important. First, we can determine the *average level of return* generated by this investment over the past 10 years. The total return earned by Exxon's shareholders (column 6) over this period averaged 11.6%, performance that put Exxon well ahead of most other stocks for the same period. Second, observe that there was considerable variation in Exxon's return from one year to the next. The

TABLE 4.3	Historical Investment Data for ExxonMobil Corp. (XOM)					EXCEL With Spreadsheets
	Market Value (Price)*				Total Return	
Year	(1) Dividend Income	(2) Beginning of Year	(3) End of Year	(4) (3)−(2) Capital Gain	(5) (1) + (4)	(6) (5)/(2)
1999	$0.84	$36.56	$40.28	$3.72	$4.56	12.5%
2000	0.88	40.28	43.47	3.19	4.07	10.1
2001	0.91	43.47	39.30	−4.17	−3.26	−7.5
2002	0.92	39.30	34.94	−4.36	−3.44	−8.8
2003	0.98	34.94	41.00	6.06	7.04	20.1
2004	1.06	41.00	51.26	10.26	11.32	27.6
2005	1.14	51.26	56.17	4.91	6.05	11.8
2006	1.28	56.17	76.63	20.46	21.74	38.7
2007	1.37	76.63	93.69	17.06	18.43	24.1
2008	1.55	93.69	79.83	−13.86	−12.31	−13.1
Average						11.6%

(Source: Dividends and prices are obtained from Yahoo! Finance.)

*Prices reflect author adjustments for stock splits.

firm's best year was 2006, during which its investors earned a total return of 38.7%. But in 2008, Exxon's worst year, shareholders lost 13.1%.

Expected Return In the final analysis, of course, it's the future that matters when we make investment decisions. Therefore, **expected return** is a vital measure of performance. It's what you think the investment will earn in the future that determines what you should be willing to pay for it.

To demonstrate, let's return to the data in Table 4.3. A naive investor might estimate Exxon's expected return to be the same as its average return from the prior decade, 11.6%. That's not necessarily a bad starting point, but it would be wise to ask, "What contributed to Exxon's past success, and is it likely that the same factors will occur again in the future?" Central to Exxon's success in the recent past was a generally upward trend in oil prices. Crude oil fluctuated in the relatively narrow range of $15–$20 per barrel from 1986–1998, but in 1999 oil began to rise steadily. An investor who believed that oil prices would not continue to move up indefinitely, but rather would stabilize, might estimate Exxon's expected return by looking at its historical performance during a period of relatively stable oil prices.

Level of Return

The level of return achieved or expected from an investment will depend on a variety of factors. The key factors are internal characteristics and external forces.

Internal Characteristics Certain characteristics of an investment affect its return. For investments issued by companies, the characteristics that are important include things such as the type of investment (e.g., stocks or bonds), the quality of the firm's management, and whether the firm finances its operations with debt or equity. For example, investors might expect a different return on the common stock of a large, well-managed, completely equity-financed plastics manufacturer than they would anticipate from the common stock of a small, poorly managed, largely debt-financed clothing manufacturer. As we will see in later chapters, assessing internal factors and their impact on return is one important step in analyzing potential investments.

MARKETS in CRISIS

Recession Pushes Prices Down

For most of your lifetime, prices of most goods and services have been rising. There are important exceptions, such as the prices of consumer electronics and computers, but from one year to the next, the overall price level rose continuously in the United States from 1955–2007. However, as the recession deepened in 2008, consumer prices in the United States began to decline, falling in each of the last five months that year. By May 2009, the year-over-year change in consumer prices was −1.3%, the largest 12-month drop in nearly 60 years. The news raised fears among some investors that the recession might turn into a depression like the one that brought about a price decline of −27% from November 1929 to March 1933.

External Forces   External forces such as Federal Reserve actions, shortages, war, price controls, and political events may also affect an investment's return. None of these are under the control of the issuer of the investment vehicle, and investments react differently to these forces. For example, if investors expect oil prices to rise, they may raise their expected return for Exxon stock and lower it for the stock of an automobile manufacturer that specializes in gas guzzlers. Likewise, the economies of various countries respond to external forces in different ways.

Another external force is the *general level of price changes,* either up—**inflation**—or down—**deflation.** Inflation tends to have a positive impact on investments such as real estate and a negative impact on stocks and fixed-income securities. Rising interest rates, which normally accompany increasing rates of inflation, can significantly affect returns. The actions, if any, the Federal Reserve takes to control inflation can also have significant effects on investments. Furthermore, the return on each type of investment vehicle exhibits its own unique response to inflation.

Historical Returns

Returns vary both over time and between different types of investments. By averaging historical returns over a long period of time, it is possible to observe the differences in returns earned by various types of investments. Table 4.4 shows the arithmetic average annual rates of return for a number of popular security investments (and inflation) in

TABLE 4.4	Historical Returns for Select Asset Classes (1900–2008)		
	Average Annual Return		
Asset Class	U.S.	U.K.	Germany
Stocks	11.2%	11.2%	13.2%
Treasury Bonds	5.5	6.0	4.9
T-Bills	4.0	5.1	4.5
Inflation	3.1	4.2	5.6

(Source: Elroy Dimson, Paul Marsh, and Mike Staunton. *Triumph of the Optimists: 101 Years of Global Investment Returns.* Princeton, NJ: Princeton University Press. *Additional updates provided by Dimson et al.)*

three countries over the 108-year period from 1900–2008. With more than 100 years of data to draw on, some clear patterns emerge. You can see that significant differences exist among the average annual rates of return realized on stocks, long-term government bonds, and short-term government bills. In all three countries, stocks earn higher returns than government bonds, which in turn earn higher average returns than short-term government bills. Later in this chapter, we will see how we can link these differences in return to differences in the risk of each of these investments.

We now turn our attention to the role that time value of money concepts play in determining investment returns.

Time Value of Money and Returns

As a general rule, *the sooner you receive cash the better.* For example, two investments each requiring a $1,000 outlay and each expected to return $100 interest over a two-year holding period are *not necessarily* equally desirable. If the first investment returns $50 at the end of the first year, and the second investment returns nothing the first year and $100 at the end of the second year, the first investment is preferable because the initial $50 it pays could be *reinvested to earn more interest* in the second year. You should not fail to consider time value concepts when making investment decisions.

We now review the key computational aids available for streamlining time value of money calculations, and then we demonstrate the application of time value of money techniques to determine an acceptable investment.

Computational Aids for Use in Time Value Calculations The often time-consuming calculations involved in applying time value of money techniques can be simplified with a number of computational aids. Throughout this book we will demonstrate the use of hand-held financial calculators and electronic spreadsheets. *Financial calculators* include numerous preprogrammed financial routines. To demonstrate the calculator keystrokes for various financial computations, we show a keypad in the margin of the book, with the keys as defined at the left. *Electronic spreadsheet* use has become a prime skill for today's investors. Like financial calculators, electronic spreadsheets have built-in routines that simplify time value calculations. For most time value calculations in the book, we show spreadsheet solutions that identify cell entries.

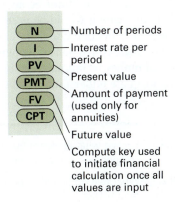

Determining a Satisfactory Investment Time value of money techniques can be used to determine whether an investment's return is satisfactory given the investment's cost. Ignoring risk at this point, a **satisfactory investment** would be one for which the present

TABLE 4.5	Present Value Applied to an Investment		EXCEL With Spreadsheets
End of Year	(1) Income	(2) Present Value Calculation at 8%	(3) Present Value at 8%
1	$ 90	$ 90/(1 + 0.08)^1	$ 83.33
2	100	100/(1 + 0.08)^2	85.73
3	110	110/(1 + 0.08)^3	87.32
4	120	120/(1 + 0.08)^4	88.20
5	100	100/(1 + 0.08)^5	68.06
6	100	100/(1 + 0.08)^6	63.02
7	1,200	1,200/(1 + 0.08)^7	700.19
		Total Present Value	$1,175.85

value of benefits (discounted at the appropriate rate) *equals* or *exceeds* its cost. The three possible benefit–cost relationships and their interpretations follow:

1. If the present value of the benefits *just equals the cost,* you would earn a rate of return equal to the discount rate.

2. If the present value of benefits *exceeds the cost,* you would earn a rate of return greater than the discount rate.

3. If the present value of benefits is *less than the cost,* you would earn a rate of return less than the discount rate.

You would prefer only those investments for which the present value of benefits equals or exceeds its cost—situations 1 and 2. In these cases, the rate of return would be equal to or greater than the discount rate.

The information in Table 4.5 demonstrates the application of present value to investment decision making. (*Note:* You can use a financial calculator or an Excel spreadsheet to convert the algebraic expression in column 2 to the numeric value in column 3.) The present value of the benefits (i.e., the income) provided by this investment over its seven-year life is $1,175.85. If the cost of the investment today is $1,175.85 or less then the investment is acceptable. At that cost, an investor would earn a rate of return equal to at least 8%. At a cost above the $1,175.85 present value, the investment would not be acceptable because the rate of return would be less than 8%. In that case it would be preferable to find an alternative investment with a present value of benefits that equals or exceeds its cost.

For your convenience, **Appendix 4A provides a complete review of the key time value of money techniques.** Be sure to review it before reading ahead, to make sure you have adequate understanding of this important financial concept.

CONCEPTS IN REVIEW

Answers available at
www.pearsonhighered.com/
gitman

4.1   Explain what is meant by the *return* on an investment. Differentiate between the two components of return—income and capital gains (or losses).

4.2   What role do historical performance data play in estimating an investment's expected return? Discuss the key factors affecting investment returns—internal characteristics and external forces.

4.3   What is a *satisfactory investment?* When the present value of benefits exceeds the cost of an investment, what can you conclude about the rate of return earned by the investor relative to the discount rate?

Measuring Return

LG3 LG4 Thus far, we have discussed the concept of return in terms of its two components (income and capital gains) and the key factors that affect the level of return (internal characteristics and external forces). These discussions intentionally oversimplified the computations involved in determining the historical or expected return. To compare returns from different investments, we need to incorporate time value of money concepts that explicitly consider differences in the timing of investment income and capital gains. We must also be able to calculate the present value of future benefits. Here we will look at several measures that enable us to compare alternative investment vehicles. First, we must define and consider the relationships among various rates of return.

Real, Risk-Free, and Required Returns

Inflation and Returns Glance back at Table 4.4 (on page 122), which reports that in the United States, the average return on a short-term Treasury bill was 4.0% between 1900–2008. The table also shows that the average inflation rate was 3.1%. It's no coincidence that the T-bill rate of return exceeds the inflation rate. Inflation erodes the purchasing power of money. For example, with 3% inflation, $1 buys about 3% fewer goods and services at the end of the year than at the beginning. Thus, if investors seek to increase their purchasing power over time, they must earn returns that exceed the inflation rate.

The **nominal return** on an investment is the actual return that the investment earns expressed in current dollars. The **real rate of return** equals the nominal return minus the inflation rate, and it measures the increase in purchasing power provided by an investment. For instance, suppose a bag of groceries costs $50 today. With 2% annual inflation, in a year's time the same groceries would cost $51. If you deposit $50 in a bank account earning 2% interest, at the end of the year you will have $51, just enough to buy one bag of groceries. But if you earn 3%, by year's end you will have $51.50, enough to buy a bag of groceries and a candy bar as you leave the store.

Risk and Returns Rational investors will choose investments that fully compensate them for the risk involved. The greater the risk, the greater the return required by investors. The rate of return that fully compensates for an investment's risk is called the **required return**.

The required return on any investment j consists of three basic components: the real rate of return, an expected inflation premium, and a risk premium, as noted in Equation 4.1.

Equation 4.1

$$\text{Required return on investment } j = \text{Real rate of return} + \text{Expected inflation premium} + \text{Risk premium for investment } j$$

Equation 4.1a

$$r_j = r^* + IP + RP_j$$

The **expected inflation premium** represents the average rate of inflation expected in the future. Although the historical average inflation rate in the United States has been close to 3%, investors' expectations may deviate from the historical norm for many reasons. For instance, most inflation forecasts for 2010 projected very low inflation due to the lingering effects of the global recession. By adding the first two terms in Equation 4.1, we obtain the **risk-free rate**. This is the rate of return that can be earned on a risk-free investment, such as a short-term U.S. Treasury bill. The formula for this rate appears in Equation 4.2.

Equation 4.2 $$\text{Risk-free rate} = \frac{\text{Real rate}}{\text{of return}} + \frac{\text{Expected inflation}}{\text{premium}}$$

Equation 4.2a $$R_F = r^* + IP$$

The required return can be found by adding to the risk-free rate a **risk premium**, which varies depending on specific issue and issuer characteristics. *Issue characteristics* are the type of investment (stock, bond, etc.), its maturity (two years, five years, infinity, etc.), and its features (voting/nonvoting, callable/noncallable, etc.). *Issuer characteristics* are industry and company factors such as the line of business and financial condition of the issuer. Together, the issue and issuer factors contribute to the overall risk of an investment and cause investors to require a risk premium above the risk-free rate.

Substituting the risk-free rate, R_F, from Equation 4.2a into Equation 4.1a for the first two terms to the right of the equal signs $(r^* + IP)$, we get Equation 4.3.

Equation 4.3 $$\frac{\text{Required return}}{\text{on investment } j} = \frac{\text{Risk-free}}{\text{rate}} + \frac{\text{Risk premium}}{\text{for investment } j}$$

Equation 4.3a $$r_j = R_F + RP_j$$

For example, if the required return on Nike common stock is 11% when the risk-free rate is 6%, investors require a 5% risk premium (11% – 6%) as compensation for the risk associated with common stock (the issue) and Nike (the issuer). Notice also that if investors expect 3% inflation, then the real required rate on Nike is 8% (11% – 3%). Later, in Chapter 5, we will explore further the relationship between the risk premium and required returns.

Next, we consider the specifics of return measurement. We look at two return measures—one used primarily for short-term investments and the other for longer-term vehicles.

Holding Period Return

The return to a *saver* is the amount of interest earned on a given deposit. Of course, the amount "invested" in a savings account does not change in value, as does the amount invested in stocks, bonds, and mutual funds. Because we are concerned with a broad range of investment vehicles, we need a measure of return that captures both periodic income and changes in value. One such measure is the *holding period return*.

The **holding period** is the period of time over which one wishes to measure the return on an investment. When comparing returns, be sure to use holding periods of the same length. For example, comparing the return on a stock over a six-month period with the return on a bond over a one-year period could result in a poor investment decision. To avoid this problem, be sure you define the holding period. It is common practice to annualize the holding period and use that as a standard.

Understanding Return Components   Earlier in this chapter we identified the two components of investment return: income and capital gains (or losses). The portion of

Smart's Tour of the Web
To watch author Scott
Smart discuss key websites
for this chapter visit
www.myfinancelab.com

income received by the investor during the period is a **realized return**. Most but not all of an investment's income is realized. (Accrued interest on taxable zero-coupon bonds is treated as current income for tax purposes but is not a realized return until the bond is sold or matures.) Capital gains and losses, on the other hand, are realized only when the investors sells an asset at the end of the holding period. Until the sale occurs the capital gain is merely a **paper return**.

For example, the capital gain return on an investment that increases in market value from $50 to $70 during a year is $20. For that capital gain to be realized, you would sell the investment for $70 at the end of that year. An investor who purchased the same investment but plans to hold it for another three years would also experience the $20 capital gain return during the first year, but he or she *would not have realized the gain* by collecting the $20 profit in cash. However, *even if the capital gain is not realized, it must be included in the total return calculation.*

A second point to recognize about returns is that both the income and the capital gains components can have a negative value. Occasionally, an investment may have negative income. That is, you may be required to pay out cash to meet certain obligations. (This situation is most likely to occur in various types of property investments that require periodic maintenance.) A capital loss can occur on *any* investment: Stocks, bonds, mutual funds, options, futures, real estate, and gold can all decline in value.

Computing the Holding Period Return (HPR) The **holding period return** (**HPR**) is the total return earned from holding an investment for a specified time (the holding period). Analysts typically use the *HPR with holding periods of one year or less.* (We'll explain why later.) It represents the sum of income and capital gains (or losses) achieved over the holding period, divided by the beginning investment value (market price). The equation for HPR is

Equation 4.4

$$\text{Holding period return} = \frac{\text{Income during period} + \text{Capital gain (or loss) during period}}{\text{Beginning investment value}}$$

Equation 4.4a

$$\text{HPR} = \frac{\text{Inc} + \text{CG}}{V_0}$$

where

Equation 4.5

$$\text{Capital gain (or loss) during period} = \text{Ending investment value} - \text{Beginning investment value}$$

Equation 4.5a

$$\text{CG} = V_n - V_0$$

The HPR equation provides a convenient method for either measuring the total return realized or estimating the total return expected. For example, Table 4.6 (on page 128) summarizes the key financial variables for four investment vehicles over the past year. The total income and capital gain or loss during the holding period are given in the lines labeled (1) and (3), respectively. The total return over the year is calculated, as shown in line (4), by adding these two sources of return. Dividing the total return value [line (4)] by the beginning-of-year investment value [line (2)], we find the holding

TABLE 4.6	Key Financial Variables for Four Investment Vehicles				EXCEL With Spreadsheets

	Investment Vehicle			
	Savings Account	Common Stock	Bond	Real Estate
Cash Received				
1st quarter	$ 15	$ 10	$ 0	$ 0
2nd quarter	15	10	70	0
3rd quarter	15	10	0	0
4th quarter	15	15	70	0
(1) Total income	$ 60	$ 45	$ 140	$ 0
Investment Value				
End-of-year	$1,000	$2,200	$ 970	$3,300
(2) Beginning-of-year	1,000	2,000	1,000	3,000
(3) Capital gain (loss)	$ 0	$ 200	($ 30)	$ 300
(4) Total return [(1) + (3)]	$ 60	$ 245	$ 110	$ 300
(5) Holding period return [(4) ÷ (2)]	6.00%	12.25%	11.00%	10.00%

period return, given in line (5). Over the one-year holding period the common stock had the highest HPR (12.25%). The savings account had the lowest (6%).

As these calculations show, to find the HPR we need the beginning- and end-of-period investment values, along with income received during the period. Note that if the current income and capital gain (or loss) values in lines (1) and (3) of Table 4.6 had been drawn from a six-month rather than a one-year period, the HPR values calculated in line 5 would have been *the same.*

Holding period return can be negative or positive. HPRs can be calculated with Equation 4.4 using either historical data (as in the preceding example) or forecast data.

Using the HPR in Investment Decisions   The holding period return is easy to use in making investment decisions. Because it considers both income and capital gains relative to the beginning investment value, it tends to overcome any problems that might be associated with comparing investments of different size.

If we look only at the total returns calculated for each of the four investments in Table 4.6 [line (4)], the real estate investment appears best, because it has the highest total return. However, the real estate investment would require the largest dollar outlay ($3,000). The holding period return offers a *relative comparison,* by dividing the total return by the amount of the investment. Comparing HPRs [line (5)], we find the investment alternative with the *highest return per invested dollar* to be the common stock's HPR of 12.25%. Because the return per invested dollar reflects the efficiency of the investment, the HPR provides a logical method for evaluating and comparing investment returns, particularly for holding periods of one year or less.

Yield: The Internal Rate of Return

An alternative way to define a satisfactory investment is in terms of the compound annual rate of return it earns. Why do we need an alternative to the HPR? Because *HPR fails to consider the time value of money.* Although the holding period return is useful with investments held for one year or less, it is generally inappropriate for longer holding periods. Sophisticated investors typically do not use HPR when the time period is greater than one year. Instead, they use a present-value-based measure, called **yield** (or **internal rate of return**), to determine the compound annual rate of return earned on investments held for longer than one year. Yield can also be defined as the discount rate that produces a present value of benefits just equal to its cost.

Once you know the yield you can decide whether an investment is acceptable. If the yield on an investment *is equal to or greater than the required return*, then the investment is acceptable. An investment with a yield *below the required return* is unacceptable.

The yield on an investment providing a *single* future cash flow is relatively easy to calculate. The yield on an investment providing a *stream* of future cash flows generally involves more complex calculations. Many hand-held financial calculators and Excel spreadsheets are available for simplifying these calculations.

Yield for a Single Cash Flow Some investments, such as U.S. savings bonds, stocks paying no dividends, and zero-coupon bonds are purchased by paying a fixed amount up front. The investor expects them to provide *no periodic income*, but to provide a single—and, the investor hopes, a large—future cash flow at maturity or when the investment is sold. The yield on investments expected to provide a single future cash flow can be estimated using a financial calculator or an Excel spreadsheet.

CALCULATOR USE Assume you wish to find the yield on an investment that costs $1,000 today and will be worth $1,400 at the end of five years. Using a financial calculator to find the yield for this investment, we can treat the earliest value as a present value, **PV**, and the latest value as a future value, **FV**. (*Note:* Most calculators require you to key in *either* the **PV** or the **FV** value as a negative number to calculate an unknown yield.) Using the inputs shown at the left, we find the yield to be 6.96%.

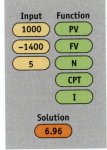

SPREADSHEET USE The yield for the single cash flow also can be calculated as shown on the following Excel spreadsheet.

	A	B
1	YIELD FOR A SINGLE CASH FLOW	
2	Point in Time	Cash Flow
3	Future	$1,400
4	Present	$1,000
5	Number of Years	5
6	Yield	6.96%
	Entry in Cell B6 is = Rate ((B5),0,–B4,B3,0), The minus sign appears before B4 because the present investment is treated as a cash outflow.	

Yield for a Stream of Income Investments such as income-oriented stocks and bonds typically provide the investor with a *stream of income*. The yield (or internal rate of return) for a stream of income (returns) is generally more difficult to estimate. The most accurate approach is based on searching for the discount rate that produces a present value of income just equal to the cost of the investment. For example, consider once more the investment presented in Table 4.5 (on page 124). That table illustrates that if the investment's cost is $1,175.85, its internal rate of return equals 8% because that's the discount rate that equates the present value of the investment's cash flows to its market price. Suppose that the cost of this investment falls to $1,100. At that price, what yield does the investment offer? Table 4.7 (on page 130) uses a trial and error approach in an attempt to find the answer. If we discount the investment's cash flows

TABLE 4.7	Present Value Applied to an Investment				EXCEL With Spreadsheets
End of Year	(1) Income	(2) Present Value Calculation at 9%	(3) Present Value at 9%	(4) Present Value Calculation at 10%	(5) Present Value at 10%
1	$ 90	$ 90/(1 + 0.09)^1	$ 82.57	$ 90/(1 + 0.1)^1	$ 81.82
2	100	100/(1 + 0.09)^2	84.17	100/(1 + 0.1)^2	82.64
3	110	110/(1 + 0.09)^3	84.94	110/(1 + 0.1)^3	82.64
4	120	120/(1 + 0.09)^4	85.01	120/(1 + 0.1)^4	81.96
5	100	100/(1 + 0.09)^5	64.99	100/(1 + 0.1)^5	62.09
6	100	100/(1 + 0.09)^6	59.63	100/(1 + 0.1)^6	56.45
7	1,200	1,200/(1 + 0.09)^7	656.44	1,200/(1 + 0.1)^7	615.79
Total Present Value			$1,117.75		$1,063.40

at 9%, its price is $1,117.75. That's above the investment's current price, so the yield must be above 9%. Table 4.7 shows that at a 10% discount rate, the investment's price is $1,063.40, so its yield must be below 10%. Therefore, we need to keep searching for the exact discount rate at which the investment's cash flows equal $1,100. We can do that using a financial calculator or an Excel spreadsheet.

CALCULATOR USE We can use a financial calculator to find the yield (or *internal rate of return*) on an investment that will produce a stream of income. This procedure typically involves three steps: (1) Punch in the cost of the investment (typically referred to as the *cash outflow* at time zero). (2) Punch in all of the income expected each period (typically referred to as the *cash inflow* in year *x*). (3) Calculate the yield (typically referred to as the *internal rate of return, IRR*).

SPREADSHEET USE We can also calculate the yield for a stream of income as shown on the following Excel spreadsheet.

	A	B
1	YIELD FOR A STREAM OF INCOME	
2	Year	Cash Flow
3	0	$ (1,100)
4	1	$ 90
5	2	$ 100
6	3	$ 110
7	4	$ 120
8	5	$ 100
9	6	$ 100
10	7	$ 1,200
11	Yield	9.32%

Entry in Cell B10 is
=IRR(B2:B10).
The initial $1,100 cost of
the investment is a cash
outflow.

Interest on Interest: The Critical Assumption The critical assumption underlying the use of yield as a return measure is an ability to earn a return equal to the yield on *all*

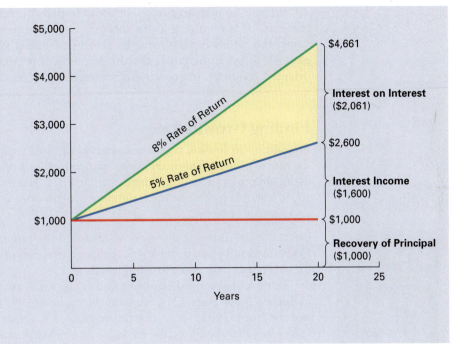

FIGURE 4.1

Earning Interest on Interest

If you invested in a $1,000, 20-year bond with an 8% coupon, you would have only $2,600 at the end of 20 years if you did not reinvest the $80 annual interest receipts—you would only have about a 5% rate of return.

If you reinvested the interest at the 8% interest rate, you would have $4,661 at the end of 20 years—an 8% rate of return. To achieve the calculated yield of 8%, you must therefore be able to earn interest on interest at that rate.

income received during the holding period. This concept can best be illustrated with a simple example. Suppose you buy a $1,000 U.S. Treasury bond that pays 8% annual interest ($80) over its 20-year maturity. Each year you receive $80, and at maturity the $1,000 in principal is repaid. There is no loss of capital, no default; all payments are made right on time. But in order to earn 8% on this investment, you must be able to reinvest the $80 annual interest receipts.

Figure 4.1 shows the elements of return on this investment to demonstrate the point. If you don't *reinvest* the interest income of $80 per year, you'll end up on the 5% line. You'll have $2,600—the $1,000 principal plus $1,600 interest income ($80/year × 20 years)—at the end of 20 years. (The yield on a single cash flow of $1,000 today that will be worth $2,600 in 20 years is about 5%.) To move to the 8% line, you have to earn 8% on the annual interest receipts. If you do, at the end of 20 years you'll have $4,661—the $1,000 principal plus the $3,661 future value of the 20-year $80 annuity of interest receipts invested at 8%. (The yield on a single cash flow of $1,000 today that will be worth $4,661 in 20 years is 8%.) The future value of the investment would be $2,061 greater ($4,661 − $2,600) with interest on interest than without reinvestment of the interest receipts. Even though we used a bond in this illustration, the same principle applies to many other investments.

It should be clear to you that if you start out with an 8% investment, *you have to earn that same rate of return when reinvesting your income.* The rate of return you start with is the required, or minimum, **reinvestment rate.** This is the rate of return earned on interest or other income received over the relevant investment horizon. By putting your income to work at this rate, you'll earn the rate of return you set out to earn. If you fail to do so, your return will decline accordingly.

The earning of interest on interest is what the market refers to as a **fully compounded rate of return.** It's an important concept: You can't start reaping the full potential from your investments until you start earning a fully compounded rate of return on them.

Interest on interest is a particularly important element of return for investment programs that involve a lot of income. You have to reinvest income. (With capital gains, the money is automatically reinvested unless you sell the asset to realize the gain.) It follows, therefore, that for investment programs that lean toward income-oriented securities, the continued reinvestment of income plays an important role in investment success.

Finding Growth Rates

In addition to finding compound annual rates of return, we frequently need to find the **rate of growth**. This is the compound annual *rate of change* in the value of a stream of income, particularly dividends or earnings. Here we use an example to demonstrate a simple technique for estimating growth rates using a financial calculator, and an Excel spreadsheet.

Input	Function
0.84	PV
−1.55	FV
9	N
	CPT
	I
Solution	
7.04	

CALCULATOR USE Imagine that you wish to find the rate of growth for the ExxonMobil Corp. dividends given in Table 4.3. Although ten years of data are presented in Table 4.3, they represent only nine years of growth.

Using a financial calculator to find the growth rate for the dividend stream shown in Table 4.3 (on page 121), we treat the earliest (1999) value as a present value, **PV**, and the latest (2008) value as a future value, **FV**. (*Note:* Most calculators require you to key in *either* the **PV** or the **FV** value as a negative number to calculate an unknown growth rate.) As noted above, although ten years of dividends are shown in Table 4.3, there are only nine years of growth (**N** = 9) because the earliest year (1999) must be defined as the base year (year 0). Using the inputs shown at the left, we calculate the growth rate to be 7.04%.

SPREADSHEET USE The growth rate for a dividend stream can also be calculated as shown on the Excel spreadsheet below.

In Chapter 8 we explore in greater detail the use of growth rates, which are often an important input to the common stock valuation process.

	A	B
1	**GROWTH RATE FOR A DIVIDEND STREAM**	
2	Year	Dividend/share
3	2008	$1.55
4	2007	$1.37
5	2006	$1.28
6	2005	$1.14
7	2004	$1.06
8	2003	$0.98
9	2002	$0.92
10	2001	$0.91
11	2000	$0.88
12	1999	$0.84
13	Annual growth rate	7.04%

Entry in Cell B13 is
=RATE((A3–A12),0,–B12,B3,0).
The expression A3–A12 in the entry
calculates the number of years of growth.
The minus sign appears before B12 because
the investment in 1999
is treated as a cash outflow.

**CONCEPTS
IN REVIEW**

Answers available at

www.pearsonhighered.com/
gitman

4.4 Define the following terms and explain how they are used to find the risk-free rate of return and the required rate of return for a given investment.

a. *Real rate of return*.
b. *Expected inflation premium*.
c. *Risk premium* for a given investment.

4.5 What is meant by the *holding period*, and why is it advisable to use holding periods of equal length when comparing alternative investment vehicles? Define the *holding period return* (*HPR*), and explain for what length holding periods it is typically used.

4.6 Define *yield* (*internal rate of return*). When is it appropriate to use yield rather than the HPR to measure the return on an investment?

4.7 Explain why you must earn 10% on *all* income received from an investment during its holding period in order for its yield actually to equal the 10% value you've calculated.

4.8 Explain how either the present value (of benefits versus cost) or the yield measure can be used to find a *satisfactory investment*. Given the following data, indicate which, if any, of these investments is acceptable. Explain your findings.

	Investment		
	A	B	C
Cost	$200	$160	$500
Required return	7%	10%	9%
Present value of income	—	$150	—
Yield	8%	—	8%

Risk: The Other Side of the Coin

LG5 LG6 Thus far, our primary concern in this chapter has been return. However, we cannot consider return without also looking at risk. Expanding a bit on its definition in Chapter 1, **risk** is the uncertainty surrounding the actual return that an investment will generate.

The risk associated with a given investment is directly related to its expected return. In general, the greater the investment's risk, the higher the expected return it must offer to attract investors. Riskier investments should provide higher levels of return. Otherwise, what incentive is there for an investor to risk his or her capital?

In general, investors attempt to minimize risk for a given level of return or to maximize return for a given level of risk. This relationship between risk and return is called the **risk-return tradeoff**. We introduce it here and will discuss it in greater detail in Chapter 5. Here we begin by examining the key sources of risk. We then consider the measurement and assessment of risk: the risk of a single asset, the assessment of risk associated with a potential investment, and the steps by which return and risk can be combined in the decision process.

Sources of Risk

The risk associated with a given investment vehicle may result from a combination of possible sources. A prudent investor considers how the major sources of risk might affect potential investment vehicles. The combined impact of the presence of any of the sources of risk, discussed following, in a given investment vehicle would be reflected in its *risk premium*. As discussed earlier in the chapter and shown in Equation 4.3, we can

MARKETS IN CRISIS

Disappearing Dividends

Investors became very familiar with business risk during the global recession from 2007–2009. Standard & Poor's reported that in 2009's first quarter, a record high number of firms cut their dividends, and a record low number announced plans to increase dividends. In fact, 2009 marked the first time since S&P began tracking dividends in 1995 that the number of firms cutting dividends was greater than the number of companies increasing dividends. Total dividend payments fell by a whopping $77 billion in one quarter.

(Source: www.usatoday.com/money/markets/
2009-04-07-companies-cut-dividends_N.htm)

find the required return on an investment by adding its risk premium to the risk-free rate. This premium in a broad sense results from the sources of risk, which derive from characteristics of both the issue and the issuer.

Business Risk In general, **business risk** is the degree of uncertainty associated with an investment's earnings and the investment's ability to pay the returns (interest, principal, dividends) owed investors. For example, business owners may receive no return if the firm's earnings are not adequate to meet obligations. Debtholders, on the other hand, are likely to receive some (but not necessarily all) of the amount owed them, because of the preferential treatment legally accorded to debt.

The business risk associated with a given investment is tied to the firm's industry. For example, the business risk in a public utility common stock differs from the risk in the stock of a high-fashion clothing manufacturer or an Internet start-up. Generally, investments in similar kinds of firms have similar business risk, although differences in management, costs, and location can cause varying levels of risk.

Financial Risk Firms that borrow money sometimes experience financial difficulties because they cannot generate enough cash to pay all of their bills, including debt payments. The uncertainty surrounding a firm's ability to meet its financial obligations because it has borrowed money is **financial risk**. The more debt used to finance a firm, the greater its financial risk. Debt financing obligates the firm to make interest and principal payments, thus increasing risk. Inability to meet debt obligations could result in business failure and in losses for bondholders and stockholders.

Purchasing Power Risk The chance that unanticipated changes in price levels (inflation or deflation) will adversely affect investment returns is **purchasing power risk**. Specifically, this risk is the chance that generally rising prices (inflation) will reduce *purchasing power* (the goods and services that can be purchased with a dollar).

In general, investments whose values move with general price levels have low purchasing power risk and are most profitable during periods of rising prices. Those that provide fixed returns have high purchasing power risk, and they are most profitable during periods of low inflation or declining price levels. The returns on stocks of durable-goods manufacturers, for example, tend to move with the general price level, whereas returns from deposit accounts and bonds do not.

Interest Rate Risk Securities are especially affected by interest rate risk. This is particularly true for those securities that offer purchasers a fixed periodic return. **Interest rate risk** is the chance that changes in interest rates will adversely affect a security's value. The interest rate changes themselves result from changes in the general relationship between the supply of and the demand for money.

As interest rates change, the prices of many securities fluctuate. As we will see in greater detail in Chapters 11, 12, and online Chapter 17, the prices of fixed-income securities (bonds and preferred stock) typically drop when interest rates rise. As interest rates rise, new securities become available in the market that pay the new, higher rates. Securities that are already outstanding make cash payments that reflect lower market rates from the past, so they are not competitive in the higher rate environment. Investors sell them, and their prices fall. The opposite occurs when interest rates fall: Prices of outstanding securities that make cash payments above the current market become more attractive, and their prices rise.

A second, more subtle aspect of interest rate risk is associated with reinvestment of income. As noted earlier, only if you can earn the initial rate of return on income received from an investment can you achieve a *fully compounded rate of return* equal to the initial rate of return. In other words, if a bond pays 8% annual interest, you must be able to earn 8% on the interest received during the bond's holding period in order to earn a fully compounded 8% rate of return over that period. This same aspect of interest rate risk applies to reinvestment of the proceeds received from an investment at its maturity or sale.

A final aspect of interest rate risk is related to investing in short-term securities such as U.S. Treasury bills and certificates of deposit (discussed in Chapter 1). Investors face the risk that when short-term securities mature, they may have to invest those proceeds in lower-yielding, new short-term securities. By initially making a long-term investment, you can lock in a return for a period of years, rather than face the risk of declines in short-term interest rates. Clearly, when interest rates are declining, the returns from investing in short-term securities are adversely affected. (On the other hand, interest rate increases have a positive impact on such a strategy.) The chance that interest rates will decline is therefore the interest rate risk of a strategy of investing in short-term securities.

Most investments are subject to interest rate risk. Although interest rate movements most directly affect fixed-income securities, they also affect other long-term vehicles such as common stock and mutual funds. *Generally, the higher the interest rate, the lower the value of an investment vehicle, and vice versa.*

Liquidity Risk The risk of not being able to sell (or liquidate) an investment quickly and at a reasonable price is called **liquidity risk**. One can generally sell an investment by significantly cutting its price. However, a liquid investment is one that investors can sell quickly without having an adverse impact on its price. For example, a security recently purchased for $1,000 would not be viewed as highly liquid if it could be quickly sold only at a greatly reduced price, such as $500.

An investment's liquidity is an important consideration. In general, investments traded in *thin markets,* where transaction volume is low, tend to be less liquid than those traded in *broad markets.* Assets such as stocks and bonds of major companies listed on the New York Stock Exchange are generally highly liquid; others, such as artwork or antique furniture, are relatively illiquid.

Tax Risk The chance that Congress will make unfavorable changes in tax laws is known as **tax risk**. The greater the chance that such changes will drive down the after-tax returns and market values of certain investments, the greater the tax risk. Undesirable changes in tax laws include elimination of tax exemptions, limitation of deductions, and increases in tax rates.

Congress has passed numerous changes in tax laws through the years. One of the most significant, the *Tax Reform Act of 1986*, contained provisions that reduced the attractiveness of many investments, particularly real estate and other tax shelters. More recently, the *Jobs and Growth Tax Relief Reconciliation Act of 2003* reduced tax rates, taxes on dividends, and taxes on capital gains. Clearly, these changes benefit investors and do not represent the unfavorable consequences of tax risk. As this book is going to press, the Obama administration has proposed numerous changes to the tax code that, if enacted, would have a significant impact on the values of many types of financial assets.

Although virtually all investments are vulnerable to increases in tax rates, certain tax-advantaged investments, such as municipal and other bonds, real estate, and natural resources, generally have greater tax risk.

Event Risk Event risk occurs when something happens to a company that has a sudden and substantial impact on its financial condition. Event risk goes beyond business and financial risk. It does not necessarily mean the company or market is doing poorly. Instead, it involves an unexpected event that has a significant and usually immediate effect on the underlying value of an investment. An example of event risk is the January 2009 announcement by Apple Inc. that its founder and CEO, Steve Jobs, was taking a leave of absence due to health concerns. The announcement, which was made after trading in Apple stock had closed for the day, provided few details as to the severity of Mr. Jobs's health issues. When Apple stock opened for trading the next morning, it was down 5.6%.

Event risk can take many forms and can affect all types of investment vehicles. Fortunately, its impact tends to be isolated in most cases.

Market Risk Market risk is the risk that investment returns will decline because of market factors independent of the given investment. Examples include political, economic, and social events, as well as changes in investor tastes and preferences. Market risk actually embodies a number of different risks: purchasing power risk, interest rate risk, and tax risk.

The impact of market factors on investment returns is not uniform. Both the degree and the direction of change in return differ among investment vehicles. For example, legislation placing restrictive import quotas on Japanese goods may result in a significant increase in the value (and therefore the return) of domestic automobile and electronics stocks. Essentially, market risk is reflected in the *price volatility* of a security—the more volatile the price of a security, the greater its perceived market risk.

Risk of a Single Asset

Most people have at some time in their lives asked themselves how risky some anticipated course of action is. In such cases, the answer is usually a subjective judgment, such as "not very" or "quite." In finance, we are able to quantify the measurement of risk, which improves comparisons between investments and enhances decision making.

We can measure statistically the risk or variability of both single assets and portfolios of assets. Here we focus solely on the risk of single assets. We first consider standard deviation, which is an absolute measure of risk. We will consider the risk and return of portfolios of assets in Chapter 5.

Standard Deviation: An Absolute Measure of Risk The most common single indicator of an asset's risk is the **standard deviation,** *s*. It measures the dispersion (variation) of returns around an asset's average or expected return. The formula is

Equation 4.6

$$\text{Standard deviation} = \sqrt{\frac{\sum_{t=1}^{n}\left(\begin{array}{c}\text{Return for}\\\text{outcome } t\end{array} - \begin{array}{c}\text{Average or}\\\text{expected return}\end{array}\right)^2}{\begin{array}{c}\text{Total number}\\\text{of outcomes}\end{array} - 1}}$$

Equation 4.6a

$$s = \sqrt{\frac{\sum_{t=1}^{n}(r_t - \bar{r})^2}{n - 1}}$$

Consider two competing investments'—shares of stock in ExxonMobil and Panera Bread—described in Table 4.8. From 1999–2008, ExxonMobil earned an average of 11.7%, but Panera Bread achieved a spectacular average return of 44.4%. Looking at the returns each year, you can see that Panera returns fluctuated over a much wider range (from −35.9% to 193.8%) than did Exxon returns (from −13.1% to 39.1%).

The standard deviation provides a quantitative tool for comparing investment risk. Table 4.9 (on page 138) demonstrates the calculation of the standard deviations for Exxon and Panera Bread. We can see that the standard deviation of 17.2% for the returns on Exxon is, not surprisingly, considerably below the standard deviation of 69.4% for Panera. The fact that Panera's stock returns fluctuate over a very wide range is reflected in its larger standard deviation and indicates that Panera is a more volatile investment than Exxon. Of course, these figures are based on *historical* data. There is no assurance that the risks of these two investments will remain the same in the future.

TABLE 4.8	Historical Annual Returns for ExxonMobil and Panera Bread	
	Annual Rate of Return* (r_t)	
Year (*t*)	ExxonMobil	Panera Bread
1999	12.6%	14.8%
2000	10.2	193.8
2001	−7.6	128.2
2002	−8.9	33.8
2003	20.6	13.5
2004	28.1	2.0
2005	11.8	62.9
2006	39.1	−14.9
2007	24.3	−35.9
2008	−13.1	45.8
Average ($\bar{r}$)	11.7	44.4

*Annual rate of return is calculated based on end-of-year prices.

(Source: End-of-year prices for ExxonMobil (XOM) and Panera Bread (PNRA) are obtained from Yahoo! Finance (prices are adjusted for dividends and stock splits).)

TABLE 4.9   Calculation of Standard Deviations of Returns for ExxonMobil and Panera Bread

	ExxonMobil			
Year (t)	(1) Return r_t %	(2) Average Return %	(3) (1) – (2) $r_t - \bar{r}$ %	(4) (3)^2 $(r_t - \bar{r})^2$ %
1999	12.6	11.7	0.9	0.8
2000	10.2	11.7	–1.5	2.1
2001	–7.6	11.7	–19.3	373.3
2002	–8.9	11.7	–20.6	423.3
2003	20.6	11.7	8.9	79.5
2004	28.1	11.7	16.4	267.8
2005	11.8	11.7	0.1	0.0
2006	39.1	11.7	27.4	748.5
2007	24.3	11.7	12.6	158.2
2008	–13.1	11.7	–24.8	616.0
			Sum	2,669.6
			Variance =	296.6
			Std. deviation =	17.2

$$S_{XOM} = \sqrt{\frac{\sum_{t=1}^{10}(r_t - \bar{r})^2}{n-1}} = \sqrt{\frac{2,669.6}{10-1}} = \sqrt{296.6} = 17.2\%$$

	Panera Bread			
Year (t)	(1) Return r_t %	(2) Average Return $\bar{r}$ %	(3) (1) – (2) $r_t - \bar{r}$ %	(4) (3)^2 $(r_t - \bar{r})^2$ %
1999	14.8	44.4	–29.6	877.3
2000	193.8	44.4	149.4	22321.1
2001	128.2	44.4	83.8	7028.1
2002	33.8	44.4	–10.6	113.0
2003	13.5	44.4	–30.9	953.7
2004	2.0	44.4	–42.4	1796.7
2005	62.9	44.4	18.5	341.7
2006	–14.9	44.4	–59.3	3515.0
2007	–35.9	44.4	–80.3	6455.3
2008	45.8	44.4	1.4	2.0
			Sum	43,403.8
			Variance =	4,822.6
			Std. deviation =	69.4

$$S_{PNRA} = \sqrt{\frac{\sum_{t=1}^{10}(r_t - \bar{r})^2}{n-1}} = \sqrt{\frac{43,403.8}{10-1}} = \sqrt{4822.6} = 69.4\%$$

Historical Returns and Risk We can now use the standard deviation as a measure of risk to assess the historical (1900–2008) investment return data in Table 4.4. Table 4.10 reports the average return and the standard deviation associated with each investment. Within each country, a close relationship exists between the average return and the standard deviation of different types of investments. Stocks earn higher returns than bonds, and bonds earn higher returns than bills. Similarly, stock returns are more

TABLE 4.10 Historical Returns and Standard Deviations for Select Asset Classes (1900–2008)						
	U.S.		U.K.		Germany	
Asset Class	Average Annual Return	Standard Deviation of Returns	Average Annual Return	Standard Deviation of Returns	Average Annual Return	Standard Deviation of Returns
Stocks	11.2%	20.2%	11.2%	21.8%	13.2%	34.0%
Government Bonds	5.5	8.3	6.0	11.9	4.9	13.2
Government Bills	4.0	2.8	5.1	3.8	4.5	3.3
Inflation	3.1	4.9	4.2	6.6	5.6	15.1

(Source: Elroy Dimson, Paul Marsh, and Mike Staunton. *Triumph of the Optimists: 101 Years of Global Investment Returns.* Princeton, NJ: Princeton University Press. *Additional updates provided by Dimson et al.*)

volatile than bond returns, with bill returns displaying the least volatility (i.e., the lowest standard deviation). The general pattern is clear: Investments with higher average returns have higher standard deviations. Because higher standard deviations are associated with greater risk, the historical data confirm the existence of a positive relationship between risk and return. That relationship reflects the fact that market participants require higher returns as compensation for greater risk.

Assessing Risk

Techniques for quantifying the risk of a given investment vehicle are quite useful. However, they will be of little use if you are unaware of your feelings toward risk. Individual investors typically seek answers to these questions: "Is the amount of perceived risk worth taking to get the expected return?" "Can I get a higher return for the same level of risk or a lower risk for the same level of return?" A look at the general risk-return characteristics of alternative investment vehicles and at the question of an acceptable level of risk will help shed light on how to evaluate risk.

Risk-Return Characteristics of Alternative Investment Vehicles A wide variety of risk-return behaviors are associated with each type of investment vehicle. Some common stocks offer low returns and low risk. Others offer high returns and high risk. A very rough generalization of the risk-return characteristics of the major investment vehicles appears in Figure 4.2 (on page 140). Of course, a broad range of risk-return behaviors exists for specific investments of each type. In other words, once you have selected the appropriate type of investment, you must still decide which specific security to acquire. (*Note:* In Chapter 5 we will present a quantitative technique for linking risk and return.)

An Acceptable Level of Risk The three basic risk preferences (risk-indifferent, risk-averse, and risk-seeking) are depicted graphically in Figure 4.3 (on page 140).

- For the **risk-indifferent** investor, the required return does not change as risk goes from x_1 to x_2. In essence, no change in return would be required for the increase in risk.

FIGURE 4.2

Risk-Return Tradeoffs for Various Investment Vehicles

A risk-return tradeoff exists such that for a higher risk one expects a higher return, and vice versa. In general, low-risk/low-return investment vehicles include U.S. government securities and deposit accounts. High-risk/high-return vehicles include real estate and other tangible investments, options, and futures.

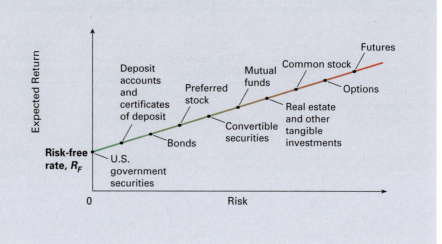

- For the **risk-averse** investor, the required return increases for an increase in risk. Because they do not like risk, these investors require higher expected returns to compensate them for taking greater risk.

- For the **risk-seeking** investor, the required return decreases for an increase in risk. Theoretically, because they enjoy risk, these investors are willing to give up some return to take more risk.

Most investors are risk-averse: For a given increase in risk, they require an increase in return, as illustrated by the green line in Figure 4.2.

Of course, the amount of return required by each investor for a given increase in risk differs depending on the investor's degree of risk aversion. A very risk-averse investor requires a great deal of compensation to take on additional risk, meaning that the green line in the figure would be very steep for such a person. Someone who is less risk-averse does not require as much compensation to be persuaded to accept risk, so for that sort of person the green line would be flatter.

FIGURE 4.3

Risk Preferences

The risk-indifferent investor requires no change in return for a given increase in risk. The risk-averse investor requires an increase in return for a given risk increase. The risk-seeking investor gives up some return for more risk. The majority of investors are risk-averse.

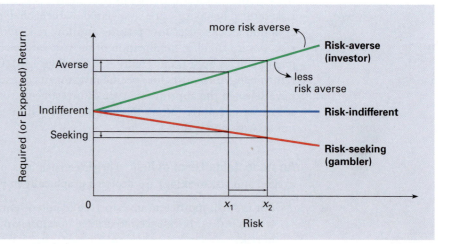

Steps in the Decision Process: Combining Return and Risk

When you are deciding among alternative investments, you should take the following steps to combine return and risk.

1. Using historical or projected return data, estimate the expected return over a given holding period. Use yield (or present-value) techniques to make sure you give the time value of money adequate consideration.

2. Using historical or projected return data, assess the risk associated with the investment. Subjective risk assessment, use of the standard deviation of returns, and use of more sophisticated measures, such as beta (developed in Chapter 5), are the primary approaches available to individual investors.

3. Evaluate the risk-return behavior of each alternative investment to make sure that the return expected is reasonable given the level of risk. If other vehicles with lower levels of risk provide equal or greater returns, the investment is not acceptable.

4. Select the investments that offer the highest returns associated with the level of risk you are willing to take. As long as you get the highest return for your acceptable level of risk, you have made a "good investment."

Probably the most difficult step in this process is assessing risk. Aside from return and risk considerations, other factors, such as portfolio considerations, taxes, and liquidity affect the investment decision. We will develop portfolio concepts in Chapter 5 and, in later chapters, will look at all of these factors as they are related to specific investment vehicles.

CONCEPTS IN REVIEW

Answers available at
www.pearsonhighered.com/
gitman

4.9 Define *risk*. Explain what we mean by the *risk-return tradeoff*. What happens to the required return as risk increases? Explain.

4.10 Define and briefly discuss each of the following sources of risk.

   a. Business risk
   b. Financial risk
   c. Purchasing power risk
   d. Interest rate risk
   e. Liquidity risk
   f. Tax risk
   g. Event risk
   h. Market risk

4.11 Briefly describe standard deviation as a measure of risk or variability.

4.12 Differentiate among the three basic risk preferences: *risk-indifferent*, *risk-averse*, and *risk-seeking*. Which of these behaviors best describes most investors?

4.13 Describe the steps involved in the investment decision process. Be sure to mention how returns and risks can be evaluated together to determine acceptable investments.

myfinancelab

Here is what you should know after reading this chapter. **MyFinanceLab** will help you identify what you know, and where to go when you need to practice.

What You Should Know	Key Terms	Where To Practice
LG1 Review the concept of return, its components, the forces that affect the level of return, and historical returns. Return is the reward for investing. The total return provided by an investment includes income and capital gains (or losses). Return is commonly calculated on a historical basis and then used to project expected returns. The level of return depends on internal characteristics and external forces, which include the general level of price changes. Significant differences exist among the average annual rates of return realized over time on various types of security investments.	deflation, *p. 122* expected return, *p. 121* income, *p. 119* inflation, *p. 122* return, *p. 119* total return, *p. 120*	MyFinanceLab Study Plan 4.1 Excel Table 4.3
LG2 Discuss the role of time value of money in measuring return and defining a satisfactory investment. Because investors have opportunities to earn interest on their funds, money has a time value. Time value concepts should be considered when making investment decisions. Financial calculators and electronic spreadsheets can be used to streamline time-value calculations. A satisfactory investment is one for which the present value of its benefits equals or exceeds the present value of its costs.	satisfactory investment, *p. 123*	MyFinanceLab Study Plan 4.2 Excel Table 4.5
LG3 Describe real, risk-free, and required returns and the calculation and application of holding period return. The required return is the rate of return an investor must earn to be fully compensated for an investment's risk. It represents the sum of the real rate of return and the expected inflation premium (which together represent the risk-free rate), plus the risk premium. The risk premium varies depending on issue and issuer characteristics. The holding period return (HPR) is the return earned over a specified period of time. It is frequently used to compare returns earned in periods of one year or less.	expected inflation premium, *p. 125* holding period, *p. 126* holding period return (HPR), *p. 127* nominal return, *p. 125* paper return, *p. 127* real rate of return, *p. 125* realized return, *p. 127* required return, *p. 125* risk-free rate, *p. 125* risk premium, *p. 126*	MyFinanceLab Study Plan 4.3 Excel Table 4.6 Video Learning Aid for Problem P4.10
LG4 Explain the concept and the calculation of yield and how to find growth rates. Yield (or internal rate of return) is the compound annual rate of return earned on investments held for more than one year. If the yield is greater than or equal to the required return, the investment is acceptable. The concept of yield assumes that the investor will be able to earn interest at the calculated yield rate on all income from the investment. Present-value techniques can be used to find a rate of growth, which is the compound annual rate of change in the value of a stream of income, particularly dividends or earnings.	fully compounded rate of return, *p. 131* rate of growth, *p. 132* reinvestment rate, *p. 131* yield (internal rate of return), *p. 128*	MyFinanceLab Study Plan 4.4 Excel Table 4.7

What You Should Know	Key Terms	Where To Practice
LG5 Discuss the key sources of risk that might affect potential investment vehicles. Risk is the chance that the actual return from an investment will differ from what is expected. Total risk results from a combination of sources: business, financial, purchasing power, interest rate, liquidity, tax, market, and event risk. These risks have varying effects on different types of investments. The combined impact of any of the sources of risk in a given investment vehicle would be reflected in its risk premium.	business risk, *p. 134* financial risk, *p. 134* interest rate risk, *p. 135* liquidity risk, *p. 135* purchasing power risk, *p. 134* risk, *p. 133* risk-return tradeoff, *p. 133* tax risk, *p. 135*	MyFinanceLab Study Plan 4.5
LG6 Understand the risk of a single asset, risk assessment, and the steps that combine return and risk. The standard deviation measures the absolute risk of both single assets and portfolios of assets. Investors require higher returns as compensation for greater risk. Generally, each type of investment vehicle displays certain risk-return characteristics. Most investors are risk-averse: for a given increase in risk, they require an increase in return. Investors estimate the return and risk of each alternative and then select investments that offer the highest returns for the level of acceptable risk.	event risk, *p. 136* market risk, *p. 136* risk-averse, *p. 140* risk-indifferent, *p. 139* risk-seeking, *p. 140* standard deviation, *s*, *p. 137*	MyFinanceLab Study Plan 4.6 Excel Table 4.9

Log into **MyFinanceLab**, take a chapter test, and get a personalized Study Plan that tells you which concepts you understand and which ones you need to review. From there, **MyFinanceLab** will give you further practice, tutorials, animations, videos, and guided solutions.
Log into **www.myfinancelab.com**

Discussion Questions

LG1   **Q4.1** Choose a publicly traded company that has been listed on a major exchange or in the over-the-counter market for at least five years. Use any data source of your choice to find the annual cash dividend, if any, paid by the company in each of the past five calendar years. Also find the closing price of the stock at the end of each of the preceding six years.
     a. Calculate the return for each of the five 1-year periods.
     b. Graph the returns on a set of year (*x*-axis)-return (*y*-axis) axes.
     c. On the basis of the graph in part **b**, estimate the return for the coming year, and explain your answer.

LG2   **Q4.2** Estimate the amount of cash you will need each year over the next 20 years to live at the standard you desire. Also estimate the rate of return you can reasonably expect to earn annually, on average, during that 20-year period by investing in a common stock portfolio similar to the S&P 500.
     a. How large a single lump sum would you need today to provide the annual cash required to allow you to live at the desired standard over the next 20 years? (*Hint:* Be sure to use the appropriate discount rate.)

b. Would the lump sum calculated in part **a** be larger or smaller if you could earn a higher return during the 20-year period? Explain.

c. If you had the lump sum calculated in part **a** but decided to delay your planned retirement in 20 years for another three years, how much extra cash would you have accumulated over the three-year period if you could invest it to earn a 7% annual rate of return?

LG4 Q4.3 Access appropriate estimates of the expected inflation rate over the next year, and the current yield on 1-year risk-free securities (the yield on these securities is referred to as the *nominal* rate of interest). Use the data to estimate the current risk-free *real* rate of interest.

LG3 LG6 Q4.4 Choose three NYSE-listed stocks and maintain a record of their dividend payments, if any, and closing prices each week over the next six weeks.

a. At the end of the six-week period, calculate the 1-week holding period returns (HPRs) for each stock for each of the six weeks.

b. For each stock, average the six weekly HPRs calculated in part **a** and compare them.

c. Use the averages you computed in part **b** and compute the standard deviation of the six HPRs for each stock. Discuss the stocks' relative risk and return behavior. Did the stocks with the highest risk earn the greatest return?

Problems

All problems are available on **www.myfinancelab.com**

LG1 P4.1 How much would an investor earn on a stock purchased one year ago for $63 if it paid an annual cash dividend of $3.75 and had just been sold for $67.50? Would the investor have experienced a capital gain? Explain.

LG1 P4.2 An investor buys a bond for $10,000. The bond pays $300 interest every six months. After 18 months, the investor sells the bond for $9,500. Describe the types of income and/or loss the investor had.

LG1 P4.3 Assuming you purchased a share of stock for $50 one year ago, sold it today for $60, and during the year received three dividend payments totaling $2.70, calculate the following.

a. Income

b. Capital gain (or loss)

c. Total return
  (1) In dollars
  (2) As a percentage of the initial investment

LG1 P4.4 Assume you purchased a bond for $9,500. The bond pays $300 interest every six months. You sell the bond after 18 months for $10,000. Calculate the following:

a. Income

b. Capital gain or loss

c. Total return in dollars and as a percentage of the original investment

LG1 P4.5 Consider the historical data given in the accompanying table.

a. Calculate the total return (in dollars) for each year.

b. Indicate the level of return you would expect in 2012 and in 2013.

c. Comment on your forecast.

		Market Value (Price)	
Year	Income	Beginning	Ending
2007	$1.00	$30.00	$32.50
2008	1.20	32.50	35.00
2009	1.30	35.00	33.00
2010	1.60	33.00	40.00
2011	1.75	40.00	45.00

LG1 P4.6 Refer to the table in Problem 4.5. What is the total return in dollars and as a percentage of your original investment if you purchased 100 shares of the investment at the beginning of 2007 and sold it at the end of 2009?

LG3 P4.7 Given a real rate of interest of 3%, an expected inflation premium of 5%, and risk premiums for investments A and B of 3% and 5%, respectively, find the following.
a. The risk-free rate of return R_F
b. The required returns for investments A and B

LG3 P4.8 The risk-free rate is 7%, and expected inflation is 4.5%. If inflation expectations change such that future expected inflation rises to 5.5%, what will the new risk-free rate be?

LG3 P4.9 Calculate the holding period return (HPR) for the following two investment alternatives. Which, if any, of the return components is likely not to be realized if you continue to hold each of the investments beyond one year? Which vehicle would you prefer, assuming they are of equal risk? Explain.

| | Investment Vehicle | |
	X	Y
Cash received		
1st quarter	$1.00	$0
2nd quarter	1.20	0
3rd quarter	0	0
4th quarter	2.30	2.00
Investment value		
End of year	$29.00	$56.00
Beginning of year	30.00	50.00

LG3 P4.10 You are considering two investment alternatives. The first is a stock that pays quarterly dividends of $0.50 per share and is trading at $25 per share; you expect to sell the stock in six months for $27. The second is a stock that pays quarterly dividends of $0.60 per share and is trading at $27 per share; you expect to sell the stock in one year for $30. Which stock will provide the better annualized holding period return?

LG3 P4.11 You are considering purchasing a bond that pays annual interest of $50 per $1,000 of par value. The bond matures in one year, when you will collect the par value and the interest payment. If you can purchase this bond for $950, what is the holding period return?

LG4 P4.12 Assume you invest $5,000 today in an investment that promises to return $9,000 in exactly 10 years.
a. Use the present-value technique to estimate the yield on this investment.
b. If a minimum return of 9% is required, would you recommend this investment?

LG4 P4.13 You invest $7,000 in stock and receive $65, $70, $70, and $65 in dividends over the following four years. At the end of the four years, you sell the stock for $7,900. What was the yield on this investment?

LG4 P4.14 Your friend asks you to invest $10,000 in a business venture. Based on your estimates, you would receive nothing for four years, at the end of year 5 you would receive interest on the investment compounded annually at 8%, and at the end of year 6 you would receive $14,500. If your estimates are correct, what would be the yield on this investment?

LG4 P4.15 Use a financial calculator or an Excel spreadsheet to estimate the yield for each of the following investments.

Investment	Initial Investment	Future Value	End of the Year
A	$ 1,000	$ 1,200	5
B	10,000	20,000	7
C	400	2,000	20
D	3,000	4,000	6
E	5,500	25,000	30

LG4 **P4.16** Sara Holliday must earn a return of 10% on an investment that requires an initial outlay of $2,500 and promises to return $6,000 in eight years.

    a. Use present-value techniques to estimate the yield on this investment.

    b. On the basis of your finding in part **a**, should Sara make the proposed investment? Explain.

LG4 **P4.17** Use a financial calculator or an Excel spreadsheet to estimate the yield for each of the following two investments.

	Investment	
	A	B
Initial Investment	$8,500	$9,500
End of Year	Income	
1	$2,500	$2,000
2	2,500	2,500
3	2,500	3,000
4	2,500	3,500
5	2,500	4,000

LG4 **P4.18** Elliott Dumack must earn a minimum rate of return of 11% to be adequately compensated for the risk of the following investment.

Initial Investment	$14,000
End of Year	Income
1	$6,000
2	3,000
3	5,000
4	2,000
5	1,000

    a. Use present-value techniques to estimate the yield on this investment.

    b. On the basis of your finding in part **a**, should Elliott make the proposed investment? Explain.

LG4 **P4.19** Assume that an investment generates the following income stream and can be purchased at the beginning of 2011 for $1,000 and sold at the end of 2017 for $1,200. Estimate the yield for this investment. If a minimum return of 9% is required, would you recommend this investment? Explain.

End of Year	Income Stream
2011	$140
2012	120
2013	100
2014	80
2015	60
2016	40
2017	20

LG4 **P4.20** For each of the following streams of dividends, estimate the compound annual rate of growth between the earliest year for which a value is given and 2011.

	Dividend Stream		
Year	A	B	C
2002		$1.50	
2003		1.55	
2004		1.61	
2005		1.68	$2.50
2006		1.76	2.60
2007	$5.00	1.85	2.65
2008	5.60	1.95	2.65
2009	6.40	2.06	2.80
2010	7.20	2.17	2.85
2011	8.00	2.28	2.90

LG4 **P4.21** A company paid dividends of $1.00 per share in 2003, and just announced that it will pay $2.21 in 2010. Estimate the compound annual growth rate of the dividends.

LG4 **P4.22** A company reported net income in 2006 of $350 million. In 2010, the company expects net income to be $441.7 million. Estimate the annual compound growth rate of net income.

LG6 **P4.23** The historical returns for two investments—A and B—are summarized in the table below for the period 2007 to 2011. Use the data to answer the questions that follow.

	Investment	
	A	B
Year	Rate of Return	
2007	19%	8%
2008	1	10
2009	10	12
2010	26	14
2011	4	16
Average	12%	12%

a. On the basis of a review of the return data, which investment appears to be more risky? Why?

b. Calculate the standard deviation for each investment's returns.

c. On the basis of your calculations in part **b**, which investment is more risky? Compare this conclusion to your observation in part **a**.

Visit **www.myfinancelab.com** for web exercises, spreadsheets, and other online resources.

Case Problem 4.1   *Coates' Decision*

 LG2 LG4 Dave Coates, a 23-year-old mathematics teacher at Xavier High School, recently received a tax refund of $1,100. Because Dave didn't need this money for his current living expenses, he decided to make a long-term investment. After surveying a number of alternative investments costing no more than $1,100, Dave isolated 2 that seemed most suitable to his needs.

Each of the investments cost $1,050 and was expected to provide income over a 10-year period. Investment A provided a relatively certain stream of income. Dave was a little less certain of the income provided by investment B. From his search for suitable alternatives, Dave found that the appropriate discount rate for a relatively certain investment was 12%. Because he felt a bit uncomfortable with an investment like B, he estimated that such an investment would have to provide a return at least 4% *higher* than investment A. Although Dave planned to reinvest funds returned from the investments in other vehicles providing similar returns, he wished to keep the extra $50 ($1,100–$1,050) invested for the full 10 years in a savings account paying 5% interest compounded annually.

As he makes his investment decision, Dave has asked for your help in answering the questions that follow the expected return data for these investments.

	Expected Returns	
Year	A	B
2011	$150	$100
2012	150	150
2013	150	200
2014	150	250
2015	150	300
2016	150	350
2017	150	300
2018	150	250
2019	150	200
2020	1,150	150

Questions

a. Assuming that investments A and B are equally risky and using the 12% discount rate, apply the present-value technique to assess the acceptability of each investment and to determine the preferred investment. Explain your findings.

b. Recognizing that investment B is more risky than investment A, reassess the 2 alternatives, adding the 4% risk premium to the 12% discount rate for investment A and therefore applying a 16% discount rate to investment B. Compare your findings relative to acceptability and preference to those found for question **a**.

c. From your findings in questions **a** and **b**, indicate whether the yield for investment A is above or below 12% and whether that for investment B is above or below 16%. Explain.

d. Use the present-value technique to estimate the yield on each investment. Compare your findings and contrast them with your response to question **c**.

e. From the information given, which, if either, of the two investments would you recommend that Dave make? Explain your answer.

f. Indicate to Dave how much money the extra $50 will have grown to by the end of 2018, assuming he makes no withdrawals from the savings account.

Case Problem 4.2   *The Risk-Return Tradeoff: Molly O'Rourke's Stock Purchase Decision*

LG3 LG6   Over the past 10 years, Molly O'Rourke has slowly built a diversified portfolio of common stock. Currently her portfolio includes 20 different common stock issues and has a total market value of $82,500.

Molly is at present considering the addition of 50 shares of one of two common stock issues— X or Y. To assess the return and risk of each of these issues, she has gathered dividend income and share price data for both over each of the last 10 years (2001–2010). Molly's investigation of the outlook for these issues suggests that each will, on average, tend to behave in the future just as it has in the past. She therefore believes that the expected return can be estimated by finding the average holding period return (HPR) over the past 10 years for each of the stocks. The historical dividend income and stock price data collected by Molly are given in the accompanying table.

| | | Stock X | | | Stock Y | |
| | | Share Price | | | Share Price | |
Year	Dividend Income	Beginning	Ending	Dividend Income	Beginning	Ending
2001	$1.00	$20.00	$22.00	$1.50	$20.00	$20.00
2002	1.50	22.00	21.00	1.60	20.00	20.00
2003	1.40	21.00	24.00	1.70	20.00	21.00
2004	1.70	24.00	22.00	1.80	21.00	21.00
2005	1.90	22.00	23.00	1.90	21.00	22.00
2006	1.60	23.00	26.00	2.00	22.00	23.00
2007	1.70	26.00	25.00	2.10	23.00	23.00
2008	2.00	25.00	24.00	2.20	23.00	24.00
2009	2.10	24.00	27.00	2.30	24.00	25.00
2010	2.20	27.00	30.00	2.40	25.00	25.00

Questions

a. Determine the holding period return (HPR) for each stock in each of the preceding 10 years. Find the expected return for each stock, using the approach specified by Molly.

b. Use the HPRs and expected return calculated in question a to find the standard deviation of the HPRs for each stock over the 10-year period 2001 to 2010.

c. Use your findings to evaluate and discuss the return and risk associated with stocks X and Y. Which stock seems preferable? Explain.

d. Ignoring her existing portfolio, what recommendations would you give Molly with regard to stocks X and Y?

Excel with Spreadsheets

From her Investment Analysis class, Laura has been given an assignment to evaluate several securities on a risk-return tradeoff basis. The specific securities to be researched are International Business Machines, Helmerich & Payne, Inc., and the S&P 500 Index. The respective ticker symbols for the stocks are IBM and HP. She finds the following (fictional) data on the securities in question. It is as follows:

Year	2005	2006	2007	2008	2009	2010
$Price_{IBM}$	$49.38	$91.63	$112.25	$112.00	$107.89	$ 92.68
$Dividend_{IBM}$	$ 0.40	$ 0.44	$ 0.48	$ 0.52	$ 0.56	$ 0.64
$Price_{HP}$	$25.56	$17.56	$ 23.50	$ 47.81	$ 30.40	$ 27.93
$Dividend_{HP}$	$ 0.28	$ 0.28	$ 0.28	$ 0.30	$ 0.30	$ 0.32
$Value_{S\&P}$	980.3	1,279.6	1,394.6	1,366.0	1,130.2	1,121.8

Note: The value of the S&P 500 Index includes dividends.

Questions

Part One

a. Use the data that Laura has found on the three securities and **create a spreadsheet** to calculate the holding period return (HPR) for each year and the average return over a five-year period. Specifically, the HPR will be based upon five unique periods of one year (i.e., 2005 to 2006, 2006 to 2007, 2007 to 2008, 2008 to 2009, 2009 to 2010). Use the following formula:

$$\text{HPR} = [\text{Inc} + (V_n - V_0)]/V_0$$

Where

> Inc = income during period
> V_n = ending investment value
> V_0 = beginning investment value

Part Two

Create a spreadsheet similar to the spreadsheet for Table 4.9 (on page 138), which can be viewed at www.myfinancelab.com, in order to evaluate the risk-return tradeoff.

b. Calculate the standard deviations of the returns for IBM, HP, and the S&P 500 Index.
c. What industries are associated with IBM and HP?
d. Based on your answer in part **c** and your results for the average return and the standard deviation, what conclusions can Laura make about investing in either IBM or HP?

Chapter-Opening Problem

The table below shows the annual change in the average U.S. home price from 1999–2008 according to the S&P/Case-Shiller index. Calculate the average annual return and its standard deviation. Compare this to the average return and standard deviation for ExxonMobil and Panera Bread shown in Table 4.9. In terms of average return and standard deviation, how does residential real estate compare as an investment relative to those two common stocks?

Year	% Change
1999	10.8%
2000	14.1%
2001	7.9%
2002	12.2%
2003	11.4%
2004	16.2%
2005	15.5%
2006	0.6%
2007	−9.0%
2008	−18.6%

The Time Value of Money

Imagine that at age 25 you begin making annual cash deposits of $1,000 into a savings account that pays 5% annual interest. After 40 years, at age 65, you will have made deposits totaling $40,000 (40 years × $1,000 per year). Assuming you made no withdrawals, what do you think your account balance will be—$50,000? $75,000? $100,000? The answer is none of the above. Your $40,000 will have grown to nearly $121,000! Why? Because the time value of money allows the deposits to earn interest, and that interest also earns interest over the 40 years. **Time value of money** refers to the fact that as long as an opportunity exists to earn interest, the value of money is affected by the point in time when the money is received.

Interest: The Basic Return to Savers

A savings account at a bank is one of the most basic forms of investment. The saver receives interest in exchange for placing idle funds in an account. **Interest** can be viewed as the "rent" paid by a borrower for use of the lender's money. The saver will experience neither a capital gain nor a capital loss, because the value of the investment (the initial deposit) will change only by the amount of interest earned. For the saver, the interest earned over a given time frame is that period's income.

Simple Interest

The income paid on investment vehicles that pay interest (such as CDs and bonds) is most often calculated using **simple interest**—interest paid only on the initial deposit for the amount of time it is held. For example, if you held a $100 initial deposit in an account paying 6% interest for $1\frac{1}{2}$ years, you would earn $9 in interest ($1\frac{1}{2}$ × 0.06 × $100) over this period. Had you withdrawn $50 at the end of half a year, the total interest earned over the $1\frac{1}{2}$ years would be $6. You would earn $3 interest on $100 for the first half-year ($\frac{1}{2}$ × 0.06 × $100) and $3 interest on $50 for the next full year (1 × 0.06 × $50).

When an investment earns simple interest, the stated rate of interest is the **true rate of interest** (**return**). This is the actual rate of interest earned. In the foregoing example, the true rate of interest is 6%. Because the interest rate reflects the rate at which current income is earned regardless of the size of the deposit, it is a useful measure of current income.

Compound Interest

Compound interest is interest paid not only on the initial deposit but also on any interest accumulated from one period to the next. This is the method typically used by savings institutions. When interest is compounded annually over a single year, compound

TABLE 4A.1	Savings Account Balance Data (5% interest compounded annually)			EXCEL With Spreadsheets
Date	(1) Deposit (Withdrawal)	(2) Beginning Account Balance	(3) 0.05 × (2) Interest for Year	(4) (2) + (3) Ending Account Balance
1/1/2010	$1,000	$1,000.00	$50.00	$1,050.00
1/1/2011	(300)	750.00	37.50	$787.50
1/1/2012	1,000	1,787.50	89.38	$1,876.88

and simple interest calculations provide similar results. In such a case, the stated interest rate and the true interest rate are equal.

The data in Table 4A.1 illustrate compound interest. In this case, the interest earned each year is left on deposit rather than withdrawn. The $50 of interest earned on the $1,000 initial deposit during 2010 becomes part of the beginning (initial) balance on which interest is paid in 2011, and so on. *Note that simple interest is used in the compounding process;* that is, interest is paid only on the initial balance held during the given time period.

When an investment earns compound interest, the stated and true interest rates are equal only when interest is compounded annually. In general, *the more frequently interest is compounded at a stated rate, the higher the true rate of interest.*

The interest calculations for the deposit data in Table 4A.1, assuming that interest is compounded semiannually (twice a year), are shown in Table 4A.2. The interest for each six-month period is found by multiplying the beginning (initial) balance for the six months by half of the stated 5% interest rate (see column 3 of Table 4A.2). You can see that larger returns are associated with more frequent compounding: Compare the end-of-2012 account balance at 5% compounded annually with the end-of-2012 account balance at 5% compounded semiannually. The semiannual compounding results in a higher balance ($1,879.19 versus $1,876.88). Clearly, with semiannual compounding, the true rate of interest is greater than the 5% annually compounded rate. Table 4A.3 (on page 153) shows the true rates of interest associated with a 5% stated rate and various compounding frequencies.

Continuous compounding calculates interest by compounding over the smallest possible interval of time. It results in the maximum true rate of interest that can be achieved with a given stated rate of interest. Table 4A.3 shows that the more frequently interest is compounded, the higher the true rate of interest. Because of the impact that differences in compounding frequencies have on return, you should evaluate the true rate of interest associated with various alternatives before making a deposit.

TABLE 4A.2	Savings Account Balance Data (5% interest compounded semiannually)			EXCEL With Spreadsheets
Date	(1) Deposit (Withdrawal)	(2) Beginning Account Balance	(3) 0.05 × 1/2 × (2) Interest for 6 Months	(4) (2) + (3) Ending Account Balance
1/1/2010	$1,000	$1,000.00	$25.00	$1,025.00
1/1/2010		1,025.00	25.63	1,050.63
1/1/2011	(300)	750.00	18.77	769.40
1/1/2011		769.40	19.24	788.64
1/1/2012	1,000	1,788.64	44.72	1,833.36
1/1/2012		1,833.36	45.83	1,879.19

TABLE 4A.3	True Rate of Interest for Various Compounding Frequencies (5% stated rate of interest)		
Compounding Frequency	True Rate of Interest	Compounding Frequency	True Rate of Interest
Annually	5.000%	Monthly	5.120%
Semiannually	5.063	Weekly	5.125
Quarterly	5.094	Continuously	5.127

Computational Aids for Use in Time Value Calculations

Time-consuming calculations are often involved in adjusting for the time value of money. Although you should understand the concepts and mathematics underlying these calculations, the application of time value techniques can be streamlined. We will demonstrate the use of financial calculators and spreadsheets as computational aids.

Financial Calculators

We can also use financial calculators for time value computations. Generally, *financial calculators* include numerous preprogrammed financial routines. Throughout this book, we show the keystrokes for various financial computations.

We focus primarily on the keys pictured and defined in Figure 4A.1. We typically use four of the five keys in the left column, plus the compute (**CPT**) key. One of the four keys represents the unknown value being calculated. (Occasionally, all five of the keys are used, with one representing the unknown value.) The keystrokes on some of the more sophisticated calculators are menu-driven: After you select the appropriate routine, the calculator prompts you to input each value; on these calculators, a compute key is not needed to obtain a solution. Regardless, any calculator with the basic time value functions can be used in lieu of financial tables. The keystrokes for other financial calculators are explained in the reference guides that accompany them.

Once you understand the basic underlying concepts, you probably will want to use a calculator to streamline routine financial calculations. With a little practice, you can increase both the speed and the accuracy of your financial computations. Note that because of a calculator's greater precision, slight differences are likely to exist between values calculated by using financial tables and those found with a financial calculator.

FIGURE 4A.1

Calculator Keys

Important financial keys on the typical calculator.

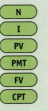

N — Number of periods
I — Interest rate per period
PV — Present value
PMT — Amount of payment (used only for annuities)
FV — Future value
CPT — Compute key used to initiate financial calculation once all values are input

Remember that *conceptual understanding of the material is the objective.* An ability to solve problems with the aid of a calculator does not necessarily reflect such an understanding, so don't just settle for answers. Work with the material until you are sure you also understand the concepts.

Computers and Spreadsheets

Like financial calculators, computers and spreadsheets have built-in routines that simplify time value calculations. We provide in the text a number of spreadsheet solutions that identify the cell entries for calculating time values. The value for each variable is entered in a cell in the spreadsheet, and the calculation is programmed using an equation that links the individual cells. If you change values of the variables, the solution automatically changes. In the spreadsheet solutions in this book, we show at the bottom of the spreadsheet the equation that determines the calculation.

The ability to use spreadsheets has become a prime skill for today's investors. As the saying goes, "Get aboard the bandwagon, or get run over." The spreadsheet solutions we present in this book will help you climb up onto that bandwagon!

We now turn to the key time value concepts, beginning with future value.

Future Value: An Extension of Compounding

Future value is the amount to which a current deposit will grow over a period of time when it is placed in an account paying compound interest. Consider a deposit of $1,000 that is earning 8% (0.08 in decimal form) compounded annually. The following calculation yields the future value of this deposit at the end of one year.

Equation 4A.1

$$\text{Future value at end of year 1} = \$1,000 \times (1 + 0.08) = \underline{\underline{\$1,080}}$$

If the money were left on deposit for another year, 8% interest would be paid on the account balance of $1,080. Thus, at the end of the second year, there would be $1,166.40 in the account. This amount would represent the beginning-of-year balance of $1,080 plus 8% of the $1,080 ($86.40) in interest. The future value at the end of the second year would be calculated as follows.

Equation 4A.2

$$\text{Future value at end of year 2} = \$1,080 \times (1 + 0.08) = \underline{\underline{\$1,166.40}}$$

To find the future value of the $1,000 at the end of year *n*, the procedure illustrated above would be repeated *n* times. Future values can be determined either mathematically or by using a financial calculator, or a spreadsheet. Here we demonstrate use of a calculator and an Excel spreadsheet.

Input	Function
1000	PV
2	N
8	I
	CPT
	FV

Solution
1,166.40

CALCULATOR USE* A financial calculator can be used to calculate the future value directly. **First punch in $1,000 and depress **PV**; next punch in 2 and depress **N**; then punch in 8 and depress **I**.† Finally, to calculate the future value, depress **CPT** and then **FV**. The future value of $1,166.40 should appear on the calculator display, as shown in the art at the left. On many calculators, this value will be preceded by a minus sign (−1,166.40). *If a minus sign appears on your calculator, ignore it here as well as in all other "Calculator Use" illustrations in this text.*‡

SPREADSHEET USE The future value of the single amount also can be calculated as shown on the following Excel spreadsheet.

	A	B
1	**FUTURE VALUE OF A SINGLE AMOUNT**	
2	Present value	$1,000
3	Interest rate, pct per year compounded annually	8%
4	Number of years	2
5	Future value	$1,166.40

Entry in Cell B5 is =FV(B3,B4,0,−B2,0).
The minus sign appears before B2 because the present value is an outflow (i.e., the initial deposit).

Future Value of an Annuity

Input	Function
1000	PMT
8	N
6	I
	CPT
	FV

Solution
9,897.47

An **annuity** is a stream of equal cash flows that occur at equal intervals over time. Receiving $1,000 per year at the end of each of the next eight years is an example of an annuity. The cash flows can be *inflows* of returns earned from an investment or *outflows* of funds invested (deposited) to earn future returns.

Investors are sometimes interested in finding the future value of an annuity. Their concern is typically with what's called an **ordinary annuity**—one for which the cash flows occur at the *end* of each period. Here we can simplify our calculations by using a financial calculator or an Excel spreadsheet.

---

*Many calculators allow the user to set the number of payments per year. Most of these calculators are preset for monthly payments—12 payments per year. Because we work primarily with annual payments—one payment per year—it is important *to be sure that your calculator is set for one payment per year.* And although most calculators are preset to recognize that all payments occur at the end of the period, it is important *to make sure that your calculator is correctly set on the END mode.* Consult the reference guide that accompanies your calculator for instructions for setting these values.

**To avoid including previous data in current calculations, *always clear all registers of your calculator before inputting values and making each computation.*

†The known values *can be punched into the calculator in any order.* The order specified in this as well as other demonstrations of calculator use included in this text merely reflects convenience and personal preference.

‡The calculator differentiates inflows from outflows with a negative sign. For example, in the problem just demonstrated, the $1,000 present value (**PV**), because it was keyed as a positive number (1000), is considered an inflow or deposit. Therefore, the calculated future value (**FV**) of −1166.40 is preceded by a minus sign to show that it is the resulting outflow or withdrawal. Had the $1,000 present value been keyed in as a negative number (−1,000), the future value of $1,166.40 would have been displayed as a positive number (1,166.40). Simply stated, *present value (PV) and future value (FV) cash flows will have opposite signs.*

CALCULATOR USE When using a financial calculator to find the future value of an annuity, we key in the annual deposit using the **PMT** key (rather than the **PV** key, which we used to find the future value of a single deposit). Use of the **PMT** key tells the calculator that a stream of **N** (the number of years input) end-of-year deposits in the amount of **PMT** dollars represents the deposit stream.

Using the calculator inputs shown on page 155, we find the future value of the $1,000, eight-year ordinary annuity earning a 6% annual rate of interest to be $9,897.47.

SPREADSHEET USE We also can calculate the future value of the ordinary annuity as shown on the following Excel spreadsheet.

	A	B
1	**FUTURE VALUE OF AN ORDINARY ANNUITY**	
2	Annual payment	$1,000
3	Annual rate of interest, compounded annually	6%
4	Number of years	8
5	Future value of an ordinary annuity	$9,897.47

Entry in Cell B5 is =FV(B3,B4,−B2)
The minus sign appears before B2 because
the annual payment is a cash outflow.

Present Value: An Extension of Future Value

Present value is the inverse of future value. That is, rather than measuring the value of a present amount at some future date, **present value** expresses the *current value of a future sum*. By applying present-value techniques, we can calculate the *value today* of a sum to be received at some future date.

When determining the present value of a future sum, we are answering the basic question, "How much would have to be deposited today into an account paying $i\%$ interest in order to equal a specified sum to be received so many years in the future?" The applicable interest rate when we are finding present value is commonly called the **discount rate** (or *opportunity cost*). It represents the annual rate of return that could be earned currently on a similar investment.

The basic present-value calculation is best illustrated using a simple example. Imagine that you are offered an opportunity that will provide you, one year from today, with exactly $1,000. If you could earn 8% on similar types of investments, how much is the most you would pay for this opportunity? In other words, what is the present value of $1,000 to be received one year from now, discounted at 8%? Letting x equal the present value, we can use Equation 4A.3 to describe this situation.

Equation 4A.3
$$x \times (1 + 0.08) = \$1,000$$

Solving Equation 4A.3 for x, we get:

Equation 4A.4
$$x = \frac{\$1,000}{(1 + 0.08)} = \$925.93$$

Thus, the present value of $1,000 to be received one year from now, discounted at 8%, is $925.93. In other words, $925.93 deposited today into an account paying 8% interest will accumulate to $1,000 in one year.

The calculations involved in finding the present value of sums to be received in the distant future are more complex than those for a one-year investment. Here we use a financial calculator or an Excel spreadsheet.

CALCULATOR USE Using the financial calculator inputs shown at the left, we find the present value of $500 to be received seven years from now, discounted at 6%, to be $332.53.

SPREADSHEET USE The present value of the single future amount also can be calculated as shown on the following Excel spreadsheet.

	A	B
1	**PRESENT VALUE OF A SINGLE FUTURE AMOUNT**	
2	Future value	$500
3	Interest rate, pct per year compounded annually	6%
4	Number of years	7
5	Present value	$332.53
	Entry in Cell B5 is =–PV(B3,B4,0,B2). The minus sign appears before PV to change the present value to a positive amount.	

The Present Value of a Stream of Returns

In the preceding paragraphs we illustrated the technique for finding the present value of a single sum to be received at some future date. Because the returns from a given investment are likely to be received at *various* future dates rather than as a single lump sum, we also need to be able to find the present value of a *stream of returns*.

A stream of returns can be viewed as a package of single-sum returns; it may be classified as a mixed stream or an annuity. A **mixed stream** of returns is one that exhibits no special pattern. As noted earlier, an *annuity* is a stream of equal periodic returns. Table 4A.4 shows the end-of-year returns illustrating each of these types of patterns. To find the present value of each of these streams (measured at the *beginning* of 2011), we must calculate the total of the present values of the individual annual returns. Because shortcuts can be used for an annuity, we will illustrate calculation of the present value of each type of return stream separately.

TABLE 4A.4	Mixed and Annuity Return Streams	EXCEL With Spreadsheets
	Returns	
End of Year	Mixed Stream	Annuity
2011	$30	$50
2012	40	50
2013	50	50
2014	60	50
2015	70	50

TABLE A4.5   Mixed-Stream Present-Value Calculation

Year	End of Year	(1) Income	(2) Present-Value Calculation at 9%	(3) Present Value at 9%
2011	1	$30	$30/(1 + 0.09)^1$	$ 27.52
2012	2	40	$40/(1 + 0.09)^2$	$ 33.67
2013	3	50	$50/(1 + 0.09)^3$	$ 38.61
2014	4	60	$60/(1 + 0.09)^4$	$ 42.51
2015	5	70	$70/(1 + 0.09)^5$	$ 45.50
			Total Present Value	$ 187.80

0.09 column (2) and (3) discount rate

Present Value of a Mixed Stream

To find the present value of the mixed stream of returns given in Table 4A.4, we must find and then total the present values of the individual returns. Assuming a 9% discount rate, we can streamline the calculation of the present value of the mixed stream using financial tables, a financial calculator, or an Excel spreadsheet.

CALCULATOR USE   You can use a financial calculator to find the present value of each individual return, as demonstrated on page 157. You then sum the present values to get the present value of the stream. However, most financial calculators have a function that allows you to punch in *all returns* (typically referred to as *cash flows*), specify the discount rate, and then directly calculate the present value of the entire return stream. Table 4A.5 shows the present value of each payment in the stream as well as the entire sum.

SPREADSHEET USE   The present value of the mixed stream of returns also can be calculated as shown on the following Excel spreadsheet.

	A	B
1	PRESENT VALUE OF A MIXED STREAM OF RETURNS	
2	Discount Rate, pct/year	9%
3	Year	Year-End Return
4	1	$30
5	2	$40
6	3	$50
7	4	$60
8	5	$70
9	Present value	$187.80
	Entry in Cell B9 is =NPV(B2,B4:B8).	

Investing about $188 would provide exactly a 9% return.

Present Value of an Annuity

We can find the present value of an annuity in the same way as the present value of a mixed stream. Fortunately, however, there are simpler approaches. Here we simplify our calculations by using either a financial calculator or an Excel spreadsheet.

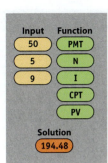

Input	Function
50	PMT
5	N
9	I
	CPT
	PV

Solution
194.48

CALCULATOR USE Using the calculator inputs shown at the left, we find the present value of the $50, five-year ordinary annuity of returns, discounted at a 9% annual rate, to be $194.48. (*Note:* Because the return stream is an annuity, the annual return is input using the **PMT** key rather than the **FV** key, which we used for finding the present value of a single return.) The value obtained with the calculator is slightly more accurate than the answer found using the table.

SPREADSHEET USE The present value of the annuity of returns also can be calculated as shown on the following Excel spreadsheet.

	A	B
1	**PRESENT VALUE OF ANNUITY RETURNS**	
2	Annual return	$50
3	Annual discount rate, compounded annually	9%
4	Number of years	5
5	Present value of an ordinary annuity	$194.48
	Entry in Cell B5 is =PV(B3,B4,–B2). The minus sign appears before B2 because the annual return is a cash outflow.	

CONCEPTS IN REVIEW

Answers available at
www.pearsonhighered.com/gitman

4A.1 What is the *time value of money?* Explain why an investor should be able to earn a positive return.

4A.2 Define, discuss, and contrast the following terms.

a. Interest   b. Simple interest
c. Compound interest   d. True rate of interest (or return)

4A.3 When interest is compounded more frequently than annually at a stated rate, what happens to the *true rate of interest?* Under what condition would the stated and true rates of interest be equal? What is *continuous compounding?*

4A.4 Describe, compare, and contrast the concepts of *future value* and *present value.* Explain the role of the *discount rate* in calculating present value.

4A.5 What is an *annuity?* How can calculation of the future value of an annuity be simplified? What about the present value of an annuity?

4A.6 What is a *mixed stream* of returns? Describe the procedure used to find the present value of such a stream.

Here is what you should know after reading this chapter. **MyFinanceLab** will help you identify what you know, and where to go when you need to practice.

What You Should Know	Key Terms	Where To Practice
Because investors have opportunities to earn interest on their funds, money has a time value. Interest can be applied using either simple interest or compound interest. The more frequently interest is compounded at a stated rate, the higher the true rate of interest. Financial tables, financial calculators, and computers and spreadsheets can be used to streamline time-value calculations. The future value of a present sum or an annuity can be found using compound interest concepts. The present value of a future sum is the amount that would have to be deposited today, into an account earning interest at a given rate, to accumulate the specified future sum. The present value of streams of future returns can be found by adding the present values of the individual returns. When the stream is an annuity, its present value can be more simply calculated.	annuity, *p. 155* compound interest, *p. 151* continuous compounding, *p. 152* discount rate, *p. 156* future value, *p. 154* interest, *p. 151* mixed stream, *p. 157* ordinary annuity, *p. 155* present value, *p. 156* simple interest, *p. 151* time value of money, *p. 151* true rate of interest (return), *p. 151*	Excel Tables 4A.1, 4A.2, 4A.4, 4A.5 Video Learning Aid for Problem P4A.12

Log into **MyFinanceLab**, take a chapter test, and get a personalized Study Plan that tells you which concepts you understand and which ones you need to review. From there, **MyFinanceLab** will give you further practice, tutorials, animations, videos, and guided solutions.
Log into **www.myfinancelab.com**

Problems

All problems are available on **www.myfinancelab.com**

P4A.1 For each of the savings account transactions in the accompanying table, calculate the following.

    a. End-of-year account balance. (Assume that the account balance at December 31, 2010, is zero.)

    b. Annual interest, using 6% simple interest and assuming all interest is withdrawn from the account as it is earned.

    c. True rate of interest, and compare it to the stated rate of interest. Discuss your finding.

Date	Deposit (Withdrawal)	Date	Deposit (Withdrawal)
1/1/11	$5,000	1/1/13	$2,000
1/1/12	(4,000)	1/1/14	3,000

P4A.2 Using a financial calculator or spreadsheet, calculate the following.
a. The future value of a $300 deposit left in an account paying 7% annual interest for 12 years.
b. The future value at the end of six years of an $800 *annual* end-of-year deposit into an account paying 7% annual interest.

P4A.3 For each of the following initial investment amounts, calculate the future value at the end of the given investment period if interest is compounded annually at the specified rate of return over the given investment period.

Investment	Investment Amount	Rate of Return	Investment Period
A	$ 200	5%	20 years
B	4,500	8	7
C	10,000	9	10
D	25,000	10	12
E	37,000	11	5

P4A.4 Using a financial calculator or spreadsheet, calculate the future value in two years of $10,000 invested today in an account that pays a stated annual interest rate of 12%, compounded monthly.

P4A.5 For each of the following annual deposits into an account paying the stated annual interest rate over the specified deposit period, calculate the future value of the *annuity* at the end of the given deposit period.

Deposit	Amount of Annual Deposit	Interest Rate	Deposit Period
A	$ 2,500	8%	10 years
B	500	12	6
C	1,000	20	5
D	12,000	6	8
E	4,000	14	30

P4A.6 If you deposit $1,000 into an account at the end of each of the next five years, and the account pays an annual interest rate of 6%, how much will be in the account after five years?

P4A.7 If you could earn 9% on similar-risk investments, what is the least you would accept at the end of a six-year period, given the following amounts and timing of your investment?
a. Invest $5,000 as a lump sum today.
b. Invest $2,000 at the end of *each* of the next five years.
c. Invest a lump sum of $3,000 today and $1,000 at the end of *each* of the next five years.
d. Invest $900 at the end of years 1, 3, and 5.

P4A.8 For each of the following investments, calculate the present value of the future sum, using the specified discount rate and assuming the sum will be received at the end of the given year.

Investment	Future Sum	Discount Rate	End of Year
A	$ 7,000	12%	4
B	28,000	8	20
C	10,000	14	12
D	150,000	11	6
E	45,000	20	8

P4A.9 A Florida state savings bond can be converted to $1,000 at maturity eight years from purchase. If the state bonds are to be competitive with U.S. savings bonds, which pay 6% interest compounded annually, at what price will the state's bonds sell, assuming they make no cash payments prior to maturity?

P4A.10 Referring to Problem 4A.9 above, at what price would the bond sell if U.S. savings bonds were paying 8% interest compounded annually? Compare your answer to your answer to the preceding problem.

P4A.11 How much should you be willing to pay for a lump sum of $10,000 five years from now if you can earn 3% every six months on other similar investments?

P4A.12 Find the present value of each of the following streams of income, assuming a 12% discount rate.

A		B		C	
End of Year	Income	End of Year	Income	End of Year	Income
1	$2,200	1	$10,000	1–5	$10,000/yr
2	3,000	2–5	5,000/yr	6–10	8,000/yr
3	4,000	6	7,000		
4	6,000				
5	8,000				

P4A.13 Consider the streams of income given in the following table.
    a. Find the present value of each income stream, using a 15% discount rate.
    b. Compare the calculated present values and discuss them in light of the fact that the undiscounted total income amounts to $10,000 in each case.

	Income Stream	
End of Year	A	B
1	$ 4,000	$ 1,000
2	3,000	2,000
3	2,000	3,000
4	1,000	4,000
Total	$10,000	$10,000

P4A.14 For each of the investments below, calculate the present value of the *annual* end-of-year returns at the specified discount rate over the given period.

Investment	Annual Returns	Discount Rate	Period
A	$ 1,200	7%	3 years
B	5,500	12	15
C	700	20	9
D	14,000	5	7
E	2,200	10	5

P4A.15 Congratulations! You have won the lottery! Would you rather have $1 million at the end of each of the next 20 years or $15 million today? (Assume an 8% discount rate.)

P4A.16 Using a financial calculator or an Excel spreadsheet, calculate the following.
    a. The present value of $500 to be received four years from now, using an 11% discount rate.
    b. The present value of the following end-of-year income streams, using a 9% discount rate and assuming it is now the beginning of 2012.

End of Year	Income Stream A	Income Stream B
2012	$80	$140
2013	80	120
2014	80	100
2014	80	80
2016	80	60
2017	80	40
2018	80	20

P4A.17 Terri Allessandro has an opportunity to make any of the following investments. The purchase price, the amount of its lump-sum future value, and its year of receipt are given below for each investment. Terri can earn a 10% rate of return on investments similar to those currently under consideration. Evaluate each investment to determine whether it is satisfactory and make an investment recommendation to Terri.

Investment	Purchase Price	Future Value	Year of Receipt
A	$18,000	$30,000	5
B	600	3,000	20
C	3,500	10,000	10
D	1,000	15,000	40

P4A.18 Kent Weitz wishes to assess whether the following two investments are satisfactory. Use his required return (discount rate) of 17% to evaluate each investment. Make an investment recommendation to Kent.

	Investment	
	A	B
Purchase price	$13,000	$8,500
End of Year	Income Stream	
1	$2,500	$4,000
2	3,500	3,500
3	4,500	3,000
4	5,000	1,000
5	5,500	500

P4A.19 You purchased a car using some cash and borrowing $15,000 (the present value) for 50 months at 12% per year. Calculate the monthly payment (annuity).

P4A.20 Referring to Problem 4A.19 above, assume you have made ten payments. What is the balance (present value) of your loan?

CHAPTER 5

Modern Portfolio Concepts

LEARNING GOALS

After studying this chapter, you should be able to:

LG1 Understand portfolio objectives and the procedures used to calculate portfolio return and standard deviation.

LG2 Discuss the concepts of correlation and diversification, and the key aspects of international diversification.

LG3 Describe the components of risk and the use of beta to measure risk.

LG4 Explain the capital asset pricing model (CAPM)—conceptually, mathematically, and graphically.

LG5 Review the traditional and modern approaches to portfolio management.

LG6 Describe portfolio betas, the risk-return tradeoff, and reconciliation of the two approaches to portfolio management.

United Rentals Inc. (URI) rents construction and industrial equipment to contractors, businesses, governments, and individuals. The company specializes in heavy equipment such as earth-moving machines and forklifts. During the recession that began in 2007, many companies found that they did not have enough work to do to keep the machines they already owned running, so naturally the demand for rental equipment suffered. URI stock reached a 2007 peak of just over $35 per share in May, but after that began a long slide, hitting bottom at $2.52 in March 2009.

That spring, the economy began to show signs of life, and URI stock surged, rising nearly 200% from its low point by August 2009. Heiko Ihle, a stock analyst for the Gabelli & Co. money management firm, issued a "buy" rating on URI despite the fact that the company had high leverage (meaning that it borrowed a lot of money to finance its operations). Ihle noted that URI stock had a high beta, meaning that it moved sharply when the broader market shifted.

In this chapter we continue to explore the tradeoff between risk and return, and we'll see that a stock's beta—it's sensitivity to movements in the overall stock market—has a big effect on both the stock's risk and the return that it offers investors.

(Sources: Yahoo! Finance; U.S. Hot Stocks: Legg Mason, JDA Software Active in Late Trading, July 20, 2009; The Wall Street Journal Digital Network, online.wsj.com/article/ BT-CO-20090720-713541.html)

Principles of Portfolio Planning

LG1 **LG2** Investors benefit from holding portfolios of investments rather than single investment vehicles. Without necessarily sacrificing returns, investors who hold portfolios can reduce risk. Surprisingly, the risk of the portfolio may be less than the risks of the individual assets that make up the portfolio. In other words, when it comes to portfolios and risk, the whole is less than the sum of its parts!

As defined in Chapter 1, a *portfolio* is a collection of investments assembled to meet one or more investment goals. Of course, different investors have different objectives for their portfolios. The primary goal of a **growth-oriented portfolio** is long-term price appreciation. An **income-oriented portfolio** is designed to produce regular dividends and interest payments.

Portfolio Objectives

Setting portfolio objectives involves definite tradeoffs, such as the tradeoff between risk and return or between potential price appreciation and income. How you evaluate these tradeoffs will depend on your tax bracket, current income needs, and ability to bear risk. The key point is that your portfolio objectives must be established *before* you begin to invest.

The ultimate goal of an investor is an **efficient portfolio**, one that provides the highest return for a given level of risk. Efficient portfolios aren't necessarily easy to identify. You usually must search out investment alternatives to get the best combinations of risk and return.

Portfolio Return and Standard Deviation

The first step in forming a portfolio is to analyze the characteristics of the securities that an investor might include in the portfolio. Two of the most important characteristics to examine are the returns that each asset might be expected to earn and the uncertainty surrounding that expected return. As a starting point, we will examine historical data to see what returns stocks have earned in the past and how much those returns have fluctuated to get a feel for what the future might hold.

The return on a portfolio is calculated as a weighted average of returns on the assets (i.e., the investments) that make up the portfolio. You can calculate the portfolio return, r_p, by using Equation 5.1. The portfolio return depends on the returns of each asset in the portfolio and on the fraction invested in each asset, w_j.

Equation 5.1

$$\begin{pmatrix} \text{Return} \\ \text{on} \\ \text{portfolio} \end{pmatrix} = \begin{pmatrix} \text{Proportion of} \\ \text{portfolio's total} \\ \text{dollar value} \\ \text{invested in} \\ \text{asset 1} \end{pmatrix} \times \begin{matrix} \text{Return} \\ \text{on asset} \\ 1 \end{matrix} + \begin{pmatrix} \text{Proportion of} \\ \text{portfolio's total} \\ \text{dollar value} \\ \text{invested in} \\ \text{asset 2} \end{pmatrix} \times \begin{matrix} \text{Return} \\ \text{on asset} \\ 2 \end{matrix} + \cdots +$$

$$\begin{pmatrix} \text{Proportion of} \\ \text{portfolio's total} \\ \text{dollar value} \\ \text{invested in} \\ \text{asset } n \end{pmatrix} \times \begin{matrix} \text{Return} \\ \text{on asset} \\ n \end{matrix} = \sum_{j=1}^{n} \begin{pmatrix} \text{Proportion of} \\ \text{portfolio's total} \\ \text{dollar value} \\ \text{invested in} \\ \text{asset } j \end{pmatrix} \times \begin{matrix} \text{Return} \\ \text{on asset} \\ j \end{matrix}$$

Equation 5.1a

$$r_p = (w_1 \times r_1) + (w_2 \times r_2) + \cdots + (w_n \times r_n) = \sum_{j=1}^{n}(w_j \times r_j)$$

Of course, $\sum_{j=1}^{n} w_j = 1$, which means that 100% of the portfolio's assets must be included in this computation.

Panel A of Table 5.1 shows the historical annual returns on two stocks, ExxonMobil (XOM) and Panera Bread (PNRA), from 1999–2008. Over that period, Exxon earned an average annual return of 11.7%, which is close to the average annual return on the U.S. stock market during the past century. Panera earned a spectacular 44.4% annual return. Although Panera is unlikely to repeat that kind of performance over the next decade, it is still instructive to examine the historical figures.

Now suppose we want to calculate the return on a portfolio containing investments in both Exxon and Panera. The first step in that calculation is to determine how much XOM and how much PNRA to hold, that is, what weight each stock should receive in the portfolio. Let's assume that we want to invest 86% of our money in XOM and 14% in PNRA. What kind of return would such a portfolio earn?

TABLE 5.1	Individual and Portfolio Returns and Standard Deviation of Returns for ExxonMobil (XOM) and Panera Bread (PNRA)	EXCEL WITH SPREADSHEETS

A. Individual and Portfolio Returns

Year (t)	(1) Historical Returns* $r_{XOM}\%$	(2) Historical Returns* $r_{PNRA}\%$	(3) Portfolio Weights $W_{XOM} = 0.86$ $\quad$ $W_{PNRA} = 0.14$	(4) Portfolio Return $r_p\%$
1999	12.6	14.8	$(0.86 \times 12.6) + (0.14 \times 14.8) =$	12.9
2000	10.2	193.8	$(0.86 \times 10.2) + (0.14 \times 193.8) =$	35.9
2001	−7.6	128.2	$(0.86 \times -7.6) + (0.14 \times 128.2) =$	11.4
2002	−8.9	33.8	$(0.86 \times -8.9) + (0.14 \times 33.8) =$	−2.9
2003	20.6	13.5	$(0.86 \times 20.6) + (0.14 \times 13.5) =$	19.6
2004	28.1	2.0	$(0.86 \times 28.1) + (0.14 \times 2.0) =$	24.4
2005	11.8	62.9	$(0.86 \times 11.8) + (0.14 \times 62.9) =$	18.9
2006	39.1	−14.9	$(0.86 \times 39.1) + (0.14 \times -14.9) =$	31.5
2007	24.3	−35.9	$(0.86 \times 24.3) + (0.14 \times -35.9) =$	15.9
2008	−13.1	45.8	$(0.86 \times -13.1) + (0.14 \times 45.8) =$	−4.9
Average Return	11.7	44.4		16.3

B. Individual and Portfolio Standard Deviations

Standard Deviation Calculation for XOM:

$$S_{XOM} = \sqrt{\frac{\sum_{t=1999}^{2008} (r_{XOM,\,t} - \bar{r})^2}{n-1}} = \sqrt{\frac{(12.6 - 11.7)^2 + \ldots + (-13.1 - 11.7)^2}{10-1}} = \sqrt{\frac{2,669.6}{10-1}} = 17.2\%$$

Standard Deviation Calculation for PNRA:

$$S_{PNRA} = \sqrt{\frac{\sum_{t=1999}^{2008} (r_{PNRA,\,t} - \bar{r})^2}{n-1}} = \sqrt{\frac{(14.8 - 44.4)^2 + \ldots + (45.8 - 44.4)^2}{10-1}} = \sqrt{\frac{43,403.8}{10-1}} = 69.5\%$$

Standard Deviation Calculation for Portfolio:

$$S_p = \sqrt{\frac{\sum_{t=1999}^{2008} (r_{Port,\,t} - \bar{r})^2}{n-1}} = \sqrt{\frac{(12.9 - 16.3)^2 + \ldots + (-4.9 - 16.3)^2}{10-1}} = \sqrt{\frac{1,553.2}{10-1}} = 13.1\%$$

*Historical return is calculated based on end of year prices.

(Source: *End-of-year prices are obtained from Yahoo! Finance (prices are adjusted for dividends and stock splits).*)

We know that over this period, Panera earned much higher returns than Exxon, so intuitively we might expect that a portfolio containing both stocks would earn a return higher than Exxon's but lower than Panera's. Furthermore, because most (86%) of the portfolio is invested in Exxon, you might guess that the portfolio's return would be closer to Exxon's than to Panera's.

Columns 3 and 4 in Panel A show the portfolio's return each year. The average annual return on this portfolio was 16.3%. As expected, that return is a little higher than the return on Exxon stock. By investing a little in Panera, an investor could earn a higher return than he or she would achieve by holding Exxon stock in isolation.

What about the portfolio's risk? One measure of a portfolio's risk is its standard deviation. The *standard deviation of a portfolio's returns* is found by applying Equation 4.6, the formula we used to find the standard deviation of a single asset. Panel B of Table 5.1 applies this formula to calculate the standard deviation of returns on Exxon and Panera stock. The standard deviation of Exxon's returns is 17.2%, and for Panera's stock returns the standard deviation is 69.45%. Here again we see evidence of the tradeoff between risk and return. Panera's stock earned much higher returns than Exxon's stock, but Panera returns fluctuate a great deal more as well.

The final calculation in Panel B inserts the Exxon-Panera portfolio return data from column 4 in Panel A into Equation 4.6 to calculate the portfolio standard deviation. Intuitively, because the portfolio contains a lot of Exxon stock and a little of Panera, you might expect the portfolio standard deviation to be slightly higher than the standard deviation of Exxon's returns. In fact, Panel B shows the surprising result that *the portfolio returns are less volatile than are the returns of either stock in the portfolio! The portfolio consisting of 86% Exxon and 14% Panera Bread displays a standard deviation of 13.1%, well below Exxon's standard deviation.*

This is great news for investors. An investor who held only Exxon shares would have earned an average return of 11.7%, but to achieve that return the investors would have had to endure Exxon's 17.2% standard deviation. By selling a few Exxon shares and using the proceeds to buy a few Panera shares (resulting in the 86% − 14% portfolio weights shown in Table 5.1), an investor could have *simultaneously increased his or her return to 16.3% and reduce the standard deviation to 13.1%.* In other words, the investor could have had more return and less risk at the same time. This means that an investor who owns nothing but Exxon shares holds an inefficient portfolio—an alternative portfolio exists that has more return and less risk. That's the power of diversification. Next, we will see that the key factor in making this possible is a low correlation between Exxon and Panera returns.

Correlation and Diversification

As noted in Chapter 2, *diversification* involves the inclusion of a number of different investment vehicles in a portfolio. It is an important aspect of creating an efficient portfolio. Underlying the intuitive appeal of diversification is the statistical concept of *correlation*. For effective portfolio planning, you need to understand the concepts of correlation and diversification and their relationship to a portfolio's total risk and return.

Correlation Correlation is a statistical measure of the relationship, if any, between two series of numbers. If two series move in the same direction, they are **positively correlated**. For instance, if each day we record the number of hours of sunshine and the average daily temperature, we would expect those two series to display positive correlation. Days with more sunshine tend to be days with higher temperatures. If the series move in opposite directions, they are **negatively correlated.** For example, if each day we record the number of hours of sunshine and the amount of rainfall, we would expect those two series to display negative correlation because, on average, rainfall is lower on days with lots of sunshine. Finally, if two series bear no relationship at all to each other, then they are **uncorrelated.** For example, we would probably expect no correlation between the number of hours of sunshine on a particular day and the change in the value of the U.S. dollar against other world currencies on the same day. There is no obvious connection between weather and world currency markets.

The degree of correlation—whether positive or negative—is measured by the **correlation coefficient.** It's easy to use Excel to calculate the correlation coefficient between Exxon and Panera returns. First, enter the returns for Exxon in a spreadsheet in column A, rows 1-10. Next, enter the returns for Panera in the first ten rows of column B.

Finally, in any empty cell, type the formula:

$$= \text{correl}(A1:A10,B1:B10)$$

Excel will quickly tell you that the correlation coefficient between Exxon and Panera during the 1999–2008 period was −0.49. This means that during a year in which Exxon stock earned below-average returns, the odds were high that Panera stock was enjoying above-average returns, and vice versa. A negative correlation between two stocks is somewhat unusual because most stocks are affected in the same way by large, macroeconomic forces. In other words, most stocks tend to move in the same direction as the overall economy, which means that most stocks will display at least some positive correlation with each other.

However, in the case of Exxon and Panera, one might try to explain the negative correlation as follows. When oil and gas prices are rising, Exxon's profits go up, but consumers have less discretionary income to spend eating out at restaurants. That's bad news for Panera stock, but when oil prices are falling, consumers have more money to spend and can afford to visit Panera more often. We would be cautious in lending too much credence to such a story as plausible as it may sound. Chances are high that the negative correlation between Exxon and Panera is something of a statistical fluke, and that in the future, Panera and Exxon, like most other pairs of stocks, will be positively correlated. For now, though, we will proceed as if we believe that Exxon and Panera shares display a tendency to move in opposite directions.

The correlation coefficient ranges from +1 for **perfectly positively correlated** series to −1 for **perfectly negatively correlated** series. These two extremes are depicted in Figure 5.1 for series M, N, and P. The perfectly positively correlated series (M and P)

FIGURE 5.1

The Correlation Between Series M, N, and P

The perfectly positively correlated series M and P in the graph on the left move exactly together. The perfectly negatively correlated series M and N in the graph on the right move in exactly opposite directions.

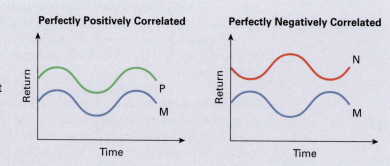

move exactly together. The perfectly negatively correlated series (M and N) move in exactly opposite directions. While these two extreme cases can be illustrative, *the correlations between most asset returns exhibit some degree (ranging from high to low) of positive correlation.* Negative correlation is the exception.

Diversification As a general rule, the lower the correlation between any two assets, the greater the risk reduction that can be achieved by combining those assets in a portfolio. Figure 5.2 shows negatively correlated assets F and G, both having the same average return, $\bar{r}$. The portfolio that contains both F and G has the same return, $\bar{r}$, but has less risk (variability) than either of the individual assets because some of the fluctuations in asset F cancel out fluctuations in G. As a result, the combination of F and G is less volatile than either F or G alone. Even if assets are not negatively correlated, the lower the positive correlation between them, the lower the resulting risk.

Table 5.2 (on page 170) shows the average return and the standard deviation of returns for many different combinations of Exxon and Panera stock. Columns 1 and 2 show the percentage of the portfolio invested in Exxon and Panera, respectively, and columns 3 and 4 show the portfolio average return and standard deviation. Notice that as you move from the top of the table to the bottom (i.e., from investing all of the portfolio in Exxon to investing all of it in Panera), the portfolio return goes up. That makes sense because as you move from top to bottom, the percentage invested in Panera increases, and Panera's average return is higher than Exxon's. The general conclusion from column 3 is that *when a portfolio contains two stocks, with one having a higher average return than the other, the portfolio's return rises the more you invest in the stock with the higher return.*

Column 4 shows the standard deviation of returns for different portfolios of Exxon and Panera. Here again we see a surprising result. A portfolio invested entirely in Exxon has a standard deviation of 17.2%. Intuitively, it might seem that reducing the investment in Exxon slightly and increasing investment in Panera would increase the portfolio's standard deviation because Panera stock is so much more volatile that Exxon. However, the opposite is true, at least up to a point. The portfolio standard deviation initially falls as the percentage invested in Panera rises. Eventually, however, increasing the amount invested in Panera does increase the portfolio's standard deviation. So the general conclusion from column 4 is *when a portfolio contains two stocks, with one*

FIGURE 5.2

Combining Negatively Correlated Assets to Diversify Risk

The risk or variability of returns, resulting from combining negatively correlated assets F and G, both having the same average return, $\bar{r}$, results in a portfolio (shown in the right-most graph) with the same level of average return but less risk.

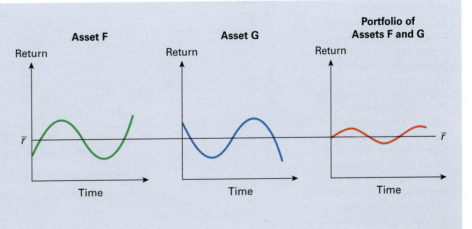

| TABLE 5.2 | Portfolio Returns and Standard Deviations for ExxonMobil (XOM) and Panera Bread (PNRA) | | | EXCEL WITH SPREADSHEETS |

(1) Portfolio Weights		(3) Portfolio Average Return%		(4) Portfolio Standard Deviations%
W_{XOM}	W_{PNRA}	$\bar{r}_{XOM}$ = 11.7%	$\bar{r}_{PNRA}$ = 44.4%	
1.0	0.0	(1.0 × 11.7) + (0.0 × 44.4) = 11.7		17.2
0.9	0.1	(0.9 × 11.7) + (0.1 × 44.4) = 15.0		13.5
0.8	0.2	(0.8 × 11.7) + (0.2 × 44.4) = 18.2		14.0
0.7	0.3	(0.7 × 11.7) + (0.3 × 44.4) = 21.5		18.3
0.6	0.4	(0.6 × 11.7) + (0.4 × 44.4) = 24.8		24.4
0.5	0.5	(0.5 × 11.7) + (0.5 × 44.4) = 28.1		31.4
0.4	0.6	(0.4 × 11.7) + (0.6 × 44.4) = 31.3		38.8
0.3	0.7	(0.3 × 11.7) + (0.7 × 44.4) = 34.6		46.3
0.2	0.8	(0.2 × 11.7) + (0.8 × 44.4) = 37.9		54.0
0.1	0.9	(0.1 × 11.7) + (0.9 × 44.4) = 41.1		61.7
0.0	1.0	(0.0 × 11.7) + (1.0 × 44.4) = 44.4		69.5

Example: Calculation of the Standard Deviation for the Equally Weighted Portfolio

S_{XOM} = 17.2%
S_{PNRA} = 69.5%
$\rho_{XOM/,PNRA}$ = −0.49

$$S_p = \sqrt{w_i^2 s_i^2 + w_j^2 s_j^2 + 2w_i w_j \rho_{i,j} s_i s_j}$$
$$S_p = \sqrt{(0.5^2 \times 17.2^2) + (0.5^2 \times 69.5^2) + (2 \times 0.5 \times 0.5 \times -0.49 \times 17.2 \times 69.5)} = 31.4$$

having a higher standard deviation than the other, the portfolio's standard deviation may rise or fall the more you invest in the stock with the higher standard deviation.

Figure 5.3 illustrates the two lessons emerging from Table 5.2. The curve plots the average return (*y*-axis) and standard deviation (*x*-axis) for each of the portfolios listed in Table 5.2. As the portfolio composition moves from 100% Exxon to a mix of Exxon and Panera, the average return rises, but the standard deviation initially falls.

FIGURE 5.3

Portfolios of ExxonMobil and Panera Bread

Because the returns of ExxonMobil and Panera Bread are not highly correlated, investors who hold only Exxon shares can simultaneously increase their portfolio return and reduce its standard deviation by holding at least some Panera shares. At some point, however, investing more in Panera does increase the portfolio volatility while also increasing its expected return.

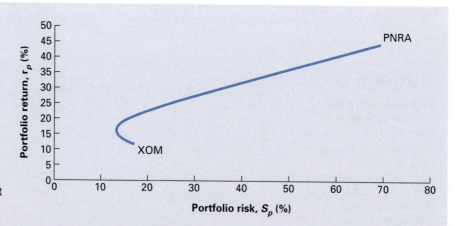

Therefore, portfolios of Exxon and Panera trace out a backward-bending arc. Clearly no investor should place all of his or her money in Exxon because a higher return and lower standard deviation can be achieved by holding at least some stock in Panera Bread. However, investors who want to earn the highest possible returns, and who therefore will invest heavily in Panera, have to accept a higher standard deviation.

The relationship between Exxon and Panera is obviously a special case, so let's look at the more general patterns that investors encounter in the markets. In addition, let's shift our focus from historical to expected returns. Table 5.3 presents the expected returns from three different assets—X, Y, and Z—over the next five years (2012–2016), along with their average expected returns and standard deviations. Asset X has an average expected return of 12% and a standard deviation of 3.16%. Assets Y and Z each have an average expected return of 16% and a standard deviation of 6.32%. Thus, we can view asset X as having a low-return, low-risk profile while assets Y and Z are high-return, high-risk stocks. The returns of assets X and Y are perfectly negatively correlated—they move in exactly opposite directions over time. The returns of assets X and Z are perfectly positively correlated—they move in precisely the same direction.

Portfolio XY (shown in Table 5.3) is constructed by investing $\frac{2}{3}$ in asset X and $\frac{1}{3}$ in asset Y. The expected return on this portfolio, 13.3%, is a weighted average of the expected returns of assets X and Y ($\frac{2}{3} \times 12\% + \frac{1}{3} \times 16\%$). To calculate the portfolio's standard deviation, use the equation shown in Table 5.2 (on page 170) with a value of −1.0 for the correlation between X and Y. Notice that portfolio XY generates a predictable 13.3% return every year. In other words, the portfolio is risk-free and has a standard deviation of zero.

Portfolio XZ uses the same proportions: $\frac{2}{3}$ invested in X and $\frac{1}{3}$ invested in Z. Like portfolio XY, portfolio XZ has an expected return of 13.3%. But unlike portfolio XY, portfolio XZ is risky. Its returns fluctuate between 8% and 18.7%.

To summarize, the two portfolios, XY and XZ, have identical expected returns, but they differ in terms of risk. The reason for that difference is correlation. Movements in X are offset by movements in Y, so by combining the two assets in a portfolio, the investor can reduce or eliminate risk. Assets X and Z move together, so movements in one cannot offset movements in the other, and the standard deviation of portfolio XZ cannot be reduced below the standard deviation of asset X.

TABLE 5.3	Expected Returns, Average Returns, and Standard Deviations for Assets X, Y, and Z and Portfolios XY and XZ					EXCEL WITH SPREADSHEETS
	Assets Expected Returns			Portfolios Expected Returns		
				$E(r_{xy})\%$		$E(r_{xz})\%$
Year (t)	$E(r_X)\%$	$E(r_Y)\%$	$E(r_Z)\%$	[2/3 × $E(r_X)\%$ + 1/3 × $E(r_Y)\%$]		[2/3 × $E(r_X)\%$ + 1/3 × $E(r_Z)\%$]
2012	8.0	24.0	8.0	13.3		8.0
2013	10.0	20.0	12.0	13.3		10.7
2014	12.0	16.0	16.0	13.3		13.3
2015	14.0	12.0	20.0	13.3		16.0
2016	16.0	8.0	24.0	13.3		18.7
Average Expected Return	12.0	16.0	16.0	13.3		13.3
Standard Deviation	3.16	6.32	6.32	0.00		4.74

FIGURE 5.4

Risk and Return for Combinations of Two Assets with Various Correlation Coefficients

This graph illustrates how a low-return, low-risk asset can be combined with a high-return, high-risk asset in a portfolio, and how the performance of that portfolio depends on the correlation between the two assets. In general, as an investor shifts the portfolio weight from the low-return to the high-return investment, the portfolio return will rise. But the portfolio's standard deviation may rise or fall depending on the correlation. In general, the lower the correlation, the greater the risk reduction that can be achieved through diversification.

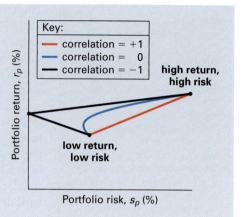

Figure 5.4 illustrates the relation between a portfolio's expected return and standard deviation and the correlation between the assets in the portfolio. The black line illustrates a case like portfolio XY where the correlation coefficient is −1.0. In that case, it is possible to combine two risky assets in just the right proportions so that the portfolio return is completely predictable (i.e., has no risk). Notice that in this situation, it would be very unwise for an investor to hold an undiversified position in the least risky asset. By holding a portfolio of assets rather than just one, the investor moves up and to the left along the black line to earn a higher return while taking less risk. Beyond some point, however, increasing the investment in the more risky asset pushes both the portfolio return and risk higher, so the investor's portfolio moves up and to the right along the second segment of the black line.

The red line in Figure 5.4 illustrates a situation like portfolio XZ in which the correlation coefficient is +1.0. In that instance, when an investor decreases their investment in the low-risk asset to hold more of the high-risk asset, the portfolio's expected return rises, but so does its standard deviation. The investor moves up and to the right along the red line. An investor might choose to invest in both assets, but making that decision is a matter of one's risk tolerance, and not all investors will make that choice. In other words, when the correlation between two assets is −1.0, diversifying is definitely the right move, but when the correlation is +1.0, whether to diversify or not is less obvious.

The blue line in Figure 5.4 illustrates an intermediate case in which the correlation coefficient is between −1.0 and +1.0. This is what investors encounter in real markets most of the time—assets are neither perfectly negatively correlated, nor are they perfectly positively correlated. When the correlation coefficient is between the extremes, portfolios of two assets lie along an arc (i.e., the blue line). When two assets have very low correlation, that arc may bend back upon itself, as was the case with Exxon and Panera Bread. When the correlation is higher, but still below 1.0, the arc merely curves up and to the right. Even then, the benefits of diversification are better than when the correlation is 1.0, meaning that portfolios along the blue arc earn higher returns for the same risk compared to portfolios along the red line.

International Diversification

Diversification is clearly a primary consideration when constructing an investment portfolio. As noted earlier, many opportunities for international diversification are now available. Here we consider three aspects of international diversification: effectiveness, methods, and benefits.

Effectiveness of International Diversification Investing internationally offers greater diversification than investing only domestically. That is true for U.S. investors. It is even truer for investors from countries with capital markets that offer much more limited diversification opportunities than are available in the United States.

However, does international diversification actually reduce risk, particularly the variability of rates of return? Two classic studies overwhelmingly support the argument that well-structured international diversification does indeed reduce the risk of a portfolio and increase the return on portfolios of comparable risk. One study looked at diversification across 12 European countries in seven different industries between 1978 and 1992. It found that an investor could actually reduce the risk of a portfolio much more by diversifying internationally *in the same industry* than by diversifying across industries within one country. If the investor diversified across both countries and industries, the opportunities for risk reduction were even greater.

Another study examined the risk-return performance between January 1984 and November 1994 of diversified stock portfolios: the S&P 500 in the United States and Morgan Stanley's Europe/Australia/Far East (EAFE) Index. It found that a 100% EAFE portfolio offered a much greater return than a 100% S&P 500 portfolio did—but at much greater risk. However, a portfolio composed of various combinations of the two indexes would have been better. It would have realized both lower risk and a higher return than did the 100% S&P 500 portfolio and less risk and a moderately lower return than did the 100% EAFE portfolio. For the U.S. investor, a portfolio consisting of 70% S&P 500 coupled with 30% EAFE would have reduced risk by about 5% and increased return by about 7% (from around 14% to more than 15%). Or, for the same degree of risk, an investor could have increased return by about 18% (from around 14% to more than 16.5%).

INVESTOR FACTS

U.S. investors benefit from a vibrant and highly competitive mutual fund industry. That industry offers investors a vast array of opportunities for diversifying their portfolios, and the fees that U.S. mutual funds charge are a bargain compared to the rest of the world. A recent study finds that the total cost to invest in an average U.S. mutual fund is about 1.04% per year of the amount invested. The country with the next most affordable mutual fund costs is Australia at 1.41% per year, followed by France (1.64%), Germany (1.79%), and Italy and Switzerland (1.94%). Mutual fund costs in the U.K. are 2.21%, more than double the costs in the U.S.

(Source: Ajay Khorana, Henri Servaes, & Peter Tufano. (2009). Mutual Fund Fees Around the World. *Review of Financial Studies* (March), 1279-1310.)

Methods of International Diversification In later chapters we will examine a wide range of alternatives for international portfolio diversification. We will see that investors can make investments in bonds and other debt instruments in U.S. dollars or in foreign currencies—either directly or via foreign mutual funds. Foreign currency investment, however, brings currency exchange risk. This risk can be hedged with contracts such as currency forwards, futures, and options. Even if there is little or no currency exchange risk, investing abroad is generally less convenient, more expensive, and riskier than investing domestically. When making direct investments abroad, you must know what you're doing. You should have a clear idea of the benefits being sought and enough time to monitor foreign markets.

International diversification can also be achieved by U.S. domestic investments. Investors can buy stock of foreign companies listed on U.S. exchanges. Many foreign issuers, both corporate and government, sell their bonds (called *Yankee bonds*) in the United States. The stocks of more than 2,000 foreign companies, from more than 50 different countries, trade in the United States in the form of American Depositary Shares (ADSs). Finally, international mutual funds (such as the Fidelity Japan Fund and the AIM Global Equity Fund) provide foreign investment opportunities.

You might wonder whether it is possible to achieve the benefits of international diversification by investing in a portfolio of U.S.-based multinational corporations. The answer is yes and no. Yes, a portfolio of U.S. multinationals is more diversified than a portfolio of wholly domestic firms. Multinationals generate revenues, costs, and profits in many different markets and currencies, so when one part of the world is doing poorly, another part may be doing well.

Investors who invest only in U.S.-based multinationals will still not enjoy the full benefits of international diversification. That's because a disproportionate share of the revenues and costs generated by these firms are still in the U.S. Thus, to fully realize the benefits of international diversification, it is necessary to invest in firms located outside the U.S.

Benefits of International Diversification Can you find greater returns overseas than in the United States? Yes! Can you reduce a portfolio's risk by including foreign investments? Yes! Is international diversification desirable for you? Maybe a successful global investment strategy depends on many things, just as a purely domestic strategy does. Included are factors such as your resources, goals, and risk tolerance. What percentage of your portfolio you allocate to foreign investments depends on your overall investment goals and risk preferences. Commonly cited allocations to foreign investments are about 20% to 30%, with two-thirds of this allocation in established foreign markets and the other one-third in emerging markets.

In general, you should avoid investing directly in foreign-currency-denominated instruments. Unless the magnitude of each foreign investment is in hundreds of thousands of dollars, the transactions costs will tend to be high. A safer choice for international diversification would be international mutual funds, which offer diversified foreign investments and the professional expertise of fund managers. ADSs can be used by those who want to make foreign investments in individual stocks. With either mutual funds or ADSs, you can obtain international diversification along with low cost, convenience, transactions in U.S. dollars, protection under U.S. security laws, and (usually) attractive markets.

We should not leave this topic without saying that some of the benefits of international diversification are diminishing over time. Technological advances in communication have greatly improved the quality of information on foreign companies. Participation by a growing number of better-informed investors in the foreign markets continues to reduce the opportunities to earn "excess" returns on the additional risk embodied in foreign investments, thereby leveling the playing field. However, the relatively low correlation of returns in Asian and emerging markets with U.S. returns continues to make international investments appealing as a way to diversify your portfolio. Today, an important motive for international investment is portfolio diversification rather than realizing sizable excess returns.

CONCEPTS IN REVIEW
Answers available at
www.pearsonhighered.com/gitman

5.1 What is an *efficient portfolio*, and what role should such a portfolio play in investing?

5.2 How can the return and standard deviation of a portfolio be determined? Compare the portfolio standard deviation calculation to that for a single asset.

5.3 What is *correlation*, and why is it important with respect to asset returns? Describe the characteristics of returns that are (a) positively correlated, (b) negatively correlated, and (c) uncorrelated. Differentiate between *perfect positive correlation* and *perfect negative correlation*.

5.4 What is *diversification?* How does the diversification of risk affect the risk of the portfolio compared to the risk of the individual assets it contains?

5.5 Discuss how the correlation between asset returns affects the risk and return behavior of the resulting portfolio. Describe the potential range of risk and return when the correlation between two assets is (a) perfectly positive, (b) uncorrelated, and (c) perfectly negative.

5.6 What benefit, if any, does international diversification offer the individual investor? Compare and contrast the methods of achieving international diversification by investing abroad versus investing domestically.

The Capital Asset Pricing Model (CAPM)

LG3 LG4   From an investor's perspective, the relevant risk is the *inescapable risk* of the firm. This risk significantly affects the returns earned and the value of the firm in the financial marketplace. As you'll learn in Chapter 8, the firm's value is directly determined by its risk and the associated return. The basic theory that links return and the relevant risk for all assets is the *capital asset pricing model (CAPM)*.

Components of Risk

The risk of an investment consists of two components: diversifiable and nondiversifiable risk. **Diversifiable risk**, sometimes called **unsystematic risk**, results from uncontrollable or random events that are firm-specific, such as labor strikes, lawsuits, and regulatory actions. It is the portion of an investment's risk that can be eliminated through diversification. **Nondiversifiable risk**, also called **systematic risk**, is the inescapable portion of an investment's risk. It is attributed to more general forces such as war, inflation, and political events that affect all investments and therefore are not unique to a given vehicle. The sum of nondiversifiable risk and diversifiable risk is called **total risk**.

Equation 5.2

$$\text{Total risk} = \text{Nondiversifiable risk} + \text{Diversifiable risk}$$

Any careful investor can reduce or virtually eliminate diversifiable risk by holding a diversified portfolio of securities. Studies have shown that investors can eliminate most diversifiable risk by carefully selecting a portfolio of 8 to 15 securities. Therefore, *the only relevant risk is nondiversifiable risk,* which is inescapable. Each security has its own unique level of nondiversifiable risk, which we can measure, as we'll show in the following section.

Beta: A Popular Measure of Risk

During the past 40 years, the finance discipline has developed much theory on the measurement of risk and its use in assessing returns. The two key components of this theory are *beta,* which is a measure of risk, and the *capital asset pricing model (CAPM),* which uses beta to estimate return.

First we will look at **beta**, a number that measures *nondiversifiable,* or *market, risk*. Beta indicates how the price of a security responds to market forces. The more responsive the price of a security is to changes in the market, the higher that security's beta. Beta is found by relating the historical returns for a security to the market return. **Market return** is the average return for all (or a large sample of) stocks. Analysts commonly use the average return on all stocks in the *Standard & Poor's 500-Stock Composite Index* or some other broad stock index to measure market return. You don't have to calculate betas yourself; you can easily obtain them for actively traded securities from a variety of published and online sources. But you should understand how betas are derived, how to interpret them, and how to apply them to portfolios.

Deriving Beta   We can demonstrate graphically the relationship between a security's return and the market return, and its use in deriving beta. Figure 5.5 plots the relationship between the returns of two securities, C and D, and the market return. Note that the horizontal (x) axis measures the historical market returns, and the vertical (y) axis measures the individual security's historical returns.

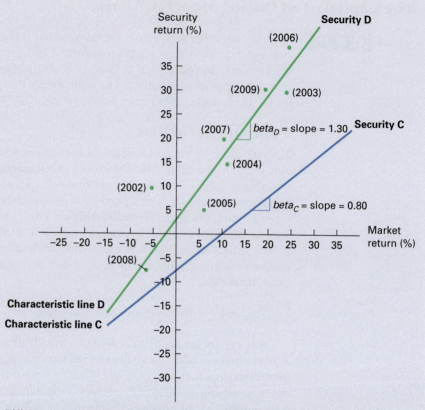

FIGURE 5.5

Graphical Derivation of Beta for Securities C and D*

Betas can be derived graphically by plotting the coordinates for the market return and security return at various points in time and using statistical techniques to fit the "characteristic line" to the data points. The slope of the characteristic line is beta. For securities C and D, the betas are 0.80 and 1.30, respectively.

*All data points shown are associated with security D. No data points are shown for security C.

The first step in deriving beta is plotting the coordinates for the market return and the security return at various points in time. Figure 5.5 shows such annual market-return and security-return coordinates *for security D* for the years 2002 to 2009 (the years are noted in parentheses). For example, in 2007, security D's return was 20% when the market return was 10%.

By use of statistical techniques, the "characteristic line" that best explains the relationship between security-return and market-return coordinates is fit to the data points. *The slope of this line is beta.* The beta for security D is 1.30. In comparison to a beta of 0.80 for security C (also shown in Figure 5.5), security D's higher beta—steeper characteristic line slope—indicates that its return is more responsive to changing market returns. *Therefore, security D is more risky than security C.*

Interpreting Beta The beta for the overall market is equal to 1.00. That also implies that the beta of the "average" stock is 1.0. All other betas are viewed in relation to this value. Table 5.4 shows some selected beta values and their associated interpretations. As you can see, betas can, in principle, be positive or negative, although *nearly all betas are positive.* The positive or negative sign preceding the beta number merely indicates whether the stock's return moves in the *same direction as the general market* (positive beta) or in the *opposite direction* (negative beta).

Most stocks have betas that fall between 0.50 and 1.75. The return of a stock that is half as responsive as the market ($b = 0.50$) is expected to change by ½ of 1% for

TABLE 5.4	Selected Betas and Associated Interpretations	
Beta	Comment	Interpretation
2.00 1.00 0.50	Move in same direction as the market	Twice as responsive as the market Same response as the market One half as responsive as the market
0		Unaffected by market movement
−0.50 −1.00 −2.00	Move in opposite direction as the market	Only half as responsive as the market Same response as the market Twice as responsive as the market

each 1% change in the return of the market portfolio. A stock that is twice as responsive as the market ($b = 2.0$) is expected to experience a 2% change in its return for each 1% change in the return of the market portfolio. Listed here, for illustration purposes, are the actual betas for some popular stocks, as reported on Yahoo! Finance on August 17, 2009:

Stock	Beta	Stock	Beta
Amazon.com	1.23	Int'l Business Machines	0.78
Molson Coors Brewing	0.84	Goldman Sachs	1.49
Bank of America Corp.	2.61	Microsoft	0.99
Procter & Gamble	0.56	Nike, Inc.	0.89
Disney	1.14	Panera Bread Co.	0.87
eBay	1.79	Qualcomm	0.8
ExxonMobil Corp.	0.38	Sempra Energy	0.64
Gap (The), Inc.	1.20	Walmart Stores	0.24
Ford Motor Co.	2.80	Xerox	1.59
Intel	1.20	Yahoo! Inc.	0.76

Many large brokerage firms, as well as subscription services like *Value Line,* publish betas for a broad range of securities. They also can be obtained online through sites such as **finance.yahoo.com.** The ready availability of security betas has enhanced their use in assessing investment risks. Later in this chapter we discuss the importance of beta in planning and building portfolios of securities.

Applying Beta Individual investors will find beta useful. It can help in assessing market risk and in understanding the impact the market can have on the return expected from a share of stock. In short, beta reveals how a security responds to market forces. For example, if the market is expected to experience a 10% *increase* in its rate of return over the next period, we would expect a stock with a beta of 1.50 to experience an *increase* in return of about 15% ($1.50 \times 10\%$). Because its beta is greater than 1.00, this stock is more volatile than the market as a whole.

For stocks with positive betas, increases in market returns result in increases in security returns. Unfortunately, decreases in market returns are translated into decreasing security returns. In the preceding example, if the market is expected to experience a 10% *decrease* in its rate of return, then a stock with a beta of 1.50 should experience a 15% *decrease* in its return. Because the stock has a beta greater than 1.00, it is more responsive than the market, either up or down.

Stocks that have betas less than 1.00 are, of course, less responsive to changing returns in the market. They are therefore considered less risky. For example, a stock

MARKETS IN CRISIS

Bulging Betas

Ford Motor Company has always been considered a cyclical stock whose fortunes rise and fall with the state of the economy. But as the table on page 177 shows, in August 2009 Yahoo! Finance reported a beta for Ford Motor of 2.80, indicating that Ford common stock was extremely sensitive to movements in the broad market. That high sensitivity was a result of the financial crisis and recession from 2007–2009, which hit automakers hard and prompted them to seek government assistance.

Ford's high beta in 2009 meant that investors believed the company would rebound quickly if and when the economy improved, but if the economy failed to improve, Ford might find itself in bankruptcy with General Motors, which had filed for bankruptcy a few months earlier. Notice that Bank of America, another firm in an industry hit hard by the recession, had a beta in 2009 of 2.61, indicating that it too was extremely sensitive to movements in the overall economy.

INVESTOR FACTS

WHICH BETA?—Working with betas is not an exact science. A researcher recently found that by browsing through 16 different financial Web sites, one could find estimates of beta for the same company (Walt Disney) ranging from 0.72 to 1.39. If you try to estimate betas on your own, you will find that your estimates will vary depending on how much historical data you use in your analysis and the frequency with which returns are measured.

(Source: Pablo Fernandez. (2009, May). *Betas used by professors: A survey with 2,500 answers*. IESE Business School.)

with a beta of 0.50 will increase or decrease its return by about half that of the market as a whole. Thus, if the market return went down by 8%, such a stock's return would probably experience only about a 4% ($0.50 \times 8\%$) decline.

Here are some important points to remember about beta:

- Beta measures the nondiversifiable (or market) risk of a security.

- The beta for the market is 1.00.

- Stocks may have positive or negative betas. Nearly all are positive.

- Stocks with betas greater than 1.00 are more responsive to changes in the market return and therefore are more risky than the market. Stocks with betas less than 1.00 are less risky than the market.

- Because of its greater risk, the higher a stock's beta, the greater its level of expected return.

The CAPM: Using Beta to Estimate Return

About 40 years ago, finance professors William F. Sharpe and John Lintner developed a model that uses beta to formally link the notions of risk and return. Called the **capital asset pricing model (CAPM)**, it attempts to explain the behavior of security prices. It also provides a mechanism whereby investors can assess the impact of a proposed security investment on their portfolio's risk and return. The CAPM predicts that a stock's expected return depends on three things: the risk-free rate, the expected return on the overall market, and the stock's beta.

The Equation With beta, b, as the measure of nondiversifiable risk, the capital asset pricing model defines the required return on an investment as follows.

Equation 5.3
$$\text{Required return on investment } j = \text{Risk-free rate} + \left[\text{Beta for investment } j \times \left(\text{Expected market return} - \text{Risk-free rate} \right) \right]$$

Equation 5.3a
$$r_j = R_F + [b_j \times (r_m - R_F)]$$

where

r_j = the required return on investment j, given its risk as measured by beta

R_F = the risk-free rate of return; the return that can be earned on a risk-free investment

b_j = beta coefficient or index of nondiversifiable risk for investment j

r_m = the expected market return; the average return on all securities (typically measured by the average return on all securities in the Standard & Poor's 500-Stock Composite Index or some other broad stock market index)

The CAPM can be divided into two parts: (1) the risk-free rate of return, R_F, and (2) the *risk premium,* $b_j \times (r_m - R_F)$. The risk premium is the return investors demand beyond the risk-free rate to compensate for the investment's nondiversifiable risk as measured by beta. The equation shows that *as beta increases, the stock's risk premium increases, thereby causing the required return to increase.*

We can demonstrate use of the CAPM with the following example. Assume you are considering security Z with a beta (b_Z) of 1.25. The risk-free rate (R_F) is 6% and the market return (r_m) is 10%. Substituting these data into the CAPM equation, Equation 5.3a, we get:

$$r_z = 6\% + [1.25 \times (10\% - 6\%)] = 6\% + [1.25 \times 4\%]$$
$$= 6\% + 5\% = \underline{11\%}$$

You should therefore expect—indeed, require—an 11% return on this investment as compensation for the risk you have to assume, given the security's beta of 1.25.

If the beta were lower, say, 1.00, the required return would be lower. In fact, in this case the required return on the stock is the same as the expected (or required) return on the market.

$$r_z = 6\% + [1.00 \times (10\% - 6\%)] = 6\% + 4\% = \underline{10\%}$$

If the beta were higher, say 1.50, the required return would be higher:

$$r_z = 6\% + [1.50 \times (10\% - 6\%)] = 6\% + 6\% = \underline{12\%}$$

Clearly, the CAPM reflects the positive tradeoff between risk and return: The higher the risk (beta), the higher the risk premium, and therefore the higher the required return.

The Graph: The Security Market Line (SML) When the capital asset pricing model is depicted graphically, it is called the **security market line (SML)**. Plotting the CAPM, we would find that the SML is, in fact, a straight line. For each level of nondiversifiable risk (beta), the SML reflects the required return the investor should earn in the marketplace.

We can plot the CAPM at a given point in time by simply calculating the required return for a variety of betas. For example, as we saw earlier, using a 6% risk-free rate and a 10% market return, the required return is 11% when the beta is 1.25. Increase the beta to 2.00, and the required return equals 14% ($6\% + 2.00 \times (10\% - 6\%)$). Similarly, we can find the required return for a number of betas and end up with the following combinations of risk (beta) and required return.

Smart's Tour of the Web
To watch author Scott Smart discuss key websites for this chapter visit www.myfinancelab.com

Risk (beta)	Required Return
0.0	6%
0.5	8
1.0	10
1.5	12
2.0	14
2.5	16

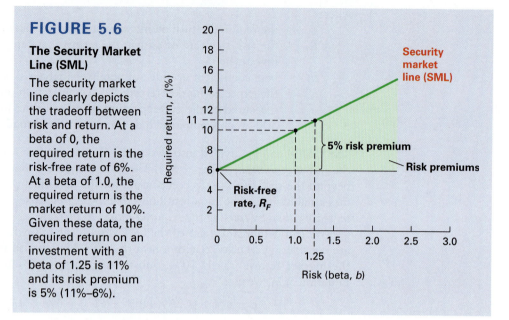

FIGURE 5.6

The Security Market Line (SML)

The security market line clearly depicts the tradeoff between risk and return. At a beta of 0, the required return is the risk-free rate of 6%. At a beta of 1.0, the required return is the market return of 10%. Given these data, the required return on an investment with a beta of 1.25 is 11% and its risk premium is 5% (11%–6%).

Plotting these values on a graph (with beta on the horizontal axis and required returns on the vertical axis) would yield a straight line like the one in Figure 5.6. The shaded area shows the amount by which the required return exceeds the risk-free rate. It represents the risk premiums. It is clear from the SML that as risk (beta) increases, so do the risk premium and required return, and vice versa.

Some Closing Comments The capital asset pricing model generally relies on historical data. The betas may or may not actually reflect the *future* variability of returns. Therefore, the required returns specified by the model can be viewed only as rough approximations. Analysts who use betas commonly make subjective adjustments to the historically determined betas to reflect their expectations of the future.

Despite its limitations, the CAPM provides a useful conceptual framework for evaluating and linking risk and return. Its simplicity and practical appeal cause beta and CAPM to remain important tools for investors who seek to measure risk and link it to required returns in security markets. The CAPM also sees widespread use in corporate finance, because before they spend large sums of money on big investment projects, companies need to know what returns their shareholders require. Many surveys show that the primary method that companies use to determine the required rate of return on their stock is the CAPM.

CONCEPTS IN REVIEW

Answers available at
www.pearsonhighered.com/
gitman

5.7 Briefly define and give examples of each of the following components of total risk. Which is the relevant risk, and why?

a. Diversifiable risk
b. Nondiversifiable risk

5.8 Explain what is meant by *beta*. What is the relevant risk measured by beta? What is the *market return?* How is the interpretation of beta related to the market return?

5.9 What range of values does beta typically exhibit? Are positive or negative betas more common? Explain.

5.10 What is the *capital asset pricing model (CAPM)?* What role does beta play in it? What is the *risk premium?* How is the *security market line (SML)* related to the CAPM?

5.11 Is the CAPM a predictive model? Why do beta and the CAPM remain important to investors?

Traditional Versus Modern Portfolio Management

LG5 LG6 Individual and institutional investors currently use two approaches to plan and construct their portfolios. The *traditional approach* refers to the less-quantitative methods that investors have been using since the evolution of the public securities markets. *Modern portfolio theory (MPT)* is a more recent, more mathematical development that relies on quantitative analysis to guide investment decisions.

The Traditional Approach

Traditional portfolio management emphasizes "balancing" the portfolio by assembling a wide variety of stocks and/or bonds. The typical emphasis is *interindustry diversification*. This produces a portfolio with securities of companies from a broad range of industries. Traditional portfolios are constructed using the security analysis techniques discussed in Chapters 7 and 8.

Table 5.5 presents the industry groupings and the percentages invested in them by a typical mutual fund that is managed by professionals using the traditional approach. This fund, The Growth Fund of America (GFA), is an open-end mutual fund.

TABLE 5.5   The Growth Fund of America, November 1, 2008

The Growth Fund of America (GFA) appears to adhere to the traditional approach to portfolio management. Its total portfolio value is about $140 billion, of which 86% ($120 billion) is common stock, including more than 200 different stocks representing a wide range of industries plus about 14% ($20 billion) in short-term securities from several dozen different issuers. In addition, the fund has a very small position in fixed-income securities ($67 million).

The Growth Fund of America Investments by Broad Industry Group as of November 1, 2008

Industry Group	Percentage
Equity Securities	**85.86%**
Information technology	21.80
Health care	9.81
Energy	13.89
Consumer discretionary	10.01
Industrials	7.76
Other Industries	22.59
Fixed-Income Securities	**0.48**
Preferred stocks	0.00
Convertible securities	0.44
Bonds and notes	0.04
Short-Term Securities and Other Assets Less Liabilities	**13.66**

(Source: Data from The Growth Fund of America, *Prospectus*, November 2008, p. 10.)

Its portfolio value in November 2008 was approximately $140 billion. Its objective is to invest in a wide range of companies that appear to offer superior opportunities for growth of capital. The GFA holds shares of more than 250 different stocks from a wide range of industries as well as short-term securities of several dozen different issuers.

Analyzing the stock position of GFA, which accounts for about 86% of the fund's total assets, we observe the traditional approach to portfolio management at work. This fund holds numerous stocks from a broad cross-section of the total universe of available stocks. The stocks are a mix of large and small companies. By far the largest industry group is information technology, representing 21.82% of the total portfolio. The fund's largest individual holding is Microsoft, which accounts for about 3% of the total portfolio. Google, one of the most frequently used Web site search engines in the world, ranks second, also at about 3%. The third largest holding—2.9%—is Oracle. Although many of the fund's stocks are those of large, recognizable companies, its portfolio does include stocks of smaller, less-recognizable firms.

Those who manage traditional portfolios want to invest in well-known companies for three reasons. First, because these are known as successful enterprises, investing in them is perceived as less risky than investing in lesser-known firms. Second, the securities of large firms are more liquid and are available in large quantities. Third, institutional investors prefer successful, well-known companies because it is easier to convince clients to invest in them. Called *window dressing,* this practice of loading up a portfolio with successful, well-known stocks makes it easier for institutional investors to sell their services.

One tendency often attributed to institutional investors during recent years is that of "herding"—investing in securities similar to those held by their competitors. These institutional investors effectively mimic the actions of their competitors. In the case of GFA, for example, its managers would buy stocks in companies that are held by other large, growth-oriented mutual funds. While we really don't know why GFA's managers bought specific stocks, it is clear that most funds with similar objectives hold many of the same well-known stocks.

Modern Portfolio Theory

During the 1950s, Harry Markowitz, a trained mathematician, first developed the theories that form the basis of modern portfolio theory. Many other scholars and investment experts have contributed to the theory in the intervening years since. **Modern portfolio theory (MPT)** utilizes several basic statistical measures to develop a portfolio plan. Included are *expected returns* and *standard deviations of returns* for both securities and portfolios, and the *correlation between returns.* According to MPT, diversification is achieved by combining securities in a portfolio *in such a way that individual securities have negative (or low-positive) correlations between each other's rates of return.* Thus, the statistical diversification is the deciding factor in choosing securities for an MPT portfolio. Two important aspects of MPT are the *efficient frontier* and *portfolio betas.*

The Efficient Frontier   At any point in time, you are faced with virtually hundreds of investments from which to choose. You can form any number of possible portfolios. In fact, using only, say, 10 different assets, you could create hundreds of portfolios by changing the proportion of each asset in the portfolio.

If we were to create all possible portfolios, calculate the return and risk of each, and plot each risk-return combination on a set of risk-return axes, we would have the *feasible* or *attainable set* of all possible portfolios. This set is represented by the shaded area in Figure 5.7 (on page 183). It is the area bounded by ABYOZCDEF. As defined

FIGURE 5.7

The Feasible or Attainable Set and the Efficient Frontier

The *feasible* or *attainable set* (shaded area) represents the risk-return combinations attainable with all possible portfolios; the *efficient frontier* is the locus of all efficient portfolios. The point O where the investor's highest possible indifference curve is tangent to the efficient frontier is the optimal portfolio. It represents the highest level of satisfaction the investor can achieve given the available set of portfolios.

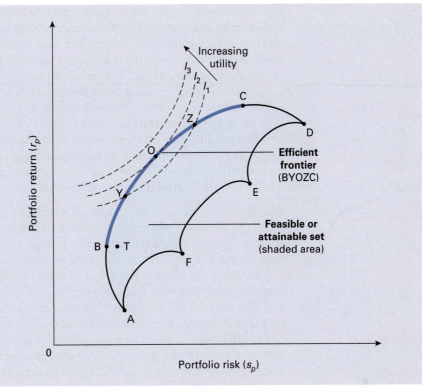

earlier, an *efficient portfolio* is a portfolio that provides the highest return for a given level of risk. For example, let's compare portfolio T to portfolios B and Y shown in Figure 5.7. Portfolio Y appears preferable to portfolio T because it has a higher return for the same level of risk. Portfolio B also "dominates" portfolio T because it has lower risk for the same level of return.

The boundary BYOZC of the feasible set of portfolios represents *all efficient portfolios*—those portfolios that provide the best tradeoff between risk and return. This boundary is called the **efficient frontier**. *All portfolios on the efficient frontier are preferable to all other portfolios in the feasible set.* Any portfolios that would fall to the left of the efficient frontier are not available for investment, because they fall outside of the attainable set. Portfolios that fall to the right of the efficient frontier are *not desirable*, because their risk-return tradeoffs are inferior to those of portfolios on the efficient frontier.

We can, in theory, use the efficient frontier to find the highest level of satisfaction the investor can achieve given the available set of portfolios. To do this, we would plot on the risk-return axes an *investor's utility function*, or *risk-indifference curves*. These curves indicate, for a given level of utility (satisfaction), the set of risk-return combinations among which an investor would be indifferent. These curves, labeled I_1, I_2, and I_3 in Figure 5.7, reflect increasing satisfaction as we move from I_1 to I_2 to I_3. The optimal portfolio, O, is the point at which indifference curve I_2 meets the efficient frontier. The higher utility provided by I_3 cannot be achieved given the best available portfolios represented by the efficient frontier.

When coupled with a risk-free asset, the efficient frontier can be used to develop the *capital asset pricing model* (introduced earlier) in terms of portfolio risk (measured by the standard deviation, s_p) and return (r_p). Rather than focus further on theory, let's shift our attention to the more practical aspects of the efficient frontier and its extensions. To do so, we consider the use of *portfolio betas*.

Portfolio Betas As we have noted, investors strive to diversify their portfolios by including a variety of noncomplementary investment vehicles so as to reduce risk while meeting return objectives. Remember that investment vehicles embody two basic types of risk: (1) *diversifiable risk,* the risk unique to a particular investment vehicle, and (2) *nondiversifiable risk,* the risk possessed by every investment vehicle.

A great deal of research has been conducted on the topic of risk as it relates to security investments. The results show that, in general, *to earn more return, you must bear more risk.* More startling, however, are research results showing that only with nondiversifiable risk is there a positive risk-return relationship. High levels of *diversifiable risk* do not result in correspondingly high levels of return. Because there is no reward for bearing diversifiable risk, investors should minimize this form of risk by diversifying the portfolio so that only nondiversifiable risk remains.

Risk Diversification As we've seen, diversification minimizes diversifiable risk by off-setting the below-average return on one vehicle with the above-average return on another. Minimizing diversifiable risk through careful selection of investment vehicles requires that the vehicles chosen for the portfolio come from a wide range of industries.

To understand better the effect of diversification on the basic types of risk, let's consider what happens when we begin with a single asset (security) in a portfolio and then expand the portfolio by randomly selecting additional securities. Using the standard deviation, s_p, to measure the portfolio's *total risk,* we can depict the behavior of the total portfolio risk as more securities are added, as done in Figure 5.8. As we add securities to the portfolio (x-axis), the total portfolio risk (y-axis) declines because of the effects of diversification, but there is a limit to how much risk reduction can be achieved.

On average, most of the risk-reduction benefits of diversification can be gained by forming portfolios containing eight to 15 carefully selected securities, but our recommendation is to hold 40 securities or more to achieve efficient diversification. This suggestion tends to support the popularity of investment in mutual funds.

Because any investor can create a portfolio of assets that will eliminate virtually all diversifiable risk, the only **relevant risk** is that which is nondiversifiable. You must

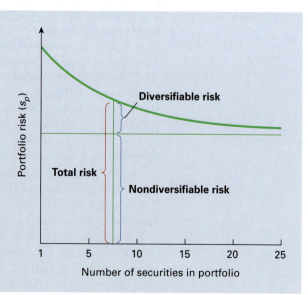

FIGURE 5.8

Portfolio Risk and Diversification

As more securities are combined to create a portfolio, the total risk of the portfolio (measured by its standard deviation, s_p) declines. The portion of the risk eliminated is the *diversifiable risk;* the remaining portion is the *nondiversifiable* or *relevant risk.*

therefore be concerned solely with nondiversifiable risk. The measurement of nondiversifiable risk is thus of primary importance.

Calculating Portfolio Betas As we saw earlier, *beta* measures the *nondiversifiable* or *relevant risk* of a security. The beta for the market is equal to 1.00. Securities with betas greater than 1.00 are more risky than the market, and those with betas less than 1.00 are less risky than the market. The beta for the risk-free asset is 0.

The **portfolio beta,** b_p, is merely the weighted average of the betas of the individual assets it includes. It can be easily estimated using the betas of the component assets. To find the portfolio beta, b_p, we can use Equation 5.4.

Equation 5.4

$$\text{Portfolio beta} = \left(\begin{array}{c} \text{Proportion of} \\ \text{portfolio's total} \\ \text{dollar value} \\ \text{asset 1} \end{array} \times \begin{array}{c} \text{Beta} \\ \text{for} \\ \text{asset 1} \end{array} \right) + \left(\begin{array}{c} \text{Proportion of} \\ \text{portfolio's total} \\ \text{dollar value} \\ \text{asset 2} \end{array} \times \begin{array}{c} \text{Beta} \\ \text{for} \\ \text{asset 2} \end{array} \right) + \ldots +$$

$$\left(\begin{array}{c} \text{Proportion of} \\ \text{portfolio's total} \\ \text{dollar value} \\ \text{asset } n \end{array} \times \begin{array}{c} \text{Beta} \\ \text{for} \\ \text{asset } n \end{array} \right) = \sum_{j=1}^{n} \left(\begin{array}{c} \text{Proportion of} \\ \text{portfolio's total} \\ \text{dollar value} \\ \text{asset } j \end{array} \times \begin{array}{c} \text{Beta} \\ \text{for} \\ \text{asset } j \end{array} \right)$$

Equation 5.4a

$$b_p = (w_1 \times b_1) + (w_2 \times b_2) + \cdots + (w_n \times b_n) = \sum_{j=1}^{n} (w_j \times b_j)$$

Of course, $\sum_{j=1}^{n} w_j = 1$, which means that 100% of the portfolio's assets must be included in this computation.

Portfolio betas are interpreted in exactly the same way as individual asset betas. They indicate the degree of responsiveness of the *portfolio's* return to changes in the market return. For example, when the market return increases by 10%, a portfolio with a beta of 0.75 will experience a 7.5% increase in its return ($0.75 \times 10\%$). A portfolio with a beta of 1.25 will experience a 12.5% increase in its return ($1.25 \times 10\%$). Low-beta portfolios are less responsive, and therefore less risky, than high-beta portfolios. Clearly, a portfolio containing mostly low-beta assets will have a low beta, and vice versa.

To demonstrate, consider the Austin Fund, a large investment company that wishes to assess the risk of two portfolios, V and W. Both portfolios contain five assets, with the proportions and betas shown in Table 5.6. We can calculate the betas for portfolios

TABLE 5.6	Austin Fund's Portfolios V and W			
	Portfolio V		Portfolio W	
Asset	Proportion	Beta	Proportion	Beta
1	0.10	1.65	0.10	0.80
2	0.30	1.00	0.10	1.00
3	0.20	1.30	0.20	0.65
4	0.20	1.10	0.10	0.75
5	0.20	1.25	0.50	1.05
Total	1.00		1.00	

V and W, b_v and b_w, by substituting the appropriate data from the table into Equation 5.4, as follows.

$b_v = (0.10 \times 1.65) + (0.30 \times 1.00) + (0.20 \times 1.30) + (0.20 \times 1.10) + (0.20 \times 1.25)$
$\quad = 0.165 + 0.300 + 0.260 + 0.220 + 0.250 = 1.195 \approx \underline{\underline{1.20}}$

$b_w = (0.10 \times 0.80) + (0.10 \times 1.00) + (0.20 \times 0.65) + (0.10 \times 0.75) + (0.50 \times 1.05)$
$\quad = 0.080 + 0.100 + 0.130 + 0.075 + 0.525 = \underline{\underline{0.91}}$

Portfolio V's beta is 1.20, and portfolio W's is 0.91. These values make sense because portfolio V contains relatively high-beta assets and portfolio W contains relatively low-beta assets. Clearly, portfolio V's returns are more responsive to changes in market returns—and therefore more risky—than portfolio W's.

Interpreting Portfolio Betas If a portfolio has a beta of +1.00, the portfolio experiences changes in its rate of return equal to changes in the market's rate of return. The +1.00 beta portfolio would tend to experience a 10% increase in return if the stock market as a whole experienced a 10% increase in return. Conversely, if the market return fell by 6%, the return on the +1.00 beta portfolio would also fall by 6%.

Table 5.7 lists the expected returns for three portfolio betas in two situations: an increase in market return of 10% and a decrease in market return of 10%. The 2.00 beta portfolio is twice as volatile as the market. When the market return increases by 10%, the portfolio return increases by 20%. When the market return declines by 10%, the portfolio's return will fall by 20%. This portfolio would be considered a high-risk, high-return portfolio.

The middle, 0.50 beta portfolio is considered a low-risk, low-return portfolio. This would be a conservative portfolio for investors who wish to maintain a low-risk investment posture. The 0.50 beta portfolio is half as volatile as the market.

A portfolio with a beta of −1.00 moves in the opposite direction from the market. A bearish investor would probably want to own a negative-beta portfolio, because this type of investment tends to rise in value when the stock market declines, and vice versa. Finding securities with negative betas is difficult, however. Most securities have positive betas, because they tend to experience return movements in the same direction as changes in the stock market.

The Risk-Return Tradeoff: Some Closing Comments Another valuable outgrowth of modern portfolio theory is the specific link between nondiversifiable risk and investment return. The basic premise is that an investor must have a portfolio of relatively risky investments to earn a relatively high rate of return. That relationship is illustrated in Figure 5.9. The upward-sloping line shows the **risk-return tradeoff**. The point where the risk-return line crosses the return axis is called the **risk-free rate, R_F**. This is the return an investor can earn on a risk-free investment such as a U.S. Treasury bill or an insured money market deposit account.

TABLE 5.7	Portfolio Betas and Associated Changes in Returns	
Portfolio Beta	Changes in Market Return	Change in Expected Portfolio Return
+2.00	+10.0%	+20.0%
	−10.0	−20.0
+0.50	+10.0	+5.0
	−10.0	−5.0
+1.00	+10.0	−10.0
	−10.0	+10.0

FIGURE 5.9

The Portfolio Risk-Return Tradeoff

As the risk of an investment portfolio increases from zero, the return provided should increase above the risk-free rate, R_F. Portfolios A and B offer returns commensurate with their risk, portfolio C provides a high return at a low-risk level, and portfolio D provides a low return for high risk. Portfolio C is highly desirable; portfolio D should be avoided.

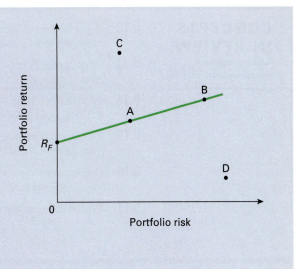

As we proceed upward along the risk-return tradeoff line, portfolios of risky investments appear, as depicted by four investment portfolios, A through D. Portfolios A and B are investment opportunities that provide a level of return commensurate with their respective risk levels. Portfolio C provides a high return at a relatively low risk level—and therefore would be an excellent investment. Portfolio D, in contrast, offers high risk but low return—an investment to avoid.

Reconciling the Traditional Approach and MPT

We have reviewed two fairly different approaches to portfolio management: the traditional approach and MPT. The question that naturally arises is which technique should you use? There is no definite answer; the question must be resolved by the judgment of each investor. However, we can offer a few useful ideas.

The average individual investor does not have the resources, computers, and mathematical acumen to implement a total MPT portfolio strategy. But most individual investors can extract and use ideas from *both* the traditional and MPT approaches. The traditional approach stresses security selection, which is discussed in Chapters 7 and 8. It also emphasizes diversification of the portfolio across industry lines. MPT stresses reducing correlations between rates of return for the securities within the portfolio. This approach calls for diversification to minimize diversifiable risk. Thus, diversification must be accomplished to ensure satisfactory performance with either strategy. Also, beta is a useful tool for determining the level of a portfolio's nondiversifiable risk and should be part of the decision-making process.

We recommend the following portfolio management policy, which uses aspects of both approaches:

- Determine how much risk you are willing to bear.

- Seek diversification among different types of securities and across industry lines, and pay attention to how the return from one security is related to that from another.

- Consider how a security responds to the market, and use beta in diversifying your portfolio as a way to keep the portfolio in line with your acceptable level of risk.

- Evaluate alternative portfolios to make sure that the portfolio selected provides the highest return for the given level of acceptable risk.

5.12 Describe *traditional portfolio management*. Give three reasons why traditional portfolio managers like to invest in well-established companies.

5.13 What is *modern portfolio theory (MPT)?* What is the *feasible* or *attainable set* of all possible portfolios? How is it derived for a given group of investment vehicles?

5.14 What is the *efficient frontier?* How is it related to the attainable set of all possible portfolios? How can it be used with an investor's utility function to find the optimal portfolio?

5.15 Define and differentiate among the diversifiable, nondiversifiable, and total risk of a portfolio. Which is considered the *relevant risk?* How is it measured?

5.16 Define *beta.* How can you find the beta of a portfolio when you know the beta for each of the assets included within it?

5.17 Explain how you can reconcile the traditional and modern portfolio approaches.

---

myfinancelab

Here is what you should know after reading this chapter. **MyFinanceLab** will help you identify what you know, and where to go when you need to practice.

What You Should Know	Key Terms	Where To Practice
LG1 **Understand portfolio objectives and the procedures used to calculate portfolio return and standard deviation.** A portfolio is a collection of investments assembled to achieve one or more investment goals. It produces potential price appreciation and current income, subject to a tradeoff between risk and return. The return on a portfolio is calculated as a weighted average of the returns of the assets from which it is formed. The standard deviation of a portfolio's returns is found by applying the same formula that is used to find the standard deviation of a single asset.	efficient portfolio, *p. 165* growth-oriented portfolio, *p. 165* income-oriented portfolio, *p. 165*	MyFinanceLab Study Plan 5.1 Excel Table 5.1 Video Learning Aid for Problem P5.5
LG2 **Discuss the concepts of correlation and diversification, and the key aspects of international diversification.** Correlation is a statistic used to measure the relationship, if any, between the returns on assets. To diversify, it is best to add assets with negatively correlated returns. In general, the less positive and more negative the correlation between asset returns, the more effectively a portfolio can be diversified to reduce its risk. Diversification can reduce the risk (standard deviation) of a portfolio below the risk of the least risky asset (sometimes to zero). The return of the resulting portfolio will be no lower than the smallest return of its component assets. For any two-asset portfolio, the ability to reduce risk depends on both the degree of correlation and proportion of each asset in the portfolio. International diversification may allow an investor to reduce portfolio risk without necessarily imposing a corresponding reduction in return. It can be achieved by investing abroad or through domestic investment in foreign companies or funds, but it typically cannot be achieved by investing in U.S. multinationals. The preferred method of	correlation, *p. 167* correlation coefficient, *p. 168* negatively correlated, *p. 168* perfectly negatively correlated, *p. 168* perfectly positively correlated, *p. 168* positively correlated, *p. 167* uncorrelated, *p. 168*	MyFinanceLab Study Plan 5.2 Excel Tables 5.2, 5.3

What You Should Know	Key Terms	Where To Practice
international diversification for individual investors is the use of ADSs or international mutual funds available in the United States. Although opportunities to earn "excess" returns in international investments are diminishing over time, they continue to be effective diversification vehicles.		
LG3 **Describe the components of risk and the use of beta to measure risk.** The two basic components of total risk are diversifiable (unsystematic) and nondiversifiable (systematic) risk. Nondiversifiable risk is the relevant risk. Beta measures the nondiversifiable, or market, risk associated with a security investment. It is derived from the historical relationship between a security's return and the market return.	beta, *p. 175* diversifiable (unsystematic) risk, *p. 175* market return, *p. 175* nondiversifiable (systematic) risk, *p. 175* total risk, *p. 175*	MyFinanceLab Study Plan 5.3 Video Learning Aid for Problem P5.22
LG4 **Explain the capital asset pricing model (CAPM)— conceptually, mathematically, and graphically.** The capital asset pricing model (CAPM) relates risk (as measured by beta) to return. It can be divided into two parts: (1) the risk-free rate of return, R_F, and (2) the risk premium, $b \times (r_m - R_F)$. The graphic depiction of the CAPM is the security market line (SML). The CAPM reflects increasing required returns for increasing risk.	capital asset pricing model (CAPM), *p. 179* security market line (SML), *p. 179*	MyFinanceLab Study Plan 5.4
LG5 **Review the traditional and modern approaches to portfolio management.** The traditional approach constructs portfolios by combining a large number of securities issued by companies from a broad cross-section of industries. Modern portfolio theory (MPT) uses statistical diversification to develop efficient portfolios. To determine the optimal portfolio, MPT finds the efficient frontier and couples it with an investor's risk-indifference curves.	efficient frontier, *p. 183* modern portfolio theory (MPT), *p. 182* portfolio beta, b_p, *p. 185* relevant risk, *p. 184* risk-return tradeoff, *p. 186* risk-free rate, R_F, *p. 186* traditional portfolio management, *p. 181*	MyFinanceLab Study Plan 5.5
LG6 **Describe portfolio betas, the risk-return tradeoff, and reconciliation of the two approaches to portfolio management.** In practice, portfolio betas can be used to develop efficient portfolios consistent with the investor's risk-return preferences. Portfolio betas are merely a weighted average of the betas of the individual assets included in the portfolio. Generally, investors use elements of both the traditional approach and MPT to create portfolios. This approach involves determining how much risk you are willing to bear, seeking diversification, using beta to diversify your portfolio, and evaluating alternative portfolios to select the one that offers the highest return for an acceptable level of risk.		MyFinanceLab Study Plan 5.6 Video Learning Aid for Problem P5.22

Log into **MyFinanceLab**, take a chapter test, and get a personalized Study Plan
that tells you which concepts you understand and which ones you need to
review. From there, **MyFinanceLab** will give you further practice, tutorials,
animations, videos, and guided solutions.
Log into www.myfinancelab.com

Discussion Questions

LG1 **Q5.1** State your portfolio objectives. Then construct a 10-stock portfolio that you feel is consistent with your objectives. (Use companies that have been public for at least five years.) Obtain annual dividend and price data for each of the past five years.

    a. Calculate the historical return for each stock for each year.

    b. Calculate the historical portfolio return for each of the five years, using your findings in part **a**.

    c. Use your findings in part **b** to calculate the average portfolio return over the five years.

    d. Use your findings in parts **b** and **c** to find the standard deviation of the portfolio's returns over the five-year period.

    e. Use the historical average return from part **c** and the standard deviation from part **d** to evaluate the portfolio's return and risk in light of your stated portfolio objectives.

LG2 **Q5.2** Using the following guidelines, choose the stocks—A, B, and C—of 3 firms that have been public for at least 10 years. Stock A should be one you are interested in buying. Stock B should be a stock, possibly in the same line of business or industry, that you feel will have the lowest possible return correlation with stock A. Stock C should be one you feel will have the highest possible return correlation with stock A.

    a. Calculate the annual rates of return for each of the past 10 years for each stock.

    b. Plot the 10 annual return values for each stock on the same set of axes, where the x-axis is the year and the y-axis is the annual return in percentage terms.

    c. Join the points for the returns for each stock on the graph. Evaluate and describe the returns of stocks A and B in the graph. Do they exhibit the expected positive correlation? Why or why not?

    d. Evaluate and describe the relationship between the returns of stocks A and C in the graph. Do they exhibit negative correlation? Why or why not?

    e. Compare and contrast your findings in parts **c** and **d** to the expected relationships among stocks A, B, and C. Discuss your findings.

LG3 **Q5.3** From the *Wall Street Journal*, a Web site such as Yahoo! Finance (**finance.yahoo.com**), or some other source, obtain a current estimate of the risk-free rate (use a 10-year Treasury bond). Use the *Value Line Investment Survey* or Yahoo! Finance to obtain the beta for each of the following stocks:

Ford (autos)
Dell (computers)
Sempra Energy (utilities)
Kroger (groceries)
Bank of America (financial services)

Use the information you gathered, along with the market risk premium on large stocks given in the chapter, to find the required return for each stock with the capital asset pricing model (CAPM).

LG3 LG4 **Q5.4** From the *Wall Street Journal*, a Web site such as Yahoo! Finance (**finance.yahoo.com**), or some other source, obtain a current estimate of the risk-free rate (use a 10-year Treasury bond). Use the *Value Line Investment Survey* or Yahoo! Finance to obtain the beta for each of the companies listed on page 177.

    a. Compare the current betas to the August 2009 betas given in the chapter for each of the companies.

    b. What might cause betas to change over time, even in a stable economic environment?

    c. Use the current betas, along with a market risk premium on stocks of 8.5%, to find the required return for each stock with the capital asset pricing model (CAPM).

    d. Compare and discuss your findings in part **c** with regard to the specific business that each company is in.

Q5.5 Obtain a prospectus and an annual report for a major mutual fund that includes some international securities. Carefully read the prospectus and annual report and study the portfolio's composition in light of the fund's stated objectives.

    a. Evaluate the amount of diversification and the types of industries and companies held. Is the portfolio well diversified?

    b. Discuss the additional risks faced by an investor in this fund compared to an investor in a domestic stock portfolio such as the S&P 500.

LG6 **Q5.6** Use *Value Line Investment Survey* or some other source to select four stocks with betas ranging from about 0.50 to 1.50. Record the current market prices of each of these stocks. Assume you wish to create a portfolio that combines all four stocks in such a way that the resulting portfolio beta is about 1.10.

    a. Through trial and error, use all four stocks to create a portfolio with the target beta of 1.10.

    b. If you have $100,000 to invest in this portfolio, on the basis of the weightings determined in part **a**, what dollar amounts would you invest in each stock?

    c. Approximately how many shares of each of the four stocks would you buy, given the dollar amounts calculated in part **b**?

    d. Repeat parts **a**, **b**, and **c** with a different set of weightings that still result in a portfolio beta of 1.10. Can only one unique portfolio with a given beta be created from a given set of stocks?

Problems

All problems are available on **www.myfinancelab.com**

LG1 **P5.1** Your portfolio had the values in the following table for the four-year period listed. Calculate your average return over the four-year period.

Year	Beginning Value	Ending Value
2007	$50,000.00	$55,000.00
2008	$55,000.00	$58,000.00
2009	$58,000.00	$65,000.00
2010	$65,000.00	$70,000.00

LG1 **P5.2** Using your data from Problem 5.1 above, calculate the portfolio standard deviation.

LG1 **LG2** **P5.3** Assume you are considering a portfolio containing two assets, L and M. Asset L will represent 40% of the dollar value of the portfolio, and asset M will account for the other 60%. The expected returns over the next 6 years, 2012–2017, for each of these assets are summarized in the following table.

	Expected Return (%)	
Year	Asset L	Asset M
2012	14	20
2013	14	18
2014	16	16
2015	17	14
2016	17	12
2017	19	10

    a. Calculate the expected portfolio return, $\bar{r}_p$, for each of the six years.

    b. Calculate the average expected portfolio return, $\bar{r}_p$, over the six-year period.

c. Calculate the standard deviation of expected portfolio returns, s_p, over the six-year period.

d. How would you characterize the correlation of returns of the two assets L and M?

e. Discuss any benefits of diversification achieved through creation of the portfolio.

 P5.4 Refer to Problem 5.3 above. Assume that asset L represents 60% of the portfolio and asset M 40%. Calculate the average expected return and standard deviation of expected portfolio returns over the 6-year period. Compare your answers to the answers from Problem 5.3.

 P5.5 You have been given the following return data on 3 assets—F, G, and H—over the period 2012–2015.

	Expected Return (%)		
Year	Asset F	Asset G	Asset H
2012	16	17	14
2013	17	16	15
2014	18	15	16
2015	19	14	17

Using these assets, you have isolated three investment alternatives:

Alternative	Investment
1	100% of asset F
2	50% of asset F and 50% of asset G
3	50% of asset F and 50% of asset H

a. Calculate the portfolio return over the four-year period for each of the three alternatives.

b. Calculate the standard deviation of returns over the four-year period for each of the three alternatives.

c. On the basis of your findings in parts a and b, which of the three investment alternatives would you recommend? Why?

 P5.6 You have been asked for your advice in selecting a portfolio of assets and have been supplied with the following data.

	Expected Return (%)		
Year	Asset A	Asset B	Asset C
2012	12	16	12
2013	14	14	14
2014	16	12	16

You have been told that you can create two portfolios—one consisting of assets A and B and the other consisting of assets A and C—by investing equal proportions (50%) in each of the two component assets.

a. What is the average expected return, $\bar{r}$, for each asset over the three-year period?

b. What is the standard deviation, s, for each asset's expected return?

c. What is the average expected return, $\bar{r}_p$, for each of the two portfolios?

d. How would you characterize the correlations of returns of the two assets making up each of the two portfolios identified in part c?

e. What is the standard deviation of expected returns, s_p, for each portfolio?

f. Which portfolio do you recommend? Why?

LG1 LG2   **P5.7** Referring to Problem 5.6 earlier, what would happen if you constructed a portfolio consisting of assets A, B, and C, equally weighted? Would this reduce risk or enhance return?

LG1 LG2   **P5.8** Assume you wish to evaluate the risk and return behaviors associated with various combinations of assets V and W under three assumed degrees of correlation: perfect positive, uncorrelated, and perfect negative. The following average return and risk values were calculated for these assets.

Asset	Average Return, $\bar{r}$ (%)	Risk (Standard Deviation), s (%)
V	8	5
W	13	10

a. If the returns of assets V and W are *perfectly positively correlated* (correlation coefficient = +1), describe the *range* of (1) return and (2) risk associated with all possible portfolio combinations.
b. If the returns of assets V and W are *uncorrelated* (correlation coefficient = 0), describe the *approximate range* of (1) return and (2) risk associated with all possible portfolio combinations.
c. If the returns of assets V and W are *perfectly negatively correlated* (correlation coefficient = −21), describe the *range* of (1) return and (2) risk associated with all possible portfolio combinations.

LG3   **P5.9** Imagine you wish to estimate the betas for two investments, A and B. You have gathered the following return data for the market and for each of the investments over the past 10 years, 2002–2011.

	Historical Returns		
		Investment	
Year	Market	A	B
2002	6%	11%	16%
2003	2	8	11
2004	−13	−4	−10
2005	−4	3	3
2006	−8	0	−3
2007	16	19	30
2008	10	14	22
2009	15	18	29
2010	8	12	19
2011	13	17	26

a. On a set of market return (*x*-axis)–investment return (*y*-axis) axes, use the data to draw the characteristic lines for investments A and B on the same set of axes.
b. Use the characteristic lines from part **a** to estimate the betas for investments A and B.
c. Use the betas found in part **b** to comment on the relative risks of investments A and B.

LG3   **P5.10** You are evaluating two possible stock investments, Buyme Co. and Getit Corp. Buyme Co. has an expected return of 14%, and a beta of 1. Getit Corp. has an expected return of 14%, and a beta of 1.2. Based only on this data, which stock should you buy and why?

LG3   **P5.11** Referring to Problem 5.10 above, if you expected a significant market rally, would your decision be altered? Explain.

LG3   **P5.12** A security has a beta of 1.20. Is this security more or less risky than the market? Explain. Assess the impact on the required return of this security in each of the following cases.
   a. The market return increases by 15%.
   b. The market return decreases by 8%.
   c. The market return remains unchanged.

LG3   **P5.13** Assume the betas for securities A, B, and C are as shown here.

Security	Beta
A	1.40
B	0.80
C	−0.90

   a. Calculate the change in return for each security if the market experiences an increase in its rate of return of 13.2% over the next period.
   b. Calculate the change in return for each security if the market experiences a decrease in its rate of return of 10.8% over the next period.
   c. Rank and discuss the relative risk of each security on the basis of your findings. Which security might perform best during an economic downturn? Explain.

LG3 LG6   **P5.14** Referring to Problem 5.13 above, assume you have a portfolio with $20,000 invested in each of Investment A, B, and C. What is your portfolio beta?

LG3 LG6   **P5.15** Referring to Problem 5.14 above, using the portfolio beta, what would you expect the value of your portfolio to be if the market rallied 20%? Declined 20%?

LG4   **P5.16** Use the capital asset pricing model (CAPM) to find the required return for each of the following securities in light of the data given.

Security	Risk-Free Rate	Market Return	Beta
A	5%	8%	1.30
B	8	13	0.90
C	9	12	−0.20
D	10	15	1.00
E	6	10	0.60

LG4   **P5.17** Jay is reviewing his portfolio of investments, which include certain stocks and bonds. He has a large amount tied up in U.S. Treasury bills paying 3%. He is considering moving some of his funds from the T-bills into a stock. The stock has a beta of 1.25. If Jay expects a return of 14% from the stock (a little better than the current market return of 13%), should he buy the stock or leave his funds in the T-bill?

LG4   **P5.18** The risk-free rate is currently 7%, and the market return is 12%. Assume you are considering the following investments.

Investment Vehicle	Beta
A	1.50
B	1.00
C	0.75
D	0
E	2.00

   a. Which vehicle is most risky? Least risky?
   b. Use the capital asset pricing model (CAPM) to find the required return on each of the investment vehicles.

    c. Draw the security market line (SML), using your findings in part **b.**

    d. On the basis of your findings in part **c,** what relationship exists between risk and return? Explain.

LG5 LG6 **P5.19** Portfolios A through J, which are listed in the following table along with their returns (r_p) and risk (measured by the standard deviation, s_p), represent all currently available portfolios in the feasible or attainable set.

Portfolio	Return (r_p)	Risk (s_p)
A	9%	8%
B	3	3
C	14	10
D	12	14
E	7	11
F	11	6
G	10	12
H	16	16
I	5	7
J	8	4

    a. Plot the *feasible* or *attainable set* represented by these data on a set of portfolio risk, s_p (x-axis)–portfolio return, r_p (y-axis) axes.

    b. Draw the *efficient frontier* on the graph in part **a.**

    c. Which portfolios lie on the efficient frontier? Why do these portfolios dominate all others in the feasible or attainable set?

    d. How would an investor's *utility function* or *risk-indifference curves* be used with the efficient frontier to find the optimal portfolio?

LG5 LG6 **P5.20** For his portfolio, Jack Cashman randomly selected securities from all those listed on the New York Stock Exchange. He began with one security and added securities one by one until a total of 20 securities were held in the portfolio. After each security was added, Jack calculated the portfolio standard deviation, s_p. The calculated values follow.

Number of Securities	Portfolio Risk, s_p (%)	Number of Securities	Portfolio Risk, s_p (%)
1	14.50	11	7.00
2	13.30	12	6.80
3	12.20	13	6.70
4	11.20	14	6.65
5	10.30	15	6.60
6	9.50	16	6.56
7	8.80	17	6.52
8	8.20	18	6.50
9	7.70	19	6.48
10	7.30	20	6.47

    a. On a set of axes showing the number of securities in the portfolio (x-axis) and portfolio risk, s_p (y-axis), plot the portfolio risk data given in the preceding table.

    b. Divide the total portfolio risk in the graph into its *nondiversifiable* and *diversifiable* risk components, and label each of these on the graph.

    c. Describe which of the two risk components is the *relevant risk,* and explain why it is relevant. How much of this risk exists in Jack Cashman's portfolio?

LG3 LG6 **P5.21** If portfolio A has a beta of +1.50 and portfolio Z has a beta of −1.50, what do the two values indicate? If the return on the market rises by 20%, what impact, if any, would this have on the returns from portfolios A and Z? Explain.

P5.22 Stock A has a beta of 0.80, stock B has a beta of 1.40, and stock C has a beta of –0.30.

  a. Rank these stocks from the most risky to the least risky.

  b. If the return on the market portfolio increases by 12%, what change in the return for each of the stocks would you expect?

  c. If the return on the market portfolio declines by 5%, what change in the return for each of the stocks would you expect?

  d. If you felt the stock market was about to experience a significant decline, which stock would you be most likely to add to your portfolio? Why?

  e. If you anticipated a major stock market rally, which stock would you be most likely to add to your portfolio? Why?

LG6 **P5.23** Jeanne Lewis is attempting to evaluate two possible portfolios consisting of the same five assets but held in different proportions. She is particularly interested in using beta to compare the risk of the portfolios and, in this regard, has gathered the following data:

Asset	Asset Beta	Portfolio Weights (%)	
		Portfolio A	Portfolio B
1	1.30	10	30
2	0.70	30	10
3	1.25	10	20
4	1.10	10	20
5	0.90	40	20
Total		100	100

  a. Calculate the betas for portfolios A and B.

  b. Compare the risk of each portfolio to the market as well as to each other. Which portfolio is more risky?

LG4 **P5.24** Referring to Problem 5.23 above, if the risk-free rate is 2% and the market return is 12%, calculate the required return for each portfolio using the CAPM.

LG5 LG6 **P5.25** Referring to Problem 5.24 above, assume you now have the following annual returns (r_j) for each investment.

Asset (j)	r_j
1	16.5%
2	12.0%
3	15.0%
4	13.0%
5	7.0%

Using your finding from Problem 5.24 and the additional return data, determine which portfolio you would choose and explain why.

Visit **www.myfinancelab.com** for web exercises, spreadsheets, and other online resources.

Case Problem 5.1   *Traditional Versus Modern Portfolio Theory: Who's Right?*

 Walt Davies and Shane O'Brien are district managers for Lee, Inc. Over the years, as they moved through the firm's sales organization, they became (and still remain) close friends. Walt, who is 33 years old, currently lives in Princeton, New Jersey. Shane, who is 35, lives in Houston, Texas.

Recently, at the national sales meeting, they were discussing various company matters, as well as bringing each other up to date on their families, when the subject of investments came up. Each had always been fascinated by the stock market, and now that they had achieved some degree of financial success, they had begun actively investing.

As they discussed their investments, Walt said he felt the only way an individual who does not have hundreds of thousands of dollars can invest safely is to buy mutual fund shares. He emphasized that to be safe, a person needs to hold a broadly diversified portfolio and that only those with a lot of money and time can achieve independently the diversification that can be readily obtained by purchasing mutual fund shares.

Shane totally disagreed. He said, "Diversification! Who needs it?" He felt that what one must do is look carefully at stocks possessing desired risk-return characteristics and then invest all one's money in the single best stock. Walt told him he was crazy. He said, "There is no way to measure risk conveniently—you're just gambling." Shane disagreed. He explained how his stockbroker had acquainted him with beta, which is a measure of risk. Shane said that the higher the beta, the more risky the stock, and therefore the higher its return. By looking up the betas for potential stock investments on the Internet, he can pick stocks that have an acceptable risk level for him. Shane explained that with beta, one does not need to diversify; one merely needs to be willing to accept the risk reflected by beta and then hope for the best.

The conversation continued, with Walt indicating that although he knew nothing about beta, he didn't believe one could safely invest in a single stock. Shane continued to argue that his broker had explained to him that betas can be calculated not just for a single stock but also for a portfolio of stocks, such as a mutual fund. He said, "What's the difference between a stock with a beta of, say, 1.20 and a mutual fund with a beta of 1.20? They both have the same risk and should therefore provide similar returns."

As Walt and Shane continued to discuss their differing opinions relative to investment strategy, they began to get angry with each other. Neither was able to convince the other that he was right. The level of their voices now raised, they attracted the attention of the company vice-president of finance, Elinor Green, who was standing nearby. She came over and indicated she had overheard their argument about investments and thought that, given her expertise on financial matters, she might be able to resolve their disagreement. She asked them to explain the crux of their disagreement, and each reviewed his own viewpoint. After hearing their views, Elinor responded, "I have some good news and some bad news for each of you. There is some validity to what each of you says, but there also are some errors in each of your explanations. Walt tends to support the traditional approach to portfolio management. Shane's views are more supportive of modern portfolio theory." Just then, the company president interrupted them, needing to talk to Elinor immediately. Elinor apologized for having to leave and offered to continue their discussion later that evening.

Questions

a. Analyze Walt's argument and explain why a mutual fund investment may be overdiversified. Also explain why one does not necessarily have to have hundreds of thousands of dollars to diversify adequately.

b. Analyze Shane's argument and explain the major error in his logic relative to the use of beta as a substitute for diversification. Explain the key assumption underlying the use of beta as a risk measure.

c. Briefly describe the traditional approach to portfolio management, and relate it to the approaches supported by Walt and Shane.

d. Briefly describe modern portfolio theory (MPT) and relate it to the approaches supported by Walt and Shane. Be sure to mention diversifiable risk, nondiversifiable risk, and total risk, along with the role of beta.

e. Explain how the traditional approach and modern portfolio theory can be blended into an approach to portfolio management that might prove useful to the individual investor. Relate this to reconciling Walt's and Shane's differing points of view.

Case Problem 5.2   *Susan Lussier's Inherited Portfolio: Does It Meet Her Needs?*

LG3 LG4
LG5 LG6

Susan Lussier is a 35-year-old divorcée currently employed as a tax accountant for a major oil and gas exploration company. She has no children and earns nearly $135,000 a year from her salary and from participation in the company's drilling activities. Divorced only a year, Susan has found being single quite exciting. An expert on oil and gas taxation, she is not worried about job security—she is content with her income and finds it adequate to allow her to buy and do whatever she wishes. Her current philosophy is to live each day to its fullest, not concerning herself with retirement, which is too far in the future to require her current attention.

A month ago, Susan's only surviving parent, her father, was killed in a sailing accident. He had retired in La Jolla, California, two years earlier and had spent most of his time sailing. Prior to retirement, he managed a children's clothing manufacturing firm in South Carolina. Upon retirement he sold his stock in the firm and invested the proceeds in a security portfolio that provided him with supplemental retirement income of over $30,000 per year. In his will, he left his entire estate to Susan. The estate was structured in such a way that in addition to a few family heirlooms, Susan received a security portfolio having a market value of nearly $350,000 and about $10,000 in cash.

Susan's father's portfolio contained 10 securities: five bonds, two common stocks, and three mutual funds. The accompanying table lists the securities and their key characteristics. The common stocks were issued by large, mature, well-known firms that had exhibited continuing patterns of dividend payment over the past five years. The stocks offered only moderate growth potential—probably no more than 2% to 3% appreciation per year. The mutual funds in the portfolio were income funds invested in diversified portfolios of income-oriented stocks and bonds. They provided stable streams of dividend income but offered little opportunity for capital appreciation.

Case 5.2 The Securities Portfolio That Susan Lussier Inherited

			Bonds			
Par Value	Issue	S&P Rating	Interest Income	Quoted Price	Total Cost	Current Yield
$40,000	Delta Power and Light 10.125% due 2029	AA	$4,050	98.000	$39,200	10.33%
30,000	Mountain Water 9.750% due 2021	A	2,925	102.000	30,600	9.56
50,000	California Gas 9.500% due 2016	AAA	4,750	97.000	48,500	9.79
20,000	Trans-Pacific Gas 10.000% due 2027	AAA	2,000	99.000	19,800	10.10
20,000	Public Service 9.875% due 2017	AA	1,975	100.000	20,000	9.88

		Common Stocks					
Number of Shares	Company	Dividend per Share	Dividend Income	Price per Share	Total Cost	Beta	Dividend Yield
2,000	International Supply	$2.40	$4,800	$22	$44,900	0.97	10.91%
3,000	Black Motor	1.50	4,500	17	52,000	0.85	8.82

		Mutual Funds					
Number of Shares	Fund	Dividend per Share Income	Dividend Income	Price per Share	Total Cost	Beta	Dividend Yield
2,000	International Capital Income A Fund	$0.80	$1,600	$10	$20,000	1.02	8.00%
1,000	Grimner Special Income Fund	2.00	2,000	15	15,000	1.10	7.50
4,000	Ellis Diversified Income Fund	1.20	4,800	12	48,00	0.90	10.00

Total annual income: **$33,400**   Portfolio value: **$338,000**   Portfolio current yield: **9.88%**

Now that Susan owns the portfolio, she wishes to determine whether it is suitable for her situation. She realizes that the high level of income provided by the portfolio will be taxed at a rate (federal plus state) of about 40%. Because she does not currently need it, Susan plans to invest the after-tax income primarily in common stocks offering high capital gain potential. During the coming years she clearly needs to avoid generating taxable income. (Susan is already paying out a sizable portion of her current income in taxes.) She feels fortunate to have received the portfolio and wants to make certain it provides her with the maximum benefits, given her financial situation. The $10,000 cash left to her will be especially useful in paying broker's commissions associated with making portfolio adjustments.

Questions

a. Briefly assess Susan's financial situation and develop a portfolio objective for her that is consistent with her needs.

b. Evaluate the portfolio left to Susan by her father. Assess its apparent objective and evaluate how well it may be doing in fulfilling this objective. Use the total cost values to describe the asset allocation scheme reflected in the portfolio. Comment on the risk, return, and tax implications of this portfolio.

c. If Susan decided to invest in a security portfolio consistent with her needs—indicated in response to question **a**—describe the nature and mix, if any, of securities you would recommend she purchase. Discuss the risk, return, and tax implications of such a portfolio.

d. Compare the nature of the security portfolio inherited by Susan, from the response to question **b**, with what you believe would be an appropriate security portfolio for her, from the response to question **c**.

e. What recommendations would you give Susan about the inherited portfolio? Explain the steps she should take to adjust the portfolio to her needs.

Excel with Spreadsheets

In the previous chapter's spreadsheet problem, you helped Laura evaluate the risk-return tradeoff for three stand-alone securities. An alternative for Laura is to look at the investment as a portfolio of both IBM and HP and not as stand-alone situations. Laura's professor suggests that she use the capital asset pricing model to define the required returns for the 2 companies (refer to Equations 5.3 and 5.3a):

$$r_j = R_F + [b_j \times (r_m - R_F)]$$

Laura measures R_F using the current long-term Treasury bond return of 5% and measures r_m using the average return on the S&P 500 Index from her calculations in the Chapter 4 spreadsheet problem. She researches a source for the beta information and follows these steps:

• Go to **moneycentral.msn.com**.

• Within the "Get Quote" box, type IBM and press "Go."

• In the left column, look under "Quote, Chart, News" and choose "Company Report."

• Under the heading of "Stock Activity," find the "Volatility (beta)" figure.

• Repeat the same steps for the HP stock.

Questions

a. What are the beta values for IBM and HP? Assume that the beta for the S&P 500 Index is 1.0. Using the CAPM, create a spreadsheet to determine the required rates of return for both IBM and HP.

b. Laura has decided that the portfolio will be distributed between IBM and HP in a 60% and 40% split, respectively. Hence, a weighted average can be calculated for both the returns and betas of the portfolio. This concept is shown in the spreadsheet for Table 5.2, which can be viewed at www.myfinancelab.com. **Create a spreadsheet** using the following models for the calculations:

$$war = w_i * r_i + w_j * r_j$$

where:
- war = weighted average required rate of return for the portfolio
- w_i = weight of security i in the portfolio
- r_i = required return of security i in the portfolio
- w_j = weight of security j in the portfolio
- r_j = required return of security j in the portfolio

$$wab = w_i * b_i + w_j * b_j$$

where:
- wab = weighted average beta for the portfolio
- w_i = weight of security i in the portfolio
- b_i = beta for security i
- w_j = weight of security j in the portfolio
- bj = beta for security j

Chapter-Opening Problem

In this problem we will revisit United Rentals Inc. (URI), which was introduced at the beginning of the chapter. The following table shows the monthly return on URI stock and on the S&P500 stock index from August 2004 to July 2009.

Month/Year	S&P 500 Return	United Rentals Return	Month/Year	S&P 500 Return	United Rentals Return
7/1/2009	2.3%	−5.2%	6/1/2007	−1.8%	−3.0%
6/1/2009	0.0%	36.6%	5/1/2007	3.3%	0.1%
5/1/2009	5.3%	−21.6%	4/2/2007	4.3%	21.8%
4/1/2009	9.4%	43.9%	3/1/2007	1.0%	−3.7%
3/2/2009	8.5%	4.0%	2/1/2007	−2.2%	10.9%
2/2/2009	−11.0%	−27.4%	1/3/2007	1.4%	1.3%
1/2/2009	−8.6%	−38.8%	12/1/2006	1.3%	1.5%
12/1/2008	0.8%	13.0%	11/1/2006	1.6%	5.8%
11/3/2008	−7.5%	−21.3%	10/2/2006	3.2%	1.9%
10/1/2008	−16.9%	−32.7%	9/1/2006	2.5%	7.3%
9/2/2008	−9.1%	−5.9%	8/1/2006	2.1%	−22.4%
8/1/2008	1.2%	0.1%	7/3/2006	0.5%	−12.7%
7/1/2008	−1.0%	−17.5%	6/1/2006	0.0%	−1.8%
6/2/2008	−8.6%	−4.8%	5/1/2006	−3.1%	−8.7%
5/1/2008	1.1%	9.3%	4/3/2006	1.2%	3.4%
4/1/2008	4.8%	0.0%	3/1/2006	1.1%	5.8%
3/3/2008	−0.6%	−6.3%	2/1/2006	0.0%	11.2%
2/1/2008	−3.5%	10.3%	1/3/2006	2.5%	25.3%
1/2/2008	−6.1%	−0.7%	12/1/2005	−0.1%	10.5%
12/3/2007	−0.9%	−21.1%	11/1/2005	3.5%	8.1%
11/1/2007	−4.4%	−31.9%	10/3/2005	−1.8%	−0.7%
10/1/2007	1.5%	6.3%	9/1/2005	0.7%	9.2%
9/4/2007	3.6%	−1.3%	8/1/2005	−1.1%	−3.0%
8/1/2007	1.3%	1.4%	7/1/2005	3.6%	−8.0%
7/2/2007	−3.2%	−1.2%	6/1/2005	0.0%	0.6%

Month/Year	S&P 500 Return	United Rentals Return	Month/Year	S&P 500 Return	United Rentals Return
5/2/2005	3.0%	9.2%	12/1/2004	3.2%	5.8%
4/1/2005	−2.0%	−9.0%	11/1/2004	3.9%	15.7%
3/1/2005	−1.9%	6.8%	10/1/2004	1.4%	−2.8%
2/1/2005	1.9%	11.2%	9/1/2004	0.9%	8.2%
1/3/2005	−2.5%	−10.0%	8/2/2004	0.2%	−26.0%

1. Calculate the average monthly return on URI stock and on the S&P 500.

2. Calculate the standard deviation of monthly returns for URI and the S&P 500. What do your answers tell you about diversifiable risk, nondiversifiable risk, and total risk?

3. Plot the returns of URI on the vertical axis and the returns of the S&P500 on the horizontal axis of a graph. Does it appear that URI and the S&P 500 are correlated? If so, are they positively or negatively correlated?

4. Draw a line that you think best fits the scatterplot of points that you created in part 3. What is the slope of this line? How can you interpret the slope? What does it say about the risk of URI compared to the risk of the S&P 500?

CFA EXAM QUESTIONS

Being certified as a Chartered Financial Analyst (CFA) is globally recognized as the highest professional designation you can receive in the field of professional money management. The CFA charter is awarded to those candidates who successfully pass a series of three levels of exams, with each exam lasting 6 hours and covering a full range of investment topics. The CFA program is administered by the CFA Institute in Charlottesville, VA (for more information about the CFA program, go to: www.cfainstitute.org).

Starting with this Part (Two) of the text, and at the end of each part hereafter, you will find a small sample of CFA questions taken from the Level I curriculum as well as *CFA Candidates Study Notes, Level 1, Volume 4* (Cengage Learning).

The Investment Environment and Conceptual Tools

Following is a sample of 11 Level-I CFA exam questions that deal with many of the topics covered in Parts One and Two of this text, including the time value of money, measures of risk and return, securities markets, and portfolio management. (When answering the questions, give yourself 1½ minutes for each question; the objective is to correctly answer 8 of the 11 questions in a period of 16½ minutes.)

1. An investor bought a stock for $50 a month ago and it is currently selling for $45. An order to sell the stock if it drops to $40 is a:
a. short sale order.
b. stop loss order.
c. stop buy order.

2. What is the leveraged return of 500 shares of a stock purchased with 40% margin at $15/share that rises to $20/share?
a. 55.56%
b. 33.33%
c. 66.67%

3. The adjustment for a stock split in the Standard & Poor's 500 is accomplished:
a. automatically through the market value calculation.
b. by deflating the numerator.
c. by the adjusted divisor.

4. An investment of $150,000 is expected to generate an after-tax cash flow of $100,000 in one year and another $120,000 in two years. The cost of capital is 10 percent. What is the internal rate of return?
a. 28.39 percent.
b. 28.59 percent.
c. 28.79 percent.

5. An analyst expects that a company's net sales will double and the company's net income will triple over the next five-year period starting now. Based on the analyst's expectations, which of the following *best* describes the expected compound annual growth?

a. Net sales will grow 15% annually and net income will grow 25% annually.
b. Net sales will grow 20% annually and net income will grow 40% annually.
c. Net sales will grow 25% annually and net income will grow 50% annually.

6. A stock has the following potential returns and the associated probabilities that each will occur.

Possible return	Probability of occurrence
3%	25%
10%	50%
25%	12.5%
40%	12.5%

What is the expected return on this stock?

a. 13.88%
b. 19.50%
c. 42.50%

7. A portfolio that is on the capital market line but to the left of the market portfolio (M) has the following characteristic:

a. a lending portfolio.
b. a borrowing portfolio.
c. higher unsystematic risk than the market portfolio.

8. In the Markowitz model, portfolio risk:

a. is equal to the simple sum of the standard deviations of each of the securities in the portfolio.
b. is equal to the product of the standard deviations of each of the securities in the portfolio.
c. is different from the simple weighted average of the risks of the individual securities in the portfolio.

9. Risk that can be diversified away is described as:

a. unsystematic risk.
b. market risk.
c. systematic risk.

10. iCorporation has a relative systematic risk level that is 40% greater than the overall market. The expected return on the market is 16%, and the risk-free rate is 7%. Using the CAPM, the required rate of return for iCorporation is *closest* to:

a. 16.0%

b. 19.6%

c. 22.4%

11. If a stock's market-implied expected return exceeds the capital asset pricing model—predicted required (expected) return, the stock plots on the security market line (SML) as follows:

a. above the SML and is underpriced.

b. below the SML and is overpriced.

c. above the SML and is overpriced.

Answers: 1. b; 2. a; 3. a; 4. c; 5. a; 6. a; 7. a; 8. c; 9. a; 10. b; 11. a.

Source: From PROFESSIONAL EXAM REVIEW. *CFA Candidate Study Notes, Level 1, Volume 4*, 2E. © 2009 Delmar Learning, a part of Cengage Learning, Inc. Reproduced by permission. www.cengage.com/permissions

Common Stocks

LEARNING GOALS

After studying this chapter, you should be able to:

LG1 Explain the investment appeal of common stocks and why individuals like to invest in them.

LG2 Describe stock returns from a historical perspective and understand how current returns measure up to historical standards of performance.

LG3 Discuss the basic features of common stocks, including issue characteristics, stock quotations, and transaction costs.

LG4 Understand the different kinds of common stock values.

LG5 Discuss common stock dividends, types of dividends, and dividend reinvestment plans.

LG6 Describe various types of common stocks, including foreign stocks, and note how stocks can be used as investment vehicles.

In recent years, the performance of stock markets in the United States and around the world have left a lot to be desired. From the summer of 2007 to the spring of 2009, U.S. stocks lost more than half their value, and in many markets around the world, the results were even worse. Those declining stock values mirrored the state of the world economy, as country after country slipped into a deep recession in 2008.

One sign of the times was that many firms that had managed to increase their dividends for many years without interruption actually cut dividend payouts in early 2009. One such company was the large-cap, blue-chip stock, General Electric, which in February 2009 announced its first dividend cut since the Great Depression. According to Standard and Poor's, about one out of every 20 dividend-paying firms in the United States cut their dividend in early 2009.

Not all the news was that bleak, however. On April 27, 2009, the board of directors of IROC Energy announced plans to pay a dividend for the very first time. The board cited reductions in the firm's outstanding debts as well as strong expected future earnings to justify their decision to distribute cash to shareholders.

(Sources: IROC Press Release, August 10, 2009, CNW Telbec, www.cnw.ca/fr/releases/archive/August2009/10/c3719.htm; Stephen Bernard, S&P: Record Number of Firms Cut Dividends in 1st Quarter, *Pittsburgh Post Gazette* (April 7, 2009).)

What Stocks Have to Offer

LG1 LG2 Common stock enables investors to participate in the profits of a firm. Every share-holder is a part owner of the firm and, as such, has a claim on the wealth created by the company. This claim is not without limitations, however, because common stock-holders are really the **residual owners** of the company. That is, their claim is sub-ordinate to the claims of other investors, such as lenders, so for stockholders to get rich, the firm must first meet all its other financial obligations. Accordingly, *as residual owners, holders of common stock have no guarantee that they will receive any return on their investment.*

The Appeal of Common Stocks

Even in spite of the steep decline in the U.S. stock market in 2008, common stocks remain a popular investment choice among both individual and institutional investors. For most investors, the allure of common stocks is the prospect that they will increase in value over time and generate significant capital gains. Many stocks do pay dividends, thereby providing investors with a periodic income stream. For most stocks, however, the dividends paid in any particular year pale in comparison to the capital gains (and capital losses) that are the natural consequence of stock price fluctuations.

Putting Stock Price Behavior in Perspective

Given the nature of common stocks, when the market is strong, investors can generally expect to benefit from steady price appreciation. A good example is the performance that took place in 2006, when the market, as measured by the Dow Jones Industrial Average (DJIA), went up by more than 16%. Unfortunately, when markets falter, so do investor returns. Just look at what happened in 2008, when the market (again, as measured by the DJIA) fell by almost 34%. Excluding dividends, that means a $100,000 investment declined in value to a little more than $66,000. That hurts!

Make no mistake about it: The market does have its bad days, and sometimes those bad days seem to go on for months. Even though it may not always appear to be so, those bad days *are the exception rather than the rule*. That was certainly the case over the 53-year period from 1956 through 2008, when the Dow went down (for the year) just 17 times—about 32% of the time. The other 68% of the time, the market was up—anywhere from 2% on the year to nearly 40%. True, there is some risk and

MARKETS in CRISIS

The Lumbering Bear

Bear markets occur when stock prices are falling. But not all falling markets end up as bears. A drop of *5% or more* in one of the major market indexes, like the Dow Jones Industrial Average (DJIA), is called a *routine decline*. Such declines are considered "routine" since they typically occur several times a year. A *correction* is a drop of *10% or more* in an index, whereas the term *bear market* is reserved for severe market declines of *20% or more*. Bear markets usually occur every three to four years, although the 1990s were totally bear-free. The most recent bear market began in July 2007 when the DJIA peaked just shy of 14,000. The next 20 months witnessed one of the worst bear markets in U.S. history, with the DJIA falling almost 55% by March 2009.

TABLE 6.1	Historical Returns on the Standard and Poor's 500, 1950-2008		
Period	Rate of Return from Dividends	Rate of Return from Capital Gains	Total Return
1950s	5.4%	13.2%	19.3%
1960s	3.3%	4.4%	7.8%
1970s	4.3%	1.6%	5.8%
1980s	4.6%	12.6%	17.3%
1990s	2.7%	15.3%	18.1%
2000–2008	1.7%	−5.3%	−3.6%
1950–2008	3.6%	7.0%	10.8%

Note: The total return is higher than the sum of the dividend return and the capital gain return because we assume dividends are reinvested when received.

(Source: www.simplestockinvesting.com/SP500-historical-real-total-returns.htm)

price volatility (even in good markets), but that's the price you pay for all the upside potential. For example, from 1982 through early 2000, in one of the longest bull markets in history, the DJIA grew (over 18 years) at an average annual rate of nearly 17%. Yet, even in this market, there were some off days, and even a few off years. But, clearly, they were the exception rather than the rule.

From Stock Prices to Stock Returns

Our discussion so far has centered on *stock prices*. What are even more important to investors are *stock returns*, which take into account both price behavior and dividend income. Table 6.1 uses the Standard and Poor's 500 Stock Index (S&P500) to illustrate how the U.S. stock market has performed since 1950. Like the DJIA, the S&P500 is a barometer of the overall stock market. As its name implies, the S&P500 tracks 500 companies (most of which are large firms), so most experts consider it to be a better indicator of the market's overall performance than the DJIA, which tracks just 30 firms. In addition to total returns, the table breaks market performance down into the two basic sources of return: dividends and capital gains. These figures, of course, reflect the *general behavior of the market as a whole,* not necessarily that of *individual stocks.* Think of them as the return behavior on a well-balanced portfolio of common stocks.

The table shows several interesting patterns. First, the returns from capital gains range from an average of 15.3% during the booming 1990s to −5.3% from 2000–2008. Returns from dividends vary too, but not nearly as much, ranging from 5.4% in the 1950s to 1.7% since 2000. Breaking down the returns into dividends and capital gains reveals, not surprisingly, that the big returns (or losses) come from capital gains.

Second, stocks generally earn positive total returns over long time periods. From 1950–2000, the average total return on the S&P500 was 13.7% per year. At that rate, investors can double their money every five or six years. To look at the figures another way, if you had invested $10,000 in the S&P500 in 1950, your investment would have grown to $6.1 million over the next 50 years. You can get rich by investing in the stock market, as long as you are patient!

Third, investing in stocks is clearly not without risk. From 2000–2008, the U.S. stock market lost 3.6% per year! In other words, if you had accumulated $6.1 million from 1950–2000, by the end of 2008 your portfolio would have been worth $4.5 million. That's still a lot of money, suggesting that stocks may be a very good investment in the long run, but that was little consolation to investors who saw their wealth fall dramatically in the early years of the 21st century.

Now keep in mind that the numbers here represent market performance; *individual* stocks can and often do perform quite differently. But at least the averages give us a benchmark against which we can assess current stock returns and our own expectations. For example, if a return of 13% to 14% can be considered a good long-term estimate for stocks, then *sustained* returns of 16% to 18% should definitely be viewed as extraordinary. (These higher returns are possible, of course, but to get them, investors very likely will have to take on more risk.) Likewise, long-run stock returns of only 6% to 8% should probably be viewed as substandard. If that's the best you think you can do, then you may want to consider sticking with bonds, where you'll earn almost as much, but with less risk.

A Real Estate Bubble Goes Bust and So Does the Market

An old investment tip is, "Buy land because they aren't making any more of it." For many years, it appeared that this advice applied to housing in the United States, as home prices enjoyed a long, upward march. According to the Standard and Poor's Case-Shiller Home Price Index, a measure of the average value of a single-family home in the United States, the average home price peaked in May 2006 at $206,170. Over the next three years, home prices fell sharply, falling 32% by the summer of 2009. As prices fell, some homeowners realized that they owed more on their mortgages than their homes were worth, and mortgage defaults began to rise. Unfortunately, some of the biggest investors in home mortgages were U.S. commercial and investment banks. As homeowners fell behind on their mortgage payments, the stock prices of financial institutions began to drop, raising serious concerns about the health of the entire U.S. financial system. Those fears seemed to have been realized when a top-tier investment bank, Lehman Brothers, filed for bankruptcy in September 2008. That event sparked a free fall in the stock market.

Figure 6.1 (on page 210) shows that U.S. stocks rose along with housing prices, but when weakness in the housing sector spilled over into banking, stock prices plummeted, and the world economy fell into a deep recession that was continuing as this book went to press. Stocks hinted that a recovery might be near, rising more than 50% from March to September. Even then, however, the real-estate meltdown and its effects on the stock market had wiped out all the gains accumulated over the prior six years.

The Pros and Cons of Stock Ownership

Investors own stocks for all sorts of reasons: the potential for capital gains, for their current income, or perhaps the high degree of market liquidity. But as with any investment vehicle, there are pros and cons to these securities.

The Advantages of Stock Ownership One reason stocks are so appealing is the substantial return opportunities they offer. As we just saw, stocks generally provide attractive, highly competitive returns over the long haul. Indeed, common stock returns compare very favorably to other investment outlets such as long-term corporate bonds and U.S. Treasury securities. For example, over the last century, high-grade corporate bonds earned annual returns that were *about half as large as the returns on common stocks*. Although long-term bonds outperform stocks in some years, the opposite is true far more often than not. Stocks typically outperform bonds, and usually by a wide

FIGURE 6.1 **A Snapshot of U.S. Stock and Housing Indexes (mid-2003 through mid-2009)**

From mid-2003 through 2005 U.S. stocks rose along with housing prices, but when crumbling U.S. housing prices began to spill over into banking, stock prices plummeted. Not until early 2009 were there signs of recovery, but even then with housing prices and stocks attempting to rebound, most of the stock and housing markets, gains accumulated over the prior six years had vanished. (Source: Data from bigcharts.com and marketwatch.com.)

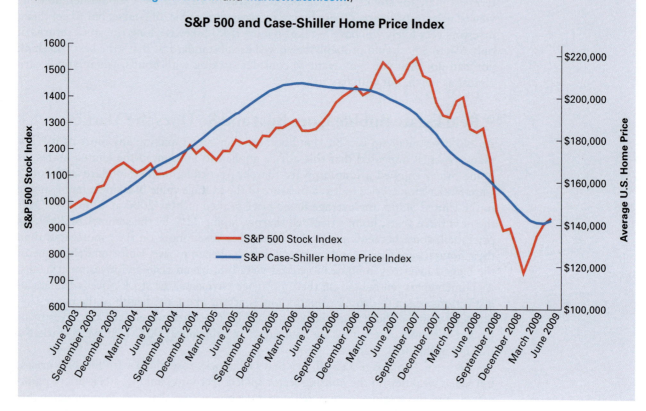

S&P 500 and Case-Shiller Home Price Index

margin. Stocks also provide investors protection from inflation because over time their returns exceed the inflation rate. In other words, by purchasing stocks, investors gradually increase their purchasing power over time.

Stocks offer other benefits as well: They are easy to buy and sell, and the transaction costs are modest. Moreover, price and market information is widely disseminated in the news and financial media. A final advantage is that the unit cost of a share of common stock is usually within the reach of most individual investors. Unlike bonds, which normally carry minimum denominations of at least $1,000, and some mutual funds that have fairly hefty minimum investments, common stocks don't have such minimums. Instead, most stocks today are priced at less than $50 or $60 a share—and any number of shares, no matter how few, can be bought or sold.

The Disadvantages There are also some disadvantages to common stock ownership. Risk is perhaps the most significant. Stocks are subject to various types of risk, including business and financial risk, purchasing power risk, market risk, and event risk. All of these can adversely affect a stock's earnings and dividends, its price appreciation, and,

FIGURE 6.2   The Current Income of Stocks and Bonds

Clearly, the level of current income (dividends) paid to stockholders falls far short of the amount of interest income paid to bondholders. Note that in most years, the dividend yield on stocks is less than half the coupon yield on bonds.

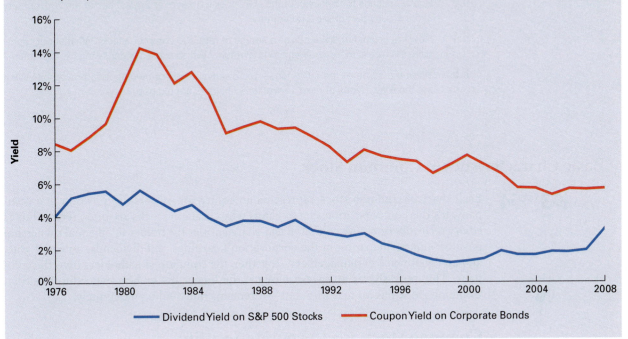

of course, the rate of return earned by an investor. Even the best of stocks possess elements of risk that are difficult to overcome, because company earnings are subject to many factors, including government control and regulation, foreign competition, and the state of the economy. Because such factors affect sales and profits, they also affect the price behavior of the stock and possibly even dividends.

All of this leads to another disadvantage: The earnings and general performance of stocks are subject to wide swings, so it is difficult to value common stocks and consistently select top performers. The selection process is complex because so many elements go into formulating expectations of stock performance. In other words, not only is the future outcome of the company and its stock uncertain, but the evaluation and selection process itself is also far from perfect.

A final disadvantage of stocks is the sacrifice in current income. Several types of investments—bonds, for instance—pay higher levels of current income and do so with much greater certainty. Figure 6.2 compares the dividend yield on common stocks with the coupon yield on high-grade corporate bonds. It shows the degree of sacrifice common stock investors make in terms of current income. Clearly, even though the yield gap has narrowed a great deal in the past few years, common stocks still have a long way to go before they catch up with the *current income levels* available from bonds and most other types of fixed-income securities.

CONCEPTS IN REVIEW

Answers available at www.pearsonhighered.com/gitman

6.1 What is a *common stock?* What is meant by the statement that holders of common stock are the *residual owners* of the firm?

6.2 What are two or three of the major investment attributes of common stocks?

6.3 Briefly describe the behavior of the U.S. stock market over the last half of the 20th century and the early part of the 21st century.

6.4 How important are dividends as a source of return to common stock? What about capital gains? Which is more important to total return? Which causes wider swings in total return?

6.5 What are some of the advantages *and* disadvantages of owning common stock? What are the major types of risk to which stockholders are exposed?

Basic Characteristics of Common Stock

Each share of common stock represents an equity (or ownership) position in a company. It's this equity position that explains why common stocks are often referred to as *equity securities* or **equity capital**. Every share entitles the holder to an equal ownership position and participation in the corporation's earnings and dividends, an equal vote, and an equal voice in management. Together, the common stockholders own the company. The more shares an investor owns, the bigger his or her ownership position. Common stock has no maturity date—it remains outstanding indefinitely.

Common Stock as a Corporate Security

All corporations "issue" common stock of one type or another. But the shares of many, if not most, corporations are never traded, because the firms either are too small or are family controlled. The stocks of interest to us in this book are **publicly traded issues**—the shares that are readily available to the general public and that are bought and sold in the open market. The firms issuing such shares range from giants like AT&T and Microsoft to much smaller regional or local firms. The market for publicly traded stocks is enormous: The value of all actively traded listed and OTC stocks in mid-2009 was more than $12 trillion.

Issuing New Shares Companies can issue shares of common stock in several different ways. The most widely used procedure is the **public offering**. When using this procedure, the corporation offers the investing public a certain number of shares of its stock at a certain price. Figure 6.3 (on page 213) shows an announcement for such an offering. Note in this case that OpenTable is offering 3,000,000 shares of stock at a price of $20 per share. Of the 3,000,000 shares being offered, 1,572,684 are newly issued shares sold by the company to investors. At $20 per share, the offering will raise almost $31.5 million. The remaining 1,427,316 shares are being sold by existing shareholders to new investors. The cash raised from selling these shares goes to the firm's existing shareholders and not to the company.

Companies also can issue new shares of stock using what is known as a **rights offering**. In a rights offering, existing stockholders are given the first opportunity to buy the new issue. In essence, a stock right gives a shareholder the right (but not the obligation) to purchase new shares of the company's stock in proportion to his or her current ownership position.

FIGURE 6.3 **An Announcement of a New Stock Issue**

This announcement indicates that the company—OpenTable—is issuing 3 million shares of stock at a price of $20.00 per share. For this leading provider of free online reservations for diners and guest management systems for restaurants, the new issue will mean more than a *quarter of a billion dollars* in fresh capital. (Source: *OpenTable*, Initial Public Offer prospectus, **investors.opentable.com/releases**. CFM, May 27, 2009.)

PROSPECTUS

Filed pursuant to Rule 424(b)(1)
Registration No. 333-157034

3,000,000 Shares ← { Number of shares offered

OpenTable® ← { Name of issuer

Common Stock

This is the initial public offering of our common stock. We are offering 1,572,684 shares of the common stock offered by this prospectus, and the selling stockholders are offering 1,427,316 shares. We will not receive any proceeds from the sale of shares to be offered by the selling stockholders. Our common stock has been approved for listing on The Nasdaq Global Market under the symbol "OPEN."

Investing in our common stock involves a high degree of risk. See "Risk Factors" on page 10 of this prospectus.

	Per Share	Total
Public offering price	$20.00	$60,000,000
Underwriting discount	$1.40	$4,200,000
Proceeds, before expenses, to OpenTable, Inc.	$18.60	$29,251,922
Proceeds, before expenses, to the selling stockholders	$18.60	$26,548,078

{ Price at which shares were offered to the public and total proceeds

The underwriters have a 30-day option to purchase up to an additional 450,000 shares of common stock from us to cover overallotments, if any.

Neither the Securities and Exchange Commission nor any state securities commission nor any other regulatory body has approved or disapproved of these securities or determined if this prospectus is truthful or complete. Any representation to the contrary is a criminal offense.

The shares will be ready for delivery on or about May 27, 2009.

Merrill Lynch & Co. ← { The lead underwriting firms handling this new issue

Allen & Company LLC

Stifel Nicolaus

ThinkEquity LLC ← { Additional underwriters

The date of this prospectus is May 21, 2009. ← Date of issue

Smart's Tour of the Web
To watch author Scott
Smart discuss key websites
for this chapter visit
www.myfinancelab.com

For instance, if a stockholder currently owns 1% of a firm's stock and the firm issues 10,000 additional shares, the rights offering will give that stockholder the opportunity to purchase 1% (100 shares) of the new issue. If the investor does not want to use the rights, he or she can sell them to someone who does. The net result of a rights offering is the same as that of a public offering: The firm ends up with more equity in its capital structure, and the number of shares outstanding increases.

Stock Spin-Offs Perhaps one of the most creative ways of bringing a new issue to the market is through a **stock spin-off**. Basically, a spin-off occurs when a company gets rid of one of its subsidiaries or divisions. For example, Ralston Purina did this when it spun off its Energizer subsidiary. The company doesn't just sell the subsidiary to some other firm. Rather, it creates a new stand-alone company and then distributes stock in that company to its existing stockholders. Thus, every Ralston Purina shareholder received a certain (prorated) number of shares in the newly created, and now publicly traded, Energizer company.

There have been hundreds of stock spin-offs in the last 10 to 15 years. Some of the more notable ones were the spin-off of Coach (the designer bag company) by Sara Lee, the Freescale Semiconductor spin-off by Motorola, the spin-off of Agilent Technologies by Hewlett-Packard, and the spin-off of Moody's by Dun & Bradstreet. Normally, companies execute stock spin-offs if they believe the subsidiary is no longer a good fit, or if they feel they've become too diversified and want to focus on their core products. The good news is such spin-offs often work very well for investors, too.

Stock Splits Companies can also increase the number of shares outstanding by executing a **stock split**. In declaring a split, a firm merely announces that it will increase the number of shares outstanding by exchanging a specified number of new shares for each outstanding share of stock. For example, in a 2-for-1 stock split, two new shares of stock are exchanged for each old share. In a 3-for-2 split, three new shares are exchanged for every two old shares outstanding. Thus, a stockholder who owned 200 shares of stock before a 2-for-1 split becomes the owner of 400 shares; the same investor would hold 300 shares if there had been a 3-for-2 split.

A company uses a stock split when it wants to enhance its stock's trading appeal by lowering its market price. Normally, the firm gets the desired result: The price of the stock tends to fall in close relation to the terms of the split (unless the stock split is accompanied by a big increase in the level of dividends). For example, using the ratio of the number of old shares to new, we can expect a $100 stock to trade at or close to $50 a share after a 2-for-1 split. Specifically, we divide the original price per share by the ratio of new shares to old. That same $100 stock would trade at about $67 after a 3-for-2 split—that is, $100 ÷ 3/2 = $100 ÷ 1.5 = $67. (Later in this chapter we will discuss a variation of the stock split, known as a stock dividend.)

Treasury Stock Instead of increasing the number of outstanding shares, corporations sometimes find it desirable to *reduce* the number of shares by buying back their own stock. Generally speaking, firms repurchase their own stock when they view it as undervalued in the marketplace. When that happens, the company's own stock becomes an attractive investment candidate.

Those firms that can afford to do so will purchase their stock in the open market, like any other individual or institution. When acquired, these shares become known as **treasury stock**. Technically, treasury stocks are simply shares of stock that have been issued and subsequently repurchased by the issuing firm. Treasury stocks are kept by the corporation and can be used at a later date for any number of reasons. For example, they could be used for mergers and acquisitions, to meet employee stock option plans, or as a means of paying stock dividends. Or the shares can simply be held in treasury for an indefinite time.

The impact of these share repurchases—or *buybacks*, as they're sometimes called—is not clear. Generally, the feeling is that if the buyback involves a significant number of shares, the stockholder's equity position and claim on income will increase. This result is likely to benefit stockholders to the extent that such action has a positive effect on the market price of the stock. However, it has also been suggested that buybacks are often used merely as a way to prop up the price of an undervalued stock.

Classified Common Stock For the most part, all the stockholders in a corporation enjoy the same benefits of ownership. Occasionally, however, a company will *issue different classes of common stock*, each of which entitles holders to different privileges and benefits. These issues are known as **classified common stock**. Hundreds of publicly traded firms have created such stock classes. Although issued by the same company, each class of common stock is different and has its own value.

Classified common stock is customarily used to denote either different voting rights or different dividend obligations. For instance, class A could designate non-voting shares, and class B would carry normal voting rights. Or the class A stock would receive no dividends, and class B would receive regular cash dividends.

Notable for its use of classified stock is Ford Motor Company, which has two classes of stock outstanding. Ford's class A stock is owned by the investing public, and class B stock is owned by the Ford family and their trusts or corporations. The two classes of stock share equally in the dividends. But class A stock has one vote per share, whereas the voting rights of the class B stock are structured to give the Ford family a 40% absolute control of the company. Similar types of classified stock are used at the *Washington Post*, Dillards Department Stores, Dow Jones & Co., Nike, and Berkshire Hathaway.

Regardless of the specifics, whenever there is more than one class of common stock outstanding, investors should take the time to determine the privileges, benefits, and limitations of each class.

Buying and Selling Stocks

Whether buying or selling stocks, you should become familiar with how stocks are quoted and with the costs of executing common stock transactions. Certainly, keeping track of *current prices* is an essential element in the buy-and-sell decisions of investors. Prices also help investors monitor the market performance of their security holdings. Similarly, *transaction costs* are important because of the impact they can have on investment returns. Indeed, the costs of executing stock transactions can sometimes consume most (or all) of the profits from an investment. These costs should not be taken lightly.

Reading the Quotes Investors in the stock market have come to rely on a highly efficient information system that quickly disseminates market prices to the public. The stock quotes that appear daily in the financial press are a vital part of that information system. To see how to read and interpret stock price quotations, consider the quotes that appear daily in the printed and online versions of the *Wall Street Journal*. As we'll see, these quotes give not only the most recent price of each stock but also a great deal of additional information.

Some NYSE stock quotes are presented in Figure 6.4 (on page 216)—let's use the Halliburton quotations for purposes of illustration. These quotes were published in the

FIGURE 6.4 Stock Quotations

This figure shows the quotations for a small sample of stocks traded on the NYSE, providing a summary of the transactions that occurred on one day.
(Source: *Wall Street Journal*, wsj.com, September 4, 2009.)

NYSE Stock Exchange
Friday, September 04, 2009

(1) Name	(2) Symbol	(3) Open	(4) High	(5) Low	(6) Close	(7) Net Chg	(8) %Chg	(9) Vol	(10) 52 Week High	(11) 52 Week Low	(12) Div	(13) Yield	(14) PE	(15) Year-To-Date %Chg
HCC INSURANCE HOLDINGS INC.	HCC	26.46	26.49	26.18	26.41	-0.03	-0.11	278,575	28.68	14.17	.54f	2.0	10	-1.3
HCP INC.	HCP	26.63	26.69	26.02	26.64	0.02	0.08	2,777,799	42.16	14.26	1.84	6.9	30	-4.1
HDFC BANK LTD. ADS	HDB	96.67	100.07	96.67	99.47	3.02	3.13	349,151	110.23	44.85	.60	.6	32	39.4
HFF INC. CL A	HF	5.90	5.92	5.81	5.90	-0.07	-1.17	63,200	6.66	1.05	...	...	dd	140.8
HNI CORP	HNI	21.37	21.61	20.96	21.43	0.06	0.28	304,861	34.37	7.70	.86	4.0	65	35.3
HRPT PROPERTIES TRUST SBI	HRP	6.47	6.58	6.31	6.58	0.11	1.70	1,633,576	8.33	1.57	.48	7.3	33	95.3
HSBC HOLDINGS PLC ADS	HBC	54.02	54.45	53.66	54.19	1.08	2.03	2,086,510	86.50	22.89	2.20e	4.1	33	11.3
HAEMONETICS CORP.	HAE	53.10	54.19	53.10	54.08	0.74	1.39	127,320	67.49	46.78	...	...	22	-4.3
HALLIBURTON CO.	HAL	23.79	24.66	23.78	24.54	0.56	2.34	9,892,699	41.54	12.80	.36	1.5	11	35.0
HANESBRANDS INC.	HBI	19.56	19.79	19.20	19.76	0.21	1.07	355,749	27.80	5.14	...	...	42	55.0
HANGER ORTHOPEDIC GROUP INC.	HGR	13.88	14.00	13.72	13.93	0.05	0.36	76,770	21.00	11.10	...	...	15	-4.0
HANOVER INSURANCE GROUP INC.	THG	40.08	40.94	40.03	40.94	0.61	1.51	193,804	55.00	28.01	.45f	1.1	34	-4.7
HARLEY-DAVIDSON INC.	HOG	22.68	23.33	22.61	23.29	0.67	2.96	2,474,440	48.05	7.99	.40	1.7	14	37.2
HARMAN INTERNATIONAL INDUSTRIES INC.	HAR	27.72	27.97	27.31	27.77	0.23	0.84	1,045,336	36.84	9.17	...	...	dd	66.0
HARMONY GOLD MINING CO. LTD. ADS	HMY	10.46	10.80	10.40	10.68	0.17	1.62	3,026,709	13.25	5.47	.06	...	25	-2.6
HARRIS CORP.	HRS	34.57	35.06	34.26	34.99	0.61	1.77	950,817	52.07	25.77	.88f	2.5	43	-2.9

1. Company name
2. Company ticker symbol
3. Opening price for the day
4. High price for the day
5. Low price for the day
6. Closing price for the day
7. Net change in closing price from the previous day's closing price
8. Percentage change in closing price from the previous day's closing price
9. Share volume for the day
10. High price for the previous 52 weeks
11. Low price for the previous 52 weeks
12. Annual dividends per share for the previous 12 months
13. Dividend yield (expressed as a percentage of the current share price)
14. Price-to-earnings ratio (expressed as the current share price divided by earnings per share)
15. Percentage change in closing price from the previous year's final closing price

online edition of the *Wall Street Journal* on September 4, 2009. They describe the trading activity that took place that day. A glance shows that stocks, like most other securities, are quoted in dollars and cents.

Working from left to right in Figure 6.4 and using Halliburton Co. as an example, we first see the company name, followed by its ticker symbol (HAL). The next four columns show Halliburton's opening price ($23.79), the high and low prices reached during the day ($24.66 and $23.78, respectively), and the closing price at the end of the trading day ($24.54). The next two columns show how Halliburton's stock changed from Thursday to Friday, both in dollar and in percentage terms. The 9th column shows how many Halliburton shares traded that day. Continuing to the left we see that over the past 52 weeks, Halliburton stock had been as high as $41.54 and as low as $12.80! Also over the past year, Halliburton paid a dividend of $0.36, which is a dividend yield of 1.5% ($0.36/$24.54 × 100). Finally, in the last two columns we learn that Halliburton's price-to-earnings ratio (PE) was 11, and the stock's value rose 35% between January 1 and September 4.

The same basic quotation system is also used for Nasdaq *Global Market* and *National Market* shares. That's not the case, however, for AMEX and small Nasdaq/OTC stocks. With those, you may get little more than the stock's name and symbol, share volume, closing price, and change in price.

Transaction Costs As explained in Chapter 3, investors can buy and sell common stock in round or odd lots. A *round lot* is 100 shares of stock or multiples thereof. An *odd lot* is a transaction involving fewer than 100 shares. For example, the sale of 400 shares of stock would be a round-lot transaction; the sale of 75 shares would be an odd-lot transaction. Trading 250 shares of stock would involve a combination of two round lots and an odd lot.

An investor incurs certain transaction costs when buying or selling stock. In addition to some modest transfer fees and taxes paid by the *seller*, the major cost is the brokerage fee paid—by both *buyer and seller*—at the time of the transaction. As a rule, brokerage fees can amount to just a fraction of 1% to as much as 2% or more, depending on whether you use the services of a discount broker or full-service broker. (Types of brokers and brokerage services were discussed in Chapter 3.) But they can go even higher, particularly for very small trades. Higher fees are connected with the purchase or sale of odd lots, which requires a specialist known as an *odd-lot dealer*. This usually results in an *odd-lot differential* of 10 to 25 cents per share, which is tacked on to the normal commission charge, driving up the costs of these small trades. Indeed, the relatively high cost of an odd-lot trade makes it better to deal in round lots whenever possible.

Common Stock Values

The worth of a share of common stock can be described in a number of ways. Terms such as *par value, book value, market value,* and *investment value* are all found in the financial media. Each designates some accounting, investment, or monetary attribute of a stock.

Par Value The term **par value** refers to the stated, or face, value of a stock. Except for accounting purposes, it is relatively useless. Par value is a throwback to the early days of corporate law, when it was used as a basis for assessing the extent of a stockholder's legal liability. Because the term has little or no significance for investors, many stocks today are issued as no-par or low-par stocks. That is, they may have par values of only a penny or two.

Book Value **Book value**, another accounting measure, represents the amount of stockholders' equity in the firm. As we will see in the next chapter, it is commonly used in stock valuation. Book value indicates the amount of stockholder funds used to finance the firm. It is calculated by subtracting the firm's liabilities and preferred stock from its assets. For example, assume that a corporation has $10 million in assets, owes $5 million in various forms of short- and long-term debt, and has $1 million worth of preferred stock outstanding. The book value of this firm would be $4 million.

Book value can be converted to a per-share basis—*book value per share*—by dividing it by the number of common shares outstanding. For example, if the firm just described has 100,000 shares of common stock outstanding, then its book value per share is $40. As a rule, most stocks have market prices that are well above their book values.

Market Value **Market value** is one of the easiest stock values to determine. It is simply *the prevailing market price of an issue*. In essence, market value indicates how the market participants as a whole have assessed the worth of a share of stock.

By multiplying the market price of the stock by the number of shares outstanding, we can also find the market value of the firm itself—or what is known as the firm's *market capitalization*. For example, if a firm has one million shares outstanding and its stock trades at $50 per share, the company has a market value (or "market cap") of

$50 million. For obvious reasons, the market value of a share of stock is generally of considerable importance to stockholders.

Investment Value **Investment value** is probably the most important measure for a stockholder. It indicates the worth investors place on the stock—in effect, what they think the stock *should* be trading for. Determining a security's investment value is a complex process based on expectations of the return and risk characteristics of a stock. Any stock has two potential sources of return: annual dividend payments and the capital gains that arise from appreciation in market price. In establishing investment value, investors try to determine how much money they will make from these two sources. They then use those estimates as the basis for formulating the return potential of the stock. At the same time, they try to assess the amount of risk to which they will be exposed by holding the stock. Such return and risk information helps them place an investment value on the stock. This value represents the *maximum* price an investor should be willing to pay for the issue. Investment value is the major topic in Chapter 8.

CONCEPTS IN REVIEW

Answers available at
www.pearsonhighered.com/gitman

6.6 What is a *stock split?* How does a stock split affect the market value of a share of stock? Do you think it would make any difference (in price behavior) if the company also changed the dividend rate on the stock? Explain.

6.7 What is a *stock spin-off?* In very general terms, explain how a stock spin-off works. Are these spin-offs of any value to investors? Explain.

6.8 Define and differentiate between the following pairs of terms.

  a. *Treasury stock* versus *classified stock.*
  b. *Round lot* versus *odd lot.*
  c. *Par value* versus *market value.*
  d. *Book value* versus *investment value.*

6.9 What is an *odd-lot differential* and what effect does it have on the cost of buying and selling stocks? How can you avoid odd-lot differentials? Which of the following transactions would involve an odd-lot differential?

  a. Buy 90 shares of stock.
  b. Sell 200 shares of stock.
  c. Sell 125 shares of stock.

Common Stock Dividends

LG5 In 2008, U.S. corporations paid out more than half a trillion dollars in dividends. Yet, in spite of these numbers, dividends still don't get much respect. Many investors, particularly younger ones, often put very little value on dividends. To a large extent, that's because capital gains provide a much bigger source of return than dividends—at least over the long haul.

But attitudes toward dividends are beginning to change. The protracted bear market of 2007–2009 revealed just how uncertain capital gains can be and, indeed, that all those potential profits can at times turn into substantial capital losses. At least with dividends, the cash flow is far more certain. Plus, dividends provide a nice cushion when the market stumbles (or falls flat on its face). Moreover, recent changes in the

INVESTOR FACTS

DIVIDENDS AROUND THE WORLD—A recent study of the dividend policies of companies from 40 countries around the world uncovered two interesting facts. First, the fraction of firms paying dividends is low in the United States compared to most other countries. Excluding financial firms and utilities, about 20% of U.S. firms paid dividends from 2000–2007. In 39 other major economies, the average fraction of dividend-paying firms was 59%. Second, in 32 of the 40 countries studied, the percentage of firms paying dividends was lower in the period 2000-2007 compared to the 1990s. In other words, there is evidence that dividends are slowly "disappearing" around the world.

(Source: Miguel Ferreira, Massimo Massa, and Pedro Matas. (2009, August). *Dividend Clienteles Around the World: Evidence from Institutional Holdings.* Working paper.)

(federal) tax laws put dividends on the same plane as capital gains. Both now are taxed at the same (maximum 15%) tax rate, although it seems likely that this provision of the tax code will change under the Obama administration. As of 2009, capital gains are no longer taxed at more attractive rates, making dividends just as attractive and perhaps even more so, as they're far less risky.

The Dividend Decision

By paying out dividends, typically on a quarterly basis, companies share with their stockholders some of the profits they've earned. Actually, a firm's board of directors decides how much to pay in dividends. The directors evaluate the firm's operating results and financial condition to determine whether dividends should be paid and, if so, in what amount. They also consider whether the firm should distribute some of its cash to investors by paying a dividend or by simply buying back some of the firm's outstanding stock. If the directors decide to pay dividends, they also establish several important payment dates. In this section we'll look at the corporate and market factors that go into the dividend decision. Then we'll briefly examine some of the key payment dates.

Corporate Versus Market Factors   When the board of directors assembles to consider the question of paying dividends, it weighs a variety of factors. First, the board looks at the firm's earnings. Even though a company does not have to show a profit to pay dividends, profits are still considered a vital link in the dividend decision.

With common stocks, the annual earnings of a firm are usually measured and reported in terms of **earnings per share** (**EPS**). Basically, EPS translates aggregate corporate profits into profits on a per-share basis. It provides a convenient measure of the amount of earnings available to stockholders. Earnings per share is found by using the following formula:

Equation 6.1

$$EPS = \frac{\text{Net profit after taxes} - \text{Preferred dividends}}{\text{Number of shares of common stock outstanding}}$$

For example, if a firm reports a net profit of $1.25 million, pays $250,000 in dividends to preferred stockholders, and has 500,000 shares of common stock outstanding, it has an EPS of $2 (($1,250,000 − $250,000)/500,000). Note in Equation 6.1 that preferred dividends are subtracted from profits, since they must be paid before any funds can be made available to common stockholders.

While assessing profits, the board also looks at the firm's growth prospects. It's very likely that the firm will need some of its present earnings for investment purposes and to help finance expected growth. In addition, the board will take a close look at the firm's cash position. Depending on the company and the firm's current dividend rate, the payment of dividends can take up a large amount of cash, so board members will want to make sure plenty of this precious resource is available. Finally, the board will want to make sure that it is meeting all legal and contractual constraints. For example, the firm may be subject to a loan agreement that legally limits the amount of dividends it can pay.

After looking at internal matters, the board will consider certain market effects and responses. Most investors feel that if a company is going to retain earnings rather than pay them out in dividends, it should exhibit proportionately higher growth and profit levels. The market's message is clear: If the firm is investing the money wisely and at a high rate of return, fine; otherwise, pay a larger portion of earnings out in the form of dividends.

Moreover, to the extent that different types of investors tend to be attracted to different types of firms, the board must make every effort to meet the dividend expectations of its shareholders. For example, income-oriented investors are attracted to firms that generally pay high dividends. Failure to meet those expectations can lead to disastrous results—a sell-off of the firm's stock—in the marketplace. Finally, the board cannot ignore the fact that investors today are placing a much higher value on dividends.

Some Important Dates   Let's assume the directors decide to declare a dividend. Once that's done, they must indicate the date of payment and other important dates associated with the dividend. Three dates are particularly important to the stockholder: date of record, payment date, and ex-dividend date. The **date of record** is the date on which the investor must be a registered shareholder of the firm to be entitled to a dividend. All investors who are official stockholders as of the close of business on that date will receive the dividends that have just been declared. These stockholders are often referred to as *holders of record*. The **payment date**, also set by the board of directors, generally follows the date of record by a week or two. It is the actual date on which the company will mail dividend checks to holders of record (and is also known as the *payable date*).

Because of the time needed to make bookkeeping entries after a stock is traded, the stock will sell without the dividend (ex-dividend) for three business days up to and including the date of record. The **ex-dividend date** will dictate whether you were an official shareholder and therefore eligible to receive the declared dividend. If you sell a stock *on or after* the ex-dividend date, you receive the dividend. The reason is that the buyer of the stock (the *new* shareholder) will not have held the stock on the date of record. Instead, you (the seller) will still be the holder of record. Just the opposite will occur if you sell the stock *before* the ex-dividend date. In this case, the new shareholder (the buyer of the stock) will receive the dividend because he or she will be the holder of record.

To see how this works, consider the following sequence of events. On June 3, the board of directors of Cash Cow, Inc., declares a quarterly dividend of 50 cents a share to holders of record on June 18. Checks will be mailed out on the payment date, June 30. The calendar below shows these dividend dates. In this case, if you bought 200 shares of the stock on June 15, you would receive a check in the mail sometime after June 30 in the amount of $100. On the other hand, if you purchased the stock on June 16, the *seller* of the stock would receive the check, because he or she would be recognized as the holder of record, not you.

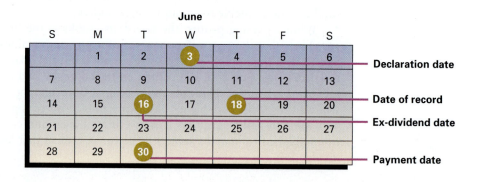

Types of Dividends

Normally, companies pay dividends in the form of cash. Sometimes they pay dividends by issuing additional shares of stock. The first type of distribution is known as a **cash dividend**; the second is called a **stock dividend**. Occasionally, companies pay dividends in other forms, such as a *stock spin-off* (discussed earlier in this chapter) or perhaps even samples of the company's products. But dividends in the form of either cash or stock remain by far the most popular.

Cash Dividends More firms pay *cash dividends* than any other type of dividend. A nice by-product of cash dividends is that *they tend to increase over time, as companies' earnings grow*. In fact, for companies that pay cash dividends, the average annual increase in dividends is around 3% to 5%. This trend represents good news for investors, because *a steadily increasing stream of dividends tends to shore up stock returns in soft markets*.

A convenient way of assessing the amount of dividends received is to measure the stock's **dividend yield**. Basically, this is a measure of dividends on a relative (percentage) basis, rather than on an absolute (dollar) basis. Dividend yield, in effect, indicates the rate of current income earned on the investment dollar. It is computed as follows:

Equation 6.2

$$\text{Dividend yield} = \frac{\text{Annual dividends received per share}}{\text{Current market price of the stock}}$$

Thus, a company that annually pays $2 per share in dividends to its stockholders, and whose stock is trading at $40, has a dividend yield of 5%.

To put dividend yield into perspective, it is helpful to look at a company's **dividend payout ratio**. The payout ratio describes that portion of earnings per share (EPS) that is paid out as dividends. It is computed as follows:

Equation 6.3

$$\text{Dividend payout ratio} = \frac{\text{Dividends per share}}{\text{Earnings per share}}$$

A company would have a payout ratio of 50% if it had earnings of $4 a share and paid annual dividends of $2 a share. Although stockholders like to receive dividends, they normally do not like to see payout ratios over 60% to 70%. Payout ratios that high are difficult to maintain and may lead the company into trouble.

The appeal of cash dividends took a giant leap forward in 2003, when the federal tax code changed to reduce the tax on dividends. Prior to this time, cash dividends were taxed as ordinary income, meaning they could be taxed at rates as high as 35%. For that reason, many investors viewed cash dividends as a highly unattractive source of income, especially since capital gains (when realized) were taxed at much lower preferential rates. Now, *both dividends and capital gains are taxed at the same low, preferential rate* (of 15% or less). That, of course, makes dividend-paying stocks far more attractive, even to investors in higher tax brackets. Other things being equal, the tax change should have a positive effect on the price behavior of dividend-paying stocks. That, in turn, should motivate companies either to begin paying dividends or to increase their dividend payout rate. However, the tax break on dividends enacted in 2003 is set to expire in 2011, and it remains to be seen whether Congress will extend the low dividend tax rates or allow them to go back to their pre-2003 levels.

Stock Dividends Occasionally, a firm may declare a *stock dividend*. A stock dividend simply means that the dividend is paid in additional shares of stock. For instance, if the board declares a 10% stock dividend, then each shareholder will receive one new share of stock for each ten shares currently owned.

Although they seem to satisfy some investors, *stock dividends really have no value*, because they represent the receipt of something already owned. The market responds to such dividends by adjusting share prices according to the terms of the stock dividend. Thus, in the example above, a 10% stock dividend normally leads to a decline of around 10% in the stock's share price. The market value of your shareholdings after a stock dividend, therefore, is likely to be about the same as it was before the stock dividend. For example, if you owned 200 shares of stock that were trading at $100 per share, the total market value of your investment would be $20,000. After a 10% stock dividend, you'd own 220 shares of stock (i.e., 200 shares × 1.10), but because of the stock dividend, they would probably be trading at around $91 per share. You would own more shares, but they would be trading at lower prices, so the total market value of your investment would remain about the same (i.e., 220 × $91 = $20,020). There is, however, one bright spot in all this: Unlike cash dividends, stock dividends are not taxed until you actually sell the stocks.

Dividend Reinvestment Plans

Do you want to have your cake and eat it too? When it comes to dividends, there is a way to do just that. You can participate in a **dividend reinvestment plan (DRIP)**. In these corporate-sponsored programs, shareholders can have their cash dividends automatically reinvested into additional shares of the company's common stock. (Similar reinvestment programs are offered by mutual funds, which we'll discuss in Chapter 12, and by some brokerage houses, such as Bank of America and Fidelity.) The basic investment philosophy is that *if the company is good enough to invest in, it's good enough to reinvest in.* As Table 6.2 demonstrates, such an approach can have a tremendous impact on your investment position over time.

TABLE 6.2	Cash or Reinvested Dividends?

Situation: You buy 100 shares of stock at $25 a share (total investment, $2,500); the stock currently pays $1 a share in annual dividends. The price of the stock increases at 8% per year; dividends grow at 5% per year.

Investment Period	Number of Shares Held	Market Value of Stock Holdings	Total Cash Dividends Holdings
Take Dividends in Cash			
5 years	100	$ 3,672	$ 552
10 years	100	5,397	1,258
15 years	100	7,930	2,158
20 years	100	11,652	3,307
Full Participation in Dividend Reinvestment Plan (100% of cash dividends reinvested)			
5 years	115.59	$ 4,245	$ 0
10 years	135.66	7,322	0
15 years	155.92	12,364	0
20 years	176.00	20,508	0

Today more than 1,000 companies (including most major corporations) offer dividend reinvestment plans. These plans provide investors with a convenient and inexpensive way to accumulate capital. Stocks in most DRIPs are acquired free of any brokerage commissions, and most plans allow *partial participation*. That is, participants may specify a portion of their shares for dividend reinvestment and receive cash dividends on the rest. Some plans even sell stocks to their DRIP investors at below-market prices—often at discounts of 3% to 5%. In addition, most plans will credit fractional shares to the investor's account, and many will even allow investors to buy additional shares of the company's stock. For example, once enrolled in the General Mills plan, investors can purchase up to $3,000 worth of the company's stock each quarter, free of commissions.

Shareholders can join dividend reinvestment plans by simply sending a completed authorization form to the company. (Generally, it takes about 30 to 45 days for all the paperwork to be processed.) Once you're in, the number of shares you hold will begin to accumulate with each dividend date. There is a catch, however: Even though these dividends take the form of additional shares of stock, you must still pay taxes on them *as though they were cash dividends*. Don't confuse these dividends with stock dividends—*reinvested dividends are treated as taxable income in the year they're received*, just as though they had been received in cash. But at least with the new preferential tax rate, even this feature is much less of a burden than it used to be.

6.10 Briefly explain how the dividend decision is made. What corporate and market factors are important in deciding whether, and in what amount, to pay dividends?

6.11 Why is the *ex-dividend date* important to stockholders? If a stock is sold on the ex-dividend date, who receives the dividend—the buyer or the seller? Explain.

6.12 What is the difference between a *cash dividend* and a *stock dividend?* Which would be more valuable to you? How does a stock dividend compare to a stock split? Is a 200% stock dividend the same as a 2-for-1 stock split? Explain.

6.13 What are *dividend reinvestment plans*, and what benefits do they offer to investors? Are there any disadvantages?

Types and Uses of Common Stock

LG6 Common stocks appeal to investors because they offer the potential for everything from current income and stability of capital to attractive capital gains. The market contains a wide range of stocks, from the most conservative to the highly speculative. Generally, the kinds of stocks that investors seek will depend on their investment objectives and investment programs. We will examine several of the more popular types of common stocks here, as well as the various ways such securities can be used in different types of investment programs.

Types of Stocks

As an investor, one of the things you will want to understand is the market system used to classify common stock. A stock's general classification reflects not only its fundamental source of return but also the quality of the company's earnings, the issue's susceptibility to market risks, the nature and stability of its earnings and dividends, and even its susceptibility to adverse economic conditions. Such insight is useful in selecting stocks that will best fit your overall investment objectives.

Among the many different types of stocks, the following are the most common: blue chips, income stocks, growth stocks, tech stocks, speculative stocks, cyclical stocks, defensive stocks, mid-cap stocks, and small-cap stocks. We will now look at each of these to see what they are and how investors might use them.

Blue-Chip Stocks

Blue-Chip Stocks Blue chips are the cream of the common stock crop. They are stocks that are unsurpassed in quality and have a long and stable record of earnings and dividends. **Blue-chip stocks** are issued by large, well-established firms that have impeccable financial credentials. These companies hold important, often leading, positions in their industries and frequently set the standards by which other firms are measured.

Not all blue chips are alike, however. Some provide consistently high dividend yields; others are more growth-oriented. Good examples of blue-chip growth stocks are Nike, Procter & Gamble, Home Depot, Walgreen's, Lowe's Companies, and United Parcel Service. Figure 6.5 (on page 225) shows some basic operating and market information about P&G's stock, as obtained from the introductory part of a typical *S&P Stock Report*. Examples of high-yielding blue chips include such companies as AT&T, Chevron, Johnson & Johnson, McDonald's, and Pfizer.

While blue-chip stocks are not immune from bear markets, they do nonetheless provide the potential for relatively attractive long-term returns. They tend to appeal to investors who are looking for quality investment outlets that offer decent dividend yields and respectable growth potential. They are often used for long-term investment purposes and, because of their relatively low risk, are a way of obtaining modest but dependable rates of return.

Income Stocks

Income Stocks Some stocks are appealing simply because of the dividends they pay. This is the case with **income stocks**. These issues have a long and sustained record of regularly paying higher-than-average dividends. Income stocks are ideal for those who seek a relatively safe and high level of current income from their investment capital. But there's more: Holders of income stocks (unlike bonds and preferred stocks) can expect the dividends they receive to increase regularly over time. Thus, a company that paid, say, $1.00 a share in dividends in 1993 would be paying just over $1.80 a share in 2008, if dividends had been growing at around 4% per year. That's a big jump in dividends, and it's something that can have a definite impact on total return.

The major disadvantage of income stocks is that some of them may be paying high dividends because of limited growth potential. Indeed, it's not unusual for income securities to exhibit only low or modest rates of growth in earnings. This does not mean that such firms are unprofitable or lack future prospects. Quite the contrary: Most firms whose shares qualify as income stocks are highly profitable organizations with excellent future prospects. A number of income stocks are among the giants of U.S. industry, and many are also classified as quality blue chips. Many public utilities, such as American Electric Power, Duke Energy, Oneok, Scana, DTE Energy, and Southern Company, are in this group. Also in this group are selected industrial and financial issues like Conagra Foods, Sara Lee, and Altria Group. By their very nature, income stocks are not exposed to a great deal of business and market risk. They are, however, subject to a fair amount of interest rate risk.

Growth Stocks

Growth Stocks Shares that have experienced, and are expected to continue experiencing, consistently high rates of growth in operations and earnings are known as

FIGURE 6.5   A Blue-Chip Stock

(Source: Standard & Poor's *Stock Reports*, August 22, 2009. ©2009 The McGraw-Hill Companies. All Rights Reserved.)

growth stocks. A good growth stock might exhibit a *sustained* rate of growth in earnings of 15% to 18% per year over a period when common stocks, on average, are experiencing growth rates of only 6% to 8%. Generally speaking, established growth companies combine steady earnings growth with high returns on equity. They also have high operating margins and plenty of cash flow to service their debt. Netflix, eBay, Research in Motion, Berkshire Hathaway, and Starbucks are all prime examples of growth stocks. As this list suggests, some growth stocks also rate as blue chips and provide quality growth, whereas others represent higher levels of speculation.

Growth stocks normally pay little or nothing in the way of dividends. Their payout ratios seldom exceed 10% to 15% of earnings. Instead, all or most of the profits are reinvested in the company and used to help finance rapid growth. Thus, the major source of return to investors is price appreciation—and that can have both a good side and a bad side. That is, with growth stocks, when the markets are good, these stocks are hot. When the markets turn down, so do these stocks, often in a big way. Growth shares generally appeal to investors who are looking for attractive capital gains rather than dividends and who are willing to assume a higher element of risk.

Tech Stocks Over the past 15 years or so, *tech stocks* have become such a dominant force in the market (both positive and negative) that they deserve to be put in a class all their own. **Tech stocks** basically represent the technology sector of the market. They include companies that produce or provide everything from computers, semiconductors, data storage, computer software, and computer hardware to peripherals, Internet services, content providers, networking, and wireless communications. These companies provide the high-tech equipment, networking systems, and online services to all lines of businesses, education, health care, communications, governmental agencies, and the home. Some of these stocks are listed on the NYSE and Amex, although the vast majority are traded on the Nasdaq. Tech stocks, in fact, dominate the Nasdaq market and, thus, the Nasdaq Composite Index and other Nasdaq measures of market performance.

These stocks would probably fall into either the *growth stock* category or the *speculative stock* class, although some of them are legitimate *blue chips*. Tech stocks today may, indeed, offer the potential for attractive (and, in some cases, phenomenal) returns. But they also involve considerable risk, and are probably most suitable for the more risk-tolerant investor. Included in the tech-stock category you'll find some big names, like Microsoft, Cisco Systems, Hewlett Packard, Intel, Dell, and Yahoo!. You'll also find many not-so-big names, like NVIDIA, SanDisk, Serena Software, Advantest, L-3 Communications, and Electronic Arts (see Figure 6.6 on page 227).

Speculative Stocks Shares that lack sustained records of success but still offer the potential for substantial price appreciation are known as **speculative stocks**. Perhaps investors' hopes are spurred by a new management team that has taken over a troubled company or by the introduction of a promising new product. Other times, it's the hint that some new information, discovery, or production technique will favorably affect the growth prospects of the firm. Speculative stocks are a special breed of securities, and they enjoy a wide following, particularly when the market is bullish.

Generally speaking, the earnings of speculative stocks are uncertain and highly unstable. These stocks are subject to wide swings in price, and they usually pay little or nothing in dividends. On the plus side, speculative stocks such as Sirius XM Radio, Dreamworks Animation, Liberty Media, NitroMed, and Under Armour offer attractive growth prospects and the chance to "hit it big" in the market. To be successful, however, an investor has to identify the big-money winners before the rest of the

FIGURE 6.6 A Tech Stock

Stock Report | August 22, 2009 | NNM Symbol: **ERTS** | **ERTS** is in the S&P 500

STANDARD &POOR'S

Electronic Arts Inc

S&P Recommendation SELL ★★☆☆☆

Price	12-Mo. Target Price	Investment Style
$19.44 (as of Aug 21, 2009)	$14.00	Large-Cap Growth

GICS Sector Information Technology
Sub-Industry Home Entertainment Software

Summary This company produces entertainment software for PCs, home video game consoles and mobile gaming devices.

Key Stock Statistics (Source S&P, Vickers, company reports)

52-Wk Range	$50.17– 14.24	S&P Oper. EPS 2010 **E**	-0.82	Market Capitalization(B)	$6.289	Beta	1.52
Trailing 12-Month EPS	$-3.82	S&P Oper. EPS 2011 **E**	-0.30	Yield (%)	Nil	S&P 3-Yr. Proj. EPS CAGR(%)	NM
Trailing 12-Month P/E	NM	P/E on S&P Oper. EPS 2010 **E**	NM	Dividend Rate/Share	Nil	S&P Credit Rating	NA
$10K Invested 5 Yrs Ago	$3,887	Common Shares Outstg. (M)	323.5	Institutional Ownership (%)	93		

Price Performance

30-Week Mov. Avg. · · · 10-Week Mov. Avg. — GAAP Earnings vs. Previous Year | Volume Above Avg. STARS
12-Mo. Target Price — Relative Strength — ▲ Up ▼ Down ► No Change | Below Avg.

2006   2007   2008   2009

Options: ASE, CBOE, P, Ph

Analysis prepared by **Jim Yin** on August 18, 2009, when the stock traded at **$ 19.67.**

Highlights

➤ We see revenue falling 10% in FY 10 (Mar.), following 15% growth in FY 09. Our forecast of a revenue decline in FY 10 reflects our view of a prolonged economic recession, which is causing consumers to reduce their spending and to focus their purchases on top-selling titles. As a result, retailers are lowering their inventories of older games. We also think sales will be hurt by the maturity of some of ERTS's game titles, lack of price cuts on video consoles, unfavorable foreign currency exchange and faster growth in non-traditional video game player segments, in which ERTS has smaller market shares.

➤ We forecast a gross margin of 50% in FY 10, the same percentage as in FY 09. We see operating expenses declining as a percentage of revenues, as ERTS curbs development of less popular titles. We project that FY 10 operating margins will improve to -9.0%, from -19.6% in FY 09, reflecting lower restructuring charges.

➤ Our loss per share estimate for FY 10 is $0.82, versus a loss of $3.40 in FY 09. The projected improvement reflects better operating margins in FY 10 and $448 million of goodwill impairment and restructuring charges in FY 09.

Investment Rationale/Risk

➤ Our sell recommendation reflects our view that the global economic slowdown will hurt sales of video games, which have been viewed as a safe haven amid weak consumer spending. We think consumers will continue to buy top-selling games, but fewer catalog titles, and believe the company's key franchises, including Madden NFL and NCAA Football, have been losing their appeal. We are concerned about ERTS's lack of new major game titles to offset this trend.

➤ Risks to our recommendation and target price include a recovery in the global economy, stronger sales of next-generation game consoles, and better-than-expected cost savings from restructuring.

➤ Our 12-month target price of $14 is based on a blend of our discounted cash flow (DCF) and enterprise value (EV) to sales analyses. Our DCF model assumes a 12.5% weighted average cost of capital and 3% terminal growth, yielding an intrinsic value of $13. We derive a value of $14 based on an EV/sales multiple of 0.6X our FY 10 revenue estimate, a discount to the industry average of 2.1X, due to ERTS's inconsistent profitability.

Qualitative Risk Assessment

LOW	MEDIUM	HIGH

Our risk assessment takes into account the worsening global economy, weak consumer spending, the volatile nature of the home entertainment software industry and our projection of ERTS's further loss in market share.

Quantitative Evaluations

S&P Quality Ranking B+

D	C	B-	B	B+	A-	A	A+

Relative Strength Rank WEAK

12

LOWEST = 1   HIGHEST = 99

Revenue/Earnings Data

Revenue (Million $)

	1Q	2Q	3Q	4Q	Year
2010	644.0	--	--	--	--
2009	804.0	894.0	1,654	860.0	4,212
2008	395.0	640.0	1,503	1,127	3,665
2007	413.0	784.0	1,281	613.0	3,091
2006	365.0	675.0	1,270	641.0	2,951
2005	431.6	715.7	1,428	553.0	3,129

Earnings Per Share ($)

	1Q	2Q	3Q	4Q	Year
2010	-0.72	E-0.49	E0.49	E-0.02	E-0.82
2009	-0.52	-0.97	-2.00	-0.13	-3.40
2008	-0.42	-0.62	-0.10	-0.29	-1.45
2007	-0.26	0.07	0.50	-0.08	0.24
2006	-0.19	0.16	0.83	-0.05	0.75
2005	0.08	0.31	1.18	0.02	1.59

Fiscal year ended Mar. 31. Next earnings report expected: Early November. EPS Estimates based on S&P Operating Earnings; historical GAAP earnings are as reported.

Dividend Data

No cash dividends have been paid.

market does. Speculative stocks are highly risky; they require not only a strong stomach but also a considerable amount of investor know-how. They are used to seek capital gains, and investors will often aggressively trade in and out of these securities as the situation demands.

Cyclical Stocks Cyclical stocks are issued by companies whose earnings are closely linked to the general level of business activity. They tend to reflect the general state of the economy and to move up and down with the business cycle. Companies that serve markets tied to capital equipment spending by business, or to consumer spending for big-ticket, durable items like houses and cars, typically head the list of cyclical stocks. Examples include Alcoa, Caterpillar, Genuine Parts, Lennar, Brunswick, and Timken.

Cyclical stocks generally do well when the economy is moving ahead, but they tend to do *especially well* when the country is in the early stages of economic recovery. They are, however, perhaps best avoided when the economy begins to weaken. Cyclical stocks are probably most suitable for investors who are willing to trade in and out of these issues as the economic outlook dictates and who can tolerate the accompanying exposure to risk.

Defensive Stocks Sometimes it is possible to find stocks whose prices remain stable or even increase when general economic activity is tapering off. These securities are known as **defensive stocks**. They tend to be less affected than the average issue by downswings in the business cycle.

Defensive stocks include the shares of many public utilities, as well as industrial and consumer goods companies that produce or market such staples as beverages, foods, and drugs. An excellent example of a defensive stock is Walmart. This recession-resistant company is the world's leading retailer. Other examples are Checkpoint Systems, a manufacturer of antitheft clothing security clips, WD-40, the maker of that famous all-purpose lubricant, and Extendicare, a leading provider of long-term care and assisted-living facilities. Defensive shares are commonly used by more aggressive investors, who tend to "park" their funds temporarily in defensive stocks while the economy remains soft, or until the investment atmosphere improves.

Mid-Cap Stocks A stock's size is based on its market value—or, more commonly, its *market capitalization*. This value is calculated as the market price of the stock times the number of shares outstanding. Generally speaking, the U.S. stock market can be broken into three segments, as measured by a stock's market "cap":

Small-cap	less than $2 billion
Mid-cap	$2 billion up to $10 billion
Large-cap	more than $10 billion

The large-cap stocks are the real biggies—the Walmarts, GMs, and Microsofts of the investment world. Although there are far fewer large-cap stocks than any other size, these companies account for 80% to 90% of the total market value of all U.S. equities. But as the saying goes, bigger isn't necessarily better. Nowhere is that statement more accurate than in the stock market. Indeed, both the small-cap and mid-cap segments of the market tend to hold their own, or even outperform large stocks over time.

Mid-cap stocks offer investors some attractive return opportunities. They provide much of the sizzle of small-stock returns, without as much price volatility. (We'll look at small-cap stocks soon.) At the same time, because mid-caps are fairly good-sized companies and many of them have been around for a long time, they offer some of the safety of the big, established stocks. Among the ranks of the mid-caps are such well-known companies as Abercrombie & Fitch, Dollar Tree, Hasbro, Nordstrom, and Whole Foods. Although these securities offer a nice alternative to large stocks without the uncertainties of small-caps, they probably are most appropriate for investors who are willing to tolerate a bit more risk and price volatility than large-caps have.

One type of mid-cap stock of particular interest is the so-called *baby blue chip*. Also known as "baby blues," these companies have all the characteristics of a regular blue chip *except size*. Like their larger counterparts, baby blues have rock-solid balance sheets, modest levels of debt, and long histories of steady profit growth. Baby blues normally pay a modest level of dividends, but like most mid-caps, they tend to emphasize growth. Thus, they're considered ideal for investors seeking quality long-term growth. Some well-known baby blues are Logitech, American Eagle Outfitters, and Garmin Ltd.

Small-Cap Stocks Some investors consider small companies to be in a class by themselves in terms of attractive return opportunities. In many cases, this has turned out to be true. Known as **small-cap stocks**, these companies generally have annual revenues of less than $250 million. But because of their size, spurts of growth can have dramatic effects on their earnings and stock prices. Callaway Golf, California Pizza Kitchen, Winn-Dixie Stores, and Shoe Carnival are some of the better-known small-cap stocks.

Although some small-caps (like Sanderson Farms, for example) are solid companies with equally solid financials, that's not the case with most of them. Indeed, because many of these companies are so small, they don't have a lot of stock outstanding, and their shares are not widely traded. In addition, small-company stocks have a tendency to be "here today and gone tomorrow." Although some of these stocks may hold the potential for high returns, investors should also be aware of the very high-risk exposure that comes with many of them.

A special category of small-cap stocks is the so-called *initial public offering (IPO)*. Most IPOs are small, relatively new companies that are going public for the first time. (Prior to their public offering, these stocks were privately held and not publicly traded.) Like other small-company stocks, IPOs are attractive because of the substantial capital gains that investors can earn. Of course, there's a catch: To stand a chance of buying some of the better, more attractive IPOs, you need to be either an active trader or a preferred client of the broker. Otherwise, the only IPOs you're likely to hear of will be the ones these investors don't want. Without a doubt, IPOs are high-risk investments, with the odds stacked against the investor. Because there's no market record to rely on, only investors who know what to look for in a company and who can tolerate substantial exposure to risk should buy these stocks.

Investing in Foreign Stocks

One of the most dramatic changes to occur in our financial markets in the past 20 years was the trend toward globalization. Indeed, globalization became the buzzword of the 1990s, and nowhere was that more evident than in the world's equity markets. Consider, for example, that in 1970 the U.S. stock market accounted for fully *two-thirds of the world market*. In essence, our stock market was twice as big as all the rest of the world's stock markets *combined*. That's no longer true: By 2008, the U.S. share of the world equity market had dropped to approximately 35%.

Today the world equity markets are dominated by just six markets, which together account for about 80% of the global total. The United States, by far, has the biggest equity market, which in 2008 had a total value of $11.6 *trillion*. In a distant second place was Japan (at less than one-third the size of the U.S. market), closely followed by the NYSE Euronext (which covers several countries), and the United Kingdom. Rounding out the list were the stock markets in Shanghai, Hong Kong, Germany, and Canada.

TABLE 6.3	Comparative Annual Returns in the World's Major Equity Markets, 1984–2008

	France	Germany	Switzerland	United Kingdom	United States
2008	−40.9%	−42.6%	−34.0%	−31.1%	−37.2%
2007	3.1	20.4	0.0	5.1	5.6
2006	22.6	24.1	20.6	16.4	15.8
2005	10.6	10.5	17.1	7.4	1.7
2004	19.2	16.7	15.6	19.6	5.3
2003	41.0	64.8	35.0	32.1	28.3
2002	−20.8	−32.9	−10.0	−15.2	−14.5
2001	−22.0	−21.9	−21.0	−14.0	−5.3
2000	−4.1	−15.3	6.4	−11.5	−4.6
1999	29.7	20.5	−6.6	12.4	26.7
1998	42.1	29.9	24.0	17.8	17.8
1997	12.4	25.0	44.8	22.6	24.4
1996	21.6	14.0	2.8	27.2	28.0
1995	14.8	17.0	45.0	21.3	35.7
1994	−7.3	3.1	30.0	−4.4	4.9
1993	19.6	34.8	41.7	19.0	16.4
1992	5.2	−2.1	26.0	14.0	7.2
1991	18.6	8.7	16.8	16.0	23.3
1990	−13.3	−8.8	−5.1	10.4	−0.4
1989	37.6	48.2	28.0	23.1	30.7
1988	37.1	19.8	5.8	4.1	15.5
1987	−13.9	−24.6	−9.2	35.2	5.9
1986	79.9	36.4	34.7	27.7	26.1
1985	84.2	138.1	109.2	53.4	31.7
1984	4.8	−5.2	−11.1	5.3	1.2
Average Annual Returns Over Extended Holding Periods					
5 years 2004–2008	5.2%	7.7%	5.8%	5.0%	0.6%
10 years 1999–2008	5.5	4.1	2.6	3.0	1.6
15 years 1994–2008	8.8	8.2	8.7	7.0	8.5
25 years 1984–2008	14.0	11.4	11.7	11.9	11.1

Note: Total return = dividend income + capital gain (or loss).

(Source: Elroy Dimson, Paul Marsh, and Mike Staunton *Triumph of the Optimists: 101 Years of Global Investment Returns.* Princeton, NJ: Princeton University Press. Additional updates provided by authors.)

Comparative Returns The United States still dominates the world equity markets in terms of sheer size, as well as in the number of listed companies (over 10,000 of them). But that leaves unanswered an important question: How has the U.S. equity market performed in comparison to the rest of the world's major stock markets? For an answer to that question, look at Table 6.3, which summarizes total annual returns (in U.S. dollars) for five large equity markets over the 25-year period from 1984 through 2008. To begin with, we can see that over the latest five years (from 2004 through 2008), the comparative performance of U.S. stocks was nothing short of dismal: They earned just 0.6% per year over that period. Looking over longer time periods or year by year we can see that while U.S. stocks have been able to generate highly competitive returns, they seldom finished on top. Translated, that means there definitely are attractive returns awaiting those investors who are willing to venture beyond our borders.

Going Global: Direct Investments Basically, there are two ways to invest in foreign stocks: through direct investments or through ADRs. (We'll discuss a third way—international mutual funds—in Chapter 12.)

Without a doubt, the most adventuresome way is to *buy shares directly in foreign markets*. Investing directly is *not* for the uninitiated, however. You have to know what you're doing and be prepared to tolerate a good deal of market risk. Although most major U.S. brokerage houses are set up to accommodate investors interested in buying foreign securities, there are still many logistical problems to be faced. To begin with, you have to cope with currency fluctuations and changing foreign exchange rates, because, as we'll see below, these can have a dramatic impact on your returns. But that's just the start: You also have to deal with different regulatory and accounting standards. The fact is that most foreign markets, even the bigger ones, are not as closely regulated as U.S. exchanges. Investors in foreign markets, therefore, may have to put up with insider trading and other practices that can cause wild swings in market prices. Finally, there are the obvious language barriers, tax problems, and general "red tape" that all too often plague international transactions. The returns from direct foreign investments can be substantial, but so can the obstacles placed in your way.

Going Global with ADRs Fortunately, there is an easier way to invest in foreign stocks, and that is to buy *American Depositary Receipts (ADRs)*. As we saw in Chapter 2, ADRs are dollar-denominated instruments (or certificates) that represent ownership of a certain number of shares in a specific foreign company (the number of shares can range from a fraction of a share to 20 shares or more). ADRs are great for investors who want to own foreign stocks but don't want the hassles that often come with them. Actually, ADRs trade in the market as *American depositary shares* (or *ADSs*). Although the terms *ADR* and *ADS* are often used interchangeably, technically there is a difference between the two: An ADR is the legal document that describes the security, whereas an ADS is the vehicle through which you invest in the security. Thus, ADSs represent shares in a given ADR and are the securities that are traded in the market. (Take a look at the stock quotes in the *Wall Street Journal*, and you will see that ADRs are listed in the quotes as ADSs. See, for example, Figure 6.4, where you will find three ADSs listed.)

American depositary receipts are bought and sold on U.S. markets just like stocks in U.S. companies. Their prices are quoted in U.S. dollars. Furthermore, dividends are paid in dollars. Although there are about 400 foreign companies *whose shares are directly listed on U.S. exchanges,* most foreign companies are registered in this country as ADRs. Indeed, shares of some 2,000 companies, from more than 50 countries, are traded as ADSs on the NYSE, Amex, Nasdaq, and OTC markets.

To see how ADRs are structured, take a look at Cadbury Schweppes, the British food and household-products firm, whose ADRs are traded on the NYSE. Each Cadbury ADR represents ownership of four shares of Cadbury stock. These shares are held in a custodial account by a U.S. bank (or its foreign correspondent), which receives dividends, pays any foreign withholding taxes, and then converts the net proceeds to U.S. dollars, which it passes on to investors. Other foreign stocks that can be purchased as ADRs include Sony (a Japanese stock), Ericsson Telephone (Sweden), Nokia (Finland), Royal Dutch Shell (Netherlands), Nestle's (Switzerland), Elan Corporation (Ireland), Suntech Power (China), BASF (Germany), Hutchison Wampoa, Ltd. (Hong Kong), Teva Pharmaceuticals (Israel), Norsk Hydro (Norway), Diageo (U.K.), and Grupo Televisa (Mexico). You can even buy ADRs on Russian companies, such as Vimpel-Communications, a Moscow-based cellular phone company whose shares trade (as ADRs) on the NYSE.

Putting Global Returns in Perspective Whether you buy foreign stocks directly or through ADRs, the whole process of global investing is a bit more complicated and more risky than domestic investing. The reason: When investing globally, *you have to pick both the right stock and the right market.* Basically, foreign stocks are valued much the same way as U.S. stocks. Indeed, the same variables that drive U.S. share prices (earnings, dividends, and so on) also drive stock values in foreign markets. On top of this, each market reacts to its own set of economic forces (inflation, interest rates, level of economic activity), which set the tone of the market. At any given time, some markets are performing better than others. The challenge facing global investors is to be in the right market at the right time.

As with U.S. stocks, foreign shares produce the same two basic sources of returns: dividends and capital gains (or losses). But with global investing, there is a third variable—*currency exchange rates*—that affects returns to U.S. investors. In particular, as the U.S. dollar weakens or strengthens relative to a foreign currency, the returns to U.S. investors from foreign stocks increase or decrease accordingly. In a global context, total return to U.S. investors in foreign securities is defined as follows:

Equation 6.4

$$\begin{matrix} \text{Total returns} \\ \text{(in U.S. dollars)} \end{matrix} = \begin{matrix} \text{Current income} \\ \text{(dividends)} \end{matrix} + \begin{matrix} \text{Capital gains} \\ \text{(or losses)} \end{matrix} \pm \begin{matrix} \text{Changes in currency} \\ \text{exchange rates} \end{matrix}$$

Because current income and capital gains are in the "local currency" (the currency in which the foreign stock is denominated, such as the euro or the Japanese yen), we can shorten the total return formula to:

Equation 6.5

$$\begin{matrix} \text{Total return} \\ \text{(in U.S. dollars)} \end{matrix} = \begin{matrix} \text{Returns from current} \\ \text{income and capital gains} \\ \text{(in local currency)} \end{matrix} \pm \begin{matrix} \text{Returns from} \\ \text{changes in currency} \\ \text{exchange rates} \end{matrix}$$

Thus, the two basic components of total return are *those generated by the stocks themselves* (dividends plus change in share prices) and *those derived from movements in currency exchange rates.*

Measuring Global Returns Employing the same two basic components noted in Equation 6.5 above, we can compute total return in U.S. dollars by using the following holding period return (HPR) formula, as modified for changes in currency exchange rates.

Equation 6.6

$$\begin{matrix} \text{Total return} \\ \text{(in U.S. dollars)} \end{matrix} = \left[\frac{\begin{matrix} \text{Ending value of} \\ \text{stock in foreign} \\ \text{currency} \end{matrix} + \begin{matrix} \text{Amount of dividends} \\ \text{received in} \\ \text{foreign currency} \end{matrix}}{\begin{matrix} \text{Beginning value of stock} \\ \text{in foreign currency} \end{matrix}} \times \frac{\begin{matrix} \text{Exchange rate} \\ \text{at } end \text{ of} \\ \text{holding period} \end{matrix}}{\begin{matrix} \text{Exchange rate} \\ \text{at } beginning \text{ of} \\ \text{holding period} \end{matrix}} \right] - 1.00$$

In Equation 6.6, the "exchange rate" represents the *value of the foreign currency in U.S. dollars*—that is, how much one unit of the foreign currency is worth in U.S. money.

This modified HPR formula is best used over investment periods of one year or less. Also, because it is assumed that dividends are received at the same exchange rate as the ending price of the stock, this equation provides only an approximate (although fairly close) measure of return. Essentially, the first component of Equation 6.6 provides returns on the stock in local currency, and the second element accounts for the impact of changes in currency exchange rates.

To see how this formula works, consider a U.S. investor who buys several hundred shares of Siemans AG, the German electrical engineering and electronics company that trades on the Frankfurt Stock Exchange. Since Germany is part of the European Common Market, its currency is the *euro*. Let's assume that the investor paid a price *per share* of 90.48 euros for the stock, at a time when the exchange rate between the U.S. dollar and the euro (U.S.\$/€) was \$0.945, meaning a euro was worth almost 95 (U.S.) cents. The stock paid *annual* dividends of 5 euros per share. Twelve months later, the stock was trading at 94.00 euros, when the U.S.\$/€ exchange rate was \$1.083. Clearly, the stock went up in price and so did the euro, so the investor must have done all right. To find out just what kind of return this investment generated (in U.S. dollars), we'll have to use Equation 6.6.

$$\begin{aligned}\text{Total return} \atop \text{(in U.S. dollars)} &= \left[\frac{€94.00 + €5.00}{€90.48} \times \frac{\$1.083}{\$0.945} \right] - 1.00 \\ &= [1.0942 \times 1.1460] - 1.00 \\ &= [1.2540] - 1.00 \\ &= \underline{\underline{25.4\%}}\end{aligned}$$

With a return of 25.4%, the investor obviously did quite well. However, *most of this return was due to currency movements, not to the behavior of the stock*. Look at just the first part of the equation, which shows the return (in local currency) *earned on the stock* from dividends and capital gains: 1.0942 − 1.00 = 9.42%. Thus, the stock itself produced a return of less than 9.50%. All the rest of the return—about 16% (i.e., 25.40 − 9.42)—came from the change in currency values. In this case, the value of the U.S. dollar went down relative to the euro and thus added to the return.

Currency Exchange Rates As we've just seen, exchange rates can have a dramatic impact on investor returns. They can convert mediocre returns or even losses into very attractive returns—and vice versa. Only one thing determines whether the so-called *currency effect* is going to be positive or negative: the behavior of the U.S. dollar relative to the currency in which the security is denominated. In essence, *a stronger dollar has a negative impact on total returns to U.S. investors, and a weaker dollar has a positive impact*. Thus, other things being equal, the best time to be in foreign securities is when the dollar is *falling*.

Of course, the greater the amount of fluctuation in the currency exchange rate, the greater the impact on total returns. The challenge facing global investors is to find not only the best-performing foreign stock(s) but also the best-performing foreign currencies. You want the *value of both the foreign stock and the foreign currency to go up over your investment horizon*. And note that this rule applies *both* to direct investment in foreign stocks and to the purchase of ADRs. (Even though ADRs are denominated in dollars, their quoted prices vary with ongoing changes in currency exchange rates.)

Alternative Investment Strategies

Basically, common stocks can be used: (1) as a "storehouse" of value, (2) as a way to accumulate capital, and (3) as a source of income. Storage of value is important to all investors, as nobody likes to lose money. However, some investors are more concerned about it than are others. They rank safety of principal as their most important stock selection criteria. These investors are more quality-conscious and tend to gravitate toward blue chips and other nonspeculative shares.

Accumulation of capital, in contrast, is generally an important goal to those with long-term investment horizons. These investors use the capital gains and/or dividends that stocks provide to build up their wealth. Some use growth stocks for this purpose, others do it with income shares, and still others use a little of both.

Finally, some investors use stocks as a source of income. To them, a dependable flow of dividends is essential. High-yielding, good-quality income shares are usually their preferred investment vehicle.

Individual investors can use various *investment strategies* to reach their investment goals. These include buy-and-hold, current income, quality long-term growth, aggressive stock management, and speculation and short-term trading. The first three strategies appeal to investors who consider storage of value important. Depending on the temperament of the investor and the time he or she has to devote to an investment program, any of these strategies might be used to accumulate capital. In contrast, the current-income strategy is the logical choice for those using stocks as a source of income.

We discuss these five strategies in more detail below. You should understand these strategies so that you can choose which one best suits your needs.

Buy-and-Hold   Buy-and-hold is the most basic of all investment strategies, and certainly one of the most conservative. The objective is to place money in a secure investment outlet (safety of principal is vital) and watch it grow over time. In this strategy, investors select high-quality stocks that offer attractive current income and/or capital gains and hold them for extended periods—perhaps as long as 10 to 15 years. This strategy is often used to finance future retirement plans, to meet the educational needs of children, or simply to accumulate capital over the long haul. Generally, investors pick a few good stocks and invest in them on a regular basis for long periods of time—until either the investment climate or corporate conditions change dramatically.

Buy-and-hold investors regularly add fresh capital to their portfolios (many treat them like savings plans). Most also plow the income from annual dividends back into the portfolio and reinvest in additional shares (often through dividend reinvestment plans). Long popular with so-called *value-oriented investors*, this approach is used by quality-conscious individuals who are looking for competitive returns over the long haul.

Current Income   Some investors use common stocks to seek high levels of current income. Common stocks are desirable for this purpose, not so much for their high dividend yields but because their *dividend levels tend to increase over time*. In this strategy, safety of principal and stability of income are vital; capital gains are of secondary importance. Quality income shares are the obvious choice for this strategy. Some investors adopt it simply as a way of earning high (and relatively safe) returns on their investment capital. More often, however, the current-income strategy is used by those who are trying to supplement their income. Indeed, many of these investors plan to use the added income for consumption purposes, such as a retired couple supplementing their retirement benefits.

Quality Long-Term Growth   This strategy is *less conservative* than either of the first two in that it *seeks capital gains as the primary source of return*. A fair amount of trading takes place with this approach. Most of the trading is confined to *quality* *growth stocks* (including some of the better tech stocks, as well as baby blues and other mid-caps). These stocks offer attractive growth prospects and the chance for considerable price appreciation. A number of growth stocks also pay dividends, which many growth-oriented investors consider *an added source of return*. But even so, this strategy still emphasizes capital gains as the principal way to earn big returns.

This approach involves greater risk, because of its heavy reliance on capital gains. Therefore, a good deal of diversification is often used. Long-term accumulation of capital is the most common reason for using this approach, but compared to the buy-and-hold tactic, the investor aggressively seeks a bigger payoff by doing considerably more trading and assuming more market risk.

A variation of this investment strategy combines quality long-term growth with high income. This is the so-called *total-return approach* to investing. Although solidly anchored in long-term growth, this approach also considers dividend income as a source of return. Investors who use the total return approach seek attractive long-term returns from *both* dividend income *and* capital gains by holding both income stocks and growth stocks in their portfolios. Or they may hold stocks that provide both dividends and capital gains. In the latter case, the investor doesn't necessarily look for high-yielding stocks, but for stocks that offer the potential for *high rates of growth in their dividend streams*.

Total-return investors are very concerned about quality. Indeed, about the only thing that separates them from current-income and quality long-term growth investors is that total-return investors care more about the *amount of return* than about the *source of return*. For this reason, total-return investors seek the most attractive returns wherever they can find them—be it from a growing stream of dividends or from appreciation in the price of a stock.

Aggressive Stock Management Aggressive stock management also seeks attractive rates of return through a fully managed portfolio. An investor using this strategy aggressively trades in and out of stocks to achieve eye-catching returns, primarily from capital gains. Blue chips, growth stocks, big-name tech stocks, mid-caps, and cyclical issues are the primary investment vehicles. More aggressive investors might even consider small-cap stocks, including some of the more speculative tech stocks, foreign shares, and ADRs.

This approach is similar to the quality long-term growth strategy. However, it involves considerably more trading, and the investment horizon is generally much shorter. For example, rather than waiting two or three years for a stock to move, an aggressive stock trader would go after the same investment payoff in six months to a year. Timing security transactions and turning investment capital over fairly rapidly are both key elements of this strategy. These investors try to stay fully invested in stocks when the market is bullish. When the market weakens, they put a big chunk of their money into defensive stocks or even into cash and other short-term debt instruments.

This aggressive strategy has substantial risks and trading costs. It also places real demands on the individual's time and investment skills. But the rewards can be equally substantial.

Speculation and Short-Term Trading Speculation and short-term trading characterize the least conservative of all investment strategies. The sole objective of this strategy is capital gains. The shorter the time in which the objective can be achieved, the better. Although investors who use this strategy confine most of their attention to speculative or small-cap stocks and tech stocks, they are not averse to using foreign shares (especially those in so-called *emerging markets*) or other forms of common stock if they offer attractive short-term opportunities. Many speculators feel that information about the industry or company is less important than market psychology or the general tone of the market. It is a process of constantly switching from one position to another as new opportunities unfold.

Because the strategy involves so much risk, many transactions yield little or no profit, or even substantial losses. The hope is, of course, that when one does hit, it will be in a big way, and returns will be more than sufficient to offset losses. This strategy obviously requires considerable knowledge and time. Perhaps most important, it also requires the psychological and financial fortitude to withstand the shock of financial losses.

CONCEPTS IN REVIEW

Answers available at www.pearsonhighered.com/gitman

6.14 Define and briefly discuss the investment merits of each of the following.

a. *Blue chips.*
b. *Income stocks.*
c. *Mid-cap stocks.*
d. *American Depositary Receipts.*
e. *IPOs.*
f. *Tech stocks.*

6.15 Why do most income stocks offer only limited capital gains potential? Does this mean the outlook for continued profitability is also limited? Explain.

6.16 With all the securities available in this country, why would a U.S. investor want to buy foreign stocks? Briefly describe the two ways in which a U.S. investor can buy stocks in a foreign company. As a U.S. investor, which approach would you prefer? Explain.

6.17 Which *investment approach (or approaches)* do you feel would be most appropriate for a quality-conscious investor? What kind of investment approach do you think you'd be most comfortable with? Explain.

---

myfinancelab Here is what you should know after reading this chapter. **MyFinanceLab** will help you identify what you know, and where to go when you need to practice.

What You Should Know	Key Terms	Where To Practice
LG 1 **Explain the investment appeal of common stocks and why individuals like to invest in them.** Common stocks have long been a popular investment vehicle, largely because of the attractive return opportunities they provide. From current income to capital gains, there are common stocks available to fit any investment need.	residual owners, *p. 207*	MyFinanceLab Study Plan 6.1

What You Should Know	Key Terms	Where To Practice
LG2 Describe stock returns from a historical perspective and understand how current returns measure up to historical standards of performance. Stock returns consist of both dividends and capital gains, although price appreciation is the key component. Over the long run, stocks have provided investors with annual returns of around 10% to 12%. The decade of the 1990s was especially rewarding, as stocks generated returns of anywhere from around 20% (on the Dow) to nearly 30% in the tech-heavy Nasdaq market. That situation changed in early 2000, when one of the biggest bull markets in history came to an abrupt end. From 2000 through late 2002, the DJIA fell some 38%, the S&P 500 fell nearly 50%, and the Nasdaq fell an eye-popping 77%.		MyFinanceLab Study Plan 6.2
LG3 Discuss the basic features of common stocks, including issue characteristics, stock quotations, and transaction costs. Common stocks are a form of equity capital, with each share representing partial ownership of a company. Publicly traded stock can be issued via a public offering or through a rights offering to existing stockholders. Companies can also increase the number of shares outstanding through a stock split. To reduce the number of shares in circulation, companies can buy back shares, which are then held as treasury stock. Occasionally, a company issues different classes of common stock, known as classified common stock.	classified common stock, *p. 215* equity capital, *p. 212* public offering, *p. 212* publicly traded issues, *p. 212* rights offering, *p. 212* stock spin-off, *p. 214* stock split, *p. 214* treasury stock, *p. 214*	MyFinanceLab Study Plan 6.3 Video Learning Aid for Problem P6.1
LG4 Understand the different kinds of common stock values. There are several ways to calculate the value of a share of stock. Book value represents accounting value. Market value is a security's prevailing market price. Investment value is the amount that investors think the stock should be worth.	book value, *p. 217* investment value, *p. 218* market value, *p. 217* par value, *p. 217*	MyFinanceLab Study Plan 6.4
LG5 Discuss common stock dividends, types of dividends, and dividend reinvestment plans. Companies often share their profits by paying out cash dividends to stockholders. Companies pay dividends only after carefully considering a variety of corporate and market factors. Sometimes companies declare stock dividends rather than, or in addition to, cash dividends. Many firms that pay cash dividends have dividend reinvestment plans, through which shareholders can automatically reinvest cash dividends in the company's stock.	cash dividend, *p. 221* date of record, *p. 220* dividend yield, *p. 221* dividend payout ratio, *p. 221* dividend reinvestment plan (DRIP), *p. 222* earnings per share, *p. 219* ex-dividend date, *p. 220* payment date, *p. 220* stock dividend, *p. 221*	MyFinanceLab Study Plan 6.5

What You Should Know	Key Terms	Where To Practice
LG 6 **Describe various types of common stocks, including foreign stocks, and note how stocks can be used as investment vehicles.** Depending on their needs and preferences, investors can choose blue chips, income stocks, growth stocks, tech stocks, speculative issues, cyclicals, defensive shares, mid-cap stocks, small-cap stocks, and initial public offerings. Also, U.S. investors can buy common stock of foreign companies either directly on foreign exchanges or on U.S. markets as American Depositary Shares (ADSs). Generally, common stocks can be used as a storehouse of value, as a way to accumulate capital, or as a source of income. Investors can follow different investment strategies (buy-and-hold, current income, quality long-term growth, aggressive stock management, and speculation and short-term trading) to achieve these objectives.	blue-chip stocks, *p. 224* cyclical stocks, *p. 228* defensive stocks, *p. 228* growth stocks, *p. 226* income stocks, *p. 224* mid-cap stocks, *p. 228* small-cap stocks, *p. 229* speculative stocks, *p. 226* tech stocks, *p. 226*	MyFinanceLab Study Plan 6.6 Video Learning Aid for Problem P6.14

Log into **MyFinanceLab**, take a chapter test, and get a personalized Study Plan that tells you which concepts you understand and which ones you need to review. From there, **MyFinanceLab** will give you further practice, tutorials, animations, videos, and guided solutions.
Log into **www.myfinancelab.com**

Discussion Questions

LG 1 **Q6.1** Look at the record of stock returns in Table 6.1, particularly the return performance during the 1970s, 1980s, 1990s, and 2000–2008.
  a. How would you compare the returns during the 1970s with those produced in the 1980s? How would you characterize market returns in the 1990s? Is there anything that stands out about this market? How does it compare with the market that existed from early 2000 through 2008?
  b. Considering the average annual returns that have been generated over holding periods of five years or more, what rate of return do you feel is typical for the stock market in general? Is it unreasonable to expect this kind of return, on average, in the future? Explain.

LG 2 **Q6.2** Given the information in the *Wall Street Journal* quote in Figure 6.4 (page 216), answer the following questions for Harley Davidson Inc.
  a. On what day did the trading activity occur?
  b. At what price did the stock sell at the end of the day on Thursday, September 3, 2009?
  c. What is the firm's price/earnings ratio? What does that indicate?
  d. What is the last price at which the stock traded on the date quoted?
  e. What was the dividend payout per share for the previous year?
  f. What are the highest and lowest prices at which the stock traded during the latest 52-week period?

g. How many shares of stock were traded on the day quoted?

h. How much, if any, of a change in price took place between the day quoted and the immediately preceding day? At what price did the stock close on the immediately preceding day?

Q6.3 Listed below are three pairs of stocks. Look at each pair and select the security you would like to own, given that you want to *select the one that's worth more money*. Then, *after* you make all three of your selections, use the *Wall Street Journal* or some other source to find the latest market value of the two securities in each pair.

a. 50 shares of Berkshire Hathaway (stock symbol BRKA) or 150 shares of Coca-Cola (stock symbol KO). (Both are listed on the NYSE.)

b. 100 shares of WD-40 (symbol WDFC—a Nasdaq National Market issue) or 100 shares of Nike (symbol NKE—a NYSE stock).

c. 150 shares of Walmart (symbol WMT) or 50 shares of Sears (symbol S). (Both are listed on the NYSE.)

How many times did you pick the one that was worth more money? Did the price of any of these stocks surprise you? If so, which one(s)? Does the price of a stock represent its value? Explain.

Q6.4 Assume that a wealthy individual comes to you looking for some investment advice. She is in her early forties and has $250,000 to put into stocks. She wants to build up as much capital as she can over a 15-year period and is willing to tolerate a "fair amount" of risk.

a. What types of stocks do you think would be most suitable for this investor? Come up with at least three different types of stocks, and briefly explain the rationale for each.

b. Would your recommendations change if you were dealing with a smaller amount of money—say, $50,000? What if the investor were more risk-averse? Explain.

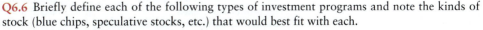

Q6.5 Identify and briefly describe the three sources of return to U.S. investors in foreign stocks. How important are currency exchange rates? With regard to currency exchange rates, when is the best time to be in foreign securities?

a. Listed below are exchange rates (for the beginning and end of a hypothetical 1-year investment horizon) for three currencies: the British pound (B£), Australian dollar (A$), and Mexican peso (Mp).

	Currency Exchange Rates at	
Currency	Beginning of Investment Horizon	End of One-Year Investment Horizon
British pound (B£)	1.55 U.S.$ per B£	1.75 U.S.$ per B£
Australian dollar (A$)	1.35 A$ per U.S.$	1.25 A$ per U.S.$
Mexican peso (Mp)	0.10 U.S.$ per Mp	0.08 U.S.$ per Mp

From the perspective of a U.S. investor holding a foreign (British, Australian, or Mexican) stock, which of the above changes in currency exchange rates would have a positive effect on returns (in U.S. dollars)? Which would have a negative effect?

b. ADRs are denominated in U.S. dollars. Are their returns affected by currency exchange rates? Explain.

Q6.6 Briefly define each of the following types of investment programs and note the kinds of stock (blue chips, speculative stocks, etc.) that would best fit with each.

a. A buy-and-hold strategy.

b. A current-income portfolio.

c. Long-term total return.

d. Aggressive stock management.

Problems

All problems are available on **www.myfinancelab.com**

LG3 **P6.1** An investor owns some stock in General Refrigeration & Cooling. The stock recently underwent a 5-for-2 stock split. If the stock was trading at $50 per share just before the split, how much is each share most likely selling for after the split? If the investor owned 200 shares of the stock before the split, how many shares would she own afterward?

LG3 **P6.2** An investor deposits $20,000 into a new brokerage account. The investor buys 1,000 shares of Tipco stock for $19 per share. Two weeks later, the investor sells the Tipco stock for $20 per share. When the investor receives his brokerage account statement, he sees that there is a balance of $20,900 in his account:

Item	Number	Price per Share	Total Transaction	Account Balance
1. Deposit			$20,000	$20,000
2. Tipco purchase	1,000 shares	$19	($19,000)	$20,000
3. Tipco sale	1,000 shares	$20	$20,000	$21,000
4.				
5. Balance				$20,900

What belongs in item 4 on this statement?

LG4 **P6.3** Kracked Pottery Company has total assets of $2.5 million, total short- and long-term debt of $1.8 million, and $200,000 worth of 8% preferred stock outstanding. What is the firm's total book value? What would its book value per share be if the firm had 50,000 shares of common stock outstanding?

LG4 **P6.4** Lots ov' Profit, Inc., is trading at $25 per share. There are 250 million shares outstanding. What is the market capitalization of this company?

LG5 **P6.5** The MedTech Company recently reported net profits after taxes of $15.8 million. It has 2.5 million shares of common stock outstanding and pays preferred dividends of $1 million per year.
    a. Compute the firm's earnings per share (EPS).
    b. Assuming that the stock currently trades at $60 per share, determine what the firm's dividend yield would be if it paid $2 per share to common stockholders.
    c. What would the firm's dividend payout ratio be if it paid $2 per share in dividends?

LG5 **P6.6** On January 1, 2010, an investor bought 200 shares of Gottahavit, Inc., for $50 per share. On January 3, 2011, the investor sold the stock for $55 per share. The stock paid a quarterly dividend of $0.25 per share. How much (in $) did the investor earn on this investment, and, assuming the investor is in the 33% tax bracket, how much will she pay in income taxes on this transaction?

LG4 **LG5** **P6.7** Consider the following information about Truly Good Coffee, Inc.

Total assets	$240 million
Total debt	$115 million
Preferred stock	$25 million
Common stockholders' equity	$100 million
Net profits after taxes	$22.5 million
Number of preferred stock outstanding	1 million shares
Number of common stock outstanding	10 million shares
Preferred dividends paid	$2/share
Common dividends paid	$0.75/share
Market price of the preferred stock	$30.75/share
Market price of the common stock	$25.00/share

Use the information above to find the following.
- **a.** The company's book value.
- **b.** Its book value per share.
- **c.** The stock's earnings per share (EPS).
- **d.** The dividend payout ratio.
- **e.** The dividend yield on the common stock.
- **f.** The dividend yield on the preferred stock.

LG5 **P6.8** East Coast Utilities is currently trading at $28 per share. The company pays a quarterly dividend of $0.28 per share. What is the dividend yield?

LG5 **P6.9** West Coast Utilities had a net profit of $900 million. It has 900 million shares outstanding and paid annual dividends of $0.90 per share. What is the dividend payout ratio?

LG5 **P6.10** Wilfred Nadeau owns 200 shares of Consolidated Glue. The company's board of directors recently declared a cash dividend of 50 cents a share payable April 18 (a Wednesday) to shareholders of record on March 22 (a Thursday).
- **a.** How much in dividends, if any, will Wilfred receive if he *sells* his stock on March 20?
- **b.** Assume Wilfred decides to hold onto the stock rather than sell it. If he belongs to the company's dividend reinvestment plan, how many new shares of stock will he receive if the stock is currently trading at $40 and the plan offers a 5% discount on the share price of the stock? (Assume that all of Wilfred's dividends are diverted to the plan.) Will Wilfred have to pay any taxes on these dividends, given that he is taking them in stock rather than cash?

LG5 **P6.11** Southern Cities Trucking Company has the following five-year record of earnings per share.

Year	EPS
2006	$1.40
2007	2.10
2008	1.00
2009	3.25
2010	0.80

Which of the following procedures would produce the greater amount of dividends to stockholders over this five-year period?
- **a.** Paying out dividends at a fixed ratio of 40% of EPS.
- **b.** Paying out dividends at a fixed rate of $1 per share.

LG4 **LG5** **P6.12** Using the resources available at your campus or public library, or on the Internet, select any three common stocks you like and determine the latest book value per share, earnings per share, dividend payout ratio, and dividend yield for each. (Show all your calculations.)

LG4 **LG5** **P6.13** In January 2006, an investor purchased 800 shares of Engulf & Devour, a rapidly growing high-tech conglomerate. Over the five-year period from 2006 through 2010, the stock turned in the following dividend and share price performance.

Year	Share Price at Beginning of Year	Dividends Paid During Year	Share Price at End of Year
2006	$42.50*	$0.82	$54.00
2007	54.00	1.28	74.25
2008	74.25	1.64	81.00
2009	81.00	1.91	91.25
2010	91.25	2.30	128.75

*Investor purchased stock in 2006 at this price.

On the basis of this information, find the annual holding period returns for 2006 through 2010. (*Hint:* See Chapter 4 for the HPR formula.)

 LG6 **P6.14** George Robbins considers himself to be an aggressive investor. At the present time, he's thinking about investing in some foreign securities. In particular, he's looking at two stocks: (1) Bayer AG, the big German chemical and health-care firm, and (2) Swisscom AG, the Swiss telecommunications company.

Bayer AG, which trades on the Frankfurt Exchange, is currently priced at 53.25 euros per share. It pays annual dividends of 1.50 euros per share. Robbins expects the stock to climb to 60.00 euros per share over the next 12 months. The current exchange rate is 0.9025 €/U.S.$, but that's expected to rise to 1.015€/U.S.$. The other company, Swisscom, trades on the Zurich Exchange and is currently priced at 71.5 Swiss francs (Sf) per share. The stock pays annual dividends of 1.5 Sf per share. Its share price is expected to go up to 76.0 Sf within a year. At current exchange rates, one Sf is worth $0.75 U.S., but that's expected to go to $0.85 by the end of the one-year holding period.

a. *Ignoring the currency effect*, which of the two stocks promises the higher total return (in its local currency)? Based on this information, which of the two stocks looks like the better investment?

b. Which of the two stocks has the better total return *in U.S. dollars*? Did currency exchange rates affect their returns in any way? Do you still want to stick with the same stock you selected in part **a**? Explain.

LG6 **P6.15** Bruce buys $25,000 of UH-OH Corporation stock. Unfortunately, a major newspaper reveals the very next day that the company is being investigated for accounting fraud, and the stock price falls by 50%. What is the percentage increase now required for Bruce to get back to $25,000 of value?

Visit **www.myfinancelab.com** for web exercises, spreadsheets, and other online resources.

Case Problem 6.1   *Sara Decides to Take the Plunge*

LG1 **LG6** Sara Thomas is a child psychologist who has built up a thriving practice in her hometown of Boise, Idaho. Over the past several years she has been able to accumulate a substantial sum of money. She has worked long and hard to be successful, but she never imagined anything like this. Even so, success has not spoiled Sara. Still single, she keeps to her old circle of friends. One of her closest friends is Terry Jenkins, who happens to be a stockbroker and who acts as Sara's financial adviser.

Not long ago, Sara attended a seminar on investing in the stock market, and since then she's been doing some reading about the market. She has concluded that keeping all of her money in low-yielding savings accounts doesn't make sense. As a result, Sara has decided to move part of her money to stocks. One evening, Sara told Terry about her decision and explained that she had found several stocks that she thought looked "sort of interesting." She described them as follows:

• *North Atlantic Swim Suit Company.* This highly speculative stock pays no dividends. Although the earnings of NASS have been a bit erratic, Sara feels that its growth prospects have never been brighter—"what with more people than ever going to the beaches the way they are these days," she says.

- *Town and Country Computer*. This is a long-established computer firm that pays a modest dividend yield (of about 1.50%). It is considered a quality growth stock. From one of the stock reports she read, Sara understands that T&C offers excellent long-term growth and capital gains potential.

- *Southeastern Public Utility Company*. This income stock pays a dividend yield of around 5%. Although it's a solid company, it has limited growth prospects because of its location.

- *International Gold Mines, Inc.* This stock has performed quite well in the past, especially when inflation has become a problem. Sara feels that if it can do so well in inflationary times, it will do even better in a strong economy. Unfortunately, the stock has experienced wide price swings in the past. It pays almost no dividends.

Questions

a. What do you think of the idea of Sara keeping "substantial sums" of money in savings accounts? Would common stocks make better investments for her than savings accounts? Explain.

b. What is your opinion of the four stocks Sara has described? Do you think they are suitable for her investment needs? Explain.

c. What kind of common stock investment program would you recommend for Sara? What investment objectives do you think she should set for herself, and how can common stocks help her achieve her goals?

Case Problem 6.1   *Wally Wonders Whether There's a Place for Dividends*

LG5 LG6 Wally Wilson is a commercial artist who makes a good living by doing freelance work—mostly layouts and illustrations—for local ad agencies and major institutional clients (such as large department stores). Wally has been investing in the stock market for some time, buying mostly high-quality growth stocks as a way to achieve long-term growth and capital appreciation. He feels that with the limited time he has to devote to his security holdings, high-quality issues are his best bet. He has become a bit perplexed lately with the market, disturbed that some of his growth stocks aren't doing even as well as many good-grade income shares. He therefore decides to have a chat with his broker, Al Fried.

During the course of their conversation, it becomes clear that both Al and Wally are thinking along the same lines. Al points out that dividend yields on income shares are indeed way up and that, because of the state of the economy, the outlook for growth stocks is not particularly bright. He suggests that Wally seriously consider putting some of his money into income shares to capture the high dividend yields that are available. After all, as Al says, "the bottom line is not so much where the payoff comes from as how much it amounts to!" They then talk about a high-yield public utility stock, Hydro-Electric Light and Power. Al digs up some forecast information about Hydro-Electric and presents it to Wally for his consideration:

Year	Expected EPS	Expected Dividend Payout Ratio
2010	$3.25	40%
2011	3.40	40
2012	3.90	45
2013	4.40	45
2014	5.00	45

The stock currently trades at $60 per share. Al thinks that within five years it should be trading at around $75 to $80 a share. Wally realizes that to buy the Hydro-Electric stock, he will have to sell his holdings of CapCo Industries—a highly regarded growth stock that Wally is disenchanted with because of recent substandard performance.

Questions

a. How would you describe Wally's present investment program? How do you think it fits him and his investment objectives?

b. Consider the Hydro-Electric stock.
   1. Determine the amount of annual dividends Hydro-Electric can be expected to pay over the years 2010 to 2014.
   2. Compute the total dollar return that Wally will make from Hydro-Electric if he invests $6,000 in the stock and all the dividend and price expectations are realized.
   3. If Wally participates in the company's dividend reinvestment plan, how many shares of stock will he have by the end of 2014? What will they be worth if the stock trades at $80 on December 31, 2014? Assume that the stock can be purchased through the dividend reinvestment plan at a net price of $50 a share in 2010, $55 in 2011, $60 in 2012, $65 in 2013, and $70 in 2014. Use fractional shares, to two decimals, in your computations. Also, assume that, as in part **b**, Wally starts with 100 shares of stock and all dividend expectations are realized.

c. Would Wally be going to a different investment strategy if he decided to buy shares in Hydro-Electric? If the switch is made, how would you describe his new investment program? What do you think of this new approach? Is it likely to lead to more trading on Wally's behalf? If so, can you reconcile that with the limited amount of time he has to devote to his portfolio?

Excel with Spreadsheets

Build a spreadsheet containing the quoted information below. Based on the information given, what is the current market cap of the firm? What was the firm's net income.

City National Corp. (CYN)   NYSE

Comprehensive Quote:	11/16/09 04:00 PM EST		
Last	Change	% Change	Volume
37.95	0.66	1.77%	658,323

Open	High	Low	Prior Day's Volume
37.57	38.40	37.57	394,981

52-Week High	52-Week Low	Prior Day's Close
48.99	22.59	37.29
(12/31/2008)	(03/05/2009)	

Snapshot quotes reflect real-time trades reported through Nasdaq only: comprehensive quotes reflect trading in all markets and are delayed at least 15 minutes. Volume updates from 4:00 a.m. - 8:00 p.m. ET. (More Info)

Other Prices

U.S. Germany Xetra

Historical Quotes

Closing prices since 1/2/1970.

date: [   ] [Go]

Stock Data

Market Cap(Mil)	1920.56
P/E Ratio	151.96
Dividend Yield	1.07%
Latest Dividend	$0.1
Pay Date of Latest Dividend	11/18/09
Last Stock Split	5 for 4 or 25% stock div.
Date of Last Split	10/17/89
Shares Outstanding (Mil)	51.5
Public Float (Mil)	43.44

All data updated daily before market opens
Source: Reuters

Chapter-Opening Problem

Note: On February 29, 2009, GE announced plans to cut its quarterly dividend from $0.31 to $0.10 per share.

a. If GE has 10.6 billion shares outstanding, how much cash will GE save each year by cutting the dividend?

b. In the two days surrounding GE's announcement, its stock fell from $9.03 to $7.54 per share. What is the decline in GE's total market value over this period?

c. Does this answer to part **b** seem appropriate given the answer to part **a**? Why or why not?

CHAPTER
7

Analyzing Common Stocks

LEARNING GOALS

After studying this chapter, you should be able to:

LG1 Discuss the security analysis process, including its goals and functions.

LG2 Understand the purpose and contributions of economic analysis.

LG3 Describe industry analysis and note how it is used.

LG4 Demonstrate a basic appreciation of fundamental analysis and why it is used.

LG5 Calculate a variety of financial ratios and describe how financial statement analysis is used to gauge the financial vitality of a company.

LG6 Use various financial measures to assess a company's performance, and explain how the insights derived form the basic input for the valuation process.

Shares of Dell Computer received a much-needed lift when Dinesh Moorjani, a prominent stock analyst, issued a report upgrading his rating on the company from "neutral" to "buy" on August 24, 2009. In his report, Moorjani cited macroeconomic factors, industry factors, and factors unique to Dell as the reasons for his optimism. At the macroeconomic level, Moorjani pointed to signs that the overall economy was showing the first signs of recovering from a deep recession. At the industry level, he noted that companies could not defer new informational technology investment forever. Microsoft planned to launch its new operating system, Windows 7, in the fall of 2009, and although Windows 7 required less processing power than its predecessor, Vista, Moorjani observed that most corporate customers were still running Microsoft's Windows XP operating system. He expected that firms that had never made the switch from XP to Vista would switch to Windows 7 after it became widely available, and Windows 7 placed more demands on computer hardware than did Vista. Finally, at the company level, Moorjani pointed out that Dell's future growth would likely come from product lines with higher profit margins. As news of the analysts' report spread, Dell shares surged, gaining about 5% in a single day.

The report issued by Dinesh Moorjani is typical of those produced by professional securities analysts every day. In forming their recommendations to clients, stock analysts have to consider broad macroeconomic trends, industry factors, and specific attributes of individual firms. This chapter, the first of two on security analysis, introduces some of the techniques and procedures you can use to evaluate the future of the economy, of industries, and of specific companies, such as Dell.

(Source: Rex Crum, *Dell shares get a lift following analyst upgrade,* MarketWatch.com, August 24, 2009; Associated Press, *Dell shares climb following upgrade on demand,* Forbes.com, August 24, 2009.)

Security Analysis

LG1 The obvious motivation for investing in stocks is to watch your money grow. Consider, for example, the case of Google, the hugely successful search engine and software company. If you had purchased $10,000 worth of Google stock when the company had its initial public offering (IPO) on August 19, 2004, five years later, in August 2009, that stock would have had a market value of about $44,400. That works out to an average annual return of almost 35%, as compared to the –1.8% annual return generated over the same period by the S&P 500. Unfortunately, for every story of great success in the market, there are dozens more that don't end so well.

More often than not, most of those investment flops can be traced to bad timing, greed, poor planning, or failure to use common sense in making investment decisions. Although these chapters on stock investments cannot offer magic keys to sudden wealth, they do provide sound principles for formulating a successful long-range investment program. The techniques described are proven methods that have been used by millions of successful investors.

Principles of Security Analysis

Security analysis consists of gathering information, organizing it into a logical framework, and then using the information to determine the intrinsic value of common stock. That is, given a rate of return that's compatible with the amount of risk involved in a proposed transaction, **intrinsic value** provides a measure of the underlying worth of a share of stock. It provides a standard for helping you judge whether a particular stock is undervalued, fairly priced, or overvalued. The entire concept of stock valuation, in fact, is based on the belief that all securities possess an intrinsic value that their market value will approach over time.

In investments, the question of value centers on return. That is, a satisfactory investment candidate is one *that offers a level of expected return proportionate to the amount of risk involved.* As a result, not only must an investment candidate be profitable, but it also must be *sufficiently* profitable—in the sense that you'd expect it to generate a return that's high enough to offset the perceived exposure to risk.

The problem, of course, is finding the right securities. One approach is to buy whatever strikes your fancy. A more rational approach is to use security analysis to look for promising candidates. Security analysis addresses the question of what to buy by determining what a stock *ought to be worth*. Presumably, an investor will buy a stock *only if its prevailing market price does not exceed its worth*—its intrinsic value. Ultimately, intrinsic value depends on several factors:

1. Estimates of the stock's future cash flows (e.g., the amount of dividends you expect to receive over the holding period and the estimated price of the stock at time of sale).

2. The discount rate used to translate those future cash flows into a present value.

3. The risk associated with future performance, which helps define the appropriate discount rate.

The Top-Down Approach to Security Analysis Traditional security analysis usually takes a "top-down" approach: It begins with economic analysis, moves to industry analysis, and then to fundamental analysis of a specific company. *Economic analysis* assesses the general state of the economy and its potential effects on businesses.

Industry analysis deals with the industry within which a particular company operates. It looks at the overall outlook for that industry and at how companies compete against each other in that industry. *Fundamental analysis* looks at the financial condition and operating results—the "fundamentals"—of a specific company. The fundamentals include the company's investment decisions, the liquidity of its assets, its use of debt, its profit margins and earnings growth. Once an analyst, or an investor, has synthesized all of the information from the economic, industry, and fundamental analysis, the analyst uses that information to estimate the intrinsic value of a company's stock and then compares that intrinsic value to the actual market value of the stock. When the intrinsic value is greater than the market price, an analyst will recommend that clients purchase the stock, and when the opposite is true, the analyst may issue a recommendation to sell.

Fundamental analysis is closely linked to the notion of intrinsic value, because it *provides the basis for projecting a stock's future cash flows*. A key part of this analytical process is *company analysis,* which takes a close look at the actual financial performance of the company. Such analysis is not meant simply to provide interesting tidbits of information about how the company has performed in the past. Rather, company analysis is done to *help investors formulate expectations about the future performance of the company and its stock*. Make no mistake about it: In investments, it's the future that matters. But to understand the future prospects of the firm, you should have a good handle on the company's current condition and its ability to produce earnings. That's what company analysis does: It helps investors predict the future by looking at the past and determining how well the company is situated to meet the challenges that lie ahead.

Who Needs Security Analysis in an Efficient Market?

The concept of security analysis in general, and fundamental analysis in particular, is based on the assumption that at least some investors are capable of identifying stocks whose intrinsic values differ from their market values. Fundamental analysis operates on the broad premise that some securities may be mispriced in the marketplace at least some of the time. If securities are occasionally mispriced, and if investors can identify mispriced securities, then fundamental analysis may be a worthwhile and profitable pursuit.

To many, those two premises seem reasonable. However, there are others who do not accept the assumptions of fundamental analysis. These so-called *efficient market* advocates believe that the market is so efficient in processing new information that securities trade very close to or at their correct values at all times and that even when securities are mispriced, it is nearly impossible for investors to determine which stocks are overvalued and which are undervalued. Thus, they argue, it is virtually impossible to consistently outperform the market. In its strongest form, the *efficient market hypothesis* asserts the following:

1. Securities are rarely, if ever, substantially mispriced in the marketplace.

2. No security analysis, however detailed, is capable of identifying mispriced securities with a frequency greater than that which might be expected by random chance alone.

Is the efficient market hypothesis correct? Is there a place for fundamental analysis in modern investment theory? Interestingly, most financial theorists and practitioners would answer "yes" to both questions.

The solution to this apparent paradox is quite simple. Basically, fundamental analysis is of value in the selection of alternative investments for two important

MARKETS in CRISIS

Lahde Earns 1000% and Retires

While most investors around the world were losing money in 2007–2008, Andrew Lahde, portfolio manager of the Lahde Capital hedge fund, earned spectacular returns betting on the collapse of the U.S. mortgage market. After earning returns close to 1000% in 2007, Lahde abruptly shut down his fund in September 2008, saying that trading with U.S. financial institutions had become too risky. In his goodbye letter to investors, Lahde skewered the leaders of companies such as AIG, Lehman Brothers, and Bear Sterns, calling them "idiots . . .

not worthy of the education they received." What led to Lahde's incredible investment success was a deep understanding of the assets underlying complex financial securities, particularly residential real estate. Lahde's fundamental analysis of the real estate business led him to believe that the United States would experience a collapse in real estate values along with the securities based on residential property. Trades based upon that analysis made Lahde one of the most successful fund managers of all time in his remarkably short-lived career.

reasons. First, financial markets are as efficient as they are because a large number of people and financial institutions invest a great deal of time and money analyzing the fundamentals of most widely held investments. In other words, markets tend to be efficient and securities tend to trade at or near their intrinsic values simply because a great many people have done the research to determine what their intrinsic values should be.

Second, although the financial markets are generally quite efficient, they are by no means *perfectly* efficient. Pricing errors are inevitable. Those individuals who have conducted the most thorough studies of the fundamentals of a given security are the most likely to profit when errors do occur. We will study the ideas and implications of efficient markets in some detail in Chapter 9. For now, however, we will assume that traditional security analysis is useful in identifying attractive equity investments.

CONCEPTS IN REVIEW
Answers available at
www.pearsonhighered.com/gitman

7.1 Identify the three major parts of security analysis and explain why security analysis is important to the stock selection process.

7.2 What is *intrinsic value?* How does it fit into the security analysis process?

7.3 How would you describe a satisfactory investment vehicle? How does security analysis help in identifying investment candidates?

7.4 Would there be any need for security analysis if we operated in an efficient market environment? Explain.

Economic Analysis

LG2 Stock prices are heavily influenced by the state of the economy and by economic events. As a rule, stock prices tend to move up when the economy is strong, and they retreat when the economy starts to weaken. It's not a perfect relationship, but it is a fairly powerful one.

The reason why the economy is so important to the market is simple: The overall performance of the economy has a significant bearing on the performance and profitability of most companies. As firms' fortunes change with economic conditions, so do the prices of their stocks. Of course, not all stocks are affected in the same way or to the same extent. Some sectors of the economy, like food retailing, may be only mildly affected by the economy. Others, like the construction and auto industries, are often hard hit when times get rough.

Economic analysis consists of a general study of the prevailing economic environment—often on both a global and domestic basis (although here we'll concentrate, for the most part, on the domestic economy). Such analysis is meant to help investors gain insight into the underlying condition of the economy and the potential impact it might have on the behavior of share prices. It can go so far as to include a detailed examination of each sector of the economy, or it may be done on a very informal basis. However, from a security analysis perspective, its purpose is always the same: to establish a sound foundation for the valuation of common stock.

Economic Analysis and the Business Cycle

Economic analysis is the first step in the top-down approach. It sets the tone for the entire security analysis process. Thus, if the economic future looks bleak, you can probably expect most stock returns to be equally dismal. If the economy looks strong, stocks should do well. The behavior of the economy is captured in the **business cycle**, which reflects changes in total economic activity over time.

Two widely followed measures of the business cycle are gross domestic product and industrial production. *Gross domestic product* (GDP) is the market value of all goods and services produced in a country over a given period. *Industrial production* is an indicator of the output produced by industrial companies. Normally, GDP and the index of industrial production move up and down with the business cycle.

Key Economic Factors

The state of the economy is affected by a wide range of factors, from the consumption, saving, and investment decisions made independently by millions of households to major government policy decisions. Some of the most important factors that analysts examine when conducting a broad economic analysis include:

Government fiscal policy
  Taxes
  Government spending
  Debt management

Monetary policy
  Money supply
  Interest rates

Other factors
  Inflation
  Consumer spending
  Business investments
  Foreign trade and foreign exchange rates

Government fiscal policies can influence how fast the economy grows through a variety of channels. When the government increases spending or reduces taxes, it is pursuing an expansionary fiscal policy. An example of this type of policy was the $787 billion stimulus bill passed by Congress and signed by President Obama in February 2009. Similarly, monetary policy is said to be expansive when interest rates are relatively low and money is readily available. An expansive economy also depends on a generous level of spending by consumers and business concerns. These same variables moving in a reverse direction can have a contractionary (recessionary) impact on the economy, as, for example, when taxes and interest rates increase or when spending by consumers and businesses falls off.

The impact of these major forces filters through the system and affects several key dimensions of the economy. The most important of these are industrial production, corporate profits, retail sales, personal income, the unemployment rate, and inflation. For example, a strong economy exists when industrial production, corporate profits, retail sales, and personal income are moving up and unemployment is down.

Thus, when conducting an economic analysis, you should keep an eye on fiscal and monetary policies, consumer and business spending, and foreign trade *for the potential impact they might have on the economy.* At the same time, you must stay abreast of the level of industrial production, corporate profits, retail sales, personal income, unemployment, and inflation *in order to assess the current state of the business cycle.*

To help you keep track of the economy, Table 7.1 (on page 252) provides a brief description of some key economic measures. These economic statistics are compiled by various government agencies and are widely reported in the financial media. Most of the reports are released monthly. Take the time to carefully read about the various economic measures and reports cited in Table 7.1. When you understand the behavior of these statistics, you can make your own educated guess as to the current state of the economy and where it's headed.

Developing an Economic Outlook

Conducting an economic analysis involves studying fiscal and monetary policies, inflationary expectations, consumer and business spending, and the state of the business cycle. Often, investors do this on a fairly informal basis. As they form their economic judgments, many rely on one or more of the popular published sources (e.g., the *Wall Street Journal, Barron's, Fortune,* and *Business Week*) as well as on periodic reports from major brokerage houses. These sources provide a convenient summary of economic activity and give investors a general feel for the condition of the economy.

Once you have developed a general economic outlook, you can use the information in one of two ways. One approach is to construct an economic outlook and then consider where it leads in terms of possible areas for further analysis. For example, suppose you uncover information that strongly suggests the outlook for business spending is very positive. On the basis of such an analysis, you might want to look more closely at capital goods producers, such as office equipment manufacturers. Similarly, if you feel that because of sweeping changes in world politics, U.S. government defense spending is likely to drop off, you might want to avoid the stocks of major defense contractors.

A second way to use information about the economy is to consider specific industries or companies and ask, "How will they be affected by expected developments in the economy?" Take, for example, an investor with an interest in *business equipment stocks.* This industry category includes companies involved in the production of everything from business machines and electronic systems to work lockers and high-fashion office furnishings. In this industry, you'll find companies like Pitney Bowes, Diebold, Herman Miller, and Steelcase. These stocks are highly susceptible to changing

TABLE 7.1   Keeping Track of the Economy

To help you sort out the confusing array of figures that flow almost daily from Washington, DC, and keep track of what's happening in the economy, here are some of the most important economic measures and reports to watch.

- **Gross domestic product (GDP).** This is the broadest measure of the economy's performance. Issued every three months by the Commerce Department, it is an estimate of the total dollar value of all the goods and services produced in this country. Movements in many areas of the economy are closely related to changes in GDP, so it is a good analytic tool. In particular, watch the annual rate of growth or decline in "real" or "constant" dollars. This number eliminates the effects of inflation and thus measures the actual volume of production. Remember, though, that frequent revisions of GDP figures sometimes change the picture of the economy.

- **Industrial production.** Issued monthly by the Federal Reserve Board, this index shows changes in the physical output of U.S. factories, mines, and electric and gas utilities. The index tends to move in the same direction as the economy; it is thus a good guide to business conditions between reports on GDP. Detailed breakdowns of the index give a reading on how individual industries are faring.

- **The index of leading indicators.** This boils down to one number, which summarizes the movement of a dozen statistics that tend to predict—or "lead"—changes in the GDP. This monthly index, issued by the Commerce Department, includes such things as layoffs of workers, new orders placed by manufacturers, changes in the money supply, and the prices of raw materials. If the index moves in the same direction for several months, it's a fairly good sign that total output will move the same way in the near future.

- **Personal income.** A monthly report from the Commerce Department, this shows the before-tax income received in the form of wages and salaries, interest and dividends, rents, and other payments, such as Social Security, unemployment compensation, and pensions. As a measure of individuals' spending power, the report helps explain trends in consumer buying habits, a major part of total GDP. When personal income rises, people often increase their buying. But note a loophole: Excluded are the billions of dollars that change hands in the so-called underground economy—cash transactions that are never reported to tax or other officials.

- **Retail sales.** The Commerce Department's monthly estimate of total sales at the retail level includes everything from cars to groceries. Based on a sample of retail establishments, the figure gives a rough clue to consumer attitudes. It can also indicate future conditions: A long slowdown in sales can lead to cuts in production.

- **Money supply.** The amount of money in circulation as reported weekly by the Federal Reserve. Actually, there are three measures of the money supply: *M1* is basically currency, demand deposits, and NOW accounts. *M2,* the most widely followed measure, equals M1 plus savings deposits, money market deposit accounts, and money market mutual funds. *M3* is M2 plus large CDs and a few other less significant types of deposits/transactions. Reasonable growth in the money supply, as measured by M2, is thought to be necessary for an expanding economy. However, too rapid a rate of growth in money is considered inflationary. In contrast, a sharp slowdown in the growth rate is viewed as recessionary.

- **Consumer prices.** Issued monthly by the Labor Department, this index shows changes in prices for a fixed market basket of goods and services. The most widely publicized figure is for all urban consumers. A second figure, used in labor contracts and some government programs, covers urban wage earners and clerical workers. Both are watched as a measure of inflation, but many economists believe that flaws cause them to be inaccurate.

- **Producer prices.** This monthly indicator from the Labor Department shows price changes of goods at various stages of production, from crude materials such as raw cotton to finished goods like clothing and furniture. An upward surge may mean higher consumer prices later. However, the index can miss discounts and may exaggerate rising price trends. Watch particularly changes in the prices of finished goods. These do not fluctuate as widely as the prices of crude materials and thus are a better measure of inflationary pressures.

- **Employment.** The percentage of the workforce that is involuntarily out of work (*unemployment*) is a broad indicator of economic health. But another monthly figure issued by the Labor Department—the number of payroll jobs—may be better for spotting changes in business. A decreasing number of jobs is a sign that firms are cutting production.

- **Housing starts.** A pickup in the pace of housing starts usually follows an easing in the availability and cost of money and is an indicator of improving economic health. This monthly report from the Commerce Department also includes the number of new building permits issued across the country, an even earlier indicator of the pace of future construction.

economic conditions. That's because when the economy starts slowing down, companies can put off purchases of durable equipment and fixtures. Especially important to this industry, therefore, is the outlook for corporate profits and business investments. As long as these economic factors look good, the prospects for business equipment stocks should be positive.

TABLE 7.2 Economic Variables and the Stock Market	
Economic Variable	Potential Effect on the Stock Market
Real growth in GDP	Positive impact—it's good for the market.
Industrial production	Continued increases are a sign of strength, which is good for the market.
Inflation	Detrimental to stock prices. Higher inflation leads to higher interest rates and lower price/earnings multiples, and generally makes equity securities less attractive.
Corporate profits	Strong corporate earnings are good for the market.
Unemployment	A downer—an increase in unemployment means business is starting to slow down.
Federal budget surplus	Budget surpluses are good for interest rates and stock prices. Budget deficits, in contrast, may be a positive sign for a depressed economy but can lead to inflation in a stronger economic environment and therefore have a negative impact.
Weak dollar	Often the result of big trade imbalances, a weak dollar has a negative effect on the market. It makes our markets less attractive to foreign investors. However, it also makes our products more affordable in overseas markets and therefore can have a positive impact on our economy.
Interest rates	Another downer—rising rates tend to have a negative effect on the market for stocks.
Money supply	Moderate growth can have a positive impact on the economy and the market. Rapid growth, however, is inflationary and therefore detrimental to the stock market.

Assessing the Potential Impact on Share Prices In this instance, our imaginary investor would first want to assess the current state of the business cycle. Using that insight, he could then formulate some expectations about the future of the economy and the potential impact it holds for the stock market in general and business equipment stocks in particular. Table 7.2 shows how some of the more important economic variables can affect the behavior of the stock market.

To see how this might be done, let's assume that the economy has just gone through a year-long recession and is now in the recovery stage of the business cycle: Employment is starting to pick up. Inflation and interest rates are low. Both GDP and industrial production have experienced sharp increases in the past two quarters. Also, Congress is putting the finishing touches on a major piece of legislation that will lead to reduced taxes. More important, although the economy is now in the early stages of a recovery, things are expected to get even better in the future. The economy is definitely starting to build steam, and all indications are that both corporate profits and business spending should undergo a sharp increase. All of these predictions should be good news for the producers of business equipment and office furnishings, as a good deal of their sales and an even larger portion of their profits depend on the level of corporate profits and business spending. In short, our investor sees an economy that's in good shape and set to become even stronger—the consequences of which are favorable not only for the market but for business equipment stocks as well.

Note that these conclusions could have been reached by relying on sources such as *Barron's* or *Business Week*. In fact, about the only "special thing" this investor would have to do is pay careful attention to those economic forces that are particularly important to the business equipment industry (e.g., corporate profits and capital spending). The economic portion of the analysis has set the stage for further evaluation by indicating the type of economic environment to expect in the near future. The next step is to narrow the focus a bit and conduct the industry phase of the analysis.

The Market as a Leading Indicator Before we continue our analysis, it is vital to clarify the relationship that normally exists between the stock market and the economy. As we just saw, investors use the economic outlook to get a handle on the market and to identify developing industry sectors. Yet it is important to note that changes in stock prices normally occur *before* the actual forecasted changes become apparent in the economy. Indeed, the current trend of stock prices is frequently used to help *predict* the course of the economy itself.

The apparent conflict here can be resolved somewhat by noting that because of this relationship, it is even more important to derive a reliable economic outlook and to be sensitive to underlying economic changes that may mean the current outlook is becoming dated. Investors in the stock market tend to look into the future to justify the purchase or sale of stock. If their perception of the future is changing, stock prices are also likely to be changing. Therefore, watching the course of stock prices as well as the course of the general economy can make for more accurate investment forecasting.

CONCEPTS IN REVIEW

Answers available at
www.pearsonhighered.com/
gitman

7.5 Describe the general concept of *economic analysis*. Is this type of analysis necessary, and can it really help the individual investor make a decision about a stock? Explain.

7.6 Why is the business cycle so important to economic analysis? Does the business cycle have any bearing on the stock market?

7.7 Briefly describe each of the following:

a. Gross domestic product.
b. Leading indicators.
c. Money supply.
d. Producer prices.

7.8 What effect, if any, does inflation have on common stocks?

Industry Analysis

LG3 Have you ever thought about buying oil stocks, or autos, or chemicals? How about computer stocks or telecommunications stocks? Looking at securities in terms of industry groupings is widely used by both individual and institutional investors. This approach makes a lot of sense because stock prices are influenced, to one degree or another, by industry conditions. Indeed, various industry forces, including the level of demand within an industry, can have a real impact on individual companies.

Industry analysis, in effect, sets the stage for a *more thorough analysis of individual companies and securities*. Clearly, if the outlook is good for an industry, then the prospects are likely to be favorable for many of the companies that make up that industry. In addition, industry analysis also helps the investor *assess the riskiness of a company* and therefore *define the appropriate risk-adjusted rate of return* to use in setting a value on the company's stock. That's true because there are always at least some similarities in the riskiness of the companies that make up an industry, so if you can gain an understanding of the risks inherent in an industry, you'll gain valuable insights about the risks inherent in individual companies and their securities.

Key Issues

Because all industries do not perform the same, the first step in **industry analysis** is to establish the competitive position of a particular industry *in relation to others*. The next step is to identify companies *within the industry* that hold particular promise. Analyzing an industry means looking at such things as its makeup and basic characteristics, the key economic and operating variables that drive industry performance, and the outlook for the industry. You will also want to keep an eye out for specific companies that appear well situated to take advantage of industry conditions. Companies with strong market positions should be favored over those with less secure positions. Such dominance indicates an ability to maintain pricing leadership and suggests that the firm will be in a position to enjoy economies of scale and low-cost production. Market dominance also enables a company to support a strong research and development effort, thereby helping it secure its leadership position for the future.

Normally, you can gain valuable insight about an industry by seeking answers to the following questions:

1. *What is the nature of the industry?* Is it monopolistic, or are there many competitors? Do a few set the trend for the rest, and if so, who are those few?

2. *To what extent is the industry regulated?* If so, how "friendly" are the regulatory bodies?

3. *What role does labor play in the industry?* How important are labor unions? Are there good labor relations within the industry? When is the next round of contract talks?

4. *How important are technological developments?* Are any new developments taking place? What impact are potential breakthroughs likely to have?

5. *Which economic forces are especially important to the industry?* Is demand for the industry's goods and services related to key economic variables? If so, what is the outlook for those variables? How important is foreign competition to the health of the industry?

6. *What are the important financial and operating considerations?* Is there an adequate supply of labor, material, and capital? What are the capital spending plans and needs of the industry?

The Industry Growth Cycle Questions like these can sometimes be answered in terms of an industry's **growth cycle**, which reflects the vitality of the industry over time. In the first stage—*initial development*—investment opportunities are usually not available to most investors. The industry is new and untried, and the risks are very high. The second stage is *rapid expansion,* during which product acceptance is spreading and investors can foresee the industry's future more clearly. At this stage, economic and financial variables have little to do with the industry's overall performance. Investors will be interested in investing almost regardless of the economic climate. This is the phase that is of substantial interest to investors, and a good deal of work is done to find such opportunities.

Unfortunately, most industries do not experience rapid growth for long. Instead, they eventually slip into the next category in the growth cycle, *mature growth,* which is the one most influenced by economic developments. In this stage, expansion comes from growth of the economy. It is a slower source of overall growth than that experienced in stage 2. In stage 3, the long-term nature of the industry becomes apparent. Industries in this category include defensive ones, like food and apparel, and cyclical industries, like autos and heavy equipment.

The last stage is either *stability* or *decline.* In the decline phase, demand for the industry's products is diminishing, and companies are leaving the industry. Investment opportunities at this stage are almost nonexistent, unless you are seeking only dividend income. Certainly, growth-oriented investors will want to stay away from industries at the decline stage of the cycle. Other investors may be able to find some investment opportunities here, especially if the industry (like, say, tobacco) is locked in the mature, stable phase. The fact is, however, that very few really good companies ever reach this final stage because they continually bring new products to the market and, in so doing, remain at least in the mature growth phase.

Developing an Industry Outlook

Individual investors can conduct industry analysis themselves. Or, as is more often the case, it can be done with the help of published industry reports, such as the popular *S&P Industry Surveys*. These surveys cover all the important economic, market, and financial aspects of an industry, providing commentary as well as vital statistics. Other widely used sources of industry information include brokerage house reports, articles in the popular financial media, and even the well-known *S&P Stock Reports, which now include a one-page write-up on the stock's industry outlook.* Figure 7.1, for example, provides a sub-industry outlook for Apple and other computer stocks. There also are scores of Web sites (like **Yahoo!.com, Finance.com, businessweek.com,** and **bigcharts.com**) that provide all sorts of useful information about various industries and sub-industries.

Let's resume our example of the imaginary investor who is thinking about buying business equipment stocks. Recall from our prior discussion that the economic phase of the analysis suggested a strong economy for the foreseeable future—one in which corporate profits and business spending will be expanding. Now the investor is ready to focus on the industry. A logical starting point is to assess the expected industry response to forecasted economic developments. Demand for the product and industry sales would be especially important. The industry is made up of many large and small competitors, and although it is labor-intensive, labor unions are not an important force. Thus, our investor may want to look closely at the potential effect of these factors on the industry's cost structure. Also worth a look is the work being done in research and development (R&D) and in industrial design within the industry. Our investor would also want to know which firms are coming out with the new products and fresh ideas, because these firms are likely to be the potential industry leaders.

Industry analysis yields an understanding of the nature and operating characteristics of an industry, which can then be used to form judgments about the prospects for industry growth. Let's assume that our investor, by using various types of published and online reports, has examined the key elements of the office equipment industry and has concluded that the industry, *particularly the office furnishings segment,* is well positioned to take advantage of the rapidly improving economy. Many new and exciting products have come out in the last several years, and more are in the R&D stage. Even more compelling is the current emphasis on new products that will contribute to long-term business productivity. Thus, the demand for office furniture and fixtures should increase, and although profit margins may tighten a bit, the level of profits should move up smartly, providing a healthy outlook for growth.

In the course of researching the industry, our imaginary investor has noticed several companies that stand out, but one looks particularly attractive: the imaginary company Universal Office Furnishings. Long regarded as one of the top design firms in the industry, Universal designs, manufactures, and sells a full line of high-end office furniture and fixtures (desks, chairs, credenzas, modular work stations, filing systems, etc.). In addition, the company produces and distributes state-of-the-art computer furniture and a specialized line of institutional furniture for the hospitality, health care,

FIGURE 7.1   An Example of a Published Industry Report

Here's an excerpt from an *S&P Stock Report* on **Apple Inc.** It provides a brief overview of the computer industry, along with comparative stock price performance, and peer group behavior of Apple stock and its major competitors in this sub-industry. (Source: Standard & Poor's *Stock Reports*, September 5, 2009. ©2009 The McGraw-Hill Companies. All Rights Reserved.)

Stock Report | September 5, 2009 | NNM Symbol: **AAPL**

STANDARD &POOR'S

Apple Inc

Sub-Industry Outlook

Our fundamental outlook for the S&P Computer Hardware sub-industry for the next 12 months is neutral. We estimate that global unit sales of personal computers will decrease about 8% in 2009, reflecting slowing economic activity. This would represent a sharp downturn from moderately healthy unit sales growth we estimate near 10% in 2008; the sales pace faded in the second half of 2008. Price competition, a long-term trend toward lower average selling prices, and growing demand for small, low-cost "ultra-portable" notebook PCs will contribute to a decline of about 17% in global PC industry revenue in 2009, in our view. Consumer preference for wireless and portable computing is helping to drive PC unit sales. With more laptops, versus desktops, in the PC sales mix, we see some help for margins for PC makers. We think computer hardware vendors will redouble their efforts to take costs out of their infrastructures in order to manage through a period of moderating demand. We expect computer makers' profitability in 2009 to benefit from modest component costs as a result of competition among semiconductor suppliers. We project the industry downturn in computer hardware will begin to fade in 2010, and believe that some share prices might rise in anticipation of a potential recovery in industry fundamentals.

We see longer-term fundamentals in the computer industry remaining attractive, albeit with lively price competition, as we think that a global appetite for technology products such as smartphones, personal digital assistants and lightweight portable computers with wireless functionality should boost productivity and communications. Many vendors have also streamlined operations in recent years, and we see this boosting longer-term profit potential.

We believe the benefits of Internet-related

computing for the computer industry are well under way. Demand for Internet-based applications is growing, as we think they offer companies opportunities to reduce costs and improve customer service. Although many deployments have been made to capitalize on these opportunities, we think the evolution of the platforms could produce additional investment as Internet use matures. In addition, as price pressures in the PC industry have remained intense, we think that hardware vendors have been seeking to offset the negative impact on profits by offering higher-margin services, servers and storage.

Year to date through August 7, the S&P Computer Hardware Index increased 48.6%, versus a 12.7% increase for the S&P 1500 Index. In 2008, the S&P Computer Hardware Index decreased 40.5%, compared to a 38.5% drop in the S&P 1500 Index.

--Thomas W. Smith, CFA

Stock Performance

GICS Sector: Information Technology
Sub-Industry: Computer Hardware

Based on S&P 1500 Indexes
Month-end Price Performance as of 08/31/09

| Sub-Industry | Sector | S&P 1500 |

NOTE: All Sector & Sub-Industry information is based on the Global Industry Classification Standard (GICS)

Sub-Industry : Computer Hardware Peer Group*: Computer Hardware - Personal Computers

Peer Group	Stock Symbol	Stk.Mkt. Cap. (Mil. $)	Recent Stock Price($)	52 Week High/Low($)	Beta	Yield (%)	P/E Ratio	Fair Value Calc.($)	Quality Ranking	S&P IQ %ile	Return on Revenue (%)	LTD to Cap (%)
Apple Inc	**AAPL**	152,567	170.31	172.49/78.20	1.64	Nil	30	159.90	B	95	14.9	NA
3PAR Inc	PAR	556	9.03	12.98/4.25	NA	Nil	NM	NA	NR	32	NA	NA
Avid Technology	AVID	469	12.55	29.91/8.40	1.04	Nil	NM	7.40	C	21	NA	NA
Cray Inc	CRAY	258	7.35	9.49/1.15	1.49	Nil	NM	7.10	C	14	NA	NA
Dell Inc	DELL	30,658	15.69	20.68/7.84	1.33	Nil	17	21.90	B+	94	4.1	30.8
Diebold, Inc	DBD	2,049	30.92	39.09/18.80	0.99	3.4	26	32.20	A-	93	3.4	37.8
Hewlett-Packard	HPQ	107,620	45.10	49.20/25.39	1.05	0.7	15	48.80	B+	94	7.0	15.4
Intl Bus. Machines	IBM	153,976	117.46	124.00/69.50	0.83	1.9	13	144.40	A	100	11.9	71.6
NCR Corp	NCR	2,093	13.17	25.72/6.62	1.60	Nil	15	12.10	B	97	4.4	0.9
Silicon Graphics International	SGI	170	5.63	11.75/3.42	1.50	Nil	NM	NA	NR	3	NA	NA
Stratasys Inc	SSYS	302	14.93	19.49/7.58	1.49	Nil	51	12.60	B	27	10.9	NA
Sun Microsystems	JAVA	6,893	9.15	9.55/2.60	1.68	Nil	NM	NA	C	32	NA	15.3
Super Micro Computer	SMCI	279	8.02	10.92/3.63	1.34	Nil	20	8.50	NR	16	3.2	5.1
Teradata Corp	TDC	4,499	26.19	28.02/11.11	NA	Nil	19	NA	NR	87	14.2	NA
Toshiba Corp	TOSBF	16,179	5.00	5.30/2.15	1.64	0.6	NM	NA	NR	17	1.7	30.9

NA-Not Available NM-Not Meaningful NR-Not Rated. *For Peer Groups with more than 15 companies or stocks, selection of issues is based on market capitalization.

and educational markets. The company was founded over 50 years ago, and its stock (which trades under the symbol UVRS) has been listed on the NYSE since the late 1970s. Universal would be considered a *mid-cap stock*, with total market capitalization of around $2 or $3 billion. The company experienced rapid growth in the 1990s, as it expanded its product line. Because of its institutional division, it was not as hard hit as others in the recent bear market. Looking ahead, the general consensus is that the company should benefit nicely from the strong economic environment now in place. Everything about the economy and the industry looks good for the stock, so our investor decides to take a closer look at Universal Office Furnishings.

We now turn our attention to fundamental analysis, which will occupy the rest of the chapter.

CONCEPTS IN REVIEW
Answers available at
www.pearsonhighered.com/gitman

7.9 What is *industry analysis,* and why is it important?

7.10 Identify and briefly discuss several aspects of an industry that are important to its behavior and operating characteristics. Note especially how economic issues fit into industry analysis.

7.11 What are the four stages of an industry's growth cycle? Which of these stages offers the biggest payoff to investors? Which stage is most influenced by forces in the economy?

Fundamental Analysis

LG4 LG5 LG6   **Fundamental analysis** is the study of the financial affairs of a business for the purpose of better understanding the company that issued the common stock. In this part of the chapter, we will deal with several aspects of fundamental analysis. We will examine the general concept of fundamental analysis and introduce several types of financial statements that provide the raw material for this type of analysis. We will then describe some key financial ratios that are widely used in company analysis and will conclude with an interpretation of those financial ratios. It's important to understand that this represents the more traditional approach to security analysis. This approach is commonly used in any situation where investors rely on financial statements and other databases to at least partially form an investment decision.

The Concept

Fundamental analysis rests on the belief that *the value of a stock is influenced by the performance of the company that issued the stock.* If a company's prospects look strong, the market price of its stock is likely to reflect that and be bid up. However, the value of a security depends not only on the return it promises but also on the amount of its risk exposure. Fundamental analysis captures these dimensions (risk and return) and incorporates them into the valuation process. It begins with a historical analysis of the financial strength of a firm: the so-called *company analysis* phase. Using the insights obtained, along with economic and industry analyses, an investor can then formulate expectations about the future growth and profitability of a company.

In the company analysis phase, the investor studies the financial statements of the firm to learn its strengths and weaknesses, identify any underlying trends and developments, evaluate operating efficiencies, and gain a general understanding of the nature and operating characteristics of the firm. The following points are of particular interest:

1. The competitive position of the company.

2. Its composition and growth in sales.

3. Profit margins and the dynamics of company earnings.

4. The composition and liquidity of corporate resources (the company's asset mix).

5. The company's capital structure (its financing mix).

This phase is in many respects the most demanding and time-consuming. Because most investors have neither the time nor the inclination to conduct such an extensive study, they rely on published reports for the background material. Fortunately, individual investors have a variety of sources to choose from. These include the reports and recommendations of major brokerage houses, the popular financial media, and financial subscription services like S&P and *Value Line*. Also available is a whole array of computer-based software and online financial sources, such as Business Week Online, Morningstar.com, Quicken, MSN.Money.com, Wall Street on Demand, CNNMoney .com, and SmartMoney.com. These are all valuable sources of information, and the paragraphs that follow are not meant to replace them. Nevertheless to be an intelligent investor you should have at least a basic understanding of financial reports and financial statement analysis, for ultimately you will be drawing your own conclusions about a company and its stock.

Financial Statements

Financial statements are a vital part of company analysis. They enable investors to develop an opinion about the operating results and financial condition of a firm. Investors use three financial statements in company analysis: the balance sheet, the income statement, and the statement of cash flows. The first two statements are essential to carrying out basic financial analysis, because they contain the data needed to compute many of the financial ratios. The statement of cash flows is used primarily to assess the cash/liquidity position of the firm.

Companies prepare financial statements on a quarterly basis (these are *abbreviated* statements, compiled for each three-month period of operation) and again at the end of each calendar year or *fiscal year*. (The fiscal year is the 12-month period the company has defined as its operating year, which may or may not end on December 31.) Annual financial statements must be fully verified by independent certified public accountants (CPAs). They then must be filed with the U.S. Securities and Exchange Commission and distributed on a timely basis to all stockholders in the form of annual reports.

By themselves, corporate financial statements are an important source of information to the investor. When used with financial ratios, and in conjunction with fundamental analysis, they become even more powerful. But to get the most from financial ratios, you must have a good understanding of the uses and limitations of the financial statements themselves.

The Balance Sheet The **balance sheet** is a statement of the company's assets, liabilities, and stockholders' equity. The *assets* represent the resources of the company (the things the company owns). The *liabilities* are its debts. *Equity* is the difference between a firm's assets and its liabilities. A balance sheet may be thought of as a summary of the firm's assets balanced against its debt and ownership positions *at a single point in time* (on the last day of the calendar or fiscal year, or at the end of the quarter). To balance, the total assets must equal the total amount of liabilities and equity.

A typical balance sheet is illustrated in Table 7.3. It shows the comparative 2009–2010 figures for Universal Office Furnishings, the firm our investor is analyzing. These tables accurately depict what real financial statements look like and how they're used in financial statement analysis.

TABLE 7.3	*Corporate Balance Sheet*		
Universal Office Furnishings, Inc. Comparative Balance Sheets December 31 ($ in millions)			
		2010	**2009**
Assets			
Current assets			
Cash and equivalents		$ 95.8	$ 80.0
Receivables		227.2	192.4
Inventories		103.7	107.5
Other current assets		73.6	45.2
Total current assets		500.3	425.1
Noncurrent assets			
Property, plant, & equipment, gross		771.2	696.6
Accumulated depreciation		(372.5)	
Property, plant, & equipment, net		398.7	316.7
Other noncurrent assets		42.2	19.7
Total noncurrent assets		440.9	336.4
Total assets		**$941.2**	**$761.5**
Liabilities and stockholders' equity			
Current liabilities			
Accounts payable		$ 114.2	$ 82.4
Short-term debt		174.3	79.3
Other current liabilities		85.5	89.6
Total current liabilities		374.0	251.3
Noncurrent liabilities			
Long-term debt		177.8	190.9
Other noncurrent liabilities		94.9	110.2
Total noncurrent liabilities		272.7	301.1
Total liabilities		**$646.7**	**$552.4**
Stockholders' equity			
Common shares		92.6	137.6
Retained earnings		201.9	71.5
Total stockholders' equity		**$294.5**	**$209.1**
Total liabilities and stockholders' equity		**$941.2**	**$761.5**

The Income Statement The **income statement** provides a financial summary of the operating results of the firm. It shows the amount of revenues generated over a period of time, the costs and expenses incurred over the same period, and the company's profits. (Profits are calculated by subtracting all costs and expenses, including taxes, from revenues.) Unlike the balance sheet, the income statement covers activities that have occurred over the course of time, or for a given operating period. Typically, this period extends no longer than a fiscal or calendar year.

Table 7.4 shows the income statements for Universal Office Furnishings for 2009 and 2010. Note that these annual statements cover operations for the 12-month period ending on December 31, which corresponds to the date of the balance sheet. The income statement indicates how successful the firm has been in using the assets listed on the balance sheet. That is, management's success in operating the firm is reflected in the profit or loss the company generates during the year.

TABLE 7.4	Corporate Income Statement		

Universal Office Furnishings, Inc. Income Statements Fiscal Year Ended December 31 ($ in millions)

	2010	2009
Net sales	$1,938.0	$1,766.2
Cost of goods sold	1,128.5	1,034.5
Gross profit	**$ 809.5**	**$ 731.7**
Selling, general, and administrative, and other operating expenses	$ 496.7	$ 419.5
Depreciation & amortization	77.1	62.1
Other expenses	0.5	12.9
Total operating expenses	**$ 574.3**	**$ 494.5**
Earnings before interest & taxes (EBIT)	**$ 235.2**	**$ 237.2**
Interest expense	$ 13.4	$ 7.3
Earnings before taxes	221.8	229.9
Income taxes	82.1	88.1
Net profit after taxes	**$ 139.7**	**$ 141.8**
Dividends paid per share	$ 0.15	$ 0.13
Earnings per share (EPS)	$ 2.26	$ 2.17
Number of common shares outstanding (in millions)	61.8	65.3

The Statement of Cash Flows The **statement of cash flows** provides a summary of the firm's cash flow and other events that caused changes in its cash position. A relatively new report, first required in 1988, this statement essentially brings together items from *both* the balance sheet and the income statement to show how the company obtained its cash and how it used this valuable liquid resource.

Unfortunately, because of certain accounting conventions (the *accrual concept* being chief among them), a company's reported earnings may bear little resemblance to its cash flow. That is, whereas profits are simply the difference between revenues and the accounting costs that have been charged against them, *cash flow is the amount of money a company actually takes in as a result of doing business.* As such, the cash flow statement is highly valued by analysts and others in the investment community, because it offers insight on the underlying financial condition of the firm. The fact is, corporate management has considerable leeway in constructing financial statements, which can, at times, lead to the manipulation of reported earnings. While it's relatively easy to manipulate an income statement, short of outright fraud, it's far more difficult to do that with a cash flow statement. That's because what doesn't show up on the income statement will most likely affect asset and/or liability accounts on the balance sheet, and therefore will impact the company's statement of cash flows (usually in a negative fashion). (Nevertheless, accounting fraud can occur, as discussed in the *Ethics in Investing* box on page 263. As suggested there, audits are an important aspect of a company's financial statements.)

Table 7.5 presents the 2009–2010 statement of cash flows for Universal Office Furnishings. The statement is broken into three parts. The most important part is the first one, labeled "Cash from operating activities." It captures the *net cash flow from operating activities*—the line highlighted on the statement. This is what people typically mean when they say "cash flow"—the amount of cash generated by the company and available for investment and financing activities.

TABLE 7.5	Statement of Cash Flows		

Universal Office Furnishings, Inc. Statements of Cash Flows Fiscal Year Ended December 31 ($ in millions)

	2010	2009
Cash from operating activities		
Net earnings	$139.7	$141.8
Depreciation and amortization	77.1	62.1
Other noncash charges	5.2	16.7
Increase (decrease) in current assets	(41.7)	14.1
Increase (decrease) in current liabilities	21.8	29.1
Net cash flow from operating activities	**$202.1**	**$205.6**
Cash from investing activities		
Acquisitions of property, plant, and equipment—net	($150.9)	($ 90.6)
Net cash flow from investing activities	**($150.9)**	**($ 90.6)**
Cash from financing activities		
Proceeds from long-term borrowing	$749.8	$ 79.1
Reduction in long-term debt, including current maturities and early retirements	(728.7)	(211.1)
Net repurchase of capital stock	(47.2)	(9.8)
Payment of dividends on common stock	(9.3)	(8.5)
Net cash flow from financing activities	**($ 35.4)**	**($150.3)**
Net increase (decrease) in cash	**$ 15.8**	**($ 35.3)**
Cash and equivalents at beginning of period	$ 80.0	$ 115.3
Cash and equivalents at end of period	$ 95.8	$ 80.3

INVESTOR FACTS

THE CASH-REALIZATION RATIO— Want to keep an eye out for signs that earnings are being propped up by financial shenanigans? Then try comparing the cash flow statement with the income statement. That can be done with the cash-realization ratio, which shows how much of a company's net income is being converted into cash. Simply divide *cash flow from operating activities* (from the cash flow statement) by *net income* (from the income statement), preferably using average figures over a two- to four-year period. Generally speaking, companies with higher cash-realization ratios have higher quality of earnings. Ideally, companies should have cash-realization ratios of at least 1.0, indicating that net income and cash flow from operations are equal. Higher ratios indicate that the company is generating more in cash flow than it is in income—*a very healthy sign.*

Note that Universal's 2010 cash flow from operating activities was over $200 million, down a bit from the year before. This amount was more than enough to cover the company's investing activities ($150.9 million) and its financing activities ($35.4 million). Thus, Universal's actual cash position (see the line near the bottom of the statement, labeled "Net increase (decrease) in cash") increased by some $15.8 million. That result was a big improvement over the year before, when the firm's cash position fell by more than $35 million. A high (and preferably increasing) cash flow means the company has enough money to service debt, finance growth, and pay dividends. In addition, you'd like to see the firm's cash position increase over time because of the positive impact that it has on the company's liquidity and its ability to meet operating needs in a prompt and timely fashion.

Financial Ratios

To see what accounting statements really have to say about the financial condition and operating results of a firm, we have to turn to *financial ratios*. Such ratios provide a different perspective on the financial affairs of the firm—particularly with regard to the balance sheet and income statement—and thus *expand the information content of the company's financial statements*. Simply stated, **ratio analysis** is the study of the relationships between various financial statement accounts. Each measure relates an item on the balance sheet (or income statement) to another, or as

ETHICS IN INVESTING

Cooking the Books: What Were They Thinking?

Recent scandals involving fraudulent accounting practices have resulted in public outrage, not only in the United States, but around the world as well. In January 2009, Ramalinga Rau, Chairman of the Indian tech company Satyam Computer Services, confessed that the firm's books had been falsified and overstated the firm's true revenues and assets while understating its expenses. Satyam's stock, which traded as an ADR on the New York Stock Exchange, lost more than 90% of its value between 2008–2009 as the scandal unfolded. This was hardly the first case of accounting fraud leading to financial ruin. It appears that creative and unethical accounting practices kept real costs and debts off the books at Enron, WorldCom, Xerox, Qwest Communications, Conseco, and dozens of other public companies. When the reality finally caught up with the fantasy, tens of thousands of investors and employees lost their life savings, while many corporate executives responsible for fraud reaped huge financial rewards. For example, "cooking the books" at Enron cost investors almost $67 billion when the company declared bankruptcy in 2001; the implosion of WorldCom wiped out $175 billion of shareholder value, the biggest corporate bankruptcy in U.S. history.

Global Crossing sought Chapter 11 protection from its creditors after the SEC started its inquiry of widespread allegations that the company had used "creative accounting" to inflate its earnings. An SEC investigation of another telecom giant, Qwest Communications, found that Qwest had booked hundreds of millions of dollars of revenue at the end of its quarterly reporting period that should have been delayed until the next quarter. At WorldCom, internal audits revealed that $3.8 billion in operating expenses had been fraudulently disguised as capital expenditures over five quarters dating back to January 2001. Accounting firm Arthur Andersen was implicated as the corporate auditor in the Enron, Global Crossing, and WorldCom investigations.

Among the common accounting tricks used in the recent corporate scandals, the following appeared to be most popular: capitalizing operating expenses on the balance sheet (WorldCom), recognizing fictitious or premature revenues (Xerox, Qwest), creating off-balance-sheet liabilities (Enron), using off-balance-sheet derivative contracts transactions and company stock to hedge risk (Enron), and writing off goodwill as extraordinary loss rather than amortizing it over time (Time Warner) to manipulate future earnings growth.

Critical Thinking Question One of the steps to strengthen corporate reporting is to separate internal and external audits of a company by requiring that an external auditor will not be permitted to provide internal audits to the same client. Will this regulation be able to eliminate conflict of interest? Discuss.

---

is more often the case, a balance sheet account to an operating (income statement) item. In this way, we can look not so much at the absolute size of the financial statement accounts, but rather at what they indicate about the liquidity, activity, or profitability of the firm.

What Ratios Have to Offer Investors use financial ratios to evaluate the financial condition and operating results of the company and to compare those results to historical or industry standards. When using historical standards, investors compare the company's ratios from one year to the next. When using industry standards, investors compare a particular company's ratios to those of other companies in the same line of business.

Remember, the reason we use ratios is *to develop information about the past that can be used to get a handle on the future*. It's only from an understanding of a company's past performance that you can forecast its future with some degree of confidence. For example, even if sales have been expanding rapidly over the past few years, you must carefully assess the reasons for the growth, rather than naively assuming that past growth-rate trends will continue into the future. Such insights are obtained from financial ratios and financial statement analysis.

Financial ratios can be divided into five groups: (1) liquidity, (2) activity, (3) leverage, (4) profitability, and (5) common-stock, or market, measures. Using the 2010 figures from the Universal financial statements (Tables 7.3 and 7.4), we will now identify and briefly discuss some of the more widely used measures in each of these five categories.

Measuring Liquidity **Liquidity measures** are concerned with the firm's ability to meet its day-to-day operating expenses and satisfy its short-term obligations as they come due. Of major concern is whether a company has adequate cash and other liquid assets on hand to service its debt and operating needs in a prompt and timely fashion. A general overview of a company's liquidity can be obtained from two simple measures: current ratio and net working capital. *Generally speaking, other things being equal, you'd like to see high or rising measures with both of these ratios.*

Current Ratio One of the most commonly cited of all financial ratios, is the *current ratio.*

Equation 7.1

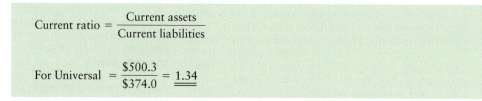

$$\text{Current ratio} = \frac{\text{Current assets}}{\text{Current liabilities}}$$

$$\text{For Universal} = \frac{\$500.3}{\$374.0} = \underline{\underline{1.34}}$$

This figure indicates that UVRS had $1.34 in short-term resources to service every dollar of current debt. That's a fairly good number and, by most standards today, would suggest that the company is carrying an adequate level of liquid assets.

Net Working Capital Although technically not a ratio, *net working capital* is often viewed as such. Actually, net working capital is an absolute measure, which indicates the dollar amount of equity in the working capital position of the firm. It is the difference between current assets and current liabilities. For 2010, the net working capital position for UVRS amounted to

Equation 7.2

$$\text{Net working capital} = \text{Current assets} - \text{Current liabilities}$$

$$\text{For Universal} = \$500.3 - \$374.0 = \underline{\$126.3 \text{ million}}$$

A net working capital figure that exceeds $125,000,000 is indeed substantial (especially for a firm this size). It reinforces our contention that the liquidity position of this firm is good—so long as it is not made up of slow-moving, obsolete inventories and/or past-due accounts receivable.

Activity Ratios Measuring general liquidity is only the beginning of the analysis. We must also assess the composition and underlying liquidity of key current assets and evaluate how effectively the company is managing these resources. **Activity ratios** compare company sales to various asset categories in order to measure how well the company is utilizing its assets. Three of the most widely used activity ratios deal with accounts receivable, inventory, and total assets. *Here again, other things being equal, you'd like to see high or rising measures with all three of these ratios.*

Accounts Receivable Turnover A glance at most financial statements will reveal that the asset side of the balance sheet is dominated by just a few accounts that make up 80% to 90%, or even more, of total resources. Certainly, this is the case with Universal Office Furnishings, where, as you can see in Table 7.3, three entries (accounts receivable, inventory, and net long-term assets) accounted for nearly 80% of total assets in 2010. Like Universal, most firms invest a significant amount of capital in accounts receivable, and for this reason they are viewed as a crucial corporate resource. *Accounts receivable turnover* is a measure of how these resources are being managed. It is computed as follows:

Equation 7.3

$$\text{Accounts receivable turnover} = \frac{\text{Annual sales}}{\text{Accounts receivable}}$$

$$\text{For Universal} = \frac{\$1,938.0}{\$227.2} = \underline{\underline{8.53}}$$

In essence, this turnover figure indicates the kind of return (in the form of sales) the company is getting from its investment in accounts receivable. Other things being equal, the higher the turnover figure, the more favorable it is. In 2010, UVRS was turning its receivables about 8.5 times a year. That excellent turnover rate suggests a very strong credit and collection policy. It also means that each dollar invested in receivables was supporting, or generating, $8.53 in sales.

Inventory Turnover Another important corporate resource—and one that requires a considerable amount of management attention—is inventory. Control of inventory is important to the well-being of a company and is commonly assessed with the *inventory turnover* measure:

Equation 7.4

$$\text{Inventory turnover} = \frac{\text{Annual sales}}{\text{Inventory}}$$

$$\text{For Universal} = \frac{\$1,938.0}{\$103.7} = \underline{\underline{18.69}}$$

Again, the more sales the company can get out of its inventory, the better the return on this vital resource. Universal's 2010 turnover of almost 19 times a year means that the firm is holding inventory for less than a month—actually, for about 20 days (365/18.69 = 19.5). That's the kind of performance you'd normally like to see. For the higher the turnover figure, the less time an item spends in inventory and the better the return the company is able to earn from funds tied up in inventory.

Note that, rather than sales, some analysts prefer to use *cost of goods sold* in the numerator of Equation 7.4, on the premise that the inventory account on the balance sheet is more directly related to cost of goods sold from the income statement. Because cost of goods sold is less than sales, using it will, of course, lead to a lower inventory turnover figure—for UVRS in 2010: $1,128.5/$103.7 = 10.88, versus 18.69 when sales is used. Regardless of whether you use sales (which we'll continue to do in this chapter) or cost of goods sold, for analytical purposes you'd still use the measure in the same way.

Total Asset Turnover *Total asset turnover* indicates how efficiently assets are being used to support sales. It is calculated as follows:

Equation 7.5

$$\text{Total asset turnover} = \frac{\text{Annual sales}}{\text{Total assets}}$$

$$\text{For Universal} = \frac{\$1,938.0}{\$941.2.7} = \underline{\underline{2.06}}$$

Note in this case that UVRS is generating more than $2 in revenues from every dollar invested in assets. This is a fairly high number and is important because it has a direct bearing on corporate profitability. The principle at work here is much like the return to an individual investor: Earning $100 from a $1,000 investment is far more desirable than earning the same amount from a $2,000 investment. A high total asset turnover figure suggests that corporate resources are being well managed and that the firm is able to realize a high level of sales (and, ultimately, profits) from its asset investments.

Leverage Measures Leverage measures look at the firm's financial structure. It indicates the amount of debt being used to support the resources and operations of the company. The amount of indebtedness within the financial structure and the ability of the firm to service its debt are major concerns to potential investors. There are two widely used leverage ratios. The first, the debt-equity ratio, measures the amount of debt being used by the company. The second, times interest earned, assesses how well the company can service its debt.

Debt-Equity Ratio The *debt-equity ratio* measures the relative amount of funds provided by lenders and owners. It is computed as follows:

Equation 7.6

$$\text{Debt-equity ratio} = \frac{\text{Long-term debt}}{\text{Stockholders' equity}}$$

$$\text{For Universal} = \frac{\$177.8}{\$294.5} = \underline{\underline{0.60}}$$

Because highly leveraged firms (those that use large amounts of debt) run an increased risk of defaulting on their loans, this ratio is particularly helpful in assessing a stock's risk exposure. The 2010 debt-equity ratio for UVRS is reasonably low (at 0.60) and shows that most of the company's capital comes from its owners. Stated another way, there was only 60 cents worth of debt in the capital structure for every dollar of equity. Unlike the other measures we've looked at so far, a *low or declining* debt-equity ratio is preferable, as that would suggest the firm has a more reasonable debt load and, therefore, less exposure to financial risk.

Times Interest Earned *Times interest earned* is a so-called coverage ratio. It measures the ability of the firm to meet ("cover") its fixed interest payments. It is calculated as follows:

Equation 7.7

$$\text{Times interest earned} = \frac{\text{Earnings before interest and taxes}}{\text{Interest expense}}$$

$$\text{For Universal} = \frac{\$235.2}{\$13.4} = \underline{\underline{17.55}}$$

MARKETS IN CRISIS

Credit Constraints Bind

A June 2009 survey of 1,309 CFOs from around the world found that credit-constrained firms, meaning those that could not obtain credit or could only do so at much higher cost than before the financial crisis began, experienced a decline in liquidity and an increase in debt from 2008 to 2009. Cash holdings as a percentage of total assets fell from 16% to 13%. Moreover, credit-constrained firms reported that they had drawn on their credit lines up to 41% of the maximum allowed. Sixty percent of these firms reported that they had attempted to negotiate better terms with their lenders, but two-thirds of these firms had been unsuccessful in obtaining better terms.

(Source: Duke/CFO Magazine Global CFO Survey, June 2009, www.cfosurvey.org)

The ability of the company to meet its interest payments (which, with bonds, are fixed contractual obligations) in a timely fashion is an important consideration in evaluating risk exposure. Universal's times interest earned ratio indicates that the firm has about $17.50 available to cover every dollar of interest expense. That's an outstanding coverage ratio—way above average! As a rule, a ratio eight to nine times earnings is considered strong. To put this number in perspective, there's usually little concern until times interest earned drops to something less than two or three times earnings. Clearly, low or declining measures definitely are *not* what you want to find here.

It's recently become popular to use an alternative earnings figure in the numerator for the times interest earned ratio. In particular, some analysts are adding back depreciation and amortization expenses to earnings and are using what is known as *earnings before interest, taxes, depreciation, and amortization* (EBITDA). Their argument is that because depreciation and amortization are both noncash expenditures (i.e., they're little more than bookkeeping entries), they should be added back to earnings to provide a more realistic "cash-based" figure. The problem is that EBITDA figures invariably end up putting performance in a far more favorable light. (Indeed, many argue that this is the principal motivation behind their use.) As a result, EBITDA tends to sharply increase ratios such as times interest earned. For example, in the case of UVRS, adding depreciation and amortization (2010: $77.1 million) to EBIT (2010: $235.2 million) results in a coverage ratio of $312.3/$13.4 = 23.31—versus 17.5 when this ratio is computed in the conventional way (with EBIT).

Measuring Profitability Profitability is a relative measure of success. Each of the various profitability measures relates the returns (profits) of a company to its sales, assets, or equity. There are three widely used profitability measures: net profit margin, return on assets, and return on equity. Clearly, the more profitable the company, the better—thus, *other things being equal, higher or increasing measures of profitability are what you'd like to see.*

Net Profit Margin This is the "bottom line" of operations. *Net profit margin* indicates the rate of profit being earned from sales and other revenues. It is computed as follows:

$$\text{Net profit margin} = \frac{\text{Net profit after taxes}}{\text{Total revenues}}$$

Equation 7.8

$$\text{For Universal} = \frac{\$139.7}{\$1,938.0} = \underline{7.2\%}$$

The net profit margin looks at profits as a percentage of sales (and other revenues). Because it moves with costs, it also reveals the type of control management has over the cost structure of the firm. Note that UVRS had a net profit margin of 7.2% in 2010. That is, the company's return on sales was better than 7 cents on the dollar. That may be about average for the large U.S. companies, but as we shall see, that's well above average for firms in the business equipment industry.

Return on Assets As a profitability measure, *return on assets (ROA)* looks at the amount of resources needed to support operations. Return on assets reveals management's effectiveness in generating profits from the assets it has available, and is perhaps *the single most important measure of return.* ROA is computed as follows:

Equation 7.9

$$ROA = \frac{\text{Net profit after taxes}}{\text{Total assets}}$$

$$\text{For Universal} = \frac{\$139.7}{\$941.2} = \underline{\underline{14.8\%}}$$

In the case of Universal Office Furnishings, the company earned almost 15% on its asset investments in 2010. That is a very healthy return, and well above average. As a rule, you'd like to see a company maintain as high an ROA as possible. The higher the ROA, the more profitable the company.

Return on Equity A measure of the overall profitability of the firm, *return on equity (ROE)* is closely watched by investors because of its direct link to the profits, growth, and dividends of the company. Return on equity—or return on investment (ROI), as it's sometimes called—measures the return to the firm's stockholders by relating profits to shareholder equity:

Equation 7.10

$$ROE = \frac{\text{Net profit after taxes}}{\text{Stockholders' equity}}$$

$$\text{For Universal} = \frac{\$139.7}{\$294.5} = \underline{\underline{47.4\%}}$$

ROE shows the annual payoff to investors, which in the case of UVRS amounts to nearly 48 cents for every dollar of equity. That, too, is an outstanding measure of performance and suggests that the company is doing what it has to do to keep its shareholders happy. Generally speaking, look out for a falling ROE, as it could mean trouble later on.

Breaking Down ROA and ROE ROA and ROE are both important measures of corporate profitability. But to get the most from these two measures, we have to break them down into their component parts. ROA, for example, is made up of two key components: the firm's net profit margin and its total asset turnover. Thus, rather than using Equation 7.9 to find ROA, we can use the net profit margin and total asset turnover figures that we computed earlier (Equations 7.8 and 7.5, respectively). Using this expanded format, we can find Univeral's 2010 ROA:

Equation 7.11

$$ROA = \text{Net profit margin} \times \text{Total asset turnover}$$

$$\text{For Universal } = 7.2\% \times 2.06 = \underline{\underline{14.8\%}}$$

Note that we end up with the same figure as that found with Equation 7.9. So why would you want to use the expanded version of ROA? *The major reason is that it shows you what's driving company profits.* As an investor, you want to know if ROA is moving up (or down) because of improvement (or deterioration) in the company's profit margin and/or its total asset turnover. Ideally, you'd like to see ROA moving up (or staying high) because the company is doing a good job in managing *both* its profits and its assets.

Going from ROA to ROE Just as ROA can be broken into its component parts, so too can the return on equity (ROE) measure. Actually, ROE is nothing more than an extension of ROA. It brings the company's financing decisions into the assessment of profitability. That is, the expanded ROE measure indicates the extent to which financial leverage (or "trading on the equity") can increase return to stockholders. The use of debt in the capital structure, in effect, means that *ROE will always be greater than ROA.* The question is how much greater. Rather than using the abbreviated version of ROE in Equation 7.10, we can compute ROE as follows:

Equation 7.12

$$\text{ROE} = \text{ROA} \times \text{Equity multiplier}$$

where

$$\text{Equity multiplier} = \frac{\text{Total assets}}{\text{Total stockholders' equity}}$$

To find ROE according to Equation 7.12, we first have to find the equity multiplier.

$$\text{Equity multiplier for Universal} = \frac{\$941.2}{\$294.5} = \underline{3.20}$$

We can now find the 2010 ROE for Universal as follows:

$$\text{ROE} = 14.8 \times 3.20 = \underline{47.4\%}$$

Here we can see that the use of debt (the equity multiplier) has magnified—in this case, tripled—returns to stockholders. (Note that small rounding errors account for the difference between the number computed here, 47.4%, and the one computed earlier, 47.4%, when we used Equation 7.10.)

An Expanded ROE Equation Alternatively, we can expand Equation 7.12 still further by breaking ROA *into its component parts.* In this case, we could compute ROE as

Equation 7.13

$$\text{ROE} = \text{ROA} \times \text{Equity multiplier}$$

$$= (\text{Net profit margin} \times \text{Total asset turnover}) \times \text{Equity multiplier}$$

$$\text{For Univeral} = 7.2\% \times 2.06 \times 3.20 = \underline{47.4\%}$$

This expanded version of ROE is especially helpful, because it enables investors to assess the company's profitability in terms of three key components: net profit margin, total asset turnover, and financial leverage. In this way, you can determine whether ROE is moving up simply because the firm is employing more debt, which isn't necessarily beneficial, or because of how the firm is managing its assets and operations, which certainly does have positive long-term implications. To stockholders, ROE is a critical measure of performance (and thus merits careful attention) because of the impact it has on growth and earnings—both of which, as we'll see in Chapter 8, play vital roles in the stock valuation process.

Smart's Tour of the Web
To watch author Scott
Smart discuss key websites
for this chapter visit
www.myfinancelab.com

Common-Stock Ratios Finally, there are a number of **common-stock ratios** that convert key bits of information about the company to a per-share basis. Also called **market ratios**, they tell the investor exactly what portion of total profits, dividends, and equity is allocated to each share of stock. Popular common-stock ratios include earnings per share, price/earnings ratio, dividends per share, dividend yield, payout ratio, and book value per share. We examined two of these measures (earnings per share and dividend yield) in Chapter 6. Let's look now at the other four.

Price/Earnings Ratio This measure, an extension of the earnings per share ratio, is used to determine how the market is pricing the company's common stock. The *price/earnings (P/E) ratio* relates the company's earnings per share (EPS) to the market price of its stock.

To compute the P/E ratio, it is necessary to first know the stock's EPS. Using the earnings per share equation from the previous chapter, we see that the EPS for UVRS in 2010 was

$$\text{EPS} = \frac{\text{Net profit after taxes} - \text{Preferred dividends}}{\text{Number of common shares outstanding}}$$

$$\text{For Universal} = \frac{\$139.7 - \$0}{61.8} = \underline{\$2.26}$$

In this case, the company's profits of $139.7 million translate into earnings of $2.26 for *each share* of outstanding common stock. (Note in this case that dividends are shown as $0 because the company has no preferred stock outstanding.) Given this EPS figure and the stock's current market price (assume it is currently trading at $41.50), we can use Equation 7.14 to determine the P/E ratio for Universal.

Equation 7.14

$$\text{P/E} = \frac{\text{Net price of common stock}}{\text{EPS}}$$

$$\text{For Universal} = \frac{\$41.50}{\$2.26} = \underline{\underline{18.4}}$$

In effect, the stock is currently selling at a multiple of about 18 times its 2010 earnings.

Price/earnings multiples are widely quoted in the financial press and are an essential part of many stock valuation models. Other things being equal, you would like to find stocks with *rising P/E ratios,* because higher P/E multiples usually translate into higher future stock prices and better returns to stockholders. But even though you'd like to see them going up, you also want to *watch out for P/E ratios that become too high* (relative either to the market or to what the stock has done in the past). When this multiple gets too high, it may be a signal that the stock is becoming overvalued (and may be due for a fall).

One way to assess the P/E ratio is to compare it to the company's rate of growth in earnings. The market has developed a measure of this comparison called the **PEG ratio**. Basically, it looks at the latest P/E relative to the three- to five-year rate of growth in earnings. (The earnings growth rate can be all historical—the last three to five years—or perhaps part historical and part forecasted.)

As we saw earlier, Universal Office Furnishings had a P/E ratio of 18.4 times earnings in 2010. If corporate earnings for the past five years had been growing at an average annual rate of, say, 15%. The PEG ratio is computed as

Equation 7.15

$$\text{PEG ratio} = \frac{\text{Stock's P/E ratio}}{\text{3- to 5-year growth rate in earnings}}$$

$$\text{For Universal} = \frac{18.4}{15.0} = \underline{\underline{1.21}}$$

A PEG ratio this close to 1.0 is certainly reasonable. It suggests that the company's P/E is not out of line with the earnings growth of the firm. In fact, the idea is to *look for stocks that have PEG ratios that are equal to or less than 1*. In contrast, a high PEG means the stock's P/E has outpaced its growth in earnings and, if anything, the stock is probably "fully valued." Some investors, in fact, won't even look at stocks if their PEGs are too high—say, more than 1.5 or 2.0. At the minimum, PEG is probably something you would want to look at, because it certainly is not unreasonable to expect some correlation between a stock's P/E and its rate of growth in earnings.

Dividends per Share The principle here is the same as for EPS: to translate total common dividends paid by the company into a per-share figure. (*Note:* If not shown on the income statement, the amount of dividends paid to common stockholders can usually be found on the statement of cash flows—see Table 7.5.) Dividends per share is measured as follows:

Equation 7.16

$$\text{Dividends per share} = \frac{\text{Annual dividends paid to common stock}}{\text{Number of common shares outstanding}}$$

$$\text{For Universal} = \frac{\$9.3}{61.8} = \underline{\underline{\$0.15}}$$

For fiscal 2010, Universal paid out dividends of $0.15 per share—at a quarterly rate of about 3.75 cents per share.

As we saw in the preceding chapter, we can relate dividends per share to the market price of the stock to determine its *dividend yield:* i.e., $0.15 ÷ $41.50 = 0.4%. Clearly, you won't find Universal Office Furnishings within the income sector of the market. It pays very little in annual dividends and has a dividend yield of less than one-half of 1%.

Payout Ratio Another important dividend measure is the dividend *payout ratio*. It indicates how much of its earnings a company pays out to stockholders in the form of dividends. Well-managed companies try to maintain target payout ratios. If earnings are going up over time, so will the company's dividends. The payout ratio is calculated as follows:

Equation 7.17

$$\text{Payout ratio} = \frac{\text{Dividends per share}}{\text{Earnings per share}}$$

$$\text{For Universal} = \frac{\$0.15}{\$2.26} = \underline{\underline{0.07}}$$

For Universal in 2010, dividends accounted for about 7% of earnings. Traditionally, most companies that pay dividends tend to pay out somewhere between 40% and 60% of earnings. By that standard, Universal's payout, like its dividend yield, is quite low. But that's not necessarily bad, as it indicates that the company is retaining most of its earnings to, at least in part, internally finance the firm's rapid growth. Indeed, it is quite common for growth-oriented companies to have low payout ratios. Some of the better-known growth companies, like Genetech, Boston Scientific, EchoStar Communications, and Starbucks, all retain 100% of their earnings. (In other words, they have dividend payout ratios of zero.)

Although low dividend payout ratios are not a cause for concern, *high payout ratios may be*. In particular, once the payout ratio reaches 70% to 80% of earnings, you should take extra care. A payout ratio that high is often an indication that the company may not be able to maintain its current level of dividends. That generally means that dividends will have to be cut back to more reasonable levels. And if there's one thing the market doesn't like, it's cuts in dividends; they're usually associated with big cuts in share prices.

Book Value per Share The last common stock ratio is *book value per share*, a measure that deals with stockholders' equity. Actually, *book value is simply another term for equity (or net worth)*. It represents the difference between total assets and total liabilities. Note that in this case we're defining equity as *common stockholders' equity*, which would *exclude* preferred stock. That is, *common stockholders' equity = total equity − preferred stocks*. (Universal has no preferred outstanding, so its total equity equals its common stockholders' equity.) Book value per share is computed as follows:

Equation 7.18

$$\text{Book value per share} = \frac{\text{Common stockholders' equity}}{\text{Number of common shares outstanding}}$$

$$\text{For Universal} = \frac{\$294.5}{61.8} = \underline{\$4.76}$$

Presumably, a stock should sell for *more* than its book value (as Universal does). If not, it could be an indication that something is seriously wrong with the company's outlook and profitability.

A convenient way to relate the book value of a company to the market price of its stock is to compute the *price-to-book-value* ratio.

Equation 7.19

$$\text{Price-to-book-value} = \frac{\text{Market price of common stock}}{\text{Book value per share}}$$

$$\text{For Universal} = \frac{\$41.50}{\$4.76} = \underline{8.72}$$

Widely used by investors, this ratio shows how aggressively the stock is being priced. Most stocks have a price-to-book-value ratio of more than 1.0—which simply indicates that the stock is selling for more than its book value. In fact, in strong bull markets, it is not uncommon to find stocks trading at four or five times their book values, or even more. Universal's price-to-book ratio of 8.7 times is definitely on the high side. That is something to evaluate closely. It may indicate that the stock is already fully priced, or perhaps even overpriced. Or it could result from nothing more than a relatively low owners' equity ratio.

Interpreting the Numbers

Rather than compute all the financial ratios themselves, most investors rely on published reports for such information. Many large brokerage houses and a variety of financial services firms publish such reports. An example is given in Figure 7.2 (on page 273). These reports provide a good deal of vital information in a convenient and easy-to-read format. Best of all, they relieve investors of the chore of computing the financial ratios

FIGURE 7.2 An Example of a Published Report with Financial Statistics

This and similar reports are widely available to investors and play an important part in the security analysis process. (Source: Standard & Poor's *Stock Reports,* September 5, 2009. ©2009 The McGraw-Hill Companies. All Rights Reserved.)

TABLE 7.6	Comparative Historical and Industry Ratios				EXCEL WITH SPREADSHEETS
	Historical Figures for Universal Office Furnishings Inc.				Industry Averages for the Office Equipment Industry in 2010
	2007	2008	2009	2010	
Liquidity measures					
Current ratio	1.55	1.29	1.69	1.34	1.45
Activity measures					
Receivables turnover	9.22	8.87	9.18	8.53	5.70
Inventory turnover	15.25	17.17	16.43	18.69	7.80
Total asset turnover	1.96	2.12	2.32	2.06	0.85
Leverage measures					
Debt-equity ratio	0.70	0.79	0.91	0.60	1.58
Times interest earned	15.37	26.22	32.49	17.55	5.60
Profitability measures					
Net profit margin	6.6%	7.5%	8.0%	7.2%	4.6%
Return on assets	9.8%	16.4%	18.6%	14.8%	3.9%
Return on equity	25.9%	55.5%	67.8%	47.4%	17.3%
Common stock measures					
Earnings per share	$1.92	$2.00	$2.17	$2.26	N/A
Price/earnings ratio	16.2	13.9	15.8	18.4	16.2
Dividend yield	0.3%	0.4%	0.4%	0.4%	1.1%
Payout ratio	5.2%	5.5%	6.0%	6.6%	24.8%
Price-to-book-value ratio	7.73	10.73	10.71	8.72	3.54

themselves. (Similar information is also available from a number of online services, as well as from various software providers.) Even so, as an investor, you must be able to evaluate this published information. To do so, you need not only a basic understanding of financial ratios but also some performance standard, or benchmark, against which you can assess trends in company performance.

Basically, financial statement analysis uses two types of performance standards: historical and industry. With *historical standards,* various financial ratios and measures are run on the company for a period of three to five years (or longer). You would use these to assess developing trends in the company's operations and financial condition. That is, are they improving or deteriorating, and where do the company's strengths and weaknesses lie? In contrast, *industry standards* enable you to compare the financial ratios of the company with comparable firms or with the average results for the industry as a whole. Here, we focus on determining the relative strengths of the firm with respect to its competitors. Using Universal Office Furnishings, we'll see how to use both of these standards of performance to evaluate and interpret financial ratios.

Using Historical and Industry Standards Look at Table 7.6. It provides a summary of historical data and average industry figures (for the latest year) for most of the ratios we have discussed. (Industry averages, such as those used in Table 7.6, are readily available from such sources as S&P, Moody's, or from many industry-specific publications.) By carefully evaluating these ratios, we should be able to draw some basic conclusions about the financial condition, operating results, and general financial health of UVRS. By comparing the financial ratios contained in Table 7.6, we can make the following observations about the company:

1. Universal's *liquidity position* is a bit below average. This doesn't seem to be a source of major concern, however, especially when you consider its receivables and inventory positions. That is, based on its respective turnover ratios (see item 2 below), both of these current assets seem to be very well controlled, which could explain the relatively low current ratio of this company. That is, the current ratio is a bit below average, not because the firm has a lot of current liabilities, but because it is doing such a good job in controlling current assets.

2. Universal's *activity measures* are all way above average. This company consistently has very high turnover measures, which in turn make significant contributions not only to the firm's liquidity position but also to its profitability. Clearly, the company has been able to get a lot more from its assets than the industry as a whole.

3. The company's *leverage position* seems well controlled. It tends to use a lot less debt in its financial structure than the average firm in the office equipment industry. The payoff for this judicious use of debt comes in the form of a coverage ratio that's well above average.

4. The *profitability picture* for Universal is equally attractive. The profit margin, return on assets, and ROE are all well above the industry norms. Clearly, the company is doing an outstanding job in managing its profits and is getting good results from its sales, assets, and equity.

In summary, our analysis shows that this firm is very well managed and highly profitable. The results of this are reflected in *common stock ratios* that are consistently equal or superior to industry averages. Universal does not pay out a lot in dividends, but that's only because it uses those valuable resources to finance its growth and to reward its investors with consistently high ROEs.

Looking at the Competition In addition to analyzing a company historically and relative to the average performance of the industry, it's useful to evaluate the firm relative to two or three of its major competitors. A lot can be gained from seeing how a company stacks up against its competitors and by determining whether it is, in fact, well positioned to take advantage of unfolding developments. Table 7.7 offers an array of comparative financial statistics for Universal and three of its major competitors. One is about the same size (Cascade Industries), one is much smaller (Colwyn Furniture), and one is much larger (High Design, Inc.).

As the data in Table 7.7 show, Universal can hold its own against other leading producers in the industry. Indeed, in virtually every category, Universal's numbers are about equal or superior to those of its three major competitors. It may not be the biggest (or the smallest), but it outperforms them all in profit margins and growth rates (in revenues and earnings). Equally important, it has the highest asset turnover, ROE, and price/earnings ratio. Tables 7.6 and 7.7 clearly show that Universal Office Furnishings is a solid, up-and-coming business that's been able to make a name for itself in a highly competitive industry. The company has done well in the past and appears to be well managed today. Our major concern at this point (and the topic of discussion in Chapter 8) is whether Universal can continue to produce above-average returns to investors.

TABLE 7.7	Comparative Financial Statistics: Universal Office Furnishings and Its Major Competitors (All figures are for year-end 2010 or for the five-year period ending in 2010; $ in millions)			
Financial Measure	Universal Office Furnishings	Cascade Industries	Colwyn Furniture	High Design, Inc.
Total assets	$ 941.2	$ 906.7	$342.7	$3,037.6
Long-term debt	$ 177.8	$ 124.2	$ 73.9	$ 257.8
Stockholders' equity	$ 294.5	$ 501.3	$183.9	$1,562.2
Stockholders' equity as a % of total assets	31.3%	55.3%	53.7%	51.4%
Total revenues	$1,938.0	$1,789.3	$642.2	$3,316.1
Net earnings	$ 139.7	$ 87.4	$ 38.5	$ 184.2
Net profit margin	7.2%	4.9%	6.0%	5.5%
5-year growth rates in:				
Total assets	14.36%	19.44%	17.25%	17.73%
Total revenues	18.84%	17.76%	15.91%	15.84%
EPS	56.75%	38.90%	21.10%	24.66%
Dividends	1.48%	11.12%	N/A	12.02%
Total asset turnover	2.063	1.973	1.883	1.093
Debt-equity ratio	0.60	0.43	1.46	0.17
Times interest earned	17.553	13.383	8.353	14.363
ROA	14.8%	9.5%	6.7%	6.7%
ROE	47.4%	18.8%	21.8%	13.0%
P/E ratio	18.43	14.43	13.33	12.43
PEG ratio	1.21	2.42	1.98	1.09
Payout ratio	6.6%	26.2%	N/A	32.4%
Dividend yield	0.4%	1.8%	N/A	2.6%
Price-to-book-value ratio	8.72	2.71	2.93	1.59

CONCEPTS IN REVIEW

Answers available at
www.pearsonhighered.com/gitman

7.12 What is *fundamental analysis?* Does the performance of a company have any bearing on the value of its stock? Explain.

7.13 Why do investors bother to look at the historical performance of a company when future behavior is what really counts? Explain.

7.14 What is *ratio analysis?* Describe the contribution of ratio analysis to the study of a company's financial condition and operating results.

7.15 Contrast historical standards of performance with industry standards. Briefly note the role of each in analyzing the financial condition and operating results of a company.

Here is what you should know after reading this chapter. **MyFinanceLab** will help you identify what you know, and where to go when you need to practice.

What You Should Know	Key Terms	Where To Practice
LG 1 Discuss the security analysis process, including its goals and functions. Success in buying common stocks is largely a matter of careful security selection and investment timing. Security analysis helps the investor make the selection decision by gauging the intrinsic value (underlying worth) of a stock.	intrinsic value, p. 247 security analysis, p. 247	MyFinanceLab Study Plan 7.1

What You Should Know	Key Terms	Where To Practice
LG2 **Understand the purpose and contributions of economic analysis.** Economic analysis evaluates the general state of the economy and its potential effects on security returns. Its purpose is to characterize the future economic environment the investor is likely to face, and to set the tone for the security analysis process.	business cycle, *p. 250* economic analysis, *p. 250*	MyFinanceLab Study Plan 7.2
LG3 **Describe industry analysis and note how it is used.** In industry analysis, the investor focuses on the activities of one or more industries. Especially important are how the competitive position of a particular industry stacks up against others and which companies within an industry hold special promise.	growth cycle, *p. 255* industry analysis, *p. 254*	MyFinanceLab Study Plan 7.3
LG4 **Demonstrate a basic appreciation of fundamental analysis and why it is used.** Fundamental analysis looks closely at the financial and operating characteristics of the company—at its competitive position, its sales and profit margins, its asset mix, its capital structure, and, eventually, its future prospects. A key aspect of this analytical process is company analysis, which involves an in-depth study of the financial condition and operating results of the company.	balance sheet, *p. 259* fundamental analysis, *p. 258* income statement, *p. 260* statement of cash flows, *p. 261*	MyFinanceLab Study Plan 7.4
LG5 **Calculate a variety of financial ratios and describe how financial statement analysis is used to gauge the financial vitality of a company.** The company's balance sheet, income statement, and statement of cash flows are all used in company analysis. An essential part of this analysis is financial ratios, which expand the perspective and information content of financial statements. There are five broad categories of financial ratios—liquidity, activity, leverage, profitability, and common-stock (market) ratios. All involve the study of relationships between financial statement accounts.	activity ratios, *p. 264* common stock (market) ratios, *p. 270* leverage measures, *p. 266* liquidity measures, *p. 264* PEG ratio, *p. 270* profitability, *p. 267* ratio analysis, *p. 262*	MyFinanceLab Study Plan 7.5 Video Learning Aid for Problems P7.7, P7.15
LG6 **Use various financial measures to assess a company's performance, and explain how the insights derived form the basic input for the valuation process.** To evaluate financial ratios properly, it is necessary to base the analysis on historical and industry standards of performance. Historical standards are used to assess developing trends in the company. Industry benchmarks enable the investor to see how the firm stacks up against its competitors. Together, they provide insight into how well the company is situated to take advantage of unfolding market conditions and opportunities.		MyFinanceLab Study Plan 7.6 Excel Table 7.6

Log into **MyFinanceLab**, take a chapter test, and get a personalized Study Plan that tells you which concepts you understand and which ones you need to review. From there, **MyFinanceLab** will give you further practice, tutorials, animations, videos, and guided solutions.
Log into **www.myfinancelab.com**

Discussion Questions

LG2 Q7.1 Economic analysis is generally viewed as an integral part of the "top-down" approach to security analysis. In this context, identify each of the following and note how each would probably behave in a strong economy.
    a. Fiscal policy
    b. Interest rates
    c. Industrial production
    d. Retail sales
    e. Producer prices

LG1 LG2 Q7.2 As an investor, what kind(s) of economic information would you look for if you were thinking about investing in the following?
    a. An airline stock
    b. A cyclical stock
    c. An electrical utility stock
    d. A building materials stock
    e. An aerospace firm, with heavy exposure in the defense industry

LG5 Q7.3 Match the specific ratios in the left-hand column with the category in the right-hand column to which it belongs.

a. Inventory turnover	1. Profitability ratios
b. Debt-equity ratio	2. Activity ratios
c. Current ratio	3. Liquidity ratios
d. Net profit margin	4. Leverage ratios
e. Return on assets	5. Common stock ratios
f. Total asset turnover	
g. Price/earnings ratio	
h. Times interest earned	
i. Price-to-book-value ratio	
j. Payout ratio	

Problems

All problems are available on **www.myfinancelab.com**

LG5 P7.1 Assume you are given the following abbreviated financial statement.

	($ in millions)
Current assets	$150.0
Fixed and other assets	200.0
Total assets	$350.0
Current liabilities	$100.0
Long-term debt	50.0
Stockholders' equity	200.0
Total liabilities and equities	$350.0
Common shares outstanding	10 million shares
Total revenues	$500.0
Total operating costs and expenses	435.0
Interest expense	10.0
Income taxes	20.0
Net profits	$ 35.0
Dividends paid to common stockholders	$ 10.0

On the basis of this information, calculate as many liquidity, activity, leverage, profitability, and common stock measures as you can. (*Note:* Assume the current market price of the common stock is $75 per share.)

 P7.2 BOOKV has $750,000,000 in total assets, no preferred stock, and total liabilities of $300,000,000. There are 300,000,000 shares of common stock outstanding. What is the book value per share?

 P7.3 BOOKV has $750,000,000 in total assets, no preferred stock, and total liabilities of $300,000,000. There are 300,000,000 shares of common stock outstanding. The stock is selling for $5.25 per share. What is the price-to-book ratio?

 P7.4 The Amherst Company has net profits of $10 million, sales of $150 million, and 2.5 million shares of common stock outstanding. The company has total assets of $75 million and total stockholders' equity of $45 million. It pays $1 per share in common dividends, and the stock trades at $20 per share. Given this information, determine the following:
   a. Amherst's EPS.
   b. Amherst's book value per share and price-to-book-value ratio.
   c. The firm's P/E ratio.
   d. The company's net profit margin.
   e. The stock's dividend payout ratio and its dividend yield.
   f. The stock's PEG ratio, given that the company's earnings have been growing at an average annual rate of 7.5%.

 P7.5 ZAPIT common stock is selling at a P/E of 15 times trailing earnings. The stock price is $25. What were the firm's earnings per share?

 P7.6 PEGCOR has a P/E ratio of 15. Earnings per share are $2.00, and the expected EPS five years from today is $3.22. Calculate the PEG ratio. (Refer to Chapter 4 if necessary.)

 P7.7 Highgate Computer Company produces $2 million in profits from $28 million in sales. It has total assets of $15 million.
   a. Calculate Highgate's total asset turnover and its net profit margin.
   b. Find the company's ROA, ROE, and book value per share, given that it has a total net worth of $6 million and 500,000 shares of common stock outstanding.

 P7.8 The following data have been gathered from the financial statements of HiFly Corporation:

	2009	2010
Operating profit	$550,000,000	$600,000.000
Interest expense	200,000,000	250,000,000
Taxes	126,000,000	126,000,000
Net profit	224,000,000	224,000,000

Calculate the times interest earned ratios for 2009 and 2010. Is the company more or less able to meet its interest payments in 2010 when measured this way?

 P7.9 Financial Learning Systems has 2.5 million shares of common stock outstanding and 100,000 shares of preferred stock. (The preferred pays annual cash dividends of $5 a share, and the common pays annual cash dividends of 25 cents a share.) Last year, the company generated net profits (after taxes) of $6,850,000. The company's balance sheet shows total assets of $78 million, total liabilities of $32 million, and $5 million in preferred stock. The firm's common stock is currently trading in the market at $45 a share.

a. Given the preceding information, find the EPS, P/E ratio, and book value per share.

b. What will happen to the price of the stock if EPS *rises* to $3.75 and the P/E ratio stays where it is? What will happen if EPS *drops* to $1.50 and the P/E doesn't change?

c. What will happen to the price of the stock if EPS rises to $3.75 and the P/E jumps to 25 times earnings?

d. What will happen if *both* EPS and the P/E ratio *drop*—to $1.50 and 10 times earnings, respectively?

e. Comment on the effect that EPS and the P/E ratio have on the market price of the stock.

LG5 **P7.10** The Buffalo Manufacturing Company has total assets of $10 million, an asset turnover of 2.0 times, and a net profit margin of 15%.

a. What is Buffalo's return on assets?

b. Find Buffalo's ROE, given that 40% of the assets are financed with stockholders' equity.

LG5 **P7.11** Find the EPS, P/E ratio, and dividend yield of a company that has 5 million shares of common stock outstanding (the shares trade in the market at $25), earns 10% after taxes on annual sales of $150 million, and has a dividend payout ratio of 35%. At what rate would the company's net earnings be growing if the stock had a PEG ratio of 2.0?

LG5 **P7.12** FigureItOut Corporation has a net profit margin of 8% and a total asset turnover of two times. What is the company's return on assets?

LG5 **P7.13** FigureItOut Corporation has a net profit margin of 8%, a total asset turnover of two times, total assets of $1 billion, and total equity of $500 million. What is the company's return on equity?

LG5 **P7.14** FigureItOut Corporation has a net profit margin of 8%, a total asset turnover of 2 times, total assets of $1 billion, and total equity of $500 million. What were the company's sales and net profit?

LG5 **P7.15** Using the resources available at your campus or public library (or on the Internet), select any common stock you like and determine as many of the profitability, activity, liquidity, leverage, and market ratios, covered in this and the preceding chapter, as you can. Compute the ratios for the latest available fiscal year. (*Note:* Show your work for all calculations.)

LG4 LG5 LG6 **P7.16** Listed below are six pairs of stocks. Pick *one of these pairs* and then, using the resources available at your campus or public library (or on the Internet), comparatively analyze the two stocks. Which is fundamentally stronger and holds more promise for the future? Compute (or obtain) as many ratios as you see fit. As part of your analysis, obtain the latest S&P and/or *Value Line* reports on both stocks, and use them for added insights about the firms and their stocks.

a. Walmart versus Target

b. Sara Lee versus Campbell Soup

c. IBM versus Intel

d. Marriott International versus Intercontinental Hotels Group

e. Liz Claiborne versus Under Armour

f. General Dynamics versus Boeing

LG4 LG5 LG6 **P7.17** Listed here are the 2009 and 2010 financial statements for Otago Bay Marine Motors, a major manufacturer of top-of-the-line outboard motors.

Otago Bay Marine Motors Balance Sheets ($ in thousands)

	As of December 31,	
	2010	2009
Assets		
Current assets		
Cash and cash equivalents	$ 56,203	$ 88,942
Accounts receivable, net of allowances	20,656	12,889
Inventories	29,294	24,845
Prepaid expenses	5,761	6,536
Total current assets	$ 111,914	$133,212
Property, plant, and equipment, at cost	$137,273	$ 85,024
Less: Accumulated depreciation and amortization	(50,574)	(44,767)
Net fixed assets	$ 86,699	$ 40,257
Other assets	$ 105,327	$ 51,001
Total assets	$303,940	$224,470
Liabilities and Shareholders' Equity		
Current liabilities		
Notes and accounts payable	$ 28,860	$ 4,927
Dividends payable	1,026	791
Accrued liabilities	20,976	16,780
Total current liabilities	$ 50,862	$ 22,498
Noncurrent liabilities		
Long-term debt	$ 40,735	$ 20,268
Shareholders' equity		
Common stock	$ 7,315	$ 7,103
Capital in excess of par value	111,108	86,162
Retained earnings	93,920	88,439
Total shareholders' equity	$ 212,343	$ 181,704
Total liabilities and equity	$ 303,940	$ 224,470
Average number of common shares outstanding	10,848,000	10,848,000

Otago Bay Marine Motors Income Statements ($ in thousands)

	For the Year Ended December 31,	
	2010	2009
Net sales	$259,593	$245,424
Cost of goods sold	133,978	127,123
Gross profit margin	$125,615	$ 118,301
Operating expenses:	72,098	70,368
Earnings from operations	$ 53,517	$ 47,933
Other income (expense), net	4,193	3,989
Earnings before income taxes	$ 57,710	$ 51,922
Provision for income taxes	22,268	19,890
Net earnings	$ 35,442	$ 32,032
Cash dividends ($0.35 and $0.27 per share)	$ 3,769	$ 2,947
Average price per share of common stock (in the fourth quarter of the year)	$ 74.25	$ 80.75

a. On the basis of the information provided, calculate the following financial ratios for 2009 and 2010.

	Otago Bay Marine Motors		Industry Averages (for 2010)
	2009	2010	
Current ratio			2.36
Total asset turnover			1.27
Debt-equity ratio			10.00
Net profit margin			9.30
ROA			15.87
ROE			19.21
EPS			1.59
P/E ratio			19.87
Dividend yield			.44
Payout ratio			.26
Price-to-book-value			6.65

b. Considering the financial ratios you computed, along with the industry averages, how would you characterize the financial condition of Otago Bay Marine Motors? Explain.

LG5 LG6 **P7.18** The following summary financial statistics were obtained from the 2009 Otago Bay Marine Motors (OBMM) annual report.

	2009 ($ in millions)
Net sales	$179.3
Total assets	$136.3
Net earnings	$ 20.2
Shareholders' equity	$109.6

a. Use the profit margin and asset turnover to compute the 2009 ROA for OBMM. Now introduce the equity multiplier to find ROE.

b. Use the summary financial information from the 2010 OBMM financial statements (see Problem 7.17) to compute the 2010 ROA and ROE. Use the same procedures to calculate these measures as you did in part **a**.

c. On the basis of your calculations, describe how *each* of the three components (profit margin, asset turnover, and leverage) contributed to the change in OBMM's ROA and ROE between 2009 and 2010. Which component(s) contributed the most to the change in ROA? Which contributed the most to the change in ROE?

d. Generally speaking, do you think that these changes are fundamentally healthy for the company?

Visit **www.myfinancelab.com** for web exercises, spreadsheets, and other online resources.

Case Problem 7.1   *Some Financial Ratios Are Real Eye-Openers*

LG5 LG6 Jack Arnold is a resident of Lubbock, Texas, where he is a prosperous rancher and businessman. He has also built up a sizable portfolio of common stock, which, he believes, is due to the fact that he thoroughly evaluates each stock he invests in. As Jack says, "Y'all can't be too careful about these things! Anytime I'm fixin' to invest in a stock, you can bet I'm gonna learn as much as I can about the company." Jack prefers to compute his own ratios even though he could easily obtain analytical reports from his broker at no cost. (In fact, Billy Bob Smith, his broker, has been volunteering such services for years.)

Recently, Jack has been keeping an eye on a small chemical stock. The firm, South Plains Chemical Company, is big in the fertilizer business—which is something Jack knows a lot about. Not long ago, he received a copy of the firm's latest financial statements (summarized here) and decided to take a closer look at the company.

South Plains Chemical Company Balance Sheet ($ thousands)

Cash	$ 1,250		
Accounts receivable	8,000	Current liabilities	$10,000
Inventory	12,000	Long-term debt	8,000
Current assets	21,250	Stockholders' equity	12,000
Fixed and other assets	8,750	Total liabilities and	
Total assets	$30,000	stockholders' equity	$30,000

South Plains Chemical Company Income Statement ($ thousands)

Sales	$ 50,000
Cost of goods sold	25,000
Operating expenses	15,000
Operating profit	10,000
Interest expense	2,500
Taxes	2,500
Net profit	$ 5,000
Dividends paid to common stockholders ($ in thousands)	$ 1,250
Number of common shares outstanding	5 million
Recent market price of the common stock	$ 25

Questions

a. Compute the following ratios, using the South Plains Chemical Company figures.

	Latest Industry Averages		Latest Industry Averages
Liquidity		*Profitability*	
a. Net working capital	N/A	h. Net profit margin	8.5%
b. Current ratio	1.95	i. Return on assets	22.5%
Activity		j. ROE	32.2%
c. Receivables turnover	5.95	*Common Stock Ratios*	
d. Inventory turnover	4.50	k. Earnings per share	$2.00
e. Total asset turnover	2.65	l. Price/earnings ratio	20.0
Leverage		m. Dividends per share	$1.00
f. Debt-equity ratio	0.45	n. Dividend yield	2.5%
g. Times interest earned	6.75	o. Payout ratio	50.0%
		p. Book value per share	$6.25
		q. Price-to-book-value ratio	6.4

b. Compare the company ratios you prepared to the industry figures given in part a. What are the company's strengths? What are its weaknesses?

c. What is your overall assessment of South Plains Chemical? Do you think Jack should continue with his evaluation of the stock? Explain.

Case Problem 7.2   *Doris Looks at an Auto Issue*

LG2 LG3 LG5   Doris Wise is a young career woman. She lives in Phoenix, Arizona, where she owns and operates a highly successful modeling agency. Doris manages her modest but rapidly growing investment portfolio, made up mostly of high-grade common stocks. Because she's young and single and has no pressing family requirements, Doris has invested primarily in stocks that offer the potential for attractive capital gains. Her broker recently recommended an auto company stock and sent her some literature and analytical reports to study. One report, prepared by the brokerage house she deals with, provided an up-to-date look at the economy, an extensive study of the auto industry, and an equally extensive review of several auto companies (including the one her broker recommended). She feels strongly about the merits of security analysis and believes it is important to spend time studying a stock before making an investment decision.

Questions

a. Doris tries to stay informed about the economy on a regular basis. At the present time, most economists agree that the economy, now well into the third year of a recovery, is healthy, with industrial activity remaining strong. What other information about the economy do you think Doris would find helpful in evaluating an auto stock? Prepare a list—and be specific. Which three items of economic information (from your list) do you feel are most important? Explain.

b. In relation to a study of the auto industry, briefly note the importance of each of the following.
  1. Auto imports
  2. The United Auto Workers union
  3. Interest rates
  4. The price of a gallon of gas

c. A variety of financial ratios and measures are provided about one of the auto companies and its stock. These are incomplete, however, so some additional information will have to be computed. Specifically, we know the following:

Net profit margin	15%
Total assets	$25 billion
Earnings per share	$3.00
Total asset turnover	1.5
Net working capital	$3.4 billion
Payout ratio	40%
Current liabilities	$5 billion
Price/earnings ratio	12.5

Given this information, calculate the following:
  1. Sales.
  2. Net profits after taxes.
  3. Current ratio.
  4. Market price of the stock.
  5. Dividend yield.

Excel with Spreadsheets

You have been asked to analyze the financial statements of the Dayton Corporation for the two years ending 2009 and 2010.

	A	B	C	D	E
1	Dayton Corporation				
2	Financial Data				
3		2009	2010		
4	Net sales	47,715	40,363		
5	Cost sales	27,842	21,485		
6	SG& A expenses	8,090	7,708		
7	Depreciation expense	628	555		
8	Interest expense	754	792		
9	Tax expense	3,120	3,002		
10	Cash & equivalents	2,144	2,536		
11	Receivables	5,215	5,017		
12	Inventory	3,579	3,021		
13	Other current assets	2,022	2,777		
14	Plant & equipment	18,956	16,707		
15	Accumulated depreciation	5,853	5,225		
16	Intangible assets	7,746	7,374		
17	Other non-current assets	10,465	7,700		
18	Payables	5,108	4,361		
19	Short-term notes payable	4,066	3,319		
20	Other current liabilities	2,369	2,029		
21	Long-term debt	4,798	3,600		
22	Other non-current liabilities	4,837	5,020		
23	Common stock	6,776	6,746		
24	Retained earnings	16,050	14,832		
25	Common shares outstanding	2,300	2,300		
26	Current market price of stock	$45	$45		

Questions

a. Create a comparative balance sheet for the years 2010 and 2009, similar to the spreadsheet for Table 7.3, which can be viewed at www.myfinancelab.com.

b. Create a comparative income statement for the years 2010 and 2009, similar to the spreadsheet for Table 7.4, which can be viewed at www.myfinancelab.com.

c. **Create a spreadsheet** to calculate the listed financial ratios for both 2010 and 2009, similar to the spreadsheet for Table 7.6, which can be viewed at www.myfinancelab.

Ratios	2009	2010
Current ratio		
Quick ratio		
Accounts receivable turnover		
Inventory turnover		
Total asset turnover		
Debt-equity ratio		
Times interest earned		
Net profit margin		
Return on equity (ROE)		
Earnings per share		
Price/earnings ratio		
Book value per share		
Price-to-book-value		

Chapter-Opening Problem

At the beginning of the chapter you read about an analyst's report on Dell Inc. Use an online sources such as Yahoo! Finance or Dell's own Web site to look up the company's income statement for the fiscal year ending in early 2010. What was Dell's net profit margin in 2009 and 2010? Did the profit margin improve as the analyst predicted?

CHAPTER
8

Stock Valuation

LEARNING GOALS

After studying this chapter, you should be able to:

LG1 Explain the role that a company's future plays in the stock valuation process.

LG2 Develop a forecast of a stock's expected cash flow, starting with corporate sales and earnings, and then moving to expected dividends and share price.

LG3 Discuss the concepts of intrinsic value and required rates of return, and note how they are used.

LG4 Determine the underlying value of a stock using the zero-growth, constant-growth, and variable-growth dividend valuation models.

LG5 Use other types of present-value-based models to derive the value of a stock, as well as alternative price-relative procedures.

LG6 Gain a basic appreciation of the procedures used to value different types of stocks, from traditional dividend-paying shares to more growth-oriented stocks.

What drives a stock's value? Many factors come into play, including how much profit the company earns, how its new products fare in the marketplace, and the overall state of the economy. But what matters most is what investors believe about the company's future.

Nothing illustrates this principle better than the behavior of Winn-Dixie stock around the firm's earnings announcement on August 24, 2009. After business hours on that day, the company released earnings figures for the quarter ended June 24. The company earned $0.17 per share, up dramatically from a $0.10 loss in the same quarter the prior year. That news sent the stock up 4% in after-hours trading. However, the next morning before the markets opened, CEO Peter Lynch held a conference call with analysts to go over the previous night's earnings report in more detail. In that call, Lynch expressed concerns that Winn-Dixie's weekend sales had been sluggish since the end of the prior quarter. His statements prompted investors to rethink their projections for the company's future earnings, and that caused the stock to plunge 8.4%.

How do you determine a stock's true value? This chapter explains how to determine a stock's intrinsic value by using dividend valuation, dividend and earnings, price/earnings, and other models.

(Sources: David Benoit, Winn-Dixie Falls as CEO Warns Sales 'Soft' to Start FY10, August 25, 2009, The Wall Street Journal Online, online.wsj.com/article/BT-CO-20090825-712005.html; Chris Jones, Winn-Dixie Does an Earnings Two-Step, August 25, 2009, The Motley Fool, www.fool.com/investing/small-cap/2009/08/25/winn-dixie-does-an-earnings-two-step.aspx.)

Valuation: Obtaining a Standard of Performance

LG1 LG2 LG3 Obtaining a performance estimate of a stock's intrinsic value that can be used to judge the investment merits of a share of stock is the underlying purpose of **stock valuation**. Investors attempt to resolve the question of whether and to what extent a stock is under- or overvalued by comparing its current market price to its intrinsic value. At any given time, the price of a share of common stock depends on investor expectations about the future behavior of the security. If the outlook for the company and its stock is good, the price will probably be bid up. If conditions deteriorate, the price of the stock will probably go down. Let's look now at the single most important issue in the stock valuation process: *the future*.

Valuing a Company and Its Future

Thus far, we have examined several aspects of security analysis: macroeconomic factors, industry factors, and company-specific factors. But as we've said, it's *not the past* that's important but *the future*. The primary reason for looking at past performance is to gain insight about the future direction of the firm. Although past performance provides no guarantees about future returns, it can give us a good idea of a company's strengths and weaknesses. For example, it can tell us how well the company's products have done in the marketplace, how the company's fiscal health shapes up, and how management tends to respond to difficult situations. In short, the past can reveal how well the company is positioned to take advantage of the things that may occur in the future.

Because *the value of a share of stock is a function of its future returns*, the investor's task is to use available historical data to project key financial variables into the future. In this way, you can assess the future prospects of the company and the expected returns from its stock.

Forecasted Sales and Profits The key to our forecast is, of course, the future behavior of the *company*, and the most important aspects to consider in this regard are the outlook for sales and profits. One way to develop a sales forecast is to assume that the company will continue to perform as it has in the past and simply extend the historical trend. For example, if a firm's sales have been growing at a rate of 10% per year, then assume they will continue at that rate. Of course, if there is some evidence about the economy, industry, or company that suggests a faster or slower rate of growth, you would want to adjust the forecast accordingly. Often, this "naive" approach will be about as effective as more complex techniques.

Once the sales forecast has been generated, we can shift our attention to the net profit margin. We want to know what profit the firm will earn on the level of sales that it achieves. One of the best ways of doing that is to use what is known as a **common-size income statement**. Basically, a common-size statement takes every entry found on a normal dollar-based financial statement and converts it to a percentage. For a common-size income statement, every item on the statement is divided by *net sales*—which, in effect, is the common denominator. An example of this can be seen in Table 8.1 (on page 288), which shows the 2010 dollar-based and common-size income statements for Universal Office Furnishings. (This is the same income statement that we first saw in Table 7.4, page 261).

To understand how these statements are constructed, let's use the *gross profit margin* (of 41.8%) as an illustration. In this case, the *gross operating profit* of $809.5 million was divided by *net sales* of $1,938.0 million; thus: $809.5 ÷ $1,938.0 = 0.4177 = 41.8%.

TABLE 8.1	Comparative Dollar-Based and Common-Size Income Statements Universal Office Furnishings, Inc. 2010 Income Statements		EXCEL With Spreadsheets

	$ (in millions)	% (Common-Size)*
Net sales	$1,938.0	100.0%
Cost of goods sold	1,128.5	58.2
Gross profit	$ 809.5	41.8%
Selling, administrative, and other operating expenses	$ 496.7	25.6%
Depreciation & amortization	77.1	4.0
Other expenses	0.5	0.1
Total operating expenses	$ 574.3	29.7%
Earnings before interest & taxes (EBIT)	$ 235.2	12.1%
Interest expense	$ 13.4	0.7%
Income taxes	$ 82.1	4.2%
Net profit after taxes	$ 139.7	7.2%

*Common-size figures are found by using "Net Sales" as the common denominator, and then dividing all entries by net sales. For example, cost of goods sold = $1,128.5 ÷ $1,938.0 = 58.2%; EBIT = $235.2 ÷ $1,938.0 = 12.1%.

Using net sales of $1,938.0 million, the same procedure was used for every other entry on the income statement. Note that a common-size statement adds up, just like its dollar-based counterpart. For example, net sales of 100.0% minus costs of goods sold of 58.2% equals a gross operating profit margin of 41.8%. (You can also work up common-size balance sheets, using total assets as the common denominator, but they are not nearly as popular or as widely used as common-size income statements.)

Comparative common-size income statements are very popular with credit and securities analysts. They enable the users to compare operating results from one year to the next and in so doing, to quickly determine what's causing, say, gross or operating profit margins to improve or deteriorate. In essence, they let the analyst know how good a job management is doing in controlling the firm's cost structure and what's driving the company's profit margins. For our purposes, we can use this statement to help us get a handle on the firm's *forecasted net profit margin* (the bottom line of the common-size income statement). Starting with the latest common-size statement (or perhaps an average of the statements that have prevailed for the past few years), we can work our way down the statement, adjusting any of the entries for likely industry or company developments. For example, if cost of goods sold is expected to fall, we might raise the gross profit margin by, say, half a percentage point. In this way, we will (hopefully) end up with a good idea of what the future net profit margin should look like. Most individual investors can obtain valuable insight about future revenues, costs, and earnings from industry or company reports put out by brokerage houses, advisory services (e.g., *Value Line*), the financial media (e.g., *Forbes*), and from various investor Web sites.

Given a satisfactory sales forecast and estimate of the future net profit margin, we can combine these two pieces of information to arrive at future earnings.

Equation 8.1

$$\begin{array}{c} \text{Future after-tax} \\ \text{earnings in year } t \end{array} = \begin{array}{c} \text{Estimated sales} \\ \text{for year } t \end{array} \times \begin{array}{c} \text{Net profit margin} \\ \text{expected in year } t \end{array}$$

The *year t* notation in this equation simply denotes a given calendar or fiscal year in the future. It can be next year, the year after that, or any other year in which we are interested.

Let's say that in the year just completed, a company reported sales of $100 million, we estimate that revenues will grow at an 8% annual rate, and the net profit margin should be about 6%. Thus, estimated sales next year will equal $108 million ($100 million × 1.08). And, with a 6% profit margin, we should expect to see earnings next year of

$$\text{Future after-tax earnings next year} = \$108 \text{ million} \times 0.06 = \underline{\$6.5 \text{ million}}$$

Using this same process, we would then estimate sales and earnings *for other years* in our forecast period.

Forecasted Dividends and Prices At this point we have an idea of the future earnings performance of the company. We are now ready to evaluate the effects of this performance on returns to common stock investors. Given a corporate earnings forecast, we need three additional pieces of information:

- An estimate of future dividend payout ratios.
- The number of common shares that will be outstanding over the forecast period.
- A future price/earnings (P/E) ratio.

For the first two pieces of information, unless we have evidence to the contrary, we can simply project the firm's recent experience into the future. Payout ratios are usually fairly stable, so there is little risk in using a recent average figure. (Or, if a company follows a fixed-dividend policy, we could use the latest dividend rate in our forecast.) It is also generally safe to assume that the number of common shares outstanding will hold at the latest level or perhaps change at some moderate rate of increase (or decrease) that's reflective of the recent past.

Getting a Handle on the P/E Ratio The only really thorny issue in this process is coming up with an estimate of the future P/E ratio—a figure that has considerable bearing on the stock's future price behavior. Generally speaking, the P/E ratio is a function of several variables, including the following:

1. The growth rate in earnings.
2. The general state of the market.
3. The amount of debt in a company's capital structure.
4. The current and projected rate of inflation.
5. The level of dividends.

As a rule, higher P/E ratios can be expected with higher rates of growth in earnings, an optimistic market outlook, and lower debt levels (less debt means less financial risk).

The link between the inflation rate and P/E multiples, however, is a bit more complex. Generally speaking, as inflation rates rise, so do bond interest rates. This, in turn, causes required returns on stocks to rise (so stock returns will remain competitive with bond returns), and higher required returns on stocks mean lower stock prices and lower P/E multiples. On the other hand, declining inflation (and interest) rates normally have positive effects on the economy and business conditions, and that translates into higher P/E ratios and stock prices. We can also argue that a high P/E ratio should be expected with high dividend payouts. In practice, however, most companies with high P/E ratios have *low dividend payouts*. The reason: Earnings growth tends to be more valuable than dividends, especially in companies with high rates of return on equity.

FIGURE 8.1   **Average P/E Ratio of S&P 500 Stocks**

The average price/earnings ratio for stocks in the S&P 500 fluctuated around a mean of 14 from the 1930s to the 1980s before starting an upward climb. Increases in the P/E ratio do not necessarily indicate a bull market. The P/E ratio spiked recently, not because prices were high, but because earnings were very low due to the recession.

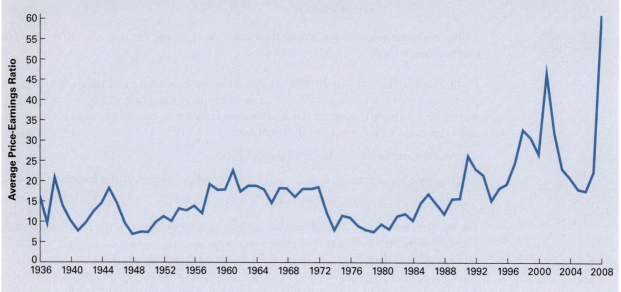

A Relative Price/Earnings Multiple   A useful starting point for evaluating the P/E ratio is the *average market multiple*. This is simply the average P/E ratio of all the stocks in a given market index, like the S&P 500 or the DJIA. The average market multiple indicates the general state of the market. It gives us an idea of how aggressively the market, in general, is pricing stocks. Other things being equal, the higher the P/E ratio, the more optimistic the market—*unless, of course, the economy is in a slump, in which case a high P/E could simply be the result of lower earnings.* Figure 8.1 plots the S&P 500 price/earnings multiple from 1936 to 2008. It shows that market multiples tend to move over a fairly wide range.

Looking at Figure 8.1, you can see that the market's P/E ratio has increased in recent years. From 1936 to 1995, the average P/E ratio was about 14, but since then the average P/E ratio has been much higher. In the latter half of the 1990s, that upward

MARKETS in CRISIS

P/E Ratios Can Be Misleading

The most recent spike in the S&P 500 P/E ratio cannot be explained by a booming economy or a rising stock market. Recall that in 2008, stock prices fell dramatically, with the overall market declining by more than 30%. Yet the P/E ratio skyrocketed that year. The reason is that with the deep recession of 2008, corporate earnings declined even more sharply than stock prices did. So, in the market P/E ratio, the denominator (earnings) declined more rapidly than the numerator (prices), and the overall P/E ratio jumped. In fact, in mid 2009, the S&P 500 P/E ratio reached an all-time high of 144!

trend could easily be explained by the very favorable state of the economy. Business was booming and new technologies were emerging at a rapid pace. There were no recessions from 1991–2000. If investors believed that the good times would continue indefinitely, then it's easy to understand why they might be willing to pay higher and higher P/E ratios over time.

With the market multiple as a benchmark, you can evaluate a stock's P/E performance relative to the market. That is, you can calculate a **relative P/E multiple** by dividing a stock's P/E by a market multiple. For example, if a stock currently has a P/E of 35 and the market multiple for the S&P 500 is, say, 25, the stock's relative P/E is 35/25 = 1.40. Looking at the relative P/E, you can quickly get a feel for how aggressively the stock has been priced in the market and what kind of relative P/E is normal for the stock.

Other things being equal, a high relative P/E is desirable—up to a point, at least. For just as *abnormally* high P/Es can spell trouble (i.e., the stock may be overpriced and headed for a fall), so too can *abnormally* high *relative P/Es*. Given that caveat, it follows that the higher the relative P/E measure, the higher the stock will be priced in the market. But watch out for the downside: High relative P/E multiples can also mean lots of price volatility, and as noted above, the potential for lots of downside risk. (Similarly, we can use average *industry* multiples to get a feel for the kind of P/E multiples that are standard for a given industry. We can then use that information, along with market multiples, to assess or project the P/E for a particular stock.)

Now we can generate a forecast of what the stock's *future* P/E will be over the anticipated *investment horizon* (the period of time over which we expect to hold the stock). For example, with the existing P/E multiple as a base, an *increase* might be justified if you believe the *market multiple* will increase (as the market becomes more bullish), and the *relative P/E* is likely to remain at its current level, or may even increase.

Estimating Earnings per Share So far we've been able to come up with an estimate for the dividend payout ratio, the number of shares outstanding, and the price/earnings multiple. We're now ready to forecast the stock's future earnings per share (EPS), which can be done as follows:

Equation 8.2

$$\text{Estimated EPS in year } t = \frac{\text{Future after-tax earnings in year } t}{\text{Number of shares of common stock outstanding in year } t}$$

Earnings per share is a critical part of the valuation process, for once you have EPS, you can combine it with (1) the dividend payout ratio to obtain (future) dividends per share and (2) the price/earnings multiple to project the (future) price of the stock.

Equation 8.2 simply converts aggregate or total corporate earnings to a per-share basis, by relating company (forecasted) profits to the expected number of shares outstanding. Although this approach works quite effectively, some investors would rather bypass the projection of aggregate sales and earnings and instead *concentrate on earnings from a per-share basis right from the start*. That can be done by looking at the major forces that drive earnings per share: ROE and book value. Quite simply, by using these two variables, we can define earnings per share as follows:

Equation 8.3

$$\text{EPS} = \text{ROE} \times \text{Book value per share}$$

This formula will produce the same results as the standard EPS equation shown first in Chapter 6 (Equation 6.1) and applied in Chapter 7 (on page 270). The major advantage of this form of the equation is that it allows you to assess the extent to which EPS is influenced by the company's book value and (especially) its ROE. As we saw in the previous chapter, ROE is a key financial measure, because it captures the amount of success the firm is having in managing its assets, operations, and capital structure. And as we see here, ROE not only is important in defining overall corporate profitability but it also plays a crucial role in defining a stock's EPS.

To produce an estimated EPS using Equation 8.3, you would go directly to the two basic components of the formula and try to get a handle on their future behavior. In particular, what kind of growth is expected in the firm's book value per share, and what's likely to happen to the company's ROE? In the vast majority of cases, ROE is really the driving force, so it's important to produce a good estimate of that variable. Investors often do that by breaking ROE into its component parts—net profit margin, total asset turnover, and the equity multiplier (see Equation 7.3, on page 265).

Once you have projected ROE and book value per share, you can plug these figures into Equation 8.3 to produce estimated EPS. The bottom line is that, one way or another (using the approach reflected in Equation 8.2 or that in Equation 8.3), you have to arrive at a forecasted EPS number that you are comfortable with. When you've done that, it's a pretty simple matter to use the forecasted payout ratio to estimate dividends per share:

Equation 8.4

$$\frac{\text{Estimated dividends}}{\text{per share in yeat } t} = \frac{\text{Estimated EPS}}{\text{for year } t} \times \frac{\text{Estimated}}{\text{payout ratio}}$$

And then the future price of the stock, which can be determined as

Equation 8.5

$$\frac{\text{Estimated share price}}{\text{at end of year } t} = \frac{\text{Estimated EPS}}{\text{in year } t} \times \frac{\text{Estimated P/E}}{\text{ratio}}$$

Pulling It All Together We've seen the various components that go into our estimates of future dividends and share prices. Now, to see how they all fit together, let's continue with the example we started above. Using the aggregate sales and earnings approach, if the company had 2 million shares of common stock outstanding and that number was expected to hold in the future, then given the estimated earnings of $6.5 million that we computed earlier, the firm should generate earnings per share (EPS) next year of

$$\frac{\text{Estimated EPS}}{\text{next year}} = \frac{\$6.5 \text{ million}}{2 \text{ million}} = \underline{\$3.25}$$

This result, of course, would be equivalent to the firm having a projected ROE of, say, 15% and an estimated book value per share of $21.67. According to Equation 8.3, those conditions would also produce an estimated EPS of $3.25 (i.e., 0.15 × $21.67). Using this EPS figure, along with an estimated payout ratio of 40%, we see that dividends per share next year should equal

$$\frac{\text{Estimated dividends}}{\text{per share next year}} = \$3.25 \times .40 = \underline{\$1.30}$$

If the firm adheres to a *fixed-dividend policy*, this estimate may have to be adjusted to reflect the level of dividends being paid. For example, if the company has been paying annual dividends at the rate of $1.25 per share *and is expected to continue doing so for the near future*, then you would adjust estimated dividends accordingly (i.e., use $1.25/share). Finally, if it has been estimated that the stock should sell at 17.5 times earnings, then a share of stock in this company should be trading at $56.88 by the *end* of next year.

$$\text{Estimated share price at the end of next year} = \$3.25 \times 17.5 = \underline{\$56.88}$$

Actually, we are interested in the price of the stock at the end of our anticipated investment horizon. Thus, the $56.88 figure would be appropriate if we had a one-year horizon. However, if we had a three-year holding period, we would have to extend the EPS figure for two more years and repeat our calculations with the new data. As we shall see, *the estimated share price is important because it has embedded in it the capital gains portion of the stock's total return.*

Developing an Estimate of Future Behavior

Using information obtained from Universal Office Furnishings (UVRS), we can illustrate the forecasting procedures we discussed above. Recall from Chapter 7 that an assessment of the economy and the office equipment industry was positive and that the company's operating results and financial condition looked strong, both historically and relative to industry standards. Because everything looks favorable for Universal, we decide to take a look at the future prospects of the company and its stock.

Assume we have chosen a three-year investment horizon because we believe (from earlier studies of economic and industry factors) that the economy and the market for office equipment stocks will start running out of steam near the end of 2013 or early 2014. (Some investors prefer to use one-year investment horizons, because they believe that trying to forecast out any further involves too many uncertainties. We use a three-year investment horizon here primarily for illustration—and because we feel comfortable forecasting the numbers out that far. Should that not be the case, then by all means use a shorter investment horizon.)

Table 8.2 provides selected historical financial data for the company, covering a five-year period (ending with the latest fiscal year) and provides the basis for much of

TABLE 8.2	Selected Historical Financial Data, Universal Office Furnishings				
	2006	**2007**	**2008**	**2009**	**2010**
Total assets (millions)	$554.2	$694.9	$755.6	$761.5	$941.2
Total asset turnover	1.72×	1.85×	1.98×	2.32×	2.06×
Net sales (millions)	$953.2	$1,283.9	$1,495.9	$1,766.2	$1,938.0
Annual rate of growth in sales*	11.5%	34.7%	16.5%	18.1%	9.7%
Net profit margin	4.2%	3.6%	5.0%	8.0%	7.2%
Payout ratio	6.8%	5.6%	5.8%	6.0%	6.6%
Price/earnings ratio	13.5×	21.7×	14.9×	15.7×	18.4×
Number of common shares outstanding (millions)	77.7	78.0	72.8	65.3	61.8

*Annual rate of growth in sales = Change in sales from one year to the next ÷ Level of sales in the base (or earliest) years. For 2007, the annual rate of growth in sales equaled 34.7% = (2007 sales − 2006 sales)/2006 sales = ($1,283.9 − $953.2)/$953.2 = 0.3469.

TABLE 8.3	Summary Forecast Statistics, Universal Office Furnishings				EXCEL With Spreadsheets

	Latest Actual Figure (Fiscal 2010)	Average for the Past Five Years (2006–2010)	Forecasted Figures		
			2011	2012	2013
Annual rate of growth in sales	9.7%	18.1%	22%	19%	15%
Net sales (millions)	$1,938.0	N/A*	$2,364.4**	$2,813.6**	$3,235.6**
× Net profit margin	7.8%	5.6%	8.0%	8.5%	8.5%
= Net after-tax earnings (millions)	$ 139.7	N/A	$ 189.2	$ 239.2	$ 275.0
÷ Common shares outstanding (millions)	61.8	71.1	61.5	60.5	59.0
= Earnings per share	$ 2.26	N/A	$ 3.08	$ 3.95	$ 4.66
× Payout ratio	6.6%	6.2%	6.0%	6.0%	6.0%
= Dividends per share	$ 0.15	$ 0.08	$ 0.18	$ 0.24	$ 0.28
Earnings per share	$ 2.26	N/A	$ 3.08	$ 3.95	$ 4.66
× P/E ratio	18.4	16.8	20	19	20
= Share price at year end	$ 41.58	N/A	$ 61.60	$ 75.00	$ 93.20

*N/A: Not applicable.

**Forecasted sales figures: Sales from *preceding* year × Growth rate in sales = Growth in sales; then Growth in sales + Sales from preceding year = Forecast sales for the year. For example, for 2011: $1,938.0 × 0.22 = $426.4 + $1938.0 = $2,364.4.

our forecast. The data reveal that, with one or two exceptions, the company has performed at a fairly steady pace and has been able to maintain a very attractive rate of growth. Our economic analysis suggests that the economy is about to pick up, and our research (from Chapter 7) indicates that the industry and company are well situated to take advantage of the upswing. Therefore, we conclude that the rate of growth in sales should pick up dramatically from the abnormally low level of 2010, attaining a growth rate of over 20% in 2011—more in line with the firm's five-year average. After a modest amount of pent-up demand is worked off, the rate of growth in sales should drop to about 19% in 2012 and to 15% in 2013.

The essential elements of the financial forecast for 2011–2013 are provided in Table 8.3. Highlights of the key assumptions and the reasoning behind them are as follows:

- *Net profit margin*. Various published industry and company reports suggest a comfortable improvement in earnings, so we decide to use a profit margin of 8.0% in 2011 (up a bit from the latest margin of 7.2% recorded in 2010). We're projecting even better profit margins (8.5%) in 2012 and 2013, as some cost improvements start to take hold.

- *Common shares outstanding*. We believe the company will continue to pursue its share buyback program, but at a substantially lower pace than in the 2007–2010 period. From a current level of 61.8 million shares, we project that the number of shares outstanding will drop to 61.5 million in 2011, to 60.5 million in 2012, and to 59.0 million in 2013.

- *Payout ratio*. We assume that the dividend payout ratio will hold at a steady 6% of earnings, as it has for most of the recent past.

- *P/E ratio*. Primarily on the basis of expectations for improved growth in revenues and earnings, we are projecting a P/E multiple that will rise from its present level of 18.4 times earnings to roughly 20 times earnings in 2011. Although this is a fairly conservative increase in the P/E, when it is coupled with the hefty growth in EPS, the net effect will be a big jump in the projected price of Universal stock.

Table 8.3 also shows the sequence involved in arriving at forecasted dividends and share price behavior; that is:

1. The company dimensions of the forecast are handled first. These include sales and revenue estimates, net profit margins, net earnings, and the number of shares of common stock outstanding. Note that after-tax earnings are derived according to the procedure described earlier in this chapter.

2. Next we estimate earnings per share, following the procedures established earlier.

3. The bottom line of the forecast is, of course, the returns in the form of dividends and capital gains expected from a share of Universal stock, given that the assumptions about net sales, profit margins, earnings per share, and so forth hold up. We see in Table 8.3 that dividends should go up to 28 cents a share, which is a big jump from where they are now (15 cents/share). Even so, with annual dividends of a little over a quarter a share, it's clear that dividends still won't account for much of the stock's return. In fact, the dividend yield in 2013 is projected to *fall* to just 0.3%. Clearly, the returns from this stock are going to come from capital gains, not dividends. That's obvious when you look at year-end share prices, which are expected to more than double over the next three years. That is, if our projections are valid, the price of a share of stock should rise from around $41.50 to over $93.00 by year-end 2013.

We now have an idea of what the future cash flows of the investment are likely to be. We can now use that information to establish an intrinsic value for Universal Office Furnishings stock.

The Valuation Process

Valuation is a process by which an investor determines the worth of a security using the risk and return concepts introduced in Chapters 4 and 5. This process can be applied to any asset that produces a stream of cash flow—a share of stock, a bond, a piece of real estate, or an oil well. To establish the value of an asset, the investor must determine certain key inputs, including the *amount* of future cash flows, the *timing* of these cash flows, and the *rate of return required* on the investment.

In terms of common stock, the essence of valuation is to determine what the stock *ought to be worth*, given estimated returns to stockholders (future dividends and price behavior) and the amount of potential risk exposure. Toward that end we employ various types of stock valuation models, the end product of which represents the elusive intrinsic value we have been seeking. That is, the stock valuation models determine either an *expected rate of return* or the *intrinsic worth of a share of stock*, which in effect represents the stock's "justified price." In this way, we obtain a standard of performance, based on forecasted stock behavior, which can be used to judge the investment merits of a particular security.

Either of two conditions would make us consider a stock a worthwhile investment candidate: (1) if the computed rate of return equals or exceeds the yield we feel is warranted, or (2) if the justified price (intrinsic worth) is equal to or greater than the current market price. Note that a security is considered acceptable even if its yield simply *equals* the required rate of return or if its intrinsic value simply *equals* the current market price of the stock. There is nothing irrational about such behavior. In either case, the security meets your minimum standards to the extent that it is giving you the rate of return you wanted.

Remember this, however, about the valuation process: Even though valuation plays an important part in the investment process, there is *absolutely no assurance* that the actual outcome will be even remotely similar to the forecasted behavior. The stock is still subject to economic, industry, company, and market risks, any one of which could negate *all* your assumptions about the future. Security analysis and stock valuation models are used not to guarantee success but to *help you better understand the return and risk dimensions of a potential transaction.*

Required Rate of Return One of the key ingredients in the stock valuation process is the **required rate of return**. Generally speaking, the amount of return required by an investor should be related to the level of risk that must be assumed to generate that return. In essence, the required return establishes a level of compensation compatible with the amount of risk involved. Such a standard helps you determine whether the expected return on a stock (or any other security) is satisfactory. Because you don't know for sure what the cash flow of an investment will be, you should expect to earn a rate of return that reflects this uncertainty. Thus, the greater the perceived risk, the more you should expect to earn. As we saw in Chapter 5, this is basically the notion behind the *capital asset pricing model* (CAPM).

Recall that using the CAPM, we can define a stock's required return as

Equation 8.6

$$\begin{array}{c}\text{Required}\\ \text{rate of return}\end{array} = \begin{array}{c}\text{Risk-free}\\ \text{rate}\end{array} + \left[\begin{array}{c}\text{Stock's}\\ \text{beta}\end{array} \times \left(\begin{array}{c}\text{Market}\\ \text{return}\end{array} - \begin{array}{c}\text{Risk-free}\\ \text{rate}\end{array}\right)\right]$$

The required inputs for this equation are readily available. You can obtain a stock's beta from *Value Line* or S&P's *Stock Reports* (or from any one of many Internet sites, such as **Quicken.com, MSN Money, Yahoo! Finance,** or **SmartMoney.com**). The risk-free rate is basically the return on Treasury bills, and a good proxy for the market return is the long-run average return on the stock market. This average return may, of course, have to be adjusted up or down a bit based on what you expect the market to do over the next year or so.

In the CAPM, the risk of a stock is captured by its beta. For that reason, the required return on a stock increases (or decreases) with increases (or decreases) in its beta. As an illustration of the CAPM at work, consider Universal's stock, which we'll assume has a beta of 1.30. Given that the risk-free rate is 5.5% and the expected market return is, say, 15%, according to the CAPM model, this stock would have a required return of

$$\text{Required return} = 5.5\% + [1.30 \times (15.0\% - 5.5\%)] = \underline{17.85\%}$$

This return—let's round it to 18%—can now be used in a stock valuation model to assess the investment merits of a share of stock.

As an alternative, or perhaps even *in conjunction with the CAPM,* you could take a more subjective approach to finding the required return. For example, if your assessment of the historical performance of the company had uncovered some volatility in

INVESTOR FACTS

HOW TO SPOT AN UNDERVALUED (OR OVERVALUED) MARKET—Just as shares of common stock can become over- or undervalued, so can the market as a whole. How can you tell if the market is overvalued? Some market observers suggest you look at comparative yields. That is, compare the so-called *earnings yield on stocks* with the yields on 10-year Treasuries. The earnings yield on stocks is the inverse of the market's P/E ratio—if the market P/E is 18 times earnings, the earnings yield would be 5.56% (1/18). If the earnings yield is *above* the yield on 10-year Treasuries, stocks are *undervalued* (cheap), especially compared to bonds. In contrast, you'd normally expect the earnings yield on stocks to be *less than* 10-year Treasury yields; as that spread continues to widen, the market is becoming more and more *overvalued*—definitely not a good thing.

sales and earnings, you could conclude that the stock is subject to a good deal of business risk. Also important is market risk, as measured by a stock's beta. A valuable reference point in arriving at a measure of risk is the rate of return available on less risky but competitive investment vehicles. Thus, you could *use the rate of return on long-term Treasury bonds or high-grade corporate issues* as a starting point in defining your desired rate of return. That is, starting with yields on long-term bonds, you could adjust those returns for the levels of business and market risk to which you believe the common stock is exposed.

To see how these elements make up the desired rate of return, let's go back to Universal Office Furnishings. Assume that it is now early 2011 and rates on high-grade corporate bonds are hovering around 9%. Given that our analysis thus far has indicated that the office equipment industry in general, and Universal in particular, is subject to a "fair" amount of business risk, we would want to adjust that figure upward—probably by around 2 or 3 points. In addition, with its beta of 1.30, we can conclude that the stock carries a good deal of market risk. Thus, we should increase our base rate of return even more—say, by another 4 or 5 points. That is, starting from a base (high-grade corporate bond) rate of 9%, we tack on, say, 3% for the company's added business risk and another 4.5 or 5% for the stock's market risk. Adding these up, we find that an appropriate required rate of return for Universal's common stock is around 17% or 17.5%. This figure is reasonably close to what we would obtain with CAPM using a beta of 1.30, a risk-free rate of 5.5%, and an expected market return of 15% (as in Equation 8.6). The fact that the two numbers are close shouldn't be surprising. If they're carefully (and honestly) done, the CAPM and the subjective approach should yield similar results. Whichever procedure you use, the required rate of return stipulates the minimum return you should expect to receive from an investment. To accept anything less means you'll fail to be fully compensated for the risk you must assume.

CONCEPTS IN REVIEW

Answers available at
www.pearsonhighered.com/gitman

8.1 What is the purpose of stock valuation? What role does *intrinsic value* play in the stock valuation process?

8.2 Are the expected future earnings of the firm important in determining a stock's investment suitability? Discuss how these and other future estimates fit into the stock valuation framework.

8.3 Can the growth prospects of a company affect its price/earnings multiple? Explain. How about the amount of debt a firm uses? Are there any other variables that affect the level of a firm's P/E ratio?

8.4 What is the *market multiple* and how can it help in evaluating a stock's P/E ratio? Is a stock's *relative P/E* the same thing as the market multiple? Explain.

8.5 In the stock valuation framework, how can you tell whether a particular security is a worthwhile investment candidate? What roles does the required rate of return play in this process? Would you invest in a stock if all you could earn was a rate of return that just equaled your required return? Explain.

Stock Valuation Models

LG4 LG5 LG6   Investors employ a number of different types of stock valuation models. Although they may all be aimed at a security's future cash benefits, their approaches to valuation are nonetheless considerably different. Some investors, for example, search for value in a company's financials—by keying in on such factors as book value, debt load, return on equity, and cash flow. These so-called *value investors* rely as much on historical performance as on earnings projections to identify undervalued stock. Then there are the *growth investors*, who concentrate primarily on growth in earnings. To them, though past growth is important, the real key lies in projected earnings—in finding companies that will produce big earnings, along with big P/E multiples.

There are still other stock valuation models in use—models that employ such variables as dividend yield, abnormally low P/E multiples, relative price performance over time, and even company size or market cap as key elements in the decision-making process. For purposes of our discussion, we'll focus on several stock valuation models that derive value from the fundamental performance of the company. We'll look first at stocks that pay dividends and at a procedure known as the dividend valuation model. From there, we'll look at several valuation procedures that can be used with companies that pay little or nothing in dividends. Finally, we'll move on to procedures that set the price of a stock based on how it behaves relative to earnings, cash flow, sales, or book value. The stock valuation procedures that we'll examine in this chapter are the same as those used by many professional security analysts, and are, in fact, found throughout the "Equity Investments" portion of the CFA exam, especially at Level-I. And, of course, as more fully discussed in the *Ethics in Investing* box on page 299, an understanding of these valuation models will enable you to better evaluate analysts' recommendations.

The Dividend Valuation Model

In the valuation process, the intrinsic value of any investment equals the *present value of its expected cash benefits*. For common stock, this amounts to the cash dividends received each year plus the future sale price of the stock. One way to view the cash flow benefits from common stock is to assume that the dividends will be received over an infinite time horizon—an assumption that is appropriate so long as the firm is considered a "going concern." Seen from this perspective, *the value of a share of stock is equal to the present value of all the future dividends it is expected to provide over an infinite time horizon.*

When a stockholder sells a stock, from a strictly theoretical point of view, what is really being sold is the right to all remaining future dividends. Thus, just as the *current* value of a share of stock is a function of future dividends, the *future* price of the stock is also a function of future dividends. In this framework, the *future* price of the stock will rise or fall as the outlook for dividends (and the required rate of return) changes. This approach, which holds that the value of a share of stock is a function of its future dividends, is known as the **dividend valuation model (DVM)**.

There are three versions of the dividend valuation model, each based on different assumptions about the future rate of growth in dividends:

1. *The zero-growth model* assumes that dividends will not grow over time.

2. *The constant-growth model*, which is the basic version of the dividend valuation model, assumes that dividends will grow by a fixed/constant rate over time.

3. *The variable-growth model* assumes that the rate of growth in dividends will vary over time.

In one form or another, the DVM is widely used in practice to value many of the larger, more mature companies.

ETHICS IN INVESTING

Stock Analysts: Don't Always Believe the Hype

Buy, sell, or hold? Unfortunately, many investors have learned the hard way not to trust these recommendations.

Consider the late 1990s stock market bubble. As the market began to fall in 2000, 95% of all publicly traded stocks were free of any sell recommendations, according to investment research firm Zacks, and 5% of stocks that did have a sell rating had exactly that: a sell rating from a *single* analyst. When the market began its climb back up, analysts missed the boat again: From 2000 to 2004, stocks that analysts told investors to sell rose 19% per annum on average, while their "buys" and "holds" rose just 7%.

Why were the all-star analysts wrong so often? Conflict of interest is one explanation. Analysts are handsomely rewarded for generating investment banking business. They often felt pressure to make positive comments to please current or prospective investment banking clients. Also, analysts are expected to generate commissions for their firms by making buy and sell recommendations.

Analyst hype is a real problem for both Wall Street and Main Street, and the securities industry has taken steps to correct it. The SEC's Regulation Fair Disclosure requires that all company information must be released *to the public* rather than quietly disseminated to analysts. Some brokerages ban analysts from owning stocks they cover. In 2003, the SEC ruled that compensation for analyst research must be separated from investment banking fees, so that the analyst's job is to research stock rather than solicit clients.

Most important, investors must learn how to read between the lines of analysts' reports. To start, they should probably lower analysts' ratings by one notch. A strong buy could be interpreted as a buy, a buy as a hold, and a hold or neutral as a sell. Also, investors should give more weight to negative ratings than to positive ones: Downgrades and those rare sell recommendations may signal future problems. Investors should also pay attention to downward revisions of earnings estimates; bad news often gets worse as changing business conditions spread beyond individual companies. Finally, when in doubt, investors should do their own homework, using the techniques taught in this book.

Critical Thinking Question Do you agree with the policies forbidding analysts to own stock of the companies they cover?

(Source: Rich Smith, Analysts Running Scared, *The Motley Fool*, April 5, 2006, www.fool.com.)

Zero Growth The simplest way to picture the dividend valuation model is to assume the stock has a fixed stream of dividends. In other words, dividends stay the same year in and year out, and they're expected to do so in the future. Under such conditions, the value of a zero-growth stock is simply *the capitalized value of its annual dividends*. To find the capitalized value, just divide annual dividends by the required rate of return, which in effect acts as the capitalization rate. That is,

Equation 8.7

$$\frac{\text{Value of a}}{\text{share of stock}} = \frac{\text{Annual dividends}}{\text{Required rate of return}}$$

For example, if a stock paid a (constant) dividend of $3 a share and you wanted to earn 10% on your investment, the value of the stock would be $30 a share ($3/0.10 = $30).

As you can see, the only cash flow variable that's used in this model is the fixed annual dividend. Given that the annual dividend on this stock never changes, does that mean the price of the stock never changes? Absolutely not! For as the required rate of return (capitalization rate) changes, so will the price of the stock. Thus, if the required rate of return goes up to, say, 15%, the price of the stock will fall to $20 ($3/0.15). Although this may be a very simplified view of the valuation model, it's actually not as far-fetched as it may appear, for this is basically the procedure used to price *preferred stocks* in the marketplace.

Constant Growth The zero-growth model is a good beginning, but it does not take into account a growing stream of dividends. The standard and more widely recognized version of the dividend valuation model assumes that dividends will grow over time at a specified rate. In this version, the value of a share of stock is still considered to be a function of its future dividends, but such dividends are expected to grow forever (to infinity) at a constant rate of growth, g. Accordingly, we can find the value of a share of stock as follows:

Equation 8.8

$$\text{Value of a share of stock} = \frac{\text{Next year's dividends}}{\text{Required rate of return} - \text{Constant rate of growth in dividends}}$$

Equation 8.8a

$$V = \frac{D_1}{k - g}$$

where

D_1 = annual dividends expected to be paid *next* year (the first year in the forecast period)

k = the capitalization rate, or discount rate (which defines the required rate of return on the investment)

g = the annual rate of growth in dividends, which is expected to hold constant to infinity

In this version of the DVM, the model assumes that dividends will grow to infinity at a constant rate. (A similar assumption also applies, by the way, to the variable-growth model.) Even so, it is important to understand that just because we assume that dividends will go on forever, *that doesn't mean we assume the investor will hold the stock forever*. Indeed, the DVM makes *no assumptions about how long the investor will hold the stock*, for the simple reason that the investment horizon has no bearing on the computed value of a stock. Thus, with the constant-growth DVM, it is irrelevant whether the investor has a one-year, five-year, or ten-year expected holding period. The computed value of the stock will be the same under all circumstances. So long as the input assumptions (k, g, and D_0) are the same, the value of the stock will be the same regardless of the intended holding period.

You'll also note that as simple as this model is, it nonetheless succinctly captures the very essence of stock valuation: *Increase* the cash flow (through D or g) and/or *decrease* the required rate of return (k), and the value of the stock will *increase*. Also note that in the DVM, k *defines* the *total return* to the stockholder, and g *represents the expected capital gains* on the investments. We know that, in practice, there are potentially two components that make up the total return to a stockholder: dividends and capital gains. As it turns out, the returns from both dividends and capital gains are captured in the DVM. That is, because k represents total returns and g defines the amount of capital gains embedded in k, it follows that if you subtract g from k ($k - g$), you'll have the expected dividend yield on the stock. Thus, the expected total return on a stock (k) equals the returns from capital gains (g) plus the returns from dividends ($k - g$).

The constant-growth DVM should not be used with just any stock. Rather, *it is best suited to the valuation of mature, dividend-paying companies* that hold established market positions. These are companies with strong track records that have reached the "mature" stage of growth. They are probably

Smart's Tour of the Web
To watch author Scott
Smart discuss key websites
for this chapter visit
www.myfinancelab.com

large-cap (or perhaps even some mature mid-cap) companies that have demonstrated an ability to generate steady—although perhaps not spectacular—rates of growth year in and year out. The growth rates *may not be identical* from year to year, but they tend to move within such a small range that they are seldom far off the average rate. These are companies that have established dividend policies and fairly predictable growth rates in earnings and dividends.

For example, in the 20 years between 1989–2009, the food company, General Mills, increased its dividend payments at the rate of 6.3% per year. The food industry is not one where we would expect explosive growth. Food consumption is closely tied to population growth, so profits in this business should grow relatively slowly over time. Traditionally, General Mills increases its dividend every summer, so in the spring of 2009, investors were expecting a modest increase in General Mills dividends over the coming year to $1.88 per share. If the required return on General Mills stock is 10%, the investors should have been willing to pay $50.81 for the stock ($1.88/(0.10 − 0.063)). In fact, General Mills stock traded in a range near $50 in the spring of 2009, so the constant growth model seems to work fairly well for that company.

In addition to its use in valuing mature, dividend-paying companies, the constant-growth DVM is also widely used to *value the market as a whole*. That is, using something like the DJIA or the S&P 500, analysts will often employ the DVM to determine the expected return on the market for the coming year—in other words, they'll use it to find the R_m in the capital asset pricing model (CAPM).

Applying the Constant-Growth DVM Use of the constant-growth DVM requires some basic information about the stock's required rate of return, its *current* level of dividends, and the expected rate of growth in dividends. A fairly simple, albeit naïve, way to find the dividend growth rate, g, is to look at the *historical* behavior of dividends. If they are growing at a relatively constant rate, you can assume they will continue to grow at (or near) that average rate in the future. You can get historical dividend data in a company's annual report, from various online sources, or from publications like *Value Line*.

With the help of a good hand-held calculator, we can use basic present value arithmetic to find the growth rate embedded in a stream of dividends. Here's how: Take the level of dividends, say, ten years ago and the level that's being paid today. Presumably, dividends today will be (much) higher than they were ten years ago, so, using your calculator, find the present value discount rate that equates the (higher) dividend today to the level paid ten years earlier. When you find that, you've found the growth rate; in this case, the *discount rate is the average rate of growth in dividends*. (See Chapter 5 for a detailed discussion of how to use present value to find growth rates.) Finding the appropriate growth rate, g, is a critical element in the DVM. Accordingly, we'll examine this variable in more detail later in this chapter, at which point we will discuss a more analytically sound procedure. For now, we will assume that the naïve approach (above) does an adequate job in defining the growth rate, so let's proceed with our illustration of the DVM.

Once you've determined the dividend growth rate, you can find next year's dividend, D_1, as $D_0 \times (1 + g)$, where D_0 equals the actual (current) level of dividends. Let's say that in the latest year, Amalgamated Anything paid $2.50 a share in dividends. If you expect those dividends to grow at the rate of 6% a year, you can find next year's dividends as follows: $D_1 = D_0(1 + g) = \$2.50 (1 + 0.06) = \$2.50(1.06) = \$2.65$. The only other information you need is the required rate of return (capitalization rate), k. (Note that k must be greater than g for the constant-growth model to be mathematically operative.)

To see this dividend valuation model at work, consider a stock that currently pays an annual dividend of $1.75 a share. Let's say that by using the present-value approach described above, you find that dividends are growing at a rate of 8% a year, and you expect they will continue to do so into the future. In addition, based on the CAPM, you determine that this investment should carry a required rate of return of 12%. Given this information, you can use Equation 8.8 to value the stock. That is, given $D_0 = \$1.75$, $g = 0.08$, and $k = 0.12$, it follows that

$$\frac{\text{Value of a}}{\text{Share of stock}} = \frac{D_0(1 + g)}{k - g} = \frac{\$1.75(1.08)}{0.12 - 0.08} = \frac{\$1.89}{0.04} = \underline{\underline{\$47.25}}$$

Thus, if you want to earn a 12% return on this investment—made up of 8% in capital gains (g), plus 4% in dividend yield (i.e., $\$1.89/\$47.25 = 0.04$)—then according to the constant-growth dividend valuation model, you should pay no more than $47.25 a share for this stock.

With this version of the DVM, *the price of the stock will increase over time* so long as k and g don't change. In fact, as we noted earlier, the growth rate (g) defines the amount of (expected) capital gains embedded in the future price of the stock. So, if $g = 8\%$, then we can expect the future price of the stock to go up around 8% per year. This will occur because the cash flow from the investment will increase as dividends grow. To see how this happens, let's carry our example a little further. Recall that $D_0 = \$1.75$, $g = 8\%$, and $k = 12\%$. On the basis of this information, we found the current value of the stock to be $47.25. Now look what happens to the price of this stock if k and g don't change:

Year	Dividend	Stock Price*
(Current year) 0	$1.75	$47.25
1	1.89	51.00
2	2.04	55.00
3	2.20	59.50
4	2.38	64.25
5	2.57	69.50

*As determined by the dividend valuation model, given $g = 0.08$, $k = 0.12$, and D_1 = next year's dividend level.

As the table shows, the price of the stock should rise from $47.25 today to around $69.50 in five years—as expected, that works out to an 8% growth rate.

Just as we can use this version of the DVM to value a stock today, so too can we find the expected price of the stock *in the future* by using the same valuation model. To do this, we simply redefine the appropriate level of dividends. For example, to find the price of the stock in year 3, we use the expected dividend in the third year, $2.20, and increase it by the factor $(1 + g)$. Thus, the stock price in year 3 $= D_3 \times (1 + g)/(k - g) = \$2.20 \times (1 + 0.08)/(0.12 - 0.08) = \$2.38/0.04 = \$59.50$. Of course, if future expectations about k or g do change, the *future price* of the stock will change accordingly. Should that occur, you could use the new information to decide whether to continue to hold the stock.

Variable Growth Although the constant-growth dividend valuation model is an improvement over the zero-growth model, it still has some shortcomings. The most obvious is the fact that it does not allow for changes in expected growth rates. To overcome this problem, we can use a form of the DVM that allows for *variable rates of growth* over time. Essentially, the *variable-growth dividend valuation model* derives, in two stages, a value based on future dividends and the future price of the stock (which price is a function of all future dividends). The variable-growth version of the model finds the value of a share of stock as follows:

Equation 8.9

$$\text{Value of a share of stock} = \text{Present value of future dividends during the initial variable-growth period} + \text{Present value of the price of the stock at the end of the variable-growth period}$$

Equation 8.9a

$$V = \frac{D_1}{(1+k)^1} + \frac{D_2}{(1+k)^2} + \cdots \frac{D_v}{(1+k)^v} + \frac{\frac{D_v(1+g)}{(k-g)}}{(1+k)^v}$$

where

D_1, D_2, etc. = future annual dividends

v = number of years in the initial variable-growth period

Note that the last element in this equation is the standard constant-growth dividend valuation model, which is used to find the price of the stock at the end of the initial variable-growth period.

This form of the DVM is appropriate for companies that are expected to experience rapid or variable rates of growth for a period of time—perhaps for the first three to five years—and then settle down to a constant (average) growth rate thereafter. This, in fact, is the growth pattern of many companies, so the model has considerable application in practice. (It also overcomes one of the operational shortcomings of the constant-growth DVM in that k does not always have to be greater than g. That is, *during the variable-growth period*, the rate of growth, g, can be greater than the required rate of return, k, and the model will still be fully operational.)

Finding the value of a stock using Equation 8.9 is actually a lot easier than it looks. To do so, follow these steps:

1. Estimate annual dividends during the initial variable-growth period and then specify the constant rate, g, at which dividends will grow after the initial period.

2. Find the present value of the dividends expected during the initial variable-growth period.

3. Using the constant-growth DVM, find the price of the stock at the end of the initial growth period.

4. Find the present value of the price of the stock (as determined in step 3). Note that the price of the stock is discounted for the same length of time as the last dividend payment in the initial growth period, because the stock is being priced (per step 3) at the end of this initial period.

5. Add the two present-value components (from steps 2 and 4) to find the value of a stock.

Applying the Variable-Growth DVM To see how this works, let's apply the variable-growth model to one of our favorite companies: Sweatmore Industries. Let's assume that dividends will grow at a variable rate for the first three years (2010, 2011, and 2012).

TABLE 8.4   **Using the Variable-Growth DVM to Value Sweatmore Stock**   `EXCEL With Spreadsheets`

Step

1. Projected annual dividends:

	2010	$2.65
	2011	3.08
	2012	3.48

Estimated annual rate of growth in dividends, g, for 2013 and beyond: 8%

2. Present value of dividends, using a required rate of return, k, of 14%, during the initial variable-growth period:

Year	Dividends	Present Value
2010	$2.65	$2.32
2011	3.08	2.37
2012	3.48	2.35
	Total	$7.04 (to step 5)

3. Price of the stock at the end of the initial growth period:

$$P_{2012} = \frac{D_{2013}}{k-g} = \frac{D_{2012} \times (1+g)}{k-g} = \frac{\$3.48 \times (1.08)}{0.14 - 0.08} = \frac{\$3.76}{0.06} = \underline{\$62.67}$$

4. Discount the price of the stock (as computed above) back to its present value, at k, of 14%:

$$\$62.67/(1.14)^3 = \$42.30 \text{ (to step 5)}$$

5. Add the present value of the initial dividend stream (step 2) to the present value of the price of the stock at the end of the initial growth period (step 4):

Value of Sweatmore stock $7.04 + $42.30 = $49.34

After that, the annual rate of growth in dividends is expected to settle down to 8% and stay there for the foreseeable future. Starting with the latest (2009) annual dividend of $2.21 a share, we estimate that Sweatmore's dividends should grow by 20% next year (in 2010), by 16% in 2011, and then by 13% in 2012 before dropping to an 8% rate.

Using these (initial) growth rates, we project that dividends in 2010 will amount to $2.65 a share ($2.21 × 1.20), and will rise to $3.08 ($2.65 × 1.16) in 2011 and to $3.48 ($3.08 × 1.13) in 2012. In addition, using CAPM, we feel that Sweatmore's stock should produce a minimum (required) rate of return (k) of at least 14%. We now have all the input we need and are ready to put a value on Sweatmore Industries. Table 8.4 shows the variable-growth DVM in action. The value of Sweatmore stock, according to the variable-growth DVM, is just under $49.34 a share. In essence, that's the maximum price you should be willing to pay for the stock if you want to earn a 14% rate of return.

Defining the Expected Growth Rate Mechanically, application of the DVM is really quite simple. It relies on just three key pieces of information: future dividends, future growth in dividends, and a required rate of return. But this model is not without its difficulties: One of the most difficult (and most important) aspects of the DVM is *specifying the appropriate growth rate*, g, *over an extended period of time*. Whether you are using the constant-growth or the variable-growth version of the dividend valuation model, the growth rate, g, has an enormous impact on the value derived from the model. Indeed, the DVM is *very sensitive* to the growth rate being used, because that rate affects both the model's numerator and its denominator. As a result, in practice analysts spend a good deal of time trying to come up with a growth rate, *g*, for a given company and its stock.

As we saw earlier in this chapter, we can define the growth rate from a strictly historical perspective (by using present value to find the past rate of growth) and then use it (or something close) in the DVM. While that approach might work in some cases, it does have some serious shortcomings. What's needed is a procedure that looks at the key forces that actually drive the growth rate. Fortunately, we have such an approach, one that's widely used in practice; it defines the growth rate, *g*, as follows:

Equation 8.10

$$g = \text{ROE} \times \text{The firm's retention rate, } rr$$

where

Equation 8.10a

$$rr = 1 - \text{dividend payout ratio}$$

Both variables in Equation 8.10 (ROE and *rr*) are *directly related to the firm's rate of growth*, and both play key roles in defining a firm's future growth. The *retention rate* represents the percentage of its profits that the firm plows back into the company. Thus, if the firm pays out 35% of its earnings in dividends (i.e., it has a dividend payout ratio of 35%), then it has a retention rate of 65%: $rr = 1 - 0.35 = 0.65$. The retention rate, in effect, indicates the amount of capital that is flowing back into the company to finance growth. Other things being equal, the more money being retained in the company, the higher the rate of growth.

The other component of Equation 8.10 is the familiar return on equity (ROE). Clearly, the more the company can earn on its retained capital, the higher the growth rate. Remember that ROE is made up of the net profit margin, total asset turnover, and equity multiplier (see Equation 7.13, page 269), so if you want to get a handle on how ROE is impacting the firm's growth rate, look to those three components.

To see how this works, consider a situation where a company retains, on average, about 80% of its earnings and generates an ROE of around 18%. (Driving the firm's ROE is a net profit margin of 7.5%, a total asset turnover of 1.20, and an equity multiplier of 2.0.) Under these circumstances, we would expect the firm to have a growth rate of around 14.5%:

$$g = \text{ROE} \times rr = 0.18 \times 0.80 = \underline{14.4\%}$$

Actually, the growth rate will probably be a bit more than 14.5%, because Equation 8.10 ignores financial leverage, which in itself will magnify growth. But at least the equation gives you a good idea of what to expect. Similarly, Equation 8.10 can serve as a starting point in assessing past and future growth. You can use it to compute expected growth and then assess the two key components of the formula (ROE and *rr*) to see whether they're likely to undergo major changes in the future. If so, then what impact is the change in ROE and/or *rr* likely to have on the growth rate, *g*? The idea is to take the time to study the forces (ROE and *rr*) that drive the growth rate, because the DVM itself is so sensitive to the rate of growth being used. Employ a growth rate that's too high and you'll end up with an intrinsic value that's way too high also. The downside, of course, is that you may end up buying a stock that you really shouldn't.

Other Approaches to Stock Valuations

In addition to the DVM, the market has also developed other ways of valuing shares of stock. Some are simply variations of the DVM; others are alternatives to it. The motivation for using these approaches is to find techniques that are compatible to given investment horizons and/or that can be used with non-dividend-paying stocks. In addition, for a variety of reasons, some investors prefer to use procedures that don't rely on corporate earnings as the basis of valuation. For these investors, it's not earnings that matter, but instead things like cash flow, sales, or book value.

One valuation procedure that is popular with many investors is the so-called *dividends-and-earnings approach*, which directly utilizes future dividends and the future selling price of the stock as the relevant cash flows. Another is the *P/E approach*, which builds the stock valuation process around the stock's price/earnings ratio. One of the major advantages of these procedures is that *they don't rely on dividends as the only input*. Accordingly, they can be used with stocks that are more growth-oriented and that pay little or nothing in dividends. Let's take a closer look at both of these approaches, as well as a technique that arrives at the expected return on the stock (in percentage terms) rather than a (dollar-based) "justified price."

A Dividends-and-Earnings Approach As we saw earlier, the value of a share of stock is a function of the amount and timing of future cash flows and the level of risk that must be taken on to generate that return. The **dividends-and-earnings (D&E) approach** (also known as the *DCF approach*) conveniently captures the essential elements of expected risk and return and does so in a present-value context. The model is as follows:

Equation 8.11
$$\text{Value of a share of stock} = \text{Present value of future dividends} + \text{Present value of the price of the stock at the date of sale}$$

Equation 8.11a
$$V = \frac{D_1}{(1 + k)^1} + \frac{D_2}{(1 + k)^2} + \ldots + \frac{D_N}{(1 + k)^N} + \frac{SP_N}{(1 + k)^N}$$

where

D_t = future annual dividend in year t
SP_N = estimated share price of the stock at date of sale, year N
N = number of years in the investment horizon

Note its similarities to the variable-growth DVM: It is present-value–based, and its value is derived from future dividends and the expected future price of the stock. The big difference between the two procedures revolves around the role that dividends play in determining the future price of the stock. That is, the D&E approach doesn't rely on dividends as the principal player in the valuation process. Therefore, it works just as well with companies that pay little or nothing in dividends as it does with stocks that pay out a lot in dividends. Along that same line, whereas the variable-growth DVM relies on future dividends to price the stock, the D&E approach employs projected earnings per share and estimated P/E multiples. These are the same two variables that drive the price of the stock in the market. Thus, the D&E approach is far more flexible than the DVM and is easier to understand and apply. Using the D&E valuation approach, we focus on projecting future dividends and share price behavior over a defined, finite investment horizon, much as we did for Universal Office Furnishings in Table 8.3 (on page 294).

Especially important in the D&E approach is finding a viable P/E multiple that you can use to project the future price of the stock. This is a critical part of this valuation process, because of the major role that capital gains (and therefore the estimated price of the stock at its date of sale) play in defining the level of security returns. Using market or industry P/E ratios as benchmarks, you should establish a multiple that you feel the stock will trade at in the future. Like the growth rate, g, in the DVM, the P/E multiple is the single most important (and most difficult) variable to project in the D&E approach.

Using this input, along with estimated future dividends and earnings per share, this present-value–based model generates a *justified price* based on estimated returns. This intrinsic value represents the price you should be willing to pay for the stock, given its expected dividend and price behavior and assuming you want to generate a return that is equal to or greater than your required rate of return.

To see how this procedure works, consider once again the case of Universal Office Furnishings. Let's return to our original three-year investment horizon. Given the fore-casted annual dividends and share price from Table 8.3, along with a required rate of return of 18% (as computed earlier using Equation 8.6 on page 294), we can see that the value of Universal's stock is

$$V = \frac{\$0.18}{1.18} + \frac{\$0.24}{1.18^2} + \frac{\$0.28}{1.18^3} + \frac{\$93.20}{1.18^3} = \$0.15 + \$0.17 + \$0.17 + \$56.76 = \$57.25$$

According to the D&E approach, Universal's stock should be valued at about $57 a share. That assumes, of course, that our projections hold up—particularly with regard to our forecasted EPS and P/E multiple in 2013. For example, if the P/E drops from 20 to 17 times earnings, then the value of a share of stock will drop to less than $50 (to around $48.75/share). Given that we have confidence in our projections, the present-value figure computed here means that we would realize our (18%) desired rate of return so long as we can buy the stock at no more than $57 a share. Because UVRS is currently trading at (around) $41.50, we can conclude that the stock at present is an *attractive investment vehicle*. That is, because we can buy the stock at *less* than its computed intrinsic value, we'll be able to earn our required rate of return, *and then some*.

Note that by most standards, Universal would be considered a highly risky invest-ment, if for no other reason than the fact that *nearly all the return is derived from cap-ital gains*. Indeed, dividends alone account for less than 1% of the value of the stock. That is, only 49 cents of the $57.25 comes from dividends. Clearly, if we're wrong about EPS or the P/E multiple, the future price of the stock (in 2013) could be way off the mark, and so, too, would our projected return.

Actually, the D&E approach to stock valuation is not an alternative to the DVM, but rather, is simply a *variation* of that model. That is, regardless of what holding period is used in the D&E approach (be it one year, three years, ten years, or whatever), the computed value will be the same as that obtained with the constant-growth (or even variable-growth) DVM, *so long as the input assumptions regarding k, g, and D_0 are the same*. Need proof? Consider the constant-growth DVM example we used earlier (see page 302). Recall that we used a stock that had a current annual dividend (D_0) of $1.75 a share, a growth rate (g) of 8%, and a required return (k) of 12%. Let's use this same stock, *with these same assumptions*, but this time we'll use the D&E approach to value the stock, assuming a three-year investment horizon. Under these conditions, with an

8% growth rate, dividends would grow to $1.89 next year ($1.75 × 1.08), $2.04 in the second year, and $2.20 a share in year 3. Also, at an 8% appreciation rate, the price of the stock would go up to $59.50 by the end of year 3. Using this information in the D&E model, the value of the stock would be:

$$Value = \frac{\$1.89}{1.12^1} + \frac{\$2.04}{1.12^2} + \frac{\$2.20}{1.12^3} + \frac{\$59.50}{1.12^3} = \$1.69 + \$1.63 + \$1.57 + \$42.36 = \$47.25$$

Note that we end up with the same value here as we did using the DVM (see page 302). So no matter what holding period or which procedure we use, D&E or DVM, so long as the input assumptions are the same, the computed share values will be the same.

Finding the Value of Non–Dividend-Paying Stocks What about *the value of a stock that does not pay dividends*—and is not expected to do so for the foreseeable future? That's not a problem with the D&E approach. Using Equation 8.11, simply set all dividends to zero, so the computed value of the stock would come solely from its projected future price. In other words, the value of the stock will equal the present value of its price at the end of the holding period.

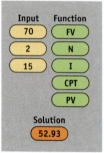

Input	Function
70	FV
2	N
15	I
	CPT
	PV

Solution
52.93

Consider, for example, an investor who's looking at a stock that pays no dividends; she estimates that at the end of a two-year holding period, this stock should be trading at around $70 a share. Using a 15% required rate of return, this stock would have a present value of $70/1.15^2 = $52.93. This value is, of course, the intrinsic value, or justified price of the stock. So long as it's trading for around $53 or less, it would be a worthwhile investment candidate. (*Note:* As shown at the left, you can just as easily *use a handheld calculator to find the value of this stock.*)

Determining Expected Return Sometimes investors find it more convenient to deal in terms of expected return than a dollar-based justified price. This is no problem, nor is it necessary to sacrifice the present-value dimension of the stock valuation model to achieve such an end. We can find expected return by using the (present-value–based) *internal rate of return (IRR)* procedure first introduced in Chapter 5. This approach to stock valuation uses forecasted dividend and price behavior, along with the *current market price*, to arrive at the fully compounded rate of return you can expect to earn from a given investment.

To see how a stock's expected return is computed, let's look once again at Universal Office Furnishings. Using 2011–2013 data from Table 8.3 (on page 294), along with the stock's current price of $41.58, we can determine Universal's expected return. To do so, we find the discount rate that equates the future stream of benefits (i.e., the future annual dividends and future price of the stock) to the stock's current market price. In other words, find the discount rate that produces a present value of future benefits equal to the price of the stock, and you have the IRR, or expected return on that stock.

Here's how it works: Using the Universal example, we know that the stock is expected to pay per-share dividends of $0.18, $0.24, and $0.28 over the next three years. At the end of that time, we hope to sell the stock for $93.20. Given that the stock is currently trading at $41.58, we're looking for the discount rate, r, that will produce a present value (of the future annual dividends and stock price) equal to $41.58. That is,

$$\frac{\$0.18}{(1+r)^1} + \frac{\$0.24}{(1+r)^2} + \frac{\$0.28}{(1+r)^3} + \frac{\$93.20}{(1+r)^3} = \$41.58$$

We need to solve for the discount rate (the present-value interest factors) in this equation. Through a process of "hit and miss" (or with the help of a personal computer or hand-held calculator), you'll find that with an interest factor of 31.3%, the present value of the future cash benefits from this investment will equal exactly $41.58. That, of course, is our expected return. Thus, Universal can be expected to earn a fully compounded annual return of about 31%, assuming that the stock can be bought at $41.58, is held for three years (during which time investors receive indicated annual dividends), and then is sold for $93.20 at the end of the three-year period. When compared to its 18% *required rate of return*, the 31.3% *expected return* makes Universal look like a very attractive investment candidate.

It's even easier to determine the return on stocks that don't pay dividends. Just *find the discount rate that equates the projected future price of the stock to its current share price*. For example, if Universal didn't pay dividends, then all we'd have to do is find the discount rate that equates the projected share price of $93.20 (three years from now) to the stock's current price of $41.58. Using a hand-held calculator as shown at the left, we arrive at an expected rate of return of about 30.9%. Given the return of 31.3% with dividends versus the 30.9% without, the cash flow from dividends clearly doesn't play much of a role in defining the potential return on this stock.

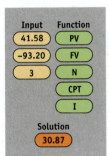

Input	Function
41.58	PV
−93.20	FV
3	N
	CPT
	I

Solution
30.87

The Price/Earnings (P/E) Approach One of the problems with the stock valuation procedures we've looked at so far is that they are fairly mechanical. They involve a good deal of "number crunching." Although such approaches are fine with some stocks, they do not work well with others. Fortunately, there is a more intuitive approach. That alternative is the **price/earnings (or P/E) approach** to stock valuation.

The P/E approach is a favorite of professional security analysts and is widely used in practice. It's relatively simple to use; it's based on the standard P/E formula first introduced in Chapter 7 (Equation 7.14 on page 270). There we showed that a stock's P/E ratio is equal to its market price divided by the stock's EPS. Using this equation and solving for the market price of the stock, we have

Equation 8.12

$$\text{Stock price} = \text{EPS} \times \text{P/E ratio}$$

Equation 8.12 basically captures the P/E approach to stock valuation. That is, given an *estimated* EPS figure, *you decide on a P/E ratio that you feel is appropriate for the stock. Then you use it in Equation 8.12 to see what kind of price you come up with and how that compares to the stock's current price.*

Actually, this approach is no different from what's used in the market every day. Look at the stock quotes in the *Wall Street Journal*. They include the stock's P/E ratio and show what investors are willing to pay for one dollar of earnings. Essentially, the *Journal* relates the company's earnings per share for the *last* 12 months (known as *trailing earnings*) to the latest price of the stock. In practice, however, investors buy stocks not for their past earnings but for their *expected future earnings*. Thus, in Equation 8.12, it's customary to use *forecasted EPS for next year*—that is, to use projected earnings one year out.

The first thing you have to do to implement the P/E approach is to come up with an expected EPS figure for next year. In the early part of this chapter, we saw how this might be done (see, for instance, Equations 8.2 and 8.3 on page 291). Given the forecasted EPS, the next step is to evaluate the variables that drive the P/E ratio. Most of that assessment is intuitive. For example, you might look at the stock's expected rate of growth in earnings, any potential major changes in the firm's capital structure or dividends, and any other factors such as relative market or industry P/E multiples that might affect the stock's multiple. You could use such inputs to come up with a base P/E ratio. Then adjust that base, as necessary, to account for the perceived state of the market and/or anticipated changes in the rate of inflation.

Along with estimated EPS, we now have the P/E ratio we need to compute (via Equation 8.12) the price at which the stock should be trading. Take, for example, a stock that's currently trading at $37.80. One year from now, it's estimated that this stock should have an EPS of $2.25 a share. If you feel that the stock should be trading at a P/E ratio of 20 times projected earnings, then it should be valued at $45 a share (i.e., $2.25 × 20). By comparing this targeted price to the current market price of the stock, you can decide whether the stock is a good buy. In this case, you would consider the stock undervalued and therefore a good buy, since the computed price of the stock ($45) is more than its market price (of $37.80).

While this is the principal application of the P/E approach, you'll find that a *variation of this procedure* is also used with the D&E and IRR approaches. That is, by using estimated figures for *both* EPS and the P/E multiple, you can come up with *the share price that's expected to prevail at the end of a given investment horizon.* Throw in any dividends that may be received, discount that cash flow (of dividends and future share price) back to the present, and you have either the *justified price*, as in the D&E approach, or the *expected rate of return*, as in the IRR approach.

Other Price-Relative Procedures

As we saw with the P/E approach, price-relative procedures base their valuations on the assumptions that *the value of a share of stock should be directly linked to a given performance characteristic of the firm*, such as earnings per share. These procedures involve a good deal of judgment and intuition, and they rely heavily on the market expertise of the analysts. Besides the P/E approach, there are several other price-relative procedures that are used by investors who, for one reason or another, want to use some measure other than earnings to value stocks. They include:

- The price-to-cash-flow (P/CF) ratio
- The price-to-sales (P/S) ratio
- The price-to-book-value (P/BV) ratio

Like the P/E multiple, these procedures determine the value of a stock by relating share price to cash flow, sales, or book value. Let's look at each of these in turn to see how they're used in stock valuation.

A Price-to-Cash-Flow (P/CF) Procedure This measure has long been popular with investors, because cash flow is felt to provide a more accurate picture of a company's earning power than net earnings. When used in stock valuation, the procedure is almost identical to the P/E approach. That is, a P/CF ratio is combined with a *projected* cash flow per share to arrive at what the stock should be trading for.

Although it is quite straightforward, this procedure nonetheless has one problem—defining the appropriate cash flow measure. While some investors use *cash flow from operating activities*, as obtained from the statement of cash flows, others use *free cash flow*. But the one measure that seems to be the most popular with professional analysts is EBITDA (earnings before interest, taxes, depreciation, and amortization), which we'll use here. EBITDA represents "cash earnings" to the extent that the major noncash expenditures (depreciation and amortization) are added back to operating earnings (EBIT).

The price-to-cash-flow (P/CF) ratio is computed as follows:

Equation 8.13
$$\text{P/CF ratio} = \frac{\text{Market price of common stock}}{\text{Cash flow per share}}$$

where cash flow per share = EBITDA ÷ number of common shares outstanding.

Before you can use the P/CF procedure *to assess the current market price of a stock*, you first have to come up with a forecasted cash flow per share one year out, and then define an appropriate P/CF multiple to use. For most firms, it is very likely that the cash flow (EBITDA) figure will be larger than net earnings available to stockholders. As a result, *the cash flow multiple will probably be lower than the P/E multiple*. In any event, once an appropriate P/CF multiple is determined (subjectively and with the help of any historical market information), simply multiply it by the expected cash flow per share one year from now to find the price at which the stock should be trading. That is, the computed price of a share of stock = cash flow per share × P/CF ratio.

To illustrate, assume a company currently is generating an EBITDA of $325 million, which is expected to increase by some 12.5% to around $365 million ($325 million × 1.125) over the course of the next 12 months. On a per-share basis, let's say that translates into a *projected* cash flow per share of nearly $6.50. If we feel this stock should be trading at about eight times its projected cash flow per share, then it should be valued at around $52 a share. Thus, if it is currently trading in the market at $45.50 (or at seven times its projected cash flow per share), we can conclude, once again, that the stock is undervalued and, therefore, should be considered a viable investment candidate.

Price-to-Sales (P/S) and Price-to-Book-Value (P/BV) Ratios Some companies, like high-tech startups, have little, if any, earnings. Or if they do have earnings, they're either unreliable or very erratic and therefore highly unpredictable. In these cases, valuation procedures based on earnings (and even cash flows) aren't much help. So investors turn to other procedures—those based on sales or book value, for example. While companies may not have much in the way of profits, they certainly have sales and, ideally, some book value. (As noted in Chapter 7, *book value* is simply another term for equity, or net worth.)

Both the price-to-sales (P/S) and price-to-book-value (P/BV) ratios are used exactly like the P/E and P/CF procedures. Recall that we defined the P/BV ratio in Equation 7.19 (on page 272) as follows:

$$\text{P/BV ratio} = \frac{\text{Market price of common stock}}{\text{Book value per share}}$$

We can define the P/S ratio in a similar fashion:

Equation 8.14
$$\text{P/S ratio} = \frac{\text{Market price of common stock}}{\text{Sales per share}}$$

where sales per share equals net annual sales (or revenues) divided by the number of common shares outstanding.

Many bargain-hunting investors look for stocks with P/S ratios of 2.0 or less. These securities are felt to offer the most potential for future price appreciation. Especially attractive to these investors are very low P/S multiples of 1.0 or less. Think about it: With a P/S ratio of, say, 0.9, you can buy $1 in sales for only 90 cents! So long as the company isn't a basket case, such low P/S multiples may well be worth pursuing.

Keep in mind that while the emphasis may be on low multiples, *high P/S ratios aren't necessarily bad*. To determine if a high multiple—more than 3.0 or 4.0, for example—is justified, look at the company's net profit margin. Companies that can consistently generate high net profit margins often have high P/S ratios. Here's a valuation rule to remember: *High profit margins should go hand-in-hand with high P/S multiples*. That makes sense, too, because a company with a high profit margin brings more of its sales down to the bottom line in the form of profits.

You would also expect the price-to-book-value measure to be low, but probably not as low as the P/S ratio. Indeed, unless the market becomes grossly overvalued (think about what happened in 1999 and 2000), most stocks are likely to trade at multiples of less than three to five times their book values. And in this case, unlike with the P/S multiple, there's usually little justification for abnormally high price-to-book-value ratios—except perhaps for firms that have abnormally *low* levels of equity in their capital structures. Other than that, high P/BV multiples are almost always caused by "excess exuberance." As a rule, when stocks start trading at seven or eight times their book values, or more, they are becoming overvalued.

CONCEPTS IN REVIEW

Answers available at
www.pearsonhighered.com/gitman

8.6 Briefly describe the *dividend valuation model* and the three versions of this model. Explain how CAPM fits into the *DVM*.

8.7 What is the difference between the variable-growth dividend valuation model and the *dividends-and-earnings approach* to stock valuation? Which procedure would work better if you were trying to value a growth stock that pays little or no dividends? Explain.

8.8 How would you go about finding the *expected return* on a stock? Note how such information would be used in the stock selection process.

8.9 Briefly describe the *P/E approach* to stock valuation and note how this approach differs from the variable-growth DVM. Describe the *P/CF approach* and note how it is used in the stock valuation process. Compare the P/CF approach to the P/E approach, noting the relative strengths and weaknesses of each.

8.10 Briefly describe the *price/sales* ratio and explain how it is used to value stocks. Why not just use the P/E multiple? How does the P/S ratio differ from the *P/BV measure*?

 Here is what you should know after reading this chapter. **MyFinanceLab** will help you identify what you know, and where to go when you need to practice.

What You Should Know	Key Terms	Where To Practice
LG1 **Explain the role that a company's future plays in the stock valuation process.** The final phase of security analysis involves an assessment of the investment merits of a specific company and its stock. The focus here is on formulating expectations about the company's prospects and the risk and return behavior of the stock. In particular, we would want some idea of the stock's future earnings, dividends, and share prices, which are ultimately the basis of return.	common-size income statement, *p. 287* relative P/E multiple, *p. 291* required rate of return, *p. 296* stock valuation, *p. 287* target price, *p. 293*	MyFinanceLab Study Plan 8.1 Excel Table 8.1
LG2 **Develop a forecast of a stock's expected cash flow, starting with corporate sales and earnings, and then moving to expected dividends and share price.** Because the value of a share of stock is a function of its future returns, investors must try to formulate expectations about what the future holds for the company. Look first at the company's projected sales and earnings, and then translate those data into forecasted dividends and share prices. These variables define an investment's future cash flow and, therefore, investor returns.	valuation, *p. 295*	MyFinanceLab Study Plan 8.2 Excel Table 8.3
LG3 **Discuss the concepts of intrinsic value and required rates of return, and note how they are used.** Information such as projected sales, forecasted earnings, and estimated dividends are important in establishing intrinsic value. This is a measure, based on expected return and risk exposure, of what the stock ought to be worth. A key element is the investor's required rate of return, which is used to define the amount of return that should be earned given the stock's perceived exposure to risk.		MyFinanceLab Study Plan 8.3 Video Learning Aid for Problem P8.18
LG4 **Determine the underlying value of a stock using the zero-growth, constant-growth, and variable-growth dividend valuation models.** The dividend valuation model (DVM) derives the value of a share of stock from the stock's future growth in dividends. There are three versions of the DVM. Zero-growth assumes that dividends are fixed and won't change in the future. Constant-growth assumes that dividends will grow at a constant rate into the future. Variable-growth assumes that dividends will initially grow at varying (or abnormally high) rates, before eventually settling down to a constant rate of growth.	dividend valuation model (DVM), *p. 298*	MyFinanceLab Study Plan 8.4 Excel Table 8.4 Video Learning Aid for Problem P8.9
LG5 **Use other types of present-value–based models to derive the value of a stock, as well as alternative price-relative procedures.** The DVM works well with some	dividends-and-earnings (D&E) approach, *p. 306*	MyFinanceLab Study Plan 8.5

What You Should Know	Key Terms	Where To Practice
types of stocks, but not so well with others. Investors may turn to other types of stock-valuation approaches, including the D&E and IRR approaches, as well as certain price-relative procedures, like the P/E, P/CF, P/S, and P/BV methods. The dividends-and-earnings approach uses a finite investment horizon to derive a present-value–based "justified price." Or, investors can determine the expected return on a stock (via IRR) by finding the discount rate that equates the stock's future cash flows to its current market price. Several price-relative procedures exist as well, such as the price/earnings approach, which uses projected EPS and the stock's P/E ratio to determine whether a stock is fairly valued.	price/earnings (P/E) approach, *p. 309*	Video Learning Aid for Problem P8.18
LG6 Gain a basic appreciation of the procedures used to value different types of stocks, from traditional dividend-paying shares to more growth-oriented stocks. All sorts of stock valuation models are used in the market; this chapter examined nine more widely used procedures. One thing that becomes apparent in stock evaluation is that one approach definitely does not fit all situations. Some approaches (like the DVM) work well with mature, dividend-paying companies. Others (like the D&E, IRR, P/E, and P/CF approaches) are more suited to growth-oriented firms, which may not pay dividends. Other price-relative procedures (like P/S and P/BV) are often used to value companies that have little or nothing in earnings, or whose earnings records are sporadic.		MyFinanceLab Study Plan 8.6

Log into **MyFinanceLab**, take a chapter test, and get a personalized Study Plan that tells you which concepts you understand and which ones you need to review. From there, **MyFinanceLab** will give you further practice, tutorials, animations, videos, and guided solutions.
Log into www.myfinancelab.com

Discussion Questions

LG1 **LG2**   Q8.1 Using the resources available at your campus or public library, select a company from *Value Line* that would be of interest to you. (*Hint*: Pick a company that's been publicly traded for at least 10 to 15 years and avoid public utilities, banks, and other financial institutions.) Obtain a copy of the latest *Value Line* report on your chosen company. Using the historical and forecasted data reported in *Value Line*, along with one of the valuation techniques described in this chapter, calculate the maximum (i.e., justified) price you'd be willing to pay for this stock. Use the CAPM to find the required rate of return on your stock. (For this problem, use a market rate of return of 12%, and for the risk-free rate, use the latest 3-month Treasury bill rate.)

     a. How does the justified price you computed compare to the latest market price of the stock?

     b. Would you consider this stock to be a worthwhile investment candidate? Explain.

LG5 **LG6** Q8.2 In this chapter, we examined nine different stock valuation procedures:
- Zero-growth DVM
- Constant-growth DVM
- Variable-growth DVM
- Dividends-and-earnings (D&E) approach
- Expected return (IRR) approach
- P/E approach
- Price-to-cash-flow ratio
- Price-to-sales ratio
- Price-to-book-value ratio

   a. Which one (or more) of these procedures would be most appropriate when trying to put a value on:
     1. A growth stock that pays little or nothing in dividends?
     2. The S&P 500?
     3. A relatively new company that has only a brief history of earnings?
     4. A large, mature, dividend-paying company?
     5. A preferred stock that pays a fixed dividend?
     6. A company that has a large amount of depreciation and amortization?

   b. Of the nine procedures listed above, which *three* do you think are the best? Explain.
   c. If you had to choose just *one* procedure to use in practice, which would it be? Explain. (*Note:* Confine your selection to the list above.)

LG1 **LG3** Q8.3 Explain the role that the future plays in the stock valuation process. Why not just base the valuation on historical information? Explain how the intrinsic value of a stock is related to its required rate of return. Illustrate what happens to the value of a stock when the required rate of return increases.

LG3 **LG4** Q8.4 Assume an investor uses the constant-growth DVM to value a stock. Listed below are various situations that could affect the computed value of a stock. Look at each one of these individually and indicate whether it would cause the computed value of a stock to go up, down, or stay the same. Briefly explain your answers.
    a. Dividend payout ratio goes up.
    b. Stock's beta rises.
    c. Equity multiplier goes down.
    d. T-bill rates fall.
    e. Net profit margin goes up.
    f. Total asset turnover falls.
    g. Market return increases.

Assume throughout that the current dividend (D_0) remains the same and that all other variables in the model are unchanged.

Problems

All problems are available on **www.myfinancelab.com**

LG2 P8.1 An investor estimates that next year's sales for New World Products should amount to about $75 million. The company has 2.5 million shares outstanding, generates a net profit margin of about 5%, and has a payout ratio of 50%. All figures are expected to hold for next year. Given this information, compute the following.
    a. Estimated net earnings for next year.
    b. Next year's dividends per share.
    c. The expected price of the stock (assuming the P/E ratio is 24.5 times earnings).
    d. The expected holding period return (latest stock price: $25 per share).

LG2   **P8.2**   GrowthCo had sales of $55 million in 2008, and is expected to have sales of $83,650,000 for 2011. The company's net profit margin was 5% in 2008, and is expected to increase to 8% by 2011. Estimate the company's net profit for 2011.

LG2   **P8.3**   Goodstuff Corporation has total equity of $500 million and 100 million shares outstanding. Its ROE is 15%. Calculate the company's EPS.

LG2   **P8.4**   Goodstuff Corporation has total equity of $500 million and 100 million shares outstanding. Its ROE is 15%. The dividend payout ratio is 33.3%. Calculate the company's dividends per share (round to the nearest penny).

LG2   **P8.5**   HighTeck has an ROE of 15%. Its earnings per share are $2.00, and its dividends per share are $0.20. Estimate HighTeck's growth rate.

LG2   **P8.6**   Last year, InDebt Company paid $75 million of interest expense, and its average rate of interest for the year was 10%. The company's ROE is 15%, and it pays no dividends. Estimate next year's interest expense assuming that interest rates will fall by 25% and the company keeps a constant equity multiplier of 20.

LG2   **P8.7**   Melissa Popp is thinking about buying some shares of Education, Inc., at $50 per share. She expects the price of the stock to rise to $75 over the next three years. During that time she also expects to receive annual dividends of $5 per share.
a. What is the intrinsic worth of this stock, given a 10% required rate of return?
b. What is its expected return?

LG4   **P8.8**   Amalgamated Aircraft Parts, Inc., is expected to pay a dividend of $1.50 in the coming year. The required rate of return is 16%, and dividends are expected to grow at 7% per year. Using the dividend valuation model, find the intrinsic value of the company's common shares.

LG4   **P8.9**   Danny is considering a stock purchase. The stock pays constant annual dividend of $2.00 per share, and is currently trading at $20. Danny's required rate of return for this stock is 12%. Should he buy this stock?

LG4 LG5   **P8.10**   Larry, Moe, and Curley are brothers. They're all serious investors, but each has a different approach to valuing stocks. Larry, the oldest, likes to use a one-year holding period to value common shares. Moe, the middle brother, likes to use multiyear holding periods. Curley, the youngest of the three, prefers the dividend valuation model.

As it turns out, right now, all three of them are looking at the same stock—American Home Care Products, Inc. (AHCP). The company has been listed on the NYSE for over 50 years and is widely regarded as a mature, rock-solid, dividend-paying stock. The brothers have gathered the following information about AHCP's stock:

Current dividend (D_0) = $2.50/share
Expected growth rate (g) = 9.0%
Required rate of return (k) = 12.0%

All three of them agree that these variables are appropriate, and they will use them in valuing the stock. Larry and Moe intend to use the D&E approach; Curley is going to use the constant-growth DVM. Larry will use a one-year holding period; he estimates that with a 9% growth rate, the price of the stock will increase to $98.80 by the end of the year. Moe will use a three-year holding period; with the same 9% growth rate, he projects the future price of the stock will be $117.40 by the end of his investment horizon. Curley will use the constant-growth DVM, so his holding period isn't needed.
a. Use the information provided above to value the stocks first for Larry, then for Moe, then for Curley.
b. Comment on your findings. Which approach seems to make the most sense?

LG5 **P8.11** Assume you've generated the following information about the stock of Bufford's Burger Barns: The company's latest dividends of $4 a share are expected to grow to $4.32 next year, to $4.67 the year after that, and to $5.04 in year 3. In addition, the price of the stock is expected to rise from $56.50 (its current price) to $77.75 in three years.

a. Use the dividends-and-earnings model and a required return of 15% to find the value of the stock.

b. Use the IRR procedure to find the stock's expected return.

c. Given that dividends are expected to grow indefinitely at 8%, use a 15% required rate of return and the dividend valuation model to find the value of the stock.

d. Assume dividends in year 3 actually amount to $5.04, the dividend growth rate stays at 8%, and the required rate of return stays at 15%. Use the dividend valuation model to find the price of the stock at the end of year 3. [*Hint:* In this case, the value of the stock will depend on dividends in year 4, which equal $D_3 \times (1 + g)$.] Do you note any similarity between your answer here and the forecasted price of the stock ($77.75) given in the problem? Explain.

LG6 **P8.12** Let's assume that you're thinking about buying stock in West Coast Electronics. So far in your analysis, you've uncovered the following information: The stock pays annual dividends of $2.50 a share (and that's not expected to change within the next few years—*nor are any of the other variables*). It trades at a P/E of 18 times earnings and has a beta of 1.15. In addition, you plan on using a risk-free rate of 7% in the CAPM, along with a market return of 14%. You would like to hold the stock for three years, at the end of which time you think EPS will peak at about $7 a share. Given that the stock currently trades at $70, use the IRR approach to find this security's expected return. Now use the present-value (dividends-and-earnings) model to put a price on this stock. Does this look like a good investment to you? Explain.

LG6 **P8.13** The price of Consolidated Everything is now $75. The company pays no dividends. Ms. Bossard expects the price three years from now to be $100 per share. Should Ms. B. buy Consolidated E. if she desires a 10% rate of return? Explain.

LG5 **P8.14** This year, Shoreline Light and Gas (SL&G) paid its stockholders an annual dividend of $3 a share. A major brokerage firm recently put out a report on SL&G stating that, in its opinion, the company's annual dividends should grow at the rate of 10% per year for each of the next five years and then level off and grow at the rate of 6% a year thereafter.

a. Use the variable-growth DVM and a required rate of return of 12% to find the maximum price you should be willing to pay for this stock.

b. Redo the SL&G problem in part **a**, this time assuming that after year 5, dividends stop growing altogether (for year 6 and beyond, $g = 0$). Use all the other information given to find the stock's intrinsic value.

c. Contrast your two answers and comment on your findings. How important is growth to this valuation model?

LG5 **P8.15** Assume there are three companies that in the past year paid exactly the same annual dividend of $2.25 a share. In addition, the future annual rate of growth in dividends for each of the three companies has been estimated as follows:

Buggies-Are-Us	Steady Freddie, Inc.	Gang Buster Group	
$g = 0$	$g = 6\%$	Year 1	$2.53
(i.e., dividends	(for the	2	$2.85
are expected	foreseeable	3	$3.20
to remain at	future)	4	$3.60
$2.25/share)		Year 5 and beyond: $g = 6\%$	

Assume also that as the result of a strange set of circumstances, these three companies all have the same required rate of return ($k = 10\%$).

   a. Use the appropriate DVM to value each of these companies.

   b. Comment briefly on the comparative values of these three companies. What is the major cause of the differences among these three valuations?

LG6 **P8.16** New Millennium Company's stock sells at a P/E ratio of 21 times earnings. It is expected to pay dividends of $2 per share in each of the next five years and to generate an EPS of $5 in year 5. Using the dividends-and-earnings model and a 12% discount rate, compute the stock's justified price.

LG6 **P8.17** A particular company currently has sales of $250 million; sales are expected to grow by 20% next year (year 1). For the year after next (year 2), the growth rate in sales is expected to equal 10%. Over each of the next two years, the company is expected to have a net profit margin of 8% and a payout ratio of 50% and to maintain the common stock outstanding at 15 million shares. The stock always trades at a P/E of 15 times earnings, and the investor has a required rate of return of 20%. Given this information:

   a. Find the stock's intrinsic value (its justified price).

   b. Use the IRR approach to determine the stock's expected return, given that it is currently trading at $15 per share.

   c. Find the holding period returns for this stock for year 1 and for year 2.

LG3 LG5 **P8.18** Assume a major investment service has just given Oasis Electronics its highest investment rating, along with a strong buy recommendation. As a result, you decide to take a look for yourself and to place a value on the company's stock. Here's what you find: This year, Oasis paid its stockholders an annual dividend of $3 a share, but because of its high rate of growth in earnings, its dividends are expected to grow at the rate of 12% a year for the next four years and then to level out at 9% a year. So far, you've learned that the stock has a beta of 1.80, the risk-free rate of return is 6%, and the expected return on the market is 11%. Using the CAPM to find the required rate of return, put a value on this stock.

LG5 **P8.19** Consolidated Software doesn't currently pay any dividends but is expected to start doing so in four years. That is, Consolidated will go three more years without paying any dividends, and then is expected to pay its first dividend (of $3 per share) in the fourth year. Once the company starts paying dividends, it's expected to continue to do so. The company is expected to have a dividend payout ratio of 40% and to maintain a return on equity of 20%. Based on the DVM, and given a required rate of return of 15%, what is the maximum price you should be willing to pay for this stock today?

LG5 **P8.20** Assume you obtain the following information about a certain company:

Total assets	$50,000,000
Total equity	$25,000,000
Net income	$3,750,000
EPS	$5.00 per share
Dividend payout ratio	40%
Required return	12%

Use the constant-growth DVM to place a value on this company's stock.

LG6 **P8.21** You're thinking about buying some stock in Affiliated Computer Corporation and want to use the P/E approach to value the shares. You've estimated that next year's earnings should come in at about $4.00 a share. In addition, although the stock normally trades at a relative P/E of 1.15 times the market, you believe that the relative P/E will rise to 1.25, whereas the market

P/E should be around 18.5 times earnings. Given this information, what is the maximum price you should be willing to pay for this stock? If you buy this stock today at $87.50, what rate of return will you earn over the next 12 months if the price of the stock rises to $110.00 by the end of the year? (Assume that the stock doesn't pay any dividends.)

LG6 **P8.22** AviBank Plastics generated an EPS of $2.75 over the last 12 months. The company's earnings are expected to grow by 25% next year, and because there will be no significant change in the number of shares outstanding, EPS should grow at about the same rate. You feel the stock should trade at a P/E of around 30 times earnings. Use the P/E approach to set a value on this stock.

LG6 **P8.23** Newco is a young company that has yet to make a profit. You are trying to place a value on the stock, but it pays no dividends and you obviously cannot calculate a P/E ratio. As a result, you decide to look at other stocks in the same industry as Newco to see if you can find a way to value this company. You find the following information:

	Per-Share Data ($)			
	Newco	Adolescentco	Middle-Ageco	Oldco
Sales	10	200	800	800
Profit	−10	10	60	80
Book Value	−2	2	5	8
Market Value	?	20	80	75

Estimate a market value for Newco. Discuss how your estimate could change if Newco was expected to grow much faster than the other companies.

LG4 **P8.24** World Wide Web Wares (4W, for short) is an online retailer of small kitchen appliances and utensils. The firm has been around for a few years and has created a nice market niche for itself. In fact, it actually turned a profit last year, albeit a fairly small one. After doing some basic research on the company, you've decided to take a closer look. You plan to use the price/sales ratio to value the stock, and you have collected P/S multiples on the following Internet retailer stocks:

Company	P/S Multiples
Amazing.com	4.5
Really Cooking.com	4.1
Fixtures & Appliances Online	3.8

Find the *average P/S ratio* for these three firms. Given that 4W is expected to generate $40 million in sales next year, and will have 10 million shares of stock outstanding, use the average P/S ratio you computed above to put a value on 4W's stock.

Visit **www.myfinancelab.com** for web exercises, spreadsheets, and other online resources

Case Problem 8.1   *Chris Looks for a Way to Invest His Newfound Wealth*

LG1 **LG2** **LG4** Chris Norton is a young Hollywood writer who is well on his way to television superstardom. After writing several successful television specials, he was recently named the head writer for one of TV's top-rated sitcoms. Chris fully realizes that his business is a fickle one and, on the advice of his dad and manager, has decided to set up an investment program. Chris will earn about a half-million dollars this year. Because of his age, income level, and desire to get as big a bang as possible from his investment dollars, he has decided to invest in speculative, high-growth stocks.

Chris is currently working with a respected Beverly Hills broker and is in the process of building up a diversified portfolio of speculative stocks. The broker recently sent him information on a hot new issue. She advised Chris to study the numbers and, if he likes them, to buy as many as 1,000 shares of the stock. Among other things, corporate sales for the next three years have been forecasted as follows:

Year	Sales (in millions)
1	$22.5
2	35.0
3	50.0

The firm has 2.5 million shares of common stock outstanding. They are currently being traded at $70 a share and pay no dividends. The company has a net profit rate of 20%, and its stock has been trading at a P/E of around 40 times earnings. All these operating characteristics are expected to hold in the future.

Questions

a. Looking first at the stock:
1. Compute the company's net profits and EPS for each of the next three years.
2. Compute the price of the stock three years from now.
3. Assuming that all expectations hold up and that Chris buys the stock at $70, determine his expected return on this investment.
4. What risks is he facing by buying this stock? Be specific.
5. Should he consider the stock a worthwhile investment candidate? Explain.

b. Looking at Chris's investment program in general:
1. What do you think of his investment program? What do you see as its strengths and weaknesses?
2. Are there any suggestions you would make?
3. Do you think Chris should consider adding foreign stocks to his portfolio? Explain.

Case Problem 8.2   *An Analysis of a High-Flying Stock*

LG2 LG6 Marc Dodier is a recent university graduate and a security analyst with the Kansas City brokerage firm of Lippman, Brickbats, and Shaft. Dodier has been following one of the hottest issues on Wall Street, C&I Medical Supplies, a company that has turned in an outstanding performance lately and, even more important, has exhibited excellent growth potential. It has 5 million shares outstanding and pays a nominal annual dividend of 5 cents per share. Dodier has decided to take a closer look at C&I to see whether it still has any investment play left. Assume the company's sales for the past five years have been as follows:

Year	Sales (in millions)
2006	$10.0
2007	12.5
2008	16.2
2009	22.0
2010	28.5

Dodier is concerned with the future prospects of the company, not its past. As a result, he pores over the numbers and generates the following estimates of future performance:

Expected net profit margin	12%
Estimated annual dividends per share	5¢
Number of common shares outstanding	No change
P/E ratio at the end of 2011	35
P/E ratio at the end of 2012	50

Questions

a. Determine the average annual rate of growth in sales over the past five years. (Assume sales in 2005 amounted to $7.5 million.)
   1. Use this average growth rate to forecast revenues for next year (2011) and the year after that (2012).
   2. Now determine the company's net earnings and EPS for each of the next two years (2011 and 2012).
   3. Finally, determine the expected future price of the stock at the end of this two-year period.

b. Because of several intrinsic and market factors, Dodier feels that 25% is a viable figure to use for a desired rate of return.
   1. Using the 25% rate of return and the forecasted figures you came up with in question **a**, compute the stock's justified price.
   2. If C&I is currently trading at $32.50 per share, should Dodier consider the stock a worthwhile investment candidate? Explain.

Excel with Spreadsheets

Fundamental to the valuation process is the determination of the intrinsic value of a security, where an investor calculates the present value of the expected future cash benefits of the investment. Specifically, in the case of common stock, these future cash flows are defined by expected future dividend payments and future potential price appreciation. A simple but useful way to view stock value is that it is equal to the present value of all expected future dividends it may provide over an infinite time horizon.

Based on this latter concept, the dividend valuation model (DVM) has evolved. It can take on any one of three versions—the zero-growth model, the constant-growth model, and the variable-growth model.

Create a spreadsheet that applies the variable-growth model to predict the intrinsic value of the Rhyhorn Company common stock. Assume that dividends will grow at a variable rate for the next three years (2010, 2011, and 2012). After that, the annual rate of growth in dividends is expected to be 7% and stay there for the foreseeable future. Starting with the latest (2009) annual dividend of $2.00 per share, Rhyhorn's earnings and dividends are estimated to grow by 18% in 2010, by 14% in 2011, and by 9% in 2012 before dropping to a 7% rate. Given the risk profile of the firm, assume a minimum required rate of return of at least 12%. The spreadsheet for Table 8.4, which you can view on www.myfinance.lab.com, is a good reference for solving this problem.

Questions

a. Calculate the projected annual dividends over the years 2010, 2011, and 2012.
b. Determine the present value of dividends during the initial variable-growth period.

c. What do you believe the price of Rhyhorn stock will be at the end of the initial growth period (2012)?

d. Having determined the expected future price of Rhyhorn stock in part c, discount the price of the stock back to its present value.

e. Determine the total intrinsic value of Rhyhorn stock based on your calculations above.

Chapter-Opening Problem

At the beginning of this chapter you read about a 2009 earnings announcement from Winn-Dixie in which earnings per share were reported as $0.17 for the quarter. Let's make a simple assumption and say that earnings for the year were four times as much, or $0.68 per share. At the time of that announcement, the average P/E for stocks in the U.S. was close to 100.

a. If you use the market's P/E and Winn-Dixie's current earnings to estimate the stock's intrinsic value, what value do you obtain?

b. The actual price of Winn-Dixie after the earnings announcement was less than $15. What does this tell you about your answer to part a?

c. Suppose Winn-Dixie paid out all of its earnings as a dividend. Suppose also that investors expected the firm to continue doing that forever, and because the company was not reinvesting any earnings, investors expected no growth in dividends. If the required return on Winn-Dixie stock is 9%, what is the stock price?

d. Comment on your answer to part c in light of Winn-Dixie's market price at the time.

CHAPTER 9

Market Efficiency, Behavioral Finance, and Technical Analysis

LEARNING GOALS

After studying this chapter, you should be able to:

LG1 Describe the characteristics of an efficient market, explain what market anomalies are, and note some of the challenges that investors face when markets are efficient.

LG2 List four "decision traps" that may lead investors to make systematic errors in their investment decisions.

LG3 Explain how behavioral finance links market anomalies to investors' cognitive biases.

LG4 Discuss the purpose of technical analysis and explain why the performance of the market is important to stock valuation.

LG5 Describe some of the approaches to technical analysis, including, among others, the Dow theory, moving averages, charting, and various indicators of the technical condition of the market.

LG6 Compute and use technical trading rules for individual stocks and the market as a whole.

In the TV show *Who Wants to be a Millionaire?*, contestants answer a series of trivia questions for a $1 million prize. One wrong answer sends the contestant home empty-handed, but when contestants are unsure of the answer to a question, they may use one of several "lifelines." One lifeline permits a phone call to a friend for help. The success rate of these "phone a friend" calls has been about 65%.

That success rate pales in comparison to the 91% success rate achieved by another of the show's lifelines—a simple poll of the audience. The poll works because members of the audience who do not know the answer simply guess, spreading their answers randomly across the four possible choices. The responses of audience members who know the answer cluster on the correct choice, which causes the correct response to receive the greatest number of votes. Thus, it is a rare contestant who ignores the wisdom of the audience and survives in the game.

What does this have to do with investments? Estimating the value of a company's stock is more difficult than answering a trivia question. Many variables affect a stock's value, and relevant information about those variables becomes available to different investors at different times. Moreover, thousands of professional investors follow the stock market, ferreting out information to gain an advantage over other investors. According to a famous theory, known as the *efficient markets hypothesis*, the end result of all this analysis is that the market price is right, just as the audience poll tends to be right most of the time. The market price of a stock reflects everything that investors know about that security, and the collective information known to the market is greater than what any single investor can replicate. Thus, when an investor buys a stock, thinking that the market price doesn't reflect the stock's true value, it's equivalent to a contestant on *Who Wants to be a Millionaire?* rejecting the results of the audience poll. The evidence is clear that such a strategy succeeds a very small percentage of the time, and if markets are efficient, investors would be wise to think twice before betting that the market has overvalued or undervalued a particular stock.

(Source: James Surowiecki, *The Wisdom of Crowds*, www.randomhouse.com.)

Efficient Markets

LG1   If a drunk were abandoned in an open field at night, where would you begin to search for him the next morning? The answer, of course, is at the spot where he was left the night before, because there's no way to predict where he will go. To some analysts, stock prices seem to wander about in a similar fashion. Observations of such erratic movements have led to a body of evidence called the **random walk hypothesis**. Its followers believe that price movements are unpredictable and therefore security analysis will not help to predict future market behavior. Although random price movements might seem to be a sign of a market gone haywire, it is actually a natural consequence of a financial market operating with a high degree of efficiency.

An **efficient market** is one in which security prices fully reflect all available information. This concept holds that investors quickly incorporate all available information into their opinions about what a particular stock is worth. Because different investors have access to different information, some will view the stock as being overvalued, and others will see it as undervalued. Stock prices move in response to investors' shifting views, which in turn are influenced by the arrival of new information. But by definition, *new information* is information that investors did not previously have and could not anticipate. In other words, because prices respond to new information, and new information is itself unpredictable, stock prices will move in a seemingly random fashion as well.

An example may help cement these ideas. Toy retailers have highly seasonal sales patterns, with most of their sales, and hence most of their profits, coming during the Christmas season. Every year in their quarterly reports, these firms show huge jumps in sales and earnings in the fourth quarter of the year. Do the stock prices of these firms behave in the same way, rising in the fourth quarter when sales peak? The answer is no, because investors have witnessed the seasonal patterns in the past, so they know to anticipate fourth-quarter jumps in sales and profits.

Efficient markets advocates take this argument further by arguing that even if stock prices *did* exhibit recurring patterns, those patterns couldn't last for long. Suppose, for example, the toy stocks increased every year around Christmas. Investors anticipating a Christmas price runup would buy the stock a few weeks before Christmas, hoping to earn unusually high short-term returns. But the surge in demand for shares ahead of Christmas would cause the price to increase earlier than it had in past years, and the seasonal pattern would be gone.

When financial experts say that stock prices follow a random walk, they mean that no matter what patterns seem to appear when we examine the behavior of past stock patterns, prices move essentially at random. The important implication of this theory is that trying to predict the future direction of a stock's price based on how that stock has performed in the past is futile. Investors who try to spot recurring trends in the stock market and use those trends to decide when to buy and sell are not likely to consistently outperform investors who adopt a more passive, buy and hold approach—at least that's the theory.

Levels of Market Efficiency

The **efficient markets hypothesis (EMH)** is concerned with *information*—not only the type and source of information, but also the quality and speed with which it is disseminated among investors and reflected in asset prices. The more information that is incorporated into stock prices, the more efficient the market becomes. One way of characterizing the extent to which markets are efficient is to define different levels of efficiency corresponding to different types of information that prices may reflect. These levels of market efficiency are known as the weak form, the semi-strong form, and the strong form.

Weak Form   The **weak form of the EMH** holds stock prices fully reflect any relevant information that can be obtained from an analysis of past price movements. Go back to the example of the toy retailer stock. If toy stocks exhibited seasonal patterns in the past, traders would learn about them, begin to trade ahead of them, and thereby eliminate them. In short, the weak form of the EMH says that past data on stock prices are of no use in predicting future price changes. If prices follow a random walk, then price changes over time are random. Tomorrow's price change is unrelated to today's, yesterday's, or to that of any other day.

The earliest research on the weak form of market efficiency appeared to confirm the prediction that prices moved at random. Using databases that contained the past prices of listed stocks in the United States, researchers constructed a variety of "trading rules," such as buying a stock when it hit a 52-week low, and then tested these rules using historical information to see what returns investors following these rules might have earned. The results were encouraging to theorists, but not to traders—none of the trading rules earned better returns than investors could earn by purchasing a diversified portfolio and holding it.

Semi-Strong Form   The **semi-strong form of the EMH** asserts that stock prices fully reflect all relevant information that investors can obtain from public sources. This means that investors cannot consistently earn abnormally high returns using publicly available information such as annual reports and other required filings, analyst recommendations, product reviews, and so on. To illustrate the idea, suppose that you see that a particular firm has just posted its latest financial results online. You read the report and see that the company reported an unexpected surge in profits in the most recent quarter. Should you call your broker and buy some shares? The semi-strong form of the EMH says that by the time you download the annual report, read it, and call your broker, the market price of the stock will have already increased, reflecting the company's latest good news.

Many tests of semi-strong efficiency have examined how stock prices respond before and after particular types of corporate announcements. A famous study involved stock splits. A stock split does not change the value of a company, so the value of the stock should not be affected by a stock split. The research indicated that there are sharp increases in the price of a stock *before* a stock split, but the changes after the split are random. Investors, therefore, cannot gain by purchasing stocks on or after the announcement of a split. To earn abnormal profits they would have to purchase before the split is announced, but then again, how would investors know that a split announcement is coming? Almost as soon as the announcement is made public, the market has already incorporated into the price any favorable information associated with the split.

Other research has examined the effects of major events on stock prices. One study looked at four companies who were major contractors in the space shuttle program. When the shuttle *Challenger* exploded shortly after liftoff in 1986, the stock prices of all four companies fell, but the one that fell the most was Morton Thiokol. That company made the booster rockets that lifted the shuttle into orbit, and months after the accident occurred, an investigation concluded that it was a problem with the O-rings in these rockets that caused the accident. In other words, the market's initial reaction within minutes of the accident seemed to point to the same conclusion as the subsequent investigation.

The overwhelming evidence indicates that stock prices react within minutes, if not seconds, to any important new information. Certainly, by the time an investor reads about the event in the newspaper, the stock price has almost completely adjusted to the news. Even hearing about the event on the radio or television usually allows too little time to complete the transaction in time to make an abnormal profit.

Strong Form The **strong form of the EMH** holds that there is no information, public or private, that allows investors to consistently earn abnormal returns. It states that stock prices rapidly adjust to any information, even if it isn't available to every investor.

One type of private information is the kind obtained by corporate insiders, such as officers or directors of a corporation. They have access to valuable information about major strategic and tactical decisions the company makes. They also have detailed information about the financial state of the firm that may not be available to other shareholders. Insiders are generally prohibited from trading the shares of their employer prior to major news releases. However, at other times corporate insiders may legally trade shares of stock in their company, if they report the transactions to the Securities and Exchange Commission (SEC). When insiders file the required forms with the SEC, they are quickly made available to the public via the Internet. Most studies of corporate insiders find that their trades are particularly well timed, meaning that they tend to buy before significant price increases and sell prior to big declines. This, of course, is contrary to what you'd expect to find if the strong form of the EMH were true.

Insiders and other market participants occasionally have inside—nonpublic—information that they obtained or traded on *illegally*. With this information, they can gain an unfair advantage that permits them to earn an excess return. Clearly, those who violate the law when they trade have an unfair advantage. Empirical research has confirmed that those with such inside information do indeed have an opportunity to earn an excess return—but there might be an awfully high price attached, such as spending time in prison, if they're caught.

Market Anomalies

Despite considerable evidence in support of the EMH, researchers have uncovered some patterns that seem inconsistent with the theory. Collectively, this body of puzzling evidence is known as **market anomalies**, a name that itself suggests that there is less evidence contradicting the EMH than there is in support of it. What all of these anomalies have in common is that they reveal patterns or trading strategies that, at least in hindsight, earned higher returns than would be expected in efficient markets.

Calendar Effects One widely cited anomaly is the so-called *calendar effect,* which holds that stock returns may be closely tied to the time of the year or the time of the week. That is, certain months or days of the week may produce better investment results than others. The most famous of the calendar anomalies is the *January effect,* which is a documented tendency for small-

---

INVESTOR FACTS

IT'S HARD TO BEAT THE MARKET—That's pretty much the message that the EMH has for investors. As such, trading in and out of securities wouldn't seem to make much sense. And that's exactly what was found in a recent study of over 66,000 investors, grouped according to annual portfolio turnover (how much of the portfolio the investor replaces each year). Buy-and-hold investors, with turnovers of less than 2% a year, earned annual returns of 18.5%. On the other end of the spectrum, the most active traders, with 258% portfolio turnover, averaged only 11.4% per year, a full 7 percentage points less than the more conservative, buy-and-hold investors.

cap stocks to outperform large-cap stocks by an unusually wide margin in the month of January. One possible explanation for this pattern has to do with taxes. Under certain conditions, investors can deduct investment losses when calculating their federal income taxes. Thus, there is an incentive for investors to sell stocks that have gone down in value during the year, and investors who recognize that incentive are particularly likely to sell in December as the tax year comes to a close. Think about what happens to the market capitalization of a firm when its stock falls during the year—the market cap gets smaller. Thus, if investors have a tax incentive to sell their loser stocks in December, and if these stocks by definition tend to be smaller than average, then their prices may be temporarily depressed due to December tax selling, and they may rebound in January. As plausible as this explanation may sound, there is at best mixed evidence that it can account for the puzzling behavior of small stocks in January.

Small-Firm Effect Another anomaly is the *small-firm effect*, or size effect, which states that the size of the firm has a bearing on the level of stock returns. Indeed, several studies have shown that small firms (or small-cap stocks) earn higher returns than large-cap stocks (and not just in January), even after taking into account the higher betas typical of most small firms. This tendency has been documented in the United States as well as in many other stock markets around the world.

Post Earnings Announcement Drift (or Momentum) Another market anomaly has to do with how stock prices react to *earnings announcements*. Obviously, earnings announcements contain important information that should, and does, affect stock prices. However, much of the information has already been anticipated by the market, and so—if EMH is correct—prices should only react to the "surprise" portion of the announcement. Studies have shown that stock prices do increase (decrease) quickly when an earnings announcement is surprisingly good (bad), but prices tend to "drift" in the same direction for many weeks after the announcement. That is, when a firm has an especially good quarterly earnings report, its stock shoots up immediately, but it keeps drifting up for many weeks. This seems to indicate that investors underreact to the information in the announcement—they don't realize just how good the good news is!

A slight variation on this story is known as the momentum anomaly. In physics, momentum refers to the tendency of an object in motion to continue moving or the tendency of an object at rest to remain at rest. Applied to stocks, momentum refers to the tendency for stocks that have gone up recently to keep going up, or the tendency for stocks that have gone down recently to continue going down. The connection to earnings announcement drift is easy to see. When a company has a particularly good quarter, it is common for some of the good news to leak out into the market prior to the official earnings announcement. So leading up to the earnings release, it is common to see the stock price moving up. As we've already discussed, when the firm releases the news that it has had a very strong quarter, the price goes up more, but then it continues to drift up for weeks. Taking the entire pattern into account, we observe that before a company releases very good earnings news, its stock price has gone up, and then it keeps going up after the earnings announcement. Hence, these stocks display positive momentum. The same thing happens in reverse for companies that have particularly bad quarters. Some of the bad news leaks out early, and the stock goes down, but then the stock continues to go down after the announcement.

The Value Effect According to the *value effect*, the best way to make money in the market is to buy stocks that have relatively low prices relative to some measure of fundamental value such as book value or earnings. An investor following a value strategy might calculate the P/E ratio or the ratio of market value to book value for many stocks, then buy the stocks with the lowest ratios (and perhaps short-sell the stocks with high P/E or market/book ratios). Studies have shown that, on average, value stocks outperform stocks with high P/E or market/book ratios (so-called growth stocks). This pattern has repeated itself decade after decade in the United States and in most stock markets around the world.

Possible Explanations

Each new discovery of an anomaly that appears to violate the EMH prompts a flurry of research that offers rational explanations for the pattern observed. The most common explanation for market anomalies is that the stocks that earn abnormally high returns are simply riskier than other stocks, so the higher returns on these stocks reflect a risk premium rather than mispricing by the market. For example, most academics and practitioners would agree that small firms are riskier than large firms, so it is not surprising that small stocks earn higher returns. The real question is, how much riskier are small firms, and how large should the risk premium be on those securities? According to the CAPM, if a small stock has a beta of 2.0 and a large stock has a beta of 1.0, the small stock should earn roughly twice the risk premium (over Treasury bills) that the large stock earns. The reason that the small firm effect is known as an anomaly is that small stocks seemed to earn higher returns than their betas can justify. Believers in the EMH argue that beta is an imperfect measure of risk and that if a better risk measure were available, the difference in returns between small and large stocks could be fully attributed to differences in risk.

Another explanation for market anomalies is that even in an efficient market where prices move essentially at random, some trading rules may appear to earn abnormally high returns simply as a matter of chance. For example, one of the more amusing market anomalies is known as the Super Bowl anomaly. This anomaly says that if the team winning the Super Bowl in a particular year is one of the original National Football League teams (prior to the merger with the old American Football League), then the stock market will rise. Otherwise, the stock market will fall. This "trading rule" correctly predicted the direction of the market more than 80% of the time in the last 40 years. But should investors rely on it in the future? Most people would agree that the connection between the Super Bowl winner and the stock market is purely a matter of chance and is unlikely to exhibit a similar track record in the next 40 years. Some EMH advocates believe that most market anomalies are similarly just an artifact of random chance. However, this explanation is less persuasive in the face of evidence that anomalies such as the small firm effect and the value effect appear in most markets around the world.

The discovery of these and other anomalies led to the development of an entirely new way of viewing the workings of financial markets that has come to be known as **behavioral finance.** In contrast to traditional finance, which starts with the assumption that investors, managers, and other actors in financial markets are rational, behavioral finance posits that market participants make systematic mistakes, and that those mistakes are inextricably linked to cognitive biases that are hard-wired into human nature. We now turn to a discussion of the basic tenets of behavioral finance and how they may help explain market anomalies.

**CONCEPTS
IN REVIEW**
Answers available at
www.pearsonhighered.com/
gitman

9.1 What is the *random walk hypothesis*, and how does it apply to stocks? What is an *efficient market*? How can a market be efficient if its prices behave in a random fashion?

9.2 Explain why it is difficult, if not impossible, to consistently outperform an efficient market.

a. Does this mean that high rates of return are not available in the stock market?
b. How can an investor earn a high rate of return in an efficient market?

9.3 What are *market anomalies* and how do they come about? Do they support or refute the EMH? Briefly describe each of the following:

a. The January effect.
b. The size effect.
c. The value effect.

Behavioral Finance: A Challenge to the Efficient Markets Hypothesis

LG2 LG3 For more than 30 years, the efficient markets hypothesis (EMH) has been an influential force in financial markets. The notion that asset prices fully reflect all available information is supported by a large body of academic research. In practitioner circles, supporters of market efficiency include John Bogle of Vanguard, who helped pioneer the development of a special type of mutual fund known as an *index* fund. Managers of index funds don't try to pick individual stocks or bonds, because they assume that the market is efficient. They recognize that any time and energy spent researching individual securities will merely serve to increase the fund's expenses, which will drag down investors' returns.

Although considerable evidence supports the concept of market efficiency, an increasing number of academic studies have begun to cast doubt on the EMH. This research documents various anomalies and draws from research on cognitive psychology to offer explanations for the anomalies. One notable event that acknowledged the importance of this field was the awarding of the 2002 Nobel Prize in economics to Daniel Kahneman, whose work integrated insights from psychology and economics. In addition to academic studies, some professional money managers are also incorporating concepts from behavioral finance into their construction and management of portfolios.

Investor Behavior and Security Prices

Researchers in behavioral finance believe that investors' decisions are affected by a number of psychological biases that lead investors to make systematic, predictable mistakes in certain decision-making situations. These mistakes, in turn, may lead to predictable patterns in asset prices that create opportunities for other investors to earn abnormally high profits without accepting abnormally high risk. Let's now take a look at some of the behavioral factors that might influence the actions of investors.

Overconfidence and Self-Attribution Bias Research in psychology provides overwhelming evidence that, on average, people tend to exhibit *overconfidence*, putting too much faith in their own ability to perform complex tasks. Try this experiment. The next time you are in a large group, ask people to indicate whether they believe they have above average, average, or below average skill in driving a car. What you will probably find is that a majority of the group believes that they have above-average ability, and almost no one will lay claim to having below-average skill. But simply by the definition of average, some people have to be above average and some must be below average.

Closely linked to overconfidence is a phenomenon known as *self-attribution bias*. Self-attribution bias roughly means that when something good happens, individuals attribute that to actions that they have taken, but when something bad happens, they attribute it to bad luck or external factors beyond their control. The connection to overconfidence is straightforward. An individual takes an action or makes a decision that leads to a favorable outcome. Self-attribution bias causes the individual to discount the role that chance may have played in determining the outcome and to put too much emphasis on his or her actions as the cause. This causes the individual to become overconfident.

What effects do overconfidence and self-attribution bias have in the investments realm? Consider an individual investor, or even a professional money manager, who analyzes stocks to determine which ones are over value and which are bargains. Suppose in a particular year the investor's portfolio earns very high returns. Perhaps the high returns are largely due to a booming stock market, but perhaps in addition the investor's stock picks performed even better than the overall market. Is this the result of good fortune or good analysis? It would take many years to be sure, but most investors would probably attribute the favorable outcome to their own investing prowess. What is the consequence if investors mistakenly attribute investment success to their own skill? One study found that investors whose portfolios had outperformed the market in the past subsequently increased their trading activity. After beating the overall market average by 2% per year for several years, these investors increased their trading activity more than 70%. The increase in trading led to much higher transactions costs and much lower returns. The same group of investors trailed the market by 3% per year after increasing their trading activity.

This tendency is not confined to individual investors. A recent study found that CEOs exhibit similar behavior when they undertake acquisitions of other firms. When a CEO acquires another firm and the acquisition target performs well, the CEO is more likely to acquire another firm. The CEO is also more likely to buy more shares in his or her employer's stock prior to the next acquisition. But these second acquisitions actually destroy shareholder value on average. In other words, it appears that CEOs become overconfident regarding their ability to acquire other firms and run them profitably.

Loss Aversion Here's an interesting series of questions. Suppose you have just won $8,500 in a game of chance. You can walk away with your winnings, or you can risk them. If you take the risk, there is a 90% chance that you will win an addition $1,500, but there is a 10% chance that you will lose everything. Would you walk away or gamble? Most people who are asked this question say that they would take the $8,500—the sure thing. They say this even though the expected value from the additional gamble is $500. That is,

$$\text{Expected value} = (\text{Probability of gain}) \times (\text{Amount of gain}) - (\text{Probability of loss}) \times (\text{Amount of loss}) = 0.90 \times \$1,500 - 0.10 \times \$8,500 = \underline{\underline{\$500}}$$

MARKETS IN CRISIS

Loss Aversion and Trading Volume

When people are *loss averse*, they are reluctant to sell investments that have lost value because doing so forces them to realize the loss. But if investors are reluctant to sell when prices are falling, trading activity can dry up. That was a finding from a recent study of residential real estate activity over several market cycles in Boston. Researchers found that when market prices were rising, homeowners were generally willing to sell their properties at market value. But when price declines left homeowners in a position such that the market value of their home was less than what they paid for it, homeowners exhibited a tendency to set asking prices above the true market value. As a consequence, homes sat on the market month after month, with very few transactions taking place.

In this case, the decision to take the $8,500 indicates that the individual making that choice is risk averse. The risk of losing $8,500 isn't worth the expected $500 gain.

However, if we reframe the question, most people respond differently. Suppose you have already lost $8,500 in a game of chance. You can walk away and cut your losses, or you can gamble again. If you gamble, there is a 90% chance that you will lose $1,500, but there is a 10% chance that you will win $8,500, thus entirely reversing your initial loss. When confronted with this choice, most people say that they will take the risk to try to "get even," even though the expected value of this gamble is –$500. In this case, people are exhibiting risk-seeking behavior. They are accepting a risk that they do not have to take, and it is a risk that has a negative expected return.

In behavioral finance, the tendency to exhibit risk-averse behavior when confronting gains and risk-seeking behavior when confronting losses is called **loss aversion**. Loss aversion simply means that people feel the pain of loss more acutely than the pleasure of gain. In an investments context, loss aversion can lead people to hold onto investments that have lost money longer than they should.

Representativeness

Overreaction In an interesting experiment, six people were asked to flip a coin 20 times and count the number of heads that came up. Another group of six was asked to imagine flipping a coin 20 times and write down the sequence of heads and tails that might occur. The table below shows the results reported by each group.

Group	Subject	Number of Heads	Group	Subject	Number of Heads
A	1	10	B	1	6
	2	10		2	13
	3	8		3	7
	4	10		4	11
	5	10		5	8
	6	10		6	14

Looking at the responses from individuals in each group, which group do you think actually flipped coins, and which imagined doing so?

The answer is that Group A only imagined flipping coins. Notice that almost everyone in the group said they expected to obtain 10 heads in 20 flips, but in the group that actually tossed the coins, the number of heads varied widely, from 6 to 14. What accounts for the differences between the two groups?

Representativeness refers to cognitive biases that occur because people have difficulty thinking about randomness in outcomes. Subjects in Group A assume (correctly) that the probability of obtaining a heads on any single flip of a coin is 50%, but they also assume (incorrectly) that this means that in 20 flips of a coin, it is very likely that heads will come up exactly 10 times. In other words, when people know the probability of a particular event occurring, they assume that a series of events will mirror that probability. As the results of Group B's coin flips clearly show, it is rather unusual to obtain exactly 10 heads in 20 flips. Lots of other outcomes are quite likely.

A similar problem occurs when people do not know whether or to what extent randomness influences the outcomes of a series of events. That is, when people observe what appears to be a systematic pattern in a series of numbers or outcomes, they underestimate the likelihood that such a pattern might be the outcome of random chance, and they overestimate the likelihood that some underlying force will cause the pattern to repeat. In other words, they overreact to a series of similar events. For example, suppose a particular mutual fund outperforms the S&P500 index three years in a row. According to the EMH, earning above-average returns is more a matter of luck than of skill, so any particular investor (individual or professional) has roughly a 50% chance of beating the market in a particular year. With so many mutual funds available, it would hardly be surprising to see some of these beat the market three years in a row, even if doing so is purely due to good luck as the EMH would suggest. In fact, there is a great deal of evidence indicating that most professional mutual fund managers fail to outperform the market average over long periods.

Even so, what do you think happens when one fund does well for three consecutive years? Research shows that investors overreact and pour money into successful funds, enriching the fund managers, but not necessarily the fund investors. Apparently, many investors see a string of good performance and overestimate the likelihood that the trend will continue. Investors overreact to the past performance of funds, even though there is little objective evidence that past performance is a good predictor of future success.

This logic may provide a behavioral explanation for the value phenomenon cited earlier. Recall that value stocks are stocks that have low prices relative to earnings or book value. These stocks generally display rather poor past performance—several years of declining prices is what puts these stocks in the value category. Similarly, growth stocks, firms with high prices relative to earnings or book value, generally have very good past performance. One of the earliest studies of the value effect studied the results of a very simple trading rule. Each year, researchers sorted all stocks based on their cumulative performance in the previous three years. The trading rule was to buy the stocks that had performed worst (the value stocks) and sell short the stocks that had performed best (the growth stocks). Researchers discovered that this strategy earned returns that beat the market by 8% per year! Why would such a simple trading rule that anyone could follow work so well?

The researchers argued that it was due to representativeness. To be specific, they proposed that investors who watched particular stocks decline in value for three years in a row eventually decided that the trend would continue indefinitely, so they bid the prices of these stocks below their true values. Similarly, after watching other stocks do very well several years in a row, investors naively assumed that this excellent performance would continue, and they bid up the prices of these stocks above their true values. Over time, the firms that had been performing poorly surprised investors by rebounding, and the firms that had been earning spectacular returns failed to sustain that performance. As a result, past price trends reversed themselves, and value investors made money.

As before, individual investors are not the only participants in markets likely to be affected by representativeness. Consider a firm that is looking to make an acquisition. What makes an acquisition target attractive? One criterion might be a firm with recent increases in sales and earnings. Would acquirers be wise to pay a premium to acquire a firm that has been growing faster than its competitors in recent years? The research evidence says no. There is almost no correlation between how fast firms have grown in the past and how fast they will grow in the future. In fact, that is a fundamental prediction of basic economic theory. When one firm enjoys great success in a particular market, other firms will enter the industry. Competition makes it more difficult for firms to sustain the high growth that attracted new entrants in the first place. Yet there is ample evidence that managers do pay a larger premium when they acquire firms that experienced rapid growth prior to the acquisition, even though the prospect of sustaining the growth is low.

Underreaction In certain instances, representativeness can cause investors to *underreact* to new information. Consider this problem from statistics. On a table are 100 sacks, each of which contains 1,000 poker chips. Forty-five of these sacks contain 70% black chips and 30% red chips. The other 55 bags hold 70% red chips and 30% black chips. If you pick one bag at random, what is the likelihood that it will contain mostly black chips?

Most people get this answer right. If 45 out of 100 bags contain mostly black chips, then the probability of picking a bag at random that has mostly black chips is 45%. Here is a much harder problem. Suppose you choose one bag at random and then take out 12 chips, without looking at the others. Of the 12 chips that you pull out, 8 are black and 4 are red. What is the probability that the bag you picked contains mostly black chips?

Intuitively, people know that if the sample of 12 chips taken from the bag has a majority of black chips, then that means the probability that the bag has mostly black chips is higher than in the first problem where we simply select a bag at random. But how much higher? Few people come close to guessing that the probability is over 95%! In other words, people tend to underreact to the new information they obtain in the second version of the question.

Let's make an analogy between drawing poker chips out of a bag and reading firms' earnings announcements. Earnings announcements contain a mix of good and bad news that varies over time. When a company announces particularly good (or bad) news, representativeness may cause investors to underreact to the new information. That is, investors may not appreciate that good earnings news this quarter probably means the likelihood of good news next quarter has gone up (and vice versa for bad news this quarter). That could explain the post-earnings announcement drift (or momentum) phenomenon discussed earlier.

A careful reader may object that we have asserted that representativeness can lead to both overreaction (in the case of value stocks) and underreaction (in the case of momentum). Keep in mind that there are important differences in the nature of the information that investors are reacting to in each case. In the value phenomenon, investors see a common string of information—several good years or several bad years in a row. This causes them to discount the role of chance in the outcome and overreact to the series of events. In the case of earning announcement drift, investors are responding to a single new piece of information that is extreme—particularly good or particularly bad. In that case, representativeness may lead investors to underreact to the new information they've received.

Narrow Framing Many people tend to analyze a situation in isolation, while ignoring the larger context. This behavior is called *narrow framing*. A common example in investments relates to the asset allocation decisions that investors make in their retirement plans. Consider Firm A that offers its employees two options for investing retirement savings—a stock fund and a bond fund. Firm B also offer two options—a stock fund and a blended fund that holds 50% stocks and 50% bonds. Research shows that most investors view this decision through the narrow frame of two choices, and they follow a simple guideline—put 50% into one fund and 50% into the other. But the narrow frame combined with the guideline produces an odd outcome. Employees of Firm A will follow an asset allocation of 50% stocks and 50% bonds, while employees of Firm B, simply by putting half of their money into each fund, will wind up with 75% of their money in stocks and 25% in bonds.

Belief Perseverance People typically ignore information that conflicts with their existing beliefs. If they believe a stock is good and purchase it, for example, they later tend to discount any signals of trouble. In many cases, they even avoid gathering new information, for fear it will contradict their initial opinion. It would be better to view each stock owned as a "new" stock when periodically reviewing a portfolio and to ask whether the information available at that time would cause you to buy or sell the stock.

Implications of Behavioral Finance for Security Analysis

Our discussion of the psychological factors that affect financial decisions suggests that behavioral finance can play an important role in investing. Naturally, the debate on the efficiency of markets rages on and will continue to do so for many years. The contribution of behavioral finance is to identify particular psychological factors that can lead investors to make systematic mistakes, and those mistakes may contribute to predictable patterns in stock prices. If that's the case, the mistakes of some investors may be the profit opportunities for others. See Table 9.1 for our advice on how to keep

---

TABLE 9.1   Using Behavioral Finance to Improve Investment Results

Studies have documented a number of behavioral factors that appear to influence investors' decisions and adversely affect their returns. By following some simple guidelines, you can avoid making mistakes and improve your portfolio's performance. A little common sense goes a long way in the financial markets!

- **Don't hesitate to sell a losing stock.** If you buy a stock at $20 and its price drops to $10, ask yourself whether you would buy that same stock if you came into the market today with $10 in cash. If the answer is yes, then hang onto it. If not, sell the stock and buy something else.

- **Don't chase performance.** The evidence suggests that there are no "hot hands" in investment management. Don't buy last year's hottest mutual fund if it doesn't make sense for you. Always keep your personal investment objectives and constraints in mind.

- **Be humble and open-minded.** Many investment professionals, some of whom are extremely well paid, are frequently wrong in their predictions. Admit your mistakes and don't be afraid to take corrective action. The fact is, reviewing your mistakes can be a very rewarding exercise—all investors make mistakes, but the smart ones learn from them. Winning in the market is often about not losing, and one way to avoid loss is to learn from your mistakes.

- **Review the performance of your investments on a periodic basis.** Remember the old saying, "Out of sight, out of mind." Don't be afraid to face the music and to make changes as your situation changes. Nothing runs on "autopilot" forever—including investment portfolios.

- **Don't trade too much.** Investment returns are uncertain, but transaction costs are guaranteed. Considerable evidence indicates that investors who trade frequently perform poorly.

your own mistakes to a minimum. In the next section we will examine technical analysis, the art and science of examining past price movements to make future investment decisions.

<table>
<tr>
<td>

CONCEPTS IN REVIEW

Answers available at
www.pearsonhighered.com/
gitman

</td>
<td>

9.4

9.5

</td>
<td>

How can behavioral finance have any bearing on investor returns? Do supporters of behavioral finance believe in efficient markets? Explain.

Briefly explain how behavioral finance can affect each of the following:

a. The trading activity of investors.
b. The tendency of value stocks to outperform growth stocks.
c. The tendency of stock prices to drift up (down) after unusually good (bad) earnings news.

</td>
</tr>
</table>

Technical Analysis

LG4 LG5 LG6   Analyzing the various forces at work in the market is known as **technical analysis**. For some investors, it's another piece of information to use when deciding whether to buy, hold, or sell a stock. For others, it's the *only* input they use in their investment decisions. Still others regard both technical analysis and fundamental analysis as a waste of time.

Analyzing market behavior dates back to the 1800s, when there was no such thing as industry or company analysis. Detailed financial information about individual companies simply was not made available to stockholders, let alone the general public. About the only thing investors could study was the market itself. Some investors used detailed charts to monitor what large market operators were doing. These charts were intended to show when major buyers were moving into or out of particular stocks and to provide information useful for profitable buy-and-sell decisions. The charts centered on stock price movements. These movements were said to produce certain "formations," indicating when the time was right to buy or sell a particular stock. The same principle is still applied today: Technical analysts argue that internal market factors, such as trading volume and price movements, often reveal the market's future direction long before it is evident in financial statistics.

Using Technical Analysis

Investors have a wide range of choices with respect to technical analysis. They can use the charts and complex ratios of the technical analysts. Or they can, more informally, use technical analysis just to get a general sense of the market. In the latter case, market behavior itself is not as important as the implications such behavior can have for the price performance of a particular stock. Thus, investors can use technical analysis in conjunction with fundamental analysis to determine when to add a particular stock to one's portfolio. Some investors and professional money managers, in fact, look at the technical side of a stock *before* doing any fundamental analysis. If they find the stock to be technically sound, then they'll look at its fundamentals; if not, they'll look for another stock. For these investors, the concerns of technical analysis are still the same: *Do the technical factors indicate that this might be a good stock to buy?*

Most investors rely on published sources, such as those put out by brokerage firms—or now widely available on the Internet—to obtain technical insights. Such information provides investors with a convenient and low-cost way of staying abreast of the market. Certainly, trying to determine the right (or best) time to get into the market is a principal objective of technical analysis—and one of the major pastimes of many investors.

Measuring the Market

If assessing the market is a worthwhile endeavor, then we need some sort of tool or measure to do it. Charts are popular with many investors because they provide a visual summary of the behavior of the market and the price movements of individual stocks. (We'll examine charting in more detail later in this chapter.) As an alternative or supplement to *charting*, some investors prefer to study various *market statistics*. They might look at the market as a whole, or track certain technical conditions that exist within the market itself, such as the volume of trading, the amount of short selling, or the buy/sell patterns of small investors (i.e., odd-lot transactions).

Let's now examine some of these approaches to technical analysis. Later, we'll look at some ratios and formulas that investors can use to measure—that is, quantify—various technical conditions in the market. One thing to keep in mind as you work your way through this material is that, whether the measures appear rational or not, many of them (like breadth of the market, or charting) involve a good deal of judgment and intuition. Thus, they rely heavily on the market expertise of the analysts.

The Big Picture

Technical analysis addresses those factors in the marketplace that can (or may) have an effect on the price movements of stocks in general. The idea is to get a handle on the general condition (or "tone") of the market, and to gain some insights into where the market may be headed over the next few months. One way to do that is to look at *the overall behavior of the market*. Several approaches try to do just that, including (1) the Dow theory, (2) trading actions, and (3) the confidence index.

The Dow Theory The **Dow theory** is based on the idea that the market's performance can be described by the long-term price trend in the overall market. Named after Charles H. Dow, one of the founders of Dow Jones, this approach is supposed to signal the end of both bull and bear markets. The theory does not indicate *when* a reversal will occur; rather, it is strictly an after-the-fact verification of what has already happened. It concentrates on the long-term trend in market behavior (known as the *primary trend*) and largely ignores day-to-day fluctuations or secondary movements.

The Dow theory uses the Dow Jones industrial *and* transportation averages to assess the position of the market. Once a primary trend in the Dow Jones industrial average has been established, the market tends to move in that direction until the trend is canceled out by *both* the industrial and transportation averages. Known as *confirmation*, this crucial part of the Dow theory occurs when secondary movements in the industrial average are confirmed by secondary movements in the transportation average. When confirmation occurs, the market has changed from bull to bear, or vice versa, and a new primary trend is established. Figure 9.1 captures the key elements of the Dow theory. Observe that in this case, the bull market comes to an end at the

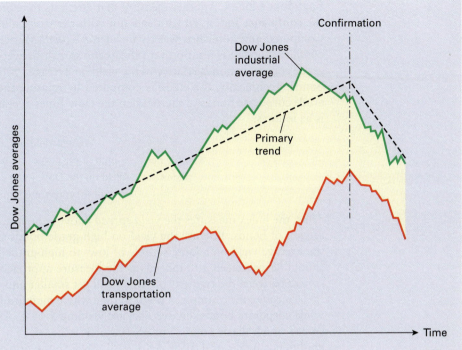

FIGURE 9.1

The Dow Theory in Operation

Secondary movements (the sharp, short fluctuations in the Dow Jones industrial and transportation lines) are largely unimportant to the Dow theory. What is of key importance, however, is the primary trend in the DJIA, which is seen to remain on the upswing until a reversal is confirmed by the transportation average.

point of confirmation—when *both* the industrial and transportation averages are dropping.

The biggest drawback of the Dow theory is that it is an after-the-fact measure with *no* predictive power. Also, the investor really does not know at any given point whether an existing primary trend has a long way to go or is just about to end.

Trading Action This approach to technical analysis concentrates on minor trading characteristics in the market. Daily trading activity over long periods of time (sometimes as long as 50 years or more) is examined to determine whether certain characteristics occur with a high degree of frequency. Although the empirical results generated from these studies are in many cases due to little more than statistical aberrations, analysts nonetheless use them to form a series of trading rules. Here are a few examples:

- If the year starts out strong (that is, if January is a good month for the market), the chances are that the whole year will be good.

- If the party in power wins the presidential election, it is also going to be a good year for the market.

- It is best to buy air conditioning stocks in October and sell the following March. (This buy-and-sell strategy was found to be significantly more profitable over the long haul than buy-and-hold.)

- Markets tend to go up or down with the hemlines on women's dresses.

Clearly, the trading action approach is based on the simple assumption that the market moves in cycles and that these cycles have a tendency to repeat themselves. As a result, the contention seems to be that whatever has happened repeatedly in the past will probably reoccur in the future.

Confidence Index Another measure that attempts to capture the tone of the market is the **confidence index**, which deals not with the stock market but with *bond* returns. Computed and published weekly in *Barron's* (see "Market Laboratory—Bonds"), the confidence index is a ratio that reflects *the spread* between the average yield on high-grade corporate bonds relative to the yield on average- or intermediate-grade corporate bonds. Technically, the index is computed by relating the average yield on ten high-grade corporate bonds to the yield on the Dow Jones average of 40 bonds. The formula is as follows:

$$\text{Confidence Index} = \frac{\text{Average yield on 10 high-grade corporate bonds}}{\text{Yield on the Dow Jones average of 40 corporate bonds}}$$

Thus, the index measures the *yield spread* between high-grade bonds and a large cross-section of bonds. Because the yield on high-grade bonds should always be lower than the average yield on a large sample of low- to high-grade bonds, the confidence index should never exceed 1.0. Indeed, as the measure approaches equality (i.e., 100%), the *spread* between the two sets of bonds will get smaller and smaller—a positive sign.

Consider, for example, a point in time where high-grade bonds are yielding 4.50%, while corporate bonds, on average, are yielding 5.15%. This would amount to a yield spread of 65 "basis points," or 65/100 of 1% (i.e., 5.15% − 4.50% = 0.65%), and a confidence index of 4.50 ÷ 5.15 = 87.38%. Now, look what happens when yields (and yield spreads) fall or rise:

	Yields (Yield Spreads)	
	Fall	Rise
Yields on high-grade bonds	4.25%	5.25%
Yields on average bonds	4.50%	6.35%
Yield spread	25 b.p.	110 b.p.
Confidence index	94.44%	82.68%

Lower yield spreads, in effect, lead to higher confidence indexes. These, in turn, *indicate that investors are demanding a lower premium in yield for the lower-rated (riskier) bonds, and in so doing, are showing more confidence in the economy.* The theory is that the trend of "smart money" is usually revealed in the bond market before it shows up in the stock market. So, a sustained rise in the confidence index suggests an increase in investor confidence and a stronger stock market; a drop in the index portends a softer tone.

Technical Conditions Within the Market

Another way to assess the market is to keep track of the variables that drive its behavior—things like the volume of trading, short sales, and odd-lot trading. Clearly, if these variables do, in fact, influence market prices, then it would be in an investor's best interest to keep tabs on them, at least informally. Let's now look at four of these market forces: (1) market volume, (2) breadth of the market, (3) short interest, and (4) odd-lot trading.

Market Volume Market volume is an obvious reflection of the amount of investor interest. Volume is a function of the supply of and demand for stock, and it indicates underlying market strengths and weaknesses. Investor eagerness to buy or sell is felt to be captured by market volume figures.

As a rule, the market is considered *strong* when volume goes up in a rising market or drops off during market declines. It is considered *weak* when volume rises during a decline or drops during rallies. For instance, the market would be considered strong if the Dow Jones industrial average went up by, say, 108 points while market volume was heavy.

The financial press regularly publishes volume data, so investors can easily watch this important technical indicator. An example of this and other vital market information is shown in Figure 9.2 (on page 340).

Breadth of the Market Each trading day, some stocks go up in price and others go down. In market terminology, some stocks *advance* and others *decline*. Breadth of the market deals with these advances and declines. The principle behind this indicator is that the number of advances and declines reflects the underlying sentiment of investors.

The idea is actually quite simple: So long as the number of stocks that advance in price on a given day exceeds the number that decline, the market is considered strong. The extent of that strength depends on the spread between the number of advances and declines. For example, if the spread narrows (the number of declines starts to approach the number of advances), market strength is said to be deteriorating. Similarly, the market is considered weak when the number of declines repeatedly exceeds the number of advances. When the mood is optimistic, advances outnumber declines. Again, data on advances and declines are published daily in the financial press.

Short Interest When investors anticipate a market decline, they sometimes sell a stock short. That is, they sell borrowed stock. The number of shares of stocks sold short in the market at any given point in time is known as the **short interest**. The more stocks are sold short, the higher the short interest. Because all short sales must eventually be "covered" (the borrowed shares must be returned), a short sale in effect ensures *future demand for the stock*. Thus, the market is viewed optimistically when the level of short interest becomes relatively high by historical standards. The logic is that as shares are bought back to cover outstanding short sales, the additional demand will push stock prices up. The amount of short interest on the NYSE, the Amex, and Nasdaq's National Market is published in the *Wall Street Journal* and *Barron's*.

Keeping track of the level of short interest can indicate future market demand, but it can also reveal *present* market optimism or pessimism. Short selling is usually done by knowledgeable investors, and a significant buildup or decline in the level of short interest is thought to reveal the sentiment of sophisticated investors about the current state of the market or a company. For example, a significant shift upward in short interest is believed to indicate pessimism concerning the *current* state of the market, even though it may signal optimism with regard to *future* levels of demand.

Odd-Lot Trading A rather cynical saying on Wall Street suggests that the best thing to do is just the opposite of whatever the small investor is doing. The reasoning behind this is that as a group, small investors are notoriously wrong in their timing of investment decisions: The investing public usually does not come into the market in force until after a bull market has pretty much run its course, and it does not get out until late in a bear market. Although its validity is debatable, this is the premise behind a widely followed technical indicator and is the basis for the **theory of contrary opinion**. This theory uses the amount and type of odd-lot trading as an indicator of the current state of the market and pending changes.

FIGURE 9.2

Some Market Statistics

Individual investors can obtain all sorts of technical information at little or no cost from brokerage houses, investment services, the popular financial media, or the Internet. Here, for example, is a sample of the type of information available daily from the *Wall Street Journal*. Note that a variety of information about market volume, new highs and lows, number of advancing and declining stocks, and the most actively traded issues is available from this one source.
(Source: *Wall Street Journal*, September 4, 2009.)

Markets Diary
5:39 p.m. EDT 09/04/09

Issues	NYSE	Nasdaq	Alternext
Advances	2,448	1,960	323
Declines	586	645	141
Unchanged	104	200	84

Issues at			
New Highs	102	31	25
New Lows	2	5	2

Share Volume			
Total	1,019,653,350	1,722,150,094	24,198,561
Advancing	875,422,240	1,444,803,824	13,999,731
Declining	126,338,390	234,364,618	8,222,830

Get this by E-mail ✉

Felcor Lodging Trust Inc. (FCH)
▸ Go to Interactive Charting

1 Day | 10 Days | 1 Month | 3 Months | 1 Year

Bridgepoint Education Inc. (BPI)
▸ Go to Interactive Charting

1 Day | 10 Days | 1 Month | 3 Months | 1 Year

Gainers   (Roll over for charts and headlines)
6:32 p.m. EDT 09/04/09
NYSE | Nasdaq | Amex | Arca

Issue	Price	Chg	% Chg	Volume
EstrlneTch (ESL)	36.41	5.91	19.38	2,130,044
Felcor (FCH)	3.94	0.51	14.87	724,238
AmBev ADS C (ABVC)	63.95	7.55	13.39	3,100
PzenaInvstMng (PZN)	7.23	0.75	11.57	45,418
AcornIntl (ATV)	3.90	0.40	11.43	76,504

See all Gainers — Get this by E-mail ✉

Decliners   (Roll over for charts and headlines)
6:32 p.m. EDT 09/04/09
NYSE | Nasdaq | Amex | Arca

Issue	Price	Chg	% Chg	Volume
Quiksilver (ZQK)	2.36	-0.50	-17.48	7,150,303
BridgepntEdu (BPI)	15.57	-2.66	-14.59	5,391,462
FstPfdCapTr IV (FBSA)	6.51	-0.76	-10.45	5,900
RylBkScot pfF (RBSF)	12.86	-0.84	-6.13	111,767
PSEG pfE (PEGE)	83.57	-5.06	-5.71	2,475

See all Decliners — Get this by E-mail ✉

Most Active Stocks   (Roll over for charts and headlines)
6:32 p.m. EDT 09/04/09
NYSE | Nasdaq | Amex | Arca

Issue	Volume	Price	Chg	% Chg
Citigroup (C)	574,950,665	4.85	0.08	1.68
FannieMae (FNM)	220,669,991	1.77	0.13	7.93
BankAm (BAC)	173,381,142	17.09	0.25	1.48
FredMac (FRE)	96,071,924	1.97	0.10	5.35
GenElec (GE)	77,211,127	13.87	0.42	3.12

See all Most Actives — Get this by E-mail ✉

Friday, September 04, 2009 - 6:34 pm ET   Find Historical Data 🖳 | WHAT'S THIS?

NYSE Volume Percentage Leaders

	Issue (Roll over for charts and headlines)	Volume	% Diff *	Price	Chg	% Chg
1	BridgepntEdu (BPI)	5,391,462	1,961.83	$15.57	-2.66	-14.59
2	NuvMA Prm (NMT)	68,750	1,104.45	13.60	-0.23	-1.66
3	BlkRkMuniBd Tr (BBK)	165,293	893.47	14.48	0.65	4.70
4	EstrlneTch (ESL)	2,130,044	813.54	36.41	5.91	19.38
5	CooperCo (COO)	4,206,044	669.20	25.66	-1.01	-3.79

Because many individual investors deal in transactions of less than 100 shares, their combined sentiments are supposedly captured in odd-lot figures. The idea is to see what odd-lot investors "on balance" are doing. So long as there is little or no difference in the spread between the volume of odd-lot purchases and sales, the theory of contrary opinion holds that the market will probably continue pretty much along its current line (either up or down). A dramatic change in the balance of odd-lot purchases and sales may be a signal that a bull or bear market is about to end. For example, if the amount of odd-lot purchases starts to exceed odd-lot sales by an ever-widening margin, speculation on the part of small investors may be starting to get out of control—an ominous signal that the final stages of a bull market may be at hand.

Trading Rules and Measures

Market technicians—analysts who believe it is chiefly (or solely) supply and demand that drive stock prices—use a variety of mathematical equations and measures to assess the underlying condition of the market. These analysts often use computers to produce the measures, plotting them on a daily basis. They then use those measures as indicators of when to get into or out of the market or a particular stock. In essence, *they develop trading rules based on these market measures*. Technical analysts almost always use several of these market measures, rather than just one (or two), because one measure rarely works the same way for all stocks. Moreover, they generally look for *confirmation* of one measure by *another*. In other words, market analysts like to see three or four of these ratios and measures all pointing in the same direction.

There are no "magic" numbers associated with these indicators. Some analysts may consider 20% and 80% to be "critical" levels for an indicator; others may use 40% and 60% for the same indicator. Market technicians often determine the critical levels by using a process known as *backtesting*, which involves using historical price data to generate buy and sell signals. That is, they compute the profits generated from a series of trading rules and then try to find the indicators that generate the greatest amount of profits. Those measures then become the buy and sell signals for the various market indicators they employ.

Although literally dozens of these market measures and trading rules exist, we'll confine our discussion here to some of the more widely used technical indicators: (1) advance-decline lines, (2) new highs and lows, (3) the arms index, (4) the mutual fund cash ratio, (5) on-balance volume and (6) the *relative strength index (RSI)*.

Advance-Decline Line Each trading day, the NYSE, Amex, and Nasdaq publish statistics on how many of their stocks closed higher on the day (i.e., *advanced* in price) and how many closed lower (*declined* in price). The *advance-decline line*, or *A/D line*, is simply the difference between these two numbers. To calculate it, you take the number of stocks that have risen in price and subtract the number that have declined, usually for the previous day. For example, if 1,000 issues advanced on a day when 450 issues declined, the day's *net number* would be 550 (i.e., 1,000 − 450). If 450 advanced and 1,000 declined, the net number would be −550 (450 − 1,000). *Each day's net number is then added to (or subtracted from) the running total, and the result is plotted on a graph.*

If the graph is rising, the advancing issues are dominating the declining issues, and the market is considered strong. When declining issues start to dominate, the graph will turn down as the market begins to soften. Technicians use the A/D line as a signal for when to buy or sell stocks.

New Highs–New Lows   This measure is similar to the advance-decline line, but looks at price movements over a longer period of time. A stock is defined as reaching a "new high" if its current price is at the highest level it has been over the past year (sometimes referred to as the "52-week high"). Conversely, a stock makes a "new low" if its current price is at the lowest level it has been over the past year.

The *new highs–new lows (NH-NL) indicator* is computed as the number of stocks reaching new 52-week highs minus the number reaching new lows. Thus, you end up with a *net number*, which can be either positive (when new highs dominate) or negative (when new lows exceed new highs), just like with the advance-decline line. To smooth out the daily fluctuations, *the net number is often added to (or subtracted from) a 10-day moving average, and then plotted on a graph.*

As you might have guessed, a graph that's increasing over time indicates a strong market, where new highs are dominating. A declining graph indicates a weak market, where new lows are more common than new highs. Technicians following a momentum-based strategy will buy stocks when new highs dominate and sell them when there are more new lows than new highs. Alternatively, they might use the indicator to rotate money into stocks when the market looks strong and to rotate out of stocks and into cash or bonds when the market looks weak.

The Arms Index   This indicator, also known as the TRIN, for *trading index*, builds on the advance-decline line by considering *the volume* in advancing and declining stocks in addition to *the number of stocks* rising or falling in price. The formula is

$$\text{TRIN} = \frac{\text{Number of up stocks}}{\text{Number of down stocks}} \div \frac{\text{Volume in up stocks}}{\text{Volume in down stocks}}$$

For example, suppose we are analyzing the S&P 500. Assume that on a given day, 300 of these stocks rose in price and 200 fell in price. Also assume that the total trading volume in the rising ("up") stocks was 400 million shares, and the total trading volume in the falling ("down") stocks was 800 million shares. The value of the TRIN for the day would be

$$\text{TRIN} = \frac{300}{200} \div \frac{400 \text{ million}}{800 \text{ million}} = 3.0$$

Alternatively, suppose the volume in up stocks was 700 million shares, and the volume in down stocks was 300 million. The value of the TRIN then would be

$$\text{TRIN} = \frac{300}{200} \div \frac{700 \text{ million}}{300 \text{ million}} = 0.64$$

Higher TRIN values are interpreted as being bad for the market, because even though more stocks rose than fell, the trading volume in the falling stocks was much greater. The underlying idea is that a strong market is characterized by more stocks rising in price than falling, *along with greater volume in the rising stocks than in the falling ones*, as in the second example.

Mutual Fund Cash Ratio   This indicator looks at the cash position of mutual funds as an indicator of future market performance. The *mutual fund cash ratio (MFCR)* measures the percentage of mutual fund assets that are held in cash. It is computed as follows:

$$\text{MFCR} = \text{Mutual fund cash position} \div \text{Total assets under management}$$

The assumption is that the higher the MFCR, the stronger the market. Indeed, the ratio is considered very bullish when it moves to abnormally high levels (i.e., when mutual fund cash exceeds 10% to 12% of total assets). It is seen as bearish when the ratio drops to very low levels (e.g., less than 5% of assets). The logic goes as follows: When fund managers hold a lot of cash (when the MFCR is high), that's good news for the market, because they will eventually have to invest that cash, buying stocks and causing prices to rise. If fund managers hold very little cash, investors might be concerned for two reasons. First, there is less demand for stocks if most of the cash is already invested. Second, if the market takes a downturn, investors might want to withdraw their money. Fund managers will then have to sell some of their stocks to accommodate these redemptions, putting additional downward pressure on prices.

On-Balance Volume Technical analysts usually consider *stock prices* to be the key measure of market activity. However, they also consider *trading volume* as a secondary indicator. *On-balance volume (OBV)* is a momentum indicator that relates volume to price change. It uses trading volume in addition to price and *tracks trading volume as a running total.* In this way, OBV indicates whether volume is flowing into or out of a security. When the security closes higher than its previous close, all the day's volume is considered "up-volume," all of which is *added to the running total.* In contrast, when a stock closes lower, all the day's volume is considered "down-volume," which is then *subtracted from the running total.*

The OBV indicator is used to *confirm* price trends. According to this measure, you want to see a lot of volume when a stock's price is rising, because that would suggest that the stock will go even higher. On the other hand, if prices are rising but OBV is falling, technical analysts would describe the situation as a *divergence* and interpret it as a sign of possible weakness.

When analyzing OBV, it is the direction or trend that is important, not the actual value. To begin the computation of OBV, you can start with an arbitrary number, such as 50,000. Suppose you are calculating the OBV for a stock that closed yesterday at a price of $50 per share, and you start with an OBV value of 50,000. Assume that the stock trades 80,000 shares today and closes at $49. Because the stock declined in price, we would subtract the full 80,000 shares from the previous balance (our starting point of 50,000); now the OBV is $50,000 - 80,000 = -30,000$. (Note that the OBV is simply the *trading volume running total.*) If the stock trades 120,000 shares on the following day and closes up at $52 per share, we would then *add* all of those 120,000 shares to the previous day's OBV: $-30,000 + 120,000 = +90,000$. This process would continue day after day. The normal procedure is to plot these daily OBVs on a graph. As long as the graph is moving up, it's bullish; when the graph starts moving down, it's bearish.

Relative Strength One of the most widely used technical indicators is the *relative strength index (RSI),* an index measuring a security's strength of advances and declines over time. The RSI indicates a security's momentum and gives the best results when used for short trading periods. It also helps identify market extremes, signaling a security is approaching its price top or bottom and may soon reverse trend. The RSI is the

Smart's Tour of the Web
To watch author Scott
Smart discuss key Web sites
for this chapter visit
www.myfinancelab.com

ratio of average price change on "up days" to the average price change on "down days" during the same period. The index formula is

$$RSI = 100 - \left[100 \Bigg/ \left(1 + \frac{\text{Average price change on up days}}{\text{Average price change on down days}} \right) \right]$$

The RSI can cover various periods of time (days, weeks, or months). The most common RSIs are 9-, 14-, and 25-day periods.

The RSI ranges between 0 and 100, with most RSIs falling between 30 and 70. Generally, values above 70 or 80 indicate an *overbought* condition (more and stronger buying than fundamentals would justify). RSI values below 30 indicate a possible *oversold* condition (more selling than fundamentals may indicate). When the RSI crosses these points, it signals a possible trend reversal. The wider 80–20 range is often used with the 9-day RSI, which tends to be more volatile than longer-period RSIs. In bull markets, 80 may be a better upper indicator than 70; in bear markets, 20 is a more accurate lower level. Different sectors and industries may have varying RSI threshold levels.

To use the RSI in their own trading, investors set buy and sell ranges—such as sell when the RSI crosses above 70 and buy when it moves below 30. Another strategy is to compare RSIs with stock charts. Most of the time both move in the same direction, but a divergence between RSI and a price chart can be a strong predictor of a changing trend.

Like many other technical indicators, the RSI should not be used alone. It works best in combination with other tools such as charting, moving averages, and trendlines. Among the Web sites that offer RSI as a charting option are BigCharts (**www.bigcharts.com**), Yahoo! Finance (**finance.yahoo.com**), and StockCharts (**www.stockcharts.com**).

Charting

Charting is perhaps the best-known activity of the technical analyst. Indeed, technical analysts use various types of charts to plot the behavior of everything from the Dow Jones industrial average and share price movements of individual stocks to moving averages (see below) and advance-decline lines. In fact, as noted above, just about every type of technical indicator is charted in one form or another. Figure 9.3 shows a typical stock chart. In this case, the chart plots the price behavior of Nike, Inc., along with a variety of supplementary technical information about the stock.

Charts are popular because they provide a visual summary of activity over time. Perhaps more important (in the eyes of technicians, at least), they contain valuable information about developing trends and the future behavior of the market and/or individual stocks. Chartists believe price patterns evolve into *chart formations* that provide signals about the future course of the market or a stock. We will now briefly review the popular types of charts, chart formations, and the use of moving averages.

Bar Charts   The simplest and probably most widely used type of chart is the **bar chart**. It shows market or share prices on the vertical axis and time on the horizontal axis. This type of chart derives its name from the fact that prices are recorded as vertical bars that depict high, low, and closing prices. A typical bar chart is shown in Figure 9.4. Note that on December 31, this particular stock had a high price of 29, a low of 27, and it closed at 27.50. Because these charts contain a time element, technicians frequently plot a variety of other pertinent information on them. For example, volume is often put at the base of bar charts (see the Nike chart in Figure 9.3).

Point-and-Figure Charts   Point-and-figure charts are used strictly to keep track of emerging price patterns. Because there is no time dimension on them, they are *not* used for plotting technical measures. (Note that while there is no indication of time on the

FIGURE 9.3

A Stock Chart

This chart for Nike, Inc., contains information about the daily price behavior of the stock, along with the stock's relative strength, its moving average, its trading volume, and several other pieces of supplementary data.
(Source: Chart courtesy of StockCharts.com, accessed September 4, 2009. *Note:* Visit this Web site's glossary for expanded definitions.)

FIGURE 9.4

A Bar Chart

Bar charts are widely used to track stock prices, market averages, and numerous other technical measures.

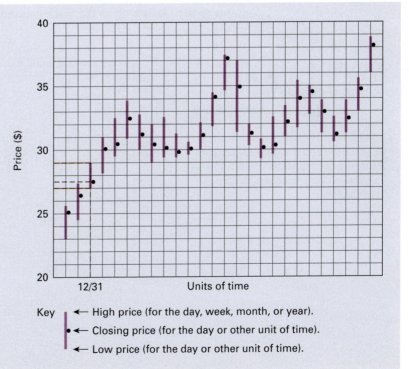

horizontal axis of point-and-figure charts, technical analysts/chartists will often keep track of significant dates or points in time by placing letters or numbers directly on the body of the chart itself.)

In addition to their treatment of time, point-and-figure charts are unique in two other ways. First, these charts record only *significant* price changes. That is, prices have to move by a certain minimum amount—usually at least a point or two—before a new price level is recognized. Second, price *reversals* show up only after a predetermined change in direction occurs. Normally, only closing prices are charted, although some point-and-figure charts use all price changes during the day. An *X* denotes an increase in price; an *O* denotes a decrease.

Figure 9.5 shows a common point-and-figure chart. In this case, the chart employs a two-point box: That is, the stock must move by a minimum of two points before any changes are recorded. The chart can cover a span of one year or less if the stock is highly active. Or it can cover a number of years if the stock is not very active. As a rule, low-priced stocks are charted with one-point boxes, moderately priced shares with increments of two to three points, and high-priced securities with three- to five-point boxes.

Here is how point-and-figure charts work: Suppose we are at point A on the chart in Figure 9.5. The stock has been hovering around this $40–$41 mark for some time. Assume, however, that it just closed at $42.25. Now, because the minimum two-point movement has been met, the chartist would place an X in the box immediately *above* point A. He or she would remain with this new box as long as the price moved (up or down) within the two-point range of 42 to 44. Although the chartist follows *daily* prices, he or she would make a new entry on the chart only after the price has changed by a certain minimum amount and moved into a new two-point box. We see that from point A, the price generally moved up over time to nearly $50 a share. At that point (point B on the chart), things began to change as a reversal set in. The price of the stock began to drift downward and in time moved out of the $48–$50 box. This reversal prompts the chartist to change columns and symbols, by moving one column to the right and recording the new price level with an O in the $46–$48 box. The chartist will continue to use Os as long as the stock continues to close on a generally lower note.

FIGURE 9.5

A Point-and-Figure Chart

Point-and-figure charts are unusual because they have no time dimension. Rather, a column of Xs is used to reflect a general upward drift in prices, and a column of Os is used when prices are drifting downward.

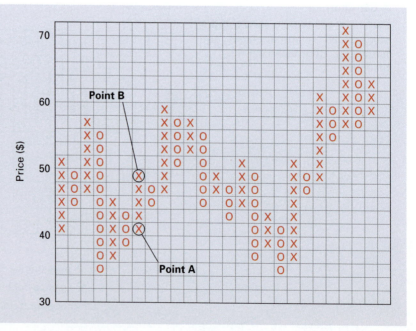

Chart Formations   A chart by itself tells you little more than where the market or a stock has been. But to chartists, those price patterns yield formations that tell them what to expect in the future. Chartists believe that history repeats itself, so they study the historical reactions of stocks (or the market) to various formations, and they devise trading rules based on these observations. It makes no difference to chartists whether they are following the market or an individual stock. *It is the formation that matters,* not the issue being plotted. If you know how to interpret charts (which is no easy task), you can see formations building and recognize buy and sell signals. These chart formations are often given exotic names, such as *head and shoulders, falling wedge, scallop and saucer, ascending triangle,* and *island reversal,* to name just a few.

Figure 9.6 shows six of these formations. The patterns form "support levels" and "resistance lines" that, when combined with the basic formations, yield buy and sell signals. Panel A is an example of a *buy* signal that occurs when prices break out above a resistance line in a particular pattern. In contrast, when prices break out below a support level, as they do at the end of the formation in panel B, a *sell* signal is said to occur. Supposedly, a sell signal means everything is in place for a major drop in the market (or in the price of a share of stock). A buy signal indicates that the opposite is about to occur.

FIGURE 9.6   **Some Popular Chart Formations**

To chartists, each of these formations has meaning about the future course of events.

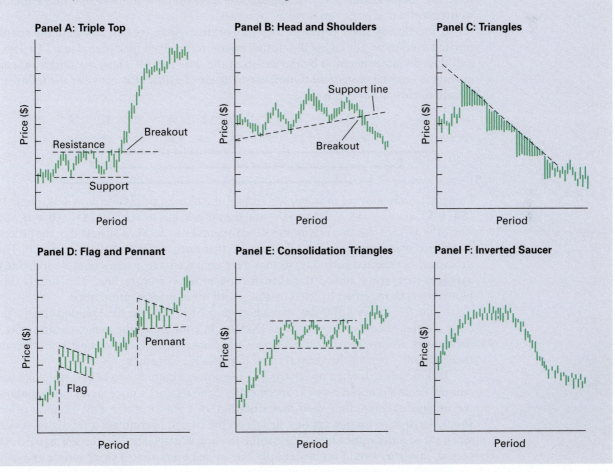

Unfortunately, one of the major problems with charting is that the formations rarely appear as neatly and cleanly as those in Figure 9.6. Rather, identifying and interpreting them often demands considerable imagination.

Moving Averages One problem with daily price charts is that they may contain a lot of often meaningless short-term price swings that mask the overall trend in prices. As a result, technical analysts will often use moving averages not only to eliminate those minor blips, but also to highlight underlying trends. A **moving average (MA)** is a mathematical procedure that records the average value of a series of prices, or other data, over time. Because they incorporate a stream of these average values, MAs will smooth out a data series and make it easier to spot trends. The moving average is one of the oldest and most popular technical indicators. It can, in fact, be used not only with share prices, but also with market indexes and even other technical measures.

Moving averages are computed over periods ranging from 10 to 200 days—meaning that from 10 to 200 data points are used in each calculation. For example, a series of 15 data points is used in a 15-day moving average. The length of the time period has a bearing on how the MA will behave. Shorter periods (10 to 30 days) are more sensitive and tend to more closely track actual daily behavior. Longer periods (say, 100 to 200 days) are smoother and do a better job of picking up the major trends. Several types of moving averages exist, with the most common (and the one we'll use here) being the *simple average*, which gives equal weight to each observation. In contrast, there are other procedures that give more weight to the most recent data points (e.g., the "exponential" and "weighted" averages) or apply more weight to the middle of the time period (e.g., "triangular" averages).

Using closing share prices as the basis of discussion, we can calculate the simple moving average by adding up the closing prices over a given time period (e.g., 10 days), and then dividing this total by the length of the time period. Thus, *the simple moving average is nothing more than the arithmetic mean*. To illustrate, consider the following stream of closing share prices:

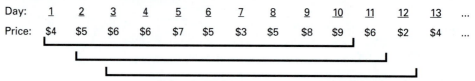

Day:	1	2	3	4	5	6	7	8	9	10	11	12	13	...
Price:	$4	$5	$6	$6	$7	$5	$3	$5	$8	$9	$6	$2	$4	...

Using a 10-day moving average, we add up the closing prices for days 1 through 10 ($4 + $5 + ... + $8 + $9 = $58) and then divide this total by 10 ($58/10 = $5.8). Thus, the average closing price for this 10-day period was $5.80. The next day, the process is repeated once again for days 2 through 11; that turns out to be $60/10 = $6.00. This procedure is repeated each day, so that over time we have a series of these individual averages that, when linked together, form a *moving-average line*. This line is then plotted on a chart, either by itself or along with other market information.

Figure 9.7 shows a 100-day moving average (the bold blue line) plotted against the daily closing prices for ExxonMobil (XOM). In contrast to the actual closing prices, the moving average provides a much smoother line, without all the short-term fluctuations; it clearly reveals the general trend in prices for this stock.

Technicians will often use charts like the one in Figure 9.7 to help them make buy and sell decisions about a stock. Specifically, if the security's price starts moving above the moving average, they read that situation as a good time to buy, because prices should be drifting up (see the buy signals on the chart). In contrast, a sell signal occurs when the security's price moves below the moving average line (see the sell signals). Of course, investors would not necessarily buy or sell every time a stock moves above or

FIGURE 9.7

A 100-Day Moving Average Line

Moving average lines are often plotted along with the actual daily (or weekly) closing prices for a stock. They're also widely used with market indexes, such as the S&P 500, and a variety of technical indicators, including the advance-decline line. (Source: Chart courtesy of Stockcharts.com, accessed September 4, 2009.)

below its moving average, and especially not when stocks are essentially moving sideways, as that could lead to little more than big transactions costs. Indeed, such a strategy is not intended to get you in at the exact bottom or out at the exact top. Instead, it's meant to indicate potential buy/sell opportunities in the early stages of a long-term change in the stock price.

CONCEPTS IN REVIEW

Answers available at
www.pearsonhighered.com/
gitman

9.6 What is the purpose of *technical analysis*? Explain how and why it is used by technicians; note how it can be helpful in timing investment decisions.

9.7 Can the market really have a measurable effect on the price behavior of individual securities? Explain.

9.8 What is the *Dow theory*, and how is it used to analyze the market? Describe the *confidence index*, and note the feature that makes it unique.

9.9 Briefly describe each of the following and explain how it is used in technical analysis:
a. Breadth of the market
b. Short interest
c. Odd-lot trading

9.10 Briefly describe each of the following and note how it is computed and how it is used by technicians:
a. Advance-decline lines.
b. Arms index.
c. On-balance volume.
d. Relative strength index.
e. Moving averages.

9.11 What is a stock chart? What kind of information can be put on charts, and what is the purpose of charting?
a. What is the difference between a bar chart and a point-and-figure chart?
b. What are chart formations, and why are they important?

 Here is what you should know after reading this chapter. **MyFinanceLab** will help you identify what you know, and where to go when you need to practice.

What You Should Know	Key Terms	Where To Practice
LG1 Describe the characteristics of an efficient market, explain what market anomalies are, and note some of the challenges that investors face when markets are efficient. An efficient market is one in which prices fully reflect all available information, and in an efficient market, price movements are nearly random. If markets are efficient, then investors should not expect to earn above-average returns consistently by using either technical or fundamental analysis.	behavioral finance, *p. 328* efficient market, *p. 324* efficient markets hypothesis (EMH), *p. 324* market anomalies, *p. 326* random walk hypothesis, *p. 324* semi-strong form (EMH), *p. 325* strong form (EMH), *p. 326* weak form (EMH), *p. 325*	MyFinanceLab Study Plan 9.1
LG2 List four "decision traps" that may lead investors to make systematic errors in their investment decisions. Behavioral finance asserts that investors are subject to a variety of decision traps which include overconfidence, loss aversion, representativeness, narrow framing, and belief perseverance. If investors do indeed make systematic errors in their investment decisions, then those errors may influence prices in financial markets.	loss aversion, *p. 331*	MyFinanceLab Study Plan 9.2
LG3 Explain how behavioral finance links market anomalies to investors' cognitive biases. A market anomaly represents a pattern in stock prices that would appear to present investors with an opportunity to earn above-average returns without taking above-average risk. Behavioral finance suggests that some market anomalies exist because investors make systematic errors, such as undervaluing stocks that have performed poorly in recent years.		MyFinanceLab Study Plan 9.3
LG4 Discuss the purpose of technical analysis and explain why the performance of the market is important to stock valuation. Technical analysis deals with the behavior of the stock market itself and the various economic forces at work in the marketplace. Technical analysis is used to assess the condition of the market and to determine whether it's a good time to be buying or selling stocks. Some investors try to keep tabs on the markets in an informal way. Others use complex mathematical formulas and rules to guide them in their buy and sell decisions.	technical analysis, *p. 335*	MyFinanceLab Study Plan 9.4
LG5 Describe some of the approaches to technical analysis, including, among others, the Dow theory, moving averages, charting, and various indicators of the technical condition of the market. Market analysts look at those factors in the marketplace that can affect the	confidence index, *p. 338* Dow theory, *p. 336* market technician, *p. 341* short interest, *p. 339*	MyFinanceLab Study Plan 9.5 Video Learning Aid for Problems P9.2, P9.6

What You Should Know	Key Terms	Where To Practice
price behavior of stocks in general. This analysis can be done by assessing the overall condition of the market (as the Dow theory does), by informally or formally studying various internal market statistics (e.g., short interest or advance-decline lines), or by charting various aspects of the market (including the use of moving averages).	theory of contrary opinion, *p. 339*	
LG6 **Compute and use technical trading rules for individual stocks and the market as a whole.** Technical analysts use a number of mathematical equations and measures to gauge the direction of the market, including advance-decline lines, new highs and lows, the trading index, the mutual fund cash ratio, on-balance volume, and the relative strength index. They test different indicators using historical price data to find those that generate profitable trading strategies, which then are developed into trading rules used to guide buy and sell decisions.	bar chart, *p. 344* charting, *p. 344* moving average (MA), *p. 348* point-and-figure charts, *p. 344*	MyFinanceLab Study Plan 9.6

Log into **MyFinanceLab**, take a chapter test, and get a personalized Study Plan that tells you which concepts you understand and which ones you need to review. From there, **MyFinanceLab** will give you further practice, tutorials, animations, videos, and guided solutions.
Log into **www.myfinancelab.com**

Discussion Questions

LG1 **Q9.1** Much has been written about the concept of an *efficient market*. It's probably safe to say that some of your classmates believe the markets are efficient and others believe they are not. Have a debate to see whether you can resolve this issue (at least among you and your classmates). Pick a side, either for or against efficient markets, and then develop your "ammunition." Be prepared to discuss these three aspects:
    a. What is an efficient market? Do such markets really exist?
    b. Are stock prices always (or nearly always) correctly set in the market? If so, does that mean little opportunity exists to find undervalued stocks?
    c. Can you cite any reasons to use fundamental and/or technical analysis in your stock selection process? If not, how would you go about selecting stocks?

LG2 **LG3** **Q9.2** Briefly define each of the following terms and describe how it can affect investors' decisions:
    a. Loss aversion
    b. Representativeness
    c. Narrow framing
    d. Overconfidence
    e. Biased self-attribution

LG2 **LG3** **Q9.3** Describe how representativeness may lead to biases in stock valuation.

LG4 Q9.4 Briefly describe how technical analysis is used as part of the stock valuation process. What role does it play in an investor's decision to buy or sell a stock?

LG4 LG5 Q9.5 Describe each of the following approaches to technical analysis and note how it would be used by investors.
   a. Confidence index
   b. Arms index
   c. Trading action
   d. Odd-lot trading
   e. Charting
   f. Moving averages
   g. On-balance volume

Which of these approaches is likely to involve some type of mathematical equation or ratio?

LG5 Q9.6 Briefly define each of the following and note the conditions that would suggest the market is technically strong.
   a. Breadth of the market
   b. Short interest
   c. Relative strength index (RSI)
   d. Theory of contrary opinion
   e. Head and shoulders

Problems

All problems are available on **www.myfinancelab.com**

LG5 LG6 P9.1 Compute the Arms index for the S&P 500 over the following three days:

Day	Number of Stocks **Rising** in Price	Number of Stocks **Falling** in Price	Volume for Stocks **Rising** in Price	Volume for Stocks **Falling** in Price
1	350	150	850 million shares	420 million shares
2	275	225	450 million shares	725 million shares
3	260	240	850 million shares	420 million shares

Which of the three days would be considered the most bullish? Explain why.

LG5 LG6 P9.2 Listed below are data that pertain to the corporate bond market. (*Note:* Each "period" below covers a span of 6 months.)

	Period 1	Period 2	Period 3	Period 4
Average yield on 10 high-grade corporate bonds	5.30%	5.70%	5.10%	?
Yield on the Dow Jones average of 40 corporate bonds	6.50%	?	6.00%	4.90%
Yield spread (in basis points)	?	155	?	25
Confidence index				

   a. Compute the confidence index for each of the four periods listed above.
   b. Assume the latest confidence index (for period 0, in effect) amounts to 86.83%, while the yield spread between high- and average-grade corporate bonds is 85 basis points. Based on your calculations, what's happening to bond yield spreads and the confidence index over the period of time covered in the problem (i.e., from period 0 through period 4)?
   c. Based on the confidence index measures you computed, what would be your overall assessment of the stock market? In which one or more of the periods (1 through 4) is the confidence index bullish? In which one(s) is it bearish?

LG5 LG6 P9.3 Compute the level of on-balance volume (OBV) for the following three-day period for a stock, if the beginning level of OBV is 50,000 and the stock closed yesterday at $25.

Day	Closing Price	Trading Volume
1	$27	70,000 shares
2	$26	45,000 shares
3	$29	120,000 shares

Does the movement in OBV appear to confirm the rising trend in prices? Explain.

LG5 LG6 P9.4 Below are figures representing the number of stocks making new highs and new lows for each month over a six-month period:

Month	New Highs	New Lows
July	117	22
August	95	34
September	84	41
October	64	79
November	53	98
December	19	101

Would a technical analyst consider the trend to be bullish or bearish over this period? Explain.

LG5 LG6 P9.5 You hear a market analyst on television say that the advance/decline ratio for the session was 1.2. What does that mean?

LG5 LG6 P9.6 At the end of a trading day you find that, on the NYSE, 2,200 stocks advanced, and 1,000 stocks declined. What is the value of the advance-decline line for that day?

LG5 LG6 P9.7 You are given the following information:

Day	New Highs	New Lows
1 (yesterday)	117	22
2	95	34
3	84	41
4	64	79
5	53	98
6	19	101
7	19	105
8	18	110
9	19	90
10	22	88

a. Calculate the 10-day moving average NH-NL indicator.
b. If there are 120 new highs and 20 new lows today, what is the new 10-day moving average NH-NL indicator?

LG5 LG6   P9.8   You have collected the following NH-NL indicator data:

Day	NH-NL Indicator
1 (yesterday)	100
2	95
3	61
4	43
5	−15
6	−45
7	−82
8	−86
9	−92
10	−71

If you are a technician following a momentum-based strategy, are you buying or selling today?

LG5 LG6   P9.9   You are presented with the following data:

Week	Mutual Fund Cash Position	Mutual Fund Total Assets
Most recent	$281,478,000.00	$2,345,650,000.00
2	258,500,000.00	2,350,000,000.00
3	234,800,000.00	2,348,000,000.00
4	211,950,000.00	2,355,000,000.00
5	188,480,000.00	2,356,000,000.00

Calculate the MFCR for each week. Based on the result, are you bullish or bearish?

LG5 LG6   P9.10   You find the closing prices for a stock you own. You want to use a 10-day moving average to monitor the stock. Calculate the 10-day moving average for days 11 through 20. Based on the data in the table below, are there any signals you should act on? Explain.

Day	Closing Price	Day	Closing Price
1	$25.25	11	$30.00
2	26.00	12	30.00
3	27.00	13	31.00
4	28.00	14	31.50
5	27.00	15	31.00
6	28.00	16	32.00
7	27.50	17	29.00
8	29.00	18	29.00
9	27.00	19	28.00
10	28.00	20	27.00

Visit www.myfinancelab.com for web exercises, spreadsheets, and other online resources.

Case Problem 9.1   *Brett Runs Some Technical Measures on a Stock*

LG4 LG5   Brett Daly is an active stock trader and an avid market technician. He got into technical analysis about 10 years ago, and although he now uses the Internet for much of his analytical work, he still enjoys running some of the numbers and doing some of the charting himself. Brett likes to describe himself as a "serious stock trader" who relies on technical analysis for some—but certainly not all—of the information he uses to make an investment decision; unlike some market technicians, he does not totally ignore a stock's fundamentals. Right now he's got his eye on a stock that he's been tracking for the past three or four months.

The stock is Nautilus Navigation, a mid-sized high-tech company that's been around for a number of years and has a demonstrated ability to generate profits year-in and year-out. The problem is that the earnings are a bit erratic, tending to bounce up and down from year to year, which causes the price of the stock to be a bit erratic as well. And that's exactly why Brett likes the stock—as a trader, the volatile prices enable him to move in and out of the stock over relatively short (three- to six-month) periods of time.

Brett has already determined that the stock has "decent" fundamentals, so he does not worry about its basic soundness. Hence, he can concentrate on the technical side of the stock. In particular, he wants to run some technical measures on the market price behavior of the security. He's obtained recent closing prices on the stock, which are shown in the table below.

Recent Price Behavior: Nautilus Navigation

14 (8/15/10)	18.55	20	17.50
14.25	17.50	20.21	18.55
14.79	17.50	20.25	19.80
15.50	17.25	20.16	19.50
16	17	20	19.25
16	16.75	20.25	20
16.50	16.50	20.50	20.90
17	16.55	20.80	21
17.25	16.15	20	21.75
17.20	16.80	20	22.50
18	17.15	20.25	23.25
18 (9/30/10)	17.22	20	24
18.55	17.31 (10/31/10)	19.45	24.25
18.65	17.77	19.20	24.15
18.80	18.23	18.25 (11/30/10)	24.75
19	19.22	17.50	25
19.10	20.51	16.75	25.50
18.92	20.15	17	25.55 (12/31/10)

Nautilus shares are actively traded on the Nasdaq Global Market and enjoy considerable market interest.

Questions

a. Use the closing share prices in the table above to compute the stock's relative strength index (RSI) for (1) the 20-day period from 9/30/10 to 10/31/10; and (2) the 22-day period from 11/30/10 to 12/31/10. [*Hint:* Use a simple (unweighted) average to compute the numerator (average price change on up days) and the denominator (average price change on down days) of the RSI formula shown on page 344.]

    1. Contrast the two RSI measures you computed. Is the index getting bigger or smaller, and is that good or bad?

    2. Is the latest RSI measure giving a buy or a sell signal? Explain.

b. Based on the above closing share prices, prepare a moving-average line covering the period shown in the table; use a 10-day time frame to calculate the individual average values.

    1. Plot the daily closing prices for Nautilus from 8/15/10 through 12/31/10 on a graph/chart.

2. On the same graph/chart, plot a moving-average line using the individual average values computed earlier. Identify any buy or sell signals.

3. As of 12/31/10, was the moving-average line giving a buy, hold, or sell signal? Explain. How does that result compare to what you found with the RSI in part **a**? Explain.

c. Prepare a point-and-figure chart of the closing prices for Nautilus Navigation. (Use a one-point system, in which each box is worth $1.) Discuss how technical analysts use this and similar charts.

d. Based on the technical measures and charts you've prepared, what course of action would you recommend that Brett take with regard to Nautilus Navigation? Explain.

Case Problem 9.2   *Deb Takes Measure of the Market*

LG4 LG5

Several months ago, Deb Forrester received a substantial sum of money from the estate of her late aunt. Deb initially placed the money in a savings account because she was not sure what to do with it. Since then, however, she has taken a course in investments at the local university. The textbook for the course was, in fact, this one, and the class just completed Chapter 9. Excited about what she has learned in class, Deb has decided that she definitely wants to invest in stocks. But before she does, she wants to use her newfound knowledge in technical analysis to determine whether now would be a good time to enter the market.

Deb has decided to use all five of the following measures to help her determine if now is, indeed, a good time to start putting money into the stock market:

- Dow theory

- Advance-decline line

- New highs-new lows (NH-NL) indicator (*Assume the current 10-day moving average is zero and the last 10 periods were each zero.*)

- Arms index

- Mutual fund cash ratio

Deb goes to the Internet and, after considerable effort, is able to put together the table of data as seen at the top of page 357.

Questions

a. Based on the data presented in the table, calculate a value (where appropriate) for periods 1 through 5, for each of the five measures listed above. (*Hint:* There are no values to compute for the Dow theory; just plot the averages.) Chart your results, where applicable.

b. Discuss each measure individually and note what it indicates for the market, as it now stands. Taken collectively, what do these five measures indicate about the current state of the market? According to these measures, is this a good time for Deb to consider getting into the market, or should she wait a while? Explain.

c. Comment on the time periods used in the table, which are not defined here. What if they were relatively long intervals of time? What if they were relatively short? Explain how the length of the time periods can affect the measures.

	Period 1	Period 2	Period 3	Period 4	Period 5
Dow Jones Industrial Average	8,300	7,250	8,000	9,000	9,400
Dow Transportation Average	2,375	2,000	2,000	2,850	3,250
New highs	68	85	85	120	200
New lows	75	60	80	75	20
Volume up	600,000,000	836,254,123	275,637,497	875,365,980	1,159,534,297
Volume down	600,000,000	263,745,877	824,362,503	424,634,020	313,365,599
Mutual fund cash (trillions of dollars)	$0.31	$0.32	$0.47	$0.61	$0.74
Total assets managed (trillions of dollars)	$6.94	$6.40	$6.78	$6.73	$7.42
Advancing issues (NYSE)	1,120	1,278	1,270	1,916	1,929
Declining issues (NYSE)	2,130	1,972	1,980	1,334	1,321

Excel with Spreadsheets

Technical analysis looks at the demand and supply for securities based on trading volumes and price studies. Charting is a common method used to identify and project price trends in a security. A well-known technical indicator is the Bollinger Band. It creates two bands, one above and one below, the price performance of a stock. The upper band is a resistance level and represents the level above which the stock is unlikely to rise. The bottom forms a support level and shows the price that a stock is unlikely to fall below.

According to technicians, if you see a significant "break" in the upper band, the expectation is that the stock price will fall in the immediate future. A "break" in the lower band signals that the security is about to rise in value. Either of these occurrences will dictate a unique investment strategy.

Replicate the following technical analysis for Amazon.com (AMZN)

- Go to **www.moneycentral.msn.com**

- Symbol(s): **AMZN**

- In the left-hand column, click on "Charts." You need to update to MSN Money Deluxe if you have not already done so.

- If download was required, fill in the Symbol box with "AMZN."

- A one-year chart appears by default.

- Click on "Analysis."

- Click on "Price Indicators."

- Choose "Bollinger Bands."

- The price performance graph for Amazon stock with an upper and lower red Bollinger Band should appear.

- Make sure that the graph covers, at a minimum, the months of June through December 2009.

Questions

a. On approximately July 7, 2009, what happened to the upper band (resistance level) of Amazon stock?

    b. During the following nine days, how did the price of the stock behave?

    c. Is this in line with what a technician would predict?

    d. What strategy would a technician have undertaken on the seventh of July?

    e. On approximately November 18, 2009, what happened to the lower band (support level) of Amazon stock?

    f. During the following 10 days, how did the price of the stock behave?

    g. Is this in line with what a technician would predict?

    h. What strategy would a technician have undertaken on the eighteenth of November?

CFA EXAM QUESTIONS

Investing in Common Stocks

Following is a sample of 11 Level-I CFA exam questions that deal with many of the topics covered in Chapters 6, 7, 8, and 9 of this text, including the use of financial ratios, various stock valuation models, and efficient market concepts. (*Note:* When answering some of the questions below, remember: "Forward P/E" is the same as a P/E based on estimated earnings 1 year out.) (When answering the questions, give yourself 1½ minutes for each question; the objective is to correctly answer 8 of the 11 questions in a period of 16½ minutes.)

1. Which of the following ratios would be *most useful* in determining a company's ability to cover its debt payments?
   a. ROA.   b. Total asset turnover.   c. Fixed charge coverage.

2. An analyst gathered the following data for a company:

	2003	2004	2005
ROE	19.8%	20.0%	22.0%
Return on total assets	8.1%	8.0%	7.9%
Total asset turnover	2.0	2.0	2.1

Based only on the information above, the *most* appropriate conclusion is that, over the period 2003 to 2005, the company's:
   a. net profit margin and financial leverage have decreased.
   b. net profit margin and financial leverage have increased.
   c. net profit margin has decreased but its financial leverage has increased.

3. In general, a creditor would consider a decrease in which of the following ratios to be positive news?
   a. Interest coverage   b. Debt to total assets.   c. Return on assets.
      (times interest earned).

4. What does the P/E ratio measure?
   a. The "multiple" that the stock market places on a company's EPS.
   b. The relationship between dividends and market prices.
   c. The earnings for one common share of stock.

5. What is the value of a $100 par preferred stock issue with an annual dividend of $7.50 and a required rate of return of 12%?
   a. $100.00   b. $62.50   c. $72.50

6. The expected return on the market for next period is 16%. The risk-free rate of return is 6%, and Zebra Company has a beta that is 20% greater than the overall market. The required rate of return for this company is closest to:
   a. 14%.   b. 15%.   c. 18%.

7. Analysts wish to value a firm with the following characteristics. Last year the firm paid a dividend of $4.00 per share. Expectations are that the firm can increase earnings and dividends at the rate of 25% for the next five years, but after that competitive forces will force the growth rate down to 6% for the foreseeable future. What is the best estimate of the stock's value if the required rate of return is 12%?
   a. $145.67   b. $150.52   c. $165.45

8. Consider a company that earned $4.00 per share last year and paid a dividend of $1.00. The firm has maintained a consistent payout ratio over the years and analysts expect this to continue. The firm is expected to earn $4.40 next year, the investor plans to hold the stock for 3 years, the required rate of return is 12%, and the expected price of the stock at the end of the third year is $45. The implied expected growth rate is expected to remain constant indefinitely. What is the *best* estimate of the stock's current value?

a. $34.92   b. $38.82   c. $55.00

9. An analyst made the following statement: "Neither price-to-book value ratios nor price-to-sales ratios are useful in valuing firms whose earnings are abnormally high or low." Is the analyst's statement correct with respect to:

	price-to-book value ratios?	price-to-sales ratios?
a.	No	No
b.	No	Yes
c.	Yes	No

10. McDonald's Corp. has a current market value of $44 per share. The earnings per share (EPS) reported in the last year was $2.02. The expected EPS for the current year is $2.42 and for the next year is $2.68. McDonalds' forward P/E ratio is *closest* to:

a.   16.42   b.   18.18   c.   21.78.

11. Each of the following represents an anomaly that challenges the semistrong-form efficient market hypothesis *except*:
a.   the January effect
b.   low P/E stocks
c.   stock splits

Answers: 1. c; 2. c; 3. b; 4. a; 5. b; 6. c; 7. b; 8. a; 9. a; 10. a; 11. c.

Investing in Fixed-Income Securities

Fixed-Income Securities

LEARNING GOALS

After studying this chapter, you should be able to:

LG1 Explain the basic investment attributes of bonds and their use as investment vehicles.

LG2 Describe the essential features of a bond, note the role that bond ratings play in the market, and distinguish among different types of call, refunding, and sinking-fund provisions.

LG3 Explain how bonds are priced in the market and why some bonds are more volatile than others.

LG4 Identify the different types of bonds and the kinds of investment objectives these securities can fulfill.

LG5 Discuss the global nature of the bond market and the difference between dollar-denominated and non-dollar-denominated foreign bonds.

LG6 Describe the basic features and characteristics of convertible securities, and measure the value of a convertible.

In a sign of the severity of the global recession, Standard and Poor's stripped General Electric of its coveted AAA bond rating in March 2009. That marked the first time in more than 50 years that GE's bonds fell below the highest possible investment-grade rating. Later the same day, another ratings company, Fitch, issued a downgrade on the debt of Warren Buffett's firm, Berkshire Hathaway, from AAA to AA. Those actions left just five U.S. corporations with AAA-rated debt: Automatic Data Processing, ExxonMobil, Johnson & Johnson, Microsoft, and Pfizer.

GE and Berkshire Hathaway had plenty of company. The number of firms receiving debt downgrades hit a record of 1,053 in March, the fifteenth consecutive monthly increase. By August 2009, downgrades eased a bit to 955 firms, but that figure was still up almost 25% from August 2008. Banking was the hardest hit sector, with 133 banks facing downgrades in August alone.

But the news wasn't all bad. Shares of Boston Scientific jumped 5% on the news that its bond rating had been upgraded by Moody's from Ba1 to Ba2, which represented a change in its credit outlook from "negative" to "stable." The satellite radio company, Sirius XM, also scored an upgrade from CCC to CCC+. Both Boston Scientific and Sirius XM still had room to improve their ratings, because both firms' bonds still fell into the broad category known as "junk" bonds.

Before you invest in debt securities, whether issued by GE or any other company, you'll want to consider credit quality, interest rates, maturity, and other factors. Chapters 10 and 11 will provide the background you need to make wise choices in the bond market.

(Sources: And Then There Were Six, Seeking Alpha, March 12, 2009, seekingalpha.com/article/ 125625-aaa-rated-companies-and-then-there-were-six; GE, Berkshire lose AAA ratings; ranks of top firms thinning, *The China Post*, March 14, 2009, www.chinapost.com.tw/business/americas/ 2009/03/14/200120/GE-Berkshire.htm; Sirius XM Scores Debt Rating Upgrade, April 14, 2009, www.marketwatch.com/story/sirius-xm-scores-debt-rating; Julie Donnelly, Boston Scientific pops on Moody's Upgrade, March 12, 2009, *Boston Business Journal*, www.bizjournals.com/ boston/stories/2009/03/09/daily55.html.)

Why Invest in Bonds?

LG1 In contrast to stocks, *bonds are liabilities*—publicly traded IOUs where the bond-holders are actually *lending money* to the issuer. Technically, **bonds** are negotiable, publicly traded, long-term debt securities. They are issued in various denominations, by a variety of borrowing organizations, including the U.S. Treasury, agencies of the U.S. government, state and local governments, and corporations. Bonds are often referred to as *fixed-income securities* because the debt payments of the issuers are usually fixed. That is, in most cases the issuing organization agrees to pay a fixed amount of interest periodically and to repay a fixed amount of principal at maturity.

Like stocks, bonds can potentially provide investors with two kinds of income: (1) current income and (2) capital gains. The current income, of course, comes from the periodic interest payments paid over the life of the issue. The capital gain component is a little different. Because the companies issuing bonds promise to repay a fixed amount when the bonds mature, bond prices do not typically rise in step with a firm's profits as stocks do. However, bond prices do rise and fall as market interest rates change. A basic relationship that bond investors must keep in mind is that *interest rates and bond prices move in opposite directions*. When interest rates rise, bond prices fall, and when rates drop, bond prices move up. We'll have more to say about this relation later in the chapter, but here's the intuition behind it. Imagine that you buy a brand-new bond issued by a company like GE paying 6% interest. Suppose that a month later, market rates have risen, and new bonds pay investors 7% interest. If you want to sell your GE bond, you're likely to experience a capital loss because investors will not want to buy a bond paying 6% interest when the going rate in the market is 7%. With fewer buyers interested in them, GE bonds will decline in value. Happily, the opposite outcome can occur if market rates fall. When the going rate on bonds is 5%, your GE bond paying 6% would command a premium in the market. Taken together, the current income and capital gains earned from bonds can lead to attractive returns.

Investors can trade a wide variety of bonds in the market, from relatively safe issues sought by conservative investors (e.g., General Electric bonds) to highly speculative securities appropriate for investors who can tolerate a great deal of risk (e.g., Sirius XM bonds). In addition, the potential risks and returns offered by *all* types of bonds depend in part upon the volatility of interest rates. Because interest rate movements cause bond prices to change, higher interest rate volatility makes bond returns less predictable.

Other bonds have special features designed to appeal to certain types of investors. Investors in high tax brackets who want to shelter income from taxes find tax-exempt bonds appealing. Municipal bonds, for example, pay interest that is not subject to federal income taxation, and interest on Treasury bonds is exempt from state income tax. Despite the term "fixed income," some bonds make interest payments that vary through time. For example, governments in the United States and many other countries issue inflation-indexed bonds with interest payments that rise with inflation. Those bonds appeal to investors who want some protection from the risk of rising inflation.

Putting Bond Market Performance in Perspective

Interest rates drive the bond market. In fact, *the behavior of interest rates is the single most important influence on bond returns*. Interest rates determine not only the current income investors will receive but also the capital gains (or losses) they will incur. It's not surprising, therefore, that bond-market participants follow interest rates closely and that when commentators in the news media describe how the market has performed on

FIGURE 10.1   **The Behavior of Interest Rates Over Time—1962–2008**

Interest rates rose dramatically from 1962 to the early 1980s before starting a long-term decline that continued into 2009. Rates on corporate bonds tend to mirror rates on government bonds, although corporate rates are higher due to the risk of default by the issuing corporation. Note that the gap or "spread" between corporate and Treasury bond yields was particularly wide in 2007–2008 during the financial crisis.

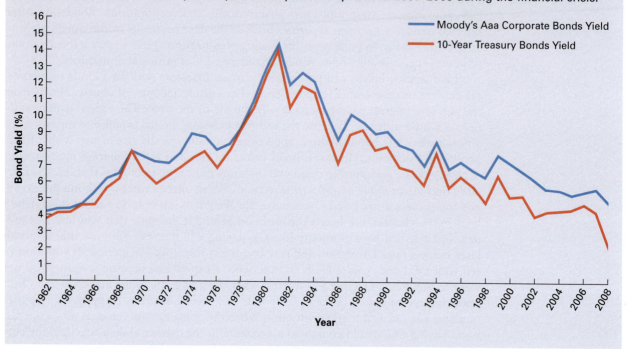

a particular day, they usually speak in terms of what happened to bond yields that day rather than what happened to bond prices.

Figure 10.1 provides a look at interest rates on bonds issued by corporations and the U.S. government from 1962–2008. It shows that rates rose steadily through the 1960s and 1970s, peaking in the early 1980s, at nearly three times their 1962 levels. Rates then began a long downward slide, and by the summer of 2009 (not shown in the figure), rates were lower than they had ever been. Keep in mind that rising interest rates lead to falling bond prices, so during the 1970s, investors who held bonds that had been issued in the 1960s endured capital losses. By the same token, investors who purchased bonds when interest rates were very high in the early 1980s earned large capital gains as market interest rates subsequently declined.

Figure 10.1 shows that rates on corporate and government bonds tend to move together, but corporate bond rates are higher. Higher rates on corporate bonds compensate investors for the risk that corporations might default on their debts. The difference between the rate on corporate bonds and the rate on government bonds is called the *yield spread* or the *credit spread*. When business conditions are weak and the risk of defaults on corporate bonds increases, the yield spread widens as it did in 2007–2008.

Historical Returns   As with stocks, *total returns* in the bond market are made up of both current income and capital gains (or losses). Table 10.1 lists *year-end market yields* and total *annual total returns* for U.S. government bonds from 1962 through 2008.

MARKETS in CRISIS

Yield Spreads Approach Records

One interesting indicator of the state of the economy is the yield spread between low-risk government bonds and high-risk corporate bonds, sometimes called junk bonds. During the 1990–1991 recession, this yield spread set a record of 10.5%. That means that if investors require a 5% interest rate on government bonds, then they will demand a 15.5% rate on the most risky corporate bonds. In 2008, the junk bond credit spread widened again, reaching 10.4%, just shy of the 1990s record.

Interestingly, both of these episodes corresponded with a major crisis in the investment banking industry. In 1990 it was the failure of Drexel Burnham Lambert and the fall of junk-bond king Michael Milken that led to wide spreads on junk bonds. In 2008, the yield spreads reflected investors' concerns following the 2007 failure of Lehman Brothers and bailouts of several other large financial institutions.

(Source: New York University Salomon Center.)

Note how total returns on bonds turned negative in 1967 as market yields began to climb. In fact, from 1967 to 1980, there were eight years when total returns on bonds were negative—which is highly unusual for the bond market. In contrast, look at the period from 1981 through 2008, when rates were in a general state of decline: There were only four years of negative returns, whereas double-digit returns occurred in 13 of the 28 years.

TABLE 10.1   Historical Annual Yields and Total Rates of Return for Treasury Bonds

Year	Year-End T-Bond Yield	T-Bond Total Rates of Return	Year	Year-End T-Bond Yield	T-Bond Total Rates of Return
1962	3.8%	6.9%	1986	7.1%	24.5%
1963	4.2	1.2	1987	8.9	−2.7
1964	4.2	3.5	1988	9.2	9.7
1965	4.6	0.7	1989	7.9	18.1
1966	4.7	3.7	1990	8.2	6.2
1967	5.7	−9.2	1991	6.9	19.3
1968	6.2	−0.3	1992	6.7	8.1
1969	7.8	−5.1	1993	5.8	18.2
1970	6.5	12.1	1994	7.8	−7.8
1971	5.9	13.2	1995	5.6	31.7
1972	6.4	5.7	1996	6.3	−0.9
1973	6.9	−1.1	1997	5.7	15.9
1974	7.4	4.4	1998	4.8	13.1
1975	7.8	9.2	1999	6.4	−9.0
1976	6.8	16.8	2000	5.1	21.5
1977	7.8	−0.7	2001	5.2	3.7
1978	9.1	−1.2	2002	3.9	17.8
1979	10.5	−1.2	2003	4.2	1.4
1980	12.3	−3.9	2004	4.3	8.5
1981	14.0	1.9	2005	4.4	7.8
1982	10.4	40.4	2006	4.7	1.2
1983	11.8	0.7	2007	4.2	9.9
1984	11.4	15.5	2008	2.2	25.9
1985	9.1	31.0			

We can use the return data from Table 10.1 to look at average bond returns over different investment horizons, as shown below:

Holding Period	Average Annual Returns
5 years: 2004–2008	10.7%
10 years: 1999–2008	8.9%
20 years: 1989–2008	10.5%

These figures show that most years in the last two decades were very good to bond investors. But that was due simply to the fact that the U.S. economy was in a sustained period of declining interest rates, *which in turn produced hefty capital gains and above-average returns*. Whether market interest rates will (or even can) continue on that path is, of course, highly doubtful. That explains in large part why most market observers caution against expecting abnormally high rates of return over the next decade or so.

Bonds Versus Stocks Compared to stocks, bonds are generally less risky and provide higher current income. Bonds, like stocks, are issued by a wide range of companies as well as various governmental bodies, so investors can construct well-diversified portfolios with bonds, just as they do with stocks. On the other hand, the potential for very high returns on bonds is much more limited compared to stocks, even though the last two decades have been exceptional for bonds.

Figure 10.2 illustrates some of the performance differences between stocks and bonds by showing how a $10,000 investment in either stocks or bonds would have grown from 1997–2008. Investors in stocks were far better off in the late 1990s as the equity market boomed. Stocks peaked in March 2000, and they fell even more after the terrorist attacks on September 11, 2001. By 2002, bond investors were back in front, although stocks gradually closed the gap, overtaking bonds in 2007. However, the financial crisis began that summer, and stocks went into a freefall in 2008.

Figure 10.2 illustrates that stock returns are much more volatile than bond returns are. If stocks are riskier, then investors should, on average, earn higher returns on stocks than on bonds, and we know from the historical evidence presented in Chapter 4 that stocks have outperformed bonds over long investment horizons. Still, Figure 10.2 shows that bonds can outperform stocks even over periods as long as a decade. The biggest differences in returns between stocks and bonds usually come during bear markets when stock returns are negative. In part, this reflects a phenomenon called "flight to quality" in which investors pull their funds out of the stock market to invest in less risky securities such as bonds. For example, Table 10.1 (on page 365) shows that while investors in stocks lost roughly 40% of their money in 2007–2008, government bond investors made nearly that much (i.e., 9.9% plus 25.9%).

Most investors would agree that even if bonds earn lower returns than stocks on average, that's a low price to pay for *the level of stability that bonds bring to a portfolio*. The fact is, bond returns are far more stable than stock returns, plus they possess *excellent portfolio diversification properties*. As a general rule, adding bonds to a portfolio will, *up to a point*, reduce the portfolio's risk without dramatically reducing its return. Investors don't buy bonds for their high returns, except when they think interest rates are heading down. Rather, investors buy them for their current income and/or for the stability they bring to a portfolio.

FIGURE 10.2 **Comparative Performance of Stocks and Bonds—1997 Through 2008**

This graph shows what happened to $10,000 invested in bonds over the 12-year period from January 1997 through December 2008, versus the same amount invested in stocks. Clearly, while stocks held a commanding lead through early 2000, the ensuing bear market more than erased that advantage. That pattern repeated itself as stocks outperformed bonds from 2003 to mid 2007, only to fall sharply through the end of 2008.

Note: Performance figures and graphs are based on fully compounded rates of return and include reinvested current income (dividends and interest) as well as capital gains (or losses); taxes have been ignored in all calculations.

	Average Annual Return	Value of $10,000 at the end of 2008
Bonds	6.18%	$20,943
Stocks	1.65%	$12,194

Exposure to Risk

Like all other investments, bonds are subject to a variety of risks. Generally speaking, bonds are exposed to five major types of risks: interest rate risk, purchasing power risk, business/financial risk, liquidity risk, and call risk.

- *Interest Rate Risk.* Interest rate risk is the most important risk that fixed-income investors must face, *because it's the major cause of price volatility in the bond market*. For bonds, interest rate risk translates into market risk, meaning that the behavior of interest rates affects nearly *all* bonds and cuts across *all* sectors of the market, even the U.S. Treasury market. When market interest rates rise, bond prices fall, and vice versa. As interest rates become more volatile, so do bond prices.

- *Purchasing Power Risk.* Inflation erodes the purchasing power of money, and that creates purchasing power risk. Investors are aware of this, of course, so market interest rates on bonds compensate investors for the rate of inflation *that they expect* over the life of a bond. When inflation is low and predictable, bonds do pretty well, because their returns exceed the inflation rate by an amount sufficient to provide investors with a positive return, even after accounting for inflation's effect on purchasing power. When inflation takes off unexpectedly, as it did in the late 1970s, bond yields start to lag behind inflation rates, and the interest payments made by bonds fail to keep up. The end result is that the purchasing power of the money that bond investors receive falls faster than they anticipated. That's what the term purchasing power risk means. Of course, risk cuts both ways, so when the inflation rate falls unexpectedly, bonds do exceptionally well.

- *Business/Financial Risk.* This is basically the risk that the *issuer will default on interest and/or principal payments.* Also known as *credit risk or default risk,* business/financial risk has to do with the quality and financial viability of the issuer. The stronger the financial position of the issuer, the less business/financial risk there is to worry about. Default risk is essentially zero for some securities (e.g., U.S. Treasuries). For others, such as corporate and municipal bonds, it's a very important consideration.

- *Liquidity Risk.* Liquidity risk is the risk that a bond will be difficult to sell at a reasonable price if the investor wants to sell it. In certain sectors of the market, this can be a big problem. Even though the U.S. bond market is enormous, many bonds do not trade actively once they are issued. U.S. Treasury bonds are the exception to the rule, but most corporate and municipal bonds are relatively illiquid.

- *Call Risk.* Call risk, or *prepayment risk,* is the risk that a bond will be "called" (retired) long before its scheduled maturity date. Issuers often prepay their bonds when interest rates fall. (We'll examine call features later in this chapter.) When issuers call their bonds, the bondholders get their cash back and have to find another place for their funds—and there's the problem. Because bonds are nearly always called for prepayment after interest rates have fallen, comparable investments just aren't available. Thus, investors have to replace high-yielding bonds with much lower-yielding bonds.

The returns on bonds are, of course, related to risk—other things being equal, the more risk embedded in a bond, the greater the expected return. The risks of investing in bonds depend upon the characteristics of the bond and the entity that issued it. For example, as we'll see later in the chapter, there's more interest rate risk with a long-term bond than with a short-term bond. In addition, for particular bonds, the characteristics that affect risk may have offsetting effects, and that makes risk comparisons between bonds difficult. That is, one issue could have *more* interest rate and call risk, but *less* credit and liquidity risk than another issue. We'll examine the various features that affect a bond's risk exposure as we work our way through this chapter.

CONCEPTS IN REVIEW

Answers available at
www.pearsonhighered.com/gitman

10.1 What appeal do bonds hold for investors? Give several reasons why bonds make attractive investment outlets.

10.2 How would you describe the behavior of market interest rates and bond returns over the last 30 to 40 years? Do swings in market interest rates have any bearing on bond returns? Explain.

10.3 Identify and briefly describe the five types of risk to which bonds are exposed. What is the most important source of risk for bonds in general? Explain.

Essential Features of a Bond

LG2 **LG3** A *bond* is a negotiable, long-term debt instrument that carries certain obligations (the payment of interest and the repayment of principal) on the part of the issuer. Because bondholders are only lending money to the issuer, they are not entitled to any of the rights and privileges associated with common stock, such as the right to vote at shareholders' meetings. But bondholders, as well as bond issuers, do have a number of well-defined rights and obligations that together define the essential features of a bond. We'll now take a look at some of these features. As you will see, when it comes to bonds, it's especially important to know what you're getting into, *for many seemingly insignificant features can have dramatic effects on price behavior and investment return.*

Bond Interest and Principal

A bond investor's return is limited to fixed interest and principal payments as long as the investor holds the bond to maturity. Most bonds pay interest every six months, although some make monthly interest payments and some pay interest annually. A bond's **coupon** defines the annual interest income that the issuer will pay to the bondholder. For instance, if a bond with a face value (or principal) of $1,000 pays $80 in interest each year, we say that $80 is the coupon and 8% is the coupon rate. If the bond makes semiannual payments, there would be two $40 payments every six months. The bond's **current yield** measures the interest component of a bond's return. The current yield equals the annual coupon divided by the bond's market price. For example, if an 8% bond is currently priced in the market at $875, then it would have a current yield of 9.14%: ($1,000 × .08)/$875 = $80/$875 = 0.0914.

The **principal** of a bond, also known as an issue's *par value*, specifies the amount of capital that must be repaid at maturity. Note that a bond's market price need not, and usually does not, equal its par value. As we have discussed, bond prices fluctuate as interest rates move, yet a bond's par value remains fixed over its life.

Maturity Date

Unlike common stock, all debt securities have limited lives and will mature on some future date, the issue's **maturity date**. Whereas bond issuers make interest payments semiannually over the life of the issue, they repay principal only at maturity. The maturity date on a bond is fixed. It not only defines the life of a new issue but also denotes the amount of time remaining for older, outstanding bonds. Such a life span is known as an issue's *term to maturity*. For example, a new issue may come out as a 25-year bond; five years later, it will have 20 years remaining to maturity.

We can distinguish two types of bonds based on the issuer's plans to mature the debt: term and serial bonds. A **term bond** has a single, fairly lengthy maturity date and is the most common type. A **serial bond**, in contrast, has a series of different maturity dates, perhaps as many as 15 or 20, within a single bond offering. For example, a 20-year term bond issued in 2010 has a single maturity date of 2030. That same issue as a serial bond might have 20 annual maturity dates, extending from 2010 through 2030. At each of these annual maturity dates, a certain portion of the issue would mature.

Debt instruments with different maturities go by different names. A debt security that's originally issued with a maturity of 2 to 10 years is known as a **note**, whereas a *bond* technically has an initial term to maturity of more than ten years. In practice, notes are often issued with maturities of five to seven years, whereas bonds normally carry maturities of 20 to 30 years, or more.

Principles of Bond Price Behavior

The price of a bond is a function of its coupon, its maturity, and the level of market interest rates. Figure 10.3 captures the relationship of bond prices to market interest rates. Basically, the graph reinforces the *inverse relationship* that exists between bond prices and market rates: *Lower* rates lead to *higher* bond prices.

Figure 10.3 also shows the difference between premium and discount bonds. A **premium bond** is one that sells for more than its par value. A premium results when market interest rates drop below the bond's coupon rate. A **discount bond**, in contrast, sells for less than par. The discount is the result of market rates being greater than the issue's coupon rate. Thus, the 10% bond in Figure 10.3 trades at a premium when market rates are at 8%, but at a discount when rates are at 12%.

When a bond is first issued, it usually sells at a price that equals or is very close to par value. Likewise, when the bond matures—some 15, 20, or 30 years later—it will once again be priced at its par value. What happens to the price of the bond in between is of considerable interest to most bond investors. In this regard, the extent to which bond prices move depends not only on the *direction* of change in interest rates but also

FIGURE 10.3   The Price Behavior of a Bond

A bond will sell at its par value so long as the prevailing market interest rate remains the same as the bond's coupon—in this case, 10%. However, even when the market rate does not equal the coupon rate, as a bond approaches its maturity, the price of the issue moves toward its par value.

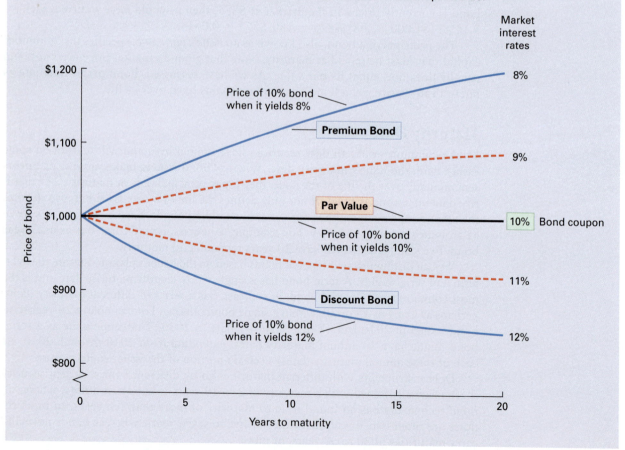

Smart's Tour of the Web
To watch author Scott
Smart discuss key Web sites
for this chapter visit
www.myfinancelab.com

on the *magnitude* of such change: the greater the moves in interest rates, the greater the swings in bond prices.

However, bond price volatility also varies according to an issue's coupon and maturity. That is, bonds with *lower coupons* and/or *longer maturities* have *lots of price volatility* and are more responsive to changes in market interest rates. (Note in Figure 10.3 that for a given change in interest rates—e.g., from 10% to 8%—the largest change in price occurs when the bond has the greatest number of years to maturity.) Therefore, if you expect a *decline* in interest rates, you should buy bonds with lower coupons and longer maturities (to maximize capital gains). When interest rates move *up*, you should do just the opposite: Purchase bonds with high coupons and short maturities. This choice will minimize price variation and act to preserve as much capital as possible.

Actually, the *maturity* of an issue has a greater impact on price volatility than the coupon does. For example, look what happens to the price of an 8% bond when market interest rates move up or down:

Bond Maturity	Percentage Change in the Price of an 8% Coupon Bond When Interest Rates Are					
	5%	6%	7%	9%	10%	11%
5 years	13.00%	8.40%	4.10%	−3.90%	−7.60%	−11.10%
25 years	42.30%	25.60%	11.70%	−9.80%	−18.20%	−25.30%

The prices of both bonds rise when interest rates fall, but the effect is much larger for the longer-term bond. Similarly, both bonds fall in value when rates rise, but the long-term bond falls a lot more than the short-term bond does. Such behavior is universal with all fixed-income securities and is very important. It means that if investors want to reduce their exposure to capital losses or, more to the point, to lower the price volatility in their bond holdings, then they should buy bonds with shorter maturities.

Pricing a Bond

Unlike stocks, the vast majority of bonds—especially corporate and municipal bonds—rarely change hands in the secondary markets. As a result, with the exception of U.S. Treasury and some agency issues, bonds are not widely quoted in the financial press, not even in the *Wall Street Journal*. So, rather than looking at how bonds are quoted, let's look at how they're priced in the marketplace. Regardless of the type, *all bond prices are usually expressed as a percent of par*, meaning that a quote of, say, 85 translates into a price of 85% of the bond's par value or $850 for a bond with a $1,000 par value (most corporate and municipal bonds have $1,000 par values). Also, the price of any bond depends on the issue's coupon and maturity, so those two features are always a part of any listed price.

In the corporate and municipal markets, bonds are expressed in decimals, using three places to the right of the decimal point. Thus, a quote of 87.562, as a percent of a $1,000 par bond, converts to a price of $875.62. Similarly, a quote of 121.683 translates into a price of $1,216.83. In contrast, U.S. Treasury and agency bond quotes are stated in *thirty-seconds of a point* (where 1 point equals $10). For example, you might see the price of a T-bond listed at 94:16. Translated, that means the bond is priced at 94 16/32, or 94.5% of par—in other words, at $945.00. With government bonds, the figures to the right of the colon (:) show the number of thirty-seconds embedded in the price. Consider another bond that's trading at 141:08. This bond is being priced at 141 8/32, or 141.25 percent of par. Thus, the price of this bond in dollars is $1,412.50.

Call Features—Let the Buyer Beware!

Consider the following situation: You've just made an investment in a high-yielding, 25-year bond. Now you can sit back and let the cash flow in, right? Well, perhaps. Certainly, that will happen for the first several years. But, if market interest rates drop, it's also likely that you'll receive a notice from the issuer that the bond is being *called*—that the issue is being retired before its maturity date. There's really nothing you can do but turn in the bond and invest your money elsewhere. Every bond is issued with a **call feature**, which stipulates whether and under what conditions a bond can be called in for retirement prior to maturity.

Basically, there are three types of call features:

1. A bond can be *freely callable*, which means the issuer can prematurely retire the bond at any time.

2. A bond can be *noncallable*, which means the issuer is prohibited from retiring the bond prior to maturity.

3. The issue could carry a *deferred call*, which means the issue cannot be called until after a certain length of time has passed from the date of issue. In essence, the issue is noncallable during the deferment period and then becomes freely callable thereafter.

Call features allow bond issuers to take advantage of declines in market interest rates. Companies usually call outstanding bonds paying high rates and then reissue new bonds at lower rates. In other words, call features work *for the benefit of the issuers. When a bond is called, the net result is that the investor is left with a much lower rate of return than anticipated.*

Investors who find their bonds called out from under them do receive a small amount of extra compensation called the **call premium**. If the issue is called, the issuer will pay the call premium to investors, along with the issue's par value. The sum of the par value plus call premium represents the issue's **call price**. This is the amount the issuer must pay to retire the bond prematurely. As a general rule, call premiums usually equal about 8 to 12 months' interest at the earliest date of call and then become progressively smaller as the issue nears maturity. Using this rule, the initial call price of a 9% bond could be as high as $1,090, where $90 represents the call premium.

In addition to call features, some bonds may carry **refunding provisions**. These are much like call features except that they prohibit just one thing: the premature retirement of an issue from the proceeds of a lower-coupon bond. For example, a bond could come out as freely callable but *nonrefundable* for five years. In this case, the bond would probably be sold by brokers as a *deferred refunding issue*, with little or nothing said about its call feature. The distinction is important, however: It means that a nonrefunding or deferred refunding issue *can still be called and prematurely retired for any reason other than refunding.* Thus, an investor could face a call on a high-yielding nonrefundable issue so long as the issuer has so-called "clean cash" to retire the bond prematurely.

Sinking Funds

Another provision that's important to investors is the **sinking fund**, which stipulates how the issuer will pay off the bond over time. This provision applies only to term bonds, of course, because serial issues already have a predetermined repayment schedule. Not all (term) bonds have sinking-fund requirements, but for those that do, the sinking fund specifies the annual repayment schedule that will be used to pay off the issue. It indicates how much principal will be retired each year.

Sinking-fund requirements generally begin one to five years after the date of issue and continue annually thereafter until all or most of the issue is paid off. Any amount not repaid (which might equal 10% to 25% of the issue) would then be retired with a single "balloon" payment at maturity. Unlike a call or refunding provision, the issuer generally does not have to pay a call premium with sinking-fund calls. Instead, the bonds are normally called at par for sinking-fund purposes.

There's another difference between sinking-fund provisions and call or refunding features. That is, whereas a call or refunding provision gives the issuer the *right* to retire a bond prematurely, a sinking-fund provision *obligates* the issuer to pay off the bond systematically over time. The issuer has no choice. It must make sinking-fund payments in a prompt and timely fashion or run the risk of being in default.

Secured or Unsecured Debt

A single issuer may have a number of different bonds outstanding at any given point in time. In addition to coupon and maturity, one bond can be differentiated from another by the type of collateral behind the issue. Issues can be either junior or senior. **Senior bonds** are secured obligations, which are backed by a legal claim on some specific property of the issuer. Such issues would include:

- **Mortgage bonds,** which are secured by real estate.

- **Collateral trust bonds,** which are backed by financial assets owned by the issuer but held in trust by a third party.

- **Equipment trust certificates,** which are secured by specific pieces of equipment (e.g., boxcars and airplanes) and are popular with railroads and airlines.

- **First and refunding bonds,** which are basically a combination of first mortgage and junior lien bonds (i.e., the bonds are secured in part by a first mortgage on some of the issuer's property and in part by second or third mortgages on other properties).

Note that first and refunding bonds are *less secure* than, and should *not* be confused with, straight first-mortgage bonds.

Junior bonds, on the other hand, are backed only by the promise of the issuer to pay interest and principal on a timely basis. There are several classes of unsecured bonds, the most popular of which is known as a **debenture.** For example, a major company like Hewlett-Packard could issue $500 million worth of 20-year debenture bonds. Being a debenture, the bond would be totally unsecured, meaning there is no collateral backing up the obligation, other than the good name of the issuer. In the final analysis, it's the quality of the issuer that matters. For that reason, highly regarded firms have no trouble selling *billion-dollar debenture bond issues* and at highly competitive rates.

Subordinated debentures can also be found in the market. These issues have a claim on income secondary to other debenture bonds. **Income bonds,** the most junior of all bonds, are unsecured debts requiring that interest be paid only after a certain amount of income is earned. With these bonds, there is no legally binding requirement to meet interest payments on a timely or regular basis so long as a specified amount of income has not been earned. These issues are similar in many respects to *revenue bonds* found in the municipal market.

Bond Ratings

To many investors, an issue's *agency rating* is just as important in defining the characteristics of a bond as are its coupon, maturity, and call features. These ratings indicate the amount of *credit risk* embedded in a bond and are widely used by fixed-income investors. **Bond ratings** are like grades: A letter grade that designates investment quality is assigned to an issue on the basis of extensive financial analysis. Ratings are an important part of the municipal and corporate bond markets, where issues are regularly evaluated and rated by one or more of the rating agencies. Even some agency issues, like the Tennessee Valley Authority (TVA), are rated, although they always receive ratings that confirm the obvious—that the issues are prime grade. The two largest and best-known rating agencies are Moody's and Standard & Poor's; another lesser known but still important bond-rating agency is Fitch Investors Service.

How Ratings Work   Every time a large new issue comes to the market, it is analyzed by a staff of professional credit analysts who estimate the likelihood that the issuer will default on its obligations to pay principal and interest. The rating agency studies the financial records of the issuing organization and assesses its future prospects. As you might expect, the firm's financial strength and stability are very important in determining the appropriate bond rating. Although there is far more to setting a rating than cranking out a few financial ratios, a strong relationship does exist between the operating results and financial condition of the firm and the rating its bonds receive. Generally, higher ratings are associated with more profitable companies that rely *less* on debt as a form of financing, are more liquid, have stronger cash flows, and have no trouble servicing their debt in a prompt and timely fashion.

Table 10.2 lists the various ratings assigned to bonds by the two major services. In addition to the standard rating categories noted in the table, Moody's uses numerical

TABLE 10.2	Bond Ratings	
Moody's	**S&P**	**Definition**
Aaa	AAA	*High-grade investment bonds.* The highest rating assigned, denoting extremely strong capacity to pay principal and interest. Often called "gilt-edge" securities.
Aa	AA	*High-grade investment bonds.* High quality by all standards but rated lower primarily because the margins of protection are not quite as strong.
A	A	*Medium-grade investment bonds.* Many favorable investment attributes, but elements may be present that suggest susceptibility to adverse economic changes.
Baa	BBB	*Medium-grade investment bonds.* Adequate capacity to pay principal and interest but possibly lacking certain protective elements against adverse economic conditions.
Ba	BB	*Speculative issues.* Only moderate protection of principal and interest in varied economic times. (This is one of the ratings carried by junk bonds.)
B	B	*Speculative issues.* Generally lacking desirable characteristics of investment bonds. Assurance of principal and interest may be small; this is another junk-bond rating.
Caa	CCC	*Default.* Poor-quality issues that may be in default or in danger of default.
Ca	CC	*Default.* Highly speculative issues, often in default or possessing other market shortcomings.
C		*Default.* These issues may be regarded as extremely poor in investment quality.
	C	*Default.* Rating given to income bonds on which no interest is paid.
	D	*Default.* Issues actually in default, with principal or interest in arrears.

(Source: Moody's *Bond Record* and Standard & Poor's *Bond Guide*.)

modifiers (1, 2, or 3) on bonds rated double-A to B, while S&P uses plus (+) or minus (−) signs on the same rating classes to show relative standing within a major rating category. For example, A+ (or A1) means a strong, high A rating, whereas A− (or A3) indicates that the issue is on the low end of the A rating scale.

Note that the top four ratings (Aaa through Baa, or AAA through BBB) designate *investment-grade* bonds. Such ratings are highly coveted by issuers, as they indicate financially strong, well-run companies. Companies and governmental bodies that want to raise money by issuing bonds save money if they have an investment-grade rating because investors will accept lower coupon rates on these bonds compared to those with lower ratings. Bonds with below investment-grade ratings are called high-yield bonds or junk bonds. The issuers of these bonds generally lack the financial strength that backs investment-grade issues. Most of the time, when Moody's and S&P assign ratings to a particular bond issue, their ratings agree. Sometimes, however, an issue carries two different ratings. These **split ratings** are viewed simply as "shading" the quality of an issue one way or another. For example, an issue might be rated Aa by Moody's but A or A+ by S&P.

Also, just because a bond receives a certain rating at the time of issue doesn't mean it will keep that rating for the rest of its life. Ratings change as the financial condition of the issuer changes. In fact, all rated issues are reviewed on a regular basis to ensure that the assigned rating is still valid. Many issues do carry a single rating to maturity, but it is not uncommon for ratings to be revised up or down. As you might expect, the market responds to rating revisions by adjusting bond yields accordingly. For example, an upward revision (e.g., from A to AA) causes the market yield on the bond to drop, as a reflection of the bond's improved quality. By the same token, if a company's financial condition deteriorates, ratings on its bonds may be downgraded. In fact, there is a special name given to junk bonds that once had investment-grade ratings—fallen angels. One final point: Although it may appear that the firm is receiving the rating, it is actually the *issue* that receives it. As a result, a firm's different issues can have different ratings. The senior securities, for example, might carry one rating and the junior issues another, lower rating.

What Ratings Mean Investors pay close attention to agency ratings, because ratings can affect not only potential market behavior but comparative market yields as well. Specifically, *the higher the rating, the lower the yield*, other things being equal. For example, whereas an A-rated bond might offer a 7.5% yield, a comparable triple-A issue would probably yield something like 7%. Furthermore, investment-grade securities are far more interest-sensitive and tend to exhibit more uniform price behavior than junk bonds and other lower-rated issues.

Perhaps most important, *bond ratings serve to relieve individual investors of the drudgery of evaluating the investment quality of an issue on their own*. Large institutional investors often have their own staff of credit analysts who independently assess the creditworthiness of various corporate and municipal issuers. Individual investors, in contrast, have little if anything to gain from conducting their own credit analysis. After all, credit analysis is time-consuming and costly, and it demands a good deal more expertise than the average individual investor possesses. Two words of caution are in order, however. First, bear in mind that bond ratings are intended to measure only an issue's *default risk*, which has no bearing whatsoever on an issue's exposure to *market risk*. Thus, if interest rates increase, even the highest-quality issues go down in price, subjecting investors to capital loss and market risk. Second, ratings agencies do make mistakes, and during the recent financial crisis, their mistakes made headlines.

MARKETS IN CRISIS

Rating Agencies Miss a Big One

Mortgage-backed securities, essentially debt instruments with returns that depended upon payments on an underlying pool of residential real estate mortgages, played a central role in the financial crisis that began in 2007 and the recession that followed. Moody's and Standard & Poor's provided ratings on these instruments, just as they did with corporate bonds. Rating these securities was much more complex than rating corporate bonds for a variety of reasons, among them the fact that rating agencies knew relatively little about the creditworthiness of the individual homeowners whose mortgages were in the pool. The rating agencies gave many mortgage-backed securities investment-grade ratings, and those ratings prompted investors of all kinds, including large financial institutions, to pour money into those assets. As real estate prices began to decline, the values of "toxic" mortgage-backed securities plummeted. That led to the failure of Lehman Brothers and bailouts of other large financial institutions.

CONCEPTS IN REVIEW

Answers available at
www.pearsonhighered.com/gitman

10.4 Can issue characteristics (such as coupon and call features) affect the yield and price behavior of bonds? Explain.

10.5 What is the difference between a *call feature* and a *sinking-fund provision*? Briefly describe the three different types of call features. Can a bond be freely callable but non-refundable?

10.6 What is the difference between a *premium bond* and a *discount bond*? What three attributes are most important in determining an issue's price volatility?

10.7 Bonds are said to be quoted "as a percent of par." What does that mean? What is 1 point worth in the bond market?

10.8 What are *bond ratings*, and how can they affect investor returns? What are *split ratings*?

10.9 From the perspective of an individual investor, what good are bond ratings? Do bond ratings indicate the amount of market risk embedded in a bond? Explain.

The Market for Debt Securities

LG4 **LG5** Thus far, our discussion has dealt with basic bond features. We now shift our attention to a review of the market in which these securities are traded. To begin with, the bond market is chiefly over-the-counter in nature, as listed bonds represent only a small portion of total outstanding obligations. In addition, this market is far more stable than the stock market. Indeed, although interest rates—and therefore bond prices—do move up and down over time, when bond price activity is measured on a daily basis, it is *remarkably stable*. Two other things that stand out about the bond market: It's big, and it has been growing rapidly. From a $250 billion market in 1950, it has grown to the point where, in 2009, the amount of bonds outstanding in the United States totaled *$33 trillion!* That makes the bond market nearly three times the size of the U.S. stock market.

Here's what the U.S. bond market looked like in January 2009:

	Amount Outstanding ($ in trillions)
U.S. Treasury securities	$6.8
Agency securities	8.2
Municipal bonds	2.7
Corporate and foreign bonds	11.6
Other	3.7
Total	$33.0

(Source: *Federal Reserve Bulletin*, "Credit Market Debt Outstanding," June 2009.)

The growth in this market has also been remarkable, as it has grown at roughly a 9% annual clip since 1992.

Major Market Segments

There are bonds available in today's market to meet almost any investment objective and to suit just about any type of investor. As a matter of convenience, the domestic bond market is normally separated into four major segments, according to type of issuer: Treasury, agency, municipal, and corporate. As we shall see, each sector has developed its own features, as well as its own trading characteristics.

Treasury Bonds "Treasuries" (or "governments," as they are sometimes called) are a dominant force in the fixed-income market. If not the most popular type of bond, they certainly are the best known. In addition to T-bills (a popular short-term debt security), the U.S. Treasury issues notes and bonds. It also issues *inflation-indexed securities*, which are the newest type of Treasury debt.

All Treasury obligations are of the highest quality because they are all backed by the "full faith and credit" of the U.S. government. This backing, along with their liquidity, makes them very popular with individual and institutional investors both here and abroad. Indeed, Treasury securities are traded in all the major markets of the world, from New York to London to Sydney and Tokyo.

Treasury notes are issued with maturities of 2, 3, 5, 7, and 10 years, whereas **Treasury bonds** carry 30-year maturities. All Treasury notes and bonds pay interest semiannually. Interest income from these securities is subject to normal federal income tax but *is exempt from state and local taxes*. The Treasury today issues only *noncallable* securities; the last time it issued callable debt was in 1984. It issues its securities at regularly scheduled auctions, the results of which are widely reported by the financial media (see Figure 10.4 on page 378). The Treasury establishes the initial yields and coupons on the securities it issues through this auction process.

Inflation-Protected Securities The newest form of Treasury security (first issued in 1997) is the **Treasury Inflation-Protected Securities**, also known as **TIPS**. They are issued with 5, 10, and 20-year maturities, and they pay interest semiannually. They offer investors the opportunity to stay ahead of inflation by periodically adjusting their returns for any inflation that has occurred. That is, if inflation causes prices to increase by 3%, then the par value of the bond also increases by 3%, so the par value of a $1,000 bond will grow to $1,030 by the end of the year. Coupon payments rise, too, because the coupon rate is paid on the inflation-adjusted principal. In the previous example, if the bond offered a 2% coupon rate when it was originally issued, the

FIGURE 10.4   Auction Results for a 30-Year Treasury Bond
Treasury auctions are closely followed by the financial media. The number of bids submitted generally far exceeds the size of the issue, so the spread between the highest and lowest bids is quite small—sometimes as small as 2 basis points, or 2/100 of 1%.
(Source: Department of the Treasury—Bureau of Public Debt—Washington, DC 20239, August 13, 2009.)

AUCTION RESULTS

Here are the results of the Treasury auction of new 30-year bonds. All bids are awarded at a single price at the market-clearing yield. Rates are determined by the difference between that price and the face value.

Applications	$38,032,046,500
Accepted bids	$15,000,001,500
Bids at market-clearing yield accepted	16.77%
Accepted noncompetitively	$21,546,500
Foreign noncompetitively	$0
Auction price (Rate)	99.331386 (4.541%)
Coupon equivalent	4.50%
CUSIP number	912810QC5

The bonds are dated Aug. 15, 2009 and mature Aug. 15, 2039.

- The amount of bids submitted.
- Size of the issue—the dollar amount of accepted bids.
- The amount of noncompetitive bids submitted (and accepted).
- The average price and yield (rate) on the issue.
- The coupon that the issue will carry, which is set after the auction.

investor would expect $20 per year in interest. But if there is 3% inflation and the bond's par value rises to $1,030, then the investor receives a coupon equal to 2% of the new par value, or $20.60. Because this type of bond offers payments that automatically adjust with inflation, investors do not have to "guess" what the inflation rate will be over the bond's life. In other words, TIPS eliminate purchasing power risk. Because they are less risky than ordinary bonds, TIPS generally offer lower coupon rates than ordinary Treasury bonds do.

Agency Bonds   **Agency bonds** are debt securities issued by various agencies and organizations of the U.S. government, such as the Federal Home Loan Bank, the Federal Farm Credit Systems, the Small Business Administration, the Student Loan Marketing Association, and the Federal National Mortgage Association. Although these securities are the closest things to Treasuries, they are not obligations of the U.S. Treasury and technically should not be considered the same as Treasury bonds. Even so, *they are very high-quality securities that have almost no risk of default.* In spite of the similar default risk, however, these securities usually provide yields that are slightly above the market rates for Treasuries. Thus, they offer a way to increase returns with little or no real difference in risk.

There are basically two types of agency issues: government-sponsored and federal agencies. Six government-sponsored organizations and more than two dozen federal agencies offer agency bonds. To overcome some of the problems in the marketing of many relatively small federal agency securities, Congress established the Federal Financing Bank to consolidate the financing activities of all federal agencies. (As a rule, the generic term *agency* is used to denote both government-sponsored and federal agency obligations.)

TABLE 10.3 Characteristics of Some Popular Agency Issues

Type of Issue	Minimum Denomination	Initial Maturity	Tax Status* Federal	State	Local
Federal Farm Credit System	$ 1,000	13 months to 15 years	T	E	E
Federal Home Loan Bank	10,000	1 to 20 years	T	E	E
Federal Land Banks	1,000	1 to 10 years	T	E	E
Farmers Home Administration	25,000	1 to 25 years	T	T	T
Federal Housing Administration	50,000	1 to 40 years	T	T	T
Federal Home Loan Mortgage Corp.** ("Freddie Mac")	25,000	18 to 30 years	T	T	T
Federal National Mortgage Association** ("Fannie Mae")	25,000	1 to 30 years	T	T	T
Government National Mortgage Association** (GNMA—"Ginnie Mae")	25,000	12 to 40 years	T	T	T
Student Loan Marketing Association ("Sallie Mae")	10,000	3 to 10 years	T	E	E
Tennessee Valley Authority (TVA)	1,000	5 to 50 years	T	E	E
U.S. Postal Service	10,000	25 years	T	E	E
Federal Financing Corp.	1,000	1 to 20 years	T	E	E

*T = taxable; E = tax-exempt.
**Mortgage-backed securities.

Table 10.3 presents selected characteristics of some of the more popular agency bonds. As the list of issuers shows, most of the government agencies support either agriculture or housing. Although agency issues are not direct liabilities of the U.S. government, a few of them do carry government guarantees and therefore represent the full faith and credit of the U.S. Treasury. Even those issues that do not carry such guarantees are viewed as *moral obligations* of the U.S. government implying it's highly unlikely that Congress would allow one of them to default. Agency issues are normally noncallable or carry lengthy call deferment features. One final point: Since 1986 *all new agency (and Treasury) securities* have been issued in *book entry form*. This means that no certificate of ownership is issued to the buyer of the bonds. Rather, the buyer receives a "confirmation" of the transaction, and his or her name is entered in a computerized logbook, where it remains as long as that investor owns the security.

MARKETS in CRISIS

Implicit Guarantee Becomes Explicit

Debt securities issued by agencies such as the Federal National Mortgage Association (Fannie Mae) and the Federal Home Loan Mortgage Corporation (Freddie Mac) have generally had an implicit guarantee from the federal government, meaning that investors believed that the government would not allow a default on any of these instruments even if they were not "officially" backed by the full faith and credit of the U.S. government as Treasury bills, notes, and bonds are. In 2007, as residential mortgage defaults began to rise, Fannie Mae and Freddie Mac came under severe financial distress. On September 7, 2008, the federal government effectively took over these institutions, injecting $100 billion of new capital into each to stabilize them and to reassure investors that these giants of the mortgage industry, who held or guaranteed about $5.5 trillion in residential mortgage debt, would not disappear.

Municipal Bonds **Municipal bonds** are the issues of states, counties, cities, and other political subdivisions (such as school districts and water and sewer districts). This is a $2.7 trillion market today, and it's the only segment of the bond market where the individual investor plays a major role: About 40% of all municipal bonds are directly held by individuals. These bonds are often issued as *serial obligations*, which means the issue is broken into a series of smaller bonds, each with its own maturity date and coupon.

Municipal bonds ("munis") are brought to the market as either general obligation or revenue bonds. **General obligation bonds** are backed by the full faith, credit, and taxing power of the issuer. **Revenue bonds**, in contrast, are serviced by the income generated from specific income-producing projects (e.g., toll roads). The vast majority of munis today come out as revenue bonds, accounting for about 70% to 75% of the new-issue volume. Municipal bonds are customarily issued in $5,000 denominations.

The distinction between a general obligation bond and a revenue bond is important for a bondholder, because the issuer of a revenue bond is obligated to pay principal and interest *only if a sufficient level of revenue is generated*. If the funds aren't there, the issuer does not have to make payment on the bond. General obligation bonds, however, are required to be serviced in a timely fashion irrespective of the level of tax income generated by the municipality. Obviously, revenue bonds involve more risk than general obligations, and because of that, they provide higher yields.

A somewhat unusual aspect of municipal bonds is the widespread use of **municipal bond guarantees**. With these guarantees, a party other than the issuer assures the bondholder that principal and interest payments will be made in a timely manner. The third party, in essence, provides an additional source of collateral in the form of insurance, placed on the bond at the date of issue, which is nonrevocable over the life of the obligation. All of this improves the quality of the bond. The two principal insurers are the Municipal Bond Investors Assurance Corporation (MBIA) and the American Municipal Bond Assurance Corporation (AMBAC). These guarantors will normally insure any general obligation or revenue bond as long as it carries an S&P rating of triple-B or better. Municipal bond insurance results in higher ratings (usually triple-A) and improved liquidity for these bonds, which are generally more actively traded in the secondary markets. Insured bonds are especially common in the revenue market, where the insurance markedly boosts their attractiveness. That is, whereas an uninsured revenue bond lacks certainty of payment, a guaranteed issue is very much like a general obligation bond because the investor knows that principal and interest payments will be made on time.

Tax Advantages Without a doubt, the thing that makes municipal securities unique is the fact that, in most cases, their interest income is exempt from federal income taxes. That's why these issues are known as *tax-free*, or *tax-exempt*, bonds. Normally, the obligations are also exempt from state and local taxes *in the state in which they were issued*. For example, a California issue is free of California tax if the bondholder lives in California, but its interest income is subject to state tax if the investor resides in Arizona. Note that *capital gains on municipal bonds are not exempt from taxes*.

Individual investors are the biggest buyers of municipal bonds, and tax-free yield is a major draw. Table 10.4 shows what a taxable bond would have to yield to equal the net yield of a tax-free bond. *It demonstrates how the yield attractiveness of municipals varies with an investor's marginal tax rate*. Clearly, the higher the individual's tax bracket and the higher the tax rate that they face on additional income, the more attractive municipal bonds become. Generally speaking, an investor has to be in one of the higher federal tax brackets (28% to 35%) before municipal bonds offer yields that are

TABLE 10.4   Taxable Equivalent Yields for Various Tax-Exempt Returns

Taxable Income*			Tax-Free Yield					
Joint Returns ($000)	Individual Returns ($000)	Federal Tax Bracket	5%	6%	7%	8%	9%	10%
$0-$16.7	$0-$8.35	10%	5.56%	6.67%	7.78%	8.89%	10.00%	11.11%
$16.7-$67.9	$8.35-$33.95	15	5.88	7.06	8.24	9.41	10.59	11.76
$67.9-$137.05	$33.95-$82.25	25	6.67	8.00	9.33	10.67	12.00	13.33
$137.05-$208.85	$82.25-$171.55	28	6.94	8.33	9.72	11.11	12.50	13.89
$208.85-$372.95	$171.55-$372.95	33	7.46	8.96	10.45	11.94	13.43	14.93
$372.95 and above	$372.95 and above	35	7.69	9.23	10.77	12.31	13.85	15.38

*Taxable income and federal tax rates effective January 1, 2009.

competitive with fully taxable issues. This is so because municipal yields are (almost always) lower than those available from fully taxable issues (such as corporates). So, unless the tax effect is sufficient to raise the yield on a municipal to a figure that equals or surpasses taxable rates, municipal bonds will not provide sufficient return.

Taxable Equivalent Yields We can determine the level of return a fully taxable bond would have to provide in order to match the after-tax return of a lower-yielding, tax-free issue by computing what is known as a municipal's **taxable equivalent yield**. Indeed, use of the taxable equivalent yield is standard convention in the market; it facilitates comparing the return on a given municipal bond to any number of fully taxable issues. This measure can be calculated according to the following simple formula:

Equation 10.1

$$\text{Taxable equivalent yield} = \frac{\text{Yield on municipal bond}}{1 - \text{Federal tax rate}}$$

For example, if a municipal offered a yield of 6.5%, then an individual in the 35% tax bracket would have to find a fully taxable bond with a yield of 10.0% (i.e., 6.5%/0.65 = 10.0%) to reap the same after-tax returns as the municipal.

Note, however, that Equation 10.1 considers *federal taxes only*. As a result, the computed taxable equivalent yield applies only to certain situations: (1) to states that have no state income tax; (2) to situations where the investor is looking at an out-of-state bond (which would be taxable by the investor's state of residence); or (3) where the investor is comparing a municipal bond to a Treasury (or agency) bond—in which case *both* the Treasury and the municipal bonds are free from state income tax. Under any of these conditions, the only tax that's relevant is federal income tax, so using Equation 10.1 is appropriate.

But what if the investor is comparing an in-state bond to, say, a corporate bond? In this case, the in-state bond would be free from both federal and state taxes, but the corporate bond would not. As a result, Equation 10.1 could not be used. Instead, the investor should use a form of the equivalent yield formula that considers *both* federal and state income taxes:

Equation 10.2

$$\text{Taxable equivalent yield for both federal and state taxes} = \frac{\text{Municipal bond yield}}{1 - [\text{Federal tax rate} + \text{State tax rate}(1 - \text{Federal tax rate})]}$$

When both federal and state taxes are included in the calculations, the net effect is to *increase* the taxable equivalent yield. Of course, the size of the increase depends on the level of state income taxes. In a high-tax state like California, for example, the impact can be substantial. Return to the 6.5% municipal bond introduced above. If a California resident in the maximum federal and state tax brackets (35% and 11%, respectively) were considering a corporate issue, she would have to get a yield of 11.25% on the corporate to match the 6.5% yield on the California bond:

$$\text{Taxable equivalent yield for both federal and state taxes} = \frac{6.5}{1 - [0.35 + 0.11(1 - 0.35)]}$$
$$= \frac{6.5}{1 - [0.35 + 0.072]}$$
$$= \underline{\underline{11.25\%}}$$

This yield compares to a taxable equivalent yield of 10.0% when only federal taxes were included in the calculation. That's a difference of more than one full percentage point.

Corporate Bonds Corporations are the major nongovernmental issuers of bonds. The market for corporate bonds is customarily subdivided into four segments: *industrials* (the most diverse of the groups), *public utilities* (the dominant group in terms of volume of new issues), *rail and transportation bonds*, and *financial issues* (e.g., banks, finance companies). In this sector of the bond market investors can find bonds from high-quality AAA-rated issues to junk bonds in or near default, and there is also a wide assortment of different types of bonds. These range from first-mortgage obligations to convertible bonds (which we'll examine later in this chapter), debentures, subordinated debentures, senior subordinated issues, capital notes (a type of unsecured debt issued by banks and other financial institutions), and income bonds. Interest on corporate bonds is paid semiannually, and sinking funds are fairly common. The bonds usually come in $1,000 denominations and are issued on a term basis with a single maturity date. Maturities usually range from 25 to 40 years or more. Many corporate bonds, especially the longer ones, carry call deferment provisions that prohibit prepayment for the first five to ten years. Corporate issues are popular with individuals because of their relatively attractive yields.

While most corporate issues fit the general description above, one that does not is the *equipment trust certificate*, a security issued by railroads, airlines, and other transportation concerns. The proceeds from equipment trust certificates are used to purchase equipment (e.g., jumbo jets and railroad engines) that serves as the collateral for the issue. These bonds are usually issued in serial form and carry uniform annual installments throughout. They normally carry maturities that range from one year to a maximum of 15 to 17 years. Despite a near-perfect payment record that dates back to pre-Depression days, these issues generally offer above-average yields to investors.

Specialty Issues

In addition to the basic bonds described above, investors can choose from a number of *specialty issues*—bonds that possess unusual issue characteristics. These bonds have coupon or repayment provisions that are out of the ordinary. Most are issued by corporations, although they are being used increasingly by other issuers as well. Four of the most actively traded specialty issues today are zero-coupon bonds, mortgage-backed securities, asset-backed securities, and

INVESTOR FACTS

WHO NEEDS LONG-TERM BONDS?—As a rule, you'd expect longer-term bonds to provide higher yields, and they usually do. But that doesn't necessarily mean they're the best investment. Consider, for example, the results of a 25-year study covering the period from 1980 through 2004. It showed that *intermediate-term bonds (those with maturities of 7 to 10 years)* typically delivered about 80% or more of the returns obtained from long bonds (with maturities of 25 to 30 years), but at roughly half the risk. This is the perfect risk-return trade-off: You give up a little return for a much bigger cut in risk.

(Source: Ibbotson Associates.)

high-yield junk bonds. All four of these rank as some of the more popular bonds on Wall Street.

Zero-Coupon Bonds As the name implies, **zero-coupon bonds** have no coupons. Rather, these securities are sold at a deep discount from their par values and then increase in value over time at a compound rate of return. Thus, at maturity, they are worth much more than their initial investment. Other things being equal, the cheaper the zero-coupon bond, the greater the return an investor can earn: For example, a bond with a 6% yield might cost $420, but one with a 10% yield might cost only $240.

Because they do not have coupons, these bonds do not pay interest semiannually. In fact, they pay *nothing* to the investor until the issue matures. As strange as it might seem, this feature is the main attraction of zero-coupon bonds. Because there are no interest payments, investors do not have to worry about reinvesting coupon income twice a year. Instead, the fully compounded rate of return on a zero-coupon bond is virtually guaranteed at the rate that existed at the time of purchase. For example, in late 2009, U.S. Treasury zero-coupon bonds with ten-year maturities were available at yields of around 3.5%. For around $700, you could buy a bond that would be worth $1,000 at maturity in ten years. That 3.5% yield is a fully compounded rate of return that's *locked in* for the life of the issue.

The foregoing advantages notwithstanding, zeros do have some serious disadvantages. One is that if rates do move up over time, you won't be able to participate in the higher return. (You'll have no coupon income to reinvest.) In addition, zero-coupon bonds are subject to tremendous price volatility: If market rates climb, you'll experience a sizable capital loss as the prices of zero-coupons plunge. (Of course, if interest rates *drop*, you'll reap enormous capital gains if you hold long-term zeros. Indeed, such issues are unsurpassed in capital gains potential.) A final disadvantage is that the IRS has ruled that zero-coupon bondholders must pay taxes on *interest as it is accrued*, even though no interest is actually received.

Zeros are issued by corporations, municipalities, and federal agencies. You can even buy U.S. Treasury notes and bonds in the form of zero-coupon securities. They're known as **Treasury strips**. Actually, the Treasury does *not* issue zero-coupon bonds. Instead, it *allows government securities dealers to sell regular coupon-bearing notes and bonds in the form of zero-coupon securities.* Essentially, the coupons are stripped from the bond, repackaged, and then sold separately as zero-coupon bonds. For example, a ten-year Treasury note has 20 semiannual coupon payments, plus one principal payment. These 21 cash flows can be repackaged and sold as 21 different zero-coupon securities, with maturities that range from six months to ten years. Because they sell at such large discounts, Treasury strips are often sold in minimum denominations (par values) of $10,000. But with their big discounts, you'll probably pay only about half that amount (or less) for $10,000 worth of ten-year strips. Because there's an active secondary market for Treasury strips, investors can get in and out of these securities with ease just about any time they want. Strips offer the maximum in issue quality, a wide array of different maturities, and an active secondary market—all of which explains why they are so popular.

Mortgage-Backed Securities Simply put, a **mortgage-backed bond** is a debt issue that is secured by a pool of residential mortgages. An issuer, such as the Government National Mortgage Association (GNMA), puts together a pool of home mortgages and then issues securities in the amount of the total mortgage pool. These securities, also known as *pass-through securities* or *participation certificates*, are usually sold in minimum denominations of $25,000. Although their maturities can go out as far as 30 years, the average life is generally much shorter (perhaps as short as eight to ten years) because many of the mortgages are paid off early.

As an investor in one of these securities, you hold an undivided interest in the pool of mortgages. When a homeowner makes a monthly mortgage payment, that payment is essentially passed through to you, the bondholder, to pay off the mortgage-backed bond you hold. Although these securities come with normal coupons, *the interest is paid monthly rather than semiannually*. Actually, the monthly payments received by bondholders are, like mortgage payments, made up of both principal and interest. Because the principal portion of the payment represents return of capital, it is considered tax-free. The interest portion, however, is subject to ordinary state and federal income taxes.

Mortgage-backed securities are issued primarily by three federal agencies. Although there are some state and private issuers (mainly big banks and S&Ls), agency issues dominate the market and account for 90% to 95% of the activity. The major agency issuers of mortgage-backed securities (MBSs) are:

- *Government National Mortgage Association (GNMA).* Known as Ginnie Mae, it is the oldest and largest issuer of MBSs.

- *Federal Home Loan Mortgage Corporation (FHLMC).* Known as Freddie Mac, it was the first to issue pools containing conventional mortgages.

- *Federal National Mortgage Association (FNMA).* Known as Fannie Mae, it's the leader in marketing seasoned/older mortgages.

One feature of mortgage-backed securities is that they are *self-liquidating investments;* that is, a portion of the monthly cash flow to the investor is repayment of principal. Thus, you are always receiving back part of the original investment capital, so that at maturity, there is *no* big principal payment. To counter this effect, a number of *mutual funds* invest in mortgage-backed securities *but* automatically reinvest the capital/principal portion of the cash flows. Mutual fund investors therefore receive only the interest from their investments and their capital remains fully invested.

Collateralized Mortgage Obligations Loan prepayments are another problem with mortgage-backed securities. In fact, it was in part an effort to diffuse some of the prepayment uncertainty in standard mortgage-backed securities that led to the creation of **collateralized mortgage obligations (CMOs)**. Normally, as pooled mortgages are prepaid, all bondholders receive a prorated share of the prepayments. The net effect is to sharply reduce the life of the bond. A CMO, in contrast, divides investors into classes (called *tranches,* which is French for "slice"), depending on whether they want a short-, intermediate-, or long-term investment. Although interest is paid to all bondholders, all principal payments go first to the shortest tranche until it is fully retired. Then the next class in the sequence becomes the sole recipient of principal, and so on, until the last tranche is retired.

Basically, CMOs are *derivative securities* created from traditional mortgage-backed bonds, which are placed in a trust. Participation in this trust is then sold to the investing public in the form of CMOs. The net effect of this transformation is that CMOs look and behave very much like any other bond: They offer predictable interest payments and have (relatively) predictable maturities. However, although they carry the same triple-A ratings and implicit U.S. government backing as the mortgage-backed bonds that underlie them, CMOs represent a quantum leap in complexity. Some types of CMOs can be as simple and safe as Treasury bonds. Others can be far more volatile—and risky—than the standard MBSs they're made from. That's because when putting CMOs together, Wall Street performs the financial equivalent of gene splicing: Investment bankers isolate the interest and principal payments from the underlying MBSs and rechannel them to the different tranches. It's not issue quality or risk of default that's the problem here, but rather prepayment, or call, risk. All the bonds will be paid off; it's just a matter of when. Different types of CMO tranches have different levels of prepayment risk. The overall risk in a CMO cannot, of course, exceed that of the underlying mortgage-backed bonds, so in order for there to be some tranches with very little (or no) prepayment risk, others have to endure a lot more. The net effect is that while some CMO tranches are low in risk, others are loaded with it.

Investors discovered just how complex and how risky these securities could be as the financial crisis unfolded in 2007–2008. As homeowner defaults on residential mortgages began to rise, the values of CMOs plummeted. Trading in the secondary market dried up, so it was difficult to know what the underlying values of some CMOs really were. Investment and commercial banks that had invested heavily in these securities came under intense pressure as doubts about their solvency grew into a near panic. Everyone wanted to know which institutions held these "toxic assets" on their balance sheets and how large their losses were on these instruments. Lehman Brothers, Bear Stearns, Merrill Lynch, and many other financial institutions went bankrupt or were acquired under distress by other institutions, and the federal government poured hundreds of billions of dollars into the banking system to try to prevent total collapse.

Asset-Backed Securities The creation of mortgage-backed securities and CMOs quickly led to the development of a new market technology—the process of **securitization**, whereby various lending vehicles are transformed into marketable securities, much like a mortgage-backed security. In recent years, investment bankers sold billions of dollars worth of pass-through securities, known as **asset-backed securities** (**ABS**), which are backed by pools of auto loans, credit card bills, and home equity lines (three of the principal types of collateral), as well as computer leases, hospital receivables, small business loans, truck rentals, and even royalty fees.

These securities, first introduced in the mid-1980s, are created when an investment bank bundles together some type of debt-linked asset (such as loans or receivables), and then sells investors—via asset-backed securities—the right to receive all or part of the future payments made on that debt. For example, GMAC, the financing arm of General Motors, is a regular issuer of collateralized *auto loan* securities. When it wants to get some of its car loans off its books, GMAC takes the monthly cash flow from a pool of auto loans and pledges them to a new issue of bonds, which are then sold to investors. In similar fashion, *credit card receivables* are regularly used as collateral for these bonds (indeed, they represent the biggest segment of the ABS market), as are *home equity loans*, the second-biggest type of ABS.

Investors are drawn to ABSs for a number of reasons. One is the relatively *high yields* they offer. Another is their *short maturities*, which often extend out no more than three to five years. A third is the *monthly, rather than semiannual, principal/interest payments* that accompany many of these securities. Also important to investors is their *high credit quality*. That's due to the fact that most of these deals are backed by generous credit protection. For example, the securities are often overcollateralized: the pool of assets backing the bonds may be 25% to 50% larger than the bond issue itself. For whatever reason, the vast majority of ABSs receive the highest credit rating possible (triple-A) from the leading rating agencies.

Junk Bonds Junk bonds (or *high-yield bonds*, as they're also called) are highly speculative securities that have received low, sub-investment-grade ratings (typically Ba or
B). These bonds are issued primarily by corporations and also by municipalities. Junk
bonds often take the form of *subordinated debentures*, which means the debt is unsecured and has a low claim on assets. These bonds are called "junk" because of their
high risk of default. The companies that issue them generally have excessive amounts
of debt in their capital structures and their ability to service that debt is subject to considerable doubt.

Probably the most unusual type of junk bond is something called a **PIK-bond**. PIK
stands for *payment in kind* and means that rather than paying the bond's coupon in
cash, the issuer can make annual interest payments in the form of additional debt. This
"financial printing press" usually goes on for five or six years, after which time the
issuer is supposed to start making interest payments in real money.

Why would any rational investor be drawn to junk bonds? The answer is simple:
They offer very high yields. Indeed, in a typical market, relative to investment-grade
bonds, you can expect to pick up anywhere from 2.5 to 5 percentage points in added
yield. For example, not long ago, investors were getting 10% or 12% yields on junk
bonds, compared to 7% or 8% on investment-grade corporates. Obviously, *such yields
are available only because of the correspondingly higher exposure to risk.*

However, there's more to bond returns than yield alone: The *returns* you actually
end up with don't always correspond to the *yields* you went in with. Junk bonds are
subject to a good deal of risk, and their prices are unstable. Indeed, unlike investment-
grade bonds, whose prices are closely linked to the behavior of market interest rates,
junk bonds tend to behave more like stocks. As a result, the returns are highly unpredictable. Accordingly, only investors who are thoroughly familiar with the risks
involved, and who are comfortable with such risk exposure, should use these securities.

A Global View of the Bond Market

Globalization has hit the bond market, just as it has the stock market. Foreign bonds
have caught on with U.S. investors because of their high yields and attractive returns.
There are risks with foreign bonds, of course, but high risk of default is *not* necessarily
one of them. Instead, the big risk with foreign bonds has to do with the impact that
currency fluctuations can have on returns in U.S. dollars.

The United States has the world's biggest debt market, accounting for about half of
the global market. Following the United States is *Euroland* (principally Germany, Italy,
and France); close behind is Japan, followed by the United Kingdom, and then Canada.
Together, these issuers account for more than 90% of the world bond market.
Worldwide, various forms of government bonds (e.g., Treasuries, agencies, and munis)
dominate the market.

U.S.-Pay Versus Foreign-Pay Bonds There are several ways to invest in foreign
bonds (*excluding* foreign bond mutual funds, which we'll examine in Chapter 12).
From the perspective of a U.S. investor, we can divide foreign bonds into two broad
categories on the basis of the currency in which the bond is denominated: *U.S.-pay* (or
dollar-denominated) bonds, and *foreign-pay* (or non-dollar-denominated) bonds. All
the cash flows—including purchase price, maturity value, and coupon income—from
dollar-denominated foreign bonds are in U.S. dollars. The cash flows from non-dollar
bonds are designated in a foreign currency, such as the euro, British pound, or Swiss
franc.

Dollar-Denominated Bonds Dollar-denominated foreign bonds are of two types: Yankee bonds and Eurodollar bonds. **Yankee bonds** are issued by foreign governments or corporations or by so-called supernational agencies, like the World Bank and the InterAmerican Bank. These bonds are issued and traded in the United States; they're registered with the SEC, and all transactions are in U.S. dollars. Not surprisingly, Canadian issuers dominate the Yankee-bond market. Buying a Yankee bond is really no different from buying any other U.S. bond: These bonds are traded on U.S. exchanges and the OTC market, and *because everything is in dollars, there's no currency exchange risk to deal with.* The bonds are generally very high in quality (which is not surprising, given the quality of the issuers) and offer highly competitive yields to investors.

Eurodollar bonds, in contrast, are issued and traded outside the United States. They are denominated in U.S. dollars, but they are not registered with the SEC, which means underwriters are legally prohibited from selling *new* issues to the U.S. public. (Only "seasoned" Eurodollar issues can be sold in this country.) The Eurodollar market today is dominated by foreign-based investors (though that is changing) and is primarily aimed at institutional investors.

Foreign-Pay Bonds From the standpoint of U.S. investors, foreign-pay international bonds encompass all those issues denominated in a currency other than dollars. These bonds are issued and traded overseas and are not registered with the SEC. Examples are German government bonds, which are payable in euros; Japanese bonds, issued in yen; and so forth. When investors speak of *foreign bonds*, it's this segment of the market that most of them are thinking of.

Foreign-pay bonds are subject to changes in currency exchange rates, which can dramatically affect total returns to U.S. investors. The returns on foreign-pay bonds are a function of three things: (1) the level of coupon (interest) income earned on the bonds; (2) the change in market interest rates, which determine the level of capital gains (or losses); and (3) the behavior of currency exchange rates. The first two variables are the same as those that drive bond returns in this country. They are, of course, just as important to foreign bonds as they are to domestic bonds. Thus, if you're investing overseas, you still want to know what the yields are today and where they're headed. *It's the third variable that separates the return behavior of dollar-denominated from foreign-pay bonds.*

We can assess returns from foreign-pay bonds by employing the same (albeit slightly modified) holding period return formula first introduced in our discussion of foreign stock returns. (See Equation 6.6 in Chapter 6.) For example, assume a U.S. investor purchased a Swedish government bond, in large part because of the attractive 7.5% coupon it carried. If the bond was bought at par and market rates fell over the course of the year, the security itself would have provided a return in excess of 7.5% (because the decline in rates would provide some capital gains). However, if the Swedish krona (SEK) fell relative to the dollar, the total return (in U.S. dollars) could have actually ended up at a lot less than 7.5%, depending on what happened to the U.S.\$/SEK exchange rate. To find out exactly how this investment turned out, you could use Equation 6.6 and make a few (very minor) modifications to it (e.g., use interest income in place of dividends received). Like foreign stocks, *foreign-pay bonds can pay off from both the behavior of the security and the behavior of the currency.* That combination, in many cases, means superior returns to U.S. investors. Knowledgeable investors find these bonds attractive not only because of their competitive returns but also because of *the positive diversification effects they have on bond portfolios.*

**CONCEPTS
IN REVIEW**
Answers available at
www.pearsonhighered.com/
gitman

10.10 Briefly describe each of the following types of bonds: (a) *Treasury bonds*, (b) *agency issues*, (c) *municipal securities*, and (d) *corporate bonds*. Note some of the major advantages and disadvantages of each.

10.11 Briefly define each of the following and note how they might be used by fixed-income investors: (a) *zero-coupon bonds*, (b) *CMOs*, (c) *junk bonds*, and (d) *Yankee bonds*.

10.12 What are the special tax features of (a) *Treasury securities*, (b) *agency issues*, and (c) *municipal bonds*?

10.13 Describe an *asset-backed security* (ABS) and identify some of the different forms of collateral used with these issues. Briefly note how an ABS differs from an MBS. What is the central idea behind securitization?

10.14 What's the difference between dollar-denominated and non-dollar-denominated (foreign-pay) bonds? Briefly describe the two major types of U.S.-pay bonds. Can currency exchange rates affect the total return of U.S.-pay bonds? Of foreign-pay bonds? Explain.

Convertible Securities

LG6

In addition to the many different types of bonds covered in the preceding material, there is still another type of fixed-income security that merits discussion at this point—namely, **convertible bonds**. Issued only by corporations, convertibles are different from most other types of corporate debt, because even though these securities may start out as bonds, they usually end up as shares of common stock. That is, while these securities are originally issued as bonds (or even preferred stock), they contain a provision that gives investors the option to convert their bonds into shares of the issuing firm's stock. Convertibles are *hybrid securities* because they contain attributes of both debt and equity. But even though they possess the features and performance characteristics of both fixed-income and equity securities, convertibles should be viewed primarily *as a form of equity*. That's because most investors commit their capital to such obligations not for the yields they provide but rather for the potential price performance of the stock side of the issue. In fact, it is always a good idea *to determine whether a corporation has convertible issues outstanding whenever you are considering a common stock investment*. In some circumstances, the convertible may be a better investment than the firm's common stock. (Preferred stocks represent another type of *hybrid security* because they too have features and characteristics of both equity and fixed-income securities.)

Convertibles as Investment Outlets

Convertible securities are popular with investors because of their **equity kicker**—i.e., the right to convert these bonds into shares of the company's common stock. Because of this feature, the market price of a convertible has a tendency to behave very much like the price of its underlying common stock.

Convertibles are used by all types of companies and are issued either as convertible *bonds* (by far the most common type) or as convertible *preferreds*. Convertibles *enable firms to raise equity capital at fairly attractive prices*. That is, when a company issues stock in the normal way (by selling more shares in the company), it does so by setting a price on the stock that's *slightly below* prevailing market prices. For example, it might be able to get $25 for a stock that's currently priced in the market at, say, $27 a share. In contrast, when it issues the stock indirectly through a convertible issue, the firm can set a price that's *above* the prevailing market—for example, it might be able to get $35 for the same stock. In this case, convertible bond investors will only choose to convert their bonds into shares if the market price of the shares subsequently increases above $35. As a result, the company can raise the *same amount of money* by issuing a lot less stock. Thus, companies issue convertibles *not* as a way of raising debt capital but as a way of raising equity. Because they are eventually converted into shares of the issuing company's common stock, convertibles are usually viewed as a form of **deferred equity**.

Convertible bonds and convertible preferreds are both linked to the equity position of the firm, so they are usually considered interchangeable for investment purposes. Except for a few peculiarities (e.g., the fact that preferreds pay dividends rather than interest and do so on a quarterly basis rather than semiannually), convertible bonds and convertible preferreds are evaluated in much the same way. Because of their similarities, the discussion that follows will be couched largely in terms of bonds, but the information and implications apply equally well to convertible preferreds.

Convertible Notes and Bonds Convertible bonds are usually issued as *subordinated debentures* and carry the provision that within a stipulated time period, *the bond may be converted into a certain number of shares of the issuing company's common stock.* (Convertibles that are issued as *notes* are just like convertible *bonds* except that the debt portion of the security carries a shorter maturity—usually of five to ten years. Other than the life of the debt, there is no real difference between the two types of issues: They're both unsecured debt obligations, and they're usually subordinated to other forms of debt.)

Generally speaking, there is little or no cash involved at the time of conversion. You merely trade in the convertible bond (or note) for a stipulated number of shares of common stock. For example, assume that a certain convertible security recently came to the market, and it carried the provision that each $1,000 note could be converted into shares of the issuing company's stock at $62.55 a share. Thus, *regardless of what happens to the market price of the stock,* you can redeem each note for 15.98 shares of the company's stock ($1,000 ÷ $62.55 = 15.98 shares). So, if the company's stock is trading in the market at, say, $125 a share at the time of conversion, then you would have just converted a $1,000 debt obligation into $1,997.50 worth of stock (15.98 × $125 = $1,997.50). Not surprisingly, this conversion privilege comes at a price: *the low coupon (or dividend) that convertibles usually carry.* That is, when new convertible issues come to the market, their coupons are normally just a fraction of those on comparable straight (nonconvertible) bonds. Indeed, the more attractive the conversion feature, the lower the coupon.

Actually, while it's the *bondholder* who has the right to convert the bond at any time, more often than not, the issuing firm initiates conversion by calling the bonds—a practice known as **forced conversion**. To provide the corporation with the flexibility to retire the debt and force conversion, most convertibles come out as freely callable issues, or they carry very short call deferment periods. To force conversion, the corporation would call for the retirement of the bond and give the bondholder one of two options: Either convert the bond into common stock, or redeem it for cash at the stipulated call price (which, in the case of convertibles, contains very little call premium). So long as the convertible is called when the market value of the stock exceeds the call price of the bond (which is almost always the case), seasoned investors would never choose the second option. Instead, they would opt to convert the bond, as the firm wants them to. Then they can hold the stocks if they want to, or they can sell their new shares in the market (and end up with more cash than they would have received by taking the call price). After the conversion is complete, the bonds no longer exist; instead, there is additional common stock in their place.

Conversion Privilege The key element of any convertible is its **conversion privilege**, which stipulates the conditions and specific nature of the conversion feature. To begin with, it states exactly when the debenture can be converted. With some issues, there may be an initial waiting period of six months to perhaps two years after the date of issue, during which time the security cannot be converted. The **conversion period** then begins, and the issue can be converted at any time. The conversion period typically extends for the remaining life of the debenture, but in some instances, it may exist for only a certain number of years. This is done to give the issuing firm more control over its capital structure. If the issue has not been converted by the end of its conversion period, it reverts to a straight-debt issue with no conversion privileges.

From the investor's point of view, the most important piece of information is the *conversion price* or the *conversion ratio*. These terms are used interchangeably and specify, either directly or indirectly, the number of shares of stock into which the bond can be converted. The **conversion ratio** denotes the number of common shares into which the bond can be converted. The **conversion price** indicates the stated value per share at which the common stock will be delivered to the investor in exchange for the bond. When you stop to think about these two measures, it becomes clear that a given conversion ratio implies a certain conversion price, and vice versa. For example, a $1,000 convertible bond might stipulate a conversion ratio of 20, which means that the bond can be converted into 20 shares of common stock. This same privilege could also be stated in terms of a conversion price: The $1,000 bond may be used to acquire the stock at a "price" of $50 per share. Here, the conversion price of $50 signifies a conversion ratio of 20. (One basic difference between a convertible debenture and a convertible preferred relates to conversion ratio: The conversion ratio of a debenture generally deals with large multiples of common stock, such as 15, 20, or 30 shares. In contrast, the conversion ratio of a preferred is generally very small, often less than one share of common and seldom more than three or four shares.)

The conversion ratio is normally adjusted for stock splits and significant stock dividends. As a result, if a firm declares, say, a 2-for-1 stock split, the conversion ratio of any of its outstanding convertible issues also doubles. And when the conversion ratio includes a fraction, such as 33.5 shares of common, the conversion privilege specifies how any fractional shares are to be handled. Usually, the investor can either put up the additional funds necessary to purchase another full share of stock at the conversion price or receive the cash equivalent of the fractional share (at the conversion price).

LYONs Leave it to Wall Street to take a basic investment product and turn it into a sophisticated investment vehicle. That's the story behind LYONs, which some refer to as "zeros on steroids": Start with a *zero-coupon bond*, throw in a *conversion feature* and a *put option*, and you have a **LYON** (the acronym stands for **liquid yield option note**). LYONs are zero-coupon convertible bonds that are convertible, at a fixed conversion ratio, for the life of the issue. Thus, they offer the built-in increase in value over time that accompanies any zero-coupon bond (as it moves toward its par value at maturity), plus full participation in the equity side of the issue via the equity kicker. Unlike most convertibles, there's no current income with a LYON (because it is a zero-coupon bond). On the other hand, however, it does carry an option feature that enables you to "put" the bonds back to the issuer (at specified values). That is, *the put* *option gives you the right to redeem your bonds periodically at prespecified prices.* Thus, you know you can get out of these securities, at set prices, if things move against you.

Although LYONs may appear to provide the best of all worlds, they do have some negatives. True, LYONs provide downside protection (via the put option feature) and full participation in the equity kicker. But being zero-coupon bonds, they don't generate current income. And you have to watch out for the put option: Depending on the type of put option, the payout does not have to be in cash—it can be in stocks or bonds/notes. One other thing: Because the conversion ratio on the LYON is fixed, while the underlying value of the zero-coupon bond keeps increasing (as it moves to maturity), *the conversion price on the stock increases over time.* Thus, the market price of the stock had better go up by more than the bond's rate of appreciation or you'll never be able to convert your LYON.

Sources of Value

Because convertibles are fixed-income securities linked to the equity position of the firm, they are normally valued in terms of *both the stock and the bond dimensions* of the issue. Thus, it is important to both analyze the underlying common stock *and* formulate interest rate expectations, when considering convertibles as an investment outlet. Let's look first at the stock dimension.

Convertible securities trade much like common stock whenever the market price of the stock starts getting close to (or exceeds) the stated conversion price. Whenever a convertible trades near, or above, its par value ($1,000), it will exhibit price behavior that closely matches that of the underlying common stock: If the stock goes up in price, so does the convertible, and vice versa. In fact, the absolute price change of the convertible will exceed that of the common because of the conversion ratio, which will define the convertible's rate of change in price. For example, if a convertible carries a conversion ratio of, say, 20, then for every point the common stock goes up (or down) in price, the price of the convertible will move *in the same direction* by roughly that same multiple (in this case, 20). In essence, whenever a convertible trades as a stock, its market price will approximate a multiple of the share price of the common, with the size of the multiple being defined by the conversion ratio.

When the market price of the common is well below the conversion price, the convertible loses its tie to the underlying common stock and begins to trade as a bond. When that happens, the convertible becomes linked to prevailing bond yields, and investors focus their attention on *market rates of interest.* However, because of the equity kicker and their relatively low agency ratings, *convertibles generally do not possess high interest rate sensitivity.* Gaining more than a rough idea of what the prevailing yield of a convertible obligation ought to be is often difficult. For example, if the issue is rated Baa and the market rate for this quality range is 9%, then the convertible should be priced to yield *something around 9%,* plus or minus perhaps half a percentage point. Even more important, however, is the fact that this bond feature sets the *price floor* on the convertible. Price floor is a key component in defining the amount of downside risk embedded in a convertible, since it provides an approximation of the price to which the convertible will drop should the stock go into a freefall. That is, the price of the convertible will not fall to much less than its price floor, because at that point, the issue's bond value will kick in. (More on this later.)

Measuring the Value of a Convertible

In order to evaluate the investment merits of convertible securities, you must consider both the bond and the stock dimensions of the issue. Fundamental security analysis of the equity position is, of course, especially important in light of the key role the equity kicker plays in defining the price behavior of a convertible. In contrast, market yields and agency ratings are used in evaluating the bond side of the issue. But there's more: *In addition to analyzing the bond and stock dimensions of the issue, it is essential to evaluate the conversion feature itself.* The two critical areas in this regard are conversion value and investment value. These measures have a vital bearing on a convertible's price behavior and therefore can have a dramatic effect on an issue's holding period return.

Conversion Value In essence, **conversion value** indicates what a convertible issue would trade for if it were priced to sell on the basis of its stock value. Conversion value is easy to find:

Equation 10.3

$$\text{Conversion value} = \text{Conversion ratio} \times \text{Current market price of the stock}$$

For example, a convertible that carries a conversion ratio of 20 would have a conversion value of $1,200 if the firm's stock traded at a current market price of $60 per share (20 × $60 = $1,200).

Sometimes analysts use an alternative measure that computes the **conversion equivalent**, also known as **conversion parity**. The conversion equivalent indicates the price at which the common stock would have to sell in order to make the convertible security worth its present market price. Conversion equivalent is calculated as follows:

Equation 10.4

$$\text{Conversion equivalent} = \frac{\text{Current market price of the convertible bond}}{\text{Conversion ratio}}$$

Thus, if a convertible were trading at $1,400 and had a conversion ratio of 20, the conversion equivalent of the common stock would be $70 per share ($1,400 ÷ 20 = $70). In effect, you would expect the current market price of the common stock in this example to be at or near $70 per share in order to support a convertible trading at $1,400.

Conversion Premium Unfortunately, convertible issues *seldom* trade precisely at their conversion values. Rather, they usually trade at prices that exceed the bond's underlying conversion value. The extent to which the market price of the convertible exceeds its conversion value is known as the *conversion premium*. The absolute size of an issue's conversion premium is found by taking the difference between the convertible's market price and its conversion value (per Equation 10.3). To place the premium on a relative basis, simply divide the dollar amount of the conversion premium by the issue's conversion value. That is,

Equation 10.5

$$\text{Conversion premium (in \$)} = \frac{\text{Current market price}}{\text{of the convertible bond}} - \frac{\text{Conversion}}{\text{value}}$$

where conversion value is found according to Equation 10.3. Then

Equation 10.6

$$\text{Conversion premium (in \%)} = \frac{\text{Conversion premium (in \$)}}{\text{Conversion value}}$$

To illustrate, if a convertible trades at $1,400 and its conversion value equals $1,200, it has a conversion premium of $200 ($1,400 − $1,200 = $200). In relation to what the convertible should be trading at, this $200 differential would amount to a conversion premium of 16.7% ($200/$1,200 = 0.167). Conversion premiums are common in the market and can often amount to as much as 30% to 40% (or more) of an issue's true conversion value.

Investors are willing to pay a premium primarily because of the added current income a convertible provides relative to the underlying common stock. An investor can recover this premium either through the added current income the convertible provides, or by selling the issue at a premium equal to or greater than that which existed at the time of purchase. Unfortunately, the latter source of recovery is tough to come by, because conversion premiums tend to fade away as the price of the convertible goes up. That means that if you purchase a convertible for its potential price appreciation (which most are), then you must accept the fact that all or a major portion of the price premium is very likely to disappear as the convertible appreciates over time and moves closer to its true conversion value. Thus, if you hope to recover any conversion premium, it will probably have to come from the added current income that the convertible provides.

Payback Period The size of the conversion premium can obviously have a major impact on investor return. When picking convertibles, one of the major questions you should ask is whether the premium is justified. One way to assess conversion premium is to compute the issue's **payback period,** a measure of the length of time it will take to recover the conversion premium from the *extra* interest income earned on the convertible. Because this added income is a principal reason for the conversion premium, it makes sense to use it to assess the premium. The payback period can be found as follows:

Equation 10.7

$$\text{Payback period} = \frac{\text{Conversion premium (in \$)}}{\begin{array}{c}\text{Annual interest} \quad \text{Annual dividend} \\ \text{income from the} \; - \; \text{income from the} \\ \text{convertible bond} \quad \text{underlying common stock}\end{array}}$$

In this equation, annual dividends are found by multiplying the stock's latest annual dividends per share by the bond's conversion ratio.

For example, in the foregoing illustration, the bond had a conversion premium of $200. Assume this bond (which carries a conversion ratio of 20) has an 8.5% coupon, and the underlying stock paid dividends this past year of 50 cents a share. Given this information, we can use Equation 10.7 to find the payback period.

$$\text{Payback period} = \frac{\$200}{\$85 - (20 \times \$0.50)}$$

$$= \frac{\$200}{\$85 - (\$10.00)} = \underline{\underline{2.7 \text{ years}}}$$

In essence, you would recover the premium in 2.7 years (a fairly decent payback period).

As a rule, everything else being equal, *the shorter the payback period, the better.* Also, watch out for excessively high premiums (of 50% or more); you may have real difficulty ever recovering such astronomical premiums. Indeed, to avoid such premiums, most experts recommend that you look for convertibles that have payback periods of around five to seven years, *or less.* Be careful when using this measure, however: Some convertibles will have *very high payback periods simply because they carry very low coupons* (of 1% to 2%, or less).

Investment Value The price floor of a convertible is defined by its bond properties and is the focus of the investment value measure. It's the point within the valuation process where we focus on current and expected market interest rates. **Investment value** is the price at which the bond would trade if it were nonconvertible and if it were priced at or near the prevailing market yields of comparable nonconvertible bonds.

While we'll cover the mechanics of bond pricing in more detail in Chapter 11, suffice it to say at this point that the investment value of a convertible is found by discounting the issue's coupon stream and its par value back to the present, using a discount rate equal to the prevailing yield on comparable nonconvertible issues. In other words, using the yields on comparable nonconvertible bonds as the discount rate, find the present value of the convertible's coupon stream, add that to the present value of its par value (usually assumed to be $1,000), and you have the issue's investment value. In practice, because the convertible's coupon and maturity are known, the only additional piece of information needed is the market yield of comparably rated issues.

For example, if comparable nonconvertible bonds were trading at 9% yields, we could use that 9% return as the discount rate in finding the present value (i.e., "investment value") of a convertible. Thus, if a particular 20-year, $1,000 par value convertible bond carried a 6% annual-pay coupon, its investment value (using a 9% discount rate) can be found as demonstrated at the left. The resulting value of the convertible would be about $726. This figure indicates how far the convertible will have to fall before it hits its price floor and begins trading as a straight-debt instrument.

Other things being equal, the greater the distance between the current market price of a convertible and its investment value, the farther the issue can fall in price and, as a result, the greater the downside risk exposure.

Input	Function
−60	PMT
−1000	FV
20	N
9	I
	CPT
	PV

Solution 726.14

CONCEPTS IN REVIEW
Answers available at
www.pearsonhighered.com/gitman

10.15 What is a *convertible debenture*? How does a convertible bond differ from a convertible preferred?

10.16 Identify the *equity kicker* of a convertible security and explain how it affects the value and price behavior of convertibles.

10.17 Explain why it is necessary to examine both the bond and stock properties of a convertible debenture when determining its investment appeal.

10.18 What is the difference between *conversion parity* and *conversion value*? How would you describe the payback period on a convertible? What is the *investment value* of a convertible, and what does it reveal?

 Here is what you should know after reading this chapter. **MyFinanceLab** will help you identify what you know, and where to go when you need to practice.

What You Should Know	Key Terms	Where To Practice
LG 1 **Explain the basic investment attributes of bonds and their use as investment vehicles.** Bonds are publicly traded debt securities that provide investors with two basic sources of return: (1) current income and (2) capital gains. Current income is derived from the coupon (interest) payments received over the life of the issue. Capital gains can be earned whenever market interest rates fall. Bonds also can be used to shelter income from taxes and for the preservation and long-term accumulation of capital. The diversification properties of bonds are such that they can greatly enhance portfolio stability.	bonds, *p. 363*	MyFinanceLab Study Plan 10.1
LG 2 **Describe the essential features of a bond, note the role that bond ratings play in the market, and distinguish among different types of call, refunding, and sinking-fund provisions.** All bonds carry some type of coupon, which specifies the annual rate of interest the issuer will pay. Bonds also have predetermined maturity dates: Term bonds carry a single maturity date, and serial bonds have a series of maturity dates. Municipal and corporate issues are rated for bond quality by independent rating agencies. These ratings indicate a bond's potential risk of default: The lower the rating, the higher the risk and the higher the expected return. Every bond is issued with some type of call feature, be it freely callable, noncallable, or deferred callable. Call features spell out whether an issue can be prematurely retired and, if so, when. Some bonds (temporarily) prohibit the issuer from paying off one bond with the proceeds from another by including a refunding provision. Others are issued with sinking-fund provisions, which specify how a bond is to be paid off over time.	bond ratings, *p. 374* call feature, *p. 372* call premium, *p. 372* call price, *p. 372* collateral trust bonds, *p. 373* coupon, *p. 369* current yield, *p. 369* debenture, *p. 373* discount bond, *p. 370* equipment trust certificates, *p. 373* first and refunding bonds, *p. 373* income bonds, *p. 373* junior bonds, *p. 373* maturity date, *p. 369* mortgage bonds, *p. 373* notes, *p. 369* premium bond, *p. 370* principal, *p. 369* refunding provisions, *p. 372*	MyFinanceLab Study Plan 10.2 Video Learning Aid for Problem P10.8
LG 3 **Explain how bonds are priced in the market and why some bonds are more volatile than others.** Bonds are priced in the market as a percent of par and are driven by the issue's coupon and maturity, along with prevailing market yields. When interest rates go down, bond prices go up, and vice versa. The extent to which bond prices move up or down depends on the coupon and maturity of an issue. Bonds with lower coupons and/or longer maturities generate larger price swings.	senior bonds, *p. 373* serial bond, *p. 369* sinking fund, *p. 372* split ratings, *p. 375* subordinated debentures, *p. 373* term bond, *p. 369*	MyFinanceLab Study Plan 10.3
LG 4 **Identify the different types of bonds and the kinds of investment objectives these securities can fulfill.** The bond market is divided into four major segments: Treasuries, agencies, municipals, and corporates. Treasury bonds are	agency bonds, *p. 378* asset-backed securities (ABS), *p. 385*	MyFinanceLab Study Plan 10.4

What You Should Know	Key Terms	Where To Practice
issued by the U.S. Treasury and are virtually default-free. Agency bonds are issued by various subdivisions of the U.S. government and make up an increasingly important segment of the bond market. Municipal bonds are issued by state and local governments in the form of either general obligation or revenue bonds. Corporate bonds make up the major nongovernment sector of the market and are backed by the assets and profitability of the issuing companies. Generally speaking, Treasuries are attractive because of their high quality, agencies and corporates because of the added returns they provide, and munis because of the tax shelter they offer.	collateralized mortgage obligation (CMO), *p. 384* Eurodollar bonds, *p. 387* general obligation bonds, *p. 380* junk bonds, *p. 386* mortgage-backed bond, *p. 383* municipal bond guarantees, *p. 380* municipal bonds, *p. 380* PIK-bond, *p. 386* revenue bonds, *p. 380* securitization, *p. 385*	
LG5 Discuss the global nature of the bond market and the difference between dollar-denominated and non-dollar-denominated foreign bonds. Foreign bonds, particularly foreign-pay securities, offer highly competitive yields and returns. Foreign-pay bonds cover all issues that are denominated in some currency other than U.S. dollars. These bonds have an added source of return: currency exchange rates. In addition, there are dollar-denominated foreign bonds—Yankee bonds and Eurodollar bonds—which have no currency exchange risk because they are issued in U.S. dollars.	taxable equivalent yield, *p. 381* Treasury bonds, *p. 377* Treasury Inflation Protected Securities (TIPS), *p. 377* Treasury notes, *p. 377* Treasury strips (strip-Ts), *p. 383* Yankee bonds, *p. 387* zero-coupon bonds, *p. 383*	MyFinanceLab Study Plan 10.5
LG6 Describe the basic features and characteristics of convertible securities, and measure the value of a convertible. Convertible securities are initially issued as bonds (or preferreds), but can subsequently be converted into shares of common stock. These securities offer investors a stream of fixed income (annual coupon payments), plus an equity kicker (a conversion feature). The value of a convertible is driven by the price behavior of the underlying common stock (when the stock price is at or above its conversion price), or by market interest rates and the behavior of bonds (when the stock's price is well below its conversion price). The two key values of a convertible are (1) its conversion (stock) value and (2) its investment (bond) value.	conversion equivalent (conversion parity), *p. 392* conversion period, *p. 390* conversion price, *p. 390* conversion privilege, *p. 390* conversion ratio, *p. 390* conversion value, *p. 392* convertible bonds, *p. 388* deferred equity, *p. 389* equity kicker, *p. 388* forced conversion, *p. 389* investment value, *p. 394* LYON (liquid yield option note), *p. 390* payback period, *p. 393*	MyFinanceLab Study Plan 10.6 Video Learning Aid for Problem P10.20

Log into **MyFinanceLab**, take a chapter test, and get a personalized Study Plan that tells you which concepts you understand and which ones you need to review. From there, **MyFinanceLab** will give you further practice, tutorials, animations, videos, and guided solutions. Log into www.myfinancelab.com

Discussion Questions

LG1 Q10.1 Using the bond returns in Table 10.1 as a basis of discussion:
a. Compare the returns during the 1970s to those produced in the 1980s. How do you explain the differences?
b. How did the bond market do in the 1990s? How does the performance in this decade compare to that in the 1980s? Explain.
c. What do you think would be a fair rate of return to expect from bonds in the future? Explain.
d. Assume that you're out of school and hold a promising, well-paying job. How much of your portfolio (in percentage terms) would you, personally, want to hold in bonds? Explain. What role do you see bonds playing in your own portfolio, particularly as you go farther and farther into the future?

LG4 LG5 Q10.2 Identify and briefly describe each of the following types of bonds.
a. Agency bonds
b. Municipal bonds
c. Zero-coupon bonds
d. Junk bonds
e. Foreign bonds
f. Collateralized mortgage obligations (CMOs)

What type of investor do you think would be most attracted to each?

LG1 LG4 Q10.3 "Treasury securities are guaranteed by the U.S. government. Therefore, there is no risk in the ownership of such bonds." Briefly discuss the wisdom (or folly) of this statement.

LG4 LG5 Q10.4 Select the security in the left-hand column that best fits the investor desire described in the right-hand column.
a. 5-year Treasury note.
b. A bond with a low coupon and a long maturity.
c. Yankee bond.
d. Insured revenue bond.
e. Long-term Treasury strips.
f. Noncallable bond.
g. CMO.
h. Junk bond.
i. ABS receivables.

1. Lock in a high-coupon yield.
2. Accumulate capital over a long period of time.
3. Generate a monthly income.
4. Avoid a lot of price volatility.
5. Generate tax-free income.
6. Invest in a foreign bond.
7. Go for the highest yield available.
8. Invest in a pool of credit card receivables.
9. Go for maximum price appreciation.

LG6 Q10.5 Why do companies like to issue convertible securities? What's in it for them?

LG6 Q10.6 Describe LYONs, and note how they differ from conventional convertible securities. Are there any similarities between LYONs and conventional convertibles? Explain.

LG6 Q10.7 Using the resources available at your campus or public library or on the Internet, find the information requested below.
a. Select any two *convertible debentures* (notes or bonds) and determine the conversion ratio, conversion parity, conversion value, conversion premium, and payback period for each.
b. Select any two *convertible preferreds* and determine the conversion ratio, conversion parity, conversion value, conversion premium, and payback period for each.
c. In what way(s) are the two convertible bonds and the two convertible preferreds you selected similar to one another? Are there any differences? Explain.

Problems

All problems are available on **www.myfinancelab.com**

LG2 **P10.1** A 6%, 15-year bond has three years remaining on a deferred call feature (the call premium is equal to one year's interest). The bond is currently priced in the market at $850. What is the issue's current yield?

LG2 **P10.2** A 12%, 20-year bond is currently trading at $1,250. What is its current yield?

LG2 **P10.3** Zack buys a 10% corporate bond with a current yield of 6%. How much did he pay for the bond?

LG4 **P10.4** An investor is in the 28% tax bracket and lives in a state with no income tax. He is trying to decide which of two bonds to purchase. One is a 7.5% corporate bond that is selling at par. The other is a municipal bond with a 5.25% coupon that is also selling at par. If all other features of these two bonds are comparable, which should the investor select? Why? Would your answer change if this were an *in-state* municipal bond and the investor lived in a place with high state income taxes? Explain.

LG4 **P10.5** An investor lives in a state where her tax rate on interest income is 8%. She is in the 33% federal tax bracket. She owns a 7% corporate bond trading at par. What is her after-tax current yield on this bond?

LG4 **P10.6** Maria Lopez is a wealthy investor who's looking for a tax shelter. Maria is in the maximum (35%) federal tax bracket and lives in a state with a very high state income tax. (She pays the maximum of $11\frac{1}{2}$% in state income tax.) Maria is currently looking at two municipal bonds, both of which are selling at par. One is a double-A-rated *in-state* bond that carries a coupon of $6\frac{3}{8}$%. The other is a double-A-rated *out-of-state* bond that carries a $7\frac{1}{8}$% coupon. Her broker has informed her that comparable fully taxable corporate bonds are currently available with yields of $9\frac{3}{4}$%. Alternatively, long Treasuries are now available at yields of 9%. She has $100,000 to invest, and because all the bonds are high-quality issues, she wants to select the one that will give her maximum after-tax returns.
　　a. Which one of the four bonds should she buy?
　　b. Rank the four bonds (from best to worst) in terms of their taxable equivalent yields.

LG4 **P10.7** Wesley Jenkins is looking for a fixed-income investment. He is considering two bond issues:
　　a. A Treasury with a yield of 5%.
　　b. An in-state municipal bond with a yield of 4%.

Wesley is in the 33% federal tax bracket and the 8% state tax bracket. Which bond would provide Wesley with a higher tax-adjusted yield?

LG2 **P10.8** Which of the following three bonds offers the highest current yield?
　　a. A $9\frac{1}{2}$%, 20-year bond quoted at $97\frac{3}{4}$.
　　b. A 16%, 15-year bond quoted at $164\frac{5}{8}$.
　　c. A $5\frac{1}{4}$%, 18-year bond quoted at 54.

LG2 **P10.9** Assume that you pay $850 for a long-term bond that carries a $7\frac{1}{2}$% coupon. Over the course of the next 12 months, interest rates drop sharply. As a result, you sell the bond at a price of $962.50.
　　a. Find the current yield that existed on this bond at the beginning of the year. What was it by the end of the one-year holding period?
　　b. Determine the holding period return on this investment. (See Chapter 5 for the HPR formula.)

LG3 **P10.10** Colwyn buys a 10% corporate bond with a current yield of 6%. When he sells the bond one year later, the current yield on the bond is 7%. How much did Col make on this investment?

LG1 **P10.11** In early January 2004, you purchased $30,000 worth of some high-grade corporate bonds. The bonds carried a coupon of 8⅛% and mature in 2018. You paid 94.125 when you bought the bonds. Over the five-year period from 2004 through 2008, the bonds were priced in the market as follows:

| | Quoted Prices | | |
Year	Beginning of the Year	End of the Year	Year-End Bond Yields
2004	94.125	100.625	8.82%
2005	100.625	102	8.70
2006	102	104.625	8.48
2007	104.625	110.125	8.05
2008	110.125	121.250	7.33

Coupon payments were made on schedule throughout the five-year period.
a. Find the annual holding period returns for 2004 through 2008. (See Chapter 4 for the HPR formula.)
b. Use the return information in Table 10.1 to evaluate the investment performance of this bond. How do you think it stacks up against the market? Explain.

LG4 **P10.12** Rhett purchased a 13% zero-coupon bond with a 15-year maturity and a $20,000 par value 15 years ago. The bond matures tomorrow. How much will Rhett receive in total from this investment, assuming all payments are made on these bonds as expected?

LG4 **P10.13** Nate purchased an interest-bearing security last year, planning to hold it until maturity. He received interest payments, and, to his surprise, a sizable amount of the principal was paid back in the first year. This happened again in year 2. What type of security did Nate purchase?

LG5 **P10.14** Letticia Garcia, an aggressive bond investor, is currently thinking about investing in a foreign (non-dollar-denominated) government bond. In particular, she's looking at a Swiss government bond that matures in 15 years and carries a 9½% coupon. The bond has a par value of 10,000 Swiss francs (CHF) and is currently trading at 110 (i.e., at 110% of par).

Letticia plans to hold the bond for a period of one year, at which time she thinks it will be trading at 117½—she's anticipating a sharp decline in Swiss interest rates, which explains why she expects bond prices to move up. The current exchange rate is 1.58 CHF/U.S.$, but she expects that to fall to 1.25 CHF/U.S.$. Use the foreign investment total return formula introduced in Chapter 6 (Equation 6.6 on page 232) to answer the questions below.
a. Ignoring the currency effect, find the bond's total return (in its local currency).
b. Now find the total return on this bond in U.S. *dollars*. Did currency exchange rates affect the return in any way? Do you think this bond would make a good investment? Explain.

LG5 **P10.15** Red Electrica España SA (E.REE) is refinancing its bank loans by issuing Eurobonds to investors. You are considering buying $10,000 of these bonds, which will yield 6%. You are also looking at a U.S. bond with similar risk that will yield 5%. You expect that interest rates will not change over the course of the next year, after which time you will sell the bonds you purchase.
a. How much will you make on each bond if you buy it, hold it for one year, and then sell it for $10,000 (or the Eurodollar equivalent)?
b. Assume the dollar/euro exchange rate goes from 1.11 to 0.98. How much will this currency change affect the proceeds from the Eurobond? (Assume you receive annual interest at the same time you sell the Eurobond.)

LG6 **P10.16** A certain convertible bond has a conversion ratio of 21 and a conversion premium of 20%. The current market price of the underlying common stock is $40. What is the bond's conversion equivalent?

LG6 **P10.17** You are considering investing $850 in Whichway Corporation. You can buy common stock at $25 per share; this stock pays no dividends. You can also buy a convertible bond that is currently trading at $850 and has a conversion ratio of 30. It pays $50 per year in interest. Given you expect the price of the stock to rise to $35 per share in one year, which instrument should you purchase if your investment horizon is one year and you do not expect the bond price to change?

LG6 **P10.18** A certain 6% annual pay convertible bond (maturing in 20 years) is convertible at the holder's option into 20 shares of common stock. The bond is currently trading at $800. The stock (which pays 75¢ a share in annual dividends) is currently priced in the market at $35 a share.
    a. What is the bond's conversion price?
    b. What is its conversion ratio?
    c. What is the conversion value of this issue? What is its conversion parity?
    d. What is the conversion premium, in dollars and as a percentage?
    e. What is the bond's payback period?
    f. If comparably rated nonconvertible bonds sell to yield 8%, what is the investment value of the convertible?

LG6 **P10.19** An 8% convertible bond carries a par value of $1,000 and a conversion ratio of 20. Assume that an investor has $5,000 to invest and that the convertible sells at a price of $1,000 (which includes a 25% conversion premium). How much total income (coupon plus capital gains) will this investment offer if, over the course of the next 12 months, the price of the stock moves to $75 per share and the convertible trades at a price that includes a conversion premium of 10%? What is the holding period return on this investment? Finally, given the information in the problem, determine what the underlying common stock is currently selling for.

LG6 **P10.20** Assume you just paid $1,200 for a convertible bond that carries a 7½% coupon and has 15 years to maturity. The bond can be converted into 24 shares of stock, which are now trading at $50 a share. Find the bond investment value of this issue, given that comparable nonconvertible bonds are currently selling to yield 9%.

LG6 **P10.21** Find the conversion value of a *convertible preferred stock* that carries a conversion ratio of 1.8, given that the market price of the underlying common stock is $40 a share. Would there be any conversion premium if the convertible preferred were selling at $90 a share? If so, how much (in dollar and percentage terms)? Also, explain the concept of conversion parity, and then find the conversion parity of this issue, given that the preferred trades at $90 per share.

Visit **www.myfinancelab.com** for web exercises,
spreadsheets, and other online resources.

Case Problem 10.1   *Max and Veronica Develop a Bond Investment Program*

LG4 Max and Veronica Shuman, along with their two teenage sons, Terry and Thomas, live in Portland, Oregon. Max is a sales rep for a major medical firm, and Veronica is a personnel officer at a local bank. Together, they earn an annual income of around $100,000. Max has just learned that his recently departed rich uncle has named him in his will to the tune of some $250,000 after taxes. Needless to say, the family is elated. Max intends to spend $50,000 of his inheritance on a number of long-overdue family items (like some badly needed remodeling of their kitchen and family room, the down payment on a new Porsche Boxster, and braces to correct Tom's overbite). Max wants to invest the remaining $200,000 in various types of fixed-income securities.

Max and Veronica have no unusual income requirements or health problems. Their only investment objectives are that they want to achieve some capital appreciation, and they want to keep their funds fully invested for a period of at least 20 years. They would rather not have to rely on their investments as a source of current income but want to maintain some liquidity in their portfolio just in case.

Questions

a. Describe the type of *bond investment program* you think the Shuman family should follow. In answering this question, give appropriate consideration to both return and risk factors.

b. List several different types of bonds that you would recommend for their portfolio and briefly indicate why you would recommend each.

c. Using a recent issue of the *Wall Street Journal* or *Barron's*, construct a $200,000 bond portfolio for the Shuman family. *Use real securities* and select any bonds (or notes) you like, given the following ground rules:
   1. The portfolio must include at least one Treasury, one agency, and one corporate bond; also, in total, the portfolio must hold at least five, but no more than eight, bonds or notes.
   2. No more than 5% of the portfolio can be in short-term U.S. Treasury bills (but note that if you hold a T-bill, that limits your selections to just seven other notes/bonds).
   3. Ignore all transaction costs (i.e., invest the full $200,000) and assume all securities have par values of $1,000 (although they can be trading in the market at something other than par).
   4. Use the latest available quotes to determine how many bonds/notes/bills you can buy.

d. Prepare a schedule listing all the securities in your recommended portfolio. *Use a form like the one shown below,* and include the information it calls for on each security in the portfolio.

e. *In one brief paragraph,* note the key investment attributes of your recommended portfolio and the investment objectives you hope to achieve with it.

Security Issuer-Coupon-Maturity	Latest Quoted Price	Number of Bonds Purchased	Amount Invested	Annual Coupon Income	Current Yield
Example: U.S. Treas - 8½%-'15	96⁸⁄₃₂	25	$ 24,062	$ 2,125	8.83%
1.					
2.					
3.					
4.					
5.					
6.					
7.					
8.					
Totals	—		$200.000	$	%

Case Problem 10.2   *The Case of the Missing Bond Ratings*

LG2 It's probably safe to say that there's nothing more important in determining a bond's rating than the underlying financial condition and operating results of the company issuing the bond. Just as financial ratios can be used in the analysis of common stocks, they can also be used in the analysis of bonds—a process we refer to as *credit analysis*. In credit analysis, attention is directed toward the basic liquidity and profitability of the firm, the extent to which the firm employs debt, and the ability of the firm to service its debt.

A Table of Financial Ratios

(All ratios are real and pertain to real companies)

Financial Ratio	Company 1	Company 2	Company 3	Company 4	Company 5	Company 6
1. Current ratio	1.13 ×	1.39 ×	1.78 ×	1.32 ×	1.03 ×	1.41 ×
2. Quick ratio	0.48 ×	0.84 ×	0.93 ×	0.33 ×	0.50 ×	0.75 ×
3. Net profit margin	4.6%	12.9%	14.5%	2.8%	5.9%	10.0%
4. Return on total capital	15.0%	25.9%	29.4%	11.5%	16.8%	28.4%
5. Long-term debt to total capital	63.3%	52.7%	23.9%	97.0%	88.6%	42.1%
6. Owners' equity ratio	18.6%	18.9%	44.1%	1.5%	5.1%	21.2%
7. Pretax interest coverage	2.3 ×	4.5 ×	8.9 ×	1.7 ×	2.4 ×	6.4 ×
8. Cash flow to total debt	34.7%	48.8%	71.2%	20.4%	30.2%	42.7%

Notes: Ratio (2)—Whereas the current ratio relates current assets to current liabilities, the quick ratio considers only the most liquid current assets (cash, short-term securities, and accounts receivable) and relates them to current liabilities.
Ratio (4)—Relates pretax profit to the total capital structure (long-term debt + equity) of the firm.
Ratio (6)—Shows the amount of stockholders' equity used to finance the firm (stockholders' equity ÷ total assets).
Ratio (8)—Looks at the amount of corporate cash flow (from net profits + depreciation) relative to the total (current + long-term) debt of the firm.
The other four ratios are as described in Chapter 6.

The financial ratios shown above are often helpful in carrying out such analysis: (1) current ratio, (2) quick ratio, (3) net profit margin, (4) return on total capital, (5) long-term debt to total capital, (6) owners' equity ratio, (7) pretax interest coverage, and (8) cash flow to total debt. The first two ratios measure the liquidity of the firm, the next two its profitability, the following two the debt load, and the final two the ability of the firm to service its debt load. (For ratio 5, the *lower* the ratio, the better. For all the others, the *higher* the ratio, the better.) The table lists each of these ratios for six different companies.

Questions

a. Three of these companies have bonds that carry investment-grade ratings. The other three companies carry junk-bond ratings. Judging by the information in the table, which three companies have the investment-grade bonds and which three have the junk bonds? Briefly explain your selections.

b. One of these six companies is an AAA-rated firm and one is B-rated. Identify those two companies. Briefly explain your selections.

c. Of the remaining four companies, one carries a AA rating, one carries an A rating, and two are BB-rated. Which companies are they?

Excel with Spreadsheets

The cash flow component of bond investments is made up of the annual interest payments and the future redemption value or its par value. Just like other time-value-of-money considerations, the bond cash flows are discounted back in order to determine their present value.

In comparing bonds to stocks, many investors look at the respective returns. The total returns in the bond market are made up of both current income and capital gains. Bond investment analysis should include the determination of the current yield as well as a specific holding period return.

On January 13, 2010, you gather the following information on three corporate bonds issued by the General Pineapple Corp (GPC). Remember that corporate bonds are quoted as a percent of their par value. Assume the par value of each bond to be $1,000. These debentures are quoted in eighths of a point. **Create a spreadsheet** that will model and answer the following three bond investment problems.

Bonds	Current Yield	Volume	Close
GPC 5.3 13	?	25	105⅞
GPC 6.65s 20	?	45	103
GPC 7.4 22	?	37	104⅝

Questions

a. Calculate the current yields for these three GPC corporate debentures.

b. Calculate the holding period returns under the following three scenarios:

1. Purchased the 5.3 bonds for 990 on January 13, 2009.

2. Purchased the 6.65s for 988 on January 13, 2009.

3. Purchased the 7.4 bonds for 985 on January 13, 2007.

c. As of January 13, 2010, GPC common stock had a close price of $26.20. The price of GPC stock in January 2007 was $25.25. The stock paid a 2007 dividend of $0.46, a 2008 dividend of $0.46, and a 2009 dividend of $0.46.

1. Calculate the current (January 13, 2010) dividend yield for this security.

2. Assuming you purchased the stock in January 2007, what is the holding period return as of January 2009?

Chapter-Opening Problem

The chart shows the number of bond issues for which Standard & Poor's issued ratings upgrades or downgrades every year from 1981–2008.

a. What is the trend in the number of ratings changes (both upgrades and downgrades) over time? Why?

b. Which type of ratings change, upgrade or downgrade, is most common in most years? Why do you think that is so?

c. In what years does the ratio of downgrades/upgrades appear to be particularly high? Why?

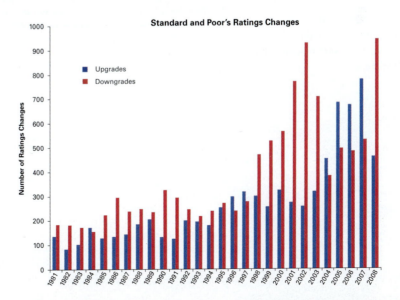

CHAPTER
11

Bond Valuation

LEARNING GOALS

After studying this chapter, you should be able to:

LG1 Explain the behavior of market interest rates and identify the forces that cause interest rates to change.

LG2 Describe the term structure of interest rates and note how yield curves can be used by investors.

LG3 Understand how bonds are valued in the marketplace.

LG4 Describe the various measures of yield and return and explain how these standards of performance are used in bond valuation.

LG5 Understand the basic concept of duration, how it can be measured, and its use in the management of bond portfolios.

LG6 Discuss various bond investment strategies and the different ways these securities can be used by investors.

For the second consecutive week, interest rates on short-term U.S. Treasury bills hit an all-time low on September 8, 2009. Investors who purchased a six-month bill in that week's Treasury auction could expect to earn less than one-quarter of one percent (0.25%) on their money. Low interest rates in the government securities markets had spillover effects in other markets. For example, the national average rate on a 30-year mortgage fell to 5.07% that week, just slightly above the record-low mark of 4.78% set in the spring of 2009.

The low interest rates were a result of actions by the U.S. Federal Reserve, which was trying to help pull the country out of one of the most severe recessions since the Great Depression. Central banks in other countries were doing much the same, and in Europe, extremely low rates on corporate bonds sparked a borrowing binge. In the first nine months of 2009, European corporations issued more than $1.23 trillion in new bonds, 11% more than the total from the prior year. The most creditworthy firms with investment-grade ratings could borrow at rates as low as 2%, and firms did not hesitate to take advantage of the easy money.

In this chapter we'll learn about the forces that move market interest rates up and down and how those movements affect bonds and the investors who buy them.

(Sources: Associated Press, Mortgage Rates Edge Down, Still Above Record Lows, September 10, 2009, www.nytimesonline.com; Associated Press, Rate on 6-month Treasury Bill Hits New Record Low, September 8, 2009, www.google.com/hostednews/ap/article/ALeqM5jWe-rhheoPn0hsiRfGSucBxdFiTwD9AJBG401; Paul Armstrong and Esteban Duarte, Corporate Bond Market on Fire in Europe as New Issues Jump, September 8, 2009, Bloomberg.com.)

The Behavior of Market Interest Rates

LG1 LG2 You will recall from Chapter 4 that rational investors try to earn a return that fully compensates them for risk. In the case of bondholders, that required return (r_i) has three components: the real rate of return (r^*), an expected inflation premium (IP), and a risk premium (RP). Thus, the required return on a bond can be expressed by the following equation:

Equation 11.1

$$r_i = r^* + IP + RP$$

The real rate of return and inflation premium are external economic factors, which *together equal the risk-free rate (R_F)*. To find the required return, we need to consider the unique features and properties of the bond issue itself that influence its level of risk. After we do this, we add a risk premium to the risk-free rate to obtain the required rate of return. A bond's risk premium (RP) will take into account key issue and issuer characteristics, including such variables as the type of bond, the issue's term-to-maturity, its call features, and bond rating.

Together, the three components in Equation 11.1 (r^*, IP, and RP) drive the required return on a bond. Recall in the previous chapter that we identified *five types of risks* to which bonds are exposed. All five of these risks are embedded in a bond's required rate of return. That is, the bond's risk premium (RP) addresses, among other things, the business and financial (credit) risk characteristics of an issue, along with its liquidity and call risks, whereas the risk-free rate (R_F) takes into account interest rate and purchasing power risks.

Viewed from the perspective of the market as a whole, it is *these investor returns in the aggregate* that define *prevailing market interest rates*. Because these interest rates have a significant bearing on bond prices and yields, investors watch them closely. For example, more conservative investors watch interest rates because one of their major objectives is to lock in high yields. Aggressive traders also have a stake in interest rates because their investment programs are often built on the capital gains opportunities that accompany major swings in rates.

Keeping Tabs on Market Interest Rates

Just as there is no single bond market but, instead, a series of different market sectors, so too there is no single interest rate that applies to all segments of the market. Rather, each segment has its own, unique level of interest rates. Granted, the various rates do tend to drift in the same direction over time, but it is also common for **yield spreads** (interest rate differentials) to exist among the various market sectors. Some of the more important market yields and yield spreads are as follows:

- Municipal bonds usually carry the lowest market rates because of their tax-exempt feature. As a rule, their market yields are about 20% to 30% lower than corporates. (There are occasional exceptions to this rule. For example, in 2008, a municipal bond fund offered by the Vanguard mutual fund family paid a yield of 5.67% while the same firm's taxable money market fund paid just 1.65%.) In the taxable sector, Treasuries have the lowest yields (because they have the least risk), followed by agencies and then corporates, which provide the highest returns.

MARKETS in CRISIS

Signs of a Recession

When short-term interest rates on Treasury bills exceed the rates on long-term Treasury bonds, watch out. That is often the precursor to a recession. This "inversion" in the relationship between short-term and long-term rates has occurred prior to each of the last five U.S. recessions. Just as important, this indicator has rarely issued a "false positive" signal.

- Issues that normally carry bond ratings (e.g., municipals or corporates) generally display the same behavior: the lower the rating, the higher the yield.

- There is generally a direct relationship between the coupon an issue carries and its yield. Discount (low-coupon) bonds yield the least, and premium (high-coupon) bonds yield the most.

- In the municipal sector, revenue bonds yield more than general obligation bonds.

- Bonds that are freely callable generally provide the highest returns, at least at date of issue. These are followed by deferred call obligations and then by noncallable bonds, which yield the least.

- As a rule, bonds with long maturities tend to yield more than short issues. However, this rule does not always hold; sometimes, as in February 2006, short-term yields equal or exceed the yields on long-term bonds. That is frequently an early signal that a recession is coming.

The preceding list can be used as a general guide to the higher-yielding segments of the market.

As an investor, you should pay close attention to interest rates and yield spreads. Try to stay abreast of both the current state of the market and the *future direction in market rates*. Thus, if you are a conservative (income-oriented) investor and think that rates have just about peaked, that should be a signal to try to lock in the prevailing high yields with some form of call protection. (For example, buy bonds, such as Treasuries or double-A-rated utilities, that are noncallable or still have lengthy call deferments.) In contrast, if you're an aggressive bond trader who thinks rates have peaked (and are about to drop), that should be a clue to buy bonds that offer maximum price appreciation potential (low-coupon bonds that still have a long time before they mature).

But how do you formulate such expectations? Unless you have considerable training in economics, you will probably have to rely on various published sources. Fortunately, a wealth of such information is available. Your broker is an excellent source for such reports, as are investor services like Moody's and Standard & Poor's. Also, of course, there are numerous online sources. Finally, there are widely circulated business and financial publications (like the *Wall Street Journal*, *Forbes*, *Business Week*, and *Fortune*) that regularly address the current state and future direction of market interest rates. Predicting the direction of interest rates is not easy. However, by taking the time to read some of these publications and reports regularly and carefully, you can at least get a handle on what experts predict is likely to occur in the near future—over, say, the next six to nine months, perhaps longer.

FIGURE 11.1 The Impact of Inflation on the Behavior of Interest Rates

The behavior of interest rates has always been closely tied to the movements in the rate of inflation. What changed in the early 1980s, however, was the spread between inflation and interest rates. Whereas a spread of roughly 3 points was common in the past, it has held at about 5 to 6 percentage points since 1982 with the exception of the period 2002–2007.

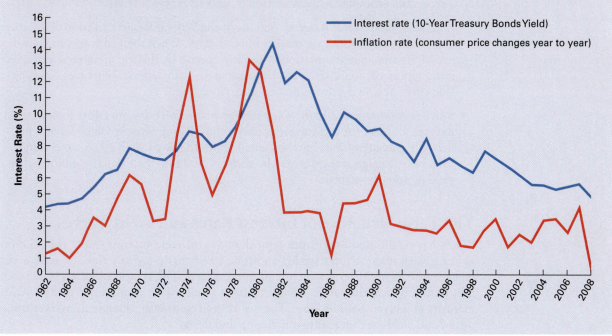

What Causes Rates to Move?

Although interest rates are a complex economic issue, we do know that certain forces are especially important in influencing their general behavior. Serious bond investors should make it a point to become familiar with the major determinants of interest rates and try to monitor those variables, at least informally.

In that regard, perhaps no variable is more important than *inflation*. Changes in the inflation rate, or even expectations about its future course, have a direct and profound effect on market interest rates. Clearly, if inflation is expected to slow down, then market interest rates should fall as well. To gain an appreciation of the extent to which interest rates are linked to inflation, look at Figure 11.1. Note that as inflation drifts up, so do interest rates. On the other hand, a drop in inflation is matched by a similar decline in interest rates.

In addition to inflation, five other important economic variables can significantly affect the level of interest rates:

- *Changes in the money supply*. An increase in the money supply pushes rates down (as it makes more funds available for loans), and vice versa. This is true only up to a point, however. If the growth in the money supply becomes excessive, it can lead to inflation, which, of course, means higher interest rates.

- *The size of the federal budget deficit*. When the U.S. Treasury has to borrow large amounts to cover the budget deficit, the increased demand for funds exerts an upward pressure on interest rates. That's why bond market participants become so concerned when the budget deficit gets bigger and bigger—*other things being equal*, that means more upward pressure on market interest rates.

- *The level of economic activity.* Businesses need more capital when the economy expands. This need increases the demand for funds, and rates tend to rise. During a recession, economic activity contracts, and rates typically fall.

- *Policies of the Federal Reserve.* Actions of the Federal Reserve to control inflation also have a major effect on market interest rates. When the Fed wants to slow actual (or anticipated) inflation, it usually does so by driving up interest rates, as it did repeatedly in 2005–2006. Unfortunately, such actions sometimes have the side effect of slowing down business activity as well.

- *The level of interest rates in major foreign markets.* Today, investors look beyond national borders for investment opportunities. Rising rates in major foreign markets put pressure on rates in the United States to rise as well; if U.S. rates don't keep pace, foreign investors may be tempted to dump their dollars to buy higher-yielding foreign securities.

The Term Structure of Interest Rates and Yield Curves

Bonds having different maturities typically have different interest rates. The relationship between interest rates (yield) and time to maturity for any class of similar-risk securities is called the **term structure of interest rates**. This relationship can be depicted graphically by a **yield curve**, which relates a bond's *term* to maturity to its *yield* to maturity at a given point in time. The yield curve constantly changes as market forces push bond yields at different maturities up and down.

Types of Yield Curves   Two different types of yield curves are illustrated in Figure 11.2. By far, the most common type is curve 1, the *upward-sloping* curve. It indicates that yields tend to increase with longer maturities. That's because the longer a bond has to

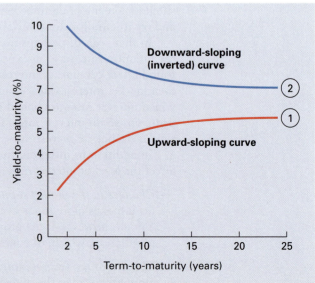

FIGURE 11.2   **Two Types of Yield Curves**

A yield curve relates term-to-maturity to yield-to-maturity at a given point in time. Although yield curves come in many shapes and forms, the most common is the *upward-sloping curve*. It shows that investor returns (yields) increase with longer maturities.

Smart's Tour of the Web
To watch author Scott Smart discuss key Web sites for this chapter visit www.myfinancelab.com

maturity, the greater the potential for price volatility and risk of loss. Investors, therefore, require higher risk premiums to induce them to buy the longer, riskier bonds. Occasionally, the yield curve becomes *inverted*, or downward-sloping, as shown in curve 2, which occurs when short-term rates are higher than long-term rates. This curve generally results from actions by the Federal Reserve to curtail inflation by driving short-term interest rates way up. In addition to these two common yield curves, two other types appear from time to time: the *flat* yield curve, when rates for short- and long-term debt are essentially the same, and the *humped* yield curve, when *intermediate-term* rates are the highest.

Plotting Your Own Curves Yield curves are constructed by plotting the yields for a group of bonds that are similar in all respects but maturity. Treasury securities (bills, notes, and bonds) are typically used to construct yield curves. There are several reasons for this: Their yields are easily found in financial publications, they have no risk of default, and they are homogeneous with regard to quality and other issue characteristics. Investors can also construct yield curves for other classes of debt securities, such as A-rated municipal bonds, Aa-rated corporate bonds, or even certificates of deposit.

Figure 11.3 (on page 410) shows the yield curves for Treasury securities on two dates, March 23, 2006, and September 4, 2009. To draw these curves, you need Treasury quotes from the *Wall Street Journal* or some other similar source. (Note that actual quoted yields for curve 2 are provided in the boxed information below the graph.) Given the required quotes, select the yields for the Treasury bills, notes, and bonds maturing in approximately 1 month, 3 months, 6 months, and 1, 2, 5, 10, 20, and 30 years. The yields used for these curves are highlighted in Figure 11.3. (You could include more points, but they would not have much effect on the general shape of the curve.) Next, plot the points on a graph whose horizontal (*x*) axis represents time to maturity in years and whose vertical (*y*) axis represents yield to maturity. Now, just connect the points to create the curves shown in Figure 11.3. You'll notice that curve 1 is relatively flat, but it lies above the upward-sloping curve 2. Curve 2 reflects the historically low interest rates that prevailed when the U.S. economy was struggling to emerge from a deep recession.

Explanations of the Term Structure of Interest Rates As we noted earlier, the shape of the yield curve can change over time. Three commonly cited theories—the expectations hypothesis, the liquidity preference theory, and the market segmentation theory—explain more fully the reasons for the general shape of the yield curve.

Expectations Hypothesis The **expectations hypothesis** suggests that the yield curve reflects investor expectations about the future behavior of interest rates. This theory argues that the relationship between short-term and long-term interest rates today reflects investors' expectations about how interest rates will change in the future. When the yield curve is upward-sloping, and long-term rates are higher than short-term rates, the expectations hypothesis interprets this as a sign that investors expect short-term rates to rise in the future. That's why long-term rates pay a premium compared to short-term rates. People will not lock their money away in a long-term investment if they think interest rates are going to rise unless the rate on the long-term investment is higher than the current rate on short-term investments.

For example, suppose the current interest rate on a one-year Treasury bill is 5%, and the current rate on a two-year Treasury note is 6%. The expectations hypothesis says that this pattern of interest rates reveals that investors believe that the rate on a one-year Treasury bill will go up to 7% next year. Why? That's the rate that makes

FIGURE 11.3

Yield Curves on U.S. Treasury Issues

Here we see two yield curves constructed from actual market data (quotes). Note the different shapes of the two curves: Curve 1 has a relatively flat slope, while curve 2 has the more common upward slope. Although it started more than 4 percent below curve 1, curve 2 ended only half-a-percent under it (the 20- and 30-year yields were about 50 to 75 basis points less). (Source: *Wall Street Journal*, September 4, 2009.)

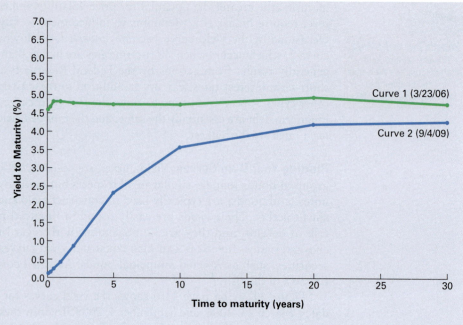

Yield Data for Curve 2 Treasury Issues—Bills, Notes, and Bonds
Friday, September 4, 2009

TREASURY BILLS
Friday, September 04, 2009

Maturity	Bid	Asked	Chg	Asked yield
2009 Sep 10	0.068	0.058	+0.003	0.058
2009 Sep 15	0.045	0.040	−0.005	0.041
2009 Sep 17	0.088	0.083	+0.007	0.084
2009 Sep 24	0.100	0.090	−0.002	0.091
2009 Oct 01	0.093	0.085	−0.003	0.086
2009 Oct 08	0.095	0.085	+0.008	0.086
1 Month→ 2009 Oct 15	0.103	0.093	+0.005	0.094
2009 Oct 22	0.113	0.105	−0.003	0.107
2009 Oct 29	0.113	0.105	unch.	0.107
2009 Nov 05	0.098	0.088	unch.	0.089
2009 Nov 12	0.115	0.105	+0.003	0.107
2009 Nov 19	0.125	0.115	+0.008	0.117
2009 Nov 27	0.115	0.105	+0.003	0.107
2009 Dec 03	0.135	0.125	+0.003	0.127
2009 Dec 10	0.135	0.125	+0.005	0.127
3 Month→ 2009 Dec 17	0.140	0.130	unch.	0.132
2009 Dec 24	0.145	0.138	+0.003	0.140
2009 Dec 31	0.150	0.140	+0.003	0.142
2010 Jan 07	0.140	0.130	+0.005	0.132
2010 Jan 14	0.138	0.130	unch.	0.132
2010 Jan 21	0.155	0.150	+0.005	0.152
2010 Jan 28	0.173	0.165	+0.005	0.167
2010 Feb 04	0.188	0.180	+0.005	0.183
2010 Feb 11	0.195	0.190	+0.005	0.193
2010 Feb 18	0.205	0.200	+0.007	0.203
2010 Feb 25	0.215	0.210	+0.005	0.213
2010 Mar 04	0.225	0.220	+0.005	0.223
6 Month→ 2010 Mar 11	0.228	0.223	+0.005	0.226
2010 Apr 01	0.245	0.240	+0.005	0.244

TREASURY NOTES & BONDS
Friday, September 04, 2009

Maturity	Coupon	Bid	Asked	Chg	Asked yield
2010 Jun 15	3.625	102:17	102:17	−1	0.3109
2010 Jun 30	2.875	102:01	102:02	−1	0.3413
2010 Jul 15	3.875	102:31	103:00	−2	0.3349
2010 Jul 31	2.750	102:03	102:04	−1	0.3797
2010 Aug 15	4.125	103:14	103:15	−2	0.3951
1 Year→ 2010 Aug 15	5.750	104:31	105:00	−2	0.4021
2010 Aug 31	2.375	101:29	101:30	−1	0.3998
2010 Sep 15	3.875	103:17	103:18	−3	0.3617
2010 Sep 30	2.000	101:20	101:21	−2	0.4322
2010 Oct 15	4.250	104:08	104:08	−2	0.3748
2010 Oct 31	1.500	101:05	101:06	−1	0.4715
2011 Jun 30	1.125	100:16	100:17	−2	0.8350
2011 Jun 30	5.125	107:23	107:24	−3	0.8064
2011 Jul 31	1.000	100:07	100:07	−1	0.8853
2011 Jul 31	4.875	107:16	107:17	−4	0.8513
2 Year→ 2011 Aug 15	5.000	107:29	107:30	−4	0.8486
2011 Aug 31	1.000	100:04	100:04	−2	0.9320
2011 Aug 31	4.625	107:07	107:08	−4	0.9176
2011 Sep 30	4.500	107:05	107:06	−3	0.9748
2011 Oct 31	4.500	107:19	107:20	−3	1.0235
2014 Jun 30	2.625	101:16	101:17	−11	2.2883
2014 Jul 31	2.625	101:11	101:12	−11	2.3275
5 Year→ 2014 Aug 15	4.250	109:00	109:01	−12	2.3015
2014 Aug 31	2.375	100:03	100:03	−11	2.3532
2014 Nov 15	4.250	108:30	109:00	−13	2.3933
2014 Nov 15	11.750	102:04	102:06	−3	−0.0435
2015 Feb 15	4.000	107:13	107:14	−13	2.5265
2015 Feb 15	11.250	144:02	144:07	−18	2.4989
2015 May 15	4.125	107:31	108:01	−14	2.5971

TREASURY NOTES & BONDS
Friday, September 04, 2009

Maturity	Coupon	Bid	Asked	Chg	Asked yield
2019 Feb 15	2.750	94:11	94:12	−27	3.4535
2019 Feb 15	8.875	143:05	143:10	−35	3.4564
2019 May 15	3.125	97:11	97:12	−28	3.4476
2019 Aug 15	3.625	101:19	101:20	−29	3.4322
10 Year→ 2019 Aug 15	8.125	137:29	138:01	−35	3.5486
2020 Feb 15	8.500	141:27	142:00	−33	3.6286
2020 May 15	8.750	144:10	144:15	−35	3.6781
2020 Aug 15	8.750	144:20	144:25	−38	3.7259
2021 Feb 15	7.875	137:11	137:15	−38	3.8032
2021 May 15	8.125	140:01	140:05	−39	3.8292
2021 Aug 15	8.125	140:12	140:17	−39	3.8567
2021 Nov 15	8.000	139:18	139:23	−41	3.8792
2022 Aug 15	7.250	132:27	133:00	−45	3.9640
2027 Feb 15	6.625	130:10	130:15	−57	4.1517
2027 Aug 15	6.375	127:20	127:25	−58	4.1622
2027 Nov 15	6.125	124:20	124:24	−56	4.1694
2028 Aug 15	5.500	116:28	117:00	−53	4.1902
2028 Nov 15	5.250	113:21	113:25	−53	4.1965
2029 Feb 15	5.250	113:19	113:25	−54	4.2049
20 Year→ 2029 Aug 15	6.125	125:23	125:28	−58	4.1962
2030 May 15	6.250	128:02	128:08	−58	4.1944
2031 Feb 15	5.375	116:01	116:07	−57	4.2178
2036 Feb 15	4.500	103:24	103:29	−58	4.2524
2037 Feb 15	4.750	107:26	107:31	−61	4.2548
2037 May 15	5.000	111:31	112:05	−64	4.2495
2038 Feb 15	4.375	101:24	101:28	−61	4.2605
2038 May 15	4.500	103:28	104:00	−61	4.2578
2039 Feb 15	3.500	87:03	87:07	−56	4.2664
2039 May 15	4.250	99:24	99:27	−61	4.2599
30 Year→ 2039 Aug 15	4.500	103:29	103:31	−64	4.2648

investors today indifferent between locking their money away for two years and earning 5% on the two-year note versus investing in the one-year T-bill today at 5% and then next year reinvesting the money from that instrument into another 1-year T-bill.

Investment Strategy	(1) Rate earned this year	(2) Rate earned next year	(3) Return over two years [(1) + (2)]
Buy two-year note today	6%	6%	12%
Buy one-year T-bill, then reinvest in another T-bill next year	5%	7%	12%

Only if the rate on a one-year T-bill rises from 5% this year to 7% next will investors be indifferent between these two strategies. Thus, according to the expectations hypothesis, an upward-sloping yield curve means that investors expect interest rates to rise, and a downward-sloping yield curve means that investors expect interest rates to fall.

Liquidity Preference Theory More often than not, yield curves have an upward slope. The expectations hypothesis would interpret this as a sign that investors expect rates to rise more often than not. That seems somewhat illogical. Why would investors expect interest rates to trend up over time? There is certainly no historical pattern to lead one to hold that view. One explanation for the frequency of upward-sloping yield curves is the **liquidity preference theory**. This theory states that, intuitively, long-term bond rates should be higher than short-term rates because of the added risks involved with the longer maturities. In other words, because of the risk differential (real or perceived) between long- and short-term debt securities, rational investors will prefer the less risky, short-term obligations *unless they can be motivated, via higher interest rates, to invest in longer bonds*.

Actually, there are a number of reasons why rational investors should prefer short-term securities. To begin with, they are more liquid (more easily converted to cash) and less sensitive to changing market rates, which means there is less price volatility. For a given change in market rates, the prices of longer-term bonds will show considerably more movement than the prices of short-term bonds. Simply put, uncertainty increases over time, and investors therefore require a premium to invest in long maturities. In addition, just as investors tend to require a premium for tying up funds for longer periods, borrowers will also pay a premium in order to obtain long-term funds. Borrowers thus assure themselves that funds will be available, and they avoid having to roll over short-term debt at unknown and possibly unfavorable rates. All of these preferences explain why higher rates of interest should be associated with longer maturities and why it's perfectly rational to expect upward-sloping yield curves.

Market Segmentation Theory Another often-cited theory, the **market segmentation theory**, suggests that the market for debt is segmented on the basis of the maturity preferences of different types of financial institutions and investors. According to this theory, the yield curve changes as the supply and demand for funds within each maturity segment determines its prevailing interest rate. The equilibrium between the financial institutions that supply the funds for short-term maturities (e.g., banks) and the borrowers of those short-term funds (e.g., businesses with seasonal loan requirements) establishes interest rates in the short-term markets. Similarly, the equilibrium between suppliers and demanders in such long-term markets as life insurance and real estate determines the prevailing long-term interest rates.

The shape of the yield curve can be either upward- or downward-sloping, as determined by the general relationship between rates in each market segment. When supply outstrips demand for short-term loans, short-term rates are relatively low. If, at the same time, the demand for long-term loans is higher than the available supply of funds, then long-term rates will move up. Thus, low rates in the short-term segment and high rates in the long-term segment cause an upward-sloping yield curve, and vice versa.

Which Theory Is Right? It is clear *that all three theories* of the term structure have merit in explaining the shape of the yield curve. From them, we can conclude that at any time, the slope of the yield curve is affected by (1) expectations regarding future interest rates, (2) liquidity preferences, and (3) the supply and demand conditions in the short- and long-term market segments. Upward-sloping yield curves result from expectations of rising interest rates, lender preferences for shorter-maturity loans, and greater supply of short- rather than of long-term loans relative to the respective demand in each market segment. The opposite behavior, of course, results in a flat or downward-sloping yield curve. At any point in time, the interaction of these forces determines the prevailing slope of the yield curve.

Using the Yield Curve in Investment Decisions Bond investors often use yield curves in making investment decisions. Analyzing the changes in yield curves over time provides investors with information about future interest rate movements and how they can affect price behavior and comparative returns. For example, if the yield curve begins to rise sharply, it usually means that inflation is starting to heat up or is expected to do so in the near future. In that case, investors can expect that interest rates, too, will rise. Under these conditions, most seasoned bond investors will turn to short or intermediate (three to five years) maturities, which provide reasonable returns and at the same time minimize exposure to capital loss when interest rates go up (and bond prices fall). A downward-sloping yield curve, although unusual, generally results from actions of the Federal Reserve to reduce inflation. As suggested by the expectations hypothesis, this would signal that rates have peaked and are about to fall.

Another factor to consider is the difference in yields on different maturities—the "steepness" of the curve. For example, a steep yield curve is one where long-term rates are *much higher* than short-term rates. This shape is often seen as an indication that long-term rates may be near their peak and are about to fall, thereby narrowing the spread between long and short rates. Steep yield curves are generally viewed as a bullish sign. For aggressive bond investors, they could be the signal to start moving into long-term securities. Flatter yield curves, on the other hand, sharply reduce the incentive for going long-term. For example, look at yield curve 1 in Figure 11.3 (on page 410). Note that the difference in yield between the five- and 30-year maturities is quite small. (In fact, it's almost nonexistent.) As a result, there's not much incentive to go long-term. Under these conditions, investors would be well advised to just stick with the five- to 10-year maturities, which will generate about the same yield as long bonds but without the risks.

**CONCEPTS
IN REVIEW**
Answers available at
www.pearsonhighered.com/
gitman

11.1 Is there a single market rate of interest applicable to all segments of the bond market, or are there a series of market yields? Explain and note the investment implications of such a market environment.

11.2 Explain why interest rates are important to both conservative and aggressive bond investors. What causes interest rates to move, and how can you monitor such movements?

11.3 What is the *term structure of interest rates* and how is it related to the *yield curve*? What information is required to plot a yield curve? Describe an upward-sloping yield curve and explain what it has to say about the behavior of interest rates. Do the same for a flat yield curve.

11.4 How might you, as a bond investor, use information about the term structure of interest rates and yield curves when making investment decisions?

The Pricing of Bonds

LG3 No matter who the issuer is, what kind of bond it is, or whether it's fully taxable or tax-free, all bonds are priced pretty much the same. That is, all bonds (including *notes* with maturities of more than one year) are priced according to the *present value of their future cash flow streams*. Indeed, once the prevailing or expected market yield is known, the whole process becomes rather mechanical.

Bond prices are driven by market yields. That's because in the marketplace, the *appropriate yield at which the bond should sell is defined first*, and then that yield is used to find the price (or market value) of the bond. As we saw earlier, the appropriate yield on a bond is a function of certain market and economic forces (e.g., the risk-free rate of return and inflation), as well as key issue and issuer characteristics (like years to maturity and the issue's bond rating). Together, these forces combine to form the *required rate of return*, which is the rate of return the investor would like to earn in order to justify an investment in a given fixed-income security. In the bond market, required return is market driven and is generally considered to be the issue's market yield. That is, the required return defines the yield at which the bond should be trading and serves as the *discount rate* in the bond valuation process.

The Basic Bond Valuation Model

Generally speaking, bond investors receive two distinct types of cash flows: (1) the periodic receipt of coupon income over the life of the bond and (2) the recovery of principal (or par value) at the end of the bond's life. Thus, in valuing a bond, you're dealing with an *annuity* of coupon payments plus a large *single cash flow*, as represented by the recovery of principal at maturity. We can use these cash flows, along with the required rate of return on the investment, in a present-value-based bond valuation model to find the dollar value, or price, of a bond. Using annual compounding, this valuation model can be expressed as follows:

Equation 11.2

$$P_0 = \sum_{t-1}^{n} \frac{I_i}{(1+i)^t} + \frac{PV_n}{(1+i)^n}$$

$$= \frac{\text{Present value of}}{\text{coupon payments}} + \frac{\text{Present value of}}{\text{bond's par value}}$$

where
P_0 = current price (or value) of the bond
I_t = annual interest (coupon) income
PV_n = par value of the bond, at maturity
n = number of years to maturity
i = prevailing market yield, or required return

In this form, we can compute the current value of the bond, or what an investor would be willing to pay for it, given that she wants to generate a certain rate of return, as defined by *i*. Or we can solve for the *i* in the equation, in which case we'd be looking for the yield embedded in the current market price of the bond.

In the discussion that follows, we will demonstrate the bond valuation process in two ways. First, we'll use *annual compounding*—that is, because of its computational simplicity, we'll assume we are dealing with coupons that are paid once a year. Second, we'll examine bond valuation under conditions of *semiannual compounding*, which is more like the way most bonds actually pay their coupon.

Annual Compounding

We need the following information to value a bond: (1) the size of the annual coupon payment, (2) the bond's par value, and (3) the number of years remaining to maturity. We then use the prevailing market yield (or an estimate of future market rates) as the discount rate to compute the price of a bond, as follows:

Equation 11.3

$$\text{Bond price} = \frac{\text{Present value of the annuity}}{\text{of annual interest income}} + \frac{\text{Present value of the bond's}}{\text{par value}}$$

Equation 11.3a

$$BP = \frac{I}{(1 + i)^1} + \frac{I}{(1 + i)^2} + \cdots + \frac{I}{(1 + i)^N} + \frac{\$1,000}{(1 + i)^N}$$

where

I = amount of annual interest income
N = number of years until the bond matures

To illustrate this bond price formula in action, consider a 20-year, 9.5% bond priced to yield 10%. That is, the bond pays an annual coupon of 9.5% (or $95), has 20 years left to maturity, and should be priced to provide a market yield of 10%. We can now use Equation 11.3 to find the price of our bond.

$$BP = \frac{\$95}{(1 + 0.10)^1} + \frac{\$95}{(1 + 0.10)^2} + \cdots + \frac{\$95}{(1 + 0.10)^{20}} + \frac{\$1,000}{(1 + 0.10)^{20}} = \underline{\$957.43}$$

Note that because this is a coupon-bearing bond, we have an annuity of coupon payments of $95 a year for 20 years, plus a single cash flow of $1,000 that occurs at the end of year 20. Thus, we find the present value of the coupon annuity and then add that amount to the present value of the recovery of principal at maturity. In this particular case, you should be willing to pay about $958 for this bond, so long as you're satisfied with earning 10% on your money.

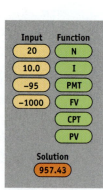

CALCULATOR USE For *annual compounding*, to price a 20-year, 9.5% bond to yield 10%, use the keystrokes shown in the margin, where:

N = number of years to maturity
I = yield on the bond (what the bond is being priced to yield)
PMT = stream of annual coupon payments
FV = par value of the bond
PV = computed price of the bond

Semiannual Compounding

Although using annual compounding simplifies the valuation process a bit, it's not the way bonds are actually valued in the marketplace. In practice, most (domestic) bonds pay interest every six months, so semiannual compounding is used in valuing bonds. Fortunately, it's relatively easy to go from annual to semiannual compounding: All you need to do is cut the annual coupon payment in half, and make two minor modifications to the present-value interest factors. Given these changes, finding the price of a bond under conditions of semiannual compounding is much like pricing a bond using annual compounding. That is,

Equation 11.4

$$\text{Bond price (with semiannual compounding)} = \text{Present value of an annuity of } \textit{semiannual} \text{ coupon payments} + \text{Present value of the bond's par value}$$

Equation 11.4a

$$BP = \frac{I/2}{\left(1 + \frac{i}{2}\right)^1} + \frac{I/2}{\left(1 + \frac{i}{2}\right)^2} + \ldots + \frac{I/2}{\left(1 + \frac{i}{2}\right)^{2N}} + \frac{\$1{,}000}{\left(1 + \frac{i}{2}\right)^{2N}}$$

where

$I/2$ = the amount of interest paid every six months
$i/2$ = the interest rate per six-month period

By simply *cutting the required return in half and doubling the number of periods to maturity*, we are, in effect, dealing with a semiannual measure of return and using the number of six-month periods to maturity (rather than *years*). For example, in our bond illustration above, we wanted to price a 20-year bond to yield 10%. With semiannual compounding, we would be dealing with a semiannual return of 10%/2 = 5%, and with 20 × 2 = 40 semiannual periods to maturity.

To see how this all fits together, consider once again the 20-year, 9.5% bond. This time assume it's priced to yield 10% *compounded semiannually*. Using Equation 11.4, you'd have:

$$BP = \frac{\$95/2}{\left(1 + \frac{0.10}{2}\right)^1} + \frac{\$95/2}{\left(1 + \frac{0.10}{2}\right)^2} + \ldots + \frac{\$95/2}{\left(1 + \frac{0.10}{2}\right)^{40}} + \frac{4{,}000}{\left(1 + \frac{0.10}{2}\right)^{40}} = \underline{\$957.10}$$

The price of the bond in this case ($957.10) is slightly less than the price we obtained with annual compounding ($957.43). Clearly, it doesn't make much difference whether we use annual or semiannual compounding, though the differences do tend to increase a bit with lower coupons and shorter maturities.

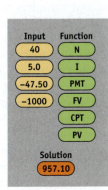

Input	Function
40	N
5.0	I
−47.50	PMT
−1000	FV
	CPT
	PV

Solution
957.10

CALCULATOR USE For *semiannual compounding*, to price a 20-year, 9.5% semiannual-pay bond to yield 10%, use the keystrokes shown in the margin, where:

N = number of 6-month periods to maturity (20 × 2 = 40),
I = yield on the bond, adjusted for semiannual compounding (10%/2 = 5%),
PMT = stream of semiannual coupon payments ($95.00/2 = $47.50), and
FV and PV = remain the same.

11.5 Explain how market yield affects the price of a bond. Could you price a bond without knowing its market yield? Explain.

11.6 Why are bonds generally priced using semiannual compounding? Does it make much difference if you use annual compounding?

Measures of Yield and Return

LG4 In the bond market, investment decisions are made more on the basis of a bond's yield than its dollar price. Not only does yield affect the price at which a bond trades, but it also serves as an important measure of return. To use yield as a measure of return, we *simply reverse the bond valuation process* described above and solve for yield rather than price. Actually, there are three widely used measures of yield: current yield, yield-to-maturity, and yield-to-call. We'll look at all three of them here, along with a concept known as *expected return*, which measures the expected (or actual) rate of return earned over a specific holding period.

Current Yield

Current yield is the simplest of all bond return measures, but it also has the most limited application. This measure looks at just one source of return: *a bond's interest income*. In particular, it indicates the amount of current income a bond provides relative to its prevailing market price. It is calculated as follows:

Equation 11.5

$$\text{Current yield} = \frac{\text{Annual interest income}}{\text{Current market price of the bond}}$$

For example, an 8% bond would pay $80 per year in interest for every $1,000 of principal. However, if the bond were currently priced at $800, it would have a current yield of 10% ($80/$800 = 0.10). Current yield is a measure of a bond's annual coupon income, so it would be of interest primarily to investors seeking high levels of current income, such as endowments or retirees.

Yield-to-Maturity

Yield-to-maturity (YTM) is the most important and most widely used bond valuation measure. It evaluates both interest income and price appreciation and considers total cash flow received over the life of an issue. Also known as **promised yield**, YTM shows the fully compounded rate of return earned by an investor, *given that the bond is held to maturity and all principal and interest payments are made in a prompt and timely fashion.* In addition, because YTM is a present-value-based measure of return, it's assumed that *all the coupons will be reinvested, for the remaining life of the issue, at an interest rate equal to the bond's yield-to-maturity.* This "reinvestment assumption" plays a vital role in YTM, and will be discussed in more detail later in this chapter (see "Yield Properties").

Yield-to-maturity is used not only to gauge the return on a single issue but also to track the behavior of the market in general. In other words, market interest rates are basically a reflection of the average promised yields that exist in a given segment of the market. Promised yield provides valuable insight into an issue's investment merits and is used to assess the attractiveness of alternative investment vehicles. Other things being equal, the higher the promised yield of an issue, the more attractive it is.

Although there are a couple of ways to compute promised yield, the best and most accurate procedure is one that is derived directly from the bond valuation model described above. That is, *assuming annual compounding*, you can use Equation 11.3 (on page 414) to measure the YTM on a bond. The difference is that now, instead of trying to determine the price of the bond, *we know its price and are trying to find the discount rate that will equate the present value of the bond's cash flow (coupon and principal payments) to its current market price*. This procedure may sound familiar: It's just like the *internal rate of return* measure described in Chapter 4. Indeed, we're basically looking for the internal rate of return on a bond. When we find that, we have the bond's yield-to-maturity.

Unfortunately, unless you have a handheld calculator or computer software that will do the calculations for you, finding yield-to-maturity is a matter of trial and error. Let's say we want to find the yield-to-maturity on a 7.5% ($1,000 par value) bond that has 15 years remaining to maturity and is currently trading in the market at $809.50. From Equation 11.3, we know that

$$BP = \$809.50 = \frac{\$75}{(1+i)^1} + \frac{\$75}{(1+i)^2} + \ldots + \frac{\$75}{(1+i)^{15}} + \frac{\$1,000}{(1+i)^{15}}$$

Notice that this bond sells below par (i.e., it sells at a discount). What do we know about the relationship between the required return on a bond and its coupon rate when the bond sells at a discount? Bonds sell at a discount when the required return (or yield to maturity) is higher than the coupon rate, so the yield to maturity on this bond must be higher than 7.5%.

Through trial and error, we might start with a discount rate of, say, 8% or 9% (or any number above the bond's coupon). Sooner or later, we'll try a discount rate of 10%. And look what happens at that point: Using Equation 11.3 to price this bond at a discount rate of 10%, we see that the price equals $809.48.

The computed price of $809.48 is reasonably close to the bond's current market price of $809.50. As a result, the 10% rate represents the yield-to-maturity on this bond. That is, 10% is the discount rate that leads to a *computed bond price that's equal (or very close) to the bond's current market price*. In this case, if you were to pay $809.50 for the bond and hold it to maturity, you would expect to earn a yield of 10.0%.

CALCULATOR USE For *annual compounding*, to find the YTM of a 15-year, 7.5% bond that is currently priced in the market at $809.50, use the keystrokes shown in the margin. The present value (*PV*) key represents the current market price of the bond, and all other keystrokes are as defined earlier.

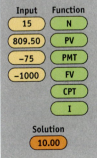

Input	Function
15	N
809.50	PV
−75	PMT
−1000	FV
	CPT
	I

Solution
10.00

Using Semiannual Compounding Given some fairly simple modifications, it's also possible to find yield-to-maturity using semiannual compounding. To do so, we cut the annual coupon in half, double the number of years (periods) to maturity, and use the bond valuation model in Equation 11.4 (on page 415). Returning to our 7.5%, 15-year bond, let's see what happens when we try a discount rate of 10%.

$$BP = \frac{\$75.00/2}{\left(1+\dfrac{0.10}{2}\right)^1} + \frac{\$75.00/2}{\left(1+\dfrac{0.10}{2}\right)^2} + \ldots + \frac{\$75.00/2}{\left(1+\dfrac{0.10}{2}\right)^{30}} + \frac{\$1,000}{\left(1+\dfrac{0.10}{2}\right)^{30}} = \$807.85$$

As you can see, a semiannual discount rate of 5% results in a computed bond value that's well short of our target price of $809.50. Given the inverse relationship between price and yield, it follows that if we need a higher price, we'll have to try a lower yield (discount rate). Therefore, we know the semiannual yield on this bond has to be something less than 5%. By trial and error, you would determine that the yield to maturity on this bond is just a shade under 5% per half year—4.987% to be more precise.

At this point, because we're dealing with semiannual cash flows, to be technically accurate, we should find the bond's "effective" annual yield. However, that's not the way it's done in practice. Rather, *market convention is to simply state the annual yield as twice the semiannual yield.* This practice produces what the market refers to as the **bond-equivalent yield.** Returning to the bond-yield problem started above, we know that the issue has a semiannual yield of 4.987%. According to the bond-equivalent yield convention, we now simply *double the solving rate in order to obtain the annual rate of return on this bond.* Doing this gives us a yield-to-maturity (or promised yield) of 4.987% × 2 = 9.97%. This is the annual rate of return we'll earn on the bond if we hold it to maturity.

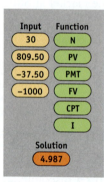

Input	Function
30	N
809.50	PV
−37.50	PMT
−1000	FV
	CPT
	I

Solution
4.987

CALCULATOR USE For *semiannual compounding,* to find the YTM of a 15-year, 7.5% semiannual-pay bond that is currently priced in the market at $809.50, use the keystrokes shown here. As before, the *PV* key is the current market price of the bond, and all other keystrokes are as defined earlier. Remember that to find the bond-equivalent yield, you have to double the computed value of *I*. That is, 4.987% × 2 = 9.974%.

Yield Properties Actually, in addition to holding the bond to maturity, there are several other critical assumptions embedded in any yield-to-maturity figure. The promised yield measure—whether computed with annual or semiannual compounding—is based on present-value concepts and therefore contains important *reinvestment assumptions.* That is, the yield-to-maturity figure itself is the *minimum required reinvestment rate the investor must subsequently earn on each of the interim coupon receipts* in order to generate a return equal to or greater than the promised yield. In essence, the calculated yield-to-maturity figure is the return "promised" only so long as the issuer meets all interest and principal obligations on a timely basis and the investor reinvests all coupon income at an average rate equal to or greater than the computed promised yield. In our example above, the investor would have to reinvest (to maturity) each of the coupons received over the next 15 years at a rate of about 10%. *Failure to do so would result in a realized yield of less than the 10% promised.* If the investor made no attempt to reinvest the coupons, he or she would earn a realized yield over the 15-year investment horizon of just over 6.5%—far short of the 10% promised return. Thus, unless it's a zero-coupon bond, it should be clear that a significant portion of a bond's total return over time is derived from the *reinvestment of coupons.*

This reinvestment assumption was first introduced in Chapter 4, when we discussed the role that "interest on interest" plays in measuring investment returns. As noted, when using present-value-based measures of return, such as YTM, there are actually three components of return: (1) coupon/interest income, (2) capital gains (or losses), and (3) interest on interest. Whereas current income and capital gains make up the profits from an investment, interest on interest is a measure of what *you* do with those profits. In the context of yield-to-maturity, the computed YTM defines the required, or minimum, reinvestment rate. Put your investment profits (i.e., coupon income) to work at this rate and you'll earn a rate of return equal to YTM. This rule applies to any coupon-bearing bond—so long as there's an annual or semiannual flow of coupon income, the reinvestment of that income and interest on interest are matters that you must deal with. Also, keep in mind that the *bigger the coupon* and/or the *longer the maturity*, the *more important the reinvestment assumption*. Indeed, for many long-term, high-coupon bond investments, interest on interest alone can account for *well over half* the cash flow.

Finding the Yield on a Zero We can also use the same promised-yield procedures described above (Equation 11.3 with annual compounding or Equation 11.4 with semiannual compounding) to find the yield-to-maturity on a zero-coupon bond. The only difference is that the coupon portion of the equation can be ignored because it will, of course, equal zero. All you have to do to find the promised yield on a zero is to solve the following expression:

$$yield = \left(\frac{\$1,000}{\text{Price}}\right)^{\frac{1}{N}} - 1$$

To illustrate, consider a 15-year zero-coupon issue that can be purchased today for $315.

$$yield = \left(\frac{\$1,000}{\$315}\right)^{\frac{1}{15}} - 1 = 0.08 = 8\%$$

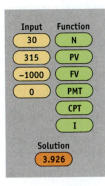

The zero-coupon bond pays an annual compound return of 8%. Had we been using semiannual compounding, we'd use the same equation except we'd substitute 30 for 15 (because there are 30 semiannual periods in 15 years). The yield would change to 3.926% per half year, or 7.845% per year.

CALCULATOR USE For *semiannual compounding*, to find the YTM of a 15-year zero-coupon bond that is currently priced in the market at $315, use the keystrokes shown in the margin. *PV* is the current market price of the bond, and all other keystrokes are as defined earlier. To find the bond-equivalent yield, double the computed value of *I*. That is, 3.926% × 2 = 7.85%.

Yield-to-Call

Bonds can be either noncallable or callable. Recall from Chapter 10 that a *noncallable bond* prohibits the issuer from calling the bond in for retirement prior to maturity. Because such issues will remain outstanding to maturity, they can be valued by using the standard *yield-to-maturity* measure. In contrast, a *callable bond* gives the issuer the right to retire the bond prematurely, so the issue may or may not remain outstanding to maturity. As a result, YTM may not always be the appropriate measure of value. Instead, we must consider the impact of the bond being called away prior to maturity. A common way to do that is to use a measure known as **yield-to-call (YTC)**, which shows the yield on a bond if the issue remains outstanding *not* to maturity, but rather until its first (or some other specified) call date.

Yield-to-call is commonly used with bonds that carry *deferred-call provisions*. Remember that such issues start out as noncallable bonds and then, after a call deferment period (of 5 to 10 years), become freely callable. Under these conditions, *YTC would measure the expected yield on a deferred-call bond assuming that the issue is retired at the end of the call deferment period* (that is, when the bond first becomes freely callable). We can find YTC by making two simple modifications to the standard YTM equation (Equation 11.3 or 11.4). First, we define the length of the investment horizon (*N*) as *the number of years to the first call date*, not the number of years to maturity. Second, instead of using the bond's par value ($1,000), we *use the bond's call price* (which is stated in the indenture and is nearly always greater than the bond's par value).

For example, assume you want to find yield-to-call on a 20-year, 10.5% deferred-call bond that is currently trading in the market at $1,204, but has five years to go to first call (that is, before it becomes freely callable), at which time it can be called in at a price of $1,085. Thus, rather than using the bond's maturity of 20 years in the valuation equation (Equation 11.3 or 11.4), we use the number of years to first call (five years), and rather than the bond's par value, $1,000, we use the issue's call price, $1,085. Note, however, we still use the bond's coupon (10.5%) and its current market price ($1,204). Thus, for annual compounding, we would have:

Equation 11.6

$$BP = \$1,204 = \frac{\$105}{(1 + i)^1} + \frac{\$105}{(1 + i)^2} + \frac{\$105}{(1 + i)^3} + \frac{\$105}{(1 + i)^4} + \frac{\$105}{(1 + i)^5} + \frac{\$1,085}{(1 + i)^5}$$

Through trial and error, we finally hit upon a discount rate of 7%. At that point, the present value of the future cash flows (coupons over the next five years, plus call price) will exactly (or very nearly) equal the bond's current market price of $1,204.

Thus, *the YTC on this bond is 7%.* In contrast, the bond's YTM is 8.37%. In practice, bond investors normally compute *both* YTM and YTC for deferred-call bonds that are *trading at a premium*. They do this to find which of the two yields is lower; market convention is to *use the lower, more conservative measure of yield (YTM or YTC) as the appropriate indicator of value*. As a result, the premium bond in our example would be valued relative to its yield-to-call. The assumption is that because interest rates have dropped so much (the YTM is 2 percentage points below the coupon rate), it will be called in the first chance the issuer gets. However, the situation is totally different when this or any bond trades at a discount. Why? Because YTM on any *discount bond*, whether callable or not, *will always be less* than YTC. Thus, YTC is a totally irrelevant measure for discount bonds—it's used only with premium bonds.

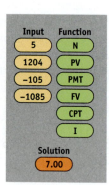

Input	Function
5	N
1204	PV
−105	PMT
−1085	FV
	CPT
	I
Solution	
7.00	

CALCULATOR USE For *annual compounding*, to find the YTC of a 20-year, 10.5% bond that is currently trading at $1,204 but can be called in five years at a call price of $1,085, use the keystrokes shown in the margin. In this computation, *N* is the number of years to first call date, and *FV* represents the bond's call price. All other keystrokes are as defined earlier.

Expected Return

Rather than just buying and holding bonds, some investors prefer to actively trade in and out of these securities over fairly short investment horizons. As a result, yield-to-maturity and yield-to-call have relatively little meaning, other than as indicators of the rate of return used to price the bond. These investors obviously need an alternative measure of return that they can use to assess the investment appeal of those bonds they intend to trade in and out of. Such an alternative measure is **expected return**. It indicates the rate of return an investor can expect to earn by holding a bond over a period of time that's less than the life of the issue. (Expected return is also known as **realized yield**, because it shows the return an investor would realize by trading in and out of bonds over short holding periods.)

Expected return lacks the precision of yield-to-maturity (and YTC), because the major cash flow variables are largely the product of investor estimates. In particular, going into the investment, both the length of the holding period and the future selling price of the bond are pure estimates and therefore subject to uncertainty. Even so, we can use pretty much the same procedure to find realized yield as we did to find promised yield. That is, with some simple modifications to the standard bond-pricing formula, we can use the following equation to find the expected return on a bond:

Equation 11.7

$$\text{Bond price} = \begin{array}{c}\text{Present value of the bond's}\\ \text{annual interest income}\\ \text{over the holding period}\end{array} + \begin{array}{c}\text{Present value of the bond's}\\ \text{future price at the}\\ \text{end of the holding period}\end{array}$$

Equation 11.7a

$$BP = \frac{I}{(1+i)^1} + \frac{I}{(1+i)^2} + \cdots + \frac{I}{(1+i)^N} + \frac{FV}{(1+i)^N}$$

where this time N represents the length of the holding period (not years to maturity), and FV is the expected future price of the bond.

As indicated above, we must determine the *future price* of the bond when computing expected realized yield; this is done by using the standard bond price formula, as described earlier. The most difficult part of deriving a reliable future price is, of course, coming up with future market interest rates that you feel will exist when the bond is sold. By evaluating current and expected market interest rate conditions, *you can estimate a promised yield that the issue is expected to carry at the date of sale and then use that yield to calculate the bond's future price.*

To illustrate, take one more look at our 7.5%, 15-year bond. This time, let's assume that you feel the price of the bond, which is now trading at a discount, will rise sharply as interest rates fall over the next few years. In particular, assume the bond is currently priced at $809.50 (to yield 10%) and you anticipate holding the bond for three years. Over that time, you expect market rates to drop, so the price of the bond should rise to around $960 by the end of the three-year holding period. (Actually, *we found the future price of the bond—$960—by assuming interest rates would fall to 8% in year 3.* We then used the standard bond-price formula—in this case Equation 11.3—to find the value of a 7.5%, *12-year obligation*, which is how many years to maturity a 15-year bond will have at the end of a three-year holding period.) Thus, we are assuming that you will buy the bond today at a market price of $809.50 and sell it three years later— after interest rates have declined to 8%—at a price of $960. Given these assumptions, the expected return (realized yield) on this bond is 14.6%, which is the discount rate in the following equation that will produce a current market price of $809.50.

$$BP = \$809.50 = \frac{\$75}{(1+i)^1} + \frac{\$75}{(1+i)^2} + \frac{\$75}{(1+i)^3} + \frac{\$960}{(1+i)^3} \quad i = 0.146 = 14.6\%$$

The better-than-14.5% return on this investment is fairly substantial, but keep in mind that this is only a measure of *expected return*. It is, of course, subject to variation if things do not turn out as anticipated, particularly with regard to the market yield expected at the end of the holding period. (*Note:* This illustration uses annual compounding, but you could just as easily have used *semiannual compounding*, which, everything else being the same, would have resulted in an expected yield of 14.4% rather than the 14.6% found with annual compounding. Also, if the anticipated horizon is one year or less, you would want to use the simple *holding period return (HPR)* measure described in Chapter 4.)

CALCULATOR USE For *semiannual compounding*, to find the expected return on a 7.5% bond that is currently priced in the market at $809.50 but is expected to rise to $960 within a three-year holding period, use the keystrokes shown in the margin. In this computation, *PV* is the current price of the bond, and *FV* is the expected price of the bond at the end of the (three-year) holding period. All other keystrokes are as defined earlier. To find the bond-equivalent yield, double the computed value of *I*: 7.217% × 2 = 14.43%.

Valuing a Bond

Depending on investor objectives, investors can determine the value of a bond by either its promised yield or its expected return. Conservative, income-oriented investors employ *promised yield* (YTM or YTC) to value bonds. Coupon income over extended periods of time is their principal objective, and promised yield provides a viable measure of return—assuming, of course, the reinvestment assumptions embedded in the yield measure are reasonable. More aggressive bond traders, on the other hand, use *expected return* to value bonds. The capital gains that can be earned by buying and selling bonds over relatively short holding periods is their chief concern, and expected return is more important to them than the promised yield at the time the bond is purchased.

In either case, promised or expected yield provides a *measure of return* that can be used to determine the relative attractiveness of fixed-income securities. But to do so, we must evaluate the measure of return in light of the *risk* involved in the investment. Bonds are no different from stocks in that the amount of return (promised or expected) should be sufficient to cover the investor's exposure to risk. Thus, the greater the amount of perceived risk, the greater the return the bond should generate. If the bond meets this hurdle, it could then be compared to other potential investments. If you find it difficult to do better in a risk–return sense, then you should seriously consider that bond as a viable investment outlet.

CONCEPTS IN REVIEW

Answers available at
www.pearsonhighered.com/
gitman

11.7 What's the difference between *current yield* and *yield-to-maturity?* Between *promised yield* and *realized yield?* How does YTC differ from YTM?

11.8 Briefly describe the term *bond-equivalent yield*. Is there any difference between promised yield and bond-equivalent yield? Explain.

11.9 Why is the reinvestment of interest income so important to bond investors?

Duration and Immunization

LG5 One of the problems with yield-to-maturity (YTM) is that it assumes you can reinvest the bond's periodic coupon payments at the same rate over time. If you reinvest this interest income at a lower rate (or if you spend it), your actual return will be lower than the YTM. Another flaw is that YTM assumes the investor will hold the bond to maturity. For bonds not held to maturity, prices will reflect prevailing interest rates, which are likely to differ from YTM. If rates have moved up since a bond was purchased, the bond will sell at a discount. If interest rates have dropped, it will sell at a premium.

The problem with yield-to-maturity, then, is that it fails to take into account the effects of *reinvestment risk and price (or market) risk*. To see how reinvestment and price risks behave relative to one another, consider a situation in which market interest rates have undergone a sharp decline. Under such conditions, bond prices will, of course, rise. You might be tempted to cash out your holdings and take some gains (i.e., do a little "profit taking"). Indeed, selling before maturity is the only way to take advantage of falling interest rates, because a bond will pay its par value at maturity, regardless of prevailing interest rates. That's the good news about falling rates, but there is a downside: When interest rates fall, so do the opportunities to reinvest at high rates. Therefore, although you gain on the price side, you lose on the reinvestment side. Even if you don't sell out, you are faced with increased reinvestment risk. In order to earn the YTM promised on your bonds, you have to reinvest each coupon payment at the same YTM rate. Obviously, as rates fall, you'll find it increasingly difficult to reinvest the stream of coupon payments at or above the YTM rate. When market rates rise, just the opposite happens: The price of the bond falls, but your reinvestment opportunities improve.

Bond investors need a measure that helps them judge just how significant these risks are for a particular bond. Such a yardstick is provided by something called **duration**. It captures in a single measure the extent to which the price of a bond will react to different interest rate environments. Because duration gauges the price volatility of a bond, it gives you a better idea of how likely you are to earn the return (YTM) you expect. That, in turn, will help you tailor your holdings to your expectations of interest rate movements.

The Concept of Duration

The concept of duration was first developed in 1938 by actuary Frederick Macaulay to help insurance companies match their cash inflows with payments. When applied to bonds, duration recognizes that the amount and frequency of interest payments, the yield-to-maturity, and the term to maturity all affect the interest rate risk of a particular bond. Term to maturity is important because it influences how much a bond's price will rise or fall as interest rates change. In general, when rates move, bonds with longer maturities fluctuate more than shorter issues. On the other hand, while the amount of price risk embedded in a bond is related to the issue's term to maturity, the amount of reinvestment risk is directly related to the size of a bond's coupon: Bonds that pay high coupons have greater reinvestment risk simply because there's more to reinvest.

As it turns out, both price and reinvestment risk are related in one way or another to interest rates, and therein lies the conflict. *Any* change in interest rates (whether up or down) will cause price risk and reinvestment risk to push and pull bonds in opposite directions. An increase in rates will produce a drop in price but will lessen reinvestment risk. Declining rates, in contrast, will boost prices but increase reinvestment risk. At some point in time, these two forces should exactly offset each other. *That point in time is a bond's duration.*

In general, bond duration possesses the following properties:

- Higher *coupons* result in shorter durations.

- Longer *maturities* mean longer durations.

- Higher *yields* (YTMs) lead to shorter durations.

Together, these three variables—coupon, maturity, and yield—interact to determine an issue's duration. *Knowing a bond's duration is helpful because it captures the bond's underlying price volatility.* That is, since *a bond's duration and volatility are directly related, it follows that the shorter the duration, the less volatility in bond prices—and vice versa, of course.*

Measuring Duration

Duration is a measure of the average maturity of a fixed-income security. The term *average maturity* may be confusing because bonds have only one final maturity date. An alternative definition of average maturity might be that it captures the average timing of the bond's cash flow. For a zero-coupon bond that makes only one cash payment on the final maturity date, the bond's duration equals its maturity. But because coupon-paying bonds make periodic interest payments, the average timing of these payments (i.e., the average maturity) is different from the actual maturity date. For instance, a 10-year bond that pays a 5% coupon each year distributes a small cash flow in year 1, in year 2, and so on up until the last and largest cash flow in year 10. Duration is a measure that puts some weight on these intermediate payments, so that the "average maturity" is a little less than 10 years.

You can think of duration as the *weighted-average life of a bond*, where the weights are the fractions of the bond's total value accounted for by each cash payment that the bond makes over its life. Mathematically, we can find the duration of a bond as follows:

Equation 11.8

$$\text{Duration} = \sum_{t=1}^{T} \left[\frac{PV(C_t)}{P_{\text{bond}}} \times t \right]$$

where

$PV(C_t)$ = present value of a future coupon or principal payment
P_{bond} = current market price of the bond
t = year in which the cash flow (coupon or principal) payment is received
T = remaining life of the bond, in years

The duration measure obtained from Equation 11.8 is commonly referred to as *Macaulay duration*—named after the actuary who developed the concept.

Although duration is often computed using semiannual compounding, Equation 11.8 uses *annual coupons and annual compounding* to keep the ensuing discussion and calculations as simple as possible. Even so, the formula looks more formidable than it really is. If you follow the basic steps noted below, you'll find that duration is not tough to calculate. Here are the steps involved:

Step 1. Find the present value of each annual coupon or principal payment [$PV(C_t)$]. *Use the prevailing YTM on the bond as the discount rate.*

Step 2. Divide this present value by the current market price of the bond (P_{bond}). This is the weight, or the fraction of the bond's total value accounted for by each individual payment. Because a bond's value is just the sum of the present values of its cash payments, these weights must sum to 1.0.

Step 3. Multiply this weight by the year in which the cash flow is to be received (t).

Step 4. Repeat Steps 1 through 3 for each year in the life of the bond, and then *add up* the values computed in Step 3.

Duration for a Single Bond Table 11.1 illustrates the four-step procedure for calculating the duration of a 7.5%, 15-year bond priced at $957 to yield 8%. Table 11.1 provide the basic input data: Column (1) shows the year (t) in which each cash payment arrives. Column (2) provides the dollar amount of each cash payment (coupons and principal) made by the bond. Column (3) lists the present value of each cash flow, given an 8% discount rate (which is equal to the prevailing YTM on the bond). For

TABLE 11.1	Duration Calculation for a 7.5%, 15-Year Bond Priced to Yield 8%			EXCEL WITH SPREADSHEETS
(1)	(2)	(3)	(4)	(5)
Year (t)	Annual Cash Flow (C_t)	Present Value at 8% of Annual Cash Flows [$PV(C_t)$] (2) × [$1/(1.08)t$]	$PV(C_t)$ Divided by Current Market Price of the Bond* (3) ÷ $957	Time-Weighted Relative Cash Flow (1) × (4)
1	$ 75	$69.45	.0726	.0726
2	75	64.27	.0672	.1343
3	75	59.55	.0622	.1867
4	75	55.12	.0576	.2304
5	75	51.08	.0534	.2668
6	75	47.25	.0494	.2962
7	75	43.72	.0457	.3198
8	75	40.50	.0423	.3386
9	75	37.50	.0392	.3527
10	75	34.72	.0363	.3628
11	75	32.18	.0336	.3698
12	75	29.78	.0311	.3734
13	75	27.60	.0288	.3749
14	75	25.50	.0266	.3730
15	1,075	338.62	.3538	5.3076
				Duration: 9.36 yrs

*If this bond is priced to yield 8%, it will be quoted in the market at $957.

example, in row 1 of Table 11.1, we see that in year 1 the bond makes a $75 coupon payment, and discounting that to the present at 8% reveals that the first coupon payment has a present value of $69.45.

Next (Step 2) we divide the present value in column 3 by the current market price of the bond (column 4). If the present value of this bond's first coupon payment is $69.45 and the total price of the bond is $957, then that first payment accounts for 7.26% of the bond's total value ($69.45 ÷ $957 = 0.0726). Therefore, 7.26% is the "weight" given to the cash payment made in year 1. If you sum the weights in column 4, you will see that they add to 1.0. Multiplying the weights from column 4 by the year (t) in which the cash flow occurs (Step 3) results in a time-weighted value for each of the annual cash flow streams (column 5). Adding up all the values in column 5 (Step 4) yields the duration of the bond. As you can see, the duration of this bond is a lot less than its maturity—a condition that would exist with any coupon-bearing bond. In addition, keep in mind *that the duration on any bond will change over time* as YTM and term to maturity change. For example, the duration on this 7.5%, 15-year bond will fall as the bond nears maturity and/or as the market yield (YTM) on the bond increases.

Duration for a Portfolio of Bonds The concept of duration is not confined to individual bonds only. It can also be applied to whole portfolios of fixed-income securities. The duration of an entire portfolio is fairly easy to calculate. All we need are the durations of the individual securities in the portfolio and their weights (i.e., the proportion that each security contributes to the overall value of the portfolio). Given this, *the duration of a portfolio is the weighted average of the durations of the individual securities in the portfolio.*

Actually, this weighted-average approach provides only an *approximate measure of duration*. But it is a reasonably close approximation and, as such, is widely used in practice—so we'll use it, too.

To see how to measure duration using this approach, consider the following five-bond portfolio:

Bond	Amount Invested*	Weight	× Bond Duration	= Portfolio Duration
Government bonds	$ 270,000	0.15	6.25	0.9375
Aaa corporates	180,000	0.10	8.90	0.8900
Aa utilities	450,000	0.25	10.61	2.6525
Agency issues	360,000	0.20	11.03	2.2060
Baa industrials	540.000	0.30	12.55	3.7650
	$1,800.000	1.00		10.4510

*Amount invested = Current market price × Par value of the bonds. That is, if the government bonds are quoted at 90 and the investor holds $300,000 in these bonds, then 0.90 × $300,000 = $270,000.

In this case, the $1.8 million bond portfolio has an *average duration* of approximately 10.5 years.

If you want to change the duration of the portfolio, you can do so by (1) changing the asset mix of the portfolio (shift the weight of the portfolio to longer- or shorter-duration bonds, as desired) and/or (2) adding new bonds to the portfolio with the desired duration characteristics. As we will see below, this approach is often used in a bond portfolio strategy known as *bond immunization*.

Bond Duration and Price Volatility

A bond's price volatility is, in part, a function of its term to maturity and, in part, a function of its coupon. Unfortunately, there is no exact relationship between bond maturities and bond price volatilities with respect to interest rate changes. There is, however, a fairly close relationship between bond duration and price volatility—at least, so long as the market doesn't experience wide swings in yield. Duration can be used as a viable predictor of price volatility *only so long as the yield swings are relatively small* (no more than 50 to 100 basis points, or so). That's because whereas duration is a straight-line relationship, the price-yield relationship of a bond is convex in nature. So when bond yields change, bond prices actually move in a curved (convex) manner rather than in a straight line, as depicted by duration.

The mathematical link between bond price and interest rate changes involves the concept of *modified duration*. To find modified duration, we simply take the (Macaulay) duration for a bond (as found from Equation 11.8 on page 424) and adjust it for the bond's yield to maturity.

Equation 11.9
$$\text{Modified duration} = \frac{\text{(Macaulay) duration in years}}{1 + \text{Yield to maturity}}$$

Thus, the modified duration for the 15-year bond discussed above is

$$\text{Modified duration} = \frac{9.36}{1 + 0.08} = \underline{8.67}$$

Note that here we use the bond's computed (Macaulay) duration of 9.36 years and the same YTM we used to compute duration in Equation 11.8; in this case, the bond was priced to yield 8%, so we use a yield-to-maturity of 8%.

To determine, in percentage terms, how much the price of this bond would change as market interest rates increased from, say, 8% to 8.5%, we multiply the modified duration value calculated above first by –1 (because of the inverse relationship between bond prices and interest rates) and then by the change in the level of the market interest rates. That is,

Equation 11.10

$$\frac{\text{Percent change}}{\text{in bond price}} = -1 \times \text{Modified duration} \times \text{Change in interest rates}$$

$$= -1 \times 8.67 \times 0.5\% = \underline{-4.33}$$

Thus, a 50-basis-point (or ½ of 1%) increase in market interest rates will lead to approximately 4.33% drop in the price of this 15-year bond. Such information is useful to bond investors seeking—or trying to avoid—price volatility.

Effective Duration

One problem with the duration measures that we've studied so far is that they do not always work well for bonds with embedded options such as callable bonds. That is, the duration measures we've been using assumes that the bond's future cash flows are paid as originally scheduled through maturity, but that may not be the case with callable bonds (or convertible bonds or bonds with other types of options attached to them). An alternative duration measure that is used for these types of bonds is the effective duration. To calculate effective duration (ED), you use Equation 11.11 below:

Equation 11.11

$$ED = \frac{P(i\downarrow) - P(i\uparrow)}{2 \times P \times \Delta r}$$

where

$P(i\uparrow)$ = the new price of the bond if market interest rates go up
$P(i\downarrow)$ = the new price of the bond if market interest rates go down
P = the original price of the bond
Δr = the change in market interest rates

Suppose you want to know the effective duration of a 25-year bond that pays a 6% coupon semiannually. The bond is currently priced at $882.72 for a yield of 7%. Now suppose the bond's yield goes up by 0.5% to 7.5%. At that yield the new price would be $831.74 (using a calculator, N = 50, I = 3.75, PMT = 30, and PV = 1,000). What if the yield drops by 0.5% to 6.5%? In that case, the price rises to $938.62 (N = 50, I = 3.25, PMT = 30, PV = 1,000). Now we can use Equation 11.11 to calculate the bond's effective duration.

Effective duration = ($938.62 − $831.74) ÷ (2 × $882.72 × 0.005) = $\underline{12.11}$

This means that if interest rates rise or fall by a full percentage point, the price of the bond would fall or rise by approximately 12.11%. Note that you can use effective duration in place of modified duration in Eqn. 11.10, above, to find the percent change in the price of a bond when interest rates move by more or less than 1.0%. When calculating the effective duration of a callable bond, one modification may be necessary. If the calculated price of the bond when interest rates fall is greater than the bond's call price, then use the call price in the equation rather than $P(i\downarrow)$ and proceed as before.

Uses of Bond Duration Measures

Bond investors have learned to use duration analysis in many ways. For example, as we saw earlier, you can use modified duration or effective duration to measure the potential price volatility of a particular issue. Another equally important use of duration is in the *structuring of bond portfolios*. That is, if you thought that interest rates were about to increase, you could reduce the overall duration of the portfolio by selling higher-duration bonds and buying shorter-duration bonds. Such a strategy could prove useful, because shorter-duration bonds do not decline in value to the same degree as longer-duration bonds. On the other hand, if you felt that interest rates were about to decline, the opposite strategy would be appropriate.

Active, short-term investors frequently use duration analysis in their day-to-day operations. Longer-term investors also employ it in planning their investment decisions. Indeed, a strategy known as *bond portfolio immunization* represents one of the most important uses of duration.

Bond Immunization   Some investors hold portfolios of bonds not for the purpose of "beating the market," but rather to *accumulate a specified level of wealth by the end of a given investment horizon*. For these investors, bond portfolio **immunization** often proves to be of great value. Immunization allows you to derive a specified rate of return from bond investments over a given investment interval *regardless of what happens to market interest rates over the course of the holding period*. In essence, you are able to "immunize" your portfolio from the effects of changes in market interest rates over a given investment horizon.

To understand how and why bond portfolio immunization is possible, you will recall from our earlier discussion that changes in market interest rates will lead to two distinct and opposite changes in bond valuation: The first effect is known as the *price effect*; the second is known as the *reinvestment effect*. The net result of both of these effects working together is that whereas an increase in rates has a negative effect on a bond's price, it has a positive effect on the reinvestment of coupons. Therefore, when interest rate changes do occur, the price and reinvestment effects work against each other from the standpoint of the investor's wealth.

When the average duration of the portfolio just equals the investment horizon, these counteracting effects offset each other and leave the investor's position unchanged. This should not come as much of a surprise, because such a property is already embedded in the duration measure itself. If that relationship applies to a single bond, it should also apply to the *weighted-average duration of a whole bond portfolio*. When such a condition (of offsetting price and reinvestment effects) exists, *a bond portfolio is said to be immunized*. More specifically, your wealth position is immunized from the effects of interest rate changes *when the weighted-average duration of the bond portfolio exactly equals your desired investment horizon*. Table 11.2 provides an example of bond immunization using a 10-year, 8% coupon bond with a duration of eight years. Here, we assume the investor's desired investment horizon is also eight years in length.

The example in Table 11.2 assumes that you originally purchased the 8% coupon bond at par. It further assumes that market interest rates for bonds of this quality drop from 8% to 6% at the end of the fifth year. Because you had an investment horizon of exactly eight years and desire to lock in an interest rate return of exactly 8%, it follows that you expect to have a terminal value of $1,850.90 [i.e., $1,000 invested at 8% for eight years = $1,000 \times (1.08)^8 = \$1,850.90$], regardless of interest rate changes in

TABLE 11.2	Bond Immunization						EXCEL WITH SPREADSHEETS

Year	Cash Flow from Bond						Terminal Value of Reinvested Cash Flow
1	$80	×	$(1.08)^4$	×	$(1.06)^3$	=	$ 129.63
2	80	×	$(1.08)^3$	×	$(1.06)^3$	=	120.03
3	80	×	$(1.08)^2$	×	$(1.06)^3$	=	111.14
4	80	×	(1.08)	×	$(1.06)^3$	=	102.90
5	80	×	$(1.06)^3$			=	95.28
6	80	×	$(1.06)^2$			=	89.89
7	80	×	(1.06)			=	84.80
8	80					=	80.00
8	$1,036.64*						1,036.64
			Total				$1,850.31
			Investor's required wealth at 8%				$1,850.90
			Difference				$ .59

*The bond could be sold at a market price of $1,036.64, which is the value of an 8% bond with two years to maturity that is priced to yield 6%.

Note: Bond interest coupons are assumed to be paid at year-end. Therefore, there are four years of reinvestment at 8% and three years at 6% for the first year's $80 coupon.

the interim. As can be seen from the results in Table 11.2, the immunization strategy netted you a total of $1,850.31—just 59 cents short of your desired goal. Note that in this case, although reinvestment opportunities declined in years 5, 6, and 7 (when market interest rates dropped to 6%), that same lower rate led to a higher market price for the bond. That higher price, in turn, provided enough capital gains to offset the loss in reinvested income. This remarkable result clearly demonstrates the power of bond immunization and the versatility of bond duration. And note that even though the table uses a single bond for purposes of illustration, the same results can be obtained from a bond *portfolio* that is maintained at the *proper weighted-average duration*.

Maintaining a fully immunized portfolio (of more than one bond) requires *continual portfolio rebalancing*. Indeed, every time interest rates change, the duration of a portfolio changes. Because effective immunization requires that the portfolio have a duration value equal in length to the *remaining investment horizon*, the composition of the portfolio must be rebalanced each time interest rates change. Further, even in the absence of interest rate changes, a bond's duration declines more slowly than its term to maturity. This, of course, means that the mere passage of time will dictate changes in portfolio composition. Such changes will ensure that the duration of the portfolio continues to match the remaining time in the investment horizon. In summary, portfolio immunization strategies can be extremely effective, but immunization is not a passive strategy and is not without potential problems, the most notable of which are associated with portfolio rebalancing.

CONCEPTS IN REVIEW

Answers available at
www.pearsonhighered.com/gitman

11.10 What does the term *duration* mean to bond investors and how does the duration of a bond differ from its maturity? What is *modified duration*, and how is it used? What is *effective duration*, and how does it differ from *modified duration*?

11.11 Describe the process of *bond portfolio immunization*, and explain why an investor would want to immunize a portfolio. Would you consider portfolio immunization a passive investment strategy comparable to, say, a buy-and-hold approach? Explain.

Bond Investment Strategies

LG6   Generally speaking, bond investors tend to follow one of three kinds of investment programs. First, there are those who live off the income: They are conservative, quality-conscious, income-oriented investors who seek to maximize current income. Second, there are the speculators (bond traders): Their investment objective is to maximize capital gains, often within a short time span. Finally, there are the serious long-term investors: Their objective is to maximize *total return*—from both current income and capital gains—over fairly long holding periods.

In order to achieve the objectives of any of these three programs, you need to adopt a strategy that is compatible with your goals. Professional money managers use a variety of techniques to manage the multimillion (or multibillion)-dollar bond portfolios under their direction. These range from passive approaches, to semiactive strategies, to active, fully managed strategies using interest rate forecasting and yield spread analysis. Most of these strategies are fairly complex and require substantial computer support. Even so, we can look briefly at some of the more basic strategies to gain an appreciation of the different ways in which you can use fixed-income securities to reach different investment objectives.

Passive Strategies

The bond immunization strategies we discussed earlier are considered to be primarily *passive* in nature. Investors using these tools typically are *not* attempting to beat the market, but to lock in specified rates of return (or terminal values) that they deem acceptable, given the risks involved. As a rule, passive investment strategies are characterized by a lack of input regarding investor expectations of changes in interest rates and/or bond prices. Further, these strategies typically do not generate significant transaction costs. A *buy-and-hold* strategy is perhaps the most passive of all investment strategies: All that is required is that the investor replace bonds that have deteriorating credit ratings, have matured, or have been called. Although buy-and-hold investors restrict their ability to earn above-average returns, they also minimize the losses that transaction costs represent.

One popular approach that is a bit more active than buy-and-hold is the use of so-called **bond ladders**. In this strategy, equal amounts are invested in a *series* of bonds with staggered maturities. Here's how a bond ladder works: Suppose you want to confine your investing to fixed-income securities with maturities of ten years or less. Given that maturity constraint, you could set up a ladder by investing (roughly) equal amounts in, say, three-, five-, seven-, and 10-year issues. When the three-year issue matures, you would put the money from it (along with any new capital) into a new 10-year note. You would continue this rolling-over process so that eventually you would hold a full ladder of staggered 10-year notes. By rolling into new 10-year issues every two or three years, you can do a kind of dollar-cost averaging and thereby lessen the impact of swings in market rates. The laddered approach is a safe, simple, and almost automatic way of investing for the long haul. A key ingredient of this or any other passive strategy is, of course, the use of high-quality investment vehicles that possess attractive features, maturities, and yields.

Trading on Forecasted Interest Rate Behavior

In contrast to passive strategies, a highly risky approach to bond investing is the *forecasted interest rate* approach. Here, the investor seeks attractive capital gains when interest rates are expected to decline and preservation of capital when an increase in interest rates is anticipated. It's risky because it relies on the imperfect forecast of future interest rates. The idea is to increase the return on a bond portfolio by making strategic moves in anticipation of interest rate changes. Such a strategy is essentially *market timing*. An unusual feature of this tactic is that most of the trading is done with *investment-grade securities*, because a high degree of interest rate sensitivity is required to capture the maximum amount of price behavior.

This strategy rests largely on technical matters. For example, when a decline in rates is anticipated, aggressive bond investors often seek to lengthen the maturity (or duration) of their bonds (or bond portfolios). The reason: Longer-term bonds rise more in price than shorter-term issues. At the same time, investors look for low-coupon and/or moderately discounted bonds, which will add to duration and increase the amount of potential price volatility. These interest swings are usually short-lived, so bond traders try to earn as much as possible in as short a time as possible. When rates start to level off and move up, these investors begin to shift their money out of long, discounted bonds and into high-yielding issues with short maturities. In other words, they do a complete reversal. During those periods when bond prices are dropping, investors are more concerned about preservation of capital, so they take steps to protect their money from capital losses. Thus, they tend to use such short-term obligations as Treasury bills, money funds, short-term (two- to five-year) notes, or even variable-rate notes.

Bond Swaps

In a **bond swap**, an investor simultaneously liquidates one position and buys a different issue to take its place. Swaps can be executed to increase current yield or yield-to-maturity, to take advantage of shifts in interest rates, to improve the quality of a portfolio, or for tax purposes. Although some swaps are highly sophisticated, most are fairly simple transactions. They go by a variety of colorful names, such as "profit takeout," "substitution swap," and "tax swap," but they are all used for one basic reason: *to seek portfolio improvement*. We will briefly review two types of bond swaps that are fairly simple and hold considerable appeal: the yield pickup swap and the tax swap.

In a **yield pickup swap**, an investor switches out of a low-coupon bond into a comparable higher-coupon issue in order to realize an instantaneous pickup of current yield and yield-to-maturity. For example, you would be executing a yield pickup swap if you sold 20-year, A-rated, 6.5% bonds (which were yielding 8% at the time) and replaced them with an equal amount of 20-year, A-rated, 7% bonds that were priced to yield 8.5%. By executing the swap, you would improve your current yield (your coupon income would increase from $65 a year to $70 a year) as well as your yield-to-maturity (from 8% to 8.5%). Such swap opportunities arise because of the *yield spreads* that normally exist between types of bonds. You can execute such swaps simply by watching for swap candidates and/or asking your broker to do so. In fact, the only thing you have to be careful of is that transaction costs do not eat up all the profits.

Another popular type of swap is the **tax swap**, which is also relatively simple and involves few risks. You can use this technique whenever you have a substantial tax liability as a result of selling some security holdings at a profit. The objective is to execute a swap to *eliminate or substantially reduce* the tax liability accompanying the capital gains. This is done by selling an issue that has undergone a capital *loss* and replacing it with a comparable obligation.

For example, assume that you had $10,000 worth of corporate bonds that you sold (in the current year) for $15,000, resulting in a capital gain of $5,000. You can eliminate the tax liability accompanying the capital gain by selling securities that have *capital losses of $5,000*. Let's assume you find you hold a 20-year, 4.75% municipal bond that has undergone a $5,000 drop in value. Thus, you have the required tax shield in your portfolio. Now you have to find a viable swap candidate. Suppose you find a comparable 20-year, 5% municipal issue currently trading at about the same price as the issue being sold. By selling the 4.75s and simultaneously buying a comparable amount of the 5s, you will not only increase your tax-free yields (from 4.75% to 5%) but also eliminate the capital gains tax liability.

The only precaution in doing tax swaps is that you cannot use *identical issues* in the swap transactions. The IRS would consider that a "wash sale" and disallow the loss. Moreover, the capital loss must occur in the same taxable year as the capital gain. Typically, at year-end, tax loss sales and tax swaps multiply as knowledgeable investors hurry to establish capital losses.

CONCEPTS IN REVIEW

Answers available at www.pearsonhighered.com/gitman

11.12 Briefly describe a *bond ladder* and note how and why an investor would use this investment strategy. What is a *tax swap* and why would it be used?

11.13 What strategy would you expect an aggressive bond investor (someone who's looking for capital gains) to employ?

11.14 Why is interest sensitivity important to bond speculators? Does the need for interest sensitivity explain why active bond traders tend to use high-grade issues? Explain.

---

myfinancelab

Here is what you should know after reading this chapter. **MyFinanceLab** will help you identify what you know, and where to go when you need to practice.

What You Should Know	Key Terms	Where To Practice
LG1 **Explain the behavior of market interest rates and identify the forces that cause interest rates to change.** The behavior of interest rates is the single most important force in the bond market. It determines not only the amount of current income an investor will receive but also the investor's capital gains (or losses). Changes in market interest rates can have a dramatic impact on the total returns obtained from bonds over time.	yield spreads, *p. 405*	MyFinanceLab Study Plan 11.1
LG2 **Describe the term structure of interest rates and note how yield curves can be used by investors.** Many forces drive the behavior of interest rates over time, including inflation, the cost and availability of funds, and the level of interest rates in major foreign markets. One particularly important force is the term structure of interest rates, which relates yield-to-maturity to term-to-maturity. Yield curves essentially plot the term structure and are	expectations hypothesis, *p. 409* liquidity preference theory, *p. 411* market segmentation theory, *p. 411* term structure of interest rates, *p. 408*	MyFinanceLab Study Plan 11.2

What You Should Know	Key Terms	Where To Practice
often used by investors as a way to get a handle on the future behavior of interest rates.	yield curve, *p. 408*	
LG3 Understand how bonds are valued in the market-place. Bonds are valued (priced) in the marketplace on the basis of their required rates of return (or market yields). The process of pricing a bond begins with the yield it should provide. Once that piece of information is known (or estimated), a standard, present-value-based model is used to find the dollar price of a bond.		MyFinanceLab Study Plan 11.3 Video Learning Aid for Problems P11.1, P11.2
LG4 Describe the various measures of yield and return and explain how these standards of performance are used in bond valuation. Four types of yields are important to investors: current yield, promised yield, yield-to-call, and expected yield (or return). Promised yield (yield-to-maturity) is the most widely used bond valuation measure. It captures both the current income and the price appreciation of an issue. Yield-to-call, which assumes the bond will be outstanding only until its first (or some other) call date, also captures both current income and price appreciation. The expected return, in contrast, is a valuation measure used by aggressive bond traders to show the total return that can be earned from trading in and out of a bond long before it matures.	bond-equivalent yield, *p. 418* current yield, *p. 416* expected return, *p. 420* promised yield, *p. 416* realized yield, *p. 420* yield-to-call (YTC), *p. 419* yield-to-maturity (YTM), *p. 416*	MyFinanceLab Study Plan 11.4
LG5 Understand the basic concept of duration, how it can be measured, and its use in the management of bond portfolios. Bond duration takes into account the effects of both reinvestment and price (or market) risks. It captures, in a single measure, the extent to which the price of a bond will react to different interest rate environments. Equally important, duration can be used to immunize whole bond portfolios from the often-devastating forces of changing market interest rates.	duration, *p. 423* immunization, *p. 428*	MyFinanceLab Study Plan 11.5 Excel Tables 11.1, 11.2
LG6 Discuss various bond investment strategies and the different ways these securities can be used by investors. Bonds can be used as a source of income, as a way to seek capital gains by speculating on interest rate move-ment, or as a way to earn long-term returns. Investors often employ one or more of the following strategies: pas-sive strategies such as buy-and-hold, bond ladders, and portfolio immunization; bond trading based on fore-casted interest rate behavior; and bond swaps.	bond ladders, *p. 430* bond swap, *p. 431* tax swap, *p. 431* yield pickup swap, *p. 431*	MyFinanceLab Study Plan 11.6

Log into **MyFinanceLab**, take a chapter test, and get a personalized Study Plan that tells you which concepts you understand and which ones you need to review. From there, **MyFinanceLab** will give you further practice, tutorials, animations, videos, and guided solutions.
Log into www.myfinancelab.com

Discussion Questions

 Q11.1 Briefly describe each of the following theories of the term structure of interest rates.
  a. Expectations hypothesis
  b. Liquidity preference theory
  c. Market segmentation theory

According to these theories, what conditions would result in a downward-sloping yield curve? What conditions would result in an upward-sloping yield curve? Which theory do *you* think is most valid, and why?

 Q11.2 Using the *Wall Street Journal* or *Barron's*, find the bond yields for Treasury securities with the following maturities: three months, six months, one year, three years, five years, 10 years, 15 years, and 20 years. Construct a yield curve based on these reported yields, putting term-to-maturity on the horizontal (*x*) axis and yield-to-maturity on the vertical (*y*) axis. Briefly discuss the general shape of your yield curve. What conclusions might you draw about future interest rate movements from this yield curve?

LG5 **Q11.3** Briefly explain what will happen to a bond's duration measure if each of the following events occur.
  a. The yield-to-maturity on the bond falls from 8.5% to 8%.
  b. The bond gets one year closer to its maturity.
  c. Market interest rates go from 8% to 9%.
  d. The bond's *modified* duration falls by half a year.

LG6 **Q11.4** Assume that an investor comes to you looking for advice. She has $200,000 to invest and wants to put it all into bonds.
  a. If she considers herself a fairly aggressive investor who is willing to take the risks necessary to generate the big returns, what kind of investment strategy (or strategies) would you suggest? Be specific.
  b. What kind of investment strategies would you recommend if your client were a very conservative investor who could not tolerate market losses?
  c. What kind of investor do you think is most likely to use:
    1. An immunized bond portfolio?
    2. A yield pickup swap?
    3. A bond ladder?
    4. A long-term zero-coupon bond when interest rates fall?

LG4 **LG5** **Q11.5** Using the resources available at your campus or public library (or on the Internet), select any six bonds you like, consisting of *two* Treasury bonds, *two* corporate bonds, and *two* agency issues. Determine the latest current yield and promised yield for each. (For promised yield, use annual compounding.) In addition, find the duration and modified duration for each bond.
    a. Assuming that you put an equal amount of money into each of the six bonds you selected, find the duration for this six-bond portfolio.
    b. What would happen to your bond portfolio if market interest rates fell by 100 basis points?
    c. Assuming that you have $100,000 to invest, use at least four of these bonds to develop a bond portfolio that emphasizes either the potential for capital gains or the preservation of capital. Briefly explain your logic.

Problems

All problems are available on **www.myfinancelab.com**

LG3 **P11.1** Two bonds have par values of $1,000. One is a 5%, 15-year bond priced to yield 8%. The other is a 7.5%, 20-year bond priced to yield 6%. Which of these two has the lower price? (Assume annual compounding in both cases.)

LG3 P11.2 Using semiannual compounding, find the prices of the following bonds:
  a. A 10.5%, 15-year bond priced to yield 8%.
  b. A 7%, 10-year bond priced to yield 8%.
  c. A 12%, 20-year bond priced at 10%.

Repeat the problem using annual compounding. Then comment on the differences you found in the prices of the bonds.

LG3 P11.3 A 15-year bond has an annual-pay coupon of 7.5% and is priced to yield 9%. Calculate the price per $1,000 par value.

LG3 P11.4 A 20-year bond has a coupon of 10% and is priced to yield 8%. Calculate the price per $1,000 par value using semiannual compounding.

LG4 P11.5 An investor buys a 10% bond for $900 and sells it in one year for $950. What is the investor's holding period return?

LG4 P11.6 A bond is priced in the market at $1,150 and has a coupon of 8%. Calculate the bond's current yield.

LG3 P11.7 An investor is considering the purchase of an 8%, 18-year corporate bond that's being priced to yield 10%. She thinks that in a year, this same bond will be priced in the market to yield 9%. Using annual compounding, find the price of the bond today and in one year. Next, find the holding period return on this investment, assuming that the investor's expectations are borne out. (If necessary, see Chapter 4 for the holding period return formula.)

LG4 P11.8 A bond is currently selling in the market for $1,170.68. It has a coupon of 12% and a 20-year maturity. Using annual compounding, calculate the promised yield on this bond.

LG4 P11.9 A bond is currently selling in the market for $1,098.62. It has a coupon of 9% and a 20-year maturity. Using annual compounding, calculate the promised yield on this bond.

LG4 P11.10 Compute the current yield of a 10%, 25-year bond that is currently priced in the market at $1,200. Use annual compounding to find the promised yield on this bond. Repeat the promised yield calculation, but this time use semiannual compounding to find yield-to-maturity.

LG4 P11.11 A 10%, 25-year bond has a par value of $1,000 and a call price of $1,075. (The bond's first call date is in five years.) Coupon payments are made semiannually (so use semiannual compounding where appropriate).
  a. Find the current yield, YTM, and YTC on this issue, given that it is currently being priced in the market at $1,200. Which of these three yields is the highest? Which is the lowest? Which yield would you use to value this bond? Explain.
  b. Repeat the three calculations above, given that the bond is being priced at $850. Now which yield is the highest? Which is the lowest? Which yield would you use to value this bond? Explain.

LG4 P11.12 Assume that an investor is looking at two bonds: Bond A is a 20-year, 9% (semiannual pay) bond that is priced to yield 10.5%. Bond B is a 20-year, 8% (annual pay) bond that is priced to yield 7.5%. Both bonds carry five-year call deferments and call prices (in five years) of $1,050.
  a. Which bond has the higher current yield?
  b. Which bond has the higher YTM?
  c. Which bond has the higher YTC?

LG4 P11.13 A zero-coupon bond that matures in 15 years is currently selling for $209 per $1,000 par value. What is the promised yield on this bond?

LG4 P11.14 A zero-coupon ($1,000 par value) bond that matures in 10 years has a promised yield of 9%. What is the bond's price?

LG4 **P11.15** A 25-year, zero-coupon bond was recently being quoted at 11.625% of par. Find the current yield *and* the promised yield of this issue, given that the bond has a par value of $1,000. Using semiannual compounding, determine how much an investor would have to pay for this bond if it were priced to yield 12%.

LG4 **P11.16** Assume that an investor pays $800 for a long-term bond that carries an 8% coupon. In three years, he hopes to sell the issue for $950. If his expectations come true, what realized yield will this investor earn? (Use annual compounding.) What would the holding period return be if he were able to sell the bond (at $950) after only nine months?

LG4 **P11.17** Using annual compounding, find the yield-to-maturity for each of the following bonds.
  a. A 9.5%, 20-year bond priced at $957.43.
  b. A 16%, 15-year bond priced at $1,684.76.
  c. A 5.5%, 18-year bond priced at $510.65.

Now assume that each of the above three bonds is callable as follows: Bond **a** is callable in seven years at a call price of $1,095; bond **b** is callable in five years at $1,250; and bond **c** is callable in three years at $1,050. Use annual compounding to find the yield-to-call for each bond.

LG5 **P11.18** A bond has a Macaulay duration equal to 9.5 and a yield to maturity of 7.5%. What is the modified duration of this bond?

LG5 **P11.19** A bond has a Macaulay duration of 8.62 and is priced to yield 8%. If interest rates go up so that the yield goes to 8.5%, what will be the percentage change in the price of the bond? Now, if the yield on this bond goes down to 7.5%, what will be the bond's percentage change in price? Comment on your findings.

LG5 **P11.20** An investor wants to find the duration of a 25-year, 6% semiannual-pay, noncallable bond that's currently priced in the market at $882.72, to yield 7%. Using a 50 basis point change in yield, find the effective duration of this bond (hint: use Eqn. 11.11).

LG5 **P11.21** Find the Macaulay duration and the modified duration of a 20-year, 10% corporate bond priced to yield 8%. According to the modified duration of this bond, how much of a price change would this bond incur if market yields rose to 9%? Using annual compounding, calculate the price of this bond in one year if rates do rise to 9%. How does this price change compare to that predicted by the modified duration? Explain the difference.

LG5 **P11.22** Which *one* of the following bonds would you select if you thought market interest rates were going to fall by 50 basis points over the next six months?
  a. A bond with a Macaulay duration of 8.46 years that's currently being priced to yield 7.5%.
  b. A bond with a Macaulay duration of 9.30 years that's priced to yield 10%.
  c. A bond with a Macaulay duration of 8.75 years that's priced to yield 5.75%.

LG5 **LG6** **P11.23** Stacy Picone is an aggressive bond trader who likes to speculate on interest rate swings. Market interest rates are currently at 9%, but she expects them to fall to 7% within a year. As a result, Stacy is thinking about buying either a 25-year, zero-coupon bond or a 20-year, 7.5% bond. (Both bonds have $1,000 par values and carry the same agency rating.) Assuming that Stacy wants to maximize capital gains, which of the two issues should she select? What if she wants to maximize the total return (interest income and capital gains) from her investment? Why did one issue provide better capital gains than the other? Based on the duration of each bond, which one should be more price volatile?

LG5 **LG6** **P11.24** Elliot Karlin is a 35-year-old bank executive who has just inherited a large sum of money. Having spent several years in the bank's investments department, he's well aware of the concept of duration and decides to apply it to his bond portfolio. In particular, Elliot intends to use $1 million of his inheritance to purchase four U.S. Treasury bonds:
  1. An 8.5%, 13-year bond that's priced at $1,045 to yield 7.47%.
  2. A 7.875%, 15-year bond that's priced at $1,020 to yield 7.60%.

3. A 20-year stripped Treasury that's priced at $202 to yield 8.22%.
4. A 24-year, 7.5% bond that's priced at $955 to yield 7.90%.

a. Find the duration and the modified duration of each bond.

b. Find the duration of the whole bond portfolio if Elliot puts $250,000 into each of the four U.S. Treasury bonds.

c. Find the duration of the portfolio if Elliot puts $360,000 each into bonds 1 and 3 and $140,000 each into bonds 2 and 4.

d. Which portfolio—**b** or **c**—should Elliot select if he thinks rates are about to head up and he wants to avoid as much price volatility as possible? Explain. From which portfolio does he stand to make more in annual interest income? Which portfolio would you recommend, and why?

Visit www.myfinancelab.com for web exercises, spreadsheets, and other online resources.

Case Problem 11.1 *The Bond Investment Decisions of Dave and Marlene Carter*

LG3 LG4 LG6 Dave and Marlene Carter live in the Boston area, where Dave has a successful orthodontics practice. Dave and Marlene have built up a sizable investment portfolio and have always had a major portion of their investments in fixed-income securities. They adhere to a fairly aggressive investment posture and actively go after both attractive current income and substantial capital gains. Assume that it is now 2010 and Marlene is currently evaluating two investment decisions: one involves an addition to their portfolio, the other a revision to it.

The Carters' first investment decision involves a short-term trading opportunity. In particular, Marlene has a chance to buy a 7.5%, 25-year bond that is currently priced at $852 to yield 9%; she feels that in two years the promised yield of the issue should drop to 8%.

The second is a bond swap. The Carters hold some Beta Corporation 7%, 2023 bonds that are currently priced at $785. They want to improve both current income and yield-to-maturity, and are considering one of three issues as a possible swap candidate: (a) Dental Floss, Inc., 7.5%, 2035, currently priced at $780; (b) Root Canal Products of America, 6.5%, 2023, selling at $885; and (c) Kansas City Dental Insurance, 8%, 2024, priced at $950. All of the swap candidates are of comparable quality and have comparable issue characteristics.

Questions

a. Regarding the short-term trading opportunity:
   1. What basic trading principle is involved in this situation?
   2. If Marlene's expectations are correct, what will the price of this bond be in two years?
   3. What is the expected return on this investment?
   4. Should this investment be made? Why?

b. Regarding the bond swap opportunity:
   1. Compute the current yield and the promised yield (use semiannual compounding) for the bond the Carters currently hold and for each of the three swap candidates.
   2. Do any of the three swap candidates provide better current income and/or current yield than the Beta Corporation bonds the Carters now hold? If so, which one(s)?
   3. Do you see any reason why Marlene should switch from her present bond holding into one of the other three issues? If so, which swap candidate would be the best choice? Why?

Case Problem 11.2 *Grace Decides to Immunize Her Portfolio*

LG4 LG5 LG6 Grace Hesketh is the owner of an extremely successful dress boutique in downtown Chicago. Although high fashion is Grace's first love, she's also interested in investments, particularly bonds and other fixed-income securities. She actively manages her own investments and over time has built up a substantial portfolio of securities. She's well versed on the latest investment techniques and is not afraid to apply those procedures to her own investments.

Grace has been playing with the idea of trying to immunize a big chunk of her bond portfolio. She'd like to cash out this part of her portfolio in seven years and use the proceeds to buy a vacation home in her home state of Oregon. To do this, she intends to use the $200,000 she now has invested in the following four corporate bonds (she currently has $50,000 invested in each one).

1. A 12-year, 7.5% bond that's currently priced at $895.

2. A 10-year, zero-coupon bond priced at $405.

3. A 10-year, 10% bond priced at $1,080.

4. A 15-year, 9.25% bond priced at $980.

(*Note:* These are all noncallable, investment-grade, nonconvertible/straight bonds.)

Questions

a. Given the information provided, find the current yield and the promised yield for each bond in the portfolio. (Use annual compounding.)

b. Calculate the Macaulay and modified durations of each bond in the portfolio and indicate how the price of each bond would change if interest rates were to rise by 75 basis points. How would the price change if interest rates were to fall by 75 basis points?

c. Find the duration of the current four-bond portfolio. Given the seven-year target that Grace has, would you consider this to be an immunized portfolio? Explain.

d. How could you lengthen or shorten the duration of this portfolio? What's the shortest portfolio duration you can achieve? What's the longest?

e. Using one or more of the four bonds described above, is it possible to come up with a $200,000 bond portfolio that will exhibit the duration characteristics Grace is looking for? Explain.

f. Using one or more of the four bonds, put together a $200,000 immunized portfolio for Grace. Because this portfolio will now be immunized, will Grace be able to treat it as a buy-and-hold portfolio—one she can put away and forget about? Explain.

Excel with Spreadsheets

All bonds are priced according to the present value of their future cash flow streams. The key components of bond valuation are par value, coupon interest rate, term to maturity, and market yield. It is market yield that drives bond prices. In the market for bonds, the appropriate yield at which the bond should sell is determined first, and then that yield is used to find the market value of the bond. The market yield can also be referred to as the required rate of return. It implies that this is the rate of return that a rational investor requires before he or she will invest in a given fixed-income security.

Create a spreadsheet to model and answer the following bond valuation questions.

Questions

a. One of the bond issues outstanding by H&W Corporation has an annual-pay coupon of 5.625% plus a par value of $1,000 at maturity. This bond has a remaining maturity of 23 years. The required rate of return on securities of similar-risk grade is 6.76%. What is the value of this corporate bond today?

b. What is the current yield for the H&W bond?

c. In the case of the H&W bond issue from question **a**, if the coupon interest payment is compounded on a semiannual basis, what would be the value of this security today?

d. How would the price of the H&W bond react to changing market interest rates? To find out, determine how the price of the issue reacts to changes in the bond's yield-to-maturity (YTM). Find the value of the security when the YTM is (1) 5.625%, (2) 8.0%, and (3) 4.5%. Label your findings as being a premium, par, or discount bond; comment on your findings.

e. The Jay & Austin Company has a bond issue outstanding with the following characteristics: par of $1,000, a semiannual-pay coupon of 6.5%, remaining maturity of 22 years, and a current price of $878.74. What is the bond's yield-to-maturity (YTM)?

CFA EXAM QUESTIONS

Investing in Fixed-Income Securities

Following is a sample of 10 Level-I CFA exam questions that deal with many of the topics covered in Chapters 10 and 11 of this text, including bond prices and yields, interest rates and risks, bond price volatility, and bond redemption provisions. (When answering the questions, give yourself 1½ minutes for each question; the objective is to correctly answer 7 of the 10 questions in a period of 15 minutes.)

1. Sinking funds are *most likely* to:
a. reduce credit risk (default risk).
b. never allow issuers to retire more than the sinking fund requirement.
c. always reduce the outstanding balance of the bond issue to zero prior to maturity.

2. An analyst stated that a callable bond has less reinvestment risk and more price appreciation potential than an otherwise identical option-free bond. The analyst's statement *most likely* is:
a. incorrect with respect to both reinvestment risk and price appreciation potential.
b. incorrect with respect to reinvestment risk, but correct with respect to price appreciation potential.
c. correct with respect to reinvestment risk, but incorrect with respect to price appreciation potential.

3. A bond portfolio manager gathered the following information about a bond issue:

Par value	$10,000,000
Current market value	$9,850,000
Duration	4.8

If yields are expected to decline by 75 basis points, which of the following would provide the *most* appropriate estimate of the price change for the bond issue?
a. 3.6% of $9,850,000.
b. 3.6% of $10,000,000.
c. 4.8% of $9,850,000.

4. A U.S. Treasury note with exactly four years to maturity *most likely* can be broken into as many as:
a. four Treasury STRIPS.
b. eight Treasury STRIPS.
c. nine Treasury STRIPS.

CFA EXAM QUESTIONS

5.   Frieda Wannamaker is a taxable investor who is currently in the 28% income-tax bracket. She is considering purchasing a tax-exempt bond with a yield of 3.75%. The taxable equivalent yield on this bond is *closest* to:
a.   1.46%.
b.   5.21%.
c.   7.47%.

6.   The present value of a $1,000 par value, zero-coupon bond with a three-year maturity assuming an annual discount rate of 6 percent compounded semiannually is *closest* to:
a. $837.48.
b. $839.62.
c. $943.40.

7.   A bond with 14 years to maturity and a coupon rate of 6.375 percent has a yield-to-maturity (YTM) of 4.5 percent. Assuming the bond's YTM remains constant, the bond's value as it approaches maturity will *most likely*:
a.   increase.
b.   decrease.
c.   remain constant.

8.   A coupon-bearing bond purchased when issued at par value was held until maturity during which time interest rates rose. The ex-post realized return of the bond investment *most likely* was:
a.   above the YTM at the time of issue.
b.   below the YTM at the time of issue.
c.   equal to the YTM at the time of issue because the bond was held until maturity.

9.   An analyst accurately calculates that the price of an option-free bond with a 9 percent coupon would experience a 12 percent change if market yields increase 100 basis points. If market yields decrease 100 basis points, the bond's price would *most likely*.
a.   increase by 12%.
b.   increase by less than 12%.
c.   increase by more than 12%.

10. A bond with a par value of $1,000 has a duration of 6.2. If the yield on the bond is expected to change from 8.80 percent to 8.95 percent, the estimated new price for the bond following the expected change in yield is *best* described as being:
a.   0.93% lower than the bond's current price.
b.   1.70% lower than the bond's current price.
c.   10.57% lower than the bond's current price.

Answers: 1. a; 2. a; 3. a; 4. c; 5. b; 6. a; 7. b; 8. a; 9. c; 10. a.

Portfolio Management

Mutual Funds: Professionally Managed Portfolios

LEARNING GOALS

After studying this chapter, you should be able to:

LG1 Describe the basic features of mutual funds and note what they have to offer as investments.

LG2 Distinguish between open- and closed-end funds, as well as other types of professionally managed investment companies, and discuss the various types of fund loads, fees, and charges.

LG3 Discuss the types of funds available and the variety of investment objectives these funds seek to fulfill.

LG4 Discuss the investor services offered by mutual funds and how these services can fit into an investment program.

LG5 Describe the investor uses of mutual funds along with the variables to consider when assessing and selecting funds for investment purposes.

LG6 Identify the sources of return and compute the rate of return earned on a mutual fund investment.

In 1976, John Bogle, founder of the Vanguard Group, had a radical idea: Create a mutual fund that would hold only stock in the Standard & Poor's 500 Stock Index and make it available to individual investors. Unlike other mutual funds, the goal of the Vanguard 500 Index fund—originally called the First Index Investment Trust—would not be to outperform the equities market, but to keep pace with the returns offered by the S&P 500 Index. Vanguard would hold down expenses by limiting itself to the small number of trades necessary to mirror changes in the S&P 500 Index.

Today, the Vanguard 500 Index fund is one of the largest mutual funds in the world, with net assets exceeding $83 billion. Investors have been rewarded with consistent returns and low operating costs. Just as Bogle predicted, the fund's emphasis on limited stock turnover has kept its operating expenses low. For every $1,000 an investor places in the fund, Vanguard extracts just $1.80 per year for operating costs, compared with a stock mutual fund average of $14.40 annually per $1,000 invested. Even more impressive to investors seeking steady, long-term growth, the Vanguard 500 Index fund has over the last 30 years produced an annual return of 10.52%, just below the 10.76% average annual return of the S&P 500 Index itself.

If the Vanguard 500 Index fund's investment strategy doesn't appeal to you, you can choose from more than 10,000 mutual funds sold by Vanguard and other mutual funds in the United States. Your choices range from funds that track other market indexes to funds focusing on companies in a particular industry sector (e.g., pharmaceutical companies) to emerging-market funds that invest in developing economies. Other options include funds that buy and sell a broad range of stocks, bonds, and even shares in other mutual funds. Before choosing a mutual fund, it's important to understand from the fund prospectus how the fund is managed and the factors affecting its performance. As you'll learn in this chapter, with this information in hand, mutual funds can help you reach your investment goals.

(Sources: Fund data from www.vanguard.com (accessed September 12, 2009), www.icifactbook.org/ (accessed September 12, 2009), and www.morningstar.com (accessed September 12, 2009).)

The Mutual Fund Concept

LG1 **LG2**   Questions of which stock or bond to select, when to buy, and when to sell have challenged investors for as long as there have been organized securities markets. These concerns lie at the very heart of the mutual fund concept and in large part explain the growth that mutual funds have experienced. Many investors lack the know-how, time, or commitment to manage their own portfolios, so instead they turn to professional money managers and allow them to decide which securities to buy and sell. More often than not, when investors look for professional help, they look to mutual funds.

Basically, a **mutual fund** is a type of financial services organization that receives money from a pool of shareholders and then invests those funds in a portfolio of securities. Thus, when investors buy shares in a mutual fund, they actually become *part owners of a portfolio of securities*. In an abstract sense, a mutual fund is the *financial product* sold to the public by an investment company. That is, the investment company builds and manages a portfolio of securities and sells ownership interests—shares—in that portfolio through a vehicle known as a mutual fund.

Recall from Chapter 5 that portfolio management deals with both asset allocation and security selection decisions. By investing in mutual funds, investors delegate some, if not all, of the *security selection decision*s to professional money managers. As a result, they can concentrate on key asset allocation decisions—which, of course, play a vital role in determining long-term portfolio returns. Indeed, it's for this reason that *many investors consider mutual funds to be the ultimate asset allocation vehicle*. All that investors have to do is decide in which fund they want to invest—and then let the professional money managers at the mutual funds do the rest.

An Overview of Mutual Funds

Mutual funds have been a part of the investment landscape in the United States for over 85 years. The first one (MFS) started in Boston in 1924 and is still in business today. By 1940 the number of mutual funds had grown to 68, and by 1980 there were 564 of them. That was only the beginning: The next 28 years saw unprecedented growth in the mutual fund industry, as assets under management grew from about $135 billion in 1980 to *$9.6 trillion* by the end of 2008. Compared to less than 6% in 1980, 45% of all U.S. households owned mutual funds in 2008. In 2008, an estimated 92 million individuals held ownership in one of the *more than 8,000 unique publicly traded mutual funds*, and their holdings accounted for 82% of the total mutual fund assets at year-end. Actually, counting all share classes, which represent multiple fund offerings from the same portfolio, there were more than *22,000 funds available* in 2008. To put that number in perspective, *there are more mutual funds in existence today than there are stocks listed on the New York and American exchanges combined*. The mutual fund industry has grown so much, in fact, that it is now *the largest financial intermediary* in this country—even ahead of banks.

Mutual funds are big business in the United States and, indeed, all over the world. Worldwide, there were more than 69,000 mutual funds in operation in 2008, which collectively held *$19 trillion* in assets. Of that amount, U.S. mutual funds held roughly half of those assets, as shown at the top of the next page.

Measured by the number of funds, stock funds clearly dominate the U.S. market, just as they do the worldwide mutual fund market. Mutual funds appeal to investors from all walks of life and all income levels. They range from inexperienced to highly experienced investors who all share a common view: Each has decided, for one reason

Type of Fund	Number of U.S. Mutual Funds	Assets Managed by U.S. Funds ($ in Billions)
Stock Funds	4,830	$3,704.5
Hybrid Funds	492	498.7
Bond Funds	1,916	1,565.7
Money Market Funds	784	3,832.2
Total	8,022	$9,601.1

(Source: Investment company institute 2009 fact book, www.ici.org.)

or another, to turn over at least a part of his or her investment management activities to professionals.

Pooled Diversification The mutual fund concept is based on the simple idea of combining the investment capital of a group of people with similar investment goals and investing that capital in a wide array of securities. In so doing, investors are able to enjoy much wider investment diversification than they could otherwise achieve on their own. It's not uncommon for a single mutual fund to hold literally hundreds of different stocks or bonds. For example, as of mid-year 2009, Fidelity Contrafund held 399 different securities, while the Dreyfus GNMA fund had over 1,171 holdings. That's far more diversification than most individual investors could ever hope to attain acting on their own. Yet each investor who owns shares in a fund is, in effect, a part owner of that fund's diversified portfolio of securities.

No matter what the size of the fund, as the securities it holds move up and down in price, the market value of the mutual fund shares moves accordingly. When the fund receives dividend and interest payments, they too are passed on to the mutual fund shareholders and distributed on the basis of prorated ownership. Thus, if you own 1,000 shares in a mutual fund and that represents 1% of all shares outstanding, you will receive 1% of the dividends paid by the fund. When the fund sells a security for a profit, it also passes the capital gain on to fund shareholders on a prorated basis. The whole mutual fund idea, in fact, rests on the concept of **pooled diversification**. This process works very much like health insurance, whereby individuals pool their resources for the collective benefit of all the contributors.

MARKETS IN CRISIS

Mutual Fund Vulnerability

The mutual fund industry is not immune to crisis. The 2008 financial crisis and accompanying economic recession delivered considerable blows to the mutual fund industry. Total net asset value for U.S. mutual funds fell by $2.4 trillion in 2008. Investor demand for mutual funds slowed in 2008 with total net new cash flow to the industry dropping more than 50% from a level of $878 billion in 2007 to some $411 billion in 2008. Largely due to rapidly declining stock prices and increasing market uncertainty, investors pulled $234 billion from U.S. stock mutual funds in 2008, while safer money market funds reached a record high level of new investment inflow of more than $636 billion. In January 2008 alone, investors parked an additional $159 billion in U.S. money market funds. The difficult times were not limited to the U.S. mutual fund market. During 2008 worldwide mutual fund assets decreased by $7.2 trillion, which represented a greater than 27% loss of the $26 trillion in total net asset value worldwide at end-of-year 2007.

Attractions and Drawbacks of Mutual Fund Ownership Among the many reasons for owning mutual funds, one of the most important is the *portfolio diversification* that they can offer. As we saw above, fund shareholders can achieve diversification benefits by spreading fund holdings over a wide variety of industries and companies, thus reducing risk. Another appeal of mutual funds is *full-time professional management,* which relieves mutual fund investors of many of the day-to-day management and record-keeping chores. What's more, the fund is probably able to offer better investment expertise than individual investors can provide for themselves. Still another advantage is that most mutual fund investments can be started with a *modest amount of investment capital.* The *services that mutual funds offer* also make them appealing to many investors: These services include automatic reinvestment of dividends, withdrawal plans, and exchange privileges. Finally, mutual funds offer *convenience.* They are relatively easy to acquire; the funds handle the paperwork and record keeping; their prices are widely quoted; and it is possible to deal in fractional shares.

There are, of course, some costs associated with mutual fund ownership. Mutual funds can be costly and involve *substantial transaction costs.* Many funds carry sizable commission fees ("load charges"). In addition, funds levy a **management fee** annually for the services provided. It is deducted right off the top, regardless of whether the fund has had a good or a bad year. And, in spite of the professional management, *mutual fund performance* over the long haul is at best about equal to what you would expect from the market as a whole. There are some notable exceptions, of course, but most funds do little more than keep up with the market. In many cases, they don't even do that.

The overarching objective of professionally managed funds is to beat a relevant market benchmark. For example, managed stock mutual funds aim to beat one or more of the stock indexes, such as the S&P 500 Index. It is often difficult to judge the true ability of professional fund managers during bull markets, since in these times the market as a whole is appreciating, and so typically is the average stock that fund managers hold. However, bear market cycles provide a sound test of fund managers' stock picking abilities—since during these times the average stock is not appreciating. Figure 12.1 (on page 448) shows the percent of professionally managed stock funds that were outperformed by their relevant market benchmark during the 2004 to 2008 bear market cycle. Across all 12 stock fund categories, more than half of the fund managers failed to beat their market benchmark. Over the five-year market cycle from 2004 to 2008, the S&P 500 outperformed 71.9% of managed large-cap funds, S&P MidCap 400 outperformed 79.1% of mid-cap funds, and S&P SmallCap 600 outperformed 85.5% of small-cap funds. For all domestic stock funds, 66.2% of professional mutual fund managers underperformed the S&P Composite 1500 Stock Index. Similar results are found for the previous five-year bear market cycle from 1999 to 2003. The message is clear: *Consistently beating the market is no easy task,* even for professional money managers. Although a handful of funds have given investors above-average and even spectacular rates of return, most mutual funds simply do not meet those levels of performance. This is not to say that the long-term returns from mutual funds are substandard or that they fail to equal what you could achieve by putting your money in, say, a savings account or some other risk-free investment outlet. Quite the contrary: The long-term returns from mutual funds have been substantial (and perhaps even better than what many individual investors could have achieved on their own), but a good deal of those returns can be traced to strong market conditions and/or to the reinvestment of dividends and capital gains.

INVESTOR FACTS

FUNDS AND TAXES—When you own shares in a mutual fund, you, not the fund, are liable for any income taxes. That's because mutual funds are tax-exempt organizations, so there's no double taxation of income. (To qualify as tax-exempt, a fund must distribute all of its realized capital gains and at least 90% of any interest and dividend income.) Although the fund may not owe any taxes, you do—unless you hold the fund in a tax-sheltered account, like an IRA or a 401(k). In that case, the taxes are deferred until you start drawing down the account. If any taxes are due, you will receive a Form 1099 from the mutual fund each year, showing how much was earned in ordinary income (dividends and interest) and/or capital gains.

FIGURE 12.1   **The Comparative Performance of Managed Mutual Funds Versus Market Benchmarks**

Even with the services of professional money managers, it's tough to outperform the market. In this case, not one fund category had a majority of funds that succeeded in beating the market during the five-year market cycle of 2004 to 2008.

(Source: *Standard & Poor's*, Standard & Poor's Indices Versus Active Funds Scorecard, Year End 2008.)

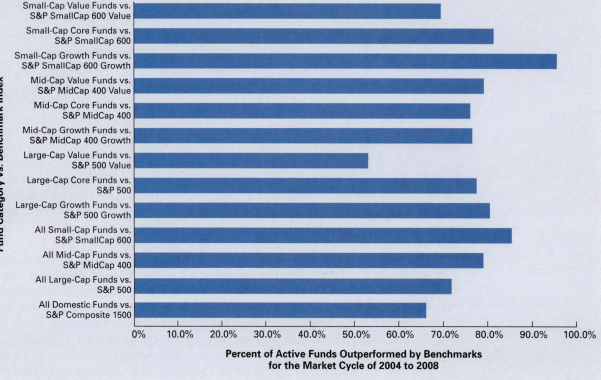

How Mutual Funds Are Organized and Run Although it's tempting to think of a mutual fund as a single large entity, that view is not really accurate. Funds split their various functions—investing, record keeping, safekeeping, and others—among two or more companies. To begin with, there's the fund itself, which is organized as a separate corporation or trust; it is *owned by the shareholders*, not by the firm that runs it. In addition, there are several other major players:

- A *management company* runs the fund's daily operations. Management companies are the firms we know as Fidelity, Vanguard, T. Rowe Price, American Century, and Dreyfus. They are the ones that create the funds in the first place. Usually, the management firm also serves as investment adviser.

- An *investment adviser* buys and sells stocks or bonds and otherwise oversees the portfolio. Usually, three parties participate in this phase of the operation: (1) *the money manager,* who actually runs the portfolio and makes the buy and sell decisions; (2) *securities analysts,* who analyze securities and look for viable investment candidates; and (3) *traders,* who buy and sell big blocks of securities at the best possible price.

- A *distributor* sells the fund shares, either directly to the public or through authorized dealers (like major brokerage houses and commercial banks). When you request a prospectus and sales literature, you deal with the distributor.

- A *custodian* physically safeguards the securities and other assets of the fund, without taking a role in the investment decisions. To discourage foul play, an independent party (usually a bank) serves in this capacity.

- A *transfer agent* keeps track of purchase and redemption requests from shareholders and maintains other shareholder records.

This separation of duties is designed to protect mutual fund shareholders. You can lose money as a mutual fund investor (if your fund's stock or bond holdings go down in value), but that's the only risk of loss you face with a mutual fund. Here's why: In addition to the separation of duties noted above, one of the provisions of the contract between the mutual fund and the company that manages it is that the fund's assets—stocks, bonds, cash, or other securities in the portfolio—can *never be in the hands of the management company*. As still another safeguard, each fund must have a board of directors, or trustees, who are elected by shareholders and are charged with keeping tabs on the management company. Nevertheless, as the *Ethics in Investing* box explains, some mutual funds have engaged in some improper trading.

Open- or Closed-End Funds

Although investing in mutual funds has been made as simple as possible, investors should have a clear understanding of what they're getting into. It's essential that you be aware of the different organizational structures, particularly with regard to open- and closed-end funds.

Open-End Investment Companies The term *mutual fund* is commonly used to describe an open-end investment company. In an **open-end investment company**, investors buy their shares from, and sell them back to, the mutual fund itself. When an investor buys shares in an open-end fund, the fund issues new shares of stock and fills the purchase order with those new shares. There is no limit, other than investor demand, to the number of shares the fund can issue. (Occasionally, funds *temporarily* close themselves to new investors—they won't open any new accounts—in an attempt to keep fund growth in check.) All open-end mutual funds stand behind their shares and buy them back when investors decide to sell. There is never any trading of shares between individuals.

Both buy and sell transactions in open-end mutual funds are carried out at prices based on the current market value of all the securities held in the fund's portfolio. Known as the fund's **net asset value (NAV)**, it is calculated at least once a day and represents the underlying value of a share of stock in a particular mutual fund. NAV is found by taking the total market value of all assets held by the fund, less any liabilities, and dividing this amount by the number of fund shares outstanding. For example, if the market value of all the assets held by XYZ mutual fund on a given day equaled $10 million, and if XYZ on that particular day had 500,000 shares outstanding, the fund's net asset value per share would be $20 ($10,000,000 ÷ 500,000). This figure, as we will see, is then used to derive the price at which the fund shares are bought and sold.

Closed-End Investment Companies Although the term *mutual fund* technically refers only to open-end funds, it is also commonly used to refer to closed-end investment companies. **Closed-end investment companies** operate with a fixed number of shares outstanding and do not regularly issue new shares of stock. In effect, they have a

ETHICS IN INVESTING

When Mutual Funds Behaved Badly

For nearly 95 million Americans who own them, mutual funds are a convenient and relatively safe place to invest money. So it came as a big shock to investors in September 2003 when New York Attorney General Eliot Spitzer shook the mutual fund industry with allegations of illegal after-hours trading, special deals for large institutional investors, market timing in flagrant violation of funds' written policies, and other abuses. Nearly 20 companies, including several large brokerages, were dragged into scandals.

Some of the abuses stemmed from *market timing*, a practice where short-term traders seek to exploit differences between hours of operations of various global markets. For example, when the U.S. market rallies on strong economic news, short-term traders buy shares of U.S.-based international funds with large Asian holdings just before the close of the market at 4:00 P.M. EST. Prices of these funds, often calculated between 4:00 and 6:00 P.M., reflect closing prices of the U.S. securities but previous-day prices of Asian stocks, which typically don't close until 2:00 A.M. When the next-day Tokyo and other Asian markets rallied following Wall Street's lead, the market-timers sold shares of Asian holdings at the higher price, pocketing the profits. Most funds prohibit this kind of activity, yet exceptions were made for large institutional investors who traded millions of dollars' worth of fund shares. According to the regulators, this practice resembles betting on a winning horse after the horse race is over. Although *late trading* is illegal, many mutual funds did not enforce that rule for some of their privileged clients.

The abuses did not stop there. The National Association of Securities Dealers and the SEC also cracked down on mutual fund sales practices that overcharged investors on sales charges, or loads. Also, several funds closed to new investors charged their existing shareholders millions of dollars in marketing and sales fees.

Some estimates put the financial damage to shareholders from the mutual fund improprieties at about 0.1% of the over $7 trillion invested in mutual funds at the time. Most of that has been recovered since—as a result of settlements reached with the regulators—many mutual funds paid large settlement amounts and have cut fees and lowered fund expenses. An odd twist, however, is that in the summer of 2009 several of the guilty mutual funds received a big check from the Fair Fund that had been set up to compensate people harmed by the market timing. As it turned out, the market-timing settlements were such that after damages were assessed and victimized shareholders compensated, leftover money was returned to the funds in amounts proportionate to the harm caused. In some cases, the size of the check was big enough to cause a noticeable return for the once unscrupulous fund—as was the case for Old Mutual Growth (formally PBHG Funds), whose fund value increased by 9 percentage points upon receipt of its check.

Critical Thinking Question The SEC has proposed several regulations intended to curb mutual trading abuses. They include strict enforcement of trading hours and the imposition of 2% redemption fees if a fund is sold in less than 90 days. Do you think this will eliminate trading abuses?

capital structure like that of any other corporation, except that the corporation's business happens to be investing in marketable securities. Shares in closed-end investment companies, like those of any other common stock, are actively traded in the secondary market. Unlike open-end funds, *all trading in closed-end funds is done between investors in the open market*. The fund itself plays no role in either buy or sell transactions. Once the shares are issued, the fund is out of the picture. Most closed-end investment companies are traded on the New York Stock Exchange, a few are traded on the American Exchange, and occasionally some are traded in the Nasdaq market. Even so, while these shares are traded like any other common stock, their quotes are listed separately—in the *Wall Street Journal* at least. Shown following is one of those quotes, for Gabelli Equity Trust, a large closed-end investment company listed on the NYSE. These quotes appear daily in the *Wall Street Journal Online*. As you can see, they pro-

Gabelli Equity Trust Inc. (GAB)   NYSE

Comprehensive Quote:		11/19/09 03:59 PM EST	
Last	Change	% Change	Volume
5.01	**-0.04**	**-0.79%**	**295,089**
Open	High	Low	Prior Day's Volume
4.95	**5.04**	**4.95**	**254,032**
52-Week High	52-Week Low	Prior Day's Close	
5.24	**2.14**		**5.05**
(09/24/2009)	(03/06/2009)		

vide only a minimal amount of information, including the fund's name, symbol, and listing exchange and the latest prices, price changes, and volume information.

A closed-end fund is, in many respects, both a common stock and an investment company. As the original form of investment company, closed-end funds have enjoyed a long history that dates back to nineteenth-century England and Scotland. In the United States, closed-end funds were actively traded during the 1920s bull market, when they far outnumbered their open-end relatives. During that freewheeling era, however, they were highly leveraged and consequently were hit hard during the crash of 1929, earning a bad reputation with investors. They remained something of an oddity for decades afterward. It wasn't until the bull market that began in the early 1980s that closed-end funds came back into fashion.

Many of the investment advisers who today run closed-end funds (like Nuveen, Eaton Vance, Dreyfus, PIMCO, and Putnam) also manage open-end funds, often with similar investment objectives. The closed- and open-end funds they offer are really *two different investment products*. Although it may not appear so at first glance, there are some major differences between these two types of funds. First, closed-end funds have a fixed amount of capital to work with. Therefore, they don't have to be concerned about keeping cash on hand (or readily available) to meet redemptions. Equally important, because there is no pressure on portfolio managers to cash in these securities at inopportune times, they can be more aggressive in their investment styles by investing in securities that may not be actively traded. And, of course, because they don't have new money flowing in all the time, portfolio managers don't have to worry about finding new investments. Instead, they can concentrate on a set portfolio of securities.

Of course, this also puts added pressure on the money managers, since their investment styles and fund portfolios are closely monitored and judged by the market. That is, the share prices of closed-end companies are determined not only by their net asset values but also by general supply and demand conditions in the market. As a result, depending on the market outlook and investor expectations, closed-end companies generally trade at a discount or premium to NAV. Share price discounts and premiums can at times become quite large. In fact, it's not unusual for such spreads to amount to as much as 25% to 30% of net asset value. (We'll discuss closed-end funds in more detail later in this chapter.)

Exchange-Traded Funds

Combine some of the operating characteristics of an open-end fund with some of the trading characteristics of a closed-end fund, and what you'll end up with is a relatively new form of investment company called an *exchange-traded fund*, or ETF for short.

ETFs can be structured in one of three ways: as *open-end funds*; as *unit investment trusts*—although far less common than open-end funds, the first ETFs were structured this way and, as such, the most popular ETFs (Qubes, Diamonds, and Spiders) are structured as unit investment trusts; and as *grantor trusts*, which legally give the shareholder certain ownership rights that are not available with the other two forms (Merrill Lynch's HOLDRS are structured this way). Because approximately 90% of all ETFs are structured as open-end funds, and because operationally, there's very little difference between ETFs organized as open-end funds or unit investment trusts, we'll couch our discussion here in terms of the open-ended variety of ETFs.

Accordingly, we can describe an **exchange-traded fund** (ETF) as a type of open-end fund that trades as a listed security on one of the stock exchanges. Until early 2008 all ETFs were structured as *index funds* set up to match the performance of a certain segment of the market. They do this by owning all, or a representative sample, of the stocks in a targeted market segment or index. (We'll examine traditional index funds in more detail later in this chapter.) In 2008 the SEC cleared the way for actively managed ETFs, which like actively managed mutual funds create a unique mix of investments to meet a specific investment objective. Thus, ETFs offer the professional money management of traditional mutual funds *and* the liquidity of an exchange-traded stock.

An ETF is created by a fund sponsor, who chooses the investment objective of the ETF. For index ETFs, the sponsor decides on the target index and tracking method. There are two tracking methods, replication or sampling. A replicate index ETF holds every security in the target index and does so by investing 100% of its assets proportionately in the securities included in the target index. Instead of investing in every security included in the target index, the sponsor of a sample index ETF selects a representative sample of securities in the target index in which to invest. A sampling index ETF provides a manageable solution for tracking a target index with thousands of securities. The sponsor of an actively managed ETF also determines the investment objectives of the fund and may also elect to trade portfolio shares; much like an actively managed mutual fund. In practice, most managed ETFs tend to trade only weekly or monthly for several reasons, including minimizing the risk of other market participants front-running the fund's trades (submitting trades in advance of the ETF to take advantage of any predictable changes in security prices).

Even though these securities are like closed-end funds in that they are traded on listed exchanges, *they are in reality open-end funds,* where the number of shares outstanding can be increased or decreased in response to market demand. That is, although ETFs can be bought or sold like any other stock on a listed exchange, *the ETF distributor can also create new shares or redeem old shares.* This is done through a special type of security known as a *payment-in-kind creation unit.* These units are created by exchange specialists, or so-called "authorized participants," who deposit with a trustee a portfolio, or market basket, of stocks that track an index. The authorized participant then receives from the trustee new ETF shares on the index to be sold in the open market. To redeem shares, the authorized participant simply turns in ETF shares in exchange for the underlying stocks. This is all done to ensure an efficient and orderly market and to help prevent the fund shares from trading at a discount or premium, thereby avoiding one of the pitfalls of closed-end funds. Individual investors, of course, are *not* involved in the creation of these fund shares (that's handled by big institutional investors). Instead, they buy and sell ETFs in the secondary market by placing orders with their brokers, as they would normally do with any stock.

By year-end 2008, there were 728 ETFs traded on U.S. markets, which together accounted for more than $531 billion in assets under management. Of these, 12 were managed ETFs with a total net asset value of less than $250 million. These funds cover a wide array of domestic and international stock indexes and sub-markets, as well as a handful of U.S. Treasury and corporate bond indexes. The biggest and oldest (dating back to 1993) is based on the S&P 500 and is known as *Spiders*. In addition, there are *Qubes* (based on the Nasdaq 100, this is the most actively traded ETF and in fact is the most actively traded stock in the world) and *Diamonds* (which is based on the DJIA). In addition, there are ETFs based on dozens of international markets (from Australia and Canada to Germany, Japan, and the United Kingdom) and a half-dozen or so that are based on various bond measures. Just about every major U.S. index, in fact, has its own ETF. So do a lot of minor indexes (some of which were created by the distributors) that cover very specialized (and sometimes fairly small) segments of the market. There are even ETFs based on gold bullion, real estate, commodities futures, clean energy, stocks with high dividend yields, tiny micro-cap stocks, and inflation-protection securities.

The net asset values of ETFs are set at a fraction of the underlying index value at any given time. For example, if the S&P 500 index stands at, say, 1042.73, the ETF on that index will trade at around 104.27 (that is, at about 1/10 of the index). Likewise, the ETF on the Dow is set at 1/100 of the DJIA. (Thus, when the DJIA is at say, 9605.41, the ETF will trade at around 96.05).

ETFs combine many of the advantages of closed-end funds with those of traditional (open-end) funds. As with closed-end funds, you can buy and sell ETFs at *any time of the day* by placing an order through your broker (and paying a standard commission, just as you would with any other stock). In contrast, you *cannot* trade a traditional open-end fund on an intraday basis; all buy and sell orders for those funds are filled at the end of the trading day, at closing prices. ETFs can also be bought on margin, and they can be sold short. Moreover, because index ETFs are passively managed, they offer all the advantages of any index fund: low cost, low portfolio turnover, and low taxes. In fact, the fund's tax liability is kept very low, because ETFs rarely distribute any capital gains to shareholders. Thus, you could hold index ETFs for decades and never pay a dime in capital gains taxes (at least not until you sell the shares).

Some Important Considerations

When you buy or sell shares in a *closed-end* investment company (or in *ETFs,* for that matter), you pay a commission, just as you would with any other listed or OTC stock. This is not the case with open-end mutual funds, however; the cost of investing in an open-end fund depends on the types of fees and load charges that the fund levies on its investors.

Load and No-Load Funds The *load charge* on an open-end fund is the commission you pay when you buy shares in a fund. Generally speaking, the term **load fund** describes a mutual fund that charges a commission when shares are bought. (Such charges are also known as *front-end loads*.) A **no-load fund** levies no sales charges. Although load charges have fallen over time, they can still be fairly substantial. The average front load that an investor might pay on the investment amount in an equity fund has fallen from 7.9% in 1980 to 5.3% in 2008. However, very few funds charge the maximum. Instead, many funds today charge commissions of only 2% or 3%. Such funds are known as **low-load funds**.

Occasionally, a fund will have a **back-end load**. This means that the fund levies commissions when shares are sold. These loads may amount to as much as 7.25% of the value of the shares sold, although back-end loads tend to decline over time and usually disappear altogether after five or six years from date of purchase. The stated purpose of back-end loads is to enhance fund stability by discouraging investors from trading in and out of the funds over short investment horizons.

Although there may be little or no difference in the performance of load and no-load funds, *the cost savings with no-load funds tend to give investors a head start in achieving superior rates of return.* Unfortunately, the true no-load fund is becoming harder to find, as more and more no-loads are becoming *12(b)-1 funds*. These funds do not directly charge commissions at the time of purchase. Instead, they *annually* assess what are known as 12(b)-1 charges to make up for any lost commissions. (These charges are more fully described below.) Overall, less than half of the funds sold today are pure no-loads; the rest charge some type of load or fee.

Known appropriately as *hidden loads*, **12(b)-1 fees** are designed to help funds (particularly the no-loads) cover their distribution and marketing costs. They can amount to as much as 1% per year of assets under management. In good markets and bad, investors pay these fees right off the top, and that can take its toll. Consider, for instance, $10,000 invested in a fund that charges a 1% 12(b)-1 fee. That translates into a charge of $100 per year—certainly not an insignificant amount of money.

To try to bring some semblance of order to fund charges and fees, the SEC instituted a series of caps on mutual fund fees. According to the latest regulations, a mutual fund cannot charge more than 8.5% in *total sales charges and fees*, including front- and back-end loads as well as 12(b)-1 fees. Thus, if a fund charges a 5% front-end load and a 1% 12(b)-1 fee, it can charge a maximum of only 2.5% in back-end load charges without violating the 8.5% cap. In addition, the SEC set a 1% cap on annual 12(b)-1 fees and, perhaps more significantly, stated that true no-load funds cannot charge more than 0.25% in annual 12(b)-1 fees. If they do, they have to drop the no-load label in their sales and promotional material.

Other Fees and Costs Another cost of owning mutual funds is the *management fee*. This is the compensation paid to the professional managers who administer the fund's portfolio. You must pay this fee regardless of whether a fund is load or no-load and whether it is an open- or closed-end fund or an exchange-traded fund. Unlike load charges, which are one-time costs, investment companies levy management and 12(b)-1 fees annually, regardless of the fund's performance. In addition, there are the administrative costs of operating the fund. These are fairly modest and represent the normal cost of doing business (e.g., the commissions paid when the fund buys and sells securities). The various fees that funds charge generally range from less than 0.5% to as much as 3% or 4% of average assets under management. In addition to these management fees, some funds may charge an *exchange fee*, assessed whenever you transfer money from one fund to another within the same fund family, or an *annual maintenance fee*, to help defer the costs of providing service to low-balance accounts.

Total expense ratios bear watching, because high expenses take their toll on performance. As a point of reference, in 2008, domestic stock funds had average expense ratios of 1.46%, foreign stock funds of 1.61%, and domestic bond funds of around 1.07%.

Keeping Track of Fund Fees and Loads Critics of the mutual fund industry have come down hard on the proliferation of fund fees and charges. Fortunately, regulators have taken steps to bring fund fees and loads out into the open. For one thing, fund charges are more widely reported now than they were in past. Most notably, today you can find detailed information about the types and amounts of fees and charges on just about any mutual fund by going to one of the dozens of Web sites that report on mutual funds, including Quicken, Kiplinger, Morningstar, Yahoo!, and a host of others. Figure 12.2 (on page 455) provides

FIGURE 12.2 Fund Fees and Charges on the Web

The Internet has become the motherlode of information on just about any topic imaginable, including mutual fund fees and charges. Here's an example of information taken from the Morningstar Web site. These excerpts show, among other things, all the fees and expenses levied by each fund. The two funds in the exhibit provide a stark contrast in fees and expenses, even though both of them are classified as large-cap value funds. The A shares of the Gabelli Blue Chip Value fund carry a high (5.75%) front-end load, a 12(b)-1 fee, and a *very high* total expense ratio (2.00%). In contrast, the Vanguard Windsor fund is a vivid example of a low-cost fund: no loads or fees and a *very low* total expense ratio (0.30%). It is projected that over a five-year period, the Gabelli fund will cost the investor about $1,600 in fees and expenses, while the Vanguard Windsor investor will pay only $208. The bottom panel shows that $10,000 invested over a recent five-year period in the Gabelli fund was worth $1,395 more than the same investment in the Vanguard Windsor fund. However, before concluding that the Gabelli fund provides the superior return, consider that the additional dollar return is just enough to offset the higher five-year projected cost of $1,392.

(Source: Data from www.morningstar.com, September 10, 2009. ©2009 Morningstar, Inc.)

Gabelli Blue Chip Value A GBCAX | ★★★★

Fees and Expenses — 04-30-09

Maximum Sales Fees %		Actual Fees %	
Initial	5.75	12b-1	0.25
Deferred	None	Management	1.00
		Net Expense Ratio: Annual Report (As of 12-31-08)	2.00
Redemption Fees %			
0 - 7 days	2.00		
More Than 7 days	0.00	Net Expense Ratio: Prospectus	2.00

Maximum Fees %		Total Cost Projections	Cost per $10,000
Administrative	0.00	3-Year	$1172
Management	1.00	5-Year	$1600
		10-Year	$2788

Vanguard Windsor VWNDX | ★★★

Fees and Expenses — 02-27-09

Maximum Sales Fees %		Actual Fees %	
Initial	None	12b-1	0.00
Deferred	None	Management	0.34
		Net Expense Ratio: Annual Report (As of 10-31-08)	0.30
Redemption Fees %	None		
		Net Expense Ratio: Prospectus	0.37

Maximum Fees %		Total Cost Projections	Cost per $10,000
Administrative	0.00	3-Year	$119
Management	0.34	5-Year	$208
		10-Year	$468

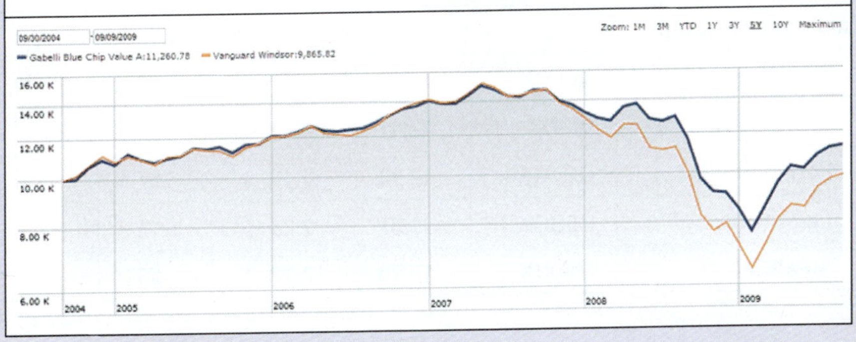

09/30/2004 - 09/09/2009   Zoom: 1M 3M YTD 1Y 3Y 5Y 10Y Maximum
■ Gabelli Blue Chip Value A:11,260.78   ■ Vanguard Windsor:9,865.82

excerpts from one of these sites and shows the kind of information that's readily available, at no charge, on the Web.

Alternatively, you can use the mutual fund quotes that appear daily in most major, large-city newspapers or in the *Wall Street Journal*. For example, look at the *Wall Street Journal* quotations in Figure 12.3. Note that right after the (abbreviated)

FIGURE 12.3   Mutual Fund Quotes

Open-end mutual funds are listed separately from other securities. They have their own quotation system, an example of which, from the *WSJ.com*, is shown here. Note that these securities are quoted in dollars and cents and that the quotes include not only the fund's NAV but year-to-date (YTD) and three-year returns as well. Also included is an indication of whether the fund charges redemption and/or 12(b)-1 fees. (Source: WSJ.com, September 09, 2009.)

Mutual Funds: Closing Quotes

Q

GO TO: A | B | C | D | E | F | G | H | I | J | K | L | M | N | O | P | R | S | T | U | V | W | X | Y | Z

Wednesday, September 09, 2009

Alphabetical listing by fund family.

Family/ Fund	Symbol	NAV	Chg	YTD % return	3-yr % chg
Quaker Funds					
MdCpValA p	QMCVX	11.00	0.10	22.4	-9.1
SmCpValA p	QUSVX	11.28	0.20	14.2	-6.6
SmCpVal I	QSVIX	11.68	0.22	14.4	-6.4
StrGwthA p	QUAGX	13.88	0.13	11.6	-5.5
StrGwthC t	QAGCX	12.71	0.11	10.9	-6.2
StrGwthI p	QAGIX	14.25	0.13	11.7	-5.2
Quantitative Group					
EmgMkts r	QFFOX	18.37	-0.02	50.7	1.7
ForeignVal I r	QFVIX	12.11	0.19	57.3	-4.6
ForeignVal O t	QFVOX	12.10	0.19	57.4	-4.8
Lg/ShtOrdy	USBOX	10.37	0.08	13.0	-10.6
SmallCp	USBNX	13.79	0.17	23.2	-11.5

names of the fund, you will often find the letters *r*, *p*, and *t*. An *r* behind a fund's name means that the fund charges some type of redemption fee, or back-end load, when you sell your shares. A *p* in the quotes means that the fund levies a 12(b)-1 fee. A *t* indicates funds that charge both redemption fees and 12(b)-1 fees. The quotations, of course, tell you only the *kinds* of fees charged by the funds. They do not tell you *how much* is charged. To get the specifics on the amount charged, you will have to turn to other sources, like a favorite Web site. Furthermore, these published quotes *tell you nothing about the front-end loads*, if any, charged by the funds. Again, to find out if a particular fund charges a front-end load, you will have to consult a Web site or some other source. (Note that the *Wall Street Journal* also publishes a *Monthly Mutual Fund Review* on the first or second Monday of each month. Among other things, it provides some specifics on front-end loads and annual expense charges, including 12(b)-1 fees.)

In addition to the public sources noted above, the SEC requires the mutual funds themselves to fully disclose all of their fees and expenses in a standardized, easy-to-understand format. Every fund profile or prospectus must contain, up front, a fairly detailed *fee table*, much like the one illustrated in Table 12.1. This table has three parts. The first specifies *all shareholder transaction costs*. This tells you what it's going to cost to buy and sell shares in the mutual fund. The next section lists the *annual operating expenses* of the fund. Showing these expenses as a percentage of average net assets, the fund must break out management fees, 12(b)-1 fees, and any other expenses. The third section provides a rundown of *the total cost over time* of buying, selling, and owning

TABLE 12.1   Mutual Fund Fee Table (Required by Federal Law)

The following table describes the fees and expenses that are incurred when you buy, hold, or sell shares of the fund.

Shareholder fees (paid by the investor directly)

Maximum sales charge (load) on purchases (as a % of offering price)	3%
Sales charge (load) on reinvested distributions	None
Deferred sales charge (load) on redemptions	None
Exchange fees	None
Annual account maintenance fee (for accounts under $2,500)	$12.00

Annual fund operating expenses (paid from fund assets)

Management fee	0.45%
Distribution and service (12b-1) fee	None
Other expenses	0.20%
Total annual fund operating expenses	0.65%

Example

This example is intended to help an investor compare the cost of investing in different funds. The example assumes a $10,000 investment in the fund for one, three, five, and ten years and then a redemption of all fund shares at the end of those periods. The example also assumes that an investment returns 5% each year and that the fund's operating expenses remain the same. Although actual costs may be higher or lower, based on these assumptions an investor's costs would be:

1 year	$364
3 years	$502
5 years	$651
10 years	$1,086

the fund. This part of the table contains both transaction and operating expenses and shows what the total costs would be over hypothetical one-, three-, five-, and 10-year holding periods. To ensure consistency and comparability, the funds must follow a rigid set of guidelines when constructing the illustrative costs.

Other Types of Investment Companies

In addition to open-end, closed-end, and exchange-traded funds, there are four other types of investment companies: (1) real estate investment trusts, (2) hedge funds, (3) unit investment trusts, and (4) annuities. Unit investment trusts, annuities, and hedge funds are similar to mutual funds to the extent that they, too, invest primarily in marketable securities, such as stocks and bonds. Real estate investment trusts, in contrast, invest primarily in various types of real estate–related investments, like mortgages. We'll look at real estate investment trusts and hedge funds in this section.

Real Estate Investment Trusts   A **real estate investment trust** (**REIT**) is a type of closed-end investment company that invests money in mortgages and various types of real estate investments. A REIT is like a mutual fund in that it sells shares of stock to the investing public and uses the proceeds, along with borrowed funds, to invest in a portfolio of real estate investments. The investor, therefore, owns a part of the real estate portfolio held by the real estate investment trust. The basic appeal of REITs is that they enable investors to receive both the capital appreciation and the current income from real estate ownership without all the headaches of property management. *REITs are also popular with income-oriented investors because of the very attractive dividend yields they provide.*

There are three basic types of REITs: those that invest in *properties*, such as shopping centers, hotels, apartments, and office buildings (the so-called *property*, or *equity*, REITs); mortgage REITs—those that invest in mortgages; and *hybrid* REITs, which invest in both properties and mortgages. Mortgage REITs tend to be more income-oriented; they emphasize their high current yields (which is to be expected from a security that basically invests in debt). In contrast, while equity REITs may promote their attractive current yields, most of them also offer the potential for earning varying amounts of capital gains (as their property holdings appreciate in value). Year-end 2008, there were 136 REITs, which together held over $191 billion in various real estate assets. Equity REITs dominated the market: There were 113 of them, accounting for some $176 billion in assets under management, or about 92% of the total market. There were 20 mortgage REITs, and just three hybrid REITs.

REITs must abide by the Real Estate Investment Trust Act of 1960, which established requirements for forming a REIT, as well as rules and procedures for making investments and distributing income. Because they are required to pay out nearly all their earnings to the owners, REITs do quite a bit of borrowing to obtain funds for their investments. A number of insurance companies, mortgage bankers, and commercial banks have formed REITs, many of which are traded on the major securities exchanges. The income earned by a REIT is not taxed, but *the income distributed to the owners is designated and taxed as ordinary income.* REITs have become very popular in the past five to 10 years, in large part because of the very attractive returns they offer. Comparative average annual returns are listed below; clearly, REITs have more than held their own against common stocks over time:

Period	REITs*	S&P 500	Nasdaq Composite
3-yr. (2006-2008)	−7.2%	−5.3%	−7.1%
5-yr. (2004-2008)	3.4	−0.1	−2.2
10-yr. (1999-2008)	9.6	0.6	3.2
20-yr. (1989-2008)	9.9	10.4	12.1
25-yr. (1984-2008)	9.5	11.5	11.2
30-yr. (1979-2008)	12.1	12.6	12.6
35-yr. (1974-2008)	12.1	11.8	11.9

(*Source: National Association of Real Estate Investment Trusts (**www.reit.com**) and Yahoo! Finance (**finance.yahoo.com**), September 2009. REIT returns measured by the *NAREIT Composite Index*.)

In addition to their highly competitive returns, REITs also offer desirable portfolio diversification properties and very attractive dividend yields (of nearly 5.0%, after taxes), which are generally well above the yields on common stock.

Hedge Funds First of all, in spite of the name similarities, it is important to understand that hedge funds are *not* mutual funds. They are totally different types of investment products! **Hedge funds** are set up as private entities, usually in the form of *limited partnerships* and, as such, are *largely unregulated*. The *general partner* runs the fund and directly participates in the fund's profits—often taking a "performance fee" of 10–20% of the profits, in addition to a base fee of 1–2% of assets under management. The *limited partners are the investors* and consist mainly of institutions, such as pension funds, endowments, and private banks, as well as high-income individual investors. Because hedge funds are unregulated, they can be sold only to "accredited investors," meaning the individual investor must have a net worth in excess of $1 million and/or an annual income (from qualified sources) of at least $200,000 to $300,000. Many hedge funds are, by choice, even more restrictive, and limit their investors to only *very*-high-net-worth individuals. In addition, some hedge funds limit the number of investors they'll let in (often to no more than 100 investors).

These practices, of course, stand in stark contrast to the way mutual funds operate: While hedge funds are largely unregulated, mutual funds are very highly regulated and monitored. Individuals do not need to qualify or be accredited to invest in mutual funds. Although some mutual funds do have minimum investments of $50,000 to $100,000 or more, they are the exception rather than the rule. Not so with hedge funds—many of them have minimum investments that can run into the millions of dollars. Also, mutual fund performance is open for all to see, whereas hedge funds simply do not divulge such information, at least not to the general public. Mutual funds are required by law to provide certain periodic and standardized pricing and valuation information to investors, as well as to the general public, whereas hedge funds are totally free from such requirements. The world of hedge funds is very secretive and about as *non*-transparent as you can get.

Hedge funds and mutual funds are similar in one respect, however: Both are pooled investment vehicles that accept investors' money and invest those funds on a collective basis. Put another way, *both sell shares (or participation) in a professionally managed portfolio of securities*. Most hedge funds structure their portfolios so as to reduce volatility and risk, while trying to preserve capital (i.e., "hedge" against market downturns) and still deliver positive returns under different market conditions. They do so by taking often very complex market positions that involve both long and short positions, the use of various arbitrage strategies (to lock in profits), as well as the use of options, futures, and other derivative securities. Indeed, hedge funds will invest in almost any opportunity in almost any market so long as impressive gains are believed to be available at reasonable levels of risk. Thus, these funds are anything but low-risk, fairly stable investment vehicles. In 2008, it was *estimated* that there were approximately 8,000 hedge funds in existence, which in total had about *$1.4 trillion* in assets under management. The top 100 hedge funds in Barron's 2009 ranking had a combined $230 billion in assets and an average three-year annualized return of 18.2%.

CONCEPTS IN REVIEW

Answers available at
www.pearsonhighered.com/
gitman

12.1 What is a *mutual fund?* Discuss the mutual fund concept, including the importance of diversification and professional management.

12.2 What are the advantages and disadvantages of mutual fund ownership?

12.3 Briefly describe how a mutual fund is organized. Who are the key players in a typical mutual fund organization?

12.4 Define each of the following:

    a. Open-end investment companies
    b. Closed-end investment companies
    c. Exchange-traded funds
    d. Real estate investment trusts
    e. Hedge funds

12.5 What is the difference between a *load fund* and a *no-load fund?* What are the advantages of each type? What is a 12(b)-1 fund? Can such a fund operate as a no-load fund?

12.6 Describe a *back-end load,* a *low load,* and a *hidden load.* How can you tell what kind of fees and charges a fund has?

Types of Funds and Services

LG3 **LG4** Some mutual funds specialize in stocks, others in bonds. Some have maximum capital gains as an investment objective; some high current income. Some funds appeal to speculators; others to income-oriented investors. Every fund has a particular investment objective, and each fund is expected to conform to its stated investment policy and objective. Categorizing funds according to their investment policies and objectives is a common practice in the mutual fund industry. The categories indicate similarities in how the funds manage their money and also their risk and return characteristics. Some of the more popular types of mutual funds are growth, aggressive growth, value, equity-income, balanced, growth-and-income, bond, money market, index, sector, socially responsible, asset allocation, and international funds.

Of course, it's also possible to define fund categories based on something other than stated investment objectives. For example, Morningstar, the industry's leading research and reporting service, has developed a *classification system based on a fund's actual portfolio position.* Essentially, it carefully evaluates the makeup of a fund's portfolio to determine where its security holdings are concentrated. It then uses that information to classify funds on the basis of investment style (growth, value, or blend), market segment (small-, mid-, or large-cap), or other factors. Such information helps *mutual fund investors make informed asset allocation decisions* when structuring or rebalancing their own portfolios. That benefit notwithstanding, let's stick with the investment-objective classification system noted above and examine the various types of mutual funds to see what they are and how they operate.

Types of Mutual Funds

Growth Funds The objective of a **growth fund** is simple: capital appreciation. Long-term growth and capital gains are the primary goals of such funds. They invest principally in well-established, large- or mid-cap companies that have above-average growth potential. They offer little (if anything) in the way of dividends and current income. Rather, growth funds mainly seek to invest in companies with above-average growth in earnings that reinvest earnings into expansion, acquisitions, or research and development. Because of the uncertain nature of their investment income, growth funds may involve a fair amount of risk exposure. They are usually viewed as long-term investment vehicles most suitable for the investor who wants to build up capital and does not require current income.

Aggressive-Growth Funds Aggressive-growth funds are the so-called performance funds that tend to increase in popularity when markets heat up. **Aggressive-growth funds** (sometimes referred to as capital appreciation funds) are highly speculative investments that seek large profits from capital gains. Most are fairly small (with average assets under management of less than $250 million), and their portfolios consist mainly of "high-flying" common stocks. These funds often buy stocks of small, unseasoned companies, stocks with relatively high price/earnings multiples, and common stocks whose prices are highly volatile. They seem to be especially fond of turnaround situations and may even use leverage in their portfolios (i.e., buy stocks on margin). They also use options fairly aggressively, various hedging techniques, and perhaps even short selling. These techniques are designed, of course, to yield big returns. In part because of their highly speculative investments, aggressive-growth funds are among the most volatile of all mutual funds. When the markets are good, aggressive-growth funds do well; conversely, when the markets are bad, these funds often experience substantial losses.

Value Funds **Value funds** confine their investing to stocks considered to be *undervalued* by the market. That is, the funds look for stocks that are fundamentally sound but overlooked by investors. These funds hold stocks as much for their underlying intrinsic value as for their *growth potential*. In stark contrast to growth funds, value funds look for stocks with relatively low price/earnings ratios, high dividend yields, and moderate amounts of financial leverage. They prefer undiscovered companies that offer the potential for growth, rather than those that are already experiencing rapid growth.

Value investing is not easy. It involves extensive evaluation of corporate financial statements and any other documents that will help fund managers uncover value (investment opportunities) *before the rest of the market does* (that's the key to the low P/Es). The approach seems to work; even though value investing is generally regarded as *less risky* than growth investing (lower P/Es, higher dividend yields, and fundamentally stronger companies all translate into reduced risk exposure), the long-term return to investors in value funds is competitive with that from growth funds and even aggressive growth funds. Thus, value funds are often viewed as a viable investment alternative for relatively conservative investors who are looking for the attractive returns that common stocks have to offer, yet want to keep share price volatility and investment risk in check.

Equity-Income Funds **Equity-income funds** emphasize current income by investing primarily in high-yielding common stocks. Capital preservation is also important, and so are capital gains, although capital appreciation is not the primary objective of equity-income funds. These funds invest heavily in high-grade common stocks, some convertible securities and preferred stocks, and occasionally even junk bonds or certain types of high-grade foreign bonds. As far as their stock holdings are concerned, they lean heavily toward blue chips (including perhaps even "baby blues"), public utilities, and financial shares. They like securities that generate hefty dividend yields but also consider potential price appreciation over the longer haul. In general, because of their emphasis on dividends and current income, these funds tend to hold higher-quality securities that are subject to less price volatility than the market as a whole. They're generally viewed as a fairly low-risk way of investing in stocks.

Balanced Funds **Balanced funds** tend to hold a balanced portfolio of both stocks and bonds for the purpose of generating a balanced return of both current income and long-term capital gains. They're much like equity-income funds, but balanced funds usually put more into fixed-income securities; generally, they keep around 30% to 40% of their portfolios in bonds. The bonds are used principally to provide current income, and stocks are selected mainly for their long-term growth potential.

The funds can shift the emphasis in their security holdings: Clearly, the more the fund leans toward fixed-income securities, the more income-oriented it will be. For the most part, balanced funds tend to confine their investing to high-grade securities, including growth-oriented blue-chip stocks, high-quality income shares, and high-yielding investment-grade bonds. Balanced funds are usually considered a relatively safe form of investing, in which you can earn a competitive rate of return without having to endure a lot of price volatility. (*Note:* Equity-income funds and the more income-oriented balanced funds, as well as certain types of bond funds, are sometimes all lumped together and referred to as *income funds*, because of their emphasis on generating high levels of current income.)

Growth-and-Income Funds **Growth-and-income funds** also seek a balanced return made up of both current income and long-term capital gains, but they place a greater emphasis on growth of capital. Unlike balanced funds, growth-and-income funds put most of their money into equities. In fact, it's not unusual for these funds to have 80% to 90% of their capital in common stocks. They tend to confine most of their investing to quality issues, so growth-oriented blue-chip stocks appear in their portfolios, along with a fair amount of high-quality income stocks. Part of the appeal of these funds is the fairly substantial returns many have generated over the long haul. These funds involve a fair amount of risk, if for no other reason than the emphasis they place on stocks and capital gains. Thus, growth-and-income funds are most suitable for those investors who can tolerate the risk and price volatility.

Bond Funds As the name implies, **bond funds** invest exclusively in various types and grades of bonds—from Treasury and agency bonds to corporate and municipal bonds and other debt securities such as mortgage-backed securities. Income from the bonds' interest payments is the primary investment objective, although capital gains are not ignored.

There are three important advantages to buying shares in bond funds rather than investing directly in bonds. First, the bond funds are generally more liquid than direct investments in bonds. Second, they offer a cost-effective way of achieving a high degree of diversification in an otherwise expensive investment vehicle. (Most bonds carry minimum denominations of $1,000 to $5,000.) Third, bond funds will automatically reinvest interest and other income, thereby allowing you to earn fully compounded rates of return.

Bond funds are generally considered to be a fairly conservative form of investment. But they are not without risk: *The prices of the bonds held in the fund's portfolio fluctuate with changing interest rates.* Many bond funds are managed pretty conservatively, but a growing number are becoming increasingly aggressive. In fact, in today's market, investors can find everything from high-grade government bond funds to highly speculative funds that invest in nothing but junk bonds or even in highly volatile derivative securities. Here's a list of the different types of domestic bond funds available to investors:

- *Government bond funds*, which invest in U.S. Treasury and agency securities.

- *High-grade corporate bond funds*, which invest chiefly in investment-grade securities rated triple-B or better.

- *High-yield corporate bond funds*, which are risky investments that buy junk bonds for the yields they offer.

- *Municipal bond funds*, which invest in tax-exempt securities. These are suitable for investors who seek tax-free income. Like their corporate counterparts, municipal bond funds can be packaged as either high-grade or high-yield funds. A special type of municipal bond fund is the so-called *single-state fund*, which invests in the municipal issues of only one state, thus producing (for residents of that state) interest income that is *fully exempt* from both federal and state taxes (and possibly even local/city taxes as well).

- *Mortgage-backed bond funds*, which put their money into various types of mortgage-backed securities of the U.S. government (e.g., GNMA issues). These funds appeal to investors for several reasons: (1) They provide diversification; (2) they are an affordable way to get into mortgage-backed securities; and (3) they allow investors to reinvest the principal portion of the monthly cash flow, thereby enabling them to preserve their capital.

- *Convertible bond funds*, which invest primarily in securities that can be converted or exchanged into common stocks. These funds offer investors some of the price stability of bonds, along with the capital appreciation potential of stocks.

- *Intermediate-term bond funds*, which invest in bonds with maturities of seven to 10 years or less and offer not only attractive yields but relatively low price volatility as well. Shorter (two- to five-year) funds are also available; these shorter-term funds are often used as substitutes for money market investments by investors looking for higher returns on their money, especially when short-term rates are way down.

Clearly, no matter what you're looking for in a fixed-income security, you're likely to find a bond fund that fits the bill. According to the *2009 Investment Company Fact Book*, in 2008 there were more than 1,900 U.S. bond funds that together had nearly $1.6 *trillion* worth of bonds under management.

Smart's Tour of the Web
To watch author Scott
Smart discuss key Web sites
for this chapter visit
www.myfinancelab.com

Money Market Funds **Money market mutual funds,** or **money funds** for short, apply the mutual fund concept to the buying and selling of short-term money market instruments—bank certificates of deposit, U.S. Treasury bills, and the like. These funds offer investors with modest amounts of capital access to the high-yielding money market, where many instruments require minimum investments of $100,000 or more. At the close of 2008, there were 784 money funds that together held more than $3.8 trillion in assets.

There are several different kinds of money market mutual funds:

- *General-purpose money funds,* which invest in any and all types of money market investment vehicles, from Treasury bills and bank CDs to corporate commercial paper. The vast majority of money funds are of this type.

- *Government securities money funds,* which effectively eliminate any risk of default by confining their investments to Treasury bills and other short-term securities of the U.S. government, or its agencies.

- *Tax-exempt money funds,* which limit their investing to very short (30- to 90-day) tax-exempt municipal securities. Because their income is free from federal income taxes, they appeal predominantly to investors in high tax brackets.

Just about every major brokerage firm has at least four or five money funds of its own, and hundreds more are sold by independent fund distributors. Because the maximum average maturity of their holdings cannot exceed 90 days, money funds are highly liquid investment vehicles, although their returns do move up and down with interest-rate conditions. They're also virtually immune to capital loss, because at least 95% of the fund's assets must be invested in top-rated/prime-grade securities. In fact, with the check-writing privileges they offer, money funds are just as liquid as checking or savings accounts. Many investors view these funds as a convenient, safe, and (reasonably) profitable way to accumulate capital and temporarily store idle funds.

Index Funds "If you can't beat 'em, join 'em." That saying pretty much describes the idea behind index funds. Essentially, an **index fund** is a type of mutual fund that buys and holds a portfolio of stocks (or bonds) equivalent to those in a market index like the S&P 500. An index fund that's trying to match the S&P 500, for example, would hold the same 500 stocks that are held in that index, in exactly (or very nearly) the same proportions. Rather than trying to beat the market, as most actively managed funds do, *index funds simply try to match the market.* That is, they seek to match the performance of the index on which the fund is based. They do this through low-cost investment management. In fact, in most cases, the whole portfolio is run almost entirely by a computer that matches the fund's holdings with those of the targeted index.

The approach of index funds is strictly buy-and-hold. Indeed, about the only time an index-fund portfolio changes is when the targeted market index alters its "market basket" of securities. A pleasant by-product of this buy-and-hold approach is that the funds have extremely low portfolio turnover rates and, therefore, very little in *realized* capital gains. As a result, aside from a modest amount of dividend income, these funds produce very little taxable income from year to year, which leads many high-income investors to view them as a type of tax-sheltered investment.

In addition to their tax shelter, these funds provide something else: By simply trying to match the market, index funds actually produce *highly competitive returns*. It's very difficult to consistently outperform the market, and the index funds don't even try to do so. The net result is that, on average, index funds produce better returns than most other types of stock funds. Granted, every now and then fully managed stock funds will have a year (or two) when they outperform index funds. But these are the exception rather than the rule, especially when you look at multi-year returns (three to five years or more). Over most multi-year periods, the vast majority of fully managed stock funds do not keep up with index funds.

The S&P 500 is the most popular index. A number of other market indexes also are used, including the S&P MidCap 400, the Russell 2000 Small Stock, and the Wilshire 5000 indexes, as well as value-stock indexes, growth-stock indexes, international-stock indexes, and even bond indexes. When picking index funds, be sure to avoid high-cost funds. Their fees significantly *reduce* the chance that the fund will be able to match the market. Also, avoid index funds that use gimmicks as a way to "enhance" yields. Rather than follow the index, these funds will "tilt" their portfolios in an attempt to outperform the market. Your best bet is to buy a *true* index fund (one that has no added "bells and whistles"), and a low-cost one at that.

At the start of 2009, 13% of U.S. households owned at least one index fund, and of households that owned mutual funds 30% owned at least one index fund. At the time there were 368 index mutual funds with total assets of $604 billion. In 2008, over 90% of $34 billion in new investment into index funds was invested in domestic equity indexes, whereas demand for global and international equity index funds declined, resulting in an aggregate outflow of investment for the first time since 1992. The lion's share of all investment in index mutual funds goes to equity index funds, and 42% of the total is invested in funds indexed to the S&P 500 Stock Index.

Sector Funds The so-called **sector fund** is a mutual fund that restricts its investments to a particular sector (or segment) of the market. These funds concentrate their investment holdings in one or more industries that make up the sector being aimed at. For example, a health care sector fund would focus on promising growth stocks from such industries as drug companies, hospital management firms, medical suppliers, and biotech concerns. Among the more popular sector funds are those that concentrate in technology, financial services, real estate (REITs), natural resources, telecommunications, and, of course, health care—all the "glamour" industries.

The overriding investment objective of a sector fund is *capital gains*. A sector fund is generally similar to a growth fund and should be considered speculative. The sector fund concept is based on the belief that the really attractive returns come from small segments of the market. It's an interesting notion that may warrant consideration by investors willing to take on the added risks that often accompany these funds.

Socially Responsible Funds For some, investing is far more than just cranking out financial ratios and calculating investment returns. To these investors, the security selection process also includes the *active, explicit consideration of moral, ethical, and environmental issues*. The idea is that social concerns should play just as big a role in investment decisions as do financial matters. Not surprisingly, a number of funds cater to such investors: Known as **socially responsible funds**, they actively and directly incorporate ethics and morality into the investment decision. Their investment decisions, in effect, revolve around *both* morality and profitability.

Socially responsible funds consider only certain companies for inclusion in their portfolios. If a company does not meet the fund's moral, ethical, or environmental tests, fund managers simply will not buy the stock, no matter how good the bottom line looks. Generally speaking, these funds refrain from investing in companies that derive revenues from tobacco, alcohol, gambling, or weapons, or that operate nuclear power plants. In addition, the funds tend to favor firms that produce "responsible" products or services, that have strong employee relations and positive environmental

INVESTOR FACTS

AGE AND ASSET ALLOCATION— Although there are several important factors to consider when determining the right asset allocation, like investment objective and market conditions, an old guideline bases the decision on your age. The rule says that the percentage of your portfolio invested in stocks should equal 100 minus your age. For example, if you are 25 then your portfolio would be 75% invested in stock—as you get older the rule shifts your portfolio from riskier stocks to less risky bond or money market instruments. However, since people are living longer now, many financial planners recommend subtracting your age from 110 or 120 in order to determine your stock allocation. Use of this larger number reflects your need to make your money last longer in retirement and the fact that you will need the extra growth that stocks can provide over a longer investment horizon.

records, and that are socially responsive to the communities in which they operate.

Asset Allocation Funds Studies have shown that the most important decision an investor can make is where to allocate his or her investment assets. *Asset allocation* involves deciding how you're going to divide up your investments among different types of securities. For example, what portion of your money do you want to devote to money market securities, what portion to stocks, and what portion to bonds? Asset allocation deals in broad terms (types of securities) and does not address individual security selection. Asset allocation has been found to be a far more important determinant of total portfolio returns than individual security selection. (See Chapter 13 for more discussion of the principles of asset allocation.)

Because many individual investors have a tough time making asset allocation decisions, the mutual fund industry has created a product to do the job for them. Known as **asset allocation funds**, these funds spread investors' money across different types of markets. Whereas most mutual funds concentrate on one type of investment—whether stocks, bonds, or money market securities—asset allocation funds put money into all these markets. Many of them also include foreign securities. Some even include inflation-resistant investments, such as gold or real estate.

These funds are designed for people who want to hire fund managers not only to select individual securities but also to allocate money among the various markets. Here's how a typical asset allocation fund works. The money manager establishes a desired allocation mix for the fund, which might look something like this: 50% to U.S. stocks, 30% to bonds, 10% to foreign securities, and 10% to money market securities. Securities are then purchased for the fund in these proportions, and the overall portfolio maintains the desired mix. Actually, each segment of the fund is managed almost as a separate portfolio. Thus, securities within, say, the stock portion are bought, sold, and held as the market dictates. However, *as market conditions change over time, the asset allocation mix changes as well*. For example, if the U.S. stock market starts to soften, the fund may reduce the (domestic) stock portion of the portfolio to, say, 35%, and simultaneously increase the foreign securities portion to 25%. There's no assurance, of course, that the money manager will make the right moves at the right time, but the expectation is that he or she will.

International Funds In their search for higher yields and better returns, U.S. investors have shown a growing interest in foreign securities. Sensing an opportunity, the mutual fund industry has been quick to respond with so-called **international funds**—a mutual fund that does all or most of its investing in foreign securities. In 1985, there were only about 40 of these funds; by 2009, the number had grown to more than 1,200. A lot of people would like to invest in foreign securities but simply do not have the know-how to do so. International funds may be just the vehicle for such investors, *provided they have at least a fundamental understanding of international economics issues* and how they can affect fund returns.

Technically, the term *international fund* describes a type of fund that invests *exclusively in foreign securities*. Such funds often confine their activities to specific geographic regions (e.g., Mexico, Australia, Europe, or the Pacific Rim). In contrast, *global funds* invest in both foreign securities and U.S. companies—usually multinational firms. As a rule, global funds provide more diversity and, with access to both foreign and domestic markets, can go wherever the action is. Regardless of whether they're global or international (we'll use the term *international* to apply to both), you can find just about any type of fund you could possibly want. There are international stock funds, international bond funds, and even international money market funds. There are aggressive growth funds, balanced funds, long-term growth funds, and high-grade bond funds. There are funds that confine their investing to large, established markets (like Japan, Germany, and Australia) and others that stick to emerging markets (such as Thailand, Mexico, Chile, and even former Communist countries like Poland).

Basically, these funds attempt to take advantage of international economic developments in two ways: (1) by capitalizing on changing *market conditions* and (2) by positioning themselves to benefit from *devaluation of the dollar*. They do so because they can make money either from rising share prices in a foreign market or from a falling dollar (which in itself produces capital gains for U.S. investors in international funds). Many of these funds, however, attempt to protect investors from currency exchange risks by using various types of *hedging strategies*. That is, by using foreign currency options and futures, or some other type of derivative product (see Chapters 14 and 15), the fund tries to reduce or eliminate the effects of fluctuating currency exchange rates. But even with currency hedging, international funds are still fairly high-risk investments and only investors who understand and are able to tolerate such risks should use them.

Investor Services

Ask most investors why they buy a particular mutual fund and they'll probably tell you that the fund provides the kind of income and return they're looking for. Now, no one would question the importance of return in an investment decision, but there are some other important reasons for investing in mutual funds, not the least of which are the valuable services they provide. Some of the most sought-after *mutual fund services* are automatic investment and reinvestment plans, regular income programs, conversion privileges, and retirement programs.

Automatic Investment Plans It takes money to make money. For an investor, that means being able to accumulate the capital to put into the market. Mutual funds have come up with a program that makes savings and capital accumulation as painless as possible. The program is the **automatic investment plan**. This service allows fund shareholders to automatically funnel fixed amounts of money *from their paychecks or bank accounts* into a mutual fund. It's much like a payroll deduction plan.

This fund service has become very popular, because it enables shareholders to invest on a regular basis without having to think about it. Just about every fund group offers some kind of automatic investment plan for virtually all of its stock and bond funds. To enroll, you simply fill out a form authorizing the fund to siphon a set amount (usually a minimum of $25 to $100 per period) from your bank account at regular intervals, such as monthly or quarterly. Once enrolled, you'll be buying more shares every month or quarter (most funds deal in fractional shares). Of course, if it's a load fund, you'll still have to pay normal sales charges on your periodic investments. You can get out of the program at any time, without penalty, by simply calling the fund. Although convenience is perhaps the chief advantage of automatic investment plans, they also make solid investment sense: One of the best ways of building up a sizable amount of capital is to *add funds to your investment program systematically over time*. The importance of making regular contributions to your investment portfolio cannot be overstated; it ranks right up there with compound interest.

Automatic Reinvestment Plans   An automatic reinvestment plan is another of the real draws of mutual funds and is offered by just about every open-end fund. Whereas automatic investment plans deal with money you are putting into a fund, automatic *reinvestment* plans deal with the dividends the funds pay to their shareholders. Much like stock dividend reinvestment plans (see Chapter 6), the **automatic reinvestment plans** of mutual funds enable you to keep your capital fully employed. This service automatically uses dividend and/or capital gains income to buy additional shares in the fund. Most funds deal in fractional shares, and such purchases are usually commission-free. Keep in mind, however, that even though you may reinvest all dividends and capital gains distributions, the IRS still treats them as cash receipts and taxes them as investment income in the year in which you received them.

Automatic reinvestment plans enable you to earn fully compounded rates of return. By plowing back profits, you can put them to work in generating even more earnings. Indeed, the effects of these plans on total accumulated capital over the long run can be substantial. Figure 12.4 shows the long-term impact of reinvested dividend and capital gain income for the S&P 500 Index. In the illustration, we assume that the investor starts with $10,000 and except for the reinvestment of dividends and capital gains distributions, *adds no new capital over time*. Even so, the initial investment of $10,000 with reinvestment grew to nearly $38,300 over the 19-year period from 1990 to 2008— which amounts to an annualized total rate of return of 7.3%. Over the same 19-year period, $10,000 invested in the S&P 500 Index without reinvestment only achieved $25,559 in value (this is an annualized price return of 5.1%). The difference reflects the

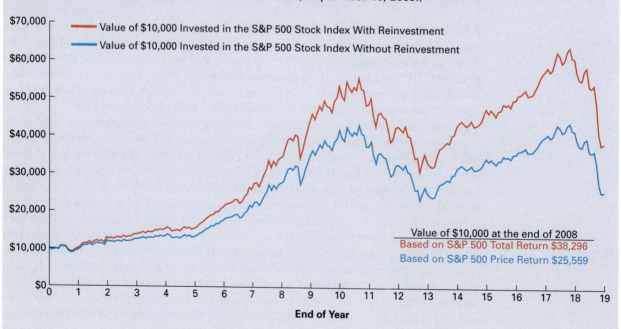

FIGURE 12.4   **The Effects of Reinvesting Income**
Reinvesting dividends or capital gains can have a tremendous impact on one's investment position. This graph shows the results of hypothetical investments of $10,000 in the S&P 500 Stock Index with and without reinvestment of all dividends and capital gains distributions, for a period of 19 years. (Source: Data from *Standard & Poor's Index Services*, September 10, 2009.)

extracted dividend income and the reinvestment return that it could have generated. Of course, not all time periods will match this performance—indeed, this time period included two separate bear market cycles—but the reinvestment strategy will typically outperform strategies without reinvestment. The point is that as long as you select an appropriate fund, you can derive *attractive benefits from the systematic accumulation of capital offered by automatic reinvestment plans.*

Regular Income Automatic investment and reinvestment plans are great for the long-term investor. But what about the investor who's looking for a steady stream of income? Once again, mutual funds have a service to meet this need. Called a **systematic withdrawal plan,** it's offered by most open-end funds. Once enrolled, an investor automatically receives a predetermined amount of money every month or quarter. Most funds require a minimum investment of $5,000 or more to participate, and the size of the minimum payment normally must be $50 or more per period (with no limit on the maximum). The funds will pay out the monthly or quarterly income first from dividends and realized capital gains. If this source proves to be inadequate and the shareholder so authorizes, the fund can then tap the principal or original paid-in capital to meet the required periodic payments.

Conversion Privileges Sometimes investors find it necessary to switch out of one fund and into another. For example, your objectives or the investment climate itself may have changed. **Conversion** (or **exchange**) **privileges** were devised to meet such needs conveniently and economically. Investment management companies that offer a number of different funds—known as **fund families**—often provide conversion privileges that enable shareholders to move money from one fund to another, either by phone or on the Internet. The only constraint is that the switches must be confined to the same *family* of funds. For example, you can switch from a Dreyfus growth fund to a Dreyfus money fund, or any other fund managed by Dreyfus.

With some fund families, the alternatives open to investors seem almost without limit. Indeed, some of the larger families offer literally hundreds of funds. Fidelity has nearly 200 different funds in its family: from high-performance stock funds to bond funds, tax-exempt funds, several dozen sector funds, and several dozen money funds. Around 200 fund families are in operation today, *not counting* the 150 to 200 families that offer only one or two funds. The two biggest—Fidelity and Vanguard—each has more than *half-a-trillion dollars* in assets under management, and that *excludes* their money market funds. Other big fund families include Franklin/Templeton ($150 billion under management), PIMCO ($160 billion), and American Century ($50 billion). All fund families provide low-cost conversion privileges. Some even provide these privileges for free, although most have limits on the number of times you can make such switches each year.

Conversion privileges are usually considered beneficial for shareholders: They allow you to meet ever-changing long-term goals, and they also permit you to manage your mutual fund holdings more aggressively by moving in and out of funds as the investment environment changes. Unfortunately, there is one major drawback: For tax purposes, the exchange of shares from one fund to another is regarded as a sale transaction followed by a subsequent purchase of a new security. As a result, if any capital gains exist at the time of the exchange, you are liable for the taxes on that profit, even though the holdings were not truly "liquidated."

Retirement Programs As a result of government legislation, self-employed individuals are permitted to divert a portion of their pretax income into self-directed retirement plans (SEPs). Also, all working Americans, whether self-employed or not, are allowed to establish individual retirement arrangements (IRAs). Indeed, with legislation passed in 1997, *qualified investors* can now choose between deductible and nondeductible (Roth) IRAs. Even those who make too much to qualify for one of these programs can set up special nondeductible IRAs. Today all mutual funds provide a service that allows individuals to set up tax-deferred retirement programs as either IRA or Keogh accounts—or, through their place of employment, to participate in a tax-sheltered retirement plan, such as a 401(k). The funds set up the plans and handle all the administrative details so that the shareholder can easily take full advantage of available tax savings.

12.7   Briefly describe each of the following types of mutual funds:

   a. Aggressive growth funds
   b. Equity-income funds
   c. Growth-and-income funds
   d. Bond funds
   e. Sector funds
   f. Socially responsible funds

12.8   What is an *asset allocation fund* and how does it differ from other types of mutual funds?

12.9   If growth, income, and capital preservation are the primary objectives of mutual funds, why do we bother to categorize funds by type? Do you think such classifications are helpful in the fund selection process? Explain.

12.10   What are *fund families?* What advantages do fund families offer investors? Are there any disadvantages?

12.11   Briefly describe some of the investor services provided by mutual funds. What are *automatic reinvestment plans,* and how do they differ from *automatic investment plans?* What is phone switching, and why would an investor want to use this service?

Investing in Mutual Funds

LG5   **LG6**   Suppose you are confronted with the following situation: You have money to invest and are trying to select the right place to put it. You obviously want to pick a security that meets your idea of acceptable risk and will generate an attractive rate of return. The problem is that you have to make the selection from a list containing literally thousands of securities. That's basically what you're facing when trying to select a suitable mutual fund. However, if you approach the problem systematically, it may not be so formidable a task. First, it might be helpful to examine more closely the various investor uses of mutual funds. With this background, we can then look at the selection process and at several measures of return that you can use to assess performance. As we will see, it is possible to whittle down the list of alternatives by matching your investment needs with the investment objectives of the funds.

Investor Uses of Mutual Funds

Mutual funds can be used in a variety of ways. For instance, performance funds can serve as a vehicle for capital appreciation, whereas bond funds can provide current income. Regardless of the kind of income a mutual fund provides, investors tend to use these securities for one of three reasons: (1) as a way to accumulate wealth, (2) as a storehouse of value, or (3) as a speculative vehicle for achieving high rates of return.

Accumulation of Wealth This is probably the most common reason for using mutual funds. Basically, the investor uses mutual funds over the long haul to build up investment capital. Depending on your goals, a modest amount of risk may be acceptable, but usually preservation of capital and capital stability are considered important. The whole idea is to form a "partnership" with the mutual fund in building up as big a pool of capital as possible: *You provide the capital by systematically investing and reinvesting in the fund, and the fund provides the return by doing its best to invest your resources wisely.*

Storehouse of Value Investors also use mutual funds as a storehouse of value. The idea is to find a place where investment capital can be fairly secure and relatively free from deterioration yet still generate a relatively attractive rate of return. Short- and intermediate-term bond funds are logical choices for such purposes, and so are money funds. Capital preservation and income over the long term are very important to some investors. Others might seek storage of value only for the short term, using, for example, money funds as a place to "sit it out" until a more attractive opportunity comes along.

Speculation and Short-Term Trading Although speculation is becoming more common, it is still not widely used by most mutual fund investors. The reason, of course, is that most mutual funds are long-term in nature and thus not meant to be used as aggressive trading vehicles. However, a growing number of funds (e.g., sector funds) now cater to speculators. Some investors have found that mutual funds are, in fact, attractive for speculation and short-term trading.

One way to do this is to aggressively trade in and out of funds as the investment climate changes. Load charges can be avoided (or reduced) by dealing in families of funds offering low-cost conversion privileges and/or by dealing only in no-load funds. Other investors might choose mutual funds as a long-term investment but seek high rates of return by investing in funds that follow very aggressive trading strategies. These are usually the fairly specialized, smaller funds such as leverage funds, option funds, emerging-market funds, small-cap aggressive growth funds, and sector funds. In essence, investors in such funds are simply letting professional money managers handle their accounts in a way they would like to see them handled: *aggressively.*

The Selection Process

When it comes to mutual funds, there is one question every investor has to answer right up front: Why invest in a mutual fund to begin with—why not "go it alone" by buying individual stocks and bonds directly? For beginning investors and investors with little capital, the answer is simple: With mutual funds, you are able to achieve far more diversification than you could ever obtain on your own. Plus, you get the help of professional money managers at a very reasonable cost. For more seasoned investors, the answers are probably more involved. Certainly, diversification and professional money management come into play, but there are other reasons as well. The competitive returns mutual funds offer are a factor, as are the services they provide. Many seasoned investors simply have decided they can get better returns by carefully selecting mutual funds than by investing on their own. Some of these investors use part of their capital to buy and sell individual securities on their own and use the rest *to buy mutual funds that invest in areas they don't fully understand or don't feel well informed about.* For example, they'll use mutual funds to get into foreign markets, or buy mortgage-backed securities.

Once you have decided to use mutual funds, you must decide which fund(s) to buy. The selection process involves putting into action all you know about mutual funds, in order to gain as much return as possible from an acceptable level of risk. It begins with an assessment of your own investment needs. Obviously, you want to select from those thousands of funds the one or two (or six or eight) that will best meet your total investment needs.

Objectives and Motives for Using Funds The place to start is with your own investment objectives. Why do you want to invest in a mutual fund, and what are you looking for in a fund? Obviously, an attractive rate of return would be desirable, but there is also the matter of a tolerable amount of risk exposure. Probably, when you look at your own risk temperament in relation to the various types of mutual funds available, you will discover that certain types of funds are more appealing to you than others. For instance, aggressive growth or sector funds are usually *not* attractive to individuals who wish to avoid high exposure to risk.

Another important factor is the intended use of the mutual fund. Do you want to invest in mutual funds as a means of accumulating wealth, as a storehouse of value, or to speculate for high rates of return? This information puts into clearer focus the question of what you want to do with your investment dollars. Finally, there is the matter of the services provided by the fund. If you are particularly interested in certain services, be sure to look for them in the funds you select.

What the Funds Offer Just as each individual has a set of investment needs, each fund has its own *investment objective,* its own *manner of operation,* and its own *range of services.* These three parameters are useful in helping you to assess investment alternatives. Where do you find such information? One obvious place is the fund's *profile,* or its prospectus. Publications such as the *Wall Street Journal, Barron's, Money, Fortune,* and *Forbes* also provide a wealth of operating and performance statistics.

There are also a number of reporting services that provide background information and assessments on funds. Among the best in this category are *Morningstar Mutual Funds* (a sample of which is shown in Figure 12.5), and *Value Line Mutual Fund Survey* (which produces a mutual fund report similar to its stock report). There also are all sorts of performance statistics available on the Internet. For example, there are scores of free finance Web sites, like **finance.yahoo.com,** where you can obtain historical information on a fund's performance, security holdings, risk profile, load charges, and purchase information. Or, you can buy, usually at very reasonable prices, quarterly or annually updated software from organizations like Morningstar or the American Association of Individual Investors (AAII).

Whittling Down the Alternatives At this point, fund selection becomes a process of elimination. You can eliminate a large number of funds from consideration simply because they fail to meet stated needs. Some funds may be too risky; others may be unsuitable as a storehouse of value. Thus, rather than trying to evaluate thousands of different funds, you can narrow down the list to two or three *types* of funds that best

FIGURE 12.5 Some Relevant Information About Specific Mutual Funds

Investors who want in-depth information about the operating characteristics, investment holdings, and market behavior of specific mutual funds, such as the Fidelity Low-Priced Stock fund profiled here, can usually find what they're looking for in publications like *Morningstar Mutual Funds* or, as shown here, from computer-based information sources like *Morningstar's Principia*.
(Source: Morningstar, Inc., *Principia*, release date: August 31, 2009.)

Data through August 31, 2009

Fidelity Low-Priced Stock

Ticker	FLPSX	
Status	Open	
Yield	0.5%	
Total Assets	$25,202 mil	
Mstar Category	Mid-Cap Blend	

Governance and Management

Stewardship Grade: B

Portfolio Manager(s)

Joel Tillinghast has managed this fund since its 1989 inception. Not only is he one of the most experienced managers around, he is also one of the best. Tillinghast receives research support from a team of small-cap analysts (both in Boston and in Fidelity's international locations) and from Fidelity's industry analysts, but he does much of the research on his own.

Historical Profile

Return: High
Risk: Average
Rating: ★★★★ Above Avg

Strategy

This fund focuses on companies with share prices of $35 or less, but that is a marketing gimmick. Manager Joel Tillinghast buys mostly smaller-cap fare with reasonable valuations and solid growth prospects. He spreads the portfolio across many hundreds of holdings. Tillinghast is also willing to devote a substantial chunk of the portfolio to foreign issues and larger-cap stocks and will let cash build if he can't find enough good investment opportunities. It does not hedge foreign-currency exposure.

History

	1998	1999	2000	2001	2002	2003	2004	2005	2006	2007	2008	08-09	
NAV	22.85	22.64	23.12	27.42	25.17	34.98	40.25	40.84	43.54	41.13	23.12	29.43	
Total Return %	0.53	5.08	18.83	26.71	-6.18	40.85	22.24	8.65	17.76	3.16	-36.17	27.29	
+/-S&P 500	-28.05	-15.96	27.93	38.60	15.92	12.17	11.36	3.74	1.97	-2.33	0.83	12.32	
+/-S&P 400 TR	-18.59	-9.64	1.32	27.32	8.35	5.23	5.76	-3.91	7.44	-4.82	0.06	4.19	
Income Return %	0.81	0.67	0.75	0.70	0.11	0.08	0.35	0.66	0.84	1.32	0.43	0.00	
Capital Return %	-0.28	4.41	18.08	26.01	-6.29	40.77	21.89	7.99	16.92	1.84	-36.60	27.29	
Total Rtn % Rank Cat	20	44	54	13	8	54	20	56	19	62	29	24	
Income $	0.20	0.15	0.16	0.16	0.03	0.02	0.12	0.26	0.33	0.57	0.17	0.00	
Capital Gains $	1.94	1.19	3.43	1.54	0.54	0.44	2.09	2.62	3.78	3.18	4.11	0.00	
Expense Ratio %	0.95	1.08	0.80	1.00	0.97	1.01	0.97	0.94	0.87	0.96	0.98		
Income Ratio %	1.10	0.52	0.58	0.92	0.34	0.05	0.15	0.57	0.72	1.36	0.68		
Turnover Rate %	47	24	15	44	26	23	28	24	26	11	36		
Net Assets $mil	9,195	6,646	6,834	12,429	15,104	26,725	35,976	36,721	39,340	35,231	18,351	22,770	

Performance 08-31-09

	1st Qtr	2nd Qtr	3rd Qtr	4th Qtr	Total
2005	-0.97	3.11	4.49	1.83	8.65
2006	8.62	-3.27	2.09	9.78	17.76
2007	2.60	6.34	-2.57	-2.94	3.16
2008	-7.63	-0.74	-12.17	-20.73	-36.17
2009	-7.87	21.60			

Trailing	Total Return%	+/- S&P 500	+/- S&P 400 TR	%Rank Cat	Growth of $10,000
3 Mo	13.54	1.87	-0.65	42	11,354
6 Mo	49.77	9.25	2.81	25	14,977
1 Yr	-11.05	7.20	7.12	13	8,895
3 Yr Avg	-2.27	3.51	0.72	16	9,334
5 Yr Avg	4.92	4.43	0.94	8	12,714
10 Yr Avg	10.39	11.18	3.85	2	26,872
15 Yr Avg	12.02	4.84	1.51	2	54,882

Tax Analysis	Tax-Adj Rtn%	%Rank Cat	Tax-Cost Rat	%Rank Cat
3 Yr (estimated)	-3.97	17	1.74	67
5 Yr (estimated)	3.33	10	1.52	63
10 Yr (estimated)	8.79	2	1.45	56

Potential Capital Gain Exposure: 12% of assets

Rating and Risk

Time Period	Load-Adj Return %	Morningstar Rtn vs Cat	Morningstar Risk vs Cat	Morningstar Risk-Adj Rating
1 Yr	-11.05			
3 Yr	-2.27	+Avg	Avg	★★★★
5 Yr	4.92	High	Avg	★★★★
10 Yr	10.39	High	-Avg	★★★★★
Incept	13.92			

Other Measures	Standard Index S&P 500	Best Fit Index Mstar Mid Core
Alpha	5.1	2.2
Beta	1.12	0.92
R-Squared	91	98

Standard Deviation	22.85
Mean	-2.27
Sharpe Ratio	-0.10

Portfolio Analysis 04-30-09

Share change since 01-09 Total Stocks:843

	Sector	PE	Tot Ret%	% Assets
Fidelity Cash Central Fu				9.96
UnitedHealth Group, Inc.	Health	9.7	5.26	3.06
Bed Bath & Beyond, Inc.	Consumer	21.6	43.51	2.77
Safeway Inc.	Consumer	8.9	-19.09	2.40
Oracle Corporation	Software	20.1	23.69	2.26
Metro Inc. A	Consumer	—	—	1.64
D.R. Horton Incorporated	Ind Mtrls	—	90.21	1.54
Hon Hai Precision Ind. C	Goods	—	—	1.22
Walgreen Company	Consumer	16.7	38.80	1.21
Unum Group	Financial	12.9	22.38	1.21
Next PLC	Consumer	—	—	1.16
Ross Stores, Inc.	Consumer	17.1	57.62	1.16
Abercrombie & Fitch Comp	Consumer	19.0	41.48	1.14
Lincare Holdings Inc.	Health	10.6	-2.01	1.12
Coventry Health Care, In	Health	13.6	46.71	1.11
Eni	Energy	—	—	0.94
Omnicom Group, Inc.	Media	12.8	36.03	0.93
Axis Capital Holdings, L	Financial	23.8	6.04	0.90
Yara International ASA	Ind Mtrls	—	—	0.85
Petro-Canada	Energy	—	—	0.84

Current Investment Style

Value Blend Growth

Market Cap %:
- Giant 6.9
- Large 19.3
- Mid 40.5
- Small 24.3
- Micro 9.0

Avg $mil: 2,389

Value Measures		Rel Category
Price/Earnings	10.80	0.78
Price/Book	1.13	0.79
Price/Sales	0.39	0.61
Price/Cash Flow	3.81	0.82
Dividend Yield %	1.84	0.76

Growth Measures	%	Rel Category
Long-Term Erngs	11.64	1.02
Book Value	2.65	11.04
Sales	7.19	0.98
Cash Flow	5.52	0.74
Historical Erngs	-0.81	NMF

Profitability	%	Rel Category
Return on Equity	12.67	1.19
Return on Assets	5.96	1.63
Net Margin	5.57	0.93

Sector Weightings

	% of Stocks	Rel S&P 500	3 Year High	Low
Info	15.10	0.64		
Software	6.94	1.70	7	3
Hardware	4.67	0.45	9	5
Media	1.88	0.77	2	0
Telecom	1.61	0.24	2	0
Service	54.32	1.36		
Health	14.72	1.15	17	9
Consumer	26.78	3.11	27	17
Business	5.94	1.76	10	6
Financial	6.88	0.45	14	7
Mfg	30.59	0.84		
Goods	12.44	1.17	12	7
Ind Mtrls	11.36	1.07	19	10
Energy	6.48	0.56	14	6
Utilities	0.31	0.08	0	0

Composition - Net

- Cash 10.0
- Stocks 89.1
- Bonds 0.0
- Other 0.9

Foreign 28.4 (% of Stock)

Morningstar's Take by Christopher Davis 05-26-09

Fidelity Low-Priced Stock holds appeal if you appreciate its old fashioned ways.

In the old days, portfolio managers ran money with a freer hand. Not confined to a narrow slot of the style box, they invested anywhere they thought they could make money. Manager Joel Tillinghast fits this earlier mold. Tillinghast, who's been at the helm for nearly two decades, employs a value-leaning strategy but invests broadly. To an extent, his wide-ranging approach is a function of the fund's girth; with $20 billion under management, Tillinghast can't limit himself to the smaller names he favored when he first took charge. Though we place his fund in the mid-blend group, his picks pepper the entire style box. Tillinghast isn't restricted by international boundaries, either, with 23% of the fund's assets overseas. The fund's sprawling nature of its 800-plus stock portfolio and its lack of concentration (its top-10 stocks soak up 19% of assets, versus 33% for the average actively managed mid-blend offering) also illustrate his broad-minded approach.

Vast portfolios like this fund's run the risk of becoming bland and marketlike, but that's anything but the case here. Tillinghast's portfolio doesn't overlap much with many of the major market benchmarks, whether it's the small-cap Russell 2000 (also the fund's bogy), the small- and mid-cap Russell 4500, or the large-cap S&P 500. It's offbeat in other respects, too. For instance, the fund is skewed toward health-care and consumer-services stocks. In fact, Tillinghast has been adding to his stake in the latter as consumer-oriented names have sunk. Such stocks now account for 26% of assets, 2.5 times the mid-blend norm.

Tillinghast has succeeded in translating his distinctive strategy into equally exceptional results, as his long-term record trounces his peers as well as the broad market. This fund won't suit investors seeking pure mid-cap exposure, but it should complement large-cap holdings well.

Address:	82 Devonshire Street, Boston, MA 02109, 800-544-9797
Web Address:	www.fidelity.com
Inception:	12-27-89
Advisor:	Fidelity Mgmt & Research Company (FMR)
Subadvisor:	FMR Co., Inc. (FMRC)
NTF Plans:	Fidelity Retail-NTF, CommonWealth NTF

Minimum Purchase:	$2500 Add: $250 IRA: $500
Min Auto Inv Plan:	$2500 Add: $100
Sales Fees:	No-load, 1.50%R
Management Fee:	0.67%
Actual Fees:	Mgt:0.79% Dist: —
Expense Projections:	3Yr:$315 5Yr:$547 10Yr:$1213
Income Distrib:	None

MORNINGSTAR Mutual Funds

match your investment needs. From here, you can whittle down the list a bit more by introducing other constraints. For example, because of cost considerations, you may want to consider only no-load or low-load funds (more on this topic below). Or you may be seeking certain services that are important to your investment goals.

Now we introduce the final element in the selection process: the *fund's investment performance*. Useful information includes:

1. How the fund has performed over the past five to seven years.

2. The type of return it has generated in good markets as well as bad.

3. The level and stability of dividend and capital gains distributions.

4. The amount of volatility/risk in the fund's return.

The dividend and capital gains distribution is an important indication not only of how much current income the fund distributes annually but also of the fund's *tax efficiency*. As a rule, funds that have low dividends and low asset turnover expose their shareholders to less taxes and therefore have higher tax-efficiency ratings. And while you're looking at performance, check out the fund's *fee structure*. Be on guard for funds that charge abnormally high management fees; they can really hurt returns over time.

Another important consideration is *how well a particular fund fits into your portfolio*. If you're trying to follow a certain asset allocation strategy, then be sure to take that into account when you're thinking about adding a fund (or two) to your portfolio. You can easily do that by using the fund categories developed by Morningstar. (For example, look in the upper-right corner of Figure 12.5 and you'll find the "Mstar Category" for Fidelity Low-Priced Stock—it's a mid-cap blend fund.)

Note that in this decision process, considerable weight is given to *past performance*. As a rule, the past is given little or no attention in the investment decision. After all, it's the future that matters. Although the *future performance* of a mutual fund is still the variable that holds the key to success, you should look carefully at past investment results to see how successful the fund's investment managers have been. In essence, the success of a mutual fund rests in large part on the *investment skills of the fund managers*. Therefore, look for consistently good performance, in up as well as down markets, over *extended* periods of time (five years or more). Most important, check whether the same key people are still running the fund. Although past success is no guarantee of future performance, a strong team of money managers can have a significant bearing on the level of fund returns.

Stick with No-Loads or Low-Loads   There's a long-standing "debate" in the mutual fund industry regarding load funds and no-load funds: Do load funds add value? If not, why pay the load charges? As it turns out, empirical results generally do not support the idea that load funds provide added value. Load-fund returns, on average, do not seem to be any better than the returns from no-load funds. In fact, in many cases, the funds with abnormally high loads and 12(b)-1 charges often produce returns that are far less than what you can get from no-load funds. In addition, because of compounding, the differential returns tend to widen with longer holding periods. These results should come as no surprise, because big load charges and/or 12(b)-1 fees reduce your investable capital—and therefore the amount of money you have working for you. In fact, the only way a load fund can overcome this handicap is to produce *superior returns*, which is no easy thing to do, year in and year out. Granted, a handful of load funds have produced very attractive returns over extended periods of time, but they are the exception rather than the rule.

Obviously, it's in your best interest to pay close attention to load charges (and other fees). As a rule, to maximize returns, you should *seriously consider sticking to no-load funds or to low-loads* (funds that have total load charges, including 12(b)-1 fees, of 3% or less). At the very minimum, you should consider a more expensive load fund *only* if it has a much better performance record (and offers more return potential) than a less expensive fund. There may well be times when the higher costs are justified, but far more often than not, you're better off trying to minimize load charges. That should not be difficult to do, because there are literally thousands of no-load and low-load funds from which to choose. What's more, most of the top-performing funds are found in the universe of no-loads or low-loads. So why would you even want to look anywhere else?

Investing in Closed-End Funds

The assets of closed-end funds (CEFs) represent only a fraction of the $9.6 trillion invested in open-end mutual funds. By year-end 2008, there were 646 CEFs, which together held total assets of $188 billion (less than 2% of the amount held by open-end mutual funds). Like open-end funds, CEFs come in a variety of types and styles, including funds that specialize in municipal bonds, taxable bonds, various types of equity securities, and international securities, as well as regional and single-country funds. Historically, unlike the open-end market, bond funds have accounted for the larger share of assets in closed-end funds. In 2008, there was $112 billion worth of bond CEFs assets, or 60 percent of total CEFs assets. Equity CEFs totaled $76 billion in assets for 2008. These proportions have been shifting gradually over time, in part because issuance by equity CEFs has exceeded that by bond CEFs from 2004 through 2008.

Some Key Differences Between Closed-End and Open-End Funds
Because closed-end funds trade like stocks, you must deal with a broker to buy or sell shares, and the usual brokerage commissions apply. Open-end funds, in contrast, are bought from and sold to the fund operators themselves. Another difference between open- and closed-end funds is their liquidity. You can buy and sell relatively large dollar amounts of an open-end mutual fund at its net asset value (NAV) without worrying about affecting the price. However, a relatively large buy or sell order for a CEF could easily bump its price up or down. Like open-end funds, most CEFs offer dividend reinvestment plans, but in many cases, that's about it. CEFs simply don't provide the full range of services that mutual fund investors are accustomed to.

All things considered, probably the most important difference is the way these funds are priced in the marketplace. This *directly affects* investor costs and returns. That is, whereas open-end funds can be bought and sold at NAV (plus any front-end load or minus any redemption charge), CEFs *have two values*—a market value (or stock price) and an NAV. The two are rarely the same, because CEFs typically trade at either a premium or a discount. A *premium* occurs when a fund trades for more than its NAV; a *discount* occurs when it trades for less. As a rule, *CEFs trade at discounts*. In addition to the normal competitive pressures in the marketplace, other factors that can lead to discounts (or premiums) include the fund's *relative performance*, its annual payout or yield, the *name recognition* of the fund's manager, the amount of *illiquid* holdings in the fund's portfolio, and/or the amount of *unrealized* appreciation sitting in the fund's portfolio. The CEFs quotations available at *WSJ.com* are available by exchange listing or fund category. Quotations by fund category report both weekly and daily statistics, including the premiums (+) and discounts (−) on CEFs, along with NAVs and market prices. The 52-week total return is also included. An example of CEFs quotations for the General Equity Funds category appears in Figure 12.6 (on page 476).

FIGURE 12.6 Selected Performance on CEFs

As can be seen here, the market prices of closed-end funds often fall short of the fund's NAV. *Premiums* occur when the fund's (closing) price is greater than its NAV; *discounts* occur when the fund's NAV is greater than its closing price. To find the "PREM/DISC %" as reported in the quotes, simply divide the fund's quoted "Mkt Price" by its quoted "NAV," and then subtract 1.
(Source: WSJ.com, September 10, 2009.)

CLOSED-END FUNDS: General Equity Funds | Return to Major Categories | Return to Expanded Categories | About Closed End Funds

Thursday, September 10, 2009

Fund	Weekly Statistics (as of 9/04/2009)			Daily Statistics (as of 9/10/2009)			52 Week Market Return %
	NAV	Mkt Price	Prem/Disc %	NAV	Mkt Price	Prem/Disc %	
Adams Express Company (ADX)	11.17	9.45	-15.40	11.49	9.73	-15.32	-13.74
Advent/Clay Enhcd G & I (LCM)	11.56	10.33	-10.64	11.81	10.89	-7.79	-7.98
BlackRock Div Achvrs (BDV)	9.04	8.09	-10.51	9.21	8.32	-9.66	-15.57
BlackRock Str Div Achvr (BDT)	9.70	8.35	-13.92	9.98	8.62	-13.63	-16.31
Blue Chip Value Fund (BLU)	3.46	2.85	-17.63	3.58	2.98	-16.76	-24.69
Boulder Growth & Income (BIF)	6.36	5.24	-17.61	N/A	5.26	N/A	-27.39
Boulder Total Return (BTF)	14.09	11.40	-19.09	N/A	11.57	N/A	-29.54
Central Securities Corp (CET)	20.85	16.28	-21.92	N/A	16.80	N/A	-24.41
Claymore Div & Inc (DCS)	14.32	12.88	-10.06	14.85	13.28	-10.57	-72.18
Cohen & Steers CE Oppty (FOF)	11.96	11.13	-6.94	12.29	11.58	-5.78	-11.44
Cohen & Steers Dvd Mjrs (DVM)	11.29	9.31	-17.54	11.66	9.66	-17.15	-33.25
Cornerstone Prog Return (CFP)	6.33	9.27	+46.45	N/A	9.52	N/A	-3.69
Cornerstone Strat Value (CLM)	8.10	12.50	+54.32	N/A	12.65	N/A	6.64
Cornerstone Total Return (CRF)	7.12	11.80	+65.73	N/A	12.70	N/A	-13.11
Defined Strategy Fund (DSF)	11.09	10.96	-1.17	11.12	11.11	-0.09	-16.69
Denali Fund (DNY)	15.07	12.08	-19.84	N/A	12.81	N/A	-23.66
DWS Dreman Val Inc Edge (DHG)	12.70	10.40	-18.11	12.95	10.62	-17.99	-43.96
Eagle Capital Growth (GRF) °	6.20	5.10	-17.74	N/A	5.34	N/A	-19.71
Eaton Vance Tax Div Inc (EVT)	15.26	13.88	-9.04	15.73	14.23	-9.54	-20.01
Engex Inc (EGX)	2.63	2.23	-15.21	N/A	2.16	N/A	-69.91
Equus Total Return (EQS)	8.24	3.18	-61.41	N/A	3.33	N/A	-53.68
Foxby Corp (FXBY)	1.49	1.01	-32.21	1.51	1.01	-33.11	-54.09
Franklin Mutual Rec;A (N/A)	8.71	N/A	N/A	8.89	N/A	N/A	N/A
Franklin Mutual Rec;Adv (N/A)	8.80	N/A	N/A	8.98	N/A	N/A	N/A
Franklin Mutual Rec;B (N/A)	8.56	N/A	N/A	N/A	N/A	N/A	N/A
Franklin Mutual Rec;C (N/A)	8.56	N/A	N/A	8.73	N/A	N/A	N/A
Gabelli Div & Inc Tr (GDV)	13.94	11.34	-18.65	14.56	12.02	-17.45	-22.67
Gabelli Equity Trust (GAB)	4.67	5.00	+7.07	4.91	5.18	5.50	-23.46

The premium or discount on CEFs is calculated as follows:

Equation 12.1

Premium (or discount) = (Share price − NAV)/NAV

Suppose Fund A has an NAV of $10. If its share price is $8, it will sell at a 20% discount. That is,

$$\text{Premium (or discount)} = (\$8 - \$10)/\$10$$
$$= -\$2/\$10 = -0.20 = \underline{-20\%}$$

This negative value indicates that the fund is trading at a *discount* (or below its NAV). On the other hand, if this same fund were priced at $12 per share, it would be trading at a *premium* of 20%—that is, ($12 − $10)/$10 = $2/$10 = 0.20. Because the value is positive, the fund is trading at a premium, above its NAV.

What to Look for in a Closed-End Fund If you know what to look for and your timing and selection are good, you may find that some *deeply discounted CEFs* provide a great way to earn attractive returns. For example, if a fund trades at a 20% discount, you pay only 80 cents for each dollar's worth of assets. If you can buy a fund at an abnormally wide discount (say, more than 10% to 15%) and then sell it when the discount narrows or turns to a premium, you can enhance your overall return. In fact, even if the discount does not narrow, your return will be improved, because the yield on your investment is higher than it would be with an otherwise equivalent open-end fund. The reason: You're investing less money. Here's a simple example. Suppose a CEF trades at $8, a 20% discount from its NAV of $10. If the fund distributed $1 in dividends for the year, it would yield 12.5% ($1 divided by its $8 price). However, if it was a no-load, open-end fund, it would be trading at its higher NAV and therefore would yield only 10% ($1 divided by its $10 NAV). Thus, when investing in CEFs, pay special attention to the size of the premium and discount. In particular, keep your eyes open for funds trading at deep discounts, because that feature alone can enhance potential returns. One final point to keep in mind about closed-end funds: Stay clear of new issues (IPOs) of closed-end funds and funds that sell at steep *premiums*. Never buy new CEFs when they are brought to the market as IPOs. Why? Because IPOs are always brought to the market at *hefty premiums*, which are necessary to cover the underwriter spread. Thus, you face the almost inevitable fate of losing money as the shares fall to a discount, or at the minimum, to their NAVs within a month or two.

For the most part, except for the premium or discount, you should analyze a CEF just like any other mutual fund. That is, check out the fund's expense ratio, portfolio turnover rate, past performance, cash position, and so on. In addition, study the history of the discount. You can find information on closed-end funds in such publications as *Morningstar Closed-End Funds* and *Value Line Investment Survey*. Also, keep in mind that with CEFs, you probably will not get a prospectus (as you might with an open-end fund), because they do not continuously offer new shares to investors.

Measuring Performance

As in any investment decision, return performance is a major dimension in the mutual fund selection process. The level of dividends paid by the fund, its capital gains, and its growth in capital are all-important aspects of return. Such return information enables you to judge the investment behavior of a fund and to appraise its performance in relation to other funds and investment vehicles. Here, we will look at different measures that investors can use to assess mutual fund return. Also, because risk is so important in defining the investment behavior of a fund, we will examine mutual fund risk as well.

Sources of Return An open-end mutual fund has three potential sources of return: (1) dividend income, (2) capital gains distribution, and (3) change in the price (or net asset value) of the fund. Depending on the type of fund, some mutual funds derive more income from one source than from another. For example, we would normally expect income-oriented funds to have much higher dividend income than capital gains distributions.

TABLE 12.2   A Report of Mutual Fund Income and Capital Changes
(For a share outstanding throughout the year)

	2010	2009	2008
1. **Net asset value, beginning of period**	$24.47	$27.03	$24.26
2. **Income from investment operations**			
3. Net investment income	$0.60	$0.66	$0.50
4. Net gains on securities (realized and unrealized)	6.37	(1.74)	3.79
5. Total from investment operations	$6.97	$(1.08)	$4.29
6. **Less distributions:**			
7. Dividends from net investment income	($0.55)	($0.64)	($0.50)
8. Distributions from realized gains	(1.75)	(.84)	(1.02)
9. Total distributions	$(2.30)	$(1.48)	$(1.52)
10. **Net asset value, end of period**	$29.14	$24.47	$27.03
11. **Total return**	28.48%	(4.00%)	17.68%
12. **Ratios/supplemental data**			
13. Net assets, end of period ($000)	$307,951	$153,378	$108,904
14. Ratio of expenses to average net assets	1.04%	0.85%	0.94%
15. Ratio of net investment income to average net assets	1.47%	2.56%	2.39%
16. Portfolio turnover rate*	85%	144%	74%

*Portfolio turnover rate relates the number of shares bought and sold by the fund to the total number of shares held in the fund's portfolio. A high turnover rate (in excess of 100%) means the fund has been doing a lot of trading.

Open-end mutual funds regularly publish reports that recap investment performance. One such report is the *Summary of Income and Capital Changes,* an example of which appears in Table 12.2. This statement, found in the fund's profile or prospectus, gives a brief overview of the fund's investment activity, including expense ratios and portfolio turnover rates. Of interest to us here is the top part of the report (which runs from "Net asset value, beginning of period" to "Net asset value, end of period"—lines 1 to 10). This part reveals the amount of dividend income and capital gains distributed to the shareholders, along with any change in the fund's net asset value.

Dividend income (see line 7 of Table 12.2) is derived from the dividend and interest income earned on the security holdings of the mutual fund. It is paid out of the *net investment income* that's left after the fund has met all operating expenses. When the fund receives dividend or interest payments, it passes these on to shareholders in the form of dividend payments. The fund accumulates all of the current income for the period and then pays it out on a prorated basis. Thus, if a fund earned, say, $2 million in dividends and interest in a given year and if that fund had one million shares outstanding, each share would receive an annual dividend payment of $2. Because the mutual fund itself is tax exempt, any taxes due on dividend earnings are payable by the individual investor. For funds that are not held in tax-deferred accounts, like IRAs or 401(k)s, the amount of taxes due on dividends will depend on the source of such dividends. That is, *if these distributions are derived from dividends earned on the fund's common stock holdings, then they are subject to a preferential tax rate of 15%, or less.* However, if these distributions are derived from interest earnings on bonds, dividends from REITs, or dividends from most types of preferred stocks, then such dividends *do not qualify for the preferential tax treatment,* and instead are taxed as ordinary income.

Capital gains distributions (see line 8) work on the same principle, except that these payments are derived from the *capital gains actually earned* by the fund. It works like this: Suppose the fund bought some stock a year ago for $50 and sold that stock in the current period for $75 per share. Clearly, the fund has achieved capital gains of $25 per share. If it held 50,000 shares of this stock, it would have realized a total capital gain of $1,250,000 ($25 × 50,000 = $1,250,000). Given that the fund has one million shares outstanding, each share is entitled to $1.25 in the form of a capital gains distribution. (From a tax perspective, if the capital gains are long-term in nature, then they qualify for the preferential tax rate of 15%, or less; if not, then they're treated as ordinary income.) Note that these (capital gains) distributions apply only to *realized* capital gains (that is, the security holdings were actually sold and the capital gains actually earned).

Unrealized capital gains (or **paper profits**) are what make up the third and final element of a mutual fund's return. When the fund's holdings go up or down in price, the net asset value of the fund moves accordingly. Suppose an investor buys into a fund at $10 per share and sometime later the fund's NAV is quoted at $12.50. The difference of $2.50 per share is the unrealized capital gains. It represents the profit that shareholders would receive (and are entitled to) if the fund were to sell its holdings. (Actually, as Table 12.2 shows, some of the change in net asset value can also be made up of undistributed income.)

For *closed-end* investment companies, the return is derived from the same three sources as that for open-end funds, and from a *fourth source* as well: changes in price discounts or premiums. But because the discount or premium is already embedded in the share price of a fund, for a closed-end fund, the third element of return—change in share price—is made up not only of change in net asset value but also of change in price discount or premium.

What About Future Performance? There's no doubt that a statement like the one in Table 12.2 provides a convenient recap of a fund's past behavior. Looking at past performance is useful, but it does not tell you what the future will be. Ideally, you want an indication of what the same three elements of return—dividend income, capital gains distribution, and change in NAV—*will be*. But it's extremely difficult—if not impossible—to get a firm grip on what the future holds in dividends, capital gains, and NAV. That's because a mutual fund's future performance is directly linked to the *future make-up of the securities in its portfolio,* something that is next to impossible to get a clear reading on. It's not like evaluating the expected performance of a share of stock, in which case you're keying in on just one company. With mutual funds, investment performance depends on the behavior of many different stocks and bonds.

Where, then, can you look for insight into future performance? Most market observers suggest that the first place to look is the market itself. In particular, try to get a fix on the future direction of *the market as a whole.* The behavior of a well-diversified mutual fund tends to reflect the general tone of the market. Thus, if the market is expected to drift up, so should the performance of mutual funds. Also spend some time evaluating the *track records* of mutual funds in which you are interested. Past performance has a lot to say about the investment skills of the fund's money managers.

Measures of Return A simple but effective measure of performance is to describe mutual fund return in terms of the three major sources noted above: dividends earned, capital gains distributions received, and change in price. When dealing with investment horizons of one year or less, we can convert these fund payoffs into a return figure by using the standard holding period return (HPR) formula. The computations necessary are illustrated following using the 2010 figures from Table 12.2. In 2010, this hypothetical no-load, open-end fund paid 55 cents per share in dividends and another $1.75 in capital gains distributions. It had a price at the beginning of the year of $24.47 that rose to $29.14 by the end of the year. Thus, summarizing this investment performance, we have

Price (NAV) at the *beginning* of the year (line 1)	$24.47
Price (NAV) at the *end* of the year (line 10)	29.14
Net increase	$ 4.67
Return for the year:	
Dividends received (line 7)	$ 0.55
Capital gains distributions (line 8)	1.75
Net increase in price (NAV)	4.67
Total return	$ 6.97
Holding period return (HPR)	**28.48%**
(Total return/beginning price)	

This HPR measure is comparable to the procedure used by the fund industry to report annual returns: This same value can be seen in Table 12.2, line 11, which shows the fund's "Total return." It not only captures all the important elements of mutual fund return but also provides a handy indication of yield. Note that the fund had a total dollar return of $6.97, and on the basis of a beginning investment of $24.47, the fund produced an annual return of nearly 28.5%.

HPR with Reinvested Dividends and Capital Gains Many mutual fund investors have their dividends and/or capital gains distributions reinvested in the fund. How do you measure return when you receive your (dividend/capital gains) payout in additional shares of stock rather than cash? With slight modifications, you can continue to use holding period return. The only difference is that you have to keep track of the number of shares acquired through reinvestment.

To illustrate, let's continue with the example above. Assume that you initially bought 200 shares in the mutual fund and also that you were able to acquire shares through the fund's reinvestment program at an average price of $26.50 a share. Thus, the $460 in dividends and capital gains distributions [($.55 + $1.75) × 200] provided you with another 17.36 shares in the fund ($460/$26.50). Holding period return under these circumstances would relate the market value of the stock holdings at the beginning of the period with the holdings at the end:

Equation 12.2

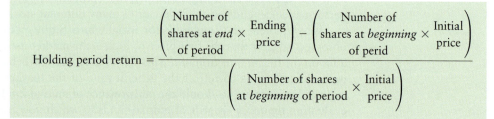

$$\text{Holding period return} = \frac{\left(\begin{array}{c}\text{Number of}\\ \text{shares at } \textit{end} \times \\ \text{of period}\end{array}\begin{array}{c}\text{Ending}\\ \text{price}\end{array}\right) - \left(\begin{array}{c}\text{Number of}\\ \text{shares at } \textit{beginning} \times \\ \text{of perid}\end{array}\begin{array}{c}\text{Initial}\\ \text{price}\end{array}\right)}{\left(\begin{array}{c}\text{Number of shares}\\ \text{at } \textit{beginning} \text{ of period}\end{array} \times \begin{array}{c}\text{Initial}\\ \text{price}\end{array}\right)}$$

Thus, the holding period return on this investment would be

$$\text{Holding period return} = \frac{(217.36 \times \$29.14) - (200 \times \$24.47)}{(200 \times \$24.47)}$$

$$= \frac{(\$6,333.87) - (\$4,894.00)}{(\$4,894.00)} = \underline{\underline{29.4\%}}$$

This holding period return, like the preceding one, provides a rate-of-return measure that you can use to compare the performance of this fund to those of other funds and investment vehicles.

Measuring Long-Term Returns Rather than using one-year holding periods, it is sometimes necessary to assess the performance of mutual funds over extended periods of time. In these cases, holding period return as a measure of performance would be inappropriate, because it ignores the time value of money. Instead, when faced with multiple-year investment horizons, we can use the present-value-based *internal rate of return* (IRR) procedure to determine the fund's average annual compound rate of return.

To illustrate, refer once again to Table 12.2. Assume that this time we want to find the annual rate of return over the full three-year period (2008 through 2010). We see that the mutual fund had the following annual dividends and capital gains distributions:

Item	2010	2009	2008
Annual dividends paid	$0.55	$0.64	$0.50
Annual capital gains distributed	$1.75	$0.84	$1.02
Total distributions	$2.30	$1.48	$1.52

Given that the fund had a price of $24.26 at the beginning of the period (1/1/08) and was trading at $29.14 at the end of 2010 (three years later), we have the following time line of cash flows:

	Subsequent Cash Flows		
Initial Cash Flow	Year 1	Year 2	Year 3
$24.26 (Beginning Price)	$1.52 (Distributions)	$1.48 (Distributions)	$2.30 + $29.14 (Distributions + Ending Price)

We want to find the discount rate that will equate the annual dividends/capital gains distributions *and* the ending price in year 3 to the beginning (2008) price of the fund ($24.26).

Using standard present-value calculations, we find that the mutual fund in Table 12.2 provided an annual rate of return of 13.1% over the three-year period. That is, at 13.1%, the present value of the cash flows in years 1, 2, and 3 equals the beginning price of the fund ($24.26). Such information helps us assess fund performance and compare the return performance of various investment vehicles.

According to SEC regulations, if mutual funds report historical return behavior, they must do so in a standardized format that employs fully compounded, total-return figures similar to those obtained from the above present value-based measure of return. The funds are not required to report such information, but if they do cite performance in their promotional material, they must follow a full-disclosure manner of presentation that takes into account not only dividends and capital gains distributions but also any increases or decreases in the fund's NAV that have occurred over the preceding one-, three-, five-, and 10-year periods.

Returns on Closed-End Funds The returns of CEFs have traditionally been reported on the basis of their NAVs. That is, *price premiums and discounts were ignored when computing return measures.* However, it is becoming increasingly common to see return performance expressed in terms of *actual market prices,* a practice that captures the impact of changing market premiums or discounts on holding period returns. As you might expect, the greater the premiums or discounts and the greater the changes in these values over time, the greater their impact on reported returns. It's not at all uncommon for CEFs to have different market-based and NAV-based holding period returns. Using NAVs, you find the returns on CEFs in exactly the same way as you do the returns on open-end funds. In contrast, when using actual market prices to measure return, all you need do *is substitute the market price of the fund* (with its embedded premium or discount) *for the corresponding NAV in the holding period or internal rate of return* measures.

Some CEF investors like to run *both* NAV-based and market-based measures of return to see how changing premiums (or discounts) have affected the returns on their mutual fund holdings. Even so, as a rule, NAV-based return numbers are generally viewed as the preferred measures of performance. Because fund managers often have little or no control over changes in premiums or discounts, NAV-based measures are felt to give a truer picture of the performance of the fund itself.

The Matter of Risk   Because most mutual funds are so diversified, their investors are largely immune to the business and financial risks normally present with individual securities. Even with extensive diversification, however, most funds are still exposed to a considerable amount of *market risk*. In fact, because mutual fund portfolios are so well diversified, they often tend to perform very much like the market—or like the segment of the market that the fund targets. Although a few funds, like gold funds, tend to be defensive (countercyclical), market risk is still an important ingredient for most types of mutual funds, both open- and closed-end. You should be aware of the effect the general market has on the investment performance of a mutual fund. For example, if the market is trending downward and you anticipate that trend to continue, it might be best to place any new investment capital into something like a money fund until the market reverses itself.

Another important risk consideration revolves around *the management practices of the fund itself*. If the portfolio is managed conservatively, the risk of a loss in capital is likely to be much less than that for aggressively managed funds. Alternatively, the more speculative are the investment goals of the fund the greater the risk of instability in the net asset value. But, a conservatively managed portfolio does not eliminate all price volatility. The securities in the portfolio are still subject to inflation, interest rate, and general market risks. However, these risks are generally less with funds whose investment objectives and portfolio management practices are more conservative.

CONCEPTS IN REVIEW

Answers available at
www.pearsonhighered.com/
gitman

12.12   How important is the general behavior of the market in affecting the price performance of mutual funds? Explain. Why is a fund's past performance important to the mutual fund selection process? Does the future behavior of the market matter in the selection process? Explain.

12.13   What is the major/dominant type of closed-end fund? How do CEFs differ from open-end funds?

12.14   Identify three potential sources of return to mutual fund investors and briefly discuss how each could affect total return to shareholders. Explain how the discount or premium of a closed-end fund can also be treated as a return to investors.

12.15   Discuss the various types of risk to which mutual fund shareholders are exposed. What is the major risk exposure of mutual funds? Are all funds subject to the same level of risk? Explain.

myfinancelab	Here is what you should know after reading this chapter. **MyFinanceLab** will help you identify what you know, and where to go when you need to practice.	

What You Should Know	Key Terms	Where To Practice
LG1 Describe the basic features of mutual funds and note what they have to offer as investments. Mutual fund shares represent ownership in a diversified, professionally managed portfolio of securities. Many investors who lack the time, know-how, or commitment to manage their own money turn to mutual funds. Mutual funds' shareholders benefit from a level of diversification and investment performance they might otherwise find difficult to achieve. They also can invest with a limited amount of capital and can obtain investor services not available elsewhere.	management fee, *p. 447* mutual fund, *p. 445* pooled diversification, *p. 446*	MyFinanceLab Study Plan 12.1
LG2 Distinguish between open- and closed-end funds, as well as other types of professionally managed investment companies, and discuss the various types of fund loads, fees, and charges. Open-end funds have no limit on the number of shares they may issue. Closed-end funds have a fixed number of shares outstanding and trade in the secondary markets like shares of common stock. Exchange-traded funds (ETFs) possess characteristics of both open-end and closed-end funds. Other types of investment companies are unit investment trusts, hedge funds (private, unregulated investment vehicles available to institutional and high-net-worth individuals), REITs (which invest in various types of real estate), and variable annuities. Mutual fund investors face an array of loads, fees, and charges, including front-end loads, back-end loads, annual 12(b)-1 charges, and annual management fees. Some of these costs are one-time charges (e.g., front-end loads). Others are paid annually (e.g., 12(b)-1 and management fees). Investors should understand fund costs, which can drag down fund performance and return.	back-end load, *p. 453* closed-end investment company, *p. 450* exchange-traded fund (ETF), *p. 452* hedge fund, *p. 459* load fund, *p. 453* low-load fund, *p. 453* net asset value (NAV), *p. 450* no-load fund, *p. 453* open-end investment company, *p. 450* real estate investment trust (REIT), *p. 458* 12(b)-1 fee, *p. 454*	MyFinanceLab Study Plan 12.2
LG3 Discuss the types of funds available and the variety of investment objectives these funds seek to fulfill. Each fund has an established investment objective that determines its investment policy and identifies it as a certain type of fund. Some popular types of funds are growth, aggressive-growth, value, equity-income, balanced, growth-and-income, asset allocation, index, bond, money, sector, socially responsible, and international funds. The different categories of funds have different risk-return characteristics.	asset allocation fund, *p. 466* aggressive-growth fund, *p. 461* automatic investment plan, *p. 467* automatic reinvestment plan, *p. 468* balanced fund, *p. 462* bond fund, *p. 462* conversion (exchange) privilege, *p. 469* equity-income fund, *p. 462* fund families, *p. 469*	MyFinanceLab Study Plan 12.3
LG4 Discuss the investor services offered by mutual funds and how these services can fit into an investment program. Mutual funds also offer special services, such as automatic		MyFinanceLab Study Plan 12.4

What You Should Know	Key Terms	Where To Practice
investment and reinvestment plans, systematic withdrawal programs, low-cost conversion and phone-switching privileges, and retirement programs.	growth-and-income fund, *p. 462* growth fund, *p. 461* index fund, *p. 464*	
LG5 Describe the investor uses of mutual funds along with the variables to consider when assessing and selecting funds for investment purposes. Investors can use mutual funds to accumulate wealth, as a storehouse of value, or as a vehicle for speculation and short-term trading. Fund selection generally starts by assessing the investor's needs and wants. The next step is to consider what the funds have to offer with regard to investment objectives, risk exposure, and investor services. The investor then narrows the alternatives by aligning his or her needs with the types of funds available and, from this short list of funds, applies the final selection tests: fund performance and cost.	international fund, *p. 466* money market mutual fund (money fund), *p. 464* sector fund, *p. 465* socially responsible fund, *p. 465* systematic withdrawal plan, *p. 469* value fund, *p. 461*	MyFinanceLab Study Plan 12.5
LG6 Identify the sources of return and compute the rate of return earned on a mutual fund investment. The payoff from investing in a mutual fund includes dividend income, distribution of realized capital gains, growth in capital (unrealized capital gains), and—for closed-end funds—the change in premium or discount. Various measures of return recognize these elements and provide simple yet effective ways of gauging the annual rate of return from a mutual fund. Risk is also important to mutual fund investors. A fund's extensive diversification may protect investors from business and financial risks, but considerable market risk still remains because most funds tend to perform much like the market, or like that segment of the market in which they specialize.	capital gains distributions, *p. 478* dividend income, *p. 478* unrealized capital gains (paper profits), *p. 479*	MyFinanceLab Study Plan 12.6 Video Learning Aid for Problems P12.11, P12.16

Log into **MyFinanceLab**, take a chapter test, and get a personalized Study Plan that tells you which concepts you understand and which ones you need to review. From there, **MyFinanceLab** will give you further practice, tutorials, animations, videos, and guided solutions.
Log into www.myfinancelab.com

Discussion Questions

LG1 LG2   Q12.1 Contrast *mutual fund ownership with direct investment in stocks and bonds.* Assume your class is going to debate the merits of investing through mutual funds versus investing directly in stocks and bonds. Develop some arguments on each side of this debate and be prepared to discuss them in class. If you had to choose one side to be on, which would it be? Why?

LG2 **Q12.2** Based on the mutual fund quotes in Figure 12.3, answer the questions listed below for each of the following 5 funds:
- (1) Quaker Funds (MdCpValA)
- (2) Quaker Funds (StrGwthC)
- (3) Quantitative Group (EmgMkts)
- (4) Quantitative Group (ForeignValO)
- (5) Quantitative Group (Lg/ShtOrdy)

Based on the information reported in Figure 12.3:
- a. How much would you receive for each fund if you were selling them?
- b. Which of the five listed funds have 12(b)-1 fees?
- c. Do any of the funds have both 12(b)-1 and redemption fees?
- d. Can you tell whether any of the funds are true no-loads?
- e. Which fund has the highest front-end load?
- f. Which fund has the highest year-to-date return? Which has the lowest?

LG3 **Q12.3** For each pair of funds listed below, select the one that is likely to be the *less* risky. Briefly explain your answer.
- a. Growth versus growth-and-income funds
- b. Equity-income versus high-grade corporate bond funds
- c. Balanced versus sector funds
- d. Global versus value funds
- e. Intermediate-term bonds versus high-yield municipal bond funds

LG2 LG3 **Q12.4** Describe an ETF and explain how these funds combine the characteristics of both open-end and closed-end funds. Consider the Vanguard family of funds. Which of its funds most closely resembles a "spider" (SPDR)? In what respects are the Vanguard fund (that you selected) and spiders the same? How are they different? If you could invest in only one of them, which would it be? Explain.

LG2 LG6 **Q12.5** In the absence of any load charges, open-end mutual funds are priced at (or very close to) their net asset values, whereas closed-end funds rarely trade at their NAVs. Explain why one type of fund would normally trade at its NAV while the other type (CEFs) usually does not. What are price premiums and discounts and in what segment of the mutual fund market will you usually find them? Look online at *WSJ.com*, and find five funds that trade at a discount and five funds that trade at a premium. List all 10 of them, including the sizes of their respective discounts and premiums. What's the biggest price discount you could find? How about the biggest price premium? What would cause a fund to trade at a discount? At a premium?

LG3 LG5 **Q12.6** Imagine that you've just inherited $20,000. Now you're faced with the "problem" of how to spend it. You could make a down payment on a condo or on that sports car you've always wanted. Or you could build a mutual fund portfolio. After some soul-searching, you decide to build a $20,000 mutual fund portfolio. Using actual mutual funds and actual quoted prices, come up with a plan to invest as much of the $20,000 as you can in a portfolio of mutual funds. (In addition to one or more open-end funds, include at least one CEF *or* one ETF.) Be specific! Briefly describe your planned portfolio, including the investment objectives you are trying to achieve.

Problems

All problems are available on **www.myfinancelab.com**

LG6 **P12.1** A year ago, an investor bought 200 shares of a mutual fund at $8.50 per share. Over the past year, the fund has paid dividends of $0.90 per share and had a capital gains distribution of $0.75 per share.
- a. Find the investor's holding period return, given that this no-load fund now has a net asset value of $9.10.

b. Find the holding period return, assuming all the dividends and capital gains distributions are reinvested into additional shares of the fund at an average price of $8.75 per share.

 P12.2 A year ago, the Really Big Growth Fund was being quoted at an NAV of $21.50 and an offer price of $23.35. Today, it's being quoted at $23.04 (NAV) and $25.04 (offer). What is the holding period return on this load fund, given that it was purchased a year ago and that its dividends and capital gains distributions over the year have totaled $1.05 per share? (*Hint:* You, as an investor, buy fund shares at the offer price and sell at the NAV.)

 P12.3 The All-State Mutual Fund has the following five-year record of performance:

	2010	2009	2008	2007	2006
Net investment income	$0.98	$0.85	$0.84	$0.75	$0.64
Dividends from net investment income	(0.95)	(0.85)	(0.85)	(0.75)	(0.60)
Net realized and unrealized gains (or losses) on security transactions	4.22	5.08	(2.18)	2.65	(1.05)
Distributions from realized gains	(1.06)	(1.00)	—	(1.00)	—
Net increase (decrease) in NAV	$3.20	$4.08	($2.19)	$1.65	($1.01)
NAV at beginning of year	$12.53	8.45	10.64	8.99	10.00
NAV at end of year	$15.73	$12.53	$8.45	$10.64	$8.99

Find this no-load fund's five-year (2006–2010) average annual compound rate of return. Also find its three-year (2008–2010) average annual compound rate of return. If an investor bought the fund in 2006 at $10.00 a share and sold it five years later (in 2010) at $15.73, how much total profit per share would she have made over the five-year holding period?

 P12.4 You've uncovered the following per-share information about a certain mutual fund:

	2009	2010	2011
Ending share prices:			
Offer	$46.20	$64.68	$61.78
NAV	43.20	60.47	57.75
Dividend income	2.10	2.84	2.61
Capital gains distribution	1.83	6.26	4.32
Beginning share prices:			
Offer	55.00	46.20	64.68
NAV	51.42	43.20	60.47

On the basis of this information, find the fund's holding period return for 2009, 2010, and 2011. (In all three cases, assume you buy the fund at the beginning of the year and sell it at the end of each year.) In addition, find the fund's average annual compound rate of return over the three-year period, 2009–2011. What would the 2010 holding period return have been if the investor had initially bought 500 shares of stock and reinvested both dividends and capital gains distributions into additional shares of the fund at an average price of $52.50 per share?

P12.5 Listed below is the 10-year, per-share performance record of Larry, Moe, & Curley's Growth Fund, as obtained from the fund's May 30, 2011, prospectus:

					Years Ended March 31					
	2011	2010	2009	2008	2007	2006	2005	2004	2003	2002
1. Net asset value, beginning of period	$58.60	$52.92	$44.10	$59.85	$55.34	$37.69	$35.21	$34.25	$19.68	$29.82
2. Income from investment operations:										
3. Net investment income	$ 1.39	$ 1.35	$ 1.09	$ 0.63	$ 0.42	$ 0.49	$ 0.79	$ 0.37	$ 0.33	$ 0.38
4. Net gains on securities	8.10	9.39	8.63	(6.64)	11.39	19.59	5.75	2.73	15.80	(0.36)
5. Total from investment	9.49	10.74	9.72	(6.01)	11.81	20.08	6.54	3.10	16.13	0.36
6. Less distributions:										
7. Dividends from net	($ 0.83)	($ 1.24)	($ 0.90)	($ 0.72)	($ 0.46)	($ 0.65)	($ 0.37)	($ 0.26)	($ 0.33)	($ 0.58)
8. Distributions from realized gains	(2.42)	(3.82)	—	(9.02)	(6.84)	(1.78)	(3.69)	(1.88)	(1.23)	(9.92)
9. Total distributions	(3.25)	(5.06)	(0.90)	(9.74)	(7.30)	(2.43)	(4.06)	(2.14)	(1.56)	(10.50)
10. Net asset value, end of period	$64.84	$58.60	$52.92	$44.10	$59.85	$55.34	$37.69	$35.21	$34.25	$19.68

Use this information to find LM&C's holding period return in 2011 and 2008. Also find the fund's rate of return over the five-year period 2007–2011, and the 10-year period 2002–2011. Finally, rework the four return figures, assuming the LM&C fund has a front-end load charge of 3% (of NAV). Comment on the impact of load charges on the return behavior of mutual funds.

 P12.6 Using the resources available at your campus or public library (or those available on the Internet), select five mutual funds—a growth fund, an equity-income fund, an international (stock) fund, an index fund, and a high-yield corporate bond fund—that you feel would make good investments. Briefly explain why you selected these funds. List the funds' holding period returns for the past year and their annual compound rates of return for the past 3 years. (Use a schedule like the one in Table 12.2 to show relevant performance figures.)

P12.7 One year ago, Super Star Closed-End Fund had an NAV of $10.40 and was selling at an 18% discount. Today, its NAV is $11.69 and it is priced at a 4% premium. During the year, Super Star paid dividends of $0.40 and had a capital gains distribution of $0.95. On the basis of the above information, calculate each of the following:
   a. Super Star's NAV-based holding period return for the year.
   b. Super Star's market-based holding period return for the year. Did the market premium/discount hurt or add value to the investor's return? Explain.
   c. Repeat the market-based holding period return calculation, except this time assume the fund started the year at an 18% *premium* and ended it at a 4% *discount*. (Assume the beginning and ending NAVs remain at $10.40 and $11.69, respectively.) Is there any change in this measure of return? Why?

P12.8 The Well Managed Closed-End Fund turned in the following performance for the year 2010.

Item	Beginning of the Year	End of the Year
NAV	$7.50	$9.25
Market price of the fund shares	$7.75	$9.00
Dividends paid over the year	—	$1.20
Capital gains distributed over the year	—	$0.90

a. Based on this information, what was the NAV-based HPR for the WMCEF in 2010?

b. Find the percentage (%) premium or discount at which the fund was trading at the beginning of the year and at the end of the year.

c. What was the market-based HPR for the fund in 2010? Did the market premium or discount add to or hurt the holding period return on this CEF? Explain.

LG6　**P12.9**　Three years ago, you invested in the Future Investco Mutual Fund by purchasing 1,000 shares of the fund at a net asset value of $20.00 per share. Because you did not need the income, you elected to reinvest all dividends and capital gains distributions. Today, you sell your 1,100 shares in this fund for $22.91 per share. What is the compounded rate of return on this investment over the three-year period?

LG6　**P12.10**　Refer to Problem 12.9 above. If there were a 3% load on this fund, assuming you purchased the same number of shares, what would your rate of return be?

LG6　**P.12.11**　You invested in the no-load OhYes Mutual Fund one year ago by purchasing 1,000 shares of the fund at the net asset value of $25.00 per share. The fund distributed dividends of $1.50 and capital gains of $2.00. Today, the NAV is $26. What was your holding period return?

LG6　**P12.12**　Refer to Problem 12.11 above. If OhYes was a load fund with a 2% front end load, what would be the HPR?

LG6　**P12.13**　Refer to Figure 12.6 (on page 476). You purchased shares of AdamsExp (**ADX**) at the end of the day quoted. Assume ADX paid out a total dividend and capital gains distribution of $1.10 for the year, and at the end of the year the fund is quoted as having a NAV of $18.50 and a close of $16.25. What is your holding period return?

LG6　**P12.14**　Refer to Problem 12.13 above. Now assume that you hold your shares of AdamsExp for three years. Each year you receive the same dividend, and at the end of year 3, the fund has a NAV of $18.50 and a close of $19.05. What is the compound annual rate of return for the three-year period?

LG6　**P12.15**　You are considering the purchase of shares in a closed end-mutual fund. The NAV is equal to $22.50 and the latest close is $20.00. Is this fund trading at a premium or a discount? How big is the premium or discount?

LG6　**P12.16**　You purchased 1,000 shares of MutualMagic one year ago for $20.00 per share. During the year, you received $2.00 in dividends, half of which were from dividends on stock the fund held and half of which was from interest earned on bonds in the fund portfolio. Assuming your federal marginal tax rate is 25%, how much will you owe in federal taxes on the distributions you received this year? (Your answer should be in dollars.)

Visit **www.myfinancelab.com** for web exercises, spreadsheets, and other online resources.

Case Problem 12.1   *Reverend Mark Thomas Ponders Mutual Funds*

LG3 LG5　Reverend Mark Thomas is the minister of a church in the San Diego area. He is married, has one young child, and earns a "modest income." Because religious organizations are not notorious for their generous retirement programs, the reverend has decided he should do some investing on his own. He would like to set up a program that enables him to supplement the church's retirement program and at the same time provide some funds for his child's college education (which is still some 12 years away). He is not out to break any investment records but wants some backup to provide for the long-run needs of his family.

Although he has a modest income, Mark Thomas believes that with careful planning, he can probably invest about $250 a quarter (and, with luck, increase this amount over time). He currently has about $15,000 in a savings account that he would be willing to use to begin this program. In view of his investment objectives, he is not interested in taking a lot of risk. Because his knowledge of investments extends to savings accounts, Series EE savings bonds, and a little bit about mutual funds, he approaches you for some investment advice.

Questions

a. In light of Reverend Mark Thomas' long-term investment goals, do you think mutual funds are an appropriate investment vehicle for him?

b. Do you think he should use his $15,000 savings to start a mutual fund investment program?

c. What type of mutual fund investment program would you set up for the reverend? Include in your answer some discussion of the types of funds you would consider, the investment objectives you would set, and any investment services (e.g., withdrawal plans) you would seek. Would taxes be an important consideration in your investment advice? Explain.

Case Problem 12.2   *Calvin Jacobs Seeks the Good Life*

LG3 LG4 Calvin Jacobs is a widower who recently retired after a long career with a major Midwestern manufacturer. Beginning as a skilled craftsman, he worked his way up to the level of shop supervisor over a period of more than 30 years with the firm. Calvin receives Social Security benefits and a generous company pension. Together, these two sources amount to over $4,500 per month (part of which is tax-free). The Jacobs had no children, so he lives alone. Calvin owns a two-bedroom rental house that is next to his home, and the rental income from it covers the mortgage payments for both the rental house and his house.

Over the years, Calvin and his late wife, Allie, always tried to put a little money aside each month. The results have been nothing short of phenomenal. The value of Calvin's liquid investments (all held in bank CDs and savings accounts) runs well into the six figures. Up to now, Calvin has just let his money grow and has not used any of his savings to supplement his Social Security, pension, and rental income. But things are about to change. Calvin has decided, "What the heck, it's time I start living the good life!" Calvin wants to travel and, in effect, start reaping the benefits of his labors. He has therefore decided to move $100,000 from one of his savings accounts to one or two high-yielding mutual funds. He would like to receive $1,000–$1,500 a month from the fund(s) for as long as possible, because he plans to be around for a long time.

Questions

a. Given Calvin's financial resources and investment objectives, what kinds of mutual funds do you think he should consider?

b. What factors in Calvin's situation should be taken into consideration in the fund selection process? How might these affect Calvin's course of action?

c. What types of services do you think he should look for in a mutual fund?

d. Assume Calvin invests in a mutual fund that earns about 10% annually from dividend income and capital gains. Given that Calvin wants to receive $1,000 to $1,500 a month from his mutual fund, what would be the size of his investment account five years from now? How large would the account be if the fund earned 15% on average and everything else remained the same? How important is the fund's rate of return to Calvin's investment situation? Explain.

Excel with Spreadsheets

In the *Wall Street Journal*, open-end mutual funds are listed separately from other securities. They have their own quotation system where two primary data variables are the net asset value (NAV) and the year-to-date returns. The NAV represents the price you get when you sell shares, or what you pay when you buy no-load funds.

Create a spreadsheet model similar to the spreadsheet for Table 12.2 (on page 478), which you can view at www.myfinancelab.com, to analyze the following three years of data relating to the MoMoney Mutual Fund. It should report the amount of dividend income and capital gains distributed to the shareholders, along with any other changes in the fund's net asset value.

	A	B	C	D	E
1		**2010**	**2009**	**2008**	
2	NAV (beginning of period)	$ 35.24	$ 37.50	$ 36.25	
3	Net investment income	$ 0.65	$ 0.75	$ 0.60	
4	Net gains on securities	$ 5.25	$ 4.75	$ (3.75)	
5	Dividends from net investment income	$ 0.61	$ 0.57	$ 0.52	
6	Distributions from realized gains	$ 1.75	$ 2.01	$ 1.55	
7					

Questions

a. What is the total income from the investment operations?

b. What are the total distributions from the investment operations?

c. Calculate the net asset value for MoMoney Fund as of the end of the years 2010, 2009, and 2008.

d. Calculate the holding period returns for each of the years 2010, 2009, and 2008.

Chapter-Opening Problem

Go to Yahoo! Finance and look up data on the Vanguard 500 Index Investor fund (ticker symbol VFINX) and the Fidelity Magellan Fund (ticker symbol FMAGX). These are two of the largest mutual funds in the United States. Pick one of these funds and click the "basic chart" link to see how it has performed over the last five years. With that chart open, enter the ticker symbol of the other fund into the box that allows you to plot another fund's performance on the same chart. Which of these two funds has performed better in recent years? Click the "holdings" link to see the top 10 holdings of each fund. Do any of the same stocks appear in the top 10 lists of both funds?

CHAPTER 13

Managing Your Own Portfolio

LEARNING GOALS

After studying this chapter, you should be able to:

LG1 Explain how to use an asset allocation scheme to construct a portfolio consistent with investor objectives.

LG2 Discuss the data and indexes needed to measure and compare investment performance.

LG3 Understand the techniques used to measure income, capital gains, and total portfolio return.

LG4 Use the Sharpe, Treynor, and Jensen measures to compare a portfolio's return with a risk-adjusted, market-adjusted rate of return, and discuss portfolio revision.

LG5 Describe the role and logic of dollar-cost averaging, constant-dollar plans, constant-ratio plans, and variable-ratio plans.

LG6 Explain the role of limit and stop-loss orders in investment timing, warehousing liquidity, and timing investment sales.

He's known as the "Oracle of Omaha" for his stock-picking prowess, and in 2008 he was ranked by *Forbes* as the richest person in the world with an estimated net worth of $62 billion. As chairman of Berkshire Hathaway, Inc., Warren Buffett has multiplied his investors' money by a factor of 2,935 since taking over the company in 1964. The Omaha-based corporation's 51 subsidiaries include insurance (GEICO), apparel (Fruit of the Loom), building products (Acme Brick Company), energy (MidAmerican Energy Holdings Company), food and gourmet retailers (International Dairy Queen, The Pampered Chef), flight services (FlightSafety International), home furnishings (Star Furniture), and jewelry retailers (Helzberg Diamonds). In addition, Berkshire Hathaway is a public investment company with major holdings in companies that read like a veritable who's who of American business: American Express, Burlington Northern, Coca-Cola, ConocoPhillips, Procter & Gamble, The Washington Post, Wells Fargo, and many others.

Owning a piece of this diversified company will cost you a pretty penny. In November 2009, the A shares were trading above $100,000 per share. Alternatively, you can buy B shares, which trade for one-thirtieth of the A shares' value. From 1965 to 2008, Berkshire Hathaway's book value per share grew from $19 to $70,530—that is a compounded annual rate of 20.3%.

What's the secret to Buffett's success? His long-term investing horizon and patience are legendary. His claim to fame has been his ability to buy businesses at prices far below what he calls their "intrinsic" value, which includes such intangibles as quality of management and the power of superior brand names. Buffett waits until a desired investment reaches his target price (perceived value) and won't buy until then. "We measure our success by the long-term progress of the companies rather than by the month-to-month movements of their stocks," he says.

As you'll see in this chapter, which introduces the basics of portfolio management, investing is a process of analysis, followed by action, followed by still more analysis. You may not be the next Warren Buffett (or maybe you will!), but understanding his techniques for building and evaluating your own portfolio will put you on the right track.

(Source: Berkshire Hathaway corporate Web site, www.berkshirehathaway.com (accessed September 2009); historical data from www.bigcharts.marketwatch.com (accessed September 2009).)

Constructing a Portfolio Using an Asset Allocation Scheme

LG1 We begin by examining the criteria for constructing a portfolio and then use them to develop a plan for allocating assets in various investment categories. This plan provides a basic, useful framework for selecting individual investments for the portfolio. In attempting to weave the concepts of risk and diversification into a solid portfolio policy, we will rely on both traditional and modern approaches (see Chapter 5).

Investor Characteristics and Objectives

Your financial and family situations are important inputs in determining portfolio policy. Vital determinants include level and stability of income, family factors, net worth, investor experience and age, and disposition toward risk. The types of investments in your portfolio depend on your relative income needs and ability to bear risk.

The size of your income and the certainty of your employment also bear on portfolio strategy. An investor with a secure job can handle more risk than one with a less secure position. Also, the higher your income, the more important the tax ramifications of an investment program become. Your investment experience also influences your investment strategy. It normally is best to "get one's feet wet" in the investment market by slipping into it gradually rather than leaping in head first. A cautiously developed investment program is likely to provide more favorable long-run results than an impulsive one.

Now you should ask yourself, "What do I want from my portfolio?" You must generally choose between high current income or significant capital appreciation. It is difficult to have both. The price of having high appreciation potential is often low potential for current income.

Your needs may determine which avenue you choose. A retired person whose income depends on his or her portfolio will probably choose a lower-risk, current-income-oriented approach. A high-income, financially secure investor may be much more willing to take on risky investments in the hope of improving net worth. Thus, a portfolio must be built around your needs, which depend on income, responsibilities, financial resources, age, retirement plans, and ability to bear risk.

Portfolio Objectives and Policies

Constructing a portfolio is a logical activity that is best done after you have analyzed your needs and the available investments. When planning and constructing a portfolio, you should consider these objectives: current income needs, capital preservation, capital growth, tax considerations, and risk.

Any one or more of these factors will play an influential role in defining the desirable type of portfolio. They can be tied together as follows: The first two items, *current income* and *capital preservation*, are consistent with a low-risk, conservative investment strategy. Normally, a portfolio with this orientation contains low-beta (low-risk) securities. The third item, a *capital growth objective*, implies increased risk and a reduced level of current income. Higher-risk growth stocks, options, futures, and other more speculative investments may be suitable for this investor. The fourth item, an investor's *tax bracket*, will influence investment strategy. A high-income investor probably wishes to defer taxes and earn investment returns in the form of capital gains. This implies a strategy of higher-risk investments and a longer holding period. Lower-bracket investors are less concerned with how they earn the income, and they may wish to invest in higher-current-income securities. The most important item, finally, is *risk*. Investors should consider the risk-return tradeoff *in all investment decisions*.

Developing an Asset Allocation Scheme

Once you have translated your needs into specific portfolio objectives, you can construct a portfolio designed to achieve these goals. Before buying any investments, however, you must develop an *asset allocation scheme*. **Asset allocation** involves dividing your portfolio into various asset classes, such as U.S. stocks, U.S. bonds, foreign securities, short-term securities, and other assets like tangibles (especially gold) and real estate. The emphasis of asset allocation is on *preservation of capital*—protecting against negative developments while taking advantage of positive developments. Asset allocation is a bit different from diversification: Its focus is on *investment in various asset classes*. Diversification, in contrast, tends to focus more on **security selection**—selecting the *specific* securities to be held *within* an asset class.

Asset allocation is based on the belief that the total return of a portfolio is influenced more by the division of investments into asset classes than by the actual investments. In fact, studies have shown that as much as 90% or more of a portfolio's *return* comes from asset allocation. Therefore, less than 10% can be attributed to the actual security selection. Furthermore, researchers have found that asset allocation has a much greater impact on reducing *total risk* than does selecting the best investment in any single asset category.

Approaches to Asset Allocation There are three basic approaches to asset allocation: (1) fixed weightings, (2) flexible weightings, and (3) tactical asset allocation. The first two differ with respect to the proportions of each asset category maintained in the portfolio. The third is a more exotic technique used by institutional portfolio managers.

Fixed Weightings The **fixed-weightings approach** allocates a fixed percentage of the portfolio to each of the asset categories, of which there typically are three to five. Assuming four categories—common stock, bonds, foreign securities, and short-term securities—a fixed allocation might be as follows.

Category	Allocation
Common stock	30%
Bonds	50
Foreign securities	15
Short-term securities	5
Total portfolio	100%

Generally, the fixed weightings do not change over time. When market values shift, you may have to adjust the portfolio annually or after major market moves to maintain the desired fixed-percentage allocations.

Fixed weights may or may not represent equal percentage allocations to each category. One could, for example, allocate 25% to each of the four categories above. Research has shown that over a long period, equal (20%) allocations to U.S. stocks, foreign stocks, long-term bonds, cash, and real estate resulted in a portfolio that outperformed the S&P 500 in terms of both return and risk. These findings add further support to the importance of even a somewhat naive "buy-and-hold" asset allocation strategy.

Flexible Weightings The **flexible-weightings approach** involves periodic adjustment of the weights for each asset category on the basis of market analysis. The use of a flexible-weighting scheme is often called *strategic asset allocation*. For example, the initial and new allocation based on a flexible-weighting scheme may be as follows.

Category	Initial Allocation	New Allocation
Common stock	30%	45%
Bonds	40	40
Foreign securities	15	10
Short-term securities	15	5
Total portfolio	100%	100%

A change from the initial to the new allocation would be triggered by shifts in market conditions or expectations. For example, the new allocation shown above may have resulted from an anticipated decline in inflation. That decline would be expected to result in increased domestic stock and bond prices and a decline in foreign and short-term security returns. The weightings were therefore changed to capture greater returns in a changing market.

Tactical Asset Allocation The third approach, **tactical asset allocation**, is a form of market timing that uses stock-index futures and bond futures (see Chapter 15) to change a portfolio's asset allocation. When stocks are forecast to be less attractive than bonds, this strategy involves selling stock-index futures and buying bond futures. Conversely, when bonds are forecast to be less attractive than stocks, the strategy results in buying stock-index futures and selling bond futures. Because this sophisticated technique relies on a large portfolio and the use of quantitative models for market timing, it is generally appropriate only for large institutional investors.

Asset Allocation Alternatives Assuming the use of a fixed-weight asset allocation plan and using, say, four asset categories, we can demonstrate three asset allocations. Table 13.1 shows allocations in each of four categories for conservative (low return/low risk), moderate (average return/average risk), and aggressive (high return/high risk) portfolios. The conservative allocation relies heavily on bonds and short-term securities to provide predictable returns. The moderate allocation consists largely of common stock and bonds and includes more foreign securities and fewer short-term securities than the conservative allocation. Its moderate risk-return behavior reflects a move away from safe, short-term securities to a larger dose of common stock and foreign securities. Finally, in the aggressive allocation, more dollars are invested in common stock, fewer in bonds, and more in foreign securities, thereby generally increasing the expected portfolio return and risk.

TABLE 13.1   Alternative Asset Allocations

Category	Allocation Alternative		
	Conservative (low return/low risk)	Moderate (average return/average risk)	Aggressive (high return/high risk)
Common stock	15%	30%	40%
Bonds	45	40	30
Foreign securities	5	15	25
Short-term securities	35	15	5
Total portfolio	100%	100%	100%

Applying Asset Allocation An asset allocation plan should consider the economic outlook and your investments, savings and spending patterns, tax situation, return expectations, and risk tolerance. Such plans must be formulated for the long run and must stress capital preservation. You also must periodically revise the plan to reflect changing investment goals. Generally, to decide on the appropriate asset mix, you must evaluate each asset category in terms of current return, growth potential, safety, liquidity, transaction costs (brokerage fees), and potential tax savings.

Many investors use mutual funds (see Chapter 12) as part of their asset allocation activities, to diversify within each asset category. Or, as an alternative to constructing your own portfolio, you can buy shares in an **asset allocation fund**—a mutual fund that seeks to reduce variability of returns by investing in the right assets at the right time. These funds, like all asset allocation schemes, emphasize diversification. They perform at a relatively consistent level by passing up the potential for spectacular gains in favor of predictability. Some asset allocation funds use fixed weightings, whereas others have flexible weights that change within prescribed limits. As a rule, investors with more than about $100,000 to invest and adequate time can justify do-it-yourself asset allocation. Those with between $25,000 and $100,000 and adequate time can use mutual funds to create a workable asset allocation. Those with less than $25,000 or with limited time may find asset allocation funds most attractive.

Most important, you should recognize that to be effective an asset allocation scheme *must be designed for the long haul*. Develop an asset allocation scheme you can live with for at least seven to 10 years, and perhaps longer. Once you have it set, stick with it. The key to success is remaining faithful to your asset allocation; that means fighting the temptation to wander.

CONCEPTS IN REVIEW

Answers available at
www.pearsonhighered.com/
gitman

13.1 What role, if any, do an investor's personal characteristics play in determining portfolio policy? Explain.

13.2 What role do an investor's portfolio objectives play in constructing a portfolio?

13.3 What is *asset allocation?* How does it differ from diversification? What role does asset allocation play in constructing an investment portfolio?

13.4 Briefly describe the three basic approaches to asset allocation: (a) fixed weightings, (b) flexible weightings, and (c) tactical asset allocation.

13.5 What role could an *asset allocation fund* play? What makes an asset allocation scheme effective?

Evaluating the Performance of Individual Investments

LG2 Imagine that one of your most important personal goals is to have accumulated $20,000 of savings three years from now in order to make the downpayment on your first house. You project that the desired house will cost $100,000 and that the $20,000 will be sufficient to make a 15% downpayment and pay the associated closing costs. Your calculations indicate that you can achieve this goal by investing existing savings plus an additional $200 per month over the next three years in an investment earning 12% per year. Projections of your earnings over the three-year period indicate that you should just be able to set aside the needed $200 per month. You consult with an invest-ment adviser, Cliff Orbit, who leads you to believe that under his management, the 12% return can be achieved.

It seems simple: Give Cliff your existing savings, send him $200 each month over the next 36 months, and at the end of that period, you will have the $20,000 needed to purchase the house. Unfortunately, there are many uncertainties involved. What if you don't set aside $200 each month? What if Cliff fails to earn the needed 12% annual return? What if in three years the desired house costs more than $100,000? Clearly, you must do more than simply devise what appears to be a feasible plan for achieving a future goal. Rarely are you guaranteed that your planned investment and portfolio outcomes will actually occur. Therefore, it is important to assess periodically your progress toward achieving your investment goals.

As actual outcomes occur, you must compare them to the *planned* outcomes and make any necessary alterations in your plans—or in your goals. Knowing how to mea-sure investment performance is therefore crucial. Here we will emphasize measures suitable for analyzing investment performance. We begin with sources of data.

Obtaining Needed Data

The first step in analyzing investment returns is gathering data that reflect the actual performance of each investment. As pointed out in Chapter 3, many sources of invest-ment information are available, both online and in print. The *Wall Street Journal*, **WSJ.com,** and **Yahoo.com,** for example, contain numerous items of information useful in assessing the performance of securities. The same type of information that you use to *make* an investment decision you also use to *evaluate* investment performance. Two key areas to stay informed about are (1) returns on owned investments and (2) economic and market activity.

Return Data The basic ingredient in analyzing investment returns is current market information, such as daily price quotations for stocks and bonds. Investors often main-tain logs or spreadsheets that contain the cost of each investment, as well as dividends, interest, and other sources of income received. By regularly recording price and return data, you can create an ongoing record of price fluctuations and cumulative returns. You should also monitor corporate earnings and dividends, which will affect a com-pany's stock price. The two sources of investment return—current income and capital gains—must of course be combined to determine total return. Later in this chapter we will demonstrate use of the techniques presented in Chapter 4 to measure some pop-ular investment vehicles.

Economic and Market Activity Changes in the economy and market will affect returns—both the level of current income and the market value of an investment. The astute investor keeps abreast of international, national, and local economic and market developments. By following economic and market changes, you should be able to assess their potential impact on returns. As economic and market conditions change, you must be prepared to make revisions in the portfolio. In essence, being a knowledgeable investor will improve your chances of generating a profit (or avoiding a loss).

Indexes of Investment Performance

In measuring investment performance, it is often worthwhile to compare your returns with broad-based market measures. Indexes useful for the analysis of common stock include the Dow Jones Industrial Average (DJIA), the Standard & Poor's 500 Stock

MARKETS in CRISIS

Baby Boomers Delay Retirement

In October of 2008, Eons.com completed a poll of its baby boomer membership that revealed a majority of U.S. boomers had to delay retirement due to the financial market crisis. Poll results indicated that only 2% of those polled anticipated a delay in retirement of less than one year, while 55% of respondents anticipated a delay in retirement of five years or more. Maybe even worse, 21% of

baby boomers expected their retirement accounts to never fully recover from the effects of the financial crisis. Seventy-three percent were more optimistic, expecting their retirement accounts to recover at some point ranging from more than a year to more than five years. (Source: eons.com, October 2, 2008.)

Composite Index (S&P 500), and the Nasdaq Composite Index. (Detailed discussions of these averages and indexes can be found in Chapter 3.) Although the DJIA is widely cited by the news media, it is *not* considered the most appropriate comparative gauge of stock price movement, because of its narrow coverage. If your portfolio is composed of a broad range of common stocks, the S&P 500 index is probably a more appropriate tool.

A number of indicators are also available for assessing the general behavior of the bond markets. These indicators consider either bond yield or bond price behavior. Bond yield data reflect the rate of return one would earn on a bond purchased today and held to maturity. Popular sources of these data include the *Wall Street Journal*, *Barron's*, Standard & Poor's, Mergent, **Yahoo.com**, and the Federal Reserve. The Dow Jones Corporate Bond Index, based on the closing prices of 32 industrial, 32 financial, and 32 utility/telecom bonds, is a popular measure of bond price behavior. It reflects the mathematical average of the closing prices of the bonds.

Indexes of bond price and bond yield performance can be obtained for specific types of bonds (industrial, utility, and municipal), as well as on a composite basis. In addition, indexes reported in terms of *total returns* are available for both stocks and bonds. They combine dividend/interest income with price behavior (capital gain or loss) to reflect total return.

Investors frequently use the Lipper indexes to assess the general behavior of mutual funds. These indexes are available for various types of equity and bond funds. Unfortunately, for most other types of funds, no widely published index or average is available. A few other indexes cover listed options and futures.

Measuring the Performance of Investments

To monitor an investment portfolio, investors need reliable techniques for consistently measuring the performance of each investment in the portfolio. In particular, the holding period return (HPR) measure, first presented in Chapter 4, can be used to determine *actual* return performance. HPR is an excellent way to assess actual return behavior, because it captures *total return* performance. It is most appropriate for holding or assessment periods of one year or less. Total return, in this context, includes the periodic cash income from the investment as well as price appreciation (or loss), whether realized or unrealized. To calculate returns for periods of more than a year, you can use yield (internal rate of return), which recognizes the time value of money. Yield can be calculated using the techniques described in Chapter 4 (pages 128–130). Because the following discussions center on the *annual* assessment of return, we will use HPR as the measure of return.

The formula for HPR, presented in Chapter 4 (Equation 4.4) and applied throughout this chapter, is restated in Equation 13.1:

Equation 13.1

$$\text{Holding period return} = \frac{\genfrac{}{}{0pt}{}{\text{Current income}}{\text{during period}} + \genfrac{}{}{0pt}{}{\text{Capital gain (or loss)}}{\text{during period}}}{\text{Beginning investment value}}$$

Equation 13.1a

$$\text{HPR} = \frac{C + CG}{V_0}$$

where

Equation 13.2

$$\genfrac{}{}{0pt}{}{\text{Capital gain (or loss)}}{\text{during period}} = \genfrac{}{}{0pt}{}{\text{Ending}}{\text{investment value}} - \genfrac{}{}{0pt}{}{\text{Beginning}}{\text{investment value}}$$

Equation 13.2a

$$CG = V_n - V_0$$

Stocks and Bonds There are several measures of investment return for stocks and bonds. *Dividend yield*, discussed in Chapter 6, measures the current yearly dividend return earned from a stock investment. It is calculated by dividing a stock's yearly cash dividend by its price. The *current yield* and *yield-to-maturity* (promised yield) for bonds, analyzed in Chapter 11, capture various components of return but do not reflect actual total return. The *holding period return* method *measures the total return (income plus change in value) actually earned on an investment over a given investment period.* We will use HPR, with a holding period of approximately one year, in the illustrations that follow.

Stocks The HPR for common and preferred stocks includes both cash dividends received and any price change in the security during the period of ownership. Table 13.2 illustrates the HPR calculation as applied to the actual performance of a common stock. Assume you purchased 1,000 shares of Dallas National Corporation in May 2010 at a cost of $27,312 (including commissions). After holding the stock for just over one year, you sold it, reaping proceeds of $32,040. In addition to the $4,728 capital gain on the sale, you also received $2,000 in cash dividends. Thus, the calculated HPR is 24.63%.

TABLE 13.2   Calculation of Pretax HPR on a Common Stock

Security: Dallas National Corporation common stock
Date of purchase: May 1, 2010
Purchase cost: $27,312
Date of sale: May 7, 2011
Sale proceeds: $32,040
Dividends received (May 2010 to May 2011): $2,000

$$\text{Holding period return} = \frac{\$2,000 + (\$32,040) - \$27,312}{\$27,312}$$

$$= \underline{\$24.63\%}$$

TABLE 13.3	Calculation of Pretax HPR on a Bond

Security: Phoenix Brewing Company 10% bonds
Date of purchase: June 2, 2010
Purchase cost: $10,000
Date of sale: June 5, 2011
Sale proceeds: $9,704
Interest earned (June 2010 to June 2011): $1,000

$$\text{Holding period return} = \frac{\$1,000 + (\$9,704 - \$10,000)}{\$10,000}$$

$$= \underline{\$7.04\%}$$

INVESTOR FACTS

BAD RECORDS?— You sold a stock this year and need to calculate your capital gain for tax purposes, but you suddenly realize you didn't keep good records. What do you do? Your best bet is to make a good-faith effort to come up with a probable cost. Ask your brokerage firm to dig into its records; it is required to keep records of transactions for six years. If you had a stock certificate, look for its date of issuance and assume that the purchase date was about two weeks before that. If you know the approximate purchase date, you can look up old stock prices in newspapers at the library or on a Web site such as **finance.yahoo.com**. Then send the IRS a letter documenting your search; chances are that they will be understanding. Finally, resolve to keep better records in the future.

This HPR was calculated without consideration for income taxes paid on the dividends and capital gain. Because many investors are concerned with both pretax and after-tax rates of return, it is useful to calculate an after-tax HPR. We assume, for simplicity, that you are in the 30% ordinary tax bracket (federal and state combined). We also assume that, for federal and state tax purposes, dividends and capital gains for holding periods of more than 12 months are taxed at a 15% rate. Thus, both your dividend and capital gain income are taxed at a 15% rate. Income taxes reduce the after-tax dividend income to $1,700 [(1 − 0.15) × $2,000] and the after-tax capital gain to $4,019 [(1 − 0.15) × ($32,040 − $27,312)]. The after-tax HPR is therefore 20.94% [($1,700 + $4,019) ÷ $27,312], a reduction of 3.69 percentage points. It should be clear that both pretax HPR and after-tax HPR are useful gauges of return.

Bonds The HPR for a bond investment is similar to that for stocks. The calculation holds for both straight debt and convertible issues. It includes the two components of a bond investor's return: interest income and capital gain or loss.

Calculation of the HPR on a bond investment is illustrated in Table 13.3. Assume you purchased Phoenix Brewing Company bonds for $10,000, held them for just over one year, and then realized $9,704 at their sale. In addition, you earned $1,000 in interest during the year. The HPR of this investment is 7.04%. The HPR is lower than the bond's current yield of 10% ($1,000 interest ÷ $10,000 purchase price) because the bonds were sold at a capital loss. Assuming a 30% ordinary tax bracket and a 15% capital gains tax rate (because the bond has been held more than 12 months), the after-tax HPR is 4.48%: {[(1 − 0.30) × $1,000] + [(1 − 0.15) × ($9,704 − $10,000)]} ÷ $10,000. This is about 2.6% less than the pretax HPR.

Mutual Funds The two basic components of return from a mutual fund investment are dividend income (including any capital gains distribution) and change in value. The basic HPR equation for mutual funds is identical to that for stocks.

Table 13.4 presents a holding period return calculation for a no-load mutual fund. Assume you purchased 1,000 shares of the fund in July 2010 at an NAV of $10.40 per share. Because it is a no-load fund, no commission was charged, so your cost was $10,400. During the one-year period of ownership, the Pebble Falls Mutual Fund distributed investment income dividends totaling $270 and capital gains dividends of $320. You redeemed (sold) this fund at an NAV of $10.79 per share, thereby realizing $10,790. As seen in Table 13.4, the pretax holding period return on this investment is 9.42%. Assuming a 30% ordinary tax bracket and a 15% dividend and capital gains

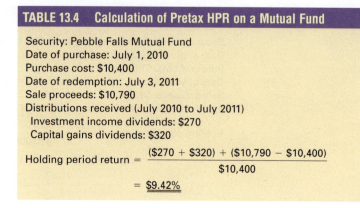

TABLE 13.4   Calculation of Pretax HPR on a Mutual Fund

Security: Pebble Falls Mutual Fund
Date of purchase: July 1, 2010
Purchase cost: $10,400
Date of redemption: July 3, 2011
Sale proceeds: $10,790
Distributions received (July 2010 to July 2011)
  Investment income dividends: $270
  Capital gains dividends: $320

$$\text{Holding period return} = \frac{(\$270 + \$320) + (\$10,790 - \$10,400)}{\$10,400}$$

$$= \underline{\underline{9.42\%}}$$

tax rate (because the fund has been held for more than 12 months), the after-tax HPR for the fund is 8.01%: {[(1 − 0.15) × ($270 + $320)] + [(1 − 0.15) × ($10,790 − $10,400)]} ÷ $10,400. This is about 1.4% below the pretax return.

Options and Futures   The only source of return on options and futures is capital gains. To calculate a holding period return for an investment in a call option, for instance, you use the basic HPR formula, but you would set current income equal to zero. If you purchased a call on 100 shares of **ecommerce.com** for $325 and sold the contract for $385 after holding it for just over 12 months, the pretax holding period return would be 18.46%. This is simply sales proceeds ($385) minus cost ($325) divided by cost. Assuming the 15% capital gains tax rate applies, the after-tax HPR would be 15.69%, which is the after-tax gain of $51 [(1 − 0.15) × $60] divided by cost ($325).

The HPRs of futures are calculated in a similar fashion. Because the return is in the form of capital gains only, the HPR analysis can be applied to any investment on a pretax or an after-tax basis. (The same basic procedure is used for securities that are sold short.)

Comparing Performance to Investment Goals

After computing an HPR (or yield) on an investment, you should compare it to your investment goal. Keeping track of an investment's performance will help you decide which investments you should continue to hold and which you might want to sell. Clearly, an investment would be a candidate for sale under the following conditions: (1) The investment failed to perform up to expectations and no real change in performance is anticipated. (2) It has met the original investment objective. (3) Better investment outlets are currently available.

Balancing Risk and Return   We have frequently discussed the basic tradeoff between investment risk and return: To earn more return, you must take more risk. In analyzing an investment, the key question is, "Am I getting the proper return for the amount of investment risk I am taking?"

Nongovernment security investments are by nature riskier than U.S. government bonds or insured money market deposit accounts. This implies that *a rational investor should invest in these riskier assets only when the expected rate of return is well in excess of what could have been earned from a low-risk investment.* Thus, one benchmark against which to compare investment returns is the rate of return on low-risk investments. If one's risky investments are outperforming low-risk investments, they are obtaining extra return for taking extra risk. If they are not outperforming low-risk investments, you should carefully reexamine your investment strategy.

Isolating Problem Investments It is best to analyze each investment in a portfolio periodically. For each, you should consider two questions: First, has it performed in a manner that could reasonably be expected? Second, if you didn't currently own it, would you buy it today? If the answers to both are negative, then the investment probably should be sold. A negative answer to one of the questions qualifies the investment for the "problem list." A *problem investment* is one that has not lived up to expectations. It may be a loss situation or an investment that has provided a return less than you expected. Many investors try to forget about problem investments, hoping the problem will go away or the investment will turn itself around. This is a mistake. Problem investments require immediate attention, not neglect. In studying a problem investment, the key question is, "Should I take my loss and get out, or should I hang on and hope it turns around?"

CONCEPTS IN REVIEW Answers available at www.pearsonhighered.com/gitman	**13.6** Why is it important to continuously manage and control your portfolio?
	13.7 What role does current market information play in analyzing investment returns? How do changes in economic and market activity affect investment returns? Explain.
	13.8 Which indexes can you use to compare your investment performance to general market returns? Briefly explain each of these indexes.
	13.9 What are indicators of bond market behavior and how are they different from stock market indicators? Name three sources of bond yield data.
	13.10 Briefly discuss *holding period return (HPR)* and *yield* as measures of investment return. Are they equivalent? Explain.
	13.11 Distinguish between the types of dividend distributions that mutual funds make. Are these dividends the only source of return for a mutual fund investor? Explain.
	13.12 Under what three conditions would an investment holding be a candidate for sale? What must be true about the expected return on a risky investment, when compared with the return on a low-risk investment, to cause a rational investor to acquire the risky investment? Explain.
	13.13 What is a *problem investment?* What two questions should one consider when analyzing each investment in a portfolio?

Assessing Portfolio Performance

LG3 LG4 A portfolio can be either passively or actively built and managed. A *passive portfolio* results from buying and holding a well-diversified portfolio over the given investment horizon. An *active portfolio* is built using the traditional and modern approaches presented in Chapter 5 and is managed and controlled to achieve its stated objectives. Passive portfolios may at times outperform equally risky active portfolios. But evidence suggests that **active portfolio management** can result in superior returns. Many of the ideas presented in this text are consistent with the belief that active portfolio management will improve your chance of earning superior returns.

TABLE 13.5 **Bob Hathaway's Portfolio (January 1, 2011)**

Number of Shares	Company	Date Acquired	Total Cost (including commission)	Cost per Share	Current Price per Share	Current Value
1,000	Bancorp West, Inc.	1/16/09	$ 21,610	$21.61	$30	$ 30,000
1,000	Dallas National Corporation	5/01/10	27,312	27.31	29	29,000
1,000	Dator Companies, Inc.	4/13/05	13,704	13.70	27	27,000
500	Excelsior Industries	8/16/08	40,571	81.14	54	27,000
1,000	Florida Southcoast Banks	12/16/08	17,460	17.46	30	30,000
1,000	Maryland-Pacific	9/27/08	22,540	22.54	26	26,000
1,000	Moronson	2/27/08	19,100	19.10	47	47,000
500	Northwest Mining and Mfg.	4/17/09	25,504	51.00	62	31,000
1,000	Rawland Petroleum	3/12/09	24,903	24.90	30	30,000
1,000	Vornox	4/16/09	37,120	37.12	47	47,000
	Total		$249,824			$324,000

Once you have built a portfolio, the first step in active portfolio management is to assess performance on a regular basis and use that information to revise the portfolio as needed. Calculating the portfolio return can be tricky. The procedures used to assess portfolio performance are based on many of the concepts presented earlier in this chapter. Here we will demonstrate how to assess portfolio performance, using a hypothetical securities portfolio over a one-year holding period. We will examine each of three measures that can be used to compare a portfolio's return with a risk-adjusted, market-adjusted rate of return.

Measuring Portfolio Return

Table 13.5 presents the investment portfolio, as of January 1, 2011, of Bob Hathaway. He is a 50-year-old widower, whose children are married. His income is $60,000 per year. His primary investment objective is long-term growth with a moderate dividend return. He selects stocks with two criteria in mind: quality and growth potential. On January 1, 2011, his portfolio consisted of 10 issues, all of good quality. Hathaway has been fortunate in his selection process: He has approximately $74,000 in unrealized price appreciation in his portfolio. During 2011, he decided to make a change in the portfolio. On May 7 he sold 1,000 shares of Dallas National Corporation for $32,040. The holding period return for that same issue was discussed earlier in this chapter (see Table 13.2). Using proceeds from the Dallas National sale, he acquired an additional 1,000 shares of Florida Southcoast Banks on May 10, because he liked the prospects for the Florida bank. Florida Southcoast is based in one of the fastest growing counties in the country.

Measuring the Amount Invested Every investor would be well advised to list his or her holdings periodically, as is done in Table 13.5. The table shows number of shares, acquisition date, cost, and current value for each issue. These data aid in continually formulating strategy decisions. The cost data, for example, are used to determine the amount invested. Hathaway's portfolio does not utilize the leverage of a margin account. Were leverage present, all return calculations would be based on the investor's *equity* in the account. (Recall from Chapter 2 that an investor's equity in a margin account equals the total value of all the securities in the account minus any margin debt.)

To measure Hathaway's return on his invested capital, we need to calculate the one-year holding period return. His invested capital as of January 1, 2011, is $324,000. He

TABLE 13.6   Dividend Income on Hathaway's Portfolio (Calendar Year 2011)

Number of Shares	Company	Annual Dividend per Share	Dividends Received
1,000	Bancorp West, Inc.	$1.20	$1,200
1,000	Dallas National Corporation*	1.80	900
1,000	Dator Companies, Inc.	1.12	1,120
500	Excelsior Industries	2.00	1,000
2,000	Florida Southcoast Banks**	1.28	1,920
1,000	Maryland-Pacific	1.10	1,100
1,000	Moronson	—	—
500	Northwest Mining and Mfg.	2.05	1,025
1,000	Rawland Petroleum	1.20	1,200
1,000	Vornox	1.47	1,470
	Total		$10,935

*Sold May 7, 2011.
**1,000 shares acquired on May 10, 2011.

made no new additions of capital in the portfolio during 2011, although he sold one stock, Dallas National, and used the proceeds to buy another, Florida Southcoast Banks.

Measuring Income There are two sources of return from a portfolio of common stocks: income and capital gains. Current income is realized from dividends or, for bonds, is earned in the form of interest. Investors must report taxable dividends and interest on federal and state income tax returns. Companies are required to furnish income reports (Form 1099-DIV for dividends and Form 1099-INT for interest) to stockholders and bondholders. Many investors maintain logs to keep track of dividend and interest income as it is received.

Table 13.6 lists Hathaway's dividends for 2011. He received two quarterly dividends of $0.45 per share before he sold the Dallas National stock. He also received two $0.32-per-share quarterly dividends on the additional Florida Southcoast Banks shares he acquired. His total dividend income for 2011 was $10,935.

Measuring Capital Gains Table 13.7 shows the unrealized gains in value for each of the issues in the Hathaway portfolio. The January 1, 2011, and December 31, 2011, values are listed for each issue except the additional shares of Florida Southcoast Banks. The amounts listed for Florida Southcoast Banks reflect the fact that 1,000 additional shares of the stock were acquired on May 10, 2011, at a cost of $32,040. Hathaway's current holdings had beginning-of-the-year values of $327,040 (including the additional Florida Southcoast Banks shares at the date of purchase) and are worth $356,000 at year-end.

During 2011, the portfolio increased in value by 8.9%, or $28,960, in unrealized capital gains. In addition, Hathaway realized a capital gain in 2011 by selling his Dallas National holding. From January 1, 2011, until its sale on May 7, 2011, the Dallas National holding rose in value from $29,000 to $32,040. This was the only sale in 2011, so the total *realized* gain was $3,040. During 2011, the portfolio had both a realized gain of $3,040 and an unrealized gain of $28,960. The total gain in value equals the sum of the two: $32,000. Put another way, Hathaway neither added nor

TABLE 13.7   Unrealized Gains in Value of Hathaway's Portfolio (January 1, 2011, to December 31, 2011)

Number of Shares	Company	Market Value (1/1/11)	Market Price (12/31/11)	Market Value (12/31/11)	Unrealized Gain (Loss)	Percentage Change
1,000	Bancorp West, Inc.	$ 30,000	$27	$ 27,000	($ 3,000)	–10.0%
1,000	Dator Companies, Inc.	27,000	36	36,000	9,000	33.3
500	Excelsior Industries	27,000	66	33,000	6,000	22.2
2,000	Florida Southcoast Banks*	62,040	35	70,000	7,960	12.8
1,000	Maryland-Pacific	26,000	26	26,000	—	—
1,000	Moronson	47,000	55	55,000	8,000	17.0
500	Northwest Mining and Mfg.	31,000	60	30,000	(1,000)	–3.2
1,000	Rawland Petroleum	30,000	36	36,000	6,000	20.0
1,000	Vornox	47,000	43	43,000	(4,000)	–8.5
	Total	$327,040**		$356,000	$28,960	8.9%

*1,000 additional shares acquired on May 10, 2011, at a cost of $32,040. The value listed is the cost plus the market value of the previously owned shares as of January 1, 2011.
**This total includes the $324,000 market value of the portfolio on January 1, 2011 (from Table 13.5) plus the $3,040 *realized* gain on the sale of the Dallas National Corporation stock on May 7, 2011. The inclusion of the realized gain in this total is necessary to calculate the *unrealized* gain on the portfolio during 2011.

withdrew capital over the year. Therefore, the total capital gain is simply the difference between the year-end market value (of $356,000, from Table 13.7) and the value on January 1 (of $324,000, from Table 13.5). This, of course, amounts to $32,000. Of that amount, for tax purposes, only $3,040 is considered realized.

Measuring the Portfolio's Holding Period Return We use the holding period return (HPR) to measure the total return on the Hathaway portfolio during 2011. The basic one-year HPR formula for portfolios appears below.

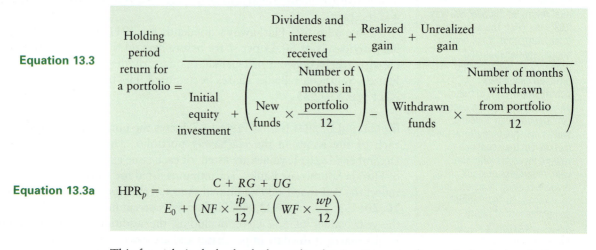

Equation 13.3

$$\text{Holding period return for a portfolio} = \frac{\text{Dividends and interest received} + \text{Realized gain} + \text{Unrealized gain}}{\text{Initial equity investment} + \left(\text{New funds} \times \frac{\text{Number of months in portfolio}}{12}\right) - \left(\text{Withdrawn funds} \times \frac{\text{Number of months withdrawn from portfolio}}{12}\right)}$$

Equation 13.3a

$$HPR_p = \frac{C + RG + UG}{E_0 + \left(NF \times \frac{ip}{12}\right) - \left(WF \times \frac{wp}{12}\right)}$$

This formula includes both the realized gains (income plus capital gains) and the unrealized yearly gains of the portfolio. Portfolio additions and deletions are time-weighted for the number of months they are in the portfolio.

Table 13.7 lays out in detail the portfolio's change in value: It lists all the issues that are in the portfolio as of December 31, 2011, and calculates the unrealized gain during the year. The beginning and year-end values are included for comparison purposes. The crux of the analysis is the HPR calculation for the year, presented in Table 13.8. All the

TABLE 13.8	Holding Period Return Calculation on Hathaway's Portfolio (January 1, 2011, to December 31, 2011, holding period)
Data	**Value**
Portfolio value (1/1/11):	$324,000
Portfolio value (12/31/11):	$356,000
Realized appreciation (1/1/11 to 5/7/11 when Dallas National Corporation was sold):	$3,040
Unrealized appreciation (1/1/11 to 12/31/11):	$28,960
Dividends received:	$10,935
New funds invested or withdrawn:	None

Portfolio HPR Calculation

$$HPR_p = \frac{\$10,935 + \$3,040 + \$28,960}{\$324,000}$$
$$= \underline{13.25\%}$$

elements of a portfolio's return are included. Dividends total $10,935 (from Table 13.6). The realized gain of $3,040 represents the increment in value of the Dallas National holding from January 1, 2011, until its sale. During 2011 the portfolio had a $28,960 unrealized gain (from Table 13.7). There were no additions of new funds, and no funds were withdrawn. Utilizing Equation 13.3 for HPR, we find that the portfolio had a total return of 13.25% in 2011.

Comparison of Return with Overall Market Measures

Bob Hathaway can compare the HPR figure for his portfolio with market measures such as stock indexes. This comparison will show how his portfolio is doing in relation to the stock market as a whole. The S&P 500 Stock Composite Index and the Nasdaq Composite Index are acceptable indexes to represent the stock market as a whole. Assume that during 2011, the return on the S&P 500 index was 10.75% (including both dividends and capital gains). The return from Hathaway's portfolio was 13.25%, which compares very favorably with the broadly based index. The Hathaway portfolio performed about 23% better than the broad indicator of stock market return.

Such a comparison factors out general market movements, but *it fails to consider risk*. Clearly, a raw return figure, such as this 13.25%, requires further analysis. A number of risk-adjusted, market-adjusted rate-of-return measures are available for use in assessing portfolio performance. Here we'll discuss three of the most popular— Sharpe's measure, Treynor's measure, and Jensen's measure—and demonstrate their application to Hathaway's portfolio.

Sharpe's Measure **Sharpe's measure** of portfolio performance, developed by William F. Sharpe, compares the risk premium on a portfolio to the portfolio's standard deviation of return. The risk premium on a portfolio is the total portfolio return minus the risk-free rate. Sharpe's measure can be expressed as the following formula:

Equation 13.4
$$\text{Sharpe's measure} = \frac{\text{Total portfolio return } - \text{ Risk-free rate}}{\text{Portfolio standard deviation of return}}$$

Equation 13.4a
$$SM = \frac{r_p - R_F}{s_p}$$

This measure allows the investor to assess the *risk premium per unit of total risk,* which is measured by the portfolio standard deviation of return.

Assume the risk-free rate, R_F, is 7.50% and the standard deviation of return on Hathaway's portfolio, s_p, is 16%. The total portfolio return, r_p, which is the HPR for Hathaway's portfolio calculated in Table 13.8 (on page 505), is 13.25%. Substituting those values into Equation 13.4, we get Sharpe's measure, SM_p.

$$SM_p = \frac{13.25\% - 7.50\%}{16\%} = \frac{5.75\%}{16\%} = \underline{\underline{0.36}}$$

Sharpe's measure is meaningful when compared either to other portfolios or to the market. In general, the higher the value of Sharpe's measure, the better—the higher the risk premium per unit of risk. If we assume that the market return, r_m, is currently 10.75% and the standard deviation of return for the market portfolio, s_{pm}, is 11.25%, Sharpe's measure for the market, SM_m, is

$$SM_m = \frac{10.75\% - 7.50\%}{11.25\%} = \frac{3.25\%}{11.25\%} = \underline{\underline{0.29}}$$

Because Sharpe's measure of 0.36 for Hathaway's portfolio is greater than the measure of 0.29 for the market portfolio, Hathaway's portfolio exhibits superior performance. Its risk premium per unit of risk is above that of the market. Had Sharpe's measure for Hathaway's portfolio been below that of the market (below 0.29), the portfolio's performance would be considered inferior to the market performance.

Treynor's Measure Jack L. Treynor developed a portfolio performance measure similar to Sharpe's measure. **Treynor's measure** uses the portfolio beta to measure the portfolio's risk. Treynor therefore focuses only on *nondiversifiable risk,* assuming that the portfolio has been built in a manner that diversifies away all diversifiable risk. (In contrast, Sharpe focuses on *total risk.*) Treynor's measure is calculated as shown in Equation 13.5.

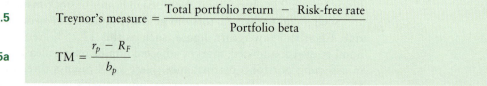

Equation 13.5
$$\text{Treynor's measure} = \frac{\text{Total portfolio return} - \text{Risk-free rate}}{\text{Portfolio beta}}$$

Equation 13.5a
$$TM = \frac{r_p - R_F}{b_p}$$

This measure gives the *risk premium per unit of nondiversifiable risk,* which is measured by the portfolio beta.

Using the data for the Hathaway portfolio presented earlier and assuming that the beta for Hathaway's portfolio, b_p, is 1.20, we can substitute into Equation 13.5 to get Treynor's measure, TM_p, for Hathaway's portfolio.

$$TM_p = \frac{13.25\% - 7.50\%}{1.20} = \frac{5.75\%}{1.20} = \underline{\underline{4.79\%}}$$

Treynor's measure, like Sharpe's measure, is useful when compared either to other portfolios or to the market. Generally, the higher the value of Treynor's measure, the better—the greater the risk premium per unit of nondiversifiable risk. Again assuming that the market return, r_m, is 10.75% and recognizing that, by definition, the beta for the market portfolio, b_m, is 1.00, we can use Equation 13.5 to find Treynor's measure for the market, TM_m.

$$\text{TM}_m = \frac{10.75\% - 7.50\%}{1.00} = \frac{3.25\%}{1.00} = \underline{\underline{3.25\%}}$$

The fact that Treynor's measure of 4.79% for Hathaway's portfolio is greater than the market portfolio measure of 3.25% indicates that Hathaway's portfolio exhibits superior performance. Its risk premium per unit of nondiversifiable risk is above that of the market. Had Treynor's measure for Hathaway's portfolio been below that of the market (below 3.25%), the portfolio's performance would be viewed as inferior to that of the market.

Jensen's Measure (Jensen's Alpha) Michael C. Jensen developed a portfolio performance measure that seems quite different from the measures of Sharpe and Treynor, yet is theoretically consistent with Treynor's measure. **Jensen's measure**, also called **Jensen's alpha**, is based on the *capital asset pricing model (CAPM)*, which was developed in Chapter 5 (see Equation 5.3 on page 179). It calculates the portfolio's *excess return*. Excess return is the amount by which the portfolio's actual return deviates from its required return, which is determined using its beta and CAPM. The value of the excess return may be positive, zero, or negative. Like Treynor's measure, Jensen's measure focuses only on the *nondiversifiable,* or *relevant, risk* by using beta and CAPM. It assumes that the portfolio has been adequately diversified. Jensen's measure is calculated as shown in Equation 13.6.

Equation 13.6

Jensen's measure = (Total portfolio return − Risk-free rate) − [Portfolio beta × (Market return − Risk-free rate)]

Equation 13.6a

$$\text{JM} = (r_p - R_F) - [b_p \times (r_m - R_F)]$$

Jensen's measure indicates the difference between the portfolio's actual return and its required return. Positive values are preferred. They indicate that the portfolio earned a return in excess of its risk-adjusted, market-adjusted required return. A value of zero indicates that the portfolio earned *exactly* its required return. Negative values indicate the portfolio failed to earn its required return.

Using the data for Hathaway's portfolio presented earlier, we can substitute into Equation 13.6 to get Jensen's measure, JM_p, for Hathaway's portfolio.

$$\text{JM}_p = (13.25\% - 7.50\%) - [1.20 \times (10.75\% - 7.50\%)]$$
$$= 5.75\% - (1.20 \times 3.25\%) = 5.75\% - 3.90\% = \underline{\underline{1.85\%}}$$

The 1.85% value for Jensen's measure indicates that Hathaway's portfolio earned an *excess return* 1.85 percentage points above its required return, given its nondiversifiable risk as measured by beta. Clearly, Hathaway's portfolio has outperformed the market on a risk-adjusted basis.

Note that unlike the Sharpe and Treynor measures, Jensen's measure, through its use of CAPM, automatically adjusts for the market return. Therefore, there is no need to make a separate market comparison. In general, the higher the value of Jensen's measure, the better the portfolio has performed. Only those portfolios with positive Jensen measures have outperformed the market on a risk-adjusted basis. Because of its computational simplicity, its reliance only on nondiversifiable risk, and its inclusion of both risk and market adjustments, Jensen's measure (alpha) tends to be preferred over those of Sharpe and Treynor for assessing portfolio performance.

Portfolio Revision

In the Hathaway portfolio we have been discussing, one transaction occurred during 2011. The reason for this transaction was that Hathaway believed the Florida Southcoast Banks stock had more return potential than the Dallas National stock. You should periodically analyze your portfolio with one basic question in mind: "Does this portfolio continue to meet my needs?" In other words, does the portfolio contain those issues that are best suited to your risk-return needs? Investors who systematically study the issues in their portfolios will occasionally find a need to sell certain issues and purchase new securities to replace them. This process is commonly called **portfolio revision**. As the economy evolves, certain industries and stocks become either less or more attractive as investments. In today's stock market, timeliness is the essence of profitability.

Given the dynamics of the investment world, periodic reallocation and rebalancing of the portfolio are a necessity. Many circumstances require such changes. For example, as an investor nears retirement, the portfolio's emphasis normally evolves from a strategy that stresses growth/capital appreciation to one that seeks to preserve capital. Changing a portfolio's emphasis normally occurs as an evolutionary process rather than an overnight switch. Individual issues in the portfolio often change in risk-return characteristics. As this occurs, you would be wise to eliminate those issues that do not meet your objectives. In addition, the need for diversification is constant. As issues rise or fall in value, their diversification effect may be lessened. Thus, you may need portfolio revision to maintain diversification.

CONCEPTS IN REVIEW

Answers available at
www.pearsonhighered.com/gitman

13.14 What is *active portfolio management?* Will it result in superior returns? Explain.

13.15 Describe the steps involved in measuring portfolio return. Explain the role of the portfolio's HPR in this process and explain why one must differentiate between realized and unrealized gains.

13.16 Why is comparing a portfolio's return to the return on a broad market index generally inadequate? Explain.

13.17 Briefly describe each of the following return measures available for assessing portfolio performance and explain how they are used.

  a. Sharpe's measure.
  b. Treynor's measure.
  c. Jensen's measure (Jensen's alpha).

13.18 Why is Jensen's measure (alpha) generally preferred over the measures of Sharpe and Treynor for assessing portfolio performance? Explain.

13.19 Explain the role of *portfolio revision* in the process of managing a portfolio.

Timing Transactions

LG5 **LG6** The essence of timing is to "buy low and sell high." This is the dream of all investors. Although there is no tried-and-true way to achieve such a goal, there are several methods you can utilize to time purchases and sales. First, there are formula plans, which we discuss next. Investors can also use limit and stop-loss orders as a timing aid, can follow procedures for warehousing liquidity, and can take into consideration other aspects of timing when selling their investments. For the story of one famous investor of the twentieth century, see the following *Ethics in Investing* box.

ETHICS IN INVESTING

The Virtues of Ethical Investing: The Remarkable Life of John Templeton

A pioneer in financial investments, John Marks Templeton has spent a lifetime encouraging ethical behavior. A naturalized British citizen living in Nassau, the Bahamas, Templeton was knighted by Queen Elizabeth II in 1987 for his many accomplishments. One of them was creating the $1 million-plus Templeton Prize for Progress toward Research or Discoveries about Spiritual Realities, presented annually in London since 1973. Mother Theresa of Calcutta was its first recipient.

John Templeton was born in 1912 in a small Tennessee town. His businessman father taught him to keep a positive attitude. By the time John was 4, he was raising beans in his mother's garden and selling them at a local store for profit. At the age of 12, he came upon an old, broken-down Ford, which he later purchased from a farmer for $10. With the help of friends he spent six months rebuilding it and drove it until he graduated from high school. Templeton never spent more than $200 on a car until he had a net worth of more than $250,000.

Qualities developed as a young man served Templeton well as he set out to become one of the world's greatest investors. Forced to live thriftily while paying for his own education at Yale University during the Depression, Templeton graduated in 1934 as a top scholar in his class. After graduation, he set out on a seven-month world tour to study global investment opportunities first-hand. Before leaving, John wrote 100 investment firms of his plans and told them he would be available for hire upon his return. His efforts landed him a job on Wall Street. When John got married,

he and his wife set a goal to save 50% of their income. To make thrift a joy rather than a burden, the Templetons became avid bargain shoppers and used to compete with their friends for bargains.

Standard stock-buying advice is "buy low, and sell high." When war began in Europe in 1939, Templeton borrowed money to buy 100 shares in each of 104 companies selling at $1 a share or less, including 34 companies that were in bankruptcy. Only four turned out to be worthless, and he turned large profits on the others after holding each for an average of four years.

Taking a less-traveled route in investing, Templeton sold advice on how to invest worldwide when Americans rarely considered foreign investment. In 1954, he launched his flagship fund, Templeton Growth. Each $100,000 invested then, with distributions reinvested, grew to total $54 million in 2009. *Money* magazine named him "arguably the greatest global stock picker of the century" (January 1999). Sir John Templeton has always been a student of *free competition:* "Competitive business has reduced costs, has increased variety, has improved quality." And if a business is not ethical, he says, "it will fail, perhaps not right away, but eventually." His progressive ideas on finance, spiritual life, and business ethics made him a distinctive figure in all these fields.

Critical Thinking Question What personal characteristic of John Templeton do you think made him an investing giant? Be ready to defend your answer.

(Source: Matthew Robinson, His Optimism and Drive Built a Financial Empire, *Investor's Business Daily*, July 24, 2006 and Franklin Templeton Investments, www.franklintempleton.com (accessed September 2009).)

Formula Plans

Formula plans are mechanical methods of portfolio management that try to take advantage of price changes that result from cyclical price movements. Formula plans are not set up to provide unusually high returns. Rather, they are conservative strategies employed by investors who do not wish to bear a high level of risk. We discuss four popular formula plans: dollar-cost averaging, the constant-dollar plan, the constant-ratio plan, and the variable-ratio plan.

Dollar-Cost Averaging **Dollar-cost averaging** is a formula plan in which a fixed dollar amount is invested in a security at fixed time intervals. In this passive buy-and-hold strategy, the periodic dollar investment is held constant. To make the plan work, you must invest on a regular basis. The goal of a dollar-cost averaging program is growth in the value of the security to which the funds are allocated. The price of the investment security will probably fluctuate over time. If the price declines, you would purchase more shares per period. Conversely, if the price rises, you would purchase fewer shares per period.

Look at the example of dollar-cost averaging in Table 13.9. The table shows investment of $500 per month in the Wolverine Mutual Fund, a growth-oriented, no-load mutual fund. Assume that during one year's time you have placed $6,000 in the mutual fund shares. (Because this is a no-load fund, shares are purchased at net asset value, NAV.) You made purchases at NAVs ranging from a low of $24.16 to a high of $30.19. At year-end, the value of your holdings in the fund was slightly less than $6,900. Dollar-cost averaging is a passive strategy; other formula plans are more active.

Constant-Dollar Plan A **constant-dollar plan** consists of a portfolio that is divided into two parts, speculative and conservative. The speculative portion consists of securities that have high promise of capital gains. The conservative portion consists of low-risk

---

TABLE 13.9 Dollar-Cost Averaging ($500 per month, Wolverine Mutual Fund shares) [EXCEL WITH SPREADSHEETS]

Transactions

Month	Net Asset Value (NAV) Month-End	Number of Shares Purchased
January	$26.00	19.23
February	27.46	18.21
March	27.02	18.50
April	24.19	20.67
May	26.99	18.53
June	25.63	19.51
July	24.70	20.24
August	24.16	20.70
September	25.27	19.79
October	26.15	19.12
November	29.60	16.89
December	30.19	16.56

Annual Summary:

Total investment: $6,000.00
Total number of shares purchased: 227.95
Average cost per share: $26.32
Year-end portfolio value: $6,881.81

TABLE 13.10 Constant-Dollar Plan

Mutual Fund NAV	Value of Speculative Portion	Value of Conservative Portion	Total Portfolio Value	Transactions	Number of Shares in Speculative Portion
$10.00	$10,000.00	$10,000.00	$20,000.00		1,000
11.00	11,000.00	10,000.00	21,000.00		1,000
12.00	12,000.00	10,000.00	22,000.00		1,000
→12.00	10,000.00	12,000.00	22,000.00	Sold 166.67 shares	833.33
11.00	9,166.63	12,000.00	21,166.63		833.33
9.50	7,916.64	12,000.00	19,916.64		833.33
→ 9.50	10,000.00	9,916.64	19,916.64	Purchased 219.30 shares	1,052.63
10.00	10,526.30	9,916.64	20,442.94		1,052.63

investments such as bonds or a money market account. The target dollar amount for the speculative portion is constant. You establish trigger points (upward or downward movement in the speculative portion) at which funds are removed from or added to that portion. The constant-dollar plan basically skims off profits from the speculative portion of the portfolio if it rises a certain percentage or amount in value and adds these funds to the conservative portion of the portfolio. If the speculative portion of the portfolio declines by a specific percentage or amount, you add funds to it from the conservative portion.

Assume that you have established the constant-dollar plan shown in Table 13.10. The beginning $20,000 portfolio consists of $10,000 invested in a high-beta, no-load mutual fund and $10,000 deposited in a money market account. You have decided to rebalance the portfolio every time the speculative portion is worth $2,000 more or $2,000 less than its initial value of $10,000. If the speculative portion of the portfolio equals or exceeds $12,000, you sell sufficient shares of the fund to bring its value down to $10,000 and add the proceeds from the sale to the conservative portion. If the speculative portion declines in value to $8,000 or less, you use funds from the conservative portion to purchase sufficient shares to raise the value of the speculative portion to $10,000.

Two portfolio-rebalancing actions are taken in the time sequence illustrated in Table 13.10. Initially, $10,000 was allocated to each portion of the portfolio. When the mutual fund's net asset value (NAV) rose to $12, the speculative portion was worth $12,000. At that point, you sold 166.67 shares valued at $2,000, and added the proceeds to the money market account. Later, the mutual fund's NAV declined to $9.50 per share, causing the value of the speculative portion to drop below $8,000. This change triggered the purchase of sufficient shares to raise the value of the speculative portion to $10,000. Over the long run, if the speculative investment of the constant-dollar plan rises in value, the conservative component of the portfolio will increase in dollar value as profits are transferred into it.

Constant-Ratio Plan The **constant-ratio plan** is similar to the constant-dollar plan except that it establishes a desired fixed *ratio* of the speculative portion to the conservative portion of the portfolio. When the actual ratio of the two differs by a predetermined amount from the desired ratio, rebalancing occurs. At that point, you make transactions to bring the actual ratio back to the desired ratio. To use the constant-ratio plan, you must decide on the appropriate apportionment of the portfolio between speculative and conservative investments. You must also choose the ratio trigger point at which transactions occur.

TABLE 13.11　Constant-Ratio Plan

Mutual Fund NAV	Value of Speculative Portion	Value of Conservative Portion	Total Portfolio Value	Ratio of Speculative Portion to Conservative Portion	Transactions	Number of Shares in Speculative Portion
$10.00	$10,000.00	$10,000.00	$20,000.00	1.000		1,000
11.00	11,000.00	10,000.00	21,000.00	1.100		1,000
12.00	12,000.00	10,000.00	22,000.00	1.200		1,000
→12.00	11,000.00	11,000.00	22,000.00	1.000	Sold 83.33 shares	916.67
11.00	10,083.00	11,000.00	21,083.00	0.917		916.67
10.00	9,166.70	11,000.00	20,166.70	0.833		916.67
9.00	8,250.00	11,000.00	19,250.00	0.750		916.67
→ 9.00	9,625.00	9,625.00	19,250.00	1.000	Purchased 152.78 shares	1,069.44
10.00	10,694.40	9,625.00	20,319.40	1.110		1,069.44

To see how this works, assume that the constant-ratio plan illustrated in Table 13.11 is yours. The initial portfolio value is $20,000. You have decided to allocate 50% of the portfolio to the speculative, high-beta mutual fund and 50% to a money market account. You will rebalance the portfolio when the ratio of the speculative portion to the conservative portion is greater than or equal to 1.20 or less than or equal to 0.80. A sequence of changes in net asset value (NAV) is listed in Table 13.11. Initially, $10,000 is allocated to each portion of the portfolio. When the fund NAV reaches $12, the 1.20 ratio triggers the sale of 83.33 shares. Then the portfolio is back to its desired 50:50 ratio. Later, the fund NAV declines to $9, lowering the value of the speculative portion to $8,250. The ratio of the speculative portion to the conservative portion is then 0.75, which is below the 0.80 trigger point. You purchase 152.78 shares to bring the desired ratio back up to the 50:50 level.

The long-run expectation under a constant-ratio plan is that the speculative securities will rise in value. When this occurs, you will sell securities to reapportion the portfolio and increase the value of the conservative portion. This philosophy is similar to the constant-dollar plan, except that it uses a ratio as a trigger point.

Variable-Ratio Plan　The **variable-ratio plan** is the most aggressive of these four fairly passive formula plans. It attempts to turn stock market movements to the investor's advantage by timing the market. That is, it tries to "buy low and sell high." The ratio of the speculative portion to the total portfolio value varies depending on the movement in value of the speculative securities. When the ratio rises a certain predetermined amount, the amount committed to the speculative portion of the portfolio is reduced. Conversely, if the value of the speculative portion declines so that it drops significantly in proportion to the total portfolio value, the amount committed to the speculative portion of the portfolio is increased.

When implementing the variable-ratio plan, you have several decisions to make. First, you must determine the initial allocation between the speculative and conservative portions of the portfolio. Next, you must choose trigger points to initiate buy or sell activity. These points are a function of the ratio between the value of the speculative portion and the value of the total portfolio. Finally, you must set adjustments in that ratio at each trigger point.

Assume that you use the variable-ratio plan shown in Table 13.12. Initially, you divide the portfolio equally between the speculative and the conservative portions. The

TABLE 13.12 Variable-Ratio Plan

Mutual Fund NAV	Value of Speculative Portion	Value of Conservative Portion	Total Portfolio Value	Ratio of Speculative Portion to Total Portfolio Value	Transactions	Number of Shares in Speculative Portion
$10.00	$10,000.00	$10,000.00	$20,000.00	0.50		1,000
15.00	15,000.00	10,000.00	25,000.00	0.60		1,000
→15.00	11,250.00	13,750.00	25,000.00	0.45	Sold 250 shares	750
10.00	7,500.00	13,750.00	21,250.00	0.35		750
→10.00	11,687.50	9,562.50	21,250.00	0.55	Purchased 418.75 shares	1,168.75
12.00	14,025.00	9,562.50	23,587.50	0.59		1,168.75

speculative portion consists of a high-beta (around 2.0) mutual fund. The conservative portion is a money market account. You decide that when the speculative portion reaches 60% of the total portfolio, you will reduce its proportion to 45%. If the speculative portion of the portfolio drops to 40% of the total portfolio, then you will raise its proportion to 55%. The logic behind this strategy is an attempt to time the cyclical movements in the mutual fund's value. When the fund moves up in value, you take profits, and you increase the proportion invested in the no-risk money market account. When the fund declines markedly in value, you increase the proportion of capital committed to the speculative portion.

A sequence of transactions is depicted in Table 13.12. When the fund net asset value (NAV) climbs to $15, the 60% ratio trigger point is reached, and you sell 250 shares of the fund. You place the proceeds in the money market account, which causes the speculative portion then to represent 45% of the value of the portfolio. Later, the fund NAV declines to $10, causing the speculative portion of the portfolio to drop to 35%. This triggers a portfolio rebalancing, and you purchase 418.75 shares, moving the speculative portion to 55%. When the fund NAV then moves to $12, the total portfolio is worth in excess of $23,500. In comparison, had the initial investment of $20,000 been allocated equally and had no rebalancing been done between the mutual fund and the money market account, the total portfolio value at this time would have been only $22,000 ($12 × 1,000 = $12,000 in the speculative portion plus $10,000 in the money market account).

Using Limit and Stop-Loss Orders

In Chapter 3 we discussed the market order, the limit order, and the stop-loss order. (See pages 99–100 to review these types of orders.) Here we will see how you can use the limit and stop-loss orders to rebalance a portfolio. These types of security orders, if properly used, can increase return by lowering transaction costs.

Limit Orders There are many ways investors can use limit orders when they buy or sell securities. For instance, if you have decided to add a stock to the portfolio, a limit order to buy will ensure that you buy only at the desired purchase price or below. A limit good-'til-canceled (GTC) order to buy instructs the broker to buy stock until the entire order is filled. The primary risk in using limit instead of market orders is that the order may not be executed. For example, if you placed a GTC order to buy 100 shares of State Oil of California at $27 per share and the stock never traded at $27 per share or less, the order would never be executed. Thus, you must weigh the need for immediate execution (market order) against the possibility of a better price with a limit order.

Limit orders, of course, can increase your return if they enable you to buy a security at a lower cost or sell it at a higher price. During a typical trading day, a stock will fluctuate up and down over a normal trading range. For example, suppose the common shares of Jama Motor traded 10 times in the following sequence: 36.00, 35.88, 35.75, 35.94, 35.50, 35.63, 35.82, 36.00, 36.13, 36.00. A market order to sell could have been executed at somewhere between 35.50 (the low) and 36.13 (the high). A limit order to sell at 36.00 would have been executed at 36.00. Thus, $0.50 per share might have been gained by using a limit order.

Stop-Loss Orders Stop-loss orders can be used to limit the downside loss exposure of an investment. For example, assume you purchase 500 shares of Easy Work at 26.00 and have set a specific goal to sell the stock if it reaches 32.00 or drops to 23.00. To implement this goal, you would enter a GTC stop order to sell with a price limit of 32.00 and another stop order at a price of 23.00. If the issue trades at 23.00 or less, the stop-loss order becomes a market order, and the broker sells the stock at the best price available. Or, if the issue trades at 32.00 or higher, the broker will sell the stock. In the first situation, you are trying to reduce your losses; in the second, you are attempting to protect a profit.

The principal risk in using stop-loss orders is **whipsawing**—a situation where a stock temporarily drops in price and then bounces back upward. If Easy Work dropped to 23.00, then 22.57, and then rallied back to 26.00, you would have been sold out at a price between 23.00 and 22.57. For this reason, limit orders, including stop-loss orders, require careful analysis before they are placed. You must consider the stock's probable fluctuations as well as the need to purchase or sell the stock when choosing among market, limit, and stop-loss orders.

Warehousing Liquidity

Investing in risky stocks or in options or futures offers probable returns in excess of those available with money market deposit accounts or bonds. However, stocks and options and futures are risky investments. One recommendation for an efficient portfolio is to keep a portion of it in a low-risk, highly liquid investment to protect against total loss. The low-risk asset acts as a buffer against possible investment adversity. A second reason for maintaining funds in a low-risk asset is the possibility of future opportunities. When opportunity strikes, an investor who has extra cash available will be able to take advantage of the situation. If you have set aside funds in a highly liquid investment, you need not disturb the existing portfolio.

There are two primary media for warehousing liquidity: money market deposit accounts at financial institutions and money market mutual funds. The money market accounts at savings institutions provide relatively easy access to funds and furnish returns competitive with (but somewhat lower than) money market mutual funds. The products offered by financial institutions are becoming more competitive with those offered by mutual funds and stock brokerage firms.

Timing Investment Sales

Knowing when to sell a stock is as important as choosing which stock to buy. Periodically, you should review your portfolio and consider possible sales and new purchases. Here we discuss two issues relevant to the sale decision: tax consequences and achieving investment goals.

Tax Consequences Taxes affect nearly all investment actions. All investors can and should understand certain basics. The treatment of capital losses is important: *A maximum of $3,000 of losses in excess of capital gains can be written off against other* *income in any one year.* If you have a loss position in an investment and have concluded that it would be wise to sell it, the best time to sell is when you have a capital gain against which you can apply the loss. Clearly, one should carefully consider the tax consequences of investment sales prior to taking action.

Achieving Investment Goals Every investor would enjoy buying an investment at its lowest price and selling it at its top price. At a more realistic level, you should sell an investment when it no longer meets your needs. In particular, if an investment has become either more or less risky than is desired, or if it has not met its return objective, it should be sold. The tax consequences mentioned above help to determine the appropriate time to sell. However, *taxes are not the foremost consideration in a sale decision.* The dual concepts of risk and return should be the overriding concerns.

Be sure to take the time periodically to examine each investment in light of its return performance and relative risk. You should sell any investment that no longer belongs in the portfolio and should buy investments that are more suitable. Finally, you should not hold out for every nickel of profit. Very often, those who hold out for the top price watch the value of their holdings plummet. If an investment looks ripe to sell, sell it, take the profit, reinvest it in an appropriate asset, and enjoy your good fortune.

CONCEPTS IN REVIEW

Answers available at
www.pearshonhighered.com/
gitman

13.20 Explain the role that *formula plans* can play in the timing of security transactions. Describe the logic underlying the use of these plans.

13.21 Briefly describe each of the following plans and differentiate among them.

  a. Dollar-cost averaging.
  b. Constant-dollar plan.
  c. Constant-ratio plan.
  d. Variable-ratio plan.

13.22 Describe how a limit order can be used when securities are bought or sold. How can a stop-loss order be used to reduce losses? To protect profit?

13.23 Give two reasons why an investor might want to maintain funds in a low-risk, highly liquid investment.

13.24 Describe the two items an investor should consider before reaching a decision to sell an investment vehicle.

 Here is what you should know after reading this chapter. **MyFinanceLab** will help you identify what you know, and where to go when you need to practice.

What You Should Know	Key Terms	What You Should Know
LG1 **Explain how to use an asset allocation scheme to construct a portfolio consistent with investor objectives.** To construct a portfolio, consider personal characteristics and establish consistent portfolio objectives such as current income, capital preservation, capital growth, tax	asset allocation, *p. 493* asset allocation fund, *p. 495* fixed-weightings approach, *p. 493*	My FinanceLab Study Plan 13.1

What You Should Know	Key Terms	What You Should Know
considerations, and level of risk. Asset allocation, which is the key influence on portfolio return, involves dividing the portfolio into asset classes. Asset allocation aims to protect against negative developments while taking advantage of positive ones. The basic approaches to asset allocation involve the use of fixed weightings, flexible weightings, and tactical asset allocation. Asset allocation can be achieved on a do-it-yourself basis, with the use of mutual funds, or by merely buying shares in an asset allocation fund.	flexible-weightings approach, *p. 493* security selection, *p. 493* tactical asset allocation, *p. 494*	
LG2 Discuss the data and indexes needed to measure and compare investment performance. To analyze the performance of individual investments, gather current market information and stay abreast of international, national, and local economic and market developments. Indexes of investment performance such as the Dow Jones Industrial Average (DJIA) and bond market indicators are available for use in assessing market behavior. The performance of individual investment vehicles can be measured on both a pretax and an after-tax basis by using the holding period return (HPR). HPR measures the total return (income plus change in value) earned on the investment during an investment period of one year or less. HPR can be compared to investment goals to assess whether the proper return is being earned for the risk involved and to isolate any problem investments.		My FinanceLab Study Plan 13.2
LG3 Understand the techniques used to measure income, capital gains, and total portfolio return. To measure portfolio return, estimate the amount invested, the income earned, and any capital gains (both realized and unrealized) over the relevant current time period. Using these values, calculate the portfolio's holding period return (HPR) by dividing the total returns by the amount of investment during the period. Comparison of the portfolio's HPR to overall market measures can provide some insight about the portfolio's performance relative to the market.	active portfolio management, *p. 501*	My FinanceLab Study Plan 13.3 Video Learning Aid for Problem P13.3
LG4 Use the Sharpe, Treynor, and Jensen measures to compare a portfolio's return with a risk-adjusted, market-adjusted rate of return, and discuss portfolio revision. A risk-adjusted, market-adjusted evaluation of a portfolio's return can be made using Sharpe's measure, Treynor's measure, or Jensen's measure. Sharpe's and Treynor's measures find the risk premium per unit of risk, which can be compared with similar market measures to assess the portfolio's performance. Jensen's measure (alpha) calculates the portfolio's excess return using beta and CAPM. Jensen's measure tends to be preferred because it is relatively easy to calculate and directly makes both risk	Jensen's measure (Jensen's alpha), *p. 507* portfolio revision, *p. 508* Sharpe's measure, *p. 505* Treynor's measure, *p. 506*	My FinanceLab Study Plan 13.4 Video Learning Aid for Problem P13.15

What You Should Know	Key Terms	What You Should Know
and market adjustments. Portfolio revision—selling certain issues and purchasing new ones to replace them—should take place when returns are unacceptable or when the portfolio fails to meet the investor's objectives.		
LG5 Describe the role and logic of dollar-cost averaging, constant-dollar plans, constant-ratio plans, and variable-ratio plans. Formula plans are used to time purchase and sale decisions to take advantage of price changes that result from cyclical price movements. The four commonly used formula plans are dollar-cost averaging, the constant-dollar plan, the constant-ratio plan, and the variable-ratio plan. All of them have certain decision rules or triggers that signal a purchase and/or sale action.	constant-dollar plan, *p. 510* constant-ratio plan, *p. 511* dollar-cost averaging, *p. 510* formula plans, *p. 510* variable-ratio plan, *p. 512*	My FinanceLab Study Plan 13.5 Excel Table 13.9
LG6 Explain the role of limit and stop-loss orders in investment timing, warehousing liquidity, and timing investment sales. Limit and stop-loss orders can be used to trigger the rebalancing of a portfolio to contribute to improved portfolio returns. Low-risk, highly liquid investment vehicles such as money market deposit accounts and money market mutual funds can warehouse liquidity. Such liquidity can protect against total loss and allow you to seize any attractive opportunities. Investment sales should be timed to obtain maximum tax benefits (or minimum tax consequences) and to contribute to the achievement of the investor's goals.	whipsawing, *p. 514*	My FinanceLab Study Plan 13.6

Log into **MyFinanceLab**, take a chapter test, and get a personalized Study Plan that tells you which concepts you understand and which ones you need to review. From there, **MyFinanceLab** will give you further practice, tutorials, animations, videos, and guided solutions.
Log into www.myfinancelab.com

Discussion Questions

LG1

Q13.1 List your personal characteristics and then state your investment objectives in light of them. Use these objectives as a basis for developing your portfolio objectives and policies. Assume that you plan to create a portfolio aimed at achieving your stated objectives. The portfolio will be constructed by allocating your money to any of the following asset classes: common stock, bonds, foreign securities, and short-term securities.

    a. Determine and justify an asset allocation to these four classes in light of your stated portfolio objectives and policies.

    b. Describe the types of investments you would choose for each of the asset classes.

c. Assume that after making the asset allocations specified in part **a**, you receive a sizable inheritance that causes your portfolio objectives to change to a much more aggressive posture. Describe the changes that you would make in your asset allocations.

d. Describe other asset classes you might consider when developing your asset allocation scheme.

LG2 LG3   **Q13.2** Choose an established local (or nearby) company whose stock is listed and actively traded on a major exchange. Find the stock's closing price at the end of each of the preceding six years and the amount of dividends paid in each of the preceding five years. Also, obtain the value of the Dow Jones Industrial Average (DJIA) at the end of each of the preceding six years.

a. Use Equation 13.1 (on page 498) to calculate the pretax holding period return (HPR) on the stock for each of the preceding five years.

b. Study the international, national, and local economic and market developments that occurred during the preceding five years.

c. Compare the stock's returns to the DJIA for each year over the five-year period of concern.

d. Discuss the stock's returns in light of the economic and market developments noted in part **b** and the behavior of the DJIA as noted in part **c** over the five preceding years. How well did the stock perform in light of these factors?

LG2 LG3   **Q13.3** Assume that you are in the 35% ordinary tax bracket (federal and state combined) and that dividends and capital gains for holding periods of more than 12 months are taxed at a 15% rate. Select a major stock, bond, and mutual fund in which you are interested in investing. For each of them, gather data for each of the past three years on the annual dividends or interest paid and the capital gain (or loss) that would have resulted had they been purchased at the start of each year and sold at the end of each year. For the mutual fund, be sure to separate any dividends paid into investment income dividends and capital gains dividends.

a. For each of the three investment vehicles, calculate the pretax and after-tax HPR for each of the 3 years.

b. Use your annual HPR findings in part **a** to calculate the average after-tax HPR for each of the investment vehicles over the three-year period.

c. Compare the average returns found in part **b** for each of the investment vehicles. Discuss the relative risks in view of these returns and the characteristics of each vehicle.

LG2 LG3   **Q13.4** Choose six actively traded stocks for inclusion in your investment portfolio. Assume the portfolio was created three years earlier by purchasing 200 shares of each of the six stocks. Find the acquisition price of each stock, the annual dividend paid by each stock, and the year-end prices for the three calendar years. Record for each stock its total cost, cost per share, current price per share, and total current value at the end of each of the three calendar years.

a. For each of the three years, find the amount invested in the portfolio.

b. For each of the three years, measure the annual income from the portfolio.

c. For each of the three years, determine the unrealized capital gains from the portfolio.

d. For each of the three years, calculate the portfolio's HPR, using the values in parts **a**, **b**, and **c**.

e. Use your findings in part **d** to calculate the average HPR for the portfolio over the three-year period. Discuss your finding.

LG4   **Q13.5** Find five actively traded stocks and record their prices at the start and the end of the most recent calendar year. Also, find the amount of dividends paid on each stock during that year and each stock's beta at the end of the year. Assume that the five stocks were held during the year in an equal-dollar-weighted portfolio (20% in each stock) created at the start of the year. Also find the current risk-free rate, R_F, and the market return, r_m, for the given year. Assume that the standard deviation for the portfolio of the five stocks is 14.25% and that the standard deviation for the market portfolio is 10.80%.

a. Use the formula presented in Chapter 5 (Equation 5.1 on page 165) to find the portfolio return, r_p, for the year under consideration.

b. Calculate Sharpe's measure for both the portfolio and the market. Compare and discuss these values. On the basis of this measure, is the portfolio's performance inferior or superior? Explain.

c. Calculate Treynor's measure for both the portfolio and the market. Compare and discuss these values. On the basis of this measure, is the portfolio's performance inferior or superior? Explain.

d. Calculate Jensen's measure (Jensen's alpha) for the portfolio. Discuss its value. On the basis of this measure, is the portfolio's performance inferior or superior? Explain.

e. Compare, contrast, and discuss your analysis using the three measures in parts **b, c,** and **d.** Evaluate the portfolio.

LG5 **Q13.6**   Choose a high-growth mutual fund and a money market mutual fund. Find and record their closing net asset values (NAVs) at the end of each *week* for the immediate past year. Assume that you wish to invest $10,400.

a. Assume you use dollar-cost averaging to buy shares in *both* the high-growth and the money market funds by purchasing $100 of each of them at the end of each week—a total investment of $10,400 (52 weeks × $200/week). How many shares would you have purchased in each fund by year-end? What are the total number of shares, the average cost per share, and the year-end portfolio value of each fund? Total the year-end fund values and compare them to the total that would have resulted from investing $5,200 in each fund at the end of the first week.

b. Assume you use a constant-dollar plan with 50% invested in the high-growth fund (speculative portion) and 50% invested in the money market fund (conservative portion). If the portfolio is rebalanced every time the speculative portion is worth $500 more or $500 less than its initial value of $5,200, what would be the total portfolio value and the number of shares in the speculative portion at year-end?

c. Assume that, as in part **b,** you initially invest 50% in the speculative portion and 50% in the conservative portion. But in this case you use a constant-ratio plan under which rebalancing to the 50:50 mix occurs whenever the ratio of the speculative to the conservative portion is greater than or equal to 1.25 or less than or equal to 0.75. What would be the total portfolio value and the number of shares in the speculative portion at year-end?

d. Compare and contrast the year-end values of the total portfolio under each of the plans in parts **a, b,** and **c.** Which plan would have been best in light of these findings? Explain.

Problems

All problems are available on **www.myfinancelab.com**

LG1 **P13.1** Refer to the table below:

	Fund A	Fund B
Beta	1.8	1.1
Investor A	20%	80%
Investor B	80%	20%

As between Investor A and Investor B, which is more likely to represent a retired couple? Why?

LG1 **P13.2** Portfolio A and Portfolio B had the same holding period return last year. Most of the returns from Portfolio A came from dividends, while most of the returns from Portfolio B came from capital gains. Which portfolio is owned by a single working person making a high salary, and which is owned by a retired couple? Why?

LG3 **P13.3** John Reardon purchased 100 shares of Tomco Corporation in December 2010, at a total cost of $1,762. He held the shares for 15 months and then sold them, netting $2,500. During the period he held the stock, the company paid him $200 in cash dividends. How much, if any, was the capital gain realized upon the sale of stock? Calculate John's pretax HPR.

LG3 **P13.4** Jeff Krause purchased 1,000 shares of a speculative stock on January 2 for $2.00 per share. Six months later on July 1, he sold them for $9.50 per share. He uses an online broker that charges him $10 per trade. What was Jeff's annualized HPR on this investment?

LG3 **P13.5** Jill Clark invested $25,000 in the bonds of Industrial Aromatics, Inc. She held them for 13 months, at the end of which she sold them for $26,746. During the period of ownership she received $2,000 interest. Calculate the pretax and after-tax HPR on Jill's investment. Assume that she is in the 31% ordinary tax bracket (federal and state combined) and pays a 15% capital gains rate on dividends and on capital gains for holding periods longer than 12 months.

LG3 **P13.6** Charlotte Smidt bought 2,000 shares of the balanced no-load LaJolla Fund exactly one year and two days ago for an NAV of $8.60 per share. During the year, the fund distributed investment income dividends of $0.32 per share and capital gains dividends of $0.38 per share. At the end of the year, Charlotte, who is in the 35% ordinary tax bracket (federal and state combined) and pays a 15% capital gains rate on dividends and on capital gains for holding periods longer than 12 months, realized $8.75 per share on the sale of all 2,000 shares. Calculate Charlotte's pretax and after-tax HPR on this transaction.

LG3 **P13.7** Linda Babeu, who is in a 33% ordinary tax bracket (federal and state combined) and pays a 15% capital gains rate on dividends and capital gains for holding periods longer than 12 months, purchased 10 options contracts for a total cost of $4,000 just over one year ago. Linda netted $4,700 upon the sale of the 10 contracts today. What are Linda's pretax and after-tax HPRs on this transaction?

LG3 **P13.8** Mom and Pop had a portfolio of long-term bonds that they purchased many years ago. The bonds pay 12% interest annually, and the face value is $100,000. If Mom and Pop are in the 25% tax bracket, what is their annual after-tax HPR on this investment? (Assume it trades at par.)

LG3 **P13.9** On January 1, 2011, Simon Love's portfolio of 15 common stocks, completely equity-financed, had a market value of $264,000. At the end of May 2011, Simon sold one of the stocks, which had a beginning-of-year value of $26,300, for $31,500. He did not reinvest those or any other funds in the portfolio during the year. He received total dividends from stocks in his portfolio of $12,500 during the year. On December 31, 2011, Simon's portfolio had a market value of $250,000. Find the HPR on Simon's portfolio during the year ended December 31, 2011. (Measure the amount of withdrawn funds at their beginning-of-year value.)

LG3 **P13.10** Congratulations! Your portfolio returned 11% last year, 2% better than the market return of 9%. Your portfolio had a standard deviation of earnings equal to 18%, and the risk-free rate is equal to 6%. Calculate Sharpe's measure for your portfolio. If the market's Sharpe's measure is .3, did you do better or worse than the market from a risk/return perspective?

LG4 **P13.11** Niki Malone's portfolio earned a return of 11.8% during the year just ended. The portfolio's standard deviation of return was 14.1%. The risk-free rate is currently 6.2%. During the year, the return on the market portfolio was 9.0% and its standard deviation was 9.4%.

  a. Calculate Sharpe's measure for Niki Malone's portfolio for the year just ended.
  b. Compare the performance of Niki's portfolio found in part **a** to that of Hector Smith's portfolio, which has a Sharpe's measure of 0.43. Which portfolio performed better? Why?

    c. Calculate Sharpe's measure for the market portfolio for the year just ended.

    d. Use your findings in parts **a** and **c** to discuss the performance of Niki's portfolio relative to the market during the year just ended.

LG4 **P13.12** Your portfolio has a beta equal to 1.3. It returned 12% last year. The market returned 10%; the risk-free rate is 6%. Calculate Treynor's measure for your portfolio and the market. Did you earn a better return than the market given the risk you took?

LG4 **P13.13** During the year just ended, Anna Schultz's portfolio, which has a beta of 0.90, earned a return of 8.6%. The risk-free rate is currently 7.3%, and the return on the market portfolio during the year just ended was 9.2%.

    a. Calculate Treynor's measure for Anna's portfolio for the year just ended.

    b. Compare the performance of Anna's portfolio found in part **a** to that of Stacey Quant's portfolio, which has a Treynor's measure of 1.25%. Which portfolio performed better? Explain.

    c. Calculate Treynor's measure for the market portfolio for the year just ended.

    d. Use your findings in parts **a** and **c** to discuss the performance of Anna's portfolio relative to the market during the year just ended.

LG4 **P13.14** Your portfolio returned 13% last year, with a beta equal to 1.5. The market return was 10%, and the risk-free rate 6%. Did you earn more or less than the required rate of return on your portfolio? (Use Jensen's measure.)

LG4 **P13.15** Chee Chew's portfolio has a beta of 1.3 and earned a return of 12.9% during the year just ended. The risk-free rate is currently 7.8%. The return on the market portfolio during the year just ended was 11.0%.

    a. Calculate Jensen's measure (Jensen's alpha) for Chee's portfolio for the year just ended.

    b. Compare the performance of Chee's portfolio found in part **a** to that of Carri Uhl's portfolio, which has a Jensen's measure of –0.24. Which portfolio performed better? Explain.

    c. Use your findings in part **a** to discuss the performance of Chee's portfolio during the period just ended.

LG4 **P13.16** The risk-free rate is currently 8.1%. Use the data in the accompanying table for the Fio family's portfolio and the market portfolio during the year just ended to answer the questions that follow.

Data Item	Fios' Portfolio	Market Portfolio
Rate of return	12.8%	11.2%
Standard deviation of return	13.5%	9.6%
Beta	1.10	1.00

    a. Calculate Sharpe's measure for the portfolio and the market. Compare the two measures, and assess the performance of the Fios' portfolio during the year just ended.

    b. Calculate Treynor's measure for the portfolio and the market. Compare the two, and assess the performance of the Fios' portfolio during the year just ended.

    c. Calculate Jensen's measure (Jensen's alpha). Use it to assess the performance of the Fios' portfolio during the year just ended.

    d. On the basis of your findings in parts **a, b,** and **c,** assess the performance of the Fios' portfolio during the year just ended.

LG5 **P13.17** Over the past two years, Jonas Cone has used a dollar-cost averaging formula to purchase $300 worth of FCI common stock each month. The price per share paid each month over the two years is given in the following table. Assume that Jonas paid no brokerage commissions on these transactions.

	Price per Share of FCI	
Month	Year 1	Year 2
January	$11.63	$11.38
February	11.50	11.75
March	11.50	12.00
April	11.00	12.00
May	11.75	12.13
June	12.00	12.50
July	12.38	12.75
August	12.50	13.00
September	12.25	13.25
October	12.50	13.00
November	11.85	13.38
December	11.50	13.50

a. How much was Jonas's total investment over the two-year period?
b. How many shares did Jonas purchase over the two-year period?
c. Use your findings in parts **a** and **b** to calculate Jonas's average cost per share of FCI.
d. What was the value of Jonas's holdings in FCI at the end of the second year?

LG5 **P13.18** Refer to the table below:

Time Period	Stock Price	Shares	MM Mutual Fund NAV	Shares
1	$20.00	1,000	$20.00	1,000
2	$25.00		$21.00	

Assume you are using a constant-dollar plan with a rebalancing trigger of $1,500. The stock price represents your speculative portfolio, and the MM mutual fund represents your conservative portfolio. What action, if any, should you take in time period 2? Be specific.

LG5 **P13.19** Refer to Problem 13.18 above. Now assume you are using a constant-ratio plan with a rebalance trigger of speculative-to-conservative of 1.25. What action, if any, should you take in time period 2? Be specific.

LG5 **P13.20** Refer to the table below:

Time Period	Stock Price	Shares	MM Mutual Fund NAV	Shares
1	$20.00	1,000	$20.00	1,000
2	$30.00	1,000	$19.00	1,000

Assume you are using a variable-ratio plan. You have decided that when the speculative portfolio reaches 60% of the total, you will reduce its proportion to 45%. What action, if any, should you take in time period 2? Be specific.

Visit **www.myfinancelab.com** for web exercises,
spreadsheets, and other online resources.

Case Problem 13.1   *Assessing the Stalchecks' Portfolio Performance*

LG3 LG4   Mary and Nick Stalcheck have an investment portfolio containing four vehicles. It was developed to provide them with a balance between current income and capital appreciation. Rather than acquire mutual fund shares or diversify within a given class of investment vehicle, they developed their portfolio with the idea of diversifying across various types of vehicles. The portfolio currently contains common stock, industrial bonds, mutual fund shares, and options. They acquired each of these vehicles during the past three years, and they plan to invest in other vehicles sometime in the future.

Currently, the Stalchecks are interested in measuring the return on their investment and assessing how well they have done relative to the market. They hope that the return earned over the past calendar year is in excess of what they would have earned by investing in a portfolio consisting of the S&P 500 Stock Composite Index. Their research has indicated that the risk-free rate was 7.2% and that the (before-tax) return on the S&P 500 portfolio was 10.1% during the past year. With the aid of a friend, they have been able to estimate the beta of their portfolio, which was 1.20. In their analysis, they have planned to ignore taxes, because they feel their earnings have been adequately sheltered. Because they did not make any portfolio transactions during the past year, all of the Stalchecks' investments have been held more than 12 months, and they would have to consider only unrealized capital gains, if any. To make the necessary calculations, the Stalchecks have gathered the following information on each of the four vehicles in their portfolio.

Common stock. They own 400 shares of KJ Enterprises common stock. KJ is a diversified manufacturer of metal pipe and is known for its unbroken stream of dividends. Over the past few years, it has entered new markets and, as a result, has offered moderate capital appreciation potential. Its share price has risen from $17.25 at the start of the last calendar year to $18.75 at the end of the year. During the year, quarterly cash dividends of $0.20, $0.20, $0.25, and $0.25 were paid.

Industrial bonds. The Stalchecks own eight Cal Industries bonds. The bonds have a $1,000 par value, have a 9.250% coupon, and are due in 2021. They are A-rated by Moody's. The bond was quoted at 97.000 at the beginning of the year and ended the calendar year at 96.375%.

Mutual fund. The Stalchecks hold 500 shares in the Holt Fund, a balanced, no-load mutual fund. The dividend distributions on the fund during the year consisted of $0.60 in investment income and $0.50 in capital gains. The fund's NAV at the beginning of the calendar year was $19.45, and it ended the year at $20.02.

Options. The Stalchecks own 100 options contracts on the stock of a company they follow. The value of these contracts totaled $26,000 at the beginning of the calendar year. At year-end the total value of the options contracts was $29,000.

Questions

a. Calculate the holding period return on a before-tax basis for each of these four investment vehicles.

b. Assuming that the Stalchecks' ordinary income is currently being taxed at a combined (federal and state) tax rate of 38%, and that they would pay a 15% capital gains tax on dividends and capital gains for holding periods longer than 12 months, determine the after-tax HPR for each of their four investment vehicles.

c. Recognizing that all gains on the Stalchecks' investments were unrealized, calculate the before-tax portfolio HPR for their four-vehicle portfolio during the past calendar year. Evaluate this return relative to its current income and capital gain components.

d. Use the HPR calculated in question **c** to compute Jensen's measure (Jensen's alpha). Use that measure to analyze the performance of the Stalchecks' portfolio on a risk-adjusted, market-adjusted basis. Comment on your finding. Is it reasonable to use Jensen's measure to evaluate a four-vehicle portfolio? Why or why not?

e. On the basis of your analysis in questions **a**, **c**, and **d**, what, if any, recommendations might you offer the Stalchecks relative to the revision of their portfolio? Explain your recommendations.

Case Problem 13.2   *Evaluating Formula Plans: Charles Spurge's Approach*

LG5 Charles Spurge, a mathematician with Ansco Petroleum Company, wishes to develop a rational basis for timing his portfolio transactions. He currently holds a security portfolio with a market value of nearly $100,000, divided equally between a very conservative, low-beta common stock, ConCam United, and a highly speculative, high-beta stock, Fleck Enterprises. On the basis of his reading of the investments' literature, Charles does not believe it is necessary to diversify one's portfolio across eight to 15 securities. His own feeling, based on his independent mathematical analysis, is that one can achieve the same results by holding a two-security portfolio in which one security is very conservative and the other is highly speculative. His feelings on this point will not be altered. He plans to continue to hold such a two-security portfolio until he finds that his theory does not work. During the past several years, he has earned a rate of return in excess of the risk-adjusted, market-adjusted rate expected on such a portfolio.

Charles's current interest centers on possibly developing his own formula plan for timing portfolio transactions. The current stage of his analysis focuses on the evaluation of four commonly used formula plans in order to isolate the desirable features of each. The four plans being considered are (1) dollar-cost averaging, (2) the constant-dollar plan, (3) the constant-ratio plan, and (4) the variable-ratio plan. Charles's analysis of the plans will involve the use of two types of data. Dollar-cost averaging is a passive buy-and-hold strategy in which the periodic investment is held constant. The other plans are more active in that they involve periodic purchases and sales within the portfolio. Thus, differing data are needed to evaluate the plans.

For evaluating the dollar-cost averaging plan, Charles decided he would assume an investment of $500 at the end of each 45-day period. He chose to use 45-day time intervals to achieve certain brokerage fee savings that would be available by making larger transactions. The $500 per 45 days totaled $4,000 for the year and equaled the total amount Charles invested during the past year. (Note: For convenience, the returns earned on the portions of the $4,000 that remain uninvested during the year are ignored.) In evaluating this plan, he would assume that half ($250) was invested in the conservative stock (ConCam United) and the other half in the speculative stock (Fleck Enterprises). The share prices for each of the stocks at the end of the eight 45-day periods when purchases were to be made are given in the accompanying table.

	Price per Share	
Period	ConCam	Fleck
1	$22.13	$22.13
2	21.88	24.50
3	21.88	25.38
4	22.00	28.50
5	22.25	21.88
6	22.13	19.25
7	22.00	21.50
8	22.25	23.63

To evaluate the three other plans, Charles decided to begin with a $4,000 portfolio evenly split between the two stocks. He chose to use $4,000, because that amount would correspond to the total amount invested in the two stocks over one year using dollar-cost averaging. He planned to use the same eight points in time given earlier to assess the portfolio and make transfers within it if required. For each of the three plans evaluated using these data, he established the following triggering points.

Constant-dollar plan. Each time the speculative portion of the portfolio is worth 13% more or less than its initial value of $2,000, the portfolio is rebalanced to bring the speculative portion back to its initial $2,000 value.

Constant-ratio plan. Each time the ratio of the value of the speculative portion of the portfolio to the value of the conservative portion is (1) greater than or equal to 1.15 or (2) less than or equal to 0.84, the portfolio is rebalanced through sale or purchase, respectively, to bring the ratio back to its initial value of 1.0.

Variable-ratio plan. Each time the value of the speculative portion of the portfolio rises above 54% of the total value of the portfolio, its proportion is reduced to 46%. Each time the value of the speculative portion of the portfolio drops below 38% of the total value of the portfolio, its proportion is raised to 50%.

Questions

a. Under the dollar-cost averaging plan, determine the total number of shares purchased, the average cost per share, and the year-end portfolio value expressed both in dollars and as a percentage of the amount invested for (1) the conservative stock, (2) the speculative stock, and (3) the total portfolio.

b. Using the constant-dollar plan, determine the year-end portfolio value expressed both in dollars and as a percentage of the amount initially invested for (1) the conservative portion, (2) the speculative portion, and (3) the total portfolio.

c. Repeat question **b** for the constant-ratio plan. Be sure to answer all parts.

d. Repeat question **b** for the variable-ratio plan. Be sure to answer all parts.

e. Compare and contrast your results from questions **a** through **d**. You may want to summarize them in tabular form. Which plan would appear to have been most beneficial in timing Charles's portfolio activities during the past year? Explain.

Excel with Spreadsheets

While most people believe that it is not possible to consistently time the market, there are several plans that allow investors to time purchases and sales of securities. These are referred to as formula plans—mechanical methods of managing a portfolio that attempt to take advantage of cyclical price movements. The objective is to mitigate the level of risk facing the investor.

One such formula plan is dollar-cost averaging. Here, a fixed dollar amount is invested in a security at fixed intervals. One objective is to increase the value of the given security over time. If prices decline, more shares are purchased; when market prices increase, fewer shares are purchased per period. The essence is that an investor is more likely not to buy overvalued securities.

Over the past 12 months, March 2011 through February 2012, Mrs. Paddock has used the dollar-cost averaging formula to purchase $1,000 worth of Neo common stock each month. The monthly price per share paid over the 12-month period is given following. Assume that Mrs. Paddock paid no brokerage commissions on these transactions.

Create a spreadsheet model similar to the spreadsheet for Table 13.9, which you can view at www.myfinancelab.com, to analyze the following investment situation for Neo common stock through dollar-cost averaging.

Year	Month	Price paid per share
2011	March	$14.30
	April	16.18
	May	18.37
	June	16.25
	July	14.33
	August	15.14
	September	15.93
	October	19.36
	November	23.25
	December	18.86
2012	January	22.08
	February	22.01

Questions

a. What is the total investment over the period from March 2011 through February 2012?
b. What is the total number of Neo shares purchased over the 12-month period?
c. What is the average cost per share?
d. What is the year-end (February 2012) portfolio value?
e. What is the profit or loss as of the end of February 2012?
f. What is the return on the portfolio after the 12-month period?

CFA EXAM QUESTIONS

Portfolio Management

Following is a sample of 9 Level-1 CFA exam questions that deal with many of the topics covered in Chapters 12 and 13 of this text, including the structure of mutual funds, portfolio diversification, portfolio returns, and the administration of personal portfolios. (*Note*: When answering some of the questions below, remember the coefficient of variation = σ/u; and for a normally distributed distribution, the safety-first ratio is basically the same as the Sharpe ratio . . .) (When answering the questions, give yourself 1½ minutes for each question; the objective is to correctly answer 6 of the 9 questions in a period of 14 minutes.)

1. An analyst compared the performance of a hedge fund index with the performance of a major stock index over the past eight years. She noted that the hedge fund index (created from a database) had a higher average return, lower standard deviation, and higher Sharpe ratio than the stock index. All the successful funds that have been in the hedge fund database continued to accept new money over the eight-year period. Are the average return and the Sharpe ratio, respectively, for the hedge fund index *most likely* overstated or understated?

	Average return for the hedge fund index	Sharpe ratio for the hedge fund index
a.	Overstated	Overstated
b.	Overstated	Understated
c.	Understated	Overstated

2. In-kind redemption is a process available to investors participating in:
    a. traditional mutual funds but not exchange traded funds.
    b. exchange traded funds but not traditional mutual funds.
    c. both traditional mutual funds and exchange traded funds.

3. Does trading take place only once a day at closing market prices in the case of:

	exchange traded funds?	traditional mutual funds?
a.	No	No
b.	No	Yes
c.	Yes	No

4. Do funds that are likely to trade at substantial discounts from their net asset values include:

	exchange traded funds?	closed-end funds?
a.	No	No
b.	No	Yes
c.	Yes	No

5. Forms of real estate investment that typically involve issuing shares that are traded on the stock market include.
    a. real estate investment trusts but not commingled funds.
    b. commingled funds but not real estate investment trusts.
    c. both real estate investment trusts and commingled funds.

CFA EXAM QUESTIONS

6. An analyst gathered the following information:

Portfolio	Mean Return (%)	Standard Deviation of Returns (%)
1	9.8	19.9
2	10.5	20.3
3	13.3	33.9

If the risk-free of return is 3.0 percent, the portfolio that had the *best* risk-adjusted performance based on the Sharpe ratio is:

a. Portfolio 1.   b. Portfolio 2.   c. Portfolio 3.

7. An analyst gathered the following information about a portfolio's performance over the past ten years:

Mean annual return	11.8%
Standard deviation of annual returns	15.7%
Portfolio beta	1.2

If the mean return on the risk-free asset over the same period was 5.0%, the coefficient of variation and Sharpe ratio, respectively, for the portfolio are *closest* to:

	Coefficient of variation	Sharpe ratio
a.	0.75	0.43
b.	1.33	0.36
c.	1.33	0.43

8. Western Investments holds a fixed-income portfolio comprised of four bonds whose market values and durations are given in the following table.

	Bond A	Bond B	Bond C	Bond D
Market value	$200,000	$300,000	$250,000	$550,000
Duration	4	6	7	8

The portfolio's duration is *closest* to:

a. 6.06.   b. 6.25.   c. 6.73.

9. At the end of the current year, an investor wants to make a donation of $20,000 to charity but does not want the year-end market value of her portfolio to fall below $600,000. If the shortfall level is equal to the risk-free rate of return and returns from all portfolios considered are normally distributed, will the portfolio that minimizes the probability of failing to achieve the investor's objective *most likely* have the:

	highest safety-first ratio?	highest Sharpe ratio?
a.	No	Yes
b.	Yes	No
c.	Yes	Yes

Answers: 1. a; 2. b; 3. b; 4. b; 5. a; 6. b; 7. c; 8. c; 9. c.

Source: From PROFESSIONAL EXAM REVIEW. *CFA Candidate Study Notes, Level 1, Volume 4, 2E.* © 2009 Delmar Learning, a part of Cengage Learning, Inc. Reproduced by permission. www.cengage.com/permissions

Derivative Securities

CHAPTER 14

Options: Puts and Calls

LEARNING GOALS

After studying this chapter, you should be able to:

LG1 Discuss the basic nature of options in general and puts and calls in particular and understand how these investment vehicles work.

LG2 Describe the options market and note key options provisions, including strike prices and expiration dates.

LG3 Explain how put and call options are valued and the forces that drive options prices in the marketplace.

LG4 Describe the profit potential of puts and calls and note some popular put and call investment strategies.

LG5 Explain the profit potential and loss exposure from writing covered call options and discuss how writing options can be used as a strategy for enhancing investment returns.

LG6 Describe market index options, puts and calls on foreign currencies, and LEAPS and discuss how these securities can be used by investors.

Would you work for $1 per year for five years? That's what Copart, Inc., Chairman and CEO Willis Johnson offered to do in April 2009 . . . well, sort of. Johnson agreed to accept a salary of $1 per year for the next five years, but in exchange, Copart's board of directors gave him a stock option grant that would allow him to buy 2 million shares of Copart stock at a fixed price of $30.21 at any time over the next five years.

If you are not familiar with Copart, think of it as the eBay for buyers and sellers of wrecked vehicles. Copart serves insurance companies, banks, car dealers, car rental companies, and other businesses that regularly have to process vehicles that are no longer serviceable. Copart's business got a tremendous push when Congress passed the "Cash for Clunkers" program in which owners of gas-guzzling older vehicles could receive a cash rebate from the federal government if they bought a new, more fuel-efficient vehicle. To obtain the rebate, car dealerships had to verify that the older cars being traded in were actually destroyed, meaning that lots of new activity would be driven to Copart's auction site.

Whether Mr. Johnson's offer to work for $1 per year in exchange for options would turn out to be a good deal for Copart shareholders or for Mr. Johnson (or perhaps both) would depend on how Copart stock performed over the subsequent five years. For each dollar by which Copart stock exceeded the $30.21 price at which the CEO could buy stock, Mr. Johnson stood to gain $2 million. On the other hand, if Copart stock fell below $30.21 and stayed there, Mr. Johnson's stock options would be worthless.

(Source: Copart Shareholders Asked to Consider Grant of Stock Options to CEO and President in Lieu of Cash and Equity Compensation for Next Five Years, www.reuters.com, March 12, 2009.)

Put and Call Options

LG1 **LG2** When investors buy shares of common or preferred stock, they are entitled to all the rights and privileges of ownership such as receiving dividends or, in the case of common stock, having the right to vote at shareholder meetings. Investors who acquire bonds or convertible issues are also entitled to certain benefits of ownership such as receiving periodic interest payments. Stocks, bonds, and convertibles are all examples of *financial assets*. They represent financial claims on the issuing organization. In contrast, investors who buy options acquire nothing more than the *right* to subsequently buy or sell other, related securities. An **option** gives the holder the right to buy or sell a certain amount of an underlying asset (such as common stocks) at a specified price over a specified period of time.

Options are *contractual instruments*, whereby two parties enter into a contract to give something of value to the other. The option *buyer* has the right to buy or sell an underlying asset for a given period of time, at a price that was fixed at the time of the contract. The option *seller* stands ready to buy or sell the underlying asset according to the terms of the contract, for which the buyer has paid seller a certain amount of money. We'll look at two basic kinds of options in this chapter: *puts* and *calls*, both of which enjoy considerable popularity as investment vehicles.

In addition, there are two other types of options: *rights* and *warrants*. Rights originate when corporations raise money by issuing new shares of common stocks. (See Chapter 6 for a discussion of *rights offerings*.) Rights enable stockholders to buy shares of the new issue at a specified price for a specified, fairly short period of time. Because their life span is so short—usually no more than a few weeks—stock rights hold very little investment appeal for the average individual investor. In contrast, warrants are long-term options that grant the right to buy shares in a certain company for a given period of time (often fairly long—five to ten years or more). Warrants are usually created as "sweeteners" to bond issues and are used to make the issues more attractive to investors. In essence, the buyer of one of these bonds also receives one or more warrants, as an *equity kicker*.

Basic Features of Puts and Calls

Stock options began trading on the Chicago Board Options Exchange in the early 1970s. Soon the interest in options spilled over to other kinds of financial assets. Today, investors can trade puts and calls on common stock, stock indexes, exchange-traded funds, foreign currencies, debt instruments, and commodities and financial futures.

As we will see, although the underlying financial assets may vary, the basic features of different types of options are very similar. Perhaps the most important feature to understand is that options allow investors to benefit from price changes in the underlying asset without investing much capital.

A Negotiable Contract Puts and calls are negotiable instruments, issued in bearer form, that allow the holder to buy or sell a specified amount of a specified security at a specified price. For example, a put or a call on common stock covers 100 shares of stock in a specific company. A **put** enables the holder to sell the underlying security at the specified price (known as the *exercise* or *strike price*) over a set period of time. A **call**, in contrast, gives the holder the right to buy the security at the stated (strike) price within a certain time period. As with any option, there are no voting rights, no privileges of ownership, and no interest or dividend income. Instead, *puts and calls possess value to the extent that they allow the holder to benefit from price movements of the underlying asset.*

Because puts and calls derive their value from the price behavior of some other real or financial asset, they are known as **derivative securities**. Rights and warrants, as well as futures contracts (which we'll study in Chapter 15), are also derivative securities. Although certain segments of this market are for big institutional investors only, there's still ample room for the individual investor. Many of these securities—especially those listed on exchanges—are readily available to, and are actively traded by, individuals as well as institutions.

The price that an investor pays to buy an option is called the **option premium**. As we will see, an option's premium depends on characteristics of the option such as its strike price and expiration date and on the price of the underlying asset. However, don't let the word "premium" confuse you. It's just the market price of the option.

One of the key features of puts and calls is the attractive **leverage** opportunities they offer. Such opportunities exist because of the low prices these options carry relative to the market prices of the underlying financial assets. What's more, the lower cost in no way affects the payoff or capital appreciation potential of your investment. To illustrate, consider a call on a common stock that gives you the right to buy 100 shares of a stock at a (strike) price of $45 a share. If that stock currently sells for $45, the call option would sell for just a few dollars—let's say $3 per option for the sake of illustration (or $300 since the option contract covers 100 shares). Next, suppose that a month or two later the stock price has increased by $10 to $55. At that point, you might exercise your right to buy 100 shares for $45 each. You pay $4,500 to acquire the shares and then immediately resell them at the market price for $5,500, pocketing a gain of $1,000. Thus, in a short period of time your $300 up-front investment grew to $1,000, a gain of 233%. The percentage increase in the stock over this period was just 22.2% ($10/$45), so the percentage gain on the option is much greater than the percentage gain on the stock. That's the benefit of the leverage the options provide.

Seller Versus Buyer Puts and calls are a unique type of security because they are *not* issued by the organizations that issue the underlying stock. Instead, they are *created by investors*. It works like this: Suppose you want to sell to another investor the right to buy 100 shares of common stock. You could do this by "writing a call." The individual (or institution) writing the option is known as the **option seller** or **writer**. As the option writer, you sell the option in the market and so are entitled to receive the price paid by the buyer for the put or call.

Puts and calls are both written (sold) and purchased through securities brokers and dealers. In fact, they're as easy to buy and sell as common stocks; a simple phone call, or a few mouse clicks, is all it takes. The writer stands behind the option, because it is the *writer* who must buy or deliver the stocks or other financial assets according to the terms of the option. (*Note:* The writers of puts and calls *have a legally binding obligation* to stand behind the terms of the contracts they have written. The buyer can just walk away from the deal if it turns sour; the writer cannot.)

Puts and calls are written for a variety of reasons, most of which we will explore following. At this point, suffice it to say that writing options can be a viable investment strategy and can be a profitable course of action because, more often than not, *options expire worthless*.

How Puts and Calls Work Taking the *buyer's* point of view, we will briefly examine how puts and calls work and how they derive their value. To start, it is best to look at their profit-making potential. For example, consider the call described earlier that has a $45 strike price and sells for $3. As the buyer of the call option, you hope for a rise in the price of the underlying security (in this case, common stock). What is the profit potential from this transaction if the price of the stock does indeed move up to, say, $75 by the expiration date on the call?

The answer is that you will earn $30 ($75 − $45) on each of the 100 shares of stock in the call, minus the original $300 cost of the option. In other words, you'll earn a gross profit of $3,000 from your $300 investment. This is so because you have the right to buy 100 shares of the stock, from the option writer, at a price of $45 each, and then immediately turn around and sell them in the market for $75 a share.

Could you have made the same gross profit ($3,000) by investing directly in the common stock? Yes, if you had purchased 100 shares of stock. Buying 100 shares of a $45 stock requires an initial investment of $4,500 compared to the $300 investment needed to buy the options. As a consequence, the rate of return from buying the shares is much less than the rate of return from buying the options. The return potential of common stocks and calls differs considerably. This difference attracts investors and speculators to calls whenever the price outlook for the underlying financial asset is positive. Such differential returns are, of course, the direct result of *leverage*, which rests on the principle of reducing the level of capital required in a given investment *without materially affecting the dollar amount of the payoff or capital appreciation from that investment*. Note that although our illustration used common stock, this same valuation principle applies to any of the other financial assets that may underlie call options, such as market indexes, foreign currencies, and futures contracts.

A similar situation can be worked out for puts. Assume that for the same stock (which has a current price of $45) you could pay $700 and buy a put to *sell* 100 shares of the stock at a strike price of $50 each. As the buyer of a put, you want the price of the stock to *drop*. Assume that your expectations are correct and the price of the stock does indeed drop, to $25 a share. Here again, when you exercise the put option you realize a gross profit of $25 per share because you can buy the stock in the open market for $25 and then exercise your right to sell it for $50.

Fortunately, put and call investors do *not* have to exercise their options and make simultaneous buy and sell transactions in order to receive their profit. That's because *the options themselves have value and can be traded in the secondary market*. The value of both puts and calls is directly linked to the market price of the underlying financial asset, so the *value of a call* increases as the market price of the underlying security *rises*. Likewise, the *value of a put* increases as the price of the security *declines*. Thus, *you can get your money out of options by selling them in the open market*, just as with any other security.

Advantages and Disadvantages The major advantage of investing in puts and calls is the leverage they offer. This feature allows investors to profit from movements in the underlying asset without investing a large amount of money up front. Also appealing is the fact that puts and calls can be used profitably when the price of the underlying security goes up *or* down.

A major disadvantage of puts and calls is that the holder enjoys neither interest or dividend income nor any other ownership benefits. Moreover, because puts and calls have limited lives, there is a limited time during which the underlying asset can move in the direction that makes the option profitable. Finally, while it is possible to buy calls and puts without investing a lot of money up front, the likelihood that an investor will lose 100% of the money that he or she does invest is much higher with options than with stocks. That's because if the underlying stock moves just a little in the wrong direction, a put or call option on that stock will be totally worthless when it expires.

Options Markets

Although the concept of options can be traced back to the writings of Aristotle, options trading in the United States did not begin until the late 1700s. Even then, up to the early 1970s, this market remained fairly small, largely unorganized, and the almost-private domain of a handful of specialists and traders. All of this changed, however, on April 26, 1973, when the Chicago Board Options Exchange (CBOE) opened.

Conventional Options Prior to the creation of the CBOE, put and call options trading was conducted in the over-the-counter market through a handful of specialized dealers. Investors who wished to purchase puts and calls contacted their own brokers, who contacted the options dealers. The dealers would find investors willing to write the options. If the buyer wished to exercise an option, he or she did so with the writer and no one else—a system that largely prohibited any secondary trading. On the other hand, there were virtually no limits to what could be written, so long as the buyer was willing to pay the price. Put and call options were written on New York and American exchange stocks, as well as on regional and over-the-counter securities, for as short a time as 30 days and for as long as a year. Over-the-counter options, known today as **conventional options**, are now used almost exclusively by institutional investors. Accordingly, our attention in this chapter will focus on listed markets, like the CBOE, where individual investors do most of their options trading.

Listed Options The creation of the CBOE signaled the birth of **listed options**, a term that describes put and call options traded on organized exchanges. The CBOE launched trading in calls on just 16 firms. From these rather humble beginnings, there evolved in a relatively short time a large and active market for listed options. Today, trading in listed options is done in both puts and calls and takes place on several exchanges, including the Boston Options Exchange (BOX), the NASDAQ, the NYSE Amex, and the NYSE ARCA. In total, *put and call options are now traded on over 3,000 different stocks, with many of those options listed on multiple exchanges.* In addition to stocks, the options exchanges also offer listed options on stock indexes, exchange-traded funds, debt securities, foreign currencies, and even commodities and financial futures.

Listed options not only provide a convenient market for puts and calls, but also standardized expiration dates and exercise prices. The listed options exchanges created a clearinghouse that eliminated direct ties between buyers and sellers of options and reduced the cost of executing put and call transactions. They also developed an active secondary market, with wide distribution of price information. As a result, it is now as easy to trade a listed option as a listed stock.

Stock Options

The advent of the CBOE and the other listed option exchanges had a dramatic impact on the trading volume of puts and calls. Today well over 3.6 billion listed options contracts are traded each year, most of which are stock options.

In 2008, *more than 90%* (or 3.3 billion contracts) *were stock options*. That year, the volume of contracts traded was divided among the options exchanges as follows:

Options Exchange	Number of Contracts Traded (millions)	Exchange Share of Trading Volume
CBOE	1,193.40	33.3%
ISE	1,007.70	28.1%
NASDAQ OMX PHLX	547.5	15.3%
NYSE ARCA	416.9	11.6%
NYSE AMEX	207.3	5.8%
BOX	178.6	5.0%
NASDAQ	31.2	0.9%
TOTAL	3,582.6	100%

Listed options exchanges have unquestionably added a new dimension to investing. In order to avoid serious (and possibly expensive) mistakes with these securities, however, you must fully understand their basic features. In the sections that follow, we will look closely at the investment attributes of stock options and the trading strategies for using them. Later, we'll explore stock-index (and ETF) options and then briefly look at other types of puts and calls, including interest rate and currency options, and long-term options. (Futures options will be taken up in Chapter 15, after we study futures contracts.)

Stock Option Provisions Because of their low unit cost, stock options (or *equity options,* as they're also called) are very popular with individual investors. Except for the underlying financial asset, they are like any other type of put or call, subject to the same kinds of contract provisions and market forces. There are two provisions that are especially important for stock options: (1) the price—known as the *strike price*—at which the stock can be bought or sold, and (2) the amount of time remaining until expiration. As we'll see below, both the strike price and the time remaining to expiration have a significant bearing on their valuation and pricing.

Strike Price The **strike price** represents the price contract between the buyer of the option and the writer. For a call, the strike price specifies the price at which each of the 100 shares of stock can be bought. For a put, it represents the price at which the stock can be sold to the writer. With conventional (OTC) options, there are no constraints on the strike price. With listed options, strike prices are *standardized*:

- Stocks selling for less than $25 per share carry strike prices that are set in $2\frac{1}{2}$ dollar increments ($7.50, $10.00, $12.50, $15, and so on.).

- In general, the increments jump to $5 for stocks selling between $25 and $200 per share, although a number of securities in the $25 to $50 range are now allowed to use $2\frac{1}{2}$ dollar increments.

- For stocks that trade at more than $200 a share, the strike price is set in $10 increments.

- Unlike most equity options, options on exchange-traded funds (discussed more fully later in this chapter) all have strike prices set in $1 increments.

In all cases, the strike price is adjusted for stock splits. Strike prices are not adjusted for cash dividends, but they are adjusted when firms pay significant stock dividends (e.g., dividends paid in additional shares rather than in cash).

Expiration Date The **expiration date** is also an important provision. It specifies the life of the option, just as the maturity date indicates the life of a bond. The expiration date, in effect, specifies the length of the contract between the holder and the writer of the option. Thus, if you hold a six-month call on Sears with a strike price of, say, $70, that option gives you the right to buy 100 shares of Sears common stock at $70 per share at any time over the next six months. *No matter what happens to the market price of the stock,* you can use your call option to buy 100 shares of Sears at $70 a share. If the price of the stock moves up, you stand to make money. If it goes down, you'll be out the cost of the option.

Expiration dates for options in the conventional market can fall on any working day of the month. In contrast, expiration dates are *standardized* in the *listed* options market. The exchanges initially created three expiration cycles for all listed options:

- January, April, July, and October.

- February, May, August, and November.

- March, June, September, and December.

Each issue is assigned to one of these three cycles. The exchanges still use the same three expiration cycles, but they've been altered so that investors are always able to trade in the two nearest (current and following) months, plus the next two closest months in the option's regular expiration cycle. For reasons that are pretty obvious, this is sometimes referred to as a *two-plus-two* schedule.

For example, if the current month (also called the *front month*) is January, then available options in the *January cycle* would be January, February, April, and July. These represent the two current months (January and February) and the next two months in the cycle (April and July). Likewise, available contracts for the *February cycle* would be January, February, May, and August; available contracts for the *March cycle* would be January, February, March, and June. The expiration dates, based on the front months, continue rolling over in this way during the course of the year. The following table demonstrates the available contracts under the two-plus-two system for the months of February and June:

Front Month	Cycle	Available Contracts
February	January	February, March, April, July
February	February	February, March, May, August
February	March	February, March, June, September
June	January	June, July, October, January
June	February	June, July, August, November
June	March	June, July, September, December

Given the month of expiration, the actual day of expiration is always the same: the Saturday following the third Friday of each expiration month. Thus, for all practical purposes, *listed options always expire on the third Friday of the month of expiration.*

Put and Call Transactions Option traders are subject to commission and transaction costs whenever they buy or sell an option or whenever they write an option. The writing of puts and calls is subject to normal transaction costs; these costs effectively represent compensation to the broker or dealer for *selling* the option.

Listed options have their own marketplace and quotation system. Finding the price (or *premium*) of a listed stock option is fairly easy. Figure 14.1 illustrates a quotation from the *Wall Street Journal Online* for an equity index option in which the Nasdaq index serves as the underlying asset. Note that quotes are provided for calls and puts

FIGURE 14.1

Quotations for Listed Stock Index Options

The quotes for puts and calls are listed side by side. In addition to the closing price of the option, the latest price of the underlying asset (in this case, $21) is shown, along with the strike price and expiration month of the option. (Source: *Wall Street Journal Online,* September 10, 2009.)

Prices at close September 10, 2009

Nasdaq (NDAQ)

Underlying stock price*: 21.00

Expiration	Strike	Call			Put		
		Last	Volume	Open Interest	Last	Volume	Open Interest
Sep	20.00	1.00	10	897	0.20	33	1425
Oct	20.00	...	...	3	0.60	61	371
Sep	21.00	0.40	149	556	0.46	20	1661
Oct	21.00	0.95	9	348	...	...	288
Oct	22.00	0.59	43	110	...	...	39
Sep	22.50	0.10	40	4553	1.80	7	540
Dec	22.50	1.15	14	1201	...	...	378
Mar	22.50	...	...	55	3.40	2	25
Oct	23.00	0.25	28	215	2.35	40	43
Sep	25.00	...	...	1809	4.10	41	431
Dec	25.00	0.45	4	441	...	...	78

*Underlying stock price represents listed exchange price only. It may not match the composite closing price.

separately. For each option, quotes are listed for various combinations of strike prices and expiration dates. Because there are so many options and a substantial number of them are rarely traded, financial publications and Web site list quotes only for the more actively traded options.

The quotes are standardized: The name of the company or index and the closing price of the underlying asset are listed at the top. The expiration month appears in the first column, followed by the strike price. Then the closing price and trading volume appear. For example, a September (2009) Nasdaq *call* with a strike price of $20 was quoted at $1.00 (which translates into a dollar price of $100 because stock options trade in 100 share lots), and a September put option with the same strike price sold for $0.20. In contrast, an October call option with a strike price of $23 is quoted at just $0.25.

CONCEPTS IN REVIEW

Answers available at
www.pearsonhighered.com/
gitman

14.1 Describe *put* and *call* options. Are they issued like other corporate securities?

14.2 What are *listed options,* and how do they differ from *conventional options?*

14.3 What are the main investment attractions of put and call options? What are the risks?

14.4 What is a *stock option?* What is the difference between a stock option and a *derivative security?* Describe a derivative security and give several examples.

14.5 What is a *strike price?* How does it differ from the market price of the stock?

14.6 Why do put and call options have expiration dates? Is there a market for options that have passed their expiration dates?

Options Pricing and Trading

LG3 LG4 LG5 The value of a put or call depends to a large extent on the price of the financial asset that underlies the option. Getting a firm grip on the current and expected future value of a put or call is extremely important to options traders and investors. Thus, to get the most from any options trading program, you must understand how options are priced in the market. *Continuing to use stock options as a basis of discussion*, let's look now at the basic principles of options valuation and pricing. We'll start with a brief review of how profits are derived from puts and calls. Then we'll take a look at several ways in which investors can use these options.

The Profit Potential from Puts and Calls

Although the quoted market price of a put or call is affected by such factors as time to expiration, stock volatility, and market interest rates, by far the most important variable is the *price behavior of the underlying common stock*. This is the variable that drives any significant moves in the price of the option and that determines the option's profit (return) potential. When the price of the underlying stock *moves up, calls do well*. When the price of the underlying stock *drops, puts do well*. Such performance also explains why it's important to get a good handle on the expected future price behavior of a stock *before* you buy or sell (write) an option.

Figure 14.2 illustrates how the ultimate payoffs that options provide depend upon the underlying stock price. By "payoff" we mean the gain that an investor would receive from exercising the option—the difference between the stock price and the strike price. The diagram on the left depicts a call, and the one on the right depicts a put. The *call* diagram assumes you pay $500 for a call option contract (i.e., 100 calls at

FIGURE 14.2   The Valuation Properties of Put and Call Options

The payoff of a call or put depends on the price of the underlying common stock (or other financial asset). The cost of the option has been recovered when the option passes its breakeven point. After that, the profit potential of a call is unlimited, but the profit potential of a put is limited because the underlying stock price cannot go lower than $0.

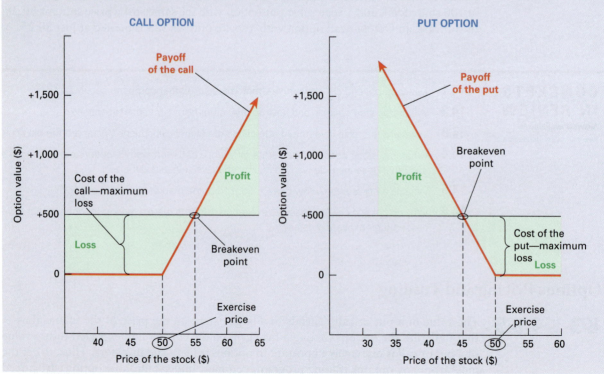

$5 per call) that has a strike price of $50. The graph shows how the option payoff increases as the stock price rises. Observe that a call provides a zero payoff unless the price of the stock *advances past the stated exercise price* ($50). If the market price of the stock is below $50, no rational investor would exercise the option and pay $50 to buy the stock—it would be cheaper to simply buy it in the open market. Also, because it costs $500 to buy the call, the stock has to move up another five points (from $50 to $55) in order for you to recover the premium and thereby reach a breakeven point. Note, however, that even if the stock price is between $50 and $55, it's still best to exercise the option because doing so reduces the option holder's net loss. For example, if the stock price is $52, exercising the option generates a cash inflow of $200, which *partially offsets* the $500 option premium. For each dollar by which the stock price exceeds this breakeven point ($55), the call option's payoff goes up by $100. The potential profit from the call position is unlimited because there is no limit on how high the underlying stock price can go.

The value of a put is also derived from the price of the underlying stock, except that the put value goes up when the stock price goes down and vice versa. The *put* diagram in Figure 14.2 assumes you buy a put for $500 and obtain the right to sell the underlying stock at $50 a share. It shows that the payoff of the put is zero unless the market price of the corresponding stock *drops below the exercise price* ($50) on the put. As the price of the stock continues to fall, the payoff of the put option increases. Again, note that because the put cost $500, you don't start making money on the investment until the price of the stock drops below the breakeven point of $45 a share. Beyond that point, the profit from the put is defined by the extent to which the price of the underlying stock continues to fall over the remaining life of the option.

Intrinsic Value

As we have seen, the payoff of a put or call depends ultimately on the exercise price stated on the option, as well as on the prevailing market price of the underlying common stock. More specifically, the *intrinsic value of a call* is determined according to the following simple formula:

Equation 14.1

$$\text{Intrinsic value of a call} = (\text{Stock price} - \text{Strike price}) \times 100$$
$$\text{or zero, whichever is greater}$$

In other words, the intrinsic value of a call is merely the difference between the stock's market price and the option's strike price. When the stock price is below the strike price, the intrinsic value is zero. As implied in Equation 14.1, a call has an intrinsic value whenever the market price of the underlying financial asset exceeds the strike price stipulated on the call. If a call option has a strike price of $50 and the underlying stock sells for $60, then the option's intrinsic value is $1,000.

A put, on the other hand, cannot be valued in the same way, because puts and calls allow the holder to do different things. To find the *intrinsic value of a put*, we must change the order of the equation a bit:

Equation 14.2

$$\text{Intrinsic value of a put} = (\text{Strike price} - \text{Stock price}) \times 100$$
$$\text{or zero, whichever is greater}$$

In this case, a put has value so long as the market price of the underlying stock (or financial asset) is less than the strike price stipulated on the put.

In-the-Money/Out-of-the-Money When a call has a strike price that is *less than* the market price of the underlying common stock, it has a positive intrinsic value and is known as an **in-the-money** option. When the strike price of the call *exceeds* the market price of the stock, the call has no intrinsic value, in which case it is known as an **out-of-the-money** option. However, an out-of-the-money call option is not worthless as long as there is still time before it expires because there is a chance that the stock price will fall below the strike price in the future. In other words, when a call is out of the money, its intrinsic value is zero but its market value is greater than zero. In such a case, we say that the option has no intrinsic value but it still has time value. In the special case when the strike price of the option and the market price of the stock are the same, we say that the call option is *at-the-money*.

As you might expect, the situation is reversed for put options: A put is in-the-money when its strike price is greater than the market price of the stock. It's considered out-of-the-money when the market price of the stock exceeds the strike price, and a put is at-the-money when the strike price equals the stock price. As with calls, an out-of-the-money put still has a positive market value as long as there is some time remaining before the expiration date.

When firms grant stock options to their employees, they typically grant at-the-money options, meaning that the strike prices of the options are set equal to the price of the underlying stock on the date of the option grant. However, as the following *Ethics in Investing* box explains, many companies got into trouble for using a bit of hindsight (and failing to disclose that) when selecting their option grant dates. This practice came to be known as options backdating.

ETHICS IN INVESTING

Extraordinarily Good Timing

In 1997, a finance professor conducting research on executive stock option grants discovered that firms awarding these grants seemed to display extraordinarily good timing, setting the exercise prices just before a large runup in the stock price. Perhaps firms were withholding good news until after they awarded stock option grants, knowing that when they released the news their stock prices would rise. A few years later, Erik Lie and Randall Heron solved the puzzle of executives' remarkable timing abilities. Some firms apparently backdated their option grants, using hindsight to set the exercise price on the one date in the prior several weeks when their stock price was at its lowest point. Backdating works like this. A firm announces on June 1 that it had granted its executives stock options on April 15, using the market price of the stock that day as the option's exercise price. In fact, the firm did not actually award the options on April 15, but rather chose that date several weeks later. That gave the firm the benefit of hindsight, meaning that the firm knew that the stock's lowest point in the prior month or two had in fact been April 15. By the time the firm announced the option grant on June 1, the options were already in-the-money because the stock price was much higher than it had been on the retroactively set grant date. In backdating options, firms failed to disclose the true value of the option grants they awarded, which in turn affected their reported earnings and taxes.

As of mid-2007, at least 257 firms had either launched their own internal investigations into options backdating or had been the subject of investigations by the Securities and Exchange Commission. Firms involved in options backdating scandals endured serious consequences. Some executives paid fines or went to prison. Other firms settled lawsuits without admitting wrongdoing, such as Broadcom, which paid $118 million to settle a shareholder lawsuit. Most of the firms investigated saw their stock prices decline by as much as 7% to 10%.

(Source: Kenneth Carow, Randall Heron, Erik Lie, and Robert Neal, Option Grant Backdating Investigations and Financial Market Discipline, *Journal of Corporate Finance,* forthcoming.)

Time Value and Option Prices Put and call intrinsic values, as found according to Equations 14.1 and 14.2, denote what an option should be worth, *in the absence of any time value*. In other words, these equations show what call and put options would be worth on their expiration dates. In fact, options rarely trade at their intrinsic values. Instead, they almost always trade at prices that exceed their intrinsic values, especially for options that still have a long time to run. Thus, puts and calls nearly always have time value. In most cases, the more time there is before an option expires, the greater is its time value.

What Drives Options Prices?

Option prices can be reduced to two separate components. The first is the *intrinsic* value of the option, which is driven by the current market price of the underlying financial asset. As we saw in Equations 14.1 and 14.2, the greater the difference between the market price of the underlying asset and the strike price on the option, the greater the fundamental value of the call or put.

The second component of an option price is customarily referred to as the **time value**. It represents the amount by which an option's price exceeds its intrinsic value. Table 14.1 lists some quoted prices for an actively traded call option. These quoted prices (panel A) are then separated into intrinsic value (panel B) and time value (panel C). Note that three strike prices are used—$65, $70, and $75. Relative to the market price of the stock ($71.75), one strike price ($65) is well below market; this is an in-the-money call. One ($70) is fairly near the market. The third ($75) is well above the market; this is an out-of-the-money call. Note the considerable difference in the makeup of the options prices as we move from an in-the-money call to an out-of-the-money call.

Panel B in the table lists the intrinsic values of the call options, as determined by Equation 14.1. For example, note that although the March 65 call (the call with the March expiration date and $65 strike price) is trading at 7.75, its intrinsic value is only 6.75. The intrinsic value (of 6.75) represents, in effect, the extent to which the option is trading in-the-money. But observe that although most of the price of the March 65 call is made up of intrinsic value, not all of it is. Now look at the calls with the $75 strike price. None of these has any fundamental value; they're all out-of-the-money, and their prices are made up solely of time value. Basically, the value of these options is determined entirely by the *belief* that the price of the underlying stock could rise to over $75 a share before the options expire.

TABLE 14.1	Option Price Components for an Actively Traded Call Option			
			Expiration Months	
Price	Strike Price	February	March	June
Panel A: Quoted Options Prices				
71.75	65	—	7.75	9.75
71.75	70	2.25	3.88	6.75
71.75	75	0.19	1.50	3.88
Panel B: Underlying Fundamental Values				
71.75	65	—	6.75	6.75
71.75	70	1.75	1.75	1.75
71.75	75	neg.	neg.	neg.
Panel C: Time Premiums				
71.75	65	—	1.00	3.00
71.75	70	0.50	2.12	5.00
71.75	75	0.19	1.50	3.88

Note: neg. indicates that options have negative fundamental values.

The Volatility Index

Because the volatility of the underlying asset plays a major role in option valuation, options traders track the volatility of individual stocks and of the market as a whole very closely. In fact, there is an index, called the VIX (which stands for volatility index), that provides an estimate of the volatility of the overall market. From about 1990 to 2007, the average volatility of the U.S. stock market as measured by VIX was close to 20% per year. But in the fall of 2008, after the failure of Lehman Brothers, the VIX index peaked at close to 80%, four times its long-run average! Since then, the VIX has been on a long, slow decline, and by the fall of 2009 it was back to a more normal level of around 25%.

Panel C shows the amount of *time value* embedded in the call prices. This represents the difference between the *quoted call price* (panel A) and the call's *intrinsic value* (panel B). It shows that the price of just about every traded option contains at least some time value. Indeed, unless the options are about to expire, you would expect them to have at least some time value. Also, note that with all three strike prices, *the longer the time to expiration, the greater the time value.*

As you might expect, *time to expiration* is an important element in explaining the time value in panel C. Several other variables also have a bearing on the behavior of this premium. One is the *price volatility of the underlying common stock.* Other things being equal, the more volatile the stock is, the more it enhances the speculative appeal of the option—and therefore the bigger the time value. In addition, the time value is *directly related to the level of interest rates.* That is, the amount of time value embedded in a call option generally increases along with interest rates (and for puts, time value increases when interest rates fall).

For the most part, then, four major forces drive the price of an option. They are, in descending order of importance, (1) the price behavior of the underlying financial asset, (2) the amount of time remaining to expiration, (3) the amount of price volatility in the underlying financial asset, and (4) the general level of interest rates. Less important variables include the dividend yield on the underlying common stock, the trading volume of the option, and the exchanges on which the option is listed.

Option-Pricing Models Some fairly sophisticated option-pricing models have been developed, notably by Myron Scholes and the late Fisher Black, to value options. Many active options traders use these formulas to identify and trade over- and undervalued options. Not surprisingly, these models are based on the same variables we identified above. For example, the five inputs used in the Black-Scholes option-pricing model are (1) the market price of the underlying stock, (2) the strike price of the option, (3) the time remaining before the option expires, (4) the risk-free rate of interest, and (5) the volatility of the underlying stock. The Black and Scholes option-pricing model prices a European call option using these equations:

Equation 14.3

Call price = (stock price) × (probability 1)
         − (present value of strike price) × (probability 2)

To get probability 1 and probability 2, you need two more equations, plus a little help from Excel.

The first equation looks like this

Equation 14.3a

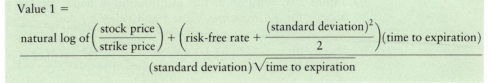

$$\text{Value 1} = \frac{\text{natural log of}\left(\dfrac{\text{stock price}}{\text{strike price}}\right) + \left(\text{risk-free rate} + \dfrac{(\text{standard deviation})^2}{2}\right)(\text{time to expiration})}{(\text{standard deviation})\sqrt{\text{time to expiration}}}$$

And the second equation is

Equation 14.3b

$$\text{Value 2} = \text{Value 1} - (\text{standard deviation}) \times \sqrt{\text{time to expiration}}$$

Equations 14.3a and 14.3b calculate numerical values that must then be converted into probabilities using the standard normal distribution function. The normal distribution is simply the familiar bell curve, and the standard normal distribution is a bell curve with a mean of zero and a standard deviation of one. The probabilities we need in Equation 14.3 represent the likelihood of drawing a number less than or equal to Value 1 (and Value 2) from this distribution. Figure 14.3 provides a graphical illustration of the probability that we seek. Suppose we use Equation 14.3a and find that Value 1 equals 0.9. To obtain "probability 1" for Equation 14.3 we need to know the area under the curve in Figure 14.3 to the left of the value 0.9.

Fortunately, Excel provides a useful function that makes it easy to calculate these standard normal probabilities. That function is denoted with =normsdist(0.9), and Excel reveals that the appropriate probability is 0.8159.

Now we are ready to price a call option using Black and Scholes. Suppose we want to price a call option that expires in three months (one-quarter of a year). The option

FIGURE 14.3

The Standard Normal Distribution

The standard normal distribution has a zero mean and a standard deviation of one. The shaded area to the left of Value 1 represents the probability of drawing a value at random from this distribution that is less than or equal to Value 1.

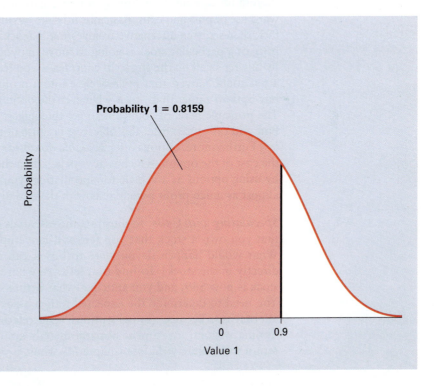

Probability 1 = 0.8159

Probability

0   0.9

Value 1

has a strike price of $45, and the market price of the underlying stock is currently $44. The standard deviation of this stock's returns is about 50% per year, and the risk-free rate is 2%. With all of this information in hand, we can price the option. Start by solving for the quantities Value 1 and Value 2.

$$\text{Value 1} = \frac{\ln\left(\frac{44}{45}\right) + \left(0.02 + \frac{0.50^2}{2}\right)0.25}{0.50\sqrt{0.25}} = \frac{-0.0225 + (0.145)0.25}{0.25} = 0.0551$$

$$\text{Value 2} = 0.0551 - 0.50\sqrt{0.25} = -0.1949$$

Next, use Excel to find the standard normal probabilities attached to these values:

$$\text{Probability 1} = \text{normsdist}(0.0551) = 0.5220$$
$$\text{Probability 2} = \text{normsdist}(-0.1949) = 0.4227$$

Finally, plug the values for Probability 1 and Probability 2 into Equation 14.3 to obtain the call price.

$$\text{Call price} = \$44(0.5220) - [\$45/(1.02)^{0.25}](0.4227) = \$22.97 - \$18.93 = \$4.04.$$

So, according to the Black-Scholes option pricing model, the call should be priced at $4.04.

Trading Strategies

For the most part, investors can use stock options in three different kinds of trading strategies: (1) buying puts and calls for speculation, (2) hedging with puts and calls, and (3) option writing and spreading.

Buying for Speculation Buying for speculation is the simplest and most straightforward use of puts and calls. Basically, it is like buying stock ("buy low, sell high") and, in fact, represents an alternative to investing in stock. For example, if you feel the market price of a particular stock is going to move up, you can capture that price appreciation by buying a call on the stock. In contrast, if you feel the stock is about to drop in price, a put could convert that price decline into a profitable situation. In essence, investors buy options rather than stock whenever the options are likely to yield a greater return. The principle here, of course, is to get the biggest return from your investment dollar. Puts and calls often meet this objective because of the added leverage they offer.

Furthermore, options offer *valuable downside protection*: The most you can lose is the cost of the option, which is always less than the cost of the underlying stock. Thus, by using options as a vehicle for speculation, you can put a cap on losses and still get almost as much profit potential as with the underlying stock.

Speculating with Calls To illustrate the essentials of speculating with options, imagine that you own a stock that you feel will move up in price over the next six months. What would happen if you were to buy a call on this stock rather than investing directly in the stock? To find out, let's see what the numbers show. The price of the stock is now $49, and you anticipate that within six months, it will rise to about $65. You need to determine the expected return associated with each of your investment alternatives. Because (most) options have relatively short lives, and because we're dealing with an investment horizon of only six months, we can use holding period return to measure yield (see Chapter 4). Thus, if your expectations about the stock are

TABLE 14.2 Speculating with Call Options			EXCEL With Spreadsheets
	100 Shares of Underlying Common Stock	Six-Month Call Options on the Stock	
		$ 40 Strike Price	$ 50 Strike Price
Today			
Market value of stock (at $49/share)	$4,900		
Market price of calls*		$1,100	$ 400
Six Months Later			
Expected value of stock (at $65/share)	$6,500		
Expected price of calls*		$2,500	$1,500
Profit	$1,600	$1,400	$1,100
Holding Period Return**	33%	127%	275%

*The price of the calls was computed according to Equation 14.1. It includes some investment premium in the purchase price but none in the expected sales price.
**Holding period return (HPR) = (Ending price of the stock or option − Beginning price of the stock or option)/Beginning price of the stock or option.

correct, it should go up by $16 a share and will provide you with a 33% holding period return: ($65 − $49)/$49 = $16/$49 = 0.33.

But there are also some listed options available on this stock. Let's see how they would do. For illustrative purposes, we will use two six-month calls that carry a $40 and a $50 strike price, respectively. Table 14.2 compares the behavior of these two calls with the behavior of the underlying common stock. Clearly, from a holding period return perspective, either call option represents a superior investment to buying the stock itself. The dollar amount of profit may be a bit more with the stock, but note that the size of the required investment ($4,900) is a lot more too, so that alternative has the lowest HPR.

Observe that one of the calls is an in-the-money option (the one with the $40 strike price). The other is out-of-the-money. The difference in returns generated by these calls is rather typical. That is, investors are usually able to generate much better rates of return with lower-priced (out-of-the-money) options, but of course there is a greater risk that these options will expire worthless. A major drawback of out-of-the-money options is that their price is made up solely of investment premium—a sunk cost that will be lost if the stock does not move in price.

Speculating with Puts To see how you can speculate in puts, consider the following situation. You're looking at a stock that's now priced at $51, but you anticipate a drop in price to about $35 per share within the next six months. If that occurs, you could sell the stock short and make a profit of $16 per share. (See Chapter 2, pages 56–59, for a discussion of short selling.)

Alternatively, you can purchase an out-of-the-money put (with a strike price of $50) for, say, $300. Again, if the price of the underlying stock drops, you will make money with the put. The profit and rate of return on the put are summarized below, along with the comparative returns from short selling the stock.

Comparative Performance Given Price of Stock Moves from $51 to $35/Share over a Six-Month Period:	Buy 1 Put ($50 strike price)	Short Sell 100 Shares of Stock
Purchase price (today)	$ 300	
Selling price (6 months later)	1,500*	
Short sell (today)		$5,100
Cover (6 months later)		3,500
Profit	$1,200	$1,600
Holding period return	400%	63%**

*The price of the put was computed according to Equation 14.2 and does not include any investment premium.
**Assumes the short sale was made with a required margin deposit of 50%.

Once again, in terms of holding period return, the stock option is the superior investment vehicle by a wide margin.

Of course, not all option investments perform as well as the ones in our examples. Success with this strategy rests on picking the right underlying common stock. Thus, *security analysis and proper stock selection are critical dimensions of this technique.* It is a highly risky investment strategy, but it may be well suited for the more speculatively inclined investor.

Hedging: Modifying Risks A **hedge** is simply a combination of two or more securities into a single investment position for the purpose of reducing risk. Let's say you hold a stock and want to reduce the amount of downside risk in this investment. You can do that by setting up a hedge. In essence, you're using the hedge as a way to *modify your exposure to risk.* To be more specific, you're trying to change not only the *chance of loss,* but also the *amount lost,* if the worst does occur. A simple hedge might involve nothing more than buying stock and simultaneously buying a put on that same stock. Or it might consist of selling some stock short and then buying a call. There are many types of hedges, some of which are very simple and others very sophisticated. Investors use them for the same basic reason: to earn or protect a profit without exposing the investor to excessive loss.

An options hedge may be appropriate if you have generated a profit from an earlier common stock investment and wish to protect that profit. Or it may be appropriate if you are about to enter into a common stock investment and wish to protect your money by limiting potential capital loss. If you hold a stock that has gone up in price, the purchase of a put would provide the type of downside protection you need; the purchase of a call, in contrast, would provide protection to a short seller of common stock. Thus, option hedging always involves two transactions: (1) the initial common stock position (long or short) and (2) the simultaneous or subsequent purchase of the option.

Protective Puts: Limiting Capital Loss Let's examine a simple option hedge in which you use a put to limit your exposure to capital loss. Assume that you want to buy 100 shares of stock. Being a bit apprehensive about the stock's outlook, you decide to use an option hedge to protect your capital against loss. Therefore, you simultaneously (1) buy the stock and (2) buy a put on the stock (which fully covers the 100 shares owned). This type of hedge is known as a *protective put.* Preferably, the put would be a low-priced option with a strike price at or near the current market price of the stock. Suppose you purchase 100 shares of the common stock at $25 a share and pay $150 for a put with a $25 strike price. Now, no matter what happens to the price of the stock over the life of the put, *you can lose no more than $150.* At the same time, *there's no limit on the gains.* If the stock does not move, you will be out the cost of a put. If it drops in price, then whatever is lost on the stock will be made up with the put. The

TABLE 14.3 Limiting Capital Loss with a Put Hedge	EXCEL With Spreadsheets

		Stock	Put*
Today			
Purchase price of the stock		$25	
Purchase price of the put			$1.50
Sometime Later			
A. **Price of common goes *up* to:**		$50	
Value of put**			$0
Profit:			
100 shares of stock ($50 − $25)	$2,500		
Less: Cost of put	−150		
	Profit: $2,350		
B. **Price of common goes *down* to:**		$10	
Value of put**			$15
Profit:			
100 shares of stock (loss: $10 − $25)	−$1,500		
Value of put (profit)	+1,500		
Less: Cost of put	−150		
	Loss: $ 150		

*The put is purchased simultaneously and carries a strike price of $25.
**See Equation 14.2.

bottom line? The most you can lose is the cost of the put ($150, in this case). However, if the price of the stock goes up (as hoped), the put becomes worthless, and you will earn the capital gains on the stock (less the cost of the put, of course).

Table 14.3 shows the essentials of this option hedge. The $150 paid for the put is sunk cost. That's lost no matter what happens to the price of the stock. In effect, it is the price paid for the insurance this hedge offers. Moreover, this hedge is good only for the life of the put. When this put expires, you will have to replace it with another put or forget about hedging your capital.

Protective Puts: Protecting Profits The other basic use of an option hedge involves entering into the options position *after* a profit has been made on the underlying stock. This could be done because of investment uncertainty or for tax purposes (to carry over a profit to the next taxable year). For example, if you bought 100 shares of a stock at $35 and it moved to $75, there would be a profit of $40 per share to protect. You could protect the profit with an option hedge by buying a put. Assume you buy a three-month put with a $75 strike price at a cost of $250. Now, regardless of what happens to the price of the stock over the life of the put, you are guaranteed a minimum profit of $3,750 (the $4,000 profit in the stock made so far, less the $250 cost of the put). This can be seen in Table 14.4 (on page 548). Note that if the price of the stock should fall, the worst that can happen is a guaranteed minimum profit of $3,750. Plus, there is still *no limit on how much profit can be made*. As long as the stock continues to go up, you will reap the benefits.

But watch out: *The cost of this kind of insurance can become very expensive just when it's needed the most*—that is, when market prices are falling. Under such circumstances, it's not uncommon to find put options trading at price premiums of 20% to 30%, or more, above their prevailing intrinsic values. Essentially, that means the price of the stock position you're trying to protect has to fall 20% to 30% before the protection even starts to kick in. Clearly, as long as high option price premiums prevail,

TABLE 14.4 Protecting Profits with a Put Hedge

EXCEL With Spreadsheets

	Stock	Three-Month Put with a $75 Strike Price
Purchase price of the stock	$ 35	
Today		
Market price of the stock	$ 75	
Market price of the put		$2.50
Three Months Later		
A. Price of common goes up to:	$100	
Value of put*		$ 0
Profit:		
100 shares of stock ($100 − $35)	$6,500	
Less: Cost of put	−250	
Profit:	$6,250	
B. Price of common goes *down* to:	$ 50	
Value of put*		$ 25
Profit:		
100 shares of stock ($50 − $35)	$1,500	
Value of put (profit)	2,500	
Less: Cost of put	−250	
Profit:	$3,750	

*See Equation 14.2.

the hedging strategies described above are a lot less attractive. They still may prove to be helpful, but only for very wide swings in value—and for those that occur over fairly short periods of time, as defined by the life of the put option.

One final point: Although the preceding discussion pertained to put hedges, call hedges can also be set up to limit the loss or protect a profit on a short sale. For example, when selling a stock short, you can purchase a call to protect yourself against a rise in the price of the stock—with the same basic results as outlined above.

Enhancing Returns: Options Writing and Spreading The advent of listed options has led to many intriguing options-trading strategies. Yet, despite the appeal of these techniques, there is one important point that all the experts agree on: *Such specialized trading strategies should be left to experienced investors who fully understand their subtleties.* Our goal at this point is not to master these specialized strategies but to explain in general terms what they are and how they operate. We will look at two types of specialized options strategies here: (1) writing options and (2) spreading options.

Writing Options Generally, investors write options because they believe the price of the underlying stock is going to move in their favor. That is, it is not going to rise as much as the buyer of a call expects, nor will it fall as much as the buyer of a put hopes. *And more often than not, the option writer is right:* He or she makes money far more often than the buyer of the put or call. Such favorable odds explain, in part, the underlying economic motivation for writing put and call options. Option writing represents an investment transaction to the writers: They receive the full option premium (less normal transaction costs) in exchange for agreeing to live up to the terms of the option.

Naked Options Investors can write options in one of two ways. One is to write **naked options**, which involves writing options on stock not owned by the writer. You simply write the put or call, collect the option premium, and hope the price of the underlying stock does not move against you. If successful, naked writing can be highly profitable because it requires essentially no capital up front. Remember, though: The amount of return to the writer is always limited to the amount of option premium received. On the other hand, there is really *no limit to loss exposure*. That's the catch: The price of the underlying stock can rise or fall by just about any amount over the life of the option and, thus, can deal a real blow to the writer of a naked put or call.

Covered Options The amount of risk exposure is a lot less for those who write **covered options**. That's because these options are written against stocks the investor (writer) already owns or has a position in. For example, you could write a call against stock you own or write a put against stock you have short sold. You thus can use the long or short position to meet the terms of the option. Such a strategy is a fairly conservative way to generate attractive rates of return. The object is to write a *slightly* out-of-the-money option, pocket the option premium, and hope the price of the underlying stock will move up or down to (but not exceed) the option's strike price. In effect, you are adding option premium to the other usual sources of return (dividends and/or capital gains). But there's more: While the option premium adds to the return, it also reduces risk. It can cushion a loss if the price of the stock moves against the investor.

There is a hitch to all this, of course: *The amount of return the covered option investor can realize is limited*. Once the price of the underlying common stock exceeds the strike price on the option, the option becomes valuable. When that happens, *you start to lose money on the options*. From this point on, for every dollar you make on the stock position, you lose an equal amount on the option position. That's a major risk of writing covered call options—if the price of the underlying stock takes off, you'll miss out on the added profits.

To illustrate the ins and outs of *covered call writing*, let's assume you own 100 shares of PFP, Inc., an actively traded, high-yielding common stock. The stock is currently trading at $73.50 and pays *quarterly* dividends of $1 a share. You decide to write a three-month call on PFP, giving the buyer the right to take the stock off your hands at $80 a share. Such options are trading in the market at 2.50, so you receive $250 for writing the call. You fully intend to hold on to the stock, so you'd like to see the price of PFP stock rise to no more than 80 by the expiration date on the call. If that happens, the call option will expire worthless. As a result, not only will you earn the dividends and capital gains on the stock, but you also get to pocket the $250 you received when you wrote the call. Basically, *you've just added $250 to the quarterly return on your stock*.

Table 14.5 (on page 550) summarizes the profit and loss characteristics of this covered call position. Note that the maximum profit on this transaction occurs *when the market price of the stock equals the strike price on the call*. If the price of the stock keeps going up, you miss out on the added profits. Even so, the $1,000 profit you earn at a stock price of 80 or above translates into a (three-month) holding period return of 13.6% ($1,000/$7,350). That represents an *annualized* return of nearly 55%! With this kind of return potential, it's not difficult to see why covered call writing is so popular. Moreover, as *situation D* in the table illustrates, covered call writing adds a little cushion to losses: The price of the stock has to drop more than $2\frac{1}{2}$ points (which is what you received when you wrote/sold the call) before you start losing money.

Besides covered calls and protective puts, there are many different ways of combining options with other types of securities to achieve a given investment objective. Probably none is more unusual than the creation of so-called *synthetic securities*. A case in point: Say you want to buy a convertible bond on a certain company, but that company doesn't have any convertibles outstanding. You can create your own customized

TABLE 14.5   Covered Call Writing

EXCEL
With
Spreadsheets

	Stock	Three-Month Put with a $75 Strike Price
Current market price of the stock		$73.50
Current market price of the call		$2.50
Three Months Later		
A. Price of the stock is *unchanged*:		$73.50
Value of the call*		$0
Profit:		
Quarterly dividends received	$ 100	
Proceeds from sale of call	250	
Total profit:	$ 350	
B. Price of the stock goes up to:		$80 — Price Where Maximum Profit Occurs
Value of the call*		$0
Profit:		
Quarterly dividends received	$ 100	
Proceeds from sale of call	250	
Capital gains on stock ($80 − $73.50)	650	
Total profit:	$1,000	
C. Price of the stock goes up to:		$90
Value of the call*		$10
Profit:		
Quarterly dividends received	$ 100	
Proceeds from sale of call	250	
Capital gains on stock ($90 − $73.50)	1,650	
Less: Loss on call	(1,000)	
Net profit:	$1,000	
D. Price of the stock drops to:		$71 — Breakeven Price
Value of the call*		$0
Profit:		
Capital loss on stock ($71 − $73.50)	($ 250) ⎫ $ 0 profit or loss	
Proceeds from sale of call	250 ⎬	
Quarterly dividends	100	
Net profit:	$ 100	

*See Equation 14.1.

convertible by combining a straight (nonconvertible) bond with a listed call option on your targeted company.

Spreading Options **Option spreading** is nothing more than the combination of two or more options into a single transaction. You could create an option spread, for example, by simultaneously buying and writing options on the same underlying stock. These would not be identical options; they would differ with respect to strike price and/or expiration date. Spreads are a very popular use of listed options, and they account for a substantial amount of the trading activity on the listed options exchanges. These spreads go by a variety of exotic names, such as *bull spreads, bear spreads, money spreads, vertical spreads,* and *butterfly spreads.* Each spread is different and each is constructed to meet a certain type of investment goal.

Consider, for example, a *vertical spread*. It would be set up by *buying* a call at one strike price and then *writing* a call (on the same stock and for the same expiration date) at a higher strike price. For instance, you could buy a February call on XYZ at a strike price of, say, 30 and simultaneously sell (write) a February call on XYZ at a strike price of 35. Strange as it may sound, such a position would generate a hefty return if the price of the underlying stock went up by just a few points. Other spreads are used to profit from a falling market. Still others try to make money when the price of the underlying stock moves either up *or* down.

Whatever the objective, most spreads are created to take advantage of differences in prevailing option prices. The payoff from spreading is usually substantial, but *so is the risk*. In fact, some spreads that seem to involve almost no risk may end up with devastating results if the market and the difference between option premiums move against the investor.

Option Straddles A variation on this theme involves an **option straddle**. This is the simultaneous purchase (or sale) of *both* a put *and* a call on the *same* underlying common stock. Unlike spreads, straddles normally involve the same strike price and expiration date. Here, the object is to earn a profit from *either* a big or a small swing in the price of the underlying common stock.

For example, in a *long straddle*, you *buy* an equal number of puts and calls. You make money in a long straddle when the underlying stock undergoes a big change in price—either up or down. If the price of the stock shoots way up, you make money on the call side of the straddle but are out the cost of the puts. If the price of the stock plummets, you make money on the puts, but the calls are useless. In either case, so long as you make more money on one side than the cost of the options for the other side, you're ahead of the game.

In a similar fashion, in a *short straddle*, you *sell/write* an equal number of puts and calls. You make money in this position *when the price of the underlying stock goes nowhere*. In effect, you get to keep all or most of the option premiums you collected when you wrote the options.

Except for obvious structural differences, the principles that underlie the creation of straddles are much like those for spreads. The object is to combine options that will enable you to capture the benefits of certain types of stock price behavior. But keep in mind that if the prices of the underlying stock and/or the option premiums do not behave in the anticipated manner, you lose. *Spreads and straddles are extremely tricky and should be used only by knowledgeable investors.*

CONCEPTS IN REVIEW

Answers available at www.pearsonhighered.com/gitman

14.7 Briefly explain how you would make money on (a) a call option and (b) a put option. Do you have to exercise the option to capture the profit?

14.8 How do you find the intrinsic (fundamental) value of a call? Of a put? Does an *out-of-the-money option* have intrinsic value?

14.9 Name at least four variables that affect the price behavior of listed options, and briefly explain how each affects prices. How important are fundamental (intrinsic) value and time value to in-the-money options? To out-of-the-money options?

14.10 Describe at least three different ways in which investors can use stock options.

14.11 What's the most that can be made from writing calls? Why would an investor want to write *covered calls*? Explain how you can reduce the risk on an underlying common stock by writing covered calls.

Stock-Index and Other Types of Options

LG6 Imagine being able to buy or sell a major stock market index like the S&P 500—and at a reasonable cost. Think of what you could do: If you felt the market was heading up, you could invest in a security that tracks the price behavior of the S&P 500 index and make money when the market goes up. No longer would you have to go through the process of selecting specific stocks that you hope will capture the market's performance. Rather, you could play the *market as a whole*. That's exactly what you can do with *stock-index options*—puts and calls that are written on major stock market indexes. Index options have been around since 1983 and have become immensely popular with both individual and institutional investors. Here we will take a closer look at these popular and often highly profitable investment vehicles.

Stock-Index Options: Contract Provisions

Basically, a **stock-index option** is a put or call written on a specific stock market index. The underlying security in this case is the specific market index. Thus, when the market index moves in one direction or another, the value of the index option moves accordingly. Because there are no stocks or other financial assets backing these options, settlement is defined in terms of cash. Specifically, the cash value of an *index option* is equal to 100 times the published market index that underlies the option. For example, if the S&P 500 is at 1,400, then the value of an S&P 500 index option will be $100 × 1,400 = $140,000. If the underlying index moves up or down in the market, so will the cash value of the option. [*Note:* Options on exchange-traded funds (ETFs) are very similar to index options and will be discussed below. For now, our attention will focus solely on index options.]

Today, put and call options are available on more than 100 different stock indexes. These include options on just about every major U.S. stock market index or average (such as the Dow Jones Industrial Average, the S&P 500, the Russell 2000, and the Nasdaq 100), options on a handful of foreign markets (e.g., China, Mexico, Japan, Hong Kong, and the Europe sector), and options on different segments of the market (pharmaceuticals, oil services, semiconductors, bank, and utility indexes). Many of these options, however, are thinly traded and do not have much of a market. As of 2009, four indexes dominated the stock-index options market, accounting for the vast majority of trading activity:

- The S&P 500 Index (SPX)
- The S&P 100 Index (OEX)
- The Dow Jones Industrial Average (DJX)
- The Nasdaq 100 Index (NDX)

The S&P 500 Index captures the market behavior of large-cap stocks. The S&P 100 is another large-cap index composed of 100 stocks, drawn from the S&P 500, that have actively traded stock options. Another popular index is the DJIA, which measures the blue-chip segment of the market and is one of the most actively traded index options. The Nasdaq 100 index tracks the behavior of the 100 largest nonfinancial stocks on the Nasdaq and is composed of mostly large, high-tech companies (such as Intel and Cisco). Options on the S&P 500 (SPX) are, by far, the most popular instruments. Indeed, there's more trading in SPX options contracts than in *all the other index options combined*. Among the options exchanges that currently deal in index options, the CBOE dominates the market, accounting for more than 85% of all trades.

FIGURE 14.4

Quotations on Index Options

The quotation system used with index options is a lot like that used with stock options: strike prices and expiration dates are shown along with closing option prices. The biggest differences are that put and call quotes are mixed together, and the closing values for the underlying indexes are shown separately. (Source: *Wall Street Journal Online*, September 11, 2009.)

Prices at close September 11, 2009

DJ Industrials (DJX)

Chicago Exchange

Underlying Index	High	Low	Close	Net Change	From Dec.31	%Change
DJ Industrials	96.50	95.72	96.05	-0.22	8.29	9.45
		Strike	Volume	Last	Net Change	Open Interest
Sep		83.00 call	40	13.15	+4.55	1,983
Sep		84.00 put	25	0.03	-0.01	3,123
Sep		84.00 call	10	12.25	+1.05	3,295
Sep		85.00 call	30	11.00	+1.64	5,279
Dec		100.00 call	6	2.02	-0.13	3,907
Dec		102.00 call	100	1.46	+0.03	1,156
Dec		103.00 put	9	8.54	-0.96	45
Dec		122.00 put	2	26.45	-2.80	2,118
Call Vol.		6,402	Open Int.			235,545
Put Vol.		6,811	Open Int.			255,862

Volume figures are unofficial. Open interest reflects previous trading day.

Both puts and calls are available on index options. They are valued and have issue characteristics like any other put or call. That is, a put lets a holder profit from a drop in the market. (When the underlying market index goes down, the value of a put goes up.) A call enables the holder to profit from a market that's going up. Also, as Figure 14.4 shows, these options even have a quotation system that is very similar to that used for puts and calls on stocks.

Putting a Value on Stock-Index Options As is true of equity options, the market price of index options is a function of the difference between the strike price on the option (stated in terms of the underlying index) and the latest published stock market index. To illustrate, consider the highly popular S&P 100 Index traded on the CBOE. Let's say this index recently closed at 587.25. Suppose there was a June call on this index that carried a strike price of 575. A stock-index *call* will have a value so long as the underlying index exceeds the index strike price (just the opposite for puts). Hence, the intrinsic value of this call would be 587.25 − 575.00 = 12.25. However, this call was actually trading at 14.90—or 2.65 points *above* the call's underlying fundamental value. This difference, of course, was the *time value*.

If the S&P 100 Index in our example (above) were to go up to, say, 600 by late June (the expiration date of the call), this option would be quoted at: 600 − 575 = 25. Because index options (like equity options) are valued in multiples of $100, this contract would be worth $2,500. Thus, if you had purchased this option when it was trading at 14.90, it would have cost you $1,490 ($14.90 × $100) and, in less than a month, would have generated a profit of: $2,500 − $1,490 = $1,010. That translates into a holding period return of a whopping 67.8% ($1,010/$1,490).

Full Value Versus Fractional Value Most broad-based index options use the full market value of the underlying index for purposes of options trading and valuation. That's not the case, however, with two of the Dow Jones measures: The option on the

Dow Jones Industrial Average is based on 1% (1/100) of the actual Industrial Average, and the Dow Transportation Average option is based on 10% (1/10) of the actual average. For example, if the DJIA is at 11,260, the index option would be valued at 1% of that amount, or 112.60. Thus, the cash value of this option is not $100 times the underlying DJIA but $100 times 1% of the DJIA, *which equals the Dow Jones Industrial Average itself*: $100 × 112.60 = $11,260.

Fortunately, the option strike prices are also based on the same 1% of the Dow, so there is no effect on option valuation: What matters is the difference between the strike price on the option and (1% of) the DJIA. For instance, note in Figure 14.4 that the DJIA option index closed at 96.05 (at the time, the actual Dow was at 9,605). Note also that there was a September call option available on this index with a strike price of 83—it was trading at 13.15 (or $1,315). Using Equation 14.1, you can see that this in-the-money option had an intrinsic value of 96.05 − 83 = 13.05. The difference between the option's market value (13.15) and its intrinsic value (13.05) is, of course, the time value. In this case, the time value is very low because the expiration date is not far away.

Another type of option that is traded at 10% (1/10) of the value of the underlying index is the "mini" index option. For example, the Mini-NDX Index (MNX) is set at 10% of the value of the Nasdaq 100. "Minis" also exist for the Nasdaq composite, the S&P 500, the Russell 2000, and the FTSE 250 (an index of mid-cap stocks in the UK), among others.

Investment Uses

Although index options, like equity options, can be used in spreads, straddles, or even covered calls, they are perhaps used most often for speculating or for hedging. When used as a speculative vehicle, index options give investors an opportunity to play the market as a whole, with a relatively small amount of capital. Like any other put or call, index options provide attractive *leverage opportunities* and at the same time *limit exposure to loss* to the price paid for the option.

Index Options as Hedging Vehicles Index options are equally effective as *hedging vehicles*. In fact, hedging is a major use of index options and accounts for a good deal of the trading in these securities. To see how these options can be used for hedging, assume that you hold a diversified portfolio of, say, a dozen different stocks and you think the market is heading down. One way to protect your capital would be to sell all of your stocks. However, that could be expensive, especially if you plan to get back into the market after it drops, and it could lead to a good deal of unnecessary taxes. Fortunately, there is a way to "have your cake and eat it too," and that is to hedge your stock portfolio with a stock index put. In this way, if the market does go down, you'll make money on your puts, which you then can use to buy more stocks at the lower prices. On the other hand, if the market continues to go up, you'll be out *only the cost of the puts*. That amount could well be recovered from the increased value of your stock holdings. The principles of hedging with stock-index options are exactly the same as those for hedging with equity options. The only difference is that with stock-index options, you're trying to protect a *whole portfolio of stocks* rather than *individual* stocks.

Like hedging with individual equity options, the cost of protecting your portfolio with index options can become very expensive (with price premiums of 20% to 30%, or more) when markets are falling and the need for this type of portfolio insurance is the greatest. That, of course, will have an impact on the effectiveness of this strategy.

Also, the amount of profit you make or the protection you obtain depends in large part on how closely the behavior of your stock portfolio is matched by the behavior of the stock-index option you employ. *There is no guarantee that the two will behave in the same way.* You should therefore select an index option that closely reflects the nature of the stocks in your portfolio. If, for example, you hold a number of small-cap stocks, you might select something like the Russell 2000 index option as the hedging vehicle. If you hold mostly blue chips, you might choose the DJIA index option. You probably can't get dollar-for-dollar portfolio protection, but you should try to get as close a match as possible.

A Word of Caution Given their effectiveness for either speculating or hedging, it's little wonder that index options have become popular with investors. But a word of caution is in order: Although trading index options appears simple and seems to provide high rates of return, these vehicles involve *high risk* and are subject to considerable price volatility. They should not be used by amateurs. True, there's only so much you can lose with these options. The trouble is that it's very easy to lose that amount. These securities are not investments you can buy and then forget about until just before they expire. With the wide market swings that are so common today, you must *monitor these securities on a daily basis.*

Other Types of Options

Options on stocks and stock indexes account for most of the market activity in listed options. But you also can obtain put and call options on various other securities. Let's now take a brief look at these other kinds of options, starting with options on ETFs.

Options on Exchange-Traded Funds In addition to various market indexes, put and call options are also available on over 225 *exchange-traded funds (ETFs)*. As more fully explained in Chapter 12, ETFs are like mutual funds that have been structured to track the performance of a wide range of market indexes—in other words, *ETFs are a type of index fund.* They trade like shares of common stock on listed exchanges, primarily the AMEX, and cover everything from broad market measures, such as the DJIA, the S&P 500, and the Nasdaq 100, to market sectors like energy, financials, health care, and semiconductors.

There's a good deal of overlap in the markets and market segments covered by index options and ETF options. In addition to their similar market coverage, they perform very much the same in the market, are valued the same, and are used for many of the same reasons (particularly for speculation and hedging). After all, an ETF option is written on an underlying *index fund* (for example, one that tracks the S&P 500) just like an index option is written on the same underlying *market index* (the S&P 500). Both do pretty much the same thing—either directly or indirectly track the performance of a market measure—so of course they should behave in the same way. The only real difference is this: Options on ETFs are operationally like stock options in that each option covers 100 shares of the underlying exchange-traded fund, rather than $100 of the underlying market index, as is the case with index options. In the end, though, both trade at 100 times the underlying index (or ETF). Thus, while operationally ETF options may be closer to stock options, they function more like index options. As such, the market views them as viable alternatives to index options. These contracts have definitely caught the fancy of investors, especially those that track the major market indexes.

Interest Rate Options Puts and calls on fixed-income (debt) securities are known as **interest rate options**. At the present time, interest rate options are written only on U.S. Treasury securities. Four maturities are used: 30-year T-bonds, 10-year and five-year T-notes, and short-term (13-week) T-bills. These options are *yield-based* rather than price-based. This means they track the yield behavior of the underlying Treasury security (rather than the price behavior). Other types of options (equity and index options) are set up so that they react to movements in the price (or value) of the underlying asset. Interest rate options, in contrast, are set up to react to *the yield of the underlying Treasury security*. Thus, when yields rise, the value of a call goes up. When yields fall, puts go up in value. In effect, because bond prices and yields move in opposite directions, the value of an interest rate call option goes up at the very time that the price (or value) of the underlying debt security is going down. (The opposite is true for puts.) This unusual characteristic may explain why the market for interest rate options remains very small. Most professional investors simply don't care for interest rate options. Instead, they prefer to use interest rate futures contracts or options on these futures contracts (both of which we will examine in Chapter 15).

Currency Options Foreign exchange options, or **currency options** as they're more commonly called, provide a way for investors to speculate on foreign exchange rates or to hedge foreign currency or foreign security holdings. Currency options are available on the currencies of most of the countries with which the United States has strong trading ties. These options are traded on the Philadelphia Exchange and include the following currencies:

- British pound
- Swiss franc
- Australian dollar
- Canadian dollar
- Japanese yen
- Euro

Puts and calls on foreign currencies give the holders the right to sell or buy large amounts of the specified currency. However, in contrast to the standardized contracts used with stock and stock-index options, the specific unit of trading in this market varies with the particular underlying currency. Table 14.6 spells out the details. Currency options are traded in full or fractional cents per unit of the underlying currency, relative to the amount of foreign currency involved. Thus, if a put or call on the British pound were quoted at, say, 6.40 (which is read as "6.4 cents"), it would be

---

TABLE 14.6   Foreign Currency Option Contracts on the Philadelphia Exchange

Underlying Currency*	Size of Contracts	Underlying Currency*	Size of Contracts
British pound	10,000 pounds	Canadian dollar	10,000 dollars
Swiss franc	10,000 francs	Japanese yen	1,000,000 yen
Euro	10,000 euros	Australian dollar	10,000 dollars

*The British pound, Swiss franc, euro, Canadian dollar, and Australian dollar are all quoted in full cents. The Japanese yen is quoted in hundredths of a cent.

valued at $2,000, because 10,000 British pounds underlie this option (that is, $10,000 \times 0.064 = \$640$).

The value of a currency option is linked to the exchange rate between the U.S. dollar and the underlying foreign currency. For example, if the Canadian dollar becomes stronger *relative to the U.S. dollar,* causing the exchange rate to go up, the price of a *call* option on the Canadian dollar will increase, and the price of a *put* will decline. [*Note:* Some cross-currency options are available in the market, but such options/trading techniques are beyond the scope of this book. Here, we will focus solely on foreign currency options (or futures) linked to U.S. dollars.]

The strike price on a currency option is stated in terms of *exchange rates*. Thus, a strike price of 150 implies that each unit of the foreign currency (such as one British pound) is worth 150 cents, or $1.50, in U.S. money. If you held a 150 call on this foreign currency, you would make money if *the foreign currency strengthened relative to the U.S. dollar* so that the exchange rate rose—say, to 155. In contrast, if you held a 150 put, you would profit from a decline in the exchange rate—say, to 145. Success in forecasting movements in foreign exchange rates is obviously essential to a profitable foreign currency options program.

LEAPS They look like regular puts and calls, and they behave pretty much like regular puts and calls, but they're not regular puts and calls. We're talking about **LEAPS**, which are puts and calls with lengthy expiration dates. Basically, LEAPS are long-term options. Whereas standard options have maturities of eight months or less, LEAPS have expiration dates as long as three years. Known formally as *Long-term Equity AnticiPation Securities,* they are listed on all of the major options exchanges. LEAPS are available on hundreds of stocks, stock indexes, and EFTs.

Aside from their time frame, LEAPS work like any other equity or index option. For example, a single (equity) LEAPS contract gives the holder the right to buy or sell 100 shares of stock at a predetermined price on or before the specified expiration date. LEAPS give you more time to be right about your bets on the direction of a stock or stock index, and they give hedgers more time to protect their positions. But there's a price for this extra time: You can expect to pay a lot more for a LEAPS than you would for a regular (short-term) option. That should come as no surprise. LEAPS, being nothing more than long-term options, are loaded with *time value*. And as we saw earlier in this chapter, other things being equal, *the more time an option has to expiration, the higher the quoted price.*

CONCEPTS IN REVIEW

Answers available at
www.pearsonhighered.com/gitman

14.12 Briefly describe the differences and similarities between *stock-index options* and *stock options*. Do the same for *foreign currency options* and stock options.

14.13 Identify and briefly discuss two different ways to use stock-index options. Do the same for foreign currency options.

14.14 Why would an investor want to use index options to hedge a portfolio of common stock? Could the same objective be obtained using *options on ETFs?* If the investor thinks the market is in for a fall, why not just sell the stock?

14.15 What are *LEAPS?* Why would an investor want to use a LEAPS option rather than a regular listed option?

myfinancelab

Here is what you should know after reading this chapter. **MyFinanceLab** will help you identify what you know, and where to go when you need to practice.

What You Should Know	Key Terms	Where To Practice
LG1 Discuss the basic nature of options in general and puts and calls in particular and understand how these investment vehicles work. An option gives the holder the right to buy or sell a certain amount of some real or financial asset at a set price for a set period of time. Puts and calls are the most widely used type of option. These derivative securities offer considerable leverage potential. A put enables the holder to *sell* a certain amount of a specified security at a specified price over a specified time period. A call gives the holder the right to *buy* the security at a specified price over a specified period of time.	call, *p. 531* derivative securities, *p. 532* leverage, *p. 532* option, *p. 531* option premium, *p. 532* option writer (or seller), *p. 532* put, *p. 531*	MyFinanceLab Study Plan 14.1
LG2 Describe the options market and note key options provisions, including strike prices and expiration dates. The options market is made up of conventional (OTC) options and listed options. OTC options are used predominantly by institutional investors. Listed options are traded on organized exchanges such as the CBOE and the AMEX. The creation of listed options exchanges led to standardized options features and to widespread use of options by individual investors. Among the option provisions are the strike price (the stipulated price at which the underlying asset can be bought or sold) and the expiration date (the date when the contract expires).	conventional options, *p. 534* expiration date, *p. 536* listed options, *p. 534* strike price, *p. 535*	MyFinanceLab Study Plan 14.2
LG3 Explain how put and call options are valued and the forces that drive options prices in the marketplace. The value of a call is the market price of the underlying security less the strike price on the call. The value of a put is its strike price less the market price of the security. The value of an option is driven by the current market price of the underlying asset. Most puts and calls sell at premium prices. The size of the premium depends on the length of the option contract (the so-called time premium), the speculative appeal and amount of price volatility in the underlying financial asset, and the general level of interest rates.	in-the-money, *p. 540* out-of-the money, *p. 540* time value, *p. 541*	MyFinanceLab Study Plan 14.3 Excel Table 4.2 Video Learning Aid for Problems P14.5, P14.11
LG4 Describe the profit potential of puts and calls and note some popular put and call investment strategies. Investors who hold puts make money when the value of the underlying asset goes down over time. Call investors make money when the underlying asset moves up in price. Aggressive investors will use puts and calls either for speculation or in highly specialized writing and spreading programs. Conservative investors like the low unit costs and the limited risk that puts and calls offer in	hedge, *p. 546*	MyFinanceLab Study Plan 14.4 Excel Tables 4.3, 4.4

What You Should Know	Key Terms	Where To Practice
absolute dollar terms. Conservative investors often use options to hedge positions in other securities.		
LG5 Explain the profit potential and loss exposure from writing covered call options and discuss how writing options can be used as a strategy for enhancing investment returns. Covered call writers have limited loss exposure because they write options against securities they already own. The maximum profit occurs when the price of the stock equals the strike price of the call. If the stock price goes above the strike price, then any loss on the option is offset by a gain on the stock position. If the stock price goes down, part of the loss on the stock is offset by the proceeds from the call option. Option writing can be combined with other securities to create investment strategies for specific market conditions.	covered options, *p. 549* naked options, *p. 548* option spreading, *p. 550* option straddle, *p. 551*	MyFinanceLab Study Plan 14.5 Excel Table 14.5 Video Learning Aid for Problem P14.11
LG6 Describe market index options, puts and calls on foreign currencies, and LEAPS and discuss how these securities can be used by investors. Standardized put and call options are available on stock-market indexes, like the S&P 500 (in the form of index options or ETF options), and on a number of foreign currencies (currency options). Also available are LEAPS, which are listed options that carry lengthy expiration dates. Although these securities can be used just like stock options, the index and currency options tend to be used primarily for speculation or to develop hedge positions.	currency options, *p. 556* interest rate options, *p. 556* LEAPS, *p. 557* stock-index option, *p. 552*	MyFinanceLab Study Plan 14.6

Log into **MyFinanceLab**, take a chapter test, and get a personalized Study Plan that tells you which concepts you understand and which ones you need to review. From there, **MyFinanceLab** will give you further practice, tutorials, animations, videos, and guided solutions.
Log into www.myfinancelab.com

Discussion Questions

LG2 **Q14.1** Using the stock option quotations in Figure 14.4 (on page 553), respectively, find the option premium, the time value, and the stock index breakeven point for the following puts and calls.
   a. The December put with a $103 strike price
   b. The December call with a $100 strike price.

LG3 **Q14.2** Prepare a schedule similar to the one in Table 14.1 (on page 541) for the call and put options listed in Figure 14.4 (on page 553). Briefly explain your findings.

LG5 **Q14.3** Alcan stock recently closed at $52.51. Assume that you write a covered call on Alcan by writing one September *call* with a strike price of $55, and buying 100 shares of stock at the market price. The option premium that you obtain from writing the call is $370. Assume the stock will pay no dividends between now and the expiration date of the option.

    a. What is the total profit if the stock price remains unchanged?

    b. What is the total profit if the stock price goes up to $55?

    c. What is the total loss if the stock price goes down to $49?

LG6 **Q14.4** Assume you hold a well-balanced portfolio of common stocks. Under what conditions might you want to use a stock-index (or ETF) option to hedge the portfolio?

    a. Briefly explain how such options could be used to hedge a portfolio against a drop in the market.

    b. Discuss what happens if the market does, in fact, go down.

    c. What happens if the market goes up instead?

LG3 LG4 **Q14.5** Using the resources available at your campus or public library (or on the Internet), complete each of the following tasks. (*Note:* Show your work for all calculations.)

    a. Find an *in-the-money call* that has two or three months to expiration. (Select an *equity option* that is at least $2 or $3 in-the-money.) What's the fundamental value of this option and how much premium is it carrying? Using the current market price of the underlying stock (the one listed with the option), determine what kind of dollar and percentage return the option would generate if the underlying stock goes up 10%. How about if the stock goes down 10%?

    b. Repeat part **a**, but this time use an *in-the-money put*. (Choose an equity option that's at least $2 or $3 in-the-money and has two or three months to expiration.) Answer the same questions as above.

    c. Repeat once more the exercise in part **a**, but this time use an *out-of-the-money call*. (Select an equity option, at least $2 or $3 out-of-the-money with two or three months to expiration.) Answer the same questions.

    d. Compare the valuation properties and performance characteristics of in-the-money calls and out-of-the-money calls [from parts **a** and **c**]. Note some of the advantages and disadvantages of each.

Problems

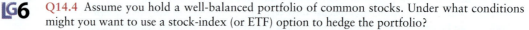

All problems are available on **www.myfinancelab.com**

LG3 **P14.1** Cisco stock is selling for $19. Call options with an $18 exercise price are priced at $2.50. What is the intrinsic value of the option, and what is the time value?

LG3 **P14.2** Gillette is trading at $31.11. Call options with a strike price of $35 are priced at $0.30. What is the intrinsic value of the option, and what is the time value?

LG3 **P14.3** Verizon is trading at $36. Put options with a strike price of $45 are priced at $10.50. What is the intrinsic value of the option, and what is the time value?

LG3 **P14.4** J. Crew is trading at $36. Put options with a strike price of $27.50 are priced at $0.85. What is the intrinsic value of the option, and what is the time value?

LG3 **P14.5** A six-month call on a certain common stock carries a strike price of $60. It can be purchased at a cost of $600. Assume that the underlying stock rises to $75 per share by the expiration date of the option. How much profit would this option generate over the six-month holding period? Using HPR, what is its rate of return?

LG4 LG6 **P14.6** You believe that oil prices will be rising more than expected and that rising prices will result in lower earnings for industrial companies that use a lot of petroleum-related products in their operations. You also believe that the effects on this sector will be magnified because consumer demand will fall as oil prices rise. You locate an exchange-traded fund, XLB, that represents a basket of industrial companies. You don't want to short the ETF because you don't have enough margin in your account. XLB is currently trading at $23. You decide to buy a put option (for 100 shares) with a strike price of $24, priced at $1.20. It turns out that you are correct. At expiration, XLB is trading at $20. Calculate your profit.

XLB: Materials—$23.00					
Calls			Puts		
Strike	Expiration	Price	Strike	Expiration	Price
$20	November	$0.25	$20	November	$1.55
$24	November	$0.25	$24	November	$1.20

LG4 LG6 **P14.7** Refer to the table for XLB in Problem 14.6. What happens if you are wrong and the price of XLB increases to $25 on the expiration date?

LG6 **P14.8** Dorothy Santosuosso does a lot of investing in the stock market and is a frequent user of stock-index options. She is convinced that the market is about to undergo a broad retreat and has decided to buy a put on the S&P 100 Index. The put carries a strike price of 690 and is quoted in the financial press at 4.50. Although the S&P Index of 100 stocks is currently at 686.45, Dorothy thinks it will drop to 665 by the expiration date on the option. How much profit will she make, and what will be her holding period return if she is right? How much will she lose if the S&P 100 goes up (rather than down) by 25 points and reaches 715 by the date of expiration?

LG3 LG4 **P14.9** Myles Houck holds 600 shares of Lubbock Gas and Light. He bought the stock several years ago at 48.50, and the shares are now trading at 75. Myles is concerned that the market is beginning to soften. He doesn't want to sell the stock, but he would like to be able to protect the profit he's made. He decides to hedge his position by buying 6 puts on Lubbock G&L. The three-month puts carry a strike price of 75 and are currently trading at 2.50.
  a. How much profit or loss will Myles make on this deal if the price of Lubbock G&L does indeed drop to $60 a share by the expiration date on the puts?
  b. How would he do if the stock kept going up in price and reached $90 a share by the expiration date?
  c. What do you see as the major advantages of using puts as hedge vehicles?
  d. Would Myles have been better off using in-the-money puts—that is, puts with an $85 strike price that are trading at 10.50? How about using out-of-the-money puts—say, those with a $70 strike price, trading at 1.00? Explain.

LG4 LG6 **P14.10** P. F. Chang holds a well-diversified portfolio of high-quality, large-cap stocks. The current value of Chang's portfolio is $735,000, but he is concerned that the market is heading for a big fall (perhaps as much as 20%) over the next three to six months. He doesn't want to sell all his stocks because he feels they all have good long-term potential and should perform nicely once stock prices have bottomed out. As a result, he's thinking about using index options to hedge his portfolio. Assume that the S&P 500 currently stands at 1,470 and among the many put options available on this index are two that have caught his eye: (1) a six-month put with a strike price of 1,450 that's trading at 26, and (2) a six-month put with a strike price of 1,390 that's quoted at 4.50.
  a. How many S&P 500 puts would Chang have to buy to protect his $735,000 stock portfolio? How much would it cost him to buy the necessary number of 1,450 puts? How much would it cost to buy the 1,390 puts?
  b. Now, considering the performance of both the put options and the Chang portfolio, determine how much *net* profit (or loss) Chang will earn from each of these put hedges if both the market (as measured by the S&P 500) and the Chang portfolio fall by 15% over

the next six months. What if the market and the Chang portfolio fall by only 5%? What if they go up by 10%?

c. Do you think Chang should set up the put hedge and, if so, using which put option? Explain.

d. Finally, assume that the DJIA is currently at 14,550 and that a six-month put option on the Dow is available with a strike price of 144, and is currently trading at 2.50. How many of these puts would Chang have to buy to protect his portfolio, and what would they cost? Would Chang be better off with the Dow options or the S&P 1,450 puts? Briefly explain.

LG3 LG5 **P14.11** Angelo Martino just purchased 500 shares of AT&E at 61.50, and he has decided to write covered calls against these stocks. Accordingly, he sells five AT&E calls at their current market price of 5.75. The calls have three months to expiration and carry a strike price of 65. The stock pays a quarterly dividend of $0.80 a share (the next dividend to be paid in about a month).

a. Determine the total profit and holding period return Angelo will generate if the stock rises to $65 a share by the expiration date on the calls.

b. What happens to Angelo's profit (and return) if the price of the stock rises to more than $65 a share?

c. Does this covered call position offer any protection (or cushion) against a drop in the price of the stock? Explain.

LG6 **P14.12** Rick owns stock in a retailer that he believes is highly undervalued. Rick expects that the stock will increase in value nicely over the long term. He is concerned, however, that the entire retail industry may fall out of favor with investors as some larger companies report falling sales. There are no options traded on his stock, but Rick would like to hedge against his fears about retail. He locates a symbol RTH, which is a Retail HOLDRS. Can Rick hedge against the risk he is concerned with by using RTH? Using options?

LG5 LG6 **P14.13** Suppose the DJIA stands at 11,200. You want to set up a long straddle by purchasing 100 calls and an equal number of puts on the index, both of which expire in three months and have strike prices of 112. The put price is listed at $1.65 and the call sells for $2.65.

a. What will it cost you to set up the straddle, and how much profit (or loss) do you stand to make if the market falls by 750 points by the expiration dates on the options? What if it goes up by 750 points by expiration? What if it stays at 11,200?

b. Repeat part **a**, but this time assume that you set up a *short straddle* by selling/writing 100 July 112 puts and calls.

c. What do you think of the use of option straddles as an investment strategy? What are the risks, and what are the rewards?

LG3 **P14.14** A stock trades for $27 per share. A call option on that stock has a strike price of $25 and an expiration date nine months in the future. The volatility of the stock's returns is 45%, and the risk-free rate is 3%. What is the Black and Scholes value of this option?

Visit **www.myfinancelab.com** for web exercises, spreadsheets, and other online resources.

Case Problem 14.1   *The Franciscos' Investment Options*

LG3 LG4 Hector Francisco is a successful businessman in Atlanta. The box-manufacturing firm he and his wife, Judy, founded several years ago has prospered. Because he is self-employed, Hector is building his own retirement fund. So far, he has accumulated a substantial sum in his investment account, mostly by following an aggressive investment posture. He does this because, as he puts it, "In this business, you never know when the bottom's gonna fall out." Hector has been following the stock of Rembrandt Paper Products (RPP), and after conducting extensive analysis, he feels the stock is about ready to move. Specifically, he believes that within the next six months, RPP could go to about $80 per share, from its current level of $57.50. The stock pays annual dividends of $2.40 per share. Hector figures he would receive two quarterly dividend payments over his six-month investment horizon.

In studying RPP, Hector has learned that the company has six-month call options (with $50 and $60 strike prices) listed on the CBOE. The CBOE calls are quoted at $8 for the options with $50 strike prices and at $5 for the $60 options.

Questions

a. How many alternative investment vehicles does Hector have if he wants to invest in RPP for no more than six months? What if he has a two-year investment horizon?

b. Using a six-month holding period and assuming the stock does indeed rise to $80 over this time frame:
   1. Find the value of both calls, given that at the end of the holding period neither contains any investment premium.
   2. Determine the holding period return for each of the three investment alternatives open to Hector Francisco.

c. Which course of action would you recommend if Hector simply wants to maximize profit? Would your answer change if other factors (e.g., comparative risk exposure) were considered along with return? Explain.

Case Problem 14.2   *Luke's Quandary: To Hedge or Not to Hedge*

LG3 LG4   A little more than 10 months ago, Luke Weaver, a mortgage banker in Phoenix, bought 300 shares of stock at $40 per share. Since then, the price of the stock has risen to $75 per share. It is now near the end of the year, and the market is starting to weaken. Luke feels there is still plenty of play left in the stock but is afraid the tone of the market will be detrimental to his position. His wife, Denise, is taking an adult education course on the stock market and has just learned about put and call hedges. She suggests that he use puts to hedge his position. Luke is intrigued by the idea, which he discusses with his broker, who advises him that the needed puts are indeed available on his stock. Specifically, he can buy three-month puts, with $75 strike prices, at a cost of $550 each (quoted at 5.50).

Questions

a. Given the circumstances surrounding Luke's current investment position, what benefits could be derived from using the puts as a hedge device? What would be the major drawback?

b. What will Luke's minimum profit be if he buys three puts at the indicated option price? How much would he make if he did not hedge but instead sold his stock immediately at a price of $75 per share?

c. Assuming Luke uses three puts to hedge his position, indicate the amount of profit he will generate if the stock moves to $100 by the expiration date of the puts. What if the stock drops to $50 per share?

d. Should Luke use the puts as a hedge? Explain. Under what conditions would you urge him *not* to use the puts as a hedge?

Excel with Spreadsheets

One of the positive attributes of investing in options is the profit potential from the puts or calls. The quoted market price of the option is influenced by the time to expiration, stock volatility, market interest rates, and the behavior of the price of the underlying common stock. The latter variable tends to drive the price movement in options and impacts its potential for profitable returns.

Create a spreadsheet model, similar to that presented below, in order to calculate the profits and/or losses from investing in the option described.

	A	B	C	D	E	F	G	H	I	J
1										
2						Long		100		3-Month Call Option
3						Position		Shares of		on the Stock
4						No		Underlying		Strike Price
5						Option		Common Stock		$$$
6										
7	Today									
8										
9	Market value of stock			$$		$$		$$		
10	Call strike price			$$						
11	Call option premium			$$						
12										
13										
14	Scenario One: 3 months later									
15	Expected market value of stock			$$		$$		$$		
16	Stock value @ strike price			$$						$$
17	Call premium			$$						$$
18	Breakeven point			$$						$$
19										
20	Profit (Loss)					$$		$$		

John has been following the stock market very closely over the past 18 months and has a strong belief that future stock prices will be significantly higher. He has two alternatives that he can follow. The first is to use a long-term strategy—purchase the stock today and sell it sometime in the future at a possibly higher price. The other alternative is to buy a three-month call option. The relevant information needed to analyze the two alternatives is presented below:

Current stock price = $49

Desires to buy one round lot = 100 shares

Three-month call option has a strike price of $51 and a call premium of $2

Questions

a. In scenario 1, if the stock price three months from now is $58:
1. What is the long-position profit or loss?
2. What is the break-even point of the call option?
3. Is the option in- or out-of-the-money?
4. What is the option profit or loss?
b. In scenario 2, if the stock price three months from now is $42:
1. What is the long-position profit or loss?
2. What is the breakeven point of the call option?
3. Is the option in- or out-of-the-money?
4. What is the option profit or loss?

Chapter-Opening Problem

In the beginning of this chapter you read about Copart CEO Willis Johnson, who agreed to work for $1 per year in exchange for the right to buy 2 million Copart shares at an exercise price of $30.21 over the next five years. Shareholders agreed to this deal on April 14, 2009. Over the next five months, Copart stock rose steadily, reaching $36.72 by mid September.

a. What was the intrinsic value of Mr. Johnson's option in mid September?

b. Would you anticipate that these options would have much time value? Why or why not?

c. Suppose that the standard deviation of Copart's stock returns is 50% per year and that as of mid-September 2009, the options had 4.5 years remaining before expiration. Assume a risk-free interest rate of 3%. What is the Black and Scholes value of Mr. Johnson's options?

d. Does it appear that this transaction was a good deal for Mr. Johnson? Is there a case to be made that it might have been good for Copart shareholders?

CHAPTER
15

Commodities and Financial Futures

LEARNING GOALS

After studying this chapter, you should be able to:

LG1 Describe the essential features of a futures contract, and explain how the futures market operates.

LG2 Explain the role that hedgers and speculators play in the futures market, including how profits are made and lost.

LG3 Describe the commodities segment of the futures market and the basic characteristics of these investment vehicles.

LG4 Discuss the trading strategies investors can use with commodities, and explain how investment returns are measured.

LG5 Explain the difference between a physical commodity and a financial future, and discuss the growing role of financial futures in the market today.

LG6 Discuss the trading techniques that can be used with financial futures and note how these securities can be used in conjunction with other investment vehicles.

In March 2005, a new commodity, ethanol, began trading on the Chicago Mercantile Exchange (CME). Ethanol (ethyl alcohol) is an alcohol produced by fermenting and distilling starch crops such as sugar cane, corn, wheat, barley, and sugar beet molasses. Ethanol has three major uses: beverages, industrial products, and increasingly, as an alternative fuel source.

With worldwide demand for energy on the rise, ethanol is becoming more attractive as a renewable, environmentally friendly fuel that enhances the nation's economy and its energy independence. Ethanol does not provide complete independence from fossil fuels since even the most popular version of ethanol-based motor fuel (E85) requires 15% gasoline and 85% ethanol. Pushed by rising demand and empowered by the U.S. *Energy Independence and Security Act of 2007*, U.S. ethanol producers operated 170 refineries in 26 states at the start of 2009, with a capacity of more than 10.5 billion gallons per year—an amount that represents nearly 9% of the U.S. gasoline supply. Both General Motors and Ford Motor Co. have committed to increasing their production of Flexible Fuel Vehicles that can run on either gasoline or E85.

The availability of the CME ethanol futures contracts, which can be traded electronically, will help the ethanol industry continue to grow. Essentially, a *future* is a contract to buy or sell a certain amount of an item—for example, agricultural products or foreign currencies—at a price for delivery on a specific future date. Before investing in individual commodities or trading financial futures, you should understand how these specialized and often high-risk investments work. This chapter will introduce you to the world of commodities and illustrate how to use futures contracts as a tool for risk management.

(Sources: Renewable Fuels Association, from Niche to Nation, Ethanol Industry Outlook 2006, downloaded from www.ethanolrfa.org on August 4, 2006; What is E85? downloaded from www.e85fuel.com on August 4, 2005; Ethanol Futures Scheduled to Launch on March 29th, March 3, 2005, downloaded from www.prnewswire.com on August 4, 2006; Renewable Fuels Association, Growing Innovation, 2009 Ethanol Industry Outlook, downloaded from www.ethanolrfa.org on September 15, 2009; What is E85? downloaded from www.e85fuel.com on August 4, 2005.)

The Futures Market

LG1 "Psst, hey buddy. Wanna buy some copper? How about some coffee, or pork bellies, or propane? Maybe the Japanese yen or Swiss franc strikes your fancy?" Sound a bit unusual? Perhaps, but these items have one thing in common: They all represent real investment vehicles. This is the more exotic side of investing—the market for commodities and financial futures—and it often involves a considerable amount of speculation. The risks are enormous, but with some luck, the payoffs can be phenomenal. Even more important than luck, however, is the need for patience and know-how. Indeed, *these are specialized investment products that require specialized investor skills.*

The amount of futures trading in the United States has mushroomed over the past two or three decades. An increasing number of investors have turned to futures trading as a way to earn attractive, highly competitive rates of return. A major reason behind the growth in futures trading has been the *number and variety of futures contracts now available for trading.* Today, markets exist for the traditional primary commodities, such as grains and metals, as well as for processed commodities, crude oil and gasoline, electricity, foreign currencies, money market securities, U.S. and foreign debt securities, Eurodollar securities, and common stocks. You can even buy listed put and call *options* on just about any actively traded futures contract. All these commodities and financial assets are traded in what is known as the *futures market.*

Market Structure

When a bushel of wheat is sold, the transaction takes place in the **cash market**. The bushel changes hands in exchange for the cash price paid to the seller. For all practical purposes the transaction is completed then and there. Most traditional securities are traded in this type of market. However, a bushel of wheat can also be sold in the **futures market**, the organized market for the trading of futures contracts. In this market, the seller would not actually deliver the wheat until some mutually agreed-upon date in the future. As a result, the transaction would not be completed for some time. The buyer, in turn, would own a highly liquid futures contract that could be held (and presented for delivery of the bushel of wheat) or traded in the futures market. No matter what the buyer does with the contract, as long as it is outstanding, the seller has a *legally binding obligation to make delivery* of the stated quantity of wheat on a specified date in the future. The buyer/holder has a similar *obligation to take delivery* of the underlying commodity.

Futures Contracts A **futures contract** is a commitment to deliver a certain amount of a specified item at a specified date at an agreed-upon price. Each market establishes its own contract specifications. These include not only the quantity and quality of the item but also the delivery procedure and delivery month. The **delivery month** on a futures contract is much like the expiration date on put and call options. It specifies when the commodity or item must be delivered and thus defines the life of the contract. For example, the Chicago Board of Trade specifies that each of its soybean contracts will involve 5,000 bushels of USDA No. 2 yellow soybeans; soybean delivery months are January, March, May, July, August, September, and November.

In addition, futures contracts have *their own trading hours.* Unlike listed stocks and bonds, which begin and end trading at the same time, normal trading hours for commodities and financial futures vary widely. For example, oats trade from 9:30 A.M. to 1:15 P.M. (central); silver, from 7:25 A.M. to 1:25 P.M.; live cattle, from 9:05 A.M. to

TABLE 15.1	Futures Contract Dimensions	
Contract	Size of a Contract*	Recent Market Value of a Single Contract**
Corn	5,000 bu	$ 16,800
Wheat	5,000 bu	23,810
Live cattle	40,000 lb	34,650
Feeder cattle	50,000 lb	49,225
Pork bellies	40,000 lb	34,320
Coffee	37,500 lb	49,913
Cotton	50,000 lb	30,595
Gold	100 troy oz	99,930
Copper	25,000 lb	70,513
Crude oil	1,000 bbls	69,660
Japanese yen	12.5 million yen	137,200
2-year Treasury notes	$200,000	216,781
Treasury bonds	$100,000	120,813
S&P 500 Stock Index	$250 times the index	260,875

*The size of some contracts may vary by exchange.
**Contract values are representative of those that existed on September 15, 2009.

1:00 P.M.; U.S. Treasury bonds, from 7:20 A.M. to 2:00 P.M.; and S&P 500 stock-index contracts, from 8:30 A.M. to 3:15 P.M. In addition, many of these contracts have one set of hours for open-outcry trading and another for electronic trading. It sounds a bit confusing, but it seems to work.

Table 15.1 lists a cross section of 13 different commodities and financial futures. The market value of a single contract, as reported in Table 15.1, is found by multiplying the size of the contract by the latest quoted price of the underlying commodity. For example, there are 37,500 pounds of coffee in a single contract, so if coffee's trading at $1.3310 a pound, then the market value of one contract is 37,500 × $1.3310 = $49,913. As you can see, the typical futures contract covers a large quantity of the underlying product or financial instrument. However, although the value of a single contract is normally quite large, the actual amount of investor capital required to deal in these vehicles is relatively small, because *all trading in this market is done on a margin basis.*

Options Versus Futures Contracts In many respects, futures contracts are closely related to the call options we studied in Chapter 14. For example, both involve the future delivery of an item at an agreed-upon price, and both are derivative securities. But there is a *significant difference* between a futures contract and an options contract. To begin with, a futures contract *obligates* a person to buy or sell a specified amount of a given commodity on or before a stated date—unless the contract is canceled or liquidated before it expires. In contrast, an option gives the holder the *right* to buy or sell a specific amount of a real or financial asset at a specific price over a specified period of time.

In addition, whereas call and put options specify the price at which investors can buy or sell the underlying asset, futures prices are not spelled out in the futures contract. Instead, the price on a futures contract is established through trading on the floor of a commodities exchange. This means that *the delivery price is set at whatever price the contract sells for.* So, if you bought a contract three months ago at $2.50 a bushel, then that's the price you'll pay to take delivery of the underlying product, even if the contract trades at, say, $3.00 a bushel at its date of expiration (i.e., delivery date). Equally important, the risk of loss with an option is limited to the price paid for it. A futures contract has *no such limit on exposure to loss*. Finally, while options have an explicit up-front cost (in the form of an option premium), futures contracts do not. Granted, the purchase of a futures contract does involve a margin deposit, but that's nothing more than a refundable *security deposit*, not a sunk cost (like an option premium).

Major Exchanges Futures contracts in this country got their start in the agricultural segment of the economy over 150 years ago, when individuals who produced, owned, and/or processed foodstuffs sought a way to protect themselves against adverse price movements. Later, futures contracts came to be traded by individuals who were not necessarily connected with agriculture, but who wanted to make money with commodities by speculating on their price swings.

The first organized commodities exchange in this country was the Chicago Board of Trade, which opened its doors in 1848. Over time, additional markets opened. There currently are more than a dozen U.S. exchanges that deal in listed futures contracts, although a number of these are small exchanges trading in only a few types of contracts. The majority of trading, in fact, occurs on only a few exchanges. The Chicago Mercantile Exchange (CME) is the most active exchange, with more trading volume than all other futures exchanges combined. The CME is followed in size by the Chicago Board of Trade (CBOT) and the New York Mercantile Exchange (NYMEX). Together, these three exchanges account for about 95% of all the trading conducted on U.S. futures exchanges. Although the exchanges continue to operate separately, in July of 2007 the CME Group was created through a merger of the CME and the CBOT. The CME Group expanded further in August of 2008 by acquiring the NYMEX.

Most exchanges deal in a number of different commodities or financial assets, and many commodities and financial futures are traded on more than one exchange. Annual volume of trading on futures exchanges has surpassed the trillion-dollar mark. Today, most exchanges conduct trading with a mix of electronic trading and **open-outcry auction**, wherein the actual trading is conducted through a series of shouts, body motions, and hand signals, as shown in Figure 15.1 (on page 570).

In 1992, CME Globex became the first global electronic futures trading platform. Currently, Globex offers trading 23 hours a day, five days a week, and provides an international link between futures exchanges. This trading platform has allowed the CME Eurodollar futures contract to become the single most actively traded futures contract in the world. Indeed, the three most actively traded contracts on CME Globex (three-month Eurodollars, the E-Mini S&P 500 Stock Index, and the Mini-Nasdaq 100 Stock Index) represent more than 40% of all futures trading volume on the U.S. exchanges.

Trading in the Futures Market

Basically, the futures market contains two types of traders: hedgers and speculators. The market could not exist and operate efficiently without either one. The **hedgers** are businesses that either produce a commodity or use it as an input to their production process. For example, a rancher might enter into a futures contract to lock in the price for his herd months before actually selling the herd. That way, the rancher's revenues are predictable and are not affected by swings in the price of cattle. In effect, the hedgers provide the underlying strength of the futures market and represent the very reason for its existence. In the case of financial futures, hedgers are companies who business is affected by swings in financial variables such as interest rates or exchange rates. Accordingly, hedgers also include financial institutions and corporate money managers.

FIGURE 15.1

The Auction Market at Work on the Floor of the Chicago Board of Trade
Traders employ a system of open-outcry and hand signals to indicate whether
they wish to buy or sell and the price at which they wish to do so. Fingers
held vertically indicate the number of contracts a trader wants to buy or sell.
Fingers held horizontally indicate the fraction of a cent above or below the
last traded full-cent price at which the trader will buy or sell.
(Source: Copyright ©2003 Board of Trade of the City of Chicago, Inc. All Rights
Reserved. Used with permission.)

Speculators, in contrast, give the market liquidity. They trade futures contracts
simply to earn a profit on expected swings in the price of a futures contract. They have
no inherent interest in the commodity or financial future other than the price action
and potential capital gains it can produce.

Trading Mechanics Once futures contracts are created, they can readily be traded in
the market. Like common stocks, futures contracts are bought and sold through local
brokerage offices, or on many Internet sites. Except for setting up a special commodities
trading account, there is no difference between trading futures and dealing in stocks or
bonds. The same types of orders are used, and margin trading is standard practice. Any
investor can buy or sell any contract, with any delivery month, at any time, so long as it
is currently being traded on one of the exchanges.

Buying a contract is referred to as *taking a long position.* Selling one is known as *taking a short position.* It is exactly like going long or short with stocks and has the same connotation: A speculator who is long wants the price to rise, and the short seller wants it to drop. Investors can liquidate both long and short positions simply by executing an offsetting transaction. The short seller, for example, would cover her position by buying an equal amount of the contract. In general, only about 1% of all futures contracts are settled by delivery. The rest are offset prior to the delivery month. All trades are subject to normal transaction costs, which include **round-trip commissions** for each contract traded. A round-trip commission includes the commission costs on both ends of the transaction—to buy and sell a contract. Although the exact size of the commission depends on the number and type of contracts being traded, trades that are executed electronically usually have round-trip commissions under $10 and are much less expensive than trades that have to be routed to a pit broker.

Margin Trading Buying on margin means putting up only a fraction of the total price in cash. Margin, in effect, is the *amount of equity* that goes into the deal. *All futures contracts are traded on a margin basis.* The margin required usually ranges from about 2% to 10% of the contract value. This is very low compared to the margin required for stocks and most other securities. Furthermore, there is *no borrowing* required on the part of the investor to finance the balance of the contract. The **margin deposit,** as margin is called with futures, represents security to cover any loss in the market value of the contract that may result from adverse price movements. It exists simply to guarantee fulfillment of the contract. The margin deposit is not a partial payment for the commodity or financial instrument, nor is it related to the value of the underlying product or item.

The dollar amount of the required margin deposit. It varies according to the type of contract and depends on the price volatility of the underlying commodity or financial asset. In some cases, it also varies according to the exchange on which the commodity is traded. Table 15.2 gives the margin requirements for the same 13 commodities

TABLE 15.2 Margin Requirements for a Sample of Commodities and Financial Futures

Contract	Initial Margin Deposit	Maintenance Margin Deposit	Exchange
Corn	$ 1,620	$ 1,200	CBOT
Wheat	2,700	2,000	CBOT
Live cattle	1,080	800	CME
Feeder cattle	1,350	1,000	CME
Pork bellies	1,620	1,200	CME
Coffee	4,400	4,000	NYMEX
Cotton	2,200	2,000	NYMEX
Gold	4,500	3,333	COMEX
Copper	6,075	4,500	COMEX
Crude oil	7,763	5,750	NYMEX
Japanese yen	2,025	1,500	IMM
2-year Treasury notes	1,080	800	CBOT
Treasury bonds	4,320	3,200	CBOT
S&P 500 Stock Index	28,125	22,500	IMM

Note: In September 2009 the exchanges identified above specified these margin requirements as outright speculative margins for nonmembers. Different margin requirements are usually set for exchange members and for hedge transactions. They are meant to be typical of the ongoing requirements that customers are expected to live up to. Depending on the volatility of the market, exchange-minimum margin requirements are changed frequently. Thus, the requirements in this table are also subject to change on short notice. The actual margin requirement for a specific type of transaction on a given exchange is typically reported on the exchange's Web site under "Contract specifications" for that futures contract.

and financial instruments listed in Table 15.1 (on page 568). Compared to the size and value of the futures contracts, margin requirements are very low. The **initial deposit** noted in Table 15.2 is the amount of capital the investor must deposit with the broker when initiating the transaction; it represents the amount of money required to make a given investment. (The margins quoted in Table 15.2 are for speculative transactions. Typically, the initial deposit amount is *slightly lower* for hedge transactions.)

After the investment is made, the market value of a contract will rise and fall as the quoted price of the underlying commodity or financial instrument goes up or down, and that triggers changes in the amount of margin on deposit. To be sure that an adequate margin is always on hand, investors are required to meet a second type of margin requirement, the **maintenance deposit**. This deposit, which is slightly less than the initial deposit, establishes the minimum amount of margin that an investor must keep in the account at all times. For instance, if the initial deposit on a commodity is $1,000 per contract, its maintenance margin might be $750. So long as the market value of the contract does not fall by more than $250 (the difference between the contract's initial and maintenance margins), the investor has no problem. But if the value of the contract drops by more than $250 the investor will receive a *margin call*. The investor must then immediately deposit enough cash to bring the position back to the *initial margin level*.

An investor's margin position is checked daily via a procedure known as **mark-to-the-market**. That is, the gain or loss in a contract's value is determined at the end of each session. At that time the broker debits or credits the account accordingly. In a falling market, an investor may receive a number of margin calls and be required to make additional margin payments. Failure to do so will mean that the broker has no choice but to close out the position—that is, to sell the contract.

CONCEPTS IN REVIEW
Answers available at
www.pearsonhighered.com/gitman

15.1 What is a futures contract? Briefly explain how it is used as an investment vehicle.

15.2 Discuss the difference between a cash market and a futures market.

15.3 What is the major source of return to commodities speculators? How important is current income from dividends and interest?

15.4 Why are both hedgers and speculators important to the efficient operation of a futures market?

15.5 Explain how margin trading is conducted in the futures market.

    a. What is the difference between an *initial deposit* and a *maintenance deposit*?
    b. Are investors ever required to put up additional margin? If so, when?

Commodities

Physical commodities like grains, metals, wood, and meat make up a major portion of the futures market. They have been actively traded in this country for well over a century. The material that follows focuses on *commodities trading*. We begin with a review of the basic characteristics and investment merits of these vehicles.

Basic Characteristics

Physical commodities are found on nearly all of the U.S. futures exchanges. In fact, several of them deal only in commodities. The market for commodity contracts is divided into four major segments: grains and oilseeds, livestock and meat, metals and petroleum, and food and fiber. Such segmentation does not affect trading mechanics and procedures. It merely provides a convenient way of categorizing commodities into groups based on similar underlying characteristics.

Table 15.3 shows the diversity of the commodities market and the variety of contracts available. Although the list changes yearly, the table indicates that investors had literally dozens of commodities to choose from in 2009. A number of these (e.g., soybeans, wheat, and sugar) are available in several different forms or grades. Actually, Table 15.3 lists only *some of the more actively traded commodities. Not included* are dozens of commodities (such as butter, cheese, boneless beef, and others) that are not widely traded but still make up a part of this market.

A Commodities Contract Every commodity (whether actively or thinly traded) has certain specifications that spell out in detail the amounts and quality of the product being traded. Figure 15.2 (on page 574) is an excerpt from the "Futures: Settlement" section of the *Wall Street Journal Online* and shows the contract and quotation system used with commodities. Each commodity quote is made up of the same six parts, and all prices are quoted in an identical fashion. In particular, the quote for each commodities contract specifies: (1) the contract commodity, (2) the delivery month and year, (3) the prices, (4) trading volume and open interest, (5) the exchange on which the contract is traded, and (6) the date and time of the quotation.

The *quotation system* used for commodities is based on the size of the contract and the pricing unit. The financial media generally report the last, open, high, low, and close prices for each delivery month. With commodities, the last price of the day, or the closing price, is known as the **settle price**. Also reported, at least by the *Wall Street Journal*, is the amount of **open interest** in each contract—that is, the number of contracts currently outstanding. Note that according to Figure 15.2, the settle price for May 2011 corn was 402'2. Since the pricing system is cents per bushel and the minimum pricing increment is $2/8$ of one cent per bushel, this means that the contract was being traded at $4.0225 per bushel. Each contract represents 5,000 bushels of corn and each bushel is worth $4.0225, thus, the market value of the contract was 5,000 × $4.0225 = $20,112.5.

TABLE 15.3	Major Classes of Commodities		
Grains and Oilseeds		**Metals and Petroleum**	
Corn	Soybean oil	Electricity	Palladium
Oats	Wheat	Copper	Gasoline
Soybeans	Canola	Gold	Heating oil
Soybean meal	Rice	Platinum	Crude oil
		Silver	Natural gas
Livestock and Meat		**Food and Fiber**	
Cattle—live	Hogs	Cocoa	Sugar
Cattle—feeder	Pork bellies	Coffee	Cotton
		Milk	Lumber
		Orange juice	

FIGURE 15.2   **Quotations on Actively Traded Commodity Futures Contracts**

Readily available online quotations quickly reveal key information about various commodities in real time (or from some sources slightly delayed). These quotations, one for corn futures contracts and one for feeder cattle futures contracts, include the latest intraday last, open, high, and low prices. They also provide the change in price from the previous day's closing price to the current day's last price update, as well as volume, open interest, and listing exchange.
(Source: *Wall Street Journal Online*, September 15, 2009, wsj.com.)

Corn Comp. - cbot

Data retrieved at Sep 15 15:42:11 GMT • All quotes are in Greenwich Mean Time • Data provided by eSignal

	Contract	Month	Last	Chg	Open	High	Low	Volume	OpenInt	Exchange	Date	Time
	CORN	Dec '09	333'6	16'0	317'0	340'0	316'0	89119	526823	CBT	09/15/09	15:32:10
	CORN	Mar '10	347'0	15'6	330'2	353'4	329'6	6989	135061	CBT	09/15/09	15:32:01
	CORN	May '10	356'6	16'2	339'2	362'2	339'2	824	32121	CBT	09/15/09	15:31:15
	CORN	Jul '10	364'6	15'2	348'2	370'0	348'2	869	66836	CBT	09/15/09	15:32:04
	CORN	Sep '10	373'4	15'6	360'0	375'0	360'0	69	12515	CBT	09/15/09	15:30:41
	CORN	Dec '10	382'4	13'6	367'6	390'4	367'4	2605	66584	CBT	09/15/09	15:31:31
	CORN	Mar '11	395'0	13'6	384'6	400'0	384'6	230	1865	CBT	09/15/09	15:30:41
	CORN	May '11	402'2	13'4	394'0	404'2	394'0	4	221	CBT	09/15/09	15:05:06
	CORN	Jul '11	409'0	14'2	400'0	415'0	400'0	69	1431	CBT	09/15/09	15:14:43
	CORN	Sep '11	399'0	9'0	397'0	399'0	397'0	4	162	CBT	09/15/09	14:52:55
	CORN	Dec '11	397'2	12'0	388'0	405'0	388'0	76	5488	CBT	09/15/09	15:13:11
	CORN	Jul '12	407'2y					0	20	CBT	09/14/09	18:41:19
	CORN	Dec '12	417'2	11'4	410'0	425'0	410'0	9	712	CBT	09/15/09	15:29:39

☑ - Chart ☑ - Options ☑ - Quotes   Save Quote Board

Feeder Cattle - cme

Data retrieved at Sep 15 15:44:10 GMT • All quotes are in Greenwich Mean Time • Data provided by eSignal

	Contract	Month	Last	Chg	Open	High	Low	Volume	OpenInt	Exchange	Date	Time
	FEEDER CATTLE	Sep '09	98.450	-0.400	98.900	98.900	98.450	0	2222	CME	09/15/09	15:27:02
	FEEDER CATTLE	Oct '09	98.200	-0.725	98.700	98.950	98.200	0	8912	CME	09/15/09	15:33:03
	FEEDER CATTLE	Nov '09	98.500	-0.900	99.200	99.250	98.450	0	10323	CME	09/15/09	15:33:59
	FEEDER CATTLE	Jan '10	99.100	-0.750	99.500	99.600	99.100	0	3166	CME	09/15/09	15:26:31
	FEEDER CATTLE	Mar '10	99.050	-0.850	99.050	99.050	99.050	0	1087	CME	09/15/09	15:25:25
	FEEDER CATTLE	Apr '10	100.500	-0.400	100.500	100.500	100.400	0	307	CME	09/15/09	14:12:43
	FEEDER CATTLE	May '10	101.050	-0.125	101.050	101.050	100.900	0	602	CME	09/14/09	18:16:56
	FEEDER CATTLE	Aug '10	101.975y					0	102	CME	09/14/09	18:16:56

☑ - Chart ☑ - Options ☑ - Quotes   Save Quote Board

Price Behavior Commodity prices react to a unique set of economic, political, and international pressures—as well as to the weather. The explanation of *why* commodity prices change is beyond the scope of this book. But they do move up and down just like any other investment vehicle, which is precisely what speculators want. Because we are dealing in such large trading units (5,000 bushels of this or 40,000 pounds of that), even a modest price change can have an enormous impact on the market value of a contract and therefore on investor returns or losses. For example, if the price of corn goes up or down by just $0.20 per bushel, the value of a *single contract* will change by $1,000. A corn contract can be bought with a $1,620 initial margin deposit, so it is easy to see the effect this kind of price behavior can have on investor return.

Do commodity prices really move all that much? Judge for yourself: The price change columns in Figure 15.2 show some excellent examples of price changes that occur from the previous day's closing price to the current day's last price. For example, relative to the previous day's closing price, May 2010 corn rose $825 (5,000 bushels × $0.165 = $825) and November 2009 feeder cattle fell $450 (50,000 pounds × 0.009). Keeping in mind that these are intraday price swings that occurred on *single* contracts, these are sizable changes even by themselves. But when you look at them relative to the (very small) original investment required (sometimes as low as $1,080), they quickly add up to serious returns (or losses)!

Clearly, such price behavior is one of the magnets that draws investors to commodities. The exchanges recognize the volatile nature of commodities contracts and try to put lids on price fluctuations by imposing daily price limits and maximum daily price ranges. (Similar limits also are put on some financial futures.) The **daily price limit** restricts the interday change in the price of the underlying commodity. For example, the price of corn can change by no more than $0.30 per bushel from one day to the next. The daily limit on feeder cattle is $0.03 per pound. Such limits, however, still leave plenty of room to turn a quick profit. For example, the daily limits on corn and feeder cattle translate into per-day changes of $1,500 for one corn contract and $1,500 for a feeder cattle contract. The **maximum daily price range**, in contrast, limits the amount the price can change *during* the day and is usually equal to twice the daily limit restrictions. For example, the daily price limit on corn is $0.30 per bushel and its maximum daily range is $0.60 per bushel.

Return on Invested Capital Futures contracts have only one source of return: the capital gains that result when prices move in a favorable direction. There is no current income of any kind. The volatile price behavior of futures contracts is one reason why high returns are possible; the other is leverage. Because all futures trading is done on margin, it takes only a small amount of money to control a large investment position—and to participate in the price swings that accompany futures contracts. Of course, the use of leverage also means that an investment can be wiped out in just a matter of days.

We can measure investment return on a commodities contract by calculating **return on invested capital**. This variation of the standard holding period return formula bases return on the *amount of money actually invested in the contract*, rather than on the value of the contract itself. The return on invested capital for a commodities position can be determined according to the following simple formula:

Equation 15.1

$$\text{Return on invested capital} = \frac{\text{Selling price of commodity contract} - \text{Purchase price of commodity contract}}{\text{Amount of margin deposit}}$$

We can use Equation 15.1 for both long and short transactions. To see how it works, assume you just bought two September 2011 corn contracts at 399'0 ($3.99 per bushel) by depositing the required initial margin of $3,240 ($1,620 for each contract). Your investment, therefore, amounts to only $3,240, but you control 10,000 bushels of corn worth $39,900 at the time of purchase. Now, assume that September 2011 corn has just closed at 420, so you decide to sell out and take your profit. Your return on invested capital is

$$\text{Return on invested capital} = \frac{\$42,000 - \$39,900}{\$3,240}$$

$$= \frac{\$2,100}{\$3,240} = \underline{\underline{64.8\%}}$$

Clearly, this high rate of return was due not only to an increase in the price of the commodity but also to the fact that you were using very low margin. (The initial margin in this particular transaction equaled about 8% of the underlying value of the contract.)

Trading Commodities

Investing in commodities takes one of three forms. The first, *speculating,* involves using commodities as a way to generate capital gains. In essence, speculators try to capitalize on the wide price swings that are characteristic of so many commodities. As explained in the accompanying *Ethics in Investing* box, this is basically what Enron was doing—until things started turning nasty.

While volatile price movements may appeal to speculators, they frighten many other investors. As a result, some of these more cautious investors turn to *spreading,* the second form of commodities investing. Futures investors use this trading technique as a way to capture some of the benefits of volatile commodities prices but without all the exposure to loss.

Finally, commodities futures can be used as *hedging* vehicles. A hedge in the commodities market is more of a technical strategy that is used almost exclusively by producers and processors to protect a position in a product or commodity. For example, a producer or grower would use a commodity hedge to obtain as *high a price* as possible for its goods. The processor or manufacturer who uses the commodity would use a hedge for the opposite reason: to obtain the goods at as *low a price* as possible. A successful hedge, in effect, means added income to producers or lower costs to processors.

Let's now look briefly at the two trading strategies that are most used by individual investors—speculating and spreading—to gain a better understanding of how to use commodities as investment vehicles.

Speculating Speculators hope to capitalize on swings in commodity prices by going long or short. To see why a speculator would go long when prices are expected to rise, assume you buy a June 2014 gold contract at 1130.60 by depositing the required initial margin of $4,500. One gold contract involves 100 troy ounces of gold, so it has a market value of $113,060. If gold goes up, you make money. Assume that one month after you purchased the June 2014 contract, its price is 1143.45. You then liquidate the contract and make a profit of $12.85 per ounce (1143.45 − 1130.60). That means a total profit of $1,285 on the long gold contract position with an investment of just $4,500—this translates into a return on invested capital of 28.6%. Not bad for a month of speculation.

Of course, instead of rising, the price of gold could have dropped by $12.85 per ounce. On a 100-ounce contract, that amounts to $1,285 loss on the position. As a result, you would have lost a good bit of your original investment: $4,500 − $1,285 leaves $3,215.

But a drop in price would be just what a *short seller* is after. Here's why: You sell "short" the June 2014 gold contract at 1130.60 and buy it back sometime later at 1117.75. Clearly, the difference between the selling price and the purchase price is the

ETHICS IN INVESTING

Trading Energy Futures at Enron

Before it was known for its financial problems, Enron, a utility firm operating pipelines and shipping natural gas, had become famous as a business pioneer, blazing new trails in the market for trading risk. In the 1980s, the price of natural gas was deregulated, which meant that its price could go down and up, exposing producers and consumers to risks. Enron decided to exploit new opportunities in the commodities business by trading natural gas futures. The natural gas futures traded on the New York Mercantile Exchange did not take into account regional discrepancies in gas prices. Enron filled this void by agreeing to deliver natural gas to any location in the United States at any time.

In addition to trading natural gas and other energy contracts, in the late 1990s Enron began trading weather derivatives for which no underlying commodities existed. These were just bets on the weather. Its weather-derivatives transactions were worth an estimated $3.5 billion in the United States alone. Thanks to its near-monopoly position in derivatives products, Enron's trading business was initially highly profitable. At one point, the company offered more than 1,800 different contracts for 16 product categories, ranging from oil and natural gas to weather derivatives, broadband services, and emissions rights, and earned 90% of its revenues from trading derivatives. And unlike traditional commodity and futures exchanges and brokers, Enron's online commodity and derivative business was not subject to federal regulations.

However, Enron eventually lost its unique position as the energy business started to mature.

When other firms entered the online derivatives-trading business, they competed by charging lower commissions and exploiting the same regional price discrepancies that had been Enron's bread and butter. Enron's trading operations became less profitable. To find new markets and products, the company expanded into areas such as water, foreign power sources, telecommunications, and broadband services. The farther it moved from its core businesses of supplying gas, the more money Enron lost.

The company sought to hide those losses by entering into more risky and bizarre financial contracts. When financial institutions began to realize that Enron was essentially a shell game, they withdrew their credit. At that point, despite rosy assurances from its founder and CEO Ken Lay, Enron went into a death spiral that ended in bankruptcy on December 2, 2001.

In July 2004, Lay was indicted on 11 counts of securities fraud and related charges. He was found guilty on May 25, 2006, of all but one of the counts. Each count carried a maximum five- to 10-year sentence and legal experts said Lay could face 20 to 30 years in prison. However, about three and a half months before his scheduled sentencing, Ken Lay died on July 5, 2006 while vacationing in Snowmass, Colorado. On October 17, 2006, as a result of his death, the federal district court judge who presided over the case vacated Lay's conviction.

Critical Thinking Questions Could the Enron debacle have been prevented? If so, what actions should have been taken by auditors, regulators, and lawmakers?

---

same $12.85. But in this case it is *profit,* because the selling price exceeds the purchase price. (See Chapter 2, pages 56–59, for a discussion of short selling.)

Spreading Instead of attempting to speculate on the price behavior of a futures contract, you might follow the more conservative tactic of *spreading.* Much like spreading with put and call options, the idea is to combine two or more different contracts into one position that offers the potential for a modest amount of profit but restricts your exposure to loss. One very important reason for spreading in the commodities market is that, unlike options, *there is no limit to the amount of loss that can occur with a futures contract.*

You set up a spread by buying one contract and simultaneously selling another. Although one side of the transaction will lead to a loss, you hope that the profit earned from the other side will more than offset the loss, and that the net result will be at least

MARKETS IN CRISIS

Oil Isn't Recession Proof

Economic activity and commodity prices have long been linked; in particular, as economies grow, so does the demand for commodities, putting upward pressure on prices. This relationship is most acute for oil, since historically oil consumption tends to be very sensitive to macroeconomic activity. The chart below shows that in 2007–2008, fueled in part by strong economic growth throughout most of the world, crude oil futures prices were reaching all-time highs. The volume of oil futures exploded; the average daily trading volume in 2008 was about 15 times the daily world production of oil. But as the global economy turned south and began to slip into recession, demand for oil and other commodities fell off sharply. After peaking at about $147 per barrel in July 2008, the price of oil responded true to form, falling precipitously to $40 a barrel by December. Commodity trading can be a perilous business, especially in times of economic uncertainty.

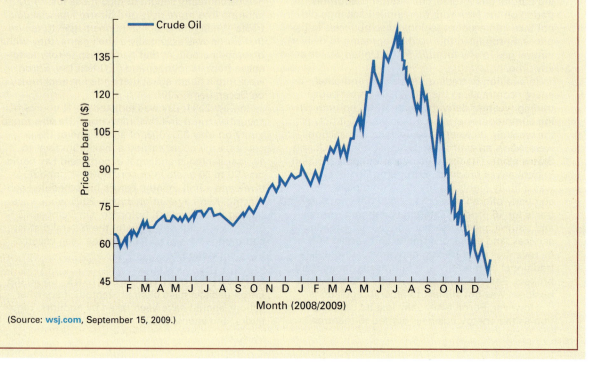

(Source: **wsj.com**, September 15, 2009.)

a modest amount of profit. If you're wrong, the spread will limit, but not eliminate, any losses.

Here is a simple example of how a spread might work: Suppose you buy contract A at 533.50 and at the same time short-sell contract B for 575.50. Sometime later, you close out your position in contract A by selling it at 542, and you simultaneously cover your short position in B by purchasing a contract at 579. Although you made a profit of 8.50 points (542 − 533.50) on the long position (contract A), you lost 3.50 points (575.50 − 579) on the contract you shorted (B). The net effect, however, is a profit of five points. If you were dealing in cents per pound, those five points would mean a profit of $250 on a 5,000-pound contract.

All sorts of commodity spreads can be set up for almost any type of investment situation. Most of them, however, are highly sophisticated and require specialized skills.

15.6 List and briefly define the five essential parts of a commodities contract. Which parts have a direct bearing on the price behavior of the contract?

15.7 Briefly define each of the following:

a. Settle price.
b. Daily price limit.
c. Open interest.
d. Maximum daily price range.
e. Delivery month.

15.8 What is the one source of return on futures contracts? What measure is used to calculate the return on a commodities contract?

15.9 Note several approaches to investing in commodities and explain the investment objectives of each.

Financial Futures

LG5 LG6 Another dimension of the futures market is **financial futures**, a segment of the market in which futures contracts are traded on *financial instruments*. Financial futures are an extension of the commodities concept. They were created for much the same reason as commodities futures, they are traded in the same market, their prices behave a lot like commodities, and they have similar investment merits. But financial futures are unique because of the underlying assets. Let's now look more closely at financial futures and see how investors can use them.

The Financial Futures Market

Although relatively young, financial futures are the dominant type of futures contract. The level of trading in financial futures far surpasses that of traditional commodities. Much of the interest in financial futures is due to hedgers and institutional investors who use these contracts as portfolio management tools. But individual investors can also use financial futures to speculate on the behavior of interest rates and to speculate in the stock market. They even offer a convenient way to speculate in the highly specialized foreign currency markets.

The financial futures market was established in response to the economic turmoil the United States experienced in the 1970s. The instability of the dollar on the world market was causing serious problems for multinational firms. Interest rates were highly volatile, which caused severe difficulties for corporate treasurers, financial institutions, and money managers. All of these parties needed a way to protect themselves from the wide fluctuations in the value of the dollar and interest rates. Thus, a market for financial futures was born. Hedging provided the economic rationale for the market, but speculators were quick to join in.

Most of the financial futures trading in this country occurs on just two exchanges—the Chicago Board of Trade and the Chicago Mercantile Exchange. Financial futures also are traded on several foreign exchanges, the most noteworthy of which is the London International Financial Futures Exchange. The three basic types of financial futures include foreign currencies, debt securities, and stock indexes.

Foreign Currencies, Interest Rates, and Stock Indexes The financial futures market started rather inconspicuously in May 1972, with the listing of a handful of foreign

INVESTOR FACTS

SINGLE STOCK FUTURES—
Several years ago, single stock futures (SSF) began trading on an exchange called OneChicago. SSFs allow investors to buy or sell futures contracts written on 100-share lots of a given common stock. SSFs today are available on more than 1,200 well-known companies, including most big-name stocks. In 2008 OneChicago's traded contract volume was over 4 million, representing more than 400 million shares of common stock. Because of their lower margin requirements (20% for SSFs versus 50% for regular stock trades), SSFs are a highly leveraged investment, with substantial risk, but also with very attractive return potential. Depending on their risk profiles, investors can use this futures version of a stock to support both speculative and hedging investment strategies.
(Source: OneChicago, LLC, Press Release PR09-001 01/06/2009, www.onechicago.com/index.html, downloaded September 15, 2009.)

currency contracts. Known as **currency futures**, they have become a major hedging vehicle as international trade has mushroomed. Most of the trading in this market is conducted in major market currencies such as the British pound, Swiss franc, Canadian dollar, Japanese yen, and the euro—all of which are issued by countries or regions with strong international trade and economic ties to the United States.

The first futures contract on debt securities, or **interest-rate futures**, began trading in October 1975. Today, trading is carried out in a variety of interest-rate-based securities, including U.S. Treasury securities, Federal Funds, interest rate swaps, Euromarket deposits (e.g., Eurodollar and Euroyen), and foreign government bonds. Interest-rate futures were immediately successful, and their popularity continues to grow.

In February 1982, still another type of trading vehicle was introduced: the stock-index futures contract. **Stock-index futures** are contracts pegged to broad-based measures of stock market performance. Today, trading is done in most of the (major) U.S. stock indexes, including the Dow Jones Industrial Average, the S&P 500, the Nasdaq 100, and the Russell 2000, among others.

In addition to U.S. indexes, investors can trade stock-index futures contracts based on the London, Tokyo, Paris, Sydney, Berlin, Zurich, and Toronto stock exchanges. Stock-index futures, which are similar to the stock-index options we discussed in Chapter 14, allow investors to participate in the general movements of the entire stock market.

Stock-index futures, and other futures contracts, are a type of *derivative security*. Like options, they derive their value from the price behavior of the assets that underlie them. In the case of stock-index futures, they reflect the general performance of the stock market as a whole, or various segments of the market. Thus, when the market for large-cap stocks, as measured by the S&P 500, goes up, the value of an S&P 500 futures contract should go up as well. Accordingly, investors can use stock-index futures as a way to buy or sell the market—or reasonable proxies thereof—and thereby participate in broad market moves.

Contract Specifications In principle, financial futures contracts are like commodities contracts. They control large sums of the underlying financial instrument and are issued with a variety of delivery months. Figure 15.3 shows quotes for a foreign currency, an interest rate, and a stock-index futures contract. Looking first at currency futures quotation, we see that the currency contracts entitle holders to 100,000 Canadian dollars. In effect, the owner of a currency futures contract holds a claim on a certain amount of foreign money, in this case 100,000 Canadian dollars. Underlying currency amounts can vary widely across currency futures contracts, such as 62,500 British pounds or 12.5 million Japanese yen. Similarly, holders of interest rate futures have a claim on a certain amount of the underlying debt security. The interest rate futures contract shown in Figure 15.3 represents a claim to $100,000 worth of U.S. Treasury bonds.

Stock-index futures, however, are a bit different because the seller of one of these contracts is *not* obligated to deliver the *underlying stocks* at the expiration date. Instead, ultimate delivery is in the form of *cash*. (This is fortunate as it would indeed be a task to make delivery of the 2,000 small-cap stocks that are in the Russell 2000 Index

FIGURE 15.3

Quotations on Selected Actively Traded Financial Futures

The trading exchange, size of the trading unit, pricing unit, and delivery months are all vital pieces of information included as part of the quotation system used with financial futures.
(Source: *Wall Street Journal Online*, September 15, 2009, wsj.com.)

Currency Futures | Index | Interest Rate | Agricultural | Metals & Petroleum

Monday, September 14, 2009 — Find Historical Data | WHAT'S THIS?

KEY TO EXCHANGES: CBT: Chicago Board of Trade; CME: Chicago Mercantile Exchange; CMX: Comex; DME: Dubai Mercantile Exchange; ENXT: Euronext.liffe; EUREX: EUREX; ICE-EU: ICE Futures Europe; ICE-US: ICE Futures U.S.; KC: Kansas City Board of Trade; ME: Montreal Exchange; MPLS: Minneapolis Grain Exchange; NYM: New York Mercantile Exchange, or Nymex; SGX-DT: Singapore Exchange Derivatives Trading Ltd

Canadian Dollar (CME)-CAD 100,000; $ per CAD

	Open	High	Low	Settle	Chg	LIFETIME High	(▲ ▼)	Low	Open Int
Sep 09	.9287	.9287	.9152	.9222	-.0063	1.0140		.7699	38,268
Dec 09	.9291	.9291	.9153	.9224	-.0064	.9937		.7712	85,185
Mar 10	.9267	.9267	.9171	.9222	-.0063	.9400		.7731	1,110
Sep 10	.9192	.9233	.9192	.9219	-.0062	.9391		.8548	360
Dec 10	.9222	.9229	.9201	.9217	-.0061	.9280		.8680	13

Est vol 71,095; vol Fri 101,019; open int, 125,196, +7,017.

Sources: Thomson Reuters; WSJ Market Data Group

Interest Rate Futures | Index | Agricultural | Currency | Metals & Petroleum

Monday, September 14, 2009 — Find Historical Data | WHAT'S THIS?

KEY TO EXCHANGES: CBT: Chicago Board of Trade; CME: Chicago Mercantile Exchange; CMX: Comex; DME: Dubai Mercantile Exchange; ENXT: Euronext.liffe; EUREX: EUREX; ICE-EU: ICE Futures Europe; ICE-US: ICE Futures U.S.; KC: Kansas City Board of Trade; ME: Montreal Exchange; MPLS: Minneapolis Grain Exchange; NYM: New York Mercantile Exchange, or Nymex; SGX-DT: Singapore Exchange Derivatives Trading Ltd

Treasury Bonds (CBT)-$100,000; pts 32nds of 100%

	Open	High	Low	Settle	Chg	LIFETIME High	(▲ ▼)	Low	Open Int
Sep 09	121-230	122-010	121-010	121-080	-20.0	136-160		111-215	25,636
Dec 09	120-150	120-230	119-190	119-270	-21.0	136-300		110-000	730,165

Est vol 130,704; vol Fri 204,248; open int, 755,960, +7,800.

Sources: Thomson Reuters; WSJ Market Data Group

Index Futures | Interest Rate | Agricultural | Currency | Metals & Petroleum

Monday, September 14, 2009 — Find Historical Data | WHAT'S THIS?

KEY TO EXCHANGES: CBT: Chicago Board of Trade; CME: Chicago Mercantile Exchange; CMX: Comex; DME: Dubai Mercantile Exchange; ENXT: Euronext.liffe; EUREX: EUREX; ICE-EU: ICE Futures Europe; ICE-US: ICE Futures U.S.; KC: Kansas City Board of Trade; ME: Montreal Exchange; MPLS: Minneapolis Grain Exchange; NYM: New York Mercantile Exchange, or Nymex; SGX-DT: Singapore Exchange Derivatives Trading Ltd

DJ Industrial Average (CBT)-$10 x index

	Open	High	Low	Settle	Chg	LIFETIME High	(▲ ▼)	Low	Open Int
Sep 09	9510	9630	9498	9611	+19	9635		6548	10,797
Dec 09	9490	9565	9437	9550	+19	9580		8025	3,471
Mar 10	9400	9401	9399	9492	+19	9558		8046	753

Est vol 4,233; vol Fri 628; open int, 15,021, +86. Idx prl: Hi 9631.11; Lo 9535.96; Close 9626.80, +21.39.

Sources: Thomson Reuters; WSJ Market Data Group

or the 500 issues in the S&P Index.) Basically, the amount of underlying cash is set at a certain multiple of the value of the underlying stock index. For example:

Index	Multiple
DJIA	$10 × index
S&P 500	$250 × index
Nasdaq 100	$100 × index
S&P 400	$500 × index
Russell 2000	$500 × index

Thus, if the March 2010 DJIA stock-index futures contract stood at 9492 (as indicated in Figure 15.3), then the amount of cash underlying a single DJIA stock-index futures contract would be $10 × 9,492 = $94,920. Again, the amount is substantial. In terms of delivery months, the lives of financial futures contracts run from about 12 months or less for most stock-index and currency futures to two to three years or more for interest-rate instruments.

Prices and Profits Not surprisingly, the price of each type of financial futures contract is quoted somewhat differently.

- *Currency futures.* All currency futures are quoted in dollars or cents per unit of the underlying foreign currency (e.g., dollars per British pound or cents per Japanese yen). Thus, according to the closing ("settle") prices in Figure 15.3, one September 2010 Canadian dollar contract is worth $92,190 (100,000 CAD × 0.9219). At the same time, a September 2009 Japanese yen contract with a settle price of 1.1010 (not shown in Figure 15.3) is valued at $137,625 (12,500,000 yen × $0.011010).

- *Interest-rate futures.* Except for the quotes on Treasury bills and other short-term securities, interest-rate futures contracts are priced as a percentage of the par value of the underlying debt instrument (e.g., Treasury notes or bonds). Because these instruments are quoted in increments of 1/32 of 1%, a quote of 121–080 for the settle price of the September 2009 U.S. Treasury bonds (in Figure 15.3) translates into 121–8/32, which converts to a quote of 121.25% of par. Apply this rate to the $100,000 par value of the underlying security, and we see that this contract is worth $121,250 ($100,000 × 1.2125). The pricing conventions for the variety of other interest-rate futures contracts are typically included with their quotations, as is the case with those quoted at **wsj.com**.

- *Stock-index futures.* Stock-index futures are quoted in terms of the actual underlying index. As noted above, they carry a face value of anywhere from $10 to $500 times the index. Thus, according to the settle price in Figure 15.3, the September 2009 DJIA contract would be worth $96,110, because the value of this particular contract is equal to $10 times the settle price of the index (9,611 × $10). The value of a March 2010 S&P 500 Stock Index contract with a settle price of 1,039.00 is 1,039 × $250 = $259,750. For the S&P 500 contract, the face value is $250 times the settle price.

The value of an interest-rate futures contract responds to interest rates exactly as the debt instrument that underlies the contract. That is, when interest rates go up, the value of an interest-rate futures contract goes down, and vice versa. The quote system used for interest rate as well as currency and stock-index futures is set up to reflect the *market value of the contract* itself. Thus, when the price or quote of a financial futures contract increases (for example, when interest rates fall or a stock-index goes up), then the investor who is long makes money. In contrast, when the price decreases, the short seller makes money.

Price behavior is the only source of return to speculators. Financial futures contracts have no claim on the dividend and interest income of the underlying issues. Even so, huge profits (or losses) are possible with financial futures because of the equally large size of the contracts. For instance, if the price of Swiss francs goes up by just $0.02 against the dollar, the investor is ahead $2,500. Likewise, a three-point drop in the Russell 2000 means a $1,500 loss to an investor (3 × $500). When related to the relatively small initial margin deposit required to make transactions in the financial futures markets, such price activity can mean very high rates of return—or very high risk of a total wipeout.

Trading Techniques

Investors can use financial futures, like commodity futures, for hedging, spreading, and speculating. Multinational companies and firms that are active in international trade might *hedge* with currency or Euromarket futures. Various financial institutions and corporate money managers often use interest-rate futures for hedging purposes. In either case, the objective is the same: to lock in the best monetary exchange or interest rate possible. In addition, individual investors and portfolio managers often hedge with stock-index futures to protect their security holdings against temporary market declines. Financial futures can also be used for *spreading*. This tactic is popular with investors who simultaneously buy and sell combinations of two or more contracts to form a desired investment position. Finally, financial futures are widely used for *speculation*.

Although investors can employ any one of the three trading strategies noted above, we will focus primarily on the use of financial futures by speculators and hedgers. We will first examine speculating in currency and interest rate futures. Then we'll look at how investors can use futures to hedge investments in stocks, bonds, and foreign securities.

Speculating in Financial Futures Speculators are especially interested in financial futures because of the size of the contracts. For instance, in mid-2009, euro currency contracts were worth over $175,500, Treasury notes interest-rate contracts were going for around $116,266, and 30-day Federal Funds contracts were being quoted at more than $4.98 million each. With contracts of this size, even small movements in the underlying asset can produce big price swings—and therefore big profits.

Currency and interest-rate futures can be used for just about any speculative purpose. For example, if you expect the dollar to be devalued relative to the euro, you could buy euro currency futures, because the contracts should go up in value, right along with the appreciation of the euro. If you anticipate a rise in interest rates, you might "go short" (sell) interest-rate futures, since they should go down in value. Because margin is used and financial futures have the same source of return as commodities (price appreciation), we can measure the profitability of these contracts using return on invested capital (Equation 15.1 on page 575.)

 Going Long a Foreign Currency Contract Suppose you believe that the Swiss franc (CHF) is about to appreciate in value relative to the dollar. You decide to go long (buy) three December 2012 CHF contracts at 0.9728—i.e., at a quote of just under $1.00 a franc. Each contract would be worth $121,600 (125,000 CHF × 0.9728), so the total underlying value of the three contracts would be $364,800. Given an initial margin requirement of, say, $2,500 per contract, you would have to deposit only $7,500 to acquire this position.

Now, if Swiss francs do appreciate and move up from 0.9728 to, say, 0.9965, the value of the three contracts will rise to $373,687.50. In a matter of months, you will have made a profit of $8,887.50. Using Equation 15.1 for return on invested capital, we find that such a profit translates into a 118.5% rate of return. Of course, an even smaller fractional change in the other direction would have wiped out this investment. Clearly, these *high returns are not without equally high risk*.

Going Short an Interest Rate Contract Let's assume that you're anticipating a sharp rise in long-term rates. A rise in rates translates into a drop in the value of interest-rate futures. You decide to short-sell two June T-bond contracts at 115-00, which means that the contracts are trading at 115% of par. Thus, the two contracts are worth $230,000 ($100,000 × 1.15 × 2). You need only $8,640 (the initial margin deposit is $4,320 per contract) to make the investment.

Assume that interest rates do, in fact, move up. As a result, the price on Treasury bond contracts drops to 106-16 (or $106\frac{1}{2}$). You could now buy back the two June 2014 T-bond contracts (to cover the short position) and in the process make a profit of $17,000. You originally sold the two contracts at $230,000 and bought them back sometime later at $213,000. As with any investment, such a difference between what you pay for a security and what you sell it for is profit. In this case, the return on invested capital amounts to 197%. Again, this return is due in no small part to the *enormous risk of loss* you assumed.

Trading Stock-Index Futures Most investors use stock-index futures for speculation or hedging. (Stock-index futures are similar to the *index options* introduced in Chapter 14. Therefore, much of the discussion that follows also applies to index options.) Whether speculating or hedging, the key to success is *predicting the future course of the stock market*. Because you are "buying the market" with stock-index futures, it is important to get a handle on the future direction of the market via technical analysis (as discussed in Chapter 9) or some other technique. Once you have a feel for the market's direction, you can formulate a stock-index futures trading or hedging strategy. For example, if you feel that the market is headed up, you would want to go long (buy stock-index futures). In contrast, if your analysis suggests a drop in equity values, you could make money by going short (selling stock-index futures).

Assume, for instance, that you believe the market is undervalued and a move up is imminent. You can try to identify one or a handful of stocks that should go up with the market (and assume the stock selection risks that go along with this approach). Or you can buy an S&P 500 stock-index futures contract currently trading at, say, 1,047.90. To execute this speculative transaction, you would need to deposit an initial margin of $28,125. Now, if the market does rise so that the S&P 500 Index moves to, say, 1,122.85 by the expiration of the futures contract, you earn a profit of $18,737.50—that is, $(1,122.85-1,047.90) \times \$250 = \$18,737.50$. Given the $28,125 investment, your return on invested capital would amount to a hefty 67%. Of course, keep in mind that if the market drops by around 113 points (or 10.8%) the investment will be a *total loss.*

Hedging with Stock-Index Futures Stock-index futures also make excellent hedging vehicles. They provide investors with a highly effective way of protecting stock holdings in a declining market. Although this tactic is not perfect, it does enable investors to obtain desired protection against a decline in market value without disturbing their equity holdings.

Here's how a so-called *short hedge* would work: Assume that you hold a total of 2,000 shares of stock in a dozen different companies and that the market value of this portfolio is around $235,000. If you think the market is about to undergo a temporary sharp decline, you can do one of two things: Sell all of your shares or buy puts on each of the stocks. Clearly, these alternatives are cumbersome and/or costly and therefore undesirable for protecting a widely diversified portfolio. The desired results could also be achieved, however, by *short selling stock-index futures*. (You also could obtain the same protection by turning to options and buying *stock-index puts*.)

Suppose for purposes of our illustration that you short-sell two DJIA stock-index futures contracts at 11,375. These contracts would provide a close match to the current value of your portfolio (they would be valued at $2 \times 11,375 \times \$10 = \$227,500$). Yet these stock-index futures contracts would require an initial margin deposit of only $7,500 per contract, or a total deposit of $2 \times \$7,500 = \$15,000$. Now, if the DJIA drops to 10,868, you will make a profit of a little over $10,000 from this short sale. That is, because the index fell 507 points (11,375 − 10,868), the total profit will be $10,140 (2 × 507 × $10). Ignoring taxes, you can add this profit to the portfolio (by purchasing additional shares of stock at their new lower prices). The net result will be a new portfolio position that will approximate the one that existed prior to the decline in the market.

How well the "before" and "after" portfolio positions match will depend on how far the portfolio dropped in value. If the average price dropped about $5 per share in our example, the positions will closely match. But this does not always happen. The price of some stocks will change more than others, so the amount of protection provided by this type of short hedge depends on how sensitive the stock portfolio is to movements in the market. Thus, the types of stocks held in the portfolio are an important consideration in structuring a stock-index short hedge.

A key to success with this kind of hedging is to make sure that the characteristics of the hedging vehicle (the futures contract) closely match those of the portfolio (or security position) being protected. If the portfolio is made up mostly (or exclusively) of large-cap stocks, use something like the S&P 500 Stock Index futures contract as the hedging vehicle. If the portfolio is mostly blue-chip stocks, use the DJIA contracts. If the portfolio holds mostly tech stocks, consider the Nasdaq 100 Index contract. Again, the point is to pick a hedging vehicle that closely reflects the types of securities you want to protect. If you keep that caveat in mind, hedging with stock-index futures can be a low-cost yet effective way of obtaining protection against loss in a declining stock market.

Hedging Other Securities Just as you can use stock-index futures to hedge stock portfolios, you can use *interest-rate futures* to hedge bond portfolios. Or, you can use *currency futures* with foreign securities as a way to protect against foreign exchange risk. *Let's consider an interest rate hedge:* If you held a substantial portfolio of bonds, the last thing you would want to see is a big jump in interest rates, which could cause a sharp decline in the value of your portfolio. Assume you hold around $300,000 worth of Treasury and agency bonds, with an average maturity of about 18 years. If you believe that market rates are headed up, you can hedge your bond portfolio by short-selling three U.S. Treasury bond futures contracts. (Each T-bond futures contract is worth about $100,000, so it would take three of them to cover a $300,000 portfolio.) If rates do head up, you will have protected the portfolio against loss. As noted above, the exact amount of protection will depend on how well the T-bond futures contracts parallel the price behavior of your particular bond portfolio.

There is, of course, a downside: If market interest rates go down, rather than up, you will miss out on potential profits *as long as the short hedge position remains in place*. This is so because the profits being made in the portfolio will be offset by losses from the futures contracts. Actually, this will occur with any type of portfolio (stocks, bonds, or anything else) that is tied to an offsetting short hedge; when you create the short hedge you essentially lock in a position at that point. Although you do not lose anything when the market falls, you also do not make anything when the market goes up. In either case, the profits you make from one position are offset by losses from the other.

Hedging Foreign Currency Exposure Now let's see how you can use futures contracts to hedge foreign exchange risk. Let's assume that you have just purchased $200,000 of British government one-year notes. (You did this because higher yields were available on the British notes than on comparable U.S. Treasury securities.) Because these notes are denominated in pounds, this investment is subject to loss if currency exchange rates move against you (if the value of the dollar rises relative to the pound).

If all you wanted was the higher yield offered by the British note, you could eliminate most of the currency exchange risk by setting up a currency hedge. Here's how: Let's say that at the current exchange rate, one U.S. dollar will "buy" 0.60 of a British pound. This means that pounds are worth about $1.65 (i.e., $1.00/0.60£ = $1.65). So, if currency contracts on British pounds were trading at around $1.65 a pound, you would have to *sell* two contracts to protect the $200,000 investment. Each contract covers 62,500 pounds; if they're being quoted at 1.65, then each contract is worth $1.65 × 62,500 = $103,125.

Assume that one year later, the value of the dollar has increased relative to the pound, so that one U.S. dollar will now "buy" 0.65 pound. Under such conditions, a British pound futures contract would be quoted at around 1.54 (i.e., $1.00/.065£ = $1.54). At this price, each futures contract would be worth $96,250 (62,500 × $1.54). Each contract, in effect, would be worth $6,875 less than it was a year ago. But because the contract was sold short when you set up the hedge, you will make a profit of $6,875 per contract—for a total profit of $13,750 on the two contracts. Unfortunately, that's not *net profit,* because this profit will offset the loss you will incur on the British note investment. In very simple terms, when you sent $200,000 overseas to buy the British notes, the money was worth about £121,000. However, when you brought the money back a year later, those 121,000 pounds purchased only about 186,500 U.S. dollars. Thus, you are out some $13,500 on your original investment. Were it not for the currency hedge, you would be out the full $13,500, and the return on this investment would be a lot lower. The hedge covered the loss (plus a little extra), and the net effect was that you were able to enjoy the added yield of the British note without having to worry about potential loss from currency exchange rates.

Financial Futures and the Individual Investor

Like commodities, financial futures can play an important role in your portfolio so long as three factors apply: (1) You thoroughly understand these investment vehicles. (2) You clearly recognize the tremendous risk exposure of these vehicles. (3) You are fully prepared (financially and emotionally) to absorb some losses.

Financial futures are highly volatile securities that have enormous potential for profit and for loss. For instance, in 2009, during the six-month period from March 13 to September 14, the September 2009 S&P 500 futures contract changed in price from 752.2 to 1,047.9. This range of 295.7 points for a single contract translated into a *potential* profit—or loss—of some $74,000, and all from an initial investment of only $28,000. Investment diversification is obviously essential as a means of reducing the potentially devastating impact of price volatility. Financial futures are exotic investment vehicles, but if properly used, they can provide generous returns.

Options on Futures

The evolution that began with listed stock options and financial futures spread, over time, to interest-rate options and stock-index futures. Eventually, it led to the creation

TABLE 15.4   Futures Options: Puts and Calls on Futures Contracts

Commodities

Corn	Pork bellies	Sugar	Gold
Soybeans	Lean hogs	Wheat	Silver
Soybean meal	Feeder cattle	Oats	Crude oil
Soybean oil	Orange juice	Rice	Natural gas
Cotton	Cocoa	Platinum	Heating oil
Live cattle	Coffee	Copper	Gasoline

Financial Futures

British pound	Treasury notes
Euro	Treasury bonds
Swiss franc	30-day Federal Funds
Japanese yen	London Interbank Offering Rate (LIBOR)
Canadian dollar	NYSE Composite Index
Mexican peso	S&P 500 Stock Index
U.S. dollar index	Dow Jones Industrial Average
Eurodollar deposits	Nasdaq 100 Index
Treasury bills	Russell 2000

of the ultimate leverage vehicle: *options on futures contracts*. **Futures options**, as they are called, represent listed puts and calls on actively traded futures contracts. In essence, they give the holders the right to buy (with calls) or sell (with puts) a single standardized futures contract for a specific period of time at a specified strike price.

Table 15.4 lists many of the actively traded futures options available. Such options can be found on both commodities and financial futures. For the most part, these puts and calls cover the same amount of assets as the underlying futures contracts—for example, 112,000 pounds of sugar, 100 ounces of gold, 62,500 British pounds, or $100,000 in Treasury bonds. Thus, they also involve the same amount of price volatility as is normally found with commodities and financial futures.

Futures options have the same standardized strike prices, expiration dates, and quotation system as other listed options. Depending on the strike price on the option and the market value of the underlying futures contract, these options can also be in the money or out of the money. Futures options are valued like other puts and calls—by the difference between the option's strike price and the market price of the underlying futures contract (see Chapter 14). They can also be used like any other listed option—for speculating or hedging, in options writing programs, or for spreading. The biggest difference between a futures option and a futures contract is that *the option limits the loss exposure* to the price of the option. The most you can lose is the price paid for the put or call option. With the futures contract, there is no real limit to the amount of loss you can incur.

To see how futures options work, assume that you want to trade some gold contracts. You believe that the price of gold will increase over the next four or five months from its present level of $1,147 an ounce. You can enter into a futures contract to buy gold at $1,150.10 an ounce by depositing the required initial margin of $4,500. Alternatively, you can buy a futures call option with a $1,140 strike price that is currently being quoted at $10.90. (Because the underlying futures contract covers 100 ounces of gold, the total cost of this option would be $10.90 × 100 = $1,090.) The call is an in-the-money option, because the market price of gold exceeds the exercise price on the option. The table below summarizes what happens to both investments if the value of the gold futures contract *increases* to $1,192 an ounce by the expiration date and also what happens if the value of the gold futures contract *drops* to $1,102 an ounce.

	Futures Contract		Futures Option	
Price Change	Dollar Profit (or Loss)	Return on Invested Capital	Dollar Profit (or Loss)	Return on Invested Capital
If futures contract value *increases* to $1,192 an ounce	$4,190	93.1%	$4,110	377.1%
If futures contract value *decreases* to $1,102 an ounce	($4,810)	−106.9%	($1,090)	−100%

Clearly, the futures option provides not only a competitive rate of return, but also a reduced exposure to loss. Futures options offer interesting investment opportunities. But as always, *they should be used only by knowledgeable commodities and financial futures investors.*

CONCEPTS IN REVIEW
Answers available at www.pearsonhighered.com/gitman

15.10 What is the difference between physical commodities and financial futures? What are their similarities?

15.11 Describe a currency future and contrast it with an interest-rate future. What is a stock-index future, and how can it be used by investors?

15.12 Discuss how stock-index futures can be used for speculation and for hedging. What advantages are there to speculating with stock-index futures rather than specific issues of common stock?

15.13 What are futures options? Explain how they can be used by speculators. Why would an investor want to use an option on an interest-rate futures contract rather than the futures contract itself?

myfinancelab
Here is what you should know after reading this chapter. **MyFinanceLab** will help you identify what you know, and where to go when you need to practice.

What You Should Know	Key Terms	Where To Practice
LG1 Describe the essential features of a futures contract and explain how the futures market operates. Commodities and financial futures are traded in futures markets. Today, more than 12 U.S. exchanges deal in futures contracts, which are commitments to make (or take) delivery of a certain amount of some real or financial asset at a specified date in the future.	cash market, *p. 567* delivery month, *p. 567* futures contract, *p. 567* futures market, *p. 567* hedgers, *p. 569* initial deposit, *p. 572* maintenance deposit, *p. 572* margin deposit, *p. 571* mark-to-the-market, *p. 572* open-outcry auction, *p. 569* round-trip commission, *p. 571*	MyFinanceLab Study Plan 15.1

What You Should Know	Key Terms	Where To Practice
LG2 Explain the role that hedgers and speculators play in the futures market, including how profits are made and lost. Futures contracts control large amounts of the underlying commodity or financial instrument. They can produce wide price swings and very attractive rates of return (or very unattractive losses). Such returns (or losses) are further magnified because all trading in the futures market is done on margin. A speculator's profit is derived directly from the wide price fluctuations that occur in the market. Hedgers derive their profit from the protection they gain against adverse price movements.		MyFinanceLab Study Plan 15.2
LG3 Describe the commodities segment of the futures market and the basic characteristics of these investment vehicles. Commodities such as grains, metals, and meat make up the traditional (commodities) segment of the futures market. A large portion of this market is concentrated in agricultural products. There's also a very active market for various metals and petroleum products. As the prices of commodities go up and down in the market, the respective futures contracts behave in much the same way. Thus, if the price of corn goes up, the value of corn futures contracts rises as well.	daily price limit, *p. 575* maximum daily price range, *p. 575* open interest, *p. 573* settle price, *p. 573*	MyFinanceLab Study Plan 15.3 Video Learning Aid for Problem P15.1
LG4 Discuss the trading strategies that investors can use with commodities and explain how investment returns are measured. The trading strategies used with commodities contracts are speculating, spreading, and hedging. Regardless of whether investors are in a long or a short position, they have only one source of return from commodities and financial futures: appreciation (or depreciation) in the price of the contract. Rate of return on invested capital is used to assess the actual or potential profitability of a futures transaction.	return on invested capital, *p. 575*	MyFinanceLab Study Plan 15.4 Video Learning Aid for Problem P15.1
LG5 Explain the difference between a physical commodity and a financial future and discuss the growing role of financial futures in the market today. Whereas commodities deal with physical assets, financial futures deal with financial assets, such as stocks, bonds, and currencies. Both are traded in the same place: the futures market. Financial futures are the newcomers, but the volume of trading in financial futures now far exceeds that of commodities.	currency futures, *p. 580* financial futures, *p. 579* interest-rate futures, *p. 580* stock-index futures, *p. 580*	MyFinanceLab Study Plan 15.5 Video Learning Aid for Problem P15.12
LG6 Discuss the trading techniques that can be used with financial futures and note how these securities can be used in conjunction with other investment vehicles. There are three major types of financial futures: currency futures, interest-rate futures, and stock-index futures. The first type deals in different kinds of foreign currencies.	futures options, *p. 587*	MyFinanceLab Study Plan 15.6

What You Should Know	Key Terms	Where To Practice
Interest-rate futures involve various types of short- and long-term debt instruments. Stock-index futures are pegged to broad movements in the stock market, as measured by such indexes as the S&P 500. These securities can be used for speculating, spreading, or hedging. They hold special appeal as hedges against other security positions. For example, interest-rate futures are used to protect bond portfolios against a jump in market interest rates. Currency futures are used to hedge the foreign currency exposure that accompanies investments in foreign securities.		

Log into **MyFinanceLab**, take a chapter test, and get a personalized Study Plan that tells you which concepts you understand and which ones you need to review. From there, **MyFinanceLab** will give you further practice, tutorials, animations, videos, and guided solutions.
Log into **www.myfinancelab.com**

Discussion Questions*

LG1 **Q15.1** Three of the biggest U.S. commodities exchanges—the CME, CBOT, and NYMEX—were identified in this chapter. Other U.S. exchanges and several foreign commodities exchanges are also closely followed in the United States. Go to the *Wall Street Journal Online*, located at **wsj.com** and look in the "Commodities & Futures" section under "Markets Data" for a list of recent futures quotes. As noted in this chapter, futures quotes include the name of the exchange on which a particular contract is traded.

a. Using these quotes, how many U.S. *commodities exchanges* can you identify? List them.

b. Are quotes from *foreign exchanges* listed in the *Wall Street Journal*? If so, list them, too.

c. For each U.S. and foreign exchange you found in parts **a** and **b**, give an example of one or two contracts traded on that exchange. For example: CBOT—Chicago Board of Trade: oats and Treasury bonds.

LG3 LG5 **Q15.2** Using settle prices from Figures 15.2 (on page 574) and 15.3 (on page 581), find the value of the following commodities and financial futures contracts.

a. July 2010 corn
b. December 2012 corn
c. April 2010 feeder cattle
d. December 2010 Canadian Dollars
e. September 2009 Treasury bonds
f. March 2010 DJIA Index

LG4 LG6 **Q15.3** Listed following are a variety of futures transactions. On the basis of the information provided, indicate how much profit or loss you would make in each of the transactions. (*Hint:* You might want to visit **wsj.com** for the size of the contract, pricing unit, and so on.)

---

*Current prices and margin requirements of futures contracts in the questions and problem below were established to make computations simpler and do not necessarily reflect current market conditions and requirements.

a. You buy three yen contracts at a quote of 1.0180 and sell them a few months later at 1.0365 (12,500,000 yen per contract; prices quoted in $ per 100 yen).

b. The price of oats (5,000 bushels/contract; cents/bu) goes up $0.60 a bushel, and you hold three contracts.

c. You short-sell two feeder cattle contracts (50,000 lbs/contract; cents/lb) at $1.24 a pound, and the price drops to $1.03 per pound.

d. You recently purchased a Swiss franc contract (CHF 125,000/contract; $/CHF) at 0.7272, and six weeks later the contract is trading at 0.685.

e. You short-sell S&P 500 contracts ($250 × index) when the index is at 1,396.55 and cover when the index moves to 1,371.95.

f. You short three corn contracts (5,000 bushels/contract; cents/bu) at $2.34 a bushel, and the price of corn goes to $2.495 a bushel.

Problems

All problems are available on **www.myfinancelab.com**

LG3 LG4 **P15.1** Josh Rink considers himself a shrewd commodities investor. Not long ago he bought one July cotton contract at $0.54 a pound, and he recently sold it at $0.58 a pound. How much profit did he make? What was his return on invested capital if he had to put up a $1,260 initial deposit?

LG3 LG4 **P15.2** You just heard a news story about mad cow disease in a neighboring country, and you believe that feeder cattle prices will rise dramatically in the next few months as buyers of cattle shift to U.S. suppliers. Someone else believes that prices will fall in the next few months because people will be afraid to eat beef. You go to the CME and find out that feeder cattle futures for delivery in April are currently quoted at 88.8. The contract size is 50,000 lbs. What is the market value of one contract?

LG3 LG4 **P15.3** You decide to act on your hunches about feeder cattle, so you purchase four contracts for April delivery at 88.8. You are required to put down 10%. How much equity/capital did you need to make this transaction?

LG3 LG4 **P15.4** As it turns out, you were correct when you purchased four contracts for feeder cattle at 88.8, as the spot price on cattle rose to 101.2 on the delivery date given in your contracts. How much money did you make? What was your return on invested capital?

LG4 **P15.5** Taryn Arsenault is a regular commodities speculator. She is currently considering a short position in July oats, which are now trading at 248. Her analysis suggests that July oats should be trading at about 240 in a couple of months. Assuming that her expectations hold up, what kind of return on invested capital will she make if she shorts three July oats contracts (each contract covers 5,000 bushels of oats) by depositing an initial margin of $540 per contract?

LG5 LG6 **P15.6** You were just notified that you will receive $100,000 in two months from the estate of a deceased relative. You want to invest this money in safe, interest-bearing instruments, so you decide to purchase five-year Treasury notes. You believe, however, that interest rates are headed down, and you will have to pay a lot more in two months than you would today for five-year Treasury notes. You decide to look into futures and find a quote of 111–08 for five-year Treasuries deliverable in two months (contracts trade in $100,000 units). What does the quote mean in terms of price, and how many contracts will you need to buy? How much money will you need to buy the contract, and how much will you need to settle the contract?

LG5 LG6 **P15.7** George Seby is thinking about doing some speculating in interest rates. He thinks rates will fall and, in response, the price of Treasury bond futures should move from 92–15, their present quote, to a level of about 98. Given a required margin deposit of $1,350 per contract, what would George's return on invested capital be if prices behave as he expects?

LG5 LG6 **P15.8** Tori Reynolds has been an avid stock market investor for years. She manages her portfolio fairly aggressively and likes to short-sell whenever the opportunity presents itself. Recently, she has become fascinated with stock-index futures, especially the idea of being able to play the market as a whole. Tori thinks the market is headed down, and she decides to short-sell some S&P 500 stock-index futures. Assume she shorts three contracts at 1,387.95 and has to make a margin deposit of $19,688 for each contract. How much profit will she make, and what will her return on invested capital be if the market does indeed drop so that the CME contracts are trading at 1,352.00 by the time they expire?

LG6 **P15.9** A wealthy investor holds $500,000 worth of U.S. Treasury bonds. These bonds are currently being quoted at 105% of par. The investor is concerned, however, that rates are headed up over the next six months, and he would like to do something to protect this bond portfolio. His broker advises him to set up a hedge using T-bond futures contracts. Assume these contracts are now trading at 111–06.
  a. Briefly describe how the investor would set up this hedge. Would he go long or short? How many contracts would he need?
  b. It's now six months later, and rates have indeed gone up. The investor's Treasury bonds are now being quoted at $93\frac{1}{2}$, and the T-bond futures contracts used in the hedge are now trading at 98–00. Show what has happened to the value of the bond portfolio and the profit (or loss) made on the futures hedge.
  c. Was this a successful hedge? Explain.

LG6 **P15.10** Not long ago, Vanessa Woods sold her company for several million dollars (after taxes). She took some of that money and put it into the stock market. Today, Vanessa's portfolio of blue-chip stocks is worth $3.8 million. Vanessa wants to keep her portfolio intact, but she's concerned about a developing weakness in the market for blue chips. She decides, therefore, to hedge her position with six-month futures contracts on the Dow Jones Industrial Average (DJIA), which are currently trading at 11,960.
  a. Why would she choose to hedge her portfolio with the DJIA rather than the S&P 500?
  b. Given that Vanessa wants to cover the full $3.8 million in her portfolio, describe how she would go about setting up this hedge.
  c. If each contract required a margin deposit of $4,875, how much money would she need to set up this hedge?
  d. Assume that over the next six months, stock prices do fall, and the value of Vanessa's portfolio drops to $3.3 million. If DJIA futures contracts are trading at 10,400, how much will she make (or lose) on the futures hedge? Is it enough to offset the loss in her portfolio? That is, what is her net profit or loss on the hedge?
  e. Will she now get her margin deposit back, or is that a "sunk cost"— gone forever?

LG5 LG6 **P15.11** A quote for a futures contract for British pounds is 1.6683. The contract size for British pounds is 62,500. What is the dollar equivalent of this contract?

 LG5 **P15.12** You have purchased a futures contract for euros. The contract is for 125,000 euros, and the quote was 1.1636. On the delivery date, the exchange quote is 1.1050. Assuming you took delivery of the euros, how many dollars would you have after converting back to dollars? What is your profit or loss (before commissions)?

 LG4 **P15.13** An American currency speculator feels strongly that the value of the Canadian dollar is going to fall relative to the U.S. dollar over the short run. If he wants to profit from these expectations, what kind of position (long or short) should he take in Canadian dollar futures contracts? How much money would he make from each contract if Canadian dollar futures contracts moved from an initial quote of 0.6775 to an ending quote of 0.6250?

LG6 **P15.14** With regard to futures options, how much profit would an investor make if she bought a call option on gold at 7.20 when gold was trading at $482 an ounce, given that the price of gold went up to $525 an ounce by the expiration date on the call? (*Note:* Assume the call carried a strike price of 480.)

Visit **www.myfinancelab.com** for web exercises, Spreadsheets, and other online resources.

Case Problem 15.1   *T. J.'s Fast-Track Investments: Interest Rate Futures*

LG5 LG6 T. J. Patrick is a young, successful industrial designer in Portland, Oregon, who enjoys the excitement of commodities speculation. T. J. has been dabbling in commodities since he was a teenager—he was introduced to this market by his dad, who is a grain buyer for one of the leading food processors. T. J. recognizes the enormous risks involved in commodities speculating but feels that because he's young, he can afford to take a few chances. As a principal in a thriving industrial design firm, T. J. earns more than $150,000 a year. He follows a well-disciplined investment program and annually adds $15,000 to $20,000 to his portfolio.

Recently, T. J. has started playing with financial futures—interest-rate futures, to be exact. He admits he is no expert in interest rates, but he likes the price action these investment vehicles offer. This all started several months ago, when T. J. met Vinnie Banano, a broker who specializes in financial futures, at a party. T. J. liked what Vinnie had to say (mostly how you couldn't go wrong with interest-rate futures) and soon set up a trading account with Vinnie's firm, Banano's of Portland.

The other day, Vinnie called T. J. and suggested he get into five-year Treasury note futures. He reasoned that with the Fed pushing up interest rates so aggressively, the short to intermediate sectors of the term structure would probably respond the most—with the biggest jump in yields. Accordingly, Vinnie recommended that T. J. short-sell some five-year T-note contracts. In particular, Vinnie thinks that rates on these T-notes should go up by a full point (moving from about 5.5% to around 6.5%), and that T. J. should short four contracts. This would be a $5,400 investment, because each contract requires an initial margin deposit of $1,350.

Questions

a. Assume T-note futures ($100,000/contract; 32's of 1%) are now being quoted at 103–16.
   1. Determine the current underlying value of this T-note futures contract.
   2. What would this futures contract be quoted at if Vinnie is right and the yield does go up by 1 percentage point, to 6.5%, on the date of expiration? (*Hint:* It'll be quoted at the same price as its underlying security, which in this case is *assumed to be a five-year, 6% semiannual-pay U.S. Treasury note.* If necessary, refer back to Chapter 11 and review the material on pricing semiannual-pay bonds.)

b. How much profit will T. J. make if he shorts four contracts at 103–16 and then covers when five-year T-note contracts are quoted at 98–00? Also, calculate the return on invested capital from this transaction.

c. What happens if rates go down? For example, how much will T. J. make if the yield on T-note futures goes down by just 3/4 of 1%, in which case these contracts would be trading at 105–8?

d. What risks do you see in the recommended short-sale transaction? What is your assessment of T. J.'s new interest in financial futures? How do you think it compares to his established commodities investment program?

Case Problem 15.2   *Jim and Polly Pernelli Try Hedging with Stock-Index Futures*

LG5 LG6   Jim Pernelli and his wife, Polly, live in Augusta, Georgia. Like many young couples, the Pernellis are a two-income family. Jim and Polly are both college graduates and hold high-paying jobs. Jim has been an avid investor in the stock market for a number of years and over time has built up a portfolio that is currently worth nearly $375,000. The Pernellis' portfolio is well diversified, although it is heavily weighted in high-quality, mid-cap growth stocks. The Pernellis reinvest all dividends and regularly add investment capital to their portfolio. Up to now, they have avoided short-selling and do only a modest amount of margin trading.

Their portfolio has undergone a substantial amount of capital appreciation in the last 18 months or so, and Jim is eager to protect the profit they have earned. And that's the problem: Jim feels the market has pretty much run its course and is about to enter a period of decline. He has studied the market and economic news very carefully and does not believe the retreat will cover an especially long period of time. He feels fairly certain, however, that most, if not all, of the stocks in his portfolio will be adversely affected by these market conditions—although some will drop more in price than others.

Jim has been following stock-index futures for some time and believes he knows the ins and outs of these securities pretty well. After careful deliberation, Jim and Polly decide to use stock-index futures—in particular, the S&P MidCap 400 futures contract—as a way to protect (hedge) their portfolio of common stocks.

Questions

a. Explain why the Pernellis would want to use stock-index futures to hedge their stock portfolio and how they would go about setting up such a hedge. Be specific.

    1. What alternatives do Jim and Polly have to protect the capital value of their portfolio?

    2. What are the benefits and risks of using stock-index futures as hedging vehicles?

b. Assume that S&P MidCap 400 futures contracts are priced at $500 × the index, and are currently being quoted at 769.40. How many contracts would the Pernellis have to buy (or sell) to set up the hedge?

    1. Say the value of the Pernelli portfolio dropped 12% over the course of the market retreat. To what price must the stock-index futures contract move in order to cover that loss?

    2. Given that a $16,875 margin deposit is required to buy or sell a single S&P 400 futures contract, what would be the Pernellis' return on invested capital if the price of the futures contract changed by the amount computed in part **b1**, above?

c. Assume that the value of the Pernelli portfolio declined by $52,000, while the price of an S&P 400 futures contract moved from 769.40 to 691.40. (Assume that Jim and Polly short-sold one futures contract to set up the hedge.)

    1. Add the profit from the hedge transaction to the new (depreciated) value of the stock portfolio. How does this amount compare to the $375,000 portfolio that existed just before the market started its retreat?

    2. Why did the stock-index futures hedge fail to give complete protection to the Pernelli portfolio? Is it possible to obtain *perfect* (dollar-for-dollar) protection from these types of hedges? Explain.

d. What if, instead of hedging with futures contracts, the Pernellis decide to set up the hedge by using *futures options?* Fortunately, such options are available on the S&P MidCap 400 Index. These futures options, like their underlying futures contracts, are also valued/priced at $500 times the underlying S&P 400 Index. Now, suppose a put on the S&P MidCap 400 futures contract (with a strike price of 769) is currently quoted at 5.80, and a comparable call is quoted at 2.35. Use the same portfolio and futures price conditions as set out in part **c** to determine how well the portfolio would be protected if these futures *options* were used as the hedge vehicle. (*Hint:* Add the net profit from the hedge to the new depreciated value of the stock portfolio.)

What are the advantages and disadvantages of using futures options, rather than the stock-index futures contract itself, to hedge a stock portfolio?

Excel with Spreadsheets

One of the unique features of futures contracts is that they have only one source of return—the capital gains that can accrue when price movements have an upward bias. Remember that there are no current cash flows associated with this financial asset. These instruments are known for their volatility due to swings in prices and the use of leverage upon purchase. With futures trading done on margin, small amounts of capital are needed to control relatively large investment positions.

Assume that you are interested in investing in commodity futures—specifically, oats futures contracts. Refer to the contract terms of oats: "**OATS (CBOT) 5000 bu.; cents per bushel.**" Suppose you had purchased five December oats contracts at the settle price of 186.75. The required amount of investor capital to be deposited with a broker at the time of the initial transaction is 5.35% of a contract's value. **Create a spreadsheet** to model and answer the following questions concerning the investment in futures contracts.

Questions

a. What is the total amount of your initial deposit for the five contracts?

b. What is the total amount of bushels of oats that you control?

c. What is the purchase price of the oats commodity contracts you control according to the December settlement date?

d. Assume that the December oats actually settle at 186.75; you decide to sell and take your profit. What is the selling price of the oats commodity contracts?

e. Calculate the return on invested capital earned on this transaction (remember that the return is based on the amount of funds actually invested in the contract, rather than on the value of the contract itself).

CFA EXAM QUESTIONS

Derivative Securities

Following is a sample of 12 Level-I CFA exam questions that deal with many of the topics covered in Chapters 14 and 15 of this text; including basic properties of options and futures, pricing characteristics, return behavior and various option strategies. (When answering the questions, give yourself 1½ minutes for each question; the objective is to correctly answer 8 of the 12 questions in a period of 18 minutes.)

1. For derivative contracts, the notional principal is *best* described as:
a. the amount of the underlying asset covered by the contract.
b. a measure of the actual payments made and received in the contract.
c. tending to underestimate the actual payments made and received in the contract.

2. By volume, the most widely used group of derivatives is the one with contracts written on which of the following types of underlying assets?
a. Financial.
b. Commodities.
c. Energy-related

3. The *most likely* reason derivative markets have flourished is that:
a. derivatives are easy to understand and use.
b. derivatives have relatively low transaction costs.
c. the pricing of derivatives is relatively straightforward.

4. Consider the following statements about a futures clearinghouse:

Statement 1: "A clearinghouse in futures contracts allows for the offsetting of contracts prior to delivery."

Statement 2: "A clearinghouse in futures contracts collects initial margin (performance bonds) from both the long and short sides in the contract."

Are the statements *most likely* correct or incorrect?
a. Both statements are correct.
b. Statement 1 is incorrect, but Statement 2 is correct.
c. Statement 1 is correct, but Statement 2 is incorrect.

5. Consider the following statements regarding futures contracts that may be settled by delivery:

Statement 1: "The long initiates the delivery process."

Statement 2: "For many such contracts, delivery can take place any business day during the delivery month."

Are the statements *most likely* correct or incorrect?
a. Both statements are correct.
b. Statement 1 is incorrect, but Statement 2 is correct.
c. Statement 1 is correct, but Statement 2 is incorrect.

6. Unless far out-of-the-money or far in-the-money, for otherwise identical call options, the longer the term to expiration, the lower the price for:
a. American call options, but not European call options.
b. both European call options and American call options.
c. neither European call options nor American call options.

7. Compare an American call with a strike of 50 which expires in 90 days to an American call on the same underlying asset which has a strike of 60 and expires in 120 days. The underlying asset is selling at 55. Consider the following statements:

CFA EXAM QUESTIONS

Statement 1: "The 50 strike call is in-the-money and the 60 strike call is out-of-the-money."

Statement 2: "The time value of the 60 strike call, as a proportion of the 60 strike call's premium, exceeds the time value of the 50 strike call as a proportion of the 50 strike call's premium."

Are the statements *most likely* correct or incorrect?
a. Both statements are correct.
b. Statement 1 is incorrect, but Statement 2 is correct.
c. Statement 1 is correct, but Statement 2 is incorrect.

8. A call with a strike price of $40 is available on a stock currently trading for $35. The call expires in one year and the risk-free rate of return is 10%.

The lower bound on this call's value:
a. is zero.
b. is $5 if the call is American-style.
c. is $1.36 if the call is European-style.

9. An investor writes a call option priced at $3 with an exercise price of $100 on a stock that he owns. The investor paid $85 for the stock. If at expiration of the call option the stock price has risen to $110, the profit for the investor's position would be *closest* to:
a. $3.   b. $12.   c. $18.

10. An investor paid $10 for an option that is currently in-the-money $5. If the underlying is priced at $90, which of the following *best* describes that option?
a. Call option with an exercise price of $80.
b. Put option with an exercise price of $95.
c. Call option with an exercise price of $95.

11. The recent price per share of Dragon Vacations Inc. is $50 per share. Calls with exactly six months left to expiration are available on Dragon with strikes of $45, $50, and $55. The prices of the calls are $8.75, $6.00, and $4.00, respectively. Assume that each call contract is for 100 shares of stock and that at initiation of the strategy the investor purchases 100 shares of Dragon at the current market price. Further assume that the investor will close out the strategy in six months when the options expire, including the sale of any stock not delivered against exercise of a call, whether the stock price goes up or goes down. If the closing price of Dragon stock in six months is exactly $60, the profit to a covered call using the $50 strike call is *closest* to:
a. $400.   b. $600.   c. $1,600.

12. The recent price per share of Win Big, Inc., is €50 per share. Verna Hillsborough buys 100 shares at €50. To protect against a fall in price, Hillsborough buys one put, covering 100 shares of Win Big, with a strike price of €40. The put premium is €1 per share. If Win Big closes at €45 per share at the expiration of the put and Hillsborough sells her shares at €45, Hillsborough's profit from the stay/put is *closest* to:
a. −€1,100   b. −€600.   c. €900.

Answer 1. a; 2. a; 3. b; 4. a; 5. b; 6. c; 7. a; 8. a; 9. c; 10. b; 11. b; 12. b.

Source: From PROFESSIONAL EXAM REVIEW. *CFA Candidate Study Notes, Level 1, Volume 4, 2E.* © 2009 Delmar Learning, a part of Cengage Learning, Inc. Reproduced by permission. www.cengage.com/permissions

Glossary

A

active portfolio management   Building a portfolio using traditional and modern approaches and managing and controlling it to achieve its objectives; a worthwhile activity that can result in superior returns. (Chapter 13)

activity ratios   Financial ratios that are used to measure how well a firm is managing its assets. (Chapter 7)

agency bonds   Debt securities issued by various agencies and organizations of the U.S. government. (Chapter 10)

aggressive-growth fund   A highly speculative mutual fund that attempts to achieve the highest capital gains. (Chapter 12)

American depositary receipts (ADRs)   U.S. dollar-denominated receipts for the stocks of foreign companies that are held in the vaults of banks in the companies' home countries. Serve as backing for *American depositary shares (ADSs)*. (Chapter 2)

American depositary shares (ADSs)   Securities created to permit U.S. investors to hold shares of non-U.S. companies and trade them on U.S. stock exchanges. They are backed by *American depositary receipts (ADRs)*. (Chapter 2)

AMEX composite index   An index that measures the current price behavior of all shares traded on the NYSE-AMEX, relative to a base of 550 set at December 29, 1995. (Chapter 3)

analytical information   Projections and recommendations about potential investments based on available current data. (Chapter 3)

annuity   A stream of equal cash flows that occur at equal intervals over time. (Chapter 4)

arbitration   A formal dispute-resolution process in which a client and a broker present their arguments before a panel, which then decides the case. (Chapter 3)

ask price   The lowest price offered to sell a security. (Chapter 2)

asset allocation   A scheme that involves dividing one's portfolio into various asset classes to preserve capital by protecting against negative developments while taking advantage of positive ones. (Chapter 13)

asset allocation fund   A mutual fund that spreads investors' money across stocks, bonds, money market securities, and possibly other asset classes. (Chapter 12)

asset-backed securities (ABS)   Securities similar to mortgage-backed securities that are backed by a pool of bank loans, leases, and other assets. (Chapter 10)

automatic investment plan   A mutual fund service that allows shareholders to automatically send fixed amounts of money from their paychecks or bank accounts into the fund. (Chapter 12)

automatic reinvestment plan   A mutual fund service that enables shareholders to automatically buy additional shares in the fund through the reinvestment of dividends and capital gains income. (Chapter 12)

averages   Numbers used to measure the general behavior of stock prices by reflecting the arithmetic average price behavior of a representative group of stocks at a given point in time. (Chapter 3)

B

back-end load   A commission charged on the *sale* of shares in a mutual fund. (Chapter 12)

back-office research reports   A brokerage firm's analyses of and recommendations on investment prospects; available on request at no cost to existing and potential clients or for purchase at some Web sites. (Chapter 3)

balance sheet   A financial summary of a firm's assets, liabilities, and shareholders' equity at a single point in time. (Chapter 7)

balanced fund   A mutual fund whose objective is to generate a balanced return of both current income and long-term capital appreciation. (Chapter 12)

bar chart   The simplest kind of chart, on which share price is plotted on the vertical axis and time on the horizontal axis; stock prices are recorded as vertical bars showing high, low, and closing prices. (Chapter 9)

Barron's   A weekly business newspaper; a popular source of financial news. (Chapter 3)

basic discount broker   Typically, a deep-discount broker through which investors can execute trades electronically online via a commercial service, on the Internet, or by phone. (Also called *online brokers* or *electronic brokers*.) (Chapter 3)

bear markets   Markets normally associated with falling prices, investor pessimism, economic slowdown, and government restraint. (Chapter 2)

behavioral finance   The body of research into the role that emotions and other subjective factors play in investment decisions. (Chapter 9)

beta   A measure of *nondiversifiable,* or *market, risk* that indicates how the price of a security responds to market forces. (Chapter 5)

bid price   The highest price offered to purchase a security. (Chapter 2)

blue-chip stocks   Financially strong, high-quality stocks with long and stable records of earnings and dividends. (Chapter 6)

bond fund   A mutual fund that invests in various kinds and grades of bonds, with interest income as the primary objective. (Chapter 12)

bond ladders   An investment strategy wherein equal amounts of money are invested in a series of bonds with staggered maturities. (Chapter 11)

bond ratings   Letter grades that designate investment quality and are assigned to a bond issue by rating agencies. (Chapter 10)

bond swap   An investment strategy wherein an investor simultaneously liquidates one bond holding and buys a different issue to take its place. (Chapter 11)

bond yield   The return an investor would receive on a bond if it were purchased and held to maturity; reported as an annual rate of return. (Chapter 3)

bond-equivalent yield   The annual yield on a bond, calculated as twice the semiannual yield. (Chapter 11)

bonds   Long-term debt instruments (IOUs), issued by corporations and governments, that offer a known interest return plus return of the bond's *face value* at maturity. (Chapter 1)

book value   The amount of stockholders' equity in a firm; equals the amount of the firm's assets minus the firm's liabilities and preferred stock. (Chapter 6)

broker market   The market in which the two sides of a transaction, the buyer and seller, are brought together to execute trades. (Chapter 2)

bull markets   Markets normally associated with rising prices, investor optimism, economic recovery, and government stimulus. (Chapter 2)

business cycle   An indication of the current state of the economy, reflecting changes in total economic activity over time. (Chapter 7)

business risk   The degree of uncertainty associated with an investment's earnings and the investment's ability to pay the returns owed to investors. (Chapter 4)

C

call   A negotiable instrument that gives the holder the right to buy securities at a stated price within a certain time period. (Chapter 14)

call feature   Feature that specifies whether and under what conditions the issuer can retire a bond prior to maturity. (Chapter 10)

call premium   The amount added to a bond's par value and paid to investors when a bond is retired prematurely. (Chapter 10)

call price   The price the issuer must pay to retire a bond prematurely; equal to par value plus the call premium. (Chapter 10)

capital asset pricing model (CAPM)   Model that formally links the notions of risk and return; it uses beta, the risk-free rate, and the market return to help investors define the required return on an investment. (Chapter 5)

capital gains   The amount by which the sale price of an asset *exceeds* its original purchase price. (Chapter 1)

capital gains distributions   Payments made to mutual fund shareholders that come from the profits that a fund makes from the sale of its securities. (Chapter 12)

capital loss   The amount by which the proceeds from the sale of a capital asset are *less than* its original purchase price. (Chapter 1)

capital market   Market in which *long-term* securities (with maturities greater than one year) such as stocks and bonds are bought and sold. (Chapter 2)

cash account   A brokerage account in which a customer can make only cash transactions. (Chapter 3)

cash dividend   Payment of a dividend in the form of cash. (Chapter 6)

cash market   A market where a product or commodity changes hands in exchange for a cash price paid when the transaction is completed. (Chapter 15)

charting   The activity of charting price behavior and other market information and then using the patterns these charts form to make investment decisions. (Chapter 9)

churning   An illegal and unethical practice engaged in by a broker to increase commissions by causing excessive trading of clients' accounts. (Chapter 3)

classified common stock   Common stock issued by a company in different classes, each of which offers different privileges and benefits to its holders. (Chapter 6)

closed-end investment company   A type of investment company that operates with a fixed number of shares outstanding. (Chapter 12)

collateral trust bonds   Senior bonds backed by securities owned by the issuer but held in trust by a third party. (Chapter 10)

collateralized mortgage obligation (CMO)   Mortgage-backed bond whose holders are divided into classes based on the length of investment desired; principal is channeled to investors in order of maturity, with short-term classes first. (Chapter 10)

common stock   Equity investment that represents ownership in a corporation; each share represents a fractional ownership interest in the firm. (Chapter 1)

common stock (market) ratios   Financial ratios that convert key information about a firm to a per-share basis. (Chapter 7)

common-size income statement   A type of financial report that uses a common denominator (net sales) to convert all entries on a normal income statement from dollars to percentages. (Chapter 8)

compound interest   Interest paid not only on the initial deposit but also on any interest accumulated from one period to the next. (Chapter 4)

confidence index   A ratio of the average yield on high-grade corporate bonds to the average yield on average- or intermediate-grade corporate bonds; a technical indicator based on the theory that market trends usually appear in the bond market before they do in the stock market. (Chapter 9)

constant-dollar plan   A formula plan for timing investment transactions, in which the investor establishes a target dollar amount for the speculative portion of the portfolio and establishes trigger points at which funds are transferred to or from the conservative portion as needed to maintain the target dollar amount. (Chapter 13)

constant-ratio plan   A formula plan for timing investment transactions, in which a desired fixed ratio of the speculative portion to the conservative portion of the portfolio is established; when the actual ratio differs by a predetermined amount from the desired ratio, transactions are made to rebalance the portfolio to achieve the desired ratio. (Chapter 13)

continuous compounding   Interest calculation in which interest is compounded over the smallest possible interval of time. (Chapter 4)

conventional options   Put and call options sold over the counter. (Chapter 14)

conversion (exchange) privilege   Feature of a mutual fund that allows shareholders to move money from one fund to another, within the same family of funds. (Chapter 12)

conversion equivalent (conversion parity)   The price at which the common stock would have to sell in order to make the convertible security worth its present market price. (Chapter 10)

conversion period   The time period during which a convertible issue can be converted. (Chapter 10)

conversion price   The stated price per share at which common stock will be delivered to the investor in exchange for a convertible issue. (Chapter 10)

conversion privilege   The conditions and specific nature of the conversion feature on convertible securities. (Chapter 10)

conversion ratio   The number of shares of common stock into which a convertible issue can be converted. (Chapter 10)

conversion value   An indication of what a convertible issue would trade for if it were priced to sell on the basis of its stock value. (Chapter 10)

convertible bonds   Fixed-income obligations that have a feature permitting the holder to convert the security into a specified number of shares of the issuing company's common stock. (Chapter 10)

convertible security A fixed-income obligation with a feature permitting the investor to convert it into a specified number of shares of common stock. (Chapter 1)

correlation A statistical measure of the relationship, if any, between series of numbers representing data of any kind. (Chapter 5)

correlation coefficient A measure of the degree of correlation between two series. (Chapter 5)

coupon Feature on a bond that defines the amount of annual interest income. (Chapter 10)

covered options Options written against stock owned (or short-sold) by the writer. (Chapter 14)

crossing markets After-hours trading in stocks that involve filling buy and sell orders by matching identical sell and buy orders at the desired price. (Chapter 2)

currency exchange rate The relationship between two currencies on a specified date. (Chapter 2)

currency exchange risk The risk caused by the varying exchange rates between the currencies of two countries. (Chapter 2)

currency futures Futures contracts on foreign currencies, traded much like commodities. (Chapter 15)

currency options Put and call options written on foreign currencies. (Chapter 14)

current yield Measure of the annual interest income a bond provides relative to its current market price. (Chapter 10)

custodial account The brokerage account of a minor; requires a parent or guardian to be part of all transactions. (Chapter 3)

cyclical stocks Stocks whose earnings and overall market performance are closely linked to the general state of the economy. (Chapter 6)

D

daily price limit Restriction on the day-to-day change in the price of an underlying commodity. (Chapter 15)

date of record The date on which an investor must be a registered shareholder to be entitled to receive a dividend. (Chapter 6)

day trader An investor who buys and sells stocks quickly throughout the day in hopes of making quick profits. (Chapter 3)

dealer market The market in which the buyer and seller are not brought together directly but instead have their orders executed by *dealers* that make markets in the given security. (Chapter 2)

debenture An unsecured (junior) bond. (Chapter 10)

debit balance The amount of money being borrowed in a margin loan. (Chapter 2)

debt Funds lent in exchange for interest income and the promised repayment of the loan at a given future date. (Chapter 1)

defensive stocks Stocks that tend to hold their own, and even do well, when the economy starts to falter. (Chapter 6)

deferred equity Securities issued in one form and later redeemed or converted into shares of common stock. (Chapter 10)

deflation A period of generally declining prices. (Chapter 4)

delivery month The time when a commodity must be delivered; defines the life of a futures contract. (Chapter 15)

derivative securities Securities that are structured to exhibit characteristics similar to those of an underlying security or asset and that derive their value from the underlying security or asset. (Chapter 1)

descriptive information Factual data on the past behavior of the economy, the market, the industry, the company, or a given investment. (Chapter 3)

designated market maker (DMM) NYSE member who specializes in making transactions in one or more stocks and manages the auction process. (Chapter 2)

direct investment Investment in which an investor directly acquires a claim on a security or property. (Chapter 1)

discount basis A method of earning interest on a security by purchasing it at a price below its redemption value; the difference is the interest earned. (Chapter 1)

discount bond A bond with a market value lower than par; occurs when market rates are greater than the coupon rate. (Chapter 10)

discount rate The annual rate of return that could be earned currently on a similar investment; used when finding present value; also called *opportunity cost*. (Chapter 4)

diversifiable (unsystematic) risk The portion of an investment's risk that results from uncontrollable or random events that are firm-specific; can be eliminated through diversification. (Chapter 5)

diversification The inclusion of a number of different investment vehicles in a portfolio to increase returns or reduce risk. (Chapter 1)

dividend income Income derived from the dividends and interest earned on the security holdings of a mutual fund. (Chapter 12)

dividend payout ratio The portion of earnings per share (EPS) that a firm pays out as dividends. (Chapter 6)

dividend reinvestment plan (DRIP) Plan in which shareholders have cash dividends automatically reinvested into additional shares of the firm's common stock. (Chapter 6)

dividend valuation model (DVM) A model that values a share of stock on the basis of the future dividend stream it is expected to produce; its three versions are zero-growth, constant-growth, and variable-growth. (Chapter 8)

dividend yield A measure that relates dividends to share price and puts common stock dividends on a relative (percentage) rather than absolute (dollar) basis. (Chapter 6)

dividends Periodic payments made by firms to their shareholders. (Chapter 1)

dividends-and-earnings (D&E) approach Stock valuation approach that uses projected dividends, EPS, and P/E multiples to value a share of stock; also known as the *DCF approach*. (Chapter 8)

DJ U.S. Total Stock Market Index An index that measures the performance of all equity securities issued by U.S. companies that have readily available price data; as of July 31, 2009, it is comprised of 4,376 stocks. (Chapter 3)

dollar-cost averaging A formula plan for timing investment transactions, in which a fixed dollar amount is invested in a security at fixed time intervals. (Chapter 13)

domestic investments Debt, equity, and derivative securities of U.S.-based companies. (Chapter 1)

Dow Jones Corporate Bond Index Mathematical averages of the *closing prices* for 96 bonds—32 industrial, 32 financial, and 32 utility/telecom. (Chapter 3)

Dow Jones Industrial Average (DJIA) A stock market average made up of 30 high-quality stocks selected for total market value and broad public ownership and believed to reflect overall market activity. (Chapter 3)

Dow theory A technical approach based on the idea that the market's performance can be described by the long-term price trend in the DJIA, as confirmed by the Dow transportation average. (Chapter 9)

dual listing Listing of a firm's shares on more than one exchange. (Chapter 2)

duration A measure of bond price volatility that captures both price and reinvestment risks and that is used to indicate how a bond will react in different interest rate environments. (Chapter 11)

E

earnings per share (EPS) The amount of annual earnings available to common stockholders, as stated on a per-share basis. (Chapter 6)

economic analysis A study of general economic conditions that is used in the valuation of common stock. (Chapter 7)

efficient frontier The leftmost boundary of the *feasible (attainable) set* of portfolios that includes all *efficient portfolios*—those providing the best attainable tradeoff between risk (measured by the standard deviation) and return. (Chapter 5)

efficient market A market in which securities reflect all possible information quickly and accurately. (Chapter 9)

efficient markets hypothesis (EMH) Basic theory of the behavior of efficient markets, in which there are a large number of knowledgeable investors who react quickly to new information, causing securities prices to adjust quickly and accurately. (Chapter 9)

efficient portfolio A portfolio that provides the highest return for a given level of risk. (Chapter 5)

electronic communications networks (ECNs) Electronic trading networks that automatically match buy and sell orders that customers place electronically. (Chapter 2)

equipment trust certificates Senior bonds secured by specific pieces of equipment; popular with transportation companies such as airlines. (Chapter 10)

equity Ongoing ownership in a business or property. (Chapter 1)

equity capital Evidence of ownership position in a firm, in the form of shares of common stock. (Chapter 6)

equity kicker Another name for the conversion feature, giving the holder of a convertible security a deferred claim on the issuer's common stock. (Chapter 10)

equity-income fund A mutual fund that emphasizes current income and capital preservation and invests primarily in high-yielding common stocks. (Chapter 12)

ethics Standards of conduct or moral judgment. (Chapter 2)

Eurodollar bonds Foreign bonds denominated in dollars but not registered with the SEC, thus restricting sales of new issues. (Chapter 10)

event risk Risk that comes from an unexpected event that has a significant and usually immediate effect on the underlying value of an investment. (Chapter 4)

ex-dividend date Three business days up to the date of record; determines whether one is an official shareholder and thus eligible to receive a declared dividend. (Chapter 6)

excess margin More equity than is required in a margin account. (Chapter 2)

exchange-traded fund (ETF) An open-end fund that trades as a listed security on a stock exchange. (Chapter 12)

expectations hypothesis Theory that the shape of the yield curve reflects investor expectations of future interest rates. (Chapter 11)

expected inflation premium The average rate of inflation expected in the future. (Chapter 4)

expected return The return an investor thinks an investment will earn in the future. (Chapter 4)

expiration date The date at which an option expires. (Chapter 14)

F

fair disclosure rule (Regulation FD) Rule requiring senior executives to disclose critical information simultaneously to investment professionals and the public via press releases or SEC filings. (Chapter 3)

financial futures A type of futures contract in which the underlying "commodity" is a financial asset, such as debt securities, foreign currencies, or common stocks. (Chapter 15)

financial institutions Organizations that channel the savings of governments, businesses, and individuals into loans or investments. (Chapter 1)

financial leverage The use of debt financing to magnify investment returns. (Chapter 2)

financial markets Forums in which suppliers and demanders of funds trade financial assets. (Chapter 1)

financial portals Supersites on the Web that bring together a wide range of investing features, such as real-time quotes, stock and mutual fund screens, portfolio trackers, news, research, and transaction capabilities, along with other personal finance features. (Chapter 3)

financial risk The degree of uncertainty of payment resulting from a firm's mix of debt and equity; the larger the proportion of debt financing, the greater this risk. (Chapter 4)

first and refunding bonds Bonds secured in part with both first and second mortgages. (Chapter 10)

fixed-commission schedules Fixed brokerage commissions that typically apply to the small transactions usually made by individual investors. (Chapter 3)

fixed-income securities Investments that offer fixed periodic cash payments. (Chapter 1)

fixed-weightings approach Asset allocation plan in which a fixed percentage of the portfolio is allocated to each asset category. (Chapter 13)

flexible-weightings approach Asset allocation plan in which weights for each asset category are adjusted periodically based on market analysis. (Chapter 13)

forced conversion The calling in of convertible bonds by the issuing firm. (Chapter 10)

foreign investments Debt, equity, and derivative securities of foreign-based companies. (Chapter 1)

Form 10-K A statement that must be filed annually with the SEC by all firms having securities listed on a securities exchange or traded in the OTC market. (Chapter 3)

formula plans Mechanical methods of portfolio management that try to take advantage of price changes that result from cyclical price movements. (Chapter 13)

fourth market Transactions made directly between large institutional buyers and sellers of securities. (Chapter 2)

full-service broker Broker who, in addition to executing clients' transactions, provides them with a full array of brokerage services. (Chapter 3)

fully compounded rate of return The rate of return that includes interest earned on interest. (Chapter 4)

fund families Different kinds of mutual funds offered by a single investment management company. (Chapter 12)

fundamental analysis The in-depth study of the financial condition and operating results of a firm. (Chapter 7)

future value   The amount to which a current deposit will grow over a period of time when it is placed in an account paying compound interest. (Chapter 4)

futures   Legally binding obligations stipulating that the seller of the contract will make delivery and the buyer of the contract will take delivery of an asset at some specific date, at a price agreed on at the time the contract is sold. (Chapter 1)

futures market   The organized market for the trading of futures contracts. (Chapter 15)

futures options   Options that give the holders the right to buy or sell a single standardized futures contract for a specified period of time at a specified strike price. (Chapter 15)

G

general obligation bonds   Municipal bonds backed by the full faith, credit, and taxing power of the issuer. (Chapter 10)

growth cycle   A reflection of the amount of business vitality that occurs within an industry (or company) over time. (Chapter 7)

growth fund   A mutual fund whose primary goal is capital appreciation. (Chapter 12)

growth stocks   Stocks that experience high rates of growth in operations and earnings. (Chapter 6)

growth-and-income fund   A mutual fund that seeks both long-term growth and current income, with primary emphasis on capital gains. (Chapter 12)

growth-oriented portfolio   A portfolio whose primary objective is long-term price appreciation. (Chapter 5)

H

hedge   A combination of two or more securities into a single investment position for the purpose of reducing or eliminating risk. (Chapter 14)

hedge fund   Lightly regulated investment funds that pool resources from wealthy investors. (Chapter 1)

hedgers   Producers and processors who use futures contracts to protect their interest in an underlying commodity or financial instrument. (Chapter 15)

holding period   The period of time over which one wishes to measure the return on an investment vehicle. (Chapter 4)

holding period return (HPR)   The total return earned from holding an investment for a specified *holding period* (*usually one year or less*). (Chapter 4)

I

immunization   Bond portfolio strategy that uses duration to offset price and reinvestment effects; a bond portfolio is immunized when its average duration equals the investment horizon. (Chapter 11)

in-the-money   A call option with a strike price less than the market price of the underlying security; a put option whose strike price is greater than the market price of the underlying security. (Chapter 14)

income   Usually cash or near-cash that is periodically received as a result of owning an investment. (Chapter 4)

income bonds   Unsecured bonds requiring that interest be paid only after a specified amount of income is earned. (Chapter 10)

income statement   A financial summary of the operating results of a firm covering a specified period of time, usually a year. (Chapter 7)

income stocks   Stocks with long and sustained records of paying higher-than-average dividends. (Chapter 6)

income-oriented portfolio   A portfolio that is designed to produce regular dividends and interest payments. (Chapter 5)

index fund   A mutual fund that buys and holds a portfolio of stocks (or bonds) equivalent to those in a specific market index. (Chapter 12)

indexes   Numbers used to measure the general behavior of stock prices by measuring the current price behavior of a representative group of stocks in relation to a base value set at an earlier point in time. (Chapter 3)

indirect investment   Investment made in a collection of securities or properties. (Chapter 1)

individual investors   Investors who manage their own funds. (Chapter 1)

industry analysis   Study of industry groupings that looks at the competitive position of a particular industry in relation to others and identifies companies that show particular promise within an industry. (Chapter 7)

inflation   A period of generally rising prices. (Chapter 4)

initial deposit   The amount of investor capital that must be deposited with a broker at the time of a commodity transaction. (Chapter 15)

initial margin   The minimum amount of equity that must be provided by a margin investor *at the time of purchase*. (Chapter 2)

initial public offering (IPO)   The first public sale of a company's stock. (Chapter 2)

insider trading   The use of *nonpublic* information about a company to make profitable securities transactions. (Chapter 2)

institutional investors   Investment professionals who are paid to manage other people's money. (Chapter 1)

interest   The "rent" paid by a borrower for use of the lender's money. (Chapter 4)

interest rate options   Put and call options written on fixed-income (debt) securities. (Chapter 14)

interest rate risk   The chance that changes in interest rates will adversely affect a security's value. (Chapter 4)

interest-rate futures   Futures contracts on debt securities. (Chapter 15)

international fund   A mutual fund that does all or most of its investing in foreign securities. (Chapter 12)

intrinsic value   The underlying or inherent value of a stock, as determined through fundamental analysis. (Chapter 7)

investment   Any asset into which funds can be placed with the expectation that it will generate positive income and/or preserve or increase its value. (Chapter 1)

investment advisers   Individuals or firms that provide investment advice, typically for a fee. (Chapter 3)

investment banker   Financial intermediary that specializes in assisting companies issue new securities and advising companies with regard to major financial transactions. (Chapter 2)

investment club   A legal partnership through which a group of investors are bound to a specified organizational structure, operating procedures, and purpose, which is typically to earn favorable long-term returns from moderate-risk investments. (Chapter 3)

investment goals   The financial objectives that one wishes to achieve by investing. (Chapter 1)

investment letters   Newsletters that provide, on a subscription basis, the analyses, conclusions, and recommendations of experts in securities investment. (Chapter 3)

investment plan   A written document describing how funds will be invested and specifying the target date for achieving each investment goal and the amount of tolerable risk. (Chapter 1)

investment value   The amount that investors believe a security should be trading for, or what they think it's worth. (Chapter 6)

investment value   The price at which a convertible would trade if it were nonconvertible and priced at or near the prevailing market yields of comparable nonconvertible issues. (Chapter 10)

J

Jensen's measure (Jensen's alpha)   A measure of portfolio performance that uses the portfolio beta and CAPM to calculate its *excess return*, which may be positive, zero, or negative. (Chapter 13)

junior bonds   Debt obligations backed only by the promise of the issuer to pay interest and principal on a timely basis. (Chapter 10)

junk bonds   High-risk securities that have low ratings but high yields. (Chapter 10)

L

LEAPS   Long-term options. (Chapter 14)

leverage   The ability to obtain a given equity position at a reduced capital investment, thereby magnifying returns. (Chapter 14)

leverage measures   Financial ratios that measure the amount of debt being used to support operations and the ability of the firm to service its debt. (Chapter 7)

limit order   An order to buy at or below a specified price or to sell at or above a specified price. (Chapter 3)

liquidity   The ability of an investment to be converted into cash quickly and with little or no loss in value. (Chapter 1)

liquidity measures   Financial ratios concerned with a firm's ability to meet its day-to-day operating expenses and satisfy its short-term obligations as they come due. (Chapter 7)

liquidity preference theory   Theory that investors tend to prefer the greater liquidity of short-term securities and therefore require a premium to invest in long-term securities. (Chapter 11)

liquidity risk   The risk of not being able to liquidate an investment quickly and at a reasonable price. (Chapter 4)

listed options   Put and call options listed and traded on organized securities exchanges, such as the CBOE. (Chapter 14)

load fund   A mutual fund that charges a commission when shares are bought; also known as a *front-end load fund*. (Chapter 12)

long purchase   A transaction in which investors buy securities in the hope that they will increase in value and can be sold at a later date for profit. (Chapter 2)

long-term investments   Investments with maturities of longer than a year or with no maturity at all. (Chapter 1)

low-load fund   A mutual fund that charges a small commission when shares are bought. (Chapter 12)

LYON (liquid yield option note)   A zero-coupon bond that carries both a conversion feature and a put option. (Chapter 10)

M

maintenance deposit   The minimum amount of margin that must be kept in a margin account at all times. (Chapter 15)

maintenance margin   The absolute minimum amount of margin (equity) that an investor must maintain in the margin account at all times. (Chapter 2)

management fee   A fee levied annually for professional mutual fund services provided; paid regardless of the performance of the portfolio. (Chapter 12)

margin account   A brokerage account for which margin trading is authorized. (Chapter 2)

margin call   Notification of the need to bring the equity of an account whose margin is below the maintenance level up above the maintenance margin level or to have enough margined holdings sold to reach this standard. (Chapter 2)

margin deposit   Amount deposited with a broker to cover any loss in the market value of a futures contract that may result from adverse price movements. (Chapter 15)

margin loan   Vehicle through which borrowed funds are made available, at a stated interest rate, in a margin transaction. (Chapter 2)

margin requirement   The minimum amount of equity that must be a margin investor's own funds; set by the Federal Reserve Board (the "Fed"). (Chapter 2)

margin trading   The use of borrowed funds to purchase securities; magnifies returns by reducing the amount of equity that the investor must put up. (Chapter 2)

mark-to-the-market   A daily check of an investor's margin position, determined at the end of each session, at which time the broker debits or credits the account as needed. (Chapter 15)

market anomalies   Irregularities or deviations from the behavior one would expect in an efficient market. (Chapter 9)

market makers   *Securities dealers* that "make markets" by offering to buy or sell certain quantities of securities at stated prices. (Chapter 2)

market order   An order to buy or sell stock at the best price available when the order is placed. (Chapter 3)

market return   The average return for all (or a large sample of) stocks, such as those in the *Standard & Poor's 500-Stock Composite Index*. (Chapter 5)

market risk   Risk of decline in investment returns because of market factors independent of the given investment. (Chapter 4)

market segmentation theory   Theory that the market for debt is segmented on the basis of maturity, that supply and demand within each segment determine the prevailing interest rate, and that the slope of the yield curve depends on the relationship between the prevailing rates in each segment. (Chapter 11)

market technicians   Analysts who believe it is chiefly (or solely) supply and demand that drive stock prices. (Chapter 9)

market value   The prevailing market price of a security. (Chapter 6)

maturity date   The date on which a bond matures and the principal must be repaid. (Chapter 10)

maximum daily price range   The amount a commodity price can change during the day; usually equal to twice the daily price limit. (Chapter 15)

mediation   An informal, voluntary, dispute-resolution process in which a client and a broker agree to a mediator, who facilitates negotiations between them to resolve the case. (Chapter 3)

Mergent   Publisher of a variety of financial material, including *Mergent's Manuals*. (Chapter 3)

mid-cap stocks   Medium-sized stocks, generally with market values of less than $4 or $5 billion but more than $1 billion. (Chapter 6)

mixed stream   A stream of returns that, unlike an annuity, exhibits no special pattern. (Chapter 4)

modern portfolio theory (MPT)   An approach to portfolio management that uses several basic statistical measures to develop a portfolio plan. (Chapter 5)

money market   Market where *short-term* debt securities (with maturities less than one year) are bought and sold. (Chapter 2)

money market mutual funds   Mutual funds that invest solely in short-term investment vehicles. (Chapter 1)

mortgage bonds   Senior bonds secured by real estate. (Chapter 10)

mortgage-backed bond   A debt issue secured by a pool of home mortgages; issued primarily by federal agencies. (Chapter 10)

moving average (MA)   A mathematical procedure that computes and records the average values of a series of prices, or other data, over time; results in a stream of average values that will act to smooth out a series of data. (Chapter 9)

municipal bond guarantees   Guarantees from a party other than the issuer that principal and interest payments will be made in a prompt and timely manner. (Chapter 10)

municipal bonds   Debt securities issued by states, counties, cities, and other political subdivisions; most of these bonds are tax-exempt (free of federal income tax on interest income). (Chapter 10)

mutual fund   A company that raises money from sale of its shares and invests in and professionally manages a diversified portfolio of securities. (Chapter 1)

N

naked options   Options written on securities not owned by the writer. (Chapter 14)

Nasdaq market   A major segment of the *secondary market* that employs an all-electronic trading platform to execute trades. (Chapter 2)

Nasdaq Stock Market indexes   Indexes that measure the current price behavior of securities traded in the Nasdaq stock market, relative to a base of 100 set at specified dates. (Chapter 3)

negatively correlated   Describes two series that move in opposite directions. (Chapter 5)

negotiated commissions   Brokerage commissions agreed to by the client and the broker as a result of their negotiations; typically available to large institutional transactions and to individual investors who maintain large accounts. (Chapter 3)

net asset value (NAV)   The underlying value of a share of stock in a particular mutual fund. (Chapter 12)

net losses   The amount by which capital losses exceed capital gains; up to $3,000 of net losses can be applied against ordinary income in any year. (Chapter 1)

no-load fund   A mutual fund that does not charge a commission when shares are bought. (Chapter 12)

nominal return   The actual return earned on an investment expressed in current dollars. (Chapter 4)

nondiversifiable (systematic) risk   The inescapable portion of an investment's risk attributable to forces that affect all investments and therefore are not unique to a given vehicle. (Chapter 5)

note   A debt security originally issued with a maturity of from 2 to 10 years. (Chapter 10)

NYSE composite index   An index that measures the current price behavior of stocks listed on the NYSE, relative to a base of 5000 set at December 31, 2002. (Chapter 3)

O

odd lot   Less than 100 shares of stock. (Chapter 3)

open interest   The number of contracts currently outstanding on a commodity or financial future. (Chapter 15)

open-end investment company   A type of investment company in which investors buy shares from, and sell them back to, the mutual fund itself, with no limit on the number of shares the fund can issue. (Chapter 12)

open-outcry auction   In futures trading, an auction in which trading is done through a series of shouts, body motions, and hand signals. (Chapter 15)

option   A security that gives the holder the right to buy or sell a certain amount of an underlying financial asset at a specified price for a specified period of time. (Chapter 14)

option premium   The quoted price the investor pays to buy a listed put or call option. (Chapter 14)

option spreading   Combining two or more options with different strike prices and/or expiration dates into a single transaction. (Chapter 14)

option straddle   The simultaneous purchase (or sale) of a put and a call on the same underlying common stock (or financial asset). (Chapter 14)

option writer (or seller)   The individual or institution that writes/creates put and call options. (Chapter 14)

ordinary annuity   An annuity for which the cash flows occur at the *end* of each period. (Chapter 4)

out-of-the-money   A call option with no real value because the strike price exceeds the market price of the stock; a put option whose market price exceeds the strike price. (Chapter 14)

over-the-counter (OTC) market   A segment of the *secondary market* that involves trading in smaller, unlisted securities. (Chapter 2)

P

paper return   A return that has been achieved but not yet realized by an investor during a given period. (Chapter 4)

par value   The stated, or face, value of a stock. (Chapter 6)

payback period   The length of time it takes for the buyer of a convertible to recover the conversion premium from the extra current income earned on the convertible. (Chapter 10)

payment date   The actual date on which the company will mail dividend checks to shareholders (also known as the *payable date*). (Chapter 6)

PEG ratio   A financial ratio that relates a stock's price/earnings multiple to the company's rate of growth in earnings. (Chapter 7)

perfectly negatively correlated   Describes two negatively correlated series that have a correlation coefficient of -1. (Chapter 5)

perfectly positively correlated   Describes two positively correlated series that have a correlation coefficient of $+1$. (Chapter 5)

PIK-bond   A payment-in-kind junk bond that gives the issuer the right to make annual interest payments in new bonds rather than in cash. (Chapter 10)

point-and-figure charts   Charts used to keep track of emerging price patterns by plotting significant price changes with Xs and Os but with no time dimension used. (Chapter 9)

pooled diversification   A process whereby investors buy into a portfolio of securities for the collective benefit of the individual investors. (Chapter 12)

portfolio   Collection of securities or other investments, typically constructed to meet one or more investment goals. (Chapter 1)

portfolio beta, b_p   The beta of a portfolio; calculated as the weighted average of the betas of the individual assets it includes. (Chapter 5)

portfolio revision   The process of selling certain issues in a portfolio and purchasing new ones to replace them. (Chapter 13)

positively correlated   Describes two series that move in the same direction. (Chapter 5)

preferred stock   Ownership interest in a corporation; has a stated dividend rate, payment of which is given preference over common stock dividends of the same firm. (Chapter 1)

premium bond   A bond with a market value in excess of par; occurs when interest rates drop below the coupon rate. (Chapter 10)

premium discount broker   Broker who charges low commissions to make transactions for customers but provides limited free research information and investment advice. (Chapter 3)

present value   The *value today* of a sum to be received at some future date; the inverse of future value. (Chapter 4)

price/earnings (P/E) approach   Stock valuation approach that tries to find the P/E ratio that's most appropriate for the stock; this ratio, along with estimated EPS, is then used to determine a reasonable stock price. (Chapter 8)

primary market   The market in which *new issues* of securities are sold by the issuers to investors. (Chapter 2)

prime rate   The lowest interest rate charged to the best business borrowers. (Chapter 2)

principal   On a bond, the amount of capital that must be repaid at maturity. (Chapter 10)

private placement   The sale of new securities directly, without SEC registration, to private investors. (Chapter 2)

profitability measures   Financial ratios that measure a firm's returns by relating profits to sales, assets, or equity. (Chapter 7)

promised yield   Yield-to-maturity. (Chapter 11)

property   Investments in real property or tangible personal property. (Chapter 1)

prospectus   A portion of a security registration statement that describes the key aspects of the issue and issuer. (Chapter 2)

public offering   The sale of a firm's securities to public investors. (Chapter 2)

publicly traded issues   Shares of stock that are readily available to the general public and are bought and sold in the open market. (Chapter 6)

purchasing power risk   The chance that unanticipated changes in price levels (inflation or deflation) will adversely affect investment returns. (Chapter 4)

put   A negotiable instrument that enables the holder to sell the underlying security at a specified price over a set period of time. (Chapter 14)

pyramiding   The technique of using paper profits in margin accounts to partly or fully finance the acquisition of additional securities. (Chapter 2)

Q

quotations   Price information about various types of securities, including current price data and statistics on recent price behavior. (Chapter 3)

R

random walk hypothesis   The theory that stock price movements are unpredictable, so there's no way to know where prices are headed. (Chapter 9)

rate of growth   The compound annual rate of change in the value of a stream of income. (Chapter 4)

ratio analysis   The study of the relationships between financial statement accounts. (Chapter 7)

real estate   Entities such as residential homes, raw land, and income property. (Chapter 1)

real estate investment trust (REIT)   A type of closed-end investment company that sells shares to investors and invests the proceeds in various types of real estate and real estate mortgages; they come in three types: equity REITs, mortgage REITs, and hybrid REITs. (Chapter 12)

real rate of return   The nominal return minus the inflation rate; a measure of the increase in purchasing power that an investment provides. (Chapter 4)

realized return   Current income actually received by an investor during a given period. (Chapter 4)

realized yield   Expected return. (Chapter 11)

red herring   A preliminary prospectus made available to prospective investors while waiting for the registration statement's SEC approval. (Chapter 2)

refunding provisions   Provisions that prohibit the premature retirement of an issue from the proceeds of a lower-coupon refunding bond. (Chapter 10)

reinvestment rate   The rate of return earned on interest or other income received from an investment over its investment horizon. (Chapter 4)

relative P/E multiple   A measure of how a stock's P/E behaves relative to the average market multiple. (Chapter 8)

relevant risk   Risk that is nondiversifiable. (Chapter 5)

required return   The rate of return an investor must earn on an investment to be fully compensated for its risk. (Chapter 4)

residual owners   Owners/stockholders of a firm, who are entitled to dividend income and a prorated share of the firm's earnings only after all other obligations have been met. (Chapter 6)

restricted account   A margin account whose equity is less than the initial margin requirement; the investor may not make further margin purchases and must bring the margin back to the initial level when securities are sold. (Chapter 2)

return on invested capital   Return to investors based on the amount of money actually invested in a security, rather than the value of the contract itself. (Chapter 15)

returns   The rewards from investing, received as current income and/or increased value. (Chapter 1)

revenue bonds   Municipal bonds that require payment of principal and interest only if sufficient revenue is generated by the issuer. (Chapter 10)

rights offering   An offer of new shares of stock to existing stockholders on a pro rata basis. (Chapter 2)

risk   Reflects the uncertainty surrounding the return that an investment will generate. (Chapter 1)

risk premium   A return premium that reflects the issue and issuer characteristics associated with a given investment vehicle. (Chapter 4)

risk-averse   Describes an investor who requires greater return in exchange for greater risk. (Chapter 4)

risk-free rate   The rate of return that can be earned on a risk-free investment; the sum of the real rate of return and the expected inflation premium. (Chapter 4)

risk-indifferent   Describes an investor who does not require a change in return as compensation for greater risk. (Chapter 4)

risk-return tradeoff   The relationship between risk and return, in which investments with more risk should provide higher returns, and vice versa. (Chapter 4)

risk-seeking Describes an investor who will accept a lower return in exchange for greater risk. (Chapter 4)

round lot 100-share units of stock. (Chapter 3)

S

satisfactory investment An investment whose present value of benefits (discounted at the appropriate rate) *equals* or *exceeds* the present value of its costs. (Chapter 4)

secondary distributions The public sales of large blocks of previously issued securities held by large investors. (Chapter 2)

secondary market The market in which securities are traded *after they have been issued*; an *aftermarket*. (Chapter 2)

sector fund A mutual fund that restricts its investments to a particular segment of the market. (Chapter 12)

Securities and Exchange Commission (SEC) Federal agency that regulates securities offerings and markets. (Chapter 2)

Securities Investor Protection Corporation (SIPC) A nonprofit membership corporation, authorized by the federal government, that insures each brokerage customer's account for up to $500,000, with claims for cash limited to $100,000 per customer. (Chapter 3)

securities Investments issued by firms, governments, or other organizations that represent a financial claim on the issuer's resources. (Chapter 1)

securities markets Forums that allow suppliers and demanders of *securities* to make financial transactions. (Chapter 2)

securitization The process of transforming lending vehicles such as mortgages into marketable securities. (Chapter 10)

security analysis The process of gathering and organizing information and then using it to determine the intrinsic value of a share of common stock. (Chapter 7)

security market line (SML) The graphical depiction of the capital asset pricing model; reflects the investor's required return for each level of nondiversifiable risk, measured by beta. (Chapter 5)

security selection The procedures used to select the specific securities to be held within an asset class. (Chapter 13)

selling group A group of dealers and brokerage firms that join the investment banker(s); each member is responsible for selling a certain portion of a new security issue. (Chapter 2)

semi-strong form (EMH) Form of the EMH holding that abnormally large profits cannot be consistently earned using publicly available information. (Chapter 9)

senior bonds Secured debt obligations, backed by a legal claim on specific property of the issuer. (Chapter 10)

serial bond A bond that has a series of different maturity dates. (Chapter 10)

settle price The closing price (last price of the day) for commodities and financial futures. (Chapter 15)

Sharpe's measure A measure of portfolio performance that measures the *risk premium per unit of total risk*, which is measured by the portfolio standard deviation of return. (Chapter 13)

short interest The number of stocks sold short in the market at any given time; a technical indicator believed to indicate future market demand. (Chapter 9)

short-selling The sale of borrowed securities, their eventual repurchase by the short-seller, and their return to the lender. (Chapter 2)

short-term investments Investments that typically mature within one year. (Chapter 1)

simple interest Interest paid only on the initial deposit for the amount of time it is held. (Chapter 4)

sinking fund A provision that stipulates the amount of principal that will be retired annually over the life of a bond. (Chapter 10)

small-cap stocks Stocks that generally have market values of less than $1 billion but can offer above-average returns. (Chapter 6)

socially responsible fund A mutual fund that actively and directly incorporates ethics and morality into the investment decision. (Chapter 12)

speculation The purchase of high-risk investment vehicles that offer highly uncertain returns and future value. (Chapter 1)

speculative stocks Stocks that offer the potential for substantial price appreciation, usually because of some special situation, such as new management or the introduction of a promising new product. (Chapter 6)

split ratings Different ratings given to a bond issue by two or more rating agencies. (Chapter 10)

Standard & Poor's Corporation (S&P) Publisher of a large number of financial reports and services, including *corporation records* and *stock reports*. (Chapter 3)

Standard & Poor's indexes Indexes that measure the current price of a group of stocks relative to a base index value (set according to the specific index). (Chapter 3)

standard deviation, s A statistic used to measure the dispersion (variation) of returns around an asset's average or expected return. (Chapter 4)

statement of cash flows A financial summary of a firm's cash flow and other events that caused changes in the company's cash position. (Chapter 7)

stock dividend Payment of a dividend in the form of additional shares of stock. (Chapter 6)

stock spin-off Conversion of one of a firm's subsidiaries to a stand-alone company by distribution of stock in that new company to existing shareholders. (Chapter 6)

stock split A maneuver in which a company increases the number of shares outstanding by exchanging a specified number of new shares of stock for each outstanding share. (Chapter 6)

stock valuation The process by which the underlying value of a stock is established on the basis of its forecasted risk and return performance. (Chapter 8)

stock-index futures Futures contracts written on broad-based measures of stock market performance (e.g., the S&P 500 Stock Index), allowing investors to participate in the general movements of the stock market. (Chapter 15)

stock-index option A put or call option written on a specific stock market index, such as the S&P 500. (Chapter 14)

stockholders' (annual) report A report published yearly by a publicly held corporation; contains a wide range of information, including financial statements for the most recent period of operation. (Chapter 3)

stop-loss (stop) order An order to sell a stock when its market price reaches or drops below a specified level; can also be used to buy stock when its market price reaches or rises above a specified level. (Chapter 3)

street name Security certificates issued in the brokerage firm's name but held in trust for its client, who actually owns them. (Chapter 3)

strike price The stated price at which you can buy a security with a call or sell a security with a put. (Chapter 14)

strong form (EMH) Form of the EMH that holds that there is no information, public or private, that allows investors to consistently earn abnormal profits. (Chapter 9)

subordinated debentures   Unsecured bonds whose claim is secondary to other debentures. (Chapter 10)

systematic withdrawal plan   A mutual fund service that enables shareholders to automatically receive a predetermined amount of money every month or quarter. (Chapter 12)

T

tactical asset allocation   Asset allocation plan that uses stock-index futures and bond futures to change a portfolio's asset allocation based on forecast market behavior. (Chapter 13)

tangibles   Investment assets, other than real estate, that can be seen or touched. (Chapter 1)

target price   the price an analyst expects the stock to reach within a certain period of time, usually a year. (Chapter 8)

tax planning   The development of strategies that will defer and minimize an individual's level of taxes over the long run. (Chapter 1)

tax risk   The chance that Congress will make unfavorable changes in tax laws, driving down the after-tax returns and market values of certain investments. (Chapter 4)

tax swap   Replacement of a bond that has a capital loss for a similar security; used to offset a gain generated in another part of an investor's portfolio. (Chapter 11)

tax-advantaged investments   Investment vehicles and strategies designed to produce higher after-tax returns by reducing the amount of taxes that investors must pay. (Chapter 1)

taxable equivalent yield   The return a fully taxable bond would have to provide to match the after-tax return of a lower-yielding, tax-free municipal bond. (Chapter 10)

tech stocks   Stocks that represent the technology sector of the market. (Chapter 6)

technical analysis   The study of the various forces at work in the marketplace and their effect on stock prices. (Chapter 9)

term bond   A bond that has a single, fairly lengthy maturity date. (Chapter 10)

term structure of interest rates   The relationship between the interest rate or rate of return (yield) on a bond and its time to maturity. (Chapter 11)

theory of contrary opinion   A technical indicator that uses the amount and type of odd-lot trading as an indicator of the current state of the market and pending changes. (Chapter 9)

third market   Over-the-counter transactions typically handled by market makers and made in securities listed on the NYSE, the NYSE AMEX, or one of the other exchanges. (Chapter 2)

time value   The amount by which the option price exceeds the option's fundamental value. (Chapter 14)

time value of money   The fact that as long as an opportunity exists to earn interest, the value of money is affected by the point in time when the money is received. (Chapter 4)

total return   The sum of the current income and the capital gain (or loss) earned on an investment over a specified period of time. (Chapter 4)

total risk   The sum of an investment's nondiversifiable risk and diversifiable risk. (Chapter 5)

traditional portfolio management   An approach to portfolio management that emphasizes "balancing" the portfolio by assembling a wide variety of stocks and/or bonds of companies from a broad range of industries. (Chapter 5)

Treasury bonds   U.S. Treasury securities that are issued with 20- and 30-year maturities. (Chapter 10)

Treasury inflation-indexed obligations (TIPS)   A type of Treasury security that provides protection against inflation by adjusting investor returns for the annual rate of inflation. (Chapter 10)

Treasury notes   U.S. Treasury debt securities that are issued with maturities of 2 to 10 years. (Chapter 10)

treasury stock   Shares of stock that have been sold and subsequently repurchased by the issuing firm. (Chapter 6)

Treasury strips (strip-Ts)   Zero-coupon bonds created from U.S. Treasury securities. (Chapter 10)

Treynor's measure   A measure of portfolio performance that measures the *risk premium per unit of nondiversifiable risk*, which is measured by the portfolio beta. (Chapter 13)

true rate of interest (return)   The actual rate of interest earned. (Chapter 4)

12(b)-1 fee   A fee levied annually by many mutual funds to cover management and other operating costs. (Chapter 12)

U

uncorrelated   Describes two series that lack any relationship or interaction and therefore have a correlation coefficient close to zero. (Chapter 5)

underwriting   The role of the *investment banker* in bearing the risk of reselling the securities purchased from an issuing corporation at an agreed-on price. (Chapter 2)

underwriting syndicate   A group of investment banks formed by the originating investment banker to share the financial risk associated with *underwriting* new securities. (Chapter 2)

unrealized capital gains (paper profits)   A capital gain made only "on paper"—that is, not realized until the fund's holdings are sold. (Chapter 12)

V

valuation   Process by which an investor uses risk and return concepts to determine the value of a security. (Chapter 8)

value fund   A mutual fund that invests in stocks that are deemed to be undervalued in the market; value stocks often exhibit low P/E multiples, high dividend yields, and promising futures. (Chapter 12)

Value Line composite index   Stock index that reflects the percentage changes in share price of about 1,700 stocks, relative to a base of 100 set at June 30, 1961. (Chapter 3)

Value Line Investment Survey   One of the most popular subscription services used by individual investors; subscribers receive three basic reports weekly. (Chapter 3)

variable-ratio plan   A formula plan for timing investment transactions, in which the ratio of the speculative portion to the total portfolio value varies depending on the movement in value of the speculative securities; when the ratio rises or falls by a predetermined amount, the amount committed to the speculative portion of the portfolio is reduced or increased, respectively. (Chapter 13)

W

Wall Street Journal   A daily business newspaper; the most popular source of financial news. (Chapter 3)

weak form (EMH)   Form of the EMH holding that past data on stock prices are of no use in predicting future prices. (Chapter 9)

whipsawing   The situation where a stock temporarily drops in price and then bounces back upward. (Chapter 13)

wrap account   A brokerage account in which customers with large portfolios pay a flat annual fee that covers the cost of a money manager's services and the commissions on all trades. (Also called a *managed account*.) (Chapter 3)

Y

Yankee bonds   Bonds issued by foreign governments or corporations but denominated in dollars and registered with the SEC. (Chapter 10)

Yankee bonds   U.S. dollar-denominated debt securities issued by foreign governments or corporations and traded in U.S. securities markets. (Chapter 2)

yield (internal rate of return)   The compound annual rate of return earned by a long-term investment; the discount rate that produces a present value of the investment's benefits that just equals its cost. (Chapter 4)

yield curve   A graph that represents the relationship between a bond's term to maturity and its yield at a given point in time. (Chapter 11)

yield pickup swap   Replacement of a low-coupon bond for a comparable higher-coupon bond in order to realize an increase in current yield and yield-to-maturity. (Chapter 11)

yield spreads   Differences in interest rates that exist among various sectors of the market. (Chapter 11)

yield-to-call (YTC)   The yield on a bond if it remains outstanding only until a specified call date. (Chapter 11)

yield-to-maturity (YTM)   The fully compounded rate of return earned by an investor over the life of a bond, including interest income and price appreciation. (Chapter 11)

Z

zero-coupon bonds   Bonds with no coupons that are sold at a deep discount from par value. (Chapter 10)

Index

Credits

Page 35. Figure 2.1: LogMeIn, Inc., June 26, 2009, p.1.

Page 70. Figure 3.1: www.eSignal.com. Reprinted with permission.

Page 71. Figure 3.2: From Kiplinger's Personal Finance, © August 27, 2009 Kiplinger's Personal Finance. All rights reserved. Used by permission and protected by the Copyright Laws of the United States. The printing, copying, redistribution, or retransmission of the Material without express written permission is prohibited.

Page 72. Figure 3.3: Reprinted with permission from Zacks Investment Research, Inc.

Page 73. Figure 3.4: © 2009 Morningstar, Inc. All rights reserved. Reprinted by permission of Morningstar, Inc.

Page 76. Figure 3.5: © 2009. Reprinted by permission of Value Line Publishing, Inc.

Page 81. Figure 3.6: Reprinted from the Wal-Mart 2009 Annual Report.

Page 89. Figure 3.7: WALL STREET JOURNAL ONLINE by Wall Street Journal. Copyright 2009 by Dow Jones & Company, Inc. Reproduced with permission of Dow Jones & Company, Inc via Copyright Clearance Center.

Page 90. Figure 3.8: WALL STREET JOURNAL by Wall Street Journal. Copyright 2009 by Dow Jones & Company, Inc. Reproduced with permission of Dow Jones & Company, Inc via Copyright Clearance Center.

Page 210. Figure 6.1: Data from S&P 500 and Case-Shiller.

Page 213. Figure 6.3: © 2009. Reprinted by permission of ThinkEquity.

Page 216. Figure 6.4: *Wall Street Journal*, September 4, 2009.

Page 225. Figure 6.5: Proctor & Gamble stock report, August 22, 2009. Standard & Poor Financial Services. Reprinted by permission of The McGraw-Hill Companies, Inc.

Page 227. Figure 6.6: Electronic Arts, Inc. stock report, August 22, 2009. Standard & Poor Financial Services. Reprinted by permission of The McGraw-Hill Companies, Inc.

Page 246. Source: "Dell shares get a lift following analyst upgrade," by Rex Crum, MarketWatch.com, August 24, 2009; "Dell shares climb following upgrade on demand," Associated Press, Forbes.com, August 24, 2009.

Page 257. Figure 7.1: Apple Inc. sub-industry outlook, September 5, 2009. Standard & Poor Financial Services. Reprinted by permission of The McGraw-Hill Companies, Inc.

Page 273. Figure 7.2: Apple Inc. stock report, September 5, 2009. Standard & Poor Financial Services. Reprinted by permission of The McGraw-Hill Companies, Inc.

Page 286. Source: "Winn-Dixie Falls as CEO Warns Sales 'Soft' to Start FY10" by David Benoit, August 25, 2009, *The Wall Street Journal Online*, http://online.wsj.com; "Winn-Dixie Does an Earnings Two-Step" by Chris Jones, *The Motley Fool*, August 25, 2009, http://www.fool.com.

Page 299. Source: Adapted from Rich Smith, "Analysts Running Scared," *The Motley Fool*, April 5, 2006, www.fool.com.

Page 323. Source: Adapted from *The Wisdom of Crowds* by James Surowiecki Copyright © 2004 by James Surowiecki. Excerpted by permission of Anchor, a division of Random House, Inc. All rights reserved.

Page 340. Figure 9.2: WALL STREET JOURNAL by Wall Street Journal. Copyright 2009 by Dow Jones & Company, Inc. Reproduced with permission of Dow Jones & Company, Inc via Copyright Clearance Center.